S0-CFV-515

THE NAVARRE BIBLE

THE GOSPELS AND ACTS

EDITORIAL COMMITTEE

José María Casciaro, General Editor
Luis Alonso Martín, Santiago Ausín,
Claudio Basevi, Antonio García-Moreno,
Juan Belda, Secretary
with
P. Hípola, K. Limburg, L.F. Mateo-Seco

FOR THE ENGLISH EDITION
James Gavigan, Brian McCarthy
Thomas McGovern

VOLUMES IN THIS SERIES

Standard Edition

NEW TESTAMENT
St Matthew's Gospel
St Mark's Gospel
St Luke's Gospel
St John's Gospel
Acts of the Apostles
Romans and Galatians
Corinthians
Captivity Letters
Thessalonians and Pastoral Letters
Hebrews
Catholic Letters
Revelation

OLD TESTAMENT
The Pentateuch
Joshua–Kings [Historical Books 1]
Chronicles–Maccabees [Historical Books 2]
The Psalms and the Song of Solomon
Wisdom Books
Major Prophets
Minor Prophets

Reader's (Omnibus) Edition
The Gospels and Acts
The Letters of St Paul
Revelation, Hebrews and Catholic Letters

Single-volume, large-format New Testament

THE NAVARRE BIBLE

The Gospels and Acts of the Apostles

in the Revised Standard Version
with a commentary by members of the Faculty of Theology
of the University of Navarre

READER'S EDITION

FOUR COURTS PRESS • DUBLIN
SCEPTER PUBLISHERS • PRINCETON, NJ

Typeset by Carrigboy Typesetting Services for
FOUR COURTS PRESS
7 Malpas Street, Dublin 8, Ireland.
www.fourcourtspress.ie
and in North America for
SCEPTER PUBLISHERS, INC.
P.O. Box 211, New York, NY 10018
www.scepterpublishers.org

Nihil obstat: Martin Hogan, LSS, PhD, *censor deputatus*.
Imprimi potest: Desmond, Archbishop of Dublin, 17 February 1999

A catalogue record for this title
is available from the British Library.

ISBN 1-85182-508-8 (Four Courts Press)
ISBN 1-889334-27-8 (Scepter Publishers)

First edition 2000
Second printing 2002
Second edition (reset and repaged) 2008; reprinted 2010, 2013.

Library of Congress Cataloging-in-Publication Data

Sagrada Bible. English.
The Navarre Bible in the Revised Standard Version with a commentary by members of the Faculty of Theology of the University of Navarre – Reader's ed.
p. cm
Includes bibliographical references and index.
Contents: [1] The four Gospels and the Acts of the Apostles.
ISBN 1-889334-27-8 (hardback: v.1 alk. paper)
I. Bible – Commentaries. I. Universidad de Navarre. Facultad de Teología. II. Title.

BS497.2. S2413 2000
220.7'7—dc21 00-039349

ACKNOWLEDGMENTS

Original title: *Sagrada Biblia: Santos Evangelios* and *Sagrada Biblia: Hechos de los Apóstoles*.
Quotations from Vatican II documents are based on the translation in *Vatican Council II: The Conciliar and Post Conciliar Documents*, ed. A. Flannery, OP (Dublin 1981).

The New Vulgate text of the Bible can be accessed via http://www.vatican.va.archive/bible/index.htm

Printed and bound by CPI Group (UK) Ltd, Croydon, CR0 4YY

Contents

Preface and Preliminary Notes

The Commentary
The distinguishing feature of the *Navarre Bible* is its commentary on the biblical text. Compiled by members of the Theology faculty of the University of Navarre, Pamplona, Spain, this commentary draws on writings of the Fathers, texts of the Magisterium of the Church, and works of spiritual writers, including St Josemaría Escrivá, the founder of Opus Dei; it was he who in the late 1960s entrusted the faculty at Navarre with the project of making a translation of the Bible and adding to it a commentary of the type found here.

The commentary, which is not particularly technical, is designed to explain the biblical text and to identify its main points, the message God wants to get across through the sacred writers. It also deals with doctrinal and practical matters connected with the text.

The first volume of the *Navarre Bible* (the English edition) came out in 1985—first, twelve volumes covering the New Testament; then seven volumes covering the Old Testament. Many reprints and revised editions have appeared over the past twenty years. All the various volumes are currently in print.

The Revised Standard Version
The English translation of the Bible used in the *Navarre Bible* is the Revised Standard Version (RSV) which is, as its preface states, "an authorized revision of the American Standard Version, published in 1901, which was a revision of the King James Version [the "Authorized Version"], published in 1611".

The RSV of the entire Bible was published in 1952; its Catholic edition (RSVCE) appeared in 1966. The differences between the RSV and the RSVCE New Testament texts are listed in the "Explanatory Notes" in the end-matter of this volume. Whereas the Spanish editors of what is called in English the "Navarrre Bible" made a new translation of the Bible, for the English edition the RSV has proved to be a very appropriate choice of translation. The publishers of the *Navarre Bible* wish to thank the Division of Christian Education of the National Council of the Churches of Christ in the USA for permission to use that text.

The Latin Text
This volume also carries the official Latin version of the New Testament in the *editio typica altera* of the New Vulgate (Vatican City, 1986).

PRELIMINARY NOTES

The headings within the biblical text have been provided by the editors (they are not taken from the RSV). A full list of these headings, giving an overview of the New Testament, can be found at the back of the volume.

An asterisk *inside the biblical text* signals an RSVCE 'Explanatory Note' at the end of the volume.

References in the biblical text indicate parallel texts in other biblical books. All these marginal references come from the *Navarre Bible* editors, not the RSV.

Abbreviations

1. BOOKS OF HOLY SCRIPTURE

Acts	Acts of the Apostles	1 Kings	1 Kings
Amos	Amos	2 Kings	2 Kings
Bar	Baruch	Lam	Lamentations
1 Chron	1 Chronicles	Lev	Leviticus
2 Chron	2 Chronicles	Lk	Luke
Col	Colossians	1 Mac	1 Maccabees
1 Cor	1 Corinthians	2 Mac	2 Maccabees
2 Cor	2 Corinthians	Mal	Malachi
Dan	Daniel	Mic	Micah
Deut	Deuteronomy	Mk	Mark
Eccles	Ecclesiastes (Qoheleth)	Mt	Matthew
Esther	Esther	Nah	Nahum
Eph	Ephesians	Neh	Nehemiah
Ex	Exodus	Num	Numbers
Ezek	Ezekiel	Obad	Obadiah
Ezra	Ezra	1 Pet	1 Peter
Gal	Galatians	2 Pet	2 Peter
Gen	Genesis	Phil	Philippians
Hab	Habakkuk	Philem	Philemon
Hag	Haggai	Ps	Psalms
Heb	Hebrews	Prov	Proverbs
Hos	Hosea	Rev	Revelation (Apocalypse)
Is	Isaiah	Rom	Romans
Jas	James	Ruth	Ruth
Jer	Jeremiah	1 Sam	1 Samuel
Jn	John	2 Sam	2 Samuel
1 Jn	1 John	Sir	Sirach (Ecclesiasticus)
2 Jn	2 John	Song	Song of Solomon
3 Jn	3 John	1 Thess	1 Thessalonians
Job	Job	2 Thess	2 Thessalonians
Joel	Joel	1 Tim	1 Timothy
Jon	Jonah	2 Tim	2 Timothy
Josh	Joshua	Tit	Titus
Jud	Judith	Wis	Wisdom
Jude	Jude	Zech	Zechariah
Judg	Judges	Zeph	Zephaniah

2. OTHER ABBREVIATIONS

ad loc.	*ad locum*, commentary on this passage	f	and following (*pl*. ff)
AAS	*Acta Apostolicae Sedis*	ibid.	*ibidem*, in the same place
Apost.	Apostolic	in loc.	*in locum,* commentary on this passage
can.	canon	loc.	*locum*, place or passage
chap.	chapter	par.	parallel passages
cf.	*confer*, compare	Past.	Pastoral
Const.	Constitution	RSV	Revised Standard Version
Decl.	Declaration	RSVCE	Revised Standard Version, Catholic Edition
Dz-Sch	Denzinger-Schönmetzer, *Enchiridion Biblicum* (4th edition, Naples & Rome, 1961)	SCDF	Sacred Congregation for the Doctrine of the Faith
		sess.	session
Enc.	Encyclical	v.	verse (*pl*. vv.)
Exhort.	Exhortation		

"Sources quoted in the Commentary", which appears at the end of this book, explains other abbreviations used.

General Introduction to the Bible

WHAT IS THE BIBLE?

The Bible or Holy Scripture is the collection of books which, written under the inspiration of the Holy Spirit, have God as their author, and have been entrusted as such to the Church.[1]

Therefore, in order to understand what these sacred books essentially are, in the first place we should realize that they have two unique characteristics. Firstly, they are of divine origin, the result of a special action which is called "divine inspiration" of Scripture; and, secondly, the Bible has been entrusted by God to his Church as a sacred deposit and a divine gift which she has to keep, interpret and expound to all so that, by knowing and loving God in this life, they can obtain eternal happiness thereafter.

We should bear in mind that the reading of Holy Scripture, apart from giving us a knowledge of God as he is in himself, ought also produce in us an increase of love of God and of our neighbour; moreover, we can say that if one does not achieve this increase of charity one has not fully understood Holy Scripture: "everybody who knows that the purpose of the law is love that issues from a pure heart and a good conscience and a sincere faith (cf. 1 Tim 1:5), preferring all knowledge of the divine Scripture to other things, let him dedicate himself with confidence to expounding the divine books. If anybody thinks that he has understood the divine Scriptures or any part of them, and with this knowledge does not build up the double love of God and of his neighbour, then he has not yet understood them."[2]

Before explaining these two characteristics in more detail we should like to outline a few ideas about divine Revelation.

DIVINE REVELATION

The word "revelation" literally means to remove a veil that is hiding something. In religious language it means God' s manifestation to mankind of his own being and of those other truths necessary for or helpful to salvation. God makes himself known to us in two ways. One is through the things he has created, like an artist through his work; this is our natural knowledge of God, described with great poetic feeling in the Old Testament book of Wisdom: "For all men who were ignorant of God were foolish by nature; and they were

1. Vatican Council I, Dogm. Const. *Dei Filius*, chap. 2. **2.** St Augustine, *De doctrina christiana*, 1, 36, 40; 1, 40, 44.

unable from the good things that are seen to know him who exists; nor did they recognize the craftsman while paying heed to his works; but they supposed that either fire or wind or air, or the circle of the stars, or turbulent water, or the luminaries of heaven were the gods that rule the world. If through delight in the beauty of these things men assumed them to be gods, let them know how much better than these is their lord, for the author of beauty created them. And if men were amazed at their power and working, let them perceive from them how much more powerful is he who formed them. For from the greatness and beauty of created things comes a corresponding perception of their Creator" (Wis 13:1–5). This is what the Apostle St Paul points out to the Romans when he says that the invisible perfections of God, especially his eternal power and his divinity (cf. Rom 1:20), become visible to our intelligence through created things.

But God has not been content for man to have just this natural knowledge; he has also made himself known directly: "In many and various ways God spoke of old to our fathers through the prophets; but in these last days he has spoken to us through a Son, whom he appointed the heir of all things, through whom he created the world" (Heb 1:1–2). This action of God is supernatural or divine Revelation.

God chose the people of Israel in order to reveal himself gradually, through the prophets, in the Old Testament. This Revelation reaches its fullness in Christ, the Son of God made man, who has communicated to us all truth: "God has graciously arranged that what he had revealed for the salvation of all nations would abide perpetually in its full integrity and be handed on to all generations. Therefore, Christ the Lord, in whom the entire revelation of the most high God is brought to completion, commissioned the apostles to preach to all men that Gospel which is the source of all saving truth and moral teaching, and to impart to them heavenly gifts. This Gospel had been promised in former times through the prophets, and Christ himself had fulfilled it and promulgated it with his lips. This commission was faithfully fulfilled by the apostles who by their oral preaching, by example and by observances handed on what they had received from the lips of Christ, from living with him, and from what he did, or what they had learned through the prompting of the Holy Spirit. The commission was fulfilled, too, by those apostles and others associated with them who, under the inspiration of the same Holy Spirit, committed the message of salvation to writing."[3] And so in the Church, side by side with Scripture, there is also Tradition. Both constitute the deposit of God's Revelation on matters of faith and morals, entrusted by Christ to the apostles and by them in turn to their successors down to our day.

In this way Tradition and Scripture are the means by which we receive God's saving Revelation: "There exists a close connexion and communication between sacred Tradition and sacred Scripture. For both of them, flowing from the same divine well-spring, in a certain way merge into a unity and tend toward the same end."[4]

3. Vatican Council II, Dogm. Const. *Dei Verbum*, 7, 14. **4**. *Dei Verbum*, 9.

Thanks to Tradition, the Church knows the canon of the sacred books and understands them ever more deeply. For this reason Scripture cannot be understood without Tradition.

This Tradition is contained chiefly in the teaching of the universal Magisterium of the Church, in the writings of the Fathers, and in the words and actions of the sacred liturgy.

Both Tradition and Scripture have been entrusted to the Church, and within the Church, only the Magisterium has the role of interpreting them authentically and of preaching them with authority. And so both have to be received and interpreted with equal devotion.[5]

THE DIVINE INSPIRATION OF THE BIBLE

How does the divine action of inspiration influence the human authors of the sacred books?

Divine inspiration enlightens their intellect so that they can rightly conceive all that, and only that, which God wants them to write; it is also an infallible motion which moves the will of the sacred writer or hagiographer, though without impairing his freedom, to write faithfully what he has conceived in his intellect; and finally, it also consists in effective assistance to the sacred writer to find the correct language and expressions for describing aptly and with infallible truth all that he has conceived and has wanted to write.[6]

Thus, God is the principal author of Holy Scripture, and the sacred writers are also true, though subordinate, authors, intelligent and free instruments in the hands of God.[7]

According to this, the inspired book is the result of an action of God and of the hagiographer, in such a way that all the concepts and all the words of the sacred text can be attributed simultaneously to God and to his instrument, the hagiographer. There is nothing, then, in the Bible, that is not inspired by God.

THE MESSAGE OF THE BIBLE

The Bible does not speak about God as other books do; rather, in it *God speaks to us about himself*—which is something quite different. Both the Old and New Testament are the Word of God, a word at once living and life-giving. Apart from the narration of historical facts, the Bible contains a whole marvellous collection of teachings from which there derive a profound philosophy and a complete system of ethical principles; but all this treasure of truths is communicated by being linked to real events, God's intervention in history: for

5. Cf. Council of Trent, Decree *De libris sacris el de traditionibus recipiendis*, sess. IV. **6.** Cf. Leo XIII, Encyclical *Providentissimus Deus*, 18 November 1893. **7.** Cf. ibid. and *Dei Verbum*, 11.

example, the first chapters of Genesis, when describing the origin of the world and of man, also give us some very fundamental teaching about not only supernatural truths but also natural truths such as the creation by God of all things out of nothing. When we read that God created the heavens and the earth we see that God is the Creator and that he transcends the world, and that man is God' s creature.

The Bible contains the most important events of human history relevant to our salvation; throughout this history, like an internal motor driving it, there is something else to be seen, also historical but less perceptible, namely, the impulses, forces and sentiments which God has placed in the protagonists of that history or in the sacred authors who wrote down these events. There is, then, within human history yet another history, as it were, wrought by God on behalf of man—for us and with our cooperation or indeed in spite of us. Fundamentally the Bible is the history of salvation, or better, the history of the salvation of man by God. And in its midst we find the key to understanding all that history, namely, the death and resurrection of Jesus: the cross is the great explanation of that history: to save the world God becomes man and allows himself to be nailed to the cross like a criminal, but on the third day he rises from the dead. This is how God saves humanity from the slavery of sin, from death and from the devil. This Incarnation-Death-Resurrection, or, saying it another way, this mysterious God-Man, Jesus Christ, is the very centre of the Bible; from the opening pages of Genesis to the last pages of the Apocalypse everything at first tends towards, then afterwards derives from, Christ dead and risen again. Once the cross has been raised on Calvary and in the centre of history, neither history nor the world can have any meaning independently of it. At that moment the history of salvation reaches its climax. The great and all-powerful Love of God, humbling himself unto death, gains victory over death, over evil and over the powers of the devil. This is the mystery of the cross: to live one must die; to conquer, one must perish. Before the coming of Jesus, from the time of the original fall of our first parents, everything is promise, preparation, waiting. Afterwards everything is fulfilment, fact, although in hope and in faith, until the end of the world.

Biblical history also has a beginning, but, unlike secular history which speaks only of events that have already taken place, it also has an ending that lies in the future and that to a certain extent has already been written. The beginning is the creation of man and his immediate elevation to a state of justice, holiness and happiness, all this later being dramatically lost. The end is the vision of heaven under the image of heavenly Jerusalem, the future holy city of God. This biblical history unfolds in time and space; in it we can distinguish different periods, along the following lines:

1. After the loss of Paradise time passed slowly. Immediately after the original sin of our first parents, God promised a Saviour who would come from the lineage of the Woman (cf. Gen 3:15, the so-called "proto-evangelion", i.e. "first gospel" or good news of salvation). Afterwards came the centuries in which God did not completely abandon mankind: he showed mercy to the patriarchs, like Enoch, and especially Noah, with whom he formed a special relationship or covenant. In

his speech to the Athenians in the Areopagus, St Paul referred to this period as the "times of ignorance" (Acts 17:29–30), and, in his Letter to the Romans, as the "times of God's patience" (cf. Rom 3:26). In his speech to the citizens of Lycaonia he mentions that in those days God "allowed" the nations to follow their own devices (Acts 14:16). During this period God "has patience" and allows mankind to experience the dreadful consequence of sin and of ignorance of the true God.

2. At a certain moment God intervenes more decisively in human history: when he calls Abraham, to whom he makes the "promise": "In you [in your descendants] all the tribes of the earth will be blessed" (Gen 12:3). This is the "time of the promise" mentioned by St Stephen (cf. Acts 7:17). From here on mankind is divided: on the one hand, the race born of Abraham, and on the other the great mass of mankind, the Gentiles. Human life outside the chosen people was governed by the principles engraved by God in the individual conscience (cf. Rom 2:12–15); these could be saved by fulfilling the natural law, for God does not deny his grace to anyone who does what he can. But the great majority of people drowned the voice of their conscience and lived in sin (cf. Rom 1:18–32).

3. A new divine intervention marks the start of a third period, the "time of the Law". God chooses Moses, reveals his own intimacy to him in the episode of the burning bush (Ex 3: 14–17) and establishes a pact, the Covenant of Sinai (cf. Ex 19–24; Deut 29), in which God gives the Hebrews the Law which they have to fulfil to show their faithfulness to the Covenant. In this manner God constitutes the Hebrew clans as "his people", the people of God. From then on (thirteenth century BC) until Jesus Christ, biblical history is simply the history of the Old Covenant, the history of the Old Testament.

The Covenant and the Law given to Moses, the starting point of the chosen people, is the centre of rebirth to which they return again and again after their crises and their falls, to remain faithful to their vocation as the people of God. On occasions of special solemnity or gravity the Old Testament is renewed. Different periods can be distinguished: the conquest of Canaan under the leadership of Joshua (end of thirteenth century BC); the period of the separate tribes (twelfth century and first half of eleventh), united partially and occasionally under the judges; the long centuries of the Hebrew monarchy (eleventh to sixth centuries) in which the prophets exercise an important religious ministry and continually exhort the people and their rulers to return to the genuine spirit of the Covenant and of the Law; the great national and religious crisis of the Babylonian exile (sixth century BC), the terrible trial in which the soul of the people of Israel is re-forged thanks to the prophets and to certain deeply religious leaders like Nehemiah and Ezra; and finally the long post-exilic period (fifth to first century BC) not without its dangerous and difficult moments, such as the forced Hellenization which the Seleucid kings of Syria sought to inflict on the Jews and against which they revolted under the leadership of the Maccabees (second century BC).

During these long centuries the religion and the history of Israel were being forged simultaneously. Under the impulse of the Holy Spirit the judges, the kings and other leaders defended the nation's independence, a necessary precondition for conserving of the monotheistic purity of the revealed religion of the Old Testament. Under the impulse of the same Spirit the prophets taught the truths of Revelation: some stressed the moral and social responsibility of the people of God (for example, Amos); others, the infinite and intimate love of God for his people (for example, Hosea); or the ineffable transcendence of God's majesty (for example, Isaiah); or the need for limitless confidence in God (for example, Jeremiah); or individual responsibility as opposed to the anonymity of the crowd (Ezekiel); etc. Meanwhile hope grew steadily to form the backbone of the prophets' preaching around the messianism of the Old Testament, which was to have its fulfilment in the Person and in the work of Jesus, the Christ or Messiah. At the same time, and more so especially in the latter centuries of Old Testament history and also under the influence of the same Holy Spirit, there took place the gradual development of Hebrew "wisdom": gifted individuals, chosen by God and educated in the meditation of the Law and in the teachings of the prophets and trained to reflect on life, gradually fashion, under the inspiration of the Holy Spirit, the so-called "wisdom" literature of the Old Testament, which completes Revelation and prepares people for the coming of the messianic Saviour in the "fullness of the times" (cf. Gal 4:4).

4. Finally, the "fullness of the times": the Incarnation of the Word of God, Jesus Christ. By his life on earth and by his sacrifice on the cross followed by his glorious resurrection, Jesus gains victory over the powers and forces that have enslaved mankind. Jesus brings a new and definitive creation, quite distinct from the former one. He is the new Adam, to use St Paul's image, first-born of the renewed creation; he is the head of the new people of God, the Church, based not on "flesh and blood" but on the spirit and the charity of the New Covenant in Jesus' own blood. By his resurrection and ascension into heaven the humanity of Jesus, united to his divinity in the self-same one Person of the Word (the hypostatic union), receives from the Father lordship over all creation, visible and invisible, earthly and heavenly: the "last times" of history have begun.

THE BOOKS WHICH MAKE UP THE BIBLE

Given that the divine inspiration of the Bible is a supernatural grace, only God can reveal which books specifically are inspired by him. The list of inspired books is called the "canon" of the Bible. The revealed fact of the biblical canon is to be found in the faith of the Church from her beginnings. The most important documentary evidence that we have of this faith are the decrees of the councils of Carthage (*c.*AD 400) and some other documents of the ordinary Magisterium from the fifth century onwards. The Council of Florence (1441) in due course witnessed to this Tradition of the Church. This truth of faith was solemnly defined by the Council of Trent (1546). The First Vatican Council (1870) repeated in a solemn manner the definition of Trent, which Vatican II also adopted (cf. *Dei Verbum*, 11).

The concept of "canonicity" presupposes that of inspiration: a book is canonical when, having been written under divine inspiration, it is recognized and proclaimed as such by the Church. The Church does not define as canonical any book that has not been inspired. The criterion which the Magisterium of the Church has used in order to define exactly which books are inspired and canonical is sacred Tradition, which stems from Jesus and the apostles, interpreted with the assistance of the Holy Spirit.

The books of the biblical canon are those which are to be found in Catholic editions of the Bible.

CONSERVATION OF THE SACRED BOOKS

Once we have discussed the question of *what* the Bible is and *which* books it comprises, a third question arises, namely, what relationship do the present-day versions of Scripture have with the original writings as they came from the hands of the inspired authors? Or, in other words, do they conserve and reproduce the original inspired text?

We should point out in the first place that the original manuscripts or autographs (that is, written by the author himself) are no longer extant; instead we have only copies, either direct or indirect. The same is true of the other literary works of ancient times.

The books of the Old Testament were written originally in Hebrew, with the exception of the book of Wisdom and the second book of Maccabees which were composed in Greek; in addition some small fragments of other books were written originally in Greek or in Aramaic. The New Testament, on the other hand, was originally composed entirely in Greek with the single exception of the first redaction of the Gospel of St Matthew which was written in Aramaic.

Insofar as the dates of composition are concerned, the Old Testament began to be written down possibly towards the end of the thirteenth century BC and was finished at the beginning of the first century BC, thus spanning a long period of twelve centuries. The New Testament, by contrast, was completed in the short period of fifty years, AD 50–100 approximately.

The Bible, and especially the New Testament, is far and away the best-documented literary production of antiquity: in the case of Homer's *Iliad* and *Odyssey* and certain works of Plato and of Aristotle (for which the most manuscripts are extant) the number of manuscripts never exceeds one thousand; indeed at most there are twenty or thirty and of a rather late date (tenth to fifteenth centuries); but for the Bible we have over 6,000 manuscripts in the original languages (Hebrew and Greek) and over 40,000 in other very early versions (Coptic, Latin, Armenian, Aramaic etc.).

Hence we see that the Bible, quite apart from its divine authority, also possesses a historico-critical character immeasurably superior to any other ancient literary work.

INTERPRETATION OF THE BIBLE

"We can know the authentic meaning of Holy Scripture only through the Church, because only the interpretation given by the Church is guaranteed free from error."[8] And from the definition of Holy Scripture given by the First Vatican Council we get another of the essential conditions for interpretation of the Bible, namely, that only the Church, through her Magisterium, is the authentic interpreter of Holy Scripture. This has to be understood in both the positive and the negative sense: we have to accept as a biblical meaning one that has been proposed as such by the Church Magisterium (either directly or indirectly); and we have to reject as false any interpretation that does not agree with the meaning proposed by the Magisterium. Hence Holy Scripture cannot be understood by somebody who does not have the Christian faith. Something similar occurs with the Bible as occurs with the figure of Jesus Christ: the person who does not have faith recognizes Jesus only as a unique and extraordinary man, but falls very far short of the truth and therefore cannot comprehend that he is the Incarnate Son of God, the second Person of the Blessed Trinity, the only Saviour and Redeemer of mankind.

Likewise, the Bible, in its deeper sense, cannot be understood by somebody who does not believe in its divine inspiration and that it has God as its principal author. This fact is a necessary condition for correct interpretation of the Bible and its absence cannot be compensated for by any human technique, whether literary, historical, philosophical or of any other kind.

St Augustine, having explained some difficulties in interpretation of Scripture, replies to a friend: "Let him who asks these things become a Christian, lest in trying to solve all the questions about the holy books he should end his life before having passed from death to life. There are innumerable problems that cannot be solved before believing, at the risk of ending this life without faith. Once faith has been accepted, then they can be studied in detail as an exercise for the pious enjoyment of the faithful mind."[9]

Insofar as the Bible is also a human book of notable antiquity, our understanding of it is helped by certain explanations of a historical or literary character, as is the case with any ancient work.

At this point we should like to recall the comparison St Augustine offers: when the Israelites left Egypt they took with them valuables of gold, silver, precious stones, garments etc. which the Egyptians used either as personal ornaments or for idolatrous worship. But from these very same precious objects the Hebrews made ornaments for use in the worship of the one true God. The saintly bishop of Hippo applies this idea to the use of human sciences (philosophy, history, literature etc.) in the understanding of the Scriptures, provided they are used properly in the service of Scripture, that is to say, with humility and reverence and the invocation of divine grace: "He who applies

8. *St Pius X Catechism*, 887. **9.** *Letter* 102, 6, 380,

himself to the study of Holy Scripture [...] should not forget to consider that apostolic maxim: Knowledge puffs up, but love builds up (1 Cor 8:1); because he will realize that, although he has emerged rich from Egypt, if he does not celebrate the Pasch he cannot be saved."[10]

TRUTHFULNESS AND INERRANCY OF THE BIBLE

Everything that the hagiographer affirms, states or implies ought to be taken as affirmed, stated or implied by God, who can neither deceive nor be deceived. Truthfulness has to do with agreement between what one expresses and what one thinks or feels; inerrancy means absolute freedom from error. Consequently, in Holy Scripture there can be no errors whatsoever because, since all of it is inspired, God himself is the author of all its parts.

In the things of nature, proper to the physical sciences, God has not wished to make any supernatural revelation about the inner constitution of the visible world; hence neither have the sacred authors revealed anything on this matter. What they do teach, however, are the truths necessary for salvation: the creation of the world and of man by God, the providence and government of the world by God and his freedom and omnipotence to perform miracles. It is normal to quote two reasons of convenience that help us to understand why God has not revealed the inner constitution of the visible world: firstly, the knowledge of these things does not affect directly the doctrine of salvation; and secondly, God has left precisely these matters to the free investigation of human science. And so the hagiographers allude to the events of nature using the expressions and concepts of their own time and cultural surroundings. Because they were writing in a period long before the development of the natural sciences, the sacred authors speak about things in the manner in which they are immediately apprehended by the senses and according to the common descriptions of all ages: the sun rises, the moon sets, etc. The attitude of those writers, especially in the last century, who felt that the sacred authors ought to have spoken about the most up-to-date scientific theories (often abandoned later) is superficial and unreasonable. We should thank God that the sacred writers have spoken in simple language so that anyone can understand them by applying a little common sense.

In historical matters it is another question altogether. If the explanation of the happenings of nature is a matter in which divine Revelation has no part to play, human history nevertheless has in many ways a close connexion with revealed truth. The reason is because biblical Revelation is concerned not only with abstract truths, but also with the merciful intervention of God in certain events of human history. The foundations of Christian Revelation and the major dogmas are very firmly rooted in history. For example, the creation of the world by God underlies the whole of Revelation about the notion of God, of the

10. St Augustine, *De doctrina christiana*, 2, 9, 14.

world and of man. The birth of Jesus Christ of the Blessed Virgin Mary and the power of the Holy Spirit without the intervention of a man, is an event that has really taken place in history and which is at the centre of the Christian faith. The death and resurrection of Jesus Christ in the time of Pontius Pilate is the crucial historical event of salvation history and cannot be changed nor denied, nor can it be understood in a way that denies its real historical character.

CHRISTIAN READING OF THE BIBLE

"Here we are going to read the words, not of a lord of this world, but of the Prince of Angels. If we prepare ourselves in this manner, the grace of the Holy Spirit will guide us with all certainty and we will reach the very throne of the King, and we will attain all good things through the grace and love of our Lord Jesus Christ, to whom be the glory and the power, with the Father and the Holy Spirit, now and forever. Amen."[11]

St John Chrysostom calls the Holy Scriptures letters sent by God to men.[12] Given that this is so, the first thing that we have to do on reading Holy Scripture is to have a holy desire and longing to know and to meditate the content of these divine letters. And so St Jerome exhorted his friend: "Read very often the divine Scriptures; nay, never abandon the sacred reading."[13]

The Second Vatican Council "earnestly and especially urges all the Christian faithful [...] to learn by frequent reading of the divine Scriptures 'the surpassing knowledge of Jesus Christ' (Phil 3:8). For ignorance of the Scriptures is ignorance of Christ (St Jerome). Therefore they should gladly go to the sacred text itself, whether in the liturgy, rich in the divine words, or in spiritual reading. [...] Let them remember that prayer should accompany the reading of sacred Scripture, so that God and man may talk together; for 'we speak to him when we pray; we hear him when we read the divine sayings' (St Ambrose)."[14] And St Pius X affirms that "whereas the reading of the Bible is not required of all Christians because they are already taught by the Church, it is nevertheless very useful and is recommended to everybody."[15]

For faithful reading we have to start necessarily from *the obedience of faith of the one Church of Jesus Christ*; faith, to be precise, in all that the Church professes and teaches about the canon of the sacred books, their divine inspiration, their inerrancy and truthfulness, their historicity and their authenticity; in brief, faith that God is the principal author of the sacred books and that they contain the truth of salvation without any error.

Piety and *holiness of life* are also needed for the understanding of Holy Scripture. As one grows in the understanding of the written Word of God, one needs to prepare oneself through prayer to receive the insights that are freely given by the Holy Spirit. The person who reads, meditates or studies the Bible

11. St John Chrysostom, *In Matt. hom.*, 1, 8. **12.** Cf. *In Gen. hom.*, 2, 2. **13.** *Ad Nepotianum*, 7, 1. **14.** *Dei Verbum*, 25. **15.** *St Pius X Catechism*, 884.

needs to have recourse to constant prayer, to contact with God, for the comprehension of this holy word. The secrets of Holy Scripture are not unlocked only with the aid of linguistics, archaeology, sociology, psychology or any other human science, but rather by a desire to achieve personal holiness, and therefore in the light of God.

It is also necessary to have the virtue of humility which makes us like children before our Father God. Only in this way will the words of Christ be fulfilled in us: "I thank you, Father, Lord of heaven and of earth, because thou hast hidden these things from the wise and understanding and revealed them to babes" (Mt 11:25).

This humility and piety are manifested in the Christian by his prudence in not allowing or accepting wanton opinions that are opposed to the constant teaching of the Magisterium of the Church and Tradition; and also, by the firm conviction that we shall never manage to demonstrate truths of the supernatural order and that therefore we do not discover for ourselves, but rather accept joyfully, what God has revealed and precisely as the Church Magisterium proposes it. Faced with the grandeur of the divine mysteries, the Christian ought to experience humble joy at the fact that his intelligence cannot comprehend them. How can I, small and finite that I am, comprehend the infinity and grandeur of God? Hence Pope St Pius X quoted a passage from St Anselm: "The desire for knowledge will move our reason, and humility will subdue it when it fails to understand. No Christian ought to discuss whether something that the catholic Church believes in her heart and confesses with her mouth is indeed as she says or not; but rather, always maintaining and loving the same faith without doubting, and living in accordance with it, he will humbly investigate, as far as he is able, why it is so. If he understands, let him thank God, and if he cannot, let him not lower his horns to attack but bow his head to adore."[16]

Finally, let the reader embark with these dispositions on the reading of the Holy Bible, knowing that, if he does so, in them he will find Christ; in the words of St Augustine: "Divine Scripture is like a field in which we are going to build a house. We must not be lazy and be happy to build just on the surface: we have to dig down until we reach the living rock, and this rock is Christ."[17]

16. Encyclical *Communium rerum*, 21 April 1909. **17.** *In Ioann. Evang. tractatus*, 23, 1.

Introduction to the Books of the New Testament

WHAT IS THE NEW TESTAMENT?

What "New Testament" primarily means is the new and definitive stage in salvation history brought about by Jesus Christ, which replaced and completed the Revelation and structures of the "Old Testament"; both expressions have been in use among Christian writers since the first century.

God's promise of salvation, given in paradise after the fall of our first parents (cf. Gen 3:15), was ratified by the Covenant he made with the patriarch Abraham (cf. Gen 17) and renewed with Isaac and with Jacob (cf. Gen 26; 28:12–15); later Moses sealed this Covenant by offering victims (cf. Ex 24:1–11). In the New Testament God keeps his promise: Jesus, by his death on the cross, establishes the New and Eternal Covenant. The expression "New Testament" is taken from the words Jesus uses when instituting the eucharistic Sacrifice (cf. Mt 26:28; Mk 14:24; Lk 22:20; 1 Cor 11:25). The sacrifice which Christ offers on the cross is the new and definitive Covenant, also known as the New Alliance or New Testament.

This first meaning of the expression led to a special meaning: from the end of the second century the words "New Testament" were more and more taken also to designate the collection of divinely inspired books containing the full and definitive Revelation given by our Lord Jesus Christ.

THE BOOKS OF THE NEW TESTAMENT

The New Testament is made up of twenty-seven books, all of them written in the second half of the first century. These are often divided into three groups: (i) historical books: the four Gospels and the Acts of the Apostles; (ii) didactical books: the thirteen letters of St Paul, Hebrews, and the seven "catholic" letters; (iii) the prophetical book of the Apocalypse of St John, the book of Revelation.

These writings exactly as we have them today were from the beginning accepted by the Church as being the *new* sacred books and were placed alongside the books of the Old Testament—which the Church also accepted as God's gift. Together, these two collections constitute the Bible or Holy Scripture.

Just as Christ fulfilled the promises made by God through the patriarchs and prophets of the Old Covenant or Testament, so the books of the New Testament record the fulfillment of these promises which themselves were recorded in the sacred books of the Old Covenant: the whole Old Testament can be seen as a promise or prophecy of the New Testament, and the New Testament as the keeping of that promise.

THE GREAT RESPECT DUE THE NEW TESTAMENT

Since God is the author of the New Testament and salvation its purpose, it should be read with great respect and veneration. As the Second Vatican Council says: "The word of God, which is the power of God for salvation to everyone who has faith (cf. Rom 1:16), is set forth and displays its power in a most wonderful way in the writings of the New Testament. For when the time fully came (cf. Gal 4:4), the Word became flesh and dwelt among us full of grace and truth (cf. Jn 1:14). Christ established on earth the kingdom of God, revealed his Father and himself by deeds and words; and by his death, resurrection and glorious ascension, as well as by sending the Holy Spirit, completed his work. Lifted up from the earth he draws all men to himself (cf. Jn 12:32), for he alone has the words of eternal life (cf. Jn 6:68). This mystery was not made known to other generations as it has now been revealed to his apostles and prophets by the Holy Spirit (cf. Eph 3:4–6), that they might preach the Gospel, stir up faith in Jesus, Christ and Lord, and bring together the Church. The writings of the New Testament stand as a perpetual and divine witness to these realities."[1]

The New Testament contains the Good News, that is, the Gospel of Jesus Christ (cf. Mk 1:1)—the Gospel which our Lord himself preached and commanded his apostles to preach. God wanted the books of the New Testament to be written, so that by their being preached and authentically explained by the Church they would provide people in every generation with an excellent means of getting to know Jesus Christ, the *Way* for us to take, *Truth* for our intellects and *Life* for our souls (cf. Jn 14:6).

DOCTRINAL CONTENT OF THE NEW TESTAMENT

The New Testament proclaims the gifts and also the commands of God, Almighty Father, who sent his only-begotten Son into the world to save us ("for us men and for our salvation he came down from heaven", in the words of the Nicene-Constantinopolitan Creed). The New Testament reveals to us the unfathomable mystery of God, one and triune, a mystery which was hinted at but not clearly revealed in the Old Testament.

In Jesus Christ, the Son of God, we can see the Father: "All things have been delivered to me by my Father; and no one knows the Son except the Father, and anyone to whom the Son chooses to reveal him" (Mt 11:27). "Philip said to him, 'Lord, show us the Father, and we shall be satisfied.' Jesus said to him, 'Have I been with you so long, and yet you do not know me, Philip? He who has seen me has seen the Father'" (Jn 14:8–9).

Jesus' teaching came not only from himself but also from the Father who had sent him: "He who does not love me does not keep my words; and the word which you hear is not mine but the Father's who sent me" (Jn 14:24).

1. Vatican Council II, Dogm. Const. *Dei Verbum*, 17.

Jesus came in obedience to his Father's command: "For I have come down from heaven, not to do my own will, but the will of him who sent me" (Jn 6:38). The Father wants him to lead men to divine sonship and to the vision of the glory of God: "he has granted us his precious and very great promises, that through these you may … become partakers of the divine nature" (2 Pet 1:4).

Jesus is, then, the Saviour: in him is revealed God's tender loving-kindness towards us. Jesus is the Christ (the Messiah), the Lord, the Son of God. He not only offers people the way to satisfy their deepest yearnings: he brings something that is on an entirely different plane—supernatural grace, which makes us adoptive sons and daughters of God.

The books of the New Testament, together with those of the Old, are all part of one, single, ornate plan: "In many and various ways God spoke of old to our fathers by the prophets; but in these last days he has spoken to us by a Son, whom he appointed the heir of all things, through whom also he created the world. He reflects the glory of God and bears the very stamp of his nature, upholding the universe by his word of power. When he had made purification for sins, he sat down at the right hand of the Majesty on high" (Heb 1:1–3).

The Old Testament, then, bore witness to Christ by announcing his coming: its books, whether historical, prophetical or wisdom books, prophesied the future Christ. The Gospels, by God's design, deal with Jesus' life on earth, his words and actions, his redemptive death and his glorious resurrection. Through Christ we have been freed from sin, from death and from the power of the devil, and enabled to live in the glorious liberty of the children of God (cf. Rom 8:21). The Acts of the Apostles reports the coming of the Holy Spirit on the day of Pentecost; we see him promote the early spread of the Church among Jews and Gentiles. The letters of the apostles teach us how to practise the Christian faith, whatever our circumstances. And, finally, the Apocalypse or book of Revelation consoles and strengthens us in the midst of difficulties and keeps alive our hope of final victory (in this connexion it foretells the second coming of Christ).

Jesus established the Kingdom of God on earth, but it will not take final shape until, at the end of the world, Jesus returns in glory to judge the living and the dead and deliver the Kingdom to the Father (cf. 1 Cor 15:24). In the meantime, "some of his disciples are pilgrims on earth, others have died and are being purified, while still others are in glory, contemplating 'in full light, God himself triune and one, exactly as he is'."[2] In the Beatitudes (cf. Mt 5:1–12) our Lord promises Christians fulfilment: in heaven that fulfilment will be complete, but even on earth, whether in the midst of affliction and sorrow or joy and prosperity, in honour or in dishonour, in scarcity or in plenty, in sickness or in health, Christians always realize that they are God's children, redeemed by Christ's death, and destined to eternal life with Christ in God. Buoyed up by this hope they can face any tribulation with the serenity of a son or daughter of God, identifying themselves with Christ their Saviour.

2. Vatican Council II, Dogm. Const. *Lumen gentium*, 49.

WHEN WERE THE BOOKS OF THE NEW TESTAMENT WRITTEN?

Jesus did not command his apostles to write books; he commanded them to teach: "Go therefore and make disciples of all nations, baptizing them in the name of the Father and of the Son and of the Holy Spirit, teaching them to observe all that I have commanded you; and lo, I am with you always, to the close of the age" (Mt 28:19–20). The Spirit trained the apostles for this mission; and then he gave the Church another gift: he stirred some of them, and a few of their immediate disciples, to put into writing, under his inspiration, everything that, taken in conjunction with the Old Testament and with Sacred Tradition, would constitute the deposit of Revelation.

This writing took place more or less in the period AD 50–100. No book in the New Testament gives its date of composition; but scholars have managed to assign dates: some of these can be taken as certain; others are quite probable or at least approximate. The chronological table given below outlines the dates deduced; we would like to point out three things about it. (i) A date given in brackets is a second hypothesis, less probable than the first but certainly possible. (ii) Most of St Paul' s letters were written before the three Synoptic Gospels, with the exception of the early Hebrew or Aramaic version of St Matthew. (iii) Question marks in parentheses indicate that the date is unclear in Christian tradition or has been questioned by scholars on good grounds.

Date of composition	*Canonical writing*	*Author*	*Written in*
51–52	1 and 2 Thess	Paul	Corinth
50–55	[early Aramaic Gospel]	Matthew	Palestine(?)
50–60	Jas	James	Jerusalem(?)
54	Gal	Paul	Ephesus(?)
57 (spring)	1 Cor	Paul	Ephesus
57–58 (autumn)	2 Cor	Paul	Macedonia
57–58 (winter)	Rom	Paul	Corinth
60(?) (64–70)	Mk	Mark	Rome (?)
62(?) (54–57)	Phil	Paul	Rome (Ephesus)
62	Col, Philem, Eph	Paul	Rome
62(?) (67–70)	Lk	Luke	Rome (Achaia)
63 (75)	Acts	Luke	
64	1 Pet	Peter	Rome
64 (80)	2 Pet	Peter(?)	Rome(?)
65	1 Tim and Tit	Paul	Macedonia
65(?) (80)	Heb	Paul(?)	Rome(?) Athens(?)
66	2 Tim	Paul	Rome
68–70	Mt	Matthew	Syria(?)
70(?)	Jude	Jude Thaddeus	(?)
85–95	Rev	John	Patmos
95–100	1, 2 and 3 Jn	John	Ephesus(?)
98–100	Jn	John	Ephesus(?)

Introduction to the Holy Gospels

WHAT ARE THE GOSPELS?

The climax of God's Revelation to mankind is the incarnation of the Son of God. Jesus Christ perfected Revelation "by the total fact of his presence and self-manifestation—by words and works, signs and miracles, but above all by his death and glorious resurrection from the dead, and finally by sending the Spirit of truth."[1] By this Christ "accomplishes the saving work which his Father gave him to do."[2] The account of this saving work of the Lord, which was taught orally by the Apostles and is continually being handed on in the Tradition of the Church, was also written down under the inspiration of the Holy Spirit, in the books of the New Testament, where the word of God is given its fullest written expression.

The New Testament opens with four books, each of which is called a "Gospel"; all the other books of Holy Scripture are also inspired, but these four are of outstanding importance, for "they are our principal source for the life and teaching of the Incarnate Word, our Saviour."[3] These four books were given the name "Gospel" from the beginning of the second century: for example, around the year 150 St Justin Martyr calls them "recollections of the apostles" or "Gospels."[4] But before this time, the word "gospel" was not used in the sense of book, which it later acquired. How did these books come to be called "Gospels"?

The word "gospel" is of Greek origin (*euangélion*) and originally means "good news." It is also used in Greek antiquity to describe the reward given to the bearer of this good news, or the offering made to the gods in thanksgiving for benefits received. The Romans used the word *evangelios* to describe the contribution made by Emperor Augustus to the world.

Among the Jews, the verb "to evangelize", "to announce the good news", obtains special significance when used to refer to the messianic times when God will save his people: "How beautiful upon the mountains are the feet of him who brings good tidings, who publishes peace, who brings good tidings of good, who publishes salvation" (Is 52:7).

When, from the beginning of his public ministry, our Lord invites people to believe in the Gospel, he is referring to the good news of the arrival of the Kingdom of God which he is announcing and establishing: "The time is fulfilled, and the kingdom of God is at hand; repent, and believe in the gospel" (Mk 1:14). This good news of salvation must be proclaimed to the whole world, which is the mission our Lord entrusts to the apostles (cf. Mk 13:10).

The preaching of the Twelve concerning Christ and his work of salvation also came to be called "the Gospel": in their preaching, "gospel" covers the

1. Vatican Council II, Dogm. Const. *Dei Verbum*, 4. **2.** Ibid. **3.** *Dei Verbum*, 18. **4.** *Apology*, 1, 66.

words and actions of Jesus, but it particularly proclaims that, through his death and resurrection, he has redeemed us from our sins and fulfilled the promises of salvation which God made in the Old Testament. So, the Gospel that the apostles proclaim is the proclamation of the good news, that is to say, Jesus Christ himself.

Therefore, there is only one Gospel, only one "good news"—that preached by the apostles, which they in turn received from Christ and which they proclaim with the power of the Holy Spirit. St Paul wrote: "As we have said before, so now I say again, If anyone is preaching to you a gospel contrary to that which you received, let him be accursed" (Gal 1:9). The Gospel is immutable; it must be held on to, for it is the only route to salvation.

To sum up: the word "gospel" was first used by Christians to describe the joyous proclamation of the salvation brought by Christ. When this was later expressed in written form, the word was applied to the actual books which contained this preaching: the first four books of the New Testament are called Gospels because they transmit the "gospel" preached by the apostles, who received it from Christ himself.

THE CONTENT OF THE GOSPEL

Here is how St Peter, in one of his addresses, describes the life of our Lord: "You know … the word which was proclaimed throughout all Judea, beginning from Galilee after the baptism which John preached: how God anointed Jesus of Nazareth with the Holy Spirit and with power; how he went about doing good and healing all that were oppressed by the devil, for God was with him. And we are witnesses to all that he did both in the country of the Jews and in Jerusalem. They put him to death by hanging him on a tree; but God raised him on the third day and made him manifest; not to all the people but to us who were chosen by God as witnesses, who ate and drank with him after he rose from the dead. And he commanded us to preach to the people, and to testify that he is the one ordained by God to be the judge of the living and the dead. To him all the prophets bear witness that every one who believes in him receives forgiveness of sins through his name" (Acts 10:37–43).

The Gospels tell the story of Christ's life along the general lines of the structure of this address by St Peter. St John begins his by going right back to the eternity of the Word in the bosom of the Father and then moves on to describe the incarnation of the Son of God and his life among men (cf. Jn 1:1–14). St Luke and St Matthew start with accounts of the birth of Jesus (Mt 12; Lk 1–2). St Mark starts directly with St John the Baptist preaching the need to do penance to prepare for the Messiah.

The four Gospels then describe the prelude to Christ's public ministry: the baptism of Jesus by John in the river Jordan, with a clear Revelation of the Holy Trinity; John bearing witness that Jesus is the Christ (and the first three Gospels also give accounts of his fasting and being tempted by the devil). In reporting these events the Gospels teach that Christ is incomparably greater than John the Baptist and all the prophets of the Old Testament: Jesus is the Son of God, and his mission is divine: he has come to install the Kingdom of God (cf. Mt 3:1— 4:11; Mk 1:1–13; Lk 3:1–4, 13; Jn 1:19–51).

Most of the text of each Gospel has to do with showing us Jesus going about doing good: he healed the sick and freed those possessed by the devil, for God was with him (Acts 10:38); he preached and worked miracles by the power of God (Acts 2:22). And as he did so the Jewish authorities grew to hate him more and more, until eventually they brought about his passion and death. This section of the Gospels covers what is described as Christ's "public life". "Christ established on earth the kingdom of God and revealed his Father and himself by deeds and words."[5] The evangelists report what Jesus was constantly preaching—particularly, how his disciples must conduct themselves (the sermon on the mount); the characteristics of the Kingdom of heaven which he came to establish (the Kingdom parables); the true nourishment of the soul in the new Kingdom (discourse on the bread of life); etc. Our Lord backs up his teaching by performing many miracles, among the most outstanding of which are: changing water into wine at Cana in Galilee (Jn 2:1–11); raising the son of the widow of Naim (Lk 7:11–17) and the daughter of Jairus (Mk 5:21–43); the curing of possessed people (Mk 5:1–20), of lepers (Mk 8:22–26), and of people suffering from other diseases (Mk 1:29–31 and parallel passages in other Gospels; 2:1–12 and par.); 3:7–12 and par.); the multiplication of the loaves and fish (Mk 6:32–44 and par.). The Gospels also tell about Jesus' choice of the apostles (Mk 3:13–19 and par.): they are to be direct witnesses of his miracles and he will give them a detailed explanation of what his doctrine means, until the point comes when, with God's grace, they are able to recognize him as the Messiah and Son of God: this is a key stage in the whole Gospel narrative (cf. Mt 16:13–20; Mk 8:27–30; Lk 9:18–21; Jn 6:67–71).

From this point forward the Gospels concentrate on the lead-up to Christ's passion and death. In this section, to which St Luke gives much more space than the others, we see the hostility of the Jewish authorities growing to the point where they decide to put him to death (Mk 11:18 and par.; Jn 11:53). God has mysteriously planned that events should take this turn, and three times Jesus prophesies what will happen on the last days of his life on earth (Mk 8:31–33 and par.; Mk 9:30–32 and par.; Mk 10:32–34 and par.; Jn 10:17–18). He also manifests his divinity more clearly to his disciples (cf. Mk 9:2–10 and par.; Jn 12:28–30).

As regards Jesus' activity in Judea immediately prior to his triumphal entry into Jerusalem (Mk 11:1–11 and par.; Jn 12:12–19), what stand out are the miracles of the raising of Lazarus (Jn 11:1–45) and the curing of the blind man, Bartimaeus (Mk 10:46–52). The narratives of the last days of his ministry in Jerusalem (Mt 21–25 and par.; Jn 12:12–50) conclude the Gospels' account of his public life. In this account the evangelists have passed on to us the most important things our Lord said and did, the reason why he died on the cross

5. *Dei Verbum*, 17.

and rose in triumph—all of which constitute the core of the Gospel as preached by the apostles.

The accounts of our Lord's passion describe how he died, and they are followed by the witness of disciples who saw the risen Christ, ate with him, listened to his words and touched his glorified body. Before ascending into heaven, the risen Christ sends out the apostles to preach the Gospel and baptize all nations for the forgiveness of sins (Mt 28:18–20; Mk 16:15; Lk 24:27; cf. Jn 20:21–23).

The Gospels are "a perpetual and divine witness"[6] to all this. They were written to help fulfil Christ's commandment to preach the Gospel, the "good news", to all mankind. St John expressly states this at the end of his text: "Now Jesus did many other signs in the presence of the disciples, which are not written in this book; but these are written that you may believe that Jesus is the Christ, the Son of God, and that believing you may have life in his name" (Jn 20:30–31). God has given us the written Gospels to help ground us in the truths we already hold (cf. Lk 1:4): they are sincere, truthful accounts of the sayings and doings of Jesus Christ, true God and true Man.[7]

WHO WROTE THE GOSPELS?

God, who is the principal author of all Holy Scripture, is therefore the principal author of the four Gospels officially recognized by the Church. To compose them, "God chose certain men who, all the while he employed them in this task, made full use of their powers and faculties so that, though he acted in them and by them, it was as true authors that they consigned to writing whatever he wanted written, and no more."[8] In other words, the Holy Spirit used each evangelist as a living and intelligent instrument; he did not suspend his faculties, he raised them and applied them to compose the books, in such a way that, under divine inspiration, everything the evangelists affirm, state or imply in their writings, must be regarded as affirmed, stated or implied by the Holy Spirit.[9]

We know the names of the four evangelists through the testimony of Christian tradition, which from the beginning unanimously attributed these four books respectively to St Matthew, St Mark, St Luke and St John. In addition to Tradition, critical analysis of the literary features of the text and historical references in each Gospel support the unanimous, precise testimony of Tradition.

The earliest Christian writings which cite the Gospels go back to the last years of the first century. Thus St Clement of Rome (between 92 and 101) and St Ignatius of Antioch (who died around 107) speak of the four books but do not refer to their authors. It is Papias, bishop of Hierapolis in Asia Minor, who around 130 refers to Matthew and Mark as the authors of the first two Gospels:

6. *Dei Verbum*, 17. **7.** Cf. *Dei Verbum*, 19. **8.** *Dei Verbum*, 11. **9.** Ibid.

this is reported in Eusebius of Caesarea's *Ecclesiastical History* (around the middle of the fourth century).[10] At the end of the second century (between the years 178 and 188), St Irenaeus attests to the authenticity of the four Gospels in his book *Against Heresies*[11] (Irenaeus had wide experience of the Church; a native of Asia Minor, he lived for a time in Rome and became bishop of Lyons in Gaul: hence the importance of what he has to say). From around the same time we have the statements in the "Muratorian Canon", a document of Roman origin. Around the start of the third century Clement of Alexandria, writing in Alexandria, in Egypt, and Tertullian, who represents the tradition of the churches of the north of Africa (Carthage), give the four saints as the recognized authors of the four Gospels.

From the fourth century onwards, given the rapid spread of the Church, so many ecclesiastical writers give the same four authors that it would be tedious to list them here.

What tradition tells us is corroborated by evidence in the text of the Gospels themselves. In St John's Gospel it says that "the disciple whom Jesus loves" (cf. Jn 21:20–24) is its author. But this must be St John, as can be deduced from the text of the Gospels as a whole. As regards the Synoptics, certain evidence as to authorship can be gleaned, but nowhere are we told who precisely the human authors are. Thus, for example, we can notice that the First Gospel has a more Jewish ring about it than the others; that the Second seems to be written for people in Rome and that it treats the figure of St Peter in a very particular way; and that the Third has the same style as the Acts of the Apostles: it is as if it were the first part of a two-volume work.

Data of this type support the arguments based on Christian Tradition, which attributes the First Gospel to St Mathew, who wrote it for Palestinian Christians of Jewish origin; the Second to St Mark, who wrote it in Rome and who was the disciple of St Peter; and the Third to the Antiochene physician and disciple of St Paul, St Luke, who also wrote the Acts of the Apostles.

In the early centuries it was extremely necessary for the Church to identify which were the true Gospels and who wrote them, for there were already many apocryphal books in circulation which heretics used to help spread their errors. In replying to heresy the Christian apologists put forward the genuine apostolic tradition, making it quite clear that the Gospels officially used in the Church came either from apostles themselves—St Matthew and St John—or from their immediate disciples, so-called "apostolic men"—St Mark and St Luke.

So the Gospels' apostolic origin and authenticity—that is, that they were written precisely by those to whom they are attributed—are something that has been held in all parts of the Church from the first centuries. In his book *Against Faustus*[12] St Augustine presents the clinching argument: "You should believe that this is Matthew's because the Church has preserved this book ever since the time when Matthew lived, through an uninterrupted series of generations, in an unfailing succession, down to our own day."

10. 3, 39. **11.** 3, 1, 1. **12.** 28, 2.

WHEN WERE THE GOSPELS WRITTEN?

Christian Tradition is unanimous in attesting that St Matthew was the first to put the Gospel in writing in the Hebrew tongue. The earliest testimony to this effect is that of Papias, bishop of Hierapolis, part of whose book *An Explanation of the Sayings of the Lord* has been preserved for us by the quotations taken from it by Eusebius in his *Ecclesiastical History*.[13] Early tradition also says that some years later St Mark, in Rome, wrote down what he heard St Peter say in his preaching. Some Fathers say that he wrote it immediately after St Peter's death;[14] others, during the apostle's lifetime.[15] Of St Luke, Tradition states that, being a disciple of St Paul, he wrote down what he heard apostles say or what he had picked up indirectly and verified.[16] All concur in suggesting that St John was the last to write his Gospel, the so-called "spiritual" Gospel.[17]

Tradition clearly states that St Matthew was the first to write; but this text written in the language of the Jews has not come down to us. Our copy of the Gospel of St Matthew is the Greek edition, substantially the same as the original Hebraic and definitely later than the Gospel according to St Mark, as we shall see later when we discuss the connexion among the first three Gospels.

We do not know the exact year in which each Gospel was written: it was not literary practice at the time for writings to carry the author's name or the date; but we can certainly establish limits within which the Gospels must have been written by inferring from the data of tradition and from the texts themselves. We have already noted that some early ecclesiastic authors say that St Mark wrote in Rome, a little before or a little after the death of St Peter, which occurred in the year 64 (or 67 at the latest). Added to this there is the fact that the first three Gospels speak prophetically of the destruction of Jerusalem, which had not yet taken place: they mention that it will happen but they are imprecise about when it will happen. There are grounds, therefore, for thinking that the first three Gospels could have been written before the year 70, that is, before the destruction of the Holy City.

Another argument which confirms this is an inference drawn from the Acts of the Apostles: that book goes up as far as St Paul's imprisonment in Rome, which lasted from 61 to 63, and it seems more than reasonable to deduce that Acts was composed immediately after this imprisonment or fairly soon after it. Then, if, as we have said, the Third Gospel contains features which make it look like volume one of a work extending to the Acts of the Apostles, we might conclude that Luke wrote his Gospel sometime before he wrote Acts. These arguments point to dates prior to the year 70.

However, the Gospel of St John is in a different position. Tradition attests that it was written by the apostle St John in Ephesus after his exile on the island

13. 3, 39. **14.** *Against Heresies*, 3, 2, 1. **15.** Clement of Alexandria, as quoted by Eusebius, *Ecclesiastical History*, 6, 14. **16.** Cf. *Against Heresies*, 3, 1, 1. **17.** *Ecclesiastical History*, 6, 25.

of Patmos, that is, around the year 100, perhaps a very short time before he died.[18] For more documentation on this subject see the special introduction provided for each Gospel.[19]

HOW DID THE GOSPELS COME TO BE WRITTEN?

We have seen what the Gospels are, their general content, who wrote them, and when. At this point we should ask about how God arranged for the Gospel of Jesus Christ to be written down in the four books the Church possesses. The evangelists, whom the Holy Spirit chose for this work, were direct witnesses of Jesus (in the case of St Matthew and St John) or indirect (in the case of St Mark and St Luke, disciples respectively of St Peter and St Paul). Before being written down, the content of these was handed on orally, starting on the day of Pentecost.[20]

We can distinguish three stages in the shaping of the Gospels: (i) our Lord's preaching; (ii) the preaching and catechesis of the apostles; (iii) the work of writing done by the evangelists under the inspiration of the Holy Spirit.

(i) The Sower of the word, the divine Master who chose the apostles, instructed them in his teaching, made them the pillars, the foundation, of his Church, with St Peter at their head, and sent them out to preach the Gospel to the whole world. Our Lord took pains to get his teaching across to them in such a way that they could easily grasp it and be able to remember it. The net result was that, even before the Resurrection, the apostles already understood that one of the reasons Jesus performed miracles was to move people to have faith in him. Our Lord not only proclaimed the Gospel: he actually carried it out through his presence on earth, through what he said and did and especially through his death, resurrection, ascension into heaven and sending of the Holy Spirit.[21]

18. *Against Heresies*, 3, 1, 1. **19.** The apostolicity of the Gospels is an undeniable fact. As to when exactly each was written, there is a number of possible answers. As to the process whereby they came to be written, what Vatican II's Constitution *Dei Verbum,* 19 says should be followed. *Dei Verbum,* 19 reads: "Holy Mother Church has firmly and with absolute constancy maintained and continues to maintain, that the four Gospels just named, whose historicity she unhesitatingly affirms, faithfully hand on what Jesus, the son of God, while he lived among men, really did and taught for their eternal salvation, until the day when he was taken up (cf. Acts 1:1–2). For, after the ascension of the Lord, the apostles handed on to their hearers what he had said and done, but with that fuller understanding which they, instructed by the glorious events of Christ and enlightened by the Spirit of truth, now enjoyed. The sacred authors, in writing the four Gospels, selected certain of the many elements which had been handed on, either orally or already in written form, others they synthesized or explained with an eye to the situation of the churches, the while sustaining the form of preaching, but always in such a fashion that they have told us the honest truth about Jesus. Whether they relied on their own memory and recollections or on the testimony of those who 'from the beginning were eyewitnesses and ministers of the Word' their purpose in writing was that we might know the 'truth' concerning the things of which we have been informed (cf Lk. 1:2–4)." **20.** *Dei Verbum*, 19. **21.** Cf. *Dei Verbum,* 17; Pontifical Biblical Commission, Instruction *Sancta Mater Ecclesia* (21 April 1964), 2.

When our Lord arose from the dead, the apostles clearly realized his divinity: thus, Thomas confesses his faith by saying to Jesus, "My Lord and my God!" The risen Jesus opened their minds and explained to them the Scriptures—the Old Testament—causing their hearts to burn when he showed how what the prophets had foretold, and what he himself had foretold, had been fulfilled in him (Lk 24:44–48). Now they grasped the inner meaning of everything they had heard and seen Jesus do. When passing on to us our Lord's words "Destroy this temple, and in three days I will raise it up," in which he refers to his death and resurrection, St John comments that "when he was raised from the dead, his disciples remembered that he had said this and they believed the scripture and the word which Jesus had spoken" (Jn 2:19, 22).

(ii) The Holy Spirit, the Spirit of Truth whom our Lord promised to send reminded the apostles of everything Jesus said, and enabled them to understand the whole truth concerning Christ and his saving mission, and the meaning of his words and miracles, which prior to this they had failed to grasp fully (Jn 14:26; 16:13). And in addition to this the Holy Spirit constantly guided the apostles in their teaching and moved them boldly to preach the truth concerning Christ (cf. Acts 2:36).

"The apostles proclaimed particularly the death and resurrection of the Lord; in bearing witness to Christ they accurately described his life and repeated his words, suiting them to the capacity of their audiences to understand what he meant" (cf. Acts 2:33–36).[22] As well as this "first preaching" aimed at the conversion of both Jews and Gentiles, which proclaimed the fact of the death and resurrection of Christ and the main features of his life on earth (cf. Acts 10:36), the apostles also devoted time to improving the formation of those already converted, to help them deepen their faith and shape their lifestyle to that faith: this "apostolic catechesis" trained Christians to explain to enquirers the reason for their faith and their hope (1 Pet 2:5).

It is only reasonable to presume that the early Christians were very keen to know as much as possible about our Lord's life, his miracles, his meetings with the crowds and with individuals, the circumstances of his birth, of his passion and death, his appearances after his resurrection, etc.: and the more they learned the more their piety increased. The apostles were aware that they constituted the foundation on which the Church was built and that their writings would be read by Christians in every era, and not just their own; however, they did try to meet the needs of their listeners. The faithful "devoted themselves to the apostles' teaching and fellowship, to the breaking of the bread and the prayers" (Acts 2:42): this undoubtedly was the setting for which the apostles' first accounts of Christ were devised. They do not all tell the same things or tell them in the same way; but they do agree on basics, because they were witnesses of the same events and heard the same words spoken by Jesus. St John expressly says this when he writes: "That which was from the beginning, which we have heard, which we have seen with our own eyes, which we have looked upon and

22. Pontifical Biblical Commission, Instruction *Sancta Mater Ecclesia*, 2.

touched with our hands, concerning the word of life … we proclaim also to you, so that you may have fellowship with us" (1 Jn 1:1–3).

Although the apostles had helpers in this task, it is they who were primarily responsible, as qualified witnesses of Christ and people whom he sent out to continue his saving work. They were very careful to make sure that nothing inaccurate about Jesus was taught, and they made sure to omit nothing important. By continuing Jesus' teaching in this way, they were not only the immediate source of oral Tradition: they were the zealous custodians of that Tradition, and were guided by the Holy Spirit. St Peter, whom our Lord placed at the head of the apostolic college, took the initiative in preaching the Gospel, as we see in the Acts of the Apostles, and his teaching had a decisive influence on the way our Lord's words and deeds have been passed on to us in the first three Gospels: he preached the Gospel in Jerusalem, Antioch and Rome, the places where the Gospels of Matthew, Luke and Mark, respectively originated.

(iii) What were the evangelists doing when they produced their Gospels, under the inspiration of the Holy Spirit? St Luke gives us the answer to this question at the start of his book: "Inasmuch as many have undertaken to compile a narrative of the things which have been accomplished among us, just as they were delivered to us by eyewitnesses and ministers of the word, it seemed good to me also, having followed all things closely for some time past, to write an orderly account for you, most excellent Theophilus, that you may know the truth concerning the things of which you have been informed" (Lk 1:1–4). The evangelists gave of their very best when writing their books, intent as they were on the good of the Church and seeking to strengthen their readers in the faith and encourage them to do the will of Christ. To this purpose, they used the best sources available—what the apostles preached, or their own personal recollections. Naturally they availed themselves of any earlier writings which recorded parts of Christ's life or things he said. They collected all the oral and written material they could lay their hands on, and then each author organized it to suit his purpose. They took account of their immediate readership and how best to communicate with it. Depending on their own personal qualities and their readers' needs, they put the emphasis on some or other aspects of our Lord's life and teaching. But in all this process the Holy Spirit was influencing them: God, as we have said, is the principal author of these documents.[23]

We do know that they selected what they considered most important—whether intrinsically more important, or because previous writers had omitted it. We read in John's Gospel that "There are also many other things which Jesus did; were every one of them to be written, I suppose that the world itself could not contain the books that would be written" (Jn 21:25). At other times they provide a summary of what our Lord did, or collect together everything he said about one particular subject or said in one particular place. And sometimes they explain something which readers might otherwise find confusing, or point out the

23. Cf. *Dei Verbum*, 11.

significance of certain events, showing that they were foretold in the Old Testament.[24] The evangelists, therefore, were not merely re-compilers of material which was already being handed on; no: using the material available to them they applied their minds, aided by the Holy Spirit through the charism of divine inspiration, in such a way that, although they were instruments subordinate to God, the principal author, they themselves were true authors of their books and each left on his book the mark of his own personality.

THE SYNOPTIC GOSPELS

The first three Gospels have many passages in common, even word for word. But they also contain many striking differences. By setting out their content in three parallel columns we can see these differences and similarities at a glance (*synopsis*), which is why they have come to be called "synoptic" Gospels. They are also said to share a *concordia discors*, a discordant agreement: in general they coincide, but in particulars they can differ. Thus, all three share about 350 verses. St Matthew and St Luke coincide in an *additional* 230–240 verses; St Matthew and St Mark in 170–180 and St Mark and St Luke in about 50. The study of the possible causes of these coincidences and differences is usually called the "synoptic question". Many different and complicated theories have been devised to solve this problem.

Here we can only outline the question in broad terms. Recalling what we said about the date of composition of the Gospels, we know from Church Tradition that the first to write a Gospel was St Matthew, who wrote it in the language of the Jews. A little later St Mark and St Luke wrote theirs: if they had access to St Matthew's text at the time this would explain how the three have so many verses in common.

It is also possible that very early on there were in existence certain short texts containing sayings of our Lord, which St Luke would have used and which could also have been used for the Greek edition of St Matthew. If the latter did happen it could explain the similarities (especially in parts where our Lord's words are given) between the Gospel of St Matthew and that of St Luke. Besides, in the production of the Greek edition of St Matthew, the writer must have also had access to the Gospel of St Mark, which would explain why there are verses common to Matthew and Mark not found in Luke (Luke also used St Mark's Gospel, but independently of the Greek Matthew, which would explain why there are verses common to Mark and Luke which are not found in Matthew). But in addition to all this borrowing, each of the three had his own particular sources of inspiration: St Matthew, his personal recollections; St Mark, St Peter's catechesis and very personal accounts; St Luke, who never met Jesus, seems to have been the one who consulted the greatest number of

24. Cf. *Dei Verbum*, 19.

eyewitnesses and written documents—all of which helps us understand the differences and similarities in the synoptic Gospels.

THE GOSPELS ARE TRUE HISTORY

When scholars speak of the "historicity" of the Gospels they mean that the accounts they give are true accounts of what Jesus said and did. In other words, the evangelists are writing real history; they are telling of events which really happened, which people have actually witnessed and which impact on human history; and they are reporting things which were actually said. Although the Gospels are not a systematic history aiming at covering *all* events referring to Jesus Christ, this does not mean that they are not genuine history.

The Gospels also contain doctrinal teaching: in other words, the evangelists were not only concerned to record mere facts for posterity; they sought also to explain what those facts meant in God's plan of salvation, and how man is supposed to respond to them.

For example: St Matthew reports that when Joseph was puzzled on finding that Mary was expecting a child, "an angel of the Lord appeared to him in a dream, saying, 'Joseph, son of David, do not fear to take Mary your wife, for that which is conceived in her is of the Holy Spirit; she will bear a son, and you shall call his name Jesus, for he will save his people from their sins'" (Mt 1:20–21). But St Matthew does not stop there; he goes further than just report on the event, adding: "All this took place to fulfil what the Lord had spoken by the prophet: 'behold, a virgin shall conceive and bear a son, and his name shall be called Emmanuel' (which means, God with us)" (Mt 1:22–23). So the description of the event is followed by an explanation of it: God has already foretold through Isaiah the future virginal birth of the Saviour, and now the divine oracle is coming true. Showing that it has come true is obviously not a matter of anecdotal interest: it is a call to the readers to respond in faith and to commit their lives to Jesus Christ.

Hence the special importance of the *historicity* of the Gospels: it is a matter that involved and will always involve the eternal destiny of man, and therefore no one should be indifferent to it. The Gospels were written for man's salvation; as the fourth evangelist puts it so well: "Now Jesus did many other signs in the presence of the disciples, which are not written in this book; but these are written that you may believe that Jesus is the Christ, the Son of God, and that believing you may have life in his name" (Jn 20:30–31).

Since the historicity of the Gospels is so important, we can appreciate how historical sciences can help us go deeper into the text; but we also realize that to decide on the *truthfulness* of what the Gospels contain is not something to be left to the mercy of developments in these sciences or to the opinion of specialists: it is faith that decides that, though faith avails itself of human reason and the tools it uses.

The Church, who has by God' s command the duty and right of protecting, handing on and interpreting Holy Scripture, "has firmly and with absolute constancy maintained and continues to maintain, that the four Gospels just named, whose historicity she unhesitatingly affirms, faithfully hand on what Jesus, the Son of God, while he lived among men, really did and taught for their eternal salvation."[25] Every effort made to understand the Gospel better is highly praiseworthy, but any interpretation is always subordinate to what the Church, aided by the Holy Spirit, taught from the very beginning, about this divine treasure entrusted to her by God. For, as St Augustine put it, "I would not believe in the Gospel were I not moved to do so by the authority of the Church."[26]

Down the centuries Christian Tradition shows that the historical character of the Gospels has always been taken as an undisputed truth. Their historicity is, in the first instance, part of our faith: the Gospels are books which narrate history and, like all the books of the Bible, they are inspired by God. Hence, since they have God as their principal author (which is a matter of faith), the history which they contain is, without doubt, true history, for God cannot deceive or be deceived. At the same time, the Church has always maintained that this historicity, which our faith assures us of, has also a solid basis in reason: competent historico-literary critical scholarship, even if pursued on the margin of faith, provided it really uses serious, scientific arguments, fully supports faith in the historical truthfulness of the Gospels.

The Gospels narrate the life of our Lord Jesus Christ, the Son of God become man. And just as the most holy humanity of our Lord can be seen and contemplated with the physical eye, whereas his divinity can be discovered only with the eye of faith, similarly, the Gospel accounts can be checked by historico-critical methods only in those areas which are verifiable by human tools. And just as Jesus' miracles and words were, for those who experienced them, signs of his divine mission, so those Gospel accounts which can be tested by historical science are a guarantee of the veracity of those others which cannot be tested by reason and are accepted on faith.

Let us take some examples. Historical research can show that Christ was crucified in the time of Pontius Pilate; that he preached in Palestine; that he gathered disciples around him; that he founded the Church; that on the third day after his death he began to appear to certain of his disciples and this led to an enormous change in their lives; that he raised Lazarus from the dead; etc. But what history on its own cannot do is provide any ultimate explanations of these historically verifiable facts; only the light of faith can explain them.

On the other hand, many episodes in Jesus' life are so concrete and so tiny in the framework of world history that it is very difficult to check them (or even the Gospels themselves) by referring to non-Christian sources. This does not mean that these details are not historically checkable, that is, theoretically possible to check, but that in practice it would be very difficult to find any

25. *Dei Verbum*, 19. **26.** *Contra Epist. Fundamenti*, 5,6; cf. *Confessions*, 6, 5, 7; 6, 7, 11.

documentation to support them, other than the Gospels themselves. In cases like this, as in so many others in world history, historical science can assess at least the degree of credibility which such accounts merit by critical examination of the testimonies themselves. Historians tend to require (i) that the authors be sincere, that is, that they are striving to tell the truth; and (ii) that they be well-informed on the matters in question. If careful study shows that these or similar requirements are met, then the document is historically acceptable. Well, in the case of the Gospels these requirements are in fact met.

(i) The human authors of the Gospels did write in order to pass on to us the truth about what they had seen and heard (cf. Lk 1:1–4; Jn 21:24). Although they did not write their histories in exactly the same way as modern historians (for example, as far as chronological and topographical exactness goes), they still really did try to tell the facts just as they happened. Thus in the case of St Matthew and St Luke, when they tell about the temptations Christ underwent in the desert, they give them in a different order but both of them tell us what really happened. It is also true that the evangelists were enlightened by the Holy Spirit when they wrote and that their purpose was to strengthen the faith of their readers; but that did not lead them to falsify events or neglect historical accuracy; on the contrary: the very articles of our faith include some which are historical facts, such as those to do with Christ's life (his incarnation, death, resurrection etc.), which is why St Paul asserts that if Christ had not risen, then our faith would be in vain (cf. 1 Cor 15:14, 17). Hence the evangelists do what they set out to do precisely by telling the true story of what happened.

However, each evangelist, under the inspiration of the Spirit, tries to lay special emphasis on particular aspects of Jesus and his work: and to this end each plans his book differently. The evangelists, even those who were witnesses of Jesus' public life, each remember things differently depending on their mentality and the circumstances in which they are operating. The Holy Spirit does help them to remember and to understand everything they have seen and heard (Jn 14:16) but this does not cancel out their human faculties or the use of memory. Also, each evangelist drew on different sources, and these sources had peculiarities of their own—thus explaining the different order in which they narrate words and events in our Lord's life, and the differences which we find between Gospel and Gospel. But this does not in any way take from their historicity; on the contrary, as St Augustine explains, "it is quite likely that the evangelists believed they had a duty to tell things in the order in which God suggested them to their memory, at least in matters where the order in which they were reported in no way took from the truth and authority of the Gospel. For the Holy Spirit distributes gifts to each individually as he wills (1 Cor 12:11). He directed and ruled the minds of the saints [the sacred writers] to ensure that the books would have full authority; in bringing to their minds the things they should write, the Holy Spirit would allow each to plan his narrative as he thought fit and in such away that anyone who read it carefully and devoutly would be able to read it with God's help."[27]

27. *De consensu Evangelistarum*, 2, 21, 51.

Another proof of the evangelists' sincerity is their fortitude in bearing persecution, even to the point of giving their lives to bear witness to the truth they pass on to us in their writings. From what has been said, it is clear that the human authors of the Gospels were sincere and strove to tell the truth.

(ii) But investigation into the historicity of the Gospels needs to go further than that: were the writers well-informed about the subject in question, or were they, unintentionally, mistaken or misled? In reply to this question we must say that, humanly speaking, they were very well-informed, because they have been eyewitnesses of the events they describe or had been in contact with eyewitnesses. We should also add that the educational method used by Jesus — which was similar to rabbinical method of the time—consisted in repeating the same teachings time and again, to ensure his disciples got a good grasp of them. This learning method, based on exercising memory, meant that the apostles could remember many sayings of Jesus which the evangelists later put down in writing. The fact that they sometimes do not pass on exactly the same wording must be due to (a) the fact that Jesus said these things often, on different occasions and in different ways in the course of his preaching in various parts of Palestine; (b) the evangelists being more concerned about getting the meaning right than giving his exact words; (c) differences naturally arising in translations from the original into Greek.

Another factor which gives us the guarantee that the evangelists were not mistaken is that their narratives coincide in essentials with the preaching of St Peter after Pentecost, as reported in the Acts of the Apostles. There are no grounds, therefore, for thinking that the Gospel story was the product of the fertile hyper-imagination of the first generation of Christians: from the very first moment, fifty days after the Resurrection, the very same things were still being proclaimed, and the apostles, in their zeal to perform the mission of preaching entrusted to them by our Lord, were extremely careful not to pass on anything which was not true. A proof of this is that the Church never accepted as authentic later outpourings of popular imagination such as the apocryphal gospels.

The evangelists, then, were well-informed about the material they were transmitting; and the fact that their books were received by the Church as divinely inspired indicates that their content concurred with what the apostles, in their preaching about Jesus, had spread everywhere. It is true that the evangelists do not present our Lord's life in the way a modern biography would; but they do give us reliable information about what Jesus, the Son of God, taught and did when he was living among us. They do not tell us everything about Christ, but they have left us a permanent and divine witness to the truth we need to know about our Lord and his teaching. After the meticulous research the Gospels have been subjected to over the past two centuries, any serious critic must accept that the sacred books are true history. The main difficulty which some people experience is the fact that supernatural phenomena, the miracles of Jesus, appear frequently in the Gospels. Ultimately this involves questions of faith: either one accepts the supernatural or one does not. So in fact we find that one of two things happens: if a person accepts the supernatural and God's direct intervention in human and physical events, that is, the possibility of miracles, the key question of the historical truthfulness of the Gospels is solved in the affirmative; if a person does not accept the possibility of God's directly intervening in history in this way, then from the outset he denies the historicity of the Gospels, because if he denies the possibility of miracles he cannot accept as true writings which report miracles even if those documents are historical according to the criteria of scholarship.

Summing up what we have said, we can assert that when our faith tells us that the Holy Gospels "faithfully hand on what Jesus, the Son of God, while he lived among men, really did and taught for their eternal salvation, until the day of his ascension,"[28] this faith is based on a solid, reasonable foundation; it is not a blind option; it is based on certain facts which are part of history and which have been passed down to us in reliable documents (the Gospels) in the bosom of a society which authenticates them (the Church), and which has faithfully conserved them and which offers us a correct interpretation of them. But these historical facts can only be deeply understood and fully accepted if one has the divine gift of faith. We have already quoted (see p. 18, note 9) St Augustine's advice to those who find some passages in the Gospels an obstacle to their conversion.

This concludes our general introduction to the four Gospels. The characteristics of each particular Gospel will be dealt with briefly in the introduction which precedes it.

28. *Dei Verbum*, 19.

Introduction to the Gospel according to Matthew

With the help of God we are going to enter a golden city, more precious than all the gold the world contains. Let us notice what its foundations are made of, and find its gates to be composed of sapphires and precious stones. In Matthew we have the best of guides. Matthew is the door by which we enter, and we must enter eagerly, for if the guide notices that someone is distracted, he will exclude him from the city. What a magnificent and truly stately city it is; not like our cities, which are a mixture of streets and palaces. Here all are palaces. Let us, then, open the gates of our soul, let us open our ears, and as we prepare reverently to cross its threshold, let us adore the King who holds sway therein. What immense splendour shall we not find when we enter![1]

THE AUTHOR

As is the case with many other sacred books, the name of the author does not appear in the text of this Gospel. This fact is significant in itself: it indicates that the author was not writing a book of his own; he was bearing witness, briefly and in written form, to Jesus' life on earth, his teachings, his redemptive passion and death, and his glorious resurrection. He was seeking to show that Jesus of Nazareth, a descendant of David, a descendant of Abraham according to the flesh, who was virginally conceived in the pure womb of Mary by the working of the Holy Spirit, was the Messiah promised in the Old Testament prophecies; that he was the Incarnate Son of God, the Saviour of mankind, who had come to set men free from the slavery of sin, from the devil and from eternal death. In the presence of the divine and human majesty of Jesus Christ, St Matthew makes no appearance. Jesus is what matters, and what he said, and what he did.

However, the constant Tradition of the Church from earliest times identifies the human author of this Gospel as the apostle St Matthew, one of the first

1. St John Chrysostom, *Hom. on St Matthew*, 1, 8.

Twelve, whom Jesus himself called when he was working at his job as a "publican", that is, as a tax collector.

We have referred to St Matthew as being the "human author" of the first Gospel, the reason being that the principal author of the sacred books is God himself, who "inspired" the human authors, or hagiographers, in their literary work and "by supernatural power so moved and impelled them to write—he so assisted them when writing—that the things which he ordered, and those only, they, first, rightly understood, then willed faithfully to write down, and finally expressed in apt words and with infallible truth".[2]

However, when he communicates his grace to men, God, in his providence, does not destroy nature—in this case, the human qualities of the writers; rather, he raises nature on to a new level, perfects it and uses it to suit his purpose, in the same kind of way as a musician brings out all the qualities of a good violin. In two important respects, however, the comparison does not fit: firstly, because God, as well as using the writer as his instrument, also created him and endowed him with those qualities which he wanted him to have, to equip him to perform the task he planned for him; and secondly, because the sacred writer is not an inert instrument in God's hands: he is a living instrument, gifted with all his faculties. By virtue of this divine inspiration, a sacred book—in its entirety—is the end-product of close collaboration between God and the particular writer: each and every part of the book is really and in the proper sense of the word a work composed by God and a work composed by his instrument, the hagiographer; but, first and foremost, it is God's book, because God is its principal author.

St Matthew's Gospel, therefore—like any other biblical text—has characteristics of its own, which we will later examine. These help to identify the human author and they combine perfectly with the divine hallmark that is to be found in all the books of Holy Scripture.

Much less is known about St Matthew than about certain other New Testament authors, such as St Peter, St Paul and St John. We do know that very soon after being called to be an apostle, the immense joy he felt over his vocation led him to give a large dinner-party for his old friends and colleagues, a party attended by Jesus and by Matthew's new companions in the apostolate (cf. Mt 9:10–13; Mk 2:15–17; Lk 5:29–32). St Luke describes it as a "great feast" for "a large company": this shows that Matthew was well-to-do, had many friends and was held in high regard in Capernaum, despite the low opinion the Jews generally had of tax collectors.

St Matthew himself tells about how Jesus first called him (cf. Mt 9:9–12). When Jesus addressed him personally, in affectionate and at the same time imperative terms, Matthew immediately left his position as a tax collector and "followed him" (cf. Mt 9:9; Mk 2:14; Lk 5:27). From St Luke (5:27) we learn

2. Leo XIII, Enc. *Providentissimus Deus*.

that Matthew was also known as Levi, and St Mark (2:14) further specifies him as "Levi the son of Alphaeus".

Later on, St Matthew received a further call from our Lord: after spending a night in prayer Jesus chose him to be one of the twelve apostles (cf. Mt 10:1–14; Mk 3:13–19; Lk 6:12–16; 9:1–2; Acts 1:13). We find him involved in those episodes of our Lord's life where the Twelve are present—or the Eleven after Judas' betrayal. He was, therefore, an eye-witness of the life of Christ.

After the events reported in the Gospels and in the Acts of the Apostles, the New Testament tells us nothing further about Matthew's life. According to an ancient tradition reflected in Christian writers of the second to fourth centuries (St Irenaeus, Clement of Alexandria, Eusebius etc.), Matthew stayed in Palestine for some years, working with the other apostles, preaching the Gospel and ministering to the early Church. He would have written his Gospel towards the end of that period.

In later years he evangelized other countries, but no hard historical evidence is available in this connexion. Some documents speak of his ministering mainly in Abyssinia and Persia. The place, circumstances and date of his martyrdom are unclear.

DATE OF COMPOSITION

Written testimonies going back as early as the beginning of the second century assure us that St Matthew was the first to write down the Gospel of Jesus Christ "in the language of the Hebrews". This would have been the language spoken at that time by the Jews of Palestine; it is difficult to say exactly whether the evangelist used Hebrew or Aramaic, because no copy of the original text is extant nor any description of it—merely references to its existence. All we can say is that most scholars think that it must have been written in Aramaic. However, the Greek text of this Gospel was very soon accepted as canonical; Christian documents going back to the end of the first century show that it was widely known and used; these are: the *Didache*, written between AD 80 and 100; the *First Letter* of Pope St Clement of Rome, written between 92 and 101; the so-called *Letter of Barnabas*, written between 96 and 98; the *Letters* of St Ignatius of Antioch, martyred around the year 107; the writings of St Polycarp, who died in 156; etc.

We know that St Matthew wrote his (Aramaic) Gospel before the other evangelists wrote theirs; the estimated date is around the year 50. We do not know the date of composition of the Greek text, which is the one we have. Nor do we know whether the Greek editor was St Matthew himself or some other early Christian. The most likely date for this text is around the year 70.

In any event, the original text (Aramaic or Hebrew) of St Matthew is to be dated prior to the destruction of Jerusalem (the year 70) and indeed prior to St Paul's journey to Rome (the year 60). In view of the general agreement among the Fathers and ancient ecclesiastical writers and the unanimous tradition of the Church from the beginning, our Greek Matthew, the only Matthew text used as canonical, is substantially identical with the original Matthew written in the language of the Jews.

AUTHENTICITY AND CANONICITY

The authenticity of the original Jewish-language text of St Matthew has never been questioned by the Church: in other words, it was always held that the apostle St Matthew is the author of the Gospel which bears his name. Similarly the Church has always regarded the Greek text as canonical.

THE PURPOSE OF THIS GOSPEL

The primary purpose of St Matthew's Gospel is identical with that of the other three. St John sums up this purpose very well in these words: "Now Jesus did many other signs in the presence of his disciples, which are not written in this book; but these are written that you may believe that Jesus is the Christ, the Son of God, and that believing you may have life in his name" (Jn 20:30–31). His purpose is also to show, in the first place, that Jesus of Nazareth is the Christ or Messiah promised and announced in the Old Testament, that is, that the ancient prophecies find their fulfilment in Christ; and that this messiahship consists in Jesus being the Son of God, that is, that Jesus Christ is God. This truth is illustrated and explained by providing a rich account of our Lord's teaching and reporting certain aspects or episodes of his life among men. Finally, "the Kingdom of God" or "the Kingdom of heaven", predicted in the Old Testament, has now come to pass and been made visible in the life of Jesus and in that of the messianic people he founded and convoked—the Church. That Church is the perfecting of the ancient people of God—Israel—and is the visible beginning of the definitive and perfect Kingdom of heaven, to which all are called; but only those will be finally chosen who have responded generously to God's call.

To put it another way, the first Gospel sets out to proclaim in writing the "Good News", which the apostles preached orally—news to the effect that the salvation of Israel and of mankind, promised by God in the Old Testament, has now been brought into the world by Jesus Christ, the Messiah and the Son of

God; men are enabled to know this by the marvellous account given in the Gospel, in which Jesus' words and works explain each other and reach their climax in his redemptive sacrifice, his passion and death, followed by his glorious resurrection.

CONTENT

In broad outline the content of the first Gospel can be summed up as follows: the birth and infancy of Jesus; the announcement by John the Baptist, the Precursor, that Christ is about to begin his mission; Jesus' public ministry in Galilee and the calling of the twelve apostles: here he begins to reveal his messiahship and divinity, through his teaching and miracles; journeys Jesus makes with his disciples, doing good, curing the sick, teaching—in other words fulfilling what the Old Testament prophecies said about him; the last stage of his public ministry in Judea and Jerusalem; the account of his passion and death; his glorious resurrection; and post-resurrection appearances.

An outstanding feature of this Gospel is its account of five long discourses of Jesus; these, and the narrative parts of the Gospel, shed light on each other and lead the reader into the drama of Christ's death and the joy of his resurrection.

It is really not possible to fit St Matthew's Gospel into any kind of rigid structure. However, the following outline may be of some help:

1. *Birth and infancy of Jesus* (chaps. 1–2). A selection of the basic historical facts which illustrate and explain the following truths of faith: Jesus is the Messiah descended from David, the Saviour promised in the Old Testament; the Son of God, conceived by the action of the Holy Spirit and born of the Virgin Mary; the *Emmanuel* or *God-with-us* prophesied by Isaiah, protected during his infancy by a special providence of God (the fatherly care given him by St Joseph and the maternal affection of the Blessed Virgin Mary); the King of Israel, adored even by Gentiles (the wise men). The sober accounts—simple yet profound—comprising these two chapters already bring in quite a number of the basic truths about the divine and human mystery of Jesus Christ.

2. *Prelude to the public ministry of Jesus* (3:1—4:11). This takes place in regions which for centuries lived in hope of salvation—the Judean desert and the river Jordan. Here we find the Baptist's prophetic announcement of the imminence of the Kingdom of God; his exhortation to conversion and penance; the baptism of Jesus, accompanied by the revelation that he is the Son of God made man; and the temptations of Jesus in the wilderness.

PART ONE: JESUS' MINISTRY IN GALILEE

The beginnings of the message of salvation, the calling of the disciples and the convocation of the new people of God (4:12–25).

3. *The sermon on the mount.* Jesus, the supreme Teacher, Lawgiver and Prophet: the "discourse on the mount" (chaps. 5–7), the first of the five great discourses and a summary of the new Law of the Kingdom of God; Jesus, God made man, teaches a most sublime doctrine never heard before, in words simple yet totally demanding; this is the way of salvation which man must follow. This discourse is a kind of distillate of the teachings of Jesus the Messiah on evangelical holiness.

4. *The miracles of the Messiah* (chaps. 8–9). Following on these words or teachings, St Matthew's Gospel presents an array of miracles, whereby our Lord backs up his teaching with divine authority. These miracles also mean that the salvation promised in the Old Testament has come about in the person of Jesus. Also, the curing of the sick shows that men are being set free from sin, because sin is the ultimate cause of illness and mortality in man. These two chapters are, then, a kind of summary of "the words of the Messiah".

5. *From the old to the new people of God.* The first sending forth of the disciples, the "apostolic discourse", the hardening of the hearts of the religious leaders of Israel against Jesus' messiahship (chaps. 10–12); Jesus trains his twelve apostles for their immediate mission and for the future (chap. 10). In reaction to the proclamation of Jesus as Messiah—through his words and works and his convocation of the new messianic people (chaps. 3–10)—the Jewish leaders grow more and more opposed to him (chaps. 11–12). The scene is being set for their rejection of him, their plotting of his death, and the foundation of the Church as the new people of God.

6. *The parables of the Kingdom* (chap. 13). Despite this, Jesus continues to reveal to the people the mystery of the Kingdom of God, or Kingdom of heaven. This he does by means of parables—a teaching method suited to the capacity of his listeners. These parables contain a substantial proportion of his teaching concerning the Church which he will found; from a small beginning it will grow until the end of time. This "parabolic discourse" ends with a visit to Nazareth, where Jesus encounters the incredulity of his fellow-townsmen. This brings to an end what we might call the first part of St Matthew's Gospel.

7. *Jesus withdraws to the border country* (13:53—16:20). In view of the growing antagonism of the Jewish religious authorities and the martyrdom of John the Baptist, Jesus makes a series of evangelical journeys in the regions

adjoining Israel. His disciples accompany him. These journeys are an advance indication of the universality of the Gospel; but they also act as a form of retreat, enabling Jesus to continue his ministry undisturbed, and to avoid precipitating his passion. Jesus teaches his disciples, with an eye to founding his Church. Outside Israel proper, in Caesarea Philippi, Peter makes a confession of faith in Jesus as Messiah, and Jesus promises to make Peter the head of his Church (Mt 16:13–20).

PART TWO: JESUS' MINISTRY ON THE WAY TO JERUSALEM

8. *Towards Judea and Jerusalem* (16:21—17:27). The transfiguration of Jesus and new teachings (chap. 17): Jesus' divinity is revealed to his disciples.

9. *The discourse on the Church* (chap. 18): so called because it contains specific teaching about the life of the future Church, and the authority of the apostles and their successors.

Various teachings of Jesus—on marriage and virginity, poverty, humility, etc. (chap. 19); the parable of the labourers in the vineyard; the third announcement of the Passion, etc. (chap. 20).

PART THREE: JESUS' MINISTRY IN JERUSALEM

10. *Cleansing of the temple. Controversies* (21:1—23:39). This begins with his messianic entry into the Holy City and the temple (21:1–17), followed by teaching concerning Christ's authority (21:18–27) and three great allegorical parables (21:28—22:14) on salvation history and the mystery of the Church. Then comes an account of controversies with the Pharisees (22:15–46) in which they bring up various questions in the hope that Jesus will provide them with grounds for indicting him. These events lead to Jesus' invective against the scribes and Pharisees ("Woe to him …": 23:13–36) and his lament over the destruction of Jerusalem (23:37–39).

11. *The eschatological discourse.* This section ends with Jesus' prophecies about the destruction of Jerusalem and the end of the world—the "eschatological discourse" (chaps. 24–25): the prophecies (24:1–36) are followed by teaching about the vigilance required of a Christian (24:37—25:30). Our Lord illustrates his teaching by three parables—that of the unjust servant (24:45–51), that of the ten virgins (25:1–13), and the parable of the talents (25:14–30). The eschatological discourse ends with teaching on the Last Judgment, where Jesus himself will be the judge (25:31–46).

12. *The passion, death and resurrection of Jesus* (chaps. 26–28). Like the other three Gospels, St Matthew's devotes considerable space to its account of the passion and death of the Son of God, which embraces the truths

every Christian should know regarding the sacrifice of the Messiah. Two chapters cover the period from the anointing at Bethany (26:6–13), to the death of Jesus on the cross (27:45–56), his burial (27:57–61) and the placing of the guard over the tomb (27:62–66). At various points the Passion account throws light on Old Testament prophecies which predicted the Passion in one way or another.

Also like the other Gospels, St Matthew's ends with Jesus' victory over death through his glorious resurrection—a message of immense joy, hope and faith. It tells how the tomb was found to be empty (28:1–8, 11–15) and of the appearances of the risen Jesus to the holy women (28:9–10) and to the apostles (28:16–17). The Gospel ends with the proclamation of the absolute lordship of Jesus Christ, now glorified (28:18), and his charge to his disciples to preach the Gospel throughout the world, baptizing in the name of the three divine persons (28:19–20).

SPECIAL FEATURES

The Gospel of St Matthew is a divine and human work. God is the principal author of the book, and his purpose goes beyond that of the human author, his instrument. St Matthew—man, apostle and evangelist—does speak to us through these pages: but, above all, God himself is speaking. This means that no matter how much honest effort is put into studying and explaining this Gospel—or any other part of Holy Scripture—we can never grasp its full meaning. God's purpose in inspiring a particular man to write this book is to reveal to us something about himself and to entrust this text to his Church, which will make it comprehensible to us and helpful to our sanctification and eternal salvation. St Matthew's Gospel is one of the most precious of all the many gifts God has given us in Scripture; we should thank God for it, in the first instance; but we should also be grateful to the man who, with the help of divine inspiration, took pains to write it.

THE GOSPEL OF THE DISCOURSES OF THE LORD

St Matthew's Gospel has been called "the Gospel of the Discourses of the Lord" because of the five long discourses it contains. Through these we can hear Jesus' words and be present when he preaches. However, we should not forget that, since the Gospel was written under the inspiration of the Holy Spirit and has God as its principal author, the entire text—not just these discourses—is truly the word of God, and "all that the hagiographer (or sacred writer) affirms should be regarded as affirmed by the Holy Spirit".[3]

These five discourses are: the discourse on the mount (chaps. 5–7); the apostolic discourse (chap. 10); the parabolic discourse (chap. 13); the discourse on the Church (chap. 18); and the eschatological discourse (chaps. 24–25). There are also shorter discourses—such as Christ's indictment of the Pharisees and scribes (23:13–36) and some of his controversies with the Pharisees (12:25–45). Usually these discourses are preceded by other passages describing the development of events; the discourse part and narrative part of the account combine to help us understand the deep meaning of the works and words of Jesus.

THE GOSPEL OF FULFILMENT

Although each of the four Gospels was written for all men in all ages, God also wrote them for a particular immediate readership. In the case of Matthew, the text was obviously written in a manner suited to Christians of Jewish background—its immediate readers—as well as for later generations. Matthew, for example, is at pains to show that all the Old Testament finds its fulfilment in the person and work of Christ: at particularly important points in Jesus' life, the evangelist expressly points out that "this took place to fulfil what the Lord had spoken by the prophet" or words to that effect (cf., e.g., Mt 1:23; 2:6, 15, 17–18; 3:3–4; 4:4, 14–16; 5:17; 21:4–5, 16; 26:31; 27:9–10). This feature of his Gospel has led to its being called "the Gospel of fulfilment". Insight into the Old Testament in the light of the New is not unique to St Matthew's Gospel, for it was something Jesus was always teaching to his disciples and something that the Holy Spirit also revealed to them—it is the science of "understanding the Scriptures" (cf., e.g., Lk 24:32, 45; Acts 8:35)—but it was clearly an important factor in the evangelization of Jews and in their subsequent catechesis.

JESUS, THE REJECTED MESSIAH

In countless ways all the books of the New Testament show that Jesus is the promised Messiah, the Christ, the Lord (*Kyrios*) and the Son of God; and they also reveal the mystery of God, one essence and three persons.

But within this general teaching common to them all, it is clear from the particular accents it carries that Matthew's Gospel was addressed in the first instance to Christians of Jewish background. In keeping with what has been said about the "Gospel of fulfilment", it points out that the beginning of Christ's public preaching is the dawn of messianic light (cf. Mt 4:13–17) foretold by the prophet Isaiah (cf. Is 8:23—9:1); similarly the first cures Jesus performs (cf. Mt 8:16–17) are presented as fulfilling the words of the prophets, particularly Isaiah (cf. Is 53:4–5).

3. Vatican II, *Dei Verbum*, 11.

And, above all, the first Gospel contains teaching and events which dramatically emphasize the mystery of the rejection of Jesus, the promised Messiah, by the rulers of the Jews, and by many of the people, whom those rulers succeeded in misleading. Guided by the light of divine inspiration, the evangelist confronts this mystery in various ways: sometimes, when reporting how the scribes, Pharisees and chief priests react against Jesus, or when narrating the way he suffers during his passion, he stresses that all this, far from frustrating God's plan, was foreseen and predicted by the Old Testament prophets and fulfils what they predicted would happen (cf. Mt 12:17; 13:35; 26:54, 56; 27:9; etc.). At other times he explains that this rejection of the Messiah by Israel is in line with and a culmination of a whole history of infidelity to God's generosity and love (cf., e.g., Mt 21:28–44; 23:9–33). In any event the Gospel shows the pain Christ feels over Israel's failure to respond to his love and the punishment that lies in store for it if it fails to mend its ways (cf. Mt 23:37–39).

THE GOSPEL OF THE KINGDOM

St Matthew refers 51 times to "the Kingdom", St Mark 14 times and St Luke 39. But whereas the two last-mentioned speak of "the Kingdom of God", Matthew on all but five occasions uses the phrase "the Kingdom of heaven". This must certainly have been the phrase Jesus normally used, given the Jewish custom of the time not to utter the name of God—out of respect—but instead to use other equivalent terms such as "of heaven". The Kingdom of God comes into being with the arrival of Christ (cf. note on Mt 3:2) and, especially in the parables, Jesus explains what its features are (cf. note on Mt 13:3). The first Gospel is called the "Gospel of the Kingdom" because it throws so much light on these features.

THE DIVINITY OF JESUS

Christ's divinity is affirmed in various ways in this Gospel. From the conception of Jesus by the action of the Holy Spirit (Mt 1:20) to the trinitarian formula for Baptism at the end (Mt 28:19), the first Gospel asserts and stresses that Jesus, the Christ, is the Son of God. In numerous passages it mentions the relationship between the Father and the Son: Jesus is the Son of the Father, the Father is God, and the Son is equal to the Father. Some passages also place the Father, the Son and the Holy Spirit on the same level (the most famous being that just mentioned: Mt 28:19). What this means is that the revelation of the Blessed Trinity, a revelation expressly made by Jesus Christ, is affirmed in St Matthew's Gospel by the revelation that Jesus is the Son of the Father, and God like him.

In the light of this essential truth, that Jesus is the Son of God, all the other messianic titles which the Old Testament used in prophecies about the Saviour fall into place—Son of David, Son of man, Messiah, Lord.

THE GOSPEL OF THE CHURCH

This Gospel has also been called the "ecclesiastical Gospel" or the "Gospel of the Church". One reason for this is that the actual word "church" appears three times (cf. Mt 16:18; 18:17 twice). Another is that the Church, even without being expressly named, can be seen to be in the background of the narrative: it is hinted at in different ways in quite a few parables; its foundation is announced and explicitly expressed when Peter is promised the primacy (cf. Mt 16:17–19); its beginning can in some way be seen in the discourse in chapter 18; it is figuratively depicted in some episodes such as that of the calming of the storm (cf. Mt 8:23–27); it is cast in the role of the new, true Israel in the parable of the wicked tenants of the vineyard (cf. Mt 21:33–45); and its role as universal vessel of salvation is based on the apostolic charge which our Lord gives at the end of the Gospel. In effect, the Church forms a background to the entire text of this Gospel and is ever-present in the mind and heart of the evangelist—as it is in the mind and heart of Jesus Christ.

LITERARY STYLE

From what has been said about its content and structure it can be seen that the Gospel also has strong literary unity: every paragraph is written in line with the writer's purpose; this affects both the content of the writing and the context in which it is placed. As the reader grows more familiar with the text he notices more hints, more symbolism and additional teaching developing themes already covered quite elaborately.

The precision with which Matthew articulates Jesus' teaching comes across very clearly. He writes in a concise, sober and thoughtful style, and a person making his way through the book will find that it enters into his soul and brings him face to face with the powerful yet tender mystery of Jesus Christ.

Many commentators have pointed out that St Matthew's particular style has the effect of making many of his phrases easy to recognize: we often find ourselves quoting Matthew's version in preference to other Gospel accounts. For this reason his Gospel has been called the first Gospel of Christian catechesis.

ST MATTHEW'S GOSPEL IN THE LIFE OF THE CHURCH

From the end of the first century—in references by Pope St Clement—there is overwhelming evidence of predominant use of the St Matthew text in the teachings of the Church's Magisterium. The early Fathers are forever quoting it and many later Fathers commented on it (for example, there are ninety long homilies by St John Chrysostom) as did the great teachers of the Middle Ages (for example, St Thomas Aquinas) and later ecclesiastical writers.

1. BIRTH AND INFANCY OF JESUS

The ancestry of Jesus Christ Lk 3:23–38
1 1The book of the genealogy of Jesus Christ, the son of David, 1 Chron 17:11 Gen 5:1; 22:1
the son of Abraham.*
2Abraham was the father of Isaac, and Isaac the father of Gen 21:3, 12; 25:26; 29:35;
Jacob, and Jacob the father of Judah and his brothers, 3and Judah 49:10
the father of Perez and Zerah by Tamar, and Perez the father of 1 Chron 1:34
Hezron, and Hezron the father of Ram,[a] 4and Ram[a] the father of 1 Chron 2:5, 9
Amminadab, and Amminadab the father of Nahson, and Nahson Gen 38:29f
the father of Salmon, 5and Salmon the father of Boaz by Rahab, Ruth 4:18–22 1 Chron 2:10f
and Boaz the father of Obed by Ruth, and Obed the father of Ruth 4:13–17
Jesse, 6and Jesse the father of David the king. 2 Sam 12:24
And David was the father of Solomon by the wife of Uriah,
7and Solomon the father of Rehoboam, and Rehoboam the father 1 Chron
of Abijah, and Abijah the father of Asa,[b] 8and Asa[b] the father of 3:10–16

1:1. This verse is a kind of title to St Matthew's entire Gospel. The promises God made to Abraham for the salvation of mankind (Gen 12:3) are fulfilled in Jesus Christ, as is Nathan's prophecy to King David of an everlasting kingdom (2 Sam 7:12–16).

The genealogy presented here by St Matthew shows Jesus' human ancestry and also indicates that salvation history has reached its climax with the birth of the Son of God through the working of the Holy Spirit. Jesus Christ, true God and true man, is the expected Messiah.

The genealogy is presented in a framework of three series, each consisting of fourteen links which show the progressive development of salvation history.

For the Jews (and for other Eastern peoples of nomadic origin) genealogical trees were of great importance because a person's identity was especially linked to family and tribe, with place of birth taking secondary importance. In the case of the Jewish people there was the added religious significance of belonging by blood to the chosen people.

In Christ's time each family still kept a careful record of its genealogical tree, since because of it people acquired rights and duties.

1:6. Four women are named in these genealogies—Tamar (cf. Gen 38; 1 Chron 2:4), Rahab (cf. Josh 2:6, 17). Bathsheba (cf. 2 Sam 11:12, 24) and Ruth (cf. Book of Ruth). These four foreign women, who in one way or another are brought into the history of Israel, are one sign among many others of God's design to save all men.

By mentioning sinful people, God's ways are shown to be different from man's. God will sometimes carry out his plan of salvation by means of people whose conduct has not been just. God saves us, sanctifies us and chooses us to do good despite our sins and infidelities—and he chose to leave evidence of this at various stages in the history of our salvation.

a. Greek *Aram* **b.** Greek *Asaph*

Jehoshaphat, and Jehoshaphat the father of Joram, and Joram the
father of Uzziah, 9 and Uzziah the father of Jotham, and Jotham
the father of Ahaz, and Ahaz the father of Hezekiah, 10 and Hezekiah the father of Manasseh, and Manasseh the father of Amos,[c]
Ezra 1:32 and Amos[c] the father of Josiah, 11 and Josiah the father of Jechoniah and his brothers, at the time of the deportation to Babylon.
1 Chron 3:17 12 And after the deportation to Babylon: Jechoniah was the
Ezra 3:2 father of Shealtiel,[d] and Shealtiel[d] the father of Zerubbabel, 13 and
Zerubbabel the father of Abiud, and Abiud the father of Eliakim,
and Eliakim the father of Azor, 14 and Azor the father of Zadok, and
Zadok the father of Achim, and Achim the father of Eliud, 15 and
Eliud the father of Eleazar, and Eleazar the father of Matthan, and
Matthan the father of Jacob, 16 and Jacob the father of Joseph the
husband of Mary, of whom Jesus was born, who is called Christ.*

1:11. The deportation to Babylon, described in 2 Kings 24–25, fulfilled the prophets' warning to the people of Israel and their kings that they would be punished for their infidelity to the commandments of the Law of God, especially the first commandment.

1:16. Jewish genealogies followed the male line. Joseph, being Mary's husband, was the legal father of Jesus. The legal father is on a par with the real father as regards rights and duties. This fact provides a sound basis for recognizing St Joseph as Patron of the whole Church, since he was chosen to play a very special role in God's plan for our salvation; with St Joseph as his legal father, Jesus the Messiah has David as his ancestor.

Since it was quite usual for people to marry within their clan, it can be concluded that Mary belonged to the house of David. Several early Fathers of the church testify to this—for example, St Ignatius of Antioch, St Irenaeus, St Justin and Tertullian, who base their testimony on an unbroken oral tradition.

It should also be pointed out that when St Matthew comes to speak of the birth of Jesus, he uses an expression which is completely different from that used for the other people in the genealogy. With these words the text positively teaches that Mary conceived Jesus while still a virgin, without the intervention of man.

1:18. St Matthew relates here how Christ was conceived (cf. Lk 1:25–38): "We truly honour and venerate (Mary) as Mother of God, because she gave birth to a person who is at the same time both God and man" (St Pius V, *Catechism*, 1, 4, 7).

According to the provisions of the Law of Moses, engagement took place about one year before marriage and enjoyed almost the same legal validity. The marriage proper consisted, among other ceremonies, in the bride being brought solemnly and joyously to her husband's house (cf. Deut 20:7)

From the moment of engagement onwards, a certificate of divorce was needed in the event of a break in the relationship between the couple. The entire account of Jesus' birth teaches, through

c. Other authorities read *Amon* **d.** Greek *Salathiel*

[17]So all the generations from Abraham to David were fourteen
generations, and from David to the deportation to Babylon fourteen generations, and from the deportation to Babylon to the
Christ fourteen generations.

The virginal conception of Jesus, and his birth

[18]Now the birth of Jesus Christ[f] took place in this way. When his Lk 1:35
mother Mary had been betrothed to Joseph, before they came
together she was found to be with child of the Holy Spirit; [19]and
her husband Joseph, being a just man and unwilling to put her to
shame, resolved to send her away quietly. [20]But as he considered
this, behold, an angel of the Lord appeared to him in a dream,
saying, "Joseph, son of David, do not fear to take Mary your wife,

---

the fulfilment of the prophecy of Isaiah 7:14 (which is expressly quoted in vv. 22–23) that: 1) Jesus has David as his ancestor since Joseph is his legal father; 2) Mary is the Virgin who gives birth according to the prophecy; 3) the Child's conception without the intervention of man was miraculous.

1:19. "St Joseph was an ordinary sort of man on whom God relied to do great things. He did exactly what the Lord wanted him to do, in each and every event that went to make up his life. That is why Scripture praises Joseph as a 'just man' (Mt 1:19). In Hebrew a just man means a good and faithful servant of God, someone who fulfils the divine will (cf. Gen 7:1; 18:23–32; Ezek 18:5ff; Prov 12:10), or who is honourable and charitable towards his neighbour (cf. Tob 7:6; 9:6). So a just man is someone who loves God and proves his love by keeping God's commandments and directing his whole life towards the service of his brothers, his fellow men" (St Josemaría Escrivá, *Christ Is Passing By*, 40).

Joseph considered his spouse to be holy despite the signs that she was going to have a child. He was therefore faced with a situation he could not explain. Precisely because he was trying to do God's will, he felt obliged to put her away; but to shield her from public shame he decided to send her away quietly.

Mary's silence is admirable. Her perfect surrender to God even leads her to the extreme of not defending her honour or innocence. She prefers to suffer suspicion and shame rather than reveal the work of grace in her. Faced with a fact which was inexplicable in human terms she abandons herself confidently to the love and providence of God. God certainly subjected the holy souls of Joseph and Mary to a severe trial. We ought not be surprised if we also undergo difficult trials in the course of our lives. We ought to trust in God during them, and remain faithful to him, following the example Mary and Joseph gave us.

1:20. God gives his light to those who act in an upright way and who trust in his power and wisdom when faced with situations which exceed human understanding. By calling him the son of David, the angel reminds Joseph that he is the prov-

f. Other ancient authorities read *of the Christ*

Lk 1:31; 2:21 Acts 4:12 for that which is conceived in her is of the Holy Spirit; [21]she will
bear a son, and you shall call his name Jesus, for he will save his
Is 7:14 Lk 2:7 people from their sins." [22]All this took place to fulfil what the
Lord had spoken by the prophet:

[23]"Behold, a virgin shall conceive and bear a son,
and his name shall be called Emmanuel"

---

idential link which joins Jesus with the family of David, according to Nathan's messianic prophecy (cf. 2 Sam 7:12). As St John Chrysostom says: "At the very start he straightaway reminds him of David, of whom the Christ was to spring, and he does not wish him to be worried from the moment he reminds him, through naming his most illustrious ancestor, of the promise made to all his lineage" (*Hom. on St Matthew*, 4).

"The same Jesus Christ, our only Lord, the Son of God, when he assumed human flesh for us in the womb of the Virgin, was not conceived like other men, from the seed of man, but in a manner transcending the order of nature, that is, by the power of the Holy Spirit, so that the same person, remaining God as he was from eternity, became man, which he was not before" (St Pius V, *Catechism*, 1, 4, 1).

1:21. According to the Hebrew root, the name of Jesus means "saviour". After our Lady, St Joseph is the first person to be told by God that salvation has begun. "Jesus is the proper name of the God-man and signifies 'Saviour', a name given him not accidentally, or by the judgment or will of man, but by the counsel and command of God" [...]. All other names which prophecy gave to the Son of God—Wonderful Counsellor, Mighty God, Everlasting Father, Prince of Peace (cf. Is 9:6)—are comprised in this one name Jesus; for while they partially signified the salvation which he was to bestow on us, this name included the force and meaning of all human salvation" (St Pius V, *Catechism*, 1, 3, 5 and 6).

1:23. "Emmanuel": the prophecy of Isaiah 7:14, quoted in this verse, foretold about seven hundred years in advance that God's salvation would be marked by the extraordinary event of a virgin giving birth to a child. The Gospel here, therefore, reveals two truths.

The first is that Jesus is in fact the God-with-us foretold by the prophet. This is how Christian tradition has always understood it. Indeed the Church has officially condemned an interpretation denying the messianic sense of the Isaiah text (cf. Pius VI, Brief *Divina*, 1779). Christ is truly God-with-us, therefore, not only because of his God-given mission but because he is God made man (cf. Jn 1:14). This does not mean that Jesus should normally be called Emmanuel, for this name refers more directly to the mystery of his being the Incarnate Word. At the Annunciation the angel said that he should be called Jesus, that is, Saviour. And that was the name St Joseph gave him.

The second truth revealed to us by the sacred text is that Mary, in whom the prophecy of Isaiah 7:14 is fulfilled, was a virgin before and during the birth itself. The miraculous sign given by God that salvation had arrived was precisely that a woman would be a virgin and a mother at the same time. "Jesus Christ came forth from his mother's womb without injury

(which means God with us). [24]When Joseph woke from sleep, he
did as the angel of the Lord commanded him; he took his wife,
[25]but knew her not until she had borne a son;* and he called his
name Jesus.

---

to her maternal virginity. This immaculate and perpetual virginity forms, therefore, the just theme of our eulogy. Such was the work of the Holy Spirit, who at the conception and birth of the Son so favoured the Virgin Mother as to impart fruitfulness to her while preserving inviolate her perpetual virginity" (St Pius V, *Catechism*, 1, 4, 8).

1:25. St John Chrysostom, addressing himself to St Joseph, comments: "Christ's conception was the work of the Holy Spirit, but do not think this divine economy has nothing to do with you. For although it is true that you had no part in the generation of Christ, and that the Virgin remained inviolate, nevertheless, what pertains to a father (not injuring the honour of virginity) that do I give you—the naming of the child. For 'you shall call his name'. Although you have not generated him, you will act as a father to him. Hence it is that, beginning with giving him his name, I associate you intimately with the one who is to be born" (*Hom. on St Matthew*, 4).

Following the Greek text strictly, the New Vulgate version says: "et non cognoscebat eam, *donec* peperit filium". The literal English translation is: "and he knew her not *until* she had borne a son". The word "*donec*" (until) of itself does not direct our attention to what happened afterwards; it simply points out what has happened up to that moment, that is, the virginal conception of Jesus Christ by a unique intervention of God. We find the same word in John 9:18, where it says that the Pharisees did not believe in the miraculous cure of the man blind from birth "until" (*donec*) they called his parents. However, neither did they believe afterwards. Consequently, the word "until" does not refer to what happens later.

The Vulgate adds after "*filium*" the words "*suum primogenitum*", which in the Bible simply means "the first son", without implying that there are any other children (cf. Ex 13:2). This Latin variant gives no ground whatsoever for thinking that our Lady had other children later. See the note on Lk 2:7.

The Church has always taught that the perpetual virginity of our Lady is a truth to be held by Catholics. For example, the following are the words of the Lateran Council of AD 649: "If anyone does not profess according to the holy Fathers, that in the proper and true sense, the holy, ever-virgin, immaculate Mary is the Mother of God, since in this last age not with human seed but of the Holy Spirit she properly and truly conceived the Divine Word, who was born of God the Father before all ages, and gave him birth without any detriment to her virginity, which remained inviolate even after his birth: let such a one be condemned" (can. 3).

St Jerome gives the following reasons why it was fitting that the Mother of God, as well as being a virgin, should also be married: first, so that Mary's child would be clearly a descendant of King David (through the genealogy of St Joseph); second, to ensure that on having a son her honour would not be questioned nor any legal penalty be imposed on her; third, so that during the flight into Egypt she would have the help and pro-

The adoration of the Magi

Lk 2:1–7 2 [1]Now when Jesus was born in Bethlehem of Judea in the days
of Herod the king, behold, wise men from the East came to
Num 24:17 Jerusalem, saying, [2]"Where is he who has been born king of the
Jews? For we have seen his star in the East, and have come to

---

tection of St Joseph. He even points to a fourth possible reason, expressly taken from St Ignatius Martyr, and to which he seems to give less importance—that the birth of Jesus would go unnoticed by the devil, who would have no knowledge of the virginal conception of our Lord (cf. *Comm. on Matthew*, 1, 1).

2:1. "King Herod": four different Herods are mentioned in the New Testament. The first is Herod the Great, referred to in this passage and in the next; the second, his son, Herod Antipas, who had St John the Baptist beheaded (Mt 14:1–12) and who abused our Lord during his passion (Lk 23:7–11); the third, Herod Agrippa I, a grandson of Herod the Great, who executed the apostle St James the Greater (Acts 12: 1–3), imprisoned St Peter (Acts 12:4–7), and died suddenly and mysteriously (Acts 12:20–23). The fourth, Herod Agrippa II, was Herod Agrippa I's son. It was before him that St Paul answered Jewish accusations when he was a prisoner in Caesarea (Acts 25:23).

Herod the Great, who appears here, was the son of non-Jewish parents. He came to power with the aid and as a vassal of the Romans. He was a consummate politician and among other things he rebuilt the temple in Jerusalem on a lavish scale. Herod the Great had a persecution complex; everywhere he saw rivals to his throne. He was notorious for his cruelty: he killed over half of his ten wives, some of his children and many people of standing. This information derives largely from the Jewish historian Flavius Josephus, who wrote towards the end of the first century, and it confirms the cruel picture drawn in the Gospels.

"Wise men": these were learned men, probably from Persia, who devoted themselves to the study of the stars. Since they were not Jews, they can be considered to be the very first Gentiles to receive the call to salvation in Christ. The adoration of the wise men forms part of the very earliest documented tradition: the scene is already depicted at the beginning of the second century in the paintings in the catacombs of St Priscilla in Rome.

2:2. The Jews had made known throughout the East their hope of a Messiah. The wise men knew about this expected Messiah, king of the Jews. According to ideas widely accepted at the time, this sort of person, because of his significance in world history, would have a star connected with his birth. God made use of these ideas to draw to Christ these representatives of the Gentiles who would later be converted

"The star had been hidden from them so that, on finding themselves without their guide, they would have no alternative but to consult the Jews. In this way the birth of Jesus would be made known to all" (St John Chrysostom, *Hom. on St Matthew*, 7). Chrysostom also points out that "God calls them by means of the things they are most familiar with: and he shows them a large and extraordinary star so that they would be impressed by its size and beauty" (ibid., 6). God called the wise men in the midst of their ordinary occupations, and he still calls people in

worship him." [3]When Herod the king heard this, he was troubled,
and all Jerusalem with him; [4]and assembling all the chief priests
and scribes of the people, he inquired of them where the Christ
was to be born. [5]They told him, "In Bethlehem of Judea; for so it Mic 5:2
is written by the prophet: Jn 7:42

---

that way. He called Moses when he was shepherding his flock (Ex 3:1–3), Elisha the prophet ploughing his land with oxen (1 Kings 19:19–20), Amos looking after his herd (Amos 7:15). … "What amazes you seems natural to me: that God has sought you out in the practice of your profession! That is how he sought the first, Peter and Andrew, James and John, beside their nets, and Matthew, sitting in the custom-house. And—wonder of wonders!—Paul, in his eagerness to destroy the seeds of Christianity" (St Josemaría Escrivá, *The Way*, 799).

"Like the Magi we have discovered a star—a light and a guide in the sky of our soul. 'We have seen his star in the East and have come to worship him (Mt 2:2).' We have had the same experience. We too noticed a new light shining in our soul and growing increasingly brighter. It was a desire to live a fully Christian life, a keenness to take God seriously" (St J. Escrivá, *Christ Is Passing By*, 32).

2:4. In all Jewish circles at the time of Jesus, the hope was widespread that the Messiah would come soon. The general idea was that he would be a king, like a new and even greater David. Herod's worry is therefore all the more understandable: he governed the Jews with the aid of the Romans and cruelly and jealously guarded his crown. Due to his political ambition and his lack of religious sense, Herod saw a potential Messiah-King as a dangerous rival to his own worldly power.

In the time of our Lord, both Herod's monarchy and the occupying Romans (through their procurators) recognized the Sanhedrin as the representative body of the Jewish people. The Sanhedrin was, therefore, the nation's supreme council which ruled on day-to-day affairs, both religious and civil. The handling of the more important questions needed the approval of either the king (under Herod's monarchy) or the Roman procurator (at the time of the direct Roman occupation of Palestine). Following Exodus 24:1–9 and Numbers 11:16, the Sanhedrin was composed of seventy-one members presided over by the high priest. The members were elected from three groupings: 1) the chief priests, that is, the leaders of the principal priestly families; it was these families who appointed the high priest (the chief priests also included anybody who had formerly held the high priesthood); 2) the elders, or the leaders of the most important families; 3) the scribes, who were teachers of the Law or experts on legal and religious matters; the majority of these scribes belonged to the party or school of the Pharisees. In this passage of St Matthew only the first and third of the above groups are mentioned. This is understandable since the elders would have no authority in the matter of the birth of the Messiah—a purely religious question.

2:5–6. The prophecy referred to in this passage is Micah 5:1. It is worth noting that Jewish tradition interpreted this prophecy as predicting the Messiah's exact place of birth and as referring to a particular person. The second text thus teaches us once more that the prophecies of the Old Testament are fulfilled in Jesus Christ.

[6] 'And you, O Bethlehem, in the land of Judah,
are by no means least among the rulers of Judah;
for from you shall come a ruler
who will govern my people Israel.'"

[7] Then Herod summoned the wise men secretly and ascertained
from them what time the star appeared; [8] and he sent them to
Bethlehem, saying, "Go and search diligently for the child, and
when you have found him bring me word, that I too may come
and worship him." [9] When they had heard the king they went their
way; and lo, the star which they had seen in the East went before
them, till it came to rest over the place where the child was.
[10] When they saw the star, they rejoiced exceedingly with great

---

2:8. Herod tried to find out exactly where the Child was—not, of course, to adore him, as he said, but to dispose of him. Such was Herod's exclusively political view of things. Yet neither his shrewdness nor his wickedness could prevent God's plans from being fulfilled. Despite Herod's ambition and his scheming, God's wisdom and power were going to bring salvation about.

2:9. "It might happen at certain moments of our interior life—and we are nearly always to blame—that the star disappears, just as it did to the wise kings on their journey. [...] What should we do if this happens? Follow the example of those wise men and ask. Herod used knowledge to act unjustly. The Magi use it to do good. But we Christians have no need to go to Herod nor to the wise men of this world. Christ has given his Church sureness of doctrine and a flow of grace in the sacraments. He has arranged things so that there will always be people to guide and lead us, to remind us constantly of our way" (St Josemaría Escrivá, *Christ Is Passing By*, 34).

2:10. "Why were they so happy? Because those who had never doubted received proof from the Lord that the star had not disappeared. They had ceased to contemplate it visibly, but they kept it always in their souls. Such is the Christian's vocation. If we do not lose faith, if we keep our hope in Christ who will be with us 'until the consummation of the world' (Mt 28:20), then the star reappears. And with this fresh proof that our vocation is real, we are conscious of a greater joy which increases our faith, hope and love" (*Christ Is Passing By*, 35).

2:11. The gifts they offered—gold, frankincense and myrrh—were those most valued in the East. People feel the need to give gifts to God to show their respect and faith. Since they cannot give themselves as a gift, which is what they would wish, they give instead what is most valuable and dear to them.

The prophets and the psalmists foretold that the kings of the earth would pay homage to God at the time of the Messiah (Is 49:23). They would offer him their treasures (Is 60:5) and adore him (Ps 72:10–15). Through this action of the wise men and the offering of their gifts to Jesus, these prophecies begin to be fulfilled.

The Council of Trent expressly quotes this passage when it underlines the veneration that ought to be given to Christ in the Eucharist: "The faithful of Christ venerate this most holy sacrament with

joy; 11and going into the house they saw the child with Mary his Ps 72:10–15
mother, and they fell down and worshipped him. Then, opening Is 60:6
their treasures, they offered him gifts, gold and frankincense and
myrrh. 12And being warned in a dream not to return to Herod, they
departed to their own country by another way.

The flight into Egypt. The massacre of the Innocents

13Now when they had departed, behold, an angel of the Lord Ex 2:15
appeared to Joseph in a dream and said, "Rise, take the child and
his mother, and flee to Egypt, and remain there till I tell you; for
Herod is about to search for the child, to destroy him." 14And he
rose and took the child and his mother by night, and departed to

---

the worship of latria which is due to the true God. [...] For in this sacrament we believe that the same God is present whom the eternal Father brought into the world, saying of him, 'Let all God's angels worship him' (Heb 1:6; cf. Ps 97:7). It is the same God whom the Magi fell down and worshipped (cf. Mt 2:11) and, finally, the same God whom the apostles adored and worshipped (cf. Mt 28:17)" (*De SS. Eucharistia*, chap. 5).

St Gregory Nazianzen has also commented on this verse, as follows: "Let us remain in adoration; and to him, who, in order to save us, humbled himself to such a degree of poverty as to take our flesh, let us offer him not only incense, gold and myrrh (the first as God, the second as king, and the third as one who sought death for our sake), but also spiritual gifts, more sublime than those which can be seen with the eyes" (*Oratio*, 19).

2:12. The involvement of the wise men in the events at Bethlehem ends with yet another act of respectful obedience and cooperation with God's plans. Christians also should be receptive to the specific grace and mission God has given them. They should persevere in this even if it means having to change any personal plans they may have made.

2:14. St John Chrysostom, commenting on this passage, draws particular attention to Joseph's faithfulness and obedience: "On hearing this, Joseph was not scandalized, nor did he say, 'This is hard to understand. You yourself told me not long ago that he would save his people, and now he is not able to save even himself. Indeed, we have to flee and undertake a journey and be away for a long time...'. But he does not say any of these things, because Joseph is a faithful man. Neither does he ask when they will be coming back, even though the angel had left it open when he said 'and remain there till I tell you'. This does not hold him back: on the contrary, he obeys, believes and endures all the trials with joy" (*Hom. on St Matthew*, 8).

It is worth noting also how God's way of dealing with his chosen ones contains light and shade: they have to put up with intense sufferings side by side with great joy: "It can be clearly seen that God, who is full of love for man, mixes pleasant things with unpleasant ones, as he did with all the saints. He gives us neither dangers nor consolations in a continual way, but rather he makes the lives of the just a mixture of both. This is what he did with Joseph" (ibid.).

Hos 11:1 Egypt, 15and remained there until the death of Herod. This was to
fulfil what the Lord had spoken by the prophet, "Out of Egypt
have I called my son."
16Then Herod, when he saw that he had been tricked by the
wise men, was in a furious rage, and he sent and killed all the
male children in Bethlehem and in all that region who were two
years old or under, according to the time which he had ascertained
Jer 31:15 from the wise men. 17Then was fulfilled what was spoken by the
prophet Jeremiah:
Gen 35:19 18"A voice was heard in Ramah,
wailing and loud lamentation,
Rachel weeping for her children;
she refused to be consoled,
because they were no more."

Return to Nazareth

19But when Herod died, behold, an angel of the Lord appeared in
Ex 4:19 a dream to Joseph in Egypt, saying, 20"Rise, take the child and his

---

2:15. The text of Hosea 11:1 speaks of a child who comes out of Egypt and is a son of God. This refers in the first place to the people of Israel whom God brought out of Egypt under Moses' leadership. But this event was a symbol or prefiguration of Jesus, the head of the Church, the new people of God. It is in him that this prophecy is principally fulfilled. The sacred text gives a quotation from the Old Testament in the light of its fulfilment in Jesus Christ. The Old Testament achieves its full meaning in Christ, and, in the words of St Paul, to read it without keeping in mind Jesus is to have one's face covered by a veil (cf. 2 Cor 3:12–18).

2:16–17. Concerning Herod, see the note on Matthew 2:1. God permitted Herod to be wicked and cruel in trying to kill the Child. His cruel behaviour also fulfils the prophecy of Jeremiah 31:15. The Church regards these children as the first martyrs to give their lives for Christ. Martyrdom brought them justification (that is, salvation) and gave them the same grace as Baptism gives; their martyrdom is, in fact, Baptism by blood. St Thomas Aquinas comments on this passage in the following way: "How can it be said that they died for Christ, since they could not use their freedom? […] God would not have allowed that massacre if it had not been of benefit to those children. St Augustine says that to doubt that the massacre was good for those children is the same as doubting that Baptism is of use to children. For the Holy Innocents suffered as martyrs and confessed Christ *non loquendo, sed moriendo*, not by speaking, but by dying" (*Comm. on St Matthew*, 2, 16).

2:18. Ramah was the city in which Nebuchadnezzar, king of Babylon, concentrated the Israelites he had taken prisoner. Since Ramah was in the land of Benjamin, Jeremiah puts this lament for the children of Israel in the mouth of Rachel, the mother of Benjamin and Joseph. So great was the misfortune of those exiled to Babylon that Jeremiah says poetically that Rachel's sorrow is too great to allow

mother, and go to the land of Israel, for those who sought the
child's life are dead." 21And he rose and took the child and his
mother, and went to the land of Israel. 22But when he heard that
Archelaus reigned over Judea in place of his father Herod, he was
afraid to go there, and being warned in a dream he withdrew to
the district of Galilee. 23And he went and dwelt in a city called Lk 1:26; 2:39
Nazareth, that what was spoken by the prophets might be fulfilled, Is 11:1; 53:2 Jn 1:46
"He shall be called a Nazarene."

2. PRELUDE TO THE PUBLIC MINISTRY OF JESUS

John the Baptist preaching in the wilderness

3 1In those days came John the Baptist, preaching in the Mk 1:2–8 Lk 3:3–18;
wilderness of Judea, 2"Repent,* for the kingdom of heaven 1:13; 4:17

---

of consolation. "Rachel was buried in the racecourse near Bethlehem. Since her grave was nearby and the property belonged to her son, Benjamin (Ramah was of the tribe of Benjamin), the children beheaded in Bethlehem could reasonably be called Rachel's children" (St John Chrysostom, *Hom. on St Matthew*, 9).

2:22. History tells us that Archelaus was ambitious and cruel like his father. By the time Joseph returned from Egypt, the new king was quite notorious. "In the different circumstances of his life, St Joseph never refuses to think, never neglects his responsibilities. On the contrary, he puts his human experience at the service of faith. When he returns from Egypt, learning 'that Archelaus reigned over Judea in place of his father Herod, he was afraid to go there'. In other words, he had learned to work within the divine plan. And to confirm that he was doing the right thing, Joseph received an instruction to return to Galilee" (St J. Escrivá, *Christ Is Passing By*, 42).

2:23. Nazareth, where the Annunciation had taken place (Lk 1:26), was a tiny and insignificant Palestinian village. It was located in Galilee, the most northerly part of the country. The term "Nazarene" refers to Jesus' geographic origin, but his critics used it as a term of abuse when he began his mission (Jn 1:46). Even in the time of St Paul the Jews tried to humiliate the Christians by calling them Nazarenes (Acts 24:5). Many prophets predicted that the Messiah would suffer poverty and contempt (Is 52:2ff.; Jer 11:19; Ps 22) but the words "he shall be called a Nazarene" are not to be found as such in any prophetic text. They are, rather, as St Jerome points out, a summary of the prophets' teaching in a short and expressive phrase. However, St Jerome himself (cf. *Comm. in Isaiah*, 11:1) says that the name "Nazarene" fulfils the prophecy of Isaiah 11:1: Christ is the "shoot" (*nezer*, in Hebrew) of the entire race of Abraham and David.

3:1. The expression "in those days" does not specify the exact time of the event in question. It is sometimes used merely as an opening phrase to mark the beginning

Is 40:3 Jn 1:23

is at hand." 3For this is he who was spoken of by the prophet
Isaiah when he said,

"The voice of one crying in the wilderness:
Prepare the way of the Lord,
make his paths straight."

---

of a new episode. In this case, in fact, it can be calculated that some twenty-five years have elapsed since the Holy Family's return from Egypt. This is only an estimate, because the exact date of their return has not been established.

On the date of the start of John the Baptist's preaching, see Luke 3:1–3.

The word "wilderness" has a wider meaning here than we give it today. It does not refer to a sandy or rocky desert, but rather to arid regions, low in vegetation.

3:2. "Repent": Christ's redeeming work ushers in a new era in the Kingdom of God. This brings such advance in salvation history, that what is required from now on is a radical change in man's behaviour towards God. The coming of the Kingdom means that God has intervened in a special way to save mankind, but it also implies that we must be open to God's grace and reform our ways. Christ's life on earth compels people to take a stand—either for God or against him ("He who is not with me is against me, and he who does not gather with me scatters": Lk 11:23). Given man's sinful state after original sin, the newly-arrived Kingdom requires that all men repent of their past life. To put it another way, they have to stop going away from God and instead try to get closer to him. Since sin hinders this conversion, it is impossible to turn back to God without performing acts of penance. Conversion is not simply a question of making a good resolution to mend our ways; we have to fulfil that resolution, even if we find it difficult. Penance grows only where there is humility—and everyone should admit sincerely that he is a sinner (cf. 1 Jn 1:8–10). Obedience also goes hand in hand with penance; everyone ought to obey God and keep his commandments (cf. 1 Jn 2:3–6).

The literal translation of the Greek is "Repent". But precisely because the very essence of conversion consists in doing penance, as we have said, the New Vulgate has *paenitentaim agite* ("do penance"). This translation conveys the deeper meaning of the text.

Man's whole life, in fact, consists in constantly correcting his behaviour, and therefore implies a continual doing of penance. This turning back to God was preached continually by the prophets in the Old Testament. Now, however, with the coming of Christ, this penance and turning to God are absolutely essential. That Christ took on our sins and suffered for us does not excuse us from making a true conversion; on the contrary, it demands it of us (cf. Col 1:24).

"Kingdom of heaven": this expression is identical to "Kingdom of God". The former is the one most used by St Matthew, and is more in line with the Jewish turn of phrase. Out of reverence, the Jews avoided pronouncing the name of God and substituted other words for it, as in this case. "Kingdom of God" or "Kingdom of heaven" was a concept used already in the Old Testament and in religious circles at the time of Christ. But it occurs particularly frequently in Jesus' preaching.

The phrase "Kingdom of God" can refer in a general way to God's dominion

[4]Now John wore a garment of camel's hair, and a leather girdle 2 Kings 1:18
around his waist; and his food was locusts and wild honey. [5]Then
went out to him Jerusalem and all Judea and all the region about
the Jordan, [6]and they were baptized by him in the river Jordan,
confessing their sins.*

---

over creatures; but normally, as in this text, it refers to God's sovereign and merciful involvement in the life of his people. Man's rebellion and sin broke the order originally established in creation. To re-establish it, God's intervention was needed again; this consisted in the redeeming work of Christ, Messiah and Son of God. It was preceded by a series of preliminary stages in salvation history throughout the Old Testament. Consequently, the Kingdom of God, announced as imminent by John the Baptist, is brought into being by Jesus. However, this is an entirely spiritual one and does not have the nationalistic dimension expected by Jesus' contemporaries. He comes to save his people and all mankind from the slavery of sin, from death and from the devil, thereby opening up the way of salvation.

In the period between the first and second comings of Christ, this Kingdom of God (or Kingdom of heaven) is, in fact, the Church. The Church makes Christ (and therefore also God) present among all peoples and calls them to eternal salvation. The Kingdom of God will be brought to completion only at the end of this world, that is, when our Lord comes to judge the living and the dead at the end of time. Then God will reign over the blessed in a perfect way.

In the passage we are considering, John the Baptist, the last of the Old Testament prophets, preaches the imminence of the Kingdom of God, ushered in by the coming of the Messiah.

3:3. By quoting Isaiah 40:3, St Matthew makes it clear that St John the Baptist has a mission as a prophet. This mission has two purposes—first, to prepare the people to receive the Kingdom of God; second, to testify before the people that Jesus is the Messiah who is bringing that Kingdom.

3:4. The Gospel gives a brief outline of the extremely austere life of St John the Baptist. His style of life is in line with that of certain Old Testament prophets and is particularly reminiscent of Elijah (cf. 2 Kings 1:8; 2:8–13ff). The kinds of food and dress described are of the most rudimentary for the region in question. The locust was a kind of grasshopper; the wild honey probably refers to substances excreted by certain local shrubs rather than to bees' honey. In view of the imminent coming of the Messiah, John underlines, with his example, the attitude of penance preceding great religious festivals (similarly, in its Advent liturgy the Church puts John before us as a model and invites us to practise mortification and penance). In this way, the point made in the previous verse (concerning John's view of his mission as precursor of Christ) is fulfilled. A Christian's entire life is a preparation for his meeting with Christ. Consequently, mortification and penance play a significant part in his life.

3:6. John's baptism did not have the power to cleanse the soul from sin as Christian baptism does. The latter is a sacrament, a sign, which produces the grace it signifies. Concerning the value of John's baptism, see the note on Mt 3:11.

Gen 3:15

[7]But when he saw many of the Pharisees and Sadducees
coming for baptism, he said to them, "You brood of vipers! Who
warned you to flee from the wrath to come? [8]Bear fruit that befits
repentance, [9]and do not presume to say to yourselves, 'We have
Abraham as our father'; for I tell you, God is able from these
stones to raise up children to Abraham. [10]Even now the axe is laid
to the root of the trees; every tree therefore that does not bear
good fruit is cut down and thrown into the fire.

[11]"I baptize you with water for repentance, but he who is
coming after me is mightier than I, whose sandals I am not worthy

Rom 2:28f; 4:12
Jn 8:33, 39
Lk 13:7–9
Jn 15:6
Jn 1:15, 26f, 33
Acts 1:5

3:7. St John reproaches the Pharisees and Sadducees for their attitude towards him. His preaching and baptism are not simply one more purification rite. Rather, they demand a true interior conversion of the soul, as a necessary predisposition to reach the grace of faith in Jesus. In the light of this explanation, we can understand why the prophetic words of St John the Baptist were so hard-hitting; as it turned out, most of these people did not accept Jesus as the Messiah.

"Pharisees": these constituted the most important religious group in Jesus' time. They kept the Law of Moses rigorously and also the oral traditions which had built up around it. They gave as much importance to these latter, indeed, as to the Law itself. They strongly opposed the influence of Greek paganism and totally rejected the homage paid to the Roman emperor. Among them there were men of great spiritual eminence and sincere piety; but there were many others who exaggerated pharisaical religiosity to the extreme of fanaticism, pride and hypocrisy. It was this perversion of the true Israelite religion that John the Baptist (and later our Lord) castigated.

"Sadducees": the Sadducees constituted a smaller religious group than the Pharisees, but they included many influential people, most of them from the main priestly families. They accepted the written Law, but, unlike the Pharisees, they rejected oral tradition. They also rejected certain important truths, such as the resurrection of the dead.

On the political front, they went along easily with the terms dictated by the Romans, and they acquiesced in the introduction of pagan customs into the country. Their opposition to Christ was even more pronounced than that of the Pharisees.

3:9–10. St John the Baptist's listeners believe their salvation is assured because they are descendants of Abraham according to the flesh. But St John warns them that to pass God's judgment it is not enough to belong to the chosen people; they must also yield the good fruit of a holy life. If they fail to do this, they will be thrown into the fire, that is, into hell, the eternal punishment, because they did not do penance for their sins. See the note on Mt 25:46.

3:11. St John the Baptist did not limit himself to preaching penance and repentance; he encouraged people to receive his baptism. This baptism was a way of interiorly preparing them and helping them to realize that the coming of Christ was imminent. By his words of encouragement and by their humble recognition of their sins, they were prepared to

to carry; he will baptize you with the Holy Spirit and with fire.
12His winnowing fork is in his hand, and he will clear his threshing floor and gather his wheat into the granary, but the chaff he
will burn with unquenchable fire."

Jesus is baptized

13Then Jesus came from Galilee to the Jordan to John, to be baptized by him. 14John would have prevented him, saying, "I need to

Mk 1:9–11
Lk 3:21f
Jn 1:31–34

---

receive Christ's grace through Baptism with fire and the Holy Spirit. To put it another way, John's baptism did not produce justification, whereas Christian Baptism is the sacrament of initiation, which forgives sin and bestows sanctifying grace. The effectiveness of the sacrament of Christian Baptism is expressed in Catholic teaching when it says that the sacrament gives grace *ex opere operato*. This means that grace is given by virtue of Christ who acts through the sacrament, and not by virtue of the merits of either the minister or the recipient of the sacrament. "When Peter baptizes, it is Christ who baptizes [...]. When Judas baptizes, it is Christ who baptizes" (St Augustine, *In Ioann. Evang.*, 6).

The word "fire" points in a metaphorical way to the effectiveness of the Holy Spirit's action in totally wiping out sins. It also shows the life-giving power of grace in the person baptized. Foremost among the personal qualities of St John the Baptist is his remarkable humility; he resolutely rejects the temptation of accepting the dignity of Messiah which the crowds apparently wanted to bestow on him. Carrying the sandals of one's master was a job for the lowest of servants.

3:12. Verses 10 and 12 refer to judgment by the Messiah. This judgment has two parts: the first occurs throughout each man's life and ends in the Particular Judgment immediately after death; the second occurs at the time of the Last Judgment. Christ is the judge in both instances. Let us remember the words of St Peter in Acts 10:42: "And he commanded us to preach to the people, and to testify that he [Jesus] is the one ordained by God to be judge of the living and the dead." The judgment will give to each person the reward or punishment merited by his good or bad actions.

It is worth noting that the word "chaff" does not refer only to bad deeds; it refers also to useless ones, for example, lives lacking in service to God and men. God will judge us, therefore, for our omissions and our lost opportunities.

"Don't let your life be barren. Be useful. Make yourself felt. Shine forth with the torch of your faith and your love. With your apostolic life, wipe out the trail of filth and slime left by the unclean sowers of hatred. And set aflame all the ways of the earth with the fire of Christ that you bear in your heart" (St Josemaría Escrivá, *The Way*, 1).

3:13. Jesus spent about thirty years (Lk 3:23) in what is normally called his "hidden life". We should marvel at the silence of the Incarnate Word of God during this period. There may be many reasons why he waited so long before beginning his public ministry, but one factor may have been the Jewish custom whereby rabbis did not carry out their function as teachers until they were thirty

be baptized by you, and do you come to me?" 15But Jesus
answered him, "Let it be so now; for thus it is fitting for us to
1 Pet 4:14 fulfil all righteousness." Then he consented.* 16And when Jesus
Ezek 1:1 was baptized, he went up immediately from the water, and behold,
the heavens were opened[g] and he saw the Spirit of God descend-
Mt 17:5 Ps 2:7 ing like a dove, and alighting on him; 17and lo, a voice from

---

years old. Whatever the reason, by his long years of work beside St Joseph, our Lord teaches all Christians the sanctifying value of ordinary life and work.

The Baptist prepares the people to receive the Messiah, according to God's plan; and it is only then that Jesus commences his public life.

3:14. St. John's reluctance to baptize Jesus is not surprising since he had given such forthright witness to Him. Jesus did not need to be baptized by John since he had no sin, but he chose to receive this baptism (see the note on v. 15) before beginning to preach, so to teach us to obey all God's commands (he had already subjected himself to circumcision, presentation to the temple and being redeemed as the first-born). God wished to humble himself even to the extent of submitting to the authority of others.

3:15. "Righteousness" (or "justice") has a very deep meaning in the Bible; it refers to the plan which God, in his infinite goodness and wisdom, has marked out for man's salvation. Consequently, "to fulfil all righteousness" should be understood as fulfilling God's will and designs. Thus we could translate "fulfil all righteousness" as; "fulfil everything laid down by God". Jesus comes to receive John's baptism and hence recognizes it as a stage in salvation history—a stage foreseen by God as a final and immediate preparation for the messianic era. The fulfilment of any one of these stages can be called an act of righteousness. Jesus, who has come to fulfil his Father's will (Jn 4:34), is careful to fulfil that saving plan in all its aspects. See the note on Mt 5:6.

3:16. Jesus possessed the fullness of the Holy Spirit from the moment of his conception. This is due to the union of human nature and divine nature in the person of the Word (the dogma of the hypostatic union). Catholic teaching says that in Christ there is only one person (who is divine) but two natures (divine and human). The descent of the Spirit of God spoken of in the text indicates that just as Jesus was solemnly commencing his messianic task, so the Holy Spirit was beginning his action through him. There are many texts in the Old Testament which speak of the showing forth of the Holy Spirit in the future Messiah. This sign of the Spirit gave St John the Baptist unmistakable proof of the genuineness of his testimony concerning Christ (cf. Jn 1:29–34). The mystery of the Holy Trinity is revealed in the baptism of Jesus: the Son is baptized; the Holy Spirit descends on him in the form of a dove; and the voice of the Father gives testimony about his Son. Christians must be baptized in the name of the three divine persons. "If you have sincere piety, the Holy Spirit will descend on you also and you will hear the voice of the Father saying to you from above: 'This was not

g. Other ancient authorities add *to him* **h.** Or *my Son, my* (or *the*) *Beloved*

heaven, saying, "This is my beloved son,[h] with whom I am well pleased." Is 42:1

Jesus fasts and is tempted

Mk 1:12f
Lk 4:1–13

4 [1]Then Jesus was led up by the Spirit into the wilderness to be Heb 4:15
tempted by the devil. [2]And he fasted forty days and forty Ex 34:28
1 Kings 19:8

---

my son, but now after Baptism he has been made my son'" (St Cyril of Jerusalem, *De Baptismo*, 14).

3:17. Literally, as the RSV points out, "This is my Son, my (*or* the) Beloved". When the expression "the beloved" goes with "the son", normally it refers to an only son (cf. Gen 16; Jer 6:26; Amos 8:10; Zech 12:10). Repetition of the article and the solemnity of the passage show that, in the language of the Bible, Jesus is not just one more among the adopted sons of God, nor even the greatest of them. Rather, it declares strongly and correctly that Jesus is "the Son of God", the Only-begotten, who is totally different from other men because of his divine nature (cf. Mt 7:21; 11:27; 17:5; Jn 3:35; 5:20; 20:17; etc.).

Here we can see the fulfilment of the messianic prophecies, especially Isaiah 42:1, which is applied now to Jesus through the voice of the Father speaking from heaven.

4:1. Jesus, our Saviour, allowed himself to be tempted because he so chose; and he did so out of love for us and to instruct us. However, since he was perfect, he could only be tempted externally. Catholic teaching tells us that there are three levels of temptation: 1) suggestion, that is, external temptation, which we can undergo without committing any sin; 2) temptation, in which we take a certain delight, whether prolonged or not, even though we do not give clear consent; this level of temptation has now become internal and there is some sinfulness in it; 3) temptation to which we consent; this is always sinful, and, since it affects the deepest part of the soul, is definitely internal. By allowing himself to be tempted, Jesus wanted to teach us how to fight and conquer our temptations. We will do this by having trust in God and prayer, with the help of God's grace and by having fortitude.

Jesus' temptations in the desert have a deep significance in salvation history. All the most important people throughout sacred history were tempted—Adam and Eve, Abraham, Moses, and the chosen people themselves. Similarly with Jesus. By rejecting the temptations of the devil, our Lord atones for the falls of those who went before him and those who come after him. He is an example for us in all the temptations we were subsequently to have, and also for the battles between the Church and the power of the devil. Later Jesus teaches us in the Our Father to ask God to help us with his grace not to fall at the time of temptation.

4:2. Before beginning his work as Messiah, that is, before promulgating the New Law or New Testament, Jesus prepares himself by prayer and fasting in the desert. Moses acted in the same way before proclaiming, in God's name, the Old Law on Mount Sinai (Ex 34:28), Elijah, too, journeyed for forty days in the desert to fulfil the Law (1 Kings 19:5–8).

The Church follows Jesus' footsteps by prescribing the yearly Lenten fast. We

Gen 3:1–7 nights, and afterward he was hungry. 3And the tempter came and
said to him, "If you are the Son of God, command these stones to
Deut 8:3 become loaves of bread." 4But he answered, "It is written,
Wis 16:26 'Man shall not live by bread alone,
but by every word that proceeds from the mouth of God.'"
5Then the devil took him to the holy city, and set him on the pin-
Ps 91:11f nacle of the temple, 6and said to him, "If you are the Son of God,
throw yourself down; for it is written,

---

should practise Lent each year with this spirit of piety. "It can be said that Christ introduced the tradition of forty days fast into the Church's liturgical year, because he himself 'fasted forty days and forty night' before beginning to teach. By this Lenten fast the Church is in a certain sense called every year to follow her Master and Lord if she wishes to preach his Gospel effectively" (John Paul II, General Audience, 28 February 1979). In the same way, Jesus' withdrawal into the desert invites us to prepare ourselves by prayer and penance before any important decision or action.

4:3. Jesus has fasted for forty days and forty nights. Naturally he is very hungry and the devil makes use of this opportunity to tempt him. Our Lord rejects the temptation and in doing so he uses a phrase from Deuteronomy (8:3). Although he could do this miracle, he prefers to continue to trust his Father since performing the miracle is not part of his plan of salvation. In return for this trust, angels come and minister to him (Mt 4:11).

Miracles in the Bible are extraordinary and wonderful deeds done by God to make his words or actions understood. They do not occur as isolated outpourings of God's power but rather as part of the work of Redemption. What the devil proposes in this temptation would be for Jesus' benefit only and therefore could not form part of the plan for Redemption. This suggests that the devil, in tempting him in this way, wanted to check if Jesus is the "Son of God". For, although he seems to know about the voice from heaven at Jesus' baptism, he cannot see how the Son of God could be hungry. By the way he deals with the temptation, Jesus teaches us that when we ask God for things we should not ask in the first place for what we can obtain by our own efforts. Neither should we ask for what is exclusively for our own convenience, but rather for what will help towards our holiness or that of others.

4:4. Jesus' reply is an act of trust in God's fatherly providence. God led him into the desert to prepare him for his messianic work, and now he will see to it that Jesus does not die. This point is underlined by the fact that Jesus' reply evokes Deuteronomy 8:3, where the sons of Israel are reminded how Yahweh fed them miraculously with manna in the desert. Therefore, in contrast to the Israelites who were impatient when faced with hunger in the desert, Jesus trustingly leaves his well-being to the Father's providence. The words of Deuteronomy 8:3, repeated here by Jesus, associate "bread" and "word" as having both come from the mouth of God: God speaks and gives his Law; God speaks and makes manna appear as food.

Also, manna is commonly used in the New Testament (see, for example, Jn 6:32–58) and throughout Tradition as a symbol of the Eucharist.

'He will give his angels charge of you,'
and
'On their hands they will bear you up,
lest you strike your foot against a stone.'"
7Jesus said to him, "Again it is written, 'You shall not tempt the Deut 6:16
Lord your God.'" 8Again, the devil took him to a very high moun- Deut 34:1
tain, and showed him all the kingdoms of the world and the glory Rev 21:10

The Second Vatican Council points out another interesting aspect of Jesus' word when it proposes guidelines for international cooperation in economic matters: "In many instances there exists a pressing need to reassess economic and social structures, but caution must be exercised with regard to proposed solutions which may be untimely, especially those which offer material advantage while militating against man's spiritual nature and advancement. For 'man shall not live by bread alone, but by every word that proceeds from the mouth of God'" (*Gaudium et spes*, 86).

4:5. Tradition suggests that this temptation occurred at the extreme southeast corner of the temple wall. At this point, the wall was at its highest, since the ground beneath sloped away steeply to the Cedron river. Looking down from this point one could easily get a feeling of vertigo. St Gregory the Great (*In Evangelia homiliae*, 16) says that if we consider how our Lord allowed himself to be treated during his passion, it is not surprising that he allowed the devil also to treat him as he did.

4:6. "Holy Scripture is good, but heresies arise through its not being understood properly" (St Augustine, *In Ioann. Evang.*, 18, 1). Catholics should be on their guard against arguments which, though they claim to be founded on Scripture, are nevertheless untrue. As we can see in this passage of the Gospel, the devil can also set himself up at times as an interpreter of Scripture, quoting it to suit himself. Therefore, any interpretation which is not in line with the teaching contained in the Tradition of the Church should be rejected. The error proposed by a heresy normally consists in stressing certain passages to the exclusion of others, interpreting them at will, losing sight of the unity that exists in Scripture and the fact that the faith is all of a piece.

4:7. Jesus rejects the second temptation as he did the first; to do otherwise would have been to tempt God. In rejecting it, he uses a phrase from Deuteronomy (6:16): "You shall not put the Lord your God to the test". In this way he alludes also to the passage in Exodus where the Israelites demand a miracle of Moses. The latter replies, "Why do you put the Lord to the proof?" (Ex 17:2).

To tempt God is the complete opposite of having trust in him. It means presumptuously putting ourselves in the way of an unnecessary danger, expecting God to help us by an exceptional use of his power. We would also tempt him if, by our unbelief and arrogance, we were to ask him for signs of proof. The very first lesson from this passage of the Gospel is that if ever a person were to ask or demand extraordinary proofs or signs from God, he would clearly be tempting him.

4:8–10. The third temptation is the most pseudo-messianic of the three: Jesus is

of them; [9]and he said to him, "All these I will give you, if you will
Deut 6:13 fall down and worship me." [10]Then Jesus said to him, "Begone,
Satan! for it is written,

'You shall worship the Lord your God
and him only shall you serve.'"

Jn 1:51 [11]Then the devil left him, and behold, the angels came and minis-
Heb 1:6, 14 tered to him.

PART ONE

Jesus' ministry in Galilee

Jesus begins to preach

Mk 1:14f
Lk 4:14f [12]Now when he heard that John had been arrested, he withdrew
Jn 2:12; 4:43 into Galilee; [13]and leaving Nazareth he went and dwelt in

---

urged to appropriate to himself the role of an earthly messianic king of the type so widely expected at the time. Our Lord's vigorous reply, "Begone, Satan!" is an uncompromising rejection of an earthly messianism—an attempt to reduce his transcendent, God-given mission to a purely human and political use. By his attitude, Jesus, as it were, rectifies and makes amends for the worldly views of the people of Israel. And, for the same reason, it is a warning to the Church, God's true Israel, to remain faithful to its God-given mission of salvation in the world. The Church's pastors should be on the alert and not allow themselves to be deceived by this temptation of the devil.

"We should learn from Jesus' attitude in these trials. During his life on earth he did not even want the glory that belonged to him. Though he had the right to be treated as God, he took the form of a servant, a slave (cf. Phil 2:6–7). And so the Christian knows that all glory is due to God and that he must not make use of the sublimity and greatness of the Gospel to further his own interests or human ambitions.

"We should learn from Jesus. His attitude in rejecting all human glory is in perfect balance with the greatness of his unique mission as the beloved Son of God who takes flesh to save men […]. And the Christian, who, following Christ, has this attitude of complete adoration of the Father, also experiences our Lord's loving care: 'because he cleaves to me in love. I will deliver him; I will protect him, because he knows my name' (Ps 90:14)" (St Josemaría Escrivá, *Christ Is Passing By*, 62).

4:11. If we struggle constantly, we will attain victory. And nobody is crowned without having first conquered: "Be faithful unto death, and I will give you the crown of life" (Rev 2:10). By coming to minister to Jesus after he rejects the

Capernaum by the sea, in the territory of Zebulun and Naphtali,
[14]that what was spoken by the prophet Isaiah might be fulfilled:
[15]"The land of Zebulun and the land of Naphtali, Is 8:23; 9:1
toward the sea, across the Jordan, Galilee of the Gentiles Jn 7:52
—[16] the people who sat in darkness have seen a great light Lk 1:78f
and for those who sat in the region and shadow of death Jn 1:9
light has dawned."
[17]From that time Jesus began to preach, saying, "Repent, for the
kingdom of heaven is at hand."

---

temptations, the angels teach us the interior joy given by God to the person who fights energetically against the temptation of the devil. God has given us also powerful defenders against such temptations—our guardian angels, on whose aid we should call.

4:15–16. Here St Matthew quotes the prophecy of Isaiah 8:23—9:1. The territory referred to (Zebulun, Naphtali, the way of the sea, the land beyond the Jordan), was invaded by the Assyrians in the period 734–721 BC, especially during the reign of Tilgathpilneser III. A portion of the Jewish population was deported and sizeable numbers of foreigners were planted in the region to colonize it. For this reason it is referred to in the Bible henceforward as the "Galilee of the Gentiles".

The evangelist, inspired by God, sees Jesus' coming to Galilee as the fulfilment of Isaiah's prophecy. This land, devastated and abused in Isaiah's time, will be the first to receive the light of Christ's life and preaching. The messianic meaning of the prophecy is, therefore, clear.

4:17. See the note on Mt 3:2. This verse indicates the outstanding importance of the first step in Jesus' public ministry, begun by proclaiming the imminence of the Kingdom of God. Jesus' words echo John the Baptist's proclamation: the second part of this verse is the same, word for word, as Matthew 3:2. This underlines the role played by St John the Baptist as prophet and precursor of Jesus. Both St John and our Lord demand repentance, penance, as a prerequisite to receiving the Kingdom of God, now beginning. God's rule over mankind is a main theme in Christ's Revelation, just as it was central to the whole Old Testament. However, in the latter, the Kingdom of God had an element of theocracy about it: God reigned over Israel in both spiritual and temporal affairs and it was through him that Israel subjected other nations to her rule. Little by little, Jesus will unfold the new-style Kingdom of God, now arrived at its fullness. He will show it to be a Kingdom of love and holiness, thereby purifying it of the nationalistic misconceptions of the people of this time.

The King invites everyone without exception to this Kingdom (cf. Mt 22:1–14). The banquet of the Kingdom is held on this earth and has certain entry requirements which must be preached by the proponents of the Kingdom: "Therefore the eucharist celebration is the centre of the assembly of the faithful over which the priest presides. Hence priests teach the faithful to offer the divine Victim to God the Father in the sacrifice of the Mass, and with the Victim to make an offering of their whole lives. In the

The first disciples are called

Mk 1:16–20 [18]As he walked by the Sea of Galilee, he saw two brothers, Simon
Lk 5:1–11 Jn 1:40f who is called Peter and Andrew his brother, casting a net into the
Ezek 47:10 sea; for they were fishermen. [19]And he said to them, "Follow me,
Mt 19:27 and I will make you fishers of men." [20]Immediately they left their
nets and followed him. [21]And going on from there he saw two
other brothers, James the son of Zebedee and John his brother, in
the boat with Zebedee their father, mending their nets, and he
called to them. [22]Immediately they left the boat and their father,
and followed him.

Mk 1:39 [23]And he went about all Galilee, teaching in their synagogues
Lk 4:15, 44 Acts 10:38 and preaching the gospel of the kingdom and healing every disease and every infirmity among the people. [24]So his fame spread

---

spirit of Christ the pastor, they instruct them to submit their sins to the Church with a contrite heart in the sacrament of Penance, so that they may be daily more and more converted to the Lord, remembering his words: 'Repent, for the Kingdom of heaven is at hand'" (Vatican II, *Presbyterorum ordinis*, 5).

4:18–22. These four disciples had already met our Lord (Jn 1:35–42), and their brief meeting with him seems to have had a powerful effect on their souls. In this way Christ prepared their vocation, a fully effective vocation which moved them to leave everything behind so as to follow him and be their disciples. Standing out above their human defects (which the Gospels never conceal), we can see the exemplary generosity and promptness of the apostles in answering God's call.

The thoughtful reader cannot fail to be struck by the delightful simplicity with which the evangelists describe the calling of these men in the midst of their daily work. "God draws us from the shadows of our ignorance, our groping through history, and, no matter what our occupation in the world, he calls us in a loud voice, as he once called Peter and Andrew" (St Josemaría Escrivá, *Christ Is Passing By*, 45).

"This divine and human dialogue completely changed the lives of John and Andrew, and Peter and James and so many others. It prepared their hearts to listen to the authoritative teaching which Jesus gave them beside the Sea of Galilee" (ibid., 108).

We should notice the words Sacred Scripture uses to describe the alacrity with which these apostles follow our Lord. Peter and Andrew "immediately" left their nets and followed him. Similarly, James and John "immediately" left their boats and their father and followed him. God passes by and calls us. If we do not answer him "immediately", he may continue on his way and we could lose sight of him. When God passes us by, he may do so rapidly; it would be sad if we were to fall behind because we wanted to follow him while still carrying many things that are only a dead weight and a nuisance.

Concerning Christ's call to men in the midst of their ordinary work, see the note on Mt 2:2.

4:23. "Synagogue": this word comes from the Greek and designates the build-

throughout all Syria and they brought him all the sick, those Mk 6:55
afflicted with various diseases and pains, demoniacs, epileptics,
and paralytics, and he healed them. [25]And great crowds followed Mk 3:7f
him from Galilee and the Decapolis and Jerusalem and Judea and Lk 6:17–19
from beyond the Jordan.

3. THE SERMON ON THE MOUNT

The Beatitudes

5 [1]Seeing the crowds, he went up on the mountain, and when he Lk 6:20–49
sat down his disciples came to him. [2]And he opened his
mouth and taught them, saying:

---

ing where the Jews assembled for religious ceremonies on the sabbath and other feast days. Such ceremonies were non-sacrificial in character (sacrifices could be performed only in the temple of Jerusalem). The synagogue was also the place where the Jews received their religious training. The word was also used to designate local Jewish communities within and without Palestine.

4:24. "Epileptic" (or, in some translations, "lunatic"): this word was applied in a very general way to those who had illnesses related to epilepsy. The disease was popularly regarded as being dependent on the phases of the moon (Latin: *luna*).

4:23–25. In these few lines, the evangelist gives us a very fine summary of the various aspects of Jesus' work. The preaching of the gospel or "good news" of the Kingdom, the healing of diseases, and the casting out of devils are all specific signs of the Messiah's presence, according to Old Testament prophecies (Is 35:5–6; 61:1; 40:9; 52:7).

5:1. The discourse, or sermon, on the mount takes up three full chapters of St Matthew's Gospel—chapters 5–7. It is the first of the five great discourses of Jesus which appear in this Gospel and contains a considerable amount of our Lord's teaching.

It is difficult to reduce this discourse to one single theme, but the various teachings it contains could be said to deal with these five points: 1) the attitude a person must have for entering the Kingdom of heaven (the Beatitudes, the salt of the earth, the light of the world, Jesus and his teaching, the fullness of the Law); 2) uprightness of intention in religious practices (here the Our Father would be included); 3) trust in God's fatherly providence; 4) how God's children should behave towards one another (not judging one's neighbour, respect for holy things, the effectiveness of prayer and the golden rule of charity); 5) the conditions for entering the Kingdom (the narrow gate, false prophets and building on rock).

5:2. "He taught them": this refers both to the disciples and to the multitude, as can be seen at the end of the Sermon.

5:3–12. The Beatitudes form, as it were, the gateway to the Sermon on the Mount. In order to understand the Beatitudes properly, we should bear in mind that

Is 57:15; 61:1 Mt 11:5 Lk 4:18 3“Blessed are the poor in spirit, for theirs is the kingdom of
heaven.
Ps 126:6 Is 61:2 4“Blessed are those who mourn, for they shall be comforted.
Ps 37:11 5“Blessed are the meek, for they shall inherit the earth.

---

they do not promise salvation only to the particular kinds of people listed here: they cover everyone whose religious dispositions and moral conduct meet the demands which Jesus lays down. In other words, the poor in spirit, the meek, those who mourn, those who hunger and thirst after righteousness, the merciful, the pure in heart, the peacemakers and those who suffer persecution in their search for holiness—these are not different people or kinds of people but different demands made on everyone who wants to be a disciple of Christ.

Similarly, salvation is not being promised to different groups in society but to everyone, no matter what his or her position in life, who strives to follow the spirit and to meet the demands contained in the Beatitudes.

All the Beatitudes have an eschatological meaning, that is, they promise us definitive salvation, not in this world, but in the next. But the spirit of the Beatitudes does give us, in this life, peace in the midst of tribulation. The Beatitudes imply a completely new approach, quite at odds with the usual way man evaluates things: they rule out any kind of pharisaical religiosity, which regards earthly happiness as a blessing from God and a reward for good behaviour, and unhappiness and misfortune as a form of punishment. In all ages the Beatitudes put spiritual good on a much higher plane than material possessions. The healthy and the sick, the powerful and the weak, the rich and the poor—all are called, independently of their circumstances, to the deep happiness that is experienced by those who live up to the Beatitudes which Jesus teaches.

The Beatitudes do not, of course, contain the entire teaching of the Gospel, but they do contain, in embryo, the whole programme of Christian perfection.

5:3. This text outlines the connexion between poverty and the soul. This religious concept of poverty was deeply rooted in the Old Testament (cf., e.g., Zeph 2:3ff). It was more to do with a religious attitude of neediness and of humility towards God than with material poverty: that person is poor who has recourse to God without relying on his own merits and who trusts in God’s mercy to be saved. This religious attitude of poverty is closely related to what is called “spiritual childhood”. A Christian sees himself as a little child in the presence of God, a child who owns nothing: everything he has comes from God and belongs to God. Certainly, spiritual poverty, that is, Christian poverty, means one must be detached from material things and practise austerity in using them. God asks certain people—religious—to be legally detached from ownership and thereby bear witness to others of the transitoriness of earthly things.

5:4. “Those who mourn”: here our Lord is saying that those are blessed who suffer from any kind of affliction—particularly those who are genuinely sorry for their sins, or are pained by the offences which others offer God, and who bear their suffering with love and with a spirit of atonement.

“You are crying? Don’t be ashamed of it. Yes, cry: men also cry like you, when they are alone and before God.

6"Blessed are those who hunger and thirst for righteousness, for they shall be satisfied. Rev 7:16f

7"Blessed are the merciful, for they shall obtain mercy. Jas 2:13

8"Blessed are the pure in heart, for they shall see God. Ps 24:4; 51:10; 73:1 Jn 3:2f

---

Each night, says King David, I soak my bed with tears. With those tears, those burning manly tears, you can purify your past and supernaturalize your present life" (St J. Escrivá, *The Way*, 216).

The Spirit of God will console with peace and joy, even in this life, those who weep for their sins, and later he will give them a share in the fullness of happiness and glory in heaven: these are the blessed.

5:5. "The meek": those who patiently suffer unjust persecution; those who remain serene, humble and steadfast in adversity, and do not give way to resentment or discouragement. The virtue of meekness is very necessary in the Christian life. Usually irritableness, which is very common, stems from a lack of humility and interior peace.

"The earth": this is usually understood as meaning our heavenly fatherland.

5:6. The notion of righteousness (or justice) in Holy Scripture is an essentially religious one (cf. notes on Mt 1:19 and 3:15; Rom 1:17; 1:18–32; 3:21–22 and 24). A righteous person is one who sincerely strives to do the will of God, which is discovered in the commandments, in one's duties of state in life and through one's life of prayer. Thus, righteousness, in the language of the Bible, is the same as what nowadays is usually called "holiness" (1 Jn 2:29; 3:7–10; Rev 22:11; Gen 15:6; Deut 9:4).

As St Jerome comments (*Comm. on Matthew*, 5, 6), in the fourth Beatitude our Lord is asking us not simply to have a vague desire for righteousness: we should hunger and thirst for it, that is, we should love and strive earnestly to seek what makes a man righteous in God's eyes. A person who genuinely wants to attain Christian holiness should love the means that the Church, the universal vehicle of salvation, offers all men and teaches them to use—frequent use of the sacraments, an intimate relationship with God in prayer, a valiant effort to meet one's social, professional and family responsibilities.

5:7. Mercy is not just a matter of giving alms to the poor but also of being understanding towards other people's defects, overlooking them, helping them cope with them and loving them despite whatever defects they may have. Being merciful also means rejoicing and suffering with other people.

5:8. Christ teaches us that the source of the quality of human acts lies in the heart, that is, in a man's soul, in the depth of his spirit. "When we speak of a person's heart, we refer not just to his sentiments, but to the whole person in his loving dealings with others. In order to help us understand divine things, Scripture uses the expression 'heart' in its full meaning, as the summary and source, expression and ultimate basis, of one's thoughts, words and actions. A man is worth what his heart is worth" (St J. Escrivá, *Christ Is Passing By*, 164).

Cleanness of heart is a gift of God, which expresses itself in a capacity to love, in having an upright and pure attitude to everything noble. As St Paul says, "whatever is true, whatever is honourable, whatever is just, whatever is pure, whatever is lovely, whatever is gracious,

Rev 22:4 Heb 12:14 Sir 4:11 1 Pet 3:14

9"Blessed are the peacemakers, for they shall be called sons of
God.
10"Blessed are those who are persecuted for righteousness'
sake, for theirs is the kingdom of heaven.

1 Pet 4:14

11"Blessed are you when men revile you and persecute you and
utter all kinds of evil against you falsely on my account.

Jas 5:10 Heb 11:33–38

12"Rejoice and be glad, for your reward is great in heaven, for
so men persecuted the prophets who were before you.

Salt of the earth and light of the world

Mk 9:50 Lk 14:34f

13"You are the salt of the earth; but if salt has lost its taste, how
shall its saltness be restored? It is no longer good for anything
except to be thrown out and trodden under foot by men.

---

if there is any excellence, if there is anything worthy of praise, think about these things" (Phil 4:8). Helped by God's grace, a Christian should strive to cleanse his heart and acquire this purity, the reward for which is the vision of God.

5:9. The translation "peacemakers" well conveys the active meaning of the original text—those who foster peace, in themselves and in others and, as a basis for that, try to be reconciled and to reconcile others with God. Being at peace with God is the cause and the effect of every kind of peace. Any peace on earth not based on this divine peace would be vain and misleading.

"They shall be called sons of God": this is an Hebraicism often found in Sacred Scripture; it is the same as saying "they will be sons of God". St John's first letter (3:1) provides a correct exegesis of this Beatitude: "See what love the Father has given us, that we should be called children of God; and so we are".

5:10. What this Beatitude means, then, is: blessed are those who are persecuted because they are holy, or because they are striving to be holy, for theirs is the Kingdom of heaven.

Thus, blessed is he who suffers persecution for being true to Jesus Christ and who does so not only patiently but joyfully. Circumstances arise in a Christian's life that call for heroism—where no compromise is admissible: either one stays true to Jesus Christ whatever the cost in terms of reputation, life or possessions, or one denies him. St Bernard (*Sermon on the Feast of All Saints*) says that the eighth Beatitude is as it were the prerogative of Christian martyrs. Every Christian who is faithful to Jesus' teaching is in fact a "martyr" (a witness) who reflects or acts in accordance with this Beatitude, even if he does not undergo physical death.

5:11–12. The Beatitudes are the conditions Jesus lays down for entering the Kingdom of heaven. This verse, in a way summing up the preceding ones, is an invitation to everyone to put this teaching into practice. The Christian life, then, is no easy matter, but it is worthwhile, given the reward that Jesus promises.

5:13–16. These verses are calling to that apostolate which is part and parcel of being a Christian. Every Christian has to strive for personal sanctification, but he also has to seek the sanctification of others. Jesus teaches us this, using the very expressive simile of salt and light. Salt preserves food from corruption; it

[14]"You are the light of the world. A city set on a hill cannot be Jn 8:12 Rev 21:10f
hid. [15]Nor do men light a lamp and put it under a bushel, but on a Mk 4:21
stand, and it gives light to all the house. [16]Let your light so shine Lk 8:16; 11:33
before men, that they may see your good works and give glory to Eph 5:8f 1 Pet 2:12
your Father who is in heaven.

Jesus and his teaching, the fullness of the Law

[17]"Think not that I have come to abolish the law and the prophets; Lk 4:21
I have come not to abolish them but to fulfil them.* [18]For truly I Rom 3:31; 10:4

---

also brings out its flavour and makes it more pleasant; and it disappears into the food; the Christian should do the same among the people around him.

"You are salt, apostolic soul. '*Bonum est sal*: salt is a useful thing', we read in the holy Gospel; '*si autem sal evanuerit*: but if the salt loses its taste', it is good for nothing, neither for the land nor for the manure heap; it is thrown out as useless. You are salt, apostolic soul. But if you lose your taste …" (St Josemaría Escrivá, *The Way*, 921).

Good works are the fruit of charity, which consists in loving others as God loves us (cf. Jn 15:12). "I see now," St Thérèse of Lisieux writes, "that true charity consists in bearing with the faults of those about us, never being surprised at their weaknesses, but edified at the least sign of virtue. I see above all that charity must not remain hidden in the bottom of our hearts: 'nor do men light a lamp and put it under a bushel, but on a stand, and it gives light to all in the house.' It seems to me that this lamp is the symbol of charity; it must shine out not only to cheer up those we love best but all in the house" (*The Autobiography of a Saint*, chap. 9).

Apostolate is one of the clearest expressions of charity. The Second Vatican Council emphasized the Christian's duty to be apostolic. Baptism and Confirmation confer this duty, which is also a right (cf. *Lumen gentium*, 33), so much so that, because the Christian is part of the Mystical Body, "a member who does not work at the growth of the body to the extent of his possibilities must be considered useless both to the Church and to himself" (*Apostolicam actuositatem*, 2). "Laymen have countless opportunities for exercising the apostolate of evangelization and sanctification. The very witness of a Christian life, and good works done in a supernatural spirit, are effective in drawing men to the faith and to God; and that is what the Lord has said: 'Let your light shine before men, that they may see your good works and give glory to your Father who is in heaven'" (ibid., 6).

"The Church must be present to these groups [those who do not even believe in God] through those of its members who live among them or have been sent to them. All Christians by the example of their lives and the witness of their word, wherever they live, have an obligation to manifest the new man, which they put on in Baptism, and to reveal the power of the Holy Spirit by whom they were strengthened at Confirmation, so that others, seeing their good works, might glorify the Father and more perfectly perceive the true meaning of human life and the universal solidarity of mankind" (*Ad gentes*, 11; cf. 36).

5:17–19. In this passage Jesus stresses the perennial value of the Old Testament, it is the word of God; because it has a

Lk 16:17; 21:33 say to you, till heaven and earth pass away, not an iota, not a dot,
will pass from the law until all is accomplished. 19Whoever then
Jas 2:10 relaxes one of the least of these commandments and teaches men
1 Cor 15:9 so, shall be called least in the kingdom of heaven; but he who
does them and teaches them shall be called great in the kingdom
of heaven. 20For I tell you, unless your righteousness exceeds that
of the scribes and Pharisees, you will never enter the kingdom of
heaven.

Ex 20:13; 21:12 21"You have heard that it was said to the men of old, 'You shall
Lev 24:17 Deut 17:8 not kill; and whoever kills shall be liable to judgment.' 22But I say
1 Jn 3:15 to you that every one who is angry with his brother[i] shall be liable

---

divine authority it deserves total respect. The Old Law enjoined precepts of a moral, legal and liturgical type. Its moral precepts still hold good in the New Testament because they are for the most part specific, divine-positive, promulgations of the natural law. However, our Lord gives them greater weight and meaning. But the legal and liturgical precepts of the Old Law were laid down by God for a specific stage in salvation history, that is, up to the coming of Christ; Christians are not obliged to observe them (cf. St Thomas Aquinas, *Summa theologiae*, 1–2, 108, 3 ad 3).

The law promulgated through Moses and explained by the prophets was God's gift to his people, a kind of anticipation of the definitive Law which the Christ or Messiah would lay down. Thus, as the Council of Trent defined, Jesus not only "was given to men as a redeemer in whom they are to trust, but also as lawgiver whom they are to obey" (*De iustificatione*, can. 21).

5:20. "Righteousness": see the note on Mt 5:6. This verse clarifies the meaning of the preceding verses. The scribes and Pharisees had distorted the spirit of the Law, putting the whole emphasis on its external, ritual observance. For them exact and hyper-detailed but external fulfilment of the precepts of the Law was a guarantee of a person's salvation: "if I fulfil this I am righteous, I am holy and God is duty bound to save me". For someone with this approach to sanctification it is really not God who saves: man saves himself through external works of the Law. That this approach is quite mistaken is obvious from what Christ says here; in effect what he is saying is: to enter the Kingdom of God the notion of righteousness or salvation developed by the scribes and Pharisees must be rejected. In other words, justification or sanctification is a grace from God; man's role is one of cooperating with that grace by being faithful to it. Elsewhere Jesus gives the same teaching in an even clearer way (cf. Lk 18:9–14, the parable of the Pharisee and the tax collector).

It was also the origin of one of St Paul's great battles with the "Judaizers" (see Gal 3 and Rom 2–5).

5:21–26. Verses 21–26 give us a concrete example of the way that Jesus Christ brought the Law of Moses to its fulfilment, by explaining the deeper meaning of the commandments of that law.

i. Other ancient authorities insert *without cause*

to judgment; whoever insults[j] his brother shall be liable to the
council, and whoever says, 'You fool!' shall be liable to the hell[k]
of fire. 23So if you are offering your gift at the altar, and there Mk 11:25
remember that your brother has something against you, 24leave
your gift there before the altar and go; first be reconciled to your
brother, and then come and offer your gift. 25Make friends quickly Mt 18:35
with your accuser, while you are going with him to court, lest Lk 12:58f
your accuser hand you over to the judge, and the judge to the 1 Pet 5:8
guard, and you be put in prison; 26truly, I say to you, you will
never get out till you have paid the last penny.

5:22. By speaking in the first person ("but I say to you") Jesus shows that his authority is above that of Moses and the prophets; that is to say, he has divine authority. No mere man could claim such authority.

"Insults": practically all translations of this passage transcribe the original Aramaic words, *raca* (cf. RSV note below). It is not an easy word to translate. It means "foolish, stupid, crazy". The Jews used it to indicate utter contempt; often, instead of verbal abuse they would show their feelings by spitting on the ground.

"Fool" translates an even stronger term of abuse than *raca*—implying that a person has lost all moral and religious sense, to the point of apostasy.

In this passage our Lord points to three faults which we commit against charity, moving from internal irritation to showing total contempt. St Augustine comments that three degrees of faults and punishments are to be noted. The first is the fault of feeling angry; to this corresponds the punishment of "judgment". The second is that of passing an insulting remark, which merits the punishment of "the council". The third arises when anger quite blinds us: this is punished by "the hell of fire" (cf. *De Serm. Dom. in monte*, 2, 9).

"The hell of fire": literally, "*Gehenna* of fire", meaning, in the Jewish language of the time, eternal punishment. This shows the gravity of external sins against charity—gossip, backbiting, calumny etc. However, we should remember that these sins stem from the heart; our Lord focusses our attention, first, on internal sins—resentment, hatred etc.—to make us realize that that is where the root lies and that it is important to nip anger in the bud.

5:23–24. Here our Lord deals with certain Jewish practices of his time, and in doing so gives us perennial moral teaching of the highest order. Christians, of course, do not follow these Jewish ritual practices; to keep our Lord's commandment we have ways and means given us by Christ himself. Specifically, in the New and definitive Covenant founded by Christ, being reconciled involves going to the sacrament of Penance. In this sacrament the faithful "obtain pardon from God's mercy for the offence committed against him, and are, at the same time, reconciled with the Church which they have wounded by their sins" (Vatican II, *Lumen gentium*, 11).

In the New Testament, the greatest of all offerings is the Eucharist. Although

j. Greek *says Raca to* (an obscure term of abuse) **k.** Greek *Gehenna*

Ex 20:14 27"You have heard that it was said, 'You shall not commit adul-
Job 31:1; 2 Pet 2:14 tery.' 28But I say to you that every one who looks at a woman lust-
Mt 18:8f fully has already committed adultery with her in his heart. 29If
Mk 9:43, 47 your right eye causes you to sin, pluck it out and throw it away; it
Col 3:5 is better that you lose one of your members than that your whole

---

one has a duty to go to Mass on Sundays and holy days of obligation, an essential condition before receiving Holy Communion is that one be in the state of grace.

It is not our Lord's intention here to give love of neighbour priority over love of God. There is an order in charity: "You shall love the Lord your God with all your heart, with all your soul and with all your strength. This is the great and first commandment" (Mt 22:37–38). Love of one's neighbour, which is the second commandment in order of importance (cf. Mt 22:39), derives its meaning from the first. Brotherhood without parenthood is inconceivable. An offence against charity is, above all, an offence against God.

5:27–30. This refers to a sinful glance at any woman, be she married or not. Our Lord fills out the precepts of the Old Law, where only adultery and the coveting of one's neighbour's wife were considered sinful.

"Lustfully": feeling is one thing, consenting another. Consent presupposes that one realizes the evil of these actions (looking, imagining, having impure thoughts) and freely engages in them.

Prohibition of vices always implies a positive aspect—the contrary virtue. Holy purity, like every other virtue, is something eminently positive; it derives from the first commandment and is also directed to it: "You shall love the Lord your God *with all* your heart, *with all* your soul, and *with all* your mind" (Mt 22:37). "Purity is a consequence of the love that prompts us to commit to Christ our soul and body, our faculties and senses. It is not something negative; it is a joyful affirmation" (St Josemaría Escrivá, *Christ Is Passing By*, 5). This virtue demands that we use all the resources available to us, to the point of heroism if necessary.

"Right eye", "right hand", refers to whatever we value most. Our Lord lays it on the line and is not exaggerating. He obviously does not mean that we should physically mutilate ourselves, but that we should fight hard without making any concessions, being ready to sacrifice anything which clearly could put us in the way of offending God. Jesus' graphic words particularly warn us about one of the most common occasions of sin, reminding us of how careful we need to be guarding our sight. King David, by indulging his curiosity, went on to commit adultery and crime. He later wept over his sins and led a holy life in the presence of God (cf. 2 Sam 11 and 12).

"The eyes! Through them many iniquities enter the soul. So many experiences like David's! If you guard your sight you will have assured the guard of your heart" (St Josemaría Escrivá, *The Way*, 183).

Among the ascetical methods of protecting the virtue of holy purity are: frequent Confession and Communion; devotion to our Lady; a spirit of prayer and mortification; guarding of the senses; flight from occasions of sin; and striving to avoid idleness by always being engaged in doing useful things. There are two further means which are particularly relevant today: "Decorum and modesty are younger brothers of purity" (ibid.,

body be thrown into hell.[k]* 30And if your right hand causes you to
sin, cut it off and throw it away; it is better that you lose one of
your members than that your whole body go into hell.[k]
31"It was also said, 'Whoever divorces his wife, let him give
her a certificate of divorce.' 32But I say to you that every one who

Mk 10:4–12
Deut 24:1

128). Decorum and modesty are a sign of good taste, of respect for others and of human and Christian dignity. To act in accord with this teaching of our Lord, the Christian has to row against the current in a paganized environment and bring his influence for good to bear on it.

"There is need for a crusade of manliness and purity to counteract and undo the savage work of those who think that man is a beast. And that crusade is your work" (ibid., 121).

5:31–32. The Law of Moses (Deut 24:1), which was laid down in ancient times, had tolerated divorce due to the hardness of heart of the early Hebrews. But it had not specified clearly the ground on which divorce might be obtained. The rabbis worked out different sorts of interpretations, depending on which schools they belonged to—solutions ranging from very lax to quite rigid. In all cases, only husbands could repudiate wife, not vice versa. A woman's inferior position was eased somewhat by the device of a written document whereby the husband freed the repudiated woman to marry again if she wished. Against these rabbinical interpretations, Jesus re-establishes the original indissolubility of marriage as God instituted it (Gen 1:27; 2:24; cf. Mt 19:4–6; Eph 1:31; 1 Cor 7:10).

[The RSVCE carries a note which reads: "unchastity": The Greek word used here appears to refer to marriages which were not legally marriages, because they were either within the forbidden degrees of consanguinity (Lev 18:6–16) or contracted with a Gentile. The phrase "except on the ground of unchastity" does not occur in the parallel passage in Lk 16:18. See also Mt 19:9 (Mk 10:11–12), and especially 1 Cor 7:10–11, which shows that the prohibition is unconditional.] The phrase "except on the ground of unchastity" should not be taken as indicating an exception to the principle of the absolute indissolubility of marriage that Jesus has just re-established. It is almost certain that the phrase refers to unions accepted as marriage among some pagan peoples, but prohibited as incestuous in the Mosaic Law (cf. Lev 18) and in rabbinical tradition. The reference, then, is to unions radically invalid because of some impediment. When persons in this position were converted to the true faith, it was not that their union could be dissolved; it was declared that they had never in fact been joined in true marriage. Therefore, this phrase does not go against the indissolubility of marriage, but rather reaffirms it.

On the basis of Jesus' teaching and guided by the Holy Spirit, the Church has ruled that in the specially grave case of adultery it is permissible for a married couple to separate, but without the marriage bond being dissolved; therefore, neither party may contract a new marriage.

The indissolubility of marriage was unhesitatingly taught by the Church from the very beginning; she demanded practi-

k. Greek *Gehenna*

Lk 16:18 divorces his wife, except on the ground of unchastity,* makes her
1 Cor 7:10f an adulteress; and whoever marries a divorced woman commits
adultery.

Ex 20:7 33"Again you have heard that it was said to the men of old,
Lev 19:12 'You shall not swear falsely, but shall perform to the Lord what
Num 30:2
Mt 23:16–22 you have sworn.' 34But I say to you, Do not swear at all, either by

---

cal and legal recognition of this doctrine, expounded with full authority by Jesus (Mt 19:3–9; Mk 10:1–12; Lk 16:18) and by the apostles (1 Cor 6:16; 7:10–11, 39; Rom 7:2–8; Eph 5:31f). Here, for example, are just a few texts from the Magisterium on this subject: "Three blessings are ascribed to matrimony [...]. The third is the indissolubility of matrimony—indissoluble because it signifies the indivisible union of Christ with the Church. Although a separation from bed maybe permitted by reason of marital infidelity, nevertheless it is not permitted to contract another matrimony since the bond of a marriage lawfully contracted is perpetual" (Council of Florence, *Pro Armeniis*).

"If anyone says that the marriage bond can be dissolved by reason of heresy, domestic incompatibility, or willful desertion by one of the parties, let him be anathema" (Council of Trent, *De Sacram. matr.*, can. 5).

"If anyone says that the Church is in error when she has taught and does teach according to the doctrine of the Gospels and apostles that the marriage bond cannot be dissolved because of adultery on the part of either the husband or the wife; and that neither party, not even the innocent one who gave no cause for the adultery, can contract another marriage while the other is still living; and that adultery is committed both by the husband who dismisses the adulterous wife and marries again and by the wife who dismisses her adulterous husband and marries again: let him be anathema" (ibid., can. 7).

"Taking our starting point from that Encyclical, which is concerned almost entirely with vindicating the divine institution of matrimony, its dignity as a Sacrament, and its perpetual stability, let us first recall this immutable, inviolable and fundamental truth: matrimony was not instituted or re-established by men but by God; not men, but God, the Author of nature, and Christ our Lord, the restorer of nature, provided marriage with its laws, confirmed it and elevated it; and consequently those laws can in no ways be subject to human wills or to any contrary pact made even by the contracting parties themselves. This is the teaching of Sacred Scripture; it is the constant and universal Tradition of the Church; it is the solemnly defined doctrine of the Council of Trent, which uses the words of Holy Scripture to proclaim and establish that the perpetual indissolubility of the marriage bond, its unity and stability, derive from God himself" (Pius XI, *Casti connubii*).

"It is true that before the coming of Christ the perfection and strictness of the original law were modified to the extent that Moses, because of the hardness of their hearts, allowed even the members of God's people to give a bill of divorce for certain reasons. But Christ, by virtue of his power as supreme Lawgiver, revoked this concession and restored the law to its original perfection by those words which must never be forgotten: 'What God hath jointed together let no man put asunder'" (ibid.).

heaven, for it is the throne of God, [35]or by the earth, for it is his Is 66:1
footstool, or by Jerusalem, for it is the city of the great King. Acts 7:49 Ps 48:2
[36]And do not swear by your head, for you cannot make one hair
white or black. [37]Let what you say be simply 'Yes' or 'No'; any- 2 Cor 1:17
thing more than this comes from evil.[l] Jas 5:12
[38]"You have heard that it was said, 'An eye for an eye and a Lev 24:19f
tooth for a tooth.' [39]But I say to you, Do not resist one who is evil. Jn 18:22f

---

"For the good of the parties, of the children, and of society this sacred bond no longer depends on human decision alone. For God himself is the author of marriage [...]. The intimate union of marriage (as a mutual giving of two persons) and the good of the children demand total fidelity from the spouses and require an unbreakable unity between them" (Vatican II, *Gaudium et spes*, 48).

5:33–37. The Law of Moses absolutely prohibited perjury or violation of oaths (Ex 20:7; Num 30:3; Deut 23:22). In Christ's time, the making of sworn statements was so frequent and the casuistry surrounding them so intricate that the practice was being grossly abused. Some rabbinical documents of the time show that oaths were taken for quite unimportant reasons. Parallel to this abuse of oath-taking there arose no less ridiculous abuses to justify non-fulfilment of oaths. All this meant great disrespect for the name of God. However, we do know from Holy Scripture that oath-taking is lawful and good in certain circumstances: "If you swear, 'As the Lord lives', in truth, in justice, and in uprightness, then nations shall bless themselves in him, and in him shall they glory" (Jer 4:2).

Jesus here lays down the criterion that his disciples must apply in this connexion. It is based on re-establishing mutual trust, nobility and sincerity. The devil is "the father of lies" (Jn 8:44). Therefore, Christ's Church cannot permit human relationships to be based on deceit and insincerity. God is truth, and the children of the Kingdom must, therefore, base mutual relationships on truth. Jesus concludes by praising sincerity. Throughout his teaching he identifies hypocrisy as one of the main vices to be combatted (cf., e.g., Mt 23:13–32), and sincerity as one of the finest of virtues (cf. Jn 1:47).

5:38–42. Among the Semites, from whom the Israelites stemmed, the law of vengeance ruled. It led to interminable strife and countless crimes. In the early centuries of the chosen people, the law of retaliation was recognized as an ethical advance, socially and legally: no punishment could exceed the crime, and any punitive retaliation was outlawed. In this way, the honour of the clans and families was satisfied, and endless feuds avoided.

As far as New Testament morality is concerned, Jesus establishes a definitive advance: a sense of forgiveness and absence of pride play an essential role. Every legal framework for combating evil in the world, every reasonable defence of personal rights, should be based on morality. The last three verses refer to mutual charity among the children of the Kingdom, a charity which presupposes and enhances justice.

l. Or *the evil one*

Lev 19:18 But if any one strikes you on the right cheek, turn to him the other
1 Cor 6:7 also; [40]and if any one would sue you and take your coat, let him
have your cloak as well; [41]and if any one forces you to go one
mile, go with him two miles. [42]Give to him who begs from you,
and do not refuse him who would borrow from you.

Lev 19:18 [43]"You have heard that it was said, 'You shall love your neigh-
Ex 23:4f bour and hate your enemy.' [44]But I say to you, Love your enemies
Rom 12:14, 20 Lk 23:34 and pray for those who persecute you, [45]so that you may be sons
Acts 7:59 of your Father who is in heaven; for he makes his sun rise on the
Eph 5:1 evil and on the good, and sends rain on the just and on the unjust.
[46]For if you love those who love you, what reward have you? Do
not even the tax collectors do the same? [47]And if you salute only
your brethren, what more are you doing than others? Do not even
Lev 19:2 the Gentiles do the same? [48]You, therefore, must be perfect, as
your heavenly Father is perfect.

5:43. The first part of this verse—"You shall love your neighbour"—is to be found in Leviticus 19:18. The second part—"hate your enemy"—is not in the Law of Moses. However, Jesus' words refer to a widespread rabbinical interpretation which understood "neighbours" as meaning "Israelites". Our Lord corrects this misinterpretation of the Law: for him everyone is our neighbour (cf. the parable of the Good Samaritan in Lk 10:25–37).

5:43–47. This passage sums up the teaching which precedes it. Our Lord goes so far as to say that a Christian has no personal enemies. His only enemy is evil as such—sin—but not the sinner. Jesus himself puts this into practice with those who crucified him, and he continues to act in the same way towards sinners who rebel against him and despise him. Consequently, the saints have always followed his example—like St Stephen, the first martyr, who prayed for those who were putting him to death. This is the apex of Christian perfection—to love, and pray for, even those who persecute and calumniate us. It is the distinguishing mark of the children of God.

5:46. "Tax collectors": the Roman Empire had no officials of its own for the collection of taxes; in each country it used local people for this purpose. These were free to engage agents (hence we find references to "chief tax collectors": cf. Lk 19:2). The global amount of tax for each region was specified by the Roman authorities; the tax collectors levied more than this amount, keeping the surplus for themselves: this led them to act rather arbitrarily, which was why the people hated them. In the case of the Jews, insult was added to injury by the fact that the chosen people were being exploited by Gentiles.

5:48. Verse 48 is, in a sense, a summary of the teaching in this entire chapter, including the Beatitudes. Strictly speaking, it is quite impossible for a created being to be as perfect as God. What our Lord means here is that God's own perfection should be the model that every faithful Christian tries to follow, even though he realizes that there is an infinite distance between himself and his Creator. However, this does not reduce the force of this commandment; it sheds more light

An upright intention in almsgiving, prayer and fasting

6 1“Beware of practising your piety before men in order to be
seen by them; for then you will have no reward from your
Father who is in heaven.
2“Thus, when you give alms, sound no trumpet before you, as
the hypocrites do in the synagogues and in the streets, that they
may be praised by men. Truly, I say to you, they have their
reward. 3But when you give alms, do not let your left hand know Rom 12:8
what your right hand is doing, 4so that your alms may be in secret;
and your Father who sees in secret will reward you.
5“And when you pray, you must not be like the hypocrites; for
they love to stand and pray in the synagogues and at the street corners, that they may be seen by men. Truly, I say to you, they have
their reward. 6But when you pray, go into your room and shut the 2 Sam 4:33 Is 26:20

---

on it. It is a difficult commandment to live up to, but also with this we must take account of the enormous help grace gives us to go so far as to tend towards divine perfection. Certainly, the perfection that we should imitate does not refer to the power and wisdom of God, which are totally beyond our scope; here the context seems to refer primarily to love and mercy. Along the same lines, St Luke quotes these words of our Lord: “Be merciful, even as your Father is merciful” (Lk 6:36; cf. the note on Lk 6:20–49).

Clearly, the “universal call to holiness” is not a recommendation but a commandment of Jesus Christ. “Your duty is to sanctify yourself. Yes, even you. Who thinks that this task is only for priests and religious? To everyone, without exception, our Lord said: ‘Be ye perfect, as my heavenly Father is perfect’ ” (St J. Escrivá, *The Way*, 291). This teaching is sanctioned by chapter 5 of Vatican II’s Constitution *Lumen gentium*, where it says (at no. 40): “The Lord Jesus, divine teacher and model of all perfection, preached holiness of life (of which he is the author and maker) to each and every one of his disciples without distinction: ‘You, therefore, must be perfect, as your heavenly Father is perfect’ […]. It is therefore quite clear that all Christians in any state or walk of life are called to the fullness of Christian life and to the perfection of love, and by this holiness a more human manner of life is fostered also in earthly society.”

6:1–18. “Piety”, here, means good works (cf. the note on Mt 5:6). Our Lord is indicating the kind of spirit in which we should do acts of personal piety. Almsgiving, fasting and prayer were the basic forms taken by personal piety among the chosen people—which is why Jesus refers to these three subjects. With complete authority he teaches that true piety must be practised with an upright intention, in the presence of God and without any ostentation. Piety practised in this way implies exercising our faith in God who sees us—and also in the safe knowledge that he will reward those who are sincerely devout.

6:5–6. Following the teaching of Jesus, the Church has always taught us to pray even when we were infants. By saying “you” (singular) our Lord is stating quite unequivocally the need for personal pray-

door and pray to your Father who is in secret; and your Father
who sees in secret will reward you.*
Is 1:15 [7]"And in praying do not heap up empty phrases as the Gentiles
do; for they think that they will be heard for their many words.
[8]Do not be like them, for your Father knows what you need before
you ask him. [9]Pray then like this:

---

er—relating as child to Father, alone with God.

Public prayer, for which Christ's faithful assemble together, is something necessary and holy; but it should never displace obedience to this clear commandment of our Lord: "When you pray, go into your room and shut the door and pray to your Father."

The Second Vatican Council reminds us of the teaching and practice of the Church in its liturgy, which is "the summit towards which the activity of the Church is directed; it is also the fount from which all her power flows [...]. The spiritual life, however, is not limited solely to participation in the liturgy. The Christian is indeed called to pray with others, but he must also enter into his bedroom to pray to his Father in secret; furthermore, according to the teaching of the apostle, he must pray without ceasing (1 Thess 5:17)" (*Sacrosanctum Concilium*, 10 and 12).

A soul who really puts his Christian faith into practice realizes that he needs frequently to get away and pray alone to his Father, God. Jesus, who gives us this teaching about prayer, practised it during his own life on earth: the holy Gospel reports that he often went apart to pray on his own: "At times he spent the whole night in an intimate conversation with his Father. The apostles were filled with love when they saw Christ pray" (St J. Escrivá, *Christ Is Passing By*, 119; cf. Mt 14:23; Mk 1:35; Lk 5:16; etc.). The apostles followed the Master's example, and so we see Peter going up to the rooftop of the house to pray in private, and receiving a revelation (cf. Acts 10:9–16). "Our life of prayer should also be based on some moments that are dedicated exclusively to our conversation with God, moments of silent dialogue" (*Christ Is Passing By*, 119).

6:7–8. Jesus condemns the superstitious notion that long prayers are needed to attract God's attention. True piety is not so much a matter of the amount of words as of the frequency and the love with which the Christian turns towards God in all the events, great or small, of his day. Vocal prayer is good, and necessary; but the words count only if they express our inner feelings.

6:9–13. The Our Father is, without any doubt, the most commented-on passage in all Holy Scripture. Numerous great Church writers have left us commentaries full of poetry and wisdom. The early Christians, taught by the precepts of salvation, and following the divine commandment, centred their prayer on this sublime and simple form of words given them by Jesus. And the last Christians, too, will raise their hearts to say the Our Father for the last time when they are on the point of being taken to heaven. In the meantime, from childhood to death, the Our Father is a prayer which fills us with hope and consolation. Jesus fully realized how helpful this prayer would be to us. We are grateful to him for giving it to us,

Our Father who art in heaven, Lk 11:2–4
Hallowed be thy name. Jn 17:6 Mt 7:11
10Thy kingdom come,
Thy will be done, Lk 22:42
On earth as it is in heaven.

---

to the apostles for passing it on to us and, in the case of most Christians, to our mothers for teaching it to us in our infancy. So important is the Lord's Prayer that from apostolic times it has been used, along with the Creed, the Ten Commandments and the Sacraments, as the basis of Christian catechesis. Catechumens were introduced to the life of prayer by the Our Father, and our catechisms today use it for that purpose. St Augustine says that the Lord's Prayer is so perfect that it sums up in a few words everything man needs to ask God for (cf. *Sermons*, 56). It is usually seen as being made up of an invocation and seven petitions—three to do with praise of God and four with the needs of men.

6:9. It is a source of great consolation to be able to call God "our Father"; Jesus, the Son of God, teaches men to invoke God as Father because we are indeed his children, and should feel towards him in that way.

"The Lord [...] is not a tyrannical master or a rigid and implacable judge; he is our Father. He speaks to us about our lack of generosity, our sins, our mistakes; but he does so in order to free us from them, to promise us his friendship and his love [...]. A child of God treats the Lord as his Father. He is not obsequious and servile, he is not merely formal and well-mannered: he is completely sincere and trusting" (St J. Escrivá, *Christ Is Passing By*, 64).

"Hallowed be thy name": in the Bible a person's "name" means the same as the person himself. Here the name of God means God himself. Why pray that his name be hallowed, sanctified? We do not mean sanctification in the human sense—leaving evil behind and drawing closer to God—for God is holiness itself. God, rather, is sanctified when his holiness is acknowledged and honoured by his creatures—which is what this first petition of the Our Father means (cf. *St Pius V Catechism*, 4, 10).

6:10. "Thy kingdom come": this brings up again the central idea of the Gospel of Jesus Christ—the coming of the Kingdom. The Kingdom of God is so identical with the life and work of Jesus Christ that the Gospel is referred to now as the Gospel of Jesus Christ, now as the Gospel of the Kingdom (Mt 9:35). On the notion of Kingdom of God see the commentary on Matthew 3:2 and 4:17. The coming of the Kingdom of God is the realization of God's plan of salvation in the world. The Kingdom establishes itself in the first place in the core of man's being, raising him up to share in God's own inner life. This elevation has, as it were, two stages—the first, in this life, where it is brought about by grace; the second, definitive stage in eternal life, where man's elevation to the supernatural level is fully completed. We for our part need to respond to God spontaneously, lovingly and trustingly.

"Thy will be done": this third petition expresses two desires. The first is that man identify humbly and unconditionally with God's will—abandonment in the arms of his Father God. The second is that the will of God be fulfilled, that man

11 Give us this day our daily bread;[m]
12 And forgive us our debts,
As we also have forgiven our debtors;
Jn 17:11, 15 13 And lead us not into temptation,
But deliver us from evil.[n]

---

cooperate with it in full freedom. For example, God's will is to be found in the moral aspect of the divine law—but this law is not forced on man. One of the signs of the coming of the Kingdom is man's loving fulfilment of God's will. The second part of the petition, "on earth as it is in heaven", means that, just as the angels and saints in heaven are fully at one with God's will, so—we desire—should the same thing obtain on earth.

Our effort to do God's will proves that we are sincere when we say the words, "Thy will be done." For our Lord says, "Not every one who says to me, 'Lord, Lord' shall enter the kingdom of heaven, but he who does the will of my Father who is in heaven" (Mt 7:21). "Anyone, then, who sincerely repeats this petition, 'Fiat voluntas tua', must, at least in intention, have done this already" (St Teresa of Avila, *Way of Perfection*, chap. 36).

6:11. In making this fourth petition, we are thinking primarily of our needs in this present life. The importance of this petition is that it declares that the material things we need in our lives are good and lawful. It gives a deep religious dimension to the support of life: what Christ's disciple obtains through his own work is also something for which he should implore God—and he should receive it gratefully as a gift from God. God is our support in life: by asking God to support him and by realizing that it is God who is providing this support, the Christian avoids being worried about material needs. Jesus does not want us to pray for wealth or to be attached to material things, but to seek and make sober use of what meets our needs. Hence, in Matthew as well as in Luke (Lk 11:2), there is reference to having enough food for every day. This fourth petition, then, has to do with moderate use of food and material things—far from the extremes of opulence and misery, as God already taught in the Old Testament: "Give me neither poverty nor riches; feed me with the food which is needful for me, lest I be full, and deny thee, and say, 'Who is the Lord?' or lest I be poor, and steal, and profane the name of my God" (Prov 30:8).

The Fathers of the Church interpreted the bread asked for here not only as material food but also as referring to the Blessed Eucharist, without which our spirit cannot stay alive.

According to the *St Pius V Catechism* (cf. 4, 13, 21) the Eucharist is called our daily bread because it is offered daily to God in the Mass and because we should worthily receive it, every day if possible, as St Ambrose advises: "If the bread is daily, why do you take it only once a year [...]? Receive daily what is of benefit to you daily! So live that you may deserve to receive it daily!" (*De Sacramentis*, 5, 4).

6:12. "Debts": clearly, here, in the sense of sin. In the Aramaic of Jesus' time the same word was used for offence and debt. In this fifth petition, then, we admit

m. Or *our bread for the morrow*

[14]For if you forgive men their trespasses, your heavenly Father
also will forgive you; [15]but if you do not forgive men their tres- Mk 11:25f
passes, neither will your Father forgive your trespasses.

---

that we are debtors because we have offended God. The Old Testament is full of references to man's sinful condition. Even the "righteous" are sinners. Recognizing our sins is the first step in every conversion to God. It is not a question of recognizing that we have sinned in the past but of confessing our present sinful condition. Awareness of our sinfulness makes us realize our religious need to have recourse to the only One who can cure it. Hence the advantage of praying insistently, using the Lord's Prayer to obtain God's forgiveness time and again.

The second part of this petition is a serious call to forgive our fellow-men, for we cannot dare to ask God to forgive us if we are not ready to forgive others. The Christian needs to realize what this prayer implies: unwillingness to forgive others means that one is condemning oneself (see the notes on Mt 5:23–24 and 18:21–35).

6:13. "And lead us not into temptation": "We do not ask to be totally exempt from temptation, for human life is one continuous temptation (cf. Job 7:1). What, then, do we pray for in this petition? We pray that the divine assistance may not forsake us, lest having been deceived, or worsted, we should yield to temptation; and that the grace of God may be at hand to succour us when our strength fails, to refresh and invigorate us in our trials" (St Pius V, *Catechism*, 4, 15, 14).

In this petition of the Our Father we recognize that our human efforts alone do not take us very far in trying to cope with temptation, and that we need to have humble recourse to God, to get the strength we need. For, "God is strong enough to free you from everything and can do you more good than all the devils can do you harm. All that God decrees is that you confide in him, that you draw near him, that you trust him and distrust yourself, and so be helped; and with this help you will defeat whatever hell brings against you. Never lose hold of this firm hope [...] even if the demons are legion and all kinds of severe temptations harass you. Lean upon Him, because if the Lord is not your support and your strength, then you will fall and you will be afraid of everything" (St John of Avila, *Sermons*, 9, First Sunday of Lent).

"But deliver us from evil": in this petition, which, in a way, sums up the previous petitions, we ask the Lord to free us from everything our enemy does to bring us down; we cannot be free of him unless God himself frees us, in response to our prayers.

This sentence can also be translated as "Deliver us from the evil one", that is to say, the devil, who is in the last analysis the author of all evils to which we are prone.

In making this request we can be sure that our prayer will be heard because Jesus Christ, when he was on the point of leaving this world, prayed to the Father for the salvation of all men: "I do not pray that thou shouldst take them out of the world, but that thou shouldst keep them from the evil one" (Jn 17:15).

6:14–15. In vv. 14 and 15 St Matthew gives us a sort of commentary of our Lord on the fifth petition of the Our Father.

n. Or *the evil one*. Other authorities, some ancient, add, in some form, *For thine is the kingdom and the power and the glory, for ever. Amen*

Is 58:5–9 16“And when you fast, do not look dismal, like the hypocrites,
for they disfigure their faces that their fasting may be seen by
men. Truly, I say to you, they have their reward. 17But when you
fast, anoint your head and wash your face, 18that your fasting may
not be seen by men but by your Father who is in secret; and your
Father who sees in secret will reward you.

Trust in God’s fatherly providence

19“Do not lay up for yourselves treasures on earth, where moth
Lk 12:33f and rust[o] consume and where thieves break in and steal, 20but lay
Col 3:1f up for yourselves treasures in heaven, where neither moth nor
rust[o] consumes and where thieves do not break in and steal. 21For
where your treasure is, there will your heart be also.
Lk 11:34–36 22“The eye is the lamp of the body. So, if your eye is sound,
your whole body will be full of light; 23but if your eye is not

---

A God who forgives is a wonderful God. But if God, who is thrice-holy, has mercy on the sinner, how much more ought we forgive others—we sinners, who know from our own experience the wretchedness of sin. No one on earth is perfect. Just as God loves us, even though we have defects, and forgives us, we should love others, even though they have defects, and forgive them. If we wait to love people who have no defects, we shall never love anyone. If we wait until others mend their ways or apologize, we will scarcely ever forgive them. But then we ourselves will never be forgiven. “All right: that person has behaved badly towards you. But, haven’t you behaved worse towards God?” (St Josemaría Escrivá, *The Way*, 686).

Thus, forgiving those who have offended us makes us like our Father, God: “In loving our enemies there shines forth in us some likeness to God our Father, who, by the death of his Son, ransomed from everlasting perdition and reconciled to himself the human race, which before was most unfriendly and hostile to him” (St Pius V, *Catechism*, 4, 14, 19).

6:16–18. Starting from the traditional practice of fasting, our Lord tells us the spirit in which we should practise mortification of our senses: we should do so without ostentation, avoiding praise, discreetly; that way Jesus’ words will not apply to us: “they have their reward”; it would have been a very bad deal. “The world admires only spectacular sacrifice, because it does not realize the value of sacrifice that is hidden and silent” (St Josemaría Escrivá, *The Way*, 185).

6:19–21. The idea here is very clear: man’s heart yearns for a treasure that will give him security and happiness. However, every treasure in the form of earthly goods—wealth, property—becomes a constant source of worry, because there is always the risk we will lose it or because the effort to protect it is such a strain.

Against this, Jesus teaches us here that our true treasure lies in good works and an upright life, which will be eter-

o. Or *worm*

sound, your whole body will be full of darkness. If then the light
in you is darkness, how great is the darkness!
[24]"No one can serve two masters; for either he will hate the Lk 16:9, 13
one and love the other, or he will be devoted to the one and
despise the other. You cannot serve God and mammon.*
[25]"Therefore I tell you, do not be anxious about your life, what Lk 12:22–31
you shall eat or what you shall drink, nor about your body, what Phil 4:6
you shall put on. Is not life more than food, and the body more 1 Pet 5:7
than clothing? [26]Look at the birds of the air; they neither sow nor 1 Tim 6:6 Heb 13:5
reap nor gather into barns, and yet your heavenly Father feeds
them. Are you not of more value than they? [27]And which of you by
being anxious can add one cubit to his span of life?[p] [28]And why are
you anxious about clothing? Consider the lilies of the field, how
they grow; they neither toil nor spin; [29]yet I tell you, even Solomon 1 Kings 10
in all his glory was not arrayed like one of these. [30]But if God so

---

nally rewarded by God in heaven. That indeed is a treasure which one never loses, a treasure on which Christ's disciple should put his heart.

Jesus closes the teaching contained in the preceding verses with a kind of refrain (v. 21). He is not saying that people should be unconcerned about earthly things; what he does say is that no created thing can be "the treasure", the ultimate aim, of man. What man should do is make his way to God, sanctify himself and give all glory to God, by making right use of the noble things of the earth: "Whether you eat or drink, or whatever you do, do all to the glory of God" (1 Cor 10:31; cf. Col 3:17).

6:22–23. Here is another jewel of Jesus' wisdom teaching. It begins with a sentence that is then immediately explained. The Master uses the simile of the eye as a lamp which provides the body with light. Christian exegesis has seen this "eye", this "lamp", as meaning the motivation behind our behaviour. St Thomas explains it in this way: "The eye refers to motive. When a person wants to do something, he first forms an intention: thus, if your intention is sound—simple and clear—that is to say, if it is directed towards God, your whole body, that is, all your actions, will be sound, sincerely directed towards good" (St Thomas Aquinas, *Comm. on St Matthew*, 6, 22–23).

6:24. Man's ultimate goal is God; to attain this goal he should commit himself entirely. But in fact some people do not have God as their ultimate goal, and instead choose wealth of some kind—in which case wealth becomes their god. Man cannot have two absolute and contrary goals.

6:25–32. In this beautiful passage Jesus shows us the value of the ordinary things of life, and teaches us to put our trust in God's fatherly providence. Using simple examples and comparisons taken from everyday life, he teaches us to abandon ourselves into the arms of God.

6:27. The word "span" could be translated as "stature", but "span" is closer to

p. Or *to his stature*

clothes the grass of the field, which today is alive and tomorrow is
thrown into the oven, will he not much more clothe you, O men of
little faith? [31]Therefore do not be anxious, saying, 'What shall we
eat?' or 'What shall we drink?' or 'What shall we wear?' [32]For the
Gentiles seek all these things; and your heavenly Father knows that
Rom 14:17 you need them all. [33]But seek first his kingdom and his righteous-
1 Kings 3:13f Ps 37:4, 25 ness, and all these things shall be yours as well.

[34]"Therefore do not be anxious about tomorrow, for tomorrow
Ex 16:19 will be anxious for itself. Let the day's own trouble be sufficient
for the day.

Various precepts. Do not judge

Rom 2:1 1 Cor 4:5 **7** [1]"Judge not, that you be not judged. [2]For with the judgment
Mk 4:24 you pronounce you will be judged, and the measure you give

---

the original (cf. Lk 12:25). A "cubit" is a measure of length which can metaphorically refer to time.

6:33. Here again the righteousness of the Kingdom means the life of grace in man—which involves a whole series of spiritual and moral values and can be summed up in the notion of "holiness". The search for holiness should be our primary purpose in life. Jesus is again insisting on the primacy of spiritual demands. Commenting on this passage, Pope Paul VI says: "Why poverty? It is to give God, the Kingdom of God, the first place in the scale of values which are the object of human aspirations. Jesus says: 'Seek first his kingdom and his righteousness.' And he says this with regard to all the other temporal goods, even necessary and legitimate ones, with which human desires are usually concerned. Christ's poverty makes possible that detachment from earthly things which allows us to place the relationship with God at the peak of human aspirations" (General Audience, 5 January 1977).

6:34. Our Lord exhorts us to go about our daily tasks serenely and not to worry uselessly about what happened yesterday or what may happen tomorrow. This is wisdom based on God's fatherly providence and on our own everyday experience: "He who observes the wind will not sow; and he who regards the clouds will not reap" (Eccles 11:4).

What is important, what is within our reach, is to live in God's presence and make good use of the present moment: "Do your duty 'now', without looking back on 'yesterday', which has already passed, or worrying over 'tomorrow', which may never come for you" (St Josemaría Escrivá, *The Way*, 253).

7:1. Jesus is condemning any rash judgments we make maliciously or carelessly about our brothers' behaviour or feelings or motives. "Think badly and you will not be far wrong" is completely at odds with Jesus' teaching.

In speaking of Christian charity St Paul lists its main features: "Love is patient and kind [...]. Love bears all things, believes all things, hopes all things, endures all things" (1 Cor 13:4, 5, 7). Therefore, "Never think badly of anyone, not even if the words or conduct of the person in question give you good

will be the measure you get. 3Why do you see the speck that is in your brother's eye, but do not notice the log that is in your own eye? 4Or how can you say to your brother, 'Let me take the speck out of your eye,' when there is the log in your own eye? 5You hypocrite, first take the log out of your own eye, and then you will see clearly to take the speck out of your brother's eye.

Respect for holy things

6"Do not give dogs what is holy; and do not throw your pearls before swine, lest they trample them under foot and turn to attack you.

Effectiveness of prayer

7"Ask, and it will be given you; seek, and you will find; knock, Mk 11:24 Lk 11:9–13
and it will be opened to you. 8For every one who asks receives, Jer 29:13f Jn 14:13; 16:23

---

grounds for doing so" (St Josemaría Escrivá, *The Way*, 442).

"Let us be slow to judge. Each one sees things from his own point of view, as his mind, with all its limitations, tells him, and through eyes that are often dimmed and clouded by passion" (ibid., 451).

7:1–2. As elsewhere, the verbs in the passive voice ("you will be judged", "the measure you will be given") have God as their subject, even though he is not explicitly mentioned: "Do not judge *others*, that you be not judged *by God*." Clearly the judgment referred to here is always a condemnatory judgment; therefore, if we do not want to be condemned by God, we should never condemn our neighbour. "God measures out according as we measure out and forgives as we forgive, and comes to our rescue with the same tenderness as he sees us having towards others" (Fray Luis de León, *Exposición del Libro de Job*, chap. 29).

7:3–5. A person whose sight is distorted sees things as deformed, even though in fact they are not deformed. St Augustine gives this advice: "Try to acquire those virtues which you think your brothers lack, and you will no longer see their defects, because you will not have them yourselves" (*Enarrationes in Psalmos*, 30, 2, 7). In this connexion, the saying "A thief thinks that everyone else is a thief" is in line with this teaching of Jesus.

Besides: "To criticize, to destroy, is not difficult; any unskilled labourer knows how to drive his pick into the noble and finely-hewn stone of a cathedral. To construct: that is what requires the skill of a master" (St Josemaría Escrivá, *The Way*, 456).

7:6. Jesus uses a popular saying to teach discernment in the preaching of the word of God and distribution of the means of sanctification. The Church has always heeded this warning, particularly in the sense of respect with which she administers the sacraments—especially the Holy Eucharist. Filial confidence does not exempt us from the sincere and profound respect that should imbue our relations with God and with holy things.

7:7–11. Here the Master teaches us in a number of ways about the effectiveness of prayer. Prayer is a raising of mind and heart to God to adore him, to praise him,

and he who seeks finds, and to him who knocks it will be opened.
[9]Or what man of you, if his son asks him for bread, will give him
Jas 1:17 a stone? [10]Or if he asks for a fish, will give him a serpent? [11]If you
then, who are evil, know how to give good gifts to your children,
how much more will your Father who is in heaven give good
things to those who ask him!

The golden rule

Lk 6:31 Rom 13:8–10 [12]So whatever you wish that men would do to you, do so to them;
for this is the law and the prophets.

The narrow gate

Lk 13:24 Jn 10:7, 9 [13]"Enter by the narrow gate; for the gate is wide and the way is
easy,[q] that leads to destruction, and those who enter by it are

---

to thank him and to ask him for what we need (cf. St Pius X, *Catechism*, 255). Jesus emphasizes the need for petitionary prayer, which is the first spontaneous movement of a soul who recognizes God as his Creator and Father. As God's creature and child, each of us needs to ask him humbly for everything.

In speaking of the effectiveness of prayer, Jesus does not put any restriction: "Every one who asks receives", because God is our Father. St Jerome comments: "It is written, to everyone who asks it will be given; so, if it is not given to you, it is not given to you because you do not ask; so, ask and you will receive" (*Comm. on Matthew*, 7). However, even though prayer in itself is infallible, sometimes we do not obtain what we ask for. St Augustine says that our prayer is not heard because we ask "aut mali, aut male, aut mala." "*Mali*" (= evil people): because we are evil, because our personal dispositions are not good; "*male*" (= badly): because we pray badly, without faith, not persevering, not humbly; "*mala*" (= bad things): because we ask for bad things, that is, things which are not good for us, things which can harm us (cf. *De civitate Dei*, 20, 22 and 27; *De Serm. Dom. in monte*, 2, 27, 73). In the last analysis, prayer is ineffective when it is not true prayer. Therefore, "Pray. In what human venture could you have greater guarantees of success?" (St Josemaría Escrivá, *The Way*, 96).

7:12. This "golden rule" gives us a guideline to realize our obligations towards and the love we should have for others. However, if we interpreted it superficially it would become a selfish rule; it obviously does not mean "*do ut des*" ("I give you something so that you will give me something") but that we should do good to others unconditionally: we are clever enough not to put limits on how much we love ourselves. This rule of conduct will be completed by Jesus' "new commandment" (Jn 13:34), where he teaches us to love others as he himself has loved us.

7:13–14. "Enter": in St Matthew's Gospel this verb often has as its object the "Kingdom of heaven" or equivalent

q. Other ancient authorities read *for the way is wide and easy*

many. [14]For the gate is narrow and the way is hard, that leads to Acts 14:22
life, and those who find it are few.

False prophets

[15]"Beware of false prophets, who come to you in sheep's clothing Acts 20:29
but inwardly are ravenous wolves. [16]You will know them by their Gal 5:19–22
fruits. Are grapes gathered from thorns, or figs from thistles? [17]So, Jas 3:12
every sound tree bears good fruit, but the bad tree bears evil fruit.
[18]A sound tree cannot bear evil fruit, nor can a bad tree bear good
fruit. [19]Every tree that does not bear good fruit is cut down and Jn 15:2, 6
thrown into the fire. [20]Thus you will know them by their fruits.

---

expressions (life, the marriage feast, the joy of the Lord, etc.). We can interpret "enter" as an imperious invitation.

The way of sin is momentarily pleasant and calls for no effort, but it leads to eternal perdition. Following the way of a generous and sincere Christian life is very demanding—here Jesus speaks of a narrow gate and a hard way—but it leads to Life, to eternal salvation.

The Christian way involves carrying the cross. "For if a man resolve to submit himself to carrying this cross—that is to say, if he resolve to desire in truth to meet trials and to bear them in all things for God's sake, he will find in them all great relief and sweetness wherewith he may travel upon this road, detached from all things and desiring nothing. Yet, if he desire to possess anything—whether it comes from God or from any other source—with any feeling of attachment, he has not stripped and denied himself in all things; and thus he will be unable to walk along this narrow path or to climb upward by it" (St John of the Cross, *Ascent of Mount Carmel*, book 2, chap. 7, 7).

7:15–20. There are many references in the Old Testament to false prophets, perhaps the best-known being Jeremiah 23:9–40 which condemns the impiety of those prophets who "prophesied by Baal and led my people Israel astray"; "who prophesy to you, filling you with vain hopes; they speak visions of their own minds, not from the mouth of the Lord […]. I did not send the prophets, yet they ran. I did not speak to them, yet they prophesied"; they "lead my people astray by their lies and their recklessness, when I did not send them or charge them; so that they do not profit this people at all".

In the life of the Church the Fathers see these false prophets, as of whom Jesus speaks, in heretics, who apparently are pious and reformist but who in fact do not have Christ's sentiments (cf. St Jerome, *Comm. on Matthew*, 7). St John Chrysostom applies this teaching to anyone who appears to be virtuous but in fact is not, and thereby misleads others.

How are false prophets and genuine prophets to be distinguished? By the fruit they produce. Human nobility and divine inspiration combine to give the things of God a savour of their own. A person who truly speaks the things of God sows faith, hope, charity, peace and understanding; whereas a false prophet in the Church of God, in his preaching and behaviour, sows division, hatred, resentment, pride and sensuality (cf. Gal 5:16–25). However, the main characteristic of a false prophet is that he separates the people of

Doing the will of God

Rom 2:13 Jas 1:22, 25; 2:14 21“Not every one who says to me, ‘Lord, Lord,’ shall enter the
1 Cor 12:3 kingdom of heaven, but he who does the will of my Father who is
Lk 13:25–27 in heaven. 22On that day many will say to me, ‘Lord, Lord, did we
1 Cor 13:1f Jer 14:14; 27:15 not prophesy in your name, and cast out demons in your name, and
2 Tim 2:19 do many mighty works in your name?’ 23And then will I declare to
Ps 6:8 them, ‘I never knew you; depart from me, you evildoers.’

Building on rock

24“Every one then who hears these words of mine and does them
will be like a wise man who built his house upon the rock; 25and
the rain fell, and the floods came, and the winds blew and beat

---

God from the Magisterium of the Church, through which Christ’s teaching is declared to the world. Our Lord also indicates that these deceivers are destined to eternal perdition.

7:21–23. To be genuine, prayer must be accompanied by a persevering effort to do God’s will. Similarly, in order to do his will it is not enough to speak about the things of God: there must be consistency between what one preaches—what one says—and what one does: “The kingdom of God does not consist in talk but in power” (1 Cor 4:20); “Be doers of the word, and not hearers only, deceiving yourselves” (Jas 1:22).

Christians, “holding loyally to the Gospel, enriched by its resources, and joining forces with all who love and practise justice, have shouldered a weighty task on earth and they must render an account of it to him who will judge all men on the last day. Not every one who says ‘Lord, Lord’ will enter the Kingdom of heaven, but those who do the will of the Father, and who manfully put their hands to the work” (Vatican II, *Gaudium et spes*, 93).

To enter the Kingdom of heaven, to be holy, it is not enough, then, to speak eloquently about holiness. One has to practise what one preaches, to produce fruit that accords with one’s words. Fray Luis de León puts it very graphically: “Notice that to be a good Christian it is not enough just to pray and fast and hear Mass; God must find you faithful, like another Job or Abraham, in times of tribulation” (*Guide for Sinners*, book 1, part 2, chap. 21).

Even if a person exercises an ecclesiastical ministry that does not assure his holiness; he needs to practise the virtues he preaches. Besides, we know from experience that any Christian (clerical, religious or lay) who does not strive to act in accordance with the demands of the faith he professes, begins to weaken in his faith and eventually parts company also with the teaching of the Church. Anyone who does not live in accordance with what he says, ends up saying things that are contrary to faith.

The authority with which Jesus speaks in these verses reveals him as sovereign Judge of the living and the dead. No Old Testament prophet ever spoke with this authority.

7:22. “That day”: a technical formula in biblical language meaning the day of the Judgment of the Lord or the Last Judgment.

upon that house, but it did not fall, because it had been founded on
the rock. [26]And every one who hears these words of mine and
does not do them will be like a foolish man who built his house
upon the sand; [27]and the rain fell, and the floods came, and the Ezek 33:10f
winds blew and beat against that house, and it fell; and great was
the fall of it."

Jesus teaches with authority

[28]And when Jesus finished these sayings, the crowds were aston- Mk 1:22 Lk 4:32
ished at his teaching, [29]for he taught them as one who had author- Jn 7:46
ity, and not as their scribes.

7:23. This passage refers to the Judgment where Jesus will be the Judge. The sacred text uses a verb which means the public proclamation of a truth. Since in this case Jesus Christ is the Judge who makes the declaration, it takes the form of a judicial sentence.

7:24–27. These verses constitute the positive side of the previous passage. A person who tries to put Christ's teaching into practice, even if he experiences personal difficulties or lives during times of upheaval in the life of the Church or is surrounded by error, will stay firm in the faith, like the wise man who builds his house on rock.

Also, if we are to stay strong in times of difficulty, we need, when things are calm and peaceful, to accept little contradictions with a good grace, to be very refined in our relationship with God and with others, and to perform the duties of our state in life in a spirit of loyalty and abnegation. By acting in this way we are laying down a good foundation, maintaining the edifice of our spiritual life and repairing any cracks that make their appearance.

7:28–29. Jesus' listeners could clearly see the radical difference between the style of teaching of the scribes and Pharisees, and the conviction and confidence with which Jesus spoke. There is nothing tentative about his words; they leave no room for doubt; he is clearly not giving a mere opinion. Jesus spoke with absolute command of the truth and perfect knowledge of the true meaning of the Law and the Prophets; indeed he often spoke on his own authority (cf. Mt 5:22, 28, 32, 38, 44), and with the very authority of God (cf. Mk 2:10; Mt 28:18). All this conferred a singular force and authority on his words, such as had never been known in Israel (cf. Lk 19:48; Jn 7:46).

Chapters 8 and 9 of St Matthew deal with a series of miracles worked by our Lord. The first Christians had vivid experience of the fact that the glorified Jesus was still present in his Church, confirming its teaching by signs, by miracles (Mk 16:20; Acts 14:3).

And so, St Matthew, after giving the nucleus of Jesus' public teaching in the Sermon on the Mount (chapters 5–7), goes on now to gather a number of miracles to support our Lord's words. Some commentators call this section— chaps. 8 and 9—"the works of the Messiah", parallelling what they called "the words of the Messiah" (the discourse on the mount). In chapters 5–7 we see Jesus as the supreme lawgiver and master who

4. MIRACLES OF THE MESSIAH

Curing of a leper

Mk 1:40–44 **8** [1]When he came down from the mountain, great crowds fol-
Lk 5:12–14 lowed him; [2]and behold, a leper came to him and knelt before
him, saying, "Lord, if you will, you can make me clean." [3]And he
stretched out his hand and touched him, saying, "I will; be clean."
Mk 7:36 And immediately his leprosy was cleansed.* [4]And Jesus said to
Lk 17:14 him, "See that you say nothing to any one; but go, show yourself
Lev 13:49; 14:2–32 to the priest, and offer the gift that Moses commanded, for a proof
to the people."[r]

The centurion's faith

Lk 7:1–10 [5]As he entered Capernaum, a centurion came forward to him,
Jn 4:47 beseeching him [6]and saying, "Lord, my servant is lying paralyzed
at home, in terrible distress." [7]And he said to him, "I will come and
heal him." [8]But the centurion answered him, "Lord, I am not

---

teaches with divine authority, a unique authority superior to that held by Moses and the prophets. Now, in chapters 8 and 9, he is shown as endowed with divine authority over disease, death, the elements and evil spirits. These miracles worked by Jesus Christ accredit the divine authority of his teaching.

8:1. The Gospel draws attention, for the third time, to the huge crowds that flocked to Jesus: literally, "many multitudes followed him". This shows the popularity he had achieved: he was so popular that the Sanhedrin (the great council of the Jewish nation) dared not arrest him for fear of what the people would do (cf. Mt 21:46; 26:5; Mk 14:2). Later on, they would accuse him before Pilate of stirring up the whole country from Judea to Galilee. And we will see Herod Antipas' eagerness to meet Jesus, of whom he has heard so much (cf. Mt 14:1). In contrast to this huge popularity, we find the elders opposing him and deceiving the people into calling for Jesus' execution (cf. Mt 27:20–22).

8:2. The Fathers have taken the following meaning from this cure: leprosy is a vivid image of sin; it is ugly, disgusting, very contagious and difficult to cure. We are all sinners and we are all in need of God's forgiveness and grace (cf. Rom 3:23–24). The leper in the Gospel knelt down before Jesus, in all humility and trust, begging to be made clean. If we have recourse to our Saviour with that kind of faith, we can be sure that he will cure the wretchedness of our souls. We should often address Christ with this short prayer, borrowed from the leper: "Lord, if you will, you can make me clean."

8:4. According to the Law of Moses (Lev 14), if a leper is cured of his disease, he should present himself to a priest, who will register the cure and give him a certificate which he needs to be reintegrated into the civil and religious life of Israel.

r. Greek *to them*

worthy to have you come under my roof; but only say the word,
and my servant will be healed. 9For I am a man under authority,
with soldiers under me; and I say to one, 'Go,' and he goes, and to
another, 'Come,' and he comes, and to my slave, 'Do this,' and he
does it." 10When Jesus heard him, he marvelled, and said to those
who followed him, "Truly, I say to you, not even[s] in Israel have I
found such faith. 11I tell you, many will come from east and west Lk 13:28f Is 49:12; 59:19
and sit at table with Abraham, Isaac, and Jacob in the kingdom of Mal 1:11
heaven, 12while the sons of the kingdom will be thrown into the Ps 107:3
outer darkness; there men will weep and gnash their teeth." 13And
to the centurion Jesus said, "Go; be it done for you as you have
believed." And the servant was healed at that very moment.

Curing of Peter's mother-in-law

14And when Jesus entered Peter's house, he saw his mother-in-law Mk 1:29–34
lying sick with a fever; 15he touched her hand, and the fever left Lk 4:38–41
her, and she rose and served him. 1 Cor 9:5

Other cures

16That evening they brought to him many who were possessed
with demons; and he cast out the spirits with a word, and healed

---

Leviticus also prescribes the purifications and sacrifice he should offer. Jesus' instruction to the leper is, then, in keeping with the normal way of fulfilling what the laws laid down.

8:5–13. "Centurion": an officer of the Roman army in control of one hundred men. This man's faith is still an example to us. At the solemn moment when a Christian is about to receive Jesus in the Blessed Eucharist, the Church's liturgy places on his lips and in his heart these words of the centurion, to enliven his faith: "Lord, I am not worthy …".

The Jews of this time regarded any Jew who entered a Gentile's house as contracting legal impurity (cf. Jn 19:28; Acts 11:2–3). This centurion has the deference not to place Jesus in an embarrassing position in the eyes of his fellow Israelites. He shows that he is convinced that Jesus has power over disease and illness; he suggests that if Jesus just says the word, he will do what is needed without having actually to visit the house; he is reasoning, in a simple, logical way, on the basis of his own professional experience. Jesus avails of this meeting with a Gentile believer to make a solemn prophecy to the effect that his Gospel is addressed to the world at large; all men, of every nation and race, of every age and condition, are called to follow Christ.

8:14–15. After his body—or soul—is healed, everyone is called to "rise up" from his previous position, to serve Jesus Christ. No laments, no delays; instead one should make oneself immediately available to the Lord.

8:16–17. The expulsion of evil spirits is one of the main signs of the establish-

s. Other ancient authorities read *with no one*

Is 53:4 all who were sick. 17This was to fulfil what was spoken by the
Jn 1:29, 36 prophet Isaiah, "He took our infirmities and bore our diseases."

Following Christ is not easy

Mk 4:35 Lk 8:22 18Now when Jesus saw great crowds around him, he gave orders
Lk 9:57–60 to go over to the other side. 19And a scribe came up and said to
2 Cor 8:9 him, "Teacher, I will follow you wherever you go." 20And Jesus
said to him, "Foxes have holes, and birds of the air have nests; but
1 Kings 19:20 the Son of man has nowhere to lay his head." 21Another of the disciples said to him, "Lord let me first go and bury my father." 22But

---

ment of the Kingdom of God (cf. Mt 12:8). Similarly, the healing of diseases, which ultimately are the result of sin, is one of the signs of the "works of the Messiah" proclaimed by the prophets (cf. Is 29:18; 35:5–6).

8:18–22. From the very outset of his messianic preaching, Jesus rarely stays in the same place; he is always on the move. He "has nowhere to lay his head" (Mt 8:20). Anyone who desires to be with him has to "follow him". This phrase "following Jesus" has a very precise meaning: it means being his disciple (cf. Mt 19:28). Sometimes the crowds "follow him"; but Jesus' true disciples are those who "follow him" in a permanent way, that is, who keep on following him: being a "disciple of Jesus" and "following him" amount to the same thing. After our Lord's ascension, "following him" means being a Christian (cf. Acts 8:26). By the simple and sublime fact of Baptism, every Christian is called, by a divine vocation, to be a full disciple of our Lord, with all that that involves.

The evangelist here gives two specific cases of following Jesus. In the case of the scribe our Lord explains what faith requires of a person who realizes that he has been called; in the second case—that of the man who has already said "yes" to Jesus—he reminds him of what his commitment entails. The soldier who does not leave his position on the battlefront to bury his father, but instead leaves that to those in the rearguard, is doing his duty. If service to one's country makes demands like that on a person, all the more reason for it to happen in the service of Jesus Christ and his Church.

Following Christ, then, means we should make ourselves totally available to him; whatever sacrifice he asks of us we should make: the call to follow Christ means staying up with him, not falling behind; we either follow him or lose him. In the sermon on the mount (Mt 5–7) Jesus explained what following him involves—a teaching that we find summarized in even the most basic catechism of Christian doctrine: a Christian is a man who believes in Jesus Christ—a faith he receives at Baptism—and is duty bound to serve him. Through prayer and friendship with the Lord every Christian should try to discover the demands which this service involves as far as he personally is concerned.

8:20. "The Son of man": this is one of the expressions used in the Old Testament to refer to the Messiah. It appeared first in Daniel 7:14 and was used in Jewish writings in the time of Jesus. Until our Lord began to preach, it had not been understood in all its depth. The title "the Son

Jesus said to him, "Follow me, and leave the dead to bury their Jn 1:43; 5:25
own dead." Rom 16:13

The calming of the storm

23 And when he got into the boat, his disciples followed him. 24 And Mk 4:36–41
behold, there arose a great storm on the sea, so that the boat was Lk 8:23–35
being swamped by the waves; but he was asleep. 25 And they went Ps 4:8
and woke him, saying, "Save us, Lord; we are perishing." 26 And Ps 107:25ff
he said to them, "Why are you afraid, O men of little faith?" Then
he rose and rebuked the winds and the sea; and there was a great
calm. 27 And the men marvelled, saying, "What sort of man is this,
that even winds and sea obey him?"

---

of man" did not fit in very well with Jewish hopes of an earthly Messiah; this was why it was Jesus' favourite way of indicating that he was the Messiah—thereby avoiding any tendency to encourage Jewish nationalism. In the prophecy of Daniel just mentioned this messianic title has a transcendental meaning; by using it Jesus was able discreetly to proclaim that he was the Messiah and yet avoid people interpreting his role in a political sense. After the Resurrection the apostles at last realized that "Son of man" meant nothing less than "Son of God".

8:22. "Leave the dead to bury their own dead": although this sounds very harsh, it is a style of speaking which Jesus did sometimes use. Here the "dead" clearly refers to those whose interest is limited to perishable things and who have no aspirations towards the things that last forever.

"If Jesus forbade him," St John Chrysostom comments, "it was not to have us neglect the honour due to our parents, but to make us realize that nothing is more important than the things of heaven and that we ought to cleave to these and not to put them off even for a little while, though our engagements be ever so indispensable and pressing" (*Hom. on St Matthew*, 27).

8:23–27. This remarkable miracle left a deep impression on Jesus' disciples, as can be seen from the fact that the first three evangelists all report it. Christian Tradition has applied this miracle in various ways to the life of the Church and the experience of the individual soul. From earliest times Christian art and literature have seen the boat as representing the Church, which also has to make its way around hazards which threaten to capsize it. Indeed, very early on, Christians were persecuted in various ways by Jews of their time, and were misunderstood by the public opinion of a pagan society—which also began to persecute them. Jesus' sleeping through the storm has been applied to the fact that sometimes God seems not to come to the Church's rescue during persecution. Following the example of the apostles in the boat, Christians should seek Jesus' help, borrowing their words, "Save us, Lord; we are perishing". Then, when it seems we can bear it no longer, Jesus shows his power: "He rose and rebuked the winds and the sea; and there was a great calm"—but first rebuking us for being men of little faith. Quite often Gospel

The demoniacs of Gadara

Mk 5:1–17 Lk 8:26–37
28And when he came to the other side, to the country of the
Gadarenes,[t] two demoniacs met him, coming out of the tombs, so
Lk 4:41 2 Pet 2:4
fierce that no one could pass that way. 29And behold, they cried
out, "What have you to do with us, O Son of God? Have you
come here to torment us before the time?"* 30Now a herd of many
swine was feeding at some distance from them. 31And the demons
begged him, "If you cast us out, send us away into the herd of
swine." 32And he said to them, "Go." So they came out and went
into the swine; and behold, the whole herd rushed down the steep
bank into the sea, and perished in the waters. 33The herdsmen fled,
and going into the city they told everything, and what had happened to the demoniacs. 34And behold, all the city came out to

---

accounts are meant to serve as examples to us: they epitomize the future history of the Church and of the individual Christian soul.

8:28. Most Gospel codexes and the New Vulgate say "Gadarenes"; but the Vulgate and parallel texts in Mark and Luke have "Gerasenes". Both names are possible; the two main towns in the area were Gerasa and Gadara. The event reported here could have happened close to both towns (limits were not very well defined), though the swine running down into the lake or sea of Galilee makes Gadara somewhat more likely. "Gergesenes" was a suggestion put forward by Origen.

8:28–34. In this episode Jesus once more shows his power over the devil. That it occurred in Gentile territory (Gerasa and Gadara were in the Decapolis, east of Jordan) is borne out by the fact that Jews were forbidden to raise swine, which the Law of Moses declared to be unclean. This and other instances of expulsion of demons narrated in the Gospel are referred to in the Acts of the Apostles, when St Peter addresses Cornelius and his household: "he went about doing good and healing all that were oppressed by the devil" (Acts 10:38). It was a sign that the Kingdom of God had begun (cf. Mt 12:28).

The attitude of local people towards this miracle reminds us that meeting God and living a Christian life require us to subordinate personal plans to God's designs. If we have a selfish or materialistic outlook we fail to appreciate the value of divine things and push God out of our lives, begging him to go away, as these people did.

9:1. "His own city": Capernaum (cf. Mt 4:13 and Mk 2:1).

9:2–6. The sick man and those who bring him to Jesus ask him to cure the man's physical illness; they believe in his supernatural powers. As in other instances of miracles, our Lord concerns himself more with the underlying cause of illness, that is, sin. With divine largesse he gives more than he is asked for, even though people do not appreciate this. St Thomas Aquinas says that Jesus Christ

t. Other ancient authorities read *Gergesenes*; some, *Gerasenes*

meet Jesus; and when they saw him, they begged him to leave their neighbourhood.

Curing of a paralyzed man

9 1And getting into a boat he crossed over and came to his own Mk 2:1–12
city. 2And behold, they brought to him a paralytic, lying on his Lk 5:16–26
bed; and when Jesus saw their faith he said to the paralytic, "Take
heart, my son; your sins are forgiven." 3And behold, some of the Mk 2:7
scribes said to themselves, "This man is blaspheming." 4But Jn 2:25
Jesus, knowing[u] their thoughts, said, "Why do you think evil in
your hearts? 5For which is easier, to say, 'Your sins are forgiven,'
or to say, 'Rise and walk'? 6But that you may know that the Son
of man has authority on earth to forgive sins"—he then said to

---

acts like a good doctor: he cures the cause of the illness (cf. *Comm. on St Matthew*, 9, 1–6).

9:2. The parallel passage of St Mark adds a detail that helps us understand this scene better and explains why the text refers to "their faith": in Mark 2:2–5 we are told that there was such a crowd around Jesus that the people carrying the bed could not get near him. So they had the idea of going up onto the roof and making a hole and lowering the bed down in front of Jesus. This explains his "seeing their faith".

Our Lord was pleased by their boldness, a boldness which resulted from their lively faith which brooked no obstacles. This nice example of daring indicates how we should go about putting charity into practice—also how Jesus feels towards people who show real concern for others: he cures the paralytic who was so ingeniously helped by his friends and relatives; even the sick man himself showed daring by not being afraid of the risk involved.

St Thomas comments on this verse as follows: "This paralytic symbolizes the sinner lying in sin"; just as the paralytic cannot move, so the sinner cannot help himself. The people who bring the paralytic along represent those who, by giving him good advice, lead the sinner to God" (*Comm. on St Matthew*, 9, 2). In order to get close to Jesus the same kind of holy daring is needed, as the saints show us. Anyone who does not act like this will never make important decisions in his life as a Christian.

9:3–7. Here "to say" obviously means "to say and mean it", "to say producing the result which your words imply". Our Lord is arguing as follows: which is easier—to cure the paralytic's body or to forgive the sins of his soul? Undoubtedly, to cure his body; for the soul is superior to the body and therefore diseases of the soul are the more difficult to cure. However, a physical cure can be seen, whereas a cure of the soul cannot. Jesus proves the hidden cure by performing a visible one.

The Jews thought that any illness was due to personal sin (cf. Jn 9:1–3); so when they heard Jesus saying, "Your sins are forgiven", they reasoned in their

u. Other ancient authorities read *seeing*

the paralytic—"Rise, take up your bed and go home." 7And he
rose and went home. 8When the crowds saw it, they were afraid,
and they glorified God, who had given such authority to men.

The call of Matthew

Mk 2:13–17 Lk 5:27–32

9As Jesus passed on from there, he saw a man called Matthew sitting at the tax office; and he said to him, "Follow me." And he
rose and followed him.
10And as he sat at table[v] in the house, behold, many tax collectors and sinners came and sat down with Jesus and his disciples.

---

minds as follows: only God can forgive sins (cf. Lk 5:21); this man says that he has power to forgive sins; therefore, he is claiming a power that belongs to God alone—which is blasphemy. Our Lord, however, forestalls them, using their own arguments: by curing the paralytic by just saying the word, he shows them that since he has the power to cure the effects of sin (which is what they believe disease to be), then he also has power to cure the cause of illness (sin); therefore, he has divine power.

Jesus Christ passed on to the apostles and their successors in the priestly ministry the power to forgive sins: "Receive the Holy Spirit. If you forgive sins of any, they are forgiven; if you retain the sins of any, they are retained" (Jn 20:22–23). "Truly, I say to you, whatever you bind on earth shall be bound in heaven, and whatever you loose on earth shall be loosed in heaven" (Mt 18:18). Priests exercise this power in the sacrament of Penance: in doing so they act not in their own name but in Christ's—*in persona Christi*, as instruments of the Lord.

Hence the respect, veneration and gratitude with which we should approach Confession: in the priest we should see Christ himself, God himself, and we should receive the words of absolution firmly believing that it is Christ who is uttering them through the priest. This is why the minister does not say: "Christ absolves you ...", but rather "I absolve you from your sins ...": he speaks in the first person, so fully is he identified with Jesus Christ himself (cf. St Pius V, *Catechism*, 2, 5, 10).

9:9. "Tax office": a public place for the payment of taxes. On "following Jesus", see the note on Mt 8:18–22.

The Matthew whom Jesus calls here is the apostle of the same name and the human author of the first Gospel. In Mark 2:14 and Luke 5:27 he is called Levi the son of Alphaeus or simply Levi.

In addition to Baptism, through which God calls all Christians (cf. the note on Mt 8:18–22), the Lord can also extend, to whomever he chooses, a further calling to engage in some specific mission in the Church. This second calling is a special grace (cf. Mt 4:19–21; Mk 1:17-20; Jn 1:39; etc.) additional to the earlier calling through Baptism. In other words, it is not man who takes the initiative; it is Jesus who calls, and man who responds to this call by his free personal decision: "You did not choose me, but I chose you" (Jn 15:16).

v. Greek *reclined*

11And when the Pharisees saw this, they said to his disciples, Lk 15:2
"Why does your teacher eat with tax collectors and sinners?"
12But when he heard it, he said, "Those who are well have no need
of a physician, but those who are sick. 13Go and learn what this Hos 6:6
means, 'I desire mercy, and not sacrifice.' For I came not to call 1 Sam 15:22 Mt 18:11
the righteous, but sinners."

A discussion on fasting

14Then the disciples of John came to him, saying, "Why do we Mk 2:18–22
and the Pharisees fast,[w] but your disciples do not fast?" 15And Lk 5:33–38; 18:12

Matthew's promptitude in "following" Jesus' call is to be noted. When God speaks, a soul may be tempted to reply, "Tomorrow; I'm not ready yet." In the last analysis this excuse, and other excuses, are nothing but a sign of selfishness and fear (different from that fear which can be an additional symptom of vocation: cf. Jon 1). "Tomorrow" runs the risk of being too late.

As in the case of the other apostles, St Matthew is called in the midst of the ordinary circumstances of his life: "What amazes you seems natural to me: that God has sought you out in the practice of your profession! That is how he sought the first, Peter and Andrew, James and John, beside their nets, and Matthew, sitting in the custom-house. And—wonder of wonders!—Paul, in his eagerness to destroy the seeds of Christianity" (St Josemaría Escrivá, *The Way*, 799).

9:10–11. The attitude of these Pharisees, who are so prone to judge others and classify them as just men or sinners, is at odds with the attitude and teaching of Jesus. Earlier on, he said, "Judge not, that you be not judged" (Mt 7:1), and elsewhere he added, "Let him who is without sin among you be the first to throw a stone at her" (Jn 8:7). The fact is that all of us are sinners; and our Lord has come to redeem all of us. There is no basis, therefore, for Christians to be scandalized by the sins of others, since any one of us is capable of committing the vilest of sins unless God's grace were to come to our aid.

9:12. There is no reason why anyone should be depressed when he realizes he is full of failings: recognition that we are sinners is the only correct attitude for us to have in the presence of God. He has come to seek all men, but if a person considers himself to be righteous, by so doing he is closing the door to God; all of us in fact are sinners.

9:13. Here Jesus quotes Hosea 6:6, keeping the hyperbole of the Semitic style. A more faithful translation would be "I desire mercy *more than* sacrifice". It is not that our Lord does not want the sacrifices we offer him: he is stressing that every sacrifice should come from the heart, for charity should imbue everything a Christian does—especially his worship of God (see 1 Cor 13:1–13; Mt 5:23–24).

9:14–17. This passage is interesting, not so much because it tells us about the sort of fasting practised by the Jews of the time—particularly the Pharisees and

w. Other ancient authorities add *much* or *often*

Jn 3:29 Jesus said to them, "Can the wedding guests mourn as long as the
bridegroom is with them? The days will come, when the bride-
Jn 1:17 groom is taken away from them, and then they will fast. 16And no
one puts a piece of unshrunk cloth on an old garment, for the
patch tears away from the garment, and a worse tear is made.
17Neither is new wine put into old wineskins; if it is, the skins
burst, and the wine is spilled, and the skins are destroyed; but new
wine is put into fresh wineskins, and so both are preserved."

The raising of Jairus' daughter and the curing of the woman with a haemorrhage

Mk 5:22–43 Lk 8:41–56 18While he was thus speaking to them, behold, a ruler came in and
knelt before him, saying, "My daughter has just died; but come
and lay your hand on her, and she will live." 19And Jesus rose and
followed him, with his disciples.

20And behold, a woman who had suffered from a hemorrhage
for twelve years came up behind him and touched the fringe of his

---

John the Baptist's disciples—but because of the reason Jesus gives for not requiring his disciples to fast in that way. His reply is both instructive and prophetic. Christianity is not a mere mending or adjusting of the old suit of Judaism. The redemption wrought by Jesus involves a total regeneration. Its spirit is too new and too vital to be suited to old forms of penance, which will no longer apply.

We know that in our Lord's time Jewish theology schools were in the grip of a highly complicated casuistry to do with fasting, purifications etc, which smothered the simplicity of genuine piety. Jesus' words point to that simplicity of heart with which his disciples might practise prayer, fasting and almsgiving (cf. Mt 6:1–18 and notes to same). From apostolic times onwards it is for the Church, using the authority given it by our Lord, to set out the different forms fasting should take in different periods and situations.

9:15. "The wedding guests": literally, "the sons of the house where the wedding is being celebrated"—an expression meaning the bridegroom's closest friends. This is an example of how St Matthew uses typical Semitic turns of phrase, presenting Jesus' manner of speech.

This "house" to which Jesus refers has a deeper meaning; set beside the parable of the guests at the wedding (Mt 22:1ff), it symbolizes the Church as the house of God and the body of Christ: "Moses was faithful in all God's house as a servant, to testify to the things that were to be spoken later, but Christ was faithful over God's house as a son. And we are his house if we hold fast our confidence and pride in our hope" (Heb 3:5–6). The second part of the verse refers to the violent death Jesus would meet.

9:18–26. Here are two miracles which occur almost simultaneously. From parallel passages in Mark (5:21–43) and Luke (8:40–56) we know that the "ruler" (of the synagogue) referred to here was called Jairus. The Gospels report Jesus raising three people to life— this girl, the son of the widow of Nain, and Lazarus.

garment; [21]for she said to herself, "If I only touch his garment, I
shall be made well." [22]Jesus turned, and seeing her he said, "Take
heart, daughter; your faith has made you well." And instantly the
woman was made well. [23]And when Jesus came to the ruler's
house, and saw the flute players, and the crowd making a tumult,
[24]he said, "Depart; for the girl is not dead but sleeping." And they Jn 11:11, 14,
laughed at him. [25]But when the crowd had been put outside, he 25
went in and took her by the hand, and the girl arose. [26]And the
report of this went through all that district.

Curing of two blind men. The dumb devil

[27]And as Jesus passed on from there, two blind men followed him,
crying aloud, "Have mercy on us, Son of David." [28]When he
entered the house, the blind men came to him; and Jesus said to
them, "Do you believe that I am able to do this?" They said to
him, "Yes, Lord." [29]Then he touched their eyes, saying, "According to your faith be it done to you." [30]And their eyes were opened.

In each case the identity of the person is clearly given.

This account shows us, once again, the role faith plays in Jesus' saving actions. In the case of the woman with the hemorrhage we should note that Jesus is won over by her sincerity and faith: she does not let obstacles get in her way. Similarly, Jairus does not care what people will say; a prominent person in his city, he humbles himself before Jesus for all to see.

9:18. "Knelt before him": the eastern way of showing respect to God or to important people. In the liturgy, especially in the presence of the Blessed Eucharist, reverences are a legitimate and appropriate external sign of internal faith and adoration.

9:23. "The flute players": engaged to provide music at wakes and funerals.

9:24. "Depart, for the girl is not dead, but sleeping": Jesus says the same thing about Lazarus: "Our friend Lazarus has fallen asleep, but I go to awaken him" (Jn 11:11).

Although Jesus speaks of sleep, there is no question of the girl—or Lazarus, later—not being dead. For our Lord there is only one true death—that of eternal punishment (cf. Mt 10:28).

9:27–34. The evangelist shows people's different reactions to miracles. Everyone admits that God is at work in these events—everyone, that is, except the Pharisees who attribute them to the power of the devil. A pharisaical attitude so hardens a person's heart that he becomes closed to any possibility of salvation. The fact that the blind men recognize Jesus as the Messiah (they call him "Son of David": v. 27) may have exasperated the Pharisees. Despite Jesus' sublime teaching, despite his miracles, they remain entrenched in their opposition.

In the light of this episode it is easy enough to see that the paradox is true: there are blind people who in fact see God and seers who see no trace of him.

9:30. Why did our Lord not want them to publicize the miracle? Because his

And Jesus sternly charged them, "See that no one knows it." 31But
they went away and spread his fame through all that district.
32As they were going away, behold, a dumb demoniac was
brought to him. 33And when the demon had been cast out, the
dumb man spoke; and the crowds marvelled, saying, "Never was
anything like this seen in Israel." 34But the Pharisees said, "He
casts out demons by the prince of demons."

The need for good pastors

35And Jesus went about all the cities and villages, teaching in their
synagogues and preaching the gospel of the kingdom, and healing
Mk 6:34 every disease and every infirmity. 36When he saw the crowds, he
had compassion for them, because they were harassed and help-

---

plan was to gradually manifest himself as the Messiah, the Son of God. He did not want to anticipate events which would occur in their own good time; nor did he want the crowd to start hailing him as Messiah King, because their notion of messiah was a nationalistic, not a spiritual one. However, the crowd did in fact proclaim him when he worked the miracles of the loaves and the fish (Jn 6:14–15): "When the people saw the sign which he had done, they said, 'This is indeed the prophet who is to come into the world!' Perceiving then that they were about to come and take him by force to make him king, Jesus withdrew again to the hills by himself."

9:31. St Jerome (cf. *Comm. on Matthew*, 9, 31) says that the blind men spread the news of their cure, not out of disobedience to Jesus, but because it was the only way they could find to express their gratitude.

9:35. The Second Vatican Council uses this passage when teaching about the message of Christian charity which the Church should always be spreading: "Christian charity is extended to all without distinction of race, social condition or religion, and seeks neither gain nor gratitude. Just as God loves us with a gratuitous love, so too the faithful, in their charity, should be concerned for mankind, loving it with that same love with which God sought man. As Christ went about all the towns and villages healing every sickness and infirmity, as a sign that the Kingdom of God had come, so the Church, through its children, joins itself with men of every condition, but especially with the poor and afflicted, and willingly spends herself for them" (*Ad gentes*, 12).

9:36. "He had compassion for them": the Greek verb is very expressive; it means "he was deeply moved". Jesus was moved when he saw the people, because their pastors, instead of guiding them and tending them, led them astray, behaving more like wolves than genuine shepherds of their flock. Jesus sees the prophecy of Ezekiel 34 as now being fulfilled; in that passage God, through the prophet, upbraids the false shepherds of Israel and promises to send them the Messiah to be their new leader.

"If we were consistent with our faith when we looked around us and contemplated the world and its history, we

less, like sheep without a shepherd. [37]Then he said to his disciples, Num 27:17
"The harvest is plentiful, but the labourers are few; [38]pray Ezek 34:5 Lk 10:2
therefore the Lord of the harvest to send out labourers into his
harvest."

5. FROM THE OLD TO THE NEW PEOPLE OF GOD

The calling of the twelve apostles

10 [1]And he called to him his twelve disciples and gave them Mk 6:7–13
authority over unclean spirits, to cast them out, and to heal Lk 9:1–5
every disease and every infirmity. [2]The names of the twelve apos- Mk 3:14–19 Lk 6:13–16
tles are these: first, Simon, who is called Peter, and Andrew his Jn 1:40–49

---

would be unable to avoid feeling in our own hearts the same sentiments that filled the heart of our Lord" (St J. Escrivá, *Christ Is Passing By*, 133). Reflection on the spiritual needs of the world should lead us to be tirelessly apostolic.

9:37–38. After contemplating the crowds neglected by their shepherds, Jesus uses the image of the harvest to show us that that same crowd is ready to receive the effects of Redemption: "I tell you, lift up your eyes, and see now the fields are already white for harvest" (Jn 4:35). The field of the Jewish people cultivated by the prophets—most recently by John the Baptist—is full of ripe wheat. In farmwork, the harvest is lost if the farmer does not reap at the right time; down the centuries the Church feels a similar need to be out harvesting because there is a big harvest ready to be won.

However, as in the time of Jesus, there is a shortage of labourers. Our Lord tells us how to deal with this: we should pray God, the Lord of the harvest, to send the necessary labourers. If a Christian prays hard, it is difficult to imagine his not feeling urged to play his part in this apostolate. In obeying this commandment to pray for labourers, we should pray especially for there to be no lack of good shepherds, who will be able to equip others with the necessary means of sanctification needed to back up the apostolate.

In this connexion Paul VI reminds us: "the responsibility for spreading the Gospel that saves belongs to everyone—to all those who have received it! The missionary duty concerns the whole body of the Church; in different ways and to different degrees, it is true, but we must all of us be united in carrying out this duty. Now let the conscience of every believer ask himself: Have I carried out my missionary duty? Prayer for the Missions is the first way of fulfilling this duty" (Angelus Address, 23 October 1977).

10:1–4. Jesus calls his twelve apostles after recommending to them to pray to the Lord to send labourers into his harvest (cf. Mt 9:38). Christians' apostolic action should always, then, be preceded and accompanied by a life of constant prayer: apostolate is a divine affair, not a merely human one. Our Lord starts his Church by calling twelve men to be, as it were, twelve patriarchs of the new people of God, the Church. This new people is

brother; James the son of Zebedee, and John his brother; 3Philip
and Bartholomew; Thomas and Matthew the tax collector; James
the son of Alphaeus, and Thaddaeus;[x] 4Simon the Cananaean, and
Judas Iscariot, who betrayed him.

The apostles' first mission

Acts 13:46 5These twelve Jesus sent out, charging them, "Go nowhere among
Jer 50:6 Lk 10:9 the Gentiles, and enter no town of the Samaritans,* 6but go rather

---

established not by physical but by spiritual generation. The names of those apostles are specifically mentioned here. They were not scholarly, powerful or important people: they were average, ordinary people who responded faithfully to the grace of their calling—all of them, that is, except Judas Iscariot. Even before his death and resurrection Jesus confers on them the power to cast out unclean spirits and cure illnesses—as an earnest sign of and as training for the saving mission which he will entrust to them.

The Church reveres these first Christians in a very special way and is proud to carry on their supernatural mission, and to be faithful to the witness they bore to the teaching of Christ. The true Church is absent unless there is uninterrupted apostolic succession and identification with the spirit which the apostles made their own.

"Apostle": this word means "sent"; Jesus sent them out to preach his Kingdom and pass on his teaching. The Second Vatican Council, in line with Vatican I, "confesses" and "declares" that the Church has a hierarchical structure: "The Lord Jesus, having prayed at length to the Father, called to himself those whom he willed and appointed twelve to be with him, whom he might send to preach the Kingdom of God (cf. Mk 3:13–19; Mt 10:1–10). These apostles (cf. Lk 6:13) he constituted in the form of a college or permanent assembly, at the head of which he placed Peter, chosen from among them (cf. Jn 21:15–17). He sent them first of all to the children of Israel and then to all peoples (cf. Rom 1:16), so that, sharing in his power, they might make all peoples his disciples and sanctify and govern them (cf. Mt 28:16–20; Mk 16:15; Lk 24:45–48; Jn 20:21–23) and thus spread the Church and, administering it under the guidance of the Lord, shepherd it all days until the end of the world (cf. Mt 28:28)" (*Lumen gentium*, 19).

10:1. In this chapter St Matthew describes how Jesus, with a view to the spreading of the Kingdom of God which he inaugurates, decides to establish a Church, which he does by giving special powers and training to these twelve men who are its seed.

10:5–15. After revealing his intention to found the Church by choosing the Twelve (vv. 1–4), in the present passage he shows that he intends to start training these first apostles. In other words, from early on in his public ministry he began to lay the foundations of his Church. Everyone needs doctrinal and apostolic training to follow his Christian calling. The Church has a duty to teach, and the faithful have a parallel duty to make that teaching their own. Therefore, every

x. Other ancient authorities read *Lebbaeus* or *Lebbaeus called Thaddaeus*

to the lost sheep of the house of Israel. 7And preach as you go,
saying, 'The kingdom of heaven is at hand.' 8Heal the sick, raise Acts 20:33
the dead, cleanse lepers, cast out demons. You received without
pay, give without pay. 9Take no gold, nor silver, nor copper in Lk 10:4
your belts, 10no bag for your journey, nor two tunics, nor sandals, 1 Tim 5:18

Christian should avail himself or herself of the facilities for training which the Church offers—which will vary according to a person's circumstances.

10:5–6. In his plan of salvation God gave certain promises (to Abraham and the patriarchs), a Covenant and a Law (the Law of Moses), and sent the prophets. The Messiah would be born into this chosen people, which explains why the Messiah and the Kingdom of God were to be preached to the house of Israel before being preached to Gentiles. Therefore, in their early apprenticeship, Jesus restricts the apostles' area of activity to the Jews, without this taking from the worldwide scope of the Church's mission. As we will see, much later on he charges them to "go and make disciples of all nations" (Mt 28:19); "Go into all the world and preach the Gospel to the whole creation" (Mk 16:16). The apostles also, in the early days of the spread of the Church, usually sought out the Jewish community in any new city they entered, and preached first to them (cf. Acts 13:46).

10:7–8. Previously, the prophets, when speaking of the messianic times, had used imagery suited to the people's spiritual immaturity. Now, Jesus, in sending his apostles to proclaim that the promised Kingdom of God is imminent, lays stress on its spiritual dimension. The powers mentioned in verse 8 are the very sign of the Kingdom of God or the reign of the Messiah proclaimed by the prophets. At first (chaps. 8 and 9) it is Jesus who exercises these messianic powers; now he gives them to his disciples as proof that his mission is divine (Is 35:5–6; 40:9; 52:7; 61:1).

10:9. "Belts": twin belts, stitched together leaving space where coins and other small, heavy objects could be secreted and carried.

10:9–10. Jesus urges his disciples to set out on their mission without delay. They should not be worried about material or human equipment: God will make up any shortfall. This holy audacity in setting about God's work is to be found throughout the history of the Church: if Christians had bided their time, waiting until they had the necessary material resources, many, many souls would never have received the light of Christ. Once a Christian is clear in his mind about what God wants him to do, he should not stay at home checking to see if he has the wherewithal to do it. "In your apostolic undertakings you are right—it's your duty—to consider what means the world can offer you (2 + 2 = 4), but don't forget—ever!—that, fortunately, your calculations must include another term: God + 2 + 2 …" (St Josemaría Escrivá, *The Way*, 471).

However, that being said, we should not try to force God's hand, to have him do something exceptional, when in fact we can meet needs by our own efforts and work. This means that Christians should generously support those who, because they are totally dedicated to the spiritual welfare of their brethren, have

Num 18:31 nor a staff; for the labourer deserves his food. [11]And whatever
town or village you enter, find out who is worthy in it, and stay
Lk 10:5f with him until you depart. [12]As you enter the house, salute it.
[13]And if the house is worthy, let your peace come upon it; but if it
Lk 10:10–12 is not worthy, let your peace return to you. [14]And if any one will
Acts 13:51; 18:6 not receive you or listen to your words, shake off the dust from
your feet as you leave that house or town. [15]Truly, I say to you, it
Lk 20:47 shall be more tolerable on the day of judgment for the land of
Sodom and Gomorrah than for that town.

Lk 10:3
Jn 10:12

Acts 20:29 **Jesus' instructions to the apostles**

Rom 16:19 [16]"Behold, I send you out as sheep in the midst of wolves; so be
Eph 5:15 wise as serpents and innocent as doves. [17]Beware of men; for they
Mk 13:9–13 Lk 21:12–17 will deliver you up to councils, and flog you in their synagogues,
Mt 24:9; 24:14 Acts 25:23; 27:24 [18]and you will be dragged before governors and kings for my

---

no time left over to provide for themselves: in this connexion see Jesus' promise in Mt 10:40–42.

10:11–15. "Peace" was, and still is, the normal Jewish form of greeting. On the apostles' lips it is meant to have a deeper meaning—to be a sign of God's blessing which Jesus' disciples, who are his envoys, pour out on those who receive them. The commandment our Lord gives here affects not only this specific mission; it is a kind of prophecy which applies to all times. His messenger does not become discouraged if his word is not well received. He knows that God's blessing is never ineffective (cf. Is 55:11), and that every generous effort a Christian makes will always produce fruit. The word spoken in apostolate always brings with it the grace of conversion: "Many of those who heard the word believed; and the number of the men came to about five thousand" (Acts 4:4; cf. 10:44; Rom 10:17).

Man should listen to this word of the Gospel and believe in it (Acts 13:48; 15:7). If he accepts it and stays faithful to it his soul is consoled, he obtains peace (Acts 8:39) and salvation (Acts 11:4–18). But if he rejects it, he is not free from blame and God will judge him for shutting out the grace he was offered.

10:16–23. The instructions and warnings Jesus gives here apply right through the history of the Church. It is difficult for the world to understand the way of God. Sometimes there will be persecutions, sometimes indifference to the Gospel or failure to understand it. Genuine commitment to Jesus always involves effort—which is not surprising, because Jesus himself was a sign of contradiction; indeed, if that were not the experience of a Christian, he would have to ask himself whether he was not in fact a worldly person. There are certain worldly things a Christian cannot compromise about, no matter how much they are in fashion. Therefore, Christian life inevitably involves nonconformity with anything that goes against faith and morals (cf. Rom 12:2). It is not surprising that a Christian's life often involves choosing between heroism and treachery. Difficulties of this sort should not make us afraid: we are not alone, we can count on

sake, to bear testimony before them and the Gentiles. 19When they Lk 12:11f
deliver you up, do not be anxious how you are to speak or what
you are to say; for what you are to say will be given to you in that
hour; 20for it is not you who speak, but the Spirit of your Father Jn 14:26; 1 Cor 2:4
speaking through you. 21Brother will deliver up brother to death, Mic 7:6
and the father his child, and children will rise against parents and
have them put to death; 22and you will be hated by all for my Jn 15:21
name's sake. But he who endures to the end will be saved. 23When
they persecute you in one town, flee to the next; for truly, I say to
you, you will not have gone through all the towns of Israel, before
the Son of man comes.

24"A disciple is not above his teacher, nor a servant[y] above his
master; 25it is enough for the disciple to be like his teacher, and the Lk 6:40; Jn 13:16; 15:20
servant[y] like his master. If they have called the master of the house Mt 12:24
Beelzebul, how much more will they malign those of his household.

---

the powerful help of our Father God to give us strength and daring.

10:20. Here Jesus teaches the completely supernatural character of the witness he asks his disciples to bear. The documented accounts of a host of Christian martyrs prove that he has kept this promise: they bear eloquent witness to the serenity and wisdom of often uneducated people, some of them scarcely more than children. The teaching contained in this verse provides the basis for the fortitude and confidence a Christian should have whenever he has to profess his faith in difficult situations. He will not be alone, for the Holy Spirit will give him words of divine wisdom.

10:23. In interpreting this text, the first thing is to reject the view of rationalists who argue that Jesus was convinced that soon he would come in glory and the world would come to an end. That interpretation is clearly at odds with many passages of the Gospel and the New Testament. Clearly, Jesus refers to himself when he speaks of the "Son of man", whose glory will be manifested in this way. The most cogent interpretation is that Jesus is referring here, primarily, to the historical event of the first Jewish war against Rome, which ended with the destruction of Jerusalem and of the temple in the year 70, and which led to the scattering of the Jewish people. But this event, which would occur a few years after Jesus' death, is an image or a prophetic symbol of the end of the world (cf. the note on Mt 24:1). The coming of Christ in glory will happen at a time which God has not revealed. Uncertainty about the end of the world helps Christians and the Church to be ever-vigilant.

10:24–25. Jesus uses these two proverbs to hint at the future that awaits his disciples: their greatest glory will consist in imitating the Master, being identified with him, even if this means being despised and persecuted as he was before them: his example is what guides a Christian; as he himself said, "I am the way, and the truth, and the life" (Jn 14:6).

y. Or *slave*

Lk 12:2–9 Mk 4:22 Lk 8:17 [26]"So have no fear of them; for nothing is covered that will not
be revealed, or hidden that will not be known. [27]What I tell you in
the dark, utter in the light; and what you hear whispered, proclaim
Jas 4:12 upon the housetops. [28] And do not fear those who kill the body but
cannot kill the soul; rather fear him who can destroy both soul and
body in hell.[z] [29]Are not two sparrows sold for a penny? And not
one of them will fall to the ground without your Father's will.
[30]But even the hairs of your head are all numbered. [31]Fear not,
therefore; you are of more value than many sparrows. [32]So every
one who acknowledges me before men, I also will acknowledge

Beelzebul (cf. Lk 11:15) was the name of the idol of the ancient Philistine city of Ekron. The Jews later used the word to describe the devil or the prince of devils (cf. Mt 12:24), and their hatred of Jesus led them to the extreme of applying it to him.

To equip them for the persecution and misunderstanding which Christians will suffer (Jn 15:18), Jesus encourages them by promising to stay close to them. Towards the end of his life he will call them his friends (Jn 15:15) and little children (Jn 13:33).

10:26–27. Jesus tells his disciples not to be afraid of calumny and detraction. A day will come when everyone will come to know the whole truth about everyone else, their real intentions, the true dispositions of their souls. In the meantime, those who belong to God may be misrepresented by those who resort to lies, out of malice or passion. These are the hidden things which will be made known.

Christ also tells the apostles to speak out clearly. Jesus' divine teaching method led him to speak to the crowds in parables so that they came to discover his true personality by easy stages. After the coming of the Holy Spirit (cf. Acts 1:8), the apostles would have to preach from the rooftops about what Jesus had taught them.

We too have to make Christ's doctrine known in its entirety, without any ambiguity, without being influenced by false prudence or fear of the consequences.

10:28. Using this and other Gospel texts (Mt 5:22, 29; 18:9; Mk 9:43, 45, 47; Lk 12:5), the Church teaches that hell exists; there those who die in mortal sin suffer eternal punishment (cf. St Pius V, *Catechism*, 1, 6, 3), in a manner not known to us in this life (cf. St Teresa of Avila, *Life*, chap. 32). See the notes on Lk 16:19–31.

Therefore, our Lord warns his disciples against false fear. We should not fear those who can only kill the body. Only God can cast body and soul into hell. Therefore God is the only one we should fear and respect; he is our Prince and Supreme Judge—not men. The martyrs have obeyed this precept of the Lord in the fullest way, well aware that eternal life is worth much more than earthly life.

10:29–31. An *as* (translated here as "penny") was a small coin of very little value. Christ uses it to illustrate how much God loves his creatures. As St Jerome says (*Comm. on Matthew*, 10:29–31): "If little birds, which are of such

z. Greek *Gehenna*

before my Father who is in heaven; [33]but whoever denies me Lk 9:26
before men, I also will deny before my Father who is in heaven.
[34]"Do not think that I have come to bring peace on earth; I have Lk 12:51–53
not come to bring peace, but a sword. [35]For I have come to set a Mic 7:6
man against his father, and a daughter against her mother, and a
daughter-in-law against her mother-in-law; [36]and a man's foes will be
those of his own household. [37]He who loves father or mother more Deut 33:9
than me is not worthy of me; and he who loves son or daughter Lk 14:26f

---

little value, still come under the providence and care of God, how is it that you, who, given the nature of your soul, are immortal, can fear that you are not looked after carefully by him whom you respect as your Father?" Jesus again teaches us about the fatherly providence of God, which he spoke about at length in the Sermon on the Mount (cf. Mt 6:19–34).

10:32–33. Here Jesus tells us that public confession of our faith in him—whatever the consequences—is an indispensable condition for eternal salvation. After the Judgment, Christ will welcome those who have given testimony of their faith and condemn those whom fear caused to be ashamed of him (cf. Mt 7:23; 25:41; Rev 21:8). The Church honours as "confessors" those saints who have not undergone physical martyrdom but whose lives bore witness to the Catholic faith. Although every Christian should be ready to die for his faith, most Christians are called to be confessors of the faith.

10:34–37. Our Lord has not come to bring a false and earthly peace—the sort of tranquillity the self-seeking person yearns for; he wants us to struggle against our own passions and against sin and its effects. The sword he equips us with for this struggle is, in the words of Scripture, "the sword of the Spirit which is the word of God" (Eph 6:17), "lively and active, sharper than any two-edged sword, piercing to the division of soul and spirit, of joints and marrow, and discerning the thoughts and intentions of the heart" (Heb 4:12).

The word of God in fact leads to these divisions mentioned here. It can lead, even within families, to those who embrace the faith being regarded as enemies by relatives who resist the word of truth. This is why our Lord goes on (v. 37) to say that nothing should come between him and his disciple—not even father, mother, son or daughter: any and every obstacle (cf. Mt 5:29–30) must be avoided.

Obviously these words of Jesus do not set up any opposition between the first and fourth commandments (love for God above all things and love for one's parents): he is simply indicating the order of priorities. We should love God with all our strength (cf. Mt 22:37), and make a serious effort to be saints; and we should also love and respect—in theory and in practice—the parents God has given us; they have generously cooperated with the creative power of God in bringing us into the world and there is so much that we owe them. But love for our parents should not come before love of God; usually there is no reason why these two loves should clash, but if that should ever happen, we should be quite clear in mind and in heart about what Jesus says here. He has in fact given us an example to follow on this point: "How is it that you sought me? Did you not know that I must

more than me is not worthy of me; [38]and he who does not take his
Lk 17:33 cross and follow me is not worthy of me. [39]He who finds his life
Jn 12:25 will lose it, and he who loses his life for my sake will find it.
[40]"He who receives you receives me, and he who receives me
Lk 10:16 receives him who sent me. [41]He who receives a prophet because
Jn 12:44; 13:20 he is a prophet shall receive a prophet's reward, and he who
receives a righteous man because he is a righteous man shall
Mk 9:41 receive a righteous man's reward. [42]And whoever gives to one of
these little ones even a cup of cold water because he is a disciple,
truly, I say to you, he shall not lose his reward."

Messengers from John the Baptist

11 [1]And when Jesus had finished instructing his twelve disciples, he went on from there to teach and preach in their cities.

---

be in my Father's house?" (Lk 2:49)—his reply when, as a youth, Mary and Joseph found him in the temple of Jerusalem after a long search. This event in our Lord's life is a guideline for every Christian—parent or child. Children should learn from it that their affection for their parents should never come before their love for God, particularly when our Creator asks us to follow him in a way that implies special self-giving on our part; parents should take the lesson that their children belong to God in the first place, and therefore he has a right to do with them what he wishes, even if this involves sacrifice, even heroic sacrifice. This teaching of our Lord asks us to be generous and to let God have his way. In fact, however, God never lets himself be outdone in generosity. Jesus has promised a hundredfold gain, even in this life, and later on eternal life (cf. Mt 19:29), to those who readily respond to his holy will.

10:38–39. The teaching contained in the preceding verses is summed up in these two succinct sentences. Following Christ, doing what he asks, means risking this present life to gain eternal life.

"People who are constantly concerned with themselves, who act above all for their own satisfaction, endanger their eternal salvation and cannot avoid being unhappy even in this life. Only if a person forgets himself and gives himself to God and to others, in marriage as well as in any other aspect of life, can he be happy on this earth, with a happiness that is a preparation for, and a foretaste of, the joy of heaven" (St Josemaría Escrivá; *Christ Is Passing By*, 24). Clearly, Christian life is based on self-denial: there is no Christianity without the cross.

10:40. To encourage the apostles and to persuade others to receive them, our Lord affirms that there is an intimate solidarity, or even a kind of identity, between himself and his disciples. God in Christ, Christ in the apostles: this is the bridge between heaven and earth (cf. 1 Cor 3:21–23).

10:41–42. A prophet's mission is not essentially one of announcing future events; his main role is that of communicating the word of God (cf. Jer 11:2; Is 1:2). The righteous man, the just man, is

2Now when John heard in prison about the deeds of the Christ, Lk 7:18–35 Mt 14:3
he sent word by his disciples 3and said to him, "Are you he who is Mal 3:1
to come, or shall we look for another?"* 4And Jesus answered Dan 9:26
them, "Go and tell John what you hear and see: 5the blind receive Is 35:5f; 61:1
their sight and the lame walk, lepers are cleansed and the deaf Lk 4:18
hear, and the dead are raised up, and the poor have good news
preached to them. 6And blessed is he who takes no offence at me."
7As they went away, Jesus began to speak to the crowds concerning John: "What did you go out into the wilderness to behold?
A reed shaken by the wind? 8Why then did you go out? To see a
man[a] clothed in soft raiment? Behold, those who wear soft raiment are in kings' houses. 9Why then did you go out? To see a Lk 1:76
prophet?[b] Yes, I tell you, and more than a prophet. 10This is he of Mal 3:1
whom it is written, Mk 1:2 Jn 3:28

> 'Behold, I send my messenger before thy face,
> who shall prepare thy way before thee.'

---

he who obeys the Law of God and follows his paths (cf. Gen 6:9; Is 3:10). Here Jesus tells us that everyone who humbly listens to and welcomes prophets and righteous men, recognizing God in them, will receive the reward of a prophet and a righteous man. The very fact of generously receiving God's friends will gain one the reward that they obtain. Similarly, if we should see God in the least of his disciples (v. 42), even if they do not seem very important, they are important, because they are envoys of God and of his Son. That is why he who gives them a glass of cold water—an alms, or any small service—will receive a reward, for he has shown generosity to our Lord himself (cf. Mt 25:40).

11:1. In chapters 11 and 12 the Gospel records the obduracy of the Jewish leaders towards Jesus, despite hearing his teaching (chaps. 5–7) and seeing the miracles which bear witness to the divine nature of his person and his doctrine (chaps. 8–9).

11:2. John knew that Jesus was the Messiah (cf. Mt 3:13–17). He sent his disciples to him so that they could shed their mistaken notions about the kind of Messiah to expect, and come to recognize Jesus.

11:3–6. Jesus replies to the Baptist's disciples by pointing to the fact that they are witnessing the signs that the ancient prophecies said would mark the advent of the Messiah and his Kingdom (cf. Is 35:5, 61:1; etc.). He says, in effect, that he is the prophet who "was to come". The miracles reported in the Gospel (chaps. 8–9) and the teaching given to the people (chaps. 5–7) prove that Jesus of Nazareth is the expected Messiah.

11:6. Jesus here corrects the mistaken idea which many Jews had of the Messiah, casting him in the role of a powerful earthly ruler—a far cry from the humble attitude of Jesus. It is not surprising that he was a stumbling block to Jews (cf. Is 8:14–15; 1 Cor 1:23).

a. Or *What then did you go out to see? A man ...* **b.** Other ancient authorities read *What then did you go out to see? A prophet?*

11 Truly, I say to you, among those born of women there has risen
Lk 16:16; 13:24; Jn 6:15 — no one greater than John the Baptist; yet he who is least in the
kingdom of heaven is greater than he. 12 From the days of John the
Baptist until now the kingdom of heaven has suffered violence,[c]
and men of violence take it by force. 13 For all the prophets and the
Mal 3:23; Mt 17:10–13 — law prophesied until John; 14 and if you are willing to accept it, he
is Elijah who is to come. 15 He who has ears to hear,[d] let him hear.

Jesus reproaches his contemporaries

16 "But to what shall I compare this generation? It is like children
sitting in the market places and calling to their playmates,
Prov 29:9 — 17 'We piped to you, and you did not dance;
we wailed, and you did not mourn.'

11:11. With John the Old Testament is brought to a close and we are on the threshold of the New. The Precursor had the honour of ushering Christ in, making him known to men. God had assigned him the exalted mission of preparing his contemporaries to hear the Gospel. The Baptist's faithfulness is recognized and proclaimed by Jesus. The praise he receives is a reward for his humility: John, realizing what his role was, had said, "He must increase, but I must decrease" (Jn 3:30).

St John the Baptist was the greatest in the sense that he had received a mission unique and incomparable in the context of the Old Testament. However, in the Kingdom of heaven (the New Testament) inaugurated by Christ, the divine gift of grace makes the least of those who faithfully receive it greater than the greatest in the earlier dispensation. Once the work of our redemption is accomplished, God's grace will also be extended to the just of the Old Alliance. Thus, the greatness of John the Baptist, the Precursor and the last of the prophets, will be enhanced by the dignity of being made a son of God.

11:12. "The Kingdom of heaven has suffered violence": once John the Baptist announces that the Christ is already come, the powers of hell redouble their desperate assault, which continues right through the lifetime of the Church (cf. Eph 6:12). The situation described here seems to be this: the leaders of the Jewish people, and their blind followers, were waiting for the Kingdom of God the way people wait for a rightful legacy to come their way; but while they rest on the laurels of the rights and rewards they think their race entitles them to, others, the men of violence (literally, attackers) are taking it, as it were, by force, by fighting the enemies of the soul—the world, the flesh and the devil.

"This violence is not directed against others. It is a violence used to fight your own weaknesses and miseries, a fortitude, which prevents you from camouflaging your own infidelities, a boldness to own up to the faith even when the environment is hostile" (St Josemaría Escrivá, *Christ Is Passing By*, 82).

This is the attitude of those who fight their passions and do themselves violence, thereby attaining the Kingdom of

c. Or *has been coming violently* **d.** Other ancient authorities omit *to hear*

[18]For John came neither eating nor drinking, and they say, 'He has
a demon'; [19]the Son of man came eating and drinking, and they
say, 'Behold, a glutton and a drunkard, a friend of tax collectors
and sinners!' Yet wisdom is justified by her deeds."[e]

Jesus reproaches cities for their unbelief

[20]Then he began to upbraid the cities where most of his mighty Lk 10:12–15
works had been done, because they did not repent. [21]"Woe to you, Jn 3:6
Chorazin! woe to you, Bethsaida! for if the mighty works done in
you had been done in Tyre and Sidon, they would have repented
long ago in sackcloth and ashes. [22]But I tell you, it shall be more
tolerable on the day of judgment for Tyre and Sidon than for you.
[23]And you, Capernaum, will you be exalted to heaven? You shall Is 14:13, 15

---

heaven and becoming one with Christ. As Clement of Alexandria puts it: "The Kingdom of heaven does not belong to those who sleep and who indulge all their desires, but to those who fight against themselves" (*Quis dives salvetur?*, 21).

11:14. John the Baptist is Elijah, not in person, but by virtue of his mission (cf. Mt 17:10–13; Mk 9:10–12).

11:16–19. Making reference to a popular song or a child's game of his time, Jesus reproaches those who offer groundless excuses for not recognizing him. From the beginning of human history the Lord has striven to attract all men to himself: "What more was there to do for my vineyard, that I have not done in it?" (Is 5:4), and often he has been rejected: "When I looked for it to yield grapes, why did it yield wild grapes?" (Is 5:4).

Our Lord also condemns calumny: some people do try to justify their own behaviour by seeing sin where there is only virtue. "When they find something which is quite obviously good," St Gregory the Great says, "they pry into it to see if there is not also some badness hidden in it" (*Moralia*, 6, 22). The Baptist's fasting they interpret as the work of the devil; whereas they accuse Jesus of being a glutton. The evangelist has to report these calumnies and accusations spoken against our Lord; otherwise, we would have no notion of the extent of the malice of those who show such furious opposition to Him who went about doing good (Acts 10:38). On other occasions Jesus warned his disciples that they would be treated the same way as he was (cf. Jn 15:20).

The works of Jesus and John the Baptist, each in their own way, lead to the accomplishment of God's plan for man's salvation: the fact that some people do not recognize him does not prevent God's plan being carried into effect.

11:21–24. Chorazin and Bethsaida were thriving cities on the northern shore of the lake of Gennesaret, not very far from Capernaum. During his public ministry Jesus often preached in these cities and worked many miracles there; in Capernaum he revealed his teaching about the Blessed Eucharist (cf. Jn 6:51ff).

e. Other ancient authorities read *children* (Luke 7:35)

be brought down to Hades. For if the mighty works done in you
had been done in Sodom, it would have remained until this day.
24But I tell you that it shall be more tolerable on the day of judgment for the land of Sodom than for you."

Lk 10:21f **Jesus thanks his Father**

1 Cor 1:26–29 25At that time Jesus declared, "I thank thee, Father, Lord of
Sir 51:1 Acts 17:24 heaven and earth, that thou hast hidden these things from the wise
Jn 3:35; 17:2 and understanding and revealed them to babes; 26yea, Father, for
Phil 2:9 such was thy gracious will.[f] 27All things have been delivered to me
Mt 16:7 Gal 1:15f by my Father; and no one knows the Son except the Father, and
no one knows the Father except the Son and any one to whom the
Mt 12:20 Jer 31:24 Son chooses to reveal him.* 28Come to me, all who labour and are

---

Tyre, Sidon, Sodom and Gomorrah, the main cities of Phoenicia—all notorious for loose living—were classical examples of divine punishment (cf. Ezek 26–28; Is 23).

Here Jesus is pointing out the ingratitude of people who could know him but who refuse to change. On the day of Judgment (vv. 22 and 24) they will have more explaining to do: "Every one to whom much is given, of him will much be required" (Lk 12:48).

11:25–26. The wise and understanding of this world, that is, those who rely on their own judgment, cannot accept the revelation which Christ has brought us. Supernatural outlook is always connected with humility. A humble person, who gives himself little importance, sees; a person who is full of self-esteem fails to perceive supernatural things.

11:27. Here Jesus formally reveals his divinity. Our knowledge of a person shows our intimacy with him, according to the principle given by St Paul: "For what person knows a man's thoughts except the spirit of the man which is in him?" (1 Cor 2:11). The Son knows the Father by the same knowledge as that by which the Father knows the Son. This identity of knowledge implies oneness of nature; that is to say, Jesus is God just as the Father is God.

11:28–30. Our Lord calls everyone to come to him. We all find things difficult in one way or another. The history of souls bears out the truth of these words of Jesus. Only the Gospel can fully satisfy the thirst for truth and justice that sincere people feel. Only our Lord, our Master—and those to whom he passes on his power—can sooth the sinner by telling him, "Your sins are forgiven" (Mt 9:2). In this connexion Pope Paul VI teaches: "Jesus says now and always, 'come to me, all who labour and are heavy laden, and I will give you rest.' His attitude towards us is one of invitation, knowledge and compassion; indeed, it is one of offering, promise, friendship, goodness, remedy of our ailments; he is our comforter; indeed, our nourishment, our bread, giving us energy and life" (Homily on Corpus Christi, 13 June 1974).

f. Or *so it was well-pleasing before thee*

heavy laden, and I will give you rest. [29]Take my yoke upon you, Sir 51:33f
and learn from me; for I am gentle and lowly in heart, and you Jer 6:16
will find rest for your souls. [30]For my yoke is easy, and my burden 1 Kings 12:4 Ps 2:3
is light." 1 Jn 5:3

The law of the sabbath

12 [1]At that time Jesus went through the grainfields on the sab- Mk 2:23–28
bath; his disciples were hungry, and they began to pluck Lk 6:1–5 Deut 5:14;
ears of grain and to eat. [2]But when the Pharisees saw it, they said 23:26
to him, "Look, your disciples are doing what is not lawful to do Ex 20:10
on the sabbath." [3]He said to them, "Have you not read what David 1 Sam 21:7
did, when he was hungry, and those who were with him: [4]how he Lev 24:9
entered the house of God and ate the bread of the Presence, which

---

"Come to me": the Master is addressing the crowds who are following him, "harassed and helpless, like sheep without a shepherd" (Mt 9:36). The Pharisees weighed them down with an endless series of petty regulations (cf. Acts 15:10), yet they brought no peace to their souls. Jesus tells these people, and us, about the kind of burden he imposes: "Any other burden oppresses and crushes you, but Christ's actually takes weight off you. Any other burden weighs down, but Christ's gives you wings. If you take a bird's wings away, you might seem to be taking weight off it, but the more weight you take off, the more you tie it down to the earth. There it is on the ground, and you wanted to relieve it of a weight; give it back the weight of its wings and you will see how it flies" (St Augustine, *Sermons*, 126). "All you who go about tormented, afflicted and burdened with the burden of your cares and desires, go forth from them, come to me, and I will refresh you and you shall find for your souls the rest which your desires take from you" (St John of the Cross, *Ascent of Mount Carmel*, book 1, chap. 7, 4).

12:2. "The sabbath": this was the day the Jews set aside for worshipping God. God himself, the originator of the sabbath (Gen 2:3), ordered the Jewish people to avoid certain kinds of work on this day (Ex 20:8–11; 21:13; Deut 5:14) to leave them free to give more time to God. As time went by, the rabbis complicated this divine precept: by Jesus' time they had extended to thirty-nine the list of kinds of forbidden work.

The Pharisees accuse Jesus' disciples of breaking the sabbath. In the casuistry of the scribes and the Pharisees, plucking ears of corn was the same as harvesting, and crushing them was the same as milling—types of agricultural work forbidden on the sabbath.

12:3–8. Jesus rebuts the Pharisees' accusation by four arguments—the example of David, that of the priests, a correct understanding of the mercy of God and Jesus' own authority over the sabbath.

The first example, which was quite familiar to the people, who were used to listening to the Bible being read, comes from 1 Samuel 21:2–7: David, in flight from the jealousy of King Saul, asks the priest of the shrine at Nob for food for his men; the priest gave them the only bread he had, the holy bread of the Presence; this was the twelve loaves that were

it was not lawful for him to eat nor for those who were with him,
Num 28:9 but only for the priests? 5Or have you not read in the law how on
the sabbath the priests in the temple profane the sabbath, and are
guiltless? 6I tell you, something greater than the temple is here.
Hos 6:6 7And if you had known what this means, 'I desire mercy, and not
sacrifice,' you would not have condemned the guiltless. 8For the
Son of man is lord of the sabbath."

Curing of the man with a withered hand

Mk 3:1–6 9And he went on from there, and entered their synagogue. 10And
Lk 6:6–11; 14:3 behold, there was a man with a withered hand. And they asked
him, "Is it lawful to heal on the sabbath?" so that they might
accuse him. 11He said to them, "What man of you, if he has one
sheep and it falls into a pit on the sabbath, will not lay hold of it
Lk 14:5 and lift it out? 12Of how much more value is a man than a sheep!
So it is lawful to do good on the sabbath." 13Then he said to the
man, "Stretch out your hand." And the man stretched it out, and it
Jn 5:16 was restored, whole like the other. 14But the Pharisees went out
and took counsel against him, how to destroy him.*

Jesus, the servant of God

Mk 3:7–12 15Jesus, aware of this, withdrew from there. And many followed
him, and he healed them all, 16and ordered them not to make him

---

placed each week on the golden altar of the sanctuary as a perpetual offering from the twelve tribes of Israel (Lev 24:5–9). The second example refers to the priestly ministry to perform the liturgy, priests had to do a number of things on the sabbath but did not thereby break the law of sabbath rest (cf. Num 28:9). On the two other arguments, see the notes on Mt 9:13 and Mk 2:26–27, 28.

12:9–13. Jesus corroborates his teaching by performing this miracle: it is lawful to do good on the sabbath; no law should get in the way of doing good. He therefore rejects the interpretation given by the Pharisees; they are polarized on the letter of the law, to the detriment of God's honour and men's welfare. The very same people who are scandalized by our Lord's miracle are quite ready to plot his death, even on the sabbath (v. 14).

12:17–21. Once again the sacred text points out the contrast between the contemporary mistaken Jewish notion of a spectacular messianic kingdom and the discernment which Jesus asks of those who witness and accept his teaching and miracles. By providing this long quotation from Isaiah (42:1–4), the evangelist is giving us the key to the teaching contained in chapters 11 and 12: in Jesus the prophecy of the Servant of Yahweh is fulfilled: the lovable and gentle teacher has come to bring the light of truth.

When narrating the passion of our Lord, the Gospels will once again remind us of the figure of the Servant of Yahweh, to show that in Jesus the suffering and

known. [17]This was to fulfil what was spoken by the prophet Is 42:1–4; 41:9
Isaiah:

[18]"Behold my servant whom I have chosen,
my beloved with whom my soul is well pleased.
I will put my Spirit upon him,
and he shall proclaim justice to the Gentiles.
[19]He will not wrangle or cry aloud,
nor will any one hear his voice in the streets;
[20]he will not break a bruised reed
or quench a smouldering wick,
till he brings justice to victory;
[21]and in his name will the Gentiles hope."

Allegations by the Pharisees. The sin against the Holy Spirit

Mk 3:22–30 Lk 11:14–26, 20, 32

[22]Then a blind and dumb demoniac was brought to him, and he
healed him, so that the dumb man spoke and saw. [23]And all the
people were amazed, and said, "Can this be the Son of David?"
[24]But when the Pharisees heard it they said, "It is only by Beelzebul,* the prince of demons, that this man casts out demons."
[25]Knowing their thoughts, he said to them, "Every kingdom
divided against itself is laid waste, and no city or house divided
against itself will stand; [26]and if Satan casts out Satan, he is
divided against himself; how then will his kingdom stand? [27]And

---

expiatory aspect of the death of the Servant finds fulfilment (cf. Mt 27:30, with reference to Is 50:6; Mt 8:17 and Is 53:4; Jn 1:38 and Is 53:9–12; etc.).

12:17. Isaiah 42:1–4 speaks of a humble servant, beloved of God, chosen by God. And in fact Jesus, without ceasing to be the Son of God, one in substance with the Father, took the form of a servant (cf. Phil 2:6). This humility led him to cure and care for the poor and afflicted of Israel, without seeking acclaim.

12:18. See the note on Mt 3:16.

12:19. The justice proclaimed by the Servant, who is filled with the Holy Spirit, is not a noisy virtue. We can see the loving, gentle way Jesus worked his miracles, performing righteousness in all humility. This is how he brings about the triumph of his Father's justice, his plan of revelation and salvation—very quietly and very effectively.

12:20. According to many Fathers, including St Augustine and St Jerome, the bruised reed and the smouldering wick refer to the Jewish people. They also stand for every sinner, for our Lord does not seek the sinner's death but his conversion, and his life (cf. Ezek 33:11). The Gospels often bear witness to this reassuring truth (cf. Lk 15:11–32, the parable of the prodigal son; Mt 18:12–24, the parable of the lost sheep; etc.).

12:22–24. Here is a case of possession by the devil. This consists in an evil spirit taking over a human body. Possession is normally accompanied by certain forms

1 Jn 3:8
1 Thess 2:16
Is 49:24
1 Jn 4:4
Mk 9:40
Jn 11:52
Heb 6:4, 6; 10:26
1 Jn 5:16
Lk 12:10
1 Tim 1:13

if I cast out demons by Beelzebul, by whom do your sons cast
them out? Therefore they shall be your judges. 28 But if it is by the
Spirit of God that I cast out demons, then the kingdom of God has
come upon you. 29 Or how can one enter a strong man's house and
plunder his goods, unless he first binds the strong man? Then
indeed he may plunder his house. 30 He who is not with me is
against me, and he who does not gather with me scatters.
31 Therefore I tell you, every sin and blasphemy will be forgiven
men, but the blasphemy against the Spirit will not be forgiven.*
32 And whoever says a word against the Son of man will be forgiven; but whoever speaks against the Holy Spirit will not be forgiven, either in this age or in the age to come.
33 "Either make the tree good, and its fruit good; or make the
tree bad, and its fruit bad; for the tree is known by its fruit. 34 You

---

of illness or disease—epilepsy, dumbness, blindness … . Possessed people have lost their self-control; when they are in the trance of possession they are tools of the devil. The evil spirit who has mastery over them sometimes gives them supernatural powers; at other times he torments the person, and may even drive him to suicide (cf. Mt 8:16; 8:28–34; 17:14–21; Mk 1:26; Lk 7:21).

The expulsion of devils by invoking Jesus' name has special significance in the history of salvation. It proves that the coming of Jesus marks the beginning of the Kingdom of God and that the devil has been dispossessed of his territory (Jn 12:31). "The seventy returned with joy, saying 'Lord, even the demons are subject to us in your name!' And he said to them, 'I saw Satan fall like lightning from heaven'" (Lk 10:17–18). Ever since Christ's coming, the devil is on the retreat—which is not to say that there are not still instances of diabolic possession.

12:30. Here Jesus sums up his whole argument against the Pharisees: they are either for him or for the devil. He said the same thing in the Sermon on the Mount: "No one can serve two masters" (Mt 6:24). Those who are not united to Jesus through faith, hope and charity, are against him—and therefore they are on the side of the devil, Jesus' enemy.

Our Lord does not mince words when it comes to asking people to adopt an attitude to his person and his Kingdom. A Christian cannot temporize; if he wants to be a true Christian he must not entertain ideas or approaches which are not in keeping with the content of Revelation and with the teaching of the Church.

Therefore, we must not compromise on matters of faith, trying to adapt Jesus' teaching to suit our convenience or because we are afraid of how other people will react to it. Our Lord wants us to adopt a clear attitude to his person *and* to his teaching.

12:31–32. God wants all men to be saved (1 Tim 2:4) and he calls everyone to repentance (2 Pet 3:9). The Redemption won by Christ is superabundant: it atones for all sins and extends to every man and woman (Rom 5:12–21). Christ gave his Church the power to forgive sins by means of the sacraments of Baptism and Penance. This power is unlimited, that is to say, the Church can pardon all sins of

brood of vipers! how can you speak good, when you are evil? For Jn 8:43
out of the abundance of the heart the mouth speaks. 35The good Rom 8:7 Lk 6:45
man out of his good treasure brings forth good, and the evil man
out of his evil treasure brings forth evil. 36I tell you, on the day of
judgment men will render account for every careless word they
utter; 37for by your words you will be justified, and by your words
you will be condemned."

The sign of Jonah

38Then some of the scribes and Pharisees said to him, "Teacher, we 1 Cor 1:22
wish to see a sign from you." 39But he answered them, "An evil and
adulterous generation seeks for a sign; but no sign shall be given to
it except the sign of the prophet Jonah. 40For as Jonah was three Jn 2:1f
days and three nights in the belly of the whale, so will the Son of

---

all the baptized as often as they confess their sins with the right disposition. This teaching is a dogma of faith (cf. Council of Trent, *De Paenitentia*, can. 1).

The sin Jesus speaks about here is termed "sin against the Holy Spirit", because external expressions of God's goodness are specially attributed to the third person of the Blessed Trinity. Sin against the Holy Spirit is said to be unforgivable not so much because of its gravity or malice but because of the subjective disposition of the sinner in this case: his attitude shuts the door on repentance. Sin against the Holy Spirit consists in maliciously attributing to the devil the miracles and signs wrought by Christ. Thus, the very nature of this sin blocks the person's route to Christ, who is the only one who can take away the sin of the world (Jn 1:29), and the sinner puts himself outside the range of God's forgiveness. In this sense the sins against the Holy Spirit cannot be forgiven.

12:33–37. Our Lord continues his case against the Pharisees: because he is evil, the devil cannot do good things. And if the works that I do are good, as you can see they are, then they cannot have been done by the devil; "a sound tree cannot bear evil fruit, nor can a bad tree bear good fruit" (Mt 7:18).

As on other occasions Jesus reminds people that there is a Judgment. The Magisterium of the Church explains that there is a "particular" judgment immediately after one dies, and a "general" judgment at the end of the world (cf. Benedict XII, *Benedictus Deus*).

12:39–40. This sign the Jews were asking for would have been a miracle or some other prodigy; they wanted Jesus, incongruously, to confirm his preaching—given with such simplicity—by dramatic signs. Our Lord replies by announcing the mystery of his death and resurrection, using the parallel of the case of Jonah: "No sign shall be given to it except the sign of the prophet Jonah." Jesus' glorious resurrection is the "sign" *par excellence*, the decisive proof of the divine character of his person, of his mission and of his teaching.

When St Paul (1 Cor 15:3–4) confesses that Jesus Christ "was raised on the third day in accordance with the scriptures" (words that later found their way into the Nicene-Constantinopolitan Creed, the Creed used in the Mass), he

Jn 3:5 man be three days and three nights in the heart of the earth. 41The
men of Nineveh will arise at the judgment with this generation and
condemn it; for they repented at the preaching of Jonah, and
1 Kings 10:1–10 behold, something greater than Jonah is here. 42The queen of the
South will arise at the judgment with this generation and condemn
it; for she came from the ends of the earth to hear the wisdom of
Solomon, and behold, something greater than Solomon is here.

43"When the unclean spirit has gone out of a man, he passes
through waterless places seeking rest, but he finds none. 44Then he
says, 'I will return to my house from which I came.' And when he
2 Pet 2:20 comes he finds it empty, swept, and put in order. 45Then he goes
and brings with him seven other spirits more evil than himself, and
they enter and dwell there; and the last state of that man becomes
worse than the first. So shall it be also with this evil generation."

---

must have had this passage particularly in mind. We can see another allusion to Jonah in the words our Lord spoke shortly before his ascension: "Thus it is written, that the Christ should suffer and on the third day rise from the dead" (Lk 24:45–46).

12:41–42. Nineveh was a city in Mesopotamia (modern Iraq) to which the prophet Jonah was sent. The Ninevites did penance (Jn 3:6–9) because they recognized the prophet and accepted his message; whereas Jerusalem does not wish to recognize Jesus, of whom Jonah was merely a figure. The queen of the South was the queen of Sheba in southwestern Arabia, who visited Solomon (1 Kings 10:1–10) and was in awe of the wisdom with which God had endowed the King of Israel. Jesus is also prefigured in Solomon, whom Jewish tradition saw as the epitome of the wise man. Jesus' reproach is accentuated by the example of pagan converts, and gives us a glimpse of the universal scope of Christianity, which will take root among the Gentiles.

There is a certain irony in what Jesus says about "something greater" than Jonah or Solomon having come: really, he is infinitely greater, but Jesus prefers to tone down the difference between himself and any figure, no matter how important, in the Old Testament.

12:43. Jesus says that when demons are driven out of men they retreat into the wilderness; but that if they repossess a man they torment him in a worse way. St Peter also says that the devil prowls around like a lion seeking someone to devour (1 Pet 5:8) and that people who have been converted and revert to the depravities of their past life become worse than they were before (2 Pet 2:20). Jesus is solemnly warning the Jews of his time that if they continue to reject the light they will end up worse than they were before. The same sad truth applies to the Christian who, after being converted and reconciled to God, allows the devil to enter his soul again.

12:46–47. "Brethren": ancient Hebrew, Aramaic and other languages had no special words for different degrees of relationship, such as are found in more modern languages. In general, all those belonging to the same family, clan and even tribe were "brethren".

The true kinsmen of Jesus

46While he was still speaking to the people, behold, his mother Mk 3:31–35 Lk 8:19–21
and his brethren* stood outside, asking to speak to him.[g] 48But he Mt 13:55
replied to the man who told him, "Who is my mother, and who Lk 2:49
are my brethren?"* 49And stretching out his hand toward his disciples, he said, "Here are my mother and my brethren! 50For who- Rom 8:29
ever does the will of my Father in heaven is my brother, and sister, Jn 15:14
and mother."

6. THE PARABLES OF THE KINGDOM

Parable of the sower. The meaning of parables

13 1That same day Jesus went out of the house and sat beside Mk 4:1–20
the sea. 2And great crowds gathered about him, so that he Lk 8:4–15
got into a boat and sat there; and the whole crowd stood on the
beach. 3And he told them many things in parables, saying: "A

In the particular case we have here, we should bear in mind that Jesus had different kinds of relatives, in two groups—some on his mother's side, others on St Joseph's. Matthew 13:55–56 mentions, as living in Nazareth, James, Joseph, Simon and Judas ("his brethren") and elsewhere there is reference to Jesus' "sisters" (cf. Mk 6:3). But in Matthew 27:56 we are told that the James and Joseph were sons of a Mary distinct from the Blessed Virgin, and that Simon and Judas were not brothers of James and Joseph, but seemingly children of a brother of St Joseph.

Jesus, on the other hand, was known to everyone as "the son of Mary" (Mk 6:3) or "the carpenter's son" (Mt 13:55).

The Church has always maintained as absolutely certain that Jesus had no brothers or sisters in the full meaning of the term: it is a dogma that Mary was ever-Virgin (cf. the note on Mt 1:25).

12:48–50. Jesus obviously loved his Mother and St Joseph. He uses this episode to teach us that in his Kingdom human ties do not take precedence. In Luke 8:19 the same teaching is to be found. Jesus regards the person who does the will of his heavenly Father as a member of his own family. Therefore, even though it means going against natural family feelings, a person should do just that when needs be in order to perform the mission the Father has entrusted to him (cf. Lk 2:49).

We can say that Jesus loved Mary more because of the bonds between them created by grace than because he was her son by natural generation: Mary's divine motherhood is the source of all our Lady's other prerogatives; but this very motherhood is, in its turn, the first and greatest of the graces with which Mary was endowed.

13:3. Chapter 13 of St Matthew includes as many as seven of Jesus' parables,

g. Other ancient authorities insert verse 47, *Some one told him "Your mother and your brothers are standing outside, asking to speak to you"*

sower went out to sow. [4]And as he sowed, some seeds fell along
the path, and the birds came and devoured them. [5]Other seeds fell
on rocky ground, where they had not much soil, and immediately
they sprang up, since they had no depth of soil, [6]but when the sun
rose they were scorched; and since they had no root they withered
away. [7]Other seeds fell upon thorns, and the thorns grew up and
choked them. [8]Other seeds fell on good soil and brought forth

---

which is the reason why it is usually called "the parable discourse" or the "parabolic discourse". Because of their similarity of content and setting these parables are often called the "Kingdom parables", and also the "parables of the Lake", because Jesus taught them on the shore of Lake Gennesaret. Jesus uses these elaborate comparisons (parables) to explain certain features of the Kingdom of God, which he has come to establish (cf. Mt 3:2)—its tiny, humble origins; its steady growth; its worldwide scope; its salvific force. God calls everyone to salvation but only those attain it who receive God's call with good dispositions and who do not change their attitude; the value of the spiritual benefits the Kingdom brings—so valuable that one should give up everything to obtain them; the fact that good and bad are all mixed together until the harvest-time, or the time of God's judgment; the intimate connexion between earthly and heavenly aspects of the Kingdom, until it reaches its point of full development at the end of time.

On Jesus' lips, parables are exceptionally effective. By using parables he keeps his listeners' attention, whether they are uneducated or not, and by means of the most ordinary things of daily life he sheds light on the deepest supernatural mysteries. He used the parable device in a masterly way; his parables are quite unique; they carry the seal of his personality; through them he has graphically shown us the riches of grace, the life of the Church, the demands of the faith and even the mystery of God's own inner life.

Jesus' teaching continues to provide every generation with light and guidance on moral conduct. By reading and reflecting on his parables one can savour the adorable humanity of the Saviour, who showed such kindness to the people who crowded around to hear him—and who shows the same readiness to listen to our prayers, despite our dullness, and to reply to our healthy curiosity when we try to make out his meaning.

13:3–8. Anyone who has visited the fertile plain to the west of the lake of Gennesaret will appreciate Jesus' touching description in the parable of the sower. The plain is crisscrossed by paths; it is streaked with rocky ground, often with the rocks lying just beneath the surface, and with the courses of rivulets, dry for most of the year but still retaining some moisture. Here and there are clumps of large thorn bushes. When the agricultural worker sows seed in this mixed kind of land, he knows that some seed will fare better than others.

13:9. Jesus did not explain this parable there and then. It was quite usual for parables to be presented in the first instance as a kind of puzzle to gain the listener's attention, excite his curiosity and fix the parable in his memory. It may well be that Jesus wanted to allow his more interested listeners to identify themselves by coming back to hear him again—as happened with his disciples.

grain, some a hundredfold, some sixty, some thirty. [9]He who has
ears,[h] let him hear."
[10]Then the disciples came and said to him, "Why do you speak
to them in parables?" [11]And he answered them, "To you it has
been given to know the secrets of the kingdom of heaven, but to
them it has not been given. [12]For to him who has will more be Mk 4:25
given, and he will have abundance; but from him who has not, Lk 8:18

The rest—who listened out of idle curiosity or for too human reasons (to see him work miracles)—would not benefit from hearing a more detailed and deeper explanation of the parable.

13:10–13. The kind of kingdom Jesus was going to establish did not suit the Judaism of his time, largely because of the Jews' nationalistic, earthbound idea of the Messiah to come. In his preaching Jesus takes account of the different outlooks of his listeners, as can be seen in the attitudes described in the parable of the sower. If people were well disposed to him, the enigmatic nature of the parable would stimulate their interest; and Jesus later did give his many disciples a fuller explanation of its meaning; but there was no point in doing this if people were not ready to listen.

Besides, parables—as indeed any type of comparison or analogy—are used to reveal or explain something that is not easy to understand, as was the case with the supernatural things Jesus was explaining. One has to shade one's eyes to see things if the sun is too bright; otherwise, one is blinded and sees nothing. Similarly, parables help to shade supernatural brightness to allow the listener to grasp meaning without being blinded by it.

These verses also raise a very interesting question: how can divine revelation and grace produce such widely differing responses in people? What is at work here is the mystery of divine grace —which is an unmerited gift—and of man's response to this grace. What Jesus says here underlines man's responsibility to be ready to accept God's grace and to respond to it. Jesus' reference to Isaiah (Mt 13:14–15) is a prophecy of that hardness of heart which is a punishment meted out to those who resist grace.

These verses need to be interpreted in the light of three points: 1) Jesus Christ loved everyone, including the people of his own hometown: he gave his life in order to save all men; 2) the parable is a literary form designed to get ideas across clearly: its ultimate aim is to teach, not to mislead or obscure; 3) lack of appreciation for divine grace is something blameworthy, which does merit punishment; however, Jesus did not come directly to punish anyone, but rather to save everyone.

13:12. Jesus is telling his disciples that, precisely because they have faith in him and want to have a good grasp of his teaching, they will be given a deeper understanding of divine truths. But those who do not "follow him" (cf. the note on Mt 4:18–22) will later lose interest in the things of God and will grow ever blinder: it is as if the little they have is being taken away from them.

This verse also helps us understand the meaning of the parable of the sower, a parable which gives a wonderful expla-

h. Other ancient authorities add here and in verse 43 *to hear*

Deut 29:4 even what he has will be taken away.* 13 This is why I speak to
Is 6:9f them in parables, because seeing they do not see, and hearing they
Jn 12:40 do not hear, nor do they understand. 14 With them indeed is ful-
Acts 28:26f filled the prophecy of Isaiah which says:

'You shall indeed hear but never understand,
and you shall indeed see but never perceive.
15 For this people's heart has grown dull,
and their ears are heavy of hearing,
and their eyes they have closed,
lest they should perceive with their eyes,
and hear with their ears,
and understand with their heart,
and turn for me to heal them.'

Lk 10:23f 16 But blessed are your eyes, for they see, and your ears, for they
hear. 17 Truly, I say to you, many prophets and righteous men
longed to see what you see, and did not see it, and to hear what
you hear, and did not hear it.

---

nation of the supernatural economy of divine grace: God gives grace, and man freely responds to that grace. The result is that those who respond to grace generously receive additional grace and so grow steadily in grace and holiness; whereas those who reject God's gifts become closed up within themselves; through their selfishness and attachment to sin they eventually lose God's grace entirely. In this verse, then, our Lord gives a clear warning: with the full weight of his divine authority he exhorts us—without taking away our freedom—to act responsibly: the gifts God keeps sending us should yield fruit; we should make good use of the opportunities for Christian sanctification which are offered us in the course of our lives.

13:14–15. Only well-disposed people grasp the meaning of God's words. It is not enough just to hear them physically. In the course of Jesus' preaching the prophetic words of Isaiah come true once again.

However, we should not think that not wanting to hear or to understand was something exclusive to certain contemporaries of Jesus; each one of us is at times hard of hearing, hard-hearted and dull-minded in the presence of God's grace and saving word. Moreover, it is not enough to be familiar with the teaching of the Church: it is absolutely necessary to put the faith into practice, with all that that implies, morally and ascetically. Jesus was fixed to the wood of the cross not only by nails and by the sins of certain Jews but also by our sins—sins committed centuries later but which afflicted the most sacred humanity of Jesus Christ, who bore the burden of our sins. See the note on Mk 4:11–12.

13:16–17. In contrast with the closed attitude of many Jews who witnessed Jesus' life but did not believe in him, the disciples are praised by our Lord for their docility to grace, their openness to recognizing him as the Messiah and to accepting his teaching.

He calls his disciples blessed, happy. As he says, the prophets and just men

18“Hear then the parable of the sower. 19When any one hears
the word of the kingdom and does not understand it, the evil one
comes and snatches away what is sown in his heart; this is what
was sown along the path. 20As for what was sown on rocky
ground, this is he who hears the word and immediately receives it
with joy; 21yet he has no root in himself, but endures for a while,
and when tribulation or persecution arises on account of the word,
immediately he falls away.[i] 22As for what was sown among thorns, 1 Tim 6:9
this is he who hears the word, but the cares of the world and the
delight in riches choke the word, and it proves unfruitful. 23As for
what was sown on good soil, this is he who hears the word and
understands it; he indeed bears fruit, and yields, in one case a hundredfold, in another sixty, and in another thirty.”

The parable of the weeds

24Another parable he put before them, saying, “The kingdom of
heaven may be compared to a man who sowed good seed in his

---

and women of the Old Testament had for centuries lived in hope of enjoying one day the peace the future Messiah would bring, but they had died without experiencing this good fortune. Simeon, towards the end of his long life, was filled with joy on seeing the infant Jesus when he was presented in the temple: “he took him up in his arms and blessed God and said, ‘Lord, now lettest thou thy servant depart in peace, according to thy word; for mine eyes have seen thy salvation’ ” (Lk 2:28–30). During our Lord’s public life, his disciples were fortunate enough to see and be on close terms with him; later they would recall that incomparable gift, and one of them would begin his first letter in these words: “That which was from the beginning, which we have heard, which we have seen with our eyes, which we have looked upon and touched with our hands, concerning the word of life; [...] that which we have seen and heard we proclaim also to you, so that you may have fellowship with us; and our fellowship is with the Father and with his Son Jesus Christ. And we are writing this that our [or: your] joy may be complete” (1 Jn 1:1–4).

This exceptional good fortune was, obviously, not theirs because of special merit: God planned it; it was he who decided that the time had come for the Old Testament prophecies to be fulfilled. In any event, God gives every soul opportunities to meet him: each of us has to be sensitive enough to grasp them and not let them pass. There were many men and women in Palestine who saw and heard the Incarnate Son of God but did not have the spiritual sensitivity to see in him what the apostles and disciples saw.

13:19. He does not understand because he does not love—not because he is not clever enough: lack of love opens the door of the soul to the devil.

13:24–25. “The situation is clear: the field is fertile and the seed is good; the

i. Or *stumbles*

field; [25]but while men were sleeping, his enemy came and sowed
weeds among the wheat, and went away. [26]So when the plants
came up and bore grain, then the weeds appeared also. [27]And the
servants [j] of the householder came and said to him, 'Sir, did you
not sow good seed in your field? How then has it weeds?' [28]He
said to them, 'An enemy has done this.' The servants [j] said to him,
'Then do you want us to go and gather them?' [29]But he said, 'No;
lest in gathering the weeds you root up the wheat along with
them. [30]Let both grow together until the harvest; and at harvest
time I will tell the reapers, Gather the weeds first and bind them
in bundles to be burned, but gather the wheat into my barn.' "

Mk 4:30–32
Lk 13:18–19; 17:6

The mustard seed; the leaven

[31]Another parable he put before them saying, "The kingdom of
heaven is like a grain of mustard seed which a man took and
sowed in his field; [32]it is the smallest of all seeds, but when it has

Ezek 17:23; 31:6

Lord of the field has scattered the seed at the right moment and with great skill. He even has watchmen to make sure that the field is protected. If, afterwards, there are weeds among the wheat, it is because men have failed to respond, because they—and Christians in particular—have fallen asleep and allowed the enemy to approach" (St Josemaría Escrivá, *Christ Is Passing By*, 123).

13:25. This weed—cockle—looks very like wheat and can easily be mistaken for it until the ears appear. If it gets ground up with wheat it contaminates the flour and any bread made from that flour causes severe nausea when eaten. In the East personal vengeance sometimes took the form of sowing cockle among an enemy's wheat. Roman law prescribed penalties for this crime.

13:28. "When the careless servants ask the Lord why weeds have grown in his field, the explanation is obvious: '*inimicus homo hoc fecit*: an enemy has done this.' We Christians should have been on guard to make sure that the good things placed in this world by the Creator were developed in the service of truth and good. But we have fallen asleep—a sad thing, that sluggishness of our heart! while the enemy and all those who serve him worked incessantly. You can see how the weeds have grown abundantly everywhere" (ibid., 123).

13:29–30. The end of this parable gives a symbolic explanation of why God allows evil to have its way for a time—and for its ultimate extirpation. Evil is to run its course on earth until the end of time; therefore, we should not be scandalized by the presence of evil in the world. It will be obliterated not in this life, but after death; at the Judgment (the harvest) the good will go to heaven and the bad to hell.

13:31–32. Here, the man is Jesus Christ and the field, the world. The grain of mustard seed is the preaching of the

j. Or *slaves*

grown it is the greatest of shrubs and becomes a tree, so that the Ps 104:12
birds of the air come and make nests in its branches."
[33]He told them another parable. "The kingdom of heaven is Lk 13:20f
like leaven which a woman took and hid in three measures of
meal, till it was all leavened."
[34]All this Jesus said to the crowds in parables; indeed he said Mk 4:33f
nothing to them without a parable. [35]This was to fulfil what was Ps 78:2
spoken by the prophet:[k]

"I will open my mouth in parables,
I will utter what has been hidden
since the foundation of the world."

The parable of the weeds explained

[36]Then he left the crowds and went into the house. And his disciples came to him, saying, "Explain to us the parable of the weeds
of the field." [37]He answered, "He who sows the good seed is the

---

Gospel and the Church, which from very small beginnings will spread throughout the world. The parable clearly refers to the universal scope and spread of the Kingdom of God: the Church, which embraces all mankind of every kind and condition, in every latitude and in all ages, is forever developing in spite of obstacles, thanks to God's promise and aid.

13:33. This comparison is taken from everyday experience: just as leaven gradually ferments all the dough, so the Church spreads to convert all nations. The leaven is also a symbol of the individual Christian. Living in the middle of the world and retaining his Christian quality, he wins souls for Christ by his word and example: "Our calling to be children of God, in the midst of the world, requires us not only to seek our own personal holiness, but also to go out onto all the ways of the earth, to convert them into roadways that will carry souls over all obstacles and lead them to the Lord. As we take part in all temporal activities as ordinary citizens, we are to become leaven acting on the mass" (ibid., 120).

13:34–35. Revelation, God's plans, are hidden (cf. Mt 11:25) from those who are not disposed to accept them. The evangelist wishes to emphasize the need for simplicity and for docility to the Gospel. By recalling Psalm 78:2, he tells us once more, under divine inspiration, that the Old Testament prophecies find their fulfilment in our Lord's preaching.

13:36–43. While making its way on earth, the Church is composed of good and bad people, just men and sinners: they are mixed in with one another until the harvest time, the end of the world, when the Son of man, in his capacity as Judge of the living and the dead, will divide the good from the bad at the Last Judgment—the former going to eternal glory, the inheritance of the saints; the latter, to the eternal fire of hell. Although the just and the sinners are now side by side, the

k. Other ancient authorities read *the prophet Isaiah*

1 Cor 3:9 Son of man; [38]the field is the world, and the good seed means the
sons of the kingdom; the weeds are the sons of the evil one, [39]and
the enemy who sowed them is the devil; the harvest is the close of
Jn 15:6 the age, and the reapers are angels. [40]Just as the weeds are gath-
ered and burned with fire, so will it be at the close of the age.
Zeph 1:3 [41]The Son of man will send his angels, and they will gather out of
Mt 25:31–46; 7:23 his kingdom all causes of sin and all evildoers, [42]and throw them
into the furnace of fire; there men will weep and gnash their teeth.
Dan 12:3 [43]Then the righteous will shine like the sun in the kingdom of their
Father. He who has ears, let him hear.

The hidden treasure; the pearl; the net

Lk 14:33 Phil 3:7 Prov 2:4 [44]"The kingdom of heaven is like treasure hidden in a field, which
a man found and covered up; then in his joy he goes and sells all
that he has and buys that field.
[45]"Again, the kingdom of heaven is like a merchant in search
Prov 8:10f of fine pearls, [46]who, on finding one pearl of great value, went and
sold all that he had and bought it.

Church has the right and the duty to exclude those who cause scandal, especially those who attack its doctrine and unity; this it can do through ecclesiastical excommunication and other canonical penalties. However, excommunication has a medicinal and pastoral function—to correct those who are obstinate in error, and to protect others from them.

13:44–46. In these two parables Jesus shows the supreme value of the Kingdom of heaven, and the attitude people need if they are to attain it. The parables are very alike, but it is interesting to note the differences: the treasure means abundance of gifts; the pearl indicates the beauty of the Kingdom. The treasure is something stumbled upon; the pearl, the result of a lengthy search; but in both instances the finder is filled with joy. Faith, vocation, true wisdom, desire for heaven, are things that sometimes are discovered suddenly and unexpectedly, and sometimes after much searching (cf. St Gregory the Great, *In Evangelia homiliae*, 11). However, the man's attitude is the same in both parables and is described in the same terms: "he goes and sells all that he has and buys it": detachment, generosity, is indispensable for obtaining the treasure.

"Anyone who understands the Kingdom which Christ proposes realizes that it is worth staking everything to obtain it [...]. The Kingdom of heaven is difficult to win. No one can be sure of achieving it, but the humble cry of a repentant man can open wide its doors" (St Josemaría Escrivá, *Christ Is Passing By*, 180).

13:47. "Fish of every kind": almost all the Greek manuscripts and early translations say "All kinds of things". A dragnet is very long and about two metres wide; when it is extended between two boats it forms double or triple mesh with the result that when it is pulled in it collects all sorts of things in addition to fish—algae, weeds, rubbish etc.

This parable is rather like the parable of the cockle, but in a fishing context: the net is the Church, the sea the world.

[47]"Again, the kingdom of heaven is like a net which was
thrown into the sea and gathered fish of every kind; [48]when it was
full, men drew it ashore and sat down and sorted the good into
vessels but threw away the bad. [49]So it will be at the close of the
age. The angels will come out and separate the evil from the righteous, [50]and throw them into the furnace of fire; there men will
weep and gnash their teeth.

[51]"Have you understood all this?" They said to him, "Yes."
[52]And he said to them, "Therefore every scribe who has been
trained for the kingdom of heaven is like a householder who
brings out of his treasure what is new and what is old."*

7. JESUS WITHDRAWS TO THE BORDER COUNTRY

No one is a prophet in his own country

[53]And when Jesus had finished these parables he went away from Mk 6:1–6
there, [54]and coming to his own country he taught them in their Lk 4:15–30

We can easily find in this parable the dogmatic truth of the Judgment: at the end of time God will judge men and separate the good from the bad. It is interesting to note our Lord's repeated references to the last things, especially Judgment and hell: he emphasizes these truths because of man's great tendency to forget them: "All these things are said to make sure that no one can make the excuse that he does not know about them: this excuse would be valid only if eternal punishment were spoken about in ambiguous terms" (St Gregory the Great, *In Evangelia homiliae*, 11).

13:52. "Scribe": among the Jews a scribe was a religious teacher, a specialist in Holy Scripture and its application to life. Our Lord here uses this old word to refer to the apostles, who will have the role of teachers in his Church. Thus, the apostles and their successors, the bishops, are the *Ecclesia docens*, the teaching Church; they have the authority and the mission to teach. The Pope and the Bishops exercise this authority directly and are also helped in this by priests. The other members of the Church form the *Ecclesia discens*, the learning Church. However, every disciple of Christ, every Christian who has received Christ's teaching, has a duty to pass this teaching on to others, in language they can understand; therefore, he should make sure he has a good grasp of Christian doctrine. The treasure of Revelation is so rich that it can provide teaching that applies to all times and situations. It is for the word of God to enlighten all ages and situations—not the other way around. Therefore, the Church and its pastors preach, not new things, but a single unchanging truth contained in the treasure of Revelation: for the past two thousand years the Gospel has always been "good news".

13:53–58. The Nazarenes' surprise is partly due to people's difficulty in recognizing anything exceptional and supernatural in those with whom they have been on familiar terms. Hence the

synagogue, so that they were astonished, and said, "Where did
this man get this wisdom and these mighty works? [55]Is not this the
carpenter's son? Is not his mother called Mary? And are not his
Jn 7:15, 52 brethren James and Joseph and Simon and Judas?* [56]And are not
all his sisters with us? Where then did this man get all this?"
Jn 4:44 [57]And they took offence at him. But Jesus said to them, "A
prophet is not without honour except in his own country and in his
own house." [58]And he did not do many mighty works there,
because of their unbelief.

The martyrdom of John the Baptist

Mk 6:14, 17–30 Lk 9:7–9; 3:19f **14** [1]At that time Herod the tetrarch heard about the fame of
Jesus; [2]and he said to his servants, "This is John the
Baptist, he has been raised from the dead; that is why these
powers are at work in him." [3]For Herod had seized John and
bound him and put him in prison, for the sake of Herodias, his
Lev 18:16; 20:21 brother Philip's wife;[l] [4]because John said to him, "It is not lawful
for you to have her." [5]And though he wanted to put him to death,
he feared the people, because they held him to be a prophet. [6]But
when Herod's birthday came, the daughter of Herodias danced
before the company, and pleased Herod, [7]so that he promised with
an oath to give her whatever she might ask. [8]Prompted by her
mother, she said, "Give me the head of John the Baptist here on a

---

saying, "No one is a prophet in his own country." These old neighbours were also jealous of Jesus. Where did he acquire this wisdom? Why him rather than us? They were unaware of the mystery of Jesus' conception; surprise and jealousy cause them to be shocked, to look down on Jesus and not to believe in him: "He came to his own home, and his own people received him not" (Jn 1:11).

"The carpenter's son": this is the only reference in the Gospel to St Joseph's occupation (in Mk 6:3 Jesus himself is described as a "carpenter"). Probably in a town like Nazareth the carpenter was a general tradesman who could turn his hand to jobs ranging from metalwork to making furniture or agricultural implements.

For an explanation of Jesus' "brethren", see the note on Mt 12:46–47.

14:1. Herod the tetrarch, Herod Antipas (see the note on Mt 2:1), is the same Herod as appears later in the account of the Passion (cf. Lk 23:7ff). A son of Herod the Great, Antipas governed Galilee and Perea in the name of the Roman emperor; according to Flavius Josephus, the Jewish historian (*Jewish Antiquities*, 18, 5, 4), he was married to a daughter of an Arabian king, but in spite of this he lived in concubinage with Herodias, his brother's wife. St John the Baptist, and Jesus himself, often criticized the tetrarch's immoral life, which was in conflict with the sexual morality laid down in the Law (Lev 18:16; 20:21) and was a cause of scandal.

l. Other ancient authorities read *his brother's wife*

platter." [9]And the king was sorry; but because of his oaths and his
guests he commanded it to be given; [10]he sent and had John
beheaded in the prison, [11]and his head was brought on a platter
and given to the girl, and she brought it to her mother. [12]And his
disciples came and took the body and buried it; and they went and
told Jesus.

First miracle of the loaves and fish

[13]Now when Jesus heard this, he withdrew from there in a boat to Mk 6:31–44
a lonely place apart. But when the crowds heard it, they followed Lk 9:10–17
him on foot from the towns. [14]As he went ashore he saw a great Jn 6:1–13
throng; and he had compassion on them, and healed their sick.
[15]When it was evening, the disciples came to him and said, "This
is a lonely place, and the day is now over; send the crowds away
to go into the villages and buy food for themselves." [16]Jesus said,
"They need not go away; you give them something to eat." [17]They
said to him, "We have only five loaves here and two fish." [18]And
he said, "Bring them here to me." [19]Then he ordered the crowds to
sit down on the grass; and taking the five loaves and the two fish
he looked up to heaven, and blessed, and broke and gave the
loaves to the disciples, and the disciples gave them to the crowds.
[20]And they all ate and were satisfied. And they took up twelve 2 Kings 4:44
baskets full of the broken pieces left over. [21]And those who ate Mk 6:45–56
were about five thousand men, besides women and children. Jn 6:15–21

14:3–12. Towards the end of the first century Flavius Josephus wrote of these same events. He gives additional information—specifying that it was in the fortress of Makeronte that John was imprisoned (this fortress was on the eastern bank of the Dead Sea, and was the scene of the banquet in question) and that Herodias' daughter was called Salome.

14:9. St Augustine comments: "Amid the excesses and sensuality of the guests, oaths are rashly made, which then are unjustly kept" (*Sermons*, 10). It is a sin against the second commandment of God's Law to make an oath to do something unjust; any such oath has no binding force. In fact, if one keeps it—as Herod did—one commits an additional sin. The Catechism also teaches that one offends against this precept if one swears something untrue, or swears needlessly (cf. St Pius V, *Catechism*, 3, 3, 24). Cf. the note on Mt 5:33–37.

14:14–21. This episode must have occurred in the middle of springtime, because the grass was green (Mk 6:40; Jn 6:10). In the Near East loaves were usually made very thin, which meant it was easy to break them by hand and distribute them to those at table; this was usually done by the head of the household or the senior person at the meal. Our Lord follows this custom, and the miracle occurs when Jesus breaks the bread. The disciples then distribute it among the crowd.

Jesus walks on the water

[22]Then he made the disciples get into the boat and go before him
Lk 6:12; 9:18 to the other side, while he dismissed the crowds. [23]And after he
had dismissed the crowds he went up into the hills by himself to
pray. When evening came, he was there alone, [24]but the boat by
this time was many furlongs distant from the land,[m] beaten by the
waves; for the wind was against them. [25]And in the fourth watch
Lk 24:37 of the night he came to them, walking on the sea. [26]But when the
disciples saw him walking on the sea, they were terrified, saying,
"It is a ghost!" And they cried out for fear. [27]But immediately he
spoke to them, saying, "Take heart, it is I; have no fear."

[28]And Peter answered him, "Lord, if it is you, bid me come to
you on the water." [29]He said, "Come." So Peter got out of the boat
and walked on the water and came to Jesus; [30]but when he saw the
wind,[n] he was afraid, and beginning to sink he cried out, "Lord,
save me." [31]Jesus immediately reached out his hand and caught
him, saying to him, "O man of little faith, why did you doubt?"

Here again we can see Jesus' desire to have people cooperate with him.

14:22–23. It has been a very full day, like so many others. First Jesus works many cures (14:14) and then performs the remarkable miracle of the multiplication of the loaves and the fish, a symbol of the future Eucharist. The crowds who have been following him were avid for food, teaching and consolation. Jesus "had compassion on them" (14:14), curing their sick and giving them the comfort of his teaching and the nourishment of food. He continues to do the same, down the centuries, tending to our needs and comforting us with his word and with the nourishment of his own body. Jesus must have been very moved, realizing the vivifying effect the Blessed Sacrament would have on the lives of Christians—a sacrament which is a mystery of life and faith and love. It is understandable that he should feel the need to spend some hours in private to speak to his Father. Jesus' private prayer, in an interlude between one demanding activity and another, teaches us that every Christian needs to take time out for recollection, to speak to his Father, God. On Jesus' frequent personal prayer see, for example, Mk 1:35; 6:47; Lk 5:16; 6:12. See the notes on Mt 6:5–6 and Mt 7:7–11.

14:24–33. This remarkable episode of Jesus walking on the sea must have made a deep impression on the apostles. It was one of their outstanding memories of the life they shared with the Master. It is reported not only by St Matthew, but also by St Mark (6:45–52), who would have heard about it from St Peter, and by St John (6:14–21).

Storms are very frequent on Lake Gennesaret; they cause huge waves and are very dangerous to fishing boats. During his prayer on the hill, Jesus is still mindful of his disciples; he sees them trying to cope with the wind and the

m. Other ancient authorities read *was out on the sea* **n.** Other ancient authorities read *strong wind*

[32]And when they got into the boat, the wind ceased. [33]And those
in the boat worshipped him, saying, "Truly you are the Son of
God."*

Cures in Gennesaret

[34]And when they had crossed over, they came to land at
Gennesaret. [35]And when the men of that place recognized him,
they sent round to all that region and brought to him all that were
sick, [36]and besought him that they might only touch the fringe of Lk 6:19
his garment; and as many as touched it were made well.

The tradition of the elders. True cleanness

15 [1]Then Pharisees and scribes came to Jesus from Jerusalem Mk 7:1–23
and said, [2]"Why do your disciples transgress the tradition Deut 4:2 Lk 11:38
of the elders? For they do not wash their hands when they eat."
[3]He answered them, "And why do you transgress the commandment of God for the sake of your tradition? [4]For God commanded,

---

waves and comes to their rescue once he has finished praying. This episode has applications to Christian life. The Church, like the apostles' boat, also gets into difficulties, and Jesus who watches over his Church comes to its rescue also, after allowing it wrestle with obstacles and be strengthened in the process. He gives us encouragement: "Take heart, it is I; have no fear" (14:27); and we show our faith and fidelity by striving to keep an even keel, and by calling on his aid when we feel ourselves weakening: "Lord, save me" (14:30), words of St Peter which every soul uses when he has recourse to Jesus, his Saviour. Then our Lord does save us, and we urgently confess our faith: "Truly you are the Son of God" (14:33).

14:29–31. St John Chrysostom (*Hom. on St Matthew*, 50) comments that in this episode Jesus taught Peter to realize, from his own experience, that all his strength came from our Lord and that he could not rely on his own resources, on his own weakness and wretchedness. Chrysostom goes as far as to say that "if we fail to play our part, God ceases to help us." Hence the reproach, "O man of little faith" (14:31). When Peter began to be afraid and to doubt, he started to sink, until again, full of faith, he called out, "Lord, save me." If at any time we, like Peter, should begin to weaken, we too should try to bring our faith into play and call on Jesus to save us.

14:34–36. Learning from the faith of these people on the shore of Lake Gennesaret, every Christian should approach the adorable humanity of the Saviour. Christ—God and Man—is accessible to us in the sacrament of the Eucharist. "When you approach the tabernacle remember that *he* has been awaiting you for twenty centuries" (St Josemaría Escrivá, *The Way*, 537).

15:3–4. "For God commanded": it is interesting to note the respect and formality with which Jesus refers to the commandments of the Law of God given through Moses—in this case, the fourth

Ex 20:12; 21:17 'Honour your father and your mother,' and, 'He who speaks evil
Deut 5:16 of father or mother, let him surely die.' 5But you say, 'If any one
tells his father or his mother, What you would have gained from
me is given to God,[o] he need not honour his father.'* 6So, for the
sake of your tradition, you have made void the word[p] of God.
Is 29:13 7You hypocrites! Well did Isaiah prophesy of you, when he said:
8'This people honours me with their lips,
but their heart is far from me;
9in vain do they worship me,
teaching as doctrines the precepts of men.' "
10And he called the people to him and said to them, "Hear and
1 Tim 4:4 understand: 11not what goes into the mouth defiles a man, but
what comes out of the mouth, this defiles a man." 12Then the disciples came and said to him, "Do you know that the Pharisees
Jn 15:2 were offended when they heard this saying?" 13He answered,
Lk 6:39 "Every plant which my heavenly Father has not planted will be
Jn 9:40 Rom 2:19 rooted up. 14Let them alone; they are blind guides. And if a blind

---

commandment (cf. Ex 20:12; 21:17). Following its divine Master, the Church sees the ten commandments summing up all human and Christian morality, as the divine-positive formulation of basic natural law. Each and every one of the ten commandments of the Law of God should be lovingly kept, even if this calls for heroism.

15:5–6. Over the years teachers of the Law (scribes) and priests of the temple had distorted the true meaning of the fourth commandment. In Jesus' time, they were saying that people who contributed to the temple in cash or in kind were absolved from supporting their parents: it would be sacrilegious for parents to lay claim to this *corban* (offerings for the altar). People educated in this kind of thinking felt that they were keeping the fourth commandment—in fact, fulfilling it in the best way possible—and they were praised for their piety by the religious leaders of the nation. But what in fact it meant was that, under the cloak of piety, they were leaving elderly parents to fend for themselves. Jesus, who is Messiah and God, is the one who can correctly interpret the Law. Here he explains the proper scope of the fourth commandment, exposing the error of Jewish practice at the time.

For Christians, therefore, the fourth commandment includes affectionate help of parents if they are old or needy, even if one has other family, social or religious obligations to attend to. Children should check regularly on whether they are looking after their parents properly.

15:6–9. Jewish man-made tradition was forever adding extra little precepts or interpretations onto the Law of God; by Jesus' time these constituted almost another law. This tradition was so incredibly detailed (and sometimes quite ridiculous) that it tended to suffocate the spirit of the Law of God instead of helping a

o. Or *an offering* **p.** Other ancient authorities read *law*

man leads a blind man, both will fall into a pit." [15]But Peter said
to him, "Explain the parable to us." [16]And he said, "Are you also
still without understanding? [17]Do you not see that whatever goes
into the mouth passes into the stomach, and so passes on?[q] [18]But
what comes out of the mouth proceeds from the heart, and this
defiles a man. [19]For out of the heart come evil thoughts, murder, Gen 8:21
adultery, fornication, theft, false witness, slander. [20]These are what
defile a man; but to eat with unwashed hands does not defile a
man."

The Canaanite woman

[21]And Jesus went away from there and withdrew to the district of Mk 7:24–30
Tyre and Sidon. [22]And behold, a Canaanite woman from that
region came out and cried, "Have mercy on me, O Lord, Son of
David; my daughter is severely possessed by a demon." [23]But he
did not answer her a word. And his disciples came and begged

---

person fulfil that Law. This is what our Lord is referring to here so bluntly. God himself, through Moses, sought to protect his Law by ordering that nothing be added to or taken from what he had commanded (cf. Deut 4:2).

15:10–20. Our Lord proclaims the true meaning of moral precepts and makes it clear that man has to answer to God for his actions. The scribes' mistake consisted in concentrating on externals and not giving pride of place to interior purity of heart. For example, they saw prayer in terms of exact recital of fixed forms of words rather than as a raising of the soul to God (cf. Mt 6:5–6). The same thing happened in the case of dietary regulations.

Jesus avails himself of the particular cases dealt with in this passage to teach us where to find the true centre of moral action: it lies in man's personal decision, good or evil, a decision that is shaped in his heart and then expressed in the form of action. For example, the sins which our Lord lists are sins committed in the human heart prior to being acted out. In the Sermon on the Mount he already said this: "Every one who looks at a woman lustfully has already committed adultery with her in his heart" (Mt 5:28).

15:21–22. Tyre and Sidon were Phoenician cities on the Mediterranean coast, in present-day Lebanon. They were never part of Galilee but they were near its northwestern border. In Jesus' time they were outside the territory of Herod Antipas (see the note on Mt 2:1). Jesus withdrew to this area to escape persecution from Herod and from the Jewish authorities and to concentrate on training his apostles.

Most of the inhabitants of the district of Tyre and Sidon were pagans. St Matthew calls this woman a "Canaanite"; according to Genesis (10:15), this district was one of the first to be settled by the Canaanites; St Mark describes the woman as a "Syrophoenician" (Mk 7:26).

q. Or *is evacuated*

him, saying, "Send her away, for she is crying after us." 24He
answered, "I was sent only to the lost sheep of the house of
Israel."* 25But she came and knelt before him, saying, "Lord, help
me." 26And he answered, "It is not fair to take the children's bread
and throw it to the dogs." 27She said, "Yes, Lord, yet even the dogs
eat the crumbs that fall from their master's table." 28Then Jesus
answered her, "O woman, great is your faith! Be it done for you
as you desire." And her daughter was healed instantly.

Curing of many sick people

Mk 7:31 29And Jesus went on from there and passed along the Sea of
Mk 3:10 Galilee. And he went up into the hills, and sat down there. 30And
great crowds came to him, bringing with them the lame, the
maimed, the blind, the dumb, and many others, and they put
Mk 7:37 them at his feet, and he healed them, 31so that the throng wondered, when they saw the dumb speaking, the maimed whole, the
lame walking, and the blind seeing; and they glorified the God of
Israel.

Both Gospels point out that she is a pagan, which means that her faith in our Lord is more remarkable; the same applies in the case of the centurion (Mt 8:5–13).

The Canaanite woman's prayer is quite perfect: she recognizes Jesus as the Messiah (the Son of David)—which contrasts with the unbelief of the Jews; she expresses her need in clear, simple words; she persists, undismayed by obstacles; and she expresses her request in all humility: "Have mercy on me." Our prayer should have the same qualities of faith, trust, perseverance and humility.

15:24. What Jesus says here does not take from the universal reference of his teaching (cf. Mt 28:19–20; Mk 16:15–16). Our Lord came to bring his Gospel to the whole world, but he himself addressed only the Jews; later on he will charge his apostles to preach the Gospel to pagans. St Paul, in his missionary journeys, also adopted the policy of preaching in the first instance to the Jews (Acts 13:46).

15:25–28. This dialogue between Jesus and the woman is especially beautiful. By appearing to be harsh he so strengthens the woman's faith that she deserves exceptional praise: "Great is your faith!" Our own conversation with Christ should be like that: "Persevere in prayer. Persevere, even when your efforts seem barren. Prayer is always fruitful" (St Josemaría Escrivá, *The Way*, 101).

15:29–31. Here St Matthew summarizes Jesus' activity in this border area where Jews and pagans were living side by side. As usual he teaches and heals the sick; the Gospel account clearly echoes the prophecy of Isaiah which Christ himself used to prove that he was the Messiah (Lk 7:22): "the eyes of the blind shall be opened, and the ears of the deaf unstopped …" (Is 35:5). "They glorified the God of Israel": this clearly refers to the Gentiles, who thought that

Second miracle of the loaves and fish

32 Then Jesus called his disciples to him and said, "I have compas- Mk 8:1–10
sion on the crowd, because they have been with me now three
days, and have nothing to eat; and I am unwilling to send them
away hungry, lest they faint on the way." 33 And the disciples said
to him, "Where are we to get bread enough in the desert to feed so
great a crowd?" 34 And Jesus said to them, "How many loaves
have you?" They said, "Seven, and a few small fish." 35 And com-
manding the crowd to sit down on the ground, 36 he took the seven
loaves and the fish, and having given thanks he broke them and
gave them to the disciples, and the disciples gave them to the
crowds. 37 And they all ate and were satisfied; and they took up
seven baskets full of the broken pieces left over. 38 Those who ate
were four thousand men, besides women and children. 39 And
sending away the crowds, he got into the boat and went to the
region of Magadan.

God could give the power to work miracles to Jews only. Once again the Gentiles are seen to have more faith than the Jews.

15:32. The Gospels speak of our Lord's mercy and compassion towards people's needs: here he is concerned about the crowds who are following him and who have no food. He always has a word of consolation, encouragement and forgiveness: he is never indifferent. However, what hurts him most are sinners who go through life without experiencing light and truth: he waits for them in the sacraments of Baptism and Penance.

15:33–38. As in the case of the first multiplication (14:13–20), the apostles provide our Lord with the loaves and the fish. It was all they had. He also avails of the apostles to distribute the food—the result of the miracle—to the people. In distributing the graces of salvation God chooses to rely on the faithfulness and generosity of men. "Many great things depend—don't forget it—on whether you and I live our lives as God wants" (St Josemaría Escrivá, *The Way*, 755).

It is interesting to note that in both miracles of multiplication of loaves and fish Jesus provides food in abundance but does not allow anything to go to waste. All Jesus' miracles, in addition to being concrete historical events, are also symbols of supernatural realities. Here abundance of material food also signifies abundance of divine gifts on the level of grace and glory: it refers to spiritual resources and eternal rewards; God gives people more graces than are strictly necessary. This is borne out by Christian experience throughout history. St Paul tells us that "where sin increased, grace abounded all the more" (Rom 5:20); he speaks of "the riches of his grace which he lavished upon us" (Eph 1:8) and tells his disciple Timothy that "the grace of our Lord overflowed for me with the faith and love that are in Christ Jesus" (1 Tim 1:14).

15:39. St Mark calls Magadan Dalmanutha (8:10). These are the only references to this place; we do not know its exact location.

The Pharisees and Sadducees try to test Jesus

Mk 8:11–21 Mt 12:38 Lk 12:54–56

16 [1]And the Pharisees and Sadducees came, and to test him
they asked him to show them a sign from heaven. [2]He
answered them,[r] "When it is evening, you say, 'It will be fair
weather; for the sky is red.' [3]And in the morning, 'It will be stormy
today, for the sky is red and threatening.' You know how to interpret the appearance of the sky, but you cannot interpret the signs
Jn 2:1 Mt 12:39f of the times. [4]An evil and adulterous generation seeks for a sign,
but no sign shall be given to it except the sign of Jonah." So he left
them and departed.

[5]When the disciples reached the other side, they had forgotten
Lk 12:1 to bring any bread. [6]Jesus said to them, "Take heed and beware of
the leaven of the Pharisees and Sadducees." [7]And they discussed
it among themselves, saying, "We brought no bread." [8]But Jesus,
aware of this, said, "O men of little faith, why do you discuss
among yourselves the fact that you have no bread? [9]Do you not
yet perceive? Do you not remember the five loaves of the five
thousand, and how many baskets you gathered? [10]Or the seven
loaves of the four thousand, and how many baskets you gathered?
[11]How is it that you fail to perceive that I did not speak about

---

16:1–4. On Jesus' reply to the Pharisees and the meaning of the sign of Jonah, see the note on Mt 12:39–40.

16:3. "The signs of the times": Jesus uses man's ability to forecast the weather to speak about the signs of the advent of the Messiah.

He reproaches the Pharisees for not recognizing that the messianic times have in fact arrived: "For the Lord Jesus inaugurated his Church by preaching the Good News, that is, the coming of the Kingdom of God, promised over the ages in the Scriptures: 'The time is fulfilled, and the kingdom of God is at hand' (Mk 1:15; cf. Mt 4:17). This Kingdom shone out before men in the world, in the works and in the presence of Christ. The word of the Lord is compared to a seed that is sown in a field (Mk 4:14); those who hear it with faith and are numbered among the little flock of Christ (Lk 12:32) have truly received the Kingdom. Then, by its own power the seed sprouts and grows until the harvest (cf. Mk 4:26–29). The miracles of Jesus also demonstrate that the Kingdom has already come on earth: 'If it be by the finger of God that I cast out demons, then the kingdom of God has come upon you' (Lk 11:20; cf. Mt 12:28). But principally the Kingdom is revealed in the person of Christ himself, Son of God and Son of man, who came 'to serve, and to give his life as a ransom for many' (Mk 10:45)" (Vatican II, *Lumen gentium*, 5).

16:13–20. In this passage St Peter is promised primacy over the whole Church, a primacy which Jesus will confer on him after his resurrection, as we learn in the Gospel of St John (cf. Jn 21:15–18). This supreme authority is given to Peter for

r. Other ancient authorities omit the following words to the end of verse 3

bread? Beware of the leaven of the Pharisees and Sadducees."
12Then they understood that he did not tell them to beware of the Jn 6:27
leaven of bread, but of the teaching of the Pharisees and Sadducees.

Peter's profession of faith and his primacy

13Now when Jesus came into the district of Caesarea Philippi, he Mk 8:27–30
asked his disciples, "Who do men say that the Son of man is?" Lk 9:18–21
14And they said, "Some say John the Baptist, others say Elijah,
and others Jeremiah or one of the prophets."* 15He said to them,
"But who do you say that I am?" 16Simon Peter replied, "You are Jn 6:69
the Christ, the Son of the living God."* 17And Jesus answered Gal 1:15f
him, "Blessed are you, Simon Bar-Jona! For flesh and blood has Mt 17:4–5
not revealed this to you, but my Father who is in heaven. 18And I Jn 1:42
tell you, you are Peter,[s] and on this rock[t] I will build my church, Eph 2:20 Job 38:17
and the powers of death[u] shall not prevail against it.* 19I will give Is 38:10
you the keys of the kingdom of heaven,* and whatever you bind Ps 9:13; 107:18
on earth shall be bound in heaven, and whatever you loose on Wis 16:30
earth shall be loosed in heaven." 20Then he strictly charged the Mt 18:18 Rev 1:18
disciples to tell no one that he was the Christ.

---

the benefit of the Church. Because the Church has to last until the end of time, this authority will be passed on to Peter's successors down through history. The Bishop of Rome, the Pope, is the successor of Peter.

The solemn Magisterium of the Church, in the First Vatican Council, defined the doctrine of the primacy of Peter and his successors in these terms:

"We teach and declare, therefore, according to the testimony of the Gospel that the primacy of jurisdiction over the whole Church was immediately and directly promised to and conferred upon the blessed apostle Peter by Christ the Lord. For to Simon, Christ had said, 'You shall be called Cephas' (Jn 1:42). Then, after Simon had acknowledged Christ with the confession, 'You are the Christ, the Son of the living God' (Mt 16:16), it was to Simon alone that the solemn words were spoken by the Lord: 'Blessed are you, Simon Bar-Jona. For flesh and blood has not revealed this to you, but my Father who is in heaven. And I tell you, you are Peter, and on this rock I will build my church, and the powers of hell shall not prevail against it. I will give you the keys of the kingdom of heaven, and whatever you bind on earth shall be bound in heaven, and what you loose on earth shall be loosed in heaven' (Mt 16:17–19). And after his resurrection, Jesus conferred upon Simon Peter alone the jurisdiction of supreme shepherd and ruler over all his fold with the words, 'Feed my lambs.... Feed my sheep' (Jn 21:15–17) [...].

"(Canon) Therefore, if anyone says that the blessed apostle Peter was not constituted by Christ the Lord as the Prince of all the apostles and the visible head of the whole Church militant, or that he received

s. Greek *Petros* **t.** Greek *petra* **u.** Greek *the gates of Hades*

PART TWO

Jesus' ministry on the way to Jerusalem

8. TOWARDS JUDEA AND JERUSALEM

Jesus foretells his passion and resurrection. The law of Christian renunciation

Mk 8:31–9:1 Lk 9:22–27 Mt 12:40 Jn 2:19

21From that time Jesus began to show his disciples that he must go
to Jerusalem and suffer many things from the elders and chief

---

immediately and directly from Jesus Christ our Lord only a primacy of honour and not a true and proper primacy of jurisdiction: let him be condemned.

"Now, what Christ the Lord, supreme shepherd and watchful guardian of the flock, established in the person of the blessed apostle Peter for the perpetual safety and everlasting good of the Church must, by the will of the same, endure without interruption in the Church which was founded on the rock and which will remain firm until the end of the world. Indeed, 'no one doubts, in fact it is obvious to all ages, that the holy and most blessed Peter, Prince and head of the apostles, the pillar of faith, and the foundation of the Catholic Church, received the keys of the kingdom from our Lord Jesus Christ, the Saviour and the Redeemer of the human race; and even to this time and forever he lives', and governs, 'and exercises judgment in his successors' (cf. Council of Ephesus), the bishops of the holy Roman See, which he established and consecrated with his blood. Therefore, whoever succeeds Peter in this Chair holds Peter's primacy over the whole Church according to the plan of Christ himself [...]. For this reason, 'because of its greater sovereignty', it was always 'necessary for every church, that is, the faithful who are everywhere, to be in agreement' with the same Roman Church [...].

"(Canon) Therefore, if anyone says that it is not according to the institution of Christ our Lord himself, that is, by divine law, that St Peter has perpetual successors in the primacy over the whole Church; or if anyone says that the Roman Pontiff is not the successor of St Peter in the same primacy: let him be condemned [...].

"We think it extremely necessary to assert solemnly the prerogative which the only-begotten Son of God deigned to join to the highest pastoral office. And so, faithfully keeping to the tradition received from the beginning of the Christian faith, for the glory of God our Saviour, for the exaltation of the Catholic religion, and for the salvation of Christian peoples, We, with the approval of the sacred council, teach and define that it is a divinely revealed dogma: that the Roman Pontiff, when he speaks *ex cathedra*, that is, when, acting in the office of shepherd and teacher of all Christians, he defines, by virtue of his supreme apostolic authority, doctrine concerning faith or morals to be held by the universal Church, possesses through the divine assistance promised to him in the person of St Peter, the infallibility with which the divine Redeemer willed his Church to be endowed in defining doctrine concerning faith or morals;

priests and scribes, and be killed, and on the third day be raised.
[22]And Peter took him and began to rebuke him, saying, "God
forbid, Lord! This shall never happen to you." [23]But he turned and Is 8:14
said to Peter, "Get behind me, Satan! You are a hindrance[v] to me;
for you are not on the side of God, but of men."

[24]Then Jesus told his disciples, "If any man would come after
me, let him deny himself and take up his cross and follow me.
[25]For whoever would save his life* will lose it, and whoever loses
his life for my sake will find it. [26]For what will it profit a man, if Jn 5:29 Rom 2:6

---

and that such definitions of the Roman Pontiff are therefore irreformable because of their nature, but not because of the agreement of the Church.

"(Canon) But if anyone presumes to contradict this our definition (God forbid that he do so): let him be condemned" (Vatican I, *Pastor aeternus*, chaps. 1, 2 and 4).

16:23. Jesus rejects St Peter's well-intentioned protestations, giving us to understand the capital importance of accepting the cross if we are to attain salvation (cf. 1 Cor 1:23–25). Shortly before this (Mt 16:17) Jesus had promised Peter: "Blessed are you, Simon"; now he reproves him: "Get behind me, Satan." In the former case Peter's words were inspired by the Holy Spirit, whereas what he says now comes from his own spirit, which he has not yet sloughed off.

16:24. "Divine love, 'poured into our hearts by the Holy Spirit who has been given to us' (Rom 5:5), enables lay people to express concretely in their lives the spirit of the Beatitudes. Following Jesus in his poverty, they feel no depression in want, no pride in plenty; imitating the humble Christ, they are not greedy for vain show (cf. Gal 5:26). They strive to please God rather than men, always ready to abandon everything for Christ (cf. Lk 14:26) and even to endure persecution in the cause of right (cf. Mt 5:10), having in mind the Lord's saying: 'If any man wants to come after me, let him deny himself and take up his cross and follow me' (Mt 16:24)" (Vatican II, *Apostolicam actuositatem*, 4).

16:25. A Christian cannot ignore these words of Jesus. He has to risk, to gamble, this present life in order to attain eternal life: "How little a life is to offer to God!" (St Josemaría Escrivá, *The Way*, 420).

Our Lord's requirement means that we must renounce our own will in order to identify with the will of God; and so to ensure that, as St John of the Cross comments, we do not follow the way of those many people who "would have God will that which they themselves will, and are fretful at having to will that which he wills, and find it repugnant to accommodate their will to that of God. Hence it happens to them that oftentimes they think that that wherein they find not their own will and pleasure is not the will of God; and that, on the other hand, when they themselves find satisfaction, God is satisfied. Thus they measure God by themselves and not themselves by God" (*Dark Night of the Soul*, book 1, chap. 7, 3).

16:26–27. Christ's words are crystal-clear: every person has to bear in mind

v. Greek *stumbling block*

Ps 62:12 he gains the whole world and forfeits his life? Or what shall a
Prov 24:12 man give in return for his life? [27]For the Son of man is to come
with his angels in the glory of his Father, and then he will repay
every man for what he has done. [28]Truly, I say to you, there are
some standing here who will not taste death before they see the
Son of man coming in his kingdom."

The Transfiguration

Mk 9:2–13 **17** [1]And after six days Jesus took with him Peter and James
Lk 5:28–36 and John his brother, and led them up a high mountain
2 Pet 1:16–18 apart. [2]And he was transfigured before them, and his face shone
like the sun, and his garments became white as light. [3]And behold,
there appeared to them Moses and Elijah, talking with him. [4]And

---

the Last Judgment. Salvation, in other words, is something radically personal: "he will repay every man for what he has done" (v. 27).

Man's goal does not consist in accumulating worldly goods; these are only means to an end; man's last end, his ultimate goal, is God himself; he possesses God in advance, as it were, here on earth by means of grace, and possesses him fully and for ever in heaven. Jesus shows the route to take to reach this destination—denying oneself (that is, saying no to ease, comfort, selfishness and attachment to temporal goods) and taking up the cross. For no earthly—impermanent—good can compare with the soul's eternal salvation. As St Thomas expresses it with theological precision, "the least good of grace is superior to the natural good of the entire universe" (*Summa theologiae*, 1–2, 113, 9).

16:28. Here Jesus is referring not to his last coming (which he speaks about in the preceding verse) but to other events which will occur prior to that and which will be a sign of his glorification after death. The coming he speaks of here may refer firstly to his resurrection and his appearances thereafter; it could also refer to his transfiguration, which is itself a manifestation of his glory. This coming of Christ in his Kingdom might also be seen in the destruction of Jerusalem—a sign of the end of the ancient people of Israel as a form of the Kingdom of God and its substitution by the Church, the new Kingdom.

17:1–13. Realizing that his death will demoralize his disciples, Jesus forewarns them and strengthens their faith. Not content with telling them in advance about his death and resurrection on the third day, he wants two of the three future pillars of the Church (cf. Gal 2:9) to see his transfiguration and thereby glimpse the glory and majesty with which his holy human nature will be endowed in heaven.

The Father's testimony (v. 5), expressed in the same words as he used at Christ's baptism (cf. Mt 3:17), reveals to the three apostles that Jesus Christ is the Son of God, the beloved Son, God himself. To these words—also spoken at Christ's baptism—he adds, "Listen to him", as if to indicate that Jesus is also the supreme prophet foretold by Moses (cf. Deut 18:15–18).

Peter said to Jesus, "Lord, it is well that we are here; if you wish,
I will make three booths here, one for you and one for Moses and
one for Elijah."* 5He was still speaking, when lo, a bright cloud Deut 18:15
overshadowed them, and a voice from the cloud said, "This is my
beloved Son,[w] with whom I am well pleased; listen to him."
6When the disciples heard this, they fell on their faces, and were
filled with awe. 7But Jesus came and touched them, saying, "Rise,
and have no fear." 8And when they lifted up their eyes, they saw
no one but Jesus only.

9And as they were coming down the mountain, Jesus commanded them, "Tell no one the vision, until the Son of man is
raised from the dead." 10And the disciples asked him, "Then why Mal 3:23f
do the scribes say that first Elijah must come?" 11He replied,
"Elijah does come, and he is to restore all things; 12but I tell you Lk 23:25

17:3. Moses and Elijah are the two most prominent representatives of the Old Testament—the Law and the Prophets. The fact that Christ occupies the central position points up his pre-eminence over them, and the superiority of the New Testament over the Old.

This dazzling glimpse of divine glory is enough to send the apostles into a rapture; so happy are they that Peter cannot contain his desire to prolong this experience.

17:5. In Christ God speaks to all men; through the Church his voice resounds in all ages: "The Church does not cease to listen to his words. She rereads them continually. With the greatest devotion she reconstructs every detail of his life. These words are listened to also by non-Christians. The life of Christ speaks, also, to many who are not capable of repeating with Peter, 'You are the Christ, the Son of the living God' (Mt 16:16). He, the Son of the living God, speaks to people also as Man: it is his life that speaks, his humanity, his fidelity to the truth, his all-embracing love. Furthermore, his death on the Cross speaks—that is to say the inscrutable depth of his suffering and abandonment. The Church never ceases to relive his death on the Cross and his resurrection, which constitute the content of the Church's daily life [...]. The Church lives his mystery, draws unwearyingly from it and continually seeks ways of bringing this mystery of her Master and Lord to humanity—to the peoples, the nations, the succeeding generations, and every individual human being" (John Paul II, *Redemptor hominis*, 7).

17:10–13. Malachi 4:5 (3:23 in the Hebrew) speaks of the coming of Elijah the prophet before "the great and terrible day of the Lord", the Judgment Day. When Jesus says that Elijah has already come, he is referring to St John the Baptist, whose mission it was to prepare the way for the first coming of the Lord, the same as Elijah will have to do prior to his last coming. The scribes failed to grasp the meaning of the prophecy of Malachi; they thought it referred simply to the coming of the Messiah, the first coming of Christ.

w. Or *my Son, my* (or *the*) *Beloved*

that Elijah has already come, and they did not know him, but did
to him whatever they pleased. So also the Son of man will suffer
Lk 1:17 at their hands." 13Then the disciples understood that he was speaking to them of John the Baptist.

Curing of an epileptic boy

Mk 9:14–29 14And when they came to the crowd, a man came up to him and
Lk 9:37–42 kneeling before him said, 15"Lord, have mercy on my son, for he is
an epileptic and he suffers terribly; for often he falls into the fire,
and often into the water. 16And I brought him to your disciples, and
Deut 32:5 they could not heal him." 17And Jesus answered, "O faithless and
Jn 14:9 perverse generation, how long am I to be with you? How long am I
to bear with you? Bring him here to me." 18And Jesus rebuked him,
and the demon came out of him, and the boy was cured instantly.
19Then the disciples came to Jesus privately and said, "Why could
Lk 17:16 we not cast it out?" 20He said to them, "Because of your little faith.
Mk 11:23 For truly, I say to you, if you have faith as a grain of mustard seed,
you will say to this mountain, 'Move hence to yonder place,' and it
will move; and nothing will be impossible to you."[x]

Second announcement of the Passion. The temple tax

Mk 9:30–32 22As they were gathering[y] in Galilee, Jesus said to them. "The Son
Lk 9:43–45
Mt 16:21 of man is to be delivered into the hands of men, 23and they will

---

17:14–21. This episode of the curing of the boy shows both Christ's omnipotence and the power of prayer full of faith. Because of his deep union with Christ, a Christian shares, through faith, in God's own omnipotence, to such an extent that Jesus actually says on another occasion, "he who believes in me will also do the works that I do; and greater works than these will he do, because I go to the Father" (Jn 14:12).

Our Lord tells the apostles that if they had faith they would be able to work miracles, to move mountains. "Moving mountains" was probably a proverbial saying. God would certainly let a believer move a mountain if that were necessary for his glory and for the edification of one's neighbour; however, Christ's promise is fulfilled everyday in a much more exalted way. Some Fathers of the Church (St Jerome, St Augustine) say that "a mountain is moved" every time someone is divinely aided to do something which exceeds man's natural powers. This clearly happens in the work of our sanctification, which the Paraclete effects in our souls when we are docile to him and receive with faith and love the grace given us in the sacraments: we benefit from the sacraments to a greater or lesser degree depending on the dispositions with which we receive them. Sanctification is something much more sublime than moving mountains, and it is something which is happening every day in so many holy souls, even though most people do not notice it.

x. Other ancient authorities insert verse 21, *But this kind never comes out except by prayer and fasting*
y. Other ancient authorities read *abode*

kill him, and he will be raised on the third day." And they were
greatly distressed.
[24]When they came to Capernaum, the collectors of the half- Ex 30:13
shekel tax went up to Peter and said, "Does not your teacher pay
the tax?" [25]He said, "Yes." And when he came home, Jesus spoke
to him first, saying, "What do you think, Simon? From whom do
kings of the earth take toll or tribute? From their sons or from
others?" [26]And when he said, "From others," Jesus said to him,
"Then the sons are free. [27]However, not to give offence to them,
go to the sea and cast a hook, and take the first fish that comes up,
and when you open its mouth you will find a shekel; take that and
give it to them for me and for yourself."

9. THE DISCOURSE ON THE CHURCH

The "little ones" and the Kingdom. On leading others astray. The lost sheep

18 [1]At that time, the disciples came to Jesus, saying, "Who is Mk 9:33–47
the greatest in the kingdom of heaven?" [2]And calling to Lk 9:46–48

The apostles and many saints down the centuries have in fact worked amazing material miracles; but the greatest and most important miracles were, are and will be the miracles of souls dead through sin and ignorance being reborn and developing in the new life of the children of God.

17:20. Here and in the parable of Matthew 13:31–32 the main force of the comparison lies in the fact that a very small seed—the mustard seed—produces a large shrub up to three metres (ten feet) high: even a very small act of genuine faith can produce surprising results.

17:21. See the RSV note and Mk 9:29.

17:24–27. "Half-shekel", or *didrachma*: a coin equal in value to the annual contribution every Jew had to make for the upkeep of the temple—a day's wage of a labourer. The shekel or stater which our Lord refers to in v. 27 was a Greek coin worth two didrachmas. Jesus uses things great and small to get his teaching across to his disciples. Peter, who is to be the rock on which he will found his Church (Mt 16:18–19), he prepares by letting him see his dramatic transfiguration (17:1–8); now he gives Peter another inkling of his divinity through an apparently unimportant miracle. We should take note of Jesus' teaching method: after his second announcement of his passion, his disciples are downhearted (Mt 17:22–23); here he lifts Peter's spirits with this friendly little miracle.

17:26. This shows how conscientiously our Lord fulfilled his civic duties. Although the half-shekel tax had to do with religion, given the theocratic structure of Israel at the time payment of this tax also constituted a civic obligation.

18:1–35. The teachings of Jesus recorded in chapter 18 of St Matthew are often

Jn 3:3–5

him a child, he put him in the midst of them, [3]and said, "Truly, I
say to you, unless you turn and become like children, you will
never enter the kingdom of heaven. [4]Whoever humbles himself
like this child, he is the greatest in the kingdom of heaven.

---

called the "discourse on the Church" or "ecclesiastical discourse" because they are a series of instructions on the way in which his Church is to be administered.

The first passage (Mt 18:1–5), addressed to leaders, that is, the future hierarchy of the Church, warns them against natural tendencies to pride and ambition: even though they have positions of government, they must act with humility. In verses 6–10 Jesus emphasizes the fatherly care that pastors of the Church should have for the "little ones"—a term which covers everyone in need of special care for whatever reason (because they are recent converts, or are not well grounded in Church teaching, or are not yet adults, etc.). He makes a special point of warning them about the harm that scandal—leading others to commit sin—can do: Christians' fraternal charity requires that all, and particularly pastors, should avoid doing anything— even anything that in itself is quite legitimate—which could endanger the spiritual health of those who are less robust: God takes special care of the weak and will punish those who harm them.

Our Lord shows similar concern for those who are experiencing spiritual difficulties. Every effort, even an heroic effort, must be made to seek out the "lost sheep" (vv. 12–14). If the Church in general and each Christian in particular should be concerned to spread the Gospel, all the more reason for them to try and see that those who have already embraced the faith do not go astray.

The following passage (vv. 15–18) on fraternal correction has special doctrinal relevance: here Jesus uses the term "the Church" in the sense of a social structure, an actual community, visible and compact, directly dependent on him and his twelve apostles and their successors, who have an all-embracing "power of the keys", a spiritual authority that God himself backs up. Among their powers is that of forgiving or retaining sins, of receiving people into the Church or cutting them off from communion with the Church—a remarkable divine power given by Jesus to the hierarchy and protected by a special kind of divine providence in the form of Jesus' continuous presence in the Church and the Holy Spirit's support of its hierarchical Magisterium.

This is followed by a passage (vv. 19–20) in which Jesus promises to be present whenever a number of Christians come together to pray (v. 20), and teaches the need to forgive any offences committed by one brother against another (vv. 21–22). The chapter ends with the parable of the unforgiving debtor (vv. 23–35), in which our Lord shows what forgiveness involves.

Thus, the whole of chapter 18, the "discourse on the Church", is a survey of the future history of the Church during its earthly stage, and a series of practical rules of conduct for Christians—a kind of complement to the Sermon on the Mount (chaps. 5–7), which is a "magna charta" for the new Kingdom established by Christ.

18:1–6. Clearly the disciples still suffer from human ambition: they want to occupy key positions when Jesus comes to establish his Kingdom on earth (cf. Acts 1:6). To correct their pride, our Lord

5"Whoever receives one such child in my name receives me; Jn 13:20
6but whoever causes one of these little ones who believe in me to Lk 17:1f
sin,[z] it would be better for him to have a great millstone fastened
round his neck and to be drowned in the depth of the sea.

---

shows them a child and tells them that if they want to enter the Kingdom of heaven, they must decide to be like children: children are incapable of hating anyone and are totally innocent of vice, particularly of pride, the worst vice of all. They are simple and full of trust.

Humility is one of the main pillars of the Christian life. "If you ask me", St Augustine says, "what is the essential thing in the religion and discipline of Jesus Christ, I shall reply: first humility, second humility and third humility" (*Letters*, 118).

18:3–4. Applying these words to our Lord's virtues, Fray Luis de Granada makes the point that humility is superior to virginity: "If you cannot imitate the virginity of the humble, then imitate the humility of the virgin. Virginity is praiseworthy, but humility is more necessary. The former is recommended to us, the latter is an obligation for us; to the former we are invited, to the latter we are obliged […]. And so we see that the former is celebrated as a voluntary sacrifice, the latter required as an obligatory sacrifice. Lastly, you can be saved without virginity, but not without humility" (*Suma de la vida cristiana*, book 3, part 2, chap. 10).

18:5. Receiving a child in Jesus' name is the same as receiving Jesus himself. Because children reflect the innocence, purity, simplicity and tenderness of our Lord, "In children and in the sick a soul in love sees him" (St Josemaría Escrivá, *The Way*, 419).

18:6–7. The holy, pained indignation sounding in Jesus' words shows the seriousness of the sin of scandal, which is defined as "something said, done or omitted which leads another person to commit sin" (cf. St Pius X, *Catechism*, 417).

"Millstone": our Lord is referring to a form of punishment used in ancient times, which consisted in throwing a person into the sea with a heavy weight attached to his neck to prevent his body floating to the surface; this was regarded as a particularly ignominious form of death because it was inflicted only on the worst criminals and also because it meant deprival of burial.

Although Jesus affirms that people will cause others to sin, this does not mean that everyone, personally, should not ensure that this does not happen. Therefore, everyone who does cause another to sin is responsible for his action. Here he refers directly to scandal given to children—an action that is particularly malicious given the weakness and innocence of children. The evil of the world as enemy of the soul consists mainly in the harm it does in this way. Its evil maxims and bad example create an environment which draws people away from God, from Christ and from his Church.

The scandal given by those whose function it is to educate others is particularly serious. "If ordinary folk are lukewarm, that is bad; but it can be remedied, and the only one they harm is themselves; but if the teachers are lukewarm, then the Lord's 'Woe to the world'

z. Greek *causes … to stumble*

7"Woe to the world for temptations to sin![a] For it is necessary
that temptations come, but woe to the man by whom the temptation comes! 8And if your hand or your foot causes you to sin,[z] cut
it off and throw it from you; it is better for you to enter life
maimed or lame than with two hands or two feet to be thrown into
the eternal fire. 9And if your eye causes you to sin,[z] pluck it out
and throw it from you; it is better for you to enter life with one
eye than with two eyes to be thrown into the hell[b]* of fire.
Heb 1:14 10"See that you do not despise one of these little ones; for I tell
you that in heaven their angels always behold the face of my
Lk 15:4–7 Father who is in heaven.[c] 12What do you think? If a man has a
hundred sheep, and one of them has gone astray, does he not leave
the ninety-nine on the hills and go in search of the one that went

---

applies because of the great evil that results from this lukewarmness; this 'woe' threatens those lukewarm teachers who spread their lukewarmness to others and even suffocate their fervour completely" (St Augustine, *Sermons*, 55).

18:8–9. Entering life means entering the Kingdom of heaven. "The fire of hell": eternal punishment, merited by anyone who does not distance himself from what causes sin. Cf. the note on Mt 9:43.

18:8. Jesus is speaking figuratively. His teaching here can guide us in making moral decisions. If something or someone—however much we love them—is liable to cause us to commit sin, we have to stay away from them; it is as simple as that. "If thy right eye scandalize thee, pluck it out and cast it from thee! Your poor heart, that's what scandalizes you! Press it, squeeze it tight in your hands: give it no consolations. And when it asks for them, say to it slowly and with a noble compassion—in confidence, as it were: 'Heart, heart on the Cross, heart on the Cross!'" (St J. Escrivá, *The Way*, 163).

10. Jesus warns that giving scandal to little children is a very serious matter, for they have angels who guard them, who will plead a case before God against those who led them to commit sin.

In this context he speaks of children having guardian angels. However, everyone, adult or child, has a guardian angel. "By God's providence angels have been entrusted with the office of guarding the human race and of accompanying every human being so as to preserve him from any serious dangers [...]. Our heavenly Father has placed over each of us an angel under whose protection and vigilance we are" (St Pius V, *Catechism*, 4, 9, 4).

This means that we should have a trusting relationship with our guardian angel. "Have confidence in your guardian Angel. Treat him as a lifelong friend — that is what he is—and he will render you a thousand services in the ordinary affairs of each day" (*The Way*, 562).

18:11–14. This parable clearly shows our Lord's loving concern for sinners. It expresses in human terms the joy God feels when a wayward child comes back to him.

a. Greek *stumbling blocks* **z.** Greek *causes ... to stumble* **b.** Greek *Gehenna* **c.** Other ancient authorities add verse 11, *For the Son of man came to save the lost*

astray? [13]And if he finds it, truly, I say to you, he rejoices over it
more than over the ninety-nine that never went astray. [14]So it is
not the will of my[d] Father who is in heaven that one of these little
ones should perish.

Fraternal correction. The apostles' authority Lev 19:17

[15]"If your brother sins against you, go and tell him his fault, Lk 17:3
between you and him alone. If he listens to you, you have gained Gal 6:1 Deut 19:15
your brother. [16]But if he does not listen, take one or two others
along with you, that every word may be confirmed by the evidence
of two or three witnesses. [17]If he refuses to listen to them, tell it to 1 Cor 5:13
the church; and if he refuses to listen even to the church, let him be
to you as a Gentile and a tax collector. [18]Truly, I say to you, what- Mt 16:19 Jn 20:23

Seeing so many souls living away from God, Pope John Paul II comments: "Unfortunately we witness the moral pollution which is devastating humanity, disregarding especially those very little ones about whom Jesus speaks.

"What must we do? We must imitate the Good Shepherd and give ourselves without rest for the salvation of souls. Without forgetting material charity and social justice, we must be convinced that the most sublime charity is spiritual charity, that is, the commitment for the salvation of souls. And souls are saved with prayer and sacrifice. This is the mission of the Church!" (Homily to the Poor Clares of Albano, 14 August 1979).

As the RSV points out, "other ancient authorities add verse 11, *For the Son of man came to save the lost*"—apparently taken from Lk 19:10.

18:15–17. Here our Lord calls on us to work with him for the sanctification of others by means of fraternal correction, which is one of the ways we can do so. He speaks as sternly about the sin of omission as he did about that of scandal (cf. Chrysostom, *Hom. on St Matthew*, 61).

There is an obligation on us to correct others. Our Lord identifies three stages in correction: 1) alone; 2) in the presence of one or two witnesses; and 3) before the Church. The first stage refers to causing scandal and to secret or private sins; here correction should be given privately, just to the person himself, to avoid unnecessarily publicizing a private matter and also to avoid hurting the person and to make it easier for him to mend his ways. If this correction does not have the desired effect, and the matter is a serious one, resort should be had to the second stage—looking for one or two friends, in case they have more influence on him. The last stage is formal judicial correction by reference to the Church authorities. If a sinner does not accept this correction, he should be excommunicated that is, separated from communion with the Church and sacraments.

18:18. This verse needs to be understood in connexion with the authority previously promised to Peter (cf. Mt 16:13–19): it is the hierarchy of the Church that exercises this power given by Christ to Peter, to the

d. Other ancient authorities read *your*

ever you bind on earth shall be bound in heaven, and whatever you
Mk 11:24 loose on earth shall be loosed in heaven.* 19Again I say to you, if
two of you agree on earth about anything they ask, it shall be done
Jn 14:23 for them by my Father in heaven. 20For where two or three are
gathered in my name, there am I in the midst of them."

Forgiveness of injuries. Parable of the unforgiving servant

21Then Peter came up and said to him, "Lord, how often shall my
brother sin against me, and I forgive him? As many as seven
Lk 17:4 times?" 22Jesus said to him, "I do not say to you seven times, but
seventy times seven.[e]
23"Therefore the kingdom of heaven may be compared to a
king who wished to settle accounts with his servants. 24When he
began the reckoning, one was brought to him who owed him ten
thousand talents;[f] 25and as he could not pay, his lord ordered him
to be sold, with his wife and children and all that he had, and payment to be made. 26So the servant fell on his knees, imploring
him, 'Lord, have patience with me, and I will pay you everything.'
27And out of pity for him the lord of that servant released him and
forgave him the debt. 28But that same servant, as he went out,
came upon one of his fellow servants who owed him a hundred
denarii;[g] and seizing him by the throat he said, 'Pay what you

---

apostles and their lawful successors—the Pope and the bishops.

18:19–20. "Ubi caritas et amor, Deus ibi est: where charity and love resides, there God is", the Holy Thursday liturgy entones, drawing its inspiration from the sacred text of 1 Jn 4:12. For it is true that love is inconceivable if there is only one person: it implies the presence of two or more (cf. St Thomas Aquinas, *Comm. on St Matthew*, 18:19–20). And so it is that when Christians meet together in the name of Christ for the purpose of prayer, our Lord is present among them, pleased to listen to the unanimous prayer of his disciples: "All those with one accord devoted themselves to prayer, together with the women and Mary the mother of Jesus" (Acts 1:14). This is why the Church from the very beginning has practised communal prayer (cf. Acts 12:5). There are religious practices—few, short, daily "that have always been lived in Christian families and which I think are marvellous—grace at meals, morning and night prayers, the family rosary (even though nowadays this devotion to our Lady has been criticized by some people). Customs vary from place to place, but I think one should always encourage some acts of piety which the family can do together in a simple and natural fashion" (St Josemaría Escrivá, *Conversations*, 103).

e. Or *seventy-seven times* **f.** A talent was more than fifteen years' wages of a labourer **g.** The denarius was a day's wage for a labourer

owe.' [29]So his fellow servant fell down and besought him, 'Have
patience with me, and I will pay you.' [30]He refused and went and
put him in prison till he should pay his debt. [31]When his fellow
servants saw what had taken place, they were greatly distressed,
and they went and reported to their lord all that had taken place.
[32]Then his lord summoned him and said to him, 'You wicked servant! I forgave you all that debt because you besought me; [33]and
should not you have had mercy on your fellow servant, as I had
mercy on you?' [34]And in anger his lord delivered him to the jail-
ers,[h] till he should pay all his debt. [35]So also my heavenly Father
will do to every one of you, if you do not forgive your brother
from your heart."

Marriage and virginity

19 [1]Now when Jesus had finished these sayings, he went away Mk 10:1–12
from Galilee and entered the region of Judea beyond the Mt 7:28; 11:1; 13:53; 26:1
Jordan; [2]and large crowds followed him, and he healed them
there.

[3]And Pharisees came up to him and tested him by asking, "Is it
lawful to divorce one's wife for any cause?" [4]He answered, "Have Gen 1:27
you not read that he who made them from the beginning made
them male and female, [5]and said, 'For this reason a man shall leave Gen 2:24 Eph 5:31

18:21–35. Peter's question and particularly Jesus' reply prescribe the spirit of understanding and mercy which should govern Christians' behaviour.

In Hebrew the figure of seventy times seven means the same as "always" (cf. Gen 4:24): "Therefore, our Lord did not limit forgiveness to a fixed number, but declared that it must be continuous and forever" (St John Chrysostom, *Hom. on St Matthew*, 6). Here also we can see the contrast between man's ungenerous, calculating approach to forgiveness, and God's infinite mercy. The parable also clearly shows that we are totally in God's debt. A talent was the equivalent of six thousand denarii, and a denarius a working man's daily wage. Ten thousand talents, an enormous sum, gives us an idea of the immense value attaching to the pardon we receive from God. Overall, the parable teaches that we must always forgive our brothers, and must do so wholeheartedly.

"Force yourself, if necessary, always to forgive those who offend you, from the very first moment. For the greatest injury or offence that you can suffer from them is as nothing compared with what God has pardoned you" (St Josemaría Escrivá, *The Way*, 452).

19:4–5. "Marriage and married love are by nature ordered to the procreation and education of children. Indeed children are the supreme gift of marriage and greatly contribute to the good of the parents themselves. God himself said: 'It is not good that man should be alone' (Gen 2:18), and 'from the beginning (he) made

h. Greek *torturers*

his father and mother and be joined to his wife, and the two shall
1 Cor 7:10f become one'?[i] 6So they are no longer two but one.[i] What therefore
Deut 24:1 God has joined together, let no man put asunder." 7They said to
him, "Why then did Moses command one to give a certificate of
divorce, and to put her away?" 8He said to them, "For your hardness of heart Moses allowed you to divorce your wives, but from
Lk 16:18 the beginning it was not so. 9And I say to you: whoever divorces his
wife, except for unchastity,[j] and marries another, commits adultery;
and he who marries a divorced woman commits adultery."[k]*

10The disciples said to him, "If such is the case of a man with
1 Cor 7:7, 17 his wife, it is not expedient to marry." 11But he said to them, "Not
all men can receive this precept, but only those to whom it is
given. 12For there are eunuchs who have been so from birth, and
there are eunuchs who have been made eunuchs by men, and

---

them male and female' (Mt 19:4); wishing to associate them in a special way with his own creative work, God blessed man and woman with the words: 'Be fruitful and multiply' (Gen 1:28). Without intending to underestimate the other ends of marriage, it must be said that true married life and the whole structure of family life which results from it is directed to disposing the spouses to cooperate valiantly with the love of the Creator and Saviour, who through them will increase and enrich his family from day to day" (Vatican II, *Gaudium et spes*, 50).

19:9. Our Lord's teaching on the unity and indissolubility of marriage is the main theme of this passage, apropos of which St John Chrysostom comments that marriage is a lifelong union of man and woman (cf. *Hom. on St Matthew*, 62). On the meaning of "except for unchastity", see the note on Mt 5:31–32.

19:11. "Not all men can receive this precept": our Lord is fully aware that the demands involved in his teaching on marriage and his recommendation of celibacy practised out of love of God run counter to human selfishness. That is why he says that acceptance of this teaching is a gift from God.

19:12. Our Lord speaks figuratively here, referring to those who, out of love for him, renounce marriage and offer their lives completely to him. Virginity embraced for the love of God is one of the Church's most precious charisms (cf. 1 Cor 7); the lives of those who practise virginity evoke the state of the blessed in heaven, who are like the angels (cf. Mt 22:30). This is why the Church's Magisterium teaches that the state of virginity for the sake of the Kingdom of heaven is higher than the married state (cf. Council of Trent, *De Sacram. matr.*, can. 10; cf. also Pius XII, *Sacra virginitas*). On virginity and celibacy the Second Vatican Council teaches: "The Church's holiness is also fostered in a special way by the manifold counsels which the Lord proposes to his disciples in the Gospel for

i. Greek *one flesh* **j.** Other ancient authorities, after *unchastity*, read *makes her commit adultery*
k. Other ancient authorities omit *and he who marries a divorced woman commits adultery*

there are eunuchs who have made themselves eunuchs for the sake of the kingdom of heaven. He who is able to receive this, let him receive it."*

Jesus blesses the children

[13]Then children were brought to him that he might lay his hands Mk 10:13–16
on them and pray. The disciples rebuked the people; [14]but Jesus Lk 18:15–17
said, "Let the children come to me, and do not hinder them; for to
such belongs the kingdom of heaven." [15]And he laid his hands on
them and went away.

The rich young man. Christian poverty and renunciation

[16]And behold, one came up to him, saying, "Teacher, what good Mk 10:17–31
deed must I do, to have eternal life?" [17]And he said to him, "Why Lk 18:18–30

---

them to observe. Towering among these counsels is that precious gift of divine grace given to some by the Father (cf. Mt 19:11; 1 Cor 7:7) to devote themselves to God alone more easily in virginity or celibacy [...]. This perfect continence for love of the Kingdom of heaven has always been held in high esteem by the Church as a sign and stimulus of love, and as a singular source of spiritual fertility in the world" (*Lumen gentium*, 42; cf. *Perfectae caritatis*, 12). And, on celibacy specifically, see Vatican II's *Presbyterorum ordinis*, 16 and *Optatam totius*, 10.

However, both virginity and marriage are necessary for the growth of the Church, and both imply a specific calling from God: "Celibacy is precisely a gift of the Spirit. A similar though different gift is contained in the vocation to true and faithful married love, directed towards procreation according to the flesh, in the very lofty context of the sacrament of Matrimony. It is obvious that this gift is fundamental for the building up of the great community of the Church, the people of God. But if this community wishes to respond fully to its vocation in Jesus Christ, there will also have to be realized in it, in the correct proportion, that other gift, the gift of celibacy 'for the sake of the kingdom of heaven'" (John Paul II, *Letter to all priests*, 8 April 1979).

19:13–14. Once again (see Mt 18:1–6) Jesus shows his special love for children, by drawing them close and blessing them. The Church, also, shows special concern for children by urging the need for Baptism: "That this law extends not only to adults but also to infants and children, and that the Church has received this from Apostolic tradition, is confirmed by the unanimous teaching and authority of the Fathers.

"Besides, it is not to be supposed that Christ the Lord would have withheld the sacrament and grace of Baptism from children, of whom he said: 'Let the little children come to me, and do not hinder them; for to such belongs the kingdom of heaven' whom also he embraced, upon whom he imposed hands, to whom he gave his blessing" (St Pius V, *Catechism*, 2, 2, 32).

19:17. The Vulgate and other translations, supported by a good many Greek

Lk 10:26–28 do you ask me about what is good? One there is who is good. If
Ex 20:12–16 you would enter life, keep the commandments." [18]He said to him,
Deut 5:17–20 "Which?" And Jesus said, "You shall not kill, You shall not
commit adultery, You shall not steal, You shall not bear false wit-
Ex 20:12 Lev 19:18 ness, [19]Honour your father and mother, and, You shall love your
Deut 5:16 neighbour as yourself." [20]The young man said to him, "All these I
Lk 12:33 have observed; what do I still lack?" [21]Jesus said to him, "If you
would be perfect, go, sell what you possess and give to the poor,
and you will have treasure in heaven; and come, follow me."
Ps 62:10 [22]When the young man heard this he went away sorrowful; for he
had great possessions.

[23]And Jesus said to his disciples, "Truly, I say to you, it will be
hard for a rich man to enter the kingdom of heaven. [24]Again I tell
you, it is easier for a camel to go through the eye of a needle than
for a rich man to enter the kingdom of God." [25]When the disciples
heard this they were greatly astonished, saying, "Who then can be
Gen 18:14 Job 42:2 saved?" [26]But Jesus looked at them and said to them, "With men
Zech 8:6 this is impossible, but with God all things are possible." [27]Then

---

codexes, fill this verse out by saying, "One alone is good, God."

19:20–22. "What do I still lack?" The young man kept the commandments that were necessary for salvation. But there is more. This is why our Lord replies, "if you would be perfect …" that is to say, if you want to acquire what is still lacking to you. Jesus is giving him an additional calling: "Come, follow me"; he is showing that he wants him to follow him more closely, and therefore he requires him, as he does others (cf. Mt 4:19–22), to give up anything that might hinder his full dedication to the Kingdom of God.

The scene ends rather pathetically: the young man goes away sad. His attachment to his property prevails over Jesus' affectionate invitation. Here is sadness of the kind that stems from cowardice, from failure to respond to God's calling with personal commitment.

In reporting this episode, the evangelists are actually giving us a case-study which describes a situation and formulates a law, a case-study of specific divine vocation to devote oneself to God's service and the service of all men.

This young man has become a symbol of the kind of Christian whose mediocrity and shortsightedness prevent him from turning his life into a generous, fruitful self-giving to the service of God and neighbour. What would this young man have become, had he been generous enough to respond to God's call? A great apostle, surely.

19:24–26. By drawing this comparison Jesus shows that it is simply not possible for people who put their hearts on worldly things to obtain a share in the Kingdom of God. "With God all things are possible": that is, with God's grace man can be brave and generous enough to use wealth to promote the service of God and man. This is why St Matthew, in chapter 5, specifies that the poor *in spirit* are blessed (Mt 5:3).

19:28. "In the new world", in the "regeneration": a reference to the renewal

Peter said in reply, "Lo, we have left everything and followed you. Lk 5:11
What then shall we have?" [28]Jesus said to them, "Truly, I say to Lk 22:30
you, in the new world, when the Son of man shall sit on his glori- Dan 7:9–18
ous throne, you who have followed me will also sit on twelve
thrones, judging the twelve tribes of Israel. [29]And every one who Heb 10:34
has left houses or brothers or sisters or father or mother or children or lands, for my name's sake, will receive a hundredfold,[l]
and inherit eternal life. [30]But many that are first will be last, and Lk 13:30
the last first.

Parable of the labourers in the vineyard

20 [1]"For the kingdom of heaven is like a householder who
went out early in the morning to hire labourers for his
vineyard. [2]After agreeing with the labourers for a denarius[m] a day,
he sent them into his vineyard. [3]And going out about the third
hour he saw others standing idle in the market place; [4]and to them
he said, 'You go into the vineyard too, and whatever is right I will
give you.' So they went. [5]Going out again about the sixth hour and

---

of all things which will take place when Jesus Christ comes to judge the living and the dead. The resurrection of the body will be an integral part of this renewal.

The ancient people of God, Israel, was made up of twelve tribes. The new people of God, the Church, to which all men are called, is founded by Jesus Christ on the twelve apostles under the primacy of Peter.

19:29. These graphic remarks should not be explained away. They mean that love for Jesus Christ and his Gospel should come before everything else. What our Lord says here should not be interpreted as conflicting with the will of God himself, the creator and sanctifier of family bonds.

20:1–16. This parable is addressed to the Jewish people, whom God called at an early hour, centuries ago. Now the Gentiles are also being called—with an equal right to form part of the new people of God, the Church. In both cases it is a matter of a gratuitous, unmerited, invitation; therefore, those who were the "first" to receive the call have no grounds for complaining when God calls the "last" and gives them the same reward—membership of his people. At first sight the labourers of the first hour seem to have a genuine grievance—because they do not realize that to have a job in the Lord's vineyard is a divine gift. Jesus leaves us in no doubt that although he calls us to follow different ways, all receive the same reward—heaven.

20:2. "Denarius": a silver coin bearing an image of Caesar Augustus (Mt 22:19–21).

20:3. The Jewish method of calculating time was different from ours. They divided the whole day into eight parts, four night parts (called "watches") and four

l. Other ancient authorities read *manifold* **m.** The denarius was a day's wage for a labourer

the ninth hour, he did the same. 6And about the eleventh hour he
went out and found others standing; and he said to them, 'Why do
you stand here idle all day?' 7They said to him, 'Because no one
has hired us.' He said to them, 'You go into the vineyard too.'
8And when evening came, the owner of the vineyard said to his
steward, 'Call the labourers and pay them their wages, beginning
with the last, up to the first.' 9And when those hired about the
eleventh hour came, each of them received a denarius. 10Now
when the first came, they thought they would receive more; but
each of them also received a denarius. 11And on receiving it they
grumbled at the householder, 12saying, 'These last worked only
one hour, and you have made them equal to us who have borne
the burden of the day and the scorching heat.' 13But he replied to
one of them, 'Friend, I am doing you no wrong; did you not agree
with me for a denarius? 14Take what belongs to you, and go; I
Rom 9:16, 21 choose to give to this last as I give to you. 15Am I not allowed to
do what I choose with what belongs to me? Or do you begrudge
Mt 19:30 my generosity?'[n] 16So the last will be first, and the first last."

---

day parts (called "hours")—the first, third, sixth and ninth hour.

The first hour began at sunrise and ended around nine o'clock; the third ran to twelve noon; the sixth to three in the afternoon; and the ninth from three to sunset. This meant that the first and ninth hours varied in length, decreasing in autumn and winter and increasing in spring and summer and the reverse happening with the first and fourth watches.

Sometimes intermediate hours were counted—as for example in v. 6 which refers to the eleventh hour, the short period just before sunset, the end of the working day.

20:16. The Vulgate, other translations and a good many Greek codexes add: "For many are called, but few are chosen" (cf. Mt 22:14).

20:18–19. Once again our Lord prophesies to his apostles about his death and resurrection. The prospect of judging the world (cf. Mt 19:28) might have misled them into thinking in terms of an earthly messianic kingdom, an easy way ahead, leaving no room for the ignominy of the cross.

Christ prepares their minds so that when the testing time comes they will remember that he prophesied his passion and not be totally scandalized by it; he describes his passion in some detail.

Referring to Holy Week, St Josemaría Escrivá writes: "All the things brought to our mind by the different expressions of piety which characterize these days are of course directed to the Resurrection, which is, as St Paul says, the basis of our faith (cf. 1 Cor 15:14). But we should not tread this path too hastily, lest we lose sight of a very simple fact which we might easily overlook. We will not be able to share in our Lord's Resurrection unless we unite ourselves with him in his Passion and Death. If we are to accom-

n. Or *is your eye evil because I am good?*

Third announcement of the Passion

17And as Jesus was going up to Jerusalem, he took the twelve dis- Mk 10:32–34 Lk 18:31–33
ciples aside, and on the way he said to them, 18"Behold, we are Mt 16:21; 17:22f
going up to Jerusalem; and the Son of man will be delivered to the
chief priests and scribes, and they will condemn him to death,
19and deliver him to the Gentiles to be mocked and scourged and
crucified, and he will be raised on the third day."

The mother of the sons of Zebedee makes her request

20Then the mother of the sons of Zebedee came up to him, with her Mk 10:34–45 Mt 10:2
sons, and kneeling before him she asked him for something. 21And
he said to her, "What do you want?" She said to him, "Command Mt 19:28
that these two sons of mine may sit, one at your right hand and one
at your left, in your kingdom." 22But Jesus answered, "You do not Jn 18:11
know what you are asking. Are you able to drink the cup that I am
to drink?" They said to him, "We are able." 23He said to them, Acts 12:2
"You will drink my cup, but to sit at my right hand and at my left Rev 1:9
is not mine to grant, but it is for those for whom it has been prepared by my Father." 24And when the ten heard it they were indig- Lk 22:24–28

---

pany Christ in his glory at the end of Holy Week, we must first enter into his holocaust and be truly united to him, as he lies dead on Calvary" (*Christ Is Passing By*, 95).

20:20. The sons of Zebedee are James the Greater and John. Their mother, Salome, thinking that the earthly reign of the Messiah is about to be established, asks that her sons be given the two foremost positions in it. Christ reproaches them for not grasping the true —spiritual—nature of the Kingdom of heaven and not realizing that government of the Church he is going to found implies service and martyrdom. "If you are working for Christ and imagine that a position of responsibility is anything but a burden, what disillusionment awaits you!" (St Josemaría Escrivá, *The Way*, 950).

20:22. "Drinking the cup" means suffering persecution and martyrdom for following Christ. "We are able": the sons of Zebedee boldly reply that they can drink the cup; their generous expression evokes what St Paul will write years later: "I can do all things in him who strengthens me" (Phil 4:13).

20:23. "You will drink my cup": James the Greater will die a martyr's death in Jerusalem around the year 44 (cf. Acts 12:2); and John, after suffering imprisonment and the lash in Jerusalem (cf. Acts 4:3; 5:40–41), will spend a long period of exile on the island of Patmos (cf. Rev 1:9).

From what our Lord says here we can take it that positions of authority in the Church should not be the goal of ambition or the subject of human intrigue, but the outcome of a divine calling. Intent on doing the will of his heavenly Father, Christ was not going to allocate positions of authority on the basis of human considerations but, rather, in line with God's plans.

nant at the two brothers. [25]But Jesus called them to him and said,
"You know that the rulers of the Gentiles lord it over them, and
their great men exercise authority over them. [26]It shall not be so
among you; but whoever would be great among you must be your
Mk 9:35 servant, [27]and whoever would be first among you must be your
Lk 22:27 slave; [28]even as the Son of man came not to be served but to serve,
Phil 2:7 and to give his life as a ransom for many."
1 Tim 2:6

Mk 10:46–52 **Curing of the blind men of Jericho**

Lk 18:35–43 [29]And as they went out of Jericho, a great crowd followed him.
Mt 15:22 [30]And behold, two blind men sitting by the roadside, when they
heard that Jesus was passing by, cried out,[o] "Have mercy on us,
Son of David!" [31]The crowd rebuked them, telling them to be
silent; but they cried out the more, "Lord, have mercy on us, Son
of David!" [32]And Jesus stopped and called them, saying, "What
do you want me to do for you?" [33]They said to him, "Lord, let our
eyes be opened." [34]And Jesus in pity touched their eyes, and
immediately they received their sight and followed him.

20:26. Vatican II puts a marked emphasis on this *service* which the Church offers to the world and which Christians should show as proof of their Christian identity: "In proclaiming the noble destiny of man and affirming an element of the divine in him, this sacred Synod offers to co-operate unreservedly with mankind in fostering a sense of brotherhood to correspond to this destiny of theirs. The Church is not motivated by an earthly ambition but is interested in one thing only—to carry on the work of Christ under the guidance of the Holy Spirit, for he came into the world to bear witness to the truth, to save and not to judge, to serve and not to be served" (*Gaudium et spes*, 3; cf. *Lumen gentium*, 32; *Ad gentes*, 12; *Unitatis redintegratio*, 7).

20:27–28. Jesus sets himself as an example to be imitated by those who hold authority in the Church. He who is God and Judge of all men (cf. Phil 2:5–11; Jn 5:22–27; Acts 10:42; Mt 28:18) does not impose himself on us: he renders us loving service to the point of giving his life for us (cf. Jn 15:13); that is his way of being the first. St Peter understood him right; he later exhorted priests to tend the flock of God entrusted to them, not domineering over them but being exemplary in their behaviour (cf. 1 Pet 5:1–3); and St Paul also was clear on this *service*: though he was "free from all men", he became the servant of all in order to win all (cf. 1 Cor 9:19ff; 2 Cor 4:5).

Christ's "service" of mankind aims at salvation. The phrase "to give his life as a ransom for many" is in line with the terminology of liturgical sacrificial language. These words were used prophetically in chapter 53 of Isaiah.

Verse 28 also underlines the fact that Christ is a priest, who offers himself as priest and victim on the altar of the cross. The expression "as a ransom for many"

o. Other ancient authorities insert *Lord*

PART THREE

Jesus' ministry in Jerusalem

10. CLEANSING OF THE TEMPLE. CONTROVERSIES

The Messiah enters the Holy City

21 [1]And when they drew near to Jerusalem and came to Bethphage, to the Mount of Olives, then Jesus sent two disciples, Mk 11:1–10 Lk 19:29–38 Jn 12:12–19
[2]saying to them, "Go into the village opposite you, and immediately you will find an ass tied, and a colt with her; untie them and bring them to me.
[3]If any one says anything to you, you shall say, 'The Lord has need of them,' and he will send them immediately."
[4]This took place to fulfil what was spoken by the prophet, saying,

---

should not be interpreted as implying that God does not will the salvation of all men. "Many", here, is used in contrast with "one" rather than "all": there is only one Saviour, and salvation is offered to all.

20:30–34. These blind men, who seize their opportunity as Christ is passing by, give us a lesson in the kind of boldness and persistence with which we should entreat God to listen to us (cf. commentary on the characteristics of petitionary prayer in note on the Sermon on the Mount: Mt 7:7–8). Chrysostom comments: "Clearly these blind men deserved to be cured: first, because they cried out; and then, because after they received the gift they did not hasten away, the way most people, in their ingratitude, are inclined to do once they have got what they wanted. No, they were not like that: they were both persevering before the gift and grateful after it, for they 'followed him' (*Hom. on St Matthew*, 66).

21:1–5. In his triumphant entry into Jerusalem Jesus reveals himself as the Messiah, as St Matthew and St John (12:14) stress by quoting the prophecy of Zechariah 9:9. Although the Latin translation says "mounted on a [female] ass", the original Hebrew text says "mounted on a [male] ass", and the latter is the text followed in this translation (in the Greek translation of the Septuagint no sex is specified). The other two Synoptic Gospels limit themselves to giving the key fact of Jesus' messianic entry into the Holy City mounted on the colt (Mk 11:2; Lk 19:30). St Matthew sees in the fact that the colt is with the ass a further detail of the prophecy, which refers to the colt being the foal of an ass (that seems to be why the ass is referred to throughout the account, the ass being with the colt, although Jesus was mounted only on the colt).

In the prophecy in Zechariah 9:9 (which in the original Old Testament text is longer than the quotation in Matthew) the future messianic king is described as

Zech 9:9 Is 62:11 [5]"Tell the daughter of Zion,
Behold, your king is coming to you,
humble, and mounted on an ass,
and on a colt, the foal of an ass."
[6]The disciples went and did as Jesus had directed them; [7]they
brought the ass and the colt, and put their garments on them, and
2 Kings 9:13 he sat thereon. [8]Most of the crowd spread their garments on the
road, and others cut branches from the trees and spread them on
Ps 118:25f the road. [9]And the crowds that went before him and that followed
2 Sam 14:4 him shouted, "Hosanna to the Son of David! Blessed is he who
comes in the name of the Lord! Hosanna in the highest!"* [10]And
when he entered Jerusalem, all the city was stirred, saying, "Who
is this?" [11]And the crowds said, "This is the prophet Jesus from
Nazareth of Galilee."

Jesus in the temple

Mk 11:11–24 [12]And Jesus entered the temple of God[p] and drove out all who sold
Lk 19:45–48 and bought in the temple, and he overturned the tables of the
Jn 2:14–15 money-changers and the seats of those who sold pigeons. [13]He

---

"humble". The ass, originally a noble mount (cf. Gen 22:3; Ex 4:20; Num 22:21; Jud 5:10), was replaced by the horse in the period of the Israelite monarchy (cf. 1 Kings 4:26; 10:28; etc.). The prophecy, by referring to an ass, shows that the king of peace wins his victory by humility and gentleness, not by force of arms.

The Fathers have read a deeper meaning into this episode. They see the ass as symbolizing Judaism, for long subject to the yoke of the Law, and the foal, on which no one has ridden, as symbolizing the Gentiles. Jesus leads both Jews and Gentiles into the Church, the new Jerusalem.

21:9. The Hebrew word "*Hosanna*", which the people use to acclaim our Lord, was originally an appeal to God meaning "Save us". Later it was used as a shout of joy, an acclamation, meaning something like "Long live …". The people are demonstrating their enthusiasm by shouting, "Long live the Son of David!" The phrase "Blessed is he who comes in the name of the Lord" comes from Psalm 118:26 and is a jubilant and appreciative greeting to someone entrusted with a mission from God. The Church takes up these acclamations, incorporating them into the preface of the Mass, to proclaim the kingship of Christ.

21:12–13. Although God is present everywhere and cannot be confined within the walls of temples built by man (Acts 17:24–25), God instructed Moses to build a tabernacle where he would dwell among the Israelites (Ex 25:40). Once the Jewish people were established in Palestine, King Solomon, also in obedience to a divine instruction, built the temple of Jerusalem (1 Kings 6–8), where people went to render public worship to God (Deut 12).

Exodus (23:15) commanded the Israelites not to enter the temple empty-handed, but to bring some victim to be

said to them, "It is written, 'My house shall be called a house of Is 56:7
prayer'; but you make it a den of robbers." Jer 7:11
[14]And the blind and the lame came to him in the temple, and
he healed them. [15]But when the chief priests and the scribes saw Ps 118:25
the wonderful things that he did, and the children crying out in the
temple, "Hosanna to the Son of David!" they were indignant;
[16]and they said to him, "Do you hear what these are saying?" And Ps 8:2
Jesus said to them, "Yes; have you never read,

'Out of the mouth of babes and sucklings
thou hast brought perfect praise'?"

[17]And leaving them, he went out of the city to Bethany and lodged
there.

The cursing of the fig tree

[18]In the morning, as he was returning to the city, he was hungry.
[19]And seeing a fig tree by the wayside he went to it, and found Lk 13:6
nothing on it but leaves only. And he said to it, "May no fruit ever
come from you again!" And the fig tree withered at once. [20]When
the disciples saw it they marvelled, saying, "How did the fig tree

---

sacrificed. To make this easier for people who had to travel a certain distance, a veritable market developed in the temple courtyards with animals being bought and sold for sacrificial purposes. Originally this may have made sense, but seemingly as time went on commercial gain became the dominant purpose of this buying and selling of victims; probably the priests themselves and temple servants benefited from this trade or even operated it. The net result was that the temple looked more like a livestock mart than a place for meeting God.

Moved by zeal for his Father's house (Jn 2:17), Jesus cannot tolerate this deplorable abuse and in holy anger he ejects everyone—to show people the respect and reverence due to the temple as a holy place. We should show much greater respect in the Christian temple—Christian churches—where the eucharistic sacrifice is celebrated and where Jesus Christ, God and Man, is really and truly present, reserved in the tabernacle. For a Christian, proper dress, liturgical gestures and postures, genuflections and reverence to the tabernacle etc. are expressions of the respect due to the Lord in his temple.

21:15–17. The children's acclamations please God and infuriate the proud. This episode fulfils something which Jesus said earlier: "I thank thee, Father, Lord of heaven and earth, that thou hast hidden these things from the wise and understanding and revealed them to babes" (Mt 11:25). Only an attitude of simplicity and humility can grasp the greatness of the King of peace and understand the things of God.

21:18–22. The cursing of the fig tree is a parable in action; Jesus acts in this dra-

p. Other ancient authorities omit *of God*

wither at once?" [21]And Jesus answered them, "Truly, I say to you,
if you have faith and never doubt, you will not only do what has
been done to the fig tree, but even if you say to this mountain, 'Be
taken up and cast into the sea,' it will be done. [22]and whatever you
ask in prayer, you will receive, if you have faith."

Mk 11:27–33 **The authority of Jesus is questioned**

Lk 20:1–8 [23]And when he entered the temple, the chief priests and the
Jn 2:18 elders of the people came up to him as he was teaching, and said,
"By what authority are you doing these things, and who gave
you this authority?"* [24]Jesus answered them, "I also will ask you
a question; and if you tell me the answer, then I also will tell you
Jn 1:25 by what authority I do these things. [25]The baptism of John,
whence was it? From heaven or from men?" And they argued
with one another, "If we say, 'From heaven,' he will say to us,
'Why then did you not believe him?' [26]But if we say, 'From
men,' we are afraid of the multitude; for all hold that John was a
prophet." [27]So they answered Jesus, "We do not know." And he
said to them, "Neither will I tell you by what authority I do these
things.

---

matic way to show people the power of faith. The disciples marvel not because he curses the fig tree but because it shrivels up instantly.

This is an example of God's omnipotence, which is something we should always keep before our minds. Jesus is explaining the enormous power of faith. A person with faith can do anything; he can do much more difficult things, such as moving a mountain. Jesus goes on to show that one effect of faith is that it makes prayer all-powerful. He also gives us a lesson on genuine and apparent faithfulness in the spiritual life. "I want you to make use of your time. Don't forget the fig tree cursed by our Lord. And it was doing something: sprouting leaves. Like you ... Don't tell me you have excuses. It availed the fig tree little, relates the evangelist, that it was not the season for figs when our Lord came to it to look for them. And barren it remained for ever" (St Josemaría Escrivá, *The Way*, 354).

21:23–27. When the chief priests and elders ask "By what authority are you doing these things?" they are referring both to his teaching and to his self-assured public actions—throwing the traders out of the temple, entering Jerusalem in triumph, allowing the children to acclaim him, curing the sick, etc. What they want him to do is to prove that he has authority to act in this way or to admit openly that he is the Messiah. However, Jesus knows that they are not well-intentioned and he declines to give them a direct answer; he prefers to put a question to them that forces them to make their own attitude clear. He seeks to provoke them into examining their consciences and changing their whole approach.

21:32. St John the Baptist had shown the way to sanctification by proclaiming the imminence of the Kingdom of God and by preaching conversion. The scribes and Pharisees would not believe him, yet they

Parable of the two sons

28“What do you think? A man had two sons; and he went to the first
and said, ‘Son, go and work in the vineyard today.’ 29And he
answered, ‘I will not’; but afterward he repented and went. 30And he
went to the second and said the same; and he answered, ‘I go, sir,’
but did not go. 31Which of the two did the will of his father?” They Lk 18:14
said, “The first.” Jesus said to them, “Truly, I say to you, the tax collectors and the harlots go into the kingdom of God before you. 32For Lk 7:29
John came to you in the way of righteousness, and you did not
believe him, but the tax collectors and the harlots believed him; and
even when you saw it, you did not afterward repent and believe him.

Parable of the wicked tenants

33“Hear another parable.* There was a householder who planted a Mk 12:1–12
vineyard, and set a hedge around it, and dug a wine press in it, Lk 20:9–19 Mt 25:14
and built a tower, and let it out to tenants, and went into another Is 5:1f
country. 34When the season of fruit drew near, he sent his servants
to the tenants, to get his fruit; 35and the tenants took his servants
and beat one, killed another, and stoned another. 36Again he sent
other servants, more than the first; and they did the same to them.

---

boasted of their faithfulness to God's teaching. They were like the son who says “I will go” and then does not go; the tax collectors and prostitutes who repented and corrected the course of their lives will enter the Kingdom before them: they are like the other son who says “I will not”, but then does go. Our Lord stresses that penance and conversion can set people on the road to holiness even if they have been living apart from God for a long time.

21:33–46. This very important parable completes the previous one. The parable of the two sons simply identifies the indocility of Israel; that of the wicked tenants focusses on the punishment to come.

Our Lord compares Israel to a choice vineyard, specially fenced, with a watchtower, where a keeper is on the look-out to protect it from thieves and foxes. God has spared no effort to cultivate and embellish his vineyard. The vineyard is in the charge of tenant farmers; the householder is God, and the vineyard, Israel (Is 5:3–5; Jer 2:21; Joel 1:7).

The tenants to whom God has given the care of his people are the priests, scribes and elders. The owner's absence makes it clear that God really did entrust Israel to its leaders; hence their responsibility and the account he demands of them.

The owner used to send his servants from time to time to collect the fruit; this was the mission of the prophets. The second despatch of servants to claim what is owing to the owner—who meet the same fate as the first—refers to the way God's prophets were ill-treated by the kings and priests of Israel (Mt 23:37; Acts 7:42; Heb 11:36–38). Finally he sent his Son to them, thinking that they would have more respect for him; here we can see the difference between Jesus and the prophets, who were servants, not

[37]Afterward he sent his son to them, saying, 'They will respect my
son.' [38]But when the tenants saw the son, they said to themselves,
'This is the heir; come, let us kill him and have his inheritance.'
[39]And they took him and cast him out of the vineyard, and killed
him. [40]When therefore the owner of the vineyard comes, what will
he do to those tenants?" [41]They said to him, "He will put those
wretches to a miserable death, and let out the vineyard to other
tenants who will give him the fruits in their seasons."

Ps 118:22f
Acts 4:11
Rom 9:33
1 Pet 2:6–8

[42]Jesus said to them, "Have you never read in the scriptures:

> 'The very stone which the builders rejected
> has become the head of the corner;
> this was the Lord's doing,
> and it is marvellous in our eyes'?

[43]Therefore I tell you, the kingdom of God will be taken away
Dan 2:34f; 44f — from you and given to a nation producing the fruits of it. [44]And he
who falls on this stone will be broken to pieces; but when it falls
on any one, it will crush him."[q]

[45]When the chief priests and the Pharisees heard his parables,
they perceived that he was speaking about them. [46]But when they
tried to arrest him, they feared the multitudes, because they held
him to be a prophet.

"the Son": the parable indicates singular, transcendental sonship, expressing the divinity of Jesus Christ.

The malicious purpose of the tenants in murdering the son and heir to keep the inheritance for themselves is the madness of the leaders in expecting to become undisputed masters of Israel by putting Christ to death (Mt 12:14; 26:4). Their ambition blinds them to the punishment that awaits them. Then "they cast him out of the vineyard, and killed him": a reference to Christ's crucifixion, which took place outside the walls of Jerusalem.

Jesus prophesies the punishment God will inflict on the evildoers: he will put them to death and rent the vineyard to others. This is a very significant prophecy. St Peter later repeats it to the Sanhedrin: "this is the stone which was rejected by you builders, but which has become the head of the corner" (Acts 4:11; 1 Pet 2:4). The stone is Jesus of Nazareth, but the architects of Israel, who build up and rule the people, have chosen not to use it in the building. Because of their unfaithfulness the Kingdom of God will be turned over to another people, the Gentiles, who *will* give God the fruit he expects his vineyard to yield (cf. Mt 3:8–10; Gal 6:16).

For the building to be well built, it needs to rest on this stone. Woe to him who trips over it! (cf. Mt 12:30; Lk 2:34), as first Jews and later the enemies of Christ and his Church will discover through bitter experience (cf. Is 8:14–15).

Christians in all ages should see this parable as exhorting them to build faithfully upon Christ and make sure they do not fall into the sin of this Jewish genera-

q. Other ancient authorities omit verse 44

Parable of the marriage feast

22 [1]And again Jesus spoke to them in parables, saying, Lk 14:16–24
[2]"The kingdom of heaven may be compared to a king Jn 3:29
who gave a marriage feast for his son, [3]and sent his servants to
call those who were invited to the marriage feast; but they would
not come. [4]Again he sent other servants, saying, 'Tell those who
are invited, Behold, I have made ready my dinner, my oxen and
my fat calves are killed, and everything is ready; come to the
marriage feast.' [5]But they made light of it and went off, one to
his farm, another to his business, [6]while the rest seized his servants, treated them shamefully, and killed them. [7]The king was
angry, and he sent his troops and destroyed those murderers and
burned their city. [8]Then he said to his servants, 'The wedding is
ready, but those invited were not worthy. [9]Go therefore to the
thoroughfares, and invite to the marriage feast as many as you
find.' [10]And those servants went out into the streets and gathered
all whom they found, both bad and good; so the wedding hall
was filled with guests.

[11]"But when the king came in to look at the guests, he saw
there a man who had no wedding garment;* [12]and he said to him,
'Friend, how did you get in here without a wedding garment?'

---

tion. We should also be filled with hope and a sense of security; for, although the building—*the Church*—at some times seems to be breaking up, its sound construction, with Christ as its cornerstone, is assured.

22:1–14. In this parable Jesus reveals how intensely God the Father desires the salvation of all men—the banquet is the Kingdom of heaven—and the mysterious malice that lies in willingly rejecting the invitation to attend, a malice so vicious that it merits eternal punishment. No human arguments make any sense that go against God's call to conversion and acceptance of faith and its consequences.

The Fathers see in the first invitees the Jewish people: in salvation history God addresses himself first to the Israelites and then to all the Gentiles (Acts 13:46).

Indifference and hostility cause the Israelites to reject God's loving call and therefore to suffer condemnation. But the Gentiles also need to respond faithfully to the call they have received; otherwise they will suffer the fate of being cast "into outer darkness".

"The marriage", says St Gregory the Great (*In Evangelia homiliae*, 36) "is the wedding of Christ and his Church, and the garment is the virtue of charity: a person who goes into the feast without a wedding garment is someone who believes in the Church but does not have charity."

The wedding garment signifies the dispositions a person needs for entering the Kingdom of heaven. Even though he may belong to the Church, if he does not have these dispositions he will be condemned on the day when God judges all mankind. These dispositions essentially mean responding to grace.

And he was speechless. [13]Then the king said to the attendants,
'Bind him hand and foot, and cast him into the outer darkness;
there men will weep and gnash their teeth.' [14]For many are called,
but few are chosen."

Paying tax to Caesar

Mk 12:13–17 [15]Then the Pharisees went and took counsel how to entangle him
Lk 20:20–26 Jn 8:6 in his talk. [16]And they sent their disciples to him, along with the
Mk 3:6 Herodians, saying, "Teacher, we know that you are true, and teach
Jn 3:2 the way of God truthfully, and care for no man; for you do not
regard the position of men. [17]Tell us, then, what you think. Is it
lawful to pay taxes to Caesar, or not?" [18]But Jesus, aware of their
malice, said, "Why put me to the test, you hypocrites? [19]Show me
the money for the tax." And they brought him a coin.[r] [20]And Jesus
Rom 13:7 said to them, "Whose likeness and inscription is this?" [21]They
said, "Caesar's." Then he said to them, "Render therefore to

22:13. Vatican II reminds us of the doctrine of the "last things", one aspect of which is covered in this verse. Referring to the eschatological dimension of the Church, the Council recalls our Lord's warning about being on the watch against the wiles of the devil, in order to resist in the evil day (cf. Eph 6:11–13). "Since we know neither the day nor the hour, we should follow the advice of the Lord and watch constantly so that, when the single course of our earthly life is completed (cf. Heb 9:27), we may merit to enter with him into the marriage feast and be numbered among the blessed (cf. Mt 25:31–46) and not, like the wicked and slothful servants (cf. Mt 25:26), be ordered to depart into the eternal fire (cf. Mt 25:41), into the outer darkness where 'men will weep and gnash their teeth'" (*Lumen gentium*, 48).

22:14. These words in no way conflict with God's will that all should be saved (cf. 1 Tim 2:4). In his love for men, Christ patiently seeks the conversion of every single soul, going as far as to die on the cross (cf. Mt 23:37; Lk 15:4–7). St Paul teaches this when he says that Christ loved us and "gave himself up for us, a fragrant offering and sacrifice to God" (Eph 5:2). Each of us can assert with the apostle that Christ "loved me and gave himself for me" (Gal 2:20). However, God in his infinite wisdom respects man's freedom: man is free to reject grace (cf. Mt 7:13–14).

22:15–21. The Pharisees and Herodians join forces to plot against Jesus. The Herodians were supporters of the regime of Herod and his dynasty. They were quite well disposed to Roman rule and, as far as religious matters were concerned, they held the same kind of materialistic ideas as the Sadducees. The Pharisees were zealous keepers of the Law; they were anti-Roman and regarded the Herods as usurpers. It is difficult to imagine any two groups more at odds with each other: their amazing pact shows how much they hated Jesus.

r. Greek *a denarius*

Caesar the things that are Caesar's, and to God the things that are
God's." [22]When they heard it, they marvelled; and they left him Jn 8:9
and went away.

The resurrection of the dead

[23]The same day Sadducees came to him, who say that there is no Mk 12:18–27
resurrection; and they asked him a question, [24]saying, "Teacher, Lk 20:27–40
Moses said, 'If a man dies, having no children, his brother must Acts 23:6, 8
marry the widow, and raise up children for his brother.' [25]Now Gen 38:8
there were seven brothers among us; the first married, and died, Deut 25:5f
and having no children left his wife to his brother. [26]So too the
second and third, down to the seventh. [27]After them all, the
woman died. [28]In the resurrection, therefore, to which of the seven
will she be wife? For they all had her."

Had Jesus replied that it was lawful to pay taxes to Caesar, the Pharisees could have discredited him in the eyes of the people, who were very nationalistic; if he said it was unlawful, the Herodians would have been able to denounce him to the Roman authorities.

Our Lord's answer is at once so profound that they fail to grasp its meaning, and it is also faithful to his preaching about the Kingdom of God: give Caesar what is his due, but no more, because God must assuredly be given what *he* has a right to (the other side of the question, which they omitted to put). God and Caesar are on two quite different levels, because for an Israelite God transcends all human categories. What has Caesar a right to receive? Taxes, which are necessary for legitimate state expenses. What must God be given? Obviously, obedience to *all* his commandments—which implies personal love and commitment. Jesus' reply goes beyond the human horizons of these temptors, far beyond the simple yes or no they wanted to draw out of him.

The teaching of Jesus transcends any kind of political approach, and if the faithful, using the freedom that is theirs, chose one particular method of solving temporal questions, they "ought to remember that in those cases no one is permitted to identify the authority of the Church exclusively with his own opinion" (Vatican II, *Gaudium et spes*, 43).

Jesus' words show that he recognized civil authority and its rights, but he made it quite clear that the superior rights of God must be respected (cf. Vatican II, *Dignitatis humanae*, 11), and pointed out that it is part of God's will that we faithfully fulfil our civic duties (cf. Rom 13:1–7).

22:23–33. The Sadducees argue against belief in the resurrection of the dead on the basis of the levirate law, a Jewish law which laid down that when a married man died without issue, one of his brothers, according to a fixed order, should marry his widow and the first son of that union be given the dead man's name. By outlining an extreme case the Sadducees make the law and belief in resurrection look ridiculous. In his reply Jesus shows up the frivolity of their objections and asserts the truth of the resurrection of the dead.

29But Jesus answered them, "You are wrong, because you
know neither the scriptures nor the power of God. 30For in the resurrection they neither marry nor are given in marriage, but are like
angels[s] in heaven. 31And as for the resurrection of the dead, have
Ex 3:6 you not read what was said to you by God, 32'I am the God of
Abraham, and the God of Isaac, and the God of Jacob'? He is not
God of the dead, but of the living." 33And when the crowd heard
it, they were astonished at his teaching.

The greatest commandment of all

Mk 12:28–31 34But when the Pharisees heard that he had silenced the Sad-
Lk 10:25–28 ducees, they came together. 35And one of them, a lawyer, asked

---

22:30. Jesus explains quite unequivocally that the blessed have transcended the natural condition of man and the institution of marriage therefore no longer has any raison d'etre in heaven. The primary aim of marriage—the procreation and education of children—no longer applies because once immortality is reached there is no need for procreation to renew the human race (cf. St Thomas Aquinas, *Comm. on St Matthew*, 22:30). Similarly, mutual help—another aim of marriage—is no longer necessary, because the blessed enjoy an eternal and total happiness by possessing God.

22:34–40. In reply to the question, our Lord points out that the whole law can be condensed into two commandments: the first and more important consists in unconditional love of God; the second is a consequence and result of the first, because when man is loved, St Thomas says, God is loved, for man is the image of God (cf. ibid., 22:4).

A person who genuinely loves God also loves his fellows because he realizes that they are his brothers and sisters, children of the same Father, redeemed by the same blood of our Lord Jesus Christ: "this commandment we have from him, that he who loves God should love his brother also" (1 Jn 4:21). However, if we love man for man's sake without reference to God, this love will become an obstacle in the way of keeping the first commandment, and then it is no longer genuine love of our neighbour. But love of our neighbour for God's sake is clear proof that we love God: "If anyone says, 'I love God', and hates his brother, he is a liar" (1 Jn 4:20).

"You shall love your neighbour as yourself ": here our Lord establishes as the guideline for our love of neighbour the love each of us has for himself; both love of others and love of self are based on love of God. Hence, in some cases it can happen that God requires us to put our neighbour's need before our own; in others, not: it depends on what value, in the light of God's love, needs to be put on the spiritual and material factors involved.

Obviously spiritual goods take absolute precedence over material ones, even over life itself. Therefore, spiritual goods, be they our own or our neighbour's, must be the first to be safeguarded. If the spiritual good in question is the supreme one of the salvation of the soul, no one is justified in putting his own soul into certain danger of being condemned in order to save another,

s. Other ancient authorities add *of God*

him a question, to test him. 36“Teacher, which is the great com- Deut 6:5
mandment in the law?” 37And he said to him, “You shall love the
Lord your God with all your heart, and with all your soul, and
with all your mind. 38This is the great and first commandment.
39And a second is like it, You shall love your neighbour as your- Lev 19:18
self. 40On these two commandments depend all the law and the Rom 13:10
prophets.” Gal 4:14

The divinity of the Messiah

41Now while the Pharisees were gathered together, Jesus asked Mk 12:25–37
them a question, 42saying, “What do you think of the Christ? Lk 20:41–44
Whose son is he?” They said to him, “The son of David.” 43He Jn 7:42

---

because given human freedom we can never be absolutely sure what personal choice another person may make: this is the situation in the parable (cf. Mt 25:1–13), where the wise virgins refuse to give oil to the foolish ones; similarly St Paul says that he would wish himself to be rejected if that could save his brothers (cf. Rom 9:3)—an unreal theoretical situation. However, what is quite clear is that we have to do all we can to save our brothers, conscious that, if someone helps to bring a sinner back to the way, he will save himself from eternal death and cover a multitude of his own sins (Jas 5:20). From all this we can deduce that self-love of the right kind, based on God’s love for man, necessarily involves forgetting oneself in order to love God and our neighbour for God.

22:37–38. The commandment of love is the most important commandment because by obeying it man attains his own perfection (cf. Col 3:14). “The more a soul loves,” St John of the Cross writes, “the more perfect is it in that which it loves; therefore this soul that is now perfect is wholly love, if it may thus be expressed, and all its actions are love and it employs all its faculties and possessions in loving, giving all that it has, like the wise merchant, for this treasure of love which it has found hidden in God […]. For, even as the bee extracts from all plants the honey that is in them, and has no use for them for aught else save for that purpose, even so the soul with great facility extracts the sweetness of love that is in all the things that pass through it; it loves God in each of them, whether pleasant or unpleasant; and being, as it is, informed and protected by love, it has neither feeling nor taste nor knowledge of such things, for, as we have said, the soul knows naught but love, and its pleasure in all things and occupations is ever, as we have said, the delight of the love of God” (*Spiritual Canticle*, stanza 27, 8).

22:41–46. God promised King David that one of his descendants would reign forever (2 Sam 7:12ff); this was obviously a reference to the Messiah, and was interpreted as such by all Jewish tradition, which gave the Messiah the title of “Son of David”. In Jesus’ time this messianic title was understood in a very nationalistic sense: the Jews were expecting an earthly king, a descendant of David, who would free them from Roman rule. In this passage Jesus shows the Pharisees that the Messiah has a higher origin: he is not only “Son of David”; his nature is

said to them, "How is it then that David, inspired by the Spirit,[t]
calls him Lord, saying,
Ps 110:1 44'The Lord said to my Lord,
Acts 2:34f Sit at my right hand,
till I put thy enemies under thy feet'?
45If David thus calls him Lord, how is he his son?" 46And no one
was able to answer him a word, nor from that day did any one
dare to ask him any more questions.

Jesus berates the scribes and Pharisees

Mk 12:38–40 **23** 1Then said Jesus to the crowds and to his disciples, 2"The
Lk 20:45–47; 11:39–52 scribes and the Pharisees sit on Moses' seat; 3so practise
Mal 2:7f and observe whatever they tell you, but not what they do; for they

---

more exalted than that, for he is the Son of God and transcends the purely earthly level. The reference to Psalm 110:1 which Jesus uses in his argument explains that the Messiah is God: which is why David calls him Lord—and why he is seated at the right hand of God, his equal in power, majesty and glory (cf. Acts 33–36; 1 Cor 6:25).

23:1–39. Throughout this chapter Jesus severely criticizes the scribes and Pharisees and demonstrates the sorrow and compassion he feels towards the ordinary mass of the people, who have been ill-used, "harassed and helpless, like sheep without a shepherd" (Mt 9:36). His address may be divided into three parts: in the first (vv. 1–12) he identifies their principal vices and corrupt practices; in the second (vv. 13–36) he confronts them and speaks his famous "woes", which in effect are the reverse of the beatitudes he preached in chapter 5: no one can enter the Kingdom of heaven—no one can escape condemnation to the flames—unless he changes his attitude and behaviour; in the third part (vv. 37–39) he weeps over Jerusalem, so grieved is he by the evils into which the blind pride and hardheartedness of the scribes and Pharisees have misled the people.

23:2–3. Moses passed on to the people the Law received from God. The scribes, who for the most part sided with the Pharisees, had the function of educating the people in the Law of Moses; that is why they were said to "sit on Moses' seat". Our Lord recognized that the scribes and Pharisees did have authority to teach the Law; but he warns the people and his disciples to be sure to distinguish the Law as read out and taught in the synagogues from the practical interpretations of the Law to be seen in their leaders' lifestyles. Some years later, St Paul—a Pharisee like his father before him—faced his former colleagues with exactly the same kind of accusations as Jesus makes here: "You then who teach others, will you not teach yourself? While you preach against stealing, do you steal? You who say that one must not commit adultery, do you commit adultery? You who abhor idols, do you rob temples? You who boast in the law, do you dishonour God by breaking the law?

t. Or *David in the Spirit*

preach, but do not practise. 4They bind heavy burdens, hard to
bear,[u] and lay them on men's shoulders; but they themselves will
not move them with their finger. 5They do all their deeds to be Ex 13:9
seen by men; for they make their phylacteries* broad and their Num 15:38f
fringes long, 6and they love the place of honour at feasts and the Lk 14:7
best seats in the synagogues, 7and salutations in the market places, Jn 5:44
and being called rabbi by men. 8But you are not to be called rabbi,
for you have one teacher, and you are all brethren. 9And call no
man your father on earth, for you have one Father, who is in
heaven.* 10Neither be called masters, for you have one master, the
Christ. 11He who is greatest among you shall be your servant; Prov 29:23
12whoever exalts himself will be humbled, and whoever humbles Job 22:29
himself will be exalted. Ezek 21:26 Lk 18:14 1 Pet 5:5

For, as it is written, 'The name of God is blasphemed among the Gentiles because of you'" (Rom 2:21–24).

23:5. "Phylacteries": belts or bands carrying quotations from Holy Scripture which the Jews used to wear fastened to their arms or foreheads. To mark themselves out as more religiously observant than others, the Pharisees used to wear broader phylacteries. The fringes were light-blue stripes on the hems of cloaks; the Pharisees ostentatiously wore broader fringes.

23:8–10. Jesus comes to teach the Truth; in fact, he is the Truth (cf. Jn 14:6). As a teacher, therefore, he is absolutely unique and unparallelled. "The whole of Christ's life was a continual teaching: his silences, his miracles, his gestures, his prayer, his love for people, his special affection for the little and the poor, his acceptance of the total sacrifice on the cross for the redemption of the world, and his resurrection are the actualization of his word and the fulfilment of revelation. Hence for Christians the crucifix is one of the most sublime and popular images of Christ the Teacher.

"These considerations are in line with the great traditions of the Church and they all strengthen our fervour with regard to Christ, the Teacher who reveals God to man and man to himself, the Teacher who saves, sanctifies and guides, who lives, who speaks, rouses, moves, redresses, judges, forgives, and goes with us day by day on the path of history, the Teacher who comes and will come in glory" (John Paul II, *Catechesi tradendae*, 9).

23:11. The Pharisees were greedy for honour and recognition: our Lord insists that every form of authority, particularly in the context of religion, should be exercised as a form of service of others; it must not be used to indulge personal vanity or greed. "He who is greatest among you shall be your servant".

23:12. A spirit of pride and ambition is incompatible with being a disciple of Christ. Here our Lord stresses the need for true humility, for anyone who is to follow him. The verbs "will be humbled", "will be exalted" have "God" as their active agent. Along the same lines, St James preaches that "God opposes the proud, but gives

u. Other ancient authorities omit *hard to bear*

13“But woe to you, scribes and Pharisees, hypocrites! because
you shut the kingdom of heaven against men; for you neither
enter yourselves, nor allow those who would enter to go in.[v]
15Woe to you, scribes and Pharisees, hypocrites! for you traverse
sea and land to make a single proselyte, and when he becomes a
proselyte, you make him twice as much a child of hell[w] as yourselves.

16“Woe to you, blind guides, who say, ‘If any one swears by the
temple, it is nothing; but if any one swears by the gold of the
temple, he is bound by his oath.’ 17You blind fools! For which is
greater, the gold or the temple that has made the gold sacred?
18And you say, ‘If any one swears by the altar, it is nothing; but if
any one swears by the gift that is on the altar, he is bound by his
Ezek 29:37 oath.’ 19You blind men! For which is greater, the gift or the altar
that makes the gift sacred? 20So he who swears by the altar, swears

---

grace to the humble” (Jas 4:6). And in the *Magnificat*, the Blessed Virgin explains that the Lord “has put down the mighty from their thrones, and exalted those of low degree [the humble]” (Lk 1:52).

23:13. Now comes our Lord’s invective against the behaviour of the scribes and Pharisees: his “woes” condemn their past conduct and threaten them with punishment if they do not repent and mend their ways.

23:14. See the RSV note below. Our Lord is not reproaching them for praying long prayers but for their hypocrisy and cupidity. By going in for a lot of external religious practices, the Pharisees wanted to be recognized as devout men and then trade on that reputation particularly with vulnerable people. Widows, for example, would ask them to say prayers; the Pharisees in turn would ask for alms. What Jesus means here is that prayer should always come from an upright heart and a generous spirit. See the notes on Mt 6:5–8.

23:15. “Proselyte”: a pagan convert to Judaism. The root of the word means “he who comes”, he who—coming from idolatry—joins the chosen people in response to a calling from God. The Pharisees spared no effort to gain converts. Our Lord reproaches them not for this, but because they were concerned only about human success, their motivation being vainglory.

The sad thing about these proselytes was that, after receiving the light of Old Testament revelation, they remained under the influence of scribes and Pharisees, who passed on to them their own narrow outlook.

23:22. Our Lord’s teaching about taking oaths is given in the Sermon on the Mount (Mt 5:33–37). Jesus does away with the nitpicking casuistry of the Pharisees by focussing directly on the uprightness of the intention of the oath-taker and by stressing the respect due to God’s majesty and dignity. What Jesus wants is a pure heart, with no element of deceit. Our Lord

v. Other authorities add here (or after verse 12) verse 14, *Woe to you, scribes and Pharisees, hypocrites! for you devour widows’ houses and for a pretence you make long prayers; therefore you will receive the greater condemnation* **w.** Greek *Gehenna*

by it and by everything on it; [21]and he who swears by the temple,
swears by it and by him who dwells in it; [22]and he who swears by
heaven, swears by the throne of God and by him who sits upon it.
[23]"Woe to you, scribes and Pharisees, hypocrites! for you tithe Lev 27:30
mint and dill and cummin, and have neglected the weightier mat- Mic 6:8
ters of the law, justice and mercy and faith; these you ought to
have done, without neglecting the others. [24]You blind guides,
straining out a gnat and swallowing a camel!
[25]"Woe to you, scribes and Pharisees, hypocrites! for you cleanse Mk 7:4
the outside of the cup and of the plate, but inside they are full of
extortion and rapacity. [26]You blind Pharisee! first cleanse the inside Tit 1:15
of the cup and of the plate, that the outside also may be clean. Jn 9:40
[27]"Woe to you, scribes and Pharisees, hypocrites! for you are Acts 23:2
like whitewashed tombs, which outwardly appear beautiful, but
within they are full of dead men's bones and all uncleanness. [28]So

---

particularly reproves any tendency to undermine the content of an oath, as the doctors of the Law tended to do, thereby failing to respect holy things and especially the holy name of God. He therefore draws attention to the commandment of the Law which says, "You shall not take the name of the Lord your God in vain" (Ex 20:7; Lev 19:12; Deut 5:11).

23:23. Mint, dill (aniseed) and cummin were herbs the Jews used in cooking or to perfume rooms. They were such insignificant items that they were not covered by the Mosaic precept on paying tithes (Lev 27:30–33; Deut 14:22ff); the precept did not apply to domestic animals and the more common agricultural products such as wheat, wine and olive oil. However, the Pharisees, being so intent on showing their scrupulous observance of the Law, paid tithes even of these herbs. Our Lord does not despise or reject the Law; he is simply telling people to get their priorities right: there is no point in attending to secondary details if one is neglecting what is really basic and important—justice, mercy and faith.

23:24. The Pharisees were so scrupulous about not swallowing any insect which the Law declared to be unclean that they went as far as to filter drinks through a linen cloth. Our Lord criticizes them for being so inconsistent—straining mosquitos, being so scrupulous about little things, yet quite happily "swallowing a camel", committing serious sins.

23:25–26. After reproaching the Pharisees for their hypocrisy in religious practice, our Lord now goes on to indict their twofacedness in matters of morality. The Jews used to perform elaborate washings of plates, cups and other tableware, in line with the regulations on legal cleansing (cf. Mk 7:1–4).

The example he chooses suggests a deeper level of meaning—concern for that moral purity which should characterize man's interior life. What is of prime importance is cleanness of heart, an upright intention, consistency between what one says and what one does, etc.

23:27–28. The Jews used to whitewash tombs annually, shortly before the feast of the Passover. The whitewash made the

Lk 16:15 you also outwardly appear righteous to men, but within you are
full of hypocrisy and iniquity.
29“Woe to you, scribes and Pharisees, hypocrites! for you build
the tombs of the prophets and adorn the monuments of the righteous, 30saying, ‘If we had lived in the days of our fathers, we
would not have taken part with them in shedding the blood of the
Acts 7:52 prophets.’ 31Thus you witness against yourselves, that you are sons
of those who murdered the prophets. 32Fill up, then, the measure
of your fathers. 33You serpents, you brood of vipers, how are you
1 Thess 2:15 to escape being sentenced to hell?[w] 34Therefore I send you
prophets and wise men and scribes, some of whom you will kill
and crucify, and some you will scourge in your synagogues and
Gen 4:8 persecute from town to town, 35that upon you may come all the
2 Chron 24:20f
Mt 27:25 righteous blood shed on earth, from the blood of innocent Abel to
the blood of Zechariah the son of Barachiah, whom you murdered
between the sanctuary and the altar. 36Truly, I say to you, all this
will come upon this generation.

---

tombs more visible and helped to avoid people brushing against them, which would have meant incurring legal uncleanness for seven days (Num 19:16; cf. Lk 11:44). In the sunlight, these tombs sparkled radiantly white, but inside they still held corruption.

23:29–32. Our Lord shows them that they are cut from the same cloth as their ancestors—not because they erect mausoleums in honour of prophets and just men but because they are guilty of the same sin as those who killed the prophets. Hence their hypocrisy, which makes them even worse than their fathers. With pained irony Jesus tells them that they are compounding the sins of their ancestors.

Clearly this is referring to his passion and death: if the ancients killed the prophets, by causing him to suffer and die our Lord’s contemporaries will be still more cruel.

23:34. The New Testament does in fact refer to prophets (cf. 1 Cor 12:28; Acts 13:1), wise men (cf. 1 Cor 2:6; Mt 13:52) and teachers (cf. Acts 13:1; 1 Cor 12:28), because the people in question are indeed full of the Holy Spirit and teach in Christ’s name. The history of the Church shows that what Jesus says here came true, for it was in the synagogue that the first persecutions of the Christians occurred.

23:35. This Zechariah was different from the last but one of the main prophets. Apparently Jesus is referring to the Zechariah who suffered death by stoning during the reign of King Joash (2 Chron 24:16–22). “Between the sanctuary and the altar”: within the sacred precincts, marked off by a wall, was the building which may be called the temple proper, in front of which was the great altar of holocausts.

23:37–39. Jesus’ moving remarks seem almost to sum up the entire history of salvation and are a testimony to his divinity. Who if not God was the source of all these acts of mercy which mark the stages of the history of Israel? The image of

w. Greek *Gehenna*

Jerusalem admonished

37"O Jerusalem, Jerusalem, killing the prophets and stoning those Lk 13:3f
who are sent to you! How often would I have gathered your chil- Acts 7:59 1 Thess 2:15
dren together as a hen gathers her brood under her wings, and you
would not! 38Behold, your house is forsaken and desolate.[x] 39For I Jer 22:5; 12:7
tell you, you will not see me again, until you say, 'Blessed is he 1 Kings 9:7f Mt 21:9
who comes in the name of the Lord.' " Ps 118:26

11. THE ESCHATOLOGICAL DISCOURSE

Announcement of the destruction of the temple

24 1Jesus left the temple and was going away, when his disci- Mk 13
ples came to point out to him the buildings of the temple.* Lk 21:5–36
2But he answered them, "You see all these, do you not? Truly, I Lk 19:44
say to you, there will not be left here one stone upon another, that
will not be thrown down."

---

being protected by wings, which occurs often in the Old Testament, refers to God's love and protection of his people. It is to be found in the prophets, in the canticle of Moses (cf. Deut 32:11), and in many psalms (cf. 17:8; 36:8; 57:2; 61:5; 63:8). "And you would not": the Kingdom of God has been preached to them unremittingly for centuries by the prophets; in these last few years by Jesus himself, the Word of God made man. But the "Holy City" has resisted all the unique graces offered it. Jerusalem should serve as a warning to every Christian: the freedom God has given us by creating us in his image and likeness means that we have this terrible capacity to reject him. A Christian's life is a continuous series of conversions—repeated instances of repentance, of turning to God, who, loving Father that he is, is ever ready to forgive.

24:1. In this discourse in which our Lord tells us about the last things, three prophecies seem to be interwoven—the destruction of Jerusalem (by the armies of the Emperor Titus in the year 70); the end of the world; and the last coming of Christ. Our Lord invites us to be watchful and pray, as we await these three events.

The headings and side headings added into the Gospel text may be of some help in working out what Jesus is referring to at different stages in the discourse. It is quite easy to confuse the signs and times of the destruction of Jerusalem and those of the end of the world and the last coming—which is not all that surprising, given that the destruction of Jerusalem itself symbolizes the end of the world. Our Lord is speaking here very much in the style and language used by the prophets, who announced future events without specifying the order in which they would happen and who used a profusion of images and symbols. Every prophecy about the future seems quite obscure at first but as the events unfold everything fits into place. The Old Testament prophecies were not well understood until they were fulfilled during Christ's first coming; and the New Testament prophecies will

x. Other ancient authorities omit *and desolate*

The beginning of tribulations. Persecution on account of the Gospel

Jn 5:43
Acts 5:36f
1 Jn 2:18
Dan 2:28
Is 19:2
2 Chron 15:6
Mt 10:17–22
Jn 16:2
Dan 11:41
1 Jn 4:1
2 Thess 2:10
2 Tim 3:1–5
Mt 10:22
Rev 13:10

3 As he sat on the Mount of Olives, the disciples came to him privately, saying, "Tell us, when will this be, and what will be the
sign of your coming and of the close of the age?" 4 And Jesus
answered them, "Take heed that no one leads you astray. 5 For
many will come in my name, saying, 'I am the Christ,' and they
will lead many astray. 6 And you will hear of wars and rumours of
wars; see that you are not alarmed; for this must take place, but
the end is not yet. 7 For nation will rise against nation, and kingdom against kingdom, and there will be famines and earthquakes
in various places: 8 all this is but the beginning of the sufferings.
9 "Then they will deliver you up to tribulation, and put you to
death; and you will be hated by all nations for my name's sake.
10 And then many will fall away,[y] and betray one another, and hate
one another. 11 And many false prophets will arise and lead many
astray. 12 And because wickedness is multiplied, most men's love
will grow cold. 13 But he who endures to the end will be saved.
14 And this gospel of the kingdom will be preached throughout the

---

not become clear until his second coming. The notes which follow should be read against this background.

24:3. This dramatic prophecy makes such an impression on Christ's disciples that they want to know when it will happen; they see the end of the temple and the end of the world as coinciding (as yet the Holy Spirit has not yet come; he will make many things plain to them: cf. Jn 14:26).

24:4–14. Our Lord says that between then and the end of the world, the Gospel will be preached to every creature. In the intervening period, the Church will experience all kinds of tribulations. These are not signs of the end of the world; they are simply the normal context in which Christian preaching takes place.

24:15. "The desolating sacrilege": Jesus is referring to a prophecy in Daniel (Dan 9:27; 11:31; 12:11) where the prophet foretold that the king (Antiochus IV) would occupy the temple and erect images of false gods on the altar of holocausts. This came to pass, and the idol was set up on the altar—a sign of "abomination" (idolatry) and desolation. Our Lord applies this episode in the history of Israel to the future destruction of Jerusalem—asking people ("let the reader understand") to pay more heed to the text in Daniel. Jesus tells them that a new abomination will occur, ruining the temple to make way for idolatrous worship—as happened in AD 70, when the Roman armies destroyed and profaned the temple, and later under Hadrian, who ordered the erection of a statue of Jupiter on the ruins.

"Having spoken of the ills that were to overtake the city, and of the trials of the apostles, and having said that they should remain unsubdued, and should conquer the whole world, he mentions again the Jews' calamities, showing that when the one [the Church] should be glorious,

y. Or *stumble*

whole world, as a testimony to all nations; and then the end will
come.

The great tribulation

15“So when you see the desolating sacrilege spoken of by the Dan 9:27;
prophet Daniel, standing in the holy place (let the reader under- 12:11
stand), 16then let those who are in Judea flee to the mountains; 17let Lk 17:31
him who is on the housetop not go down to take what is in his
house; 18and let him who is in the field not turn back to take his
mantle. 19And alas for those who are with child and for those who
give suck in those days! 20Pray that your flight may not be in Acts 1:12
winter or on a sabbath. 21For then there will be great tribulation, Dan 12:1
such as has not been from the beginning of the world until now, Joel 2:2
no, and never will be. 22And if those days had not been shortened,
no human being would be saved; but for the sake of the elect those
days will be shortened. 23Then if any one says to you, ‘Lo, here is
the Christ!’ or ‘There he is!’ do not believe it. 24For false Christs Deut 13:1–3
and false prophets will arise and show great signs and wonders, so 2 Thess 2:8f

---

having taught the whole world, the other [Israel] should suffer calamity” (St John Chrysostom, *Hom. on St Matthew*, 76).

24:15–20. People really did have to flee to escape the Romans (cf. Lk 21:20–21): the Christians had to leave the plains of Judea to take refuge in mountain caves. Many fled into present-day Transjordan (cf. Eusebius, *Ecclesiastical History*, 3, 5). Palestinian houses used to have a ladder directly from the terrace to the outside. On the sabbath, one was not allowed to walk more than two thousand paces—a little more than a kilometre (less than one mile).

Flavius Josephus, a contemporary Jewish historian, says that one million, one hundred thousand people died during the siege of Jerusalem in the year 70 (cf. *The Jewish War*, 6, 420)—which gives some idea of the scale of these events. The siege began when the city was full of pilgrims from all over the world, who had come to celebrate the Passover; therefore, Flavius Josephus’ figure may not be all that far off the truth.

24:22. What salvation is our Lord referring to here? First, physical safety: if God in his mercy had not come to the rescue everyone would have died. Second, eternal salvation: this test will be so severe that God will have to cut the time short to avoid the elect being overcome by temptation, to ensure their salvation. We should bear in mind that tribulation has a physical dimension (earthquakes, upheavals, wars) and a spiritual one (false prophets, heresies, etc.).

24:23–28. Interwoven with the prophecy of the destruction of Jerusalem comes Jesus’ announcement of his second coming. He uses mysterious words, whose meaning is obscure. Many events he speaks of in a very general way; they remain mere shadows.

The main thing we should do is grow in trust of Jesus and his teaching—“Lo, I have told you beforehand” (v. 25), as he has just said—and persevere until the end.

The same pattern as in vv. 4–13: between the fall of Jerusalem and the end

as to lead astray, if possible, even the elect. 25Lo, I have told you
Lk 17:23–24 beforehand. 26So, if they say to you, 'Lo, he is in the wilderness,'
Job 39:30 Heb 1:18 do not go out; if they say, 'Lo, he is in the inner rooms,' do not
Lk 17:37 believe it. 27For as the lightning comes from the east and shines as
Is 13:10; 34:4 far as the west, so will be the coming of the Son of man.
2 Pet 3:10 28Wherever the body is, there the eagles[z] will be gathered together.

The coming of the Son of man

29"Immediately after the tribulation of those days the sun will be
darkened, and the moon will not give its light, and the stars will fall
from heaven, and the powers of the heavens will be shaken; 30then
Rev 1:7 Mt 26:64 will appear the sign of the Son of man in heaven, and then all the
Dan 7:13f tribes of the earth will mourn, and they will see the Son of man
Zech 12:10ff Rev 19:11 coming on the clouds of heaven with power and great glory; 31and he

of the world, Christians will experience suffering time and time again—persecution, false prophets, false messiahs who will lead others to perdition (vv. 23–24). Verse 28 is difficult to interpret; it looks like a proverb based on the speed with which birds of prey swoop down on their quarry. There may be a suggestion that at Christ's second coming all mankind will gather round him—good and bad, living and dead, all irresistibly attracted to Christ in triumph, some drawn by love, others forced by justice. St Paul has described the force of attraction in the Son of man when he says that the just "will be caught up ... in the clouds to meet the Lord in the air" (1 Thess 4:17).

24:29. Nature itself will tremble in the presence of this supreme Judge when he appears vested in all his power.

24:30. "The sign of the Son of man" has been traditionally interpreted as the cross in glory, which will shine like the sun (cf. St John Chrysostom, *Hom. on St Matthew*, 76). The liturgy of the cross contains the same interpretation: "this sign will appear in the heavens, when the Lord comes to judge". This instrument of our Lord's passion will be a sign of condemnation for those who have despised it, and of joy for those who have borne a share of it.

24:32–35. Seeing in the destruction of Jerusalem a symbol of the end of the world, St John Chrysostom applies to it this parable of the fig tree: "Here he also foretells a spiritual spring and a calm which, after the storm of the present life, the righteous will experience; whereas for sinners there will be a winter after the spring they have had [...]. But this was not the only reason why he put before them the parable of the fig tree, to tell them of the interval before his coming; he wanted to show them that his word would assuredly come true. As sure as the coming of spring is the coming of the Son of man" (ibid., 77).

"This generation": this verse is a clear example of what we say in the note on Mt 24:1 about the destruction of Jerusalem being itself a symbol. "This generation" refers firstly to the people alive at the time of the destruction of Jerusalem. But, since that event is symbolic of the end of the world, we can say

z. Or *vultures*

will send out his angels with a loud trumpet call, and they will gather
his elect from the four winds, from one end of heaven to the other.

1 Cor 15:52
1 Thess 4:16
Rev 8:1f
Is 27:13

The end will surely come. The lesson of the fig tree

32"From the fig tree learn its lesson: as soon as its branch becomes
tender and puts forth its leaves, you know that summer is near.
33So also, when you see all these things, you know that he is near,
at the very gates. 34Truly, I say to you, this generation will not
pass away till all these things take place. 35Heaven and earth will
pass away, but my words will not pass away.

Deut 30:4

The time of the second coming of Christ

36"But of that day and hour no one knows, not even the angels of
heaven, nor the Son,[a] but the Father only. 37As were the days of

1 Thess 5:1f
Gen 6:11–13
Lk 17:26f

---

with St John Chrysostom that "the Lord was speaking not only of the generation then living, but also of the generation of the believers; for he knows that a generation is distinguished not only by time but also by its mode of religious worship and practice: this is what the Psalmist means when he says that 'such is the generation of those who seek him'(Ps 24:6)" (ibid.).

24:35. This is further confirmation that the prophecies he has just made will be fulfilled; it is as if he were saying: it is easier for heaven and earth, which seem so stable, to disappear, than for my words not to come true. Also he is making a formal statement about the value attaching to God's word: "heaven and earth, since they are created things, are not necessarily unchangeable: it is possible for them to cease to exist; whereas, Christ's words, which originate in eternity, have such power and force that they will last forever"(St Hilary, *In Matth.*, 26).

24:36. Every revelation about the end of the world is clothed in mystery; Jesus, being God, knows every detail of the plan of salvation but he refrains from revealing the date of the Last Judgment. Why? To ensure that his apostles and disciples stay on the alert, and to underline the transcendence of this mysterious design. This phrase carries echoes of Jesus' reply to the sons of Zebedee: "to sit at my right hand and at my left is not mine to grant, but it is for those for whom it has been prepared by my Father" (Mt 20:23)—not because he does not know the details, but because it is not for him to reveal them.

"That day": the way the Bible usually refers to the day when God will judge all men (cf. Amos 2:26; 8:9, 12; Is 2:20; Mic 2:4; Mal 3:19; Mt 7:22; Mk 13:32; Lk 10:12; 2 Tim 1:12; etc.).

24:37–39. In a few strokes our Lord sketches man's perennial insensitivity and carelessness towards the things of God. Man thinks it is more important to eat and drink, to find a husband or wife; but if that is his attitude he is forgetting about the most important thing—eternal life. Our Lord also foretells that the end of the world will be like the great flood; the Son of man's second coming will happen

a. Other ancient authorities omit *nor the Son*

2 Pet 3:5f Noah, so will be the coming of the Son of man. 38For as in those
Gen 7:7 days before the flood they were eating and drinking, marrying and
giving in marriage, until the day when Noah entered the ark, 39and
they did not know until the flood came and swept them all away,
Lk 17:35f so will be the coming of the Son of man. 40Then two men will be
in the field; one is taken and one is left. 41Two women will be
grinding at the mill; one is taken and one is left. 42Watch therefore,
Lk 12:39–46 for you do not know on what day your Lord is coming. 43But
know this, that if the householder had known in what part of the
night the thief was coming, he would have watched and would not
Rev 16:15 have let his house be broken into. 44Therefore you also must be
ready; for the Son of man is coming at an hour you do not expect.

Parable of the faithful servant

45"Who then is the faithful and wise servant, whom his master has
set over his household, to give them their food at the proper time?
46Blessed is that servant whom his master when he comes will
find so doing. 47Truly, I say to you, he will set him over all his
Eccles 8:11 possessions. 48But if that wicked servant says to himself, 'My
master is delayed,' 49and begins to beat his fellow servants, and
eats and drinks with the drunken, 50the master of that servant will
come on a day when he does not expect him and at an hour he
does not know, 51and will punish[b] him, and put him with the hypocrites; there men will weep and gnash their teeth.

---

unexpectedly, taking people by surprise, whether they are doing good or evil.

24:40. It is in the context of the ordinary affairs of life—farmwork, housework etc.—that God calls man, and man responds: that is where his eternal happiness or eternal punishment is decided. To be saved, one does not need to meet any special conditions, or to be in a special position in life: one simply has to be faithful to the Lord in the middle of ordinary everyday affairs.

24:42. Jesus himself draws from this revelation about the future the practical moral that a Christian needs to be on the watch, living each day as if it were his last. The important thing is not to be speculating about when these events will happen and what form they will take, but to live in such a way that they find us in the state of grace.

24:51. "And will punish him [or, cut him in pieces]": this can be understood as a metaphor for "will cast him away". "Weeping and gnashing of teeth": the pains of hell.

25:1–46. The whole of chapter 25 is a practical application of the teaching contained in chapter 24. With these parables of the wise and foolish virgins and of the talents, and his teaching on the Last

b. Or *cut him in pieces*

Parable of the wise and foolish maidens

25 1"Then the kingdom of heaven shall be compared to ten Lk 12:35f
maidens who took their lamps and went to meet the bride- Rev 19:7
groom.[c] 2Five of them were foolish, and five were wise. 3For when
the foolish took their lamps, they took no oil with them; 4but the
wise took flasks of oil with their lamps. 5As the bridegroom was
delayed, they all slumbered and slept. 6But at midnight there was
a cry, 'Behold, the bridegroom! Come out to meet him.' 7Then all
those maidens rose and trimmed their lamps. 8And the foolish said
to the wise, 'Give us some of your oil, for our lamps are going
out.' 9But the wise replied, 'Perhaps there will not be enough for
us and for you; go rather to the dealers and buy for yourselves.'
10And while they went to buy, the bridegroom came, and those
who were ready went in with him to the marriage feast; and the
door was shut. 11Afterward the other maidens came also, saying, Lk 13:25–27
'Lord, lord, open to us.' 12But he replied, 'Truly, I say to you, I do
not know you.' 13Watch therefore, for you know neither the day
nor the hour.

Parable of the talents

14"For it will be as when a man going on a journey called his ser- Lk 19:12–27
vants and entrusted to them his property; 15to one he gave five tal-

---

Judgment, our Lord is again emphasizing the need for vigilance (cf. the note on Mt 24:42). In this sense, chapter 25 makes chapter 24 more intelligible.

25:1–13. The main lesson of this parable has to do with the need to be on the alert: in practice, this means having the light of faith, which is kept alive with the oil of charity. Jewish weddings were held in the house of the bride's father. The virgins are young unmarried girls, bridesmaids who are in the bride's house waiting for the bridegroom to arrive. The parable centres on the attitude one should adopt up to the time when the bridegroom comes. In other words, it is not enough to know that one is "inside" the Kingdom, the Church: one has to be on the watch and be preparing for Christ's coming by doing good works. This vigilance should be continuous and unflagging, because the devil is forever after us, prowling around "like a roaring lion, seeking someone to devour" (1 Pet 5:8). "Watch with the heart, watch with faith, watch with love, watch with charity, watch with good works […]; make ready the lamps, make sure they do not go out […], renew them with the inner oil of an upright conscience; then shall the Bridegroom enfold you in the embrace of his love and bring you into his banquet room, where your lamp can never be extinguished" (St Augustine, *Sermons*, 93).

25:14–30. A talent was not any kind of coin but a measure of value worth about fifty kilos (one hundred pounds) of silver.

In this parable the main message is the need to respond to grace by making a gen-

c. Other ancient authorities add *and the bride*

Rom 12:6 ents,[d] to another two, to another one, to each according to his ability. Then he went away. 16He who had received the five talents went at once and traded with them; and he made five talents more.
17So also, he who had the two talents made two talents more. 18But he who had received the one talent went and dug in the ground and hid his master's money. 19Now after a long time the master of those servants came and settled accounts with them. 20And he who received the five talents came forward, bringing five talents more, saying, 'Master, you delivered to me five talents; here I have made five talents more.' 21His master said to him, 'Well done, good and
Lk 16:10 faithful servant; you have been faithful over a little, I will set you
Heb 12:2 over much; enter into the joy of your master.' 22And he also who had the two talents came forward, saying, 'Master, you delivered to me two talents; here I have made two talents more.' 23His master said to him, 'Well done, good and faithful servant; you have been faithful over a little, I will set you over much; enter into the joy of your master.' 24He also who had received the one talent came forward, saying, 'Master, I knew you to be a hard man, reaping where you did not sow, and gathering where you did not winnow; 25so I was afraid, and I went and hid your talent in the ground. Here you have what is yours.' 26But his master answered him, 'You wicked and slothful servant! You knew that I reap where I have not sowed, and gather where I have not winnowed?

---

uine effort right through one's life. All the gifts of nature and grace which God has given us should yield a profit. It does not matter how many gifts we have received; what matters is our generosity in putting them to good use. A person's Christian calling should not lie hidden and barren: it should be outgoing, apostolic and self-sacrificial. "Don't lose your effectiveness; instead, trample on your selfishness. You think your life is for yourself? Your life is for God, for the good of all men, through your love for our Lord. Your buried talent, dig it up again! Make it yield" (St Josemaría Escrivá, *Friends of God*, 47).

An ordinary Christian cannot fail to notice that Jesus chose to outline his teaching in response to grace by using the simile of men at work. Here we have a reminder that the Christian normally lives out his vocation in the context of ordinary, everyday affairs. "There is just one life, made of flesh and spirit. And it is this life which has to become, in both soul and body, holy and filled with God. We discover the invisible God in the most visible and material things. There is no other way. Either we learn to find our Lord in ordinary, everyday life, or else we shall never find him" (St Josemaría Escrivá, *Conversations*, 114).

25:31–46. The three parables (Mt 24:42–51; 25:1–13; and 25:14–30) are completed by the announcement of a rigorous last judgment, a last act in a

d. A talent was more than fifteen years' wages of a labourer

[27]Then you ought to have invested my money with the bankers,
and at my coming I should have received what was my own with
interest. [28]So take the talent from him, and give it to him who has
the ten talents. [29]For to every one who has will more be given, and
he will have abundance; but from him who has not, even what he
has will be taken away.* [30]And cast the worthless servant into the
outer darkness; there men will weep and gnash their teeth.'

The Last Judgment

[31]"When the Son of man comes in his glory, and all the angels Zech 14:5
with him, then he will sit on his glorious throne. [32]Before him will Rev 20:11–33
be gathered all the nations, and he will separate them one from Rom 14:10
another as a shepherd separates the sheep from the goats, [33]and he Ezek 34:17
will place the sheep at his right hand, but the goats at the left.
[34]Then the King will say to those at his right hand, 'Come, O
blessed of my Father, inherit the kingdom prepared for you from
the foundation of the world; [35]for I was hungry and you gave me Is 58:7
food, I was thirsty and you gave me drink, I was a stranger and
you welcomed me, [36]I was naked and you clothed me, I was sick
and you visited me, I was in prison and you came to me.' [37]Then
the righteous will answer him, 'Lord, when did we see thee
hungry and feed thee, or thirsty and give thee drink? [38]And when

---

drama, in which all matters of justice are resolved. Christian tradition calls it the Last Judgment, to distinguish it from the "Particular Judgment" which everyone undergoes immediately after death. The sentence pronounced at the end of time will simply be a public, formal confirmation of that already passed on the good and the evil, the elect and the reprobate.

In this passage we can discover some basic truths of faith: 1) that there will be a last judgment at the end of time; 2) the way Christ identifies himself with everyone in need—the hungry, the thirsty, the naked, the sick, the imprisoned; and 3) confirmation that the sinful will experience an eternal punishment, and the just an eternal reward.

25:31–33. In the Prophets and in the Book of Revelation the Messiah is depicted on a throne, like a judge. This is how Jesus will come at the end of the world, to judge the living and the dead. The Last Judgment is a truth spelt out in the very earliest credal statements of the Church and a dogma of faith solemnly defined by Benedict XII in the Constitution *Benedictus Deus* (29 January 1336).

25:35–46. All the various things listed in this passage (giving people food and drink, clothing them, visiting them) become works of Christian charity when the person doing them sees Christ in these "least" of his brethren.

Here we can see the seriousness of sins of omission. Failure to do something which one should do means leaving Christ unattended.

"We must learn to recognize Christ when he comes out to meet us in our

did we see thee a stranger and welcome thee, or naked and clothe
thee? 39And when did we see thee sick or in prison and visit thee?'
Prov 19:17 Heb 2:11 40And the King will answer them, 'Truly I say to you, as you did
it to one of the least of my brethren, you did it to me.' 41Then he
Mt 7:23 Rev 20:10, 15 will say to those at his left hand, 'Depart from me, you cursed,
into the eternal fire prepared for the devil and his angels; 42for I
was hungry and you gave me no food; I was thirsty and you gave
me no drink, 43I was a stranger and you did not welcome me,
naked and you did not clothe me, sick and in prison and you did
not visit me.' 44Then they also will answer, 'Lord, when did we
see thee hungry or thirsty or a stranger or naked or sick or in
prison, and did not minister to thee?' 45Then he will answer them,
'Truly, I say to you, as you did it not to one of the least of these,
Jn 5:29 Dan 12:2 you did it not to me.' 46And they will go away into eternal punishment, but the righteous into eternal life."

---

brothers, the people around us. No human life is ever isolated. It is bound up with other lives. No man or woman is a single verse; we all make up one divine poem which God writes with the cooperation of our freedom" (St Josemaría Escrivá, *Christ Is Passing By*, 111).

We will be judged on the degree and quality of our love (cf. St John of the Cross, *Spiritual Sentences and Maxims*, 57). Our Lord will ask us to account not only for the evil we have done but also for the good we have omitted. We can see that sins of omission are a very serious matter and that the basis of love of neighbour is Christ's presence in the least of our brothers and sisters.

St Teresa of Avila writes: "Here the Lord asks only two things of us: love for his Majesty and love for our neighbour. It is for these two virtues that we must strive, and if we attain them perfectly we are doing his will [...]. The surest sign that we are keeping these two commandments is, I think, that we should really be loving our neighbour; for we cannot be sure if we are loving God, although we may have good reasons for believing that we are, but we can know quite well if we are loving our neighbour. And be certain that, the farther advanced you find you are in this, the greater the love you will have for God; for so dearly does his Majesty love us that he will reward our love for our neighbour by increasing the love which we bear to himself, and that in a thousand ways: this I cannot doubt" (*Interior Castle*, 5, 3).

This parable clearly shows that Christianity cannot be reduced to a kind of agency for "doing good". Service of our neighbour acquires supernatural value when it is done out of love for Christ, when we see Christ in the person in need. This is why St Paul asserts that "if I give away all I have ... but have not love, I gain nothing" (1 Cor 13:3). Any interpretation of Jesus' teaching on the Last Judgment would be wide of the mark if it gave it a materialistic meaning or confused mere philanthrophy with genuine Christian charity.

25:40–45. In describing the exigencies of Christian charity which gives meaning to "social aid", the Second Vatican Council says: "Wishing to come down to topics that are practical and of some urgency, the

12. THE PASSION, DEATH AND RESURRECTION OF JESUS

Last announcement of the Passion. The conspiracy against Jesus

26 1When Jesus had finished all these sayings, he said to his Mk 14:1f
disciples, 2"You know that after two days the Passover is Lk 22:1f
coming, and the Son of man will be delivered up to be crucified." Mk 20:18
3Then the chief priests and the elders of the people gathered in
the palace of the high priest, who was called Caiaphas, 4and took
counsel together in order to arrest Jesus by stealth and kill him.

Council lays stress on respect for the human person: everyone should look upon his neighbour (without any exception) as another self, bearing in mind, above all, his life and the means necessary for living it in a dignified way 'lest he follow the example of the rich man who ignored Lazarus, the poor man' (cf. Lk 16:18–31).

"Today there is an inescapable duty to make ourselves the neighbour of every man, no matter who he is, and if we meet him, to come to his aid in a positive way, whether he is an aged person abandoned by all, a foreign worker despised without reason, a refugee, an illegitimate child wrongly suffering for a sin he did not commit, or a starving human being who awakens our conscience by calling to mind the words of Christ: 'As you did it to one of the least of these my brethren, you did it to me' " (*Gaudium et spes*, 27).

25:46. The eternal punishment of the reprobate and the eternal reward of the elect are a dogma of faith solemnly defined by the Magisterium of the Church in the Fourth Lateran Council (1215): "He [Christ] will come at the end of the world; he will judge the living and the dead; and he will reward all, both the lost and the elect, according to their works. And all these will rise with their own bodies which they now have so that they may receive according to their works, whether good or bad; the wicked, a perpetual punishment with the devil; the good, eternal glory with Christ."

26:1. The Gospel account of the Passion (Mt 26 and 27 and par.) is far more detailed than that of any other event in Christ's life—which is not surprising because the passion and death of our Lord are the culmination of his life on earth and his work of redemption; they constitute the sacrifice which he offers to God the Father to atone for our sins. Moreover, the terrible suffering he undergoes vividly demonstrates his infinite love for each and every one of us, and the gravity of our sins.

26:2. The Passover was the principal national festival, held to commemorate the liberation of Israel from slavery in Egypt and the protection Yahweh gave the Israelites when he castigated the Egyptians by causing their first born to die (cf. Ex 12). For a long time the festival was celebrated within the confines of the home, the essential ceremonies being the sacrifice of an unblemished lamb, whose blood was then smeared on the jambs and lintel of the front door of the house, and a thanksgiving meal. In our Lord's time the sacrifice was carried out

[5]But they said, "Not during the feast, lest there be a tumult among
the people."

The anointing at Bethany. Judas betrays Jesus

Mk 14:3–9 [6]Now when Jesus was at Bethany in the house of Simon the leper,
Lk 7:36–50 Jn 12:18 [7]a woman came up to him with an alabaster jar of very expensive
ointment, and she poured it on his head, as he sat at table. [8]But
when the disciples saw it, they were indignant saying, "Why this
waste? [9]For this ointment might have been sold for a large sum,
Lk 11:7 and given to the poor." [10]But Jesus, aware of this, said to them,
"Why do you trouble the woman? For she has done a beautiful
Deut 15:11 thing to me. [11]For you always have the poor with you, but you will
not always have me. [12]In pouring this ointment on my body she
has done it to prepare me for burial. [13]Truly, I say to you, wher-
ever this gospel is preached in the whole world, what she has done
Mk 14:10f will be told in memory of her."
Lk 22:3–6 Jn 11:57 [14]Then one of the twelve, who was called Judas Iscariot, went
Zech 11:12 to the chief priests [15]and said, "What will you give me if I deliver

---

in the temple of Jerusalem, while the meal took place in private houses, with the whole family attending.

Christ uses this to provide the setting for the new Passover, in which he himself will be the spotless lamb who will set all men free from the slavery of sin by shedding his blood on the cross.

26:3–5. This describes the rulers' final plot to do away with Jesus. The crime they are planning will provide the vehicle for Christ to fulfil to the very end his Father's plan of redemption (cf. Lk 24:26–27; Acts 2:23). This passage also shows that it was not the whole Jewish nation that plotted the death of the Lord, but only its leaders.

26:6. Bethany, where Lazarus and his sisters lived, was a small town to the east of the Mount of Olives, on the way from Jerusalem to Jericho. It is different from the other town of the same name where John the Baptist baptized people (cf. Jn 1:28).

26:8–11. The disciples criticize the generosity of this woman because they fail to understand the true meaning of poverty. They see her action as a waste of money—for, as St John tells us (12:5), the perfume cost more than three hundred denarii—that is, a labourer's annual earnings. They do not yet realize the love which motivated the woman's actions.

"The woman in the house of Simon the leper in Bethany, who anoints the Master's head with precious ointment, reminds us of our duty to be generous in the worship of God.

"All beauty, richness and majesty seem little to me. And against those who attack the richness of sacred vessels, of vestments and altars, stands the praise given by Jesus: '*opus enim bonum operata est in me*: she has acted well towards me' " (St Josemaría Escrivá, *The Way*, 527). See the note on Mt 21:12–13.

26:12. Wealthier Jews had bodies embalmed before burial, using rich ointments and perfumes. This woman is

him to you?" And they paid him thirty pieces of silver. 16And from 1 Tim 6:9f
that moment he sought an opportunity to betray him.

Preparations for the Last Supper and announcement of Judas' treachery

17Now on the first day of Unleavened Bread the disciples came to Mk 14:12–16
Jesus, saying, "Where will you have us prepare for you to eat the Lk 22:7–13
passover?"* 18He said, "Go into the city to such a one, and say to Ex 12:18–20
him, 'The Teacher says, My time is at hand; I will keep the
passover at your house with my disciples.' " 19And the disciples
did as Jesus had directed them, and they prepared the passover.

20When it was evening, he sat at table with the twelve disci- Mk 14:17–26
ples;[e] 21and as they were eating, he said, "Truly, I say to you, one Lk 22:14–23
of you will betray me." 22And they were very sorrowful, and Jn 13:21–26
began to say to him one after another, "Is it I, Lord?" 23He
answered, "He who has dipped his hand in the dish with me, will
betray me. 24The Son of man goes as it is written of him, but woe
to that man by whom the Son of man is betrayed! It would have

---

anticipating our Lord's death. She saw her action as a generous gesture and a recognition of Jesus' dignity; additionally it becomes a prophetic sign of his redemptive death.

26:15. It is disconcerting and sobering to realize that Judas Iscariot actually went as far as to sell the man whom he had believed to be the Messiah and who had called him to be one of the apostles. Thirty shekels or pieces of silver were the price of a slave (cf. Ex 21:32), the same value as Judas put on his Master.

26:17. This unleavened bread, azymes, took the form of loaves which had to be eaten over a seven-day period, in commemoration of the unleavened bread which the Israelites had to take with them in their hurry to leave Egypt (cf. Ex 12:34). In Jesus' time the passover supper was celebrated on the first day of the week of the Unleavened Bread.

26:18. Although the reference is to an unnamed person, probably our Lord gave the person's actual name. In any event, from what other evangelists tell us (Mk 14:13; Lk 22:10), Jesus gave the disciples enough information to enable them to find the house.

26:22. Although the glorious events of Easter have yet to occur (which will teach the apostles much more about Jesus), their faith has been steadily fortified and deepened in the course of Jesus' public ministry (cf. Jn 2:11; 6:68–69) through their contact with him and the divine grace they have been given (cf. Mt 16:17). At this point they are quite convinced that our Lord knows their internal attitudes and how they are going to act: each asks in a concerned way whether he will prove to be loyal in the time ahead.

26:24. Jesus is referring to the fact that he will give himself up freely to suffering

e. Other authorities omit *disciples*

been better for that man if he had not been born." 25Judas, who
betrayed him, said, "Is it I, Master?"[f] He said to him, "You have
said so."

The institution of the Eucharist

1 Cor 11:23–25 26Now as they were eating,* Jesus took bread, and blessed, and
broke it, and gave it to the disciples and said, "Take, eat; this is
my body." 27And he took a cup, and when he had given thanks he
gave it to them, saying, "Drink of it, all of you; 28for this is my

---

and death. In so doing he would fulfil the will of God, as proclaimed centuries before (cf. Ps 41:10; Is 53:7). Although our Lord goes to his death voluntarily, this does not reduce the seriousness of Judas' treachery.

26:25. This advance indication that Judas is the traitor is not noticed by the other apostles (cf. Jn 13:26–29).

26:26–29. This short scene, covered also in Mk 14:22–25, Lk 22:19–20 and 1 Cor 11:23–26, contains the essential truths of faith about the sublime mystery of the Eucharist—1) the institution of this sacrament and Jesus' real presence in it; 2) the institution of the Christian priesthood; and 3) the Eucharist, the sacrifice of the New Testament or the Mass.

1) In the first place, we can see the institution of the Eucharist by Jesus Christ, when he says, "This is my body … , this is my blood …". What up to this point was nothing but unleavened bread and wine, now—through the words and by the will of Jesus Christ, true God and true Man—becomes the true body and true blood of the Saviour. His words, which have such a realism about them, cannot be interpreted as being merely symbolic or explained in a way which obscures the mysterious fact that Christ is really present in the Eucharist: all we can do is humbly subscribe to the faith "which the Catholic Church has always held and which she will hold until the end of the world" (Council of Trent, *De SS. Eucharistia*). Paul VI expresses this faith in these words in his encyclical letter *Mysterium fidei*, 5: "The continuous teaching of the Catholic Church, the traditions delivered to catechumens, the perception of the Christian people, the doctrine defined by the Council of Trent, and the very words of Christ as he instituted the most holy Eucharist, all insist that we profess: 'The Eucharist is the flesh of our Saviour Jesus Christ; the flesh which suffered for our sins and which the Father, of his kindness, brought to life.' To these words of St Ignatius of Antioch may be added the statement addressed to the people by Theodore of Mopsuestia, a faithful witness of the Church's belief on this subject: 'The Lord did not say: "This is the symbol of my body and this the symbol of my blood." He said: "This is my body and my blood".'"

This sacrament, which not only has the power to sanctify but actually contains the very Author of holiness, was instituted by Jesus Christ to be spiritual nourishment of the soul, to strengthen it in its struggle to attain salvation. The Church teaches that it also confers pardon of venial sins and helps the Christian not

f. Or *Rabbi*

blood of the[g] covenant, which is poured out for many for the for- Ex 24:8
giveness of sins. 29 I tell you I shall not drink again of this fruit of Jer 31:31
the vine until that day when I drink it new with you in my Father's Zech 9:11
kingdom."

The disciples' desertion foretold Ps 113–118 Lk 22:39

30 And when they had sung a hymn, they went out to the Mount of Jn 18:1 Mk 14:27–31
Olives. 31 Then Jesus said to them, "You will all fall away because of Lk 22:31–34 Zech 13:7
me this night; for it is written, 'I will strike the shepherd, and the Jn 16:32

---

to fall into mortal sin: it unites us to God and thereby is a pledge of future glory.

2) In instituting the Blessed Eucharist our Lord laid down that it should be repeated until the end of time (cf. 1 Cor 11:24–25; Lk 22:19) by giving the apostles the power to perform it. From this passage, and the accounts in St Paul and St Luke (loc. cit.), we can see that Christ also instituted the priesthood, giving the apostles the power to confect the Eucharist, a power which they in turn passed on to their successors. This making of the Eucharist takes place at Mass when the priest, with the intention of doing what the Church does, says Christ's words of consecration over the bread and the wine. At this very moment, "a change takes place in which the whole substance of bread is changed into the substance of the body of Christ our Lord and the whole substance of the wine into the substance of his blood" (*De SS. Eucharistia*). This amazing change is given the name of "transubstantiation". Through transubstantiation the unleavened bread and the fruit of the vine disappear, becoming the body, blood, soul and divinity of Jesus Christ. Christ's real presence is to be found also in any little particles which become detached from the host, or the smallest drop from the chalice, after the consecration. It continues when the sacred species are reserved in the tabernacle, as long as the appearances (of bread and wine) last.

3) At the Last Supper, Christ—miraculously, in an unbloody manner—brought forward his passion and death. Every Mass celebrated from then on renews the sacrifice of our Saviour on the cross—Jesus once again giving his body and blood, offering himself to God the Father as a sacrifice on man's behalf, as he did on Calvary—with this clear difference: on the cross he gave himself shedding his blood, whereas on the altar he does so in an unbloody manner. "He, then, our Lord and our God, was once and for all to offer himself by his death on the altar of the cross to God the Father, to accomplish for them an everlasting redemption. But death was not to end his priesthood. And so, at the Last Supper, [...] in order to leave for his beloved spouse, the Church, a sacrifice that was visible, [...] he offered his body and blood under the species of bread and wine to God the Father and he gave his body and blood under the same species to the apostles to receive, making them priests of the New Testament at that time. This sacrifice was to represent the bloody sacrifice which he accomplished on the cross once and for all" (Council of Trent, *De SS. Missae sacrificio*, chap. 1).

The expression "which is poured out for many for the forgiveness of sins"

g. Other ancient authorities insert *new*

sheep of the flock will be scattered.’ 32But after I am raised up, I will
Jn 13:38 go before you to Galilee.” 33Peter declared to him, “Though they all
fall away because of you, I will never fall away.” 34Jesus said to him,
“Truly, I say to you, this very night, before the cock crows, you will
deny me three times.” 35Peter said to him, “Even if I must die with
you, I will not deny you.” And so did all the disciples.

Gethsemane—the agony in the garden

Mk 14:32–42 36Then Jesus went with them to a place called Gethsemane, and he
Lk 22:40–46 said to his disciples, “Sit here, while I go yonder and pray.” 37And
Heb 5:7 taking with him Peter and the two sons of Zebedee, he began to be
Ps 43:5 sorrowful and troubled. 38Then he said to them, “My soul is very
Jn 12:27 sorrowful, even to death; remain here, and watch[h] with me.” 39And
Jn 18:11 going a little farther he fell on his face and prayed, “My Father, if
Heb 5:8 it be possible, let this cup pass from me; nevertheless, not as I will,
but as thou wilt.” 40And he came to the disciples and found them
sleeping; and he said to Peter, “So, could you not watch[h] with me

---

means the same as “which is poured out for all” (cf. the note on Mt 20:27–28). Here we have the fulfilment of the prophecies of Isaiah (chap. 53), which spoke of the atoning death of Christ for all men. Only Christ’s sacrifice is capable of atoning to the Father; the Mass has this power because it is that very sacrifice: “The priest offers the Holy Sacrifice *in persona Christi*; this means more than offering ‘in the name of’ or ‘in the place of’ Christ. *In persona* means in specific sacramental identification with the eternal High Priest, who is the Author and principal Subject of this sacrifice of his, a sacrifice in which, in truth, nobody can take his place. Only he—only Christ—was able and is always able to be the true and effective ‘expiation for our sins and … for the sins of the whole world’ (1 Jn 2:2; cf. 4:10)” (John Paul II, *Letter to all bishops*, on the Eucharist, 24 November 1980).

Finally, we should notice that this sublime sacrament should be received with proper dispositions of soul and body—in the state of grace, in a spirit of adoration, respect and recollection, for it is God himself whom one is receiving. “Let a man examine himself, and so eat of the bread and drink of the cup. For anyone who eats and drinks without discerning the body eats and drinks judgment upon himself” (1 Cor 11:28–29).

26:30–35. At the celebration of the Passover, Psalms 113–118 were recited: this is what the reference to the “hymn” means. Our Lord knows what is going to happen—the main events (his death and resurrection) and the lesser ones (such as Peter’s denials).

Peter becomes so afraid that he denies his Master three times—a fall which Jesus allowed to happen in order to teach him humility. “Here we learn a great truth: that a man’s resolution is not sufficient unless he relies on the help of God” (St John Chrysostom, *Hom. on St Matthew*, 83).

h. Or *keep awake*

one hour? [41]Watch[h] and pray that you may not enter into tempta- Heb 2:14; 4:15
tion; the spirit indeed is willing, but the flesh is weak." [42]Again, for
the second time, he went away and prayed, "My Father, if this
cannot pass unless I drink it, thy will be done." [43]And again he
came and found them sleeping, for their eyes were heavy. [44]So, 2 Cor 12:8
leaving them again, he went away and prayed for the third time, 2 Sam 24:14
saying the same words. [45]Then he came to the disciples and said to
them, "Are you still sleeping and taking your rest? Behold, the
hour is at hand, and the Son of man is betrayed into the hands of
sinners. [46]Rise, let us be going; see, my betrayer is at hand." Jn 14:31

Arrest of Jesus

[47]While he was still speaking, Judas came, one of the twelve, and Mk 14:43–50
with him a great crowd with swords and clubs, from the chief Lk 22:47–53
priests and the elders of the people. [48]Now the betrayer had given Jn 18:3–12
them a sign, saying, "The one I shall kiss is the man; seize him."
[49]And he came up to Jesus at once and said, "Hail, Master!"[i] And

---

26:36–46. Here our Lord allows us to glimpse the full reality and exquisite sensitivity of his human nature. Strictly speaking, Christ, because he had complete self-control, could have avoided showing these limitations. However, by letting them express themselves, we are better able to understand the mystery of his genuine humanness—and to that extent, better able to imitate it. After tempting Jesus in the wilderness, the devil "departed from him until an opportune time" (Lk 4:13). Now, with the passion, he attacks again, using the flesh's natural repugnance to suffering; this is his hour "and the power of darkness" (Lk 22:53).

"Remain here": as if he did not want them to be depressed by seeing his agony; and "watch with me": to keep him company and to prepare themselves by prayer for the temptations that will follow. He goes a little farther away—about a stone's throw, St Luke tells us (22:41). Because there was a full moon, the apostles may have been able to see Jesus; they may also have heard some words of his prayers; but that could hardly explain how they were able to report this scene in such detail. It is more likely that our Lord, after his resurrection, told his disciples about his agony (cf. Acts 1:3), as he must also have told them about the time he was tempted in the wilderness (Mt 4:1).

26:47–56. Jesus again demonstrates that he is giving himself up of his own free will. He could have asked his Father to send angels to defend him, but he does not do so. He knows why this is all happening and he wants to make it quite clear that in the last analysis it is not force which puts him to death but his own love and his desire to fulfil his Father's will. His opponents fail to grasp Jesus' supernatural way of doing things; he had done his best to teach them but their hardness of heart came in the way and prevented them from accepting his teaching.

i. Or *Rabbi* **j.** Or *do that for which you have come*

he kissed him. 50Jesus said to him, “Friend, why are you here?”[j]
Then they came up and laid hands on Jesus and seized him. 51And
behold, one of those who were with Jesus stretched out his hand
and drew his sword, and struck the slave of the high priest, and
Gen 9:6 cut off his ear.* 52Then Jesus said to him, “Put your sword back
Rev 13:10 into its place; for all who take the sword will perish by the sword.
53Do you think that I cannot appeal to my Father, and he will at
once send me more than twelve legions of angels? 54But how then
should the scriptures be fulfilled, that it must be so?” 55At that
hour Jesus said to the crowds, “Have you come out as against a
robber, with swords and clubs to capture me? Day after day I sat
in the temple teaching, and you did not seize me. 56But all this has
taken place, that the scriptures of the prophets might be fulfilled.”
Then all the disciples forsook him and fled.

Jesus before the chief priests

Mk 14:53–72 57Then those who had seized Jesus led him to Caiaphas the high
Lk 22:54–27 priest, where the scribes and the elders had gathered. 58But Peter
Jn 18:12–27 followed him at a distance, as far as the courtyard of the high
priest, and going inside he sat with the guards to see the end.
59Now the chief priests and the whole council sought false testimony against Jesus that they might put him to death,* 60but they
found none, though many false witnesses came forward. At last
Jn 2:19–21 two came forward 61and said, “This fellow said, ‘I am able to
destroy the temple of God, and to build it in three days.’ ” 62And
the high priest stood up and said, “Have you no answer to make?

26:50. To effect his betrayal Judas uses a sign of friendship and trust. Although he knows what Judas is about, Jesus treats him with great gentleness: he gives him a chance to open his heart and repent. This shows us that we should respect even people who harm us and should treat them with a refined charity.

26:61. As we know from St John’s Gospel (2:19), Jesus had said, “Destroy this temple, and in three days I will raise it up”, referring to the destruction of his own body, that is, his death and resurrection. They misunderstood him (Jn 2:20), thinking he referred to the temple of Jerusalem.

26:69. The houses of well-to-do Jews had a front lobby or porter’s office; going through the lobby one came into a patio and by crossing the patio one could enter the rooms proper. Peter goes through the lobby but he is afraid to follow the mill of people around Jesus, so he stays in the patio, with the servants.

26:70–75. When they went to arrest Jesus in the Garden of Olives, Peter set about defending him and, sword in hand, he struck at the head of the first to lay a hand on his Master, but he only succeeded in cutting off his ear. Our Lord’s reaction (“Put your sword back into its place”: Mt 26:52) disconcerts Peter. His

What is it that these men testify against you?" 63But Jesus was
silent. And the high priest said to him, "I adjure you by the living
God, tell us if you are the Christ, the Son of God." 64Jesus said to Ps 110:1; 68:35
him, "You have said so. But I tell you, hereafter you will see the Mt 16:27;
Son of man seated at the right hand of Power, and coming on the 24:30 Dan 7:13
clouds of heaven." 65Then the high priest tore his robes, and said, Acts 7:56
"He has uttered blasphemy. Why do we still need witnesses? You Jn 10:33 Mk 16:19
have now heard his blasphemy.* 66What is your judgment?" They
answered, "He deserves death." 67Then they spat in his face, and Jn 19:7 Lev 24:16
struck him; and some slapped him, 68saying, "Prophesy to us, you Is 50:6
Christ! Who is it that struck you?"

Peter's denials

69Now Peter was sitting outside in the courtyard. And a maid came
up to him, and said, "You also were with Jesus the Galilean."
70But he denied it before them all, saying, "I do not know what
you mean." 71And when he went out to the porch, another maid
saw him, and she said to the bystanders, "This man was with
Jesus of Nazareth." 72And again he denied it with an oath, "I do Jn 8:55
not know the man." 73After a little while the bystanders came up
and said to Peter, "Certainly you are also one of them, for your
accent betrays you." 74Then he began to invoke a curse on himself
and to swear, "I do not know the man." And immediately the cock
crowed. 75And Peter remembered the saying of Jesus, "Before the
cock crows, you will deny me three times." And he went out and
wept bitterly.

---

faith is not in doubt—Jesus himself had praised him above the other apostles (Mt 16:17)—but it is still too human and needs a profound purification. On Jesus' arrest, all the disciples flee in disarray; thereby the prophecy is fulfilled which says "Strike the shepherd, that the sheep may be scattered" (Zech 13:7). However, Peter keeps following our Lord, though at a distance (Mt 26:58); he is quite demoralized and disconcerted yet brave enough to enter Caiaphas' house, where Malchus, the man whose ear he cut off, works (Jn 18:10–11).

Peter's faith is put to the supreme test. A few hours before Jesus' arrest Peter had assured him, "Lord, I am ready to go with you to prison and to death" (Lk 22:33); and now, as Jesus predicted, he three times denies that he ever knew him. In the midst of his confusion, our Lord's serene glance reinforces his faith (Lk 22:61) and Peter's tears purify it. What our Lord had said a few hours earlier, in the intimacy of the Last Supper, has come true: "Simon, Simon, behold, Satan demanded to have you, that he might sift you like wheat, but I have prayed for you that your faith may not fail; and when you have turned again, strengthen your brethren" (Lk 22:31–32).

Peter has committed a grave sin, but his repentance also is deep. His faith, now put to the test, will become the basis

Jesus is brought before Pilate

Mk 15:1 **27** [1]When morning came, all the chief priests and the elders
Lk 22:66 of the people took counsel against Jesus to put him to
Jn 18:28 death; [2]and they bound him and led him away and delivered him
Lk 23:1 Jn 18:31f to Pilate the governor.

Judas' despair and death

[3]When Judas, his betrayer, saw that he was condemned, he
repented and brought back the thirty pieces of silver to the chief
priests and the elders, [4]saying, "I have sinned in betraying innocent blood." They said, "What is that to us? See to it yourself."
Acts 1:18 [5]And throwing down the pieces of silver in the temple, he
2 Sam 17:23 Mk 12:41 departed; and he went and hanged himself. [6]But the chief priests,
taking the pieces of silver, said, "It is not lawful to put them into
the treasury, since they are blood money." [7]So they took counsel,
and bought with them the potter's field, to bury strangers in.
Acts 1:19 [8]Therefore that field has been called the Field of Blood to this day.
Zech 11:12f [9]Then was fulfilled what had been spoken by the prophet Jere-
Jer 32:6–9 miah, saying, "And they took the thirty pieces of silver, the price
of him on whom a price had been set by some of the sons of
Israel, [10]and they gave them for the potter's field, as the Lord
directed me."

---

on which Christ will build his Church (Mt 16:18).

As regards our own lives we should remember that no matter how low we may have fallen, God in his mercy, which is infinite, is ever ready to forgive us, because he does not despise a broken and contrite heart (Ps 51:19). If we sincerely repent, God will use us, sinners though we be, as his faithful instruments.

27:2. During this period the governor or procurator was the senior official in Judea. Although he was subordinate to the Roman legate in Syria, he had the *ius gladii*, the authority to condemn a criminal to death—which was why the Jewish leaders brought Jesus before Pilate: they were seeking a public sentence of death, to counteract Jesus' reputation and erase his teaching from people's minds.

27:3–5. Judas' remorse does not lead him to repent his sins and be converted; he cannot bring himself to turn trustingly to God and be forgiven. He despairs, mistrusting God's infinite mercy, and takes his own life.

27:6. Once again the chief priests and elders show their hypocrisy. They behave inconsistently: they worry about exact fulfilment of a precept of the Law—not to put into the temple treasury money resulting from an evil action—yet they themselves have instigated that action.

27:9. By recalling the prophecy of Jeremiah (cf. Jer 18:2; 19:1; 32:6–15) and completing it with that of Zechariah (Zech 11:12–13), the Gospel shows that this incident was foreseen by God.

27:14. The evangelist possibly wishes to indicate that this silence was foretold in

Jesus' trial before Pilate

[11]Now Jesus stood before the governor; and the governor asked Mk 15:2–5 Lk 23:2f
him, "Are you the King of the Jews?" Jesus said to him, "You Jn 18:29–38
have said so." [12]But when he was accused by the chief priests and Mt 26:63 Is 53:7
elders, he made no answer. [13]Then Pilate said to him, "Do you not
hear how many things they testify against you?" [14]But he gave Jn 19:9
him no answer, not even to a single charge; so that the governor
wondered greatly.

[15]Now at the feast the governor was accustomed to release for Mk 15:6–15
the crowd any one prisoner whom they wanted. [16]And they had then Lk 23:13–25
a notorious prisoner, called Barabbas.[k] [17]So when they had gathered, Jn 18:29–19:1
Pilate said to them, "Whom do you want me to release for you, Mt 31:38
Barabbas[k] or Jesus who is called Christ?" [18]For he knew that it was Jn 11:47f;
out of envy that they had delivered him up. [19]Besides, while he was 12:19
sitting on the judgment seat, his wife sent word to him, "Have noth- Acts 7:9
ing to do with that righteous man, for I have suffered much over him
today in a dream." [20]Now the chief priests and the elders persuaded
the people to ask for Barabbas and destroy Jesus. [21]The governor
again said to them, "Which of the two do you want me to release for
you?" And they said, "Barabbas." [22]Pilate said to them, "Then what
shall I do with Jesus who is called Christ?" They all said, "Let him
be crucified." [23]And he said, "Why, what evil has he done?" But
they shouted all the more, "Let him be crucified."

---

the Old Testament when Isaiah 53:7 speaks of his being "afflicted, yet he opened not his mouth; like a lamb that is led to the slaughter, and like a sheep that before its shearers is dumb."

Sometimes the right thing for a Christian to do is to remain silent, bearing out what Isaiah says elsewhere: "in quietness and in trust shall be your strength" (Is 30:15).

"'Jesus remained silent. *Jesus autem tacebat.*' Why do you speak, to console yourself or to excuse yourself? Say nothing. Seek joy in contempt; you will always receive less than you deserve. Can you, by any chance, ask: '*Quid enim mali feci?* What evil have I done?' " (St Josemaría Escrivá, *The Way*, 671).

27:18. The chief priests and elders had seen how the crowd followed Jesus. This caused them to be envious of him, an envy which grew into a hatred that sought his death (Jn 11:47).

St Thomas observes that just as at the beginning it was envy that caused man's death (Wis 2:24), so it was envy that condemned Christ (cf. *Comm. on St Matthew*, 27:18).

Envy is indeed one of the causes of hatred (Gen 37:8). "So put away all malice and all guile and insincerity and envy and all slander" (1 Pet 2:1).

27:23. "It is hard to read that question of Pilate's in the holy Gospel: 'Whom do you wish me to release to you, Barabbas or Jesus, who is called Christ?' But it is

k. Other ancient authorities read *Jesus Barabbas*

Deut 21:6 24So when Pilate saw that he was gaining nothing, but rather
that a riot was beginning, he took water and washed his hands
before the crowd, saying, "I am innocent of this righteous man's
Acts 5:28 blood;[1] see to it yourselves." 25And all the people answered, "His
Mt 23:35 blood be on us and on our children!" 26Then he released for them
Barabbas, and having scourged Jesus, delivered him to be crucified.

The crowning with thorns

Mk 15:16–19 Jn 19:2f 27Then the soldiers of the governor took Jesus into the praetorium,
and they gathered the whole battalion before him. 28And they

---

more painful to hear the answer: 'Barabbas!' And more terrible still when I realize that very often by going astray I too have said 'Barabbas' and added 'Christ? ... *Crucifige eum!* Crucify him!'" (St Josemaría Escrivá, *The Way*, 296).

27:24. Pilate tries publicly to justify his lack of courage, even though he has all the material necessary for giving an honest verdict. His cowardice, which he disguises by this external gesture, ends up condemning Christ to death.

27:26–50. Meditation on the passion of our Lord has made many saints in the course of Church history. Few things are of more benefit to a Christian than contemplation—slow and devout, to the point of being amazed—of the saving events surrounding the death of the Son of God made man. Our mind and heart will be overwhelmed to see the suffering of him who created the angels, men, heaven and earth; who is the Lord of all creation; the Almighty who humbles himself to this extent (something quite unimaginable, were it not that it happened). He suffers in this way because of sin—the original sin of our first parents, the personal sins of all men, of those who have gone before us and those who will come after us, and each one's own sins. Christ's terrible sufferings spell out for us, as nothing else can, the infinite gravity of sin, which has called for the death of God himself made man; moreover, this physical and moral suffering which Jesus undergoes is also the most eloquent proof of his love for the Father, which seeks to atone to him for man's incredible rebellion by the punishment inflicted on his own innocent humanity; and of his love for mankind, his brothers and sisters; he suffers what we deserve to suffer in just punishment for our sins. Our Lord's desire to atone was so great that there was no part of his body that he did not permit to be inflicted with pain—his hands and feet pierced by the nails; his head torn by the crown of thorns; his face battered and spat upon; his back pitted by the terrible scourging he received; his chest pierced by the lance; finally, his arms and legs utterly exhausted by such pain and weariness that he dies. His spirit, also, is saturated with suffering—the pain caused by his being abandoned and betrayed by his disciples, the hatred his own people turn on him, the jeers and brutality of the Gentiles, the mysterious way his divinity permits his soul to suffer.

Only one thing can explain why Christ undergoes this redemptive passion—love, immense, infinite, indescribable love. As he himself taught, the entire Law of God and the Prophets are sum-

1. Other ancient authorities omit *righteous* or *man's*

stripped him and put a scarlet robe upon him, [29]and plaiting a
crown of thorns they put it on his head, and put a reed in his right
hand. And kneeling before him they mocked him, saying, "Hail,
King of the Jews!" [30]And they spat upon him, and took the reed Is 50:6
and struck him on the head. [31]And when they had mocked him, Mk 15:20–41
they stripped him of the robe, and put his own clothes on him, and Lk 23:26, 33–49
led him away to crucify him. Jn 19:16–30

The crucifixion and death of Jesus

[32]As they were marching out, they came upon a man of Cyrene,
Simon by name; this man they compelled to carry his cross. [33]And

---

med up in the divine comandment of love (cf. Mt 22:36–40).

The four evangelists have filled many pages with their account of the sufferings of our Lord. Contemplation of Jesus' passion, identification with the suffering Christ, should play a key role in the life of every Christian, if he is to share later in the resurrection of his Lord: "Don't hinder the work of the Paraclete: seek union with Christ, so as to be purified, and feel with him the insults, the spits, and the blows, and the thorns, and the weight of the cross … , and the nails tearing through your flesh, and the agony of a forsaken death.

"And enter through our Lord's open side until you find sure refuge there in his wounded Heart" (St Josemaría Escrivá, *The Way*, 58).

27:27. A cohort, or battalion, consisted of some 625 soldiers. In Jesus' time there was always a cohort garrisoned in Jerusalem, quartered in the Antonia Tower, adjoining the temple. This reported to the governor and was recruited from non-Jewish inhabitants of the region.

27:28–31. The Gospel describes very soberly how Jesus puts up no resistance to being beaten and ridiculed; the facts are allowed to speak for themselves. He takes upon himself, out of love for the Father and for us, the punishment we deserve to suffer for our sins. This should make us very grateful and, at the same time, cause us to have sorrow for sin, to desire to suffer in silence at Jesus' side and atone for our sins and those of others: Lord, I want never to sin again; but you must help me to stay true to you.

27:32. Seeing how much Jesus has suffered, the soldiers realize that he is incapable of carrying the cross on his own as far as the top of Golgotha. There he is, in the centre of the crowd, with not a friend in sight. Where are all the people who benefitted from his preaching and healing and miracles? None of them is there to help him. He had said, "If any man would come after me, let him deny himself and take up his cross and follow me" (Mt 16:24). But cowardice and fear have taken over. The soldiers resort to laying hold of a stranger and forcing him to carry the cross. Our Lord will reward this favour done to him: God's grace will come down on "Simon of Cyrene, … the father of Alexander and Rufus" (Mk 15:21), who will soon be prominent members of the early Church. The experience of pain proves to be the best route to Christian discipleship.

Christ's disciples must try to ensure that cowardice does not undermine their

when they came to a place called Golgotha (which means the
Ps 69:21 place of a skull), 34 they offered him wine to drink, mingled with
Ps 22:18 gall; but when he tasted it, he would not drink it. 35 And when they
had crucified him, they divided his garments among them by cast-
ing lots; 36 then they sat down and kept watch over him there.
37 And over his head they put the charge against him, which read,
"This is Jesus the King of the Jews." 38 Then two robbers were cru-
Ps 22:7; cified with him, one on the right and one on the left. 39 And those
109:25 who passed by derided him, wagging their heads 40 and saying,
Mt 26:61 "You who would destroy the temple and build it in three days,
Jn 2:19 save yourself! If you are the Son of God, come down from the
cross." 41 So also the chief priests, with the scribes and elders,
mocked him, saying, 42 "He saved others; he cannot save himself.

---

commitment: "See how lovingly he embraces the Cross. Learn from him. Jesus carries the Cross for you: you … carry it for Jesus. But don't drag the Cross … Carry it squarely on your shoulder, because your Cross, if you carry it like that, will not be just any Cross.… It will be the Holy Cross. Don't carry your Cross with resignation: resignation is not a generous word. Love the Cross. When you really love it, your Cross will be … a Cross without a Cross" (St J. Escrivá, *Holy Rosary*, fourth sorrowful mystery).

27:33. On the outskirts of Jerusalem there was a little hill called "Golgotha", or "the place of a skull", as the evangelist expressly states. It was used as a site for executing criminals. The name "Golgotha" comes from a transcription of an Aramaic word meaning "head". The name "Calvary" comes from a Latin word with the same meaning.

27:34. They offered Jesus a drink consisting of a mixture of wine, honey and myrrh (cf. Mk 15:23); this was usually given to people condemned to death, as a narcotic to lessen the pain. Our Lord chooses not to take it, because he wants to suffer the full rigour of his passion.

"Let us drink to the last drop the chalice of pain in this poor present life. What does it matter to suffer for ten years, twenty, fifty … if afterwards there is heaven forever, forever … forever? And, above all—rather than because of the reward, *propter retributionem*—what does suffering matter if we suffer to console, to please God our Father, in a spirit of reparation, united to him on his cross; in a word: if we suffer for Love? …" (St Josemaría Escrivá, *The Way*, 182).

27:35. Some manuscripts add to this verse the following words taken from John 19:24: "This was to fulfil the scripture, 'They parted my garments among them, and for my clothing they cast lots'" (cf. Ps 22:18).

27:45. Approximately from twelve midday to three o'clock in the afternoon. See the note on Mt 20:3.

27:46. Words from Psalm 22:1, which our Lord uses to show the physical and moral pain he is suffering. In no sense should these words be taken as a complaint against God's plans. "Suffering does not consist in not feeling since that is proper to those who have no feelings;

He is the King of Israel; let him come down now from the cross,
and we will believe in him. [43]He trusts in God, let God deliver him Ps 22:8 Wis 2:13, 18–20
now, if he desires him; for he said, 'I am the Son of God.'" [44]And
the robbers who were crucified with him also reviled him in the
same way.

[45]Now from the sixth hour there was darkness over all the
land[m] until the ninth hour. [46]And about the ninth hour Jesus cried Ps 22:1
with a loud voice, "Eli, Eli, lama sabachthani?" that is, "My God,
my God, why hast thou forsaken me?"* [47]And some of the
bystanders hearing it said, "This man is calling Elijah." [48]And one
of them at once ran and took a sponge, filled it with vinegar, and Ps 69:21
put it on a reed, and gave it to him to drink. [49]But the others said,
"Wait, let us see whether Elijah will come to save him."[n] [50]And
Jesus cried again with a loud voice and yielded up his spirit.

---

nor does it lie in not showing that one feels pain: rather, suffering means that in spite of pain one does not set aside the law or obedience to God. For feeling is natural to the flesh, which is not like bronze; and so reason does not remove it, because reason gives to everything what its nature demands; and our sensitivity is very soft and tender; when it is wounded it of necessity feels, and when it feels it has to cry out" (Fray Luis de León, *Exposición del Libro de Job*).

In his agony in the garden (cf. note on Mt 26:36–46), Jesus experienced a kind of anticipation of the pain and abandonment he feels at this point in his passion. In the context of the mystery of Jesus Christ, God-and-Man, we should notice how his humanity—body and soul—suffers without his divinity assuaging that suffering, as it could have done. "Here before the cross, we should have sorrow for our sins and for those of all men, for they are responsible for Jesus' death. We should have faith to penetrate deep into this sublime truth which surpasses our understanding and to fill ourselves with amazement at God's love. And we should pray so that Christ's life and death may become the model and motivation for our own life and self-giving. Only thus will we earn the name of conquerors: for the risen Christ will conquer in us, and death will be changed into life" (St Josemaría Escrivá, *Christ Is Passing By*, 101).

27:50. The phrase "yielded up his spirit" (literally, "released, exhaled") is a way of saying that Christ really died; like any other man, his death meant the separation of soul and body. The fact that he genuinely did die—something that everyone, even his enemies, acknowledged— will show that his resurrection was a real resurrection, a miraculous, divine fact.

This is the climax of Christ's surrender to the will of the Father. Here he accomplishes the salvation of mankind (Mt 26:27–28; Mk 10:45; Heb 9:14) and gives us the greatest proof of God's love for us (Jn 3:16). The saints usually explain the expiatory value of Christ's sacrifice by underlining that he voluntarily "yielded up his spirit". "Our Saviour's death was a sacrifice of holocaust which

m. Or *earth* **n.** Other ancient authorities insert *And another took a spear and pierced his side, and out came water and blood*

Ex 26:31 Heb 10:19f 51And behold, the curtain of the temple was torn in two, from
top to bottom; and the earth shook, and the rocks were split; 52the
tombs also were opened, and many bodies of the saints who had
Acts 26:23 fallen asleep were raised, 53and coming out of the tombs after his
Dan 12:2 resurrection they went into the holy city and appeared to many.
54When the centurion and those who were with him, keeping
watch over Jesus, saw the earthquake and what took place, they
were filled with awe, and said, "Truly this was the Son[x] of God!"
Lk 8:2f 55There were also many women there, looking on from afar,
who had followed Jesus from Galilee, ministering to him;
56among whom were Mary Magdalene, and Mary the mother of
James and Joseph, and the mother of the sons of Zebedee.

The burial of Jesus

Mk 15:42–47 57When it was evening, there came a rich man from Arimathea,
Lk 23:50–55 Jn 19:38–42 named Joseph, who also was a disciple of Jesus. 58He went to
Ex 34:25 Pilate and asked for the body of Jesus. Then Pilate ordered it to be

---

he himself offered to his Father for our redemption; for though the pains and sufferings of his passion were so great and violent that anyone else would have died of them, Jesus would not have died of them unless he so chose and unless the fire of his infinite charity had consumed his life. He was, then, himself the sacrificer who offered himself to the Father and immolated himself, dying in love, to love, by love, for love and of love" (St Francis de Sales, *Treatise on the Love of God*, book 10, chap. 17). This fidelity of Christ to the point of dying should be a permanent encouragement to us to persevere until the end, conscious of the fact that only he who is true until death will receive the crown of life (cf. Rev 2:10).

27:51–53. The rending of the temple veil indicates that the way to God the Father has been opened up to all men (cf. Heb 9:15) and that the New Covenant, sealed with the blood of Christ, has begun to operate. The other portents which attend Jesus' death are signs of the divine character of that event: it was not just one more man who was dying, but the Son of God.

27:52–53. These events are undoubtedly difficult to understand. No explanation should say what the text does not say. Nor does any other part of Holy Scripture, or the Magisterium of the Church, help to clarify what actually happened.

The great Church writers have suggested three possible explanations. First: that it was not a matter of resurrections in the strict sense, but of apparitions of these dead people. Second: they would have been dead people who arose in the way Lazarus did, and then died again. Third: their resurrection would have been definitive, that is glorious, in this way anticipating the final universal resurrection of the dead.

The first explanation does not seem to be very faithful to the text, which does use the words "were raised" (*surrexerunt*). The third is difficult to recon-

x. Or *a son*

given to him. [59]And Joseph took the body, and wrapped it in a
clean linen shroud, [60]and laid it in his own new tomb, which he Is 53:9
had hewn in the rock; and he rolled a great stone to the door of the
tomb, and departed. [61]Mary Magdalene and the other Mary were
there, sitting opposite the sepulchre.
[62]Next day, that is, after the day of Preparation, the chief 2 Cor 6:8
priests and the Pharisees gathered before Pilate [63]and said, "Sir,
we remember how that imposter said, while he was still alive,
'After three days I will rise again.' [64]Therefore order the sepulchre
to be made secure until the third day, lest his disciples go and steal
him away, and tell the people, 'He has risen from the dead,' and
the last fraud will be worse than the first." [65]Pilate said to them, Dan 6:18
'You have a guard[o] of soldiers; go, make it as secure as you can."[p]
[66]So they went and made the sepulchre secure by sealing the stone
and setting a guard.*

---

cile with the clear assertion of Scripture that Christ was the first-born from the dead (cf. 1 Cor 15:20; Col 1:18). St Augustine, St Jerome and St Thomas are inclined towards the second explanation because they feel it fits in best with the sacred text and does not present the theological difficulties which the third does (cf. *Summa theologiae*, 3, 53, 3). It is also in keeping with the solution proposed by the *St Pius V Catechism*, 1, 6, 9.

27:55–56. The presence of the holy women beside Christ on the cross gives an example of stoutheartedness to all Christians.

"Woman is stronger than man, and more faithful, in the hour of suffering: Mary Magdalene and Mary Cleophas and Salome! With a group of valiant women like these, closely united to our Lady of Sorrows, what work for souls could be done in the world!" (St Josemaría Escrivá, *The Way*, 982).

27:60. It was customary for well-to-do Jews to build tombs for themselves on their own property. Most of these tombs were excavated out of rock, in the form of a cavern; they would have had a small hall or vestibule leading to the tomb proper. At the end of the hall, which would only have been a few metres long, a very low doorway gave access to the burial chamber. The first entrance door, which was at ground level, was closed off by a huge stone which could be rolled (it was called a "gobel"), fitted into a groove to make rolling easier.

27:62. The Day of Preparation (the Greek word *parasceve* means "preparation") was the day prior to the sabbath (cf. Lk 23:54). It got its name from the fact that it was the day when everything needed for the sabbath was prepared, the sabbath being a day of rest, consecrated to God, on which no work was permitted.

27:66. All these preventive measures (sealing the entrance to the tomb, placing the guard there, etc.)—measures taken by Christ's enemies—became factors which helped people believe in his resurrection.

o. Or *take a guard* **p.** Greek *know*

Mk 16:1–10 Lk 24:1–10 Jn 20:1–18 Mt 27:61

Jesus rises from the dead and appears to the women

28 * [1]Now after the sabbath, toward the dawn of the first day
of the week, Mary Magdalene and the other Mary went to
see the sepulchre. [2]And behold, there was a great earthquake; for
Acts 1:10 an angel of the Lord descended from heaven and came and rolled
back the stone, and sat upon it. [3]His appearance was like lightning, and his raiment white as snow. [4]And for fear of him the
guards trembled and became like dead men. [5]But the angel said to
Acts 2:36 the women. "Do not be afraid; for I know that you seek Jesus who
Mt 26:32 was crucified. [6]He is not here; for he has risen, as he said. Come,
see the place where he[q] lay. [7]Then go quickly and tell his disciples
that he has risen from the dead, and behold, he is going before
you to Galilee; there you will see him. Lo, I have told you." [8]So
they departed quickly from the tomb with fear and great joy, and

---

28:1–15. The resurrection of Jesus, which happened in the early hours of the Sunday morning, is a fact which all the evangelists state clearly and unequivocally. Some holy women discover to their surprise that the tomb is open. On entering the hall (cf. Mk 16:5–6), they see an angel who says to them, "He is not here; for he has risen, as he said." The guards who were on duty when the angel rolled back the stone go to the city and report what has happened to the chief priests. These, because of the urgency of the matter, decide to bribe the guards; they give them a considerable sum of money on condition that they spread the word that his disciples came at night and stole the body of Jesus when they were asleep. "Wretched craftiness," says St Augustine, "do you give us witnesses who were asleep? It is you who are really asleep if this is the only kind of explanation you have to offer!" (*Enarrationes in Psalmos*, 63, 15). The apostles, who a couple of days before fled in fear, will, now that they have seen him and have eaten and drunk with him, become tireless preachers of this great event: "This Jesus", they will say, "God raised up, and of that we are all witnesses" (Acts 2:32).

Just as he foretold he would go up to Jerusalem and be delivered to the leaders of the Jews and put to death, he also prophesied that he would rise from the dead (Mt 20:17–19; Mk 10:32–34; Lk 18:31–34). By his resurrection he completes the sign he promised to give unbelievers to show his divinity (Mt 12:40).

The resurrection of Christ is one of the basic dogmas of the Catholic faith. In fact, St Paul says, "If Christ has not been raised, then our preaching is in vain and your faith is in vain" (1 Cor 15:14); and, to prove his assertion that Christ rose, he tells us "that he appeared to Cephas, then to the Twelve. Then he appeared to more than five hundred brethren at one time, most of whom are still alive, though some have fallen asleep. Then he appeared to James, then to all the apostles. Last of all, as to one untimely born, he appeared also to me" (1 Cor 15:5–8). The creeds state that Jesus rose from the dead on the third day (*Nicene Creed*), by his own power (Ninth Council of Toledo, *De Redemptione*), by a true resurrection

q. Other ancient authorities read *the Lord*

ran to tell his disciples. 9And behold, Jesus met them and said,
"Hail!" And they came up and took hold of his feet and wor- Heb 2:11 Gen 45:4;
shipped him. 10Then Jesus said to them, "Do not be afraid; go and 50:19
tell my brethren to go to Galilee; and there they will see me."

The soldiers are bribed

11While they were going, behold, some of the guard went into the
city and told the chief priests all that had taken place. 12And when
they had assembled with the elders and taken counsel, they gave a
sum of money to the soldiers 13and said, "Tell people, 'His disciples
came by night and stole him away while we were asleep.' 14And if
this comes to the governor's ears, we will satisfy him and keep you
out of trouble." 15So they took the money and did as they were
directed; and this story has been spread among the Jews to this day.

---

of the flesh (*Creed* of St Leo IX), reuniting his soul with his body (Innocent III, *Eius exemplo*), and that this fact of the resurrection is historically proven and provable (St Pius X, *Lamentabili*).

"By the word 'resurrection' we are not merely to understand that Christ was raised from the dead … but that he rose by his own power and virtue, a singular prerogative peculiar to him alone. Our Lord confirmed this by the divine testimony of his own mouth when he said: 'I lay down my life, that I may take it again.[…] I have power to lay it down: and I have power to take it up again' (Jn 10:17–18). To the Jews he also said, in corroboration of his doctrine: 'Destroy this temple, and in three days I will raise it up' (Jn 2:19–20) […]. We sometimes, it is true, read in Scripture that he was raised by the Father (cf. Acts 2:24; Rom 8:11); but this refers to him as man, just as those passages on the other hand, which say that he rose by his own power, relate to him as God" (St Pius V, *Catechism*, 1, 6, 8).

Christ's resurrection was not a return to his previous earthly existence; it was a "glorious" resurrection, that is to say, attaining the full development of human life—immortal, freed from all limitations of space and time. As a result of the resurrection, Christ's body now shares in the glory which his soul had from the beginning. Here lies the unique nature of the historical fact of the resurrection. He could be seen not by anyone but only by those to whom he granted that grace, to enable them to be witnesses of this resurrection, and to enable others to believe in him by accepting the testimony of the seers.

Christ's resurrection was something necessary for the completion of the work of our redemption. For, Jesus Christ through his death freed us from sins; but by his resurrection he restored to us all that we had lost through sin and, moreover, opened for us the gates of eternal life (cf. Rom 4:25). Also, the fact that he rose from the dead by his own power is a definitive proof that he is the Son of God, and therefore his resurrection fully confirms our faith in his divinity.

The resurrection of Christ, as has been pointed out, is the most sublime truth of our faith. That is why St Augustine exclaims: "It is no great thing to believe that Christ died; for this is something that is also believed by pagans and Jews and by all the wicked: everyone believes that he died. The Christians'

Appearance in Galilee. The mission to the world

Eph 1:20–22 [16]Now the eleven disciples went to Galilee, to the mountain to
Dan 7:14 which Jesus had directed them. [17]And when they saw him they
Mk 16:15f worshipped him; but some doubted. [18]And Jesus came and said to
them, "All authority in heaven and on earth has been given to me.
[19]Go therefore and make disciples of all nations, baptizing them in

---

faith is in Christ's resurrection; this is what we hold to be a great thing—to believe that he rose" (*Enarrationes in Psalmos*, 120).

The mystery of the Redemption wrought by Christ, which embraces his death and resurrection, is applied to every man and woman through Baptism and the other sacraments, by means of which the believer is as it were immersed in Christ and in his death, that is to say, in a mystical way he becomes part of Christ, he dies and rises with Christ: "We were buried therefore with him by baptism unto death, so that as Christ was raised from the dead by the glory of the Father, we too might walk in newness of life" (Rom 6:4).

An ardent desire to seek the things of God and an interior taste for the things that are above (cf. Col 3:1–3) are signs of our resurrection with Christ.

28:16–20. This short passage, which brings to a close the Gospel of St Matthew, is of great importance. Seeing the risen Christ, the disciples adore him, worshipping him as God. This shows that at last they are fully conscious of what, from much earlier on, they felt in their heart and confessed by their words—that their Master is the Messiah, the Son of God (cf. Mt 16:18; Jn 1:49). They are overcome by amazement and joy at the wonder their eyes behold: it seems almost impossible, were he not before their very eyes. Yet he is completely real, so their fearful amazement gives way to adoration. The Master addresses them with the majesty proper to God: "All authority in heaven and on earth has been given to me." Omnipotence, an attribute belonging exclusively to God, belongs to him: he is confirming the faith of his worshippers; and he is also telling them that the authority which he is going to give them to equip them to carry out their mission to the whole world, derives from his own divine authority.

On hearing him speak these words, we should bear in mind that the authority of the Church, which is given it for the salvation of mankind, comes directly from Jesus Christ, and that this authority, in the sphere of faith and morals, is above any other authority on earth.

The apostles present on this occasion, and after them their lawful successors, receive the charge of teaching all nations what Jesus taught by word and work: he is the only path that leads to God. The Church, and in it all Christian faithful, has the duty to proclaim until the end of time, by word and example, the faith that she has received. This mission belongs especially to the successors of the apostles, for on them devolves the power to teach with authority, "for, before Christ ascended to his Father after his resurrection, he […] entrusted them with the mission and power to proclaim to mankind what they had heard, what they had seen with their eyes, what they had looked upon and touched with their hands, concerning the Word of Life (1 Jn 1:1). He also entrusted them with the mission and power to explain with authority what he had taught them, his words and actions, his signs and com-

the name of the Father and of the Son and of the Holy Spirit, Jn 14:23
20teaching them to observe all that I have commanded you; and lo,
I am with you always, to the close of the age."

---

mandments. And he gave them the Spirit to fulfil their mission" (John Paul II, *Catechesi tradendae*, 1). Therefore, the teachings of the Pope and of the bishops united in communion with him should always be accepted by everyone with assent and obedience.

Here Christ also passes on to the apostles and their successors the power to baptize, that is, to receive people into the Church, thereby opening up to them the way to personal salvation.

The mission which the Church is definitively given here at the end of St Matthew's Gospel is one of continuing the work of Christ—teaching men and women the truths concerning God and the duty incumbent on them to identify with these truths, to make them their own by having constant recourse to the grace of the sacraments. This mission will endure until the end of time and, to enable the Church to do this work, the risen Christ promises to stay with it and never leave it. When Holy Scripture says that God is with someone, this means that that person will be successful in everything he undertakes. Therefore, the Church, helped in this way by the presence of its divine Founder, can be confident of never failing to fulfil its mission down the centuries until the end of time.

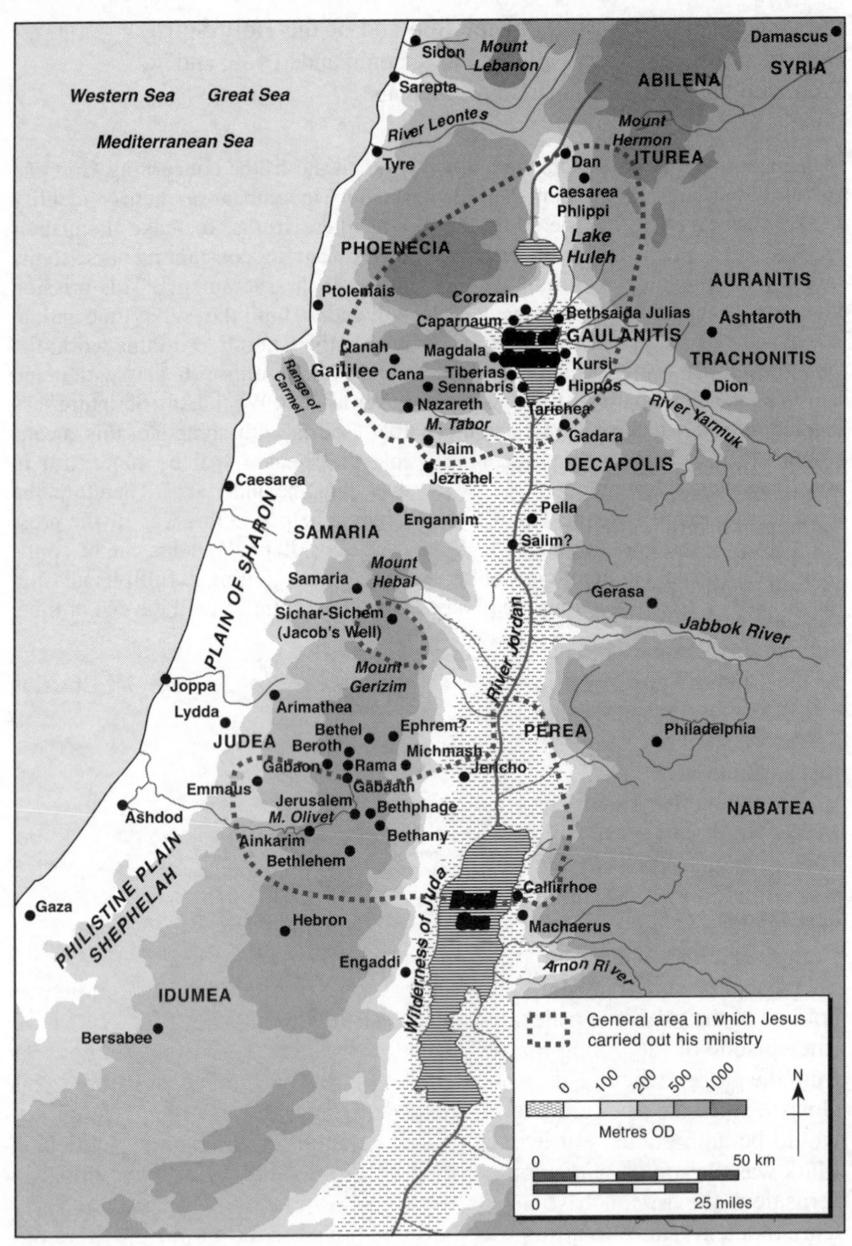

Palestine in the time of Jesus

Introduction to the Gospel according to Mark

THE AUTHOR

Christian tradition has always attributed the Second Gospel to St Mark, disciple of St Peter, St Paul and St Barnabas. Written testimonies of this attribution date back to around the year 125, with a text of Papias, bishop of Hierapolis (Asia Minor), preserved for us by Eusebius, the great church historian.[1] St Justin Martyr (*c.*155)[2] gives the same report, as does an ancient document, Roman in origin, called the "Muratorian Canon" (written *c.*180), and various references in St Irenaeus' *Against Heresies*[3] (written around the end of the second century). From the third century onwards so many writings—from both east and west—bear similar witness that it would be tedious to cite them. The authenticity of the Gospel of St Mark has also been stated by the Magisterium of the Church. The Pontifical Biblical Commission, in its reply of 26 June 1914,[4] expressly teaches that Mark is the author.

As we shall see later the internal evidence in the Gospel itself corroborates this attribution.

The New Testament gives us a certain amount of information about St Mark. He is called Mark in Acts 15:39 and John Mark in Acts 12:12 and 15:37, whereas in Acts 13:5–13 he is referred to as John. This double naming was common practice among the Jews at the time. Thus he used one Jewish name, John (Yohannan), and another hellenized Latin name, *Marcus* (Markos). Compare St Paul: Saul–Paul (the Latin name eventually prevailing).

We can be sure that Mark knew Jesus Christ personally, although he was not one of the twelve apostles: most ecclesiastical writers see Mark 14:51–52 (the episode of the young man who leaves his sheet behind him as he flees from the garden when Jesus is arrested), as Mark's own veiled signature to his Gospel, since only he refers to this episode. If this were the only reference it would be ambiguous, but it is supported by other circumstantial evidence: Mark was the son of Mary, apparently a well-to-do widow, in whose house in Jerusalem the first Christians used to gather (cf. Acts 12:12). An early Christian text[5] states that this was the same house as the Cenacle, where our Lord celebrated the Last Supper and instituted the Holy Eucharist. It also seems probable that the Garden of Olives belonged to this same Mary, which

1. Cf. *Ecclesiastical History*, 3, 39, 15. **2.** Cf. *Dialogue with Tryphon*, 106. **3.** Cf. *Against Heresies*, 3, 1, 1; 3, 10, 5. **4.** *EB*, 390–398. **5.** Cf. *Acta Sanctorum*, 2, 1867, 434.

would explain Mark's presence there. We also know from the Acts of the Apostles that Mark was a cousin of Barnabas, one of the great evangelizers of the early days, though not one of the Twelve.

THE APOSTOLIC FIGURE OF ST MARK

From his early youth, Mark shared the vibrant, intimate life of the first Christians of Jerusalem, close to the Blessed Virgin and the apostles: Mark's mother and her family were among the first to help Jesus and the Twelve. It was quite natural for Barnabas to choose Mark, his cousin, to initiate him into the task of spreading the Gospel, in company with and under the direction of himself and St Paul. Thus, Barnabas took him with him after visiting Jerusalem with St Paul to bring the first collection for the members of the mother church (cf. Acts 12:25); Mark went back with them to Antioch in Syria. When Paul and Barnabas were sent by the Holy Spirit on the first missionary journey, they brought Mark along with them (cf. Acts 13:1–6). But at the end of the first phase of evangelization in Cyprus, it seems that Mark was not very keen on the discomforts of such adventurous apostolic work; he left them and returned home (cf. Acts 13:13). Paul was not at all pleased by Mark's lack of commitment. When the second missionary journey was being planned Barnabas wanted to bring Mark with them again, but St Paul would not agree to this, given his previous experience. The result of this difference of opinion was that Paul and Barnabas decided to divide the work that lay ahead of them, Barnabas taking Mark as his assistant and sailing to Cyprus to visit the communities established there earlier (cf. Acts 15:36–39).

Some ten years later we find Mark in Rome, this time helping St Peter as "interpreter". This is also easy enough to explain because Peter, after being miraculously freed from prison by an angel, made his way precisely to the house of Mary, Mark's mother (cf. Acts 12:11–17). Peter calls Mark his son (cf. 1 Pet 5:13), which implies a long-standing and deep relationship. Mark's stay in Rome as St Peter's co-worker must have been shortly before St Paul arrived in the city, under arrest, to appeal his case to Caesar (the year 61, cf. Acts 25:11–12; 28:11–15). Tradition attributes to Mark this position of being "Peter's interpreter", which is very relevant to his writing his Gospel, as we shall see later when we discuss the Gospel in more detail.

St Paul's letters tell us more things about Mark in the years that follow: Mark, therefore, must have stayed on in Rome, and around the year 62 we find him again as an aide of St Paul (cf. Philem 24), to whom he is a source of great consolation (cf. Col 4:10ff), because of his fidelity. Later still, around the year 66, St Paul asks Timothy to come to him bringing Mark, because he is very useful to him in spreading the Gospel (cf. 2 Tim 4:11).

That is what we know about Mark's apostolic itinerary: in contrast to his softness in the early years, we find him later on as a faithful and effective co-worker of prominent apostles (Peter, Paul, Barnabas), one of their most constant and valuable assistants, in all spheres of apostolic work. Among his most outstanding contributions is his work as "interpreter of St Peter in Rome", which probably consisted of translating into Greek and Latin (many Latinisms are noticeable in the Greek of his Gospel) the oral Galilean-Aramaic preaching and teaching of the head of the apostles in the capital of the empire. This was the way the Holy Spirit chose to train Mark, whom he would inspire later to write the second canonical Gospel, a Gospel which would faithfully reflect the preaching and vivid account of Christ's life given by St Peter in Rome. Mark's progress in Christian holiness should be a great encouragement to us. Despite our weaknesses, despite failures in years past, we too can be confident that God's grace, the care we receive from our Mother the Church and the self-sacrificing service we render her in the future will enable us to do fruitful apostolic work.

From the year 66 onwards (Mark would have been a little over fifty years old), the information we have about him is less reliable but it is in line with what we know of his earlier life. For example, Eusebius (around the middle of the fourth century) in his *Ecclesiastical History* (2, 16) and St Jerome (towards the end of the same century) in his *On Famous Men* (chap. 8) pass on the tradition that Mark founded the church of Alexandria in Egypt, a tradition which is also supported by the fact that the liturgy of that church is associated with his name; another ancient tradition, mentioned in various documents (some of which go back to the fifth century), claims that Mark died a martyr in the town of Bucoli, very near Alexandria, and that in 825 his relics were devoutly transferred from Alexandria to Venice, which adopted him as patron and later erected the huge basilica dedicated to him.

DATE OF COMPOSITION

St Mark does not indicate when he wrote his Gospel. The Fathers of the Church and the ecclesiastical authors did their best to fix a date, on the basis of information given in documented tradition and on the likely biographical dates of the author. They also noted the relationships his Gospel holds to other texts in the New Testament, especially the Gospels of St Matthew and St Luke, and the Acts of the Apostles and some of St Paul's letters.

A first approximation indicates the decade 60–70, or perhaps 58–68. Taking account of the data of tradition, from which it can be inferred that the Gospel of St Mark is prior to that of St Luke, and that both were written before the year 70, scholars deduce, as a second approximation, that the latest date for this Gospel would be around the year 67.

A third line of research takes 63 as a base year—the most probable date of the redaction of the Acts, "the second book" of St Luke (Acts 1:1), written after his Gospel. This approach suggests that St Luke's Gospel should be dated around the year 62, in which case Mark's would be a little earlier, which would bring us to around the year 60. This date fits in with the biography of St Mark: by that time he would have been in Rome and have worked as St Peter's interpreter.

The scholars who suggest that Mark's Gospel was composed around 64–67 also place the Acts later, around 70. They draw support for this by referring to the passage in St Irenaeus[6] which says: "After his departure [the death of St Peter], Mark, the disciple and interpreter of Peter, transmitted to us in writing what Peter had preached."

To sum up: it should be taken as probable that the Gospel of St Mark was written before the year 70; and the two possible more precise dates are: around the year 60, or else between 64 and 67.

PLACE OF COMPOSITION AND IMMEDIATE READERSHIP

Ancient tradition states that St Mark wrote his Gospel in Italy (cf., for example, Clement of Alexandria, +211; the ancient *Latin Prologue*, second to third century; the *Monarchian Prologue*, fourth century); or, more specifically, in Rome itself (this can be inferred from Irenaeus' *Against Heresies*, around 175–189; Tertullian, who died in 220, in his *Against Marcion*, and many other writers expressly make the same claim: Clement of Alexandria, St Jerome, etc.).

Internal examination of the text corroborates what tradition says: it uses many Latin words, simply translating them from Greek (census, centurion, denarius, legion, *speculator* or watch tower, flagellum, etc.); it says that Simon of Cyrene was the father of Alexander and Rufus, who were prominent among the Christians in Rome (cf. Rom 16:13); the narrative generally is so vivid and, we might say, so characteristic that scholars are in agreement in claiming to hear St Peter's voice in such phrases as: "then we arrived, we saw, we went, he tells us, etc." These words were transcribed by St Mark with simply a change of first person singular to third person plural. The content fits in perfectly with the Gospel preaching of St Peter, as can be seen from his teaching in the Acts of the Apostles: St Mark's is the Gospel which most closely follows the structure of Peter's addresses as reported in Acts. The way in which the author treats the figure of St Peter is also very characteristic: he gives us a more detailed account than the other evangelists of Peter's less happy interventions, which must clearly indicate Peter's humility in wanting to see them recorded. And, on the other side, he omits some episodes which highlight the greater dignity Jesus conferred on Peter, such as the promise of the primacy (cf Mt 16:17–18) and his dedication to the Church (cf. Jn 21:15–17).

All this ties in with the tradition that Mark wrote his Gospel "on the insistence of the Christians of Rome" (Clement of Alexandria, according to a text preserved by Eusebius in his *Ecclesiastical History*, 6, 15, 5). This, of course, does not detract from the Second Gospel's divine inspiration, since the Holy Spirit, as well as internally moving the Evangelist's will, could also stimulate the faithful to ask him to write (which fitted in very well with Mark's circumstances at the time).

6. *Against Heresies*, 3, 1, 1.

It is very reasonable, therefore, to say, in keeping with ancient tradition reaffirmed by recent scholarship, that St Mark wrote in the first instance for the faithful in Rome, though of course his Gospel has perennial value for the whole Church. Internal evidence also supports this view: he explains Jewish rites and customs with which Gentiles would be unfamiliar (cf., e.g., Mk 7:1–5), and he translates Aramaic words used by Jesus (cf. Mk 5:41; 7:34).

STRUCTURE

The Second Gospel is basically a detailed development of St Peter's discourses in the Acts of the Apostles (cf. Acts 2:22–26; 3:12–26; 10:36–43). In it we can distinguish six major sections, as follows:

1. *Prelude to the public ministry of Jesus* (1:1–13). St Mark's account, shorter than in the other Synoptics, covers: the ministry of John the Baptist (1:1–8), Jesus is baptized (1:9–11) and the tempting of Jesus (1:12–13).

PART ONE: JESUS' MINISTRY IN GALILEE

2. *Jesus' begins his ministry* (1:14—3:35); 3. *Parables of the Kingdom of God* (4:1–34); 4. *Miracles and activity in Galilee* (4:35—6:6). Mark's report here is fairly extensive. From it we can deduce that this initial ministry certainly lasted some months, with the city of Capernaum, on the shore of Lake Gennesaret, acting as the centre of Jesus' activity throughout Galilee.

The healing and miracles performed by our Lord, his preaching, a number of disputes with Pharisees, his teaching in parables: all combine to increase his following; however, Jesus wants to wean the people away from earth-bound messianism; he wants them to recognize his as a divine and transcendent messianism. He acts very prudently in this regard.

In the meantime he gathers a group of disciples around him. His popularity provokes envy on the part of Pharisees and Herodians, who begin to plot against him. This fact, and his rejection by people of his hometown, Nazareth, leads him to make a number of evangelical journeys into border areas.

5. *Jesus journeys with his apostles* (6:6—8:30). Jesus now concentrates on training the Twelve. He initiates them into their mission of evangelization. He leads them north and then east, away from the borders of Galilee—to where the multiplication of the loaves and other miracles take place. He journeys to the Phoenician region of Tyre (6:6—7:37).

He then turns back and follows the western shore of Lake Gennesaret; the second multiplication of the loaves and other miracles take place; new plots are hatched by the Pharisees; other apostolic journeys (8:1–21).

Jesus heads towards Syria, via the Golan region; in Caesarea Philippi a significant event occurs: Peter, speaking for the Twelve, acknowledges Jesus' divinity (8:27–30). This episode constitutes, as it were, a central point dividing St Mark's Gospel into two parts.

PART TWO: JESUS' MINISTRY ON THE WAY TO JERUSALEM

6. *Teachings on the Christian life* (6:31—9:50). Then Jesus foretells his death for the first time: from this point onwards he prepares his disciples for his passion, though they fail to understand him; Peter is severely reprimanded (8:31—9:1). The transfiguration. Return to Galilee (9:2–50).

7. *Heading for Judea and Jerusalem* (10:1–52). This section covers the journey to Jerusalem, and a detour to Perea and Jericho; teaching on marriage and its indissolubility; episodes about the demands involved in following Jesus; the faith of the blind man, Bartimaeus.

PART THREE: JESUS' MINISTRY IN JERUSALEM

8. *Cleansing of the temple. Controversies* (11:1—12:44).

9. *Eschatological discourse* (13:1–37). Our Lord predicts the destruction of Jerusalem; he speaks about the end of the world and calls for vigilance.

10. *Passion, death and resurrection of Jesus* (14:1—16:20). The Sanhedrin decide to dispose of Jesus. Judas' betrayal. The Last Supper takes place and the institution of the Blessed Eucharist (14:1–26).

This is followed by Jesus' prayer in the Garden of Olives; his arrest; interrogations; Peter's denials; and the trial before Pilate (14:26—15:15).

The Way of the Cross. Crucifixion and death. Burial. (15:16–47)

The risen Jesus. The angel's announcement to the holy women. Appearances to Mary Magdalen, to the disciples at Emmaus and to the Twelve. The commandment to the apostles to preach the Gospel to the whole world. Jesus' ascension (16:1–20).

DOCTRINAL CONTENT

We could say that the special characteristic of St Mark's Gospel is that it gives us a direct picture of Jesus: the main episodes in his life are reported in a straightforward way, without any further explanation; unlike the other Gospels there are no long discourses in Jesus' words, no detailed explanations of his teachings. For example, St Mark does not give us the great Sermon on the Mount which we find in chapters 5–7 of St Matthew (half of the content of which is to be found in various places in St Luke); in his fourth chapter, he does give the parables discourse, but quite briefly by comparison with chapter 13 of Matthew; he omits many of the rulings and teachings on the life of the Church, which we are given in Matthew 18; etc. St Mark's Gospel contains only two of Jesus' great discourses, properly speaking: the one on the parables, which we have just mentioned (Mk 4:1–34) and the eschatological discourse (Mk 13:1–37), which is the equivalent of Matthew 24:1–44 and Luke 21:5–38. To compensate for these omissions Mark has left us something different but quite delightful—his vivid description of episodes of Jesus' life with his disciples. Revelation through Mark allows us to see aspects of Jesus which fill out the picture given by the other evangelists.

Introduction to St Mark's Gospel

St Mark's Gospel takes us out into the little towns on the shore of Lake Gennesaret; we can sense the hubbub of the crowd of people following Jesus and almost exchange remarks with some of them; we can see Christ's loving gestures, the somewhat over-spontaneous reactions of the Twelve, and so forth: we can watch the Gospel story unfold before our very eyes. This is not to say that Mark's account is naive: he has achieved what he set out to do; he has managed to make Jesus attractive to us; Jesus, who is both serene and demanding, exercises on us the same kind of influence the apostles felt when they lived with him. St Mark is passing on to us what St Peter communicated in his preaching, a preaching which, as the years went by, must have grown in emotion, depth, insight and love. Mark is the living mirror, we could say, of St Peter's preaching, of which St Luke also has left us faithful records in the Acts of the Apostles (cf. Acts 2:22–26; 3:12–26; 10:36–43).

LITERARY STYLE

St Mark's vocabulary and sentence structure are simple and effective. There is a predominance of *parataxis*—phrases linked together by the continuous use of the conjunction "and" or, occasionally, "then" or "immediately". Also, very often he uses direct speech in the middle of his narrative: in addition to making it vivid, this gives us very many phrases of Jesus which are a literal translation into Greek of the very words our Lord used in the Palestinian Aramaic dialect of his time. Another feature is his use of the historical present tense ("he comes", "he says", "they go"), which occurs over 150 times and his unexpected jumping from one tense to another within the same passage, but this is not reflected in the RSV.

A particular feature of St Mark is the fine detail he gives in certain episodes which are more soberly covered by St Matthew or St Luke (for example, the curing of the paralytic, Mk 2:3–12, compared with Mt 9:1–8 and Lk 5:17–26; the curing of the possessed man at Gerasa, Mk 5:1–20, Mt 8:28–34, Lk 8:26–29). Also St Mark is the only one to give us other little pieces of information: for example, only he tells us that during the storm on the lake Jesus was in the stern asleep on a cushion (Mk 4:38); or that he named the sons of Zebedee "sons of thunder" (Mk 3:17); or that the blind man of Jericho was named Bartimaeus (Mk 10:46). These things must surely reflect not simply Mark's preference for detail but also St Peter's vivid oral account of these events.

JESUS, THE PROMISED MESSIAH

In perfect harmony with the other three Gospels, St Mark's depicts Jesus as the Messiah (Mk 14:61–62). Jesus required people to follow him, and being his disciple means accepting that he is the Messiah (Mk 8:27–30). Also, whenever people asked him to do anything for them, he required them to believe that he could do it; whether it was a matter of the instantaneous curing of a paralytic and the forgiving of his sins (Mk 2:5–12) or the raising of Jairus' daughter (Mk 5:35–36), etc., these were powers which Jesus exercised in his own name, by his word alone.

However, as regards making known that he was the Messiah, Jesus acted very prudently. He wanted to make sure that people did not confuse him with some sort of nationalistic, political leader who would liberate the Jews from Roman domination. Thus, when addressing crowds he preferred to call himself "the Son of man" (Mk 2:10; 2:28; 8:31, 38 etc.). This expression, to be found in the prophecies of Daniel (cf. Dan 7:13–14), left no scope for a nationalistic interpretation: it clearly had a very transcendental religious meaning. Other messianic titles, such as "Son of David", or simply "Messiah" (Christ), could, at the time, have led to an interpretation of Jesus' mission as one of predominantly earthly messianism.

By acting in this way Jesus revealed himself gradually, preparing his disciples to recognize him as the Saviour who would redeem men and reconcile them to God, not through force of violence or political power, but through his sacrifice on Calvary, "for the Son of man also came not to be served but to serve, and to give his life as a ransom for many" (Mk 10:45).

JESUS, THE SON OF GOD

The first words of St Mark's Gospel clearly assert the divinity of Christ: "The beginning of the gospel of Jesus Christ, the Son of God" (Mk 1:1). In many passages his divinity is confessed in an implicit way (cf., e.g., Mk 2:11; 4:41). In others it is formally revealed, as when Jesus is baptized: "a voice came from heaven, 'Thou art my beloved Son'" (Mk 1:11); the same revelation is made again at the transfiguration (Mk 9:7).

We can be quite sure that the assertion that Jesus is the Son of God, made by St Mark at the very beginning of his Gospel, is a summary of everything he plans to tell us in his book; and it also provides the reader with a key to understand everything he is going to find there: if we do not believe that Jesus is the Messiah and the Son of God, we will not be able to understand the Gospel. Therefore St Mark points out at the very beginning that in Jesus Christ we must see someone who is fully God and fully man. (In the last analysis every form of heterodoxy falls into one or other of these extremes—denying Christ's divinity or denying his humanity.) The Holy Spirit has wanted to preserve those words of the Roman officer on Calvary—which also provide a sort of summary of the Gospel according to St Mark: "When the centurion, who stood facing him, saw that he thus breathed his last, he said, 'Truly this man was the Son of God!'" (Mk 15:39).

1. PRELUDE TO THE PUBLIC MINISTRY OF JESUS

The ministry of John the Baptist Mt 3:1–12 Lk 3:3–18

1 1 The beginning of the gospel of Jesus Christ, the Son of God.[a] Jn 1:19–34
2 As it is written in Isaiah the prophet,[b] Mal 3:1
"Behold, I send my messenger before thy face, Mt 11:10 Jn 3:28
who shall prepare the way; Is 40:3

1:1. With these words St Mark gives us the title of his book and emphasizes that Jesus is the Messiah foretold by the prophets and that he is the only Son of the Father, whose nature he shares. The title summarizes the content of the Second Gospel: Jesus Christ, true God and true Man.

The word "gospel" means good tidings, the good news God sends to mankind through his Son. The content of this good news is, in the first place, Jesus Christ himself, his words and his actions. "During the Synod [the 1974 Synod of Bishops], the Bishops very frequently referred to this truth: Jesus himself, the Good News of God (Mk 1:1, Rom 1:13), was the very first and the greatest evangelizer: he was so through and through, to perfection and to the point of the sacrifice of his earthly life" (Paul VI, *Evangelii nuntiandi*, 7). The apostles, who were chosen by our Lord to be the basis of his Church, fulfilled his commandment to present to Jews and Gentiles, by means of oral preaching, the witness of what they had seen and heard—the fulfilment in Jesus Christ of the prophecies of the Old Testament, and the forgiveness of sins, adoptive sonship and inheritance of heaven offered by God to all men. For this reason the word "gospel" can also be used in the case of the apostles' preaching. Later, the evangelists, inspired by the Holy Spirit, wrote down part of this oral teaching; and thus, through Holy Scripture and apostolic Tradition, the voice of Christ is perpetuated throughout the centuries to reach all generations and all nations.

The Church, which carries on the mission of the apostles, must make the "gospel" known. This it does, for example, by means of catechesis: "The primary and essential object of catechesis is, to use an expression dear to St Paul and also to contemporary theology, 'the mystery of Christ.' […] It is therefore to reveal in the Person of Christ the whole of God's eternal design reaching fulfilment in that Person. It is to seek to understand the meaning of Christ's actions and words and of the signs worked by him, for they simultaneously hide and reveal his mystery. Accordingly, the definitive aim of catechesis is to put people not only in touch but in communion, in intimacy, with Jesus Christ: only he can lead us to the love of the Father in the Spirit and make us share in the life of the Holy Trinity" (John Paul II, *Catechesi tradendae*, 5).

1:2–3. The Gospel quotes Isaiah in particular perhaps because he was the most important of the prophets who foretold the coming of the Messiah: that is why St Jerome called Isaiah the "Evangelist of the Old Testament".

a. Other ancient authorities omit *the Son of God* **b.** Other ancient authorities read *in the prophets*

³the voice of one crying in the wilderness:
Prepare the way of the Lord,
make his paths straight—"

Acts 19:4 ⁴John the baptizer appeared[c] in the wilderness, preaching a baptism of repentance for the forgiveness of sins. ⁵And there went out
to him all the country of Judea, and all the people of Jerusalem;
and they were baptized by him in the river Jordan, confessing
2 Kings 1:8 their sins. ⁶Now John was clothed in camel's hair, and had a
leather girdle around his waist, and ate locusts and wild honey.

1:4. St John the Baptist presents himself to the people after spending five years in the desert. He invites the Israelites to prepare for the coming of the Messiah by doing penance. The figure of St John points to the continuity between the Old and New Testaments: he is the last of the prophets and the first of the witnesses to Jesus. Whereas the other prophets announced Jesus from afar, John the Baptist was given the special privilege of actually pointing him out (cf. Jn 1:29; Mt 11:9–11).

The baptism given by the Precursor was not Christian Baptism: it was a penitential rite, but it prefigured the dispositions needed for Christian Baptism—faith in Christ, the Messiah, the source of grace, and voluntary detachment from sin.

1:5. "Confessing their sins": by seeking John's baptism a person showed that he realized he was a sinner: the rite which John performed announced forgiveness of sins through a change of heart and helped remove obstacles in the way of a person's acceptance of the Kingdom (Lk 3:10–14).

This confessing of sin was not the same as the Christian sacrament of Penance. But it was pleasing to God because it was a sign of interior repentance and the people performed genuine penitential acts (Mt 3:7–10; Lk 3:7–9). In the sacrament of Penance, in order to obtain God's forgiveness one must confess one's sins orally. In this connexion John Paul II has said: "And keep in mind that the teaching of the Council of Trent on the need for confession of all mortal sins still holds and will always hold (sess. XIV, chap. 5 and can. 7). The norm taught by St Paul and by the same Council of Trent, according to which the worthy reception of the Eucharist must be preceded by the confession of sins when one is conscious of mortal sin, is and always will be in force in the Church (sess. XIII, chap. 7 and can. 11)" (*Address to penitentiaries of the four major basilicas in Rome*, 30 January 1981).

1:8. "Baptizing with the Holy Spirit" refers to the Baptism Jesus will institute and shows how it differs from the baptism of John. In John's baptism, as in the other rites of the Old Testament, grace was only signified, symbolized. "By the baptism of the New Law men are baptized inwardly by the Holy Spirit, and this is accomplished by God alone. But by the baptism of John the body alone was cleansed by the water" (St Thomas Aquinas, *Summa theologiae*, 3, 38, 2 ad 1). In Christian Baptism, instituted by our Lord, the baptismal rite not only signifies grace but is the effective cause of grace, that is, it con-

c. Other ancient authorities omit *John was baptizing*

7And he preached, saying, "After me comes he who is mightier Acts 13:25
than I, the thong of whose sandals I am not worthy to stoop down
and untie. 8I have baptized you with water, but he will baptize you
with the Holy Spirit."

Jesus is baptized

9In those days Jesus came from Nazareth of Galilee and was bap- Mt 3:13–17
tized by John in the Jordan. 10And when he came up out of the Lk 3:21–22
water, immediately he saw the heavens opened and the Spirit Jn 1:31–34

---

fers grace. "Baptism confers the first sanctifying grace and the supernatural virtues, taking away original sin and also personal sins if there are any, together with the entire debt of punishment which the baptized person owes for sin. In addition, Baptism impresses the Christian character in the soul and makes it able to receive the other sacraments" (St Pius X, *Catechism*, 295). The effects of Christian Baptism, like everything to do with the sanctification of souls, are attributed to the Holy Spirit, the "Sanctifier". It should be pointed out, however, that like all the *ad extra* actions of God (that is, actions external to the intimate life of the Blessed Trinity), the sanctification of souls is the work of all three divine Persons.

1:9. Our Lord's hidden life takes place (apart from his birth at Bethlehem and the time he was in Egypt) in Nazareth of Galilee, from where he comes to receive John's baptism.

Jesus had no need to receive this baptism of conversion. However, it was appropriate that he who was going to establish the New Alliance should recognize and accept the mission of his Precursor by being baptized with his baptism: this would encourage people to prepare to receive the Baptism which *was* necessary. The Fathers comment that our Lord went to receive John's baptism in order to fulfil all righteousness (cf. Mt 3:15), to give us an example of humility, to become widely known, to have people believe in him and to give life-giving strength to the waters of Baptism.

"Ever since the Baptism of Christ in the water, Baptism removes the sins of all" (St Augustine, *Sermons*, 135).

"There are two different periods of time which relate to Baptism—one the period of its institution by the Redeemer; the other the establishment of the law regarding its reception. [...] The second period to be distinguished, that is, the time when the law of Baptism was made, also admits of no doubt. Holy writers are unanimous in saying that after the Resurrection of our Lord, when he gave to his apostles the command to go and 'make disciples of all nations, baptizing them in the name of the Father and of the Son and of the Holy Ghost' (Mt 28:19) the law of Baptism became obligatory on all who were to be saved" (St Pius V, *Catechism*, part 2).

1:10. The visible presence of the Holy Spirit in the form of a dove marks the beginning of Christ's public ministry. The Holy Spirit will also appear, in the form of tongues of fire, on the occasion when the Church begins its mission to all the world on the day of Pentecost (cf. Acts 2: 3–21).

The Fathers usually interpret the dove as a symbol of peace and reconciliation between God and men. It first appears in the account of the flood (Gen 8: 10–11)

Mk 9:7 Ps 2:7 Is 42:1 Mt 4:1–17 Lk 4:1–13 Jn 1:51 Job 5:22f

descending upon him like a dove; 11and a voice came from
heaven, "Thou art my beloved Son;[d] with thee I am well pleased."

The tempting of Jesus

12The Spirit immediately drove him out into the wilderness. 13And
he was in the wilderness forty days, tempted by Satan; and he was
with the wild beasts; and the angels ministered to him.

---

as a sign that God's punishment of mankind has come to an end. Its presence at the beginning of Christ's public ministry symbolizes the peace and reconciliation he will bring.

1:11. At the very beginning of his public life the mystery of the Holy Trinity is made manifest: "The Son is baptized, the Holy Spirit descends in the form of a dove and the voice of the Father is heard" (St Bede, *In Marci Evangelium expositio*, in loc.). "The Holy Spirit dwells in him," the same author goes on, "but not from the moment of his Baptism, but from the moment he became man." In other words, Jesus did not become God's son at his Baptism; he is the Son of God from all eternity. Nor did he become the Messiah at this point; he was the Messiah from the moment he became man.

Baptism is the public manifestation of Jesus as Son of God and as Messiah, ratified by the presence of the Blessed Trinity.

"The Holy Spirit descended visibly in bodily form upon Christ when he was baptized so that we may believe him to descend invisibly upon all those who are baptized afterwards" (St Thomas Aquinas, *Summa theologiae*, 3, 39, 6 ad 3).

1:13. St Matthew (4: 1–11) and St Luke (4: 1–13) relate the temptations of Jesus in more detail. By submitting to temptation, Jesus wanted to show us that we should not be afraid of temptations: on the contrary, they give us an opportunity to progress in the interior life.

"Yet the Lord sometimes permits that souls, which are dear to him, should be tempted with some violence, in order that they may better understand their own weakness, and the necessity of grace to prevent them from falling […]; God permits us to be tempted, that we may be more detached from the things of earth, and conceive a more ardent desire to behold him in heaven […]; God also permits us to be tempted, in order to increase our merits. […] When it is disturbed by temptation, and sees itself in danger of committing sin, the soul has recourse to the Lord and to his divine Mother; it renews its determination to die rather than offend God; it humbles itself and takes refuge in the arms of divine mercy. By this means, as is proved by experience, it acquires more strength and is united more closely to God" (St Alphonsus Mary de Liguori, *The Love of our Lord Jesus Christ*, chap. 17).

Besides, as in our Lord's own case, we will always have God's help to overcome temptation: "Jesus has stood up to the test. And it was a real test […]. The devil, with twisted intention, quoted the Old Testament: 'God will send his angels to protect the just man wherever he goes' (Ps 91:11). But Jesus refuses to tempt his Father; he restores true meaning to this passage from the Bible. And, as a reward for his fidelity, when the time comes, ministers of God the Father appear and

d. Or *my Son, my* (or *the*) *Beloved*

PART ONE

Jesus' ministry in Galilee

2. JESUS BEGINS HIS MINISTRY

Jesus begins to preach

[14]Now after John was arrested, Jesus came into Galilee, preaching Mt 4:12–17 Lk 4:14–15
the gospel of God, [15]and saying, "The time is fulfilled, and the Gal 4:4
kingdom of God is at hand; repent, and believe in the Gospel."

Jesus calls his first disciples

[16]And passing along by the Sea of Galilee, he saw Simon and Mt 4:18–22
Andrew the brother of Simon casting a net in the sea; for they Lk 5:1–11

---

wait upon him [...]. We have to fill ourselves with courage, for the grace of God will not fail us. God will be at our side and will send his angels to be our travelling companions, our prudent advisers along the way, our cooperators in all that we take on" (St Josemaría Escrivá, *Christ Is Passing By*, 63).

1:14–15. "The gospel of God": this expression is found in St Paul (Rom 1:1; 2 Cor 11:7; etc.) where it means the same as "the gospel of Jesus Christ" (2 Thess 1:8; etc.), thereby implying the divinity of Jesus Christ. The imminence of the Kingdom requires a genuine conversion of man to God. The prophets had already spoken of the need for conversion and for Israel to abandon its evil ways (Jer 3:22; Is 30:15; Hos 14:2; etc.).

Both John the Baptist and Jesus and his apostles insist on the need for conversion, the need to change one's attitude and conduct as a prerequisite for receiving the Kingdom of God. John Paul II underlines the importance of conversion: "Therefore, the Church professes and proclaims conversion. Conversion to God always consists *in discovering his mercy*, that is, in discovering that love which is patient and kind (cf. 1 Cor 13:4) as only the Creator and Father can be; the love to which the 'God and Father of our Lord Jesus Christ' (2 Cor 1:3) is faithful to the uttermost consequences in the history of his covenant with man: even to the Cross and to the death and resurrection of the Son. Conversion to God is always the fruit of the 'rediscovery' of this Father, who is rich in mercy.

"Authentic knowledge of the God of mercy, the God of tender love, is a constant and inexhaustible source of conversion, not only as a momentary interior act but also as a permanent attitude, as a state of mind. Those who come to know God in this way, who 'see' him in this way, can live only in a state of being continually converted to him. They live, therefore, *in statu conversionis* and it is this state of conversion which marks out the most profound element of the pilgrimage of every man and woman on earth in *statu viatoris*" (John Paul II, *Dives in misericordia*, 13).

1:16–20. In these verses the evangelist describes how Jesus called some of those

were fishermen. [17]And Jesus said to them, "Follow me and I will
Mt 13:47 make you become fishers of men." [18]And immediately they left
their nets and followed him. [19]And going on a little farther, he saw
James the son of Zebedee and John his brother, who were in their
boat mending the nets. [20]And immediately he called them; and
they left their father Zebedee in the boat with the hired servants,
and followed him.

Jesus in the synagogue of Capernaum

Lk 4:31:37 Mt 4:13 [21]And they went into Capernaum; and immediately on the sabbath
he entered the synagogue and taught. [22]And they were astonished
Mt 7:28–29 at his teaching, for he taught them as one who had authority, and

---

who would later form part of the Apostolic College (3:16ff). From the start of his public ministry in Galilee the Messiah seeks co-workers to help him in his mission as Saviour and Redeemer. He looks for them among people used to hard work, people for whom life is a struggle and whose lifestyle is plain. In human terms they are obviously at a disadvantage *vis-à-vis* many of those to whom they will preach; but this in no way prevents their self-surrender from being generous and free. The light lit in their hearts was enough to lead them to give up everything. A simple invitation to follow the Master was enough for them to put themselves completely at his disposal.

It is Jesus who chooses them: he interfered in the lives of the apostles just as he interferes in ours, without seeking our permission: he is our Lord. Cf. the note on Mt 4:18–22.

1:21. "Synagogue" means meeting, assembly, community. It was—and is—used by the Jews to describe the place where they met to hear the Scriptures read, and to pray. Synagogues seem to have originated in the social gatherings of the Jews during their exile in Babylon, but this phenomenon did not spread until much later. In our Lord's time there were synagogues, in Palestine, in every city and town of any importance; and, outside Palestine, wherever the Jewish community was large enough. The synagogue consisted mainly of a rectangular room built in such a way that those attending were facing Jerusalem when seated. There was a rostrum or pulpit from which Holy Scripture was read and explained.

1:22. Here we can see how Jesus showed his authority to teach. Even when he took Scripture as his basis—as in the Sermon on the Mount—he was different from other teachers, for he spoke in his own name: "But I say to you" (cf. the note on Mt 7:28–29). Our Lord speaks about the mysteries of God, and about human relationships; he teaches in a simple and authoritative way because he speaks of what he knows and testifies to what he has seen (Jn 3:11). The scribes also taught the people, St Bede comments, about what is written in Moses and the prophets; but Jesus preached to them as God and Lord of Moses himself (cf. St Bede, *In Marci Evangelium expositio*, in loc.). Moreover, first he does and then he preaches (Acts 1:1)—not like the scribes who teach and do not do (Mt 23:1–5).

1:23–26. The Gospels give us many accounts of miraculous cures, among the

not as the scribes. 23And immediately there was in their synagogue a man with an unclean spirit; 24and he cried out, "What Mk 5:7
have you to do with us, Jesus of Nazareth? Have you come to
destroy us? I know who you are, the Holy One of God." 25But
Jesus rebuked him saying, "Be silent, and come out of him!"
26And the unclean spirit, convulsing him and crying out with a
loud voice, came out of him. 27And they were all amazed, so that
they questioned among themselves, saying, "What is this? A new
teaching! With authority he commands even the unclean spirits,
and they obey him." 28And at once his fame spread everywhere
throughout all the surrounding region of Galilee.

---

most outstanding of which are those of people possessed by the devil. Victory over the unclean spirit, as the devil is usually described, is a clear sign that God's salvation has come: by overcoming the Evil One, Jesus shows that he is the Messiah, the Saviour, more powerful than the demons: "Now is the judgment of this world, now shall the ruler of this world be cast out" (Jn 12:31). Throughout the Gospel we see many accounts of this continuous and successful struggle of our Lord against the devil.

As time goes on the devil's opposition to Jesus becomes ever clearer; in the wilderness it is hidden and subtle; it is noticeable and violent in the case of possessed people; and radical and total during the Passion, the devil's "hour, and the power of darkness" (Lk 22:53). And Jesus' victory also becomes ever clearer, until he triumphs completely by rising from the dead.

The devil is called unclean, St John Chrysostom says, because of his impiety and withdrawal from God. In some ways he does recognize Christ's holiness, but this knowledge is not accompanied by charity. In addition to the historical fact of this cure, we can also see, in this possessed man, those sinners who must be converted to God and freed from the slavery to sin and the devil. They may have to struggle for a long time but victory will come: the Evil One is powerless against Christ (cf. the note on Mt 12:22–24).

1:27. The same authority that Jesus showed in his teaching (1:22) is now to be seen in his actions. His will is his command: he has no need of long prayers or incantations. Jesus' words and actions already have a divine power which provokes wonder and fear in those who hear and see him.

Jesus continues to impress people in this way (Mk 2:12; 5:20–42; 7:37; 15:39; Lk 19:48; Jn 7:46). Jesus of Nazareth is the long-awaited Saviour. He knows this himself and he lets it be known by his actions and by his words; according to the gospel accounts (Mk 1:38–39; 2:10–11; 4:39) there is complete continuity and consistency between what he says and what he does. As Vatican II teaches (*Dei Verbum*, 2), Revelation is realized by deeds and words intimately connected with each other: the words proclaim the deeds and clarify the mystery contained in them; the deeds confirm the teaching. In this way Jesus progressively reveals the mystery of his Person: first the people sense his exceptional authority; later on, the apostles, enlightened by God's grace, recognize the deepest source of this authority: "You are the Christ, the Son of the living God" (Mt 16:16).

Curing of Peter's mother-in-law

29And immediately he[e] left the synagogue, and entered the house
Mt 8:14–16 Lk 4:38–41 of Simon and Andrew, with James and John. 30Now Simon's
mother-in-law lay sick with a fever, and immediately they told
Acts 28:8 him of her. 31And he came and took her by the hand and lifted her
up, and the fever left her; and she served them.

Jesus cures many sick people

32That evening, at sundown, they brought to him all who were sick
Lk 4:41 or possessed with demons. 33And the whole city was gathered
Acts 16:17–18 together about the door. 34And he healed many who were sick

---

1:34. Demons possess a supernatural type of knowledge and therefore they recognize Jesus as the Messiah (Mk 1:24). Through the people they possess they are able to publish this fact. But our Lord, using his divine powers, orders them to be silent. On other occasions he also silences his disciples (Mk 8:30; 9:9), and he instructs people whom he has cured not to talk about their cure (Mk 1:4; 5:43; 7:36; 8:26). He may have acted in this way to educate the people away from a too human and political idea of the Messiah (cf. the note on Mt 9:30). Therefore, he first awakens their interest by performing miracles and gradually, through his preaching, gives them a clearer understanding of the kind of Messiah he is.

Some Fathers of the Church point out that Jesus does not want to accept, in support of the truth, the testimony of him who is the father of lies. Cf. the note on Jn 8:44.

1:35. Many passages of the New Testament make reference to Jesus praying. The evangelists point to him praying only on specially important occasions during his public ministry: Baptism (Lk 3:1), the choosing of the Twelve (Lk 6:12), the first multiplication of the loaves (Mk 6:46), the transfiguration (Lk 9:29), in the garden of Gethsemane prior to his passion (Mk 26:39), etc. St Mark, for his part, refers to Jesus' prayer at three solemn moments: at the beginning of his public ministry (1:35), in the middle of it (6:46), and at the end, in Gethsemane (14:32).

Jesus' prayer is prayer of perfect praise to the Father; it is prayer of petition for himself and for us; and it is also a model for his disciples. It is a prayer of perfect praise and thanksgiving because he is God's beloved Son in whom the Father is well pleased (cf. Mk 1:11). It is a prayer of petition because the first spontaneous movement of a soul who recognizes God as Father is to ask him for things. Jesus' prayer, as we see in very many Gospel passages (e.g., Jn 17:9ff) was a continuous petition to the Father for the work of redemption which he, Jesus, had to achieve through prayer and sacrifice (cf. the notes on Mk 14:32–42 and Mt 7:7–11).

Our Lord wants to give us an example of the kind of attitude a Christian should have: he should make a habit of addressing God as son to Father in the midst of and through his everyday activities—work, family life, personal relationships, apostolate—so as to give his

e. Other ancient authorities read *they*

with various diseases, and cast out many demons; and he would
not permit the demons to speak, because they knew him.*

Jesus goes to a lonely place to pray

[35]And in the morning, a great while before day, he rose and went Lk 4:42–44
out to a lonely place, and there he prayed. [36]And Simon and those
who were with him followed him, [37]and they found him and said
to him, "Every one is searching for you." [38]And he said to them,
"Let us go on to the next towns, that I may preach there also; for
that is why I came out." [39]And he went throughout all Galilee, Mt 4:23
preaching in their synagogues and casting out demons.

---

life a genuinely Christian meaning, for, as Jesus will point out later on, "apart from me you can do nothing" (Jn 15:5).

"You write: 'To pray is to talk with God. But about what?' About what? About him, about yourself: joys, sorrows, successes and failures, noble ambitions, daily worries, weaknesses! And acts of thanksgiving and petitions and love and reparation. In a word: to get to know him and to get to know yourself: 'to get acquainted!' " (St Josemaría Escrivá, *The Way*, 91; cf. the notes on Mt 6:5–6; 7:11; and 14:22–23).

1:38. Jesus tells us here that his mission is to preach, to spread the Good News. He was sent for this purpose (cf. also Lk 4:43). The apostles, in turn, were chosen by Jesus to be preachers (Mk 3:14; 16:15). Preaching is the method selected by God to effect salvation: "it pleased God through the folly of what we preach to save those who believe" (1 Cor 1:21). This is why St Paul says to Timothy: "Preach the word, be urgent in season and out of season, convince, rebuke, and exhort, be unfailing in patience and teaching" (2 Tim 4:1–2). Faith comes from hearing, we are told in Romans 10:17, where St Paul enthusiastically quotes Isaiah: "How beautiful are the feet of those who preach good news!" (Rom 10:15; Is 52:7).

The Church identifies preaching the Gospel as one of the main tasks of bishops and priests. St Pius X went so far as saying that "for a priest there is no duty more grave or obligation more binding (to dispel ignorance)" (*Acerbo nimis*). In this connexion Vatican II states: "The people of God is formed into one in the first place by the Word of the living God (cf. 1 Pet 1:23; Acts 6:7; 12:24), which is quite rightly sought from the mouths of priests (cf. 2 Cor 11:7). For since nobody can be saved who has not first believed (Mk 16:16), it is the first task of priests as co-workers of the bishops to preach the Gospel of God to all men (cf. 2 Cor 11:7). In this way they carry out the Lord's command 'Go into all the world and preach the Gospel to every creature' (Mk 16:15) (cf. Mal 2:7; 1 Tim 4:11–13; etc.) and thus set up and increase the people of God" (*Presbyterorum ordinis*, 4).

Jesus' preaching is not just limited to words: he backs up his teaching with his authority and with deeds. The Church also has been sent to preach salvation *and* to effect the work of salvation which it proclaims—a work done through the sacraments and especially through the renewal of the sacrifice of Calvary in the Mass (cf. Vatican II, *Sacrosanctum Concilium*, 6).

In the Church of God all of us should listen devoutly to the preaching of the

Curing of a leper

Mt 8:2–4 Lk 5:12–16 40And a leper came to him, beseeching him, and kneeling said to
him, "If you will, you can make me clean." 41Moved with pity, he
stretched out his hand and touched him, and said to him, "I will;
be clean." 42And immediately the leprosy left him, and he was
made clean. 43And he sternly charged him, and sent him away at
Lev 13:49; 14:2–32 once, 44and said to him, "See that you say nothing to any one; but
go, show yourself to the priest, and offer for your cleansing what
Moses commanded, for a proof to the people."[f] 45But he went out
and began to talk freely about it, and spread the news, so that
Jesus[g] could no longer openly enter a town, but was out in the
country; and people came to him from every quarter.

Curing of a paralyzed man

Mt 9:1–8 Lk 5:17–26 2 1And when he returned to Capernaum after some days, it was
reported that he was at home. 2And many were gathered
Mk 3:20 together, so that there was no longer room for them, not even

---

Gospel and we all should feel a responsibility to spread the Gospel by our words and actions. It is the responsibility of the hierarchy of the Church to teach the Gospel authentically—on the authority of Christ.

1:40–44. Leprosy was seen as a punishment from God (cf. Num 12:10–15). The disappearance of the disease was regarded as one of the blessings of the messianic times (Is 35:8; cf. Mt 11:5; Lk 7:22). Because leprosy was contagious the Law declared that lepers were impure and that they transmitted impurity to those who touched them and to places they entered. Therefore, they had to live apart (Num 5:2; 12:14ff) and to show that they were lepers by certain external signs. On the rite of purification, see the note on Mt 8:4.

The passage shows us the faithful and confident prayer of a man needing Jesus' help and begging him for it, confident that, if our Lord wishes, he can free him from the disease (cf. Mt 8:2). "This man prostrated himself on the ground, as a sign of humility and shame, to teach each of us to be ashamed of the stains of his life. But shame should not prevent us from confessing: the leper showed his wound and begged for healing. If you will, he says, you can make me clean: that is, he recognized that the Lord had the power to cure him" (St Bede, *In Marci Evangelium expositio*, in loc.).

On the discretion and prudence Jesus required regarding his person, see the note on Mk 1:34 and Mt 9:30.

2:4. Many houses had a terraced roof accessible by steps at the back. The same structure can be found even today.

2:5. Here Jesus emphasizes the connexion between faith and the forgiveness of sins. The boldness of the people who brought in the paralytic shows their faith in Christ, and this faith moves Jesus to forgive the man's sins. We should question how God views our faith: the faith of these people leads to the instantaneous physical and

f. Greek *to them* **g.** Greek *he*

about the door; and he was preaching the word to them. 3And they
came, bringing to him a paralytic carried by four men. 4And when
they could not get near him because of the crowd, they removed
the roof above him; and when they had made an opening, they let
down the pallet on which the paralytic lay. 5And when Jesus saw
their faith, he said to the paralytic, "My son, your sins are forgiven." 6Now some of the scribes were sitting there, questioning Is 43:25
in their hearts, 7"Why does this man speak thus? It is blasphemy!
Who can forgive sins but God alone?" 8And immediately Jesus, Lk 6:8; 9:47 Jn 16:19
perceiving in his spirit that they thus questioned within themselves, said to them, "Why do you question thus in your hearts?
9Which is easier, to say to the paralytic, 'Your sins are forgiven,'
or to say, 'Rise, take up your pallet and walk'? 10But that you may
know that the Son of man has authority on earth to forgive sins"—
he said to the paralytic—11"I say to you, rise, take up your pallet Jn 5:8
and go home." 12And he rose, and immediately took up the pallet
and went out before them all; so that they were all amazed and
glorified God, saying, "We never saw anything like this!"

---

spiritual curing of this man; we should notice also that one person's need can be helped by the merits of another.

In this man's physical paralysis St Jerome sees a type or figure of spiritual paralysis: the cripple was unable to return to God by his own efforts. Jesus, God and Man, cured him of both kinds of paralysis (cf. *Comm. on Mark*, in loc.). Cf. the notes on Mt 9:2–7.

Jesus' words to the paralytic—"Your sins are forgiven"—reflect the fact that his pardon involves a personal encounter with Christ; the same happens in the sacrament of Penance: "In faithfully observing the centuries-old practice of the sacrament of Penance—the practice of individual confession with a personal act of sorrow and an intention to amend and make satisfaction—the Church is defending the human soul's individual right: man's right to a more personal encounter with the crucified forgiving Christ, with Christ saying, through the minister of the sacrament of Reconciliation: 'Your sins are forgiven'; 'Go, and do not sin again' (Jn 8:11). As is evident, this is also a right on Christ's part with regard to every human being redeemed by him: his right to meet each one of us in that key moment in the soul's life constituted by the moment of conversion and forgiveness" (John Paul II, *Redemptor hominis*, 20).

2:7–12. Here we find a number of indicators of Jesus' divinity: he forgives sins, he can read the human heart and has the power to instantly cure physical illnesses. The scribes know that only God can forgive sins; this is why they take issue with our Lord's statement and call it blasphemous. They require a sign to prove the truth of what he says. And Jesus offers them a sign: thus just as no one can deny that the paralytic has been cured, so no one can reasonably deny that he has been forgiven his sins. Christ, God and man, exercised power to forgive sins and, in his infinite mercy, he chose to extend this power to his Church. Cf. the note on Mt 9:3–7.

The calling of Matthew

Mt 9:9–13 Lk 5:27–32 Jn 1:43

13He went out again beside the sea; and all the crowd gathered
about him, and he taught them. 14And as he passed on, he saw
Levi* the son of Alphaeus sitting at the tax office, and he said to
him, "Follow me." And he rose and followed him.
15And as he sat at table in his house, many tax collectors and
sinners were sitting with Jesus and his disciples; for there were
many who followed him. 16And the scribes of[h] the Pharisees,
when they saw that he was eating with sinners and tax collectors,
said to his disciples, "Why does he eat[i] with tax collectors and

---

2:14. St Mark and St Luke (5:27–32) both call him "Levi"; the First Gospel, on the other hand, calls him "Matthew" (Mt 9:9–13); but they are all referring to the same person. All three accounts describe the same event. Later on, St Mark and St Luke, when giving the list of apostles (Mk 3:13–19; Lk 6:12–16), include Matthew, not Levi. The Fathers identify Matthew with Levi. Besides it was quite common for Jews to have two names: Jacob-Israel, Simon-Peter, Saul-Paul; Joseph-Caiaphas; John-Mark ... Frequently, the name and surname were connected with some significant change in the life and mission of the person concerned. Did Jesus' saving intervention in this apostle's life lead to a change of name? The Gospel does not tell us.

Levi-Matthew, as a publican or tax collector (Mt 9:9–13), was sitting at the "tax office", a special place where one went to pay tribute. Publicans were tax-collectors appointed by the Romans. It was, therefore, an occupation hated and despised by the people; but it was also a much-coveted position because it was an easy way to become prosperous. Matthew leaves everything behind when Jesus calls him. He immediately responds to his vocation, because Jesus gives him the grace to accept his calling.

Jesus is the basis of our confidence in being able to change, provided we cooperate with his grace, no matter how unworthy our previous conduct may have been. And he is also the source of the confidence we need in order to be apostolic—helping others to be converted and to seek holiness of life. Because he is the Son of God he is able to raise up children of God even from stones (cf. Mt 3:9). Cf. the note on Mt 9:9.

2:17. The scribes and Pharisees reproach the disciples, and Jesus replies with a popular proverb: "Those who are well have no need of a physician, but those who are sick." He is the doctor of souls, come to cure sinners of their spiritual ailments.

Our Lord calls everyone, his redemptive mission extends to everyone; he affirms this on other occasions, using parables such as that of the marriage feast (Mt 22:1–14; Lk 14:16–24). How, then, can we explain the restriction he seems to place here by saying that he has not come to call the righteous? It is not really a restriction. Jesus uses the opportunity to reproach the scribes and Pharisees for their pride: they consider themselves just, and their reliance on their apparent virtue prevents them from hearing the call to conversion; they think

h. Other ancient authorities read *and* **i.** Other ancient authorities add *and drink*

sinners?" [17]And when Jesus heard it, he said to them, "Those who
are well have no need of a physician, but those who are sick; I
came not to call the righteous, but sinners."

A discussion on fasting

[18]Now John's disciples and the Pharisees were fasting; and people Mt 9:14–17
came and said to him, "Why do John's disciples and the disciples Lk 5:33–38
of the Pharisees fast, but your disciples do not fast?" [19]And Jesus Jn 3:29
said to them, "Can the wedding guests fast while the bridegroom

---

they can be saved by their own efforts (cf. Jn 9:41). This explains the proverb Jesus quotes; certainly his preaching makes it quite clear that "no one is good but God alone" (Mk 10:18) and that everyone must have recourse to the mercy and forgiveness of God in order to be saved. In other words, mankind is not divided into two—the just and the unjust. We are all sinners, as St Paul confirms: "all have sinned and fall short of the glory of God" (Rom 3:23). Precisely because of this, Christ came to call all of us; he justifies those who respond to his call.

Our Lord's words should also move us to pray humbly and confidently for people who seem to want to continue living in sin. As St Teresa beseeched God: "Ah, how hard a thing am I asking of thee, my true God! I ask thee to love one who loves thee not, to open to one who has not called upon thee, to give health to one who prefers to be sick and who even goes about in search of sickness. Thou sayest, my Lord, that thou comest to seek sinners; these, Lord, are the true sinners. Look not upon our blindness, my God, but upon all the blood that was shed for us by thy Son. Let thy mercy shine out amid such tremendous wickedness. Behold, Lord, we are the works of thy hands" (*Exclamations of the Soul to God*, 8).

The Fathers of the Church see this calling by Jesus as an invitation to repentance and penance. St John Chrysostom (*Hom. on St Matthew*, 30:3), for example, explains the phrase by putting these words in Jesus' mouth: "I am not come that they should continue sinners but that they should change and become better."

2:18–22. Using a particular case, Christ's reply tells us about the connexion between the Old and New Testaments. In the Old Testament the bridegroom has not yet arrived; in the New Testament he is present, in the person of Christ. With him began the messianic times, a new era distinct from the previous one. The Jewish fasts, therefore, together with their system of religious observances, must be seen as a way of preparing the people for the coming of the Messiah. Christ shows the difference between the spirit he has brought and that of the Judaism of his time. This new spirit will not be something extra, added on to the old; it will bring to life the perennial teachings contained in the older Revelation. The newness of the Gospel—just like new wine—cannot fit within the moulds of the Old Law.

But this passage says more: to receive Christ's new teaching people must inwardly renew themselves and throw off the strait-jacket of old routines. Cf. the note on Mt 9:14–17.

2:19–20. Jesus describes himself as the bridegroom (cf. also Lk 12:35–36; Mt

is with them? As long as they have the bridegroom with them,
Jn 16:20 they cannot fast. 20 The days will come, when the bridegroom is
taken away from them, and then they will fast in that day. 21 No
one sews a piece of unshrunk cloth on an old garment; if he does,
the patch tears away from it, the new from the old, and a worse
tear is made. 22 And no one puts new wine into old wineskins; if he
does, the wine will burst the skins, and the wine is lost, and so are
the skins; but new wine is for fresh skins.”[j]

The law of the sabbath

Mt 12:1–8 23 One sabbath he was going through the grainfields; and as they
Lk 6:1–5 made their way his disciples began to pluck ears of grain. 24 And
the Pharisees said to him, “Look, why are they doing what is not
lawful on the sabbath?” 25 And he said to them, “Have you never
read what David did, when he was in need and hungry, he and

25:1–13; Jn 3:29), thereby fulfilling what the prophets had said about the relationship between God and his people (cf. Hos 2:18–22; Is 54:5ff). The apostles are the guests at the wedding, invited to share in the wedding feast with the bridegroom, in the joy of the Kingdom of heaven (cf. Mt 22:1–14).

In v. 20 Jesus announces that the bridegroom will be taken away from them: this is the first reference he makes to his passion and death (cf. Mk 8:31; Jn 2:19; 3:14). The vision of joy and sorrow we see here epitomizes our human condition during our sojourn on earth.

2:24. Cf. the note on Mt 12:2.

2:26–27. The bread of the Presence consisted of twelve loaves or cakes placed each morning on the table in the sanctuary, as homage to the Lord from the twelve tribes of Israel (cf. Lev 24:5–9). The loaves withdrawn to make room for the fresh ones were reserved to the priests.

Abiathar’s action anticipates what Christ teaches here. Already in the Old Testament God had established a hierarchy in the precepts of the Law so that the lesser ones yielded to the main ones.

This explains why a ceremonial precept (such as the one we are discussing) should yield before a precept of the natural law. Similarly, the commandment to keep the sabbath does not come before the duty to seek basic subsistence. Vatican II uses this passage of the Gospel to underline the value of the human person over and above economic and social development: “The social order and its development must constantly yield to the good of the person, since the order of things must be subordinate to the order of persons and not the other way around, as the Lord suggested when he said that the sabbath was made for man and not man for the sabbath. The social order requires constant improvement: it must be founded in truth, built on justice, and enlivened by love” (*Gaudium et spes*, 26).

Finally in this passage Christ teaches God’s purpose in instituting the sabbath: God established it for man’s good, to

j. Other ancient authorities omit *but new wine is for fresh skins*

those who were with him: [26]how he entered the house of God, 1 Sam 21:6
when Abiathar was high priest, and ate the bread of the Presence, Lev 24:5–9
which it is not lawful for any but the priests to eat, and also gave
it to those who were with him?" [27]And he said to them, "The sab- Deut 5:14
bath was made for man, not man for the sabbath; [28]so the Son of
man is lord even of the sabbath."

Curing of the man with a withered hand

3 [1]Again he entered the synagogue, and a man was there who Mt 12:9–14
had a withered hand. [2]And they watched him, to see whether Lk 6:6–11
he would heal him on the sabbath, so that they might accuse him.
[3]And he said to the man who had the withered hand, "Come
here." [4]And he said to them, "Is it lawful on the sabbath to do
good or to do harm, to save life or to kill?" But they were silent.
[5]And he looked around at them with anger, grieved at their hard- Lk 14:4

---

help him rest and devote himself to divine worship in joy and peace. The Pharisees, through their interpretation of the Law, had turned this day into a source of anguish and scruple due to all the various prescriptions and prohibitions they introduced.

By proclaiming himself "lord of the sabbath", Jesus affirms his divinity and his universal authority. Because he is lord he has the power to establish other laws, as Yahweh had in the Old Testament.

2:28. The sabbath had been established not only for man's rest but also to allow him to give glory to God: that is the correct meaning of the expression "the sabbath was made for man." Jesus has every right to say he is lord of the sabbath, because he is God. Christ restores to the weekly day of rest its full, religious meaning: it is not just a matter of fulfilling a number of legal precepts or of concern for physical well-being: the sabbath belongs to God; it is one way, suited to human nature, of rendering glory and honour to the Almighty. The Church, from the time of the apostles onwards, transferred the observance of this precept to the following day, Sunday—the Lord's day—in celebration of the resurrection of Christ.

"Son of man": the origin of the messianic meaning of this expression is to be found particularly in the prophecy in Dan 7:13ff, where Daniel, in a prophetic vision, contemplates "one like a son of man" coming down on the clouds of heaven, who even goes right up to God's throne and is given dominion and glory and royal power over all peoples and nations. This expression appears sixty-nine times in the Synoptic Gospels; Jesus prefers it to other ways of describing the Messiah—such as Son of David, Messiah, etc.—thereby avoiding the nationalistic overtones those expressions had in Jewish minds at the time (cf. "Introduction to the Gospel according to St Mark", pp. 221–222 above).

3:5. The evangelists refer a number of times to the way Jesus looks at people (e.g. at the young man: Mk 10:21; at St Peter: Lk 22:61; etc.). This is the only time we are told he showed indignation—provoked by the hypocrisy shown in v. 2.

ness of heart, and said to the man, "Stretch out your hand." He
Mt 22:16 stretched it out, and his hand was restored. 6The Pharisees went
Mk 12:13 out, and immediately held counsel with the Herodians against
him, how to destroy him.

Cures beside the Sea of Galilee

Mt 12:15–16 Lk 6:17–19 7Jesus withdrew with his disciples to the sea, and a great multitude
Mt 4:25 from Galilee followed; also from Judea 8and Jerusalem and
Idumea and from beyond the Jordan and from about Tyre and
Sidon a great multitude, hearing all that he did, came to him. 9And
he told his disciples to have a boat ready for him because of the

---

3:6. The Pharisees were the spiritual leaders of Judaism; the Herodians were those who supported the regime of Herod, benefitting politically and financially thereby. The two were completely opposed to one another and avoided each other's company, yet they combined forces against Jesus.

The Pharisees wanted to see the last of him because they considered him a dangerous innovator. The most recent occasion may have been when he pardoned sins (Mk 2:1ff) and interpreted with full authority the law of the sabbath (Mk 3:2); they also want to get rid of him because they consider that he lowered their own prestige in the eyes of the people by the way he cured the man with the withered hand. The Herodians, for their part, despised the supernatural and eschatological tone of Christ's message, since they looked forward to a purely political and temporal Messiah.

3:10. During our Lord's public life people were constantly crowding round him to be cured (cf. Lk 6:19; 8:45; etc.). As in the case of many other cures, St Mark gives us a graphic account of what Jesus did to these people (cf. Mk 1:31, 41; 7:31–37; 8:22–26; Jn 9:1–7, 11, 15). By working these cures our Lord shows that he is both God and Man: he cures by virtue of his divine power and using his human nature. In other words, only in the Word of God become man is the work of our Redemption effected, and the instrument God used to save us was the human nature of Jesus—his body and soul—in the unity of the person of the Word (cf. Vatican II, *Sacrosanctum Concilium*, 5).

This crowding round Jesus is repeated by Christians of all times: the holy human nature of our Lord is our only route to salvation; it is the essential means we must use to unite ourselves to God. Thus, we can today approach our Lord by means of the sacraments, especially and pre-eminently the Eucharist. And through the sacraments there flows to us, from God, through the human nature of the Word, a strength which cures those who receive the sacraments with faith (cf. St Thomas Aquinas, *Summa theologiae*, 3, 62, 5).

3:13. "He called to him those whom he desired": God wants to show us that calling, vocation, is an initiative of God. This is particularly true in the case of the apostles, which is why Jesus could tell them, later on, that "you did not choose me, but I chose you" (Jn 15:16). Those who will have power and authority in the Church will not obtain this because first they offer their services and then Jesus accepts their offering: on the contrary,

crowd, lest they should crush him; [10]for he had healed many, so Mt 15:30
that all who had diseases pressed upon him to touch him. [11]And Lk 4:41
whenever the unclean spirits beheld him, they fell down before
him and cried out, "You are the Son of God." [12]And he strictly Mk 1:31
ordered them not to make him known.

Jesus chooses twelve apostles

[13]And he went up into the hills, and called to him those whom he Mt 10:1–4
desired; and they came to him. [14]And he appointed twelve,[k] to be Lk 6:12–16
with him, and to be sent out to preach [15]and have authority to cast

"not through their own initiative and preparation, but rather by virtue of divine grace, would they be called to the apostolate" (St Bede, *In Marci Evangelium expositio*, in loc.).

3:14–19. The Twelve chosen by Jesus (cf. 3:14) receive a specific vocation to be "people sent out", which is what the word "apostles" means. Jesus chooses them for a mission which he will give them later (6:6–13) and to enable them to perform this mission he gives them part of his power. The fact that he chooses *twelve* is very significant. This is the same number as the twelve patriarchs of Israel, and the apostles represent the new people of God, the Church founded by Christ. Jesus sought in this way to emphasize the continuity that exists between the Old and New Testaments. The Twelve are the pillars on which Christ builds his Church (cf. Gal 2:9); their mission to make disciples of the Lord (to teach) all nations, sanctifying and governing the believers (Mt 28:16–20; Mk 16:15; Lk 24:45–48; Jn 20:21–23).

The very designation of them as the Twelve shows that they form a well-defined and complete group; therefore, after Judas' death Matthias is elected to take his place (Acts 1:15–26).

3:14. The Second Vatican Council sees in this text the establishment of the College of apostles: "The Lord Jesus, having prayed at length to the Father, called to himself those whom he willed and appointed twelve to be with him, whom he might send to preach the Kingdom of God (cf. Mk 3:13–19; Mt 10:1–42). These apostles (cf. Lk 6:13) he constituted in the form of a college or permanent assembly, at the head of which he placed Peter, chosen from amongst them" (cf. Jn 21:15–17). "That divine mission, which was committed by Christ to the apostles, is destined to last until the end of the world (cf. Mt 28:20), since the Gospel, which they were charged to hand on, is, for the Church, the principle of all its life for all time. For that very reason the apostles were careful to appoint successors in this hierarchically constituted society" (*Lumen gentium*, 19–20). Therefore, the Pope and the bishops, who succeed the College of the Twelve, are also called by our Lord to be always with Jesus and to preach the Gospel, aided by priests. Life in union with Christ and apostolic zeal must be very closely linked together; in other words, effectiveness in apostolate always depends on union with our Lord, on continuous prayer and on sacramental life: "Apostolic zeal is a divine craziness I want you to have. Its

k. Other ancient authorities add *whom also he named apostles*

Jn 1:42 out demons: 16Simon whom he surnamed Peter; 17James the son of
Lk 9:54 Zebedee and John the brother of James, whom he surnamed
Boanerges, that is, sons of thunder; 18Andrew, and Philip, and
Bartholomew, and Matthew, and Thomas, and James the son of
Alphaeus, and Thaddaeus, and Simon the Cananaean, 19and Judas
Iscariot, who betrayed him.

Jesus' relatives are concerned about him

Mk 6:31 Then he went home; 20and the crowd came together again, so that
Jn 7:20; 8:48, 52; 10:20 they could not even eat. 21And when his friends heard it, they went
out to seize him, for they said, "He is beside himself."

Allegations of the scribes. Sin against the Holy Spirit

22And the scribes who came down from Jerusalem said, "He is
Mt 12:24–32 Lk 11:15–22; 12:10 possessed by Beelzebul, and by the prince of demons he casts out
the demons." 23And he called them to him, and said to them in
parables, "How can Satan cast out Satan? 24If a kingdom is
divided against itself, that kingdom cannot stand. 25And if a house

---

symptoms are: hunger to know the Master; constant concern for souls; perseverance that nothing can shake" (St Josemaría Escrivá, *The Way*, 934).

3:16. At this point, before the word "Simon", the sentence "He formed the group of the twelve" occurs in many manuscripts (it is similar to "he appointed twelve" in v. 14), but it is not included in the New Vulgate. The repetition of the same expression and the article in "*the* twelve" show the importance of the establishment of the apostolic college.

3:20–21. Some of his relatives, whose outlook was too human, regarded Jesus' total commitment to apostolate as excessive: the only explanation, they thought, was that he was out of his mind. On reading these words of the Gospel, we cannot help being moved, realizing what Jesus did for love of us: people even thought him mad. Many saints, following Christ's example, have been taken for madmen—but they were mad with love, mad with love for Jesus Christ.

3:22–23. Even Jesus' miracles were misunderstood by these scribes, who accuse him of being a tool of the prince of devils, Beelzebul. This name may be connected with Beelzebub (which spelling is given in some codexes), the name of a god of the Philistine city of Eqron (Accaron), which means "god of the flies". But it is more likely that the prince of devils is called Beelzebul, which means "god of excrement": "excrement" is the word the Jews used to describe pagan sacrifices. Whether Beelzebub or Beelzebul, in the last analysis it refers to him to whom these sacrifices were offered, the devil (1 Cor 10:20). He is the same mysterious but real person whom Jesus calls Satan, which means "the enemy", whose dominion over the world Christ has come to wrest from him (1 Cor 15:24–28; Col 1:13f) in an unceasing struggle (Mt 4:1–10; Jn 16:11). These names show us that the devil really exists: he is a real person who has at his beck and call others of his kind (Mk 5:9).

is divided against itself, that house will not be able to stand. 26And
if Satan has risen up against himself and is divided, he cannot
stand, but is coming to an end. 27But no one can enter a strong
man's house and plunder his goods, unless he first binds the
strong man; then indeed he may plunder his house.
28"Truly, I say to you, all sins will be forgiven the sons of men, Lk 12:10
and whatever blasphemies they utter; 29but whoever blasphemes 1 Jn 5:16
against the Holy Spirit never has forgiveness, but is guilty of an
eternal sin"—30for they had said, "He has an unclean spirit." Mk 3:22

The true kinsmen of Jesus

31And his mother and his brethren* came; and standing outside
they went to him and called him. 32And a crowd was sitting about Mt 12:46–50
him: and they said to him, "Your mother and your brethren[l] are Lk 8:19–21
outside, asking for you." 33And he replied, "Who are my mother
and my brethren?" 34And looking around on those who sat about
him, he said, "Here are my mother and my brethren! 35Whoever
does the will of God is my brother, and sister, and mother."

3:24–27. Our Lord invites the Pharisees, who are blind and obstinate, to think along these lines: if someone expels the devil this means that he is stronger than the devil: once more we are exhorted to recognize in Jesus the God of strength, the God who uses his power to free man from enslavement to the devil. Satan's dominion has come to an end: the prince of this world is about to be cast out. Jesus' victory over the power of darkness, which is completed by his death and resurrection, shows that the light has already entered the world, as our Lord himself told us: "Now is the judgment of this world, now shall the ruler of this world be cast out; and I, when I am lifted up from the earth, will draw all men to myself" (Jn 12:31–32).

3:28–30. Jesus has just worked a miracle but the scribes refuse to recognize it "for they had said 'He has an unclean spirit'" (v. 30). They do not want to admit that God is the author of the miracle. In this attitude lies the special gravity of blasphemy against the Holy Spirit—attributing to the prince of evil, to Satan, the good works performed by God himself. Anyone acting in this way will become like the sick person who has so lost confidence in the doctor that he rejects him as if an enemy and regards as poison the medicine that can save his life. That is why our Lord says that he who blasphemes against the Holy Spirit will not be forgiven: not because God cannot forgive all sins, but because that person, in his blindness towards God, rejects Jesus Christ, his teaching and his miracles, and despises the graces of the Holy Spirit as if they were designed to trap him (cf. St Pius V, *Catechism*, 2, 5, 19; St Thomas Aquinas, *Summa theologiae*, 2–2, 14, 3). Cf. the note on Mt 12:31–32.

3:31–35. In Aramaic, the language used by the Jews, the word "brethren" is a broad term indicating kinship: nephews,

l. Other ancient authorities add *and your sisters*

3. PARABLES OF THE KINGDOM OF GOD

Parable of the sower. The meaning of parables

Mt 13:1–23 Lk 8:4–15

4 [1]Again he began to teach beside the sea. And a very large
crowd gathered about him, so that he got into a boat and sat in
it on the sea; and the whole crowd was beside the sea on the land.
[2]And he taught them many things in parables, and in his teachings
he said to them: [3]"Listen! A sower went out to sow. [4]And as he
sowed, some seed fell along the path, and the birds came and
devoured it. [5]Other seed fell on rocky ground, where it had not
much soil, and immediately it sprang up, since it had no depth of

---

first cousins and relatives in general are called "brethren" (for further explanation see the note on Mk 6:1–3). "Jesus did not say this to disown his mother, but to show that she is worthy of honour not only on account of having given birth to Jesus, but also because she has all the virtues" (Theophylact, *Enarratio in Evangelium Marci*, in loc.).

Therefore, the Church reminds us that the Blessed Virgin "in the course of her Son's preaching received the words whereby, in extolling a kingdom beyond the concerns and ties of flesh and blood, he declared blessed those who heard and kept the word of God as she was faithfully doing" (Vatican II, *Lumen gentium*, 58).

Our Lord, then, is also telling us that if we follow him we will share his life more intimately than if we were a member of his family. St Thomas explains this by saying that Christ "had an eternal generation and a generation in time, and gave preference to the former. Those who do the will of the Father reach him by heavenly generation [...]. Everyone who does the will of the Father, that is to say, who obeys him, is a brother or sister of Christ, because he is like him who fulfilled the will of his Father. But he who not only obeys but converts others, begets Christ in them, and thus becomes like the Mother of Christ" (*Comm. on St Matthew*, 12:49–50).

4:1–34. Parables are a special method of preaching used by Jesus. By means of them he gradually unfolds before his listeners the mysteries of the Kingdom of God. Cf. the note on Mt 13:3. Chapter 4 of St Mark, although much shorter, is the equivalent of chapter 13 of St Matthew and chapter 8:4–18 of St Luke, which is the shortest synoptic account of the Kingdom parables.

4:1–9. The ordinary Christian, who seeks holiness in his ordinary work, must be moved to find how often our Lord uses in his parables examples taken from work situations: "In his parables on the Kingdom of God, Jesus Christ constantly refers to human work: that of the shepherd (e.g. Jn 10:1–6), the farmer (cf. Mk 12:1–12), the doctor (cf. Lk 4:32), the sower (cf. Mk 4:1–9), the householder (cf. Mt 13:52), the servant (cf. Mt 24:25; Lk 12:42–48), the steward (cf. Lk 16:1–8), the fisherman (cf. Mt 13:47–50), the merchant (cf. Mt 13:45–46), the labourer (cf. Mt 20:1–16). He also speaks of the various forms of women's work (cf. Mt 13:33; Lk 15:8–9). He compares the apostolate to the manual work of harvesters (cf. Mt 9:37; Jn 4:35–38) or fish-

soil; 6and when the sun rose it was scorched, and since it had no
root it withered away. 7Other seed fell among thorns and the
thorns grew up and choked it, and it yielded no grain. 8And other
seeds fell into good soil and brought forth grain, growing up and
increasing and yielding thirtyfold and sixtyfold and a hundredfold." 9And he said, "He who has ears to hear, let him hear."
10And when he was alone, those who were about him with the
twelve asked him concerning the parables. 11And he said to them, 1 Cor 5:12
"To you has been given the secret of the kingdom of God, but for
those outside everything is in parables; 12so that* they may indeed Is 6:9–10
see but not perceive, and may indeed hear but not understand; lest Jn 12:40 Acts 28:26

---

ermen (cf. Mt 4:19). He refers to the work of scholars too (cf. Mt 13:52)" (John Paul II, *Laborem exercens*, 26).

4:3–9. With the parable of the sower Jesus wants to move his listeners to open their hearts generously to the word of God and put it into practice (cf. Lk 11:28). God expects the same docility also from each of us: "It is a vivid scene. The divine sower is also sowing his seed today. The work of salvation is still going on, and our Lord wants us to share that work. He wants Christians to open to his love all the paths of the earth. He invites us to spread the divine message, by both teaching and example, to the farthest corners of the earth [...]. If we look around, if we take a look at the world, which we love because it is God's handiwork, we will find that the parable holds true. The word of Jesus Christ is fruitful, it stirs many souls to dedication and fidelity. The life and conduct of those who serve God have changed history. Even many of those who do not know our Lord are motivated, perhaps unconsciously, by ideals which derive from Christianity.

"We can also see that some of the seed falls on barren ground or among thorns and thistles; some hearts close themselves to the light of faith. Ideals of peace, reconciliation and brotherhood are widely accepted and proclaimed, but all too often the facts belie them. Some people are futilely bent on smothering God's voice. To drown it out they use brute force or a method which is more subtle but perhaps more cruel because it drugs the spirit—indifference" (St J. Escrivá, *Christ Is Passing By*, 150).

The parable of the sower also shows us the wonderful economy of divine Providence, which distributes various graces among men but gives each person enough to reach salvation: "There was then in the eternal providence an incomparable privilege for the queen of queens, Mother of fair Love, and most singularly all perfect. There were also for certain others some special favours. But after this the sovereign goodness poured an abundance of graces and benedictions over the whole race of mankind and upon the angels; [...] every one received his portion as of seed which falls not only upon the good ground but upon the highway, amongst thorns, and upon rocks, that all might be inexcusable before the Redeemer, if they employ not this most abundant redemption for their salvation" (St Francis de Sales, *Treatise on the Love of God*, book 2, chap. 7).

4:11–12. The Kingdom of God is a mystery. If the Twelve know it, it is simply because the mercy of God has revealed it to them, not because they are better able,

they should turn again, and be forgiven." [13]And he said to them,
"Do you not understand this parable? How then will you understand all the parables? [14]The sower sows the word. [15]And these are
the ones along the path, where the word is sown; when they hear,
Satan immediately comes and takes away the word which is sown
in them. [16]And these in like manner are the ones sown upon rocky
ground, who, when they hear the word, immediately receive it
with joy; [17]and they have no root in themselves, but endure for a
while; then, when tribulation or persecution arises on account of
the word, immediately they fall away.[m] [18]And others are the ones
Mk 10:23–24 sown among thorns; they are those who hear the word, [19]but the
cares of the world, and the delight in riches, and the desire for
other things, enter in and choke the word, and it proves unfruitful.
[20]But those that were sown upon the good soil are the ones who
hear the word and accept it and bear fruit, thirtyfold and sixtyfold
and a hundredfold."

---

by themselves, to understand the meaning of the parables.

Jesus' use of parables had many advantages: firstly, because typically the human mind grasps concepts by first working on sense-information: in his teaching Christ often clothes spiritual things in corporal images. Secondly, Holy Scripture is written for everyone, as St Paul says: "I am under obligation ... both to the wise and to the foolish" (Rom 1:4): this meant it made sense for him to put forward even the deepest truths by using comparisons—so that people could more easily grasp what he meant (cf. St Thomas Aquinas, *Summa theologiae*, 1, 1, 9).

The disciples are distinguished here from "those outside" (v. 11)—an expression which Jews applied to Gentiles, and which Jesus here applies to those Jews who do not want to understand the signs which he performs (cf. Lk 12:41).

Later on, our Lord does give his disciples even more exact instruction about the content of the parables. But, since the Jews do not want to accept the signs he performs, in them are fulfilled the words of the prophet Isaiah (6:9–10). The parables, which were an expression of our Lord's mercy, were the occasion for his condemning incredulous Jews, whose sins he cannot forgive because they do not wish to see or listen or be converted.

4:17. "They fall away": they are "scandalized": the word "scandal" originally refers to a stone or obstacle which could easily cause one to trip. Here, in the language of morality, it is used to refer to anything which leads others to commit sin (cf. the note on Mt 18:1–7). The word is also applied in a broader sense to anything which could be an occasion of sin—for example, sorrow and tribulation. In this passage, falling away or being scandalized means being demoralized, stumbling, giving in and falling. If a person maliciously professes to be shocked by a good action, he is guilty of "pharisaical" scandal: that is what St Paul means when he says that the cross of

m. Or *stumble*

Parables of the lamp and the measure

21And he said to them, "Is a lamp brought in to be put under a Lk 8:16–18 Mt 5:15
bushel, or under a bed, and not on a stand? 22For there is nothing Mt 10:26
hid, except to be made manifest; nor is anything secret, except to Lk 8:17
come to light. 23If any man has ears to hear, let him hear." 24And Mt 7:2
he said to them, "Take heed what you hear; the measure you give Lk 6:38
will be the measure you get, and still more will be given you.
25For to him who has will more be given; and from him who has Mt 13:12
not, even what he has will be taken away." Lk 8:18

Parables of the seed and of the mustard seed

26And he said, "The kingdom of God is as if a man should scatter
seed upon the ground, 27and should sleep and rise night and day, Jas 5:7
and the seed should sprout and grow, he knows not how. 28The
earth produces of itself, first the blade, then the ear, then the full
grain in the ear. 29But when the grain is ripe, at once he puts in the Joel 3:13
sickle, because the harvest has come." Rev 14:15

Christ was a stumbling-block to Jews, who refused to grasp that the saving plans of God were to be effected through pain and sacrifice (cf. 1 Cor 1:23; cf. also Mk 14:27; Mt 16:23).

4:21. A "bushel" was a container used for measuring cereals and vegetables. It held a little over eight litres (two gallons).

4:22. This parable contains a double teaching. Firstly, it says that Christ's doctrine should not be kept hidden; rather, it must be preached throughout the whole world. We find the same idea elsewhere in the Gospels: "What you hear whispered, proclaim it upon the housetops" (Mt 10:27); "Go into all the world and preach the Gospel to the whole of creation …" (Mk 16:15). The other teaching is that the Kingdom which Christ proclaims has such ability to penetrate all hearts that, at the end of time, when Jesus comes again, not a single human action, in favour or against Christ, will not become public and manifest (cf. Mt 25:31–46).

4:24–25. Our Lord never gets tired of asking the apostles, the seeds which will produce the Church, to listen carefully to the teaching he is giving: they are receiving a treasure for which they will be held to account. "To him who has will more be given …": he who responds to grace will be given more grace and will yield more and more fruit; but he who does not will become more and more impoverished (cf. Mt 25:14–30). Therefore, there is no limit to the development of the theological virtues: "If you say 'Enough,' you are already dead" (St Augustine, *Sermons*, 51). A soul who wants to make progress in the interior life will pray along these lines: "Lord, may I have due measure in everything, except in Love" (St Josemaría Escrivá, *The Way*, 427).

4:26–29. Farmers spare no effort to prepare the ground for the sowing; but once the grain is sown there is nothing more they can do until the harvest; the grain develops by itself. Our Lord uses this comparison to describe the inner strength that causes the Kingdom of God on earth

Mt 13:31–32, 34 Lk 13:18–19 [30]And he said, "With what can we compare the kingdom of
God, or what parable shall we use for it? [31]It is like a grain of
mustard seed, which, when sown upon the ground, is the smallest
Ezek 17:23; 31:6 of all the seeds on earth; [32]yet when it is sown it grows up and
becomes the greatest of all shrubs, and puts forth large branches,
so that the birds of the air can make nests in its shade."

The end of the Parables Discourse

[33]With many such parables he spoke the word to them, as they
were able to hear it; [34]he did not speak to them without a parable,
but privately to his own disciples he explained everything.

4. MIRACLES AND ACTIVITY IN GALILEE

The calming of the storm

Mt 8:18, 23–27 Lk 8:22–25 [35]On that day, when evening had come, he said to them, "Let us
go across to the other side." [36]And leaving the crowd, they took

---

to grow until the day of harvest (cf. Joel 3:13 and Rev 14:15), that is, the day of the Last Judgment.

Jesus is telling his disciples about the Church: the preaching of the Gospel, the generously sown seed, will unfailingly yield its fruit, independently of who sows or who reaps: it is God who gives the growth (cf. 1 Cor 3:5–9). It will all happen "he knows not how", without men being fully aware of it.

The Kingdom of God also refers to the action of grace in each soul: God silently works a transformation in us, whether we sleep or watch, causing resolutions to take shape in our soul—resolutions to be faithful, to surrender ourselves, to respond to grace—until we reach "mature manhood" (cf. Eph 4:13). Even though it is necessary for man to make this effort the real initiative lies with God, "because it is the Holy Spirit who, with his inspirations, gives a supernatural tone to our thoughts, desires and actions. It is he who leads us to receive Christ's teaching and to assimilate it in a profound way. It is he who gives us the light by which we perceive our personal calling and the strength to carry out all that God expects of us. If we are docile to the Holy Spirit, the image of Christ will be found more and more fully in us, and we will be brought closer every day to God the Father. 'For whoever are led by the Spirit of God, they are the children of God' (Rom 8:14)" (St Josemaría Escrivá, *Christ Is Passing By*, 135).

4:30–32. The main meaning of this parable has to do with the contrast between the great and the small. The seed of the Kingdom of God on earth is something very tiny to begin with (Lk 12:32; Acts 1:15); but it will grow to be a big tree. Thus we see how the small initial group of disciples grows in the early years of the Church (cf. Acts 2:47; 6:7; 12:24), and spreads down the centuries and becomes a great multitude "which no man could number" (Rev 7:9).

This mysterious growth which our Lord refers to also occurs in each soul:

him with them just as he was, in the boat. And other boats were
with him. [37]And a great storm of wind arose, and the waves beat
into the boat, so that the boat was already filling. [38]But he was in
the stern, asleep on the cushion; and they woke him and said to
him, "Teacher, do you not care if we perish?" [39]And he awoke and Ps 89:9;
rebuked the wind, and said to the sea, "Peace! Be still!" And the 107:23–32
wind ceased, and there was a great calm. [40]He said to them, "Why
are you afraid? Have you no faith?" [41]And they were filled with Mk 1:27
awe, and said to one another, "Who then is this, that even wind
and sea obey him?"

The Gerasene demoniac

5 [1]They came to the other side of the sea, to the country of the Mt 8:28–34
Gerasenes.[n] [2]And when he had come out of the boat, there Lk 8:26–40
met him out of the tombs a man with an unclean spirit, [3]who lived
among the tombs; and no one could bind him any more, even with
a chain; [4]for he had often been bound with fetters and chains, but
the chains he wrenched apart, and the fetters he broke in pieces;

"the Kingdom of God is in the midst of you" (Lk 17:21); we can see a prediction of this in the words of Psalm 92:12: "The righteous grow like a cedar in Lebanon." To allow the mercy of God to exalt us, to make us grow, we must make ourselves small, humble (Ezek 17:22–24; Lk 18:9–14).

4:35–41. The episode of the calming of the storm, the memory of which must often have helped the apostles regain their serenity in the midst of struggles and difficulties, also helps us never lose the supernatural way of looking at things: a Christian's life is like a ship: "As a vessel on the sea is exposed to a thousand dangers—pirates, quicksands, hidden rocks, tempests—so man in this life, is encompassed with perils, arising from the temptations of hell, from the occasions of sin, from the scandals or bad counsels of men, from human respect, and, above all from the passions of corrupt nature […]. This should not cause him to lose confidence. Rather […] when you find yourself assaulted by a violent passion […] take whatever steps you can to avoid the occasions [of sin] and place your reliance on God […]: when the tempest is violent, the pilot never takes his eyes from the light which guides him to port. In like manner, we should keep our eyes always turned to God, who alone can deliver us from the many dangers to which we are exposed" (St Augustine, *Sermons*, 51; for the fourth Sunday after Epiphany).

5:1–20. The inhabitants of Gerasa were mostly pagans, as one can gather from the fact that there was such a huge herd of swine there (which must have belonged to a number of different people). Jews were forbidden to raise pigs or eat pork (Lev 11:7).

This miracle emphasizes, once more, the existence of the devil and his influ-

n. Other ancient authorities read *Gergesenes*; some, *Gadarenes*

and no one had the strength to subdue him. 5Night and day among
the tombs and on the mountains he was always crying out, and
bruising himself with stones. 6And when he saw Jesus from afar,
Mk 1:24 Jas 2:19 he ran and worshipped him; 7and crying out with a loud voice, he
said, "What have you to do with me, Jesus, Son of the Most High
God? I adjure you by God, do not torment me." 8For he had said
to him, "Come out of the man, you unclean spirit!" 9And Jesus[o]
asked him, "What is your name?" He replied, "My name is
Legion; for we are many." 10And he begged him eagerly not to
send them out of the country. 11Now a great herd of swine was
feeding there on the hillside; 12and they begged him, "Send us to
the swine, let us enter them." 13So he gave them leave. And the
unclean spirits came out, and entered the swine; and the herd,
numbering about two thousand, rushed down the steep bank into
the sea, and were drowned in the sea.

14The herdsmen fled, and told it in the city and the country.
And people came to see what it was that had happened. 15And
they came to Jesus, and saw the demoniac sitting there, clothed
and in his right mind, the man who had had the legion; and they

---

ence over men's lives: if God permits it, the devil can harm not only humans but also animals. When Christ allows the demons to enter the swine, the malice of the demons becomes obvious: they are tormented at not being able to do men harm and therefore they ask Christ to let them, at least, inflict themselves on animals. This he does, in order to show that they would have the same effect on men as they have on these swine, if God did not prevent them.

Clearly it was not Jesus' intention to punish the owners of the swine by the loss of the herd: since they were pagans they were not subject to the precepts of the Jewish law. Rather, the death of the swine is visible proof that the demon has gone out of the possessed man.

Jesus permitted the loss of some material goods because these were of infinitely less value than the spiritual good involved in the cure of the possessed man. Cf. the note on Mt 8:28–34.

5:15–20. Notice the different attitudes to Jesus Christ: the Gerasenes beg him to go away; the man freed from the devil wants to stay with him and follow him. The inhabitants of Gerasa have had our Lord near them, they have seen his divine powers, but they are very self-centred: all they can think about is the material damage they have suffered through the loss of the herd; they do not realize the marvel Jesus has worked. Christ has invited them and offered them his grace but they do not respond: they reject him. The man who has been cured wants to follow Jesus with the rest of his disciples but our Lord refuses; instead he gives him a task which shows Christ's unlimited compassion for all men, even for those who reject him: the man is to stay in Gerasa and proclaim to the whole neighbourhood what the Lord has done for him.

o. Greek *he*

were afraid. [16]And those who had seen it told what had happened
to the demoniac and to the swine. [17]And they began to beg Jesus[p]
to depart from their neighbourhood. [18]And as he was getting into
the boat, the man who had been possessed with demons begged
him that he might be with him. [19]But he refused, and said to him,
"Go home to your friends, and tell them how much the Lord has
done for you, and how he has had mercy on you." [20]And he went Mk 7:31
away and began to proclaim in the Decapolis how much Jesus had
done for him; and all men marvelled.

Jairus' daughter is restored to life. Curing of the woman with a haemorrhage

[21]And when Jesus had crossed again in the boat to the other side, Mt 9:18–26
a great crowd gathered about him; and he was beside the sea. Lk 8:41–56
[22]Then came one of the rulers of the synagogue, Jairus by name,
and seeing him, he fell at his feet, [23]and besought him, saying, Mk 7:32
"My little daughter is at the point of death. Come and lay your
hands on her, so that she may be made well, and live." [24]And he
went with him.

Perhaps they will think again and realize who he is who has visited them, and escape from the sins their greed has led them to commit. These two attitudes are to be found whenever Christ passes by—as are Jesus' mercy and continuous offer of grace: our Lord does not want the death of the sinner but rather that he should turn from his way and live (cf. Ezek 18:23).

5:20. The "Decapolis" or "country of the ten cities", among the more famous of which are Damascus, Philadelphia, Scythopolis, Gadara, Pella and Gerasa. The region was located to the east of the lake of Gennesaret and was inhabited mainly by pagans of Greek and Syrian origin. This territory came under the Roman governor of Syria.

5:21–43. Both Jairus and the woman with the flow of blood give us an example of faith in Christ's omnipotence, for only a miracle can cure Jairus' daughter, who is on her death-bed, and heal this lady, who has done everything humanly possible to get better. Similarly, the Christian should always expect God to help him overcome the obstacles in the way of his sanctification. Normally, God's help comes to us in an unspectacular way, but we should not doubt that, if it is necessary for our salvation, God will again work miracles. However, we should bear in mind that what the Lord expects of us is that we should every day fulfil his will.

5:22. At the head of each synagogue was the archisynagogist, whose function it was to organize the meetings of the synagogue on sabbaths and holy days, to lead the prayers and hymns and to indicate who should explain the Sacred Scripture. He was assisted in his task by a council and also had an aide who looked after the material side of things.

p. Green *him*

And a great crowd followed him and thronged about him.
[25]And there was a woman who had a flow of blood for twelve
years, [26]and who had suffered much under many physicians, and
had spent all that she had, and was no better but rather grew
worse. [27]She had heard the reports about Jesus, and came up
Mk 6:56 behind him in the crowd and touched his garment. [28]For she said,
"If I touch even his garments, I shall be made well." [29]And immediately the hemorrhage ceased; and she felt in her body that she
was healed of her disease. [30]And Jesus, perceiving in himself that
Lk 6:19 power had gone forth from him, immediately turned about in the
crowd, and said, "Who touched my garments?" [31]And his disciples said to him, "You see the crowd pressing around you, and
yet you say, 'Who touched me?'" [32]And he looked around to see
who had done it. [33]But the woman, knowing what had been done
to her, came in fear and trembling and fell down before him, and
Lk 7:50 told him the whole truth. [34]And he said to her, "Daughter, your

---

5:25. This woman suffered from an illness which implied legal impurity (Lev 15:25ff). Medical attention had failed to cure her; on the contrary, as the Gospel puts it so realistically, she was worse than ever. In addition to her physical suffering—which had gone on for twelve years—she suffered the shame of feeling unclean according to the Law. The Jews not only regarded a woman in this position as being impure: everything she touched became unclean as well. Therefore, in order not to be noticed by the people, the woman came up to Jesus from behind and, out of delicacy, touched only his garment. Her faith is enriched by her expression of humility: she is conscious of being unworthy to touch our Lord. "She touched the hem of his garment, she approached him in a spirit of faith, she believed, and she realized that she was cured [...]. So we too, if we wish to be saved, should reach out in faith to touch the garment of Christ" (St Ambrose, *Expositio Evangelii sec. Lucam*, 6, 56 and 58).

5:30. In all that crowd pressing around him only this woman actually touched Jesus—and she touched him not only with her hand but with the faith she bore in her heart. St Augustine comments: "She touches him, the people crowd him. Is her touching not a sign of her belief?" (*In Ioann. Evang*., 26, 3). We need contact with Jesus. We have been given no other means under heaven by which to be saved (cf. Acts 4:12). When we receive Jesus in the Holy Eucharist, we obtain this physical contact through the sacramental species. We too need to enliven our faith if these encounters with our Lord are to redound to our salvation (cf. Mt 13:58).

5:37. Jesus did not want more than these three apostles to be present: three was the number of witnesses laid down by the Law (Deut 19:15). "For Jesus, being humble, never acted in an ostentatious way" (Theophylact, *Enarratio in Evangelium Marci*, in loc.). Besides these were the three disciples closest to Jesus: later, only they will be with him at the transfiguration (cf. 9:2) and at his agony in the Garden of Gethsemane (cf. 14:33).

faith has made you well; go in peace, and be healed of your disease."
35While he was still speaking, there came from the ruler's
house some who said, "Your daughter is dead. Why trouble the
Teacher any further?" 36But ignoring[q] what they said, Jesus said to
the ruler of the synagogue, "Do not fear, only believe." 37And he
allowed no one to follow him except Peter and James and John
the brother of James. 38When they came to the house of the ruler
of the synagogue, he saw a tumult, and people weeping and wailing loudly. 39And when he had entered, he said to them, "Why do Jn 11:11
you make a tumult and weep? The child is not dead but sleeping." Acts 20:10
40And they laughed at him. But he put them all outside, and took Acts 9:40
the child's father and mother and those who were with him, and
went in where the child was. 41Taking her by the hand he said to Lk 7:14
her, "Talitha cumi"; which means, "Little girl, I say to you, arise."
42And immediately the girl got up and walked; for she was twelve

---

5:39. Jesus' words are in contrast with those of the ruler's servants; they say: "Your daughter is dead"; whereas he says: "She is not dead but sleeping." "To men's eyes she was dead, she could not be awoken; in God's eyes she was sleeping, for her soul was alive and was subject to God's power, and her body was resting, awaiting the resurrection. Hence the custom which arose among Christians of referring to the dead, whom we know will rise again, as those who are asleep" (St Bede, *In Marci Evangelium expositio*, in loc.). What Jesus says shows us that, for God, death is only a kind of sleep, for he can awaken anyone from the dead whenever he wishes. The same happens with the death and resurrection of Lazarus. Jesus says: "Our friend Lazarus has fallen asleep, but I go to awaken him out of sleep." And, when the disciples think that it is ordinary sleep he is referring to, our Lord tells them plainly: "Lazarus is dead" (cf. Jn 11:11ff).

5:40–42. Like all the Gospel miracles the raising of the daughter of Jairus demonstrates Christ's divinity. Only God can work miracles; sometimes he does them in a direct way, sometimes by using created things as a medium. The exclusively divine character of miracles—especially the miracle of raising the dead—is noticed in the Old Testament: "The Lord wills and brings to life; he brings down to Sheol and raises up" (1 Sam 2:6), because he has "power over life and death" (Wis 16:13). And also in the Old Testament God uses men to raise the dead to life: the prophet Elijah revives the son of the widow of Sarepta by "crying to the Lord" (cf. 1 Kings 17:21), and Elisha prevails on him to raise the son of the Shunammite (2 Kings 4:33).

In the same way, in the New Testament the apostles do not act by their own power but by that of Jesus to whom they first offer fervent prayer: Peter restores to life a Christian woman of Joppa named Tabitha (Acts 9:36ff); and Paul, in Troas, brings Eutychus back to life after he falls from a high window (Acts 20:7ff). Jesus does not refer to any superior power; his authority is sovereign: all he has to do is

q. Or *overhearing*. Other ancient authorities read *hearing*

years old. And immediately they were overcome with amazement.
Mk 1:44 [43]And he strictly charged them that no one should know this,* and
told them to give her something to eat.

No prophet is honoured in his own country

Mt 13:53–58 6 [1]He went away from there and came to his own country; and
Lk 4:16–30 his disciples followed him. [2]And on the sabbath he began to
Jn 7:15 teach in the synagogue; and many who heard him were astonished,
saying, "Where did this man get all this? What is the wisdom given
Lk 2:34f to him? What mighty works are wrought by his hands! [3]Is not this
the carpenter, the son of Mary and brother of James and Joses and
Judas and Simon, and are not his sisters here with us?" And they
Jn 4:44 took offence[r] at him. [4]And Jesus said to them, "A prophet is not

---

give the order and the daughter of Jairus is brought back to life; this shows that he is God.

6:1–3. Jesus is here described by his occupation and by the fact that he is the son of Mary. Does this indicate that St Joseph is dead already? We do not know, but it is likely. In any event, the description is worth underlining: in the Gospels of St Matthew and St Luke we are told of the virginal conception of Jesus. St Mark's Gospel does not deal with our Lord's infancy, but there may be an allusion here to his virginal conception and birth, in his being described as "the son of Mary".

"Joseph, caring for the child as he had been commanded, made Jesus a craftsman, transmitting his own professional skill to him. So the neighbours of Nazareth will call Jesus both *faber* and *fabri filius*: the craftsman and the son of the craftsman" (St J. Escrivá, *Christ Is Passing By*, 55). This message of the Gospel reminds us that our vocation to work is not marginal to God's plans.

"The truth that by means of work man participates in the activity of God himself, his Creator, was *given particular prominence by Jesus Christ*—the Jesus at whom many of his first listeners in Nazareth 'were astonished, saying, "Where did this man get all this? What is the wisdom given to him? … Is not this the carpenter?"' (Mk 6:2–3). For Jesus not only proclaimed but first and foremost fulfilled by his deeds the 'gospel', the word of eternal Wisdom, that had been entrusted to him. Therefore this was also 'the gospel of work', because *he who proclaimed it was himself a man of work*, a craftsman like Joseph of Nazareth (cf. Mt 13:55). And if we do not find in his words a special command to work—but rather on one occasion a prohibition against too much anxiety about work and life (Mt 6:25–34)—at the same time the eloquence of the life of Christ is unequivocal: he belongs to the 'working world', he has appreciation and respect for human work. It can indeed be said that *he looks with love upon human work* and the different forms that it takes, seeing in each one of these forms a particular facet of man's likeness with God, the Creator and Father" (John Paul II, *Laborem exercens*, 26).

St Mark mentions by name a number of brothers of Jesus, and refers in general

r. Or *stumbled*

without honour, except in his own country, and among his own kin,
and in his own house." 5And he could do no mighty work there,
except that he laid his hands upon a few sick people and healed
them. 6And he marvelled because of their unbelief.

5. JESUS JOURNEYS WITH HIS APOSTLES

And he went about among the villages teaching.

The mission of the Twelve

7And he called to him the twelve, and began to send them out two Mt 10:1, 9–15
by two, and gave them authority over the unclean spirits. 8He Lk 9:1–6; 10:1

---

to his sisters. But the word "brother" does not necessarly mean son of the same parents. It can also indicate other degrees of relationship—cousins, nephews, etc. Thus in Genesis 13:8 and 14:14 and 16 Lot is called the brother of Abraham (translated as "kinsman" in RSV), whereas we know that he was Abraham's nephew, the son of Abraham's brother Haran. The same is true of Laban, who is called the brother of Jacob although he was his mother's brother (Gen 29:15); there are other instances: cf. 1 Chronicles 23:21–22, etc. This confusion is due to the poverty of Hebrew and Aramaic language: in the absence of distinct terms, the same word, brother, is used to designate different degrees of relationship.

From other Gospel passages we know that James and Joses, who are mentioned here, were sons of Mary of Clophas (Jn 19:25). We know less about Judas and Simon: it seems that they are the apostles Simon the Cananaean (Mt 10:4) and Judas the son of James (Lk 6:16), the author of the Catholic Letter, in which he describes himself as "brother" of James. In any event, although James, Simon and Judas are referred to as brothers of Jesus, it is nowhere said they were "sons of Mary"—which would have been the natural thing if they had been our Lord's brothers in the strict sense. Jesus always appears as an only son: to the people of Nazareth, he is "the son of Mary" (Mt 13:55). When he was dying Jesus entrusted his mother to St John (cf. Jn 19:26–27), which shows that Mary had no other children. To this is added the constant belief of the Church, which regards Mary as the ever-virgin: "a perfect virgin before, while, and forever after she gave birth" (Paul IV, *Cum quorumdam*).

6:5–6. Jesus worked no miracles here: not because he was unable to do so, but as punishment for the unbelief of the townspeople. God wants man to use the grace offered him, so that, by cooperating with grace, he become disposed to receive further graces. As St Augustine neatly puts it, "He who made you without your own self, will not justify you without yourself" (*Sermons*, 169).

6:7. Cf. the note on Mk 1:27; 3:14–19.

6:8–9. Jesus requires them to be free of any form of attachment if they are to preach the Gospel. A disciple, who has the mission of bringing the Kingdom of God to souls through preaching, should not rely

charged them to take nothing for their journey except a staff; no
bread, no bag, no money in their belts; 9but to wear sandals and
not put on two tunics. 10And he said to them, "Where you enter a
house, stay there until you leave the place. 11And if any place will
not receive you and they refuse to hear you, when you leave,
shake off the dust that is on your feet for a testimony against
them." 12So they went out and preached that men should repent.
Jas 5:14–15 13And they cast out many demons, and anointed with oil many
that were sick and healed them.

Opinions about Jesus

Mt 14:1–12 Lk 9:7–9; 3:19–20 14King Herod heard of it; for Jesus's[s] name had become known.
Some[t] said, "John the baptizer has been raised from the dead; that
is why these powers are at work with him." 15But others said, "It
is Elijah." And others said, "It is a prophet, like one of the
prophets of old." 16But when Herod heard of it, he said, "John,
whom I beheaded, has been raised."

---

on human resources but on God's providence. Whatever he does need in order to live with dignity as a herald of the Gospel, he must obtain from those who benefit from his preaching, for the labourer deserves his upkeep (cf. Mt 10:10).

"The preacher should so trust in God that he is convinced that he will have everything he needs to support life, even if he cannot himself obtain it; for he should not neglect eternal things through worrying about temporal things" (St Bede, *In Marci Evangelium expositio*, in loc.). "By these instructions the Lord did not mean that the evangelists should not seek to live in any other way than by depending on what was offered them by those to whom they preached the Gospel; otherwise this very apostle [St Paul] would have acted contrary to this precept when he earned his living by the labours of his own hands" (St Augustine, *De consensu Evangelistarum*, 2, 30).

6:13. St Mark is the only evangelist who speaks of anointing the sick with oil. Oil was often used for treating wounds (cf. Is 1:6; Lk 10:34), and the apostles also use it for the miraculous cure of physical illnesses by virtue of the power given them by Jesus. Hence the use of oil as the matter of the sacrament of the Anointing of the Sick, which cures wounds of the soul and even, if appropriate, bodily diseases. As the Council of Trent teaches—*Doctrina de sacramento extremae unctionis*, chap. 1—in this verse of St Mark there can be seen a "hint" of the sacrament of Anointing of the Sick, which our Lord will institute and which later on "is recommended and promulgated to the faithful by St James the apostle" (cf. Jas 5:14ff).

6:14. Following popular custom, St Mark called Herod "king", but in strict legal terminology he was only tetrarch, which is the way St Matthew (14:1) and St Luke (9:7) describe him, that is, a governor of certain consequence. The Herod referred

s. Greek *his* **t.** Other ancient authorities read *he*

The martyrdom of John the Baptist

17 For Herod had sent and seized John, and bound him in prison for
the sake of Herodias, his brother Philip's wife; because he had
married her. 18 For John said to Herod, "It is not lawful for you to Lev 18:16
have your brother's wife." 19 And Herodias had a grudge against
him, and wanted to kill him. But she could not, 20 for Herod feared Acts 24:24
John, knowing that he was a righteous and holy man, and kept
him safe. When he heard him, he was much perplexed; and yet he
heard him gladly. 21 But an opportunity came when Herod on his
birthday gave a banquet for his courtiers and officers and the leading men of Galilee. 22 For when Herodias' daughter came in and
danced, she pleased Herod and his guests; and the king said to the
girl, "Ask me for whatever you wish, and I will grant it." 23 And he
vowed to her, "Whatever you ask me, I will give you, even half of Esther 5:3, 6
my kingdom." 24 And she went out, and said to her mother, "What
shall I ask?" And she said, "The head of John the baptizer." 25 And
she came in immediately with haste to the king, and asked,
saying, "I want you to give me at once the head of John the baptizer on a platter." 26 And the king was exceedingly sorry; but Lk 18:23

---

to here was Herod Antipas, the son of Herod the Great who was king of the Jews at the time of Jesus' birth. Cf. the note on Mt 2:1.

6:16–29. It is interesting that the extensive account of the death of John the Baptist is inserted here in the Gospel narrative. The reason is St John the Baptist's special relevance in the history of salvation: he is the Precursor, entrusted with the task of preparing the way for the Messiah. Besides, John the Baptist had a great reputation among the people: they believed him to be a prophet (Mk 11:32); some even thought he was the Messiah (Lk 3:15; Jn 1:20); and they flocked to him from many places (Mk 1:5). Jesus himself said: "Among those born of women there has risen no one greater than John the Baptist" (Mt 11:11). Later, the apostle St John will speak of him in the Gospel: "There was a man sent from God, whose name was John" (Jn 1:6); but the sacred text points out that, despite this, he was not the light, but rather the witness to the light (Jn 1:6–8). More correctly, he was the lamp carrying the light (Jn 5:35). We are told here that he was a righteous man and preached to everyone what had to be preached: he had a word for people at large, for publicans, for soldiers (Lk 3:10–14); for Pharisees and Sadducees (Mt 3:7–12); for King Herod himself (Mk 6:18–20). This humble, upright and austere man paid with his life for the witness he bore to Jesus the Messiah (Jn 1:29 and 36–37).

6:26. Oaths and promises immoral in content should never be made, and, if made, should never be kept. This is the teaching of the Church, which is summed up in the *St Pius X Catechism*, 383, in the following way: "Are we obliged to keep oaths we have sworn to do unjust and unlawful things? Not only are we not obliged: we sin by making such oaths, for they are prohibited by the Law of God or of the Church."

because of his oath and his guests he did not want to break his
word to her. [27]And immediately the king sent a soldier of the
guard and gave orders to bring his head. He went and beheaded
him in the prison, [28]and brought his head on a platter, and gave it
to the girl; and the girl gave it to her mother. [29]When his disciples
heard of it, they came and took his body, and laid it in a tomb.

The apostles return. First miracle of the loaves and fish

Lk 9:10; 10:17 [30]The apostles returned to Jesus, and told him all that they had
Mk 2:2 done and taught. [31]And he said to them, "Come away by your-
selves to a lonely place, and rest a while." For many were coming
Mt 14:13–21 and going, and they had no leisure even to eat. [32]And they went
Lk 9:11–17 Jn 6:1–13 away in the boat to a lonely place by themselves. [33]Now many
saw them going, and knew them, and they ran there on foot from
Num 27:17 Ezek 34:5 the towns, and got there ahead of them. [34]As he landed he saw a
Mt 9:36 great throng, and he had compassion on them, because they were

---

6:30–31. We can see here the intensity of Jesus' public ministry. Such was his dedication to souls that St Mark twice mentions that the disciples did not even have time to eat (cf. Mk 3:20). A Christian should be ready to sacrifice his time and even his rest in the service of the Gospel. This attitude of availability will lead us to change our plans whenever the good of souls so requires.

But Jesus also teaches us here to have common sense and not to go to such extremes that we physically cannot cope: "The Lord makes his disciples rest, to show those in charge that people who work or preach cannot do so without breaks" (St Bede, *In Marci Evangelium expositio*, in loc.). "He who pledges himself to work for Christ should never have a free moment, because to rest is not to do nothing: it is to relax in activities which demand less effort" (St Josemaría Escrivá, *The Way*, 357).

6:34. Our Lord had planned a period of rest, for himself and his disciples, from the pressures of the apostolate (Mk 6:31–32). And he has to change his plans because so many people come, eager to hear him speak. Not only is he not annoyed with them: he feels compassion on seeing their spiritual need. "My people are destroyed for lack of knowledge" (Hos 4:6). They need instruction and our Lord wants to meet this need by preaching to them. "Jesus is moved by hunger and sorrow, but what moves him most is ignorance" (St Josemaría Escrivá, *Christ Is Passing By*, 109).

6:37. A denarius was what an artisan earned for a normal day's work. The disciples must, therefore, have thought it little less than impossible to fulfil the Master's command, because they would not have had this much money.

6:41. This miracle is a figure of the Holy Eucharist: Christ performed it shortly before promising that sacrament (cf. Jn 6:1ff), and the Fathers have always so interpreted it. In this miracle Jesus shows

like sheep without a shepherd; and he began to teach them many
things. 35And when it grew late, his disciples came to him and Mk 8:1–9
said, "This is a lonely place, and the hour is now late; 36send them
away, to go into the country and villages round about and buy
themselves something to eat." 37But he answered them, "You give
them something to eat." And they said to him, "Shall we go and
buy two hundred denarii[u] worth of bread, and give it to them to
eat?" 38And he said to them, "How many loaves have you? Go and
see." And when they had found out, they said, "Five, and two
fish." 39Then he commanded them all to sit down by companies
upon the green grass. 40So they sat down in groups, by hundreds
and by fifties. 41And taking the five loaves and the two fish he Mk 7:34
looked up to heaven, and blessed, and broke the loaves, and gave
them to the disciples to set before the people; and he divided the
two fish among them all. 42And they all ate and were satisfied.
43And they took up twelve baskets full of broken pieces and of the
fish. 44And those who ate the loaves were five thousand men.

---

his supernatural power and his love for men—the same power and love as make it possible for Christ's one and only body to be present in the eucharistic species to nourish the faithful down the centuries. In the words of the sequence composed by St Thomas Aquinas for the Mass of Corpus Christi: "Sumit unus, sumunt mille, quantum isti, tantum ille, nec sumptus consumitur" (Be one or be a thousand fed, they eat alike that living bread which, still received, ne'er wastes away).

This gesture of our Lord—looking up to heaven—is recalled in the Roman canon of the Mass: "Et elevatis oculis in caelum, ad Te Deum Patrem suum omnipotentem" (and looking up to heaven, to you, his almighty Father). At this point in the Mass we are preparing to be present at a miracle greater than that of the multiplication of the loaves—the changing of bread into his own body, offered as food for all men.

6:42. Christ wanted the left-overs to be collected (cf. Jn 6:12) to teach us not to waste things God gives us, and also to have them as a tangible proof of the miracle.

The collecting of the left-overs is a way of showing us the value of little things done out of love for God—orderliness, cleanliness, finishing things completely. It also reminds the sensitive believer of the extreme care that must be taken of the eucharistic species. Also, the generous scale of the miracle is an expression of the largesse of the messianic times. The Fathers recall that Moses distributed the manna for each to eat as much as he needed but some left part of it for the next day and it bred worms (Ex 16:16–20). Elijah gave the widow just enough to meet her needs (1 Kings 17:13–16). Jesus, on the other hand, gives generously and abundantly.

u. The denarius was a day's wage for a labourer

Jesus walks on water

Mt 14:22–36 45 Immediately he made his disciples get into the boat and go
Jn 6:15–21 before him to the other side, to Bethsaida, while he dismissed the
crowd. 46 And after he had taken leave of them, he went into the
hills to pray. 47 And when evening came, the boat was out on the
Ps 77:19 sea, and he was alone on the land. 48 And he saw that they were
Job 9:8 distressed in rowing, for the wind was against them. And about
Is 43:16 the fourth watch of the night he came to them, walking on the sea.
He meant to pass by them, 49 but when they saw him walking on
the sea they thought it was a ghost, and cried out; 50 for they all
saw him, and were terrified. But immediately he spoke to them
and said, "Take heart, it is I; have no fear." 51 And he got into the
Mk 4:39 boat with them and the wind ceased. And they were utterly
astounded, 52 for they did not understand about the loaves, but their
Mk 8:17 hearts were hardened.

Cures at Gennesaret

53 And when they had crossed over, they came to land at
Gennesaret, and moored to the shore. 54 And when they got out of
the boat, immediately the people recognized him, 55 and ran about

---

6:48. The Romans divided the night into four parts or watches, whose length varied depending on the season. St Mark (13:35) gives the popular names for these watches: evening, midnight, cockcrow, morning. Therefore, it is towards dawn that Jesus comes to the disciples.

He wishes to teach us that even when we are in very pressurized and difficult situations, he is nearby, ready to help us; but he expects us to make an effort, to strengthen our hope and temper our resolve. As an early Greek commentator puts it: "The Lord allowed his disciples to enter danger to make them suffer, and he did not immediately come to their aid; he left them in peril for the whole night, to teach them to be patient and not to be accustomed to receiving immediate succour in tribulation" (Theophylact, *Enarratio in Evangelium Marci*, in loc.).

6:52. The disciples do not yet see Jesus' miracles as signs of his divinity. They witness the multiplication of the loaves and the fish (Mk 6:33–44) and the second multiplication of the loaves (Mk 8:17), but their hearts and minds are still hardened; they fail to grasp the full import of what Jesus is teaching them through his actions—that he is the Son of God. Jesus is patient and understanding with their defects, even when they fail to grasp what he says when he speaks about his own passion (Lk 18:34). Our Lord will give them further miracles and further teaching to enlighten their minds, and, later, he will send the Holy Spirit to teach them all things and remind them of everything he said (cf. Jn 14:26). St Bede comments on this episode (Mk 6:45–52) in this way: "In a mystical sense, the disciples' efforts to row against the wind point to the efforts the Holy Church must make against the waves of the enemy world and the outpourings of evil spirits in order to reach the haven of its heavenly home. It is rightly said that the boat

the whole neighbourhood and began to bring sick people on their
pallets to any place where they heard he was. [56]And wherever he Mk 5:27–28
came, in villages, cities, or country, they laid the sick in the Acts 5:15; 19:11f
market places, and besought him that they might touch even the
fringe of his garment; and as many as touched it were made well.

The traditions of the elders. What defiles a man

7 [1]Now when the Pharisees gathered together to him, with some Mt 15:1–20
of the scribes, who had come from Jerusalem, [2]they saw that Lk 11:38
some of his disciples ate with hands defiled, that is, unwashed.
[3](For the Pharisees, and all the Jews, do not eat unless they wash
their hands,[v] observing the tradition of the elders;* [4]and when they
come from the market place, they do not eat unless they purify[w]
themselves; and there are many other traditions which they
observe, the washing of cups and pots and vessels of bronze.[x])
[5]And the Pharisees and the scribes asked him, "Why do your disciples not live[y] according to the tradition of the elders, but eat with
hands defiled?" [6]And he said to them, "Well did Isaiah prophesy Is 29:13
of you hypocrites, as it is written,

---

was out on the sea and he alone on the land, because the Church has never been so intensely persecuted by the Gentiles that it seemed as if the Redeemer had abandoned it completely. But the Lord sees his disciples struggling, and to sustain them he looks at them compassionately and sometimes frees them from peril by clearly coming to their aid" (*In Marci Evangelium expositio*, in loc.).

7:1–2. Hands were washed not for reasons of hygiene or good manners but because the custom had religious significance: it was a rite of purification. In Exodus 30:17ff the Law of God laid down how priests should wash before offering sacrifice. Jewish tradition had extended this to all Jews before every meal, in an effort to give meals a religious significance, which was reflected in the blessings which marked the start of meals. Ritual purification was a symbol of the moral purity a person should have when approaching God (Ps 24:3ff; 51:2 and 7); but the Pharisees had focussed on the mere external rite. Therefore Jesus restores the genuine meaning of these precepts of the Law, whose purpose is to teach the right way to render homage to God (cf. Jn 4:24).

7:3–5. We can see clearly from this text that very many of those to whom St Mark's Gospel was first addressed were Christians who had been pagans and were unfamiliar with Jewish customs. The Evangelist explains these customs in some detail, to help them realize the significance of the events and teachings reported in the Gospel story.

Similarly, Holy Scripture needs to be preached and taught in a way which puts it within reach of its hearers. This is why

v. One Greek word is of uncertain meaning and is not translated **w.** Other ancient authorities read *baptize* **x.** Other ancient authorities add *and beds* **y.** Greek *walk*

'This people honours me with their lips,
but their heart is far from me;
7 in vain do they worship me,
teaching as doctrines the precepts of men.'
8 You leave the commandment of God, and hold fast the tradition
of men."
9 And he said to them, "You have a fine way of rejecting the
commandment of God, in order to keep your tradition! 10 For
Ex 20:12; 21:17 Moses said, 'Honour your father and your mother'; and 'He who
Deut 5:16 Lev 20:9 speaks evil of father or mother, let him surely die'; 11 but you say,
'If a man tells his father or his mother, What you would have
gained from me is Corban' (that is, given to God)[z]—12 then you no
longer permit him to do anything for his father or mother, 13 thus
making void the word of God through your tradition which you
hand on. And many such things you do."
14 And he called the people to meet him, and said to them,
Acts 10:14–15 "Hear me, all of you, and understand: 15 there is nothing outside a
man which by going into him can defile him; but the things that
come out of a man are what defile him."[a] 17 And when he had
entered the house, and left the people, his disciples asked him
about the parable. 18 And he said to them, "Then are you also with-

---

Vatican II teaches that "it is for the bishops suitably to instruct the faithful [...] by giving them translations of the sacred texts which are equipped with necessary and really adequate explanations. Thus the children of the Church can familiarize themselves safely and profitably with the Sacred Scriptures, and become steeped in their spirit" (*Dei Verbum*, 25).

7:11–13. For an explanation of this text see the note on Mt 15:5–6. Jesus Christ, who is the authentic interpreter of the Law, because as God he is its author, explains the scope of the fourth commandment and points out the mistakes made by Jewish casuistry. There were many other occasions when he corrected mistaken interpretations offered by the Jewish teachers: for example, when he recalls that phrase of the Old Testament, "Go and learn what this means, I desire mercy, and not sacrifice" (Hos 6:6; 1 Sam 15:22; Sir 35:4) in Matthew 9:13.

7:15. See the RSV note.

7:18–19. We know from Tradition that St Mark was the interpreter of St Peter and that, in writing his Gospel under the inspiration of the Holy Spirit, he gathered up the Roman catechesis of the head of the apostles.

The vision which St Peter had in Joppa (Acts 10:10–16) showed him the full depth of what Jesus teaches here about food. When he returns to Jerusalem, St Peter himself tells us this in his report on the conversion of Cornelius: "I remembered the word of the Lord" (Acts 11:16). The now non-obligatory charac-

z. Or *an offering* **a.** Other ancient authorities add verse 16, *If any man has ears to hear, let him hear*

out understanding? Do you not see that whatever goes into a man
from outside cannot defile him, [19]since it enters, not his heart but Col 2:16, 21–22
his stomach, and so passes on?"[b] (Thus he declared all foods
clean.) [20]And he said, "What comes out of a man is what defiles a
man. [21]For from within, out of the heart of man, come evil
thoughts, fornication, theft, murder, adultery, [22]coveting, wicked- Mt 6:23; 20:15
ness, deceit, licentiousness, envy, slander, pride, foolishness. [23]All
these evil things come from within, and they defile a man."

The Syrophoenician woman

[24]And from there he arose and went away to the region of Tyre Mt 15:21–28
and Sidon.[c] And he entered a house, and would not have any one
know it; yet he could not be hid. [25]But immediately a woman,
whose little daughter was possessed by an unclean spirit, heard of
him, and came and fell down at his feet. [26]Now the woman was a
Greek, a Syrophoenician by birth. And she begged him to cast the
demon out of her daughter. [27]And he said to her, "Let the children
first be fed, for it is not right to take the children's bread and
throw it to the dogs." [28]But she answered him, "Yes, Lord; yet
even the dogs under the table eat the children's crumbs." [29]And he
said to her, "For this saying you may go your way; the demon has

---

ter of such prescriptions laid down by God in the Old Testament (cf. Lev 11) would have been something St Peter included in his preaching. For interpretation of this text see also the note on Mt 15:10–20.

7:20–23. "In order to help us understand divine things, Scripture uses the expression 'heart' in its full human meaning, as the summary and source, expression and ultimate basis, of one's thoughts, words and actions" (St Josemaría Escrivá, *Christ Is Passing By*, 164).

The goodness or malice, the moral quality, of our actions does not depend on their spontaneous, instinctive character. The Lord himself tells us that sinful actions can come from the human heart.

We can understand how this can happen if we realize that, after original sin, man "was changed for the worse" in both body and soul and was, therefore, prone to evil (cf. Council of Trent, *De peccato originali*). Our Lord here restores morality in all its purity and intensity.

7:24. The region of Tyre and Sidon is nowadays the southern part of Lebanon-Phoenicia in ancient times. The distance from the lake of Gennesaret to the frontier of Tyre and Sidon is not more than 50 kms (30 miles). Jesus withdrew from Palestine to avoid persecution by the Jewish authorities and to give the apostles more intensive training.

7:27. Our Lord actually uses the diminutive—"little dogs" to refer to the Gentiles—thereby softening a scornful expression which Jews used. On the episode of

b. Or *is evacuated* **c.** Other ancient authorities omit *and Sidon*

left your daughter." 30And she went home, and found the child
lying in bed, and the demon gone.

Curing of a deaf man

Mt 15:29–31 31Then he returned from the region of Tyre, and went through Sidon
Mk 5:23 to the Sea of Galilee, through the region of the Decapolis. 32And
they brought him a man who was deaf and had an impediment in
Mk 8:23 his speech; and they besought him to lay his hand upon him. 33And
taking him aside from the multitude privately, he put his fingers
Jn 11:41 into his ears, and he spat and touched his tongue; 34and looking up
to heaven, he sighed, and said to him, "Ephphatha," that is, "Be
opened." 35And his ears were opened, his tongue was released, and
Mk 1:43–45 he spoke plainly. 36And he charged them to tell no one; but the
more he charged them, the more zealously they proclaimed it.
Is 35:5 37And they were astonished beyond measure, saying, "He has done
all things well; he even makes the deaf hear and the dumb speak."

Second miracle of the loaves

Mt 15:32–39 8 1In those days, when again a great crowd had gathered, and
they had nothing to eat, he called his disciples to him, and said
to them, 2"I have compassion on the crowd, because they have
Mk 6:34–44 been with me now three days, and have nothing to eat; 3and if I

---

the Canaanite woman see the notes on parallel passages, Mt 15:21–28.

7:32–33. Holy Scripture quite often shows the laying on of hands as a gesture indicating the transfer of power or blessing (cf. Gen 48:14ff; 2 Kings 5:11; Lk 13:13). Everyone knows that saliva can help heal minor cuts. In the language of Revelation fingers symbolized powerful divine action (cf. Ex 8:19; Ps 8:3; Lk 11:20). So Jesus uses signs which suit in some way the effect he wants to achieve, though we can see from the text that the effect—the instantaneous cure of the deaf and dumb man—far exceeds the sign used.

In the miracle of the deaf and dumb man we can see a symbol of the way God acts on souls: for us to believe, God must first open our heart so we can listen to his word. Then, like the apostles, we too can proclaim the *magnalia Dei*, the mighty works of God (cf. Acts 2:11). In the Church's liturgy (cf. the hymn *Veni Creator*) the Holy Spirit is compared to the finger of the right hand of God the Father (*Digitus paternae dexterae*). The Consoler produces in our souls, in the supernatural order, effects comparable to those which Christ produces in the body of the deaf and dumb man.

8:1–9. Jesus repeats the miracle of the multiplication of the loaves and the fish: the first time (Mk 6:33–44) he acted because he saw a huge crowd like "sheep without a shepherd"; now he takes pity on them because they have been with him for three days and have nothing to eat.

This miracle shows how Christ rewards people who persevere in following him: the crowd had been hanging on his words, forgetful of everything else. We

send them away hungry to their homes, they will faint on the way;
and some of them have come a long way." [4]And his disciples
answered him, "How can one feed these men with bread here in
the desert?" [5]And he asked them, "How many loaves have you?"
They said, "Seven." [6]And he commanded the crowd to sit down
on the ground; and he took the seven loaves, and having given
thanks he broke them and gave them to his disciples to set before
the people; and they set them before the crowd. [7]And they had a
few small fish; and having blessed them, he commanded that
these also should be set before them. [8]And they ate, and were satisfied; and they took up the broken pieces left over, seven baskets
full. [9]And there were about four thousand people. [10]And he sent
them away; and immediately he got into the boat with his disciples, and went to the district of Dalmanutha.[d]

The leaven of the Pharisees and Herod

[11]The Pharisees came and began to argue with him, seeking from Mt 16:1–12
him a sign from heaven, to test him. [12]And he sighed deeply in his Jn 6:30 1 Cor 1:22

---

should be like them, attentive and ready to do what he commands, without any vain concern about the future, for that would amount to distrusting divine providence.

8:10. "Dalmanutha": this must have been somewhere near the lake of Gennesaret, but it is difficult to localize it more exactly. This is the only time it is mentioned in Holy Scripture. In the parallel passage in St Matthew (15:39) Magadan (sometimes Magdala) is mentioned.

8:11–12. Jesus expresses the deep sadness he feels at the hard-heartedness of the Pharisees: they remain blind and unbelieving despite the light shining around them and the wonderful things Christ is doing. If someone rejects the miracles God has offered him, it is useless for him to demand new signs, because he asks for them not because he is sincerely seeking the truth but out of ill will: he is trying to tempt God (cf. Lk 16:27–31). Requiring new miracles before one will believe, not accepting those already performed in the history of salvation, amounts to asking God to account for himself before a human tribunal (cf. Rom 2:1–11). Unfortunately, many people do act like this. But God can only be found if we have an open and humble attitude to him. "I have no need of miracles: there are more than enough for me in the Gospel. But I do need to see you fulfilling your duty and responding to grace" (St J. Escrivá, *The Way*, 362).

8:12. The generation to which Jesus refers does not include all the people of his time, but only the Pharisees and their followers (cf. Mk 8:38; 9:19; Mt 11:16), who do not want to see in Jesus' miracles the sign and guarantee of his messianic mission and dignity: they even attribute his miracles to Satan (Mt 12:28).

If they do not accept the signs offered to them, they will be given no other sign

d. Other ancient authorities omit *Magadan* or *Magdala*

spirit, and said, "Why does this generation seek a sign? Truly, I
say to you, no sign shall be given to this generation." 13And he left
them, and getting into the boat again he departed to the other side.
14Now they had forgotten to bring bread; and they had only
Lk 12:1 one loaf with them in the boat. 15And he cautioned them, saying,
"Take heed, beware of the leaven of the Pharisees and the leaven
of Herod."[e] 16And they discussed it with one another, saying, "We
Mk 6:52 have no bread." 17And being aware of it, Jesus said to them, "Why
do you discuss the fact that you have no bread? Do you not yet
Jer 5:21 Ezek 12:2 perceive or understand? Are your hearts hardened? 18Having eyes
do you not see, and having ears do you not hear? And do you not
Mk 6:41–44 remember? 19When I broke the five loaves for the five thousand,
how many baskets full of broken pieces did you take up?" They
Mk 8:6–9 said to him, "Twelve." 20"And the seven for the four thousand,
how many baskets full of broken pieces did you take up?" And
they said to him, "Seven." 21And he said to them, "Do you not yet
understand?"

---

of the spectacular kind they seek, for the Kingdom of God does not come noisily (Lk 17:20–21) and even if it did they in their twisted way would manage to misinterpret the event (Lk 16:31). According to Matthew 12:38–42 and Luke 11:29–32, they are offered yet another sign—the miracle of Jonah, the sign of the death and resurrection of Christ; but not even this remarkable proof will lead the Pharisees to shed their pride.

8:15–16. In another Gospel passage (Lk 13:20–21; Mt 13:33) Jesus uses the simile of the leaven to show the vitality of his teaching. Here "leaven" is used in the sense of bad disposition. In the making of bread, leaven is what causes the dough to rise; the Pharisees' hypocrisy and Herod's dissolute life, stemming from their personal ambition, were the "leaven" which was poisoning from within the "dough" of Israel and which would eventually corrupt it. Jesus seeks to warn his disciples about these dangers, and to have them understand that if they are to take in his doctrine they need a pure and simple heart.

But the disciples fail to understand: "They weren't educated; they weren't very bright, if we judge from their reaction to supernatural things. Finding even the most elementary examples and comparisons beyond their reach, they would turn to the Master and ask: 'Explain the parable to us.' When Jesus uses the image of the 'leaven' of the Pharisees, they think that he's reproaching them for not having purchased bread… . These were the disciples called by our Lord. Such stuff is what Christ chose. And they remain just like that until they are filled with the Holy Spirit and thus become pillars of the Church. They are ordinary people, full of defects and shortcomings, more eager to say than to do. Nevertheless, Jesus calls them to be fishers of men, co-redeemers, dispensers of the grace of God" (St J. Escrivá, *Christ Is Passing By*, 2). The same thing can happen to us. Although we may not be very gifted, the Lord calls us, and love of

e. Other ancient authorities read *the Herodians*

Curing of a blind man at Bethsaida

[22]And they came to Bethsaida. And some people brought to him a Mk 6:56
blind man, and begged him to touch him. [23]And he took the blind Mk 7:32–33
man by the hand, and led him out of the village; and when he had Jn 9:6
spit on his eyes and laid his hands upon him, he asked him, "Do
you see anything?" [24]And he looked up and said, "I see men; but
they look like trees, walking." [25]Then again he laid his hands upon
his eyes; and he looked intently and was restored, and saw everything clearly. [26]And he sent him away to his home, saying, "Do Mk 7:36
not even enter the village."

Peter's profession of faith

[27]And Jesus went on with his disciples, to the villages of Caesarea Mt 16:13–28
Philippi; and on the way he asked his disciples, "Who do men say Lk 9:18–27
that I am?" [28]And they told him, "John the Baptist; and others say, Mk 6:15
Elijah; and others one of the prophets." [29]And he asked them, "But Jn 6:67–69
who do you say I am?" Peter answered him, "You are the Christ."
[30]And he charged them to tell no one about him. Mk 9:9

God and docility to his words will cause to grow in our souls unsuspected fruit of holiness and supernatural effectiveness.

8:23. Cf. the note on Mk 7:32–33.

8:22–25. Normally the cures which Jesus worked were instantanteous; not so in this case. Why? Because the blind man's faith was very weak, it would seem, to begin with. Before curing the eyes of his body, Jesus wanted the man's faith to grow; the more it grew and the more trusting the man became, the more sight Jesus gave him. He acted in keeping with his usual pattern: not working miracles unless there was a right predisposition, yet encouraging a good disposition in the person and giving more grace as he responds to the grace already given.

God's grace is essential even for desiring holy things: "Give us light, Lord. Behold, we need it more than the man who was blind from his birth, for he wished to see the light and could not, whereas nowadays, Lord, no one wishes to see it. Oh, what a hopeless ill is this! Here, my God, must be manifested thy power and thy mercy" (St Teresa, *Exclamations of the Soul to God*, 8).

8:29. Peter's profession of faith is reported here in a shorter form than in Matthew 16:18–19. Peter seems to go no further than say that Jesus is the Christ, the Messiah. Eusebius of Caesarea, in the fourth century, explains the Evangelist's reserve by the fact that he was the interpreter of St Peter, who omitted from his preaching anything which might appear to be self-praise. The Holy Spirit, when inspiring St Mark, wanted the Gospel to reflect the preaching of the prince of the apostles, leaving it to other evangelists to fill out certain important details to do with the episode of the confession of Peter.

The sketchiness of the narrative still shows Peter's role quite clearly: he is the first to come forward affirming the messiahship of Jesus. Our Lord's question,

PART TWO

Jesus' ministry on the way to Jerusalem

6. TEACHINGS ON THE CHRISTIAN LIFE

Jesus foretells his passion and resurrection. Christian renunciation

Mk 9:31; 10:32–34 [31]And he began to teach them that the Son of man must suffer
many things, and be rejected by the elders and the chief priests
and the scribes, and be killed, and after three days rise again.
[32]And he said this plainly. And Peter took him, and began to
rebuke him. [33]But turning and seeing his disciples, he rebuked
Peter, and said, "Get behind me, Satan! For you are not on the
side of God, but of men."

"But who do you say that I am?", shows what Jesus is asking the apostles for—not an opinion, more or less favourable, but firm faith. It is St Peter who expresses this faith (cf. the note on Mt 16:13–20).

8:31–33. This is the first occasion when Jesus tells his disciples about the sufferings and death he must undergo. He does it twice more, later on (cf. Mk 9:31 and 10:32). The apostles are surprised, because they cannot and do not want to understand why the Master should have to suffer and die, much less that he should be so treated "by the elders and the chief priests and the scribes". But Peter, with his usual spontaneity, immediately begins to protest. And Jesus replies to him using the same words as he addressed to the devil when he tempted him (cf. Mt 4:10); he wants to affirm, once again, that his mission is spiritual, not earthly, and that therefore it cannot be understood by using mere human criteria: it is governed by God's designs, which were that Jesus should redeem us through his passion and death. So too, for a Christian, suffering, united with Christ, is also a means of salvation.

8:34. When Jesus said "If any man would come after me …", he was well aware that in fulfilling his mission he would be brought to death on a cross; this is why he speaks clearly about his passion (vv: 31–32). The Christian life, lived as it should be lived, with all its demands, is also a cross which one has to carry, following Christ.

Jesus' words, which must have seemed extreme to his listeners, indicate the standard he requires his followers to live up to. He does not ask for short-lived enthusiasm or occasional dedication; he asks everyone to renounce himself, to take up his cross and follow him. For the goal he sets for men is eternal life. This whole Gospel passage has to do with man's eternal destiny. The present life should be evaluated in the light of this eternal life: life on earth is not definitive, but transitory and relative; it is a means to be used to achieve definitive life in

[34]And he called to him the multitude with his disciples, and
said to them, "If any man would come after me, let him deny himself and take up his cross and follow me. [35]For whoever would Mt 10:39
save his life will lose it: and whoever loses his life for my sake
and the gospel's will save it. [36]For what does it profit a man to
gain the whole world and forfeit his life?* [37]For what can a man
give in return for his life? [38]For whoever is ashamed of me and of Mt 10:33
my words in this adulterous and sinful generation, of him will the
Son of man also be ashamed, when he comes in the glory of his
Father with the holy angels."

---

heaven: "All that, which worries you for the moment, is of relative importance. What is of absolute importance is that you be happy, that you be saved" (St Josemaría Escrivá, *The Way*, 297).

"There is a kind of fear around, a fear of the Cross, of our Lord's Cross. What has happened is that people have begun to regard as crosses all the unpleasant things that crop up in life, and they do not know how to take them as God's children should, with supernatural outlook. So much so, that they are even removing the roadside crosses set up by our forefathers … !

"In the Passion, the Cross ceased to be a symbol of punishment and became instead a sign of victory. The Cross is the emblem of the Redeemer: *in quo est salus, vita et resurrectio nostra*: there lies our salvation, our life and our resurrection" (St Josemaría Escrivá, *The Way of the Cross*, II, 5).

8:35. "Life": in the original text and the New Vulgate the word literally means "soul". But here, as in many other cases, "soul" and "life" are equivalent. The word "life" is used, clearly, in a double sense: earthly life and eternal life, the life of man here on earth and man's eternal happiness in heaven. Death can put an end to earthly life, but it cannot destroy eternal life (cf. Mt 10:28), the life which can only be given by him who brings the dead back to life.

Understood in this way, we can grasp the paradoxical meaning of our Lord's phrase: whoever wishes to save his (earthly) life will lose his (eternal) life. But whoever loses his (earthly) life for me and the Gospel, will save his (eternal) life. What, then, does saving one's (earthly) life mean? It means living this life as if there were none other—letting oneself be controlled by the lust of the flesh and the lust of the eyes and the pride of life (cf. 1 Jn 2:16). And losing one's (earthly) life means mortifying, by continuous ascetical effort, this triple concupiscence—that is, taking up one's cross (v. 34)—and consequently seeking and savouring the things that are God's and not the things of the earth (cf. Col 3:1–2).

8:36–37. Jesus promises eternal life to those who are willing to lose earthly life for his sake. He has given us example: he is the Good Shepherd who lays down his life for his sheep (Jn 10:15); and he fulfilled in his own case what he said to the apostles on the night before he died: "Greater love has no man than this that a man lay down his life for his friends" (Jn 15:13).

8:38. Each person's eternal destiny will be decided by Christ. He is the Judge who will come to judge the living and the

9 [1]And he said to them, "Truly, I say to you, there are some
standing here who will not taste death before they see the
kingdom of God come with power."

The Transfiguration

Mt 17:1–13 [2]And after six days Jesus took with him Peter and James and
Lk 9:28–36 John, and led them up a high mountain apart by themselves; and

---

dead (Mt 16:27). The sentence will depend on how faithful each has been in keeping the Lord's commandments—to love God and to love one's neighbour, for God's sake. On that day Christ will not recognize as his disciple anyone who is ashamed to imitate Jesus' humility and example and follow the precepts of the Gospel for fear of displeasing the world or worldly people: he has failed to confess by his life the faith which he claims to hold. A Christian, then, should never be ashamed of the Gospel (Rom 1:16); he should never let himself be drawn away by the worldliness around him; rather he should exercise a decisive influence on his environment, counting on the help of God's grace. The first Christians changed the ancient pagan world. God's arm has not grown shorter since their time (cf. Is 59:1). Cf. Mt 10:32–33 and the note on same.

9:1. The coming of the Kingdom of God with power does not seem to refer to the second, glorious coming of Jesus at the end of time (the Parousia); it may, rather, indicate the amazing spread of the Church in the lifetime of the apostles. Many of those present here will witness this. The growth and spread of the Church in the world can be explained only by the divine power God gives to the mystical body of Christ. The transfiguration of our Lord, which is recounted in the next passage, is a sign, given to the apostles, of Jesus' divinity and of the divine powers which he will give his Church.

9:2–10. We contemplate in awe this manifestation of the glory of the Son of God to three of his disciples. Ever since the Incarnation, the divinity of our Lord has usually been hidden behind his humanity. But Christ wishes to show, to these three favourite disciples, who will later be pillars of the Church, the splendour of his divine glory, in order to encourage them to follow the difficult way that lies ahead, fixing their gaze on the happy goal which is awaiting them at the end. This is why, as St Thomas comments (cf. *Summa theologiae*, 3, 45, 1), it was appropriate for him to give them an insight into his glory. The fact that the transfiguration comes immediately after the first announcement of his passion, and his prophetic words about how his followers would also have to carry his cross, shows us that "through many tribulations we must enter the kingdom of God" (Acts 14:22).

What happened at the transfiguration? To understand this miraculous event in Christ's life, we must remember that in order to redeem us by his passion and death our Lord freely renounced divine glory and became man, assuming flesh which was capable of suffering and which was not glorious, becoming like us in every way except sin (cf. Heb 4:15). In the transfiguration, Jesus Christ willed that the glory which was his as God and which his soul had from the moment of the Incarnation, should miraculously become present in his body. "We should learn from Jesus' attitude in these trials.

he was transfigured before them, 3and his garments became glis-
tening, intensely white, as no fuller on earth could bleach them.
4And there appeared to them Elijah with Moses; and they were
talking to Jesus. 5And Peter said to Jesus, "Master,[f] it is well that
we are here; let us make three booths, one for you and one for
Moses and one for Elijah." 6For he did not know what to say, for Mk 14:40
they were exceedingly afraid. 7And a cloud overshadowed them,

During his life on earth he did not even want the glory that belonged to him. Though he had the right to be treated as God, he took the form of a servant, a slave (cf. Phil 2:6)" (St Josemaría Escrivá, *Christ Is Passing By*, 62). Bearing in mind *who* became man (the divinity of the person and the glory of his soul), it was appropriate for his body to be glorious; given the *purpose* of his incarnation, it was not appropriate, usually, for his glory to be evident. Christ shows his glory in the transfiguration in order to move us to desire the divine glory which will be given us so that, having this hope, we too can understand "that the sufferings of this present time are not worth comparing with the glory that is to be revealed to us" (Rom 8:18).

9:2. According to Deuteronomy (19:15), to bear witness to anything the evidence of two or three must concur. Perhaps this is why Jesus wanted three apostles to be present. It should be pointed out that these three apostles were specially loved by him; they were with him also at the raising of the daughter of Jairus (Mk 5:37) and will also be closest to him during his agony at Gethsemane (Mk 14:33). Cf. the note on Mt 17:1–13.

9:7. This is how St Thomas Aquinas explains the meaning of the the transfiguration: "Just as in the Baptism, where the mystery of the first regeneration was proclaimed, the operation of the whole Trinity was made manifest, because the Son Incarnate was there, the Holy Spirit appeared under the form of a dove, and the Father made himself known in the voice; so also in the transfiguration, which is the sign of the second regeneration [the Resurrection], the whole Trinity appears—the Father in the voice, the Son in the man, the Holy Spirit in the bright cloud; for just as in Baptism he confers innocence, as signified by the simplicity of the dove, so in the Resurrection will he give his elect the clarity of glory and refreshment from every form of evil, as signified by the bright cloud" (*Summa theologiae*, 3, 45, 4 ad 2). For, really, the transfiguration was in some way an anticipation not only of Christ's glorification but also of ours. As St Paul says, "it is the same Spirit himself bearing witness with our spirit that we are children of God, and if children, then heirs, heirs of God and fellow heirs with Christ, provided we suffer with him in order that we may also be glorified with him" (Rom 8:16–17).

"Beloved": this reveals that Christ is the only-begotten Son of the Father in whom are fulfilled the prophecies of the Old Testament. Fray Luis de León comments: "Christ is the Beloved, that is to say, he has always been, is now and ever shall be loved above all else [...] for no single creature or all created things taken together are as loved by God, and

f. Or *Rabbi*

Mk 1:11 2 Pet 1:17 — and a voice came out of the cloud, “This is my beloved Son;[g]
Deut 18:15 Acts 3:22 — listen to him.” [8]And suddenly looking around they no longer saw
any one with them but Jesus only.
Mk 8:30 — [9]And as they were coming down the mountain, he charged
them to tell no one what they had seen, until the Son of man
should have risen from the dead. [10]So they kept the matter to
themselves, questioning what the rising from the dead meant.
[11]And they asked him, “Why do the scribes say that first Elijah
Mal 3:1f, 23 — must come?” [12]And he said to them, “Elijah does come first to
Is 53:3 — restore all things; and how is it written of the Son of man, that he
Mt 11:14 — should suffer many things and be treated with contempt? [13]But I
1 Kings 19:2, 10 — tell you that Elijah has come,* and they did to him whatever they
pleased, as it is written of him.”

Curing of an epileptic boy

Mt 17:14–21 Lk 9:37–42 — [14]And when they came to the disciples, they saw a great crowd
about them, and scribes arguing with them. [15]And immediately all
the crowd, when they saw him, were greatly amazed, and ran up
to him and greeted him. [16]And he asked them, “What are you discussing with them?” [17]And one of the crowd answered him,
“Teacher, I brought my son to you, for he has a dumb spirit; [18]and
wherever it seizes him, it dashes him down; and he foams and

---

because only he is the object of true adoration” (*The Names of Christ*, book 3, The Beloved).

9:10. That the dead would rise was already revealed in the Old Testament (cf. Dan 12:2–3; 2 Mac 7:9; 12:43) and was believed by pious Jews (cf. Jn 11:23–25). However, they were unable to understand the profound truth of the death and resurrection of the Lord: they expected a glorious, triumphant Messiah, despite the prophecy that he would suffer and die (cf. Is 53). Hence the apostles’ oblique approach; they too do not dare to directly question our Lord about his resurrection.

9:11–13. The scribes and Pharisees interpret the messianic prophecy in Malachi (3:1–2) as meaning that Elijah will appear in person, dramatically, to be followed by the all-triumphant Messiah, with no shadow of pain or humiliation. Jesus tells them that Elijah has indeed come, in the person of John the Baptist (Mt 17:13) and has prepared the way of the Messiah, a way of pain and suffering.

Verse 12 is a question which Jesus puts to his disciples, but they should really have asked it themselves, had they realized that Christ’s resurrection presupposed the Messiah’s suffering and death. Since they fail to ask it, Jesus does, to teach them that he like Elijah (that is, John the Baptist) must experience suffering before entering his glory.

9:17. The demon who possessed this boy is described as a “dumb spirit” because dumbness was the main feature

g. Or *my Son, my* (or *the*) *Beloved*

grinds his teeth and becomes rigid; and I asked your disciples to
cast it out, and they were not able." [19]And he answered them, "O
faithless generation, how long am I to be with you? How long am
I to bear with you? Bring him to me." [20]And they brought the boy
to him; and when the spirit saw him, immediately it convulsed the
boy, and he fell on the ground and rolled about, foaming at the
mouth. [21]And Jesus[h] asked his father, "How long has he had this?"
And he said, "From childhood. [22]And it has often cast him into the
fire and into the water, to destroy him; but if you can do anything,
have pity on us and help us." [23]And Jesus said to him, "If you can! Mk 11:23
All things are possible to him who believes." [24]Immediately the Lk 17:5
father of the child cried out[i] and said, "I believe; help my unbelief!" [25]And when Jesus saw that a crowd came running together,
he rebuked the unclean spirit, saying to it, "You dumb and deaf
spirit, I command you, come out of him, and never enter him
again." [26]And after crying out and convulsing him terribly, it came Mk 1:26
out, and the boy was like a corpse; so that most of them said, "He
is dead." [27]But Jesus took him by the hand and lifted him up, and Mk 5:41
he arose. [28]And when he had entered the house, his disciples
asked him privately, "Why could we not cast it out?" [29]And he
said to them, "This kind cannot be driven out by anything but
prayer and fasting."[j]

---

of the possession. On diabolic possession see the note on Mt 12:22–24.

9:19–24. As on other occasions, Jesus requires submission of faith before he works the miracle. The exclamation of Jesus refers to the request of the boy's father (v. 22), which seemed to suggest some doubt about God's omnipotence. The Lord corrects this way of asking and requires him to have firm faith. In v. 24 we can see that the father has quite changed; then Jesus does the miracle. The man's strengthened faith made him all-powerful, for someone with faith relies not on himself but on Jesus Christ. Through faith, then, we become sharers in God's omnipotence. But faith is a gift of God, which man, especially at times when he is wavering, should ask for humbly and tenaciously, like the father of this boy: "I believe, help my unbelief," and like the apostles: "Increase our faith!" (Lk 17:5).

9:28–29. "In teaching the apostles how to expel a spirit as evil as this he is teaching all of us how we should live, and telling us that prayer is the resource we should use to overcome even the severest temptations, whether they come from unclean spirits or from men. Prayer does not consist only in the words we use to invoke God's clemency but also in everything we do, out of faith, as homage to God. The apostle bears witness to this when he says: 'Pray constantly' (1 Thess 5:7)" (St Bede, *In Marci Evangelium expositio*, in loc.).

h. Greek *he* **i.** Other ancient authorities add *with tears* **j.** Other ancient authorities omit *and fasting*

Second announcement of the Passion

Mt 17:22–23 Lk 9:43–45 30 They went on from there and passed through Galilee. And he
Jn 7:1 Mk 8:31; would not have any one know it; 31 for he was teaching his disci-
10:32–34 ples, saying to them, "The Son of man will be delivered into the
hands of men, and they will kill him; and when he is killed, after
Lk 9:45; 18:34 three days he will rise." 32 But they did not understand the saying,
and they were afraid to ask him.

Service to others. On leading others astray

Mt 18:1–9 33 And they came to Capernaum; and when he was in the house he
Lk 9:46–50 asked them, "What were you discussing on the way?" 34 But they
were silent; for on the way they had discussed with one another
Mk 10:44 who was the greatest. 35 And he sat down and called the twelve;
and he said to them, "If any one would be first, he must be last of
Mk 10:16 all and servant of all." 36 And he took a child, and put him in the

---

9:30–32. Although moved when he sees the crowds like sheep without a shepherd (Mt 9:36), Jesus leaves them, to devote time to careful instruction of the apostles. He retires with them to out-of-the-way places, and there he explains points of his public preaching which they had not understood (Mt 13:36). Here, specifically, for a second time, he announces his death and resurrection.

In his relationships with souls Jesus acts in the same way: he calls man to be with him in the quiet of prayer and there he teaches him about his more intimate plans and about the more demanding side of the Christian life. Later, like the apostles, Christians were to spread this teaching to the ends of the earth.

9:34–35. Jesus uses this argument going on behind his back to teach his disciples about how authority should be exercised in his Church—not by lording it over others, but by serving them. In fulfilling his own mission to found the Church whose head and supreme lawgiver he is, he came to serve and not to be served (Mt 20:28).

Anyone who does not strive to have this attitude of self-forgetful service, not only lacks one of the main pre-requisites for proper exercise of authority but also runs the risk of being motivated by ambition or pride. "To be in charge of an apostolic undertaking demands readiness to suffer everything, from everybody, with infinite charity" (St Josemaría Escrivá, *The Way*, 951).

9:36–37. To demonstrate to his apostles the abnegation and humility needed in their ministry, he takes a child into his arms and explains the meaning of this gesture: if we receive for Christ's sake those who have little importance in the world's eyes, it is as if we are embracing Christ himself and the Father who sent him. This little child whom Jesus embraces represents every child in the world, and everyone who is needy, helpless, poor or sick—people who are not naturally attractive.

9:38–40. Our Lord warns the apostles, and through them all Christians, against exclusivism in the apostolate—the notion that "good is not good unless I am the one who does it". We must assimilate this

midst of them; and taking him in his arms, he said to them,
37“Whoever receives one such child in my name receives me; and Mt 10:40
whoever receives me, receives not me but him who sent me.” Jn 13:20
38John said to him, “Teacher, we saw a man casting out Num 11:27–28
demons in your name,[k] and we forbade him, because he was not
following us.” 39But Jesus said, “Do not forbid him; for no one 1 Cor 12:3
who does a mighty work in my name will be able soon after to
speak evil of me. 40For he that is not against us is for us. 41For Mt 12:30
truly, I say to you, whoever gives you a cup of water to drink Mt 10:42
because you bear the name of Christ, will by no means lose his
reward.
42“Whoever causes one of these little ones who believe in me
to sin,[l] it would be better for him if a great millstone were hung
round his neck and he were thrown into the sea. 43And if your Mt 5:30
hand causes you to sin,[l] cut it off; it is better for you to enter life

---

teaching of Christ's: good is good, even if it is not I who do it. Cf. the note on Lk 9:49–50.

9:41. The value and merit of good works lies mainly in the love of God with which they are done: “A little act, done for love, is worth so much” (St J. Escrivá, *The Way*, 814). God regards in a special way acts of service to others, however small: “Do you see that glass of water or that piece of bread which a holy soul gives to a poor person for God's sake; it is a small matter, God knows, and in human judgment hardly worthy of consideration: God, notwithstanding, recompenses it, and forthwith gives for it some increase of charity” (St Francis de Sales, *Treatise on the Love of God*, book 2, chap. 2).

9:42. “Scandal is anything said, done or omitted which leads another to commit sin” (St Pius X, *Catechism*, 417). Scandal is called, and is, diabolical when the aim of the scandal-giver is to provoke his neighbour to sin, understanding sin as offence against God. Since sin is the greatest of all evils, it is easy to understand why scandal is so serious and, therefore, why Christ condemns it so roundly. Causing scandal to children is especially serious, because they are so less able to defend themselves against evil. What Christ says applies to everyone, but especially to parents and teachers, who are responsible before God for the souls of the young.

9:43–48. After teaching the obligation everyone has to avoid giving scandal to others, Jesus now gives the basis of Christian moral teaching on the subject of “occasions of sin”—situations liable to lead to sin. He is very explicit: a person is obliged to avoid proximate occasions of sin, just as he is obliged to avoid sin itself; as God already put it in the Old Testament: “Whoever lives in danger will perish by it” (Sir 3:26–27). The eternal good of our soul is more important than any temporal good. Therefore, anything that places us in proximate danger of committing sin should be cut off and thrown away. By putting things in this

k. Other ancient authorities add *who does not follow us* **l.** Greek *stumble*

maimed than with two hands to go to hell,[m] to the unquenchable
fire.[n] 45 And if your foot causes you to sin,[l] cut it off; it is better for
you to enter life lame than with two feet to be thrown into hell.[m,n]
Mt 5:29 47 And if your eye causes you to sin, [l]pluck it out; it is better for
you to enter the kingdom of God with one eye than with two eyes
to be thrown into hell,[m] 48 where their worm does not die, and the
Lev 2:13 fire is not quenched. 49 For every one will be salted with fire.[o]
Mt 5:13 50 Salt is good; but if the salt has lost its saltness, how will you
Lk 14:34 season it? Have salt in yourselves, and be at peace with one
Col 4:6 another."

---

way our Lord makes sure we recognize the seriousness of this obligation.

The Fathers see, in these references to hands and eyes and so forth, people who are persistent in evil and ever-ready to entice others to evil behaviour and erroneous beliefs. These are the people we should distance ourselves from, so as to enter life, rather than accompany them to hell (cf. St Augustine, *De consensu Evangelistarum*, 4, 16; St John Chrysostom, *Hom. on St Matthew*, 60).

9:43. "Hell", literally "Gehenna" or *Gehinnom*, was a little valley south of Jerusalem, outside the walls and below the city. For centuries it was used as the city dump. Usually garbage was burned to avoid it being a focus of infection. Gehenna was, proverbially, an unclean and unhealthy place: our Lord used this to explain in a graphic way the unquenchable fire of hell.

9:44. "Where their worm does not die, and the fire is not quenched": these words constituting v. 44 are not in the better manuscripts. They are taken from Isaiah 66:24 and are repeated as a kind of refrain in vv. 46 (omitted for the same reason as v. 44) and 48. Our Lord uses them to refer to the torments of hell. Often "the worm that does not die" is explained as the eternal remorse felt by those in hell; and the "fire which is not quenched", as their physical pain. The Fathers also say that both things may possibly refer to physical torments. In any case, the punishment in question is terrible and unending.

9:49–50. "Every one will be salted with fire." St Bede comments on these words: "Everyone will be salted with fire, says Jesus, because spiritual wisdom must purify all the elect of any kind of corruption through carnal desire. Or he may be speaking of the fire of tribulation, which exercises the patience of the faithful to enable them to reach perfection" (*In Marci Evangelium expositio*, in loc.).

Some codexes add: "and every sacrifice will be salted with salt". This phrase in Leviticus (2:12), prescribed that all sacrificial offerings should be seasoned with salt to prevent corruption. This prescription of the Old Testament is used here to teach Christians to offer themselves as pleasing victims, impregnated with the spirit of the Gospel, symbolized by salt. Our Lord's address, which arises out of a dispute over who is the greatest, ends with a lesson about fraternal peace and charity. On salt which has lost its taste see the note on Mt 5:13.

m. Greek *Gehenna* **n.** Verses 44 and 46 (which are identical with verse 48) are omitted by the best ancient authorities **o.** Other ancient authorities add *and every sacrifice will be salted with salt*

7. HEADING FOR JUDEA AND JERUSALEM

The indissolubility of marriage

10 [1]And he left there and went to the region of Judea and beyond the Jordan, and crowds gathered to him again; and again, as his custom was, he taught them. Mt 19:1–9
[2]And Pharisees came up and in order to test him asked, "Is it
lawful for a man to divorce his wife?" [3]He answered them, "What
did Moses command you?" [4]They said, "Moses allowed a man to Deut 24:1 Mt 5:31–32
write a certificate of divorce, and to put her away." [5]But Jesus said

---

10:1–12. This kind of scene occurs often in the Gospel. The malice of the Pharisees contrasts with the simplicity of the crowd, who listen attentively to Jesus' teaching. The Pharisees' questions are aimed at tricking Jesus into going against the Law of Moses. But Jesus Christ, Messiah and Son of God, has perfect understanding of that Law. Moses had permitted divorce because of the hardness of that ancient people: women had an ignominious position in those primitive tribes (they were regarded almost as animals or slaves); Moses, therefore, protected women's dignity against these abuses by devising the certificate of divorce; this was a real social advance. It was a document by which the husband repudiated his wife and she obtained freedom. Jesus restores to its original purity the dignity of man and woman in marriage, as instituted by God at the beginning of creation. "A man leaves his father and his mother and cleaves to his wife, and they become one flesh" (Gen 2:24): in this way God established from the very beginning the unity and indissolubility of marriage. The Church's Magisterium, the only authorized interpreter of the Gospel and of the natural law, has constantly guarded and defended this teaching and has proclaimed it solemnly in countless documents (Council of Florence, *Pro Armeniis*; Council of Trent, *De Sacram. matr.*; Pius XI, *Casti connubii*; Vatican II, *Gaudium et spes*, 48; etc.).

Here is a good summary of this doctrine: "The indissolubility of marriage is not a caprice of the Chuch nor is it merely a positive ecclesiastical law. It is a precept of natural law, of divine law, and responds perfectly to our nature and to the supernatural order of grace" (St Josemaría Escrivá, *Conversations*, 97). Cf. the note on Mt 5:31–32.

10:5–9. When a Christian realizes that this teaching applies to everyone at all times, he should not be afraid about people reacting against it: "It is a fundamental duty of the Church to reaffirm strongly [...] the doctrine of the indissolubility of marriage. To all those who, in our times, consider it too difficult, or indeed impossible, to be bound to one person for the whole of life, and to those caught up in a culture that rejects the indissolubility of marriage and openly mocks the commitment of spouses to fidelity, it is necessary to reaffirm the good news of the definitive nature of that conjugal love that has in Christ its foundation and strength (cf. Eph 5:25).

"Being rooted in the personal and total self-giving of the couple, and being required by the good of the children, the indissolubility of marriage finds its ulti-

to them, "For your hardness of heart he wrote you this command-
Gen 1:27 ment. 6But from the beginning of creation, 'God made them male
Gen 2:24 and female.' 7'For this reason a man shall leave his father and
mother and be joined to his wife,[p] 8and the two shall become
one.'[q] So they are no longer two but one.[q] 9What therefore God
has joined together, let not man put asunder."
10And in the house the disciples asked him again about this
Lk 16:18 matter. 11And he said to them, "Whoever divorces his wife and
marries another, commits adultery against her; 12and if she
divorces her husband and marries another, she commits adultery."

Jesus and the children

Mt 19:13–15 Lk 18:15–17 13And they were bringing children to him, that he might touch
them; and the disciples rebuked them. 14But when Jesus saw it he

---

mate truth in the plan that God has manifested in his revelation: he wills and he communicates the indissolubility of marriage as a fruit, a sign and a requirement of the absolutely faithful love that God has for man and that the Lord Jesus has for the Church.

"Christ renews the first plan that the Creator inscribed in the hearts of man and woman, and in the celebration of the sacrament of matrimony offers 'a new heart': thus the couples are not only able to overcome 'hardness of heart' (Mt 19:8), but also and above all they are able to share the full and definitive love of Christ, the new and eternal Covenant made flesh. Just as the Lord Jesus is the 'faithful witness' (Rev 3:14), the 'yes' of the promises of God (cf. 2 Cor 1:20) and thus the supreme realization of the unconditional faithfulness with which God loves his people, so Christian couples are called to participate truly in the irrevocable indissolubility that binds Christ to the Church, his bride, loved by him to the end (cf. Jn 13:1).

"To bear witness to the inestimable value of the indissolubility and fidelity of marriage is one of the most precious and most urgent tasks of Christian couples in our time" (John Paul II, *Familiaris consortio*, 20).

10:13–16. This Gospel account has an attractive freshness and vividness about it which may be connected with St Peter, from whom St Mark would have taken the story. It is one of the few occasions when the Gospels tell us that Christ became angry. What provoked his anger was the disciples' intolerance: they felt that these people bringing children to Jesus were a nuisance: it meant a waste of his time; Christ had more serious things to do than be involved with little children. The disciples were well-intentioned; it was just that they were applying the wrong criteria. What Jesus had told them quite recently had not registered: "Whoever receives one such child in my name receives me; and whoever receives me, receives not me but him who sent me" (Mk 9:37).

Our Lord also stresses that a Christian has to become like a child to enter the Kingdom of heaven. "To be little you

p. Other ancient authorities omit *and be joined to his wife* **q.** Greek *one flesh*

was indignant, and said to them, "Let the children come to me, do
not hinder them; for to such belongs the kingdom of God. [15]Truly, Mt 18:3
I say to you, whoever does not receive the kingdom of God like a
child shall not enter it." [16]And he took them in his arms and Mk 9:36
blessed them, laying his hands upon them.

The rich young man. Poverty and renunciation

[17]And as he was setting out on his journey, a man ran up and knelt Mt 19:16–30
before him, and asked him, "Good Teacher, what must I do to Lk 18:18–30
inherit eternal life?" [18]And Jesus said to him, "Why do you call
me good? No one is good but God alone. [19]You know the com- Ex 20:12–17
mandments: 'Do not kill, Do not commit adultery, Do not steal, Deut 5:16–20; 24:14
Do not bear false witness, Do not defraud, Honour your father and
mother.'" [20]And he said to him, "Teacher, all these I have obser-

---

have to believe as children believe, to love as children love, to abandon yourself as children do ... , to pray as children pray" (St Josemaría Escrivá, *Holy Rosary*, Prologue).

Our Lord's words express simply and graphically the key doctrine of man's divine sonship: God is our Father and we are his sons and daughters, his children; the whole of religion is summed up in the relationship of a son with his good Father. This awareness of God as Father involves a sense of dependence on our Father in heaven and trusting abandonment to his loving providence—in the way a child trusts its father or mother; the humility of recognizing that we can do nothing by ourselves; simplicity and sincerity, which make us straightforward and honest in our dealings with God and man.

10:17–18. As Matthew 19:16 makes clear, the young man approaches Jesus as an acknowledged teacher of the spiritual life, in the hope that he will guide him towards eternal life. It is not that Christ rejects the praise he is offered: he wants to show the depth of the young man's words: he is good, not because he is a good man but because he is God, who is goodness itself. So, the young man has spoken the truth, but he has not gone far enough. Hence the enigmatic nature of Jesus' reply and its profundity. The young man's approach is upright but too human; Jesus tries to get him to see things from an entirely supernatural point of view. If this man is to really attain eternal life he must see in Christ not just a good master but the divine Saviour, the only Master, the only one who, because he is God, is goodness itself. Cf. the note on Mt 19:16–22.

10:19. Our Lord has not come to abolish the Law but to fulfil it (Mt 5:17). The commandments are the very core of the Law and keeping them is necessary for attaining eternal life. Christ brings these commandments to fulfilment in a double sense. First, because he helps us discover their full implications for our lives. The light of Revelation makes it easy for us to grasp the correct meaning of the precepts of the Decalogue—something that human reason, on its own, can only achieve with difficulty. Second, his grace gives us strength to counter our evil inclinations, which stem from original

Mk 8:34 Mt 10:38 ved from my youth." 21And Jesus looking upon him loved him,
and said to him, "You lack one thing; go, sell what you have, and
give to the poor, and you will have treasure in heaven; and come,
follow me." 22At that saying his countenance fell, and he went
away sorrowful; for he had great possessions.
Mk 4:19 23And Jesus looked around and said to his disciples, "How
Ps 62:10 hard it will be for those who have riches to enter the kingdom of

---

sin. The commandments, therefore, still apply in the Christian life: they are like signposts indicating the way that leads to heaven.

10:21–22. Our Lord knows that this young man has a generous heart. This is why he treats him so affectionately and invites him to greater intimacy with God. But he explains that this means renunciation—leaving his wealth behind so as to give his heart whole and entire to Jesus. God calls everyone to holiness, but holiness is reached by many different routes. It is up to every individual to take the necessary steps to discover which route God wants him to follow. The Lord sows the seed of vocation in everyone's soul, to show him the way to go to reach the goal of holiness, which is common to all.

In other words, if a person does not put obstacles in the way, if he responds generously to God, he feels a desire to be better, to give himself more generously. As fruit of this desire he seeks to know God's will; he prays to God to help him, and asks people to advise him. In responding to this sincere search, God uses a great variety of instruments. Later, when a person thinks he sees the way God wants him to follow, he may still not make the decision to go that way: he is afraid of the renunciation it involves. At this point he should pray and deny himself if the light—God's invitation—is to win out against human calculation. For, although God is calling, man is always free, and therefore he can respond generously or be a coward, like the young man we are told about in this passage. Failure to respond generously to one's vocation always produces sadness.

10:21. "In its precise eloquence", John Paul II points out, commenting on this passage, "this deeply penetrating event expresses a great lesson in a few words: it touches upon substantial problems and basic questions that have in no way lost their relevance. Everywhere young people are asking important questions—questions on the meaning of life, on the right way to live, on the scale of values: 'What must I do …?' 'What must I do to share in everlasting life?' … To each one of you I say therefore: heed the call of Christ when you hear him saying to you: 'Follow me!' Walk in my path! Stand by my side! Remain in my love! There is a choice to be made: a choice for Christ and his way of life, and his commandment of love.

"The message of love that Christ brought is always important, always relevant. It is not difficult to see how today's world, despite its beauty and grandeur, despite the conquests of science and technology, despite the refined and abundant material goods that it offers, is yearning for more truth, for more love, for more joy. And all of this is found in Christ and in his way of life.… Faced with problems and disappointments, many people will try to escape from their responsibility: escape in selfishness, escape in sexual pleasure, escape in

God!" 24And the disciples were amazed at his words.* But Jesus 1 Tim 6:17
said to them again, "Children, how hard it is for those who trust in
riches[r] to enter the kingdom of God! 25It is easier for a camel to go
through the eye of a needle than for a rich man to enter the kingdom of God." 26And they were exceedingly astonished, and said
to him,[s] "Then who can be saved?" 27Jesus looked at them and Gen 18:14
said, "With men it is impossible, but not with God; for all things

---

drugs, escape in violence, escape in indifference and cynical attitudes. But today, I propose to you the option of love, which is the opposite of escape. If you really accept that love from Christ, it will lead you to God. Perhaps in the priesthood or religious life; perhaps in some special service to your brothers and sisters: especially to the needy, the poor, the lonely, the abandoned, those whose rights have been trampled upon, or those whose basic needs have not been provided for. Whatever you make of your life, let it be something that reflects the love of Christ" (Homily on Boston Common, 1 October 1979).

10:22. "The sadness of the young man makes us reflect. We could be tempted to think that many possessions, many of the goods of this world, can bring happiness. We see instead in the case of the young man in the Gospel that his many possessions had become an obstacle to accepting the call of Jesus to follow him. He was not ready to say *yes* to Jesus and *no* to self, to say *yes* to love and *no* to escape. Real love is demanding. I would fail in my mission if I did not clearly tell you so. For it was Jesus—Jesus himself—who said: 'You are my friends if you do what I command you' (Jn 15:14). Love demands effort and a personal commitment to the will of God. It means discipline and sacrifice, but it also means joy and human fulfilment.

"Dear young people: do not be afraid of honest effort and honest work; do not be afraid of the truth. With Christ's help, and through prayer, you can answer his call, resisting temptations and fads, and every form of mass manipulation. Open your hearts to the Christ of the Gospels—to his love and his truth and his joy. Do not go away sad! …

"Follow Christ! You who are married: share your love and your burdens with each other; respect the human dignity of your spouses; accept joyfully the life that God gives through you; make your marriage stable and secure for your children's sake.

"Follow Christ! You who are single or who are preparing for marriage. Follow Christ! You who are young or old. Follow Christ! You who are sick or ageing; who are suffering or in pain. You who feel the need for healing, the need for love, the need for a friend—follow Christ!

"To all of you I extend—in the name of Christ—the call, the invitation, the plea: 'Come and follow Me'" (John Paul II, *Homily on Boston Common*).

10:23–27. The reaction of the rich young man gives our Lord another opportunity to say something about the way to use material things. In themselves they are good: they are resources God has made available to people for their development

r. Other ancient authorities omit *for those who trust in riches* **s.** Other ancient authorities read *to one another*

are possible with God." [28]Peter began to say to him, "Lo, we have
left everything and followed you." [29]Jesus said, "Truly, I say to
you, there is no one who has left house or brothers or sisters or
mother or father or children or lands, for my sake and for the
gospel, [30]who will not receive a hundredfold now in this time,
houses and brothers and sisters and mothers and children and
lands, with persecutions, and in the age to come eternal life.*
[31]But many that are first will be last, and the last first."

Third announcement of the Passion

Mt 20:17–19 Lk 18:31–34 Jn 11:16, 55

[32]And they were on the road, going up to Jerusalem, and Jesus
was walking ahead of them; and they were amazed, and those

---

in society. But excessive attachment to things is what makes them an occasion of sin. The sin lies in "trusting" in them, as if they solve all life's problems, and in turning one's back on God. St Paul calls covetousness idolatry (Col 3:5). Christ excludes from the Kingdom of God anyone who becomes so attached to riches that his life is centred around them. Or, more accurately, that person excludes himself.

Possessions can seduce both those who already have them and those who are bent on acquiring them. Therefore, there are—paradoxically—poor people who are really rich, and rich people who are really poor. Since absolutely everyone has an inclination to be attached to material things, the disciples see salvation as an impossible goal: "Then who can be saved?" No one, if we rely on human resources. But God's grace makes everything possible. Cf. the note on Mt 6:11.

Also, not putting our trust in riches means that anyone who does have wealth should use it to help the needy. This "demands great generosity, much sacrifice and unceasing effort on the part of the rich man. Let each one examine his conscience, a conscience that conveys a new message for our times. Is he prepared to support out of his own pocket works and undertakings organized in favour of the most destitute? Is he ready to pay higher taxes so that the public authorities can intensify their efforts in favour of development?" (Paul VI, *Populorum progressio*, 47).

10:28–30. Jesus Christ requires every Christian to practise the virtue of poverty: he also requires us to practise real and effective austerity in the possession and use of material things. But of those who have received a specific call to apostolate—as in the case, here, of the Twelve—he requires absolute detachment from property, time, family etc. so that they can be fully available, imitating Jesus himself who, despite being Lord of the universe, became so poor that he had nowhere to lay his head (cf. Mt 8:20). Giving up all these things for the sake of the Kingdom of heaven also relieves us of the burden they involve: like a soldier shedding some encumbrance before going into action, to be able to move with more agility. This gives one a certain lordship over all things: no longer the slave of things, one experiences that feeling St Paul referred to: "As having nothing, and yet possessing everything" (2 Cor 6:10). A Christian who sheds his selfishness in this way has acquired charity and,

who followed were afraid. And taking the twelve again, he began Mt 9:31
to tell them what was to happen to him, [33]saying, "Behold, we are
going up to Jerusalem; and the Son of man will be delivered to the
chief priests and the scribes, and they will condemn him to death,
and deliver him to the Gentiles; [34]and they will mock him, and spit
upon him, and scourge him, and kill him; and after three days he
will rise."

The sons of Zebedee make a request

[35]And James and John, the sons of Zebedee, came forward to him, Mt 20:20–28
and said to him, "Teacher, we want you to do for us whatever we
ask of you." [36]And he said to them, "What do you want me to do

---

having charity, he has everything: "All are yours; you are Christ's; and Christ is God's" (1 Cor 3:22–23).

The reward for investing completely in Christ will be fully obtained in eternal life: but we will also get it in this life. Jesus says that anyone who generously leaves behind his possessions will be rewarded a hundred times over in this life.

He adds "with persecutions" (v. 30) because opposition is part of the reward for giving things up out of love for Jesus Christ. A Christian's glory lies in becoming like the Son of God, sharing in his cross so as later to share in his glory: "provided we suffer with him in order that we may also be glorified with him" (Rom 8:17); "all who desire to live a godly life in Christ Jesus will be persecuted" (2 Tim 3:12).

10:29. These words of our Lord particularly apply to those who by divine vocation embrace celibacy, giving up their right to form a family on earth. By saying "for my sake and for the Gospel" Jesus indicates that his example and the demands of his teaching give full meaning to this way of life: "This, then, is the mystery of the newness of Christ, of all that he is and stands for; it is the sum of the highest ideals of the Gospel and of the kingdom; it is a particular manifestation of grace, which springs from the paschal mystery of the Saviour and renders the choice of celibacy desirable and worthwhile on the part of those called by our Lord Jesus. Thus, they intend not only to participate in Christ's priestly office, but also to share with him his very condition of living" (Paul VI, *Sacerdotalis coelibatus*, 23).

10:32. Jesus was making his way to Jerusalem with a burning desire to see fulfilled everything that he had foretold about his passion and death. He had already told his disciples that he would suffer there, which is why they cannot understand his eagerness. By his own example he is teaching us to carry the cross gladly, not to try to avoid it.

10:35–44. We can admire the apostles' humility: they do not disguise their earlier weakness and shortcomings from the first Christians. God also has wanted the Holy Gospel to record the earlier weaknesses of those who will become the unshakeable pillars of the Church. The grace of God works wonders in people's souls, so we should never be pessimistic in the face of our own wretchedness: "I can do all things in him who strengthens me" (Phil 4:13).

for you?" [37]And they said to him, "Grant us to sit, one at your
Mk 14:36 Lk 12:50 right hand and one at your left, in your glory." [38]But Jesus said to
Rom 6:3 them, "You do not know what you are asking. Are you able to
drink the cup that I drink, or to be baptized with the baptism with
Acts 12:2 which I am baptized?" [39]And they said to him, "We are able." And
Rev 1:9 Jesus said to them, "The cup that I drink you will drink; and with
the baptism with which I am baptized, you will be baptized; [40]but
to sit at my right hand or at my left is not mine to grant, but it is
for those for whom it has been prepared." [41]And when the ten
Lk 22:25–27 heard it, they began to be indignant at James and John. [42]And
Jesus called them to him and said to them, "You know that those
who are supposed to rule over the Gentiles lord it over them, and

---

10:38. When we ask for anything in prayer, we should be ready, always, to accept God's will, even if it does not coincide with our own: "His Majesty knows best what is suitable for us; it is not for us to advise him what to give us, for he can rightly reply that we know not what we ask" (St Teresa, *Interior Castle*, 2, 8).

10:43–45. Our Lord's word and example encourage in us a genuine spirit of Christian service. Only the Son of God who came down from heaven and freely submitted to humiliation (at Bethlehem, Nazareth, Calvary, and in the Sacred Host) can ask a person to make himself last, if he wishes to be first.

The Church, right through history, continues Christ's mission of service to mankind: "Experienced in human affairs, the Church, without attempting to interfere in any way in the politics of States, 'seeks but a solitary goal: to carry forward the work of Christ himself under the lead of the befriending Spirit. And Christ entered this world to give witness to the truth, to rescue and not to sit in judgment, to serve and not to be served' (Vatican II, *Gaudium et spes*, 3). Sharing the noblest aspirations of men and suffering when she sees them not satisfied, she wishes to help them attain their full flowering, and that is why she offers men what she possesses as her characteristic attribute: a global vision of man and of the human race" (Paul VI, *Populorum progressio*, 13).

Our attitude should be that of our Lord: we should seek to serve God and men with a truly supernatural outlook, not expecting any return; we should serve even those who do not appreciate the service we do them. This undoubtedly does not make sense, judged by human standards. However, the Christian identified with Christ takes "pride" precisely in serving others; by so doing he shares in Christ's mission and thereby attains his true dignity: "This dignity is expressed in readiness to serve, in keeping with the example of Christ, who 'came not to be served but to serve.' If, in the light of this attitude of Christ's, 'being a king' is truly possible only by 'being a servant', then 'being a servant' also demands so much spiritual maturity that it must really be described as 'being a king'. In order to be able to serve others worthily and effectively we must be able to master ourselves, possess the virtues that make this mastery possible" (John Paul II, *Redemptor hominis*, 21). Cf. the note on Mt 20:27–28.

10:46–52. "Hearing the commotion the crowd was making, the blind man asks,

their great men exercise authority over them. 43But it shall not be Mk 9:35
so among you; but whoever would be great among you must be
your servant, 44and whoever would be first among you must be
slave of all. 45For the Son of man also came not to be served but
to serve, and to give his life as a ransom of many."

Bartimeus, the blind man of Jericho

46And they came to Jericho; and as he was leaving Jericho with Mt 20:29–34
his disciples and a great multitude, Bartimaeus, a blind beggar, the Lk 18:35–43
son of Timaeus, was sitting by the roadside. 47And when he heard
that it was Jesus of Nazareth, he began to cry out and say, "Jesus,
Son of David, have mercy on me!" 48And many rebuked him,

'What is happening?' They told him, 'It is Jesus of Nazareth.' At this his soul was so fired with faith in Christ that he cried out, 'Jesus, Son of David, have mercy on me!'

"Don't you feel the same urge to cry out? You who also are waiting at the side of the way, of this highway of life that is so very short? You who need more light, you who need more grace to make up your mind to seek holiness? Don't you feel an urgent need to cry out, 'Jesus, Son of David, have mercy on me'? What a beautiful aspiration for you to repeat again and again! …

" 'Many rebuked him, telling him to be silent.' As people have done to you, when you sensed that Jesus was passing your way. Your heart beat faster and you too began to cry out, prompted by an intimate longing. Then your friends, the need to do the done thing, the easy life, your surroundings, all conspired to tell you: 'Keep quiet, don't cry out. Who are you to be calling Jesus? Don't bother him.'

"But poor Bartimaeus would not listen to them. He cried out all the more: 'Son of David, have mercy on me.' Our Lord, who had heard him right from the beginning, let him persevere in his prayer. He does the same with you. Jesus hears our cries from the very first, but he waits. He wants us to be convinced that we need him. He wants us to beseech him, to persist, like the blind man waiting by the road from Jericho. 'Let us imitate him. Even if God does not immediately give us what we ask, even if many people try to put us off our prayers, let us still go on praying' (St John Chrysostom, *Hom. on St Matthew*, 66).

" 'And Jesus stopped, and told them to call him.' Some of the better people in the crowd turned to the blind man and said, 'Take heart; rise, he is calling you.' Here you have the Christian vocation! But God does not call only once. Bear in mind that our Lord is seeking us at every moment: get up, he tells us, put aside your indolence, your easy life, your petty selfishness, your silly little problems. Get up from the ground, where you are lying prostrate and shapeless. Acquire height, weight and volume, and a supernatural outlook.

"And throwing off his mantle the man sprang up and came to Jesus. He threw off his mantle! I don't know if you have ever lived through a war, but many years ago I had occasion to visit a battlefield shortly after an engagement. There, strewn all over the ground, were greatcoats, water bottles, haversacks stuffed with family souvenirs, letters, photographs of loved ones … which belonged, moreover, not to the vanquished but to

telling him to be silent; but he cried out all the more, "Son of
David, have mercy on me!" 49And Jesus stopped and said, "Call
him." And they called the blind man, saying to him, "Take heart;
rise, he is calling you." 50And throwing off his mantle he sprang
up and came to Jesus. 51And Jesus said to him, "What do you
want me to do for you?" And the blind man said to him, "Master,[t]
let me receive my sight." 52And Jesus said to him, "Go your way;
your faith has made you well." And immediately he received his
sight and followed him on the way.

---

the victors! All these items had become superfluous in the bid to race forward and leap over the enemy defences. Just as happened to Bartimaeus, as he raced towards Christ.

"Never forget that Christ cannot be reached without sacrifice. We have to get rid of everything that gets in the way—greatcoat, haversack, water bottle. You have to do the same in this battle for the glory of God, in this struggle of love and peace by which we are trying to spread Christ's kingdom. In order to serve the Church, the Pope and all souls, you must be ready to give up everything superfluous. ...

"And now begins a dialogue with God, a marvellous dialogue that moves us and sets our hearts on fire, for you and I are now Bartimaeus. Christ, who is God, begins to speak and asks, *Quid tibi vis faciam?* 'What do you want me to do for you?' The blind man answers: 'Lord, that I may see.' How utterly logical! How about yourself, can you really see? Haven't you too experienced at times what happened to the blind man of Jericho? I can never forget how, when meditating on this passage many years back, and realizing that Jesus was expecting something of me, though I myself did not know what it was, I made up my own aspirations: 'Lord, what is it you want! What are you asking of me?' I had a feeling that he wanted me to take on something new and the cry, *Rabboni, ut videam*, 'Master, that I may see,' moved me to beseech Christ again and again, 'Lord, whatever it is that you wish, let it be done.'

"Pray with me now to our Lord: *doce me facere voluntatem tuam, quia Deus meus es tu* (Ps 142:10) ('teach me to do thy will, for you art my God'). In short, our lips should express a true desire on our part to correspond effectively to our Creator's promptings, striving to follow out his plans with unshakeable faith, being fully convinced that he cannot fail us. ...

"But let us go back to the scene outside Jericho. It is now to you that Christ is speaking. He asks you, 'What do you want me to do for you?' 'Master, let me receive my sight.' Then Jesus answers, 'Go your way. Your faith has made you well.' And immediately he received his sight and followed him on his way. Following Jesus on his way. You have understood what our Lord was asking from you and you have decided to accompany him on his way. You are trying to walk in his footsteps, to clothe yourself in Christ's clothing, to be Christ himself: well, your faith, your faith in the light our Lord is giving you, must be both operative and full of sacrifice. Don't fool yourself. Don't think you are going to find

t. Or *Rabbi*

PART THREE
Jesus' ministry in Jerusalem

8. CLEANSING OF THE TEMPLE. CONTROVERSIES

The Messiah enters the Holy City

11 [1]And when they drew near to Jerusalem, to Bethphage and Mt 21:1–9
Lk 19:29–38
Bethany, at the Mount of Olives, he sent two of his disci- Jn 12:12–16
ples, [2]and said to them, "Go into the village opposite you, and Lk 23:53
immediately as you enter it you will find a colt tied, on which no
one has ever sat; untie it and bring it. [3]If any one says to you, Mk 14:14

---

new ways. The faith he demands of us is as I have said. We must keep in step with him, working generously and at the same time uprooting and getting rid of everything that gets in the way" (St Josemaría Escrivá, *Friends of God*, 195–198).

11:1–11. Jesus had visited Jerusalem various times before, but he never did so in this way. Previously he had not wanted to be recognized as the Messiah; he avoided the enthusiasm of the crowd; but now he accepts their acclaim and even implies that it is justified, by entering the city in the style of a pacific king. Jesus' public ministry is about to come to a close: he has completed his mission; he has preached and worked miracles; he has revealed himself as God wished he should; now in this triumphant entry into Jerusalem he shows that he is the Messiah. The people, by shouting "Blessed is he who comes in the name of the Lord! Blessed is the kingdom of our father David that is coming!", are proclaiming Jesus as the long-awaited Messiah. When the leaders of the people move against him some days later, they reject this recognition the people have given him. Cf. the notes on Mt 21:1–5 and 21:9.

11:3. Although, absolutely speaking, our Lord has no need of man, in fact he does choose to use us to carry out his plans just as he made use of the donkey for his entry into Jerusalem. "Jesus makes do with a poor animal for a throne. I don't know about you; but I am not humiliated to acknowledge that in the Lord's eyes I am a beast of burden: 'I am like a donkey in your presence; nevertheless I am continually with you. You hold my right hand' (Ps 73:22–23), you take me by the bridle.

"Try to remember what a donkey is like—now that so few of them are left. Not an old, stubborn, vicious one that would give you a kick when you least expected, but a young one with his ears up like antennae. He lives on a meagre diet, is hard-working and has a quick, cheerful trot. There are hundreds of animals more beautiful, more deft and strong. But it was a donkey Christ chose when he presented himself to the people as king in response to their acclamation.

'Why are you doing this?' say, 'The Lord has need of it and will
send it back here immediately.'" 4And they went away, and found
a colt tied at the door out in the open street; and they untied it.
5And those who stood there said to them, "What are you doing,
untying the colt?" 6And they told them what Jesus had said; and
they let them go. 7And they brought the colt to Jesus, and threw
their garments on it; and he sat upon it. 8And many spread their
garments on the road, and others spread leafy branches which
Ps 118:26 they had cut from the fields. 9And those who went before and
those who followed cried out, "Hosanna! Blessed is he who
Lk 1:32 comes in the name of the Lord! 10Blessed is the kingdom of our
father David that is coming! Hosanna in the highest!"
Mt 21:12–22 Lk 19:45–48 11And he entered Jerusalem, and went into the temple; and
when he had looked around at everything, as it was already late,
he went out to Bethany with the twelve.

The barren fig tree. Expulsion of the money-changers

12On the following day, when they came from Bethany, he was
Lk 3:9; 13:6–9 hungry. 13And seeing in the distance a fig tree in leaf, he went to

---

For Jesus has no time for calculations, for astuteness, for the cruelty of cold hearts, for attractive but empty beauty. What he likes is the cheerfulness of a young heart, a simple step, a natural voice, clean eyes, attention to his affectionate word of advice. That is how he reigns in the soul" (St J. Escrivá, *Christ Is Passing By*, 181).

11:12. Jesus' hunger is another sign of his being truly human. When we contemplate Jesus we should feel him very close to us; he is true God and true man. His experience of hunger shows that he understands us perfectly: he has shared our needs and limitations. "How generous our Lord is in humbling himself and fully accepting his human condition! He does not use his divine power to escape from difficulties or effort. Let's pray that he will teach us to be tough, to love work, to appreciate the human and divine nobility of savouring the consequences of self-giving" (ibid., 161).

11:13–14. Jesus, of course, knew that it was not the right time for figs; therefore, he was not looking for figs to eat. His action must have a deeper meaning. The Fathers of the Church, whose interpretation St Bede reflects in his commentary on this passage, tell us that the miracle has an allegorical purpose: Jesus had come among his own people, the Jews, hungry to find fruit of holiness and good works, but all he found were external practices—leaves without fruit. Similarly, when he enters the temple, he upbraids those present for turning the temple of God, which is a house of prayer (prayer is the fruit of piety), into a place of commerce (mere leaves). "So you", St Bede concludes, "if you do not want to be condemned by Christ, should guard against being a barren tree, by offering to Jesus, who made himself poor, the fruit of piety which he expects of you" (*In Marci Evangelium expositio,* in loc.).

God wants both fruit and foliage; when, because the right intention is miss-

see if he could find anything on it. When he came to it, he found
nothing but leaves, for it was not the season for figs. [14]And he said
to it, "May no one ever eat fruit from you again." And his disciples heard it.

[15]And they came to Jerusalem. And he entered the temple and Jn 2:14–16
began to drive out those who sold and those who bought in the
temple, and he overturned the tables of the money-changers and
the seats of those who sold pigeons; [16]and he would not allow any
one to carry anything through the temple. [17]And he taught, and Is 56:7
said to them, "Is it not written, 'My house shall be called a house Jer 7:11
of prayer for all the nations'? But you have made it a den of robbers." [18]And the chief priests and the scribes heard it and sought a
way to destroy him; for they feared him, because all the multitude
was astonished at his teaching. [19]And when evening came they[u]
went out of the city.

[20]As they passed by in the morning, they saw the fig tree with- Mk 11:14
ered away to its roots. [21]And Peter remembered and said to him,
"Master,[v] look! The fig tree which you cursed has withered." Jn 14:1
[22]And Jesus answered them, "Have faith in God. [23]Truly, I say to Mt 17:20 Lk 17:6

---

ing, there are only leaves, only appearances, we must suspect that there is nothing but purely human action, with no supernatural depth—behaviour which results from ambition, pride and a desire to attract attention.

"We have to work a lot on this earth and we must do our work well, since it is our daily tasks that we have to sanctify. But let us never forget to do everything for God's sake. If we were to do it for ourselves, out of pride, we would produce nothing but leaves, and no matter how luxuriant they were, neither God nor our fellow man would find any good in them" (St Josemaría Escrivá, *Friends of God*, 202).

11:15–18. Our Lord does not abide lack of faith or piety in things to do with the worship of God. If he acts so vigorously to defend the temple of the Old Law, it indicates how we should conduct ourselves in the Christian temple, where he is really and truly present in the Blessed Eucharist. "Piety has its own good manners. Learn them. It's a shame to see those 'pious' people who don't know how to attend Mass—even though they go daily—nor how to bless themselves (they throw their hands about in the weirdest fashion), nor how to bend the knee before the tabernacle (their ridiculous genuflections seem a mockery), nor how to bow their heads reverently before a picture of our Lady" (St Josemaría Escrivá, *The Way*, 541). Cf. the note on Mt 21:12–13.

11:20–25. Jesus speaks to us here about the power of prayer. For prayer to be effective, absolute faith and trust are required: "A keen and living faith. Like Peter's. When you have it—our Lord has said so—you will move mountains, the humanly insuperable obstacles that rise

u. Other ancient authorities read *he* **v.** Or *Rabbi*

you, whoever says to this mountain, 'Be taken up and cast into the
sea,' and does not doubt in his heart, but believes that what he says
Mt 7:7 will come to pass, it will be done for him. [24]Therefore I tell you,
Jn 14:13; 16:23 whatever you ask in prayer, believe that you receive it, and you
Mt 5:23 will. [25]And whenever you stand praying, forgive, if you have anything against any one; so that your Father also who is in heaven
may forgive you your trespasses."[w]

Jesus' authority

Mt 21:23–27 [27]And they came again to Jerusalem. And as he was walking in the
Lk 20:1–8 temple, the chief priests and the scribes and the elders came to
him, [28]and they said to him, "By what authority are you doing
these things, or who gave you this authority to do them?" [29]Jesus
said to them, "I will ask you a question; answer me, and I will tell
you by what authority I do these things. [30]Was the baptism of John
from heaven or from men? Answer me." [31]And they argued with
one another, "If we say, 'From heaven,' he will say, 'Why then did
you not believe him?' [32]But shall we say, 'From men'?"—they

---

up against your apostolic undertakings" (St Josemaría Escrivá, *The Way*, 489).

For prayer to be effective, we also need to love our neighbour, forgiving him everything: if we do, then God our Father will also forgive us. Since we are all sinners we need to admit the fact before God and ask his pardon (cf. Lk 18:9–14). When Christ taught us to pray he required that we have these predispositions (cf. Mt 6:12; also Mt 5:23 and notes on same). Here is how Theophylact (*Enarratio in Evangelium Marci*, in loc.) puts it: "When you pray, if you have anything against anyone, forgive him, so that your Father who is in heaven may forgive you [...]. He who believes with great affection raises his whole heart to God and, in David's words, opens his soul to God. If he expands his heart before God in this way, he becomes one with him, and his burning heart is surer of obtaining what he desires."

Even when he is in the state of sin, man should seek God out in prayer; Jesus places no limitations at all: "Whatever you ask ...". Therefore, our personal unworthiness should not be an excuse for not praying confidently to God. Nor should the fact that God already knows our needs be an excuse for not turning to him. St Teresa explains this when she prays: "O my God, can it be better to keep silent about my necessities, hoping that Thou wilt relieve them? No, indeed, for Thou, my Lord and my Joy, knowing how many they must be and how it will alleviate them if we speak to Thee of them, dost bid us pray to Thee and say that Thou will not fail to give" (St Teresa, *Exclamations*, 5). Cf. the notes on Mt 6:5–6 and Mt 7:7–11.

11:26. As the RSV note points out, many ancient manuscripts add a verse 26: but it is clearly an addition, taken straight from

w. Other ancient authorities add verse 26, *"But if you do not forgive, neither will your Father who is in heaven forgive your trespasses"*

were afraid of the people, for all held that John was a real prophet.
33So they answered Jesus, "We do not know." And Jesus said to
them, "Neither will I tell you by what authority I do these things."

Parable of the wicked tenants

12 1And he began to speak to them in parables. "A man Mt 21:33–46
planted a vineyard, and set a hedge around it, and dug a pit Lk 20:9–19 Is 5:1–2
for the wine press, and built a tower, and let it out to tenants, and
went into another country. 2When the time came, he sent a servant
to the tenants, to get from them some of the fruit of the vineyard.
3And they took him and beat him, and sent him away empty-
handed. 4Again he sent to them another servant, and they
wounded him in the head, and treated him shamefully. 5And he
sent another, and him they killed; and so with many others, some
they beat and some they killed. 6He had still one other, a beloved
son; finally he sent him to them, saying, 'They will respect my
son.' 7But those tenants said to one another, 'This is the heir;
come, let us kill him, and the inheritance will be ours.' 8And they Heb 13:12
took him and killed him, and cast him out of the vineyard. 9What

---

Mt 6:15. This addition was included by the editors of the Old Vulgate.

11:27–33. Those who put this question to Jesus are the same people as, some days earlier, sought to destroy him (cf. Mk 11:18). They represent the official Judaism of the period (cf. the note on Mt 2:4). Jesus had already given proofs and signs of being the Messiah, in his miracles and preaching; and St John the Baptist had borne witness about who Jesus was. This is why, before replying, our Lord asks them to recognize the truth proclaimed by the Precursor. But they do not want to accept this truth; nor do they want to reject it publicly, out of fear of the people. Since they are not ready to admit their mistake, any further explanation Jesus might offer would serve no purpose.

This episode has many parallels in everyday life: anyone who seeks to call God to account will be confounded.

12:1–12. This parable is a masterly summary of history of salvation. To explain the mystery of his redemptive death, Jesus makes use of one of the most lovely allegories of the Old Testament: the so-called "song of the vineyard", in which Isaiah (5:1–7) prophesied Israel's ingratitude for God's favours. On the basis of this Isaiah text, Jesus reveals the patience of God, who sends one messenger after another—the prophets of the Old Testament—until at last, as the text says, he sends "his beloved son", Jesus, whom the tenants will kill. This expression, as also that which God himself uses to describe Christ at Baptism (1:11) and the transfiguration (9:7), points to the divinity of Jesus, who is the cornerstone of salvation, rejected by the builders in their selfishness and pride. To the Jews listening to Jesus telling this parable, his meaning must have been crystal clear. The rulers "perceived that he had told the parable against them" (v. 12) and that it was about the fulfilment of the Isaiah prophecy (cf. the note on Mt 21:33–46).

will the owner of the vineyard do? He will come and destroy the
tenants, and give the vineyard to others. 10Have you not read this
scripture:

Ps 118:22–23 'The very stone which the builders rejected
has become the head of the corner;
11this was the Lord's doing,
and it is marvellous in our eyes'?"

12And they tried to arrest him, but feared the multitude, for
they perceived that he had told the parable against them; so they
left him and went away.

Paying tax to Caesar

Mt 22:15–22 13And they sent to him some of the Pharisees and some of the
Lk 20:20–26 Herodians, to entrap him in his talk. 14And they came and said to
Mk 3:6 him, "Teacher, we know that you are true, and care for no man;
for you do not regard the position of men, but truly teach the way
of God. Is it lawful to pay taxes to Caesar, or not? 15Should we
pay them, or should we not?" But knowing their hypocrisy, he
said to them, "Why put me to the test? Bring me a coin,[x] and let
me look at it." 16And they brought one. And he said to them,
"Whose likeness and inscription is this?" They said to him,
"Caesar's." 17Jesus said to them, "Render to Caesar the things that
Rom 13:7 are Caesar's, and to God the things that are God's." And they were
amazed at him.

12:13–17. Jesus uses this situation to teach that man belongs totally to his Creator: "You must perforce give Caesar the coin which bears his likeness, but let you give your whole being to God, because it is his likeness, not Caesar's, that you bear" (St Jerome, *Comm. in Marcum*, in loc.).

Our Lord here asserts a principle which should guide the action of Christians in public life. The Church recognizes the rightful autonomy of earthly realities, but this does not mean that she has not a responsibility to light them up with the light of the Gospel. When they work shoulder to shoulder with other citizens to develop society, Christian lay people should bring a Christian influence to bear: "If the role of the Hierarchy is to teach and to interpret authentically the norms of morality to be followed in this matter, it belongs to lay people, without waiting passively for orders and directives, to take the initiative freely and to infuse a Christian spirit into the mentality, customs, laws and structures of the community in which they live. Changes are necessary, basic reforms are indispensable; lay people should strive resolutely to permeate them with the spirit of the Gospel" (Paul VI, *Populorum progressio*, 81).

12:18–27. Before answering the difficulty proposed by the Sadducees, Jesus

x. Greek *a denarius*

The resurrection of the dead

18 And Saducees came to him, who say that there is no resurrec- Mt 22:23–33
tion; and they asked him a question, saying, 19 "Teacher, Moses Lk 20:27–38
wrote for us that if a man's brother dies and leaves a wife, but Deut 25:5–6
leaves no child, the man[y] must take the wife, and raise up children Gen 28:8
for his brother. 20 There were seven brothers; the first took a wife,
and when he died left no children; 21 and the second took her, and
died, leaving no children; and the third likewise; 22 and the seven
left no children. Last of all the woman also died. 23 In the resurrection whose wife will she be? For the seven had her as wife."
24 Jesus said to them, "Is not this why you are wrong, that you
know neither the scriptures nor the power of God? 25 For when
they rise from the dead, they neither marry nor are given in marriage, but are like angels in heaven. 26 And as for the dead being Ex 3:2, 6
raised, have you not read in the book of Moses, in the passage Mt 8:11
about the bush, how God said to him, 'I am the God of Abraham, Lk 16:22
and the God of Isaac, and the God of Jacob'? 27 He is not God of
the dead, but of the living; you are quite wrong."

The greatest commandment of all

28 And one of the scribes came up and heard them disputing with Mt 22:34–40
one another, and seeing that he answered them well, asked him, Lk 20:39–40; 10:25–28
"Which commandment is the first of all?" 29 Jesus answered, "The

---

wants to identify the source of the problem—man's tendency to confine the greatness of God inside a human framework through excessive reliance on reason, not giving due weight to divine Revelation and the power of God. A person can have difficulty with the truths of faith; this is not surprising, for these truths are above human reason. But it is ridiculous to try to find contradictions in the revealed word of God; this only leads away from any solution of difficulty and may make it impossible to find one's way back to God. We need to approach Sacred Scripture, and, in general, the things of God, with the humility which faith demands. In the passage about the burning bush, which Jesus quotes to the Sadducees, God says this to Moses: "Put off your shoes from your feet, for the place on which you are standing is holy ground" (Ex 3:5).

12:28–34. The doctor of the law who asks Jesus this question is obviously an upright man who is sincerely seeking the truth. He was impressed by Jesus' earlier reply (vv. 18–27) and he wants to learn more from him. His question is to the point and Jesus devotes time to instructing him, though he will soon castigate the scribes, of whom this man is one (cf. Mk 12:38ff).

Jesus sees in this man not just a scribe but a person who is looking for the truth. And his teaching finds its way into

y. Greek *his brother*

Deut 6:4–5 first is, 'Hear, O Israel: The Lord our God, the Lord is one; [30]and
you shall love the Lord your God with all your heart, and with all
your soul, and with all your mind, and with all your strength.'
Lev 19:18 Jn 15:12 [31]The second is this, 'You shall love your neighbour as yourself.'
Deut 6:4; 4:35 There is no other commandment greater than these." [32]And the
scribe said to him, "You are right, Teacher; you have truly said that
1 Sam 15:22 he is one, and there is no other than he; [33]and to love him with all
the heart, and with all the understanding, and with all the strength,
and to love one's neighbour as oneself, is much more than all
Acts 26:27–29 whole burnt offerings and sacrifices." [34]And when Jesus saw that
he answered wisely, he said to him, "You are not far from the kingdom of God." And after that no one dared to ask him any question.

The divinity of the Messiah

Mt 22:41–46 Lk 20:41–44 [35]And as Jesus taught in the temple, he said, "How can the scribes
say that the Christ is the son of David? [36]David himself, inspired
by[z] the Holy Spirit, declared,

---

the man's heart. The scribe repeats what Jesus says, savouring it, and our Lord offers him an affectionate word which encourages his definitive conversion: "You are not far from the kingdom of God." This encounter reminds us of his meeting with Nicodemus (cf. Jn 3:1ff). On the doctrinal content of these two commandments see the note on Mt 22:34–40.

12:30. This commandment of the Old Law, ratified by Jesus, shows, above all, God's great desire to engage in intimate conversation with man: "Would it not have sufficed to publish a permission giving us leave to love him? [...] He makes a stronger declaration of his passionate love of us, and commands us to love him with all our power, lest the consideration of his majesty and our misery, which make so great a distance and inequality between us, or some other pretext, divert us from his love. In this he well shows that he did not leave in us for nothing the natural inclination to love him, for to the end that it may not be idle, he urges us by his general commandment to employ it, and that this commandment may be effected, there is no living man he has not furnished him abundantly with all means requisite thereto" (St Francis de Sales, *Treatise on the Love of God*, book 2, chap. 8).

12:35–37. Jesus here bears witness, with his special authority, to the fact that Scripture is divinely inspired, when he says that David was inspired by the Holy Spirit when writing Psalm 110. We can see from here that Jews found it difficult to interpret the beginning of the Psalm. Jesus shows the messianic sense of the words "The Lord said to my Lord": the second "Lord" is the Messiah, with whom Jesus implicitly identifies himself. The mysteriously transcendental character of the Messiah is indicated by the paradox of his being the son, the descendant, of David, and yet David

z. Or *himself, in*

'The Lord said to my Lord,
Sit at my right hand,
till I put thy enemies under thy feet.'
37David himself calls him Lord; so how is he his son?" And the
great throng heard him gladly.

Ps 101:1
2 Sam 23:2
Mt 9:27
Jn 7:42
Lk 19:48;
21:38

Jesus censures the scribes

38And in his teaching he said, "Beware of the scribes, who like to
go about in long robes, and to have salutations in the market
places 39and the best seats in the synagogues and the places of
honour at feasts, 40who devour widows' houses and for a pretence
make long prayers. They will receive the greater condemnation."

Mt 23:6–7
Lk 20:45–47

The widow's mite

41And he sat down opposite the treasury, and watched the multitude putting money into the treasury. Many rich people put in
large sums. 42And a poor widow came, and put in two copper
coins, which make a penny. 43And he called his disciples to him,
and said to them, "Truly, I say to you, this poor widow has put in

Lk 21:1–4
2 Kings 12:10

---

calls him his Lord. Cf. the note on Mt 22:41–46.

12:38–40. Our Lord reproves disordered desire for human honours: "We should notice that salutations in the marketplace are not forbidden, nor people taking the best seats if that befits their position; rather, the faithful are warned to avoid, as they would evil men, those who set too much store by such honours" (St Bede, *In Marci Evangelium expositio*, in loc.). See also the notes on Mt 23:2–3, 5, 11 and 14.

12:41–44. Our Lord uses this little event to teach us the importance of things which apparently are insignificant. He puts it somewhat paradoxically; the poor widow has contributed more than all the rich. In God's sight the value of such an action lies more in upright intention and generosity of spirit than in the quantity one gives. "Didn't you see the light in Jesus' eyes as the poor widow left her little alms in the temple? Give him what you can: the merit is not in whether it is big or small, but in the intention with which you give it" (St Josemaría Escrivá, *The Way*, 829).

By the same token, our actions are pleasing to God even if they are not as perfect as we would like. St Francis de Sales comments: "Now as among the treasures of the temple, the poor widow's mite was much esteemed, so the least little good works, even though performed somewhat coldly and not according to the whole extent of the charity which is in us, are agreeable to God, and esteemed by him; so that though of themselves they cannot cause any increase in the existing love [...] yet divine providence, counting on them and, out of his goodness, valuing them, forthwith rewards them with increase of charity for the present, and assigns to them a greater heavenly glory for the future" (*Treatise on the Love of God*, book 3, chap. 2).

2 Cor 8:12 more than all those who are contributing to the treasury. 44For they
all contributed out of their abundance; but she out of her poverty
has put in everything she had, her whole living."

9. THE ESCHATOLOGICAL DISCOURSE

Announcement of the destruction of the temple

Mt 24:1–3 **13** 1And as he came out of the temple, one of his disciples
Lk 21:5–7 said to him, "Look, Teacher, what wonderful stones and
what wonderful buildings!" 2And Jesus said to him, "Do you see
these great buildings? There will not be left here one stone upon
another, that will not be thrown down."

13:1. The temple of Jerusalem was the pride of the Jews, awe-inspiring in scale and magnificence. Its enormous blocks of cut stone gave it an overwhelming sense of permanence. Using here, as always, everyday incidents as examples to engrave his teaching on people's minds, Jesus Christ prophesied that soon the temple would be toppled, leaving not one stone upon another. The contrast between reality and prophecy left the apostles dumbfounded.

The prophecy was fulfilled to the letter in the year 70, when Titus conquered Jerusalem. The Roman soldiers set fire to the temple. Titus, who wanted to preserve it, tried to put out the blaze, but when he failed to do so he ordered its total destruction. The walls which exist today were the foundations of the building and part of the exterior wall: of the sanctuary itself not one stone remained standing on another. In the reign of Julian the Apostate (AD 363) some Jews tried in vain to rebuild the temple; since then no such attempts have been made.

13:4. The prophecy of the destruction of the temple was clearly contrary to the nationalistic ideas of the Jews. To their minds such a catastrophe could only happen as part of the end of the world (cf. Mt 24:3). After remaining silent for a while (cf. Mk 13:2–3), the apostles ask when this will happen and what signs will indicate that the temple is about to be destroyed.

This destruction, Jesus explains, prefigures the end of the world, but does not imply that the latter is imminent; each event has characteristics of its own. Thus, the destruction of the temple will have its own signals and will happen in the next generation. The end of the world, however, is a secret known to God alone, and not even the Son wishes to reveal when this final event will happen (cf. Mk 13:32–33; Mt 24:36).

The apostles ask Jesus about the end of the temple of Jerusalem and he notifies them of something more important: a time is approaching when they will need to be on the alert, in order not to be led into temptation or be deceived by false prophets.

Jesus replies to his disciples' questions in the form of a sermon, called the "eschatological discourse", which takes up all chapter 13 of St Mark. It is also called the "synoptic apocalypse", because it deals, mainly, with the last days of history, which will be marked by great

The beginning of tribulation. Persecution on account of the Gospel

[3]And as he sat on the Mount of Olives opposite the temple, Peter
and James and John and Andrew asked him privately, [4]"Tell us,
when will this be, and what will be the sign when these are all to
be accomplished?" [5]And Jesus began to say to them, "Take heed Mt 24:4–14
that no one leads you astray. [6]Many will come in my name, Lk 21:8–19
saying, 'I am he!' and they will lead many astray. [7]And when you
hear of wars and rumours of wars, do not be alarmed; this must
take place, but the end is not yet. [8]For nation will rise against Is 19:2
nation, and kingdom against kingdom; there will be earthquakes 2 Chron 15:6
in various places, there will be famines; this is but the beginning
of the sufferings.

[9]"But take heed to yourselves; for they will deliver you up to Mt 10:17–22
councils, and you will be beaten in synagogues; and you will Lk 21:12–17
stand before governors and kings for my sake, to bear testimony
before them. [10]And the gospel must first be preached to all Mk 16:15

---

catastrophes. Jesus uses this style of language to encourage us to be vigilant.

13:9. Jesus prophesies to the apostles that they will undergo persecutions because they preach the Gospel. These will be set in motion by the Jews (cf. Acts 4:5ff; 5:21ff; 6:12ff; 22:30; 23:1ff; 2 Cor 11:24), whose synagogues Tertullian called "fountains of persecution" (*Scorpiace*, 10, 143), and continued by the Gentiles. These words of Jesus came true even in the lifetime of the apostles. Appearance before the courts gave Christians a very valuable opportunity to bear witness to the Gospel (Acts 4:1–21; 5:17–42) and sometimes stirred the conscience of those who wielded authority, as the imprisonment of St Paul clearly shows (Acts 16:19–38; 22:24–26; 28:30–31).

13:10. This is one of the occasions on which our Lord proclaims that the Gospel, the good news of salvation, is destined to spread all over the world; and indeed, before the destruction of Jerusalem, the apostles had already preached it all over the known world. Similarly, before the end of time all peoples will have heard the news and been given an opportunity to be converted, through the preaching of the Church; but this does not mean that everyone will accept and remain faithful to Christ's teaching. In any event, persecutions and difficulties should not lessen the apostolic zeal of his disciples but rather urge it on, for Christ's promise should always act as an effective stimulus. Our Lord, in fact, counts on us to engage in the truly apostolic task of spreading the Gospel.

The Second Vatican Council lays stress on the missionary character of the Church: "Even in the secular history of mankind the Gospel has acted as a leaven in the interests of liberty and progress, and it always offers itself as a leaven with regard to brotherhood, unity and peace. So it is not without reason that Christ is hailed by the faithful as 'the hope of the nations and their saviour' (Antiphon, 23 December). The period, therefore, between the first and second comings of the Lord is the time of missionary activity, when, like the harvest, the Church will be gathered

nations. 11And when they bring you to trial and deliver you up, do
not be anxious beforehand what you are to say; but say whatever
is given you in that hour, for it is not you who speak, but the Holy
Mic 7:6 Spirit. 12And brother will deliver up brother to death, and the
father his child, and children will rise against parents and have
Jn 15:21 them put to death; 13and you will be hated by all for my name's
sake. But he who endures to the end will be saved.

The great tribulation

Dan 9:27; 12:4, 10 14"But when you see the desolating sacrilege set up where it ought
not to be (let the reader understand), then let those who are in

---

from the four winds into the kingdom of God. For the Gospel must be preached to all peoples before the Lord comes" (*Ad gentes*, 8–9).

13:11. The natural fear this prophecy causes in the disciples provides our Lord with an opportunity to encourage them, by promising them the help of the Holy Spirit, who will suggest to them what to say in these circumstances.

The lives of the martyrs are full of examples of how ordinary people find words of wisdom far above their natural ability.

Supported by Jesus' promise, so often fulfilled, we should never be afraid, no matter what difficulties arise; on the contrary, we should have a holy daring, leading us to confess, spread and defend the faith, thereby fulfilling our obligation to be apostolic in our own environment.

13:13. In the first three centuries of the Church the mere fact of being a Christian was reason enough to be hauled before the courts. St Justin (2nd century) went as far as saying that "in our case you use the mere name as proof against us" (*Apology*, 1, 4, 44). There have been, and are, countless Christians whose lives, reputations and property have been attacked out of hatred of the Gospel; in them are fulfilled these words of Jesus: "Blessed are those who are persecuted for righteousness' sake, for theirs is the kingdom of heaven. Blessed are you when men revile you and persecute you and utter all kinds of evil against you falsely on my account" (Mt 5:10–11; cf. Acts 5:41; 1 Pet 4:12–14). Nothing compares with the glory which will be the reward of those who persevere (cf. Rom 8:18).

Our Lord's final words in Mark 13:13 are an exhortation to persevere to the very end: "He who endures to the end will be saved." For each person this "end" is the moment of death. As the Magisterium of the Church teaches, each person, *immediately* after dying, passes on to enjoy his or her eternal reward or to suffer eternal punishment—though some must undergo purification in purgatory before entering the joy of heaven: "We make the following definition: In the usual providence of God the souls of all the saints who departed from this world before the Passion of our Lord Jesus Christ, and also those of the holy apostles, martyrs, confessors, virgins, and others of the faithful who died after receiving the Baptism of Christ—provided that they had no need of purification at the time of their death, or will not have such need when they die at some future time; [...] and that the souls of children who have been reborn with the

Judea flee to the mountains; [15]let him who is on the housetop not
go down, nor enter his house, to take anything away; [16]and let him Mt 24:15–25
who is in the field not turn back to take his mantle. [17]And alas for Lk 21:20–24
those who are with child and for those who give suck in those
days! [18]Pray that it may not happen in winter. [19]For in those days Dan 12:1
there will be such tribulation as has not been from the beginning Joel 2:2
of the creation which God created until now, and never will be.
[20]And if the Lord had not shortened the days, no human being
would be saved; but for the sake of the elect, whom he chose, he
shortened the days. [21]"And then if any one says to you, 'Look,
here is the Christ!' or 'Look, there he is!' do not believe it. [22]False Deut 13:1
Christs and false prophets will arise and show signs and wonders,

---

Baptism of Christ […] when they die before attaining the use of free will: all these souls immediately after death, or in the case of those needing it, after the purification we have mentioned, have been, are, and will be in heaven […] with Christ, joined to the company of the holy angels […]. We also define that […] the souls of those who die in actual mortal sin go down into hell soon after their death, and there suffer the pains of hell. Nevertheless, on the Day of Judgment, all men will appear with their bodies before the tribunal of Christ to render an account of their personal deeds, that 'each one may receive good or evil, according to what he has done in the body' (2 Cor 5:10)" (Benedict XII, *Benedictus Deus*).

13:14–19. From v. 14 on, the discourse refers to the events which will happen at the time of the destruction of Jerusalem. For interpretation of this passage see the note on Mt 24:15–20.

13:14. "The desolating sacrilege", the "abomination of desolation", a phrase taken from Daniel (9:27), is normally used to designate any idolatrous and sacrilegous person, thing or act outrageous to the religious faith and worship of the Jewish people (1 Mac 1:5).

From the parallel passage in St Matthew (24:25) we can see that Jesus explicitly cited the prophecy of Daniel 9:27. Hence, the phrase "let the reader understand", which occurs in both Gospels, should be seen as an exhortation by Jesus to attentively read the prophetic text in the light of his words. Cf. the note on Mt 24:15.

13:19–20. Verse 19 evokes a passage in Daniel (12:1). In this way Jesus moves on to describe the signals of the imminent end of the world, and the great distress that will obtain at the time. This distress, although it covers the entire history of the Church from its beginnings, will become especially severe at the time of the End. Despite being fearsome times, these are times of salvation, arranged by divine providence for the good of those who love God (cf. Rom 8:28). Therefore, they have to be faced with total confidence in God: he will shorten these days and will save us.

13:21–22. Life is a testing-time to prove our fidelity to God, and fidelity consists in acting on foot of this capital truth: there is no Saviour other than Jesus Christ (cf. Acts 4:12; 1 Tim 2:5). Anyone else who puts himself forward as a sav-

to lead astray, if possible, the elect. [23]But take heed; I have told
you all things beforehand.

The coming of the Son of man

Is 13:10 [24]"But in those days, after that tribulation, the sun will be dark-
Is 34:4 ened, and the moon will not give its light, [25]and the stars will be
falling from heaven, and the powers in the heavens will be shaken.
Dan 7:13 [26]And then they will see the Son of man coming in clouds with
Zech 2:6 great power and glory. [27]And then he will send out the angels, and
Deut 30:4 gather his elect from the four winds, from the ends of the earth to
Mt 13:41 the ends of heaven.

The end will surely come: the lesson of the fig tree

[28]"From the fig tree learn its lesson: as soon as its branch becomes
tender and puts forth its leaves, you know that summer is near.
[29]So also, when you see these things taking place, you know that

---

iour sent by God is a liar or a fool: whether he be a person, an ideology or a political system. Forewarned by what Jesus says here, a Christian knows that these false messiahs who try to take God's place can be successfully resisted by clinging to revealed Truth, which is guarded by the Magisterium of the Church.

13:23. "Not only did he foretell the good things which his saints and faithful would attain, but also the many bad experiences they would undergo in this life; his purpose being to give us a surer hope of reaching the good things which will come at the end of time, despite the evils which must precede them" (St Augustine, *Letters*, 127).

13:24–25. It would seem that at the end of time even irrational creatures will shrink before the Supreme Judge, Jesus Christ, coming in the majesty of his glory, thus fulfilling the prophecies of the Old Testament (cf., e.g., Is 13:10; 34:4; Ezek 32:7). Some Fathers, such as St Jerome (*Comm. in Matthew*, in loc.) and St John Chrysostom (*Hom. on St Matthew*, 77) understand "the powers in the heavens" to mean the angels, who will be in awe at these events. This interpretation is supported by the liturgical use of describing the angels, taken together, as "*virtutes caelorum*" (cf. *Roman Missal*, Preface of Martyrs). But many other commentators think the phrase, like the preceding words in the text, could mean "cosmic forces" or "stars of the firmament."

13:26–27. Christ here describes his second coming, at the end of time, as announced by the prophet Daniel (7:13). He discloses the deeper meaning of the words of the ancient prophet: the "one like a son of man", whom Daniel saw and to whom "was given dominion and glory and kingdom, that all peoples, nations and languages should serve him", is Jesus Christ himself, who will gather the saints around him.

13:28–30. As already pointed out in the note on Mark 13:4, Jesus' disciples, following the ideas current among Jews at

he is near, at the very gates. [30]Truly, I say to you, this generation
will not pass away before all these things take place. [31]Heaven and
earth will pass away, but my words will not pass away.

The time of Christ's second coming

[32]"But of that day or that hour no one knows, not even the angels Mt 24:36
in heaven, nor the Son, but only the Father. [33]Take heed, watch
and pray;[a] for you do not know when the time will come. [34]It is Mt 25:14
like a man going on a journey, when he leaves home and puts his Lk 19:12
servants in charge, each with his work, and commands the door-
keeper to be on the watch. [35]Watch therefore—for you do not Lk 12:38
know when the master of the house will come, in the evening, or
at midnight, or at cockcrow, or in the morning—[36]lest he come
suddenly and find you asleep. [37]And what I say to you I say to all:
Watch."

---

the time, could not conceive the destruction of Jerusalem as separate from the end of the world; and, also, there is a connexion between the two events, in that the former is a prefigurement of the latter. Our Lord answers his disciples in Mark 13:20 by saying that the destruction of Jerusalem will happen in the lifetime of their generation (as in fact occurred in the year 70, at the hands of the Roman legions). For further explanation of the ruin of Jerusalem as a figure of the end of the world, see the note on Mt 24:32–35.

13:31. With this sentence our Lord adds a special solemnity to what he is saying: all this will definitely come to pass.

God has only to speak and his words come true, only he who is Lord of the Universe has all existence in his power, and Jesus has received from the Father all power over heaven and earth (cf. Mt 11:27 and 28:18).

13:32. Referring to this verse, St Augustine explains (*On the Psalms*, 36:1): "Our Lord Jesus Christ was sent to be our Master, yet he declared that even the Son of Man was ignorant of that day, because it was not part of his office as Master to acquaint us with it."

Regarding the knowledge Christ had during his life on earth, see the note on Lk 2:52.

13:33–37. "Watch": since we do not know when the Lord will come, we must be prepared. Vigilance is, above all, love. A person who loves keeps the commandments and looks forward to Christ's return; for life is a period of hope and waiting. It is the way towards our encounter with Christ the Lord. The first Christians often tenderly repeated the aspiration: "Come, Lord Jesus" (1 Cor 16:22; Rev 22:20). By expressing their faith and charity in this way, those Christians found the interior strength and optimism necessary for fulfilling their family and social duties, and interiorly detached themselves from earthly goods, with the self-mastery that came from hope of eternal life.

a. Other ancient authorities omit *and pray*

10. PASSION, DEATH AND RESURRECTION OF JESUS

The conspiracy against Jesus

Mt 26:1–5
Lk 22:1–2

14 [1]It was now two days before the Passover and the feast of
Unleavened Bread. And the chief priests and the scribes
were seeking how to arrest him by stealth, and kill him; [2]for they
said, "Not during the feast, lest there be a tumult of the people."

The anointing at Bethany and the treachery of Judas

Mt 26:6–13
Jn 12:1–8
Lk 7:36

[3]And while he was at Bethany in the house of Simon the leper, as
he sat at table, a woman came with an alabaster jar of ointment of
pure nard, very costly, and she broke the jar and poured it over his
head. [4]But there were some who said to themselves indignantly,
"Why was the ointment thus wasted? [5]For this ointment might
have been sold for more than three hundred denarii,[b] and given to

---

14:1. The Passover was the main national and religious festival. It lasted one week, during which the eating of leavened bread was forbidden, which is why the period was known as the Azymes, the feast of the Unleavened Bread. The celebration opened with the passover meal on the night of the 14th to 15th of the month of Nisan. The essential rite of the meal consisted in eating the paschal lamb sacrificed in the temple the afternoon before. During the meal the youngest member of the family asked what was the meaning of the ceremony; and the head of the household explained to those present that it commemorated God's liberation of the Israelites when they were slaves in Egypt, and specifically the passing of the angel of Yahweh, doing no harm to the first-born of the Hebrews but destroying the first-born of the Egyptians (cf. Ex 12).

14:2. The chief priests and the scribes sought every means to ensure the condemnation and death of the Lord prior to the Passover, for during the festival Jerusalem would be thronged with pilgrims and they feared that Jesus' popularity might cause the complications referred to in the Gospel text. Cf. the note on Mt 26:3–5.

14:3–9. It was a custom at the time to honour distinguished guests by offering them scented water. This woman treated the Lord with exquisite refinement by pouring a flask of nard over his head; and we can see that he was very appreciative. Three hundred denarii was approximately what a worker would earn in a year: so her action was very generous. Breaking the flask to allow the last drop to flow, so that no one else could use it, implies that Jesus merited everything.

It is important to notice the significance our Lord gave to this gesture: it was an anticipation of the pious custom of embalming bodies prior to burial. This woman would never have thought that her action would become famous throughout the world, but Jesus knew the transcendence and universal dimension

b. The denarius was a day's wage for a labourer

the poor." And they reproached her. [6]But Jesus said, "Let her
alone; why do you trouble her? She has done a beautiful thing to
me. [7]For you always have the poor with you, and whenever you Deut 15:11
will, you can do good to them; but you will not always have me.
[8]She has done what she could; she has anointed my body before- Acts 3:6
hand for burying. [9]And truly, I say to you, wherever the gospel is
preached in the whole world, what she has done will be told in
memory of her."

[10]Then Judas Iscariot, who was one of the twelve, went to the Mt 26:14–16
chief priests in order to betray him to them. [11]And when they Lk 22:3–6
heard it they were glad, and promised to give him money. And he
sought an opportunity to betray him."

Preparations for the Last Supper. Judas' treachery foretold

[12]And on the first day of Unleavened Bread, when they sacrificed Mk 26:17–19
the passover lamb, his disciples said to him, "Where will you have Lk 22:7–13

---

of even the smallest episodes in the Gospel story. His prophecy has been fulfilled: "Certainly we hear her story told in all the churches … . Wherever in the world you may go, everyone respectfully listens to the story of her good service … . And yet hers was not an extraordinary deed, nor was she a distinguished person, nor was there a large audience, nor was the place one where she could easily be seen. She made no entrance onto a theatre stage to perform her service but did her good deed in a private house. Nevertheless … , today she is more illustrious than any king or queen; no passage of years has buried in oblivion this service she performed" (St John Chrysostom, *Adversus Iudaeos*, 5, 2).

This episode teaches us the refinement with which we should treat the holy humanity of Jesus; it also shows that generosity in things to do with sacred worship is always praiseworthy, for it is a sign of our love for the Lord. Cf. the note on Mt 26:8–11.

14:10–11. In contrast with the generous anointing by the woman, the Gospel now reports Judas' sad treachery. Her magnaminity highlights the covetousness of Jesus' false friend. "O folly, or rather ambition, of the traitor, for ambition spawns every kind of evil and enslaves souls by every sort of device; it causes forgetfulness and mental derangement. Judas, enslaved by his mad ambition, forgot all about the years he had spent alongside Jesus, forgot that he had eaten at his table, that he had been his disciple; forgot all the counsel and persuasion Jesus had offered him" (St John Chrysostom, *Hom. de prodit. Judae*).

Judas' sin is always something Christians should be mindful of: "Today many people are horrified by Judas' crime—that he could be so cruel and so sacrilegious as to sell his Master and his God; and yet they fail to realize that when they for human reasons dismiss the rights of charity and truth, they are betraying God, who is charity and truth" (St Bede, *Super Qui audientes …*).

14:12–16. At first sight our Lord's behaviour described here seems quite out of character. However, if we think about it,

us go and prepare for you to eat the passover?" [13]And he sent two
of his disciples, and said to them, "Go into the city, and a man
Mk 11:3 carrying a jar of water will meet you; follow him,* [14]and wherever
he enters, say to the householder, 'The Teacher says, Where is my
guest room, where I am to eat the passover with my disciples?'
[15]And he will show you a large upper room furnished and ready;
there prepare for us." [16]And the disciples set out and went to the
city, and found it as he had told them; and they prepared the
passover.

Mt 26:20–29 Lk 22:14–23 Jn 13:21–26 Ps 41:9

[17]And when it was evening he came with the twelve. [18]And as
they were at table eating, Jesus said, "Truly, I say to you, one of
you will betray me, one who is eating with me." [19]They began to
be sorrowful, and to say to him one after another, "Is it I?" [20]He

---

it is quite consistent: probably Jesus wanted to avoid Judas knowing in advance the exact place where the Supper will be held, to prevent him notifying the Sanhedrin. And so God's plans for that memorable night of Holy Thursday were fulfilled: Judas was unable to advise the Sanhedrin where they could find Jesus until after the celebration of the passover meal (during which Judas left the Cenacle): cf. Jn 13:30.

St Mark describes in more detail than the other evangelists the place where the meal took place: he says it was a large, well-appointed room—a dignified place. There is an ancient Christian tradition that the house of the Cenacle was owned by Mary the mother of St Mark, to whom, it seems, the Garden of Olives also belonged.

14:17–21. Jesus shows that he knows in advance what is going to happen and is acting freely and deliberately, identifying himself with the will of his Father. The words of vv. 18 and 19 are a further call to Judas to repent; our Lord refrained from denouncing him publicly, so making it easier for him to change his mind. But he did not want to remain silent about the incipient treachery; they should realize that the Master knew everything (cf. Jn 13:23ff).

14:22. The word "this" does not refer to the act of breaking the bread but to the "thing" which Jesus gives his disciples, that is, something which looked like bread and which was no longer bread but the body of Christ. "This is my body. That is to say, what I am giving you now and what you are taking is my body. For the bread is not only a symbol of the body of Christ; it becomes his very body, as the Lord has said: the bread which I shall give for the life of the world is my flesh. Therefore, the Lord conserves the appearances of bread and wine but changes the bread and wine into the reality of his flesh and his blood" (Theophylact, *Enarratio in Evangelium Marci*, in loc.). Therefore, any interpretation in the direction of symbolism or metaphor does not fit the meaning of the text. The same applies to the "This is my blood" (v. 24). On the realism of these expressions, see the first part of the note on Mt 26:26–29.

14:24. The words of consecration of the chalice clearly show that the Eucharist is a sacrifice: the blood of Christ is poured

said to them, "It is one of the twelve, one who is dipping bread in
the same dish with me. 21For the Son of man goes as it is written
of him, but woe to that man by whom the Son of man is betrayed!
It would have been better for that man if he had not been born."

The institution of the Eucharist

22And as they were eating, he took bread, and blessed, and broke 1 Cor 11:23–25
it, and gave it to them, and said, "Take; this is my body." 23And he
took a cup, and when he had given thanks he gave it to them, and
they all drank of it. 24And he said to them, "This is my blood of Ex 24:8
the[c] covenant, which is poured out for many. 25Truly, I say to you, Zech 9:11
I shall not drink again of the fruit of the vine until that day when
I drink it new in the kingdom of God."

---

out, sealing the new and definitive Covenant of God with men. This Covenant remains sealed forever by the sacrifice of Christ on the cross, in which Jesus is both Priest and Victim. The Church has defined this truth in these words: "If anyone says that in the Mass a true and proper sacrifice is not offered to God, or that to be offered is nothing else but that Christ is given us to eat, let him be anathema" (Council of Trent, *De S. Missae sacrificio*, chap. 1, can. 1).

These words pronounced over the chalice must have been very revealing for the apostles, because they show that the sacrifices of the Old Covenant were in fact a preparation for and anticipation of Christ's sacrifice. The apostles were able to grasp that the Covenant of Sinai and the various sacrifices of the temple were merely an imperfect pre-figurement of the definitive sacrifice and definitive Covenant, which would take place on the cross and which they were anticipating in this Supper.

A clear explanation of the sacrificial character of the Eucharist can be found in the inspired text in chapters 8 and 9 of the Letter to the Hebrews. Similarly, the best preparation for understanding the real presence and the Eucharist as food for the soul is a reading of chapter 6 of the Gospel of St John.

At the Last Supper, then, Christ already offered himself voluntarily to his Father as a victim to be sacrificed. The Supper and the Mass constitute with the cross one and the same unique and perfect sacrifice, for in all these cases the victim offered is the same—Christ; and the priest is the same—Christ. The only difference is that the Supper, which takes place prior to the cross, anticipates the Lord's death in an unbloody way and offers a victim soon to be immolated; whereas the Mass offers, also in an unbloody manner, the victim already immolated on the cross, a victim who exists forever in heaven.

14:25. After instituting the Holy Eucharist, our Lord extends the Last Supper in intimate conversation with his disciples, speaking to them once more about his imminent death (cf. Jn, chaps. 13–17). His farewell saddens the apostles, but he promises that the day will come when he will meet with them again, when the

c. Other ancient authorities insert *new*

The disciples will desert Jesus

Mt 26:30–35
Lk 22:31–34, 39 26And when they had sung a hymn, they went out to the Mount of
Ps 113–118 Zech 13:7 Olives. 27And Jesus said to them, "You will all fall away; for it is
written, 'I will strike the shepherd, and the sheep will be scat-
Mk 16:7 tered.' 28But after I am raised up, I will go before you to Galilee."
29Peter said to him, "Even though they all fall away, I will not."
Jn 13:38 30And Jesus said to him, "Truly, I say to you, this very night,
before the cock crows twice, you will deny me three times." 31But

---

Kingdom of God will have come in all its fullness: he is referring to the beatific life in heaven, so often compared to a banquet. Then there will be no need of earthly food or drink; instead there will be a new wine (cf. Is 25:6). Definitively, after the resurrection, the apostles and all the saints will be able to share the delight of being with Jesus.

The fact that St Mark brings in these words after the institution of the Eucharist indicates in some way that the Eucharist is an anticipation here on earth of possession of God in eternal blessedness, where God will be everything to everyone (cf. 1 Cor 15:28). "At the Last Supper," Vatican II teaches, "on the night he was betrayed, our Saviour instituted the eucharistic sacrifice of his body and blood. This he did in order to perpetuate the sacrifice of the Cross throughout the ages until he should come again, and so to entrust to his beloved Spouse, the Church, a memorial of his death and resurrection: a sacrament of love, a sign of unity, a bond of charity, a paschal banquet in which Christ is consumed, the mind is filled with grace, and a pledge of future glory is given to us" (*Sacrosanctum Concilium*, 47).

14:26. "When they had sung a hymn": it was a custom at the passover meal to recite prayers, called "Hallel", which included Psalms 113 to 118; the last part was recited at the end of the meal.

14:30–31. Only St Mark gives us the exact detail of the two cockcrows (v. 30), and Peter's insistence that he would never betray Jesus (v. 31). This is another sign of the connexion between St Mark's Gospel and St Peter's preaching; only Peter, full of contrition and humility, would so deliberately tell the first Christians about these episodes in which his presumption and failures contrasted with Jesus' mercy and understanding. The other evangelists, surely out of respect for the figure of Peter, pass over these incidents more quickly.

This account shows us that our Lord takes into account the weaknesses of those whom he calls to follow him and be his apostles. Peter is too self-confident; very soon he will deny him. Jesus knows this well and, in spite of everything, chooses him as head of the Church. "They [the disciples] remain just like that until they are filled with the Holy Spirit and thus become pillars of the Church. They are ordinary men, complete with defects and shortcomings, more eager to say than to do. Nevertheless, Jesus calls them to be fishers of men, co-redeemers, dispensers of the grace of God. Something similar has happened to us. … But I also realize that human logic cannot possibly explain the world of grace. God usually seeks out deficient instruments so that the work can more clearly be seen to be his" (St J. Escrivá, *Christ Is Passing By*, 2 and 3).

14:32–42. The very human way Jesus approaches his passion and death is note-

he said vehemently, "If I must die with you, I will not deny you." Jn 11:16
And they all said the same.

Jesus' prayer and agony in the garden

32And they went to a place which was called Gethsemane; and he Mt 26:36–46
said to his disciples, "Sit here, while I pray." 33And he took with Lk 22:40–46 Jn 18:1
him Peter and James and John, and began to be greatly distressed
and troubled. 34And he said to them, "My soul is very sorrowful, Jn 12:27 Ps 43:5

---

worthy. He feels everything any man would feel in those circumstances. "He takes with him only the three disciples who had seen his glorification on Mount Tabor, that these who saw his power should also see his sorrow and learn from that sorrow that he was truly man. And, because he assumed human nature in its entirety, he assumed the properties of man—fear, strength, natural sorrow; for it is natural that men approach death unwillingly" (Theophylact, *Enarratio in Evangelium Marci*, in loc.).

Jesus' prayer in the garden shows us, as nothing else in the Gospel does, that he prayed the prayer of petition—not only for others, but also for himself. For, in the unity of his Person there were two natures, one human and one divine; and, since his human will was not omnipotent, it was appropriate for Christ to ask the Father to strengthen that will (cf. St Thomas Aquinas, *Summa theologiae*, 3, 21, 1).

Once more, Jesus prays with a deep sense of his divine sonship (cf. Mt 11:25; Lk 23:46; Jn 17:1). Only St Mark retains in the original language his filial exclamation to the Father: "Abba", which is how children intimately addressed their parents. Every Christian should have a similar filial trust, especially when praying. At this moment of climax, Jesus turns from his private dialogue with his Father to ask his disciples to pray so as not to fall into temptation. It should be noted that the evangelists, inspired by the Holy Spirit, give us both Jesus' prayer and his commandment to us to pray. This is not a passing anecdote, but an episode which is a model of how Christians should act: prayer is indispensable for staying faithful to God. Anyone who does not pray should be under no illusions about being able to cope with the temptations of the devil: "If our Lord had said only *watch*, we might expect that our own power would be sufficient, but when he adds *pray*, he shows that *if he keeps not* our souls in time of temptation, in vain shall they watch who keep them (cf. Ps 127:1)" (St Francis de Sales, *Treatise on the Love of God*, book 11, chap. 1).

14:34. "But when he had gone on a little way, he suddenly felt such a sharp and bitter attack of sadness, grief, fear, and weariness that he immediately uttered, even in their presence, those anguished words which gave expression to his overburdened feelings: 'My soul is sad unto death.' For a huge mass of troubles took possession of the tender and gentle body of our most holy Saviour. He knew that his ordeal was now imminent and just about to overtake him: the treacherous betrayer, the bitter enemies, binding ropes, false accusations, slanders, blows, thorns, nails, the cross, and horrible tortures stretched out over many hours. Over and above these, he was tormented by the thought of his disciples' terror, the loss of the Jews, even the destruction of

even to death; remain here, and watch."[d] 35 And going a little farther, he fell on the ground and prayed that, if it were possible, the
Mk 10:38 hour might pass from him. 36 And he said, "Abba, Father, all things
Rom 8:15 Gal 4:6 are possible to thee; remove this cup from me; yet not what I will,
but what thou wilt." 37 And he came and found them sleeping, and
he said to Peter, "Simon, are you asleep? Could you not watch[d]
Rom 7:5 one hour? 38 Watch[d] and pray that you may not enter into temptation; the spirit indeed is willing, but the flesh is weak." 39 And
again he went away and prayed, saying the same words. 40 And
again he came and found them sleeping, for their eyes were very
Mk 9:6 heavy; and they did not know what to answer him. 41 And he came
a third time, and said to them, "Are you still sleeping and taking
your rest? It is enough; the hour has come; the Son of man is

---

the very man who so disloyally betrayed him, and finally the ineffable grief of his beloved Mother. The gathered storm of all these evils rushed into his most gentle heart and flooded it like the ocean sweeping through broken dikes" (St Thomas More, *De tristitia Christi*, in loc.).

14:35. "Therefore, since he foresaw that there would be many people of such a delicate constitution that they would be convulsed with terror at any danger of being tortured, he chose to enhearten them by the example of his own sorrow, his own sadness, his own weariness and unequalled fear, lest they should be so disheartened as they compare their own fearful state of mind with the boldness of the bravest martyrs that they would yield freely what they fear will be won from them by force. To such a person as this, Christ wanted his own deed to speak out (as it were) with his own living voice: 'O faint of heart, take courage and do not despair. You are afraid, you are sad, you are stricken with weariness and dread of the torment with which you have been cruelly threatened. Trust me; I conquered the world, and yet I suffered immeasurably more from fear; I was sadder, more afflicted with weariness, more horrified at the prospect of such cruel suffering drawing eagerly nearer and nearer. Let the brave man have his high-spirited martyrs, let him rejoice in imitating a thousand of them. But you, my timorous and feeble little sheep, be content to have me alone as your shepherd; follow my leadership. If you do not trust yourself, place your trust in me. See, I am walking ahead of you along this fearful road. Take hold of the border of my garment and you will feel going out from it a power which will stay your heart's blood from issuing in vain fears, and will make your mind more cheerful, especially when you remember that you are following closely in my footsteps (and I am to be trusted and will not allow you to be tempted beyond what you can bear, but I will give together with the temptation a way out that you may be able to endure it) and likewise when you remember that this light and momentary burden of tribulation will prepare for you a weight of glory which is beyond all measure. For the sufferings of this time are not worthy to be compared with the glory to come which will be revealed in you. As you reflect on such

d. Or *keep awake*

betrayed into the hands of sinners. 42Rise, let us be going; see, my betrayer is at hand." Jn 14:31

Arrest of Jesus

43And immediately, while he was still speaking, Judas came, one of the twelve, and with him a crowd with swords and clubs, from the chief priests and the scribes and the elders. 44Now the betrayer had given them a sign, saying, "The one I shall kiss is the man; seize him and lead him away safely." 45And when he came, he went up to him at once, and said, "Master!"[e] And he kissed him. 46And they laid hands on him and seized him. 47But one of those who stood by drew his sword, and struck the slave of the high priest and cut off his ear. 48And Jesus said to them, "Have you

Mt 26:47–58
Lk 22:47–55
Jn 18:2–18

---

things, take heart, and use the sign of my cross to drive away this dread, this sadness, and weariness like vain spectres of the darkness. Advance successfully and press through all obstacles, firmly confident that I will champion your cause until you are victorious and then in turn will reward you with the laurel crown of victory'" (ibid.).

14:36. "Jesus prays in the garden. *Pater mi* (Mt 26:39), *Abba Pater!* (Mk 14:36). God is my Father, even though he may send me suffering. He loves me tenderly, even while wounding me. Jesus suffers, to fulfil the Will of the Father. ... And I, who also wish to fulfil the most holy Will of God, following the footsteps of the Master, can I complain if I too meet suffering as my travelling companion?

"It will be a sure sign of my sonship, because God is treating me as he treated his own divine Son. Then I, just as he did, will be able to groan and weep alone in my Gethsemane; but, as I lie prostrate on the ground, acknowledging my nothingness, there will rise up to the Lord a cry from the depths of my soul: *Pater mi, Abba, Pater, ... fiat!*" (St Josemaría Escrivá, *The Way of the Cross*, I, 1).

14:41–42. "See now, when Christ comes back to his apostles for the third time, there they are, buried in sleep, though he commanded them to bear up with him and to stay awake and pray because of the impending danger; but Judas the traitor at the same time was so wide awake and intent on betraying the Lord that the very idea of sleep never entered his mind.

"Does not this contrast between the traitor and the apostles present to us a clear and sharp mirror image (as it were), a sad and terrible view of what has happened through the ages from those times even to our own? [...] For very many are sleepy and apathetic in sowing virtues among the people and maintaining the truth, while the enemies of Christ in order to sow vices and uproot the faith (that is, insofar as they can, to seize Christ and cruelly crucify him once again) are wide awake—so much wiser (as Christ says) are the sons of darkness in their generation than the sons of light (cf. Lk 16:8)" (St Thomas More, *De tristitia Christi*, in loc.).

14:43–50. The Gospel reports the arrest of our Lord in a matter-of-fact sort of way. Jesus, who was expecting it, offered

e. Or *Rabbi*

come out as against a robber, with swords and clubs to capture
me? 49Day after day I was with you in the temple teaching, and
you did not seize me. But let the scriptures be fulfilled." 50And
Jn 16:32 they all forsook him, and fled.

51And a young man followed him, with nothing but a linen
cloth about his body; and they seized him, 52but he left the linen
cloth and ran away naked.*

Jesus before the chief priests

53And they led Jesus to the high priest; and all the chief priests and
the elders and the scribes were assembled. 54And Peter had fol-

---

no resistance, thereby fulfilling the prophecies about him in the Old Testament, particularly this passage of the poem of the Servant of Yahweh in the Book of Isaiah: "like a lamb that is led to the slaughter, and like a sheep that before its shearers is dumb, so he opened not his mouth ... because he poured out his soul to death ..." (Is 53:7 and 12). Dejected only moments earlier at the beginning of his prayer in Gethsemane Jesus now rises up strengthened to face his passion. These mysteries of our Lord, true God and true man, are really impressive.

14:51–52. This detail about the young man in the linen cloth is found only in St Mark. Most interpreters see in it a discreet allusion to Mark himself. It is probable that the Garden of Olives belonged to Mark's family, which would explain the presence there at night-time of the boy, who would have been awakened suddenly by the noise of the crowd.

"One sees rich men—less often, it is true, than I would like—but still, thank God, one sometimes sees exceedingly rich men who would rather lose everything they have than keep anything at all by offending God through sin. These men have many clothes, but they are not tightly confined by them, so that when they need to run away from danger, they escape easily by throwing off their clothes. On the other hand we see people—and far more of them than I would wish—who happen to have only light garments and quite skimpy outfits and yet have so welded their affections to those poor riches of theirs that you could sooner strip skin from flesh than separate them from their goods. Such a person had better get going while there is still time. For once someone gets hold of his clothes, he will sooner die than leave his linen cloth behind. In summary, then, we learn from the example of this young man that we should always be prepared for troubles that arise suddenly, dangers that strike without warning and might make it necessary for us to run away; to be prepared, we ought not be so loaded with various garments, or so buttoned up in even one, that in an emergency we are unable to throw away our linen cloth and escape naked" (St Thomas More, *De tristitia Christi*, in loc.).

14:53–65. This meeting of the Sanhedrin in the house of the high priest was quite irregular. The normal thing was for it to meet during the daytime and in the temple. Everything suggests that the rulers arranged this session secretly, probably to avoid opposition from the people, which would have thwarted their plans. The direct intervention of the high priest and the ill-treatment of the prisoner

lowed him at a distance, right into the courtyard of the high priest;
and he was sitting with the guards, and warming himself at the
fire. [55]Now the chief priests and the whole council sought testi- Mt 26:59–68
mony against Jesus to put him to death, but they found none. [56]For Lk 22:63–71 Jn 18:19–24
many bore false witness against him, and their witness did not
agree. [57]And some stood up and bore false witness against him
saying, [58]"We heard him say, 'I will destroy this temple that is Jn 2:19
made with hands, and in three days I will build another, not made 2 Cor 5:1
with hands.'" [59]Yet not even so did their testimony agree. [60]And
the high priest stood up in the midst, and asked Jesus, "Have you
no answer to make? What is it that these men testify against you?"
[61]But he was silent and made no answer. Again the high priest Mk 15:5 Is 53:7

---

before sentence were also illegal. The Jewish authorities had for some time past been of a mind to do away with Jesus (cf., e.g., Mk 12:12; Jn 7:30; 11:45–50). Now all they are trying to do is give their actions an appearance of legality—that is, looking for concurring witnesses to accuse him of capital crimes. Because they do not manage to do this, the chief priest goes right to the key issue: was Jesus the Messiah, yes or no? Jesus' affirmative answer is regarded as blasphemy. Appearances are saved; they can now condemn him to death and ask the Roman procurator to ratify the sentence (cf. the note on Mt 27:2). Despite the irregularities and even though not all the members of the Sanhedrin were present, the significance of this session lies in the fact that the Jewish authorities, the official representatives of the chosen people, reject Jesus as Messiah and condemn him to death.

14:57–59. From the Gospel of St John (2:19) we know the words of Jesus which gave rise to this accusation: "Destroy the temple, and in three days I will raise it up." Now they accuse him of having said three things: that he is going to destroy the temple; that the temple of Jerusalem is the work of human hands, not something divine; and that in three days he will raise up another one, not made by hands of men. As can be seen, this is not what our Lord said. First they change his words: Jesus did not say he was going to destroy the temple; and, secondly, they apply what he said to the temple of Jerusalem, not understanding that Jesus was speaking about his own body, as is made plain in St John (2:21–22). After the Resurrection, the apostles understood the depth of Jesus' words (Jn 2:22): the temple of Jerusalem, where God's presence was manifested in a special way and where he was offered due worship, was but a sign, a prefiguring of the humanity of Christ, in which the fullness of divinity, God, dwelt (cf. Col 2:9).

The same accusation is made at the martyrdom of St Stephen: "We have heard him say that this Jesus of Nazareth will destroy this place, and will change the customs which Moses delivered to us" (Acts 6:14). In fact, St Stephen knew that the true temple was no longer that of Jerusalem but Jesus Christ; but once again they misinterpreted his meaning and accused him as they had our Lord.

14:61. As at other points during his passion, Jesus kept completely silent. He appeared defenceless before the false

asked him, "Are you the Christ, the Son of the Blessed?" [62]And
Dan 7:13 Ps 110:1 Jesus said, "I am; and you will see the Son of man sitting at the
right hand of Power, and coming with the clouds of heaven."
[63]And the high priest tore his mantle, and said, "Why do we still
Jn 19:7 need witnesses? [64]You have heard his blasphemy. What is your
decision?" And they all condemned him as deserving death. [65]And
some began to spit on him, and to cover his face, and to strike
him, saying to him, "Prophesy!" And the guards received him
with blows.

Peter's denial

Mt 26:69–75 [66]And as Peter was below in the courtyard, one of the maids of the
Lk 22:56–62 Jn 18:17, 25–27 high priest came; [67]and seeing Peter warming himself, she looked
Mt 2:23 at him, and said, "You also were with the Nazarene, Jesus." [68]But

---

accusations of his enemies. "God our Saviour," St Jerome says, "who has redeemed the world out of mercy, lets himself be led to death like a lamb, not saying a word; he does not complain, he makes no effort to defend himself. Jesus' silence obtains forgiveness for Adam's protest and excuse" (*Comm.on Mark*, in loc.). This silence is another motive and encouragement to us to be silent at times in the face of calumny or criticism. "In quietness and in trust shall be your strength," says the prophet Isaiah (30:15).

"'Jesus remained silent, *Jesus autem tacebat.*' Why do you speak, to console yourself, or to excuse yourself?

"Say nothing. Seek joy in contempt: you will always receive less than you deserve.

"Can you, by any chance, ask: '*Quid enim mali feci,* what evil have I done?'" (St Josemaría Escrivá, *The Way*, 671).

14:61–64. The high priest was undoubtedly trying to corner Jesus: if he replied that he was not the Christ, it would be equivalent to his contradicting everything he had said and done; if he answered yes, it would be interpreted as blasphemy, as we shall see later. Strictly speaking it was not blasphemy to call oneself the Messiah, or to say one was the Son of God, taking that phrase in a broad sense. Jesus' reply not only bore witness to his being the Messiah; it also showed the divine transcendence of his messianism, by applying to him the prophecy of the Son of man in Daniel (7:13–14). By making this confession, Jesus' reply opened the way for the high priest to make his theatrical gesture: he took it as a mockery of God and as blasphemy that this handcuffed man could be the transcendent figure of the Son of man. At this solemn moment Jesus defines himself by using the strongest of all the biblical expressions his hearers could understand—that which most clearly manifested his divinity. We might point out that had Jesus said simply "I am God" they would have thought it simply absurd and would have regarded him as mad: in which case he would not have borne solemn witness to his divinity before the authorities of the Jewish people.

14:63. The rending of garments was a custom in Israel to express indignation and protest against sacrilege and blas-

he denied it, saying, "I neither know nor understand what you
mean." And he went out into the gateway.[f] 69And the maid saw
him, and began again to say to the bystanders, "This man is one
of them." 70But again he denied it. And after a little while the
bystanders said to Peter, "Certainly you are one of them; for you
are a Galilean." 71But he began to invoke a curse on himself and to
swear, "I do not know this man of whom you speak." 72And Mk 14:30
immediately the cock crowed a second time. And Peter remembered how Jesus had said to him, "Before the cock crows twice,
you will deny me three times." And he broke down and wept.

Jesus before Pilate

15 1And as soon as it was morning the chief priests, with the Mt 27:1–2
elders and scribes, and the whole council held a consulta- Lk 22:66; 23:1 Jn 18:28

---

phemy. The rabbis had specified exactly how it should be done. Only a kind of seam was torn, to prevent the fabric being damaged. With this tragi-comic gesture Caiaphas brings the trial to an end, cleverly sabotaging any later procedure that might favour the prisoner and show up the truth.

14:64. Through Luke 23:51 and John 7:25–33 we know that not all the members of the Sanhedrin condemned Jesus, for Joseph of Arimathea did not consent in this act of deicide. It may be supposed, therefore, that they were not present at this meeting of the council, either because they had not been summoned or because they absented themselves.

14:66–72. Although the accounts given by the Synoptic Gospels are very alike, St Mark's narrative does have its own characteristics: the sacred text gives little details which add a touch of colour. He says that Peter was "below" (v. 66), which shows that the council session was held in an upstairs room; he also mentions the two cockcrows (v. 72), in a way consistent with our Lord's prophecy described in v. 30. On the theological and ascetical implications of this passage, see the note on Mt 26:70–75.

15:1. At daybreak the Sanhedrin holds another meeting to work out how to get Pilate to ratify the death sentence. And then Christ is immediately brought before Pilate. It is not known for certain where the governor was residing during these days. It was either in Herod's palace, built on the western hill of the city, south of the Jaffa Gate, or the Antonia fortress, which was on the north-east of the temple esplanade. It is more than likely that, for the Passover, Pilate lived in the fortress. From there he could have a full view of the whole outside area of the temple, where unrest and riots were most likely to occur. In the centre of this impressive building there was a perfectly paved courtyard of about 2,500 square metres (approximately half an acre). This may well have been the yard where Pilate judged our Lord and which St John (19:13) called The Pavement (*Lithostrotos*, in Greek). Philo, Josephus and

f. Or *fore-court.* Other ancient authorities add *and the cock crowed*

tion; and they bound Jesus and led him away and delivered him to
Mt 27:11–30 Pilate.* [2]And Pilate asked him, "Are you the King of the Jews?"
Lk 23:2–25
Jn 18:29–19:16 And he answered him, "You have said so." [3]And the chief priests
accused him of many things. [4]And Pilate again asked him, "Have
you no answer to make? See how many charges they bring against
Mk 14:61 you." [5]But Jesus made no further answer, so that Pilate wondered.
Is 53:7 [6]Now at the feast he used to release for them one prisoner
whom they asked. [7]And among the rebels in prison, who had
committed murder in the insurrection, there was a man called
Barabbas. [8]And the crowd came up and began to ask Pilate to do
as he was wont to do for them. [9]And he answered them, "Do you
Jn 11:48; want me to release for you the King of the Jews?" [10]For he per-
12:19
Mt 21:38 ceived that it was out of envy that the chief priests had delivered
him up. [11]But the chief priests stirred up the crowd to have him

---

other historians depict Pilate as having the defects of the worst type of Roman governor. The evangelists emphasize his cowardice and his sycophancy bordering on wickedness.

15:2. Jesus' reply, as given in St Mark, can be interpreted in two ways. It may mean: You say that I am king; I say nothing; or else: I am a king. The second interpretation is the more common and logical, since in other Gospel passages he affirms his kingship quite categorically (cf. Mt 27:37 and par.; Jn 18:36–38). In St John's Gospel (18:33–38) Jesus tells Pilate that he is a King and explains the special nature of his kingship: his Kingdom is not of this world; it transcends this world (cf. the note on Jn 18:35–37).

15:3–5. On three occasions the evangelists specify that Jesus remained silent in the face of these unjust accusations: before the Sanhedrin (14:61); here, before Pilate; and later on, before Herod (Lk 23:9). From the Gospel of St John we know that our Lord did say other things during this trial. St Mark says that he made no further reply, since he is referring only to the accusations made against our Lord: being false, they deserved no reply. Besides, any attempt at defence was futile, since they had decided in advance that he should die. Nor did Pilate need any further answer, since he was more concerned to please the Jewish authorities than, correctly, to find Jesus innocent.

15:6–15. Instead of simply coming to the rescue of this innocent prisoner, as was his duty and as his conscience advised him, Pilate wants to avoid a confrontation with the Sanhedrin; so he tries to deal with the people and have them set Jesus free. Since it was customary to release a prisoner of the people's choice to celebrate the Passover, Pilate offers them the chance of selecting Jesus. The priests, seeing through this manoeuvre, incite the crowd to ask for Barabbas. This was not difficult to do, since many felt disillusioned about Jesus because he had not set them free of the foreign yoke. Pilate could not oppose their choice; and so it became even more difficult for him to give a just decision. All he can do now is appeal to the people on behalf of "the King of the Jews". The humble and helpless appearance of Jesus exasperates the

release for them Barabbas instead. [12]And Pilate again said to
them, "Then what shall I do with the man whom you call the King
of the Jews?" [13]And they cried out again, "Crucify him." [14]And
Pilate said to them, "Why, what evil has he done?" But they Acts 3:13
shouted all the more, "Crucify him." [15]So Pilate, wishing to satisfy
the crowd, released for them Barabbas; and having scourged
Jesus, he delivered him to be crucified.

The crowning with thorns

[16]And the soldiers led him away inside the palace (that is, the
praetorium); and they called together the whole battalion. [17]And
they clothed him in a purple cloak, and plaiting a crown of thorns
they put it on him. [18]And they began to salute him, "Hail, King of
the Jews!" [19]And they struck his head with a reed, and spat upon

---

crowd: this is not the sort of king they want, and they ask for his crucifixion.

In the course of the trial Pilate was threatened with being reported to the emperor if he interfered in this affair (cf. Jn 19:12); he now accedes to their shouting and signs the warrant for death by crucifixion, to protect his political career.

15:15. Scourging, like crucifixion, was a degrading form of punishment applied only to slaves. The whip or *flagellum* used to punish serious crimes was strengthened with small sharp pieces of metal at the end of the thongs, which had the effect of tearing the flesh and even fracturing bones. Scourging often caused death. The condemned person was tied to a post to prevent him collapsing. People condemned to crucifixion were scourged beforehand.

These sufferings of Jesus have a redemptive value. In other passages of the Gospel our Lord made carrying the cross a condition of following him. Through self-denial a Christian associates himself with Christ's passion and plays a part in the work of redemption (cf. Col 1:24).

"Bound to the pillar. Covered with wounds. The blows of the lash sound upon his torn flesh, upon his undefiled flesh, which suffers for your sinful flesh. More blows. More fury. Still more ... It is the last extreme of human cruelty.

"Finally, exhausted, they untie Jesus. And the body of Christ yields to pain and falls limp, broken and half dead.

"You and I cannot speak. Words are not needed. Look at him, look at him ... slowly.

"After this ... can you ever fear penance?" (St Josemaría Escrivá, *Holy Rosary*, second sorrowful mystery).

15:16–19. The soldiers make Jesus an object of mockery; they accuse him of pretending to be a king, and crown him and dress him up as one.

The image of the suffering Jesus, scourged and crowned with thorns, with a reed in his hands and an old purple cloak around his shoulders, has become a vivid symbol of human pain, under the title of the "Ecce homo".

But, as St Jerome teaches, "his ignominy has blotted out ours, his bonds have set us free, his crown of thorns has won for us the crown of the Kingdom, his wounds have cured us" (*Comm. in Marcum*, in loc.).

him, and they knelt down in homage to him. [20]And when they had
mocked him, they stripped him of the purple cloak, and put his
own clothes on him. And they led him out to crucify him.

The crucifixion and death of Jesus

Mt 27:32–56 Lk 23:26–49 Jn 19:17–30

[21]And they compelled a passer-by, Simon of Cyrene, who was
coming in from the country, the father of Alexander and Rufus, to

---

"You and I … , haven't we crowned him anew with thorns and struck him and spat on him?" (St Josemaría Escrivá, *Holy Rosary*, third sorrowful mystery).

15:21. "Jesus is exhausted. His footsteps become more and more unsteady, and the soldiers are in a hurry to be finished. So, when they are going out of the city through the Judgment Gate, they take hold of a man who was coming in from a farm, a man called Simon of Cyrene, the father of Alexander and Rufus, and they force him to carry the Cross of Jesus (cf. Mk 15:21).

"In the whole context of the Passion, this help does not add up to very much. But for Jesus, a smile, a word, a gesture, a little bit of love is enough for him to pour out his grace bountifully on the soul of his friend. Years later, Simon's sons, Christians by then, will be known and held in high esteem among their brothers in the faith. And it all started with this unexpected meeting with the Cross.

"*I went to those who were not looking for me; I was found by those who sought me not* (Is 65:1).

"At times the Cross appears without our looking for it: it is Christ who is seeking us out. And if by chance, before this unexpected Cross which, perhaps, is therefore more difficult to understand, your heart were to show repugnance … don't give it consolations. And, filled with a noble compassion, when it asks for them, say to it slowly, as one speaking in confidence: 'Heart: heart on the Cross! Heart on the Cross!' " (St J. Escrivá, *The Way of the Cross*, V).

St Mark stops for a moment to say who this Simon was: he was the father of Alexander and Rufus. It appears that Rufus, years later, moved with his mother to Rome; St Paul sent them affectionate greetings in his Letter to the Romans (16:13). It seems reasonable to imagine that Simon first felt victimized at being forced to do such unpleasant work, but contact with the Holy Cross—the altar on which the divine Victim was going to be sacrificed—and the sight of the suffering and death of Jesus, must have touched his heart; and the Cyrenean, who was at first indifferent, left Calvary a faithful disciple of Christ: Jesus had amply rewarded him. How often it happens that divine providence, through some mishap, places us face to face with suffering and brings about in us a deeper conversion.

When reading this passage, we might reflect that, although our Lord has rescued us voluntarily, and although his merits are infinite, he does seek our cooperation. Christ bears the burden of the cross, but we have to help him carry it by accepting all the difficulties and contradictions which divine providence presents us with. In this way we grow in holiness, at the same time atoning for our faults and sins.

From the Gospel of St John (19:17) we know that Jesus bore the cross on his shoulders. In Christ burdened by the cross St Jerome sees, among other mean-

carry his cross. 22And they brought him to the place called Golgotha (which means the place of a skull). 23And they offered him Ps 69:21
wine mingled with myrrh; but he did not take it. 24And they cruci- Ps 22:18
fied him, and divided his garments among them, casting lots for

---

ings, the fulfilment of the figure of Abel, the innocent victim, and particularly of Isaac (cf. Gen 22:6), who carried the wood for his own sacrifice (cf. St Jerome, *Comm. in Marcum*, in loc.). Later, weakened from the scourging, Jesus can go no further on his own, which is why they compel this man from Cyrene to carry the cross.

"If anyone would follow me ... Little friend, we are sad, living the Passion of our Lord Jesus. See how lovingly he embraces the Cross. Learn from him. Jesus carries the Cross for you: you ... carry it for Jesus.

"But don't drag the Cross.... Carry it squarely on your shoulder, because the Cross, if you carry it like that, will not be just any Cross.... It will be the Holy Cross. Don't carry your Cross with resignation: resignation is not a generous word. Love the Cross. When you really love it, your Cross will be ... a Cross without a Cross. And surely you will find Mary on the way, just as Jesus did" (St J. Escrivá, *Holy Rosary*, fourth sorrowful mystery).

15:22. There is no doubt about where this place was: it was a small, bare hill, at that time outside the city, right beside a busy main road.

15:23. Following the advice of Proverbs (31:6), the Jews used to offer dying criminals wine mixed with myrrh or incense to drug them and thus alleviate their suffering.

Jesus tastes it (according to Mt 27: 34), but he does not drink it. He wishes to remain conscious to the last moment and to keep offering the chalice of the Passion, which he accepted at the Incarnation (Heb 10:9) and did not refuse in Gethsemane. St Augustine (*On the Psalms*, 21:2 and 8) explains that our Lord wanted to suffer to the very end in order to purchase our redemption at a high price (cf. 1 Cor 6:20).

Faithful souls have also experienced this generosity of Christ in embracing pain: "Let us drink to the last drop the chalice of pain in this poor present life. What does it matter to suffer for ten years, twenty, fifty ... if afterwards there is heaven for ever, for ever ... for ever?

"And, above all rather than because of the reward, 'propter retributionem' what does suffering matter if we suffer to console, to please God our Lord, in a spirit of reparation, united to him on his cross; in a word: if we suffer for Love? ..." (St J. Escrivá, *The Way*, 182).

15:24–28. Crucifixion, as well as being the most degrading of punishments, was also the most painful. By condemning him to death, Jesus' enemies try to achieve the maximum contrast with his triumphant entry into Jerusalem some days previously. Usually, the bodies of people crucified were left on the gibbet for some days as a warning to people. In the case of Christ they also sought death by crucifixion as the most convincing proof that he was not the Messiah.

Crucifixion took various forms. The usual one, and perhaps the one applied to Jesus, consisted of first erecting the upright beam and then positioning the cross-beam with the prisoner nailed to it by his hands; and finally nailing his feet to the lower part of the the upright.

them, to decide what each should take. 25And it was the third hour,
when they crucified him. 26And the inscription of the charge
against him read, "The King of the Jews." 27And with him they
crucified two robbers, one on his right and one on his left.[g] 29And
Ps 22:7; 109:25 those who passed by derided him, wagging their heads, and
Mk 14:58 saying, "Aha! You who would destroy the temple and build it in
three days, 30save yourself, and come down from the cross!" 31So
also the chief priests mocked him to one another with the scribes,

---

According to St John's Gospel (19:23–25) the seamless tunic—that is, woven in a piece—was wagered for separately from the rest of his clothes, which were divided into four lots, one for each soldier. The words of this verse reproduce those of Psalm 22:18. Any Jew versed in the Scriptures reading this passage would immediately see in it the fulfilment of a prophecy. St John expressly notes it (cf. 19:24). St Mark, without losing the thread of his account of the Passion, implicitly argues that Jesus Christ is the promised Messiah, for in him this prophecy is fulfilled.

Looking at Jesus on the cross, it is appropriate to recall that God "decreed that man should be saved through the wood of the Cross. The tree of man's defeat became his tree of victory; where life was lost, there life has been restored" (*Roman Missal*, Preface of the Holy Cross).

15:25. "The third hour": between nine o'clock and noon. St Mark is the only evangelist who specifies the time at which our Lord was nailed to the cross. For the relationship between our clock and the Jewish system in that period, see the note on Mt 20:3.

15:26. This inscription was usually put in a prominent place so that everyone could see what the prisoner was guilty of. Pilate ordered them to write "Jesus the Nazarene, King of the Jews," in Latin, Greek and Hebrew; St Mark summarizes the inscription.

Motivated by malice, these Jews accuse Jesus of a political crime, when all his life and preaching left it quite clear that his mission was not political but supernatural. On the meaning of the inscription over the cross and the circumstances surrounding it, see John 19:19–22 and note.

15:27. Jesus is thus put to further shame; his disciples will also experience the humiliation of being treated like common criminals.

But in the case of Jesus this was providential, for it fulfilled the Scripture which prophesies that he would be counted among the evildoers. The Vulgate, following some Greek codexes, adds: "And the scripture was fulfilled which says, 'He was reckoned with the transgressors' " (v. 28; cf. Lk 22:37). "Positioned between the evildoers," St Jerome teaches, "the Truth places one on his left and one on his right, as will be the case on the day of judgment. So we see how distinct the end of similar sinners can be. One precedes Peter into Paradise, the other enters hell before Judas: a brief confession brings eternal

g. Other ancient authorities insert verse 28, *And the scripture was fulfilled which says, "He was reckoned with the transgressors"*

saying, "He saved others; he cannot save himself. 32Let the Christ, Mt 16:1, 4
the King of Israel, come down now from the cross, that we may
see and believe." Those who were crucified with him also reviled
him.
33And when the sixth hour had come, there was darkness over Amos 8:9
the whole land[h] until the ninth hour. 34And at the ninth hour Jesus Ps 22:1
cried out with a loud voice, "Elo-i, Elo-i, lama sabach-thani?"

---

life, a momentary blasphemy is punished with eternal death" (*Comm. in Marcum*, in loc.).

The Christian people have from early on given various names to these thieves. The most common in the West is Dismas for the good thief and Gestas for the bad thief.

15:29–32. Christ's suffering did not finish with the crucifixion: there now follows a form of mockery worse (if possible) than the crowning with thorns. He is mocked by passers-by, by the priests chanting insults with the scribes, and even by the two crucified thieves (cf., however, the clarification in Lk 23:39–43). They combine to reproach him for his weakness, as if his miracles had been deceptions, and incite him to manifest his power.

The fact that they ask him to work a miracle does not indicate that they have any desire to believe in him. For faith is a gift from God which only those receive who have a simple heart. "You ask for very little," St Jerome upbraids the Jews, "when the greatest event in history is taking place before your very eyes. Your blindness cannot be cured even by much greater miracles than those you call for" (*Comm. on Mark*, in loc.).

Precisely because he was the Messiah and the Son of God he did not get down from the cross; in great pain, he completed the work his Father had entrusted to him. Christ teaches us that suffering is our best and richest treasure. Our Lord did not win victory from a throne or with a sceptre in his hand, but by opening his arms on the cross. A Christian, who, like any other person, will experience pain and sorrow during his life, should not flee it or rebel against it, but offer it to God, as his Master did.

15:33. The evangelist reports this as a miraculous phenomenon signalling the magnitude of the crime of deicide which was taking place. The phrase "over the whole land" means over all the immediate horizon, without specifying its limits. The normal interpretation of the meaning of this event is dual and complementary; Origen (*In Matth. comm.*, 143) sees it as an expression of the spiritual darkness which overtook the Jewish people as a punishment for having rejected—crucified—him who is the true light (cf. Jn 1:4–9). St Jerome (*Comm. on Matthew*, in loc.) explains the darkness as expressing, rather, the mourning of the universe at the death of its Creator, nature's protest against the unjust killing of its Lord (cf. Rom 8:19–22).

15:34. These words, spoken in Aramaic, are the start of Psalm 22, the prayer of the just man who, hunted and cornered, feels utterly alone, like "a worm, and no man; scorned by men and despised by the people" (v. 7). From this abyss of misery and total abandonment, the just

h. Or *earth*

which means, "My God, my God, why hast thou forsaken me?"
[35]And some of the bystanders hearing it said, "Behold, he is call-
Ps 69:21 ing Elijah." [36]And one ran and, filling a sponge full of vinegar, put
it on a reed and gave it to him to drink, saying, "Wait, let us see
whether Elijah will come to take him down." [37]And Jesus uttered
a loud cry, and breathed his last. [38]And the curtain of the temple
Mt 4:3 was torn in two, from top to bottom. [39]And when the centurion,

---

man has recourse to Yahweh: "My God, my God, why art thou so far from helping me.... Since my mother bore me thou has been my God.... But thou, O Lord, be not far off! O thou my help, hasten to my aid!" (vv. 2, 10 and 19). Thus, far from expressing a moment of despair, these words of Christ reveal his complete trust in his heavenly Father, the only one on whom he can rely in the midst of suffering, to whom he can complain like a Son and in whom he abandons himself without reserve: "Father, into thy hands I commit my spirit" (Lk 23:46; Ps 31:5).

One of the most painful situations a person can experience is to feel alone in the face of misunderstanding and persecution on all sides, to feel completely insecure and afraid. God permits these tests to happen so that, experiencing our own smallness and world-weariness, we place all our trust in him who draws good from evil for those who love him (cf. Rom 8:28).

"So much do I love Christ on the Cross that every crucifix is like a loving reproach from my God: '... I suffering, and you ... a coward. I loving you, and you forgetting me. I begging you, and you ... denying me. I, here, with arms wide open as an Eternal Priest, suffering all that can be suffered for love of you ... and you complain at the slightest misunderstanding, over the tiniest humiliation ...' " (St Josemaría Escrivá, *The Way of the Cross*, XI, 2).

15:35–36. The soldiers near the cross, on hearing our Lord speak, may have thought, wrongly, that he was calling on Elijah for help. However, it seems it is the Jews themselves who, twisting our Lord's words, find another excuse for jeering at him. There was a belief that Elijah would come to herald the Messiah, which is why they used these words to continue to ridicule Christ on the cross.

15:37. The evangelist recalls it very succinctly: "Jesus uttered a loud cry, and breathed his last." It is as if he did not dare make any comment, leaving it to the reader to pause and meditate. Although the death of Christ is a tremendous mystery, we must insist: Jesus Christ died; it was a real, not an apparent, death; nor should we forget that our sin was what caused our Lord's death. "The abyss of malice, which sin opens wide, has been bridged by his infinite charity. God does not abandon men. His plans foresee that the sacrifices of the Old Law were insufficient to repair our faults and re-establish the unity which has been lost: a man who was God must offer himself up. To help us grasp in some measure this unfathomable mystery, we might imagine the Blessed Trinity taking counsel together in its uninterrupted intimate relationship of infinite love. As a result of its eternal decision, the only-begotten Son of God the Father takes on our human condition and bears the burden of

i. Other ancient authorities insert *cried out and* **x.** Or *a son*

who stood facing him, saw that he thus[i] breathed his last, he said,
"Truly this man was the Son[x] of God!"
40 There were also women looking on from afar, among whom Lk 8:2–3
were Mary Magdalene, and Mary the mother of James the Mk 6:3
younger* and of Joses, and Salome, 41 who, when he was in
Galilee, followed him, and ministered to him; and also many other
women who came up with him to Jerusalem.

---

our wretchedness and sorrows, to end up sewn with nails to a piece of wood. ... Let us meditate on our Lord, wounded from head to foot out of love for us" (St J. Escrivá, *Christ Is Passing By*, 95).

"... Now it is all over. The work of our Redemption has been accomplished. We are now children of God, because Jesus has died for us and his death has ransomed us.

"*Empti enim estis pretio magno!* (1 Cor 6:20), you and I have been bought at a great price.

"We must bring into our lives, to make them our own, the life and death of Christ. We must die through mortification and penance, so that Christ may live in us through Love. And then follow in the footsteps of Christ, with a zeal to co-redeem all mankind.

"We must give our lives for others. That is the only way to live the life of Jesus Christ and to become one and the same thing with him" (St Josemaría Escrivá, *The Way of the Cross*, XIV).

15:38. The strictly sacred precinct of the temple of Jerusalem had two parts: the first, called "the Holy Place," where only priests could enter for specific liturgical functions; the second, called "the Holy of Holies" (*Sancta Sanctorum*). This was the most sacred room where once the Ark of the Covenant stood, containing the tablets of the Law. Above the Ark was the "propitiatory" with figures of two cherubim. Only once a year did the high priest have access to the Holy of Holies, on the great Day of Atonement, to perform the rite of purification of the people. The curtain of the temple was the great curtain which separated the Holy of Holies from the Holy Place (cf. 1 Kings 6:15f).

The prodigy of the tearing of the curtain of the temple—apparently of no great importance—is full of theological meaning. It signifies dramatically that with Christ's death the worship of the Old Covenant has been brought to an end; the temple of Jerusalem has no longer any *raison d'être*. The worship pleasing to God—in spirit and truth (cf. Jn 4:23)—is rendered him through the humanity of Christ, who is both Priest and Victim.

15:39. Regarding this passage St Bede says that this miracle of the conversion of the Roman officer is due to the fact that, on seeing the Lord die in this way, he could not but recognize his divinity; for no one has the power to surrender his spirit but he who is the Creator of souls (cf. St Bede, *In Marci Evangelium expositio*, in loc.). Christ, indeed, being God, had the power to surrender his spirit; whereas in the case of other people their spirit is taken from them at the moment of death. But the Christian has to imitate Christ, also at this supreme moment: that is, we should accept death peacefully and joyfully. Death is the point planned by God for us to leave our spirit in his hands; the difference is that Christ yielded up his spirit when he chose (cf.

The burial of Jesus

Mt 27:57–61 Lk 23:50–55 Jn 19:38–42

42And when evening had come, since it was the day of Preparation, that is, the day before the sabbath, 43Joseph of Arimathea,
a respected member of the council, who was also himself looking
for the kingdom of God, took courage and went to Pilate, and
asked for the body of Jesus. 44And Pilate wondered if he were
already dead; and summoning the centurion, he asked him
whether he was already dead.[j] 45And when he learned from the
centurion that he was dead, he granted the body to Joseph. 46And
he bought a linen shroud, and taking him down, wrapped him in
the linen shroud, and laid him in a tomb which had been hewn out
of the rock; and he rolled a stone against the door of the tomb.
47Mary Magdalene and Mary the mother of Joses saw where he
was laid.

Jn 10–18), whereas we do so when God so disposes.

"Don't be afraid of death. Accept it from now on, generously … when God wills it, where God wills it, as God wills it. Don't doubt what I say: it will come in the moment, in the place and in the way that are best: sent by your Father-God. Welcome be our sister death!" (St Josemaría Escrivá, *The Way*, 739).

15:43–46. Unlike the apostles, who fled, Joseph of Arimathea, who had not consented to the decision of the Sanhedrin (cf. Lk 23:51), had the bold and refined piety of personally taking charge of everything to do with the burial of Jesus. Christ's death had not shaken his faith. It is worth noting that he does this immediately after the debacle of Calvary and before the triumph of the glorious resurrection of the Lord. His action will be rewarded by his name being written in the Book of Life and recorded in the Holy Gospel and in the memory of all generations of Christians.

Joseph of Arimathea put himself at the service of Jesus, without expecting any human recompense and even at personal risk: he ventured his social position, his own as yet unused tomb, and everything else that was needed. He will always be a vivid example for every Christian of how one ought to risk money, position and honour in the service of God.

16:1. The sabbath rest was laid down in the Law of Moses as a day when the Israelites should devote themselves to prayer and the worship of God, and also as a form of protection for workers. As time went by the rabbis specified in miniscule detail what could and could not be done on the sabbath. This was why the holy women were unable to organize things on the sabbath for anointing the dead body of our Lord, and why they had to wait until the first day of the week.

From the earliest days of the Church, this first day is called the "dies Domini", the Lord's Day, because, St Jerome comments, "after the sorrow of the sabbath, a joyful day breaks out, the day of greatest joy, lit up by the greatest light of all, for this day saw the triumph of the risen Christ" (*Comm. in Marcum*, in loc.). This is why the Church has designated Sunday

j. Other ancient authorities read *whether he had been some time dead*

The resurrection of Jesus. The empty tomb

16 1And when the sabbath was past, Mary Magdalene, and Mt 28:1–8
Mary the mother of James, and Salome, bought spices, so Lk 24:1–12 Jn 20:1–10
that they might go and anoint him.* 2And very early on the first
day of the week they went to the tomb when the sun had risen.
3And they were saying to one another, "Who will roll away the
stone for us from the door of the tomb?" 4And looking up, they
saw that the stone was rolled back; for it was very large. 5And
entering the tomb, they saw a young man on the right side,
dressed in a white robe; and they were amazed. 6And he said to Mt 2:23
them, "Do not be amazed; you seek Jesus of Nazareth, who was
crucified. He has risen, he is not here; see the place where they

---

as the day specially consecrated to the Lord, a day of rest on which we are commanded to attend Holy Mass.

16:3–4. On the structure of Jewish tombs and the stone covering the entrance, see the note on Mt 27:60.

16:5. Like so many other passages of the Gospel this one shows the extreme sobriety with which the evangelists report historical facts. From the parallel passage of St Matthew (28:5) we know that this person was an angel. But both Mark and Luke are content to report what the women say, without any further interpretation.

16:6. These women's sensitive love urges them, as soon as the Law permits, to go to anoint the dead body of Jesus, without giving a thought to the difficulties involved. Our Lord rewarded them in kind: they were the first to hear news of his resurrection. The Church has always invoked the Blessed Virgin "pro devota femineo sexu", to intercede for devout womanhood. And it is indeed true that in the terrible moments of the passion and death of Jesus women proved stronger than men: "Woman is stronger than man, and more faithful, in the hour of suffering: Mary of Magdala and Mary of Cleophas and Salome!

"With a group of valiant women like these, closely united to our Lady of Sorrows, what work for souls could be done in the world!" (St Josemaría Escrivá, *The Way*, 982).

"Jesus of Nazareth, who was crucified": the same name as written on the inscription on the cross is used by the angel to proclaim the glorious victory of the resurrection. In this way St Mark bears witness explicitly to the crucified man and the resurrected man being one and the same. Jesus' body, which was treated so cruelly, now has immortal life.

"He has risen": the glorious resurrection of Jesus is the central mystery of our faith. "If Christ has not been raised, then our preaching is in vain and your faith is in vain" (1 Cor 15:14). It is also the basis of our hope: "if Christ has not been raised, your faith is futile and you are still in your sins. ... If for this life only we have hoped in Christ, we are of all men most to be pitied" (1 Cor 15:17 and 19).

The Resurrection means that Jesus has overcome death, sin, pain and the power of the devil. The Redemption which our Lord carried out through his death and resurrection is applied to the believer by means of the sacraments, especially by Baptism and the Eucharist: "We were buried with him by baptism and death, so that as Christ was raised

Mk 14:28 laid him. [7]But go, tell his disciples and Peter that he is going
before you to Galilee; there you will see him, as he told you."
[8]And they went out and fled from the tomb; for trembling and
astonishment had come upon them; and they said nothing to any
one, for they were afraid.

Jesus appears to Mary Magdalene

Lk 8:2 [9]Now when he rose early on the first day of the week, he appeared
Jn 20:11–18 first to Mary Magdalene, from whom he had cast out seven
demons. [10]She went and told those who had been with him, as
they mourned and wept. [11]But when they heard that he was alive
and had been seen by her, they would not believe it.

---

from the dead by the glory of the Father, we might walk in newness of life" (Rom 6:4). "He who eats my flesh and drinks my blood has eternal life, and I will raise him up at the last day" (Jn 6:54). The resurrection of Christ is also the rule of our new life: "If you have been raised with Christ, seek the things that are above, where Christ is seated at the right hand of God. Set your minds on things that are above, not on things that are on earth" (Col 3:1–2). Rising with Christ through grace means that "just as Jesus Christ through his resurrection began a new immortal and heavenly life, so we must begin a new life according to the Spirit, once and for all renouncing sin and everything that leads us to sin, loving only God and everything that leads to God" (St Pius X, *Catechism*, 77).

16:7. The designation of the apostle Peter by name is a way of focussing attention on the head of the Apostolic College, just at this time when the apostles are so discouraged. It is also a delicate way of indicating that Peter's denials have been forgiven, and of confirming his primacy among the apostles.

16:11–14. When reporting these first appearances of the risen Jesus, St Mark stresses the disciples' disbelief and their reluctance to accept the fact of the Resurrection, even though Jesus foretold it (cf. Mk 8:31; 9:31; 10:34). This resistance shown by the apostles is a further guarantee of the truth of Jesus' resurrection: they were to be direct, specially-appointed witnesses to the risen Christ, yet they were reluctant to accept this role until they had personal, direct proof of the truth of the Resurrection.

However, our Lord will say: "Blessed are those who have not seen and yet believe" (Jn 20:29). In the apostles' case, they needed, in addition to faith in the risen Christ, clear evidence of his resurrection, for they were to be the eye-witnesses, key witnesses who would proclaim it as an irrefutable fact. In this connexion St Gregory the Great comments: "The reason why the disciples were slow to believe in the Resurrection was not so much due to their weakness as to our future firmness in the faith; what other purposes does this have (the very Resurrection being demonstrated by many arguments to those who were in doubt) than that our faith should be strengthened by their doubt?" (*In Evangelia homiliae*, 16).

16:12. Our Lord's appearance to these two disciples is reported more fully by St Luke (cf. 24:13–35).

Jesus appears to two disciples

[12]After this he appeared in another form to two of them, as they Lk 24:13–35
were walking into the country. [13]And they went back and told the
rest, but they did not believe them.

Jesus appears to the Eleven. The apostles' mission

[14]Afterward he appeared to the eleven themselves as they sat at Lk 24:36–49
table; and he upbraided them for their unbelief and hardness of Jn 20:19–23 1 Cor 15:5
heart, because they had not believed those who saw him after he
had risen. [15]And he said to them, "Go into all the world and Mt 28:18–20
preach the gospel to the whole creation. [16]He who believes and is Acts 2:38
baptized will be saved; but he who does not believe will be con-

---

16:15. This verse contains what is called the "universal apostolic mandate" (parallelled by Mt 28:19–20 and Lk 24:46–48). This is an imperative command from Christ to his apostles to preach the Gospel to the whole world. This same apostolic mission applies, especially, to the apostles' successors, the bishops in communion with Peter's successor, the Pope.

But this mission extends further: the whole "Church was founded to spread the kingdom of Christ over all the earth for the glory of God the Father, to make all men partakers in redemption and salvation. … Every activity of the mystical body with this in view goes by the name of 'apostolate'; the Church exercises it through all its members, though in various ways. In fact, the Christian vocation is, of its nature, a vocation to the apostolate as well. In the organism of a living body no member plays a purely passive part, sharing in the life of the body it shares at the same time in its activity. The same is true for the body of Christ, the Church: 'the whole body achieves full growth in dependence on the full functioning of each part' (Eph 4:16). Between the members of this body there exists, further, such a unity and solidarity (cf. Eph 4:16) that a member who does not work at the growth of the body to the extent of his possibilities must be considered useless both to the Church and to himself.

"In the Church there is diversity of ministry but unity of mission. To the apostles and their successors Christ has entrusted the office of teaching, sanctifying and governing in his name and by his power. But the laity are made to share in the priestly, prophetical and kingly office of Christ; they have therefore, in the Church and in the world, their own assignment in the mission of the whole people of God" (Vatican II, *Apostolicam actuositatem*, 2).

It is true that God acts directly on each person's soul through grace, but it must also be said that it is Christ's will (expressed here and elsewhere) that men should be an instrument or vehicle of salvation for others.

Vatican II also teaches this: "On all Christians, accordingly, rests the noble obligation of working to bring all men throughout the whole world to hear and accept the divine message of salvation" (ibid., 3).

16:16. This verse teaches that, as a consequence of the proclamation of the Good News, faith and Baptism are indispensable pre-requisites for attaining salvation. Conversion to the faith of Jesus Christ should lead directly to Baptism,

Acts 2:4, 11; 10:46 Lk 10:19

demned. [17]And these signs will accompany those who believe: in
my name they will cast out demons; they will speak in new
tongues; [18]they will pick up serpents, and if they drink any deadly
thing, it will not hurt them; they will lay their hands on the sick,
and they will recover."

---

which confers on us "the first sanctifying grace, by which original sin is forgiven, and which also forgives any actual sins there may be; it remits all punishment due for these sins; it impresses on the soul the mark of the Christian; it makes us children of God, members of the Church and heirs to heaven, and enables us to receive the other sacraments" (St Pius X, *Catechism*, 553).

Baptism is absolutely necessary for salvation, as we can see from these words of the Lord. But physical impossibility of receiving the rite of Baptism can be replaced either by martyrdom (called, therefore, "baptism of blood") or by a perfect act of love of God and of contrition, together with an at least implicit desire to be baptized: this is called "baptism of desire" (cf. ibid., 567–568).

Regarding infant Baptism, St Augustine taught that "the custom of our Mother the Church of infant Baptism is in no way to be rejected or considered unnecessary; on the contrary, it is to be believed on the ground that it is a tradition from the apostles" (*De Gen. ad litt.*, 10, 23, 39). The *Code of Canon Law* also stresses the need to baptize infants: "Parents are obliged to see that their infants are baptized within the first few weeks. As soon as possible after the birth, indeed even before it, they are to approach the parish priest to ask for the sacrament for their child, and to be themselves duly prepared for it" (can. 867).

Another consequence of the proclamation of the Gospel, closely linked with the previous one, is that *the Church is necessary*, as Vatican II declares: "Christ is the one mediator and way of salvation; he is present to us in his body which is the Church. He himself explicitly asserted the necessity of faith and baptism (cf. Mk 16:16; Jn 3:5), and thereby affirmed at the same time the necessity of the Church which men enter through baptism as through a door. Hence they could not be saved who, knowing that the Church was founded as necessary by God through Christ, would refuse to enter it, or to remain in it" (*Lumen gentium*, 14; cf. *Presbyterorum ordinis*, 4; *Ad gentes*, 1–3; *Dignitatis humanae*, 11).

16:17–18. In the early days of the Church, public miracles of this kind happened frequently. There are numerous historical records of these events in the New Testament (cf., e.g., Acts 3:1–11; 28:3–6) and in other ancient Christian writings. It was very fitting that this should be so, for it gave visible proof of the truth of Christianity. Miracles of this type still occur, but much more seldom; they are very exceptional. This, too, is fitting because, on the one hand, the truth of Christianity has been attested to enough; and, on the other, it leaves room for us to merit through faith. St Jerome comments: "Miracles were necessary at the beginning to confirm people in the faith. But, once the faith of the Church is confirmed, miracles are not necessary" (*Comm. on Mark*, in loc.). However, God still works miracles through saints in every generation, including our own.

16:19. The Lord's ascension into heaven and his sitting at the right hand of the

The ascension of our Lord

19So then the Lord Jesus, after he had spoken to them, was taken up into heaven, and sat down at the right hand of God.

Lk 24:50–53 Acts 1:4–11; 7:55 2 Kings 2:11

The apostles go forth and preach

20And they went forth and preached everywhere, while the Lord worked with them and confirmed the message by the signs that attended it. Amen.[k]*

Heb 2:4 Acts 14:3

Father is the sixth article of faith confessed in the Creed. Jesus Christ went up into heaven body and soul, to take possession of the Kingdom he won through his death, to prepare for us a place in heaven (cf. Rev 3:21) and to send the Holy Spirit to his Church (cf. St Pius X, *Catechism*, 123).

To say that he "sat at the right hand of God" means that Jesus Christ, including his humanity, has taken eternal possession of heaven and that, being the equal of his Father in that he is God, he occupies the place of highest honour beside him in his human capacity (cf. ibid., 1, 7, 2–3). Already in the Old Testament the Messiah is spoken of as seated at the right hand of the Almighty, thereby showing the supreme dignity of Yahweh's Anointed (cf. Ps 110:1). The New Testament records this truth here and also in many other passages (cf. Eph 1:20–22; Heb 1:13).

As the *St Pius V Catechism* adds, Jesus went up to heaven by his own power and not by any other. Nor was it only as God that he ascended, but also as man.

16:20. Inspired by the Holy Spirit, the evangelist attests that the words of Christ have already begun to be fulfilled by the time of writing. The apostles, in other words, were faithfully carrying out the mission our Lord entrusted to them. They began to preach the Good News of salvation throughout the known world. Their preaching was accompanied by the signs and wonders the Lord had promised, which lent authority to their witness and their teaching. Yet, we know that their apostolic work was always hard, involving much effort, danger, misunderstanding, persecution and even martyrdom—like our Lord's own life.

Thanks to God and also to the apostles, the strength and joy of our Lord Jesus Christ has reached as far as us. But every Christian generation, every man and woman, has to receive the preaching of the Gospel and, in turn, pass it on. The grace of God will always be available to us: "Non est abbreviata manus Domini" (Is 59:1), the power of the Lord has not diminished.

k. Other ancient authorities omit verses 9–20. Some ancient authorities conclude Mark instead with the following: *But they reported briefly to Peter and those with him all that they had been told. And after this, Jesus himself sent out by means of them, from east to west, the sacred and imperishable proclamation of eternal salvation*

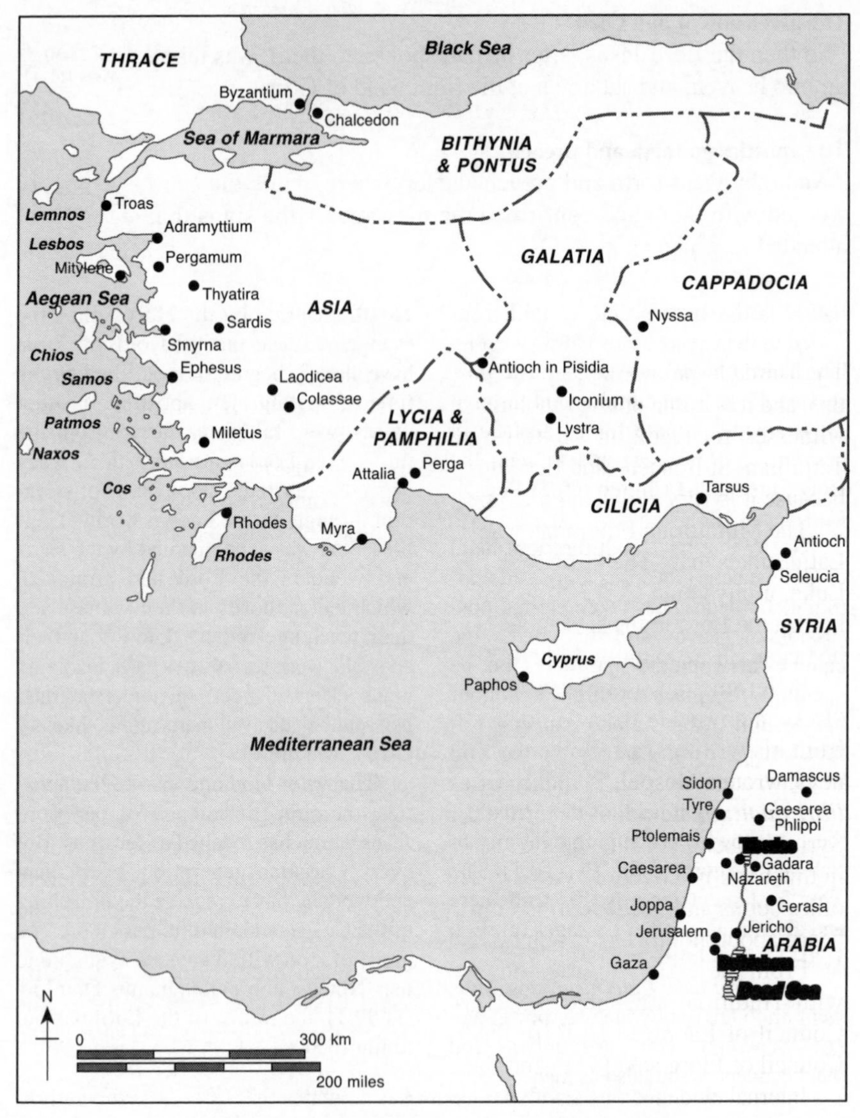

The Eastern Mediterranean Sea in the first century AD

Introduction to the Gospel according to Luke

THE AUTHOR

The Third Gospel was written by St Luke. Christian Tradition is quite clear about this, and it is borne out by scholarly study of the text. Among the more important witnesses to Tradition on this point are Origen, Clement of Alexandria, Tertullian, St Irenaeus and Eusebius; we shall cite just two sources, one chosen because it is very early, and the other, because it comes from St Jerome.

The Muratorian Fragment, a second-century Christian document written in Latin, states that "The third book of the Gospel is that according to Luke. This Luke, a physician [...], wrote down what he had heard, for [...] he had not known the Lord in the flesh, and having obtained such information as he could he began his account with the birth of John."[1]

St Jerome, around the year 400, writes in his book *On Famous Men*, 1: "Luke, a physician from Antioch, who was familiar with Greek as can be seen from his writings, a follower of St Paul, who accompanied him on his journeys, wrote a Gospel."[2] And in his *Commentariorum in Evangelium Matthaei libri quattuor* he adds: "Thirdly, Luke, a physician, a native of Antioch in Syria, a disciple of the apostle Paul, wrote his volume in Achaia and Boeotia; in this book he covered, with a broader perspective, some things contained in other books and, as he admits in his preface, he narrated things which he had heard about, not things which he had himself seen."[3]

From the early centuries onwards, the Church Magisterium, in keeping with Tradition, attributed the Third Gospel to St Luke—for example, the Council of Laodicea (*c*.360), the Decree of Pope Gelasius (492–496), the Council of Florence (1411) and the Council of Trent (1546).

Internal evidence of the Gospel itself also indicates that Luke was the author:

—the author of this Gospel writes a very elegant Greek, particularly when (as in the preface, or prologue, for example) he is writing on his own, not drawing on existing sources of information;

—in reporting cures, he shows his knowledge of medicine by the technical terms he uses and the way in which he describes particular types of illness and disease (in this respect he is generally more precise than the other evangelists);

1. *EB*, 1. **2.** *PL* 23, 650. **3.** *PL* 26, 17f.

—he was the same person who wrote the Acts of the Apostles, and the internal evidence of that work shows that only St Luke could have been its author;

—and, finally, the author was a disciple of St Paul, as witness the close affinity (in both language and doctrine) between this Gospel and St Paul's letters.

Aware of all these arguments, the Pontifical Biblical Commission on 26 June 1912 stated: "The clear verdict of Tradition—showing extraordinary unanimity from the beginnings of the Church and confirmed by manifold evidence, namely the explicit attestations of the holy Fathers and ecclesiastical writers, the quotations and allusions occurring in their writings, the use made by early heretics, the translations of the books of the New Testament, almost all the manuscripts including the most ancient, and also internal reasons drawn from the text of the sacred books—impose the definite affirmation that Mark, the disciple and interpreter of Peter, and Luke, the doctor, the assistant and companion of Paul, really were the authors of the Gospels that are attributed to them respectively."[4]

After confirming the general authenticity of the Third Gospel, the Pontifical Biblical Commission went on to re-affirm the authenticity of individual passages controverted by certain heretics and by some modern critics; on the same day, it replied that it was not "lawful to doubt the inspiration and canonicity of Luke's accounts of the infancy of Christ (chaps. 1 and 2); or of the apparition of the angel strengthening Jesus and the sweat of blood (Lk 22:43f); nor can it be shown by solid reasons—a view preferred by some ancient heretics and favoured also by certain modern critics—that the said accounts do not belong to the genuine Gospel of Luke."[5]

Thus, the first part of this document of the Magisterium states that these passages are inspired and are canonical; and the second, that they are authentic, that is, written by Luke.

THE APOSTOLIC FIGURE OF ST LUKE

Tradition tells us that Luke was born in Antioch in Syria—which is somewhat confirmed by the fact that the Acts of the Apostles shows him to have been very familiar with the church of Antioch. This suggests that he was of Gentile, not Jewish, origin, which is, besides, something St Paul tells us in Colossians 4:10–14 when he differentiates between Aristarchus, Mark and Jesus, who are "of the circumcision", and Epaphras of Colossae, "Luke the beloved physician" and Demas.

We do not know when he became a Christian; quite possibly it was very early on. In any event he was not a direct witness of the life of our Lord, because in the prologue to his Gospel he explicitly says he was not an eyewitness of Christ's preaching.

4. *EB*, 392. **5.** *EB*, 392.

The Acts of the Apostles shows Luke to have been a disciple and companion of St Paul: certain events are reported in the first person plural, implying that he himself took part in them. For example, he goes with the apostle to Macedonia to proclaim the Gospel (Acts 16:10ff); there, in the city of Philippi, Paul and Silas are beaten, imprisoned and eventually expelled from the city. In reporting these facts Luke speaks in the third person, which shows that he himself was not expelled but had stayed behind in Philippi (Acts 16:19ff). He joins up again with St Paul on his return to Philippi (Acts 20:4ff) and goes with him to Jerusalem, where he meets St James and the elders (Acts 21:15–18). Later he goes with St Paul to Rome, when Paul appeals to Caesar (Acts 27:2ff).

In his Second Letter to Timothy, St Paul refers to Luke as being his only company during his second imprisonment in Rome (2 Tim 4:11) and in v.24 of his Letter to Philemon he mentions Luke as one of his fellow workers.

An ancient tradition says that St Luke preached the Gospel in Bithynia and Achaia after the death of St Paul. And the Roman martyrology says that "having suffered much for the name of Christ, he died filled with the Holy Spirit".

CANONICITY

From the very beginning the Church has always regarded St Luke's Gospel as a sacred book: it was used for liturgical reading and is to be found in the earliest lists of canonical books, that is, books which the Church considers to be inspired by God. Thus, in the fourth century, the Council of Laodicea laid down that only canonical books of the Old and New Testaments may be read out in church and included among these the "four Gospels according to Matthew, according to Mark, according to Luke, according to John." The same regulations were issued towards the end of the century by the Council of Hippo and the Third Council of Carthage.[6]

The *Decree of Pope St Damasus*, which contains the acts of the Council of Rome (382), also includes among the sacred books "one book of the Gospels according to Matthew, one book according to Mark, one book according to Luke, one book according to John."[7]

At the beginning of the fifth century, in reply to matters on which Exuperius, bishop of Toulouse, sought his opinion, Pope St Innocent I appended in his Letter *Consulenti tibi* a list of the books which made up the canon of Holy Scripture; this list includes the four Gospels.[8]

The Decree *Pro Jacobitis* (in the papal bull *Cantate Domino*) contains a profession of faith subscribed to by the Jacobites at the Council of Florence (in the fourteenth century) in which it is stated that "the holy men of both Testaments have spoken under the inspiration of the same Holy Spirit," and then goes on to list all the books of Holy Scripture. When it starts to give those

6. *EB*, 12. **7.** *Dz-Sch*, 180.

of the New Testament it says, "the four Gospels, according to Matthew, Mark, Luke and John; the Acts of the Apostles written by Luke the Evangelist …".[9]

The Council of Trent in its *Decree on sacred books and apostolic tradition* (1546) solemnly defined the canon of Scripture; to avoid any doubt it gave a complete list of the books, in which it described the holy Gospels in the now traditional way—"the four Gospels according to Matthew, Mark, Luke and John." The decree ends with this solemn statement: "If anyone does not accept these books as sacred and canonical in their entirety according to the text usually read in the catholic Church […], let him be anathema."[10]

DATE OF COMPOSITION

Christian Tradition maintains that St Luke wrote his Gospel after the Gospels of Matthew and Mark, which is why it is listed third in documents of the Magisterium.

St Luke, in the prologue to the Acts of the Apostles, expressly mentions his first book, that is, his Gospel. Therefore, the Gospel was obviously written before Acts. Now, Acts ends with a description of St Paul's situation just before he is released from his first Roman imprisonment, which suggests that St Luke finished writing Acts at that time. Since the date of St Paul's release was the year 63, St Luke's Gospel could have been written in the year 62 or at the beginning of 63. Some scholars tend to go for a date between 67 and 70.

HISTORICAL ACCURACY

We have already discussed what Tradition and the Magisterium of the Church have to say about the historicity of the Gospels. As regards the historicity of St Luke's Gospel specifically, this was confirmed by the 1912 *Reply* of the Pontifical Biblical Commission where it said that "the words and deeds which are reported by Mark accurately and almost in verbal agreement with Peter's preaching, and those which are faithfully set forth by Luke who 'followed all things closely for some time past' through the help of entirely trustworthy witnesses 'who from the beginning were eyewitnesses and ministers of the word' (Lk 1:2f), are historical and rightly deserve that full faith which the Church has always placed in them."[11] The historical accuracy of the text is vouched for by the author's declared intention to write a true account that would enlighten and confirm the faith of his readers. The prologue, which is typical of the style of Greek and Latin historians,[12] shows that St Luke is writing as a historian. He uses (Lk 1:1) the term "narrative" (*diégesis*) to make it clear from the very outset that he is writing as a historian. This can be seen also by his reference to

8. *EB*, 21. **9.** *EB*, 47. **10.** *EB*, 59-60. **11.** *EB*, 398. **12.** Cf. e.g., Flavius Josephus, *Against Apion*.

secular history, by the chronological information he gives at the beginning of the Gospel (Lk 1:5; 2:1; 3:1–2, 23) and by the way he plans his work (he says he intends to write an "orderly" account: Lk 1:3). He is very conscientious and diligent in seeking out his sources: they have to be eyewitnesses. True, his is a higher purpose than a secular historian's: he wants to show that the catechetical teaching which has brought Christians to the faith has a solid basis in fact. But for this very reason he goes out of his way to make sure his facts are correct.

St Luke writes history not to satisfy his readers' curiosity but to teach them the history of salvation from the incarnation of Christ to the spread of Christianity among the Gentiles. His account spans two books, his Gospel and the Acts of the Apostles; indeed, they constitute one work in two volumes. He describes "the things which have been accomplished among us" (Lk 1:1) and how God's salvific action in history has been brought to completion in the way that he ordained (cf. Lk 13:33; 17:25). A glance at the language he uses shows that salvation is the underlying theme of his work: the Blessed Virgin Mary rejoices in God her Saviour (Lk 1:47); the angels announce that "to you is born this day in the city of David a Saviour, who is Christ the Lord" (Lk 2:11); God has raised up a power of salvation (cf. Lk 1:69) "that we should be saved from our enemies" (Lk 1:71); the Baptist will preach in order to lead the people to salvation, which consists in forgiveness of sins (Lk 1:77); Simeon beholds salvation when he sees the Child Jesus (Lk 2:30); all men will see salvation, as Isaiah foretold (Lk 3:6); and Zacchaeus attains it when the Master visits his house (Lk 19:9). St Luke uses the verb "to save" thirty times in the Gospel and the Acts; he sees salvation not alone in the Cross but in all the events which came at the end—Christ's death, resurrection, ascension and the preaching of the Gospel thereafter (cf. Acts 13:47; 28:28). In arranging the teaching collected from eyewitnesses of these events, St Luke works from the standpoint of salvation history. The book of the Acts is really an extension of the Gospel, showing how salvation is brought to completion with the coming of the Holy Spirit under whose impulse the Gospel will make its way throughout the world.

CONTENT

Almost half of the content of St Luke's Gospel is not to be found in the other Gospels. Among the important items exclusive to Luke are: his account of Jesus' infancy (chaps. 1 and 2); his setting of many episodes of our Lord's public ministry within the framework of a long journey from Galilee to Jerusalem;[13] and certain parables, such as for example those of the prodigal son (Lk 15:11–32), the unjust steward (Lk 16:1–13), and Lazarus and the rich man (Lk 16:19–31); and Luke is the only one who gives us an account of the appearance of the risen Jesus to the disciples at Emmaus (Lk 24:13–35).

13. Lk 9:51—19:27. This section is usually referred to as "the great Lucan insertion".

The general scheme St Luke follows is very like that of St Mark; it is along the following lines:

- A short prologue, in which he states why he has written the book and what sources he has used (Lk 1:1–4).
- Two long chapters, usually called "the Gospel of the infancy of Jesus," or "the infancy narrative" because that is what they cover (Lk 1:5—2:52). St Matthew's and St Luke's accounts of Jesus' infancy complement one another, with each Gospel concentrating on different points and events to do with the birth and early years of the Saviour.
- Jesus' preparation for his public ministry: his baptism by John and his fast in the desert, where he is tempted by the devil (Lk 3:1—4:13).
- Extensive public ministry in Galilee, where Jesus begins his preaching, works many miracles, chooses the Twelve and prepares them for their future mission. Galilee is also where Jesus begins to be rejected by the scribes and Pharisees, whereas the people flock to him. His disciples remain faithful to him and Peter confesses that Jesus is the Messiah. This section also includes such other important episodes as the transfiguration and three predictions of his passion and resurrection (Lk 4:14—9:27).
- As we have just mentioned, a feature of this Gospel is its assembly of accounts inside the framework of a long journey made by our Lord from Galilee to Jerusalem; this "journey narrative" covers ten chapters (Lk 9:51—19:27). In this section we find much of our Lord's preaching—addressed to his disciples, to crowds and even to scribes and Pharisees. Thus, he exhorts people to meekness and mercy (for example, in the parable of the lost sheep and that of the prodigal son) and to trust in God's providence. Here also we find his basic teaching on humility, sincerity, poverty (for example, in the parable about Lazarus and the rich man), repentance, acceptance of the daily cross, the need to be appreciative (the cure of the ten lepers), the importance of not causing scandal, and the duty to forgive one's neighbour. Also included in this section are other teachings of Jesus: on prayer (for example, the Our Father), on being always ready to render an account to God, on the need for faith and sincere conversion if one is to attain salvation (for example, the episode of the blind man of Jericho and that of Zacchaeus the publican), and—throughout—the living example of the Master himself, which his disciple should follow.

All this teaching is interwoven with episodes from our Lord's life (such as the mission of the seventy disciples) and accounts of miracles he worked to confirm his teaching. This long section also contains Jesus' prediction that his disciples would suffer persecution, his prophecy of the destruction of Jerusalem on account of its obstinate refusal to accept God's mercy, and the third prediction of his passion and resurrection.

- St Luke's Gospel then goes on to deal with Jesus' public ministry in Jerusalem (Lk 19:28—21:38), very much along the lines of the other two Synoptics. Jesus enters the Holy City to the acclaim of the people, ejects the dealers from the temple and defends himself against his enemies' accusations;

this gives him an opportunity to describe the real nature of the Kingdom of God (in connexion with tribute to Caesar) and to explain the resurrection of the dead. In this section comes the "eschatological discourse" on the future destruction of Jerusalem and the end of the world.

• Finally, the accounts of Christ's passion, death, resurrection and ascension (chaps. 22–24). Among the points which only St Luke gives us are: Jesus' sweating blood during his agony in Gethsemane; his promise of Paradise to the good thief; and—as we have seen—his appearance to the disciples of Emmaus.

THEOLOGICAL AND LITERARY FEATURES

In referring to the *historicity* of the Gospels, the Second Vatican Council in its Constitution *Dei Verbum* says: "The sacred authors, in writing the four Gospels, selected certain of the many elements which had been handed on, either orally or already in written form, synthesising them or explaining them with an eye to the situation of the churches, while still keeping the style of the proclamation, in such a way that they tell us the honest truth about Jesus. Whether they relied on their own memory or on the testimony of those who 'from the beginning were eyewitnesses and ministers of the word', their purpose in writing was that we might know the 'truth' concerning the things of which we have been informed (cf. Lk 1:2–4)."[14]

Each of the evangelists has given us his own portrait, as it were, of Christ; they all show us the same person, but from different perspectives. Always under the inspiration of the Holy Spirit, the sacred writers sometimes chose the very same events, the very same words (this is particularly true of the Synoptics), but occasionally they tell us things which are not to be found in any of the other Gospels. They also summarize certain items and adapt their account to their immediate readership or audience—though ultimately it is addressed to the whole Church. This explains why one evangelist stresses aspects to which another does not give such importance. When we talk of a Gospel having characteristic features we are trying to identify whom the evangelist was first addressing and what particular things he was stressing—though God is the principal author of every book in Scripture.

As regards the *literary style* of the Third Gospel, St Jerome already observed that Luke's Greek was much better and much more elegant than that of the other evangelists.[15] For example, he usually avoids bringing in Hebrew, Aramaic or Latin words or phrases, giving the Greek equivalent instead. He tends to transcribe popular jargon into more elegant language, and to omit details which might embarrass some people, or scenes which might seem a little unrefined. This sort of thing shows that he was a refined, sensitive person.

Another thing for which St Luke is noted is his concern to establish the historical framework of certain events (cf., e.g., Lk 2:1ff; 3:1; 8:3). Also he looks at

14. No. 19. **15.** Cf. *Epistola*, 20, 4.

certain things from a new angle. The most obvious example of this is the way he presents Christ's life on earth as a journey towards Jerusalem, from where, on the day of his ascension, he will go up into that heaven of which the Holy City is the earthly symbol. Other things which stand out in the Gospel are the universality, the catholicity, of the Gospel and of the Church, the divinity of Christ, Prophet and Saviour, the tender figure of the Blessed Virgin, and such aspects of the Christian life as the spirit of poverty, persevering prayer, mercy and joy.

JESUS MAKING HIS WAY TO JERUSALEM

Jerusalem occupies a very central place in St Luke's Gospel. He begins and ends his accounts of Jesus' infancy with scenes in the temple of Jerusalem—the announcement to Zechariah and the episode of the Child Jesus being lost and then found in the temple talking to the teachers. St Luke gives the temptations in the wilderness in a different order from St Matthew, with the last temptation taking place in Jerusalem. From the very outset of his public ministry Jesus begins to "make his way" towards Jerusalem, where salvation history will reach its climax. He uses this idea of his "making his way" a number of times (Lk 4:30; 9:41–53; 17:11; 19:28), to give his whole narrative the format of a long journey to the Holy City. St Luke is the only one to omit the appearances of the risen Jesus in Galilee; perhaps he does this in order to emphasize the Jerusalem appearances. Finally, the Gospel closes with a scene set exactly where it began, in the temple: "And they worshipped him, and returned to Jerusalem with great joy, and were continually in the temple blessing God" (Lk 24:52–53).

St Luke's second book, the Acts of the Apostles, begins with an account of the ascension of our Lord and the coming of the Holy Spirit in Jerusalem. It then goes on to tell of the spread of the faith and of the Church thoughout the world, under the abiding influence of the Holy Spirit. In the events which he describes in the two books, St Luke, we might say, sees the verification of the prophecy of Isaiah: "It shall come to pass in the latter days that the mountain of the house of the Lord shall be established as the highest of the mountains, and shall be raised above the hills; and all the nations shall flow to it, and many peoples shall come, and say: 'Come, let us go up to the mountain of the Lord, to the house of the God of Jacob, that he may teach us his ways and we may walk in his paths.' For out of Zion shall go forth the law, and the word of the Lord from Jerusalem" (Is 2:2–3). Jerusalem is, then, the Holy City about which God's messengers prophesied and in which Jesus, like them, is rejected (cf. Lk 4:9; 13:33).

THE IMPORTANCE OF THE ASCENSION

Only St Luke and St Mark recount the ascension of our Lord. St Mark makes the briefest of references to it (cf. Mk 16:19), but St Luke mentions it twice (Lk 24:51–53; Acts 1:1–11) and gives important details about it: in his Gospel

Jesus takes leave of his disciples, blessing them like a high priest, for the ascension marks the end of his life on earth. In the Acts of the Apostles the ascension is the point at which the risen Lord enters the glory of heaven, whence he will send the Holy Spirit to bring the Church into being.

We might say that St Luke's entire Gospel tends towards the ascension: the ascension is the final stage on Jesus' "way" to Jerusalem. The Gospel contains a number of passages which seem to refer to the ascension—the transfiguration, where Jesus speaks with Moses and Elijah (Lk 9:30–31) about his "*departure*, which he was to accomplish in Jerusalem"; the three appear "in glory"; in 9:51 it says: "When the days drew near for him to be *received up*, he [Jesus] set his face to go to Jerusalem"; in Luke 24:26 Jesus points out that it was necessary for Christ to suffer "*and enter into his glory*".

Like the other evangelists St Luke speaks of Christ's death, of its necessity, of redemption being won by the shedding of his blood (Lk 22:20; Acts 20:28), but he very definitely positions our Lord's death as a stage on the way to his glorification.

CATHOLICITY OF THE GOSPEL AND OF THE CHURCH

Throughout these two books St Luke shows the messianic largesse foretold by the prophets as coming true in Christ and in his Church, in which he lives on, and as being extended not only to Jews but to all the peoples of the world.

The Acts of the Apostles contains ample evidence of the salvation wrought by Christ spreading all over the world; but even the Gospel contains statements about this universality of salvation—particularly in prophetic passages and in the way the Gentiles are referred to. Thus, the canticle of Simeon (Lk 2:29–32) proclaims that salvation has been "prepared in the presence of all peoples" and is "a light for revelation to the Gentiles". Only St Luke applies to the mission of John the Baptist the text of Isaiah 40:5 about every man seeing the glory of the Lord (cf. Lk 3:6). And in the synagogue of Nazareth Jesus announces the forthcoming proclamation of the Gospel to the Gentiles (Lk 4:16–30). There is a parallel between this passage and Acts 13:46, where the apostles, on being rejected by the Jews, turn to the Gentiles. In Luke 24:45–47 our Lord explains to his disciples that it was prophesied that he should suffer and rise from the dead and that in his name conversion and forgiveness of sins should be preached to all nations. St Luke does not give us the text of Matthew 10:5 about the Samaritans: "Go nowhere among the Gentiles, and enter no town of the Samaritans," which seemed to limit the disciples' mission to Jewish territory. Jesus upbraids his disciples when they want the Samaritans to be punished (Lk 9:55); he sets the Good Samaritan as an example of a true neighbour (Lk 10:25–37); and of the ten lepers whom Jesus cures, the only one who comes back to thank him is a Samaritan (Lk 17:16).

All four Gospels make it clear that Christ's salvation extends to all; yet St Luke's does seem to stress this particularly. We know that our Lord preached almost exclusively to Jews; the Gentiles were to receive the Gospel later, through the apostles. Our Lord reckoned on this and said as much in his instructions to the Twelve: first the Jews, then the Gentiles (cf. Mt 10:5–6; Mk 7:27; Mt 28:18–19; Mk 16:15–16). After his resurrection Jesus made the disciples his eyewitnesses, to go out and tell the whole world (Lk 24:48).

JESUS, PROPHET AND SAVIOUR

Christ is referred to as a "prophet" in Luke 13:33; and 24:19. Because he is true God and true man Jesus Christ is the Prophet *par excellence*: like none other can he speak in God's name (cf. Lk 4:18, 43; 9:45; 19:21). In the Old Testament the prophets were moved by the Spirit of God. St Luke underlines the deep, mysterious connexion between the Holy Spirit and the prophetic ministry of our Lord: for example, at Jesus' baptism, which marks the beginning of his public ministry, the Holy Spirit descends on him in visible form (cf. Lk 3:22). After being tempted in the wilderness, Jesus returns to Galilee led by the Spirit (cf. Lk 4:14). In the synagogue of Nazareth (cf. Lk 4:16–30), when he reads the text of Isaiah 61:1, "The Spirit of the Lord is upon me, because he has anointed me to preach good news to the poor", Jesus applies the text to himself saying that in him this Scripture has been fulfilled.

Throughout this Gospel we are being told that Jesus Christ is the Saviour of men. In the infancy narrative we are constantly being shown how the prophecies of salvation find fulfilment in Christ, those promises made by God to the patriarchs and prophets of the chosen people. The Child who has been born is the long-awaited Saviour: this is the main theme of the *Benedictus*, the *Magnificat*, the announcement to the shepherds and the canticle of Simeon.

Salvation is made manifest in the healing of diseases, as in the cases of the woman with the flow of blood (Lk 8:43–48) and the blind man of Jericho (Lk 18:35–42); in the raising of Jairus' daughter (Lk 8:50–56); in freeing people from possession by the devil, as happened in the cases of the man from Gerasa (Lk 8:26–39); in forgiveness of sins, as in the cases of the sinful woman (Lk 7:36–50) and Zacchaeus, to whom Jesus announces that salvation has come (Lk 19:9–10). But in order to be saved one must believe in the power of Jesus Christ; and even though salvation is made manifest in the miracles we have just mentioned, it is not definitively obtained until the next life (cf. Lk 9:24; 13:23; 18:26). Therefore, being saved means entering the Kingdom of God, being freed by Christ from the slavery of sin, from the devil and from death.

THE BLESSED VIRGIN MARY

The Third Gospel throws special light on the Mother of Christ, a light which gently reveals the greatness and beauty of her soul. This is probably why St Luke was regarded as having actually painted our Lady in the proper sense of the word. Be that as it may, his Gospel is a basic source for doctrine of our Lady and also for devotion to the Mother of our Redeemer—and also it has inspired much Christian art in which Mary figures. With the logical exception of Jesus, no other protagonist in the Gospel story has been described with such love and admiration as Mary.

Nor has any other human creature received such sublime and singular graces as she: she is "full of grace" (*kecharitoméne*: Lk 1:28); the Lord is with her (Lk 1:28); she has found favour with God (Lk 1:30); she conceived by the work of the Holy Spirit (Lk 1:35); she is the Mother of Jesus (Lk 2:7), yet she is a Virgin (Lk 1:34); intimately involved in the redemptive mystery of the Cross (Lk 2:35); she will be blessed by all generations, for the Almighty has done great things for her (Lk 1:49). With good reason does a woman in the crowd cry out in praise of Jesus' Mother (Lk 11:27).

Our Lady responds to these gifts in a most faithful and generous way: St Elizabeth calls her blessed because she has believed (Lk 1:45); the Virgin receives with humility the archangel's announcement that she is to become the Mother of God (Lk 1:29); she asks, in all simplicity, what she has to do to obey God's will (Lk 1:34); she surrenders herself completely to God's plans (Lk 1:38; 2:50); she hastens to help others (Lk 1:39, 56); she is full of gratitude for the gifts she has received (Lk 1:46–55); she faithfully observes God's laws (Lk 2:24) and the pious customs of her people (Lk 2:41); she is very distressed when the Child is lost and makes tender complaint to him (Lk 2:48), but she meekly accepts what she does not understand (Lk 2:50–51). She has a contemplative sense of wonder towards divine mysteries, which she keeps and ponders in her heart (Lk 2:19, 51). As Paul VI said, Mary "is not only the sublime 'type' of the creature redeemed by Christ's merits, she is also the 'type' of all mankind as it makes its pilgrim way in faith."[16]

ENCOURAGEMENT OF CHRISTIAN LIVING

We said earlier that salvation in its complete form is something eschatological, that is to say, it is achieved definitively in heaven. But salvation does begin in this present life; the follower of Christ, living in this world, in the bosom of the Church, should imitate Jesus' life on earth; everything Jesus said and did constitutes both a model and a precept for the Christian. Hence eschatology and exhortation to Christian living merge into one in the Gospel; this holds good for all of the New Testament, but it is particularly noticeable in St Luke.

The phrase, "today it has been fulfilled", which is used with a certain frequency in St Luke's Gospel (cf. Lk 4:21; 19:9), shows us that the whole proclamation of the Gospel is being presented as the coming of the messianic times. The Christian must take up his cross "daily" (Lk 9:23); he must be patient (Lk 21:19). Similarly he must practise poverty if he is to respond to

16. General Audience, 30 May 1973.

Christ's call (Lk 4:18; 7:22) and attain blessedness (Lk 6:20) and eternal life (Lk 16:19–31). A person needs to be detached from "everything" to follow Jesus (Lk 18:22). Riches are of no value when they become an end in themselves (cf. Lk 12:13–21; 16:9, 14–15). One must deny oneself and practise renunciation as the first disciples did after the miraculous catch of fish on Lake Gennesaret, when "they left everything and followed him" (Lk 5:11), or like Levi (Matthew) the publican, who, on hearing the Master's call, "left everything, and rose and followed him" (Lk 5:28). Other things that the Third Gospel stresses are the need for persevering prayer, for merciful love and interior joy at all times. In this connexion, too, Jesus' words and actions provide the model. For example, there are a number of passages to be found only in St Luke's Gospel in which Christ's prayer is mentioned—and at particularly solemn moments: for example, at his baptism, before he chooses his apostles, at the transfiguration, and on the cross. And in Gethsemane Jesus exhorts his disciples to pray in order not to fall into temptation. Christians have to practise love, meekness and mercy: "Be merciful, even as your Father is merciful" (Lk 6:36). St Luke devotes a whole chapter (chap. 15) to three parables dealing with God's mercy, and the verses following the beatitudes are a discourse on love, including love of one's enemies (Lk 6:27–38).

The four Gospels, which contain the proclamation of salvation and which are, as the word "gospel" implies, "good news", are for this very reason impregnated with the joy of the Redemption wrought by Christ. This joyfulness is particularly obvious in St Luke's Gospel. He uses a range of words with a wealth of nuance to describe this joy and gladness. For example, an angel of the Lord announces to Zechariah that he will have a son and "many will rejoice at his birth" (Lk 1:14); the archangel Gabriel, in his annunciation to Mary, begins by greeting her with the word "hail", which literally means "rejoice" (Lk 1:28); and after telling them about the persecutions they will undergo for the sake of the Son of man, the Master tells the disciples to "rejoice in that day, and leap for joy" (Lk 6:23). The birth of the Baptist will bring "joy and gladness" to Zechariah (Lk 1:14); the angel announces news "of great joy" (Lk 2:10); in heaven there will be "joy" over one converted sinner (Lk 15:7); and Elizabeth declares that her son "leaped for joy" in her womb (Lk 1:44). Finally, the Gospel, after telling about the ascension, ends with these words: "And they worshipped him, and returned to Jerusalem with great joy, and were continually in the temple blessing God" (Lk 24:52–53).

Prologue

1 [1]Inasmuch as many have undertaken to compile a narrative of
the things which have been accomplished among us, [2]just as Jn 15:27
they were delivered to us by those who from the beginning were
eyewitnesses and ministers of the word, [3]it seemed good to me
also, having followed all things closely[a] for some time past, to write
an orderly account for you, most excellent Theophilus,* [4]that you
may know the truth concerning the things of which you have been Acts 1:1
informed.

1. THE INFANCY OF JOHN THE BAPTIST AND OF JESUS

The birth of John the Baptist foretold

[5] *In the days of Herod, king of Judea, there was a priest named 1 Chron 24:10
Zechariah,[b] of the division of Abijah; and he had a wife of the

---

1:1–4. St Luke is the only evangelist to give his book a preface or prologue. What is usually described as the "prologue" to St John is really a summary of what that Gospel contains. St Luke's prologue, which is very short and very elegantly written, describes why he has written the book—to provide an orderly, documented account of the life of Christ, starting at the beginning. These verses help us realize that Jesus Christ's message of salvation, the Gospel, was preached before it came to be written down: cf. the quotation from Vatican II's *Dei Verbum*, 19 (p. 333 above). God, then, wanted us to have written Gospels as a permanent, divine testimony providing a firm basis for our faith. "He does not tell Theophilus new things, things he did not previously know; he undertakes to tell him the truth concerning the things in which he has already been instructed. This he does so that you can know everything you have been told about the Lord and his doings" (St Bede, *In Lucae Evangelium expositio*, in loc.).

1:2. The "eyewitnesses" the evangelist refers to would have been the Blessed Virgin, the apostles, the holy women and others who shared Jesus' life during his time on earth.

1:3. "It seemed good to me": "When he says 'it seemed good to me' this does not exclude God's action, because it is God who prepares men's will [...]. He dedicates his Gospel to Theophilus, that is, to one whom God loves. But if you love God, it has also been written for you; and if it has been written for you, then accept this present from the evangelist, keep this token of friendship very close to your heart" (St Ambrose, *Expositio Evangelii sec. Lucam*, in loc.).

1:5ff. St Luke and St Matthew devote the first two chapters of their Gospels to episodes in the early life of our Lord (the annunciation, his birth, childhood and hidden life in Nazareth)—material not covered by the other evangelists. These chapters are usually referred to as the

a. Or *accurately* **b.** Greek *Zacharias*

daughters of Aaron, and her name was Elizabeth. 6And they were
both righteous before God, walking in all the commandments and
ordinances of the Lord blameless. 7But they had no child, because
Elizabeth was barren, and both were advanced in years. 8Now
while he was serving as priest before God when his division was

---

"infancy narrative" or "the gospel of the infancy of Jesus". The first thing one notices is that St Matthew and St Luke do not each deal with the same events.

St Luke's infancy narrative covers six episodes, structured in twos, referring to the infancy of John the Baptist and that of Jesus: two annunciations, two births, two circumcisions and two scenes in the temple; plus other episodes which have to do only with Jesus' infancy—the revelation to the shepherds and their adoration of the Child, the purification of Mary and presentation of the Child, the prophecies of Simeon and Anna, Jesus being lost and then found in the temple, and the hidden life in Nazareth.

St Luke's very poetic narrative combines simplicity and majesty, drawing us to intimate reflection on the mystery of the incarnation of our Saviour: we see the angel make the announcement to Zechariah (1:5–17); his subsequent greeting and annunciation to Mary (1:26–38); her visit to her cousin St Elizabeth (1:39–56); the birth of Jesus in Bethlehem (2:1–7); the adoration of the shepherds (2:8–20); the presentation of the Child in the temple and Simeon's blessing of Mary (2:22–38); the Child lost and found in the temple (2:41–52). St Luke also includes four prophecies in verse form, canticles, Mary's *Magnificat* (1:46 –55), Zechariah's *Benedictus* (1:67–79), the *Gloria* of the angels (2:14) and Simeon's *Nunc dimittis* (2:29–32). These canticles are interwoven with words and phrases which recall, almost word for word, different passages from the Old Testament (from Gen, Lev, Num, Judg, 1 Sam, Is, Jer, Mic and Mal). Every educated pious Jew of the time prayed either by reading the sacred books or by repeating from memory things he had read in them, so there is nothing surprising about our Lady, Zechariah, Simeon and Anna doing this. Besides, it was the same Holy Spirit as inspired the human authors of the Old Testament who now moved to speech those good people before whose very eyes the ancient prophecies were being fulfilled in the Child Jesus. This background explains why we should take these canticles as being recorded exactly as they were spoken.

1:6. After referring to the noble ancestry of Zechariah and Elizabeth, the evangelist now speaks of a higher type of nobility, that of virtue: "Both were righteous before God." "For not everyone who is righteous in men's eyes is righteous in God's; men have one way of seeing and God another; men see externals, but God sees into the heart. It can happen that someone seems righteous because his virtue is false and is practised to win people's approval; but he is not virtuous in God's sight if his righteousness is not born of simplicity of soul but is only simulated in order to appear good.

"Perfect praise consists in being righteous before God, because only he can be called perfect who is approved by him who cannot be deceived" (St Ambrose, *Expositio Evangelii sec. Lucam*, in loc.).

In the last analysis what a Christian must be is righteous before God. St Paul is advocating this when he tells the Corinthians, "But with me it is a very small thing that I should be judged by

on duty, 9according to the custom of the priesthood, it fell to him Ex 30:7
by lot to enter the temple of the Lord and burn incense. 10And the
whole multitude of the people were praying outside at the hour of
incense. 11And there appeared to him an angel of the Lord stand-

---

you or by any human court. [...] It is the Lord who judges me. Therefore do not pronounce judgment before the time, before the Lord comes, who will bring to light the things now hidden in darkness and will disclose the purposes of the heart. Then every man will receive his commendation from God" (1 Cor 4:3ff). On the notion of the just or righteous man, see the note on Mt 1:19.

1:8. There were twenty-four groups or turns of priests to which functions were allocated by the drawing of lots; the eighth group was that of the family of Abijah (cf. 1 Chron 24:7–19), to which Zechariah belonged.

1:9–10. Within the sacred precincts, in a walled-off area, stood the temple proper. Rectangular in form, there was first a large area which was called "the Holy Place", in which was located the altar of incense referred to in v. 9. Behind this was the inner sanctum, called "the Holy of Holies", where the Ark of the Covenant with the tablets of the Law used to be kept; only the high priest had access to this, the most sacred part of the temple. The veil, or great curtain, of the temple separated these two areas from one another. The sacred building was surrounded by a courtyard, called the courtyard of the priests, and outside this, at the front of the temple, was what was called the courtyard of the Israelites, where the people stayed during the ceremony of incensing.

1:10. While the priest offered incense to God, the people in the courtyard joined with him in spirit: even in the Old Testament every external act of worship was meant to be accompanied by an interior disposition of self-offering to God.

With much more reason should there be this union between external and internal worship in the liturgical rites of the New Covenant (cf. *Mediator Dei*, 8), in the liturgy of the Church. Besides, this consistency befits the nature of man, comprised as he is of body and soul.

1:11. Angels are pure spirits, that is, they have no body of any kind; therefore, "they do not appear to men exactly as they are; rather, they manifest themselves in forms which God gives them so that they can be seen by those to whom he sends them" (St John Damascene, *De fide orthodoxa*, 2, 3).

In addition to adoring and serving God, angelic spirits act as God's messengers and as channels of his providence towards men; this explains why they appear so often in salvation history and why Holy Scripture refers to them in so many passages (cf., e.g., Heb 1:14).

Christ's birth was such an important event that angels were given a very prominent role in connexion with it. Here, as at the annunciation to Mary, the archangel St Gabriel is charged with delivering God's message.

"It is no accident that the angel makes his appearance in the temple, for this announces the imminent coming of the true Priest and prepares the heavenly sacrifice at which the angels will minister. Let it not be doubted, then, that the angels will be present when Christ is immolated" (St Ambrose, *Expositio Evangelii sec. Lucam*, in loc.).

ing on the right side of the altar of incense. [12]And Zechariah was
troubled when he saw him, and fear fell upon him. [13]But the angel
said to him, "Do not be afraid, Zechariah, for your prayer is heard,
and your wife Elizabeth will bear you a son, and you shall call his
name John.

[14]And you will have joy and gladness,
and many will rejoice at his birth;
[15]for he will be great before the Lord, (Num 6:3; Judg 13:4f; 1 Sam 1:11)
and he shall drink no wine nor strong drink,
and he will be filled with the Holy Spirit,
even from his mother's womb.
[16]And he will turn many of the sons of Israel
to the Lord their God,
[17]and he will go before him in the spirit and power of Elijah, (Mt 17:11–13; Mal 3:1–23, 24; 4:5–6)
to turn the hearts of the fathers to the children,

1:12. "No matter how righteous a man be, he cannot look at an angel without feeling afraid; that is why Zechariah was alarmed: he could not but quake at the presence of the angel; he could not take the brightness that surrounded him" (St John Chrysostom, *De incomprehensibili Dei natura*). The reason for this is not so much the angel's superiority to man as the fact that the grandeur of God's majesty shines out through the angel: "And the angel said to me, 'Write this: Blessed are those who are invited to the marriage supper of the Lamb.' And he said to me, 'These are true words of God.' Then I fell down at his feet to worship him, but he said to me, 'You must not do that! I am a fellow servant with you and your brethren who hold the testimony of Jesus. Worship God'" (Rev 19:9–10).

1:13. Through the archangel God intervenes in an exceptional way in the married life of Zechariah and Elizabeth; but the message he brings has much wider reference; it has significance for the whole world. Elizabeth is already quite old but she is going to have a son who will be called John ("God is gracious") and he will be the forerunner of the Messiah. This showed that "the fulness of time" (cf. Gal 4:4) was imminent, for which all righteous people of Israel had yearned (cf. Jn 8:56; Heb 11:13).

"Your prayer is heard," St Jerome comments, "that is to say, you are given more than you asked for. You prayed for the salvation of the people, and you have been given the Precursor" (*Expositio in Evangelium sec. Lucam*, in loc.). Our Lord also sometimes gives us more than we ask for: "There is a story about a beggar meeting Alexander the Great and asking him for alms. Alexander stopped and instructed that the man be given the government of five cities. The beggar, totally confused and taken aback, exclaimed, 'I didn't ask for as much as that.' And Alexander replied, 'You asked like the man you are; I give like the man I am'" (St J. Escrivá, *Christ Is Passing By*, 160). Since God responds so generously and gives us more than we ask for, we should face up to difficulties and not be cowed by them.

1:14–17. The archangel St Gabriel gives Zechariah three reasons why he should rejoice over the birth of this child: first, because God will bestow exceptional holiness on him (v.15); second, because

and the disobedient to the wisdom of the just,
to make ready for the Lord a people prepared."
[18]And Zechariah said to the angel, "How shall I know this? For I Gen 18:11
am an old man, and my wife is advanced in years." [19]And the Dan 8:16; 9:21
angel answered him, "I am Gabriel, who stand in the presence of Heb 1:14
God; and I was sent to speak to you, and to bring you this good
news. [20]And behold, you will be silent and unable to speak until
the day that these things come to pass, because you did not
believe my words, which will be fulfilled in their time." [21]And the
people were waiting for Zechariah, and they wondered at his
delay in the temple. [22]And when he came out, he could not speak
to them, and they perceived that he had seen a vision in the
temple; and he made signs to them and remained dumb. [23]And
when his time of service was ended, he went to his home.
[24]After these days his wife Elizabeth conceived, and for five
months she hid herself, saying, [25]"Thus the Lord has done to me Gen 20:23

---

he will lead many to salvation (v.16); and third, because his whole life, everything he does, will prepare the way for the expected Messiah (v.17).

In St John the Baptist two prophecies of Malachi are fulfilled; in them we are told that God will send a messenger ahead of him to prepare the way for him (Mal 3:1; 4:5–6). John prepares the way for the first coming of the Messiah in the same way as Elijah will prepare the way for his second coming (cf. St Ambrose, *Expositio Evangelii sec. Lucam*, in loc.; St Thomas Aquinas, *Commentary on St Matthew*, 17, 11, in loc.). This is why Christ will say, "What did you go out to see? A prophet? Yes, I tell you, and more than a prophet. This is he of whom it is written, 'Behold, I send my messenger before thy face, who shall prepare thy way before thee'" (Lk 7:26–27).

1:18. Zechariah's incredulity and his sin lie not in his doubting that this message has come from God but in forgetting that God is almighty, and in thinking that he and Elizabeth are past having children. Later, referring to the conception of John the Baptist, the same angel explains to Mary that "with God nothing will be impossible" (Lk 1:37). When God asks us to take part in any undertaking we should rely on his omnipotence rather than our own meagre resources. See the note on Mt 10:9–10.

1:19–20. "Gabriel" means "might of God". God commanded the archangel Gabriel to announce the events connected with the incarnation of the Word; already in the Old Testament it was Gabriel who proclaimed to the prophet Daniel the time of the Messiah's coming (Dan 8:15–26; 9:20–27). This present passage deals with the announcement of the conception and birth of Christ's Precursor, and it is the same angel who will reveal to the Blessed Virgin the mystery of the Incarnation.

1:24. Elizabeth hid herself because of the strangeness of pregnancy at her age and out of a holy modesty, which advised her not to make known God's gifts prematurely.

1:25. Married couples who want to have children, to whom God has not yet given

in the days when he looked on me, to take away my reproach
among men."

The annunciation and incarnation of the Son of God

26In the sixth month the angel Gabriel was sent from God to a city
Lk 2:5 Mt 1:16–18 of Galilee named Nazareth, 27to a virgin betrothed to a man whose

---

any, can learn from Zechariah and Elizabeth and have recourse to them as intercessors. To couples in this situation St Josemaría Escrivá recommended that "they should not give up hope too easily. They should ask God to give them children and, if it is his will, to bless them as he blessed the Patriarchs of the Old Testament. And then it would be advisable for both of them to see a good doctor. If in spite of everything God does not give them children, they should not feel frustrated. They should be happy, discovering in this very fact God's will for them. Often God does not give children because he is 'asking more'. God asks them to put the same effort and the same kind and gentle dedication into helping their neighbours as they would have put into raising their own children, without the human joy that comes from parenthood. There is, then, no reason for feeling they are failures or for giving way to sadness" (*Conversations*, 96).

Here is the authoritative teaching of John Paul II on this subject: "It must not be forgotten, however, that, even when procreation is not possible, conjugal life does not for this reason lose its value. Physical sterility in fact can be for spouses the occasion for other important services to the life of the human person—for example, adoption, various forms of educational work, assistance to other families and to poor or handicapped children" (*Familiaris consortio*, 14).

1:26–38. Here we contemplate our Lady who was "enriched from the first instant of her conception with the splendour of an entirely unique holiness; [...] the virgin of Nazareth is hailed by the heralding angel, by divine command, as 'full of grace' (cf. Lk 1:28), and to the heavenly messenger she replies, 'Behold, I am the handmaid of the Lord, be it done unto me according to thy word' (Lk 1:38). Thus the daughter of Adam, Mary, consenting to the word of God, became the Mother of Jesus. Committing herself wholeheartedly to God's saving will and impeded by no sin, she devoted herself totally, as a handmaid of the Lord, to the person and work of her Son, under and with him, serving the mystery of Redemption, by the grace of Almighty God. Rightly, therefore, the Fathers see Mary not merely as passively engaged by God, but as freely cooperating in the work of man's salvation through faith and obedience" (Vatican II, *Lumen gentium*, 56).

The annunciation to Mary and incarnation of the Word constitute the deepest mystery of the relationship between God and men and the most important event in the history of mankind: God becomes man, and will remain so forever, such is the extent of his goodness and mercy and love for all of us. And yet on the day when the second person of the Blessed Trinity assumed frail human nature in the pure womb of the Blessed Virgin, it all happened quietly, without fanfare of any kind. St Luke tells the story in a very simple way. We should treasure these words of the Gospel and use them often, for example, practising the Christian custom of saying the Angelus every day and reflecting on the five joyful mysteries of the Rosary.

name was Joseph, of the house of David; and the virgin's name
was Mary. [28]And he came to her and said, "Hail, full of grace,[b2] Judg 5:24
the Lord is with you!"[c] [29]But she was greatly troubled at the
saying, and considered in her mind what sort of greeting this

---

1:27. God chose to be born of a virgin; centuries earlier he disclosed this through the prophet Isaiah (cf. Is 7:14; Mt 1:22–23). God "before all ages made choice of, and set in her proper place, a mother for his only-begotten Son from whom he, after being made flesh, should be born in the blessed fulness of time: and he continued his persevering regard for her in preference to all other creatures, to such a degree that for her alone he had singular regard" (Pius IX, *Ineffabilis Deus*, 2). This privilege granted to our Lady of being a virgin and a mother at the same time is a unique gift of God. This was the work of the Holy Spirit "who at the conception and the birth of the Son so favoured the Virgin Mother as to impart fruitfulness to her while preserving inviolate her perpetual virginity" (St Pius V, *Catechism*, 1, 4, 8). Paul VI reminds us of this truth of faith: "We believe that the Blessed Mary, who ever enjoys the dignity of virginity, was the Mother of the incarnate Word, of our God and Saviour Jesus Christ" (*Creed of the People of God*, 14).

Although many suggestions have been made as to what the name Mary means, most of the best scholars seem to agree that Mary means "lady". However, no single meaning fully conveys the richness of the name.

1:28. "Hail, full of grace": literally the Greek reads "Rejoice!", obviously referring to a unique joy over the news which the angel is about to communicate.

"Full of grace": by this unusual form of greeting the archangel reveals Mary's special dignity and honour. The Fathers and Doctors of the Church "taught that this singular, solemn and unheard-of greeting showed that all the divine graces reposed in the Mother of God and that she was adorned with all the gifts of the Holy Spirit", which meant that she "was never subject to the curse", that is, was preserved from all sin. These words of the archangel in this text constitute one of the sources which reveal the dogma of Mary's immaculate conception (cf. Pius IX, *Ineffabilis Deus*; Paul VI, *Creed of the People of God*).

"The Lord is with you!": these words are not simply a greeting ("the Lord be with you") but an affirmation ("the Lord is with you"), and they are closely connected with the Incarnation. St Augustine comments by putting these words on the archangel's lips: "He is more with you than he is with me: he is in your heart, he takes shape within you, he fills your soul, he is in your womb" (*Sermo de Nativitate Domini*, 4).

Some important Greek manuscripts and early translations add at the end of the verse: "Blessed are you among women!", meaning that God will exalt Mary over all women. She is more excellent than Sarah, Hannah, Deborah, Rachel, Judith, etc., for only she has the supreme honour of being chosen to be the Mother of God.

1:29–30. Our Lady is troubled by the presence of the archangel and by the confusion truly humble people experience when they receive praise.

b2. Or *O favoured one* **c.** Other ancient authorities add *"Blessed are you among women!"*

Judg 13:3 might be. 30 And the angel said to her,* "Do not be afraid, Mary, for
Is 7:14 Mt 1:21–23 you have found favour with God. 31 And behold you will conceive
Is 9:7 in your womb and bear a son, and you shall call his name Jesus.
2 Sam 7:12–16 32 He will be great, and will be called the Son of the Most High;
and the Lord God will give to him the throne of his father David,

---

1:30. The Annunciation is the moment when our Lady is given to know the vocation which God planned for her from eternity. When the archangel sets her mind at ease by saying "Do not be afraid, Mary," he is helping her to overcome that initial fear which a person normally experiences when God gives him or her a special calling. The fact that Mary felt this fear does not imply the least trace of imperfection in her: hers is a perfectly natural reaction in the face of the supernatural. Imperfection would arise if one did not overcome this fear or rejected the advice of those in a position to help—as St Gabriel helped Mary.

1:31–33. The archangel Gabriel tells the Blessed Virgin that she is to be the Mother of God by reminding her of the words of Isaiah which announced that the Messiah would be born of a virgin, a prophecy which will find its fulfilment in Mary (cf. Mt 1:22–23; Is 7:14).

He reveals that the Child will be "great": his greatness comes from his being God, a greatness he does not lose when he takes on the lowliness of human nature. He also reveals that Jesus will be the king of the Davidic dynasty sent by God in keeping with his promise of salvation; that his Kingdom will last forever, for his humanity will remain forever joined to his divinity; that "he will be called Son of the Most High", that is, he really will be the Son of the Most High and will be publicly recognized as such; in other words, the Child will be the Son of God.

The archangel's announcement evokes the ancient prophecies which foretold these prerogatives. Mary, who was well-versed in Holy Scripture, clearly realized that she was to be the Mother of God.

1:34–38. Commenting on this passage John Paul II said: "*Virgo fidelis*, the faithful Virgin. What does this faithfulness of Mary's mean? What are the dimensions of this faithfulness? The first dimension is called search. Mary was faithful first of all when she began, lovingly, to seek the deep sense of God's plan in her and for the world. *Quomodo fiet?* How shall this be?, she asked the Angel of the Annunciation […].

"The second dimension of faithfulness is called reception, acceptance. The *quomodo fiet?* is changed, on Mary's lips, to a *fiat*: Let it be done, I am ready, I accept. This is the crucial moment of faithfulness, the moment in which man perceives that he will never completely understand the 'how'; that there are in God's plan more areas of mystery than of clarity; that, however he may try, he will never succeed in understanding it completely […].

"The third dimension of faithfulness is consistency to live in accordance with what one believes; to adapt one's own life to the object of one's adherence. To accept misunderstanding, persecutions, rather than a break between what one practises and what one believes: this is consistency […].

"But all faithfulness must pass the most exacting test, that of duration.

[33]and he will reign over the house of Jacob for ever;
and of his kingdom there will be no end." Mic 4:7 Dan 7:14
[34]And Mary said to the angel, "How can this be, since I have no
husband?" [35] And the angel said to her,

"Therefore, the fourth dimension of faithfulness is constancy. It is easy to be consistent for a day or two. It is difficult and important to be consistent for one's whole life. It is easy to be consistent in the hour of enthusiasm, it is difficult to be so in the hour of tribulation. And only a consistency that lasts throughout the whole of life can be called faithfulness. Mary's 'fiat' in the Annunciation finds its fullness in the silent 'fiat' that she repeats at the foot of the Cross" (Homily in Mexico City Cathedral, 26 January 1979).

1:34. Mary believed the archangel's words absolutely; she did not doubt as Zechariah had done (cf. Lk 1:18). Her question, "How can this be?", expresses her readiness to obey the will of God even though at first sight it implied a contradiction: on the one hand, she was convinced that God wished her to remain a virgin; on the other, here was God also announcing that she would become a mother. The archangel announces God's mysterious design, and what had seemed impossible, according to the laws of nature, is explained by a unique intervention on the part of God.

Mary's resolution to remain a virgin was certainly something very unusual, not in line with the practice of righteous people under the Old Covenant, for, as St Augustine explains, "particularly attentive to the propagation and growth of the people of God, through whom the Prince and Saviour of the world might be prophesied and be born, the saints were obliged to make use of the good of matrimony"(*De bono matrimonii*, 9, 9). However, in the Old Testament there were some who, in keeping with God's plan, did remain celibate—for example, Jeremiah, Elijah, Eliseus and John the Baptist. The Blessed Virgin, who received a very special inspiration of the Holy Spirit to practise virginity, is a first-fruit of the New Testament, which will establish the excellence of virginity over marriage while not taking from the holiness of the married state, which it raises to the level of a sacrament (cf. Vatican II, *Gaudium et spes*, 48).

1:35. The "shadow" is a symbol of the presence of God. When Israel was journeying through the wilderness, the glory of God filled the Tabernacle and a cloud covered the Ark of the Covenant (Ex 40:34–36). And when God gave Moses the tablets of the Law, a cloud covered Mount Sinai (Ex 24:15–16); and also, at the transfiguration of Jesus, the voice of God the Father was heard coming out of a cloud (Lk 9:35).

At the moment of the incarnation the power of God envelopes our Lady—an expression of God's omnipotence. The Spirit of God—which, according to the account in Genesis (1:2), moved over the face of the waters, bringing things to life—now comes down on Mary. And the fruit of her womb will be the work of the Holy Spirit. The Virgin Mary, who herself was conceived without any stain of sin (cf. Pius IX, *Ineffabilis Deus*) becomes, after the incarnation, a new tabernacle of God. This is the mystery we recall every day when saying the Angelus.

Mt 1:18–20
Jn 10:36

"The Holy Spirit will come upon you,
and the power of the Most High will overshadow you;
therefore the child to be born[d] will be called holy,
the Son of God.
36And behold, your kinswoman Elizabeth in her old age has also
conceived a son; and this is the sixth month with her who was
called barren. 37For with God nothing will be impossible." 38And
Mary said, "Behold, I am the handmaid of the Lord; let it be to
me according to your word." And the angel departed from her.

1:38. Once she learns of God's plan, our Lady yields to God's will with prompt obedience, unreservedly. She realizes the disproportion between what she is going to become—the Mother of God—and what she is—a woman. However, this is what God wants to happen and for him nothing is impossible; therefore no one should stand in his way. So Mary, combining humility and obedience, responds perfectly to God's call: "Behold, I am the handmaid of the Lord; let it be done to me according to your word."

"At the enchantment of this virginal phrase, the Word became flesh" (St J. Escrivá, *Holy Rosary*, first joyful mystery). From the pure body of Mary, God shaped a new body, he created a soul out of nothing, and the Son of God united himself with this body and soul: prior to this he was only God; now he is still God but also man. Mary is now the Mother of God. This truth is a dogma of faith, first defined by the Council of Ephesus (431). At this point she also begins to be the spiritual Mother of all mankind. What Christ says when he is dying—"Behold, your son …, Behold, your mother" (Jn 19:26–27)—simply promulgates what came about silently at Nazareth. "With her generous 'fiat' (Mary) became, through the working of the Spirit, the Mother of God, but also the Mother of the living, and, by receiving into her womb the one Mediator, she became the true Ark of the Covenant and true Temple of God" (Paul VI, *Marialis cultus*, 6).

The Gospel shows us the Blessed Virgin as a perfect model of *purity* (the RSV "I have no husband" is a euphemism); of *humility* ("Behold, I am the handmaid of the Lord"); of *candour* and *simplicity* ("How can this be?"); of *obedience* and *lively faith* ("Let it be done to me according to your word"). "Following her example of obedience to God, we can learn to serve delicately without being slavish. In Mary we don't find the slightest trace of the attitude of the foolish virgins, who obey, but thoughtlessly. Our Lady listens attentively to what God wants, ponders what she doesn't fully understand and asks about what she doesn't know. Then she gives herself completely to doing the divine will: 'Behold I am the handmaid of the Lord; let it be done to me according to your word'. Isn't that marvellous? The Blessed Virgin, our teacher in all we do, shows us here that obedience to God is not servile, does not bypass our conscience. We should be inwardly moved to discover the 'freedom of the children of God' (cf. Rom 8:21)" (St Josemaría Escrivá, *Christ Is Passing By*, 173).

1:39–56. We contemplate this episode of our Lady's visit to her cousin St

d. Other ancient authorities add *of you*

The Visitation

[39]In those days Mary arose and went with haste into the hill country, to a city of Judah, [40]and she entered the house of Zechariah
and greeted Elizabeth. [41]And when Elizabeth heard the greeting of
Mary, the babe leaped in her womb; and Elizabeth was filled with Lk 1:15, 80
the Holy Spirit [42]and she exclaimed with a loud cry, "Blessed are
you among women, and blessed is the fruit of your womb! [43]And Judg 5:24 Jud 13:23
why is this granted me, that the mother of my Lord should come
to me? [44]For behold, when the voice of your greeting came to my

---

Elizabeth in the *second joyful mystery* of the Rosary: "Joyfully keep Joseph and Mary company … and you will hear the traditions of the House of David. … We walk in haste towards the mountains, to a town of the tribe of Judah (Lk 1:39).

"We arrive. It is the house where John the Baptist is to be born. Elizabeth gratefully hails the Mother of her Redeemer: Blessed are you among women, and blessed is the fruit of your womb. Why should I be honoured with a visit from the mother of my Lord? (Lk 1:42–43).

"The unborn Baptist quivers … (Lk 1:41). Mary's humility pours forth in the *Magnificat*. … And you and I, who are proud—who were proud—promise to be humble" (St J. Escrivá, *Holy Rosary*).

1:39. On learning from the angel that her cousin St Elizabeth is soon to give birth and is in need of support, our Lady in her charity hastens to her aid. She has no regard for the difficulties this involves. Although we do not know where exactly Elizabeth was living (it is now thought to be Ain Karim), it certainly meant a journey into the hill country which at that time would have taken four days.

From Mary's visit to Elizabeth Christians should learn to be caring people. "If we have this filial contact with Mary, we won't be able to think just about ourselves and our problems. Selfish personal problems will find no place in our mind" (St Josemaría Escrivá, *Christ Is Passing By*, 145).

1:42. St Bede comments that Elizabeth blesses Mary using the same words as the archangel "to show that she should be honoured by angels and by men and why she should indeed be revered above all other women" (*In Lucae Evangelium expositio*, in loc.).

When we say the *Hail Mary* we repeat these divine greetings, "rejoicing with Mary at her dignity as Mother of God and praising the Lord, thanking him for having given us Jesus Christ through Mary" (St Pius X, *Catechism*, 333).

1:43. Elizabeth is moved by the Holy Spirit to call Mary "the mother of my Lord", thereby showing that Mary is the Mother of God.

1:44. Although he was conceived in sin—original sin—like other men, St John the Baptist was born sinless because he was sanctified in his mother's womb by the presence of Jesus Christ (then in Mary's womb) and of the Blessed Virgin. On receiving this grace of God St John rejoices by leaping with joy in his mother's womb—thereby fulfilling the archangel's prophecy (cf. Lk 1:15).

St John Chrysostom comments on this scene of the Gospel: "See how new and how wonderful this mystery is. He has not yet left the womb but he speaks

Lk 1:48; 11:28 ears, the babe in my womb leaped for joy. 45And blessed is she
who believed that there would be[e] a fulfilment of what was
spoken to her from the Lord."

The Magnificat

46And Mary said,
1 Sam 2:1–10 "My soul magnifies the Lord,

---

by leaping; he is not yet allowed to cry out but he makes himself heard by his actions […]; he has not yet seen the light but he points out the Sun; he has not yet been born and he is keen to act as Precursor. The Lord is present, so he cannot contain himself or wait for nature to run its course: he wants to break out of the prison of his mother's womb and he makes sure he witnesses to the fact that the Saviour is about to come" (*Sermon recorded by Metaphrastrus*).

1:45. Joining the chorus of all future generations, Elizabeth, moved by the Holy Spirit, declares the Lord's Mother to be blessed and praises her faith. No one ever had faith to compare with Mary's; she is the model of the attitude a creature should have towards its Creator —complete submission, total attachment. Through her faith, Mary is the instrument chosen by God to bring about the Redemption; as Mediatrix of all graces, she is associated with the redemptive work of her Son: "This union of the Mother with the Son in the work of salvation is made manifest from the time of Christ's virginal conception up to his death; first when Mary, arising in haste to go to visit Elizabeth, is greeted by her as blessed because of her belief in the promise of salvation and the Precursor leaps with joy in the womb of his mother […]. The Blessed Virgin advanced in her pilgrimage of faith and faithfully persevered in her union with her Son unto the cross, where she stood (cf. Jn 19:25), in keeping with the divine plan, enduring with her only-begotten Son the intensity of his suffering, associating herself with his sacrifice in her mother's heart, and lovingly consenting to the immolation of this victim which was born of her" (Vatican II, *Lumen gentium*, 57f).

The new Latin text gives a literal rendering of the original Greek when it says "quae credidit" (RSV "she who has believed") as opposed to the Vulgate "quae credidisti" ("you who have believed") which gave more of the sense than a literal rendering.

1:46–55. Mary's *Magnificat* canticle is a poem of singular beauty. It evokes certain passages of the Old Testament with which she would have been very familiar (especially 1 Sam 2:1–10).

Three stanzas may be distinguished in the canticle: in the first (vv. 46–50) Mary glorifies God for making her the Mother of the Saviour, which is why future generations will call her blessed; she shows that the Incarnation is a mysterious expression of God's power and holiness and mercy. In the second (vv. 51–53) she teaches us that the Lord has always had a preference for the humble, resisting the proud and boastful. In the third (vv. 54–55) she proclaims that God, in keeping with his promise, has always taken special care of his chosen people—

e. Or *believed, for there will be*

[47]and my spirit rejoices in God my Saviour,
[48]for he has regarded the low estate of his handmaiden. Lk 1:38–45 1 Sam 1:11
For behold, henceforth all generations will call me blessed; Ps 113:5–6
[49]for he who is mighty has done great things for me,
and holy is his name. Ps 111:9
[50]And his mercy is on those who fear him
from generation to generation. Ps 103:13, 17

---

and now does them the greatest honour of all by becoming a Jew (cf. Rom 1:3).

"Our prayer can accompany and imitate this prayer of Mary. Like her, we feel the desire to sing, to acclaim the wonders of God, so that all mankind and all creation may share our joy" (St Josemaría Escrivá, *Christ Is Passing By*, 144).

1:46–47. "The first fruits of the Holy Spirit are peace and joy. And the Blessed Virgin had received within herself all the grace of the Holy Spirit" (St Basil, *In Psalmos homiliae*, on Ps 32). Mary's soul overflows in the words of the *Magnificat*. God's favours cause every humble soul to feel joy and gratitude. In the case of the Blessed Virgin God has bestowed more on her than on any other creature. "Virgin Mother of God, he whom the heavens cannot contain, on becoming man, enclosed himself within your womb" (*Roman Missal*, Antiphon of the common of the Mass for feasts of our Lady). The humble Virgin of Nazareth is going to be the Mother of God; the Creator's omnipotence has never before manifested itself in as complete a way as this.

1:48–49. Mary's expression of humility causes St Bede to exclaim: "It was fitting, then, that just as death entered the world through the pride of our first parents, the entry of Life should be manifested by the humility of Mary" (*In Lucae Evangelium expositio*, in loc.).

"How great is the value of humility! —*Quia respexit humilitatem.* ... It is not of her faith, nor of her charity, nor of her immaculate purity that our Mother speaks in the house of Zachary. Her joyful hymn sings: 'Since he has looked on my humility, all generations will call me blessed'" (St Josemaría Escrivá, *The Way*, 598).

God rewards our Lady's humility by mankind's recognition of her greatness: "All generations will call me blessed." This prophecy is fulfilled every time someone says the Hail Mary, and indeed she is praised on earth continually, without interruption. "From the earliest times the Blessed Virgin is honoured under the title of Mother of God, under whose protection the faithful take refuge together in prayer in all their perils and needs. Accordingly, following the Council of Ephesus, there was a remarkable growth in the cult of the people of God towards Mary, in veneration and love, in invocation and imitation, according to her own prophetic words: 'all generations will call me blessed, for he who is mighty has done great things for me'" (Vatican II, *Lumen gentium*, 66).

1:50. "And his mercy is on these who fear him from generation to generation": "At the very moment of the Incarnation, these words open up a new perspective of salvation history. After the Resurrection of Christ, this perspective is new on both the historical and the eschatological level. From that time on there is a succession of new generations of individuals

Ps 33:10; 89:10 2 Sam 22:28 Ps 147:6 Job 12:19

[51]He has shown strength with his arm,
he has scattered the proud in the imagination of their hearts,
[52]he has put down the mighty from their thrones,
and exalted those of low degree;

1 Sam 2:5 Ps 34:10; 107:9 Is 41:8 Ps 98:3

[53]he has filled the hungry with good things,
and the rich he has sent empty away.
[54]He has helped his servant Israel,
in remembrance of his mercy,

Gen 17:7; 18:18; 22:15–18 Mic 7:20

[55]as he spoke to our fathers,
to Abraham and to his posterity for ever."*

---

in the immense human family, in ever-increasing dimensions; there is also a succession of new generations of the people of God, marked with the sign of the Cross and of the Resurrection and 'sealed' with the sign of the paschal mystery of Christ, the absolute revelation of the mercy that Mary proclaimed on the threshold of her kinswoman's house: 'His mercy is […] from generation to generation' […]. Mary, then, is the one who *has the deepest knowledge of the mystery of God's mercy*. She knows its price, she knows how great it is. In this sense, we call her the *Mother of mercy*: our Lady of mercy, or Mother of divine mercy; in each one of these titles there is a deep theological meaning, for they express the special preparation of her soul, of her whole personality, so that she was able to perceive, through the complex events, first of Israel, then of every individual and of the whole of humanity, that mercy of which 'from generation to generation' people become sharers according to the eternal design of the Most Holy Trinity" (John Paul II, *Dives in misericordia*, 9).

1:51. "The proud": those who want to be regarded as superior to others, whom they look down on. This also refers to those who, in their arrogance, seek to organize society without reference to, or in opposition to, God's law. Even if they seem to do so successfully, the words of our Lady's canticle will ultimately come true, for God will scatter them as he did those who tried to build the tower of Babel, thinking that they could reach as high as heaven (cf. Gen 11:4).

"When pride takes hold of a soul, it is no surprise to find it bringing along with it a whole string of other vices—greed, self-indulgence, envy, injustice. The proud man is always vainly striving to dethrone God, who is merciful to all his creatures, so as to make room for himself and his ever cruel ways.

"We should beg God not to let us fall into this temptation. Pride is the worst sin of all, and the most ridiculous. … Pride is unpleasant, even from a human point of view. The person who rates himself better than everyone and everything is constantly studying himself and looking down on other people, who in turn react by ridiculing his foolish vanity" (St Josemaría Escrivá, *Friends of God*, 100).

1:53. This form of divine providence has been experienced countless times over the course of history. For example, God nourished the people of Israel with manna during their forty years in the wilderness (Ex 16:4–35); similarly his angel brought food to Elijah (1 Kings 19:5–8), and to Daniel in the lions' den (Dan 14:31–40); and the widow of Sarepta was given a supply of oil which

56And Mary remained with her about three months, and returned
to her home.

Birth and circumcision of John the Baptist

57Now the time came for Elizabeth to be delivered, and she gave
birth to a son. 58And her neighbours and kinsfolk heard that the
Lord had shown great mercy to her, and they rejoiced with her.
59And on the eighth day they came to circumcise the child; and Gen 17:12
they would have named him Zechariah after his father, 60but his Lev 12:3
mother said, "Not so; he shall be called John." 61And they said to

---

miraculously never ran out (1 Kings 17:8ff). So, too, the Blessed Virgin's yearning for holiness was fulfilled by the incarnation of the Word.

God nourished the chosen people with his Law and the preaching of his prophets, but the rest of mankind was left hungry for his word, a hunger now satisfied by the Incarnation. This gift of God will be accepted by the humble; the self-sufficient, having no desire for the good things of God, will not partake of them (cf. St Basil, *In Psalmos homiliae*, on Ps 33).

1:54. God led the people of Israel as he would a child whom he loved tenderly: "the Lord your God bore you, as a man bears his son, in all the way that you went" (Deut 1:31). He did so many times, using Moses, Joshua, Samuel, David etc., and now he gives them a definitive leader by sending the Messiah—moved by his great mercy which takes pity on the wretchedness of Israel and of all mankind.

1:55. God promised the patriarchs of old that he would have mercy on mankind. This promise he made to Adam (Gen 3:15), Abraham (Gen 22:18), David (2 Sam 7:12), etc. From all eternity God had planned and decreed that the Word should become incarnate for the salvation of all mankind. As Christ himself put it, "God so loved the world that he gave his only Son, that whoever believes in him should not perish but have eternal life" (Jn 3:16).

1:59. Circumcision was a rite established by God under the Old Covenant to mark out those who belonged to his chosen people: he commanded Abraham to institute circumcision as a sign of the Covenant he had made with him and all his descendants (cf. Gen 17:10–14), prescribing that it should be done on the eighth day after birth. The rite was performed either at home or in the synagogue, and, in addition to the actual circumcision, the ceremony included prayers and the naming of the child.

With the institution of Christian Baptism the commandment to circumcise ceased to apply. At the Council of Jerusalem (cf. Acts 15:1ff), the apostles definitively declared that those entering the Church had no need to be circumcised.

St Paul's explicit teaching on the irrelevance of circumcision in the context of the New Alliance established by Christ is to be found in Galatians 5:2ff; 6:12ff; and Colossians 2:11ff.

1:60–63. By naming the child John, Zechariah complies with the instructions God sent him through the angel (cf. Lk 1:13).

her, "None of your kindred is called by this name." 62And they
made signs to his father, inquiring what he would have him called.
63And he asked for a writing tablet, and wrote, "His name is
John." And they all marvelled. 64And immediately his mouth was
opened and his tongue loosed, and he spoke, blessing God. 65And
fear came on all their neighbours. And all these things were talked
about through all the hill country of Judea; 66and all who heard
them laid them up in their hearts, saying, "What then will this
child be?" For the hand of the Lord was with him.

Canticle of Zechariah

67And his father Zechariah was filled with the Holy Spirit, and
prophesied, saying,

Ps 41:13; 72:18; 106:48; 111:9

68"Blessed be the Lord God of Israel,
for he has visited and redeemed his people,

1 Sam 2:10 Ps 18:2; 132:17

69and has raised up a horn of salvation *for us
in the house of his servant David,

1:64. This miraculous event fulfils the prophecy the angel Gabriel made to Zechariah when he announced the conception and birth of the Baptist (Lk 1:19–20). St Ambrose observes: "With good reason was his tongue loosed, because faith untied what had been tied by disbelief" (*Expositio Evangelii sec. Lucam*, in loc.).

Zechariah's is a case similar to that of St Thomas, who was reluctant to believe in the resurrection of our Lord, and who believed only when Jesus gave him clear proof (cf. Jn 20:24–29). For these two men God worked a miracle and won their belief; but normally he requires us to have faith and to obey him without his working any new miracles. This was why he upbraided Zechariah and punished him, and why he reproached Thomas: "Have you believed because you have seen me? Blessed are those who have not seen and yet believe" (Jn 20:29).

1:67. Zechariah, who was a righteous man (cf. v. 6), received the special grace of prophecy when his son was born—a gift which led him to pronounce his canticle, called the *Benedictus*, a prayer so full of faith, reverence and piety that the Church has laid it down to be said daily in the Liturgy of the Hours. Prophecy has not only to do with foretelling future events; it also means being moved by the Holy Spirit to praise God. Both aspects of prophecy are to be found in the *Benedictus*.

1:68–79. Two parts can be discerned in the *Benedictus*: in the first (vv. 68–75) Zechariah thanks God for sending the Messiah, the Saviour, as he promised the patriarchs and prophets of Israel. In the second (vv. 76–79) he prophesies that his son will have the mission of being herald of the Most High and precursor of the Messiah, proclaiming God's mercy which reveals itself in the coming of Christ.

1:72–75. Again and again God promised the Old Testament patriarchs that he would take special care of Israel, giving them a land which they would enjoy undisturbed

[70]as he spoke by the mouth of his holy prophets from of old, Lk 24:25, 44
[71]that we should be saved from our enemies, Ps 106:10
and from the hand of all who hate us;
[72]to perform the mercy promised to our fathers, Ps 105:8; 106:45
and to remember his holy covenant, Gen 17:7
[73]the oath which he swore to our father Abraham, Lev 26:42
[74]to grant us that we, being delivered from the hand of our enemies, Lk 1:55
might serve him without fear,
[75]in holiness and righteousness before him all the days of our life.
[76]And you, child, will be called the prophet of the Most High; Mal 3:1
for you will go before the Lord to prepare his ways, Mt 3:3; 11:10
[77]to give knowledge of salvation to his people Jer 31:34
in the forgiveness of their sins, Num 24:17
[78]through the tender mercy of our God, Is 60:1–2
when the day shall dawn upon[f] us from on high Jer 23:5–6 Zech 3:8

---

and many descendants in whom all the peoples of the earth would be blessed. This promise he ratified by means of a covenant or alliance, of the kind commonly made between kings and their vassals in the Near East. God, as Lord, would protect the patriarchs and their descendants, and these would prove their attachment to him by offering him certain sacrifices and by doing him service. See, for example, Genesis 12:13; 17:1–8; 22:16–18 (God's promise, covenant and pledge to Abraham); and Genesis 35:11–12 (where he repeats these promises to Jacob). Zechariah realizes that the events resulting from the birth of John his son, the Precursor of the Messiah, constitute complete fulfilment of these divine purposes.

1:78–79. The "dawning", the "dayspring", is the Messiah, Jesus Christ, coming down from heaven to shed his light upon us: "the sun of righteousness shall rise, with healing on its wings" (Mal 4:2). Already in the Old Testament we were told about the glory of the Lord, the reflection of his presence—something intimately connected with light. For example, when Moses returned to the encampment after talking with God, his face so shone that the Israelites "were afraid to come near him" (Ex 34:30). St John is making the same reference when he says that "God is light and in him there is no darkness" (1 Jn 1:5) and that there will be no light in heaven "for the glory of God is its light" (cf. Rev 21:23; 22:5).

The angels (cf. Rev 1:11) and the saints (cf. Wis 3:7; Dan 2:3) partake of this divine splendour; our Lady does so in a special way. As a symbol of the Church she is revealed to us in the book of Revelation as "clothed with the sun, with the moon under her feet, and on her head a crown of twelve stars" (12:1).

Even when we live in this world, this divine light reaches us through Jesus Christ who, because he is God, is "the true light that enlightens every man" (Jn

f. Or *whereby the dayspring will visit.* Other ancient authorities read *since the dayspring has visited*

Is 9:2; 42:7; 58:8 Mt 4:16 79to give light to those who sit in darkness and in the shadow of
death,
to guide our feet into the way of peace."
Mt 3:1 80And the child grew and became strong in spirit, and he was in
the wilderness till the day of his manifestation to Israel.

The birth of Jesus

2 1In those days a decree went out from Caesar Augustus that
all the world should be enrolled. 2This was the first enrolment,

---

1:9), as Christ himself tells us: "I am the light of the world; he who follows me will not walk in darkness" (Jn 8:12).

Christians share in this light of God; Jesus tells us: "You are the light of the world" (Mt 5:14). Therefore, we must live as children of the light (cf. Lk 16:8), whose fruit takes the form of "all that is good and right and true" (Eph 5:9); our lives should shine out, thereby helping people to know God and give him glory (cf. Mt 5:16).

1:80. "Wilderness": this must surely refer to the "Judean wilderness" which stretches from the northwestern shores of the Dead Sea to the hill country of Judea. It is not a sand desert but rather a barren steppe with bushes and basic vegetation which suit bees and grasshoppers or wild locusts. It contains many caves which can provide shelter.

2:1. Caesar Augustus was Roman emperor at this time, reigning from 30 BC to AD 14. He is known to have commissioned various censuses, one of which could well be that referred to by the evangelist. Since Rome normally respected local usages, censuses were carried out in line with Jewish custom whereby every householder went to his place of origin to be listed in the census.

2:6–7. The Messiah is born, the Son of God and our Saviour. "He made himself a child [...] to enable you to become a perfect man; he was wrapped in swaddling clothes to free you from the bonds of death [...]. He came down on earth to enable you to rise up to heaven; he had no place in the inn so that you might have many mansions in heaven. He, being rich, became poor for our sake—St Paul says (2 Cor 8:9)—so as to enrich us with his poverty [...]. The tears of this crying child purify men, they wash away my sins" (St Ambrose, *Expositio Evangelii sec. Lucam*, in loc.).

The new-born Child does not yet speak, but he is the eternal Word of the Father. Even from the manger in Bethlehem he teaches us. "We must learn the lessons which Jesus teaches us, even when he is just a newly born child, from the very moment he opens his eyes on this blessed land of men" (St Josemaría Escrivá, *Christ Is Passing By*, 14). The main lesson he gives us concerns humility: "God humbled himself to allow us to get near him, so that we could give our love in exchange for his, so that our freedom might bow, not only at the sight of his power, but also before the wonder of his humility.

"The greatness of this Child who is God! His Father is the God who has made heaven and earth and there he is, in a manger, 'because there was no room at the inn' (Lk 2:7); there was nowhere else for the Lord of all creation" (*Christ Is Passing By*, 18).

when Quirinius was governor of Syria. [3]And all went to be
enrolled, each to his own city. [4]And Joseph also went up from
Galilee, from the city of Nazareth, to Judea, to the city of David,
which is called Bethlehem, because he was of the house and lineage of David, [5]to be enrolled with Mary, his betrothed, who was Lk 1:27
with child. [6]And while they were there, the time came for her to
be delivered. [7]And she gave birth to her first-born* son and Mt 1:25
wrapped him in swaddling cloths, and laid him in a manger,
because there was no place for them in the inn.

Our hearts should provide Jesus with a place where he can be born spiritually; that is, we should be born to a new life, becoming a new creature (cf. Rom 6:4), keeping that holiness and purity of soul which we were given in Baptism and which is like being born again. We contemplate the birth of our Saviour when we pray the third mystery of the Holy Rosary.

2:7. "First-born son": it is usual for Sacred Scripture to refer to the first male child as "the first-born" whether or not there were other brothers (cf., for example, Ex 13:2; 13:13; Num 15:8; Heb 1:6). The same practice is to be found in ordinary speech; take, for example, this inscription dating from approximately the same time as Christ was born, which was found near Tell-el-Jedvieh (in Egypt) in 1922, which states that a woman named Arsinoe died when giving birth to "her first-born son". Otherwise, as St Jerome explains in his letter *Adversus Helvidium*, 10, "if only he were first-born who was followed by other brothers, he would not deserve the rights of the first-born, which the Law lays down, until the other had been born"—which would be absurd, since the Law ordains that those first-born should be "redeemed" within a month of their birth (cf. Num 18:16).

However, Jesus Christ is first-born in a much deeper sense independent of natural or biological considerations—which St Bede describes in these words, summarizing a long tradition of the Fathers of the Church: "Truly the Son of God, who was made manifest in the flesh, belongs to a more exalted order not only because he is the Only-begotten of the Father by virtue of the excellence of his divinity; he is also first-born of all creatures by virtue of his fraternity with men: concerning this [his primogeniture] it is said: 'For those whom he foreknew he also predestined to be conformed to the image of his Son, in order that he might be the first-born among many brethren' (Rom 8:29). And concerning the former [his being the Only-begotten] it is said 'we have beheld his glory, glory as of the only Son from the Father' (Jn 1:14). Thus, he is only-begotten by the substance of the Godhead, and first-born through his assumption of humanity; first-born by grace, only-begotten by nature. This is why he is called brother and Lord: brother, because he is the first-born; Lord, because he is the Only-begotten" (*In Lucae Evangelium expositio*, in loc.).

Christian Tradition teaches, as a truth of faith, that Mary remained a virgin after Christ's birth, which is perfectly in keeping with Christ's status as her first-born. See, for example, these words of the Lateran Council of 649: "If anyone does not profess according to the holy Fathers that in the proper and true sense the holy, ever-Virgin, immaculate Mary is the Mother of God, since in this last age not

The adoration of the shepherds

[8]And in that region there were shepherds out in the field, keeping
watch over their flock by night. [9]And an angel of the Lord
appeared to them, and the glory of the Lord shone around them,
and they were filled with fear. [10]And the angel said to them, "Be
not afraid; for behold, I bring you good news of a great joy which
will come to all the people; [11]for to you is born this day in the city
of David a Saviour, who is Christ the Lord. [12]And this will be a

---

with human seed but of the Holy Spirit she properly and truly conceived the divine Word, who was born of God the Father before all ages, and gave him birth without any detriment to her virginity, which remained inviolate even after his birth: let such a one be condemned" (can. 3).

2:8–20. At his birth Christ's divinity and his humanity are perfectly manifested: we see his weakness—the form of a servant (Phil 2:7)—and his divine power. Christian faith involves confessing that Jesus Christ is true God and true man.

The salvation which Christ brought us is offered to everyone, without distinction: "Here there cannot be Greek and Jew, circumcised and uncircumcised, barbarian, Scythian, slave, free man, but Christ is all, and in all" (Col 3:11). That is why, even at his birth, he chose to manifest himself to different kinds of people—the shepherds, the Magi and Simeon and Anna. As St Augustine comments: "The shepherds were Israelites; the Magi, Gentiles. The first lived nearby; the latter, far away. Yet both came to the cornerstone, Christ" (*Sermo de Navitate Domini*, 202).

2:8–9. These shepherds may have been from the neighbourhood of Bethlehem or even have come from further afield in search of pasture for their flocks. It was these simple and humble people who were the first to hear the good news of Christ's birth. God has a preference for the humble (cf. Prov 3:34); he hides from those who consider themselves wise and understanding and reveals himself to "babes" (cf. Mt 11:25).

2:10–14. The angel announces that the new-born Child is the Saviour, Christ the Lord. He is the *Saviour* because he has come to save us from our sins (cf. Mt 1:21). He is *the Christ*, that is, the Messiah so often promised in the Old Testament, and now born among us in fulfilment of that ancient hope. He is *the Lord*: this shows Christ's divinity, for this is the name God chose to be known by to his people in the Old Testament, and it is the way Christians usually refer to and address Jesus and the way the Church always confesses her faith: "We believe [...] in one Lord, Jesus Christ, the only Son of God."

When the angel tells them that the Child has been born in the city of David, he reminds them that this was where the Messiah Redeemer was supposed to be born (cf. Mic 5:2; Mt 2:6), who would be a descendant of David (cf. Ps 110:1–2; Mt 22:42–46).

Christ is the Lord not only of men but also of angels, which is why the angels rejoice at his birth and render him the tribute of adoration: "Glory to God in the highest." And, since men are called to share, like them, in the happiness of heaven, the angels add: "And on earth peace among men with whom he is

sign for you: you will find a babe wrapped in swaddling cloths
and lying in a manger." [13]And suddenly there was with the angel
a multitude of the heavenly host praising God and saying,
[14]"Glory to God in the highest,
and on earth peace among men with whom he is pleased!"[g]
[15]When the angels went away from them into heaven, the
shepherds said to one another, "Let us go over to Bethlehem and
see this thing that has happened, which the Lord has made known

Lk 19:38
Is 57:19
Ezek 2:14–17

---

pleased." "They praise the Lord," St Gregory the Great comments, "putting the notes of their hymn in harmony with our redemption; they see us as already sharing in their own happy destiny and rejoice at this" (*Moralia*, 28, 7).

St Thomas explains why the birth of Christ was revealed through angels: "What is in itself hidden needs to be manifested, but not what is in itself manifest. The flesh of him who was born was manifest, but his Godhead was hidden, and therefore it was fitting that this birth should be made known by angels, who are ministers of God. This was why a certain brightness accompanied the angelic apparition, to indicate that he who was just born 'reflects the glory of the Father' (Heb 1:3)" (*Summa theologiae*, 3, 36, 5 ad 1).

The angel also tells the shepherds that Christ is a man: "You will find a babe wrapped in swaddling cloths and lying in a manger" (v. 12)—as foretold in the Old Testament: "To us a child is born, to us a son is given; and the government will be upon his shoulder" (Is 9:6).

2:14. This text can be translated in two ways, which are compatible with each other. One is the version chosen by the RSV; the other, as an RSV note points out: "other ancient authorities read *peace, good will among men*"; a variant is the translation used in the Liturgy: "Peace on earth to men who are God's friends." Essentially what the text says is that the angels ask for peace and reconciliation with God, which is not something which results from men's merits but rather comes from God's deigning to have mercy on them. The two translations are complementary, for when men respond to God's grace they are fulfilling God's good will, God's love for them: "*Iesus Christus, Deus homo*: Jesus Christ, God-man. This is one of 'the mighty works of God' (Acts 2:11), which we should reflect upon and thank him for. He has come to bring 'peace on earth to men of good will' (Lk 2:14), to all men who want to unite their wills to the holy will of God" (St Josemaría Escrivá, *Christ Is Passing By*, 13).

2:15–18. The birth of the Saviour Messiah is the key event in the history of mankind, but God wanted it to take place so quietly that the world went about its business as if nothing had happened. The only people he tells about it are a few shepherds. It was also to a shepherd, Abraham, that God gave his promise to save mankind.

The shepherds make their way to Bethlehem propelled by the sign they have received. And when they verify it they tell what they heard from the angel and about seeing the heavenly host. They are the first witnesses of the birth of the

g. Other ancient authorities read *peace, good will among men*

to us." 16And they went with haste, and found Mary and Joseph,
and the babe lying in a manger. 17And when they saw it they made
known the saying which had been told them concerning this child;
18and all who heard it wondered at what the shepherds told them.
Lk 2:51 Dan 7:28 19But Mary kept all these things, pondering them in her heart.
20And the shepherds returned, glorifying and praising God for all
they had heard and seen, as it had been told them.

Messiah. "The shepherds were not content with believing in the happy event which the angel proclaimed to them and which, full of wonder, they saw for a fact; they manifested their joy not only to Mary and Joseph but to everyone and, what is more, they tried to engrave it on their memory. 'And all who heard it wondered at what the shepherds told them.' And why would they not have wondered, seeing on earth him who is in heaven, and earth and heaven reconciled; seeing that ineffable Child who joined what was heavenly—divinity—and what was earthly—humanity—creating a wonderful covenant through this union. Not only were they in awe at the mystery of the Incarnation, but also at the great testimony borne by the shepherds, who could not have invented something they had not heard and who publish the truth with a simple eloquence" (Photius, *Ad Amphilochium*, 155).

2:16. The shepherds hasten because they are full of joy and eager to see the Saviour. St Ambrose comments: "No one seeks Christ half-heartedly" (*Expositio Evangelii sec. Lucam*, in loc.). Earlier on, the evangelist observed that our Lady, after the Annunciation, "went in haste" to see St Elizabeth (Lk 1:39). A soul who has given God entry rejoices that God has visited him and his life acquires new energy.

2:19. In very few words this verse tells us a great deal about our Lady. We see the serenity with which she contemplates the wonderful things that are coming true with the birth of her divine Son. She studies them, ponders them and stores them in the silence of her heart. She is a true teacher of prayer. If we imitate her, if we guard and ponder in our hearts what Jesus says to us and what he does in us, we are well on the way to Christian holiness and we shall never lack his doctrine and his grace. Also, by meditating in this way on the teaching Jesus has given us, we shall obtain a deeper understanding of the mystery of Christ, which is how "the Tradition that comes from the apostles makes progress in the Church, with the help of the Holy Spirit. There is a growth in insight into the realities and words that are being passed on. This comes about in various ways. It comes through the contemplation and study of believers who ponder these things in their hearts. It comes from the intimate sense of spiritual realities which they experience. And it comes from the preaching of those who have received, along with their right of succession in the episcopate, the sure charism of truth" (Vatican II, *Dei Verbum*, 8).

2:21. On the meaning and rite of circumcision, see the note on Lk 1:59. "Jesus" means "Yahweh saves" or "Yahweh is salvation," that is, Saviour. This name was given the Child not as the result of any human decision but in keeping with the commandment of God which the angel communicated to the Blessed

The circumcision of Jesus

21 And at the end of eight days, when he was circumcised, he was Lk 1:59
called Jesus, the name given by the angel before he was conceived Lev 12:3ff
in the womb. Gal 4:4

The purification of Mary and the presentation of Jesus in the temple

22 And when the time came for their purification according to the Lev 12:2–8
law of Moses, they brought him up to Jerusalem to present him to
the Lord 23 (as it is written in the law of the Lord, "Every male that Ex 13:2; 12:15

Virgin and to St Joseph (cf. Lk 1:31; Mt 1:21).

The Son of God became incarnate in order to redeem and save all men; so it is very fitting that he be called Jesus, Saviour. We confess this in the Creed: "For us men and for our salvation he came down from heaven." "There were indeed many who were called by this name [...]. But how much more appropriate it is to call by this name our Saviour, who brought light, liberty and salvation, not to one people only, but to all men, of all ages—to men oppressed, not by famine, or Egyptian or Babylonian bondage, but sitting in the shadow of death and fettered by the galling chains of sin and of the devil" (St Pius V, *Catechism*, 1, 36).

2:22–24. The Holy Family goes up to Jerusalem to fulfil the prescriptions of the Law of Moses—the purification of the mother and the presentation and then redemption or buying back of the first-born. According to Leviticus 12:2–8, a woman who bore a child was unclean. The period of legal impurity ended, in the case of a mother of a male child, after forty days, with a rite of purification. Mary most holy, ever-virgin, was exempt from these precepts of the Law, because she conceived without intercourse, nor did Christ's birth undo the virginal integrity of his Mother. However, she chose to submit herself to the Law, although she was under no obligation to do so.

"Through this example, foolish child, won't you learn to fulfil the holy Law of God, regardless of any personal sacrifice?

"Purification! You and I certainly do need purification. Atonement and, more than atonement, Love. Love as a searing iron to cauterize our soul's uncleanness, and as a fire to kindle with divine flames the wretchedness of our hearts" (St Josemaría Escrivá, *Holy Rosary*, fourth joyful mystery).

Also, in Exodus 13:2, 12–13 it is indicated that every first-born male belongs to God and must be set apart for the Lord, that is, dedicated to the service of God. However, once divine worship was reserved to the tribe of Levi, first-born who did not belong to that tribe were not dedicated to God's service, and to show that they continued to be God's special property, a rite of redemption was performed.

The Law also laid down that the Israelites should offer in sacrifice some lesser victim—for example, a lamb or, if they were poor, a pair of doves or two pigeons. Our Lord, who "though he was rich, yet for your sake he became poor, so that by his poverty you might become rich" (2 Cor 8:9), chose to have a poor man's offering made on his behalf.

Lev 12:8; 5:11 Num 6:9–10 opens the womb shall be called holy to the Lord") [24]and to offer a
sacrifice according to what is said in the law of the Lord, "a pair
of turtledoves, or two young pigeons."

Simeon's prophecy

Is 40:1; 49:13 [25]Now there was a man in Jerusalem, whose name was Simeon,
and this man was righteous and devout, looking for the consolation of Israel, and the Holy Spirit was upon him. [26]And it had been
revealed to him by the Holy Spirit that he should not see death
before he had seen the Lord's Christ. [27]And inspired by the Spirit[h]
he came into the temple; and when the parents brought in the
child Jesus, to do for him according to the custom of the law, [28]he
took him up in his arms and blessed God and said,

[29]"Lord, now lettest thou thy servant depart in peace,
according to thy word;
Is 40:5; 52:10 [30]for mine eyes have seen thy salvation
[31]which thou hast prepared in the presence of all peoples,
Is 42:6; 46:13; 49:6 Acts 13:47 [32]a light for revelation to the Gentiles,
and for glory to thy people Israel."

2:25–32. Simeon, who is described as a righteous and devout man, obedient to God's will, addresses himself to our Lord as a vassal or loyal servant who, having kept watch all his life in expectation of the coming of his Lord, sees that this moment has "now" come, the moment that explains his whole life. When he takes the Child in his arms, he learns, not through any reasoning process but through a special grace from God, that this Child is the promised Messiah, the Consolation of Israel, the Light of the nations.

Simeon's canticle (vv. 29–32) is also a prophecy. It consists of two stanzas: the first (vv. 29–30) is an act of thanksgiving to God, filled with profound joy for having seen the Messiah. The second (vv. 31–32) is more obviously prophetic and extols the divine blessings which the Messiah is bringing to Israel and to all men. The canticle highlights the fact that Christ brings redemption to all men without exception—something foretold in many Old Testament prophecies (cf. Gen 22:18; Is 2:6; 42:6; 60:3; Ps 28:2).

It is easy to realize how extremely happy Simeon was—given that many patriarchs, prophets and kings of Israel had yearned to see the Messiah, yet did not see him, whereas he now held him in his arms (cf. Lk 10:24; 1 Pet 1:10).

2:33. The Blessed Virgin and St Joseph marvelled not because they did not know who Christ was; they were in awe at the way God was revealing him. Once again they teach us to contemplate the mysteries involved in the birth of Christ.

2:34–35. After Simeon blesses them, the Holy Spirit moves him to further prophecy about the Child's future and his Mother's. His words become clearer in the light of our Lord's life and death.

Jesus came to bring salvation to all men, yet he will be a sign of contradiction because some people will obstinately

h. Or *in the Spirit*

33 And his father and his mother marvelled at what was said about Is 8:14
him; 34 and Simeon blessed them and said to Mary his mother, Mt 21:42
"Behold, this child is set for the fall* and rising of many in Israel, 1 Pet 2:8
and for a sign that is spoken against Jn 9:39 Acts 28:22
35 (and a sword will pierce through your own soul also), Jn 19:25
that thoughts out of many hearts may be revealed."

Anna the prophetess

36 And there was a prophetess Anna, the daughter of Phanuel, of
the tribe of Asher; she was of a great age, having lived with her
husband seven years from her virginity, 37 and as a widow till she 1 Tim 5:5
was eighty-four. She did not depart from the temple, worshipping
with fasting and prayer night and day. 38 And coming up at that
very hour she gave thanks to God, and spoke of him to all who Is 52:9
were looking for the redemption of Jerusalem.

The childhood of Jesus

39 And when they had performed everything according to the law
of the Lord, they returned to Galilee, to their own city, Nazareth.

---

reject him—and for this reason he will be their ruin. But for those who accept him with faith Jesus will be their salvation, freeing them from sin in this life and raising them up to eternal life.

The words Simeon addresses to Mary announce that she will be intimately linked with her Son's redemptive work. The sword indicates that Mary will have a share in her Son's sufferings; hers will be an unspeakable pain which pierces her soul. Our Lord suffered on the cross for our sins, and it is those sins which forge the sword of Mary's pain. Therefore, we have a duty to atone not only to God but also to his Mother, who is our Mother too.

The last words of the prophecy, "that thoughts out of many hearts may be revealed", link up with v. 34: uprightness or perversity will be demonstrated by whether one accepts or rejects Christ.

2:36–38. Anna's testimony is very similar to Simeon's; like him, she too has been awaiting the coming of the Messiah her whole life long, in faithful service of God, and she too is rewarded with the joy of seeing him. She spoke of him, that is, of the Child—praising God in her prayer and exhorting others to believe that this Child is the Messiah.

Thus, the birth of Christ was revealed by three kinds of witnesses in three different ways—first, by the shepherds, after the angel's announcement; second, by the Magi, who were guided by a star; third, by Simeon and Anna, who were inspired by the Holy Spirit.

All who, like Simeon and Anna, persevere in piety and in the service of God, no matter how insignificant their lives seem in men's eyes, become instruments the Holy Spirit uses to make Christ known to others. In his plan of redemption God avails of these simple souls to do much good to all mankind.

2:39. Before their return to Nazareth, St Matthew tells us (2:13–23), the Holy Family fled to Egypt where they stayed for some time.

Lk 1:80; 2:52 40And the child grew and became strong, filled with wisdom; and
the favour of God was upon him.

The finding in the temple

Ex 12:1ff; 23:14–17 41Now his parents went to Jerusalem every year at the feast of the
Passover. 42And when he was twelve years old, they went up
according to custom; 43and when the feast was ended, as they
were returning, the boy Jesus stayed behind in Jerusalem. His parents did not know it, 44but supposing him to be in the company
they went a day's journey, and they sought him among their kinsfolk and acquaintances; 45and when they did not find him, they
returned to Jerusalem, seeking him. 46After three days they found

---

2:40. "Our Lord Jesus Christ as a child, that is, as one clothed in the fragility of human nature, had to grow and become stronger but as the eternal Word of God he had no need to become stronger or to grow. Hence he is rightly described as full of wisdom and grace" (St Bede, *In Lucae Evangelium expositio*, in loc.).

2:41. Only St Luke (2:41–50) reports the event of the Child Jesus being lost and then found in the temple, which we contemplate in the fifth joyful mystery of the Rosary.

Only males aged twelve and upwards were required to make this journey. Nazareth is about 100 km (60 miles) from Jerusalem as the crow flies, but the hilly nature of the country would have made it a trip of 140 km.

2:43–44. On pilgrimages to Jerusalem, the Jews used to go in two groups—one of men, the other of women. Children could go with either group. This explains how they could go a day's journey before they discovered the Child was missing when the families regrouped to camp.

"Mary is crying. In vain you and I have run from group to group, from caravan to caravan. No one has seen him. Joseph, after fruitless attempts to keep from crying, cries too. … And you. … And I.

"Being a common little fellow, I cry my eyes out and wail to heaven and earth …, to make up for the times when I lost him through my own fault and did not cry" (St Josemaría Escrivá, *Holy Rosary*, fifth joyful mystery).

2:45. The concern which Mary and Joseph show in looking for the Child should encourage us always to seek out Jesus, particularly if we lose him through sin.

"Jesus, may I never lose you again. … Now you and I are united in misfortune and grief, as we were united in sin. And from the depths of our being come sighs of heartfelt sorrow and burning phrases which the pen cannot and should not record" (*Holy Rosary*, fifth joyful mystery).

2:46–47. The Child Jesus must have been in the courtyard of the temple, which was where the teachers usually taught. Listeners used to sit at their feet, now and again asking questions and responding to them. This was what Jesus did, but his questions and answers attracted the teachers' attention, he was so wise and well-informed.

2:48. Ever since the Annunciation our Lady had known that the Child Jesus was God. This faith was the basis of her gen-

him in the temple, sitting among the teachers, listening to them
and asking them questions; 47and all who heard him were amazed Mt 7:28
at his understanding and his answers. 48And when they saw him Jn 7:15
they were astonished; and his mother said to him, "Son, why have
you treated us so? Behold, your father and I have been looking for
you anxiously." 49And he said to them, "How is it that you sought Jn 2:16
me? Did you not know that I must be in my Father's house?"*
50And they did not understand the saying which he spoke to them.

The hidden life of Jesus at Nazareth

51And he went down with them and came to Nazareth, and was Lk 2:19
obedient to them; and his mother kept all these things in her heart.

---

erous fidelity throughout her life—but there was no reason why it should include detailed knowledge of all the sacrifices God would ask of her, nor of how Christ would go about his mission of redemption: that was something she would discover as time went by, contemplating her Son's life.

2:49. Christ's reply is a form of explanation. His words—his first words to be recorded in the Gospel—clearly show his divine Sonship; and they also show his determination to fulfil the will of his Eternal Father. "He does not upbraid them—Mary and Joseph—for searching for their son, but he raises the eyes of their souls to appreciate what he owes him whose Eternal Son he is" (St Bede, *In Lucae Evangelium expositio*, in loc.). Jesus teaches us that over and above any human authority, even that of our parents, there is the primary duty to do the will of God. "And, once we are consoled by the joy of finding Jesus—three days he was gone!—debating with the teachers of Israel (Lk 2:46), you and I shall be left deeply impressed by the duty to leave our home and family to serve our heavenly Father" (St Josemaría Escrivá, *Holy Rosary*, fifth joyful mystery). See the note on Mt 10:34–37.

2:50. We must remember that Jesus knew in detail the whole course his earthly life would take from his conception onwards (cf. the note on Lk 2:52). This is shown by what he says in reply to his parents. Mary and Joseph realized that his reply contained a deeper meaning which they did not grasp. They grew to understand it as the life of their Child unfolded. Mary's and Joseph's faith and their reverence towards the Child led them not to ask any further questions but to reflect on Jesus' words and behaviour in this instance, as they had done on other occasions.

2:51. The Gospel sums up Jesus' life in Nazareth in just three words: *erat subditus illis*, he was obedient to them. "He obeys Joseph and Mary. God has come to the world to obey, and to obey creatures. Admittedly they two are very perfect creatures—Holy Mary, our mother, greater than whom God alone; and that most chaste man Joseph. But they are only creatures, and yet Jesus, who is God, obeyed them. We have to love God so as to love his will and desire to respond to his calls. They come to us through the duties of our ordinary life—duties of state, profession, work, family, social life, our own and other people's difficulties, friendship, eagerness to do

Prov 3:4 52And Jesus increased in wisdom and in stature,[i] and in favour
with God and man.

2. PRELUDE TO THE PUBLIC MINISTRY OF JESUS

John the Baptist preaching in the wilderness

3 1In the fifteenth year of the reign of Tiberius Caesar, Pontius
Pilate being governor of Judea, and Herod being tetrarch of

---

what is right and just" (St Josemaría Escrivá, *Christ Is Passing By*, 17).

Jesus lived like any other inhabitant of Nazareth, working at the same trade as St Joseph and earning his living by the sweat of his brow. "His hidden years are not without significance, nor were they simply a preparation for the years which were to come after—those of his public life. Since 1928 I have understood clearly that God wants our Lord's whole life to be an example for Christians. I saw this with special reference to his hidden life, the years he spent working side by side with ordinary men. Our Lord wants many people to ratify their vocation during years of quiet, unspectacular living. Obeying God's will always means leaving our selfishness behind, but there is no reason why it should entail cutting ourselves off from the normal life of ordinary people who share the same status, work and social position with us.

"I dream—and the dream has come true—of multitudes of God's children, sanctifying themselves as ordinary citizens, sharing the ambitions and endeavours of their colleagues and friends. I want to shout to them about this divine truth: If you are there in the middle of ordinary life, it doesn't mean Christ has forgotten about you or hasn't called you. He has invited you to stay among the activities and concerns of the world. He wants you to know that your human vocation, your profession, your talents, are not omitted from his divine plans. He has sanctified them and made them a most acceptable offering to his Father" (ibid., 20).

2:52. As far as his human nature was concerned Jesus matured like anyone else. His growth in wisdom should be seen as referring to experiential knowledge—knowledge acquired by his mind from sense experience and general experience of life. It can also be taken as referring to the external expression of his wisdom; in this sense everything he did was done perfectly, in keeping with whatever age he was at the time.

As man Jesus had three kinds of knowledge: 1. *The knowledge of the blessed* (vision of the divine essence) by virtue of the hypostatic union (the union of his human nature with his divine nature in the one person of the Word). This knowledge did not require any increase. 2. *Infused knowledge*, which perfected his intellect and which meant that he knew everything, even hidden things; thus he was able to read men's hearts. Here again his knowledge was complete; it could not grow. 3. *Acquired knowledge*: he acquired new knowledge through sense experience and reflection; logically, this knowledge increased as time went by.

i. Or *years*

Galilee, and his brother Philip tetrarch of the region of Ituraea and
Trachonitis, and Lysanias tetrarch of Abilene, 2in the high-priesthood of Annas and Caiaphas,* the word of God came to John the
son of Zechariah in the wilderness; 3and he went into all the Mt 3:1–12
region about the Jordan, preaching a baptism of repentance for the Mk 1:2–8

As far as grace, in the strict sense of the word, was concerned, Jesus could not grow. From the first instant of his conception he possessed grace in all its fulness because he was true God by virtue of the hypostatic union. As St Thomas explains: "The end of grace is the union of the rational creature with God. But there can neither be nor be conceived a greater union of the rational creature with God than that which is in the person of Christ [...]. Hence it is clear that the grace of Christ cannot be increased on the part of grace. But neither can it be increased on the part of Christ, since Christ as man was a true and full 'comprehensor' from the first instant of his conception. Hence there could have been no increase of grace in him" (*Summa theologiae*, 3, 7, 12).

However, we can speak of his growing in grace in the sense of the *effects* of grace. In the last analysis, this matter is one of the mysteries of our faith, which our minds cannot fully grasp. How small God would be if we were able fully to fathom this mystery! That Christ should conceal his infinite power and wisdom by becoming a child teaches our pride a great lesson.

3:1. The Gospel identifies very precisely the time and place of the public appearance of John the Baptist, the Precursor of Christ. *Tiberius Caesar* was the second emperor of Rome, and the fifteenth year of his reign corresponds to AD 27 or 29, depending on which of the two possible calculations is correct.

Pontius Pilate was governor or *praefectus* of Judea from AD 26 to 36. His jurisdiction also extended to Samaria and Idumea.

The *Herod* referred to here is Herod Antipas, a son of Herod the Great, who succeeded to part of his father's territory with the title of tetrarch, not king. "Tetrarch" indicated that he exercised his power in subordination to Roman authority. It was Herod Antipas, who died in AD 39, who had St John the Baptist beheaded. On the identity of the four Herods in the New Testament, see the note on Mt 2:1.

Philip, another son of Herod the Great and stepbrother of Herod Antipas, was tetrarch in the territory mentioned here up to AD 34. He married Herodias, who is spoken about in Mark 6:17–19.

3:2. The high priest at the time was *Caiaphas*, who held the position from AD 18 to 36. Annas, his father-in-law, was still so influential that he was considered as the *de facto* head of Jewish religious and political life. That is why, when Christ was arrested, he was first interrogated before Annas (Jn 18:12–24). St Luke therefore is perfectly justified in calling him high priest.

3:2–3. Here St Luke formally introduces St John the Baptist, who appears in his gospel a number of times. When Christ praises the Baptist (cf. Mt 11:7–9) he refers particularly to his strength of will and his commitment to his God-given mission. Humility, austerity, courage and a spirit of prayer figure strongly in John's personality. So faithful was he to his mis-

Is 40:3–5 forgiveness of sins. [4]As it is written in the book of the words of
Isaiah the prophet,

"The voice of one crying in the wilderness:
Prepare the way of the Lord,
make his paths straight.
[5]Every valley shall be filled,
and every mountain and hill shall be brought low,
and the crooked shall be made straight,
and the rough ways shall be made smooth;
Acts 28:28 [6]and all flesh shall see the salvation of God."

Mt 23:33 [7]He said therefore to the multitudes that came out to be bap-
Jn 3:36 tized by him, "You brood of vipers!* Who warned you to flee
from the wrath to come? [8]Bear fruits that befit repentance, and do

---

sion of preparing the way for the Messiah that Christ praises him in a unique way: he is the greatest of those born of woman (cf. Mt 11:11), "a burning and shining lamp" (Jn 5:35). He burned with love, and shone by the witness he bore. Christ was "the true light" (Jn 1:9); the Baptist "came for testimony, to bear witness to the light, that all might believe through him" (Jn 1:7).

John the Baptist appears on the scene preaching the need for repentance. He prepares "the way of the Lord". He is the herald of salvation: but his mission does not go beyond that; he simply announces that salvation is coming. "Among you stands one … who comes after me, the thong of whose sandal I am not worthy to untie" (Jn 1:26–27). He points Christ out: "Behold, the Lamb of God" (Jn 1:29, 36), behold "the Son of God" (Jn 1:34); and he rejoices to see his own disciples leave him to follow Christ (Jn 1:37): "He must increase, but I must decrease" (Jn 3:30).

3:4–6. In the second part of the Book of Isaiah (chaps. 40–55), which is called the "Book of the Consolation of Israel", the Jewish people are told that they will once again suffer exile and a new exodus in which their guide will be, not Moses, but God himself; once again they will make their way through the desert to reach a new promised land. St Luke sees the preaching of the Baptist, who announces the arrival of the Messiah, as fulfilling this prophecy.

Because the Lord is imminent, people must prepare themselves spiritually, by doing penance for their sins, to receive the special divine grace the Messiah is bringing. This is what he means by levelling the mountains and making the Lord's path straight.

Every year in its Advent liturgy the Church proclaims the coming of Jesus Christ, our Saviour, exhorting every Christian to purify his or her soul by a new interior conversion.

3:7. The Baptist's question is aimed at getting people to realize that to obtain God's pardon—"to flee from the wrath to come"—it is not enough simply to perform external rites, not even the baptism of John: one's heart needs to be converted if one is to produce fruit of repentance pleasing to God.

3:8. Jews took enormous pride in their noble origin; they did not want to admit

not begin to say to yourselves, 'We have Abraham as our father';
for I tell you, God is able from these stones to raise up children to
Abraham. [9]Even now the axe is laid to the root of the trees; every
tree therefore that does not bear good fruit is cut down and thrown
into the fire."
[10]And the multitudes asked him, "What then shall we do?"
[11]And he answered them, "He who has two coats, let him share
with him who has none; and he who has food, let him do likewise." [12]Tax collectors also came to be baptized, and said to him,
"Teacher, what shall we do?" [13]And he said to them, "Collect no
more than is appointed you." [14]Soldiers also asked him, "And we,
what shall we do?" And he said to them, "Rob no one by violence
or by false accusation, and be content with your wages."

---

their sins, for they felt that they alone, being legitimate descendants of Abraham, were predestined to receive the salvation the Messiah would bring, without any need for them to do any other penance than the performance of external penitential practices. This is why John upbraids them, making a play on Hebrew words ("God is able from these stones (*abanim*) to raise up children (*banim*) to Abraham"); if they do not change, they will be shut out of the Kingdom of God; whereas many others, who are not of the line of Abraham according to the flesh, will be made his children by spiritual descent through faith (cf. Mt 8:11; Rom 9:8).

3:12–13. With honesty and courage St John the Baptist lays bare each person's fault. The chief sin of tax collectors lay in their using their privileged position as collaborators of the Roman authorities to acquire personal wealth at the expense of the Jewish people: Rome specified how much Israel as a whole should yield by way of taxes; the tax collectors abused their position by extorting more than was necessary. Take the case of Zacchaeus, for example, who, after his conversion, admits that he acquired wealth unjustly and, under the influence of grace, promises our Lord to make generous restitution (cf. Lk 19:1–10).

The Baptist's preaching contains a norm of natural justice which the Church also preaches. Public position should be regarded, above all, as an opportunity to serve society, not to obtain personal gain at the expense of the common good and of that justice which people holding such positions are supposed to administer. Certainly, anyone who has fallen into the temptation of unjustly appropriating what belongs to another must not only confess his sin in the sacrament of Penance if he is to obtain pardon; he must also resolve to give back what is not his.

3:14. The Baptist requires of everyone—Pharisees, tax collectors, soldiers—a deep spiritual renewal in the very exercise of their job; they have to act justly and honourably. God asks all of us to sanctify ourselves in our work and in the circumstances in which we find ourselves: "Any honest and worthwhile work can be converted into a divine occupation. In God's service there are no second-class jobs; all of them are important" (St Josemaría Escrivá, *Conversations*, 55).

Jn 1:19–28 15 As the people were in expectation, and all men questioned in
their hearts concerning John, whether perhaps he were the Christ,
Acts 13:25 16 John answered them all, "I baptize you with water; but he who
is mightier than I is coming, the thong of whose sandal I am not
worthy to untie; he will baptize you with the Holy Spirit and with
fire. 17 His winnowing fork is in his hand, to clear his threshing
floor, and to gather the wheat into his granary, but the chaff he
will burn with unquenchable fire."

18 So, with many other exhortations, he preached good news to
the people.

John the Baptist imprisoned

Mt 14:3–4 Mk 6:17–18 19 But Herod the tetrarch, who had been reproved by him for
Herodias, his brother's wife, and for all the evil things that Herod
had done, 20 added this to them all, that he shut up John in prison.

3:15–17. Using expressive imagery, John announces Christian Baptism, proclaiming that he is not the Messiah; he, who is on his way, will come with the authority of supreme Judge that belongs to God, and with the dignity of the Messiah, who has no human equal.

3:19–20. John the Baptist preached the moral requirements of the messianic kingdom with charity but without human respect. Preaching the truth can lead one to be a thorn in the side of those who are not ready to change their way of life—to such an extent that they even persecute the preacher, which was what Herod did. "Don't be afraid of the truth, even though the truth may mean your death" (St Josemaría Escrivá, *The Way*, 34).

3:21–22. In its liturgy the Church remembers the first three solemn manifestations of Christ's divinity—the adoration of the Magi (Mt 2:11), the baptism of Jesus (Lk 3:21–22; Mt 3:13–17; Mk 1:9–11) and the first miracle our Lord worked, at the wedding at Cana (Jn 2:11). In the adoration of the Magi God revealed the divinity of Jesus by means of the star. At his baptism the voice of God the Father, coming "from heaven", reveals to John the Baptist and to the Jewish people—and thereby to all men—this profound mystery of Christ's divinity. At the wedding at Cana, Jesus "manifested his glory; and his disciples believed in him" (Jn 2:11). "When he attained to the perfect age," St Thomas Aquinas comments, "when the time came for him to teach, to work miracles and to draw men to himself, then was it fitting for his Godhead to be attested to from on high by the Father's testimony, so that his teaching might be the more credible: 'The Father who sent me has himself borne witness to me' (Jn 5:37)" (*Summa theologiae*, 3, 39, 8 ad 3).

3:21. In Christ's baptism we can find a reflection of the way the sacrament of Baptism affects a person. Christ's baptism was the exemplar of our own. In it the mystery of the Blessed Trinity was revealed, and the faithful, on receiving Baptism, are consecrated by the invocation of and by the power of the Blessed Trinity. Similarly, heaven opening signifies that the power, the effectiveness, of

Jesus is baptized

21 Now when all the people were baptized, and when Jesus also Mt 3:13–17 Mk 1:9–11 Jn 1:32–34
had been baptized and was praying, the heaven was opened, 22 and Ezek 1:1
the Holy Spirit descended upon him in bodily form, as a dove, and Lk 9:35 Ps 2:7
a voice came from heaven, "Thou art my beloved Son;[j] with thee Is 42:1
I am well pleased."[k]

The ancestry of Jesus

23 Jesus, when he began his ministry, was about thirty years of age, Mt 1:1–17 Lk 4:22
being the son (as was supposed) of Joseph,* the son of Heli, 24 the
son of Matthat, the son of Levi, the son of Melchi, the son of
Jannai, the son of Joseph, 25 the son of Mattathias, the son of

---

this sacrament comes from above, from God, and that the baptized have the road to heaven opened up for them, a road which original sin had closed. Jesus' prayer after his baptism teaches us that "after Baptism man needs to pray continually in order to enter heaven; for though sins are remitted through Baptism, there still remains the inclination to sin which assails us from within, and also the flesh and the devil which assail us from without" (St Thomas Aquinas, ibid., 3, 39, 5).

3:23. St Luke tells us our Lord's age at the beginning of his public ministry. His years of "hidden life" are of great significance; they are not an interlude in his work of redemption. In going about his everyday work in Nazareth Jesus is already redeeming the world. "The fact that Jesus grew up and lived just like us shows us that human existence and all the ordinary activity of men have a divine meaning. No matter how much we may have reflected on all this, we should always be surprised when we think of the thirty years of obscurity which made up the greater part of Jesus' life among men. He lived in obscurity, but, for us, that period is full of light. It illuminates our days and fills them with meaning, for we are ordinary Christians who lead an ordinary life, just like millions of other people all over the world.

"That was the way Jesus lived for thirty years as 'the son of the carpenter' (Mt 13:55). There followed three years of public life spent among the crowds. People were surprised: 'Who is this?' they asked. 'Where has he learned these things?' For he was just like them: he had shared the life of ordinary people. He was 'the carpenter, the son of Mary' (Mk 6:3). And he was God; he was achieving the redemption of mankind and 'drawing all things to himself' (Jn 12:32)" (St J. Escrivá, *Christ Is Passing By*, 14).

Every Christian, then, can and should seek his sanctification in ordinary, everyday things, according to his state in life, his age and his work: "Therefore, all faithful are invited and obliged to holiness and the perfection of their own state of life" (Vatican II, *Lumen gentium*, 42).

3:23–28. Matthew and Luke both record our Lord's genealogy. Matthew (1:1–17) provides it as an introduction to his Gospel, showing Christ's roots in the chosen people, going right back to Abraham; he specifically shows that

j. Or *my son* (or *the*) *Beloved* **k.** Other ancient authorities read *today I have begotten thee*

Amos, the son of Nahum, the son of Esli, the son of Naggai, 26 the
son of Maath, the son of Mattathias, the son of Semein, the son of
1 Chron 3:17 Josech, the son of Joda, 27 the son of Joanan, the son of Rhesa, the
Ezra 3:2 son of Zerubbabel, the son of Shealtiel,[1] the son of Neri, 28 the son
of Melchi, the son of Addi, the son of Cosam, the son of
Elmadam, the son of Er, 29 the son of Joshua, the son of Eliezer,
the son of Jorim, the son of Matthat, the son of Levi, 30 the son of
1 Sam 16:1–13 Simeon, the son of Judah, the son of Joseph, the son of Jonam, the
2 Sam 5:14 son of Eliakim, 31 the son of Melea, the son of Menna, the son of
Ruth 4:22 Mattatha, the son of Nathan, the son of David, 32 the son of Jesse,
1 Chron 2:1ff the son of Obed, the son of Boaz, the son of Sala, the son of
Gen 29:35 Nahshon, 33 the son of Amminadab, the son of Admin, the son of
Gen 21:2–3; 11:10–26 Arni, the son of Hezron, the son of Perez, the son of Judah, 34 the

---

Jesus is the Messiah announced by the prophets, a descendant of David; he is the king of the Davidic dynasty sent by God in fulfilment of his promises of salvation.

St Luke, on the other hand, writing in the first instance for Christians of Gentile background, underlines the universality of the redemption wrought by Christ; his genealogy, therefore, goes right back to Adam, the father of all men, Gentiles and Jews, linking Christ to all mankind.

St Matthew stresses the messianic character of our Lord, St Luke his priesthood. St Thomas Aquinas, following St Augustine, sees St Luke's genealogy as teaching us about Christ's priesthood: "Luke sets forth Christ's genealogy not at the outset but after Christ's baptism, and not in the descending but in the ascending order, as though giving prominence to the Priest who expiated our sins at the point where the Baptist bore witness to him, saying, 'Behold him who takes away the sins of the world.' And in the ascending order he passes Abraham and continues up to God, to whom we are reconciled by cleansing and expiating" (St Thomas Aquinas, *Summa theologiae*, 3, 31, 3 ad 3).

Some names in these two genealogies differ. Scholars convinced of the absolute historicity of both Gospels have offered various explanations for these differences, but no particular explanation is sponsored by the Church. We must remember that Jews were very careful to keep the record of their genealogical tree—especially Jews of royal or priestly families—to guide them in the exercise of their rights, obligations and functions. For example, after the return from the Babylonian exile, priests and Levites, on production of their genealogy, were permitted to perform their temple functions; others, on the basis of the same evidence, regained possession of land which had previously been theirs; whereas those who, due to the upheaval caused by exile, were unable to prove their descent, were barred from exercising priestly functions and did not regain possession of lands to which they laid claim (cf. Ezra 2:59–62; Neh 7:64ff).

The solutions put forward to explain the differences between the two genealogies hinge on one or other of these two arguments: 1) both evangelists are quoting St Joseph's genealogy, but one follows the

1. Greek *Salathiel*

son of Jacob, the son of Isaac, the son of Abraham, the son of 1 Chron 1:24–27
Terah, the son of Nahor, [35]the son of Serug, the son of Reu, the
son of Peleg, the son of Eber, the son of Shelah, [36]the son of 1 Chron 1:1–4
Cainan, the son of Arphaxad, the son of Shem, the son of Noah, Gen 5:3–32
the son of Lamech, [37]the son of Methuselah, the son of Enoch, the Gen 11:10; 4:25
son of Jared, the son of Mahalaleel, the son of Cainan, [38]the son Gen 5:1–3
of Enos, the son of Seth, the son of Adam, the son of God.

Jesus fasts and is tempted in the wilderness

4 [1]And Jesus, full of the Holy Spirit, returned from the Jordan, Mt 4:1–11
and was led by the Spirit [2]for forty days in the wilderness, Mk 1:12–13 Lk 3:22
tempted by the devil. And he ate nothing in those days; and when
they were ended, he was hungry. [3]The devil said to him, "If you

---

levirate law (if someone died without issue his brother had to marry his widow, and the first-born of this marriage was the legal son of the deceased man: cf. Deut 25:5–6) and the other genealogy does not; 2) St Matthew is giving St Joseph's genealogy and St Luke that of the Virgin Mary. In the latter case Joseph would not be properly speaking the son of Heli but rather his son-in-law. However, this second hypothesis does not seem to have any good basis in the Gospel text.

4:1–13. Here we see the devil interfere in Jesus' life for the first time. He acts so very brazenly. Our Lord is about to begin his public ministry, so it is a particularly important point in his work of salvation.

"The whole episode is a mystery which man cannot hope to understand—God submitting to temptation, letting the evil one have his way. But we can meditate upon it, asking our Lord to help us understand the teaching it contains" (St J. Escrivá, *Christ Is Passing By*, 61).

Christ, true God and true man, made himself like us in everything except sin (cf. Phil 2:7; Heb 2:7; 4:15) and voluntarily underwent temptation. "How fortunate we are," exclaims the Curé of Ars, "how lucky to have a God as a model. Are we poor? We have a God who is born in a stable, who lies in a manger. Are we despised? We have a God who led the way, who was crowned with thorns, dressed in a filthy red cloak and treated as a madman. Are we tormented by pain and suffering? Before our eyes we have a God covered with wounds, dying in unimaginable pain. Are we being persecuted? How can we dare complain when we have a God who is being put to death by executioners? Finally, are we being tempted by the demon? We have our lovable Redeemer; he also was tempted by the demon and was twice taken up by that hellish spirit: therefore, no matter what sufferings, pains or temptations we are experiencing, we always have, everywhere, our God leading the way for us and assuring us of victory as long as we genuinely desire it" (*Selected Sermons*, First Sunday of Lent).

Jesus teaches us therefore that no one should regard himself as incorruptible and proof against temptation; he shows us how we should deal with temptation and exhorts us to have confidence in his mercy, since he himself experienced temptation (cf. Heb 2:18).

For further explanation of this passage, see the notes on Mt 4:3–11.

Deut 8:3 are the Son of God, command this stone to become bread." [4]And
Jesus answered him, "It is written, 'Man shall not live by bread
alone.' " [5]And the devil took him up, and showed him all the kingdoms of the world in a moment of time, [6]and said to him, "To you
I will give all this authority and their glory; for it has been delivered to me, and I give it to whom I will. [7]If you, then, will worship
me, it shall all be yours." [8]And Jesus answered him, "It is written,

'You shall worship the Lord your God,
Deut 6:13–14 and him only shall you serve.' "

[9]And he took him to Jerusalem, and set him on the pinnacle of the
temple, and said to him, "If you are the Son of God, throw yourself down from here; [10]for it is written,

'He will give his angels charge of you, to guard you,'
Ps 91:11–12 [11]and
'On their hands they will bear you up,
lest you strike your foot against a stone.' "

[12]And Jesus answered him, "It is said, 'You shall not tempt the
Deut 6:16 Lord your God.' " [13]And when the devil had ended every tempta-
Heb 4:15 tion, he departed from him until an opportune time.

4:13. Our Lord's temptations sum up every kind of temptation man can experience: "Scripture would not have said", St Thomas comments, "that once all the temptation ended the devil departed from him, unless the matter of all sins were included in the three temptations already related. For the causes of temptation are the causes of desires—namely, lust of the flesh, desire for glory, eagerness for power" (*Summa theologiae*, 3, 41, 4 ad 4).

By conquering every kind of temptation, Jesus shows us how to deal with the snares of the devil. It was as a man that he was tempted and as a man that he resisted: "He did not act as God, bringing his power into play; if he had done so, how could we have availed of his example? Rather, as man he made use of the resources which he has in common with us" (St Ambrose, *Expositio Evangelii sec. Lucam*, in loc.).

He wanted to show us the methods to use to defeat the devil—prayer, fasting, watchfulness, not dialoguing with temptation, having the words of God's Scripture on our lips and putting our trust in the Lord.

"Until an opportune time", that is, until it is time for Jesus to undergo his passion. The devil often appears in the course of our Lord's public life (cf., e.g., Mk 12:28), but it will be at the Passion—"this is your hour, and the power of darkness" (Lk 22:53)—that he will be most clearly seen in his role as tempter. Jesus will forewarn his disciples about this and once more assure them of victory (cf. Jn 12:31; 14:30). Through the passion, death and resurrection of Christ, the devil will be overpowered once and for all. And by virtue of Christ's victory we are enabled to overcome all temptations.

4:16–30. For the Jews the sabbath was a day of rest and prayer, as God commanded (Ex 20:8–11). On that day they

PART ONE

Jesus' ministry in Galilee

3. THE START OF HIS MINISTRY IN GALILEE

14 And Jesus returned in the power of the Spirit into Galilee, and a Mt 4:12–17
report concerning him went out through all the surrounding coun- Mk 1:14–15
try. 15 And he taught in their synagogues, being glorified by all.

Preaching in Nazareth

16 And he came to Nazareth, where he had been brought up; and he Mt 13:53–58
went to the synagogue, as his custom was, on the sabbath day.* Mk 6:1–6
And he stood up to read; 17 and there was given to him the book of
the prophet Isaiah. He opened the book and found the place where
it was written,

18 "The Spirit of the Lord is upon me, Mt 11:5
because he has anointed me to preach good news to the poor.

---

would gather together to be instructed in Holy Scripture. At the beginning of this meeting they all recited the *Shema*, a summary of the precepts of the Lord, and the "eighteen blessings". Then a passage was read from the Book of the Law—the Pentateuch—and another from the Prophets. The president invited one of those present who was well versed in the Scriptures to address the gathering. Sometimes someone would volunteer and request the honour of being allowed to give this address—as must have happened on this occasion. Jesus avails himself of this opportunity to instruct the people (cf. Lk 4:16ff), as will his apostles later on (cf. Acts 13:5, 14, 42, 44; 14:1; etc.). The sabbath meeting concluded with the priestly blessing, recited by the president or by a priest if there was one present, to which the people answered "Amen" (cf. Num 6:22ff).

4:18–21. Jesus read the passage from Isaiah 61:1–2 where the prophet announces the coming of the Lord, who will free his people of their afflictions. In Christ this prophecy finds its fulfilment, for he is the Anointed, the Messiah whom God has sent to his people in their tribulation. Jesus has been anointed by the Holy Spirit for the mission the Father has entrusted to him. "These phrases, according to Luke (vv. 18–19), are his first messianic declaration. They are followed by the actions and words known through the Gospel. By these actions and words Christ makes the Father present among men" (John Paul II, *Dives in misericordia*, 3).

The promises proclaimed in vv. 18 and 19 are the blessings God will send his people through the Messiah. According to Old Testament tradition and Jesus' own preaching (cf. the note on Mt 5:3), "the poor" refers not so much to a partic-

He has sent me to proclaim release to the captives
and recovering of sight to the blind,
to set at liberty those who are oppressed,
Lev 25:10 [19]to proclaim the acceptable year of the Lord."

---

ular social condition as to a very religious attitude of indigence and humility towards God, which is to be found in those who, instead of relying on their possessions and merits, trust in God's goodness and mercy. Thus, preaching good news to the poor means bringing them the "good news" that God has taken pity on them. Similarly, the Redemption, the release, which the text mentions, is to be understood mainly in a spiritual, transcendental sense: Christ has come to free us from the blindness and oppression of sin, which, in the last analysis, is slavery imposed on us by the devil. "Captivity can be felt", St John Chrysostom teaches in a commentary on Psalm 126, "when it proceeds from physical enemies, but the spiritual captivity referred to here is worse; sin exerts a more severe tyranny, evil takes control and blinds those who lend it obedience; from this spiritual prison Jesus Christ rescued us" (*Catena aurea*). However, this passage is also in line with Jesus' special concern for those most in need. "Similarly, the Church encompasses with her love all those who are afflicted by human misery and she recognizes in those who are poor and who suffer the image of her poor and suffering Founder. She does all in her power to relieve their need and in them she strives to serve Christ" (Vatican II, *Lumen gentium*, 8).

4:18–19. The words of Isaiah which Christ read out on this occasion describe very graphically the reason why God has sent his Son into the world—to redeem men from sin, to liberate them from slavery to the devil and from eternal death. It is true that in the course of his public ministry Christ, in his mercy, worked many cures, cast out devils, etc. But he did not cure all the sick people in the world, nor did he eliminate all forms of distress in this life, because pain, which entered the world through sin, has a permanent redemptive value when associated with the sufferings of Christ. Therefore, Christ worked miracles not so much to release the people concerned from suffering, as to demonstrate that he had a God-given mission to bring everyone eternal redemption.

The Church carries on this mission of Christ: "Go therefore and make disciples of all nations, baptizing them in the name of the Father and of the Son and of the Holy Spirit, teaching them to observe all that I have commanded you; and lo, I am with you always, to the close of the age" (Mt 28:19–20). These simple and sublime words, which conclude the Gospel of St Matthew, point out "the obligation to preach the truths of faith, the need for sacramental life, the promise of Christ's continual assistance to his Church. You cannot be faithful to our Lord if you neglect these supernatural demands—to receive instruction in Christian faith and morality and to frequent the sacraments. It is with this mandate that Christ founded his Church [...]. And the Church can bring salvation to souls only if she remains faithful to Christ in her constitution and teaching, both dogmatic and moral.

"Let us reject, therefore, the suggestion that the Church, ignoring the Sermon on the Mount, seeks a purely human happiness on earth, since we

[20]And he closed the book, and gave it back to the attendant, and
sat down; and the eyes of all in the synagogue were fixed on him.
[21]And he began to say to them, "Today this scripture has been ful- Mt 5:17
filled in your hearing." [22]And all spoke well of him, and wondered Jn 6:42

---

know that her only task is to bring men to eternal glory in heaven. Let us reject any purely naturalistic view that fails to value the supernatural role of divine grace. Let us reject materialistic opinions that exclude spiritual values from human life. Let us equally reject any secularizing theory which attempts to equate the aims of the Church with those of earthly states, distorting its essence, institutions and activities into something similar to those of temporal society" (St J. Escrivá, *In Love with the Church*, 23 and 31).

4:18. The Fathers of the Church see this verse as a reference to the three persons of the Holy Trinity: the Spirit (the Holy Spirit) of the Lord (the Father) is upon me (the Son); cf. Origen, *Homily* 32. The Holy Spirit dwelt in Christ's soul from the very moment of the Incarnation and descended visibly upon him in the form of a dove when he was baptized by John (cf. Lk 3:21–22).

"Because he has anointed me": this is a reference to the anointing Jesus received at the moment of his Incarnation, principally through the grace of the hypostatic union. "This anointing of Jesus Christ was not an anointing of the body as in the case of the ancient kings, priests and prophets; rather it was entirely spiritual and divine, because the fulness of the Godhead dwells in him substantially" (St Pius X, *Catechism*, 77). From this hypostatic union the fulness of all grace derives. To show this, Jesus Christ is said to have been anointed by the Holy Spirit *himself*—not just to have received the graces and gifts of the Spirit, like the saints.

4:19. "The acceptable year": this is a reference to the jubilee year of the Jews, which the Law of God (Lev 25:8) lays down as occurring every fifty years, symbolizing the era of redemption and liberation which the Messiah would usher in. The era inaugurated by Christ, the era of the New Law extending to the end of the world, is "the acceptable year", the time of mercy and redemption, which will be obtained definitively in heaven. The Catholic Church's custom of the "Holy Year" is also designed to proclaim and remind people of the redemption brought by Christ, and of the full form it will take in the future life.

4:20–22. Christ's words in v. 21 show us the authenticity with which he preached and explained the Scriptures: "Today this scripture has been fulfilled in your hearing." Jesus teaches that this prophecy, like the other main prophecies in the Old Testament, refers to him and finds its fulfilment in him (cf. Lk 24:44ff). Thus, the Old Testament can be rightly understood only in the light of the New—as the risen Christ showed the apostles when he opened their minds to understand the Scriptures (cf. Lk 24:45), an understanding which the Holy Spirit perfected on the day of Pentecost (cf. Acts 2:4).

4:22–29. At first the people of Nazareth listened readily to the wisdom of Jesus' words. But they were very superficial; in their narrow-minded pride they felt hurt that Jesus, their fellow-townsman, had not worked in Nazareth the wonders he had worked elsewhere. They presume they have a special entitlement and they

at the gracious words which proceeded out of his mouth; and they
Mt 4:13 said, "Is not this Joseph's son?" 23 And he said to them, "Doubtless
you will quote to me this proverb, 'Physician, heal yourself; what
we have heard you did at Capernaum, do here also in your own
Jn 4:44 country.' " 24 And he said, "Truly, I say to you, no prophet is
1 Kings 18:1 acceptable in his own country. 25 But in truth, I tell you, there were
Jas 5:17 many widows in Israel in the days of Elijah, when the heaven was
shut up three years and six months, when there came a great
famine over all the land; 26 and Elijah was sent to none of them but
only to Zarephath, in the land of Sidon, to a woman who was a
1 Kings 17:9ff widow. 27 And there were many lepers in Israel in the time of the
2 Kings 5:9ff prophet Elisha; and none of them was cleansed, but only Naaman
the Syrian." 28 When they heard this, all in the synagogue were
filled with wrath. 29 And they rose up and put him out of the city,
and led him to the brow of the hill on which their city was built,
that they might throw him down headlong. 30 But passing through
the midst of them he went away.

In the synagogue in Capernaum

Mk 1:21–28 31 And he went down to Capernaum, a city of Galilee. And he was
Mt 4:13 Jn 2:12 teaching them on the sabbath; 32 and they were astonished at his
Mt 7:28–29 teaching, for his word was with authority. 33 And in the synagogue
Jn 7:46 there was a man who had the spirit of an unclean demon; and he

---

insolently demand that he perform miracles to satisfy their vanity, not to change their hearts. In view of their attitude, Jesus performs no miracle (his normal response to lack of faith: cf., for example, his meeting with Herod in Lk 23:7–11); he actually reproaches them, using two examples taken from the Old Testament (cf. 1 Kings 17:9 and 2 Kings 5:14), which show that one needs to be well-disposed if miracles are to lead to faith. His attitude so wounds their pride that they are ready to kill him. This whole episode is a good lesson about understanding Jesus. We can understand him only if we are humble and are genuinely resolved to make ourselves available to him.

4:30. Jesus does not take flight but withdraws majestically, leaving the crowd paralysed. As on other occasions men do him no harm; it was by God's decree that he died on a cross (cf. Jn 18:32) when his hour had come.

4:33–37. Jesus now demonstrates by his actions that authority which was evident in his words.

4:34. The demon tells the truth here when he calls Jesus "the Holy One of God", but Jesus does not accept this testimony from the "father of lies" (Jn 8:44). This shows that the devil usually says something partially true in order to disguise untruth; by sowing confusion in this way, he can more readily deceive people. By silencing and expelling the demon, Jesus teaches us to be prudent and not let ourselves be deceived by half-truths.

4:38–39. In the public life of Jesus we

cried out with a loud voice, 34“Ah![m] What have you to do with us,
Jesus of Nazareth? Have you come to destroy us? I know who you
are, the Holy One of God.” 35But Jesus rebuked him, saying, “Be
silent, and come out of him!” And when the demon had thrown
him down in the midst, he came out of him, having done him no
harm. 36And they were all amazed and said to one another, “What
is this word? For with authority and power he commands the
unclean spirits, and they come out.” 37And reports of him went out
into every place in the surrounding region.

Curing of Peter’s mother-in-law

38And he arose and left the synagogue, and entered Simon’s house. Mt 8:14–17
Now Simon’s mother-in-law was ill with a high fever, and they Mk 1:21–39
besought him for her. 39And he stood over her and rebuked the
fever, and it left her; and immediately she rose and served them.

Other cures

40Now when the sun was setting, all those who had any that were
sick with various diseases brought them to him; and he laid his
hands on every one of them and healed them. 41And demons also Mt 8:29
came out of many, crying, “You are the Son of God!” But he Mk 3:11–12
rebuked them, and would not allow them to speak, because they
knew that he was the Christ.

---

find many touching episodes (cf. e.g. Lk 19:1ff; Jn 2:1ff) which show the high regard he had for everyday family life.

Here we can clearly see the effectiveness of prayer on behalf of other people: “No sooner did they pray to the Saviour”, St Jerome says, “than he immediately healed the sick; from this we learn that he also listens to the prayers of the faithful for help against sinful passions” (*Expositio in Evangelium sec. Lucam*, in loc.).

St John Chrysostom refers to this total, instantaneous cure: “Since this was a curable type of illness he displayed his power through the way he brought healing, doing what medicine could not do. Even after being cured of fever, patients need time to recover their former strength, but here the cure was instantaneous” (*Hom. on St Matthew*, 27).

The Fathers saw in this lady’s fever a symbol of concupiscence: “Peter’s mother-in-law’s fever represents our flesh affected by various illnesses and concupiscences; our fever is passion, our fever is lust, our fever is anger—vices which, although they affect the body, perturb the soul, the mind and the feelings” (St Ambrose, *Expositio evangelii sec. Lucam*, in loc.).

On the practical consequences of this St Cyril says: “Let us receive Jesus Christ, because when he visits us and we take him into our minds and hearts, even our worst passions are extinguished and we are kept safe to serve him, that is, to do what pleases him” (*Hom. 28 in Mattheum*).

m. Or *Let us alone*

Jesus preaches in other cities in Judea

42 And when it was day he departed and went into a lonely place.
And the people sought him and came to him, and would have kept
Lk 8:1 him from leaving them; 43 but he said to them, "I must preach the
good news of the kingdom of God to the other cities also; for I
Mt 4:23 was sent for this purpose." 44 And he was preaching in the syna-
gogues of Judea.[n]

The miraculous catch of fish and the calling of the first disciples

Mt 4:18–22 **5** 1 While the people pressed upon him to hear the word of God,
Mk 1:16–20 he was standing by the lake of Gennesaret. 2 And he saw two

4:43. Our Lord again stresses one of the reasons why he has come into the world. St Thomas, when discussing the purpose of the Eucharist, says that Christ "came into the world, first, to make the truth known, as he himself says: 'for this I was born, and for this I have come into the world, to bear witness to the truth' (Jn 18:37). Hence it was not fitting that he should hide himself by leading a solitary life, but rather that he should appear openly and preach in public. For this reason he tells those who wanted to detain him, 'I must preach the good news of the kingdom of God to the other cities also; for I was sent for this purpose.' Secondly, he came in order to free men from sin; as the apostle says, 'Christ Jesus came into the world to save sinners' (1 Tim 1:15). This is why Chrysostom says, 'Although Christ might, while staying in the same place, have drawn all men to himself to hear his preaching, he did not do so—in order to give us the example to go out and seek the lost sheep, as the shepherd does, or as the doctor does, who visits the sick person.' Thirdly, he came so that 'we might obtain access to God' (Rom 5:2)" (*Summa theologiae*, 3, 40, 1, c.).

5:1. "Just as they do today! Can't you see? They want to hear God's message, even though outwardly they may not show it. Some perhaps have forgotten Christ's teachings. Others, through no fault of their own, have never known them and they think that religion is something odd. But of this we can be sure, that in every man's life there comes a time sooner or later when his soul draws the line. He has had enough of the usual explanations. The lies of the false prophets no longer satisfy. Even though they may not admit it at the time, such people are longing to quench their thirst with the teachings of our Lord" (St Josemaría Escrivá, *Friends of God*, 260).

5:3. The Fathers saw in Simon's boat a symbol of the pilgrim Church on earth. "This is the boat which according to St Matthew was in danger of sinking and according to St Luke was filled with fish. Here we can see the difficult beginnings of the Church and its later fruitfulness" (St Ambrose, *Expositio Evangelii sec. Lucam*, in loc.). Christ gets into the boat in order to teach the crowds—and from the barque of Peter, the Church, he continues to teach the whole world.

Each of us can also see himself as this boat Christ uses for preaching. Externally no change is evident: "What has changed? There is a change inside our

n. Other ancient authorities read *Galilee*

boats by the lake; but the fishermen had gone out of them and
were washing their nets. [3]Getting into one of the boats, which was
Simon's, he asked him to put out a little from the land. And he sat
down and taught the people from the boat. [4]And when he had Jn 21:6
ceased speaking, he said to Simon, "Put out into the deep and let
down your nets for a catch." [5]And Simon answered, "Master, we
toiled all night and took nothing! But at your word I will let down
the nets." [6]And when they had done this, they enclosed a great
shoal of fish; and as their nets were breaking, [7]they beckoned to
their partners in the other boat to come and help them. And they

---

soul, now that Christ has come aboard, as he went aboard Peter's boat. Its horizon has opened wider. It feels a greater ambition to serve and an irrepressible desire to tell all creation about the *magnalia Dei* (Acts 2:11), the marvellous doings of our Lord, if only we let him work" (St Josemaría Escrivá, *Friends of God*, 265).

5:4. "When he had finished his catechising, he told Simon: 'Put out into the deep, and lower your nets for a catch' (Lk 5:4). Christ is the master of this boat. He it is who prepares the fishing. It is for this that he has come into the world, to do all he can so that his brothers may find the way to glory and to the love of the Father" (*Friends of God*, 260). To carry this task out, our Lord charges all of them to cast their nets, but it is only Peter he tells to put out into the deep.

This whole passage refers in some way to the life of the Church. In the Church the bishop of Rome, Peter's successor, "is the vicar of Jesus Christ because he represents him on earth and acts for him in the government of the Church" (St Pius X, *Catechism*, 195). Christ is also addressing each one of us, urging us to be daring in apostolate: " '*Duc in altum*—Put out into deep water!' Cast aside the pessimism that makes a coward of you. '*Et laxate retia vestra in capturam*—And lower your nets for a catch.' Don't you see that, as Peter said: '*In nomine tuo, laxabo rete*—At your word I will lower the net', you can say, Jesus, in your name, I will seek souls!" (St J. Escrivá, *The Way*, 792).

"If you were to fall into the temptation of wondering, 'Who's telling me to embark on this?' we would have to reply, 'Christ himself is telling you, is begging you.' 'The harvest is plentiful enough, but the labourers are few. You must ask the Lord to whom the harvest belongs to send labourers out for the harvesting' (Mt 9:37–38). Don't take the easy way out. Don't say, 'I'm no good at this sort of thing; there are others who can do it; it isn't my line.' No, for this sort of thing, there is no one else: if you could get away with that argument, so could everyone else. Christ's plea is addressed to each and every Christian. No one can consider himself excused, for whatever reason—age, health or occupation. There are no excuses whatsoever. Either we carry out a fruitful apostolate, or our faith will prove barren" (*Friends of God*, 272).

5:5. When Christ gives him these instructions, Peter states the difficulties involved. "A reasonable enough reply. The night hours were their normal time for fishing, and this time the catch had yielded nothing. What was the point of fishing by day? But Peter has faith: 'But at your word I will let down the nets' (Lk 5:5). He decides to act on Christ's sug-

came and filled both the boats, so that they began to sink. [8]But
when Simon Peter saw it, he fell down at Jesus' knees, saying,
"Depart from me, for I am a sinful man, O Lord." [9]For he was
astonished, and all that were with him, at the catch of fish which
Mt 13:47 they had taken; [10]and so also were James and John, sons of
Zebedee, who were partners with Simon. And Jesus said to
Simon, "Do not be afraid; henceforth you will be catching men."
Mt 19:27 [11]And when they had brought their boats to land, they left every-
thing and followed him.

Curing of a leper

Mt 8:1–4 [12]While he was in one of the cities, there came a man full of lep-
Mk 1:40–45 rosy; and when he saw Jesus, he fell on his face and besought

---

gestion. He undertakes the work relying entirely on the word of our Lord" (St Josemaría Escrivá, *Friends of God*, 261).

5:8. Peter does not want Christ to leave him; aware of his sins, he declares his unworthiness to be near Christ. This reminds us of the attitude of the centurion who confesses his unworthiness to receive Jesus into his house (cf. Mt 8:8). The Church requires her children to repeat these exact words of the centurion before receiving the Blessed Eucharist. She also teaches us to show due external reverence to the Blessed Sacrament when going to Communion: by falling down on his knees Peter also shows that internal adoration of God should also be expressed externally.

5:11. Perfection is not simply a matter of leaving all things but of doing so in order to follow Christ—which is what the apostles did: they gave up everything in order to be available to do what God's calling involved.

We should develop this attitude of availability, for "Jesus is never satisfied 'sharing': he wants all" (St Josemaría Escrivá, *The Way*, 155).

If we don't give ourselves generously we will find it very difficult to follow Jesus: "Detach yourself from people and things until you are stripped of them. For, says Pope Saint Gregory, the devil has nothing of his own in this world, and he goes into battle naked. If you are clothed when you fight him, you will soon be pulled to the ground, because he will have something to grab on to" (*The Way*, 149).

5:12. The words of the leper are a model prayer. First, they show his faith. "He did not say, 'If you ask God for it …', but 'If you will' " (St John Chrysostom, *Hom. on St Matthew*, 25). He rounds this off by saying, "You can"—an open confession of Christ's omnipotence. The psalmist expressed this same faith: "Whatever the Lord pleases he does, in heaven and on earth, in the seas and all deeps" (Ps 135:6). Along with this faith he shows confidence in God's mercy. "God is merciful; there is no need therefore to ask him; all we have to do is show him our need" (St Thomas Aquinas, *Comm. on St Matthew*, 8, 1). And St John Chrysostom concludes: "Prayer is perfect when it is joined to faith and confession; the leper showed his faith and confessed his need out loud" (*Hom. on St Matthew*, 25).

" '*Domine!*—Lord—*si vis, potes me mundare*—if thou wilt, thou canst make

him, "Lord, if you will, you can make me clean." [13]And he
stretched out his hand, and touched him, saying, "I will; be clean."
And immediately the leprosy left him. [14]And he charged him to Lev 13:49; 14:2–32
tell no one; but "go and show yourself to the priest, and make an
offering for your cleansing, as Moses commanded, for a proof to
the people."[o] [15]But so much the more the report went abroad concerning him; and great multitudes gathered to hear and to be
healed of their infirmities. [16]But he withdrew to the wilderness Mk 1:35
and prayed.

Curing of a paralyzed man

[17]On one of those days, as he was teaching, there were Pharisees Mt 9:1–8
and teachers of the law sitting by, who had come from every vil- Mk 2:1–12

---

me clean.' What a beautiful prayer for you to say often, with the faith of the poor leper, when there happens to you what God and you and I know may happen! You will not have to wait long to hear the Master's reply: '*Volo, mundare!* I will be clean!'" (St Josemaría Escrivá, *The Way*, 142).

5:13. Jesus listens to the leper's petition and cures him of his disease. All of us suffer from spiritual ailments and our Lord is waiting for us to approach him: "He is our physician, and he heals our selfishness, if we let his grace penetrate to the depths of our soul. Jesus has taught us that the worst sickness is hypocrisy, the pride that leads us to hide our own sins. We have to be totally sincere with him. We have to tell the whole truth, and then we have to say, 'Lord, if you will'—and you are always willing—'you can make me clean' (Mt 8:2). You know my weaknesses; I feel these symptoms; I suffer from these failings. We show him the wound, with simplicity, and if the wound is festering, we show the pus too. Lord, you have cured so many souls; help me to recognize you as the divine physician, when I have you in my heart or when I contemplate your presence in the tabernacle" (St Josemaría Escrivá, *Christ Is Passing By*, 93).

5:16. The Third Gospel frequently draws attention to Jesus going off, alone, to pray (cf. 6:12; 9:18; 11:1). By doing this Jesus teaches us the need for personal prayer in all the various situations in which we find ourselves.

"Forgive me if I insist, but it is very important to note carefully what the Messiah did, because he came to show us the path that leads to the Father. With our Lord we will discover how to give a supernatural dimension to all our actions, even those that seem least important. We will learn to live every moment of our lives with a lively awareness of eternity, and we will understand more deeply man's need for periods of intimate conversation with his God, so as to get to know him, to invoke him, to praise him, to break out into acts of thanksgiving, to listen to him or, quite simply, to be with him" (St Josemaría Escrivá, *Friends of God*, 239).

5:17. A little earlier, beside the lake, Jesus addressed his teaching to crowds

o. Greek *to them*

lage of Galilee and Judea and from Jerusalem; and the power of
the Lord was with him to heal.[p] 18And behold, men were bringing
on a bed a man who was paralyzed, and they sought to bring him
in and lay him before Jesus;[q] 19but finding no way to bring him in,
because of the crowd, they went up on the roof and let him down
with his bed through the tiles into the midst before Jesus. 20And
when he saw their faith he said, "Man, your sins are forgiven
Lk 7:49 you." 21And the scribes and the Pharisees began to question,
Is 43:25; 55:7 saying, "Who is this that speaks blasphemies? Who can forgive
sins but God only?" 22When Jesus perceived their questionings, he
answered them, "Why do you question in your hearts? 23Which is
easier, to say, 'Your sins are forgiven you,' or to say, 'Rise and
Jn 20:21–23 walk'? 24But that you may know that the Son of man has authority on earth to forgive sins"—he said to the man who was para-

---

(vv. 1ff). Here his audience includes some of the most educated of Jews. Christ desired not only to teach but also to cure everyone—spiritually and, sometimes, physically, as he will soon do in the case of the paralytic. The evangelist's observation at the end of this verse reminds us that our Lord is ever-ready to use his omnipotence for our good: "'I know the plans I have for you, plans for welfare and not for evil', was God's promise through Jeremiah (29:11). The liturgy applies these words to Jesus, for in him we are clearly shown that God does love us in this way. He did not come to condemn us, to accuse us of meanness and smallness. He came to save us, pardon us, excuse us, bring us peace and joy" (St J. Escrivá, *Christ Is Passing By*, 165). On this occasion also Jesus wanted to benefit all his listeners, even though some of them would not receive this divine gift because they were not well-disposed.

5:19–20. Our Lord is touched when he sees these friends of the paralytic putting their faith into practice: they had gone up onto the roof, taken off some of the tiles and lowered the bed down in front of Jesus. Friendship and faith combine in obtaining a miraculous cure. The paralytic himself had a like faith: he let himself be carried around, brought up onto the roof and so forth. Seeing such solid faith Jesus gives them even more than they expect: he cures the man's body and, what is much more, cures his soul. Perhaps he does this, as St Bede suggests (cf. *In Lucae Evangelium expositio*, in loc.), to show two things: that the illness was a form of punishment for his sins and therefore the paralytic could only get up once these sins had been forgiven; and that others' faith and prayer can move God to work miracles.

In some way, the paralytic symbolizes everyone whose sins prevent him from reaching God. For example, St Ambrose says: "How great is the Lord who on account of the merits of some pardons others, and while praising the former absolves the latter! [...] Therefore, let you, who judge, learn to pardon; you, who are ill, learn to beg for forgiveness. And if the gravity of your sins causes you to doubt the possibility of

p. Other ancient authorities read *was present to heal them* **q.** Greek *him*

lyzed—"I say to you, rise, take up your bed and go home." [25]And
immediately he rose before them, and took up that on which he
lay, and went home, glorifying God. [26]And amazement seized
them all, and they glorified God and were filled with awe, saying,
"We have seen strange things today."

The calling of Matthew

[27]After this he went out, and saw a tax collector, named Levi, sit- Mt 9:9–18
ting at the tax office; and he said to him, "Follow me." [28]And he Mk 2:13–17
left everything, and rose and followed him.

[29]And Levi made him a great feast in his house; and there was Lk 15:1;
a large company of tax collectors and others sitting at table[r] with 19:6–7
them. [30]And the Pharisees and their scribes murmured against his
disciples, saying, "Why do you eat and drink with tax collectors

---

being forgiven, have recourse to intercessors, have recourse to the Church, who will pray for you, and the Lord will grant you, out of love for her, what he might have refused you" (*Expositio Evangelii sec. Lucam*, in loc.).

Apostolic work should be motivated by desire to help people find Jesus Christ. Among other things it calls for daring—as we see in the friends of the paralytic; and it also needs the intercession of the saints, whose help we seek because we feel God will pay more attention to them than to us sinners.

5:24. Our Lord is going to perform a public miracle to prove that he is endowed with invisible, spiritual power. Christ, the only Son of the Father, has power to forgive sins because he is God, and he uses this power on our behalf as our Mediator and Redeemer (Lk 22:20; Jn 20:17–18, 28; 1 Tim 2:5–6; Col 2:13–14; Heb 9:14; 1 Jn 1:9; Is 53:4–5). Jesus used this power personally when he was on earth and after ascending into heaven he still uses it, through the apostles and their successors.

A sinner is like a paralytic in God's presence. The Lord is going to free him of his paralysis, forgiving him his sins and enabling him to walk by giving him grace once more. In the sacrament of Penance, if Jesus Christ "sees us cold, unwilling, rigid perhaps with the stiffness of a dying interior life, his tears will be our life: 'I say to you, my friend, Arise and walk' (cf. Jn 11:43; Lk 5:24), leave that narrow life which is no life at all" (St J. Escrivá, *Christ Is Passing By*, 93).

5:27–29. Levi, better known as Matthew, responds generously and promptly to the call from Jesus. To celebrate and to show how appreciative he is for his vocation he gives a banquet. This passage of the Gospel shows us that a vocation is something about which we should be very grateful and happy. If we see it only in terms of renunciation and giving things up, and not as a gift from God and something which will enhance us and redound to others' benefit, we can easily become depressed, like the rich young man who, not wanting to give up his possessions, went away sad (cf. Lk 18:18ff). Matthew believes in quite the opposite way, as did the Magi who, "when they saw the star, rejoiced exceedingly with great joy" (Mt

r. Greek *reclining*

and sinners?" [31]And Jesus answered them, "Those who are well
have no need of a physician, but those who are sick; [32]I have not
come to call the righteous, but sinners to repentance."

A discussion on fasting

Mt 9:14–17
Mk 2:18–22 [33]And they said to him, "The disciples of John fast often and offer
prayers, and so do the disciples of the Pharisees, but yours eat and
drink." [34]And Jesus said to them, "Can you make wedding guests
Jn 16:20
Lk 17:22 fast while the bridegroom is with them? [35]The days will come,
when the bridegroom is taken away from them, and then they will
fast in those days." [36]He told them a parable also: "No one tears a
piece from a new garment and puts it upon an old garment; if he
does, he will tear the new, and the piece from the new will not
match the old. [37]And no one puts new wine into old wineskins; if
he does, the new wine will burst the skins and it will be spilled,
and the skins will be destroyed. [38]But new wine must be put into
fresh wineskins. [39]And no one after drinking old wine desires
new; for he says, 'The old is good.'"[s]

The law of the sabbath

Mt 12:1–8
Mk 2:23–28
Deut 23:25
6 [1]On a sabbath,[t] while he was going through the grainfields, his
disciples plucked and ate some ears of grain, rubbing them in

---

2:10) and who gave much more importance to adoring the new-born God than to all the inconveniences involved in travelling to see him. See also the notes on Mt 9:9; 9:10–11; 9:12; 9:13; and Mk 2:14; 2:17.

5:32. Since this is how Jesus operates, the only way we can be saved is by admitting before God, in all simplicity, that we are sinners. "Jesus has no time for calculations, for astuteness, for the cruelty of cold hearts, for attractive but empty beauty. What he likes is the cheerfulness of a young heart, a simple step, a natural voice, clean eyes, attention to his affectionate word of advice. That is how he reigns in the soul" (St Josemaría Escrivá, *Christ Is Passing By*, 181).

5:33–35. In the Old Testament God established certain days as days of fasting—the main one being the "day of atonement" (Num 29:7; Acts 27:9). Fasting implied total or partial abstinence from food or drink. Moses and Elijah fasted (Ex 34:28; 1 Kings 19:8) and our Lord himself fasted in the desert for forty days before beginning his public ministry. In the present passage Jesus gives a deeper meaning to the word "fasting"—the deprivation of his physical presence which his apostles would experience after his death. All through his public life Jesus is trying to prepare his disciples for the final parting. At first the apostles were not very robust and Christ's physical presence did them more good than the practice of fasting.

s. Other ancient authorities read *better* **t.** Other ancient authorities read *On the second first sabbath* (on the second sabbath after the first)

their hands. [2]But some of the Pharisees said, "Why are you doing
what is not lawful to do on the sabbath?" [3]And Jesus answered, 1 Sam 21:6
"Have you not read what David did when he was hungry, he and
those who were with him: [4]how he entered the house of God, and Lev 24:9
took and ate the bread of the Presence, which it is not lawful for
any but the priests to eat, and also gave it to those with him?"
[5]And he said to them, "The Son of man is lord of the sabbath."

Curing of a man with a withered hand

Mt 12:9–14
[6]On another sabbath, when he entered the synagogue and taught, Mk 3:1–6
a man was there whose right hand was withered. [7]And the scribes Lk 14:1
and the Pharisees watched him, to see whether he would heal on
the sabbath, so that they might find an accusation against him.
[8]But he knew their thoughts, and he said to the man who had the
withered hand, "Come and stand here." And he rose and stood
there. [9]And Jesus said to them, "I ask you, is it lawful on the sabbath to do good or to do harm, to save life or to destroy it?" [10]And
he looked around on them all, and said to him, "Stretch out your
hand." And he did so, and his hand was restored. [11]But they were
filled with fury and discussed with one another what they might
do to Jesus.

Christians should sometimes abstain from food. "Fast and abstain from flesh meat when Holy Mother Church so ordains" (St Pius X, *Catechism*, 495). That is the purpose of the fourth commandment of the Church, but it has a deeper meaning, as St Leo the Great tells us: "The merit of our fasts does not consist only in abstinence from food; there is no use in depriving the body of nourishment if the soul does not cut itself off from iniquity and if the tongue does not cease to speak evil" (*Sermo IV in Quadragesima*).

6:1–5. Accused by the Pharisees of breaking the sabbath, Jesus explains the correct way of understanding the sabbath rest, using an example from the Old Testament. And, by stating that he is "Lord of the sabbath" he is openly revealing that he is God himself, for it was God who gave this precept to the people of Israel. For more on this, see the notes on Mt 12:2 and 12:3–8.

6:10. The Fathers teach us how to discover a deep spiritual meaning in apparently casual things Jesus says. St Ambrose, for example, commenting on the phrase "Stretch out your hand," says: "This form of medicine is common and general. Offer it often, in benefit of your neighbour; defend from injury anyone who seems to be suffering as a result of calumny; stretch out your hand also to the poor man who asks for your help; stretch it out also to the Lord, asking him to forgive your sins; that is how you should stretch your hand out, and that is the way to be cured" (*Expositio Evangelii sec. Lucam*, in loc.).

6:11. The Pharisees do not want to reply to Jesus' question and do not know how to react to the miracle which he goes on

4. JESUS' MIRACLES AND PREACHING IN GALILEE

Jesus chooses twelve apostles

Mk 3:13–19 Mt 10:2–4 Jn 6:70 Acts 1:13

[12]In these days he went out into the hills to pray; and all night he
continued in prayer to God. [13]And when it was day, he called his
disciples, and chose from them twelve, whom he named apostles:
[14]Simon, whom he named Peter, and Andrew his brother, and
James and John, and Philip and Bartholomew, [15]and Matthew, and
Thomas, and James the son of Alphaeus, and Simon who was

---

to work. It should have converted them, but their hearts were in darkness and they were full of jealousy and anger. Later on, these people, who kept quiet in our Lord's presence, began to discuss him among themselves, not with a view to approaching him again but with the purpose of doing away with him. In this connexion St Cyril comments: "O Pharisee, you see him working wonders and healing the sick by using a higher power, yet out of envy you plot his death" (*Commentarium in Lucam*, in loc.).

6:12–13. The evangelist writes with a certain formality when describing this important occasion on which Jesus chooses the Twelve, constituting them as the apostolic college: "The Lord Jesus, having prayed at length to the Father, called to himself those whom he willed and appointed twelve to be with him, whom he might send to preach the Kingdom of God (cf. Mk 2:13–19; Mt 10:1–42). These apostles (cf. Lk 6:13) he constituted in the form of a college or permanent assembly, at the head of which he placed Peter, chosen from among them (cf. Jn 21:15–17). He sent them first of all to the children of Israel and then to all peoples (cf. Rom 1:16), so that, sharing in his power, they might make all peoples his disciples and sanctify and govern them (cf. Mt 28:16–20; and par.) and thus spread the Church and, administering it under the guidance of the Lord, shepherd it all days until the end of the world (cf. Mt 28:20). They were fully confirmed in this mission on the day of Pentecost (cf. Acts 2:1–26) [...]. Through their preaching the Gospel everywhere (cf. Mk 16:20), and through its being welcomed and received under the influence of the Holy Spirit by those who hear it, the apostles gather together the universal Church, which the Lord founded upon the apostles and built upon Blessed Peter their leader, the chief cornerstone being Christ Jesus himself (cf. Rev 21:14; Mt 16:18; Eph 2:20). That divine mission, which was committed by Christ to the apostles, is destined to last until the end of the world (cf. Mt 28:20), since the Gospel, which they were charged to hand on, is, for the Church, the principle of all its life for all time. For that very reason the apostles were careful to appoint successors in this hierarchically constituted society" (Vatican II, *Lumen gentium*, 19–20).

Before establishing the apostolic college, Jesus spent the whole night in prayer. He often made special prayer for his Church (Lk 9:18; Jn 17:1ff), thereby preparing his apostles to be its pillars (cf. Gal 2:9). As his passion approaches, he will pray to the Father for Simon Peter, the head of the Church, and solemnly tell Peter that he has done so: "But I have

called the Zealot, 16and Judas the son of James, and Judas Iscariot,
who became a traitor.

Preaching on the plain

17And he came down with them and stood on a level place, with a Mt 4:23; 5:1 Mk 3:7–12
great crowd of his disciples and a great multitude of people from
all Judea and Jerusalem and the sea coast of Tyre and Sidon, who
came to hear him and to be healed of their diseases; 18and those
who were troubled with unclean spirits were cured. 19And all the Lk 5:17; 8:46
crowd sought to touch him, for power came forth from him and
healed them all.

---

prayed for you that your faith may not fail" (Lk 22:32). Following Christ's example, the Church stipulates that on many occasions liturgical prayer should be offered for the pastors of the Church (the Pope, the bishops in general, and priests) asking God to give them grace to fulfil their ministry faithfully.

Christ is continually teaching us that we need to pray always (Lk 18:1). Here he shows us by his example that we should pray with special intensity at important moments in our lives. "'*Pernoctans in oratione Dei*. He spent the whole night in prayer to God.' So St Luke tells of our Lord. And you? How often have you persevered like that? Well, then …" (St Josemaría Escrivá, *The Way*, 104).

On the need for prayer and the qualities our prayer should have, see the notes on Mt 6:5–6; 7:7–11; 14:22–23; Mk 1:35; Lk 5:16; 11:1–4; 22:41–42.

6:12. Since Jesus is God, why does he pray? There were two wills in Christ, one divine and one human (cf. St Pius X, *Catechism*, 91), and although by virtue of his divine will he was omnipotent, his human will was not omnipotent. When we pray, what we do is make our will known to God; therefore Christ, who is like us in all things but sin (cf. Heb 4:15), also had to pray in a human way (cf. St Thomas Aquinas, *Summa theologiae*, 3, 21, 1). Reflecting on Jesus at prayer, St Ambrose comments: "The Lord prays not to ask things for himself, but to intercede on my behalf; for although the Father has put everything into the hands of the Son, still the Son, in order to behave in accordance with his condition as man, considers it appropriate to implore the Father for our sake, for he is our Advocate […]. A Master of obedience, by his example he instructs us concerning the precepts of virtue: 'We have an advocate with the Father'(1 Jn 2:1)" (*Expositio Evangelii sec. Lucam*, in loc.).

6:14–16. Jesus chose for apostles very ordinary people, most of them poor and uneducated; apparently only Matthew and the brothers James and John had social positions of any consequence. But all of them gave up whatever they had, little or much as it was, and all of them, bar Judas, put their faith in the Lord, overcame their shortcomings and eventually proved faithful to grace and became saints, veritable pillars of the Church. We should not feel uneasy when we realize that we too are low in human qualities; what matters is being faithful to the grace God gives us.

6:19. God became man to save us. The divine person of the Word acts through

The Beatitudes and the Woes

Mt 5:3–12 20 And he lifted up his eyes on his disciples, and said:*
"Blessed are you poor, for yours is the kingdom of God.
Rev 7:16–17 Ps 126:5–6 21 "Blessed are you that hunger now, for you shall be satisfied.
Is 61:3 "Blessed are you that weep now, for you shall laugh.

---

the human nature which he took on. The cures and casting out of devils which he performed during his life on earth are also proof that Christ actually brings redemption and not just hope of redemption. The crowds of people from Judea and other parts of Israel who flock to him, seeking even to touch him, anticipate, in a way, Christians' devotion to the holy Humanity of Christ.

6:20–49. These thirty verses of St Luke correspond to some extent to the Sermon on the Mount, an extensive account of which St Matthew gives us in chapters 5–7 in his Gospel. It is very likely that in the course of his public ministry in different regions and towns of Israel Jesus preached the same things, using different words on different occasions. Under the inspiration of the Holy Spirit each evangelist would have chosen to report those things which he considered most useful for the instruction of his immediate readers—Christians of Jewish origin in the case of Matthew, Gentile converts in the case of Luke. There is no reason why one evangelist should not have selected certain items and another different ones, depending on his readership, or why one should not have laid special stress on some subjects and shortened or omitted accounts of others.

In this present discourse, we might distinguish three parts—the Beatitudes and the curses (6:20–26); love of one's enemies (6:27–38); and teaching on uprightness of heart (6:39–49).

Some Christians may find it difficult to grasp the need of practising the moral teaching of the Gospel so radically, in particular Christ's teaching in the Sermon on the Mount. Jesus is very demanding in what he says, but he is saying it to everyone, and not just to his apostles or to those disciples who followed him closely. We are told expressly that "when Jesus finished these sayings, the crowds were astonished at his teaching" (Mt 7:28). It is quite clear that the Master calls everyone to holiness, making no distinction of state-in-life, race or personal circumstances. This teaching on the universal call to holiness was a central point of the teaching of St Josemaría Escrivá de Balaguer. The Second Vatican Council expressed the same teaching with the full weight of its authority: everyone is called to Christian holiness; consider, for example, just one reference it makes, in *Lumen gentium*, 11: "Strengthened by so many and such great means of salvation, all the faithful, whatever their condition or state—though each in his or her own way—are called by the Lord to that perfection of sanctity by which the Father himself is perfect."

In the Sermon on the Mount Jesus is not proposing an unattainable ideal, useful though that might be to make us feel humble in the light of our inability to reach it. No. Christian teaching in this regard is quite clear: what Christ commands, he commands in order to have us do what he says. Along with his commandment comes grace to enable us to fulfil it. Therefore, every Christian is capable of practising the moral teaching of Christ and of attaining the full height of his calling—holiness—not by his own

[22]"Blessed are you when men hate you, and when they exclude Jn 15:19; 16:2
you and revile you, and cast out your name as evil, on account of
the Son of man! [23]Rejoice in that day, and leap for joy, for behold,
your reward is great in heaven; for so their fathers did to the
prophets.
[24]"But woe to you that are rich, for you have received your Jas 5:1
consolation.

---

efforts alone but by means of the grace which Christ has won for us, and with the abiding help of the means of sanctification which he left to his Church. "If anyone plead human weakness to excuse himself for not loving God, it should be explained that He who demands our love pours into our hearts by the Holy Spirit the fervour of his love, and this good Spirit our heavenly Father gives to those that ask him. With reason, therefore, did St Augustine pray: 'Give me what thou command, and command what you please.' As, then, God is ever ready to help us, especially since the death of Christ our Lord, by which the prince of this world was cast out, there is no reason why anyone should be disheartened by the difficulty of the undertaking. To him who loves, nothing is difficult" (St Pius V, *Catechism*, 3, 1, 7).

6:20–26. The eight Beatitudes which St Matthew gives (5:3–12) are summed up in four by St Luke, but with four opposite curses. We can say, with St Ambrose, that Matthew's eight are included in Luke's four (cf. *Expositio Evangelii sec. Lucam*, in loc.). In St Luke they are in some cases stated in a more incisive, more direct form than in the First Gospel, where they are given with more explanation: for example, the first beatitude says simply "Blessed are you poor", whereas in Matthew we read, "Blessed are the poor in spirit", which contains a brief explanation of the meaning of the virtue of poverty.

6:20. "The ordinary Christian has to reconcile two aspects of this life that can at first sight seem contradictory. There is, on the one hand, *true poverty*, which is obvious and tangible and made up of definite things. This poverty should be an expression of faith in God and a sign that the heart is not satisfied with created things and aspires to the Creator; that it wants to be filled with love of God so as to be able to give this same love to everyone. On the other hand, an ordinary Christian is and wants to be *one more among his fellow men*, sharing their way of life, their joys and happiness; working with them, loving the world and all the good things that exist in it; using all created things to solve the problems of human life and to establish a spiritual and material environment which will foster personal and social development [...].

"To my way of thinking, the best examples of poverty are those mothers and fathers of large and poor families who spend their lives for their children and who with their effort and constancy—often without complaining of their needs—bring up their family, creating a cheerful home in which everyone learns to love, to serve and to work" (St Josemaría Escrivá, *Conversations*, 111f).

6:24–26. Our Lord here condemns four things: avarice and attachment to the things of the world; excessive care of the body, gluttony; empty-headed joy and general self-indulgence; flattery, and disordered desire for human glory—four

Is 5:22 25“Woe to you that are full now, for you shall hunger.
“Woe to you that laugh now, for you shall mourn and weep.
Jas 4:4 26“Woe to you, when all men speak well of you, for so their
Mic 2:11 fathers did to the false prophets.

Love of enemies

Mt 5:39–48 27“But I say to you that hear, Love your enemies, do good to those
who hate you, 28bless those who curse you, pray for those who
abuse you. 29To him who strikes you on the cheek, offer the other
also; and from him who takes away your cloak do not withhold

---

common vices which a Christian needs to be on guard against.

6:24. In the same kind of way as in v. 20, which refers to the poor in the sense of those who love poverty, seeking to please God better, so in this verse the “rich” are to be understood as those who strive to accumulate possessions heedless of whether or not they are doing so lawfully, and who seek their happiness in those possessions, as if they were their ultimate goal. But people who inherit wealth or acquire it through honest work can be really poor provided they are detached from these things and are led by that detachment to use them to help others, as God inspires them. We can find in Sacred Scripture a number of people to whom the beatitude of the poor can be applied although they possessed considerable wealth—Abraham, Isaac, Moses, David, Job, for example.

As early as St Augustine’s time there were people who failed to understand poverty and riches properly; they reasoned as follows: The Kingdom of heaven belongs to the poor, the Lazaruses of this world, the hungry; all the rich are bad, like this rich man here. This sort of thinking led St Augustine to explain the deep meaning of wealth and poverty according to the spirit of the Gospel: “Listen, poor man, to my comments on your words. When you refer to yourself as Lazarus, that holy man covered with wounds, I am afraid your pride makes you describe yourself incorrectly. Do not despise rich men who are merciful, who are humble: or, to put it briefly, do not despise poor rich men. Oh, poor man!, be poor yourself; poor, that is, humble […]. Listen to me, then. Be truly poor, be devout, be humble; if you glory in your ragged and ulcerous poverty, if you glory in likening yourself to that beggar lying outside the rich man’s house, then you are only noticing his poverty, and nothing else. What should I notice, you ask? Read the Scriptures and you will understand what I mean. Lazarus was poor, but he to whose bosom he was brought was rich. ‘It came to pass, it is written, that the poor man died and he was brought by the angels to Abraham’s bosom.’ To where? To Abraham’s bosom or, let us say, to that mysterious place where Abraham was resting. Read […] and remember that Abraham was a very wealthy man when he was on earth: he had abundance of money, a large family, flocks, land; yet that rich man was poor, because he was humble. ‘Abraham believed God and he was reckoned righteous.’ […] He was faithful, he did good, he received the commandment to offer his son in sacrifice, and he did not refuse to offer what he had received to Him from whom he had received it. He was approved in God’s sight and set before us as an example of faith” (*Sermons*, 14).

your coat as well. [30]Give to every one who begs from you; and of
him who takes away your goods do not ask them again. [31]And as Mt 7:12
you wish that men would do to you, do so to them.
[32]"If you love those who love you, what credit is that to you?
For even sinners love those who love them. [33]And if you do good
to those who do good to you, what credit is that to you? For even
sinners do the same. [34]And if you lend to those from whom you Lev 25:35f
hope to receive, what credit is that to you? Even sinners lend to
sinners, to receive as much again. [35]But love your enemies, and do Mt 6:14
good, and lend, expecting nothing in return;[v] and your reward will

---

To sum up: poverty does not consist in something purely external, in having or not having material goods, but in something that goes far deeper, affecting a person's heart and soul; it consists in having a humble attitude to God, in being devout, in having total faith. If a Christian has these virtues and also has an abundance of material possessions, he should be detached from his wealth and act charitably towards others and thus be pleasing to God. On the other hand, if someone is not well-off he is not justified in God's sight on that account, if he fails to strive to acquire those virtues in which true poverty consists.

6:27. "In loving our enemies there shines forth in us some likeness to God our Father, who, by the death of his Son, ransomed from everlasting perdition and reconciled to himself the human race, which previously was most unfriendly and hostile to him" (St Pius V, *Catechism*, 4, 14, 19). Following the example of God our Father, we must desire for everyone (even those who say they are our enemies) eternal life, in the first place; additionally, a Christian has a duty to respect and understand everyone without exception, because of his or her intrinsic dignity as a human person, made in the image and likeness of the Creator.

6:28. Jesus Christ teaches us by example that this is a real precept and not just a pious recommendation; even when nailed to the cross he prayed to his Father for those who had brought him to such a pass: "Father, forgive them; for they know not what they do" (Lk 23:34). In imitation of the Master, St Stephen, the first martyr of the Church, when he was being stoned, prayed to our Lord not to hold the sin against his persecutors (cf. Acts 7:60). In the liturgy of Good Friday the Church offers prayers and suffrages to God on behalf of those outside the Church, asking him to give them the grace of faith; to release from their ignorance those who do not know him; to give Jews the light of the truth; to bring non-Catholic Christians, linked by true charity, into full communion with our Mother the Church.

6:29. Our Lord gives us more examples to show us how we should act if we want to imitate the mercy of God. The first has to do with one of what are traditionally called the "spiritual works of mercy"—forgiving injuries and being patient with other people's defects. This is what he means in the first instance about turning the other cheek.

To understand what our Lord is saying here, St Thomas comments that

v. Other ancient authorities read *despairing of no man*

be great, and you will be sons of the Most High; for he is kind to
the ungrateful and the selfish. [36]Be merciful, even as your Father
is merciful.

[37]"Judge not, and you will not be judged; condemn not, and
you will not be condemned; forgive, and you will be forgiven;
Mt 4:24 [38]give, and it will be given to you; good measure, pressed down,
shaken together, running over, will be put into your lap. For the
measure you give will be the measure you get back."

Integrity

Mt 15:14 [39]He also told them a parable: "Can a blind man lead a blind man?
Will they not both fall into a pit? [40]A disciple is not above his

---

"Holy Scripture needs to be understood in the light of the example of Christ and the saints. Christ did not offer the other cheek to be struck in the house of Annas (Jn 18:22f), nor did St Paul when, as we are told in the Acts of the Apostles, he was beaten in Philippi (Acts 16:22f). Therefore, we should not take it that Christ literally meant that you should offer the other cheek to someone to hit you; what he was referring to was your interior disposition; that is, if necessary we should be ready not to be intolerant of anyone who hurts us, and we should be ready to put up with this kind of treatment, or worse than that. That was how the Lord acted when he surrendered his body to death" (*Comm. on St John*, 18, 37).

6:36. The model of mercy which Christ sets before us is God himself, of whom St Paul says: "Blessed be the God and Father of our Lord Jesus Christ, the Father of mercies and God of all comfort, who comforts us in all our affliction" (2 Cor 1:3–4). "The first quality of this virtue", Fray Luis de Granada explains, "is that it makes men like God and like the most glorious thing in him, his mercy (Lk 6:36). For certainly the greatest perfection a creature can have is to be like his Creator; and the more like him he is, the more perfect he is. Certainly one of the things which is most appropriate to God is mercy, which is what the Church means when it says that prayer: 'Lord God, to whom it is proper to be merciful and forgiving …'. It says that this is proper to God, because just as a creature, as creature, is characteristically poor and needy (and therefore characteristically receives and does not give), so, on the contrary, since God is infinitely rich and powerful, to him alone does it belong to give and not to receive, and therefore it is appropriate for him to be merciful and forgiving" (*Book of Prayer and Meditation*, third part, third treatise).

This is the rule a Christian should apply: be compassionate towards other people's afflictions as if they were one's own, and try to remedy them. The Church spells out this rule by giving us a series of corporal works of mercy (visiting and caring for the sick, giving food to the hungry, drink to the thirsty …) and spiritual works of mercy (teaching the ignorant, correcting the person who has erred, forgiving injuries …): cf. St Pius X, *Catechism*, 944f.

We should also show understanding towards people who are in error: "Love and courtesy of this kind should not, of course, make us indifferent to truth and goodness. Love, in fact, impels the fol-

teacher, but every one when he is fully taught will be like his Mt 10:24–25
teacher. [41]Why do you see the speck that is in your brother's eye, Jn 15:20
but do not notice the log that is in your own eye? [42]Or how can
you say to your brother, 'Brother, let me take out the speck that is
in your eye,' when you yourself do not see the log that is in your
own eye? You hypocrite, first take the log out of your own eye,
and then you will see clearly to take out the speck that is in your
brother's eye.
[43]"For no good tree bears bad fruit, nor again does a bad tree
bear good fruit; [44]for each tree is known by its own fruit. For figs
are not gathered from thorns, nor are grapes picked from a bram-
ble bush. [45]The good man out of the good treasure of his heart Mt 12:34–35

---

lowers of Christ to proclaim to all men the truth which saves. But we must distinguish between the error (which must always be rejected) and the person in error, who never loses his dignity as a person even though he flounders amid false or inadequate religious ideas. God alone is the judge and the searcher of hearts; he forbids us to pass judgment on the inner guilt of others" (Vatican II, *Gaudium et spes*, 28).

6:38. We read in Sacred Scripture of the generosity of the widow of Zarephath, whom God asked to give food to Elijah the prophet even though she had very little left; he then rewarded her generosity by constantly renewing her supply of meal and oil (cf. 1 Kings 17:9ff). The same sort of thing happened when the boy supplied the five loaves and two fish which our Lord multiplied to feed a huge crowd of people (cf. Jn 6:9)—a vivid example of what God does when we give him whatever we have, even if it does not amount to much.

God does not let himself be outdone in generosity: "Go, generously and like a child ask him: 'What can you mean to give me when you ask me for "this"?'" (St Josemaría Escrivá, *The Way*, 153). However much we give God in this life, he will give us more in life eternal.

6:43–44. To distinguish the good tree from the bad tree we need to look at the fruit the tree produces (deeds) and not at its foliage (words). "For there is no lack of people here on earth who, on being approached, turn out to be nothing but large, shiny, glossy leaves. Foliage, just foliage and nothing more. Meanwhile, many souls are looking to us, hoping to satisfy their hunger, which is a hunger for God. We must not forget that we have all the resources we need. We have sufficient doctrine and the grace of God, in spite of our wretchedness" (St Josemaría Escrivá, *Friends of God*, 51).

6:45. Jesus is giving us two similes—that of the tree which, if it is good, produces good fruit, and that of the man, who speaks of those things he has in his heart. "The treasure of the heart is the same as the root of the tree," St Bede explains. "A person who has a treasure of patience and of perfect charity in his heart yields excellent fruit; he loves his neighbour and has all the other qualities Jesus teaches; he loves his enemies, does good to him who hates him, blesses him who curses him, prays for him who calumniates him, does not react against him who attacks him or robs him; he gives to those who ask, does not claim what they have stolen from him, wishes

produces good, and the evil man out of his evil treasure produces
evil; for out of the abundance of the heart his mouth speaks.
Mal 1:6 Mt 7:21 46“Why do you call me ‘Lord, Lord,’ and not do what I tell
you? 47Every one who comes to me and hears my words and does
them, I will show you what he is like: 48he is like a man building
a house, who dug deep, and laid the foundation upon rock; and
when a flood arose, the stream broke against that house, and could
not shake it, because it had been well built.[w] 49But he who hears
and does not do them is like a man who built a house on the
ground without a foundation; against which the stream broke, and
immediately it fell, and the ruin of that house was great.”

The centurion’s faith

Mt 8:5–13 **7** 1After he had ended all his sayings in the hearing of the
Jn 4:46 people he entered Capernaum. 2Now a centurion had a slave
who was dear[x] to him, who was sick and at the point of death.
3When he heard of Jesus, he sent to him elders of the Jews, asking
him to come and heal his slave. 4And when they came to Jesus,

---

not to judge and does not condemn, corrects patiently and affectionately those who err. But the person who has in his heart the treasure of evil does exactly the opposite: he hates his friends, speaks evil of him who loves him and does all the other things condemned by the Lord” (*In Lucae Evangelium expositio*, 2, 6).

6:46. Jesus asks us to act in a way consistent with being Christians and not to make any separation between the faith we profess and the way we live: “What matters is not whether or not we wear a religious habit; it is whether we try to practise the virtues and surrender our will to God and order our lives as His Majesty ordains, and not want to do our will but his” (St Teresa of Avila, *Interior Castle*, 2, 6).

7:1–10. “They besought him earnestly” (v. 4). Here is an example of the effectiveness of the prayer of petition, which induces almighty God to work a miracle. In this connexion St Bernard explains what we should ask God for: “As I see it, the petitions of the heart consist in three things […]. The first two have to do with the present, that is, with things for the body and for the soul; the third is the blessedness of eternal life. Do not be surprised that he says that we should ask God for things for the body: all things come from him, physical as well as spiritual things […]. However, we should pray more often and more fervently for things our souls need, that is, for God’s grace and for virtues” (*Fifth Lenten sermon*, 8f). To obtain his grace—of whatever kind—God himself expects us to ask him assiduously, confidently, humbly and persistently.

What stands out here is the centurion’s humility: he did not belong to the chosen people, he was a pagan; but he makes his request through friends, with deep humility. Humility is a route to faith,

w. Other ancient authorities read *founded upon the rock* **x.** Or *valuable*

they besought him earnestly, saying, "He is worthy to have you do
this for him, [5]for he loves our nation, and he built us our synagogue." [6]And Jesus went with them. When he was not far from
the house, the centurion sent friends to him, saying to him, "Lord,
do not trouble yourself, for I am not worthy to have you come
under my roof; [7]therefore I did not presume to come to you. But
say the word, and let my servant be healed. [8]For I am a man set
under authority, with soldiers under me: and I say to one, 'Go,'
and he goes; and to another, 'Come,' and he comes; and to my
slave, 'Do this,' and he does it." [9]When Jesus heard this he marvelled at him, and turned and said to the multitude that followed
him, "I tell you, not even in Israel have I found such faith." [10]And
when those who had been sent returned to the house, they found
the slave well.

The son of the widow of Nain restored to life

[11]Soon afterward[y] he went to a city called Nain, and his disciples
and a great crowd went with him. [12]As he drew near to the gate of 1 Kings 17:17ff

whether to receive faith for the first time or to revive it. Speaking of his own conversion experience, St Augustine says that because he was not humble, he could not understand how Jesus, who was such a humble person, could be God, nor how God could teach anyone by lowering himself to the point of taking on our human condition. This was precisely why the Word, eternal Truth, became man—to demolish our pride, to encourage our love, to subdue all things and thereby be able to raise us up (cf. *Confessions*, 7, 18, 24).

7:6–7. Such is the faith and humility of the centurion that the Church, in its eucharistic liturgy, gives us his very words to express our own sentiments just before receiving Holy Communion; we too should strive to have this interior disposition when Jesus enters under our roof, our soul.

7:11–17. "Jesus crosses paths again with a crowd of people. He could have passed by or waited until they called him. But he didn't. He took the initiative, because he was moved by a widow's sorrow. She had just lost all she had, her son.

"The evangelist explains that Jesus was moved. Perhaps he even showed signs of it, as when Lazarus died. Jesus Christ was not, and is not, insensitive to the suffering that stems from love. He is pained at seeing children separated from their parents. He overcomes death so as to give life, to reunite those who love one another. But at the same time, he requires that we first admit the pre-eminence of divine love, which alone can inspire genuine Christian living.

"Christ knows he is surrounded by a crowd which will be awed by the miracle and will tell the story all over the countryside. But he does not act artificially, merely to create an effect. Quite simply he is touched by that woman's suffering and cannot but console her. So he goes up to her and says, 'Do not weep.' It is like saying: 'I don't want to see you

y. Other ancient authorities read *Next day*

the city, behold, a man who had died was being carried out, the
only son of his mother, and she was a widow; and a large crowd
from the city was with her. 13And when the Lord saw her, he had
compassion on her and said to her, "Do not weep." 14And he came
and touched the bier, and the bearers stood still. And he said,
"Young man, I say to you, arise." 15And the dead man sat up, and
began to speak. And he gave him to his mother. 16Fear seized them
all; and they glorified God, saying, "A great prophet has arisen
among us!" and "God has visited his people!" 17And this report
concerning him spread through the whole of Judea and all the surrounding country.

Messengers from John the Baptist

Mt 11:2–19 18The disciples of John told him of all these things. 19And John,
Mal 3:1 calling to him two of his disciples, sent them to the Lord, saying,
"Are you he who is to come, or shall we look for another?" 20And
when the men had come to him, they said, "John the Baptist has
sent us to you, saying, 'Are you he who is to come, or shall we

---

crying; I have come on earth to bring joy and peace.' And then comes the miracle, the sign of the power of Christ who is God. But first came his compassion, an evident sign of the tenderness of the heart of Christ the man" (St Josemaría Escrivá, *Christ Is Passing By*, 166).

7:15. This mother's joy on being given back her son reminds us of the joy of our Mother the Church when her sinful children return to the life of grace. "The widowed mother rejoiced at the raising of that young man," St Augustine comments. "Our Mother the Church rejoices every day when people are raised again in spirit. The young man had been dead physically; the latter, dead spiritually. The young man's death was mourned visibly; the death of the latter was invisible and unmourned. He seeks them out who knew them to be dead; only he can bring them back to life" (*Sermons*, 98, 2).

7:18–23. "It was not out of ignorance that John enquired about Christ's coming in the flesh, for he had already clearly professed his belief, saying, 'I have seen and have borne witness that this is the Son of God' (Jn 1:34). That is why he does not ask, 'Are you he who has come?' but rather, 'Are you he who is to come?' thus asking about the future, not about the past. Nor should we think that the Baptist did not know about Christ's future passion, for it was John who said, 'Behold the Lamb of God, who takes away the sins of the world' (Jn 1:29), thus foretelling his future immolation, which other prophets had already foretold, particularly Isaiah (chap. 53) […]. It can also be replied, with St John Chrysostom, that John made this enquiry not from doubt or ignorance, but because he wished his disciples to be satisfied on this point by Christ. Therefore, Christ gave his reply to instruct these disciples, by pointing to the evidence of his miracles (v. 22)" (St Thomas Aquinas, *Summa theologiae*, 2–2, 2, 7 ad 2).

7:22. In his reply to these disciples of John the Baptist, Jesus points to the miracles

look for another?' " 21 In that hour he cured many of diseases and
plagues and evil spirits, and on many that were blind he bestowed
sight. 22 And he answered them, "Go and tell John what you have Is 35:5; 61:1
seen and heard: the blind receive their sight, the lame walk, lepers
are cleansed, and the deaf hear, the dead are raised up, the poor
have good news preached to them. 23 And blessed is he who takes
no offence at me."

24 When the messengers of John had gone, he began to speak to
the crowds concerning John: "What did you go out into the
wilderness to behold? A reed shaken by the wind? 25 What then did Mt 3:4
you go out to see? A man clothed in soft raiment? Behold, those
who are gorgeously apparelled and live in luxury are in kings'
courts. 26 What then did you go out to see? A prophet? Yes, I tell Lk 1:76
you, and more than a prophet. 27 This is he of whom it is written, Mal 3:1

'Behold, I send my messenger before thy face,
who shall prepare thy way before thee.'

28 I tell you, among those born of women none is greater than Lk 1:15
John; yet he who is least in the kingdom of God is greater than

---

he has worked, which show that he has inaugurated the Kingdom of God; he is, therefore, the promised Messiah. Along with miracles, one of the signs of the coming of the Kingdom is the preaching of salvation to the poor. On the meaning of "the poor", see the notes on Mt 5:3; Lk 6:20 and 6:24. Following the Lord's example, the Church has always taken special care of those in need. In our own time the Popes have stressed time and again the duties of Christians in regard to poverty caused by man's injustice to man: "Selfishness and domination are permanent temptations for men. Likewise an ever finer discernment is needed, in order to strike at the roots of newly arising situations of injustice and to establish progressively a justice which will be less and less imperfect [...]. The Church directs her attention to these new 'poor'—the handicapped, the maladjusted, the old, various groups on the fringe of society—in order to recognize them, help them, defend their place and dignity in a society hardened by competition and the attraction of success" (Paul VI, *Octogesima adveniens*, 15).

7:23. These words refer to the same thing Simeon prophesied about when he referred to Christ as a sign that is spoken against, a sign of contradiction (cf. Lk 2:34). People who reject our Lord, who are scandalized by him, will not reach heaven.

7:28. St John the Baptist is the greatest of the prophets of the Old Testament because he was the nearest to Christ and received the unique mission of actually pointing out the Messiah. Still, he belongs to the time of the promise (the Old Testament), when the work of redemption lay in the future. Once Christ did that work (the New Testament), those who faithfully accept God's gift of grace are incomparably greater than the righteous of the Old Covenant who were given, not this grace, but only the promise of it. Once the work of redemption was accomplished God's grace also

Lk 3:7–12 Mt 21:32 he."* 29(When they heard this all the people and the tax collectors
justified God, having been baptized with the baptism of John;
Acts 13:46 30but the Pharisees and the lawyers rejected the purpose of God
for themselves, not having been baptized by him.)

Jesus reproaches his contemporaries

31"To what then shall I compare the men of this generation, and
what are they like? 32They are like children sitting in the market
place and calling to one another,

'We piped to you, and you did not dance;
we wailed, and you did not weep.'

33For John the Baptist has come eating no bread and drinking no
Lk 5:30; 15:2 wine; and you say, 'He has a demon.' 34The Son of man has come
eating and drinking; and you say, 'Behold, a glutton and a drunkard, a friend of tax collectors and sinners!' 35Yet wisdom is justified by all her children."

---

reached the righteous of the Old Testament, who were waiting for Christ to open heaven and let them, too, enter.

7:31–34. See the note on Mt 11:16–19.

7:35. The wisdom referred to here is divine wisdom, especially Christ himself (cf. Wis 7:26; Prov 8:22). "Children of Wisdom" is a Hebrew way of saying "wise men"; he is truly wise who comes to know God and love him and be saved by him—in other words, a saint.

Divine wisdom is revealed in the creation and government of the universe and, particularly, in the salvation of mankind. Wise men "justifying" wisdom seems to mean that the wise, the saints, bear witness to Christ by living holy lives: "Let your light so shine before men, that they may see your good works and give glory to your Father who is in heaven" (Mt 5:16).

7:36–40. This woman, moved no doubt by grace, was attracted by Christ's preaching and by what people were saying about him. When dining, people reclined on low divans leaning on their left arm with their legs tucked under them, away from the table. A host was expected to give his guest a kiss of greeting and offer him water for his feet, and perfumes.

7:41–50. In this short parable of the two debtors Christ teaches us three things—his own divinity and his power to forgive sins; the merit the woman's love deserves; and the discourtesy implied in Simeon's neglecting to receive Jesus in the conventional way. Our Lord was not interested in these social niceties as such but in the affection which they expressed; that was why he felt hurt at Simeon's neglect.

"Jesus notices the omission of the expression of human courtesy and refinement which the Pharisee failed to show him. Christ is *perfectus Deus, perfectus homo* (*Athanasian Creed*). He is perfect God, the Second Person of the Blessed Trinity, and perfect man. He comes to save, not to destroy nature. It is from him that we learn that it is unchristian to treat our fellow men badly, for they are creatures of God, made in his image and like-

Forgiveness for a sinful woman

[36]One of the Pharisees asked him to eat with him, and he went Lk 11:37
into the Pharisee's house, and sat at table. [37]And behold, a woman
of the city, who was a sinner, when she learned that he was sitting
at table in the Pharisee's house, brought an alabaster flask of ointment, [38]and standing behind him at his feet, weeping, she began to Mt 26:7–13
wet his feet with her tears; and wiped them with the hair of her Mk 14:3–9
head, and kissed his feet, and anointed them with the ointment. Jn 12:3–8
[39]Now when the Pharisee who had invited him saw it, he said to Jn 4:19
himself, "If this man were a prophet, he would have known who
and what sort of woman this is who is touching him, for she is a
sinner." [40]And Jesus answering said to him, "Simon, I have something to say to you." And he answered, "What is it, Teacher?" [41]"A
certain creditor had two debtors; one owed five hundred denarii,
and the other fifty. [42]When they could not pay, he forgave them
both. Now which of them will love him more?" [43]Simon

---

ness (cf. Gen 1:26)" (St Josemaría Escrivá, *Friends of God*, 73).

Moreover, the Pharisee was wrong to think badly of this sinner and of Jesus: reckoning that Christ did not know anything about her, he complained inwardly. Our Lord, who could read the secret thoughts of men (which showed his divinity), intervened to point out to him his mistake. True righteousness, says St Gregory the Great (cf. *In Evangelia homiliae*, 33), is compassionate; whereas false righteousness is indignant. There are many people like this Pharisee: forgetting that they themselves were or are poor sinners, when they see other people's sin they immediately become indignant, instead of taking pity on them, or else they rush to judge them or sneer at them. They forget what St Paul says: "Let any one who thinks that he stands take heed lest he fall" (1 Cor 10:12); "Brethren, if a man is overtaken in any trespass, you who are spiritual should restore him in a spirit of gentleness [...]. Bear one another's burdens, and so fulfil the law of Christ" (Gal 6:1–2).

We should strive to have charity govern all our judgments. Otherwise, we will easily be unjust towards others. "Let us be slow to judge. Each one see things from his own point of view, and with his own mind, with all its limitations, through eyes that are often dimmed and clouded by passion.... Of what little worth are the judgments of men! Don't judge without sifting your judgment in prayer" (St J. Escrivá, *The Way*, 451).

Charity and humility will allow us to see in the sins of others our own weak and helpless position, and will help our hearts go out to the sorrow of every sinner who repents, for we too would fall into sins as serious or more serious if God in his mercy did not stay by our side.

"It was not the ointment that the Lord loved", St Ambrose comments, "but the affection; it was the woman's faith that pleased him, her humility. And you also, if you desire grace, increase your love; pour over the body of Jesus Christ your faith in the Resurrection, the perfume of the holy Church and the ointment of charity towards others" (*Expositio Evangelii sec. Lucam*, in loc.).

answered, "The one, I suppose, to whom he forgave more." And
he said to him, "You have judged rightly." 44Then turning toward
the woman he said to Simon, "Do you see this woman? I entered
your house, you gave me no water for my feet, but she has wet my
feet with her tears and wiped them with her hair. 45You gave me
no kiss, but from the time I came in she has not ceased to kiss my
feet. 46You did not anoint my head with oil, but she has anointed
my feet with ointment. 47Therefore I tell you, her sins, which are
many, are forgiven, for she loved much; but he who is forgiven
Lk 5:20–21 little, loves little."* 48And he said to her, "Your sins are forgiven."
49Then those who were at table with him began to say among
Lk 8:48; 17:19; 18:42 themselves, "Who is this, who even forgives sins?" 50And he said
to the woman, "Your faith has saved you; go in peace."

The holy women

Lk 4:43 8 1Soon afterward he went on through cities and villages,
preaching and bringing the good news of the kingdom of God.

7:47. Man cannot merit forgiveness for his sins because, since God is the offended party, they are of infinite gravity. We need the sacrament of Penance, in which God forgives us by virtue of the infinite merits of Jesus Christ; there is only one indispensable condition for winning God's forgiveness—our love, our repentance. We are pardoned to the extent that we love; when our heart is full of love there is no longer any room in it for sin because we have made room for Jesus, and he says to us as he said to this woman, "Your sins are forgiven." Repentance is a sign that we love God. But it was God who first loved us (cf.1 Jn 4:10). When God forgives us he is expressing his love for us. Our love for God is, then, always a response to his initiative. By forgiving us God helps us to be more grateful and more loving towards him. "He loves little", St Augustine comments, "who has little forgiven. You say that you have not committed many sins: but why is that the case? [...] The reason is that God was guiding you [...]. There is no sin that one man commits, which another may not commit also unless God, man's maker, guides him" (*Sermons*, 99, 6). Therefore, we ought to fall ever more deeply in love with our Lord, not only because he forgives us our sins but also because he helps us by means of his grace not to commit them.

7:50. Jesus declares that it was faith that moved this woman to throw herself at his feet and show her repentance; her repentance wins his forgiveness. Similarly, when we approach the sacrament of Penance we should stir up our faith in the fact that it is "not a human but a divine dialogue. It is a tribunal of divine justice and especially of mercy, with a loving judge who 'has no pleasure in the death of the wicked; I desire that the wicked turn back from his way and live' (Ezek 33:11)" (St Josemaría Escrivá, *Christ Is Passing By*, 78).

8:1–3. The Gospel refers a number of times to women accompanying our Lord. Here St Luke gives us the names of three

And the twelve were with him, [2]and also some women who had Mt 27:55–56
been healed of evil spirits and infirmities: Mary, called Magdal- Mk 15:40–41; 16:9
ene, from whom seven demons had gone out, [3]and Joanna, the
wife of Chuza, Herod's steward, and Susanna, and many others, Lk 24:10
who provided for them[z] out of their means.

Parable of the sower. The meaning of parables

[4]And when a great crowd came together and people from town Mt 13:1–23
after town came to him, he said in a parable: [5]"A sower went out Mk 4:1–20
to sow his seed; and as he sowed, some fell along the path, and
was trodden under foot, and the birds of the air devoured it. [6]And
some fell on the rock; and as it grew up, it withered away, because
it had no moisture. [7]And some fell among thorns; and the thorns
grew with it and choked it. [8]And some fell into good soil and
grew, and yielded a hundredfold." As he said this, he called out,
"He who has ears to hear, let him hear."

---

of them—Mary, called Magdalene, to whom the risen Christ appeared beside the holy sepulchre (Jn 20:11–18; Mk 16:9); Joanna, a lady of some position, whom we also meet among the women who went to the tomb on the morning of the Resurrection (Lk 24:10), and Susanna, whom the Gospel does not mention again. The role of these women consisted in helping Jesus and his disciples out of their own resources, thereby showing their gratitude for what Christ had done for them, and in cooperating in his ministry.

Men and women enjoy equal dignity in the Church. Within the context of that equality, women certainly have specific characteristics which must necessarily be reflected in their role in the Church: "All the baptised, men and women alike, share equally in the dignity, freedom and responsibility of the children of God. … Women are called to bring to the family, to society and to the Church, characteristics which are their own and which they alone can give—their gentle warmth and untiring generosity, their love for detail, their quick-wittedness and intuition, their simple and deep piety, their constancy. … A woman's femininity is genuine only if she is aware of the beauty of this contribution for which there is no substitute—and if she incorporates it into her own life" (St Josemaría Escrivá, *Conversations*, 14 and 87).

The Gospel makes special reference to the generosity of these women. It is nice to know that our Lord availed himself of their charity, and that they responded to him with such refined and generous detachment that Christian women feel filled with a holy and fruitful envy (cf. St J. Escrivá, *The Way*, 981).

8:4–8. Our Lord explains this parable in vv. 11–15. The seed is Jesus himself and his preaching; and the kinds of ground it falls on reflect people's different attitudes to Jesus and his teaching. Our Lord sows the life of grace in souls through the preaching of the Church and through an endless flow of actual graces.

z. Other ancient authorities read *him*

[9]And when his disciples asked him what this parable meant,
Is 6:9–10 [10]he said, "To you it has been given to know the secrets of the
kingdom of God; but for others they are in parables, so that
seeing they may not see, and hearing they may not understand.
[11]Now the parable is this: The seed is the word of God. [12]The
ones along the path are those who have heard; then the devil
comes and takes away the word from their hearts, that they may
not believe and be saved. [13]And the ones on the rock are those
who, when they hear the word, receive it with joy; but these have
no root, they believe for a while and in time of temptation fall
away. [14]And as for what fell among the thorns, they are those who
hear, but as they go on their way they are choked by the cares and
riches and pleasures of life, and their fruit does not mature. [15]And
as for that in the good soil, they are those who, hearing the word,
hold it fast in an honest and good heart, and bring forth fruit with
patience.

8:10–12. Jesus uses parables to teach people the mysteries of the supernatural life and thereby lead them to salvation. However, he foresaw that, due to the bad dispositions of some of his listeners, these parables would lead them to harden their hearts and to reject grace. For a fuller explanation of the purpose of parables see the notes on Mt 13:10–13 and Mk 4:11–12.

8:12. Some people are so immersed in a life of sin that they are like the path on which falls the seed "which suffers from two kinds of hazard: it is trodden on by wayfarers and snatched by birds. The path, therefore, is the heart, which is trodden on by the frequent traffic of evil thoughts, and cannot take in the seed and let it germinate because it is so dried up" (St Bede, *In Lucae Evangelium expositio*, in loc.). Souls hardened by sin can become good soil and bear fruit through sincere repentance and penance. We should note the effort the devil makes to prevent souls from being converted.

8:13. "Many people are pleased by what they hear, and they resolve to do good; but as soon as they experience difficulties they give up the good works they started. Stony ground has not enough soil, which is why the shoots fail to produce fruit. There are many who, when they hear greed criticized, do conceive a loathing for it and extol the scorning of it; but as soon as the soul sees something else that it desires, it forgets what it previously promised. There are also others who when they hear talk against impurity not only desire not to be stained by the filth of the flesh but are even ashamed of the stains that they already bear; but as soon as bodily beauty presents itself to their eyes, their heart is so drawn by desires that it is as if they had done or decided to do nothing against these desires, and they act in a manner deserving condemnation and in a way which they themselves previously condemned when they reflected on their behaviour. Very often we feel compunction for our faults and yet we go back and commit them even after bemoaning them" (St Gregory the Great, *In Evangelia homiliae*, 15).

Parable of the lamp

16“No one after lighting a lamp covers it with a vessel, or puts it Mk 4:21–25
under a bed, but puts it on a stand, that those who enter may see Mt 5:15
the light. 17For nothing is hid that shall not be made manifest, nor Mt 10:26
anything secret that shall not be known and come to light. 18Take Lk 19:26
heed then how you hear; for to him who has will more be given,
and from him who has not, even what he thinks that he has will be
taken away.”

The true kinsmen of Jesus

19Then his mother and his brethren* came to him, but they could Mt 12:46–50
not reach him for the crowd. 20And he was told, “Your mother and Mk 3:31–35
your brethren are standing outside, desiring to see you.” 21But he
said to them, “My mother and my brethren are those who hear the
word of God and do it.”

8:14. This is the case of people who after receiving the divine seed, the Christian calling, and having stayed on the right path for some time, begin to give up the struggle. These souls run the risk of developing a distaste for the things of God and of taking the easy, and wrong, way of seeking compensations suggested to them by their disordered ambition for power and their desire for material wealth and a comfortable life involving no suffering.

A person in this situation begins to be lukewarm and tries to serve two masters: “It is wrong to have two candles lighted—one to St Michael and another to the devil. We must snuff out the devil’s candle: we must spend our lives completely in the service of the Lord. If our desire for holiness is sincere, if we are docile enough to place ourselves in God’s hands, everything will go well. For he is always ready to give us his grace” (St Josemaría Escrivá, *Christ Is Passing By*, 59).

8:15. Jesus tells us that the good soil has three features—listening to God’s demands with the good disposition of a generous heart; striving to ensure that one does not water down these demands as time goes by; and, finally, beginning and beginning again and not being disheartened if the fruit is slow to appear. “You cannot ‘rise’. It’s not surprising: that fall!

“Persevere and you will ‘rise’. Remember what a spiritual writer has said: your poor soul is like a bird whose wings are caked with mud. Suns of heaven are needed and personal efforts, small and constant, to shake off those inclinations, those vain fancies, that depression: that mud clinging to your wings. And you will see yourself free. If you persevere, you will ‘rise’ ” (St Josemaría Escrivá, *The Way*, 991).

8:19–21. These words of our Lord show us that fulfilment of the will of God is more important than kinship and that, therefore, our Lady is more united to her Son by virtue of her perfect fulfilment of what God asked of her than by the Holy Spirit’s using her to make Christ’s body (cf. the notes on Mt 12:48–50 and Mk 3:31–35).

The calming of the storm

Mt 8:18; 23–27 22One day he got into a boat with his disciples and he said to
Mk 4:35–41 them, "Let us go across to the other side of the lake." So they set
out, 23and as they sailed he fell asleep. And a storm of wind came
down on the lake, and they were filling with water, and were in
danger. 24And they went and woke him, saying, "Master, Master,
we are perishing!" And he awoke and rebuked the wind and the
raging waves; and they ceased, and there was a calm. 25He said to
them, "Where is your faith?" And they were afraid, and they marvelled, saying to one another, "Who then is this, that he commands even wind and water, and they obey him?"

The Gerasene demoniac

Mk 8:28–34 26Then they arrived at the country of the Gerasenes,[a] which is
Mk 5:1–20 opposite Galilee. 27And as he stepped out on land, there met him
a man from the city who had demons; for a long time he had worn
no clothes, and he lived not in a house but among the tombs.
28When he saw Jesus, he cried out and fell down before him, and
said with a loud voice, "What have you to do with me, Jesus, Son
of the Most High God? I beseech you, do not torment me." 29For
he had commanded the unclean spirit to come out of the man.
(For many a time it had seized him; he was kept under guard, and
bound with chains and fetters, but he broke the bonds and was
driven by the demon into the desert.) 30Jesus then asked him,
"What is your name?" And he said, "Legion"; for many demons
had entered him. 31And they begged him not to command them to

---

8:22–25. On this passage see the note on Mt 8:23–27.

8:23. Jesus fell asleep; he was tired. In other passages the Gospel describes similar situations: he sits wearily beside a well (Jn 4:6); he is thirsty and asks the Samaritan woman for a drink (Jn 4:7). Passages of this kind show the humanity of Jesus, true God and true man. "How generous our Lord is in humbling himself and fully accepting his human condition! He does not use his divine power to escape from difficulties or effort. Let's pray that he will teach us to be tough, to love work, to appreciate the human and divine nobility of savouring the consequences of self-giving" (St Josemaría Escrivá, *Christ Is Passing By*, 61).

8:26–39. "Gerasenes": some Greek manuscripts, which the New Vulgate follows, speak of "Gergesenes". But most manuscripts say "Gerasenes" or else "Gadarenes". Gadara (cf. Mt 8:28) and Gerasa (cf. Mk 5:1) were both towns of the Decapolis, adjacent to one another. On the geographical location of these two towns, see the notes on Mt 8:28 and Mk 5:20. On this cure and on the very

a. Other ancient authorities read *Gadarenes*, others *Gergesenes*

depart into the abyss. 32 Now a large herd of swine was feeding
there on the hillside; and they begged him to let them enter these.
So he gave them leave. 33 Then the demons came out of the man
and entered the swine, and the herd rushed down the steep bank
into the lake and were drowned.

34 When the herdsmen saw what had happened, they fled, and
told it in the city and in the country. 35 Then people went out to see
what had happened, and they came to Jesus, and found the man
from whom the demons had gone, sitting at the feet of Jesus,
clothed and in his right mind; and they were afraid. 36 And those
who had seen it told them how he who had been possessed with
demons was healed. 37 Then all the people of the surrounding
country of the Gerasenes[a] asked him to depart from them; for they
were seized with great fear; so he got into the boat and returned.
38 The man from whom the demons had gone begged that he might
be with him; but he sent him away, saying, 39 "Return to your
home, and declare how much God has done for you." And he
went away, proclaiming throughout the whole city how much
Jesus had done for him.*

Jairus' daughter is restored to life. Curing of the woman with a haemorrhage

40 Now when Jesus returned, the crowd welcomed him, for they Mt 9:18–26
were all waiting for him. 41 And there came a man named Jairus, Mk 5:21–43
who was a ruler of the synagogue; and falling at Jesus' feet he
besought him to come to his house, 42 for he had an only daughter, Lk 7:12
about twelve years of age, and she was dying.

---

different attitudes of the townsfolk and the possessed man, see the notes on Mt 8:28–34 and on Mk 5:1–20 and 5:15–20.

8:40–56. Jesus Christ asks faith of those who approach him; but he does not require us all to show him respect and reverence in exactly the same way. "There are always sick people who, like Bartimaeus, pray with great faith and have no qualms about confessing their faith at the top of their voices. But notice how, among those whom Christ encounters, no two souls are alike. This woman, too, has great faith, but she does not cry aloud; she draws near to Jesus without anyone even noticing. For her it is enough just to touch his garment, because she is quite certain she will be cured. No sooner has she done so than our Lord turns round and looks at her. He already knows what is going on in the depths of her heart and has seen how sure she is: 'Take heart, daughter; your faith has made you well' (Mt 9:22)" (St Josemaría Escrivá, *Friends of God*, 199). For a more detailed description of these two miracles, see the notes on Mt 9:18–26; 9:18; 9:23; 9:24; and Mk 5:21–43; 5:25; 5:30; 5:39; 5:40–42.

As he went, the people pressed round him. [43]And a woman
who had had a flow of blood for twelve years and had spent all
her living upon physicians[b] and could not be healed by any one,
[44]came up behind him, and touched the fringe of his garment; and
immediately her flow of blood ceased. [45]And Jesus said, "Who
was it that touched me?" When all denied it, Peter[c] said, "Master,
Lk 6:19 the multitudes surround you and press upon you!" [46]But Jesus
said, "Some one touched me; for I perceive that power has gone
forth from me." [47]And when the woman saw that she was not
hidden, she came trembling, and falling down before him declared
in the presence of all the people why she had touched him, and
Lk 7:50 how she had been immediately healed. [48]And he said to her,
"Daughter, your faith has made you well; go in peace."

[49]While he was still speaking, a man from the ruler's house
came and said, "Your daughter is dead; do not trouble the Teacher
any more." [50]But Jesus on hearing this answered him, "Do not
fear; only believe, and she shall be well." [51]And when he came to
the house, he permitted no one to enter with him, except Peter and
Lk 7:13 John and James, and the father and mother of the child. [52]And all
were weeping and bewailing her; but he said, "Do not weep; for
she is not dead but sleeping." [53]And they laughed at him, knowing
that she was dead. [54]But taking her by the hand he called, saying,

---

8:43–48. Many Fathers (St Ambrose, St Augustine, St Bede etc.) see this woman with the flow of blood (cf. the note on Mk 5:25) as symbolizing the church of the Gentiles which, unlike the Jews, approached our Lord with faith and was healed; she also represents every soul who, repentant for his sins, feels sorrow and shame for his past life, and also reverence towards God and firm confidence in his help.

"This holy woman, refined, devout, most ready to believe, most prudent as can be seen from her modesty—because modesty and faith are present when one recognizes that one is sick and does not despair of forgiveness—discreetly touches the fringe of the Lord's garment, approaches him with faith, believes with devotion and knows, through wisdom, that she has been cured [...]. Christ is touched through faith, Christ is sighted through faith [...]. Therefore, if we also wish to be healed, let us touch through our faith the fringe of Christ's garment" (St Ambrose, *Expositio Evangelii sec. Lucam*, in loc.).

8:50. St John Chrysostom (*Hom. on St Matthew*, 31) observes that the curing of the woman with the haemorrhage also has the purpose of strengthening Jairus' faith because he was about to be given the news of his daughter's death. The combination of the two miracles reveals God's loving plan to cause those present to have a deeper faith.

"The Lord requires faith of those who invoke him," St Athanasius comments, "not because they really need it (for he is

b. Other ancient authorities omit *and had spent all her living upon physicians* c. Other ancient authorities add *and those who were with him*

"Child, arise." [55]And her spirit returned, and she got up at once;
and he directed that something should be given her to eat. [56]And
her parents were amazed; but he charged them to tell no one what Lk 5:14
had happened. Mk 1:44; 7:36 Mt 16:20

5. JESUS TRAVELS WITH HIS APOSTLES

The mission of the apostles

9 [1]And he called the twelve together and gave them power and Mt 10:1, 7, 9–11
authority over all demons and to cure diseases, [2]and he sent Mk 6:7–13
them out to preach the kingdom of God and to heal. [3]And he said
to them, "Take nothing for your journey, no staff, nor bag, nor
bread, nor money; and do not have two tunics. [4]And whatever Lk 10:5–7
house you enter, stay there, and from there depart. [5]And wherever Lk 10:11
they do not receive you, when you leave that town shake off the
dust from your feet as a testimony against them." [6]And they
departed and went through the villages, preaching the gospel and
healing everywhere.

Herod's opinion about Jesus

[7]Now Herod the tetrarch heard of all that was done, and he was Mt 14:1–2
perplexed, because it was said by some that John had been raised Mk 6:14–16

---

the Lord, he is the giver of faith), but in order that they do not think that he dispenses his graces in an arbitrary way; and so he shows that he favours those who believe him, to ensure that they do not receive his benefits without faith, and if they lose them it only happens through their unfaithfulness. When he does good, Christ wants grace to endure, and when he cures he wants the cure to be permanent" (*Fragmenta in Lucam*, in loc.).

8:53. "They laughed at him": when someone has no faith in God's omnipotence, he tries to measure everything by his own limited understanding and easily fails to grasp supernatural realities: instead of reacting humbly, he tries to make fun of them. St Paul is referring to someone in this position when he says, "The unspiritual man does not receive the gifts of the Spirit of God, for they are folly to him, and he is not able to understand them because they are spiritually discerned" (1 Cor 2:14).

"There are some who pass through life as through a tunnel, without ever understanding the splendour, the security and the warmth of the sun of faith" (St Josemaría Escrivá, *The Way*, 575).

9:1–4. This is the first mission the apostles were sent on. Jesus wants them to gain experience which will help them in the mission they will have after he ascends into heaven. He charges them to do what he himself did—preach the Kingdom of God and heal the sick. This scene is commented on at greater length in notes on Mt 10:7–8; 10:9–10; and Mk 6:8–9.

9:7–9. Except for the Sadducees, all Jews

from the dead, 8by some that Elijah had appeared, and by others
Lk 23:8 that one of the old prophets had risen. 9Herod said, "John I
beheaded; but who is this about whom I hear such things?" And
he sought to see him.

Return of the apostles. First miracle of the loaves and fish

Mt 14:13–21 10On their return the apostles told him what they had done. And he
Mk 6:30–44 took them and withdrew apart to a city called Bethsaida. 11When
Jn 6:1–13 the crowds learned it, they followed him; and he welcomed them
and spoke to them of the kingdom of God, and cured those who
had need of healing. 12Now the day began to wear away; and the
twelve came and said to him, "Send the crowd away, to go into
the villages and country round about, to lodge and get provisions;
for we are here in a lonely place." 13But he said to them, "You give
them something to eat." They said, "We have no more than five
loaves and two fish—unless we are to go and buy food for all
these people." 14For there were about five thousand men. And he
said to his disciples, "Make them sit down in companies, about
fifty each." 15And they did so, and made them all sit down. 16And
taking the five loaves and the two fish he looked up to heaven, and

---

believed in the resurrection of the dead, as revealed by God in Sacred Scripture (cf. Ezek 37:10; Dan 12:2 and 2 Mac 7:9). It was also commonly believed by Jews at the time that Elijah or some other prophet had to appear again (cf. Deut 19:15). This may have been why Herod began to think that perhaps John had come back to life (cf. Mt 14:1–2 and Mk 6:14–16), particularly since Jesus worked miracles and people thought this power was the prerogative of those who had risen from the dead. And yet he was aware that Christ was working miracles even before John died (cf. Jn 2:23); therefore, at first, he was disconcerted. Later, as the fame of Christ's miracles spread, to have some sort of adequate explanation he decided, as the other Gospels tell us, that John must indeed have risen.

9:10–17. Jesus replies to his disciples knowing very well what he is going to do (cf. Jn 6:5–6)—thereby teaching them little by little to trust in God's omnipotence. On this miracle see the notes on Mt 14:14–21; 15:32; 15:33–38; Mk 6:34; 6:41; 6:42; 8:1–9; and Jn 6:5–9; 6:10; 6:11; 6:12–13.

9:20. "Christ" means "anointed" and is a name indicating honour and office. In the Old Law *priests* were anointed (Ex 29:7 and 40:13), as were *kings* (1 Sam 9:16), because God laid down that they should receive anointing in view of their position; there was also a custom to anoint *prophets* (1 Sam 16:13) because they were interpreters and intermediaries of God. "When Jesus Christ our Saviour came into the world, he assumed the position and obligations of the three offices of priest, king and prophet and was therefore called Christ" (St Pius V, *Catechism*, 1, 3, 7).

9:22. Jesus prophesied his passion and

blessed and broke them, and gave them to the disciples to set
before the crowd. 17And all ate and were satisfied. And they took 2 Kings 4:42–44
up what was left over, twelve baskets of broken pieces.

Peter's profession of faith

18Now it happened that as he was praying alone the disciples were Mt 16:13–20
with him; and he asked them, "Who do the people say that I am?" Mk 8:27–30
19And they answered, "John the Baptist; but others say, Elijah; and Lk 9:7
others, that one of the old prophets has risen." 20And he said to Jn 6:68–69
them, "But who do you say that I am?" And Peter answered, "The
Christ of God."

First announcement of the Passion

21But he charged and commanded them to tell this to no one, 22say- Mt 16:21–23
ing, "The Son of man must suffer many things, and be rejected by Mk 8:31–33
the elders and chief priests and scribes, and be killed, and on the Lk 9:44; 18:23–33
third day be raised."

Mt 16:24–28 Mk 8:34–39

The need for self-denial

Lk 14:27
23And he said to all, "If any man would come after me, let him Lk 17:33 Mt 10:39
deny himself and take up his cross daily and follow me. 24For Jn 12:25

---

death in order to help his disciples believe in him. It also showed that he was freely accepting these sufferings he would undergo. "Christ did not seek to be glorified: he chose to come without glory in order to undergo suffering; and you, who have been born without glory, do you wish to be glorified? The route you must take is the one Christ took. This means recognizing him and it means imitating him both in his ignominy and in his good repute; thus you will glory in the Cross, which was his path to glory. That was what Paul did, and therefore he gloried in saying, 'Far be it from me to glory except in the cross of our Lord Jesus Christ' (Gal 6:14)" (St Ambrose, *Expositio Evangelii sec. Lucam*, in loc.).

9:23. "Christ is saying this again, to us, whispering it in our ears: the cross *each day*. As St Jerome puts it: 'Not only in time of persecution or when we have the chance of martyrdom, but in all circumstances, in everything we do and think, in everything we say, let us deny what we used to be and let us confess what we now are, reborn as we have been in Christ' (*Epistola* 121, 3) [...]. Do you see? The *daily* cross. No day without a cross; not a single day in which we are not to carry the cross of the Lord, in which we are not to accept his yoke" (St Josemaría Escrivá, *Christ Is Passing By*, 58 and 176). "There is no doubt about it: a person who loves pleasure, who seeks comfort, who flies from anything that might spell suffering, who is over-anxious, who complains, who blames and who becomes impatient at the least little thing which does not go his way—a person like that is a Christian only in name; he is only a dishonour to his religion, for Jesus Christ has said so: Anyone who wishes to come after me, let him deny himself and take up his cross

whoever would save his life will lose it; and whoever loses his life
for my sake, he will save it. [25]For what does it profit a man if he
gains the whole world and loses or forfeits himself? [26]For whoever
Mt 10:33 is ashamed of me and of my words, of him will the Son of man be
ashamed when he comes in his glory and the glory of the Father
and of the holy angels. [27]But I tell you truly, there are some standing here who will not taste death before they see the kingdom of
God."

---

every day of his life, and follow me" (St John Mary Vianney, *Selected Sermons*, Ash Wednesday).

The cross should be present not only in the life of every Christian but also at the crossroads of the world: "How beautiful are those crosses on the summits of high mountains, and crowning great monuments, and on the pinnacles of cathedrals ...! But the Cross must also be inserted in the very heart of the world.

"Jesus wants to be raised on high, there in the noise of the factories and workshops, in the silence of libraries, in the loud clamour of the streets, in the stillness of the fields, in the intimacy of the family, in crowded gatherings, in stadiums.... Wherever there is a Christian striving to lead an honourable life, he should, with his love, set up the Cross of Christ, who attracts all things to himself" (St Josemaría Escrivá, *The Way of the Cross*, XI, 3).

9:25. By this radical statement Jesus teaches us to do everything with a view to eternal life: it is well worth while to devote our entire life on earth to attaining eternal life. "We have been warned that it profits man nothing if he gains the whole world and loses or forfeits himself. Far from diminishing our concern to develop this earth, the expectancy of a new earth should spur us on, for it is here that the body of a new human family grows, foreshadowing in some way the age which is to come. That is why, although we must be careful to distinguish earthly progress clearly from the increase of the Kingdom of Christ, such progress is of vital concern to the Kingdom of God, insofar as it can contribute to the better ordering of human society" (Vatican II, *Gaudium et spes*, 39).

9:26. Our Lord is well aware how weak people can be when difficult circumstances arise in which they have to confess their faith by word or deed. To overcome this weakness he has given us a special resource—the grace of the sacrament of Confirmation, which strengthens the recipient to be a "a good soldier of Christ Jesus" (2 Tim 2:3) and to be "the aroma of Christ" (2 Cor 2:15) among men, which prevents us being led astray by an environment contrary to Christian faith and morals: "Therefore, the one to be confirmed is anointed on the forehead, where shame shows itself, lest he be ashamed to confess the name of Christ and especially his cross which was, indeed, according to the apostle, a stumbling block to the Jews and to the Gentiles foolishness (cf. 1 Cor 1:23)" (Council of Florence, *Pro Armeniis*; cf. *Lumen gentium*, 11).

This duty to confess the faith applies not only to one's private or family life but also to one's public life: "Nonsectarianism. Neutrality. Old myths that always try to seem new. Have you ever stopped to think how absurd it is to leave one's Catholicism aside on entering a univer-

The Transfiguration

[28]Now about eight days after these sayings he took with him Peter Mt 17:1–9
and John and James, and went up on the mountain to pray. [29]And Mk 9:2–9
as he was praying, the appearance of his countenance was altered,
and his raiment became dazzling white. [30]And behold, two men

---

sity, a professional association, a scholarly meeting, or Parliament, like a man leaving his hat at the door?" (St Josemaría Escrivá, *The Way*, 353). See the note on Mt 10:32–33.

9:27. Christ's words in v. 27 may refer to the destruction of Jerusalem (which occurred in the year AD 70) or to his own transfiguration, which took place shortly after this prophecy. If the former, the destruction of Jerusalem would in effect be the external sign indicating the changeover from Jewish rites to Christian rites; some of those present would actually witness this change. The second explanation is based on the fact that the transfiguration is reported in the Synoptic Gospels immediately after these words, as happening about one week later; whence some Fathers' interpretation is that the statement that some would not taste death before they see the Kingdom of God refers precisely to the apostles Peter, James and John, the witnesses of the transfiguration.

9:28–36. By his transfiguration Jesus strengthens his disciples' faith, revealing a trace of the glory his body will have after the Resurrection. He wants them to realize that his passion will not be the end but rather the route he will take to reach his glorification. "For a person to go straight along the road, he must have some knowledge of the end—just as an archer will not shoot an arrow straight unless he first sees the target […]. This is particularly necessary if the road is hard and rough, the going heavy, and the end delightful" (St Thomas Aquinas, *Summa theologiae*, 3, 45, 1).

Through the miracle of the transfiguration Jesus shows one of the qualities of glorified bodies—brightness, "by which the bodies of the saints shall shine like the sun, according to the words of our Lord recorded in the Gospel of St Matthew: 'The righteous will shine like the sun in the kingdom of their Father' (Mt 13:43). To remove the possibility of doubt on the subject, he exemplifies this in his transfiguration. This quality the apostle sometimes calls glory, sometimes brightness: He 'will change our lowly body to be like his glorious body' (Phil 3:21); and again, 'It is sown in dishonour, it is raised in glory' (1 Cor 15:43). Of this glory the Israelites beheld some image in the desert, when the face of Moses, after he had enjoyed the presence and conversation of God, shone with such lustre that they could not look on it (cf. Ex 34:29; 2 Cor 3:7). This brightness is a sort of radiance reflected by the body from the supreme happiness of the soul. It is a participation in that bliss which the soul enjoys […]. This quality is not common to all in the same degree. All the bodies of the saints will be equally impassible; but the brightness of all will not be the same, for, according to the apostle, 'There is one glory of the sun, and another glory of the moon, and another glory of the stars; for star differs from star in glory. So it is with the resurrection of the dead' (1 Cor 15:41f)" (St Pius V, *Catechism*, 1, 12 13). See also the notes on Mt 17:1–13; 17:5; 17:10–13; and Mk 9:2–10; 9:7.

talked with him, Moses and Elijah, [31]who appeared in glory and
spoke of his departure, which he was to accomplish at Jerusalem.
Jn 1:14 [32]Now Peter and those who were with him were heavy with sleep
but kept awake, and they saw his glory and the two men who
stood with him. [33]And as the men were parting from him, Peter
said to Jesus, "Master, it is well that we are here; let us make three
booths, one for you and one for Moses and one for Elijah"—not
knowing what he said. [34]As he said this, a cloud came and over-
Lk 3:22 shadowed them; and they were afraid as they entered the cloud.
2 Pet 1:15–18 Ps 2:7 [35]And a voice came out of the cloud, saying, "This is my Son, my
Is 42:1 Chosen;[d] listen to him!" [36]And when the voice had spoken, Jesus
was found alone. And they kept silence and told no one in those
days anything of what they had seen.

Curing of an epileptic boy

Mt 17:14–23 Mk 9:14–32 [37]On the next day, when they had come down from the mountain,
a great crowd met him. [38]And behold, a man from the crowd
cried, "Teacher, I beg you to look upon my son, for he is my only
child; [39]and behold, a spirit seizes him and he suddenly cries out;

9:31. "And spoke of his departure": that is, his departure from this world, in other words, his death. It can also be understood as meaning our Lord's ascension.

9:35. "Listen to him!": everything God wishes to say to mankind he has said through Christ, now that the fulness of time has come (cf. Heb 1:2) "Therefore," St John of the Cross explains, "if any now should question God or desire a vision or revelation, not only would he be acting foolishly but he would be committing an offence against God, by not fixing his gaze on Christ with no desire for any new thing. For God could reply to him in this way: 'If I have spoken all things to you in my Word, which is my Son, and I have no other word, what answer can I give you now, or what can I reveal to you that is greater than this? Fix your eyes on him alone, for in him I have spoken and revealed to you all things, and in him you will find even more than what you ask for and desire […]. Hear him, for I have no more faith to reveal, nor have I any more things to declare' " (*Ascent of Mount Carmel*, book 2, chap. 22, 5).

9:39. The power of devils over men is limited to what God permits them to have. Within these limits diabolic possession can occur. Diabolic possession involves the devil exercising a certain control over the physical and mental behaviour of the possessed person, with a parallel loss of control on the person's part; a person's body becomes a kind of tool of the devil, thereby suffering the most cruel form of slavery.

When Jesus expels devils from the bodies of possessed people it shows that the Kingdom of God has come, that the devil is beginning to be dislodged from a domain which he obtained as a result of the original sin of Adam and Eve. Our Lord won complete victory over the devil

d. Other ancient authorities read *my Beloved*

it convulses him till he foams, and shatters him, and will hardly
leave him. [40]And I begged your disciples to cast it out, but they
could not." [41]Jesus answered, "O faithless and perverse generation, how long am I to be with you and bear with you? Bring your
son here." [42]While he was coming, the demon tore him and con- Lk 7:15
vulsed him. But Jesus rebuked the unclean spirit, and healed the
boy, and gave him back to his father. [43]And all were astonished at
the majesty of God.

Second announcement of the Passion

But while they were all marvelling at everything he did, he said to
his disciples, [44]"Let these words sink into your ears; for the Son of Lk 9:22; 24:26
man is to be delivered into the hands of men." [45]But they did not Lk 18:34; 24:44
understand this saying, and it was concealed from them, that they Mk 9:32
should not perceive it; and they were afraid to ask him about this
saying.

Mk 18:1–5
Mk 9:33–40

Humility and tolerance Lk 6:8

[46]And an argument arose among them as to which of them was the Mt 9:4
Mt 10:40
greatest. [47]But when Jesus perceived the thought of their hearts, he Lk 22:26

---

through his passion and death, but the forces of hell will not be finally subdued until the second coming of Christ, or Parousia, at the end of the world.

9:41. Everyone present, in one way or other, deserved this severe reproach—the disciples, for their imperfect faith in the powers he had given them (cf. Lk 9:1); the boy's father, for his lack of confidence in the disciples; the curious spectators, who were also skeptical and who included some scribes who harassed the apostles (cf. Mk 9:14) and tried to discredit the powers Jesus gave them.

"How long am I to be with you and bear with you?": "By these words Christ means: you are enjoying my company and yet you are forever accusing me and my disciples […]. He did not say this in anger; rather, he was speaking as a doctor would who is visiting a sick person who does not want to take his prescription and that is why he says: How long will I keep coming to see you, given that you are not doing what I tell you?" (St Thomas Aquinas, *Comm. on St Matthew*, 17, 17).

9:44. Christ predicts his passion and death a number of times. Initially he does so in veiled terms (Jn 2:19; Lk 5:35) to the crowd; and later, much more explicitly, to his disciples (Lk 9:22), though they fail to understand his words, not because what he says is not clear, but because they do not have the right dispositions. St John Chrysostom comments: "Let no one be scandalized by this imperfection in the apostles; for the Cross had not yet been reached nor the grace of the Spirit given" (*Hom. on St Matthew*, 65).

9:46–48. Jesus takes a child in his arms to give his apostles example and to correct their too-human ambitions, thereby teaching all of us not to make ourselves important. "Don't try to be older. A child, always a child, even when you are dying

took a child and put him by his side, [48]and said to them, "Whoever
receives this child in my name receives me, and whoever receives
me receives him who sent me; for he who is least among you all
is the one who is great."

[49]John answered, "Master, we saw a man casting out demons
in your name, and we forbade him, because he does not follow
Lk 11:23 with us." [50]But Jesus said to him, "Do not forbid him; for he that
Phil 1:18 is not against you is for you."

PART TWO

Jesus' ministry on the way to Jerusalem

6. THE JOURNEY BEGINS

Samaritans refuse to receive Jesus

Mt 19:1 [51]When the days drew near for him to be received up, he set his
Mk 10:32 face to go to Jerusalem.* [52]And he sent messengers ahead of him,

---

of old age. When a child stumbles and falls, nobody is surprised; his father promptly lifts him up. When the person who stumbles and falls is older, the immediate reaction is one of laughter. Sometimes, after this first impulse, the laughter gives way to pity. But older people have to get up by themselves.

"Your sad experience of each day is full of stumbles and falls. What would become of you if you were not continually more of a child? Don't try to be older. Be a child; and when you stumble, may your Father God pick you up" (St Josemaría Escrivá, *The Way*, 870).

9:49–50. Our Lord corrects the exclusivist and intolerant attitude of the apostles. St Paul later learned this lesson, as we can see from what he wrote during his imprisonment in Rome: "Some indeed preach Christ from envy and rivalry, but others from good will [...]. What then? Only that in every way, whether in pretence or in truth, Christ is proclaimed; and in that I rejoice" (Phil 1:15, 18). "Rejoice when you see others working in good apostolic activities. And ask God to grant them abundant grace and correspondence to that grace. Then, you, on your way. Convince yourself that it's the only way for you" (St Josemaría Escrivá, *The Way*, 965).

9:51. "When the days drew near for him to be received up": these words refer to the moment when Jesus will leave this world and ascend into heaven. Our Lord will say this more explicitly during the Last Supper: "I come from the Father and have come into the world; again, I am leaving the world and going to the

who went and entered a village of the Samaritans, to make ready Jn 4:4–9
for him; [53]but the people would not receive him, because his face
was set toward Jerusalem.* [54]And when his disciples James and
John saw it, they said, "Lord, do you want us to bid fire come
down from heaven and consume them?"[e] [55]But he turned and
rebuked them.[f] [56]And they went on to another village. Mt 18:11 Jn 3:17; 12:47

Requirements for following Jesus

[57]As they were going along the road, a man said to him, "I will Mt 8:19–22
follow you wherever you go." [58]And Jesus said to him, "Foxes
have holes, and birds of the air have nests; but the Son of man has
nowhere to lay his head." [59]To another he said, "Follow me." But

---

Father" (Jn 16:28). By making his way resolutely to Jerusalem, towards his cross, Jesus freely complies with his Father's plan for his passion and death to be the route to his resurrection and ascension.

9:52–53. The Samaritans were hostile towards the Jews. This enmity derived from the fact that the Samaritans were descendants of marriages of Jews with Gentiles who repopulated the region of Samaria at the time of the Assyrian captivity (in the eighth century before Christ). There were also religious differences: the Samaritans had mixed the religion of Moses with various superstitious practices, and did not accept the temple of Jerusalem as the only place where sacrifices could properly be offered. They built their own temple on Mount Gerizim, in opposition to Jerusalem (cf. Jn 4:20); this was why, when they realized Jesus was headed for the Holy City, they refused him hospitality.

9:54–56. Jesus corrects his disciples' desire for revenge, because it is out of keeping with the mission of the Messiah, who has come to save men, not destroy them (cf. Lk 19:10; Jn 12:47). The apostles are gradually learning that zeal for the things of God should not be bitter or violent.

"The Lord does everything in an admirable way […]. He acts in this way to teach us that perfect virtue retains no desire for vengeance, and that where there is true charity there is no room for anger—in other words, that weakness should not be treated with harshness but should be helped. Indignation should be very far from holy souls, and desire for vengeance very far from great souls" (St Ambrose, *Expositio Evangelii sec. Lucam*, in loc.).

See the RSV footnote at v. 55. These words appear in a considerable number of early Greek manuscripts and other versions and were included in the Clementine Vulgate; but they do not appear in the best and oldest Greek codexes and have not been included in the New Vulgate.

9:57–62. Our Lord spells out very clearly what is involved in following him. Being a Christian is not an easy or

e. Other ancient authorities read *as Elijah did* **f.** Other ancient authorities add *and he said, "You do not know what manner of spirit you are of; for the Son of man came not to destroy men's lives but to save them"*

he said, "Lord, let me first go and bury my father." [60]But he said
to him, "Leave the dead to bury their own dead; but as for you, go
and proclaim the kingdom of God." [61]Another said, "I will follow
you, Lord; but let me first say farewell to those at my home."
Gen 19:17 [62]Jesus said to him, "No one who puts his hand to the plough and
looks back is fit for the kingdom of God."

Mt 10:7–16
Mk 6:7–11
Ex 24:1
Mt 9:37–38
Jn 4:35

The mission of the seventy disciples

10 [1]After this the Lord appointed seventy[g] others, and sent
them on ahead of him, two by two, into every town and

---

comfortable affair: it calls for self-denial and for putting God before everything else. See the notes on Mt 8:18–22 and Mt 8:22.

We see here the case of the man who wanted to follow Christ, but on one condition—that he be allowed to say goodbye to his family. Our Lord, seeing that he is rather undecided, gives him an answer which applies to all of us, for we have all received a calling to follow him and we have to try not to receive this grace in vain. "We receive the grace of God in vain, when we receive it at the gate of our heart, and do not let it enter our heart. We receive it without receiving it, that is, we receive it without fruit, since there is no advantage in feeling the inspiration if we do not accept it […]. It sometimes happens that being inspired to do much we consent not to the whole inspiration but only to some part of it, as did those good people in the Gospel, who upon the inspiration which our Lord gave them to follow him wished to make reservations, the one to go first and bury his father, the other to go to take leave of his people" (St Francis de Sales, *Treatise on the Love of God*, book 2, chap. 11).

Our loyalty and fidelity to the mission God has given us should equip us to deal with every obstacle we meet: "There is never reason to look back (cf. Lk 9:62). The Lord is at our side. We have to be faithful and loyal; we have to face up to our obligations and we will find in Jesus the love and the stimulus we need to understand other people's faults and overcome our own" (St Josemaría Escrivá, *Christ Is Passing By*, 160).

10:1–12. Those who followed our Lord and received a calling from him (cf. Lk 9:57–62) included many other disciples in addition to the Twelve (cf. Mk 2:15). We do not know who most of them were; but undoubtedly some of them were with him all along, from when Jesus was baptized by John up to the time of his ascension—for example, Joseph called Barsabbas, and Matthias (cf. Acts 1:21–26). We can also include Cleopas and his companion, to whom the risen Christ appeared on the road to Emmaus (cf. Lk 24:13–35).

From among these disciples, our Lord chooses seventy for a special assignment. Of them, as of the apostles (cf. Lk 9:1–5), he demands total detachment and complete abandonment to divine providence.

From Baptism onwards every Christian is called by Christ to perform a mission. Therefore, the Church, in our Lord's name, "makes to all the laity an earnest appeal in the Lord to give a will-

g. Other ancient authorities read *seventy-two*

place where he himself was about to come. 2And he said to them,
"The harvest is plentiful, but the labourers are few; pray therefore
the Lord of the harvest to send out labourers into his harvest. 3Go
your way; behold, I send you out as lambs in the midst of wolves.
4Carry no purse, no bag, no sandals; and salute no one on the Lk 9:3–5

---

ing, noble and enthusiastic response to the voice of Christ, who at this hour is summoning them more pressingly, and to the urging of the Holy Spirit. The younger generation should feel this call to be addressed in a special way to themselves; they should welcome it eagerly and generously. It is the Lord himself, by this Council, who is once more inviting all the laity to unite themselves to him ever more intimately, to consider his interests as their own (cf. Phil 2:5), and to join in his mission as Saviour. It is the Lord who is again sending them into every town and every place where he himself is to come (cf. Lk 10:1). He sends them on the Church's apostolate, an apostolate that is one yet has different forms and methods, an apostolate that must all the time be adapting itself to the needs of the moment; he sends them on an apostolate where they are to show themselves his cooperators, doing their full share continually in the work of the Lord, knowing that in the Lord their labour cannot be lost (cf. 1 Cor 15:58)" (Vatican II, *Apostolicam actuositatem*, 33).

10:3–4. Christ wants to instil apostolic daring into his disciples; this is why he says, "I send you out", which leads St John Chrysostom to comment: "This suffices to give us encouragement, to give us confidence and to ensure that we are not afraid of our assailants" (*Hom. on St Matthew*, 33). The apostles' and disciples' boldness stemmed from their firm conviction that they were on a God-given mission: they acted, as Peter the apostle confidently explained to the Sanhedrin, in the name of Jesus Christ of Nazareth, "for there is no other name under heaven ... by which we must be saved" (Acts 4:12).

"And the Lord goes on," St Gregory the Great adds, "'Carry no purse, no bag, no sandals; and salute no one on the road.' Such should be the confidence the preacher places in God that even if he is not provided with the necessities of life, he is convinced that they will come his way. This will ensure that worry about providing temporal things for himself does not distract him from providing others with eternal things" (*In Evangelia homiliae*, 17). Apostolate calls for generous self-surrender which leads to detachment; therefore, Peter, following our Lord's commandment, when the beggar at the Beautiful Gate asked him for alms (Acts 3:2–3), said, "I have no silver or gold" (ibid., 3:6), "not so as to glory in his poverty", St Ambrose points out, "but to obey the Lord's command. It is as if he were saying, 'You see in me a disciple of Christ, and you ask me for gold? He gave us something much more valuable than gold, the power to act in his name. I do not have what Christ did not give me, but I do have what he did give me: In the name of Jesus Christ, arise and walk' (cf. Acts 3:6)" (*Expositio Evangelii sec. Lucam*, in loc.). Apostolate, therefore, demands detachment from material things and it also requires us to be always available, for there is an urgency about apostolic work.

"And salute no one on the road": "How can it be", St Ambrose asks himself, "that the Lord wishes to get rid of a

road. 5Whatever house you enter, first say, 'Peace be to this
1 Pet 4:14 house!' 6And if a son of peace is there, your peace shall rest upon
1 Cor 9:5–14 him; but if not, it shall return to you. 7And remain in the same
1 Tim 5:18 house, eating and drinking what they provide, for the labourer
deserves his wages; do not go from house to house. 8Whenever
you enter a town and they receive you, eat what is set before you;
Lk 9:2–5 9heal the sick in it and say to them, 'The kingdom of God has
come near to you.' 10But whenever you enter a town and they do
not receive you, go into its streets and say, 11'Even the dust of
Acts 13:51; 18:6 your town that clings to our feet, we wipe off against you; nevertheless know this, that the kingdom of God has come near.' 12I tell
you, it shall be more tolerable on that day for Sodom than for that
town.

Jesus reproaches cities for their unbelief

Mt 11:12–23 13"Woe to you, Chorazin! woe to you, Bethsaida! for if the mighty
Jn 3:6 works done in you had been done in Tyre and Sidon, they would

---

custom so full of kindness? Notice, however, that he does not just say, 'Do not salute anyone', but adds, 'on the road.' And there is a reason for this.

"He also commanded Elisha not to salute anyone he met, when he sent him to lay his staff on the body of the dead child (2 Kings 4:29): he gave him this order so as to get him to do this task without delay and effect the raising of the child, and not waste time by stopping to talk to any passer-by he met. Therefore, there is no question of omitting the good manners to greet others; it is a matter of removing a possible obstacle in the way of service; when God commands, human considerations should be set aside, at least for the time being. To greet a person is a good thing, but it is better to carry out a divine instruction which could easily be frustrated by a delay" (ibid.).

10:6. Everyone is "a son of peace" who is disposed to accept the teaching of the Gospel which brings with it God's peace. Our Lord's recommendation to his disciples to proclaim peace should be a constant feature of all the apostolic action of Christians: "Christian apostolate is not a political programme or a cultural alternative. It implies the spreading of good, 'infecting' others with a desire to love, sowing peace and joy" (St Josemaría Escrivá, *Christ Is Passing By*, 124).

Feeling peace in our soul and in our surroundings is an unmistakeable sign that God is with us, and a fruit of the Holy Spirit (cf. Gal 5:22): "Get rid of those scruples that deprive you of peace. What robs you of your peace of soul cannot come from God. When God comes to you, you will realize the truth of those greetings: My peace I give to you … , My peace I leave you … , My peace be with you … , and this peace you will feel even in the midst of tribulation" (St Josemaría Escrivá, *The Way*, 258).

10:7. Our Lord clearly considered poverty and detachment a key feature in an apostle (vv. 3–4). But he was aware of his disciples' material needs and therefore stated the principle that apostolic ministry deserves its recompense. Vatican Council

have repented long ago, sitting in sackcloth and ashes. 14 But it
shall be more tolerable in the judgment for Tyre and Sidon than
for you. 15 And you, Capernaum, will you be exalted to heaven? Is 14:13–15
You shall be brought down to Hades.
16 "He who hears you hears me, and he who rejects you rejects Mt 10:40
me, and he who rejects me rejects him who sent me." Jn 5:23; 12:48; 15:23

The seventy return from their mission

17 The seventy[g] returned with joy, saying, "Lord, even the demons
are subject to us in your name!" 18 And he said to them, "I saw Jn 12:31
Satan fall like lightning from heaven.* 19 Behold, I have given you Rev 12:8–9
authority to tread upon serpents and scorpions, and over all the Mk 16:18 Ps 91:13
power of the enemy; and nothing shall hurt you. 20 Nevertheless do Ex 32:32
not rejoice in this, that the spirits are subject to you; but rejoice Mt 7:22
that your names are written in heaven."

II reminds us that we all have an obligation to contribute to the sustenance of those who generously devote themselves to the service of the Church: "Completely devoted as they are to the service of God in the fulfilment of the office entrusted to them, priests are entitled to receive a just remuneration. For 'the labourer deserves his wages' (Lk 10:7), and 'the Lord commanded that they who proclaim the gospel should get their living by the gospel' (1 Cor 9:14). For this reason, insofar as provision is not made from some other source for the just remuneration of priests, the faithful are bound by a real obligation of seeing to it that the necessary provision for a decent and fitting livelihood for the priests is available" (*Presbyterorum ordinis*, 20).

10:16. On the evening of the day of his resurrection, our Lord entrusts his apostles with the mission he received from the Father, endowing them with powers similar to his own (Jn 20:21). Some days later he will confer on Peter the primacy he had already promised him (Jn 21:15–17). The Pope is the successor of Peter, and the bishops the successors of the apostles (cf. *Lumen gentium*, 20). Therefore, "Bishops who teach in communion with the Roman Pontiff are to be revered by all as witnesses of divine and Catholic truth [...]. This loyal submission of the will and intellect must be given, in a special way, to the authentic teaching authority of the Roman Pontiff, even when he does not speak *ex cathedra*" (Vatican II, *Lumen gentium*, 25).

10:20. Our Lord corrects his disciples, making them see that the right reason for rejoicing lies in hope of reaching heaven, not in the power to do miracles which he gave them for their mission. As he said on another occasion, "On that day many will say to me, 'Lord, Lord, did we not prophesy in your name, and cast out demons in your name, and do many mighty works in your name?' And then will I declare to them, 'I never knew you; depart from me, you evildoers' " (Mt 7:22–23). In other words, in the eyes of God doing his holy will at all times is more important than working miracles.

g. Other ancient authorities read *seventy-two*

Jesus gives thanks

Mt 11:25–27 [21]In that same hour he rejoiced in the Holy Spirit and said, "I
thank thee, Father, Lord of heaven and earth, that thou hast hidden
these things from the wise and understanding and revealed them
to babes; yea, Father, for such was thy gracious will.[h] [22]All things
have been delivered to me by my Father; and no one knows who
the Son is except the Father, or who the Father is except the Son
and any one to whom the Son chooses to reveal him."

Mt 13:16–17 [23]Then turning to the disciples he said privately, "Blessed are
1 Pet 1:10 the eyes which see what you see! [24]For I tell you that many
prophets and kings desired to see what you see, and did not see it,
and to hear what you hear, and did not hear it."

10:21. This passage of the Gospel is usually called our Lord's "hymn of joy" and is also to be found in St Matthew (11:25–27). It is one of those moments when Jesus rejoices to see humble people understanding and accepting the word of God.

Our Lord also reveals one of the effects of humility—spiritual childhood. For example, in another passage he says: "Truly, I say to you, unless you turn and become like children, you will never enter the kingdom of heaven" (Mt 18:3). But spiritual childhood does not involve weakness, softness or ignorance: "I have often meditated on this life of spiritual childhood, which is not incompatible with fortitude, because it demands a strong will, proven maturity, an open and firm character [...]. To become children we must renounce our pride and self-sufficiency, recognizing that we can do nothing by ourselves. We must realize that we need grace, and the help of God our Father to find our way and keep to it. To be little, you have to abandon yourself as children do, believe as children believe, beg as children beg" (St Josemaría Escrivá, *Christ Is Passing By*, 10 and 143).

10:22. "This statement is a wonderful help to our faith," St Ambrose comments, "because when you read 'all' you realize that Christ is all-powerful, that he is not inferior to the Father, or less perfect than he; when you read 'have been delivered to me', you confess that Christ is the Son, to whom everything belongs by right of being one in substance [with the Father] and not by grace of gift" (*Expositio Evangelii sec. Lucam*, in loc.).

Here we see Christ as almighty Lord and God, consubstantial with the Father, and the only one capable of revealing who the Father is. At the same time, we can recognize the divine nature of Jesus only if the Father gives us the grace of faith—as he did to St Peter (cf. Mt 16:17).

10:23–24. Obviously, seeing Jesus with one's own eyes was a wonderful thing for people who believed in him. However, our Lord will say to Thomas, "Blessed are those who have not seen and yet believe" (Jn 20:29). St Peter, for his part, tells us: "Without having seen him you love him; though you do not see him you believe in him and rejoice with unutterable and exalted joy. As the outcome of your faith you obtain the salvation of your souls" (1 Pet 1:8–9).

h. Or *so it was well-pleasing before thee*

7. FURTHER PREACHING

Parable of the good Samaritan

25And behold, a lawyer stood up to put him to the test, saying, Mt 22:35–40
"Teacher, what shall I do to inherit eternal life?" 26He said to him, Mk 12:28–34 Lk 18:18–20
"What is written in the law? How do you read?" 27And he Deut 6:5
answered, "You shall love the Lord your God with all your heart, Lev 19:18
and with all your soul, and with all your strength, and with all
your mind: and your neighbour as yourself." 28And he said to him, Lev 18:5
"You have answered right; do this, and you will live." Mt 19:17

10:25–28. Our Lord's teaching is that the way to attain eternal life is through faithful fulfilment of the Law of God. The Ten Commandments, which God gave Moses on Mount Sinai (Ex 20:1–17), express the natural law in a clear and concrete way. It is part of Christian teaching that the natural law exists, that it is a participation by rational creatures in the Eternal Law and that it is impressed on the conscience of every man when he is created by God (cf. Leo XIII, *Libertas praestantissimum*). Obviously, therefore, the natural law, expressed in the Ten Commandments, cannot change or become outdated, for it is not dependent on man's will or on changing circumstances.

In this passage Jesus praises and accepts the summary of the Law given by the Jewish scribe. This reply, taken from Deuteronomy (6:4ff), was a prayer which the Jews used to say frequently. Our Lord gives the very same reply when he is asked which is the principal commandment of the Law and concludes his answer by saying, "On these two commandments depend all the law and the prophets" (Mt 22:40; cf. also Rom 13:8–9; Gal 5:14).

There is a hierarchy and order in these two commandments constituting the double precept of charity: before everything and above everything comes loving God in himself; in the second place, and as a consequence of the first commandment, comes loving one's neighbour, for God explicitly requires us to do so (1 Jn 4:21; cf. the notes on Mt 22:34–40 and 22:37–38).

This passage of the Gospel also includes another basic doctrine: the Law of God is not something negative—"Do not do this"—but something completely positive—love. Holiness, to which all baptized people are called, does not consist in not sinning, but in loving, in doing positive things, in bearing fruit in the form of love of God. When our Lord describes for us the Last Judgment he stresses this positive aspect of the Law of God (Mt 25:31–46). The reward of eternal life will be given to those who do good.

10:27. "Yes, our only occupation here on earth is that of loving God—that is, to start doing what we will be doing for all eternity. Why must we love God? Well, because our happiness consists in love of God; it can consist in nothing else. So, if we do not love God, we will always be unhappy; and if we wish to enjoy any consolation and relief in our pains, we will attain it only by recourse to love of God. If you want to be convinced of this, go and find the happiest man according to the world; if he does not love God, you

[29]But he, desiring to justify himself, said to Jesus, "And who is
my neighbour?" [30]Jesus replied, "A man was going down from
Jerusalem to Jericho, and he fell among robbers, who stripped
him and beat him, and departed, leaving him half dead. [31]Now by
chance a priest was going down that road; and when he saw him
he passed by on the other side. [32]So likewise a Levite, when he
came to the place and saw him, passed by on the other side. [33]But
a Samaritan, as he journeyed, came to where he was; and when he
Is 1:6 saw him, he had compassion, [34]and went to him and bound up his
wounds, pouring on oil and wine; then he set him on his own
beast and brought him to an inn, and took care of him. [35]And the

---

will find that in fact he is an unhappy man. And, on the contrary, if you discover the man most unhappy in the eyes of the world, you will see that because he loves God he is happy in every way. Oh my God!, open the eyes of our souls, and we will seek our happiness where we truly can find it" (St John Mary Vianney, *Selected Sermons*, Twenty-second Sunday after Pentecost).

10:29–37. In this moving parable, which only St Luke gives us, our Lord explains very graphically who our neighbour is and how we should show charity towards him, even if he is our enemy.

Following other Fathers, St Augustine (*De verbis Domini sermones*, 37) identifies the good Samaritan with our Lord, and the waylaid man with Adam, the source and symbol of all fallen mankind. Moved by compassion, he comes down to earth to cure man's wounds, making them his own (Is 53:4; Mt 8:17; 1 Pet 2:24; 1 Jn 3:5). In fact, we often see Jesus being moved by man's suffering (cf. Mt 9:36; Mk 1:41; Lk 7:13). And St John says: "In this the love of God was made manifest among us, that God sent his only Son into the world, so that we might live through him. In this is love, not that we loved God but that he loved us and sent his Son to be the expiation for our sins. Beloved, if God so loved us, we also ought to love one another" (1 Jn 4:9–11).

This parable leaves no doubt about who our neighbour is—anyone (without distinction of race or relationship) who needs our help; nor about how we should love him—by taking pity on him, being compassionate towards his spiritual and corporal needs; and it is not just a matter of having the right feelings towards him: we must do something, we must generously serve him.

Christians, who are disciples of Christ, should share his love and compassion, never distancing themselves from others' needs. One way to express love for one's neighbour is to perform the "works of mercy", which get their name from the fact that they are not duties in justice. There are fourteen such works, seven spiritual and seven corporal. The spiritual are: To convert the sinner; To instruct the ignorant; To counsel the doubtful; To comfort the sorrowful; To bear wrongs patiently; To forgive injuries; To pray for the living and the dead. The corporal works are: To feed the hungry; To give drink to the thirsty; To clothe the naked; To shelter the homeless; To visit the sick; To visit the imprisoned; To bury the dead.

10:31–32. Very probably one reason why our Lord used this parable was to

next day he took out two denarii[i] and gave them to the inn-keeper,
saying, 'Take care of him; and whatever more you spend, I will
repay you when I come back.' 36Which of these three, do you
think, proved neighbour to the man who fell among the robbers?"
37He said, "The one who showed mercy on him." And Jesus said
to him, "Go and do likewise."

Martha and Mary welcome our Lord

38Now as they went on their way, he entered a village; and a Jn 11:1;
woman named Martha received him into her house. 39And she had 12:2–3
a sister called Mary, who sat at the Lord's feet and listened to his

correct one of the excesses of false piety common among his contemporaries. According to the Law of Moses, contact with dead bodies involved legal impurity, from which one was cleansed by various ablutions (cf. Num 19:11–22; Lev 21:1–4, 11–12). These regulations were not meant to prevent people from helping the injured; they were designed for reasons of hygiene and respect for the dead. The aberration of the priest and the Levite in this parable consisted in this: they did not know for sure whether the man who had been assaulted was dead or not, and they preferred to apply a wrong interpretation of a secondary, ritualistic precept of the Law rather than obey the more important commandment of loving one's neighbour and giving him whatever help one can.

10:38–42. Our Lord was heading for Jerusalem (Lk 9:51) and his journey took him through Bethany, the village where Lazarus, Martha and Mary lived—a family for whom he had a special affection, as we see in other passages of the Gospel (cf. Jn 11:1–45; 12:1–9).

St Augustine comments on this scene as follows: "Martha, who was arranging and preparing the Lord's meal, was busy doing many things, whereas Mary preferred to find her meal in what the Lord was saying. In a way she deserted her sister, who was very busy, and sat herself down at Jesus' feet and just listened to his words. She was faithfully obeying what the Psalm said: 'Be still, and know that I am God' (Ps 46:10).

"Martha was getting annoyed, Mary was feasting; the former coping with many things, the latter concentrating on one. Both occupations were good" (*Sermon*, 103). Martha has come to be, as it were, the symbol of the active life, and Mary that of the contemplative life. However, for most Christians, called as they are to sanctify themselves in the middle of the world, action and contemplation cannot be regarded as two opposite ways of practising the Christian faith: an active life forgetful of union with God is useless and barren; but an apparent life of prayer which shows no concern for apostolate and the sanctification of ordinary things also fails to please God. The key lies in being able to combine these two lives, without either harming the other. Close union between action and contemplation can be achieved in very different ways, depending on the specific vocation each person is given by God.

Far from being an obstacle, work should be a means and an occasion for a

i. The denarius was a day's wage for a labourer

teaching. 40But Martha was distracted with much serving; and she
1 Cor 7:35 went to him and said, "Lord, do you not care that my sister has
left me to serve alone? Tell her then to help me." 41But the Lord
answered her, "Martha, Martha, you are anxious and troubled
about many things; 42one thing is needful.[j] Mary has chosen the
Mt 6:33 good portion, which shall not be taken away from her."

---

close relationship with our Lord, which is the most important thing in our life.

Following this teaching of our Lord, the ordinary Christian should strive to attain an integrated life—an intense life of piety and external activity, orientated towards God, practised out of love for him and with an upright intention, which expresses itself in apostolate, in everyday work, in doing the duties of one's state in life. "You must understand now more clearly that God is calling you to serve him *in and from* the ordinary, material and secular activities of human life. He waits for us every day, in the laboratory, in the operating room, in the army barracks, in the university chair, in the factory, in the workshop, in the fields, in the home and in all the immense panorama of work. Understand this well: there is something holy, something divine, hidden in the most ordinary situations, and it is up to each one of you to discover it [...]. There is no other way. Either we learn to find our Lord in ordinary, everyday life, or else we shall never find him. That is why I can tell you that our age needs to give back to matter and to the most trivial occurrences and situations their noble and original meaning. It needs to restore them to the service of the Kingdom of God, to spiritualize them, turning them into a means and an occasion for a continuous meeting with Jesus Christ" (St Josemaría Escrivá, *Conversations*, 114).

10:1–4. St Luke gives us a shorter form of the Lord's Prayer, or Our Father, than St Matthew (6:9–13). In Matthew there are seven petitions, in Luke only four. Moreover, St Matthew's version is given in the context of the Sermon on the Mount and specifically as part of Jesus' teaching on how to pray; St Luke's is set in one of those occasions just after our Lord has been at prayer—two different contexts. There is nothing surprising about our Lord teaching the same thing on different occasions, not always using exactly the same words, not always at the same length, but always stressing the same basic points. Naturally, the Church uses the longer form of the Lord's Prayer, that of St Matthew.

"When the disciples asked the Lord Jesus, 'Teach us to pray,' he replied by saying the words of the Our Father, thereby giving a concrete model which is also a universal model. In fact, everything that can and must be said to the Father is contained in those seven requests which we all know by heart. There is such a simplicity in them that even a child can learn them, but at the same time such a depth that a whole life can be spent meditating on their meaning. Isn't that so? Does not each of those petitions deal with something essential to our life, directing it totally towards God the Father? Doesn't this prayer speak to us about 'our daily bread', 'forgiveness of our sins, since we forgive others' and about protecting us from 'temptation' and 'delivering us from evil'?" (John Paul II, General Audience, 14 March 1979).

j. Other ancient authorities read *few things are meaningful, or only one*

The Our Father

11 [1]He was praying in a certain place, and when he ceased, one of his disciples said to him, "Lord, teach us to pray, as John taught his disciples." [2]And he said to them, "When you pray, say:

Lk 5:33; 6:12; 9:29
Mt 6:9–13

The first thing our Lord teaches us to ask for is the glorification of God and the coming of his Kingdom. That is what is really important—the Kingdom of God and his justice (cf. Mt 6:33). Our Lord also wants us to pray confidently that our Father will look after our material needs, for "your heavenly Father knows that you need them all" (Mt 6:32). However, the Our Father makes us aspire especially to possess the goods of the Holy Spirit, and invites us to seek forgiveness (and to forgive others) and to avoid the danger of sinning. Finally, the Our Father emphasizes the importance of vocal prayer. "'*Domine, doce nos orare*. Lord, teach us to pray!' And our Lord answered: 'When you pray, say: *Pater noster, qui es in coelis* … Our Father, who art in heaven …'. How can we fail to appreciate the value of vocal prayer!" (St Josemaría Escrivá, *The Way*, 84).

11:1. Jesus often went away to pray (cf. Lk 6:12; 22:39ff). This practice of the Master's causes his disciples to want to learn how to pray. Jesus teaches them to do what he himself does. Thus, when our Lord prays, he begins with the word "Father!": "Father, into thy hands I commit my spirit" (Lk 23:46; see also Mt 11:25; 26:42, 53; Lk 23:34; Jn 11:41; etc.). His prayer on the cross, "My God, my God, …" (Mt 27:46), is not really an exception to this rule, because there he is quoting Psalm 22, the desperate prayer of the persecuted just man.

Therefore, we can say that the first characteristic prayer should have is the simplicity of a son speaking to his Father, "You wrote to me: 'To pray is to talk with God. But about what?' About what? About Him, about yourself: joys, sorrows, successes and failures, noble ambitions, daily worries, even your weaknesses! And acts of thanksgiving and petition—and love and reparation. In short, to get to know him and to get to know yourself: 'to get acquainted!'" (St Josemaría Escrivá, *The Way*, 91).

11:2. "Hallowed be thy name": in this first petition of the Our Father "we pray that God may be known, loved, honoured and served by everyone and by ourselves in particular." This means that we want "unbelievers to come to a knowledge of the true God, heretics to recognize their errors, schismatics to return to the unity of the Church, sinners to be converted and the righteous to persevere in doing good." By this first petition, our Lord is teaching us that "we must desire God's glory more than our own interest and advantage". This hallowing of God's name is attained "by prayer and good example and by directing all our thoughts, affections and actions towards him" (St Pius X, *Catechism*, 290–293).

"Thy kingdom come": "By the Kingdom of God we understand a triple spiritual kingdom—the Kingdom of God in us, which is grace; the Kingdom of God on earth, which is the Catholic Church; and the Kingdom of God in heaven, which is eternal bliss […]. As regards grace, we pray that God reign in us with his sanctifying grace, by which he is pleased to dwell in us as a king in his throne-room, and that he keep us united to him by the virtues of faith, hope and charity, by which he reigns in our

"Father, hallowed be thy name. Thy kingdom come. [3]Give us
each day our daily bread;[k] [4]and forgive us our sins, for we ourselves forgive every one who is indebted to us; and lead us not
into temptation."

Effective prayer

[5]And he said to them, "Which of you who has a friend will go to
him at midnight and say to him, 'Friend, lend me three loaves; [6]for
a friend of mine has arrived on a journey, and I have nothing to set
Lk 18:5 before him'; [7]and he will answer from within, 'Do not bother me;
the door is now shut, and my children are with me in bed; I cannot

---

intellect, in our heart and in our will […]. As regards the Church, we pray that it extend and spread all over the world for the salvation of men […]. As regards heaven, we pray that one day we be admitted to that eternal bliss for which we have been created, where we will be totally happy" (ibid., 294–297).

11:3. The Tradition of the Church usually interprets the "bread" as not only material bread, since "man shall not live by bread alone, but by every word that proceeds from the mouth of God" (Mt 4:4; Deut 8:3). Here Jesus wants us to ask God for "what we need each day for soul and body […]. For our soul we ask God to sustain our spiritual life, that is, we beg him to give us his grace, of which we are continually in need […]. The life of our soul is sustained mainly by the divine word and by the Blessed Sacrament of the Altar […]. For our bodies we pray for what is needed to maintain us" (*St Pius X Catechism*, 302–305).

Christian doctrine stresses two ideas in this petition of the Our Father: the first is trust in divine providence, which frees us from excessive desire to accumulate possessions to insure us against the future (cf. Lk 12:16–21); the other idea is that we should take a brotherly interest in other people's needs, thereby moderating our selfish tendencies.

11:4. "So rigorously does God exact from us forgetfulness of injuries and mutual affection and love, that he rejects and despises the gifts and sacrifices of those who are not reconciled to one another" (*St Pius V Catechism*, 4, 14, 16).

"This, sisters, is something which we should consider carefully; it is such a serious and important matter that God should pardon us our sins, which have merited eternal fire, that we must pardon all trifling things which have been done to us. As I have so few, Lord, even of these triflings things, to offer thee, thy pardoning of me must be a free gift: there is abundant scope here for thy mercy. Blessed be thou, who endurest one that is so poor" (St Teresa of Avila, *Way of Perfection*, chap. 36).

"And leads us not into temptation": it is not a sin to *feel* temptation but to *consent* to temptation. It is also a sin to put oneself voluntarily into a situation which can easily lead one to sin. God allows us to be tempted, in order to test our fidelity, to exercise us in virtue and to increase our merits with the help of grace. In this petition we ask the Lord to give us his grace not to be overcome when put to the

k. Or *our bread for the morrow*

get up and give you anything'? [8]I tell you, though he will not get
up and give him anything because he is his friend, yet because of
his importunity he will rise and give him whatever he needs. [9]And
I tell you, Ask, and it will be given you; seek, and you will find; Mt 7:7–11
knock, and it will be opened to you. [10]For every one who asks
receives, and he who seeks finds, and to him who knocks it will be
opened. [11]What father among you, if his son asks for[l] a fish, will
instead of a fish give him a serpent; [12]or if he asks for an egg, will
give him a scorpion? [13]If you then, who are evil, know how to give
good gifts to your children, how much more will the heavenly
Father give the Holy Spirit to those who ask him!"

---

test, or to free us from temptation if we cannot cope with it.

11:5–10. One of the essential features of prayer is trusting perseverance. By this simple example and others like it (cf. Lk 18:1–8) our Lord encourages us not to desist in asking God to hear us. "Persevere in prayer. Persevere even when your efforts seem sterile. Prayer is always fruitful" (St J. Escrivá, *The Way*, 101).

11:9–10. "Do you see the effectiveness of prayer when it is done properly? Are you not convinced like me that, if we do not obtain what we ask God for, it is because we are not praying with faith, with a heart pure enough, with enough confidence, or that we are not persevering in prayer the way we should? God has never refused, nor will ever refuse, anything to those who ask for his graces in the way they should. Prayer is the great recourse available to us to get out of sin, to persevere in grace, to move God's heart and to draw upon us all kinds of blessings from heaven, whether for the souls or to meet our temporal needs" (St John Mary Vianney, *Selected Sermons*, Fifth Sunday after Easter).

11:11–13. Our Lord uses the example of human parenthood as a comparison to stress again the wonderful fact that God is our Father, for God's fatherhood is the source of parenthood in heaven and on earth (cf. Eph 3:15). "The God of our faith is not a distant being who contemplates indifferently the fate of men—their desires, their struggles, their sufferings. He is a Father who loves his children so much that he sends the Word, the Second Person of the most Blessed Trinity, so that by taking on the nature of man he may die to redeem us. He is the loving Father who now leads us gently to himself, through the action of the Holy Spirit who dwells in our hearts" (St Josemaría Escrivá, *Christ Is Passing By*, 84).

11:13. The Holy Spirit is God's best gift to us, the great promise Christ gives his disciples (cf. Jn 5:26), the divine fire which descends on the apostles at Pentecost, filling them with fortitude and freedom to proclaim Christ's message (cf. Acts 2). "The profound reality which we see in the texts of holy Scripture is not a remembrance from the past, from some golden age of the Church which has since been buried in history. Despite the weaknesses and the sins of every one of us, it is the reality of today's Church and the Church of all time. 'I will pray

l. Other ancient authorities insert *bread, will give him a stone; or if he asks for*

The Kingdom of God and the kingdom of Satan

Mt 12:22–30, 43–45 [14]Now he was casting out a demon that was dumb; when the
Mk 3:22–27 demon had gone out, the dumb man spoke, and the people marvelled. [15]But some of them said, "He casts out demons by
Mt 16:1 Beelzebul, the prince of demons"; [16]while others, to test him,
Mk 8:11 sought from him a sign from heaven. [17]But he, knowing their
thoughts, said to them, "Every kingdom divided against itself is
laid waste, and house falls upon house. [18]And if Satan also is
divided against himself, how will his kingdom stand? For you say
that I cast out demons by Beelzebul. [19]And if I cast out demons by
Beelzebul, by whom do your sons cast them out? Therefore they
shall be your judges. [20]But if it is by the finger of God that I cast
out demons, then the kingdom of God has come upon you.
[21]When a strong man, fully armed, guards his own palace, his
Col 2:15 goods are in peace; [22]but when one stronger than he assails him
Jn 12:31; 16:33 and overcomes him, he takes away his armour in which he trusted,

---

to the Father,' our Lord told his disciples, 'and he will give you another Counsellor, to be with you for ever' (Jn 14:16). Jesus has kept his promise. He has risen from the dead and, in union with the eternal Father, he sends us the Holy Spirit to sanctify us and to give us life" (St Josemaría Escrivá, *Christ Is Passing By*, 128).

11:14–23. Jesus' enemies remain obstinate despite the evidence of the miracle. Since they cannot deny that he has done something quite extraordinary, they attribute it to the power of the devil, rather than admit that Jesus is the Messiah. Our Lord answers them with a clinching argument: the fact that he expels demons is proof that he has brought the Kingdom of God. The Second Vatican Council reminds us of this truth: "The Lord Jesus inaugurated his Church by preaching the Good News, that is, the coming of the Kingdom of God, promised over the ages of the Scriptures [...]. The miracles of Jesus also demonstrate that the Kingdom has already come on earth: 'If it is by the finger of God that I cast out demons, then the Kingdom of God has come upon you' (Lk 11:20; cf. Mt 12:28). But principally the Kingdom is revealed in the person of Christ himself, Son of God and Son of man, who came 'to serve and to give his life as a ransom for many' (Mk 10:45)" (*Lumen gentium*, 5).

The strong man well armed is the devil (v. 21), who has enslaved man; but Jesus Christ, one stronger than he, has come and has conquered him and is despoiling him. St Paul will say that Christ "disarmed the principalities and powers and made a public example of them, triumphing over them" (Col 2:15).

After the victory of Christ, the "stronger one", the words of v. 23 are addressed to mankind at large; even if people do not want to recognize it, Jesus Christ has conquered and from now on no one can adopt an attitude of neutrality towards him: he who is not with him is against him.

11:18. Christ's argument is very clear. One of the worst evils that can overtake

and divides his spoil. 23He who is not with me is against me, and
he who does not gather with me scatters.
24"When the unclean spirit has gone out of a man, he passes Mt 12:43ff
through waterless places seeking rest; and finding none he says, 'I
will return to my house from which I came.' 25And when he
comes he finds it swept and put in order. 26Then he goes and Jn 5:14
brings seven other spirits more evil than himself, and they enter
and dwell there; and the last state of that man becomes worse than
the first."

Responding to the word of God

27As he said this, a woman in the crowd raised her voice and said Mt 12:46–50
to him, "Blessed is the womb that bore you, and the breasts that
you sucked!" 28But he said, "Blessed rather are those who hear the
word of God and keep it!"

---

the Church is disunity among Christians, disunity among believers. We must make Jesus' prayer our own: "That they may be one; even as thou, Father, art in me, and I in thee, that they also may be one in us, so that the world may believe that thou hast sent me" (Jn 17:21).

11:24–26. Our Lord shows us that the devil is relentless in his struggle against man; despite man rejecting him with the help of grace, he still lays his traps, still tries to overpower him. Knowing all this, St Peter advises us to be sober and vigilant, because "your adversary the devil prowls around like a roaring lion, seeking some one to devour. Resist him, firm in your faith" (1 Pet 5:8–9).

Jesus also forewarns us about the danger of being once more defeated by Satan—which would leave us worse off than we were before. The Latin proverb puts it very well: "*corruptio optimi, pessima*" (the corruption of the best is the worst of all). And St Peter, in his inspired text, inveighs against corrupt Christians, whom he compares in a graphic and frightening way to the dog turning back to his own vomit and the sow being washed and then wallowing in the mire (cf. 2 Pet 2:22).

11:27–28. These words proclaim and praise the Blessed Virgin's basic attitude of soul. As the Second Vatican Council explains: "In the course of her Son's preaching she [Mary] received the words whereby, in extolling a Kingdom beyond the concerns and ties of flesh and blood, he declared blessed those who heard and kept the word of God (cf. Mk 3:35; Lk 11:27–28) as she was faithfully doing (cf. Lk 2:19, 51)" (*Lumen gentium*, 58). Therefore, by replying in this way Jesus is not rejecting the warm praise this good lady renders his Mother; he accepts it and goes further, explaining that Mary is blessed particularly because she has been good and faithful in putting the word of God into practice. "It was a compliment to his Mother on her *fiat*, her 'be it done' (Lk 1:38). She lived it sincerely, unstintingly, fulfilling its every consequence, but never amid fanfare, rather in the hidden and silent sacrifice of each day" (St Josemaría Escrivá, *Christ Is Passing By*, 172). See the note on Luke 1:34–38.

The sign of Jonah

Mt 12:38–42 1 Cor 1:22
29When the crowds were increasing, he began to say, "This generation is an evil generation; it seeks a sign, but no sign shall be
given to it except the sign of Jonah. 30For as Jonah became a sign
to the men of Nineveh, so will the Son of man be to this genera-
1 Kings 10:1ff tion. 31The queen of the South will arise at the judgment with the
men of this generation and condemn them; for she came from the
ends of the earth to hear the wisdom of Solomon, and behold,
Jn 3:5 something greater than Solomon is here. 32The men of Nineveh
will arise at the judgment with this generation and condemn it; for
they repented at the preaching of Jonah, and behold, something
greater than Jonah is here.

The lamp of the body, the light of the soul

Mt 5:15 33"No one after lighting a lamp puts it in a cellar or under a
bushel, but on a stand, that those who enter may see the light.
Mt 6:22–23 34Your eye is the lamp of your body; when your eye is sound, your
whole body is full of light; but when it is not sound, your body is
full of darkness. 35Therefore be careful lest the light in you be

---

11:29–32. Jonah was the prophet who led the Ninevites to do penance: his actions and preaching they saw as signifying that God had sent him (cf. the note on Mt 12:41–42).

11:33–36. Jesus is using metaphors: a person who has good sight can see things well; similarly, a person whose outlook is pure and uncomplicated is in a position to appreciate the things of God.

Those who opposed our Lord saw the things he did and heard what he said, but their viewpoint was distorted and they did not want to recognize God in him. Here we have also a reproach which applies to anyone who is unwilling to accept the Gospel.

11:39–52. In this passage (one of the most severe in the Gospel) Jesus determinedly unmasks the vice which was largely responsible for official Judaism's rejection of his teaching—hypocrisy cloaked in legalism. There are many people who, under the guise of doing good, keeping the mere letter of the law, fail to keep its spirit; they close themselves to the love of God and neighbour; they harden their hearts and, though apparently very upright, turn others away from fervent pursuit of God—making virtue distasteful. Jesus' criticism is vehement because they are worse than open enemies: against open enemies one can defend oneself, but these are enemies it is almost impossible to deal with. The scribes and Pharisees were blocking the way of those who wanted to follow Jesus: they were the most formidable obstacle to the Gospel. Our Lord's invective against the scribes and Pharisees is reported even more fully in chapter 23 of St Matthew. See the note on Mt 23:1–39.

11:40–41. It is not easy to work out what these verses mean. Probably our Lord is using the idea of cleaning the inside and outside of dishes to teach that a person's heart is much more important

darkness. [36]If then your whole body is full of light, having no part
dark, it will be wholly bright, as when a lamp with its rays gives
you light."

Jesus reproaches scribes and Pharisees

[37]While he was speaking, a Pharisee asked him to dine with him; Lk 7:36; 14:1
so he went in and sat at table. [38]The Pharisee was astonished to Mt 15:2
see that he did not first wash before dinner. [39]And the Lord said to Mt 23:1–36
him, "Now you Pharisees cleanse the outside of the cup and of the
dish, but inside you are full of extortion and wickedness. [40]You
fools! Did not he who made the outside make the inside also?
[41]But give for alms those things which are within; and behold,
everything is clean for you.

[42]"But woe to you Pharisees! for you tithe mint and rue and
every herb, and neglect justice and the love of God; these you
ought to have done, without neglecting the others. [43]Woe to you Lk 20:46
Pharisees! for you love the best seat in the synagogues and salutations in the market places. [44]Woe to you! for you are like graves
which are not seen, and men walk over them without knowing it."

---

than what appears on the surface—whereas the Pharisees got it the wrong way round, as so many people tend to do. Jesus is warning us not to be so concerned about "the outside" but rather to give importance to "the inside". Applying this to the case of alms: we have to be generous with those things we are inclined to hoard; in other words, it is not enough just to give a little money (that could be a purely formal, external gesture); love is what we have to give others—love and understanding, refinement, respect for their freedom, deep concern for their spiritual and material welfare; this is something we cannot do unless our interior dispositions are right.

In an address to young people, Pope John Paul II explains what almsgiving really means: "The Greek word for alms, *eleemosyne*, comes from *éleos*, meaning compassion and mercy. Various circumstances have combined to change this meaning so that almsgiving is often regarded as a cold act, with no love in it. But almsgiving in the proper sense means realizing the needs of others and letting them share in one's own goods. Who would say that there will not always be others who need help, especially spiritual help, support, consolation, fraternity, love? The world is always very poor, as far as love is concerned" (28 March 1979).

11:42. The Law of Moses laid down that the harvest had to be tithed (cf. Lev 27:30–33; Deut 14:22ff; etc.) to provide for the worship offered in the temple. Insignificant products were not subject to this Law.

Rue is a bitter medicinal plant used by the Jews in ancient times. Did it have to be tithed?: the Pharisees, who were so nit-picking, said that it did.

11:44. According to the Old Law, anyone who touched a grave became unclean for seven days (Num 19:16), but with the passage of time a grave could

[45]One of the lawyers answered him, "Teacher, in saying this
you reproach us also." [46]And he said, "Woe to you lawyers also!
for you load men with burdens hard to bear, and you yourselves
do not touch the burdens with one of your fingers. [47]Woe to you!
for you build the tombs of the prophets whom your fathers killed.
[48]So you are witnesses and consent to the deed of your fathers; for
they killed them, and you build their tombs. [49]Therefore also the
Wisdom of God said, 'I will send them prophets and apostles,
some of whom they will kill and persecute,' [50]that the blood of all
the prophets, shed from the foundation of the world, may be
Gen 4:8 required of this generation, [51]from the blood of Abel to the blood
2 Chron 24:20 of Zechariah, who perished between the altar and the sanctuary.
Yes, I tell you, it shall be required of this generation. [52]Woe to you
lawyers! for you have taken away the key of knowledge; you did
not enter yourselves, and you hindered those who were entering."
[53]As he went away from there, the scribes and the Pharisees
began to press him hard, and to provoke him to speak of many
Lk 20:20 things, [54]lying in wait for him, to catch at something he might say.

---

become so overgrown that a person could walk on it without noticing. Our Lord uses this comparison to unmask the hypocrisy of the people he is talking to: they are very exact about very small details but they forget their basic duty—justice and the love of God (v. 42). On the outside they are clean but their hearts are full of malice and rottenness (v. 39); they pretend to be just, appearances are all that matters to them; they know that virtue is held in high regard, therefore they strive to appear highly virtuous (v. 43). Duplicity and deceit mark their lives.

11:51. Zechariah was a prophet who died by being stoned in the temple of Jerusalem around the year 800 BC because he accused the people of Israel of being unfaithful to God's law (cf. 2 Chron 24:20–22). The murder of Abel (Gen 4:8) and that of Zechariah were, respectively, the first and last murders reported in these books which the Jews regarded as Scripture. Jesus refers to a Jewish tradition which, in his own time and even later, pointed out the stain of the blood of Zechariah.

The altar referred to here was the altar of holocausts, located outside, in the courtyard of the priests, in front of the temple proper.

11:52. Jesus severely reproaches these doctors of the Law who, given their study and meditation on Scripture, were the very ones who should have recognized Jesus as the Messiah, since his coming had been foretold in the sacred books. However, as we learn from the Gospel, the exact opposite happened. Not only did they not accept Jesus: they obstinately opposed him. As teachers of the Law they should have taught the people to follow Jesus; instead, they blocked the way.

11:53–54. St Luke frequently records this attitude of our Lord's enemies (cf. 6:11; 19:47–48; 20:19–20; 22:2). The people followed Jesus and were enthusiastic

8. ANNOUNCEMENT OF THE END

Various teachings

12 [1]In the meantime, when so many thousands of the multi- Mt 16:6
tude had gathered together that they trod upon one another, Mk 8:15
he began to say to his disciples first, "Beware of the leaven of the
Pharisees, which is hypocrisy. [2]Nothing is covered up that will not Mt 10:26–27
be revealed, or hidden that will not be known. [3]Whatever you have Lk 8:17
said in the dark shall be heard in the light, and what you have
whispered in private rooms shall be proclaimed upon the housetops.

[4]"I tell you, my friends, do not fear those who kill the body, Mt 10:28–31
and after that have no more that they can do. [5]But I will warn you
whom to fear: fear him who, after he has killed, has power to cast
into hell;[m] yes, I tell you, fear him! [6]Are not five sparrows sold for
two pennies? And not one of them is forgotten before God. [7]Why, Lk 21:18
even the hairs of your head are all numbered. Fear not; you are of
more value than many sparrows.

[8]"And I tell you, every one who acknowledges me before men,
the Son of man also will acknowledge before the angels of God;

---

about his preaching and miracles, whereas the Pharisees and scribes would not accept him and would not allow the people to follow him; they tried in every way to discredit him in the eyes of the people (cf. Jn 11:48).

12:3. Most Palestinian houses had a roof in the form of a terrace. There people would meet to chat and while away the time in the hottest part of the day. Jesus points out to his disciples that just as in these get-togethers things said in private became matters of discussion, so too, despite the Pharisees' and scribes' efforts to hide their vices and defects under the veil of hypocrisy, they would become a matter of common knowledge.

12:6–7. Nothing—not even the most insignificant thing—escapes God, his providence and the judgment he will mete out. For this same reason no one should fear that any suffering or persecution he experiences in following Christ will remain unrewarded in eternity.

The teaching about fear, contained in v. 5, is filled out in vv. 6 and 7, where Jesus tells us that God is a good Father who watches over every one of us—much more than he does over these little ones (whom he also remembers). Therefore, our fear of God should not be servile (based on fear of punishment); it should be a filial fear (the fear of someone who does not want to displease his father), a fear nourished by trust in divine providence.

12:8–9. This follows logically from Christ's previous teaching: worse than physical evils, worse even than death, are evils of the soul, that is, sin. Those who out of fear of temporal suffering deny our

m. Greek *Gehenna*

Lk 9:26 Mt 12:32 Mk 3:28–29 9but he who denies me before men will be denied before the
angels of God. 10And every one who speaks a word against the
Son of man will be forgiven; but he who blasphemes against the
Lk 21:12–15 Holy Spirit will not be forgiven. 11And when they bring you
Mt 10:19–20 before the synagogues and the rulers and the authorities, do not be
anxious how or what you are to answer or what you are to say;
12for the Holy Spirit will teach you in that very hour what you
ought to say."

Parable of the rich fool

13One of the multitude said to him, "Teacher, bid my brother
divide the inheritance with me." 14But he said to him, "Man, who
1 Tim 6:9–10 made me a judge or divider over you?" 15And he said to them,
"Take heed, and beware of all covetousness; for a man's life does
not consist in the abundance of his possessions." 16And he told
them a parable, saying, "The land of a rich man brought forth
plentifully; 17and he thought to himself, 'What shall I do, for I

Lord and are unfaithful to the demands of the faith will fall into a greater evil still: they will be denied by Christ himself on the Day of Judgment; whereas those who are penalized in this life because of their faithfulness to Christ will receive the eternal reward of being recognized by him and will come to share his glory.

12:10. Blasphemy against the Holy Spirit consists in maliciously attributing to the devil actions that have God as their origin. A person who does that prevents God's pardon from reaching him: that is why he cannot obtain forgiveness (cf. Mt 12:31; Mk 3:28–30). Jesus understands and excuses the weakness of a person who makes a moral mistake, but he is not similarly indulgent to someone who shuts his eyes and his heart to the wonderful things the Spirit does; that was the way these Pharisees acted who accused Jesus of casting out demons in the name of Beelzebul; it is the way unbelieving people act who refuse to see in Christ's work a sign of the goodness of God, who reject the invitation God offers them and who thereby put themselves outside the reach of salvation (cf. Heb 6:4–6; 10:26–31). See the note on Mk 3:28–30.

12:13–14. This man is only interested in his own problems; he sees in Jesus only a teacher with authority and prestige who can help sort out his case (cf. Deut 21:17). He is a good example of those who approach religious authorities not to seek advice on the way they should go in their spiritual life, but rather to get them to solve their material problems. Jesus vigorously rejects the man's request—not because he is insensitive to the injustice which may have been committed in this family, but because it is not part of his redemptive mission to intervene in matters of this kind. By his word and example the Master shows us that his work of salvation is not aimed at solving the many social and family problems that arise in human society; he has come to give us the principles and moral standards which should inspire our actions in temporal affairs, but not to give us precise, technical solutions to problems

have nowhere to store my crops?' [18]And he said, 'I will do this: I
will pull down my barns, and build larger ones; and there I will
store all my grain and my goods. [19]And I will say to my soul,
Soul, you have ample goods laid up for many years; take your
ease, eat, drink, be merry.' [20]But God said to him, 'Fool! This
night your soul is required of you; and the things you have prepared, whose will they be?' [21]So is he who lays up treasure for
himself, and is not rich toward God."

Trust in God's fatherly providence

[22]And he said to his disciples, "Therefore I tell you, do not be anxious about your life, what you shall eat, nor about your body, what
you shall put on. [23]For life is more than food, and the body more
than clothing. [24]Consider the ravens: they neither sow nor reap, Ps 147:9
they have neither storehouse nor barn, and yet God feeds them. Of
how much more value are you than the birds! [25]And which of you
by being anxious can add a cubit to his span of life?[n] [26]If then you

---

which arise; to that end he has endowed us with intelligence and freedom.

12:15–21. After his statement in v. 15, Jesus tells the parable of the foolish rich man: what folly it is to put our trust in amassing material goods to ensure we have a comfortable life on earth, forgetting the goods of the spirit, which are what really ensure us—through God's mercy—of eternal life.

This is how St Athanasius explained these words of our Lord: "A person who lives as if he were to die every day—given that our life is uncertain by definition—will not sin, for good fear extinguishes most of the disorder of our appetites; whereas he who thinks he has a long life ahead of him will easily let himself be dominated by pleasures" (*Adversus Antigonum*).

12:19. This man's stupidity consisted in making material possession his only aim in life and his only insurance policy. It is lawful for a person to want to own what he needs for living, but if possession of material resources becomes an absolute, it spells the ultimate destruction of the individual and of society. "Increased possession is not the ultimate goal of nations nor of individuals. All growth is ambivalent. It is essential if man is to develop as a man, but in a way it imprisons man if he considers it the supreme good, and it restricts his vision. Then we see hearts harden and minds close, and men no longer gather together in friendship but out of self-interest, which soon leads to strife and disunity. The exclusive pursuit of possessions thus becomes an obstacle to individual fulfilment and to man's true greatness. Both for nations and for individuals, avarice is the most evident form of moral underdevelopment" (Paul VI, *Populorum progressio*, 19).

12:25. See the note on Mt 6:27. A "cubit", a measurement of length, was approximately half a metre or half a yard.

n. Or *to his stature*

are not able to do as small a thing as that, why are you anxious
about the rest? 27Consider the lilies, how they grow; they neither
toil nor spin;[o] yet I tell you, even Solomon in all his glory was not
arrayed like one of these. 28But if God so clothes the grass which
is alive in the field today and tomorrow is thrown into the oven,
how much more will he clothe you, O men of little faith! 29And do
not seek what you are to eat and what you are to drink, nor be of
anxious mind. 30For all the nations of the world seek these things;
and your Father knows that you need them. 31Instead, seek his[p]
kingdom, and these things shall be yours as well.

Lk 22:29 32"Fear not, little flock, for it is your Father's good pleasure to
Is 41:14 give you the kingdom. 33Sell your possessions, and give alms; pro-
Mt 6:20–21 vide yourselves with purses that do not grow old, with a treasure
Lk 16:9; 18:22 in the heavens that does not fail, where no thief approaches and no
moth destroys. 34For where your treasure is, there will your heart
be also.

12:27–28. In the history of the people of Israel, it was under King Solomon, who succeeded the great King David on the throne, that the nation reached its high point of cultural and material prosperity: in Jewish tradition, therefore, Solomon was the prototype of earthly power and splendour (cf. Mt 12:42). Jesus stresses here that divine providence looks after all those who accept his call: a person in the grace of God is far more beautiful than the lily, far more splendid than Solomon himself.

12:29–31. Our Lord here sums up his teaching on trust and abandonment to divine providence, contrasting the right attitude (seeking the Kingdom above all else) and the wrong one (seeking only temporal goods). Jesus does not condemn reasonable concern to acquire the necessities of life, but he teaches that one's efforts in this direction should be ordered towards one's last end, the possession of the Kingdom. Therefore he says that earthly things will be given us as an added extra, "not as a good on which you should fix your attention", St Augustine explains, "but as a means of enabling you to reach the true and highest good" (*De Serm. Domini in monte*, 2, 24).

The material instinct to preserve one's life is something divine providence has built into man's make-up. But this instinct should be channelled through well-organized effort and should not take the form of anxious concern which would cause one to forget the most important thing of all—inverting the Christian hierarchy of values by putting material concerns ahead of spiritual welfare.

12:33–34. Our Lord concludes this address by insisting on those imperishable goods to which we should aspire. In this connexion the Second Vatican Council concludes its teaching on the universal call to holiness saying: "Therefore all the faithful are invited and obliged to holiness and the perfection of their own state of life. Accordingly let all of them see that they direct their affections rightly, lest they be hindered in their pursuit of perfect love by

o. Other ancient authorities read *Consider the lilies; they neither spin nor weave* **p.** Other ancient authorities read *God's*

The need for vigilance; the parable of the steward Mt 24:42–51

[35]"Let your loins be girded and your lamps burning, [36]and be like Ex 12:11 1 Pet 1:13
men who are waiting for their master to come home from the mar- Mt 25:1–13
riage feast, so that they may open to him at once when he comes
and knocks. [37]Blessed are those servants whom the master finds Jn 13:4ff
awake when he comes; truly, I say to you, he will gird himself and
have them sit at table, and he will come and serve them. [38]If he
comes in the second watch, or in the third, and finds them so,
blessed are those servants! [39]But know this, that if the householder 1 Thess 5:2
had known at what hour the thief was coming, he would have
been awake and[q] would not have left his house to be broken into.
[40]You also must be ready; for the Son of man is coming at an hour
you do not expect."

---

the use of worldly things and by an adherence to riches which is contrary to the spirit of evangelical poverty, following the apostle's advice: Let those who use this world not fix their abode in it, for the form of this world is passing away (cf. 1 Cor 7:31)" (*Lumen gentium*, 42).

"When Holy Scripture refers to the heart, it does not refer to some fleeting sentiments of joy or tears. By heart it means the person who directs his whole being, soul and body, to what he considers his good, as Jesus himself indicated: 'For where your treasure is, there will your heart be also' (Mt 6:21)" (St J. Escrivá, *Christ Is Passing By*, 164). Our Lord's teaching is quite clear: man's heart yearns to possess wealth, a good social position, prestigious public or professional appointments, which he sees as providing him with security, contentment and self-affirmation; however, this kind of treasure involves endless worry and disappointment, because there is always a danger of losing it. Jesus does not mean that man should forget about earthly things, but he does teach us that no created thing should become our "treasure", our main aim in life: that should be God, our Creator and Lord, whom we should love and serve as we go about our ordinary affairs, putting our hopes on the eternal joy of heaven. See also the note on Mt 6:19–21.

12:35–39. In the preaching of Christ and of the apostles we are frequently exhorted to be watchful (cf. Mt 24:42; 25:13; Mk 14:34)—for one thing, because the enemy is always on the prowl (cf. 1 Pet 5:8), and also because a person in love is always awake (cf. Song 5:2). This watchfulness expresses itself in a spirit of prayer (cf. Lk 21:36; 1 Pet 4:7) and fortitude in faith (cf. 1 Cor 16:13). See the note on Mt 25:1–13.

12:35. To enable them to do certain kinds of work the Jews used to hitch up the flowing garments they normally wore. "Girding your loins" immediately suggests a person getting ready for work, for effort, for a journey etc. (cf. Jer 1:17; Eph 6:14; 1 Pet 1:13). And "having your lamps burning" indicates the sort of attitude a person should have who is on the watch or is waiting for someone's arrival.

12:40. God has chosen to hide from us the time of our death and the time when the world will come to an end. Immediately

q. Other ancient authorities omit *would have been awake and*

[41]Peter said, "Lord, are you telling this parable for us or for
1 Pet 4:10 all?" [42]And the Lord said, "Who then is the faithful and wise steward, whom his master will set over his household, to give them
their portion of food at the proper time? [43]Blessed is that servant
whom his master when he comes will find so doing. [44]Truly I tell
Mt 25:21 you, he will set him over all his possessions. [45]But if that servant
says to himself, 'My master is delayed in coming,' and begins to
beat the menservants and the maidservants, and to eat and drink
and get drunk, [46]the master of that servant will come on a day
when he does not expect him and at an hour he does not know,
and will punish[r] him, and put him with the unfaithful. [47]And that
Jas 4:17 servant who knew his master's will, but did not make ready or act
according to his will, shall receive a severe beating. [48]But he who
did not know, and did what deserved a beating, shall receive a
light beating. Every one to whom much is given, of him will
much be required; and of him to whom men commit much they
will demand the more.

---

after death everyone undergoes the particular judgment: "just as it is appointed for men to die once, and after that comes judgment ..." (Heb 9:27). The end of the world is when the general judgment will take place.

12:41–48. After our Lord's exhortation to vigilance, St Peter asks a question (v. 41), the answer to which is the key to understanding this parable. On the one hand, Jesus emphasizes that we simply do not know exactly when God is going to ask us to render an account of our life; on the other—answering Peter's question—our Lord explains that his teaching is addressed to every individual. God will ask everyone to render an account of his doings: everyone has a mission to fulfil in this life and he has to account for it before the judgment seat of God and be judged on what he has produced, be it much or little.

"Since we know neither the day nor the hour, we should follow the advice of the Lord and watch constantly so that, when the single course of our earthly life is completed (cf. Heb 9:27), we may merit to enter with him into the marriage feast and be numbered among the blessed (cf. Mt 25:31–46) and not, like the wicked and slothful servants (cf. Mt 25:26), be ordered to depart into the eternal fire (cf. Mt 25:41)" (Vatican II, *Lumen gentium*, 48).

12:49–50. In the Bible, fire is often used to describe God's burning love for men (cf. Deut 4:24; Ex 13:21–22; etc.). This love finds its highest expression in the Son of God become man: "God so loved the world that he gave his only Son" (Jn 3:16). Jesus voluntarily gave up his life out of love for us, and "greater love has no man than this, that a man lay down his life for his friends" (Jn 15:13).

In these words reported by St Luke, Jesus Christ reveals his abounding desire to give his life for love of us. He calls his death a baptism, because from it he will

r. Or *cut him to pieces*

Jesus brings division, not peace
49“I came to cast fire upon the earth; and would that it were
already kindled! 50I have a baptism to be baptized with; and how Jn 12:27
I am constrained until it is accomplished! 51Do you think that I Mt 10:34–36
have come to give peace on earth? No, I tell you, but rather division; 52for henceforth in one house there will be five divided, three
against two and two against three; 53they will be divided, father Mic 7:6
against son and son against father, mother against daughter and
daughter against her mother, mother-in-law against daughter-in-
law and daughter-in-law against her mother-in-law.”

The signs of the times
54He also said to the multitudes, “When you see a cloud rising in Mt 16:2–3
the west, you say at once, ‘A shower is coming’; and so it happens. 55And when you see the south wind blowing, you say,
‘There will be scorching heat’; and it happens. 56You hypocrites!

---

arise victorious never to die again. Our Baptism is a submersion in Christ’s death, in which we die to sin and are reborn to the new life of grace: “we were buried therefore with him by baptism into death, so that as Christ was raised from the dead by the glory of the Father, we too might walk in newness of life” (Rom 6:4).

Through this new life, we Christians should become set on fire in the same way as Jesus set his disciples on fire: “With the amazing naturalness of the things of God, the contemplative soul is filled with apostolic zeal. ‘My heart became hot within me, a fire blazed forth from my thoughts’ (Ps 39:3). What could this fire be if not the fire that Christ talks about: ‘I came to cast fire upon the earth, and would that it were already kindled?’ (Lk 12:49). An apostolic fire that acquires its strength in prayer: there is no better way than this to carry on, throughout the whole world, the battle of peace to which every Christian is called to fill up what is lacking in the sufferings of Christ (cf. Col 1:24)” (St Josemaría Escrivá, *Christ Is Passing By*, 120).

12:51–53. God has come into the world with a message of peace (cf. Lk 2:14) and reconciliation (cf. Rom 5:11). By resisting, through sin, the redeeming work of Christ, we become his opponents. Injustice and error lead to division and war. “Insofar as men are sinners, the threat of war hangs over them and will so continue until the coming of Christ; but insofar as they can vanquish sin by coming together in charity, violence itself will be vanquished” (Vatican II, *Gaudium et spes*, 78).

During his own life on earth, Christ was a sign of contradiction (cf. Lk 2:34). Our Lord is forewarning his disciples about the contention and division which will accompany the spread of the Gospel (cf. Lk 6:20–23; Mt 10:24).

12:56. Jesus’ listeners knew from experience how to forecast the weather. However, although they knew the signs of the Messiah’s coming announced by the prophets, and were hearing his preaching and witnessing his miracles, they did not want to draw the logical conclusion; they

You know how to interpret the appearance of earth and sky; but
why do you not know how to interpret the present time?
[57]"And why do you not judge for yourselves what is right?
Mt 5:25–26 [58]As you go with your accuser before the magistrate, make an
effort to settle with him on the way, lest he drag you to the judge,
and the judge hand you over to the officer, and the officer put you
in prison. [59]I tell you, you will never get out till you have paid the
very last copper."

The need for repentance

13 [1]There were some present at that very time who told him
of the Galileans whose blood Pilate had mingled with their
Jn 9:2 sacrifices. [2]And he answered them, "Do you think that these
Galileans were worse sinners than all the other Galileans, because
Ps 7:12 they suffered thus? [3]I tell you, No; but unless you repent you will
all likewise perish. [4]Or those eighteen upon whom the tower in
Siloam fell and killed them, do you think that they were worse
offenders than all the others who dwelt in Jerusalem? [5]I tell you,
No; but unless you repent you will all likewise perish."

---

lacked the necessary good will and upright intention, and they just closed their eyes to the light of the Gospel (cf. Rom 1:18ff).

This attitude is also found to be very widespread in our own time, in the form of certain kinds of atheism denounced by the Second Vatican Council: "Those who wilfully try to drive God from their heart and to avoid all questions about religion, not following the biddings of their conscience, are not free from blame" (*Gaudium et spes*, 19).

13:1–5. Our Lord used current events in his teaching. The Galileans referred to here may be the same as mentioned in the Acts of the Apostles (5:37). The episode was fairly typical of the times Jesus lived in, with Pilate sternly suppressing any sign of civil unrest. We do not know anything about the accident at Siloam other than what the Gospel tells us.

The fact that these people died in this way does not mean that they were worse than others, for God does not always punish sinners in this life (cf. Jn 9:3). All of us are sinners, meriting a much worse punishment than temporal misfortune: we merit eternal punishment; but Christ has come to atone for our sins, he has opened the gates of heaven. We must repent of our sins; otherwise God will not free us from the punishment we deserve. "When you meet with suffering, the cross, your thought should be: what is this compared with what I deserve?" (St Josemaría Escrivá, *The Way*, 690).

13:3. "He tells us that, without Holy Baptism, no one will enter the Kingdom of heaven (cf. Jn 3:5); and, elsewhere, that if we do not repent we will all perish (Lk 13:3). This is all easily understood. Ever since man sinned, all his senses rebel against reason; therefore, if we want the flesh to be controlled by the spirit and by reason, it must be mortified; if we do not want the body to be at war with the soul, it and all our senses need

Parable of the barren fig tree

[6]And he told this parable: "A man had a fig tree planted in his Lk 3:9
vineyard; and he came seeking fruit on it and found none. [7]And he Mt 21:19 Mk 11:13
said to the vinedresser, 'Lo, these three years I have come seeking
fruit on this fig tree, and I find none. Cut it down; why should it
use up the ground?' [8]And he answered him, 'Let it alone, sir, this 2 Pet 3:9, 15
year also, till I dig about it and put on manure. [9]And if it bears
fruit next year, well and good; but if not, you can cut it down.'"

Jesus cures a woman on the sabbath

[10]Now he was teaching in one of the synagogues on the sabbath.
[11]And there was a woman who had had a spirit of infirmity for
eighteen years; she was bent over and could not fully straighten
herself. [12]And when Jesus saw her, he called her and said to her,
"Woman, you are freed from your infirmity." [13]And he laid his Mt 9:18
hands upon her, and immediately she was made straight, and she Mk 7:32
praised God. [14]But the ruler of the synagogue, indignant because Ex 20:9
Jesus had healed on the sabbath, said to the people, "There are six Deut 5:13
days on which work ought to be done; come on those days and be

---

to be chastened; if we desire to go to God, the soul with all its faculties needs to be mortified" (St John Mary Vianney, *Selected Sermons*, Ash Wednesday).

13:6–9. Our Lord stresses that we need to produce plenty of fruit (cf. Lk 8:11–15) in keeping with the graces we have received (cf. Lk 12:48). But he also tells us that God waits patiently for this fruit to appear; he does not want the death of the sinner; he wants him to be converted and to live (Ezek 33:11) and, as St Peter teaches, he is "forbearing towards you, not wishing that any should perish, but that all should reach repentance" (2 Pet 3:9). But God's clemency should not lead us to neglect our duties and become lazy and comfort-seeking, living sterile lives. He is merciful, but he is also just and he will punish failure to respond to his grace.

"There is one case that we should be especially sorry about—that of Christians who could do more and don't; Christians who could live all the consequences of their vocation as children of God, but refuse to do so through lack of generosity. We are partly to blame, for the grace of faith has not been given us to hide but to share with others (cf. Mt 5:15f). We cannot forget that the happiness of these people, in this life and in the next, is at stake. The Christian life is a divine wonder with immediate promises of satisfaction and serenity—but on condition that we know how to recognize the gift of God (cf. Jn 4:10) and be generous, not counting the cost" (St Josemaría Escrivá, *Christ Is Passing By*, 147).

13:10–17. As was the custom, our Lord used go to the synagogue on the sabbath. Noticing this poor woman, he uses his power and mercy to cure her. The ordinary people are delighted, but the ruler of the synagogue, apparently zealous about fulfilling the Law (cf. Ex 20:8; 31:14; Lev 19:3–30), publicly upbraids our Lord. Jesus energetically censures this

healed, and not on the sabbath day." [15]Then the Lord answered
Lk 14:5 him, "You hypocrites! Does not each of you on the sabbath untie
his ox or his ass from the manger, and lead it away to water it?
Lk 19:9 [16]And ought not this woman, a daughter of Abraham whom Satan
bound for eighteen years, be loosed from this bond on the sabbath
day?" [17]As he said this, all his adversaries were put to shame; and
all the people rejoiced at all the glorious things that were done by
him.

Parables of the mustard seed and of the leaven

Mt 13:31–33 [18]He said therefore, "What is the kingdom of God like? And to
Mk 4:30–32 what shall I compare it? [19]It is like a grain of mustard seed which
a man took and sowed in his garden; and it grew and became a
tree, and the birds of the air made nests in its branches."
Ezek 17:23; [20]And again he said, "To what shall I compare the kingdom of
31:6 God? [21]It is like leaven which a woman took and hid in three measures of meal, till it was all leavened."

---

warped interpretation of the Law and stresses the need for mercy and understanding, which is what pleases God (cf. Hos 6:6; Jas 2:13).

13:18–21. The grain of mustard and the leaven symbolize the Church, which starts off as a little group of disciples and steadily spreads with the aid of the Holy Spirit until it reaches the ends of the earth. As early as the second century Tertullian claimed: "We are but of yesterday and yet we are everywhere" (*Apologeticum*, 37).

Our Lord "with the parable of the mustard seed encourages them to have faith and shows them that the Gospel preaching will spread in spite of everything. The Lord's disciples were the weakest of men, but nevertheless, because of the great power that was in them, the Gospel has been spread to every part of the world" (St John Chrysostom, *Hom. on St Matthew*, 46). Therefore, a Christian should not be discouraged if his apostolic action seems very limited and insignificant. With God's grace and his own faithfulness it will keep growing like the mustard seed, in spite of difficulties: "In the moments of struggle and tribulation, when perhaps 'the good' fill your way with obstacles, lift up your apostolic heart: listen to Jesus as he speaks of the grain of mustard seed and of the leaven. And say to him: '*Edissere nobis parabolam*—explain the parable to me.' And you will feel the joy of contemplating the victory to come: the birds of the air under the shelter of your apostolate, now only in its beginnings, and the whole of the meal leavened" (St Josemaría Escrivá, *The Way*, 695).

13:23–24. Everyone is called to form part of the Kingdom of God, for he "desires all men to be saved" (1 Tim 2:4). "Those who, through no fault of their own, do not know the Gospel of Christ or his Church, but who nevertheless seek God with a sincere heart and, moved by grace, try in their actions to do his will as they know it through the dictates of their conscience: those too may achieve eternal salvation. Nor shall divine providence

The narrow gate

22 He went on his way through towns and villages, teaching, and
journeying toward Jerusalem. 23 And some one said to him, "Lord,
will those who are saved be few?" And he said to them, 24 "Strive Mt 7:13–14
to enter by the narrow door; for many, I tell you, will seek to enter 1 Tim 6:12
and will not be able. 25 When once the householder has risen up and
shut the door, you will begin to stand outside and to knock at the Mt 25:11–12
door, saying, 'Lord, open to us.' He will answer you, 'I do not
know where you come from.' 26 Then you will begin to say, 'We ate Mt 7:22–23
and drank in your presence, and you taught in our streets.' 27 But he Ps 6:8
will say, 'I tell you, I do not know where you come from; depart
from me, all you workers of iniquity!' 28 There you will weep and Mt 8:11–12
gnash your teeth, when you see Abraham and Isaac and Jacob and
all the prophets in the kingdom of God and you yourselves thrust
out. 29 And men will come from east and west, and from north and Is 49:12; 59:19
south, and sit at table in the kingdom of God. 30 And behold, some Ps 106:3
are last who will be first, and some are first who will be last." Mt 19:30

---

deny the assistance necessary for salvation to those who, without any fault of theirs, have not yet arrived at an explicit knowledge of God, and who, not without grace, strive to lead a good life. Whatever good or truth is found among them is considered by the Church to be a preparation for the Gospel and given by him who enlightens all men that they may at length have life" (Vatican II, *Lumen gentium*, 16).

Certainly, only those who make a serious effort can reach the goal of salvation (cf. Lk 16:16; Mt 11:12). Our Lord tells us so by using the simile of the narrow gate. "A Christian's struggle must be unceasing, for interior life consists in beginning and beginning again. This prevents us from proudly thinking that we are perfect already. It is inevitable that we should meet difficulties on our way. If we did not come up against obstacles, we would not be creatures of flesh and blood. We will always have passions which pull us downwards; we will always have to defend ourselves against more or less self-defeating urges" (St J. Escrivá, *Christ Is Passing By*, 75).

13:25–28. As at other times, Jesus describes eternal life by using the example of a banquet (cf., e.g., Lk 12:35ff; 14:15ff). Knowing the Lord and listening to his preaching is not enough for getting to heaven; what God judges is how we respond to the grace he gives us: "Not every one who says to me, 'Lord, Lord,' shall enter the kingdom of heaven, but he who does the will of my Father who is in heaven" (Mt 7:21).

13:29–30. Generally speaking, the Jewish people regarded themselves as the sole beneficiaries of the messianic promises made by the prophets; but Jesus proclaims that salvation is open to everyone. The only condition he lays down is that men freely respond to God's merciful call. When Christ died on the cross the veil of the temple was torn in two (Lk 23:45 and par.), a sign of the end of the distinction between Jews and Gentiles. St Paul teaches: "For he [Christ] is our peace, who has made us both one, and

Jesus' reply to Herod

[31]At that very hour some Pharisees came, and said to him, "Get
away from here, for Herod wants to kill you." [32]And he said to
them, "Go and tell that fox, 'Behold, I cast out demons and perform cures today and tomorrow, and the third day I finish my
course. [33]Nevertheless I must go on my way today and tomorrow
and the day following; for it cannot be that a prophet should
perish away from Jerusalem.'

Jerusalem admonished

Mt 23:27–39 [34]"O Jerusalem, Jerusalem, killing the prophets and stoning those
who are sent to you! How often would I have gathered your children together as a hen gathers her brood under her wings, and you
Jer 22:5 Ps 118:26 would not! [35]Behold, your house is forsaken. And I tell you, you
will not see me until you say, 'Blessed is he who comes in the
name of the Lord.'"

Jesus cures a dropsical man on the sabbath

Lk 6:6–11; 13:10–17 **14** [1]One sabbath when he went to dine at the house of a ruler
who belonged to the Pharisees, they were watching him.

---

has broken down the dividing wall [...] that he might create in himself one new man in place of the two, so making peace, and might reconcile us both to God in one body through the cross, thereby bringing the hostility to an end" (Eph 2:14–16). Therefore, "all men are called to belong to the new people of God. This people therefore, whilst remaining one and only one, is to be spread throughout the whole world and to all ages in order that the design of God's will may be fulfilled: he made human nature one in the beginning and has decreed that all his children who were scattered should be finally gathered together as one" (Vatican II, *Lumen gentium*, 13).

13:31–33. This episode apparently took place in the Perea region which, like Galilee, was under the jurisdiction of Herod Antipas (cf. Lk 3:1), a son of Herod the Great (cf. the note on Mt 2:1). On other occasions St Luke mentions that Herod was keen to meet Jesus and see him perform a miracle (cf. Lk 9:9; 23:8). These Pharisees may be giving Jesus the warning just to get him to go away. Jesus calls Herod—and indirectly his accomplices—a "fox", once again showing his rejection of duplicity and hypocrisy.

Jesus' answer shows them he is completely in command of his life and death: he is the Son of God and his Father's will is his only governor (cf. Jn 10:18).

13:34. Jesus here shows the infinite extent of his love. St Augustine explores the meaning of this touching simile: "You see, brethren, how a hen becomes weak with her chickens. No other bird, when it is a mother, shows its maternity so clearly. We see all kinds of sparrows building their nests before our eyes; we see swallows, storks, doves, every day building their nests; but we do not know them to be

[2]And behold, there was a man before him who had dropsy. [3]And
Jesus spoke to the lawyers and Pharisees, saying, "Is it lawful to
heal on the sabbath, or not?" [4]But they were silent. Then he took
him and healed him, and let him go. [5]And he said to them, Mt 12:11
"Which of you, having an ass[s] or an ox that has fallen into a well,
will not immediately pull him out on a sabbath day?" [6]And they
could not reply to this.

A lesson about humility

[7]Now he told a parable to those who were invited, when he Mt 23:6
marked how they chose the places of honour, saying to them,
[8]"When you are invited by any one to a marriage feast, do not sit Prov 25:6f
down in a place of honour, lest a more eminent man than you be
invited by him; [9]and he who invited you both will come and say
to you, 'Give place to this man,' and then you will begin with
shame to take the lowest place. [10]But when you are invited, go and
sit in the lowest place, so that when your host comes he may say
to you, 'Friend, go up higher'; then you will be honoured in the
presence of all who sit at table with you. [11]For every one who Lk 18:14
exalts himself will be humbled, and he who humbles himself will Mt 23:12
be exalted."

---

parents, except when we see them on their nests. But the hen is so enfeebled over her brood that even if the chickens are not following her, even if you do not see the young ones, you still know her at once to be a mother. With her wings drooping, her feathers ruffled, her note hoarse, in all her limbs she becomes so sunken and abject, that, as I have said, even though you cannot see her young, you can see she is a mother. That is the way Jesus feels" (*In Ioann. Evang*., 15, 7).

13:35. Jesus shows the deep sorrow he feels over Jerusalem's resistance to the love God had so often shown it. Later St Luke will record Jesus' weeping over Jerusalem (cf. Lk 19:41). See also the note on Mt 23:37–39.

14:1–6. Fanaticism is always evil. It often causes blindness and leads a person, as in this case, to deny the principles of justice and charity and even basic humanitarianism. We should never be fanatical about anything—no matter how sacred it is.

14:11. Humility is so necessary for salvation that Jesus takes every opportunity to stress its importance. Here he uses the attitudes of people at a banquet to remind us again that it is God who assigns the places at the heavenly banquet. "Together with humility, the realization of the greatness of man's dignity—and of the overwhelming fact that, by grace, we are made children of God—forms a single attitude. It is not our own efforts that save us and give us life; it is the grace of God. This is a truth which must never be forgotten" (St Josemaría Escrivá, *Christ Is Passing By*, 133).

s. Other ancient authorities read *a son*

The right attitude to the poor

[12]He said also to the man who had invited him, "When you give a
dinner or a banquet, do not invite your friends or your brothers or
your kinsmen or rich neighbours, lest they also invite you in
return, and you be repaid. [13]But when you give a feast, invite the
Deut 14:29 poor, the maimed, the lame, the blind, [14]and you will be blessed,
because they cannot repay you. You will be repaid at the resurrection of the just."

Parable of the invited guests

Mt 22:2–10 [15]When one of those who sat at table with him heard this, he said
to him, "Blessed is he who shall eat bread in the kingdom of
God!" [16]But he said to him, "A man once gave a great banquet,
and invited many; [17]and at the time for the banquet he sent his servant to say to those who had been invited, 'Come; for all is now
ready.' [18]But they all alike began to make excuses. The first said to
him, 'I have bought a field, and I must go out and see it; I pray
you, have me excused.' [19]And another said, 'I have bought five

---

14:14. A Christian acts in the world in the same way anyone else does; but his dealings with his colleagues and others should not be based on pursuit of reward or vainglory: the first thing he should seek is God's glory, desiring heaven as his only reward (cf. Lk 6:32–34).

14:15. In biblical language the expression "to eat bread in the Kingdom of God" means sharing in eternal beatitude, of which this great banquet is a symbol (cf. Is 25:6; Mt 22:1–14).

14:16–24. If God invites someone to know him in faith, he should sacrifice any human interest which gets in the way of replying to God's call, no matter how lawful and noble it be. The objections we tend to put forward, the duties we appeal to, are really just excuses. This is why the ungrateful invitees are blameworthy.

"Compel people to come in": it is not a matter of forcing anyone's freedom—God does not want us to love him under duress—but of helping a person to make right decisions, to shrug off any human respect, to avoid occasions of sin, to do what he can to discover the truth. ... A person is "compelled to come in" through prayer, the example of a Christian life, friendship—in a word, apostolate. "If, in order to save an earthly life, it is praiseworthy to use force to stop a man from committing suicide, are we not allowed use the same force—holy coercion—to save the Lives (with a capital) of many who are stupidly bent on killing their souls?" (St Josemaría Escrivá, *The Way*, 399).

14:26. These words of our Lord should not disconcert us. Love for God and for Jesus should have pride of place in our lives and we should keep away from anything which obstructs this love: "In this world let us love everyone," St Gregory the Great comments, "even though he be our enemy; but let us hate him who opposes us on our way to God, though he be our relative [...]. We should, then, love our neighbour; we should have char-

yoke of oxen, and I go to examine them; I pray you, have me
excused.' 20And another said, 'I have married a wife, and therefore
I cannot come.' 21So the servant came and reported this to his
master. Then the householder in anger said to his servant, 'Go out
quickly to the streets and lanes of the city, and bring in the poor
and maimed and blind and lame.' 22And the servant said, 'Sir,
what you commanded has been done, and still there is room.'
23And the master said to the servant, 'Go out to the highways and
hedges, and compel people to come in, that my house may be
filled. 24For I tell you, none of these men who were invited shall
taste my banquet.' "

Conditions for following Jesus

25Now great multitudes accompanied him; and he turned and said Mt 10:37–38
to them, 26"If any one comes to me and does not hate his own Deut 33:9–10
father and mother and wife and children and brothers and sisters, Lk 18:29–30 Jn 12:25
yes, and even his own life, he cannot be my disciple.* 27Whoever
does not bear his own cross and come after me, cannot be my dis- Lk 9:23

---

ity towards all—towards relatives and towards strangers—but without separating ourselves from the love of God out of love for them" (*In Evangelia homiliae*, 37, 3). In the last analysis, it is a matter of keeping the proper hierarchy of charity: God must take priority over everything.

This verse must be understood, therefore, in the context of all our Lord's teachings (cf. Lk 6:27–35). These are "hard words. True, 'hate' does not exactly express what Jesus meant. Yet he did put it very strongly, because he doesn't just mean 'love less,' as some people interpret it in an attempt to tone down the sentence. The force behind these vigorous words does not lie in their implying a negative or pitiless attitude, for the Jesus who is speaking here is none other than that Jesus who commands us to love others as we love ourselves and who gives up his life for mankind. These words indicate simply that we cannot be half-hearted when it comes to loving God. Christ's words could be translated as 'love more, love better', in the sense that a selfish or partial love is not enough: we have to love others with the love of God" (St Josemaría Escrivá, *Christ Is Passing By*, 97). See the notes on Mt 10:34–37; Lk 2:49.

As the Second Vatican Council explains, Christians "strive to please God rather than men, always ready to abandon everything for Christ" (*Apostolicam actuositatem*, 4).

14:27. Christ "by suffering for us not only gave us an example so that we might follow in his footsteps, but he also opened up a way. If we follow that way, life and death become holy and acquire a new meaning" (Vatican II, *Gaudium et spes*, 22).

The way the Christian follows is that of imitating Christ. We can follow him only if we help him bear his cross. We all have experience of suffering, and suffering leads to unhappiness unless it is accepted with a Christian outlook. The Cross is not a tragedy: it is God's way of

ciple. 28For which of you, desiring to build a tower, does not first
sit down and count the cost, whether he has enough to complete
it? 29Otherwise, when he has laid a foundation, and is not able to
finish, all who see it begin to mock him, 30saying, 'This man
began to build, and was not able to finish.' 31Or what king, going
to encounter another king in war, will not sit down first and take
counsel whether he is able with ten thousand to meet him who
comes against him with twenty thousand? 32And if not, while the
other is yet a great way off, he sends an embassy and asks terms
of peace. 33So therefore, whoever of you does not renounce all
that he has cannot be my disciple.

Mt 5:13 34"Salt is good; but if salt has lost its taste, how shall its salt-
Mk 9:50 ness be restored? 35It is fit neither for the land nor for the dunghill;
men throw it away. He who has ears to hear, let him hear."

---

teaching us that through suffering we can be sanctified, becoming one with Christ and winning heaven as a reward. This is why it is so Christian to love pain: "Let us bless pain. Love pain. Sanctify pain. … Glorify pain!" (St Josemaría Escrivá, *The Way*, 208).

14:28–35. Our Lord uses different examples to show that if mere human prudence means that a person should try to work out in advance the risks he may run, with all the more reason should a Christian embrace the cross voluntarily and generously, because there is no other way he can follow Jesus Christ: "'*Quia hic homo coepit aedificare et non potuit consummare!*—This man started to build and was unable to finish!' A sad commentary which, if you don't want, need never be made about you: for you possess everything necessary to crown the edifice of your sanctification—the grace of God and your own will" (St Josemaría Escrivá, *The Way*, 324).

14:33. Earlier our Lord spoke about "hating" one's parents and one's very life; now he equally vigorously requires us to be completely detached from possessions. This verse is a direct application of the two foregoing parables: just as a king is imprudent if he goes to war with an inadequate army, so anyone is foolish who thinks he can follow our Lord without renouncing all his possessions. This renunciation should really bite: our heart has to be unencumbered by anything material if we are to be able to follow in our Lord's footsteps. The reason is, as he tells us later on, that it is impossible to "serve God and mammon" (Lk 16:13). Not infrequently our Lord asks a person to practise total, voluntary poverty; and he asks everyone to practise genuine detachment and generosity in the use of material things. If a Christian has to be ready to give up even life itself, with all the more reason should he renounce possessions: "As a man of God, put the same effort into scorning riches that men of the world put into possessing them" (*The Way*, 633). See the note on Lk 12:33–34.

Besides, for a soul to become filled with God it first must be emptied of everything that could be an obstacle to God's indwelling: "The doctrine that the Son of God came to teach was contempt for all things in order to receive as a reward the Spirit of God in himself. For,

9. PARABLES OF GOD'S MERCY

The lost sheep

15 [1]Now the tax collectors and sinners were all drawing near Lk 5:30; 19:7
to hear him. [2]And the Pharisees and the scribes murmured,
saying, "This man receives sinners and eats with them."
[3]So he told them this parable: [4]"What man of you, having a hun- Mt 18:12–14
dred sheep, if he has lost one of them, does not leave the ninety- Ezek 34:11–16
nine in the wilderness, and go after the one which is lost, until he Lk 19:10
finds it? [5]And when he has found it, he lays it on his shoulders,
rejoicing. [6]And when he comes home, he calls together his friends

---

as long as the soul does not reject all things, it has no capacity to receive the Spirit of God in pure transformation" (St John of the Cross, *Ascent of Mount Carmel*, book 1, chap. 5, 2).

15:1–32. Jesus' actions manifest God's mercy: he receives sinners in order to convert them. The scribes and Pharisees, who despised sinners, just cannot understand why Jesus acts like this; they grumble about him; and Jesus uses the opportunity to tell these mercy parables. "The Gospel writer who particularly treats of these themes in Christ's teaching is Luke, whose Gospel has earned the title of 'the Gospel of mercy'" (John Paul II, *Dives in misericordia*, 3).

In this chapter St Luke reports three of these parables in which Jesus describes the infinite, fatherly mercy of God and his joy at the conversion of the sinner.

The Gospel teaches that no one is excluded from forgiveness and that sinners can become beloved children of God if they repent and are converted. So much does God desire the conversion of sinners that each of these parables ends with a refrain, as it were, telling of the great joy in heaven over every sinner who repents.

15:1–2. This is not the first time that publicans and sinners approach Jesus (cf. Mt 9:10). They are attracted by the directness of our Lord's preaching and by his call to self-giving and love. The Pharisees in general were jealous of his influence over the people (cf. Mt 26:2–5; Jn 11:47), a jealousy which can also beset Christians; a severity of outlook which does not accept that, no matter how great his sins may have been, a sinner can change and become a saint; a blindness which prevents a person from recognizing and rejoicing over the good done by others. Our Lord criticized this attitude when he replied to his disciples' complaints about others casting out devils in his name: "Do not forbid him; for no one who does a mighty work in my name will be able soon after to speak evil of me" (Mk 9:39). And St Paul rejoiced that others proclaimed Christ and even overlooked the fact they did so out of self-interest, provided Christ was preached (cf. Phil 1:17–18).

15:5–6. Christian tradition, on the basis of this and other Gospel passages (cf. Jn 10:11), applies this parable to Christ, the Good Shepherd, who misses and then seeks out the lost sheep: the Word, by becoming man, seeks out mankind,

and his neighbours, saying to them, 'Rejoice with me, for I have
found my sheep which was lost.' 7Just so, I tell you, there will be
more joy in heaven over one sinner who repents than over ninety-
nine righteous persons who need no repentance.

The lost coin

8"Or what woman, having ten silver coins,[t] if she loses one coin,
does not light a lamp and sweep the house and seek diligently
until she finds it? 9And when she has found it, she calls together
her friends and neighbours, saying, 'Rejoice with me, for I have
found the coin which I had lost.' 10Just so, I tell you, there is joy
before the angels of God over one sinner who repents."

The prodigal son

11And he said, "There was a man who had two sons; 12and the
younger of them said to his father, 'Father, give me the share of

---

which has strayed through sinning. Here is St Gregory the Great's commentary: "He put the sheep on his shoulders because, on taking on human nature, he burdened himself with our sins" (*In Evangelia homiliae*, 2, 14).

The Second Vatican Council applies these verses of St Luke to the way priests should approach their pastoral work: "They should be mindful that by their daily conduct and solicitude they display the reality of a truly priestly and pastoral ministry both to believers and unbelievers alike, to Catholics and non-Catholics; that they are bound to bear witness before all men of the truth and of the life, and as good shepherds seek after those too who, whilst having been baptised in the Catholic Church, have given up the practice of the sacraments, or even fallen away from the faith" (*Lumen gentium*, 28). However, every member of the faithful should show this same kind of concern—expressed in a fraternal way—towards his brothers and sisters, towards everyone on the road to sanctification and salvation.

15:7. This does not mean that our Lord does not value the perseverance of the just: he is simply emphasizing the joy of God and the saints over the conversion of a sinner. This is clearly a call to repentance, to never doubt God's readiness to forgive. "Another fall, and what a fall! … Must you give up hope? No. Humble yourself and, through Mary, your Mother, have recourse to the merciful Love of Jesus. A *miserere*, have mercy on me, and lift up your heart! And now begin again" (St J. Escrivá, *The Way*, 711).

15:8. This silver coin was a "drachma", of about the same value as a denarius, that is, approximately a day's wage for an agricultural worker (cf. Mt 20:2).

15:11. This is one of Jesus' most beautiful parables, which teaches us once more that God is a kind and understanding Father (cf. Mt 6:8; Rom 8:15; 2 Cor 1:3). The son who asks for his part of the inheritance is a symbol of the person who cuts himself off from God through sin. "Although the word 'mercy' does not

t. The drachma, rendered here by *silver coin*, was about a day's wage for a labourer

property that falls to me.' And he divided his living between them.
[13]Not many days later, the younger son gathered all he had and took his journey into a far country, and there he squandered his property in loose living. [14]And when he had spent everything, a great famine arose in that country, and he began to be in want.
[15]So he went and joined himself to one of the citizens of that country, who sent him into his fields to feed swine. [16]And he would gladly have fed on[u] the pods that the swine ate; and no one gave him anything. [17]But when he came to himself he said, 'How many of my father's hired servants have bread enough and to spare, but I perish here with hunger! [18]I will arise and go to my father, and I will say to him, "Father, I have sinned against heaven and before you; [19]I am no longer worthy to be called your son; treat me as one of your hired servants.'" [20]And he arose and came

Prov 23:21; 29:3

Jer 3:12–13
Ps 51:4

---

appear, this parable nevertheless expresses the essence of the divine mercy in a particularly clear way" (John Paul II, *Dives in misericordia*, 5).

15:12. "That son, who receives from the father the portion of the inheritance that is due to him and leaves home to squander it in a far country 'in loose living', in a certain sense is the man of every period, beginning with the one who was the first to lose the inheritance of grace and original justice. The analogy at this point is very wide-ranging. The parable indirectly touches upon every breach of the covenant of love, every loss of grace, every sin" (*Dives in misericordia*, 5).

15:14–15. At this point in the parable we are shown the unhappy effects of sin. The young man's hunger evokes the anxiety and emptiness a person feels when he is far from God. The prodigal son's predicament describes the enslavement which sin involves (cf. Rom 1:25; 6:6; Gal 5:1): by sinning one loses the freedom of the children of God (cf. Rom 8:21; Gal 4:31; 5:13) and hands oneself over to the power of Satan.

15:17–21. His memory of home and his conviction that his father loves him cause the prodigal son to reflect and to change his life. "Human life is in some way a constant returning to our Father's house. We return through contrition, through the conversion of heart which means a desire to change, a firm decision to improve our life and which, therefore, is expressed in sacrifice and self-giving. We return to our Father's house by means of that sacrament of pardon in which, by confessing our sins, we put on Jesus Christ again and become his brothers, members of God's family" (St Josemaría Escrivá, *Christ Is Passing By*, 64).

15:20–24. God always hopes for the return of the sinner; he wants him to repent. When the young man arrives home his father does not greet him with reproaches but with immense compassion, which causes him to embrace his son and cover him with kisses.

15:20. "There is no doubt that in this simple but penetrating analogy the figure of the father reveals to us God as Father. The conduct of the father in the parable

u. Other ancient authorities read *filled his belly with*

to his father. But while he was yet at a distance, his father saw him
and had compassion, and ran and embraced him and kissed him.
21And the son said to him, 'Father, I have sinned against heaven
and before you; I am no longer worthy to be called your son.'[v]
22But the father said to his servants, 'Bring quickly the best robe,
and put it on him; and put a ring on his hand, and shoes on his
feet; 23and bring the fatted calf and kill it, and let us eat and make
Eph 2:1–5 merry; 24for this my son was dead, and is alive again; he was lost,
Lk 5:14 and is found.' And they began to make merry.
25"Now his elder son was in the field; and as he came and drew
near to the house, he heard music and dancing. 26And he called
one of the servants and asked what this meant. 27And he said to
him, 'Your brother has come, and your father has killed the fatted
calf, because he has received him safe and sound.' 28But he was
angry and refused to go in. His father came out and entreated him,
29but he answered his father, 'Lo, these many years I have served

---

and his whole behaviour, which manifests his internal attitude, enables us to rediscover the individual threads of the Old Testament vision of mercy in a synthesis which is totally new, full of simplicity and depth. The father of the prodigal son *is faithful to this fatherhood, faithful to the love* that he had always lavished on his son. This fidelity is expressed in the parable not only by his immediate readiness to welcome him home when he returns after having squandered his inheritance; it is expressed even more fully by that joy, that merrymaking for the squanderer after his return, merrymaking which is so generous that it provokes the opposition and hatred of the elder brother, who had never gone far away from his father and had never abandoned the home.

"The father's fidelity to himself [...] is at the same time expressed in a manner particularly charged with affection. We read, in fact, that when the father saw the prodigal son returning home 'he had *compassion*, ran to meet him, threw his arms around his neck and kissed him.' He certainly does this under the influence of a deep affection, and this also explains his generosity towards his son, that generosity which so angers the elder son" (John Paul II, *Dives in misericordia*, 6).

"When God runs towards us, we cannot keep silent, but with St Paul we exclaim, *Abba, Pater*: 'Father, my Father!' (Rom 8:15), for, though he is the creator of the universe, he doesn't mind our not using high-sounding titles, nor worry about our not acknowledging his greatness. He wants us to call him Father; he wants us to savour that word, our souls filling with joy [...].

"God is waiting for us, like the father in the parable, with open arms, even though we don't deserve it. It doesn't matter how great our debt is. Just like the prodigal son, all we have to do is open our heart, to be homesick for our Father's house, to wonder at and rejoice in the gift which God makes us of being able to call ourselves his children, of really being his children, even though our response to him has been so poor" (St Josemaría Escrivá, *Christ Is Passing By*, 64).

v. Other ancient authorities add *treat me as one of your hired servants*

you, and I never disobeyed your command; yet you never gave me
a kid, that I might make merry with my friends. 30But when this
son of yours came, who has devoured your living with harlots,
you killed for him the fatted calf!' 31And he said to him, 'Son, you
are always with me, and all that is mine is yours. 32It was fitting to
make merry and be glad, for this your brother was dead, and is
alive; he was lost, and is found.' "

10. VARIOUS TEACHINGS

The unjust steward

16 1He also said to the disciples, "There was a rich man who
had a steward, and charges were brought to him that this
man was wasting his goods. 2And he called him and said to him,
'What is this that I hear about you? Turn in the account of your

---

15:25–30. God's mercy is so great that man cannot grasp it: as we can see in the case of the elder son, who thinks his father loves the younger son excessively, his jealousy prevents him from understanding how his father can do so much to celebrate the recovery of the prodigal; it cuts him off from the joy that the whole family feels. "It's true that he was a sinner. But don't pass so final a judgment on him. Have pity in your heart, and don't forget that he may yet be an Augustine, while you remain just another mediocrity" (St Josemaría Escrivá, *The Way*, 675).

We should also consider that if God has compassion towards sinners, he must have much much more towards those who strive to be faithful to him. St Thérèse of Lisieux understood this very well: "What joy to remember that our Lord is just; that he makes allowances for all our shortcomings, and knows full well how weak we are. What have I to fear then? Surely the God of infinite justice who pardons the prodigal son with such mercy will be just with me 'who am always with Him'" (*The Autobiography of a Saint*, chap. 8).

15:32. "Mercy, as Christ has presented it in the parable of the prodigal son, has *the interior form of the love* that in the New Testament is called *agape*. This love is able to reach down to every prodigal son, to every human misery, and above all to every form of moral misery, to sin. When this happens, the person who is the object of mercy does not feel humiliated, but rather is found again and 'restored to value'. The father first and foremost expresses to him his joy, that he has been 'found again' and that he has 'returned to life'. This joy indicates a good that has remained intact: even if he is a prodigal, a son does not cease to be truly his father's son; it also indicates a good that has been found again, which in the case of the prodigal son was his return to the truth about himself" (John Paul II, *Dives in misericordia*, 6).

16:1–8. The unfaithful steward manages to avoid falling on hard times. Of course, our Lord presumes that we realize the immorality of the man's behaviour. What he emphasizes and praises, however, is his shrewdness and effort: he tries to

stewardship, for you can no longer be steward.' 3And the steward
said to himself, 'What shall I do, since my master is taking the
stewardship away from me? I am not strong enough to dig, and I
am ashamed to beg. 4I have decided what to do, so that people
may receive me into their houses when I am put out of the stewardship.' 5So, summoning his master's debtors one by one, he said
to the first, 'How much do you owe my master?' 6He said, 'A hundred measures of oil.' And he said to him, 'Take your bill, and sit
down quickly and write fifty.' 7Then he said to another, 'And how
much do you owe?' He said, 'A hundred measures of wheat.' He
said to him, 'Take your bill, and write eighty.' 8The master commended the dishonest steward for his prudence; for the sons of
Lk 14:14 this world[w] are wiser in their own generation than the sons of
Mt 6:20; 10:40 light.* 9And I tell you, make friends for yourselves by means of

---

derive maximum material advantage from his former position as steward. In saving our soul and spreading the Kingdom of God, our Lord wants us to apply at least the same ingenuity and effort as people put into their worldly affairs or their attempts to attain some human ideal. The fact that we can count on God's grace does not in any way exempt us from the need to employ all available legitimate human resources even if that means strenuous effort and heroic sacrifice. "What zeal people put into their earthly affairs: dreaming of honours, striving for riches, bent on sensuality! Men and women, rich and poor, old and middle-aged and young and even children: all of them alike. When you and I put the same zeal into the affairs of our souls, we will have a living and working faith. And there will be no obstacle that we cannot overcome in our apostolic works" (St J. Escrivá, *The Way*, 317).

16:9–11. "Unrighteous mammon" means temporal goods which have been obtained in some unjust, unrighteous way. However, God is very merciful: even this unjust wealth can enable a person to practise virtue by making restitution, by paying for the damage done and then by striving to help his neighbour by giving alms, by creating work opportunities etc. This was the case with Zacchaeus, the chief tax collector, who undertook to restore fourfold anything he had unjustly taken, and also to give half his wealth to the poor. On hearing that, our Lord specifically declared that salvation had that day come to that house (cf. Lk 19:1–10).

Our Lord speaks out about faithfulness in very little things, referring to riches—which really are insignificant compared with spiritual wealth. If a person is faithful and generous and is detached in the use he makes of these temporal riches, he will, at the end of his life, receive the reward of eternal life, which is the greatest treasure of all, and a permanent one. Besides, by its very nature human life is a fabric of little things: anyone who fails to give them their importance will never be able to achieve great things. "Everything in which we poor little men take a part—even holiness—is a fabric of small trifles which, depending upon one's intention,

w. Greek *age*

unrighteous mammon, so that when it fails they may receive you
into the eternal habitations.
[10]"He who is faithful in a very little is faithful also in much; Lk 19:17
and he who is dishonest in a very little is dishonest also in much.
[11]If then you have not been faithful in the unrighteous mammon,
who will entrust to you the true riches? [12]And if you have not been
faithful in that which is another's, who will give you that which is
your own? [13]No servant can serve two masters; for either he will Mt 6:24
hate the one and love the other, or he will be devoted to the one
and despise the other. You cannot serve God and mammon."
[14]The Pharisees, who were lovers of money, heard all this, and Mt 23:14
they scoffed at him. [15]But he said to them, "You are those who Lk 18:9–14
justify yourselves before men, but God knows your hearts; for Mt 23:28 Ps 7:9
what is exalted among men is an abomination in the sight of God. Prov 6:16–17

---

can form a splendid tapestry of heroism or of degradation, of virtue or of sin.

"The epic legends always related extraordinary adventures, but never fail to mix them with homely details about the hero. May you always attach great importance—faithfully—to the little things" (St J. Escrivá, *The Way*, 826).

The parable of the unjust steward is a symbol of man's life. Everything we have is a gift from God, and we are his stewards or managers, who sooner or later will have to render an account to him.

16:12. "That which is another's" refers to temporal things, which are essentially impermanent. "That which is your own" refers to goods of the spirit, values which endure, which are things we really do possess because they will go with us into eternal life. In other words: how can we be given heaven if we have proved unfaithful, irresponsible, during our life on earth?

16:13–14. In the culture of that time "service" involved such commitment to one's master that a servant could not take on any other work or serve any other master. Our service to God, our sanctification, requires us to direct all our actions towards him. A Christian does not divide up his time, allocating some of it to God and some of it to worldly affairs: everything he does should become a type of service to God and neighbour—by doing things with upright motivation, and being just and charitable.

The Pharisees jeered at what Jesus was saying, in order to justify their own attachment to material things. Sometimes people make fun of total commitment to God and detachment from material things because they themselves are not ready to practise virtue; they cannot even imagine other people really having this generosity: they think they must have ulterior motives. See also the note on Mt 6:24.

16:15. "Abomination": the original Greek word means worship of idols and, by derivation, the horror this provoked in a true worshipper of God. So the expression conveys God's disgust with the attitude of the Pharisees who, by wanting to be exalted, are putting themselves, like idols, in the place of God.

The law and the Gospel

Mt 11:12–13 16"The law and the prophets were until John; since then the good
news of the kingdom of God is preached, and every one enters it
Mt 5:18 violently. 17But it is easier for heaven and earth to pass away, than
for one dot of the law to become void.

Mt 5:32; 19:9 18"Every one who divorces his wife and marries another commits adultery, and he who marries a woman divorced from her husband commits adultery.

16:16–17. John the Baptist marks, as it were, the final point of the Old Covenant, the last of the prophets who had been preparing the way for the coming of the Messiah. With Jesus the new and definitive stage in the history of salvation has arrived; however, the moral precepts of the Old Law remain in force; they are brought to perfection by Jesus.

"Every one enters it violently": for an interpretation of these words see the note on the parallel text in Matthew (11:12).

16:18. Our Lord's teaching on the indissolubility of marriage is very clear: once a man and a woman contract a true marriage neither can marry again while the other is alive. This matter is the subject of commentaries on Matthew 5:31–32 and 19:9, to which the reader is referred. Here we will simply add that adultery is a very serious transgression of the natural moral order, frequently and expressly condemned in Sacred Scripture (e.g., Ex 20:14; Lev 20:10; Deut 5:18, 22:22; Prov 6:32; Rom 13:9; 1 Cor 6:9; Heb 13:4; etc.). The Magisterium of the Church has constantly taught this same doctrine: "Endorsed by mutual fidelity and, above all, consecrated by Christ's sacrament, this love abides faithfully in mind and body in prosperity and adversity and hence excludes both adultery and divorce" (Vatican II, *Gaudium et spes*, 49).

16:19–31. This parable disposes of two errors—that which denied the survival of the soul after death and, therefore, retribution in the next life; and that which interpreted material prosperity in this life as a reward for moral rectitude, and adversity as punishment. The parable shows that, immediately after death, the soul is judged by God for all its acts—the "particular judgment"—and is rewarded or punished; and that divine revelation is by itself sufficient for men to be able to believe in the next life.

In another area, the parable teaches the innate dignity of every human person, independent of his social, financial, cultural or religious position. And respect for this dignity implies that we must help those who are experiencing any material or spiritual need: "Wishing to come down to topics that are practical and of some urgency, the Council lays stress on respect for the human person: everyone should look upon his neighbour (without any exception) as another self, bearing in mind above all his life and the means necessary for living it in a dignified way lest he follow the example of the rich man who ignored Lazarus, the poor man" (Vatican II, *Gaudium et spes*, 27).

Another practical consequence of respect for others is proper distribution of material resources and protection of human life, even unborn life, as Paul VI pleaded with the General Assembly of the United Nations: "Respect for life, even with regard to the great problem of the birth rate, must find here in your assembly its highest affirmation and its

Lazarus and the rich man

[19]"There was a rich man, who was clothed in purple and fine linen
and who feasted sumptuously every day. [20]And at his gate lay a
poor man named Lazarus, full of sores, [21]who desired to be fed
with what fell from the rich man's table; moreover the dogs came
and licked his sores. [22]The poor man died and was carried by the
angels to Abraham's bosom. The rich man also died and was
buried; [23]and in Hades, being in torment, he lifted up his eyes, and

---

most reasoned defence. You must strive to multiply bread so that it suffices for the tables of mankind, and not rather favour an artificial control of birth, which would be irrational, in order to diminish the number of guests at the banquet of life" (Address to the UN, 4 October 1965).

16:21. Apparently this reference to the dogs implies not that they alleviated Lazarus' sufferings but increased them, in contrast with the rich man's pleasure: to the Jews dogs were unclean and therefore not generally used as domestic animals.

16:22–26. Earthly possessions, as also suffering, are ephemeral things: death marks their end, and also the end of our testing-time, our capacity to sin or to merit reward for doing good; and immediately after death we begin to enjoy our reward or to suffer punishment, as the case may be. The Magisterium of the Church has defined that the souls of all who die in the grace of God enter heaven, immediately after death or after first undergoing a purging, if that is necessary. "We believe in eternal life. We believe that the souls of all those who die in the grace of Christ—whether they must still make expiation in the fire of purgatory, or whether from the moment they leave their bodies they are received by Jesus into Paradise like the good thief—go to form that people of God which succeeds death, death which will be totally destroyed on the day of the resurrection when these souls are reunited with their bodies" (Paul VI, *Creed of the People of God*, 28).

The expression "Abraham's bosom" refers to the place or state "into which the souls of the just, before the coming of Christ the Lord were received, and where, without experiencing any sort of pain, but supported by the blessed hope of redemption, they enjoyed peaceful repose. To liberate these holy souls, who, in the bosom of Abraham were expecting the Saviour, Christ the Lord descended into hell" (St Pius V, *Catechism*, 1, 6, 3).

16:22. "Both the rich man and the beggar died and were carried before Abraham, and there judgment was rendered on their conduct. And the Scripture tells us that Lazarus found consolation, but that the rich man found torment. Was the rich man condemned because he had riches, because he abounded in earthly possessions, because he 'dressed in purple and linen and feasted sumptuously every day'? No, I would say that it was not for this reason. The rich man was condemned because he did not pay attention to the other man, because he failed to take notice of Lazarus, the person who sat at his door and who longed to eat the scraps from his table. Nowhere does Christ condemn the mere possession of earthly goods as such. Instead, he pronounces very harsh words against those who use their possessions in a selfish

saw Abraham far off and Lazarus in his bosom. 24 And he called
out, 'Father Abraham, have mercy upon me, and send Lazarus to
dip the end of his finger in water and cool my tongue; for I am in
Lk 6:24 anguish in this flame.' 25 But Abraham said, 'Son, remember that
you in your lifetime received your good things, and Lazarus in
like manner evil things, but now he is comforted here, and you are
in anguish. 26 And besides all this, between us and you a great
chasm has been fixed, in order that those who would pass from
here to you may not be able, and none may cross from there to
us.' 27 And he said, 'Then I beg you, father, to send him to my
father's house, 28 for I have five brothers, so that he may warn
2 Tim 3:16 them, lest they also come into this place of torment.' 29 But
Abraham said, 'They have Moses and the prophets; let them hear
them.' 30 And he said, 'No, father Abraham; but if some one goes

---

way, without paying attention to the needs of others […].

"The parable of the rich man and Lazarus must always be present in our memory; it must form our conscience. Christ demands openness to our brothers and sisters in need—openness from the rich, the affluent, the economically advantaged; openness to the poor, the underdeveloped and the disadvantaged. Christ demands an openness that is more than benign attention, more than token actions or half-hearted efforts that leave the poor as destitute as before or even more so […].

"We cannot stand idly by, enjoying our own riches and freedom, if, in any place, the Lazarus of the twentieth century stands at our doors. In the light of the parable of Christ, riches and freedom mean a special responsibility. Riches and freedom create a special obligation. And so, in the name of the solidarity that binds us all together in a common humanity, I again proclaim the dignity of every human person: the rich man and Lazarus are both human beings, both of them equally created in the image and likeness of God, both of them equally redeemed by Christ, at a great price, the price of the 'precious blood of Christ' (1 Pet 1:19)" (John Paul II, Homily in Yankee Stadium, 2 October 1979).

16:24–31. The dialogue between the rich man and Abraham is a dramatization aimed at helping people remember the message of the parable: strictly speaking, there is no room in hell for feelings of compassion towards one's neighbour: in hell hatred presides. "When Abraham said to the rich man 'between us and you a great chasm has been fixed', he showed that after death and resurrection there will be no scope for any kind of penance. The impious will not repent and enter the Kingdom, nor will the just sin and go down into hell. This is the unbridgable abyss" (Aphraates, *Demonstratio*, 20; *De sustentatione egenorum*, 12). This helps us understand what St John Chrysostom says: "I ask you and I beseech you and, falling at your feet, I beg you: as long as we enjoy the brief respite of life, let us repent, let us be converted, let us become better, so that we will not have to lament uselessly like that rich man when we die and tears can do us no good. For even if you have a father or a son or a friend or anyone else who might have influence

to them from the dead, they will repent.' [31]He said to him, 'If they Jn 5:46; 11:45–53
do not hear Moses and the prophets, neither will they be con-
vinced if some one should rise from the dead'."

On leading others astray

17 [1]And he said to his disciples, "Temptations to sin[x] are sure
to come; but woe to him by whom they come! [2]It would be Mt 18:6–7
better for him if a millstone were hung round his neck and he
were cast into the sea, than that he should cause one of these little
ones to sin.[y]

Forgiving offences

[3]Take heed to yourselves; if your brother sins, rebuke him, and if Mt 18:15
he repents, forgive him; [4]and if he sins against you seven times in Mt 18:21–22

---

with God, no one will be able to set you free, for your own deeds condemn you" (*Hom. on 1 Cor*).

17:1–3. Our Lord condemns scandal, that is, "any saying, action or omission which constitutes for another an occasion of sin" (St Pius X, *Catechism*, 417). Jesus is teaching two things here: the first is that scandal will *in fact* happen; the second, that it is a grave sin, as shown by the punishment it earns.

The reason why it is so serious a sin is that it "tends to destroy God's greatest work, that of Redemption, through souls being lost; it kills one's neighbour's soul by taking away the life of grace, which is more precious than the life of the body, and it is the cause of a multitude of sins. This is why God threatens with the most severe punishment those who cause others to stumble" (ibid., 418). See the notes on Mt 18:6–7; 18:8; 18:10.

"Take heed to yourselves": a serious warning, meaning that we should not be a cause of scandal to others nor should we be influenced by the bad example others give us.

People who enjoy authority of any kind (parents, teachers, politicians, writers, artists, etc.) can more easily be a cause of scandal. We need to be on the alert in this respect in view of our Lord's warning, "Take heed to yourselves."

17:2. Millstones were circular in shape with a large hole in the centre. Our Lord's description, therefore, was very graphic: it meant that the person's head just fitted through the hole and then he could not get the stone off.

17:3–4. In order to be a Christian one must always, genuinely, forgive others. Also, one has to correct an erring brother to help him change his behaviour. But fraternal correction should always be done in a very refined way, full of charity; otherwise we would humiliate the person who has committed the fault, whereas we should not humiliate him but help him to be better.

Forgiving offences—which is something we should always do—should not be confused with giving up rights which have been unjustly violated. One can claim rights without any kind of hatred being implied; and sometimes charity and justice require us to exercise our rights. "Let's not confuse the rights of the

x. Greek *stumbling blocks* **y.** Greek *stumble*

the day, and turns to you seven times, and says, 'I repent,' you
must forgive him."

The power of faith

Mk 9:24 [5]The apostles said to the Lord, "Increase our faith!" [6]And the Lord
Mt 13:31; 17:20; 21:21 said, "If you had faith as a grain of mustard seed, you could say to
this sycamine tree, 'Be rooted up, and be planted in the sea,' and
it would obey you.

Humble service

[7]"Will any one of you, who has a servant ploughing or keeping
sheep, say to him when he has come in from the field, 'Come at
once and sit down at table'? [8]Will he not rather say to him,
'Prepare supper for me, and gird yourself and serve me, till I eat
and drink; and afterward you shall eat and drink'? [9]Does he thank
the servant because he did what was commanded? [10]So you also,
when you have done all that is commanded you, say, 'We are
unworthy servants; we have only done what was our duty.'"

---

office you hold with your rights as a person. The former can never be waived" (St Josemaría Escrivá, *The Way*, 407).

Sincere forgiveness leads us to forget the particular offence and to extend the hand of friendship, which in turn helps the offender to repent.

The Christian vocation is a calling to holiness, but one of its essential requirements is that we show apostolic concern for the spiritual welfare of others: Christianity cannot be practised in an isolated, selfish way. Thus, "if any one among you wanders from the truth and some one brings him back, let him know that whoever brings back a sinner from the error of his way will save his soul from death and will cover a multitude of sins" (Jas 5:19–20).

17:5. "Increase our faith!": a good ejaculatory prayer for every Christian. "'*Omnia possibilia sunt credenti*. Everything is possible for anyone who has faith.' The words are Christ's. How is it that you don't say to him with the apostles: '*Adauge nobis fidem!* Increase my faith!'?" (*The Way*, 588).

17:6. "I'm not one for miracles. I have told you that in the holy Gospel I can find more than enough to confirm my faith. But I can't help pitying those Christians—pious people, 'apostles' many of them—who smile at the idea of extraordinary ways, of supernatural events. I feel the urge to tell them: Yes, this is still the age of miracles: we too would work them if we had faith!" (*The Way*, 583).

17:7–10. Jesus is not approving this master's abusive and arbitrary behaviour. He is using an example very familiar to his audience to show the attitude a person should have towards his Creator: everything, from our very existence to the eternal happiness promised us, is one huge gift from God. Man is always in debt to God; no matter what service he renders him he can never adequately repay the gifts God has given him. There is no sense in a creature adopting a proud atti-

Cure of ten lepers

11On the way to Jerusalem he was passing along between Samaria
and Galilee. 12And as he entered a village, he was met by ten Lev 13:34ff
lepers, who stood at a distance 13and lifted up their voices and
said, "Jesus, Master, have mercy on us." 14When he saw them he Lk 5:14
said to them, "Go and show yourselves to the priests." And as they
went they were cleansed. 15Then one of them, when he saw that he
was healed, turned back, praising God with a loud voice; 16and he
fell on his face at Jesus' feet, giving him thanks. Now he was a
Samaritan. 17Then said Jesus, "Were not ten cleansed? Where are
the nine? 18Was no one found to return and give praise to God
except this foreigner?" 19And he said to him, "Rise and go your Lk 7:50
way; your faith has made you well."

The coming of the Kingdom of God

20Being asked by the Pharisees when the kingdom of God was Jn 18:36
coming, he answered them, "The kingdom of God is not coming

---

tude towards God. What Jesus teaches us here we see being put into practice by our Lady, who replied to God's messenger, "Behold, I am the handmaid of the Lord" (Lk 1:38).

17:11–19. The setting of this episode explains how a Samaritan could be in the company of Jews. There was no love lost between Jews and Samaritans (cf. Jn 4:9), but shared pain, in the case of these lepers, overcame racial antipathy.

The Law of Moses laid down, to prevent the spread of the disease, that lepers should live away from other people and should let it be known that they were suffering from this disease (cf. Lev 13:45–46). This explains why they did not come right up to Jesus and his group, but instead begged his help by shouting from a distance. Before curing them our Lord orders them to go to the priests to have their cure certified (cf. Lev 14:2ff), and to perform the rites laid down. The lepers' obedience is a sign of their faith in Jesus' words. And, in fact, soon after setting out they are cleansed.

However, only one of them, the Samaritan, who returns praising God and showing his gratitude for the miracle, is given a much greater gift than the cure of leprosy. Jesus says as much: "Your faith has made you well" (v.19) and praises the man's gratefulness. The Gospel records this event to teach us the value of gratefulness: "Get used to lifting your heart to God, in acts of thanksgiving, many times a day. Because he gives you this and that. Because you have been despised. Because you haven't what you need or because you have.

"Because he made his Mother so beautiful, his Mother who is also your Mother. Because he created the sun and the moon and this animal and that plant. Because he made that man eloquent and you he left tongue-tied. …

"Thank him for everything, because everything is good" (St Josemaría Escrivá, *The Way*, 268).

17:20–21. Like many Jews of their time, the Pharisees imagined the establishment of the Kingdom of God in terms of exter-

Mt 24:23 with signs to be observed;* [21]nor will they say, 'Lo, here it is!' or
'There!' for behold, the kingdom of God is in the midst of you."[z]

The day of Christ's coming

[22]And he said to the disciples, "The days are coming when you
will desire to see one of the days of the Son of man, and you will
Lk 21:8 not see it. [23]And they will say to you, 'Lo, there!' or 'Lo, here!'
Mt 24:26–27 Do not go, do not follow them. [24]For as the lightning flashes and
lights up the sky from one side to the other, so will the Son of man
Lk 9:22 be in his day.[a] [25]But first he must suffer many things and be
Mt 24:37–39 rejected by this generation. [26]As it was in the days of Noah, so
Gen 7:7–23 will it be in the days of the Son of man. [27]They ate, they drank,
they married, they were given in marriage, until the day when
Noah entered the ark, and the flood came and destroyed them all.

---

nal, political authority; whereas Jesus teaches that it is something eminently spiritual, supernatural, which has been happening ever since Jesus' coming, although its climax will be after his second coming or Parousia at the end of the world; its effect is to be seen, above all, in men's hearts, although it is also something visible and external, just as the Church has a visible dimension.

The presence of the Kingdom of God in each soul is something one perceives through the affections and inspirations communicated by the Holy Spirit. St Thérèse of Lisieux says this about her own experience: "The Doctor of doctors teaches us without the sound of words. I have never heard him speak, and yet I know he is within my soul. Every moment he is guiding and inspiring me, and, just at the moment I need them, 'lights' till then unseen are granted me. Most often it is not at prayer that they come but while I go about my daily duties" (*The Autobiography of a Saint*, chap. 8).

17:22. After the apostles receive the Holy Spirit on the day of Pentecost they will devote their whole lives to preaching boldly the message of Jesus Christ, and winning all men over to the Lord. This will lead them to experience many severe contradictions; they will suffer so much that they will yearn to see even "one of the days of the Son of man", that is, one of the days of the victory of Jesus Christ. But this day will not arrive until the Lord's second coming.

17:23–36. These words of our Lord are a prophecy about the last coming of the Son of man. We should remember that prophecy often involves events on different levels, many symbols, a terminology of its own; the *chiaroscuro* which they create gives us insight into future events, but the concrete details only become clear when the events actually occur. Our Lord's last coming will be something sudden and unexpected; it will catch many people unprepared. Jesus illustrates this by giving examples from sacred history: as in the time of Noah (cf. Gen 6:9–9:7) and that of Lot (cf. Gen 18:16–19, 27) divine judgment will be visited on men without warning.

However, it is useful to recall here

z. Or *within you* **a.** Other ancient authorities omit *in his day*

28Likewise as it was in the days of Lot—they ate, they drank, they Gen 18:20
bought, they sold, they planted, they built, 29but on the day when Gen 19:15, 24–26
Lot went out from Sodom fire and brimstone rained from heaven
and destroyed them all— 30so will it be on the day when the Son
of man is revealed. 31On that day, let him who is on the housetop, Mt 24:17–18
with his goods in the house, not come down to take them away;
and likewise let him who is in the field not turn back. 32Remember
Lot's wife. 33Whoever seeks to gain his life will lose it, but who- Lk 9:24
ever loses his life will preserve it. 34I tell you, in that night there
will be two men in one bed; one will be taken and the other left.
35There will be two women grinding together; one will be taken Mt 20:40–41
and the other left."[b] 37And they said to him, "Where, Lord?" He Job 39:30
said to them, "Where the body is, there the eagles[c] will be gath- Mt 24:28
ered together."

---

that everyone will find himself before the divine Judge immediately when he dies, at the particular judgment. Thus Jesus' teaching has also a present urgency about it: *here and now* a disciple should scrutinize his own conduct, for the Lord can call him when he least expects.

17:33. "Will preserve it": what the Greek word literally means is "will engender (his life)", that is to say, "will give true life to the soul". Thus our Lord seems to mean the following: he who wants to save his life at all costs, making it his basic value, will lose eternal life; whereas he who is ready to lose his earthly life—that is, to resist even to death the enemies of God and of his soul—will obtain eternal happiness through this struggle. In content this passage is almost identical with Luke 9:24.

17:36. In the Vulgate this verse reads: "Una assumetur, et altera relinquetur. Duo in agro; unus assumetur, et alter relinquetur" ("One will be taken and the other left. Two men will be in the field; one will be taken and the other left"). These words seem to be an addition to Luke, taken from Matthew 24:40; they do not appear in the better Greek manuscripts, which is why the New Vulgate omits them. See the RSV note.

17:37. "Where, Lord?" The Pharisees had asked Jesus when the Kingdom of God was coming (v. 20). Now, after hearing the Messiah's explanation the disciples, out of natural curiosity, ask him, "Where … will this take place?" Jesus replies with a phrase which sounds very much like a proverb and which, precisely because it is enigmatic, suggests that he does not want to give a clear answer to their question. And so our Lord's short discourse on the coming of the Kingdom of God and of Christ opens and closes with questions put by his listeners, superficial questions which he uses to teach them something which they will later come to understand.

"Where the body is, there the eagles will gather": the Greek text uses a word which could mean either eagle or vulture. In any event the proverb indicates the speed with which birds of prey swoop

b. Other ancient authorities add v. 36 *"two men will be in the field; one will be taken and the other left"*
c. Or *vultures*

Persevering prayer. Parable of the unjust judge

Rom 12:13 Col 4:2 **18** 1And he told them a parable, to the effect that they ought
1 Thess 5:17 always to pray and not lose heart. 2He said, "In a certain
city there was a judge who neither feared God nor regarded man;
3and there was a widow in that city who kept coming to him and
saying, 'Vindicate me against my adversary.' 4For a while he
refused; but afterward he said to himself, 'Though I neither fear
Lk 11:7–8 God nor regard man, 5yet because this widow bothers me, I will
vindicate her, or she will wear me out by her continual coming.' "

---

down on their victims—apparently referring to the sudden, unexpected way the second coming or last judgment will happen. Holy Scripture also deals with this subject in other passages: "But as to the times and the seasons, brethren, you have no need to have anything written to you. For you yourselves know well that the day of the Lord will come like a thief in the night" (1 Thess 5:1–2). Once more Jesus is exhorting us to be watchful: we should never neglect the most important thing in life—eternal salvation. "All that, which worries you for the moment, is of relative importance. What is of absolute importance is that you be happy, that you be saved" (St Josemaría Escrivá, *The Way*, 297). So curious are the Pharisees and the disciples about the time and place of the last coming that they are distracted from Jesus' main point; the same thing happens to us: for example, we can spend a lot of time pondering the circumstances of the deaths of people we know, and fail to grasp the warning these deaths contain—that this life is going to end one way or another and that after it we too will meet God.

18:1–8. The parable of the unjust judge is a very eloquent lesson about the effectiveness of persevering, confident prayer. It also forms a conclusion to Jesus' teaching about watchfulness, contained in the previous verses (17:23–26). Comparing God with a person like this makes the point even clearer: if even an unjust judge ends up giving justice to the man who keeps on pleading his case, how much more will God, who is infinitely just, and who is our Father, listen to the persevering prayer of his children. God, in other words, gives justice to his elect if they persist in seeking his help.

18:1. "They ought always to pray and not lose heart." Why must we pray? "1. *We must pray first and foremost because we are believers*. Prayer is in fact the recognition of our limitation and our dependence: we come from God, we belong to God and we return to God! We cannot, therefore, but abandon ourselves to him, our Creator and Lord, with full and complete confidence [...]. Prayer, therefore, is first of all an act of intelligence, a feeling of humility and gratitude, an attitude of trust and abandonment to him who gave us life out of love. Prayer is a mysterious but real dialogue with God, a dialogue of confidence and love.

"2. *We, however, are Christians, and therefore we must pray as Christians*. For the Christian, in fact, prayer acquires a particular characteristic, which completely changes its innermost nature and innermost value. The Christian is a disciple of Jesus; he is one who really believes that Jesus is the Word Incarnate, the Son of God who came among us on this earth. As a man, the life of Jesus was a continual prayer, a continual act of

[6]And the Lord said, "Hear what the unrighteous judge says. [7]And
will not God vindicate his elect, who cry to him day and night?
Will he delay long over them? [8]I tell you, he will vindicate them Jer 5:3
speedily. Nevertheless, when the Son of man comes, will he find
faith on earth?"

Parable of the Pharisee and the tax collector

[9]He also told this parable to some who trusted in themselves that
they were righteous and despised others: [10]"Two men went up into

---

worship and love of the Father and since the maximum expression of prayer is sacrifice, the summit of Jesus' prayer is the Sacrifice of the Cross, anticipated by the Eucharist at the Last Supper and handed down by means of the Holy Mass throughout the centuries. Therefore, the Christian knows that his prayer is that of Jesus; every prayer of his starts from Jesus; it is he who prays in us, with us, for us. All those who believe in God, pray; but the Christian prays in Jesus Christ: Christ is our prayer!

"3. *Finally, we must also pray because we are frail and guilty.* It must be humbly and realistically recognized that we are poor creatures, confused in ideas, tempted by evil, frail and weak, in continual need of inner strength and consolation. Prayer gives the strength for great ideals, to maintain faith, charity, purity and generosity. Prayer gives the courage to emerge from indifference and guilt, if unfortunately one has yielded to temptation and weakness. Prayer gives light to see and consider the events of one's own life and of history in the salvific perspective of God and eternity. Therefore, do not stop praying! Let not a day pass without your having prayed a little! Prayer is a duty, but it is also a great joy, because it is a dialogue with God through Jesus Christ! Every Sunday, Holy Mass: if it is possible for you, sometimes during the week. Every day, morning and evening prayers, and at the most suitable moments!" (John Paul II, Audience with young people, 14 March 1979).

18:8. Jesus combines his teaching about perseverance in prayer with a serious warning about the need to remain firm in the faith: faith and prayer go hand in hand. St Augustine comments, "In order to pray, let us believe; and for our faith not to weaken, let us pray. Faith causes prayer to grow, and when prayer grows our faith is strengthened" (*Sermon*, 115).

Our Lord has promised his Church that it will remain true to its mission until the end of time (cf. Mt 28:20); the Church, therefore, cannot go off the path of the true faith. But not everyone will remain faithful: some will turn their backs on the faith of their own accord. This is the mystery which St Paul describes as "the rebellion" (2 Thess 2:3) and which Jesus Christ announces on other occasions (cf. Mt 24:12–13). In this way our Lord warns us, to help us stay watchful and persevere in the faith and in prayer even though people around us fall away.

18:9–14. Our Lord here rounds off his teaching on prayer. In addition to being persevering and full of faith, prayer must flow from a humble heart, a heart that repents of its sins: *Cor contritum et humiliatum, Deus, non despicies* (Ps 51:17), the Lord, who never despises a contrite

the temple to pray, one a Pharisee and the other a tax collector.
Is 58:2–3 [11]The Pharisee stood and prayed thus with himself, 'God, I thank
Lk 16:15 thee that I am not like other men, extortioners, unjust, adulterers,
Mt 23:23 or even like this tax collector. [12]I fast twice a week, I give tithes of
Ps 51:1 all that I get.' [13]But the tax collector, standing far off, would not
even lift up his eyes to heaven, but beat his breast, saying, 'God,
Lk 14:11 be merciful to me a sinner!' [14]I tell you, this man went down to his
Mt 23:12 house justified rather than the other; for every one who exalts him-
Ezra 21:31 self will be humbled, but he who humbles himself will be exalted."

Jesus blesses the children

Mt 19:13–15 [15]Now they were bringing even infants to him that he might touch
Mk 10:13–16 them; and when the disciples saw it, they rebuked them. [16]But

---

and humble heart, resists the proud and gives his grace to the humble (cf. 1 Pet 5:5; Jas 4:6).

The parable presents two opposite types—the Pharisee, who is so meticulous about external fulfilment of the Law; and the tax collector, who in fact is looked on as a public sinner (cf. Lk 19:7). The Pharisee's prayer is not pleasing to God, because his pride causes him to be self-centred and to despise others. He begins by giving thanks to God, but obviously it is not true gratitude, because he boasts about all the good he has done and he fails to recognize his sins; since he regards himself as righteous, he has no need of pardon, he thinks; and he remains in his sinful state; to him also apply these words spoken by our Lord to a group of Pharisees on another occasion: "If you were blind, you would have no guilt; but now that you say, 'We see,' your guilt remains" (Jn 9:41). The Pharisee went down from the temple, therefore, unjustified.

But the tax collector recognizes his personal unworthiness and is sincerely sorry for his sins: he has the necessary dispositions for God to pardon him. His ejaculatory prayer wins God's forgiveness: "It is not without reason that some have said that prayer justifies; for repentant prayer or supplicant repentance, raising up the soul to God and re-uniting it to his goodness, without doubt obtains pardon in virtue of the holy love which gives it this sacred movement. And therefore we ought all to have very many such ejaculatory prayers, said as an act of loving repentance and with a desire of obtaining reconciliation with God, so that by thus laying our tribulation before our Saviour, we may pour out our souls before and within his pitiful heart, which will receive them with mercy" (St Francis de Sales, *Treatise on the Love of God*, book 2, chap. 20).

18:15. The adverb "even" or "also" suggests that mothers were bringing little children to meet our Lord at the same time as others brought sick people to him. "That he might touch them": the sight of the curing of the sick naturally led the people to bring their children to Jesus, to be assured of good health by being touched by him—in the same way as the lady with the issue of blood thought she could be cured by touching him (cf. Mt 9:20–22). The parallel text in St Matthew (19:13) is a little more specific: "Children were brought to him that he might lay his hands on them and pray," that is, to have him bless them.

Jesus called them to him, saying, "Let the children come to me,
and do not hinder them; for to such belongs the kingdom of God.
17Truly, I say to you, whoever does not receive the kingdom of Mt 18:3
God like a child shall not enter it."

The rich young man. Christian poverty and renunciation

18And a ruler asked him, "Good Teacher, what shall I do to inherit Mt 19:16–29 Mk 10:17–30
eternal life?" 19And Jesus said to him, "Why do you call me good? Ex 20:12–16
No one is good but God alone. 20You know the commandments: Deut 5:16–20
'Do not commit adultery, Do not kill, Do not steal, Do not bear
false witness, Honour your father and mother.'" 21And he said,
"All these I have observed from my youth." 22And when Jesus Mt 6:20
heard it, he said to him, "One thing you still lack. Sell all that you Lk 12:33

18:15–17. The episode of Jesus and the children corroborates the teaching about humility contained in the parable of the Pharisee and the tax collector. "Why, then, does he say that children are fit for the Kingdom of heaven? Perhaps because usually they are without malice, nor are they deceptive, nor do they dare to avenge themselves; they have no experience of lust, do not covet riches and are not ambitious. But the virtue of all this does not lie in ignorance of evil, but in its rejection; it does not consist in not being able to sin but rather in not consenting to sin. Therefore, the Lord is not referring to childhood as such, but to the innocence which children have in their simplicity" (St Ambrose, *Expositio Evangelii sec. Lucam*, in loc.).

Receiving the Kingdom of God like children, becoming children before God, means "renouncing our pride and self-sufficiency, recognizing that we can do nothing by ourselves. We must realize that we need grace, the help of God our Father, to find our way and keep to it. To be little, you have to abandon yourself as children do, believe as children believe, beg as children beg" (St Josemaría Escrivá, *Christ Is Passing By*, 143).

18:18–27. The story of this man (Mt 19:20 tells us he was a young man) is a sad one; he trades his vocation as an apostle for material possessions. So too today, if the Lord calls us to complete self-giving, we can answer "No" and give preference to money, honour, comfort, professional prestige; in a word, to selfishness.

"You say of that friend of yours that he frequents the sacraments, that he is clean-living and a good student. But that he won't 'respond'; when you speak to him of sacrifice and apostolate, he becomes sad and tries to avoid you.

"Don't worry. It's not a failure of your zeal. It is, to the letter, the scene related by the Evangelist: 'If you wish to be perfect, go and sell what you own and give the money to the poor' (sacrifice), 'and then come, follow me' (apostolate).

"The young man also '*abiit tristis*, went away sad'; he was not willing to respond to grace" (St Josemaría Escrivá, *The Way*, 807).

18:22. The words "Come, follow me" are much more expressive in the original. A more exact translation might be: "Come on, follow me": Jesus does not offer him a gentle invitation: he imperiously calls him to follow him immediately.

have and distribute to the poor, and you will have treasure in
heaven; and come, follow me." [23]But when he heard this he
became sad, for he was very rich. [24]Jesus looking at him said,
"How hard it is for those who have riches to enter the kingdom of
God! [25]For it is easier for a camel to go through the eye of a
needle than for a rich man to enter the kingdom of God." [26]Those
who heard it said, "Then who can be saved?" [27]But he said, "What
is impossible with men is possible with God." [28]And Peter said,
"Lo, we have left our homes and followed you." [29]And he said to
them, "Truly, I say to you, there is no man who has left house or
wife or brothers or parents or children, for the sake of the kingdom of God, [30]who will not receive manifold more in this time,
and in the age to come eternal life."

18:24–26. The image of the camel and the eye of a needle is exaggeration for the sake of effect—to show how enormously difficult it is for a rich man attached to his riches to enter the Kingdom of heaven.

"Earthly goods are not bad, but they are debased when man sets them up as idols, when he adores them. They are ennobled when they are converted into instruments for good, for just and charitable Christian undertakings. We cannot seek after material goods as if they were a treasure. … Our treasure is Christ and all our love and desire must be centred on him, 'for where our treasure is, there will our hearts be also' (Mt 6:21)" (St J. Escrivá, *Christ Is Passing By*, 35).

18:27. A Christian should show daring in things to do with his sanctification and apostolate. He should not reckon on his own resources but on God's infinite power.

18:28–30. Jesus gives an answer which completely satisfies Peter and the other disciples. His words reassure those who, after giving up everything to follow the Lord, may feel at some point a certain nostalgia for the things they have left behind. Jesus' promise far exceeds what the world can give. Our Lord wants us to be happy in this world also; those who follow him generously obtain, even in this life, a joy and a peace which far exceeds human joys and consolations. To these, a foretaste of the happiness of heaven, is added eternal beatitude. Commenting on this passage St Josemaría Escrivá says in *The Way* (670): "Try to find on earth anyone who repays so generously!" On the nature of this promised reward see also Mk 10:28–30 and the note on same.

18:31–40. The apostles simply cannot understand Jesus' words; they have too human an idea of what the Messiah would be like and they do not want to accept his being handed over for execution. Later on, when they receive the Holy Spirit, they will realize very clearly that "what God foretold by the mouth of all the prophets, that his Christ should suffer, he thus fulfilled" (Acts 3:18). So, "suffering is part of God's plans. This is the truth, however difficult it may be for us to understand it" (St J. Escrivá, *Christ Is Passing By*, 168). If we cultivate the Holy Spirit, he will help us understand the meaning of suffering and the scope it

Third announcement of the Passion

31And taking the twelve, he said to them, "Behold, we are going Mt 20:17–19 Mk 10:32–34
up to Jerusalem, and everything that is written of the Son of man Lk 9:22–24
by the prophets will be accomplished. 32For he will be delivered
to the Gentiles, and will be mocked and shamefully treated and
spit upon; 33they will scourge him and kill him, and on the third
day he will rise." 34But they understood none of these things; this Mk 9:22
saying was hid from them, and they did not grasp what was said.

Curing of the blind man of Jericho

35As he drew near to Jericho, a blind man was sitting by the road- Mt 20:29–34 Mk 10:46–52
side begging; 36and hearing a multitude going by, he inquired
what this meant. 37They told him, "Jesus of Nazareth is passing

---

gives for co-redemption. And we should ask him to make us realize that only if we decide to place the cross in the centre of our lives will we experience true joy and true peace of soul. See the note on Lk 14:27.

St John Chrysostom points out that Christ's passion "had been foretold by Isaiah when he said, 'I gave my back to the smiters, and my cheeks to those who pulled out the beard; I hid not my face from shame and spitting' (Is 50:6), and the same prophet even foretold the punishment of the Cross with these words: 'He poured out his soul unto death, and was numbered with the transgressors' (Is 53:12). And therefore the text adds, 'They will scourge him and kill him'; but David had also announced his resurrection when he said, 'Thou dost not let thy godly one see the Pit' (Ps 16:10). In fulfilment of this the Lord adds, 'And on the third day he will rise' " (*Hom. on St Matthew*, 66).

18:35–43. The blind man of Jericho is quick to use the opportunity presented by Christ's presence. We should not neglect the Lord's graces, for we do not know whether he will offer them to us again. St Augustine described very succinctly the urgency with which we should respond to God's gift, to his passing us on the road: "*Timeo Jesum praetereuntem et non redeuntem*: I fear Jesus may pass by and not come back." For, at least on some occasion, in some way, Jesus passes close to everyone.

The blind man of Jericho acclaims Jesus as the Messiah—he gives him the messianic title of Son of David—and asks him to meet his need, to make him see. His is an active faith; he shouts out, he persists, despite the people getting in his way. And he manages to get Jesus to hear him and call him. God wanted this episode to be recorded in the Gospel, to teach us how we should believe and how we should pray—with conviction, with urgency, with constancy, in spite of the obstacles, with simplicity, until we manage to get Jesus to listen to us.

"Lord, let me receive my sight": this simple ejaculatory prayer should be often on our lips, flowing from the depths of our heart. It is a very good prayer to use in moments of doubt and vacillation, when we cannot understand the reason behind God's plans, when the horizon of our commitment becomes clouded. It is even a good prayer for people who are sincerely trying to find God but who do not yet have the great gift of faith. See also the note on Mk 10:46–52.

by." [38]And he cried, "Jesus, Son of David, have mercy on me!"
[39]And those who were in front rebuked him, telling him to be
silent; but he cried out all the more, "Son of David, have mercy on
me!" [40]And Jesus stopped, and commanded him to be brought to
him; and when he came near, he asked him, [41]"What do you want
me to do for you?" He said, "Lord, let me receive my sight."
[42]And Jesus said to him, "Receive your sight; your faith has made
you well." [43]And immediately he received his sight and followed
him, glorifying God; and all the people, when they saw it, gave
praise to God.

The conversion of Zacchaeus

19 [1]He entered Jericho and was passing through. [2]And there
was a man named Zacchaeus; he was a chief tax collector,
and rich. [3]And he sought to see who Jesus was, but could not, on
account of the crowd, because he was small of stature. [4]So he ran
on ahead and climbed up into a sycamore tree to see him, for he

---

19:1–10. Jesus Christ is the Saviour of mankind; he has healed many sick people, has raised the dead to life and, particularly, has brought forgiveness of sin and the gift of grace to those who approach him in faith. As in the case of the sinful woman (cf. Lk 7:36–50), here he brings salvation to Zacchaeus, for the mission of the Son of man is to save that which was lost.

Zacchaeus was a tax collector and, as such, was hated by the people, because the tax collectors were collaborators of the Roman authorities and were often guilty of abuses (cf. the note on Mt 5:46). The Gospel implies that this man also had things to seek forgiveness for (cf. vv. 7–10). Certainly he was very keen to see Jesus (no doubt moved by grace) and he did everything he could to do so. Jesus rewards his efforts by staying as a guest in his house. Moved by our Lord's presence Zacchaeus begins to lead a new life.

The crowd begin to grumble against Jesus for showing affection to a man they consider to be an evildoer. Our Lord makes no excuses for his behaviour: he explains that this is exactly why he has come—to seek out sinners. He is putting into practice the parable of the lost sheep (cf. Lk 15:4–7), which was already prophesied in Ezekiel: "I will seek the lost, and I will bring back the strayed, and I will bind up the crippled, and I will strengthen the weak" (34:16).

19:4. Zacchaeus wants to see Jesus, and to do so he has to go out and mix with the crowd. Like the blind man of Jericho he has to shed any kind of human respect. In our own search for God we should not let false shame or fear of ridicule prevent us from using the resources available to us to meet our Lord. "Convince yourself that there is no such thing as ridicule for whoever is doing what is best" (St Josemaría Escrivá, *The Way*, 392).

19:5–6. This is a very good example of the way God acts to save men. Jesus calls Zacchaeus personally, using his name, suggesting he invite him home. The Gospel states that Zacchaeus does so promptly and joyfully. This is how we

was to pass that way. 5And when Jesus came to the place, he looked
up and said to him, "Zacchaeus, make haste and come down; for I
must stay at your house today." 6So he made haste and came down,
and received him joyfully. 7And when they saw it they all mur- Lk 15:2
mured, "He has gone in to be the guest of a man who is a sinner."
8And Zacchaeus stood and said to the Lord, "Behold, Lord, the half Ex 22:1
of my goods I give to the poor; and if I have defrauded any one of Num 5:6–7
anything, I restore it fourfold." 9And Jesus said to him, "Today salvation has come to this house, since he also is a son of Abraham.
10For the Son of man came to seek and to save the lost." Ezra 34:16 Jn 3:17 1 Tim 1:15

Parable of the pounds

11As they heard these things, he proceeded to tell a parable, Mt 25:14–30 Lk 24:21
because he was near to Jerusalem, and because they supposed that Acts 1:6
the kingdom of God was to appear immediately. 12He said therefore, "A nobleman went into a far country to receive kingly
power[d] and then return. 13Calling ten of his servants, he gave them

---

should respond when God calls us by means of grace.

19:8. Responding immediately to grace, Zacchaeus makes it known that he will restore fourfold anything he obtained unjustly—thereby going beyond what is laid down in the Law of Moses (cf. Ex 21:37f). And in generous compensation he gives half his wealth to the poor. "Let the rich learn", St Ambrose comments, "that evil does not consist in having wealth, but in not putting it to good use; for just as riches are an obstacle to evil people, they are also a means of virtue for good people" (*Expositio Evangelii sec. Lucam*, in loc.). Cf. the note on Lk 16:9–11.

19:10. Jesus' ardent desire to seek out a sinner fills us with hope of attaining eternal salvation. "He chooses a chief tax collector: who can despair when such a man obtains grace?" (St Ambrose, *Expositio Evangelii sec. Lucam*, in loc.).

19:11. The disciples had a wrong concept of the Kingdom of heaven: they thought it was about to happen and they saw it in earthly terms. They envisaged Jesus conquering the Roman tyrant and immediately establishing the Kingdom in the holy city of Jerusalem, and that when that happened they would hold privileged positions in the Kingdom. There is always a danger of Christians failing to grasp the transcendent, supernatural character of the Kingdom of God in this world, that is, the Church, which "has but one sole purpose—that the Kingdom of God may come and the salvation of the human race may be accomplished" (Vatican II, *Gaudium et spes*, 45).

Through this parable our Lord teaches us that, although his reign has begun, it will only be fully manifested later on. In the time left to us we should use all the resources and graces God gives us, in order to merit the reward.

19:13. The "mina", here translated as "pound", was worth about 35 grammes of gold. This parable is very like the

d. Greek *a kingdom*

Ps 2:2f ten pounds,[e] and said to them, 'Trade with these till I come.' 14But
his citizens hated him and sent an embassy after him, saying,
'We do not want this man to reign over us.' 15When he returned,
having received the kingly power,[d] he commanded these servants,
to whom he had given the money, to be called to him, that he
might know what they had gained by trading. 16The first came
before him, saying, 'Lord, your pound has made ten pounds
Lk 16:10 more.' 17And he said to him, 'Well done, good servant! Because
you have been faithful in a very little, you shall have authority
over ten cities.' 18And the second came, saying, 'Lord, your
pound has made five pounds.' 19And he said to him, 'And you are
to be over five cities.' 20Then another came, saying, 'Lord, here is
your pound, which I kept laid away in a napkin; 21for I was afraid
of you, because you are a severe man; you take up what you did
not lay down, and reap what you did not sow.' 22He said to him,
'I will condemn you out of your own mouth, you wicked servant!
You knew that I was a severe man, taking up what I did not lay
down and reaping what I did not sow? 23Why then did you not put
my money into the bank, and at my coming I should have collected it with interest?' 24And he said to those who stood by, 'Take
the pound from him, and give it to him who has the ten pounds.'

---

parable of the talents reported in St Matthew (cf. 25:14–30).

19:14. The last part of this verse, although it has a very specific context, reflects the attitude of many people who do not want to bear the sweet yoke of our Lord and who reject him as king. "There are millions of people in the world who reject Jesus Christ in this way; or rather they reject his shadow, for they do not know Christ. They have not seen the beauty of his face; they do not realize how wonderful his teaching is. This sad state of affairs makes me want to atone to our Lord. When I hear that endless clamour—expressed more in ignoble actions than in words—I feel the need to cry out, 'He must reign!' (1 Cor 15:25)" (St J. Escrivá, *Christ Is Passing By*, 179).

19:17. God counts on our fidelity in little things, and the greater our effort in this regard the greater the reward we will receive: "Because you have been *in pauca fidelis*, faithful in small things, come and join in your master's happiness. The words are Christ's. *In pauca fidelis*! … Now will you neglect little things, if heaven itself is promised to those who keep them?" (St Josemaría Escrivá, *The Way*, 819).

19:24–26. God expects us to strive to put to good use the gifts we have received—and he lavishly rewards those who respond to his grace. The king in the parable is shown to be very generous towards these servants—and generous in rewarding those who managed to increase the money they were given. But he is very

e. The mina, rendered here by *pound*, was about three months' wages for a labourer **d.** Greek *a kingdom*

[25](And they said to him, 'Lord, he has ten pounds!') [26]'I tell you, Lk 8:18 Mt 13:12
that to every one who has will more be given; but from him who
has not, even what he has will be taken away. [27]But as for these Ps 2:9
enemies of mine, who did not want me to reign over them, bring Is 63:1–6
them here and slay them before me.'" 1 Cor 15:25

PART THREE

The Jerusalem ministry

11. CLEANSING OF THE TEMPLE. CONTROVERSIES

The Messiah enters the Holy City

[28]And when he had said this, he went on ahead, going up to Jerusalem. [29]When he drew near to Bethphage and Bethany, at the Mt 21:1–9 Mk 11:1–10
mount that is called Olivet, he sent two of the disciples, [30]saying, Jn 12:12–16

---

severe towards the lazy servant who was also the recipient of a gift from his lord, who did not let it erode but guarded it carefully—and for this his king criticizes him: he failed to fulfil the just command the king gave him when he gave him the money: "Trade till I come." If we appreciate the treasures the Lord has given us—life, the gift of faith, grace—we will make a special effort to make them bear fruit—by fulfilling our duties, working hard and doing apostolate. "Don't let your life be barren. Be useful. Make yourself felt. Shine forth with the torch of your faith and your love. With your apostolic life, wipe out the trail of filth and slime left by the corrupt sowers of hatred. And set aflame all the ways of the earth with the fire of Christ that you bear in your heart" (St Josemaría Escrivá, *The Way*, 1).

19:28. Normally in the Gospels when there is mention of going to the Holy City it is in terms of "going up" to Jerusalem (cf. Mt 20:18; Jn 7:8), probably because geographically the city is located on Mount Zion. Besides, since the temple was the religious and political centre, going up to Jerusalem had also a sacred meaning of ascending to the holy place, where sacrifices were offered to God.

Particularly in the Gospel of St Luke, our Lord's whole life is seen in terms of a continuous ascent towards Jerusalem, where his self-surrender reaches its high-point in the redemptive sacrifice of the cross. Here Jesus is on the point of entering the city, conscious of the fact that his passion and death are imminent.

19:30–35. Jesus makes use of a donkey for his entry into Jerusalem, thereby ful-

"Go into the village opposite, where on entering you will find a
colt tied, on which no one has ever yet sat; untie it and bring it
here. [31]If any one asks you, 'Why are you untying it?' you shall
say this, 'The Lord has need of it.' " [32]So those who were sent
went away and found it as he had told them. [33]And as they were
untying the colt, its owners said to them, "Why are you untying
the colt?" [34]And they said, "The Lord has need of it." [35]And they
brought it to Jesus, and throwing their garments on the colt they
set Jesus upon it. [36]And as he rode along, they spread their garments on the road. [37]As he was now drawing near, at the descent
of the Mount of Olives, the whole multitude of the disciples began
to rejoice and praise God with a loud voice for all the mighty
Ps 118:26 works that they had seen, [38]saying, "Blessed is the King who
Lk 2:14 comes in the name of the Lord! Peace in heaven and glory in the
highest!" [39]And some of the Pharisees in the multitude said to
him, "Teacher, rebuke your disciples." [40]He answered, "I tell you,
if these were silent, the very stones would cry out."

---

filling an ancient prophecy: "Rejoice greatly, O daughter of Zion! Shout aloud, O daughter of Jerusalem! Lo, your king comes to you; triumphant and victorious is he, humble and riding on an ass, on a colt the foal of an ass" (Zech 9:9).

The people, and particularly the Pharisees, were quite aware of this prophecy. Therefore, despite its simplicity of form, there was a certain solemnity about the whole episode which impressed those present, stirring the hearts of the people and irritating the Pharisees. By fulfilling the prophecy our Lord was showing everyone that he was the Messiah prophesied in the Old Testament. Other aspects of this episode are commented on in connexion with Mk 11:3.

19:38. Christ is greeted with the prophetic words referring to the enthronement of the Messiah, contained in Psalm 118:26: "Blessed be he who enters in the name of the Lord!" But the people also acclaim him as king. This is a great messianic demonstration, which infuriates the Pharisees. One of the acclamations, "Peace in heaven and glory in the highest", echoes the announcement made by the angel to the shepherds on Christmas night (cf. Lk 2:14).

19:40. To the reproaches of the Pharisees, who are scandalized by the people's shouts, our Lord replies in a phrase which sounds like a proverb: so obvious is his messiahship that if men refused to recognize it nature would proclaim it. In fact, when his friends were cowed on the hill of Calvary the earth trembled and the rocks split (cf. Mt 27:51). At other times our Lord imposed silence on those who want to proclaim him King or Messiah, but now he adopts a different attitude: the moment has come for his dignity and his mission to be made public.

19:41–44. When the procession reaches a place where there is a good view of the city, they are disconcerted by Jesus' unexpected weeping. Our Lord explains why he is weeping, by prophesying the destruction of the city which he loved so much: not one stone will remain on

Jesus weeps over Jerusalem

41And when he drew near and saw the city he wept over it,
42saying, "Would that even today you knew the things that make
for peace! But now they are hid from your eyes. 43For the days
shall come upon you, when your enemies will cast up a bank
about you and surround you, and hem you in on every side, 44and
dash you to the ground, you and your children within you, and Ps 137:9
they will not leave one stone upon another in you; because you
did not know the time of your visitation."*

Jesus in the temple

45And he entered the temple and began to drive out those who Mt 21:12–16 Mk 11:15–18
sold, 46saying to them, "It is written, 'My house shall be a house Jn 2:13–16
of prayer'; but you have made it a den of robbers." Is 56:7 Jer 7:11
47And he was teaching daily in the temple. The chief priests Jn 18:20
and the scribes and the principal men of the people sought to
destroy him; 48but they did not find anything they could do, for all
the people hung upon his words.

---

another, and its inhabitants will be massacred—a prophecy which was fulfilled in the year 70, when Titus razed the city and the temple was destroyed.

These historical events will be a punishment for Jerusalem failing to recognize the time of its visitation, that is, for closing its gates to the salvific coming of the Redeemer. Jesus loved the Jews with a very special love: they were the first to whom the Gospel was preached (cf. Mt 10:5–6); to them he directed his ministry (cf. Mt 15:24); he showed by his word and by his miracles that he was the Son of God and the Messiah foretold in the Scriptures. But the Jews for the most part failed to appreciate the grace the Lord was offering them; their leaders led them to the extreme of calling for Jesus to be crucified. Jesus visits every one of us; he comes as our Saviour; he teaches us through the preaching of the Church; he gives us forgiveness and grace through the sacraments. We should not reject our Lord, we should not remain indifferent to his visit.

19:45–48. Jesus' indignation shows his zeal for the glory of his Father, to be recognized at this time in the temple itself. He inveighs against the traders for engaging in business which has nothing to do with divine worship (cf. Mt 21:12; Mk 11:15). Even the priests allowed some of these abuses to go on—perhaps because they benefitted from them in the form of taxes. The traders did perform services necessary for divine worship but this was vitiated by their excessive desire for gain, turning the temple into a marketplace.

"My house shall be a house of prayer": Jesus uses these words from Isaiah (56:7; cf. Jer 7:11) to underline the purpose of the temple. Jesus' behaviour shows the respect the temple of Jerusalem deserved; how much more reverence should be shown our churches, where Jesus himself is really present in the Blessed Eucharist (cf. the notes on Mt 21:12–13; and Mk 11:15–18).

Jesus' authority

Mt 21:23–27
Mk 11:27–33

20 1One day, as he was teaching the people in the temple and
preaching the gospel, the chief priests and the scribes with
the elders came up 2and said to him, "Tell us by what authority
you do these things, or who it is that gave you this authority." 3He
answered them, "I also will ask you a question; now tell me, 4Was
the baptism of John from heaven or from men?" 5And they discussed it with one another, saying, "If we say, 'From heaven,' he
will say, 'Why did you not believe him?' 6But if we say, 'From
men,' all the people will stone us; for they are convinced that John
was a prophet." 7So they answered that they did not know whence
it was. 8And Jesus said to them, "Neither will I tell you by what
authority I do these things."

Parable of the wicked tenants

Mt 21:33–46
Mk 12:1–12
Is 5:1

9And he began to tell the people this parable: "A man planted a
vineyard, and let it out to tenants, and went into another country

---

20:1–40. Our Lord's public ministry is coming to an end. He has gone up from Jericho to Jerusalem on his last journey. He will stay in the city and its environs until his death. He has made his entry as Messiah into the temple and has cleansed it. And with the authority of the Messiah he now preaches in the courtyards of the temple. In this chapter the evangelist narrates a series of arguments provoked by Pharisees and Sadducees—about Jesus' authority (v. 18), about the lawfulness of giving tribute to Caesar (vv. 20–26), and about the resurrection of the dead (vv. 27–40). The chapter ends with our Lord countering, by asking them how they interpret Psalm 110:1, and by telling the parable of the murderous tenants (Lk 20:9–18). The apostles remembered with special poignancy these events prior to the Saviour's passion and death, whose transcendent meaning they later grasped in the light of the events of Easter. Jesus' long journey from Galilee to Jerusalem has reached its destination; but the authorities in the Holy City reject the Messiah and Saviour. However, there the salvation of mankind will be achieved thanks to the sacrifice of the Son of God.

20:1–8. To these sly questions Jesus replies immediately and very much to the point.

The question, "By what authority do you do these things", refers to everything our Lord has done. Therefore, the technical term "authority" must be taken in all its depth of meaning: What is the nature of Jesus' authority and power. Because of the evil motivation behind the question, our Lord avoids giving a direct answer, countering instead by asking a question about John's baptism. When the priests and scribes give an evasive reply our Lord simply closes the discussion: he asserts that he has the authority and he refuses to say how he got it. A few days later, when in the presence of the whole Sanhedrin he is solemnly asked if he is the Messiah and Son of God, he will reply by saying quite clearly that he is, thereby showing the basis of his authority and explaining why he has acted in the way he has (cf. Mt 26:63–64 and Lk 22:66–71).

for a long while. [10]When the time came, he sent a servant to the tenants, that they should give him some of the fruit of the vineyard; but the tenants beat him, and sent him away empty-handed. 2 Chron 36:15–17
[11]And he sent another servant; him also they beat and treated shamefully, and sent him away empty-handed. [12]And he sent yet
a third; this one they wounded and cast out. [13]Then the owner of
the vineyard said, 'What shall I do? I will send my beloved son; it may be they will respect him.' [14]But when the tenants saw him,
they said to themselves, 'This is the heir; let us kill him, that the
inheritance may be ours.' [15]And they cast him out of the vineyard
and killed him. What then will the owner of the vineyard do to
them? [16]He will come and destroy those tenants, and give the
vineyard to others." When they heard this, they said, "God
forbid!" [17]But he looked at them and said, "What then is this that
is written:

> 'The very stone which the builders rejected
> has become the head of the corner'? Ps 118:22

20:9–19. As the days of his passion draw near, our Lord spells out to the priests and scribes the seriousness of the sin they are committing by rejecting him, and the terrible consequences which will follow. That is the purpose of this parable, whose central theme is deeply rooted in Sacred Scripture and is very familiar to his listeners: the people of Israel are the vineyard of the Lord. Of the many places where this comparison is to be found in the Old Testament (Hos 10:1; Jer 10:21; 12:10; Ezek 19:10–14; Ps 80:7–18) one has special resonance—the Song of the vineyard which instead of yielding good grapes yielded only sour grapes (Is 5:1–7); our Lord's words seem to evoke that ancient prophetic complaint: "What more was there to do for my vineyard, that I have not done in it?" Every character in the Gospel parable is very easy to identify: the vineyard is Israel; the tenants are the leaders of Israel; the servants sent by the lord to the vineyard are the prophets, so often ill-treated; the son is Jesus Christ, the only Son of the Father. Jesus alludes to his death on the outskirts of the city; the tenants cast him out of the vineyard—Jerusalem—and put him to death. The owner of the vineyard is God. The leading priests and scribes understand what the end of the parable means and they are horrified, which is why they cry, "God forbid!" For our Lord is saying that the owner of the vineyard will put the tenants to death and hand over the vineyard to others: the leaders of the people will be rejected. To underline the teaching in the parable our Lord concludes by applying to himself the words of Psalm 118:22: "The stone which the builders rejected has become the head of the corner." The parable contains a clear lesson for all of us: it is a grave sin to reject the Lord, to despise God's grace. If our heart becomes hardened, like those priests and scribes, we will inevitably hear from our Lord's lips similar words of rejection.

The passage ends on a sad note: wounded in their pride by the clarity of what Jesus says, their hearts became even more hardened, to the point of planning to kill him.

Is 8:14 [18]Every one who falls on that stone will be broken to pieces; but
when it falls on any one it will crush him."
[19]The scribes and chief priests tried to lay hands on him at that
very hour, but they feared the people; for they perceived that he
had told this parable against them.

Tribute to Caesar

Mt 22:15–22 [20]So they watched him, and sent spies, who pretended to be sin-
Mk 12:13–17 cere, that they might take hold of what he said, so as to deliver
Lk 11:54 him up to the authority and jurisdiction of the governor. [21]They
asked him, "Teacher, we know that you speak and teach rightly,
and show no partiality, but truly teach the way of God. [22]Is it
lawful for us to give tribute to Caesar, or not?" [23]But he perceived
their craftiness, and said to them, [24]"Show me a coin.[f] Whose likeness and inscription has it?" They said, "Caesar's." [25]He said to
them, "Then render to Caesar the things that are Caesar's, and to
God the things that are God's." [26]And they were not able in the

---

20:20–26. The leaders of the people are trying to find some grounds for laying charges against Jesus, so they put to him two mischievous questions—about the legitimacy of Roman authority in Palestine and about the resurrection of the dead (vv. 21–39).

Their question about paying tribute to Caesar is malicious: if our Lord answers "Yes", they will be able to accuse him of collaboration with the Romans, whom the Jews hated because they were invaders; if he answers "No," it will allow them to report him to Pilate, the Roman ruler, as a rebel.

Our Lord's reply takes the people by surprise, it is so simple, profound and prudent. It emphasizes a duty which obliges everyone—that of giving God his due. "Render to God the things that are God's." This phrase is the key to understanding Jesus' reply in all its depth: recognition of God's sovereignty comes before everything else.

Because he is true God and true man, Christ has authority over everything, even over temporal realities, but during his life on earth "he refrained from exercising that authority, and although he himself disdained to possess or to care for earthly things, he did not, nor does he today, interfere with those who possess them" (Pius XI, *Quas primas*). Our Lord acts in this way to make sure that his Kingdom—which is spiritual—is not confused with an earthly kingdom.

At the same time Jesus' answer provides the key to the right relationship between Church and State. Each must have its own independence and sphere of action, and both should cooperate in those matters which by their very nature require the action of both authorities, as the Second Vatican Council teaches: "The political community and the Church are autonomous and independent of each other in their own fields. Nevertheless, both are devoted to the personal vocation of man, though under different titles. This service will redound the

f. Greek *denarius*

presence of the people to catch him by what he said; but marvelling at his answer they were silent.

The resurrection of the dead

[27]There came to him some Sadducees, those who say that there is Mt 22:23–33, 46
no resurrection, [28]and they asked him a question, saying, "Teacher, Mk 12:18–27, 34 Gen 38:8
Moses wrote for us that if a man's brother dies, having a wife but Deut 25:5–6
no children, the man[g] must take the wife and raise up children for
his brother. [29]Now there were seven brothers; the first took a wife,
and died without children; [30]and the second [31]and the third took
her, and likewise all seven left no children and died. [32]Afterward
the woman also died. [33]In the resurrection, therefore, whose wife
will the woman be? For the seven had her as wife."

[34]And Jesus said to them, "The sons of this age marry and are
given in marriage; [35]but those who are accounted worthy to attain Phil 3:11
to that age and to the resurrection from the dead neither marry nor
are given in marriage, [36]for they cannot die any more, because 1 Jn 3:1–2

---

more effectively to the welfare of all insofar as both institutions practise better cooperation according to the local and prevailing situation" (*Gaudium et spes*, 76).

Jesus also teaches us here that we have a duty to fulfil our obligations as citizens. In this connexion St Paul exhorted the Romans: "Pay all of them their dues, taxes to whom taxes are due, revenue to whom revenue is due, respect to whom respect is due, honour to whom honour is due" (Rom 13:7).

This was also how the first Christians acted: "As we have been instructed by him [Jesus], we before all others try everywhere to pay your appointed officials the ordinary and special taxes" (St Justin, *Apology*, 1, 17, 1).

20:27–40. The Sadducees did not believe in the resurrection of the body or the immortality of the soul. They came along to ask Jesus a question which is apparently unanswerable. According to the levirate law (cf. Deut 25:5ff), if a man died without issue, his brother was duty bound to marry his widow to provide his brother with descendants. The consequences of this law would seem to give rise to a ridiculous situation at the resurrection of the dead.

Our Lord replies by reaffirming that there will be a resurrection; and by explaining the properties of those who have risen again, the Sadducees' argument simply evaporates. In this world people marry in order to continue the species: that is the primary aim of marriage. After the resurrection there will be no more marriage because people will not die any more.

Quoting Holy Scripture (Ex 3:2, 6) our Lord shows the grave mistake the Sadducees make, and he argues: God is not the God of the dead but of the living, that is to say, there exists a permanent relationship between God and Abraham, Isaac and Jacob, who have been dead for years. Therefore, although these just men have died as far as their bodies are concerned, they are alive, truly alive, in God—

g. Greek *his brother*

they are equal to angels and are sons of God, being sons of the
Ex 3:2–6 resurrection. 37But that the dead are raised, even Moses showed,
in the passage about the bush, where he calls the Lord the God of
Rom 14:8 Abraham and the God of Isaac and the God of Jacob.* 38Now he
is not God of the dead, but of the living; for all live to him." 39And
some of the scribes answered, "Teacher, you have spoken well."
40For they no longer dared to ask him any question.

The divinity of the Messiah

41But he said to them, "How can they say that the Christ is David's
Mt 22:41–45 Mk 12:35–37 Ps 110:1 Jn 7:42 son? 42For David himself says in the Book of Psalms,

'The Lord said to my Lord,
Sit at my right hand,
43till I make thy enemies a stool for thy feet.'

44David thus calls him Lord; so how is he his son?"

Jesus condemns the scribes

Mt 23:5ff Mk 12:38–40 Lk 11:43 45And in the hearing of all the people he said to his disciples,
46"Beware of the scribes, who like to go about in long robes, and
love salutations in the market places and the best seats in the synagogues and the places of honour at feasts, 47who devour widow's
houses and for a pretence make long prayers. They will receive
the greater condemnation."

---

their souls are immortal—and they are awaiting the resurrection of their bodies.

See also the notes on Mt 22:23–33 and Mk 12:18–27.

20:41–44. Jesus states that not only is he the son of David but also he is Lord and God; he quotes Psalm 110: the Messiah, a descendant of David, seated at the right hand of God, is called Lord by David himself. In this way Jesus alludes to the mystery of his incarnation: he is David's son according to the flesh, and he is God and Lord because he is the Father's Son, equal to him in everything; which explains why he is David's Lord even though he was born long after David.

21:1–4. Our Lord, surrounded by his disciples, watches people putting offerings into the treasury. This was a place in the women's courtyard, where there were collection boxes for the offerings of the faithful. Just then, something happens whose significance Jesus wants his disciples to notice: a poor widow puts in two coins, of very little value. He describes this as the greatest offering of all, praising the giving of alms for this purpose, particularly by people who give part of what they need. Our Lord is moved by this tiny offering because in her case it implies a big sacrifice. "The Lord does not look", St John Chrysostom comments, "at the amount offered but at the affection with which it is offered" (*Hom. on Heb*, 1). Generosity is of the essence of almsgiving. This woman teaches us that we can move God's heart if we give him all we can, which will always amount to very little even if we give our very lives. "How little a life is to offer to God!" (St J. Escrivá, *The Way*, 420).

The widow's mite

21 [1]He looked up and saw the rich putting their gifts into the Mk 12:41–44
treasury; [2]and he saw a poor widow put in two copper
coins. [3]And he said, "Truly I tell you, this poor widow has put in 2 Cor 8:12
more than all of them; [4]for they all contributed out of their abun- Lk 12:15
dance, but she out of her poverty put in all the living that she had."

12. THE ESCHATOLOGICAL DISCOURSE

Announcement of the destruction of the temple

[5]And as some spoke of the temple, how it was adorned with noble Mt 24:1–21
stones and offerings, he said, [6]"As for these things which you see, Mk 13:1–19
the days will come when there shall not be left here one stone Lk 19:44
upon another that will not be thrown down."

The beginning of tribulation. Persecution on account of the Gospel

[7]And they asked him, "Teacher, when will this be, and what will
be the sign when this is about to take place?" [8]And he said, "Take Dan 7:22
heed that you are not led astray; for many will come in my name,
saying, 'I am he!' and, 'The time is at hand!' Do not go after

---

21:5–36. The disciples are in awe of the magnificence of the temple, and Jesus uses the occasion to give a long discourse, known as the "eschatological discourse" because it has to do with the last days of the world. The account given here is very similar to those in the other Synoptic Gospels. The discourse deals with three inter-connected subjects—the destruction of Jerusalem (which took place some forty years later), the end of the world, and the second coming of Christ in glory and majesty. Jesus, who also predicts here the persecution the Church will experience, exhorts his disciples to be patient, to pray and be watchful.

Our Lord speaks here in the style and language of prophecy, using images taken from the Old Testament; in this discourse, also, we find prophecies that will be fulfilled very soon, mixed in with others that have to do with the end of the world. It is not our Lord's intention to satisfy people's curiosity about future events, but to protect them from being discouraged and scandalized about what is going to happen in the days immediately ahead. This explains his exhortations in vv. 8, 9 and 36.

21:8. On hearing that Jerusalem is going to be destroyed, the disciples ask what sign will be given as a warning of these events (vv. 5–7). Jesus answers by telling them "not to be led astray," that is to say, not to expect any warning; not to be misled by false prophets; to stay faithful to him. These false prophets will come along claiming to be the Messiah ("I am he!"). Our Lord's reply in fact refers to two events which in the Jewish mind were interrelated—the destruction of the Holy City and the end of the world. This

Dan 2:28 them. 9And when you hear of wars and tumults, do not be terrified; for this must first take place, but the end will not be at
once."
Is 19:2 10Then he said to them, "Nation will rise against nation, and
2 Chron 15:6 kingdom against kingdom; 11there will be great earthquakes, and
in various places famines and pestilences; and there will be terrors
Lk 12:11 and great signs from heaven. 12But before all this they will lay
their hands on you and persecute you, delivering you up to the
synagogues and prisons, and you will be brought before kings and
governors for my name's sake. 13This will be a time for you to
Mt 10:19 bear testimony. 14Settle it therefore in your minds, not to meditate
beforehand how to answer; 15for I will give you a mouth and
Acts 6:10 wisdom, which none of your adversaries will be able to withstand
or contradict. 16You will be delivered up even by parents and
brothers and kinsmen and friends, and some of you they will put
Mt 10:21–22 to death; 17you will be hated by all for my name's sake. 18But not
Lk 12:7 a hair of your head will perish. 19By your endurance you will gain
Heb 10:36 your lives.

---

is why he goes on to speak of both events and implies that there will be a long gap between the two; the destruction of the temple and of Jerusalem are a kind of sign or symbol of the catastrophes which will mark the end of the world.

21:9–11. Our Lord does not want his disciples to confuse just any catastrophe—famine, earthquake, war—or even persecution with the signals of the end of the world. He exhorts them quite clearly: "Do not be terrified," because although all this has to happen, "the end will not be at once;" in spite of difficulties of all kinds the Gospel will spread to the ends of the earth. Difficulties should not paralyse the preaching of the faith.

21:19. Jesus foretells all kinds of persecution. Persecution itself is something inevitable: "all who desire to live a godly life in Christ Jesus will be persecuted" (2 Tim 3:12). His disciples will have need to remember the Lord's warning at the Last Supper: " 'A servant is not greater than his master.' If they persecuted me, they will persecute you" (Jn 15:20). However, these persecutions are part of God's providence: they happen because he lets them happen, which he does in order to draw greater good out of them. Persecution provides Christians with an opportunity to bear witness to Christ; without it the blood of martyrs would not adorn the Church. Moreover, our Lord promises to give special help to those who suffer persecution, and he tells them not be afraid: he will give them of his own wisdom to enable them to defend themselves; he will not permit a hair of their heads to perish, that is, even apparent misfortune and loss will be for them a beginning of heaven.

From Jesus' words we can also deduce the obligation of every Christian to be ready to lose his life rather than offend God. Only those will attain salvation who persevere until the end in faithfulness to the Lord. The three Synoptic Gospels locate his exhortation to perseverance in this discourse (cf. Mt 24:13;

The great tribulation in Jerusalem

[20]"But when you see Jerusalem surrounded by armies, then
know that its desolation has come near. [21]Then let those who
are in Judea flee to the mountains, and let those who are inside
the city depart, and let not those who are out in the country
enter it; [22]for these are days of vengeance, to fulfil all that is Deut 32:35
written. [23]Alas for those who are with child and for those who Hos 9:7 1 Thess 2:16
give suck in those days! For great distress shall be upon the Deut 28:64
earth and wrath upon this people; [24]they will fall by the edge of Zech 12:3 Is 63:18
the sword, and be led captive among all nations; and Jerusalem Ps 79:1
will be trodden down by the Gentiles, until the times of the Dan 8:10; 9:26; 12:7
Gentiles* are fulfilled. Rom 11:25

The coming of the Son of man

[25]"And there will be signs in sun and moon and stars, and upon the Mt 24:29–30
earth distress of nations in perplexity at the roaring of the sea and Mk 13:24–26
the waves, [26]men fainting with fear and foreboding of what is Ps 65:7 Is 34:4
coming on the world; for the powers of the heavens will be
shaken. [27]And then they will see the Son of man coming in a Dan 7:13 Mt 26:64

Mk 13:13) and St Matthew gives it elsewhere (Mt 10:22) as does St Peter (1 Pet 5:9)—all of which underlines the importance for every Christian of this warning from our Lord.

21:20–24. Jesus gives quite a detailed prophecy of the destruction of the Holy City. When the Christians living there saw the armies getting closer, they remembered this prophecy and fled to Transjordan (cf. Eusebius, *Ecclesiastical History*, 3, 5). Christ had advised them to flee as soon as possible because this is the time when God would punish Jerusalem for its sins, as the Old Testament predicted (Is 5:5–6).

Catholic tradition sees Israel as symbolizing the Church. In fact, in the Book of Revelation the Church triumphant is called the new Jerusalem (cf. Rev 21:2). Therefore, by applying this passage to the Church, the sufferings the Holy City experiences can symbolize the contradictions the pilgrim Church will experience due to the sins of men, for "she herself takes her place among the creatures which groan and travail yet and await the revelation of the children of God" (Vatican II, *Lumen gentium*, 48).

21:24. "The times of the Gentiles" means the period in which the Gentiles, who do not belong to the Jewish people, will become members of the new people of God, the Church, until the Jews themselves are converted at the end of the world (cf. Rom 11:11–32).

21:25–26. Jesus refers to the dramatic changes in natural elements when the world is coming to an end. "The power of the heavens will be shaken"; that is to say, the whole universe will tremble at the Lord's coming in power and glory.

21:27–28. Applying to himself the prophecy of Daniel (7:13–14), our Lord speaks of his coming in glory at the end of time. Mankind will see the power and

cloud with power and great glory. [28]Now when these things begin
to take place, look up and raise your heads, because your redemption is drawing near."

The end will surely come; the lesson of the fig tree

Mt 24:32–35 [29]And he told them a parable: "Look at the fig tree, and all the
Mk 13:28–31 trees; [30]as soon as they come out in leaf, you see for yourselves
and know that the summer is already near. [31]So also, when you see
these things taking place, you know that the kingdom of God is
near. [32]Truly, I say to you, this generation will not pass away till
Lk 16:17 all has taken place. [33]Heaven and earth will pass away, but my
words will not pass away.

The need for vigilance

Lk 17:27
Mt 29:49 [34]"But take heed to yourselves lest your hearts be weighed down
Is 5:11–13 with dissipation and drunkenness and cares of this life, and that

---

glory of the Son of man, coming to judge the living and the dead. Christ will deliver this judgment in his human capacity. Sacred Scripture describes the solemnity of this event, when the sentence passed on each person in the particular judgment will be confirmed, and God's justice and mercy to men throughout history will shine out for all to see. "It was necessary not only that rewards should await the just and punishments the wicked, in the life to come, but that they should be awarded by a public and general judgment. Thus they will become better known and will be rendered more conspicuous to all, and a tribute of praise will be offered by all to the justice and providence of God" (St Pius V, *Catechism*, 1, 8, 4).

This coming of the Lord is, then, a day of terror for evildoers and of joy for those who have remained faithful. The disciples should hold their heads high because their redemption is at hand. It is the day they will receive their reward. The victory won by Christ on the cross—victory over sin, over the devil and over death—will now be seen clearly, with all its implications. Therefore St Paul recommends that we be "awaiting our blessed hope, the appearing of the glory of our great God and Saviour Jesus Christ" (Tit 2:13).

"He [Christ] ascended into heaven whence he will come again to judge the living and the dead, each according to his merits. Those who have responded to the love and compassion of God will go into eternal life. Those who have refused them to the end will be consigned to the fire that is never extinguished" (Paul VI, *Creed of the People of God*, 12).

21:31. The Kingdom of God, announced by John the Baptist (cf. Mt 3:2) and described by our Lord in so many parables (cf. Mt 13; Lk 13:18–20), is already present among the apostles (Lk 17:20–21), but it is not yet fully manifest. Jesus here describes what it will be like when the Kingdom comes in all its fulness, and he invites us to pray for this very event in the Our Father: "Thy Kingdom come." "The Kingdom of God, which had its beginnings here on earth in the Church of Christ, is not of

day come upon you suddenly like a snare; [35]for it will come Is 24:17
upon all who dwell upon the face of the whole earth. [36]But watch 1 Thess 5:3
at all times, praying that you may have strength to escape all Mk 13:33
these things that will take place, and to stand before the Son of
man."

Jesus teaches in the temple

[37]And every day he was teaching in the temple, but at night he Jn 8:1f
went out and lodged on the mount called Olivet. [38]And early in Mk 12:37
the morning all the people came to him in the temple to hear
him.

---

this world, whose form is passing, and its authentic development cannot be measured by the progress of civilization, of science and of technology. The true growth of the Kingdom of God consists in an ever deepening knowledge of the unfathomable riches of Christ, in an ever stronger hope in eternal blessings, in an ever more fervent response to the love of God, and in an ever more generous acceptance of grace and holiness by men" (*Creed of the People of God*, 27). At the end of the world everything will be subjected to Christ and God will reign for ever more (cf. 1 Cor 15:24, 28).

21:32. Everything referring to the destruction of Jerusalem was fulfilled some forty years after our Lord's death—which meant that Jesus' contemporaries would be able to verify the truth of this prophecy. But the destruction of Jerusalem is a symbol of the end of the world; therefore, it can be said that the generation to which our Lord refers did see the end of the world, in a symbolic way. This verse can also be taken to refer to the generation of believers, that is, not just the particular generation of those Jesus was addressing (cf. the note on Mt 24:32–35).

21:34–36. At the end of his discourse Jesus emphasizes that every Christian needs to be vigilant: we do not know the day nor the hour in which he will ask us to render an account of our lives. Therefore, we must at all times be trying to do God's will, so that death, whenever it comes, will find us ready. For those who act in this way, sudden death never takes them by surprise. As St Paul recommends: "You are not in darkness, brethren, for that day to surprise you like a thief" (1 Thess 5:4). Vigilance consists in making a constant effort not to be attached to the things of this world (the concupiscence of the flesh, the concupiscence of the eyes and the pride of life: cf. 1 Jn 2:16) and in being assiduous in prayer, which keeps us close to God. If we live in this way, the day we die will be a day of joy and not of terror, for with God's help our vigilance will mean that our souls are ready to receive the visit of the Lord; they are in the state of grace: in meeting Christ we will not be meeting a judge who will find us guilty; instead he will embrace us and lead us into the house of his Father to remain there forever. "Does your soul not burn with the desire to make your Father God happy when he has to judge you?" (St Josemaría Escrivá, *The Way*, 746).

13. THE PASSION, DEATH AND RESURRECTION OF JESUS

Mk 26:1–5
Judas' treachery

Mk 14:1–2 **22** [1]Now the feast of Unleavened Bread drew near, which is
Lk 20:19 called the Passover. [2]And the chief priests and the scribes
were seeking how to put him to death; for they feared the people.
Mt 26:14–15 [3]Then Satan entered into Judas called Iscariot, who was of the
Mk 14:10–11 number of the twelve; [4]he went away and conferred with the chief
Jn 13:2–27 priests and captains how he might betray him to them. [5]And they
were glad, and engaged to give him money. [6]So he agreed and
sought an opportunity to betray him to them in the absence of the
multitude.

22:1–38. These verses report the events immediately prior to our Lord's passion, events rich in meaning. The three Synoptic Gospels all give more or less the same account, but St Luke omits certain details and adds others which fill out Mark's or Matthew's account. Take, for example, the reporting of the institution of the Eucharist: while being substantially the same in the three Synoptics and often word for word, the Matthew and Mark accounts (cf. Mt 26:26–29; Mk 14:22–25) are quite different from that of Luke taken together with the First Letter to the Corinthians (cf. Lk 22:15–20; 1 Cor 11:23–25).

22:1. The feast of the Passover, the most solemn of all the Jewish feasts, was instituted by God to commemorate the exodus of the Israelites from Egypt and to remind them of their former slavery from which he saved them (Deut 16:3). It began with the passover supper on the evening of the fourteenth day of the month of Nisan (March-April), a little after sundown, and went on until 22 Nisan, the feast of the unleavened bread. The Mosaic Law laid down (Ex 12:15–20) that on the evening of 14 Nisan the Jews had to remove any trace of leaven from their houses and eat unleavened bread for the duration of the feast—reminding them that when the moment came to leave Egypt they had to leave in such a hurry that they had no time to prepare leavened bread to take with them (Ex 12:34).

All this was a prefigurement of the renewal which Christ would bring about: "Cleanse out the old leaven that you may be a new lump, as you really are unleavened. For Christ, our paschal lamb, has been sacrificed. Let us, therefore, celebrate the festival, not with the old leaven, the leaven of malice and evil, but with the unleavened bread of sincerity and truth" (1 Cor 5:7–8).

22:3–6. Even prior to the Passion, one can sense that the behaviour of Jesus' enemies was being orchestrated by the spirit of evil, Satan. This is particularly true where Judas is concerned. Corrupt human will alone cannot explain the torrent of hatred unleashed against Jesus.

The passion of our Lord marks the climax of the struggle between God and the powers of evil. After the third temptation in the desert the devil "departed from him until an opportune time" (Lk 4:13). The time has now come: it is the hour of Christ's enemies and of the power of darkness (cf. Lk 22:53), and it is also the hour of God's definitive vic-

Preparations for the Last Supper

7Then came the day of Unleavened Bread, on which the passover Mt 26:17–20
lamb had to be sacrificed. 8So Jesus[h] sent Peter and John, saying, Mk 14:12–17 Ex 12:18–20
"Go and prepare the passover for us, that we may eat it." 9They
said to him, "Where will you have us prepare it?" 10He said to
them, "Behold, when you have entered the city, a man carrying a
jar of water will meet you; follow him into the house which he
enters, 11and tell the householder, 'The Teacher says to you,
Where is the guest room, where I am to eat the passover with my
disciples?' 12And he will show you a large upper room furnished;
there make ready." 13And they went, and found it as he had told Lk 19:32
them; and they prepared the passover.

The institution of the Eucharist

14And when the hour came, he sat at table, and the apostles with
him. 15And he said to them, "I have earnestly desired to eat this

---

tory, for he "decreed that man should be saved through the wood of the cross. The tree of man's defeat became his tree of victory; where life was lost, there life has been restored" (*Roman Missal*, Preface of the Triumph of the Cross).

22:7–13. This scene took place on 14 Nisan. Every Israelite was familiar with the details of preparations for the Passover: it involved a rite which Jewish tradition, based on God-given regulations contained in the Law (cf. the note on Lk 22:1), had spelt out in minute detail—the unleavened loaves, bitter herbs, and the lamb to be sacrificed in the courtyard of the temple in the late afternoon. Peter and John, therefore, were perfectly acquainted with all these details; the only enquiry concerns where the supper is to be held, and our Lord tells them exactly how to find the place.

The disciples think that all that is involved is the Passover meal; but Jesus is also thinking about the institution of the Holy Eucharist and the Sacrifice of the New Alliance, which will take the place of the sacrifices of the Old Testament.

22:14. The Last Supper is beginning, the meal at which our Lord is going to institute the Holy Eucharist, a mystery of faith and love: "We must therefore approach this mystery, above all, with humble reverence, not following human arguments, which ought to be hushed, but in steadfast adherence to divine revelation" (Paul VI, *Mysterium fidei*).

22:15. St John, the beloved disciple, sums up in a single phrase the sentiments welling up in Jesus' soul at the Last Supper: "when Jesus knew that his hour had come to depart out of this world to the Father, having loved his own who were in the world, he loved them to the end" (Jn 13:1). Our Lord expresses his burning desire to spend the hours prior to his death with those whom he loves most on earth and, as happens when people are taking leave of their nearest and dearest, very affectionate words are exchanged (cf. Theophylact, *Enarratio in Evangel-*

h. Greek *he*

passover with you before I suffer; [16]for I tell you I shall not eat it[i]
until it is fulfilled in the kingdom of God." [17]And he took a cup,

---

ium Ioannis, in loc.). His love is not confined to the apostles; he is thinking of all men and women. He knows that this Passover meal marks the beginning of his passion. He is going to anticipate the Sacrifice of the New Testament, which will bring such benefits to mankind.

To fulfil his Father's will, Jesus must necessarily go away, but his love, impelling him to stay with his own, moves him to institute the Eucharist, in which he stays behind, in which he remains really and truly present. "Think," St J. Escrivá writes, "of the human experience of two people who love each other, and yet are forced to part. They would like to stay together forever, but duty—in one form or another—forces them to separate. They are unable to fulfil their desire of remaining close to each other, so man's love—which, great as it may be, is limited—seeks a symbolic gesture. People who make their farewells exchange gifts or perhaps a photograph with a dedication so ardent that it seems almost enough to burn that piece of paper. They can do no more, because a creature's power is not so great as its desire.

"What we cannot do, our Lord is able to do. Jesus Christ, perfect God and perfect man, leaves us not a symbol but a reality. He himself stays with us. He will go to the Father, but he will also remain among men. He will leave us, not simply a gift that will make us remember him, not an image that becomes blurred with time, like a photograph that soon fades and yellows, and has no meaning except for those who were contemporaries. Under the appearances of bread and wine, he is really present, with his body and blood, with his soul and divinity" (*Christ Is Passing By*, 83).

22:16–20. This text contains the three basic truths of faith having to do with the sublime mystery of the Eucharist: 1) the institution of this sacrament and Jesus Christ's real presence in it; 2) the institution of the Christian priesthood; and 3) the Eucharist as the Sacrifice of the New Testament or Holy Mass (cf. the note on Mt 26:26–29). St Luke's account is substantially the same as that in the First Gospel, but it is enhanced by his more detailed description of some points (cf. the note on v.17).

Regarding the real presence of Christ in this sacrament, Paul VI stated: "In reliance on this belief of the Church, the Council of Trent 'openly and simply professes that in the bountiful sacrament of the Holy Eucharist, after the consecration of the bread and wine, our Lord and Saviour Jesus Christ, true God and true man, is contained truly, really and substantially under the appearance of the objects that the senses can perceive' (*De SS. Eucharistia*, chap. 1). Therefore our Saviour is not only present according to his humanity at the right hand of the Father, after his natural mode of existence, but at the same time he is present in the sacrament of the Eucharist also by that form of existence which is possible to God, though we can hardly express it in words. With thoughts enlightened by faith we can reach it and we must believe it with the greatest constancy" (*Mysterium fidei*). In contemplating this ineffable mystery, Christian souls have always perceived its grandeur as deriving from the fact of Christ's real presence in it. The sacrament of the Eucharist is not only an efficacious sign of Christ's loving presence in an intimate union with the faith-

i. Other ancient authorities read *never eat it again*

ful: in it he is present corporeally and substantially, as God and as man. Certainly, in order to penetrate this mystery one needs to have faith, because "there is no difficulty about Christ being present in the Sacrament as a sign; the real difficulty lies in his being as truly in the Sacrament as he is in heaven; therefore, it is very meritorious to believe this" (St Bonaventure, *In IV Sent*., d.10, q.1, a.1). This mystery cannot be perceived by the senses: it can only be grasped by faith in the words of our Saviour who, being truth itself (cf. Jn 14:6), cannot deceive or be deceived: thus, in a hymn which is traditionally attributed to St Thomas Aquinas, the *Adoro te devote*, the Christian people sing: "Seeing, touching, tasting are in thee deceived; how says trusty hearing? that shall be believed; what God's Son has told me, take for truth I do; Truth himself speaks truly or there's nothing true" (translated by G.M. Hopkins).

"If no one is to misunderstand this mode of presence, which oversteps the laws of nature and constitutes the greatest miracle of all in its kind, our minds must be docile and we must follow the voice of the Church through her teaching and prayer. This voice continually re-echoes the voice of Christ. It informs us that Christ becomes present in this sacrament precisely by a change of the bread's whole substance into his body and the wine's whole substance into his blood. This is clearly remarkable, a singular change, and the Catholic Church gives it the suitable and accurate name of transubstantiation" (Paul VI, *Mysterium fidei*).

After instituting the Eucharist, our Lord instructs the apostles to perpetuate what he has done: the Church has always taken Christ's words "Do this in remembrance of me" to mean that he thereby made the apostles and their successors priests of the New Covenant who would renew the Sacrifice of Calvary in an unbloody manner in the celebration of Holy Mass.

This means that at the centre of Christ's entire activity stands the bloody Sacrifice he offered on the cross—the Sacrifice of the New Covenant, prefigured in the sacrifices of the Old Law, in the offerings made by Abel (Gen 4:4), by Abraham (Gen 15:10; 22:13), by Melchizedek (Gen 14:18–20; Heb 7:1–28). The Last Supper is the very Sacrifice of Calvary performed in advance of the event through the words of the Consecration. Similarly the Mass renews this sacrifice which was offered once for all on the altar of the cross. Christ alone is the victim and the priest at Supper, Calvary and Mass; the only thing that varies is the way he is offered.

"We believe that the Mass which is celebrated by the priest in the person of Christ in virtue of the power he receives in the sacrament of Order, and which is offered by him in the name of Christ and of the members of his Mystical Body, is indeed the Sacrifice of Calvary sacramentally realized on our altars" (Paul VI, *Creed of the People of God*, 24).

22:16. The words "I shall not eat it [this Passover] until it is fulfilled in the kingdom of heaven," as also those in v. 18, "I shall not drink of the fruit of this vine until the kingdom of God comes," do not mean that Jesus Christ will eat the paschal lamb once his Kingdom is established, but simply that this was the last time he will celebrate the Jewish Passover. Announcing the New Passover, which is now imminent and which will last until his second coming, Jesus once and for all replaces the ancient rite with his redemptive sacrifice, which marks the beginning of the Kingdom.

22:17. The Passover meal always followed a very specific pattern. Before eating the lamb, the senior person explained, in reply

and when he had given thanks he said, "Take this, and divide it
Mt 26:26–29 among yourselves; 18for I tell you that from now on I shall not
Mk 14:22–25 drink of the fruit of the vine until the kingdom of God comes."
1 Cor 11:23–25 19And he took bread, and when he had given thanks he broke it
Acts 27:35 Ex 12:14 and gave it to them, saying, "This is my body which is given for
Ex 24:8 you. Do this in remembrance of me." 20And likewise the cup after
Jer 31:31 supper, saying, "This cup which is poured out for you is the new
Zech 9:11 covenant in my blood.[j]

The treachery of Judas foretold

Mt 26:21–25 21"But behold the hand of him who betrays me is with me on the
Mk 14:18–21 table. 22For the Son of man goes as it has been determined; but

---

to a question from the youngest present, the religious meaning of what was happening. Then the meal proceeded, interspersed with hymns and psalms. At the end came a solemn prayer of thanksgiving. Throughout the meal, marking its main stages, the diners drank four glasses of wine mixed with water. St Luke refers to two of these, the second being that which our Lord consecrated.

22:19. We should note how plainly our Lord speaks: he does not say "here is my body," or "this is the symbol of my body," but "this is my body": that is, "this bread is no longer bread, it is my body". "Some men, accordingly, not paying heed to these things, have contended that Christ's body and blood are present in this sacrament only as in a sign: this is to be rejected as heretical, since it is contrary to Christ's words" (St Thomas Aquinas, *Summa theologiae*, 3, 75, 1). Jesus' words when he promised the Eucharist reinforce what he says here: "I am the living bread which came down from heaven; if any one eats of this bread, he will live for ever; and the bread which I shall give for the life of the world is my flesh [...]. He who eats my flesh and drinks my blood has eternal life, and I will raise him up at the last day" (Jn 6:51, 54).

"Do this in remembrance of me." The solemn Magisterium of the Church teaches us the meaning and scope of these words: "If anyone says that by the words, 'Do this in remembrance of me' Christ did not make his apostles priests, or that he did not decree that they and other priests should offer his body and blood: let him be condemned" (Council of Trent, *De SS. Missae sacrificio*, c. 2).

22:24–30. This was not the first time the apostles brought up this question about which of them was the greatest. It came up when they were going towards Capernaum, after Jesus' second announcement of his passion. At that time Jesus used a child as an example of humility (cf. Mt 18:1–5; Mk 9:33–37; Lk 9:46–48). A little later, when the mother of James and John made her special request, the same subject arose: the other apostles were very annoyed with the sons of Zebedee, and our Lord intervened and put himself forward as an example: "The

j. Some ancient authorities omit *which is given for you. Do this in remembrance of me." 20And likewise the cup after supper, saying, "This cup which is poured out for you is the new covenant in my blood*

woe to that man by whom he is betrayed!" [23]And they began to Jn 13:18–30
question one another, which of them it was that would do this.

A dispute among the apostles

[24]A dispute also arose among them, which of them was to be Lk 9:46ff
regarded as the greatest. [25]And he said to them. "The kings of the Mt 20:25–27 Mk 10:42–44
Gentiles exercise lordship over them; and those in authority over
them are called benefactors. [26]But not so with you; rather let the
greatest among you become as the youngest, and the leader as one
who serves. [27]For which is the greater, one who sits at table, or Jn 13:4–14
one who serves? Is it not the one who sits at table? But I am
among you as one who serves.

Son of man also came not to be served but to serve, and to give his life as a ransom for many" (Mk 10:45; cf. Mt 20:25–28).

The apostles failed to grasp what Jesus meant. They continue to be blinded by their human outlook and the same argument starts again. Jesus had invited them to have a greater sense of responsibility by telling them that one of their number was going to betray him (vv. 21 and 22) and by charging them to renew the Eucharistic Sacrifice (v. 19). As on other occasions when the apostles boasted about their personal merits, Jesus reminds them again of the example of his own life: he was their Teacher and Lord (cf. Jn 13:13) and yet he acted as if he were the least among them and served them. To respond to a calling from God a person needs humility, which expresses itself in the form of a spirit of service. "You want to hear all that I think of 'your way'? Very well, then … , listen: if you respond to the call, you will do your utmost in your work for Christ; if you become a man of prayer, you will be granted the grace necessary to respond and, hungry for sacrifice, you will seek out the hardest tasks. … And you will be happy here, and unspeakably happy hereafter" (St J. Escrivá, *The Way*, 235).

The reward which Jesus promises those who stay faithful to him far exceeds anything human ambition can envisage: the apostles will share in divine friendship in the Kingdom of heaven and they will sit on twelve thrones to judge the twelve tribes of Israel. Christ's word and example are a basic norm of government in the Church; the Second Vatican Council explains our Lord's commandment as follows: "The bishops, vicars and legates of Christ, govern the particular Church assigned to them by their counsels, exhortations and example, but over and above that also by the authority and sacred power which indeed they exercise exclusively for the spiritual development of their flock in truth and holiness, keeping in mind that he who is greater should become as the lesser, and he who is the leader as the servant (cf. Lk 22:26–27)" (*Lumen gentium*, 27).

22:25–27. By spreading Jesus' teaching about humility and service to others, we promote the true brotherhood of man. Pope Paul VI pointed this out in his address to the United Nations: "Allow us to say this to you, as the representative of a religion which accomplishes salvation through the humility of its divine Found-

Jn 6:67 28"You are those who have continued with me in my trials; 29as
Lk 12:32 my Father appointed a kingdom for me, so do I appoint for you
Mt 19:28 30that you may eat and drink at my table in my kingdom, and sit
on thrones judging the twelve tribes of Israel.

Mt 26:31–35 Mk 14:27–31 Jn 13:36–38 2 Cor 2:11 Amon 9:9 Jn 17:11–20

Peter's denial foretold

31"Simon, Simon, behold, Satan demanded to have you,[k] that he
might sift you[k] like wheat, 32but I have prayed for you that your faith
may not fail; and when you have turned again, strengthen your
brethren." 33And he said to him, "Lord, I am ready to go with you to
prison and to death." 34He said, "I tell you, Peter, the cock will not
crow this day, until you three times deny that you know me."

---

er: men cannot be brothers if they are not humble. It is pride, no matter how legitimate it may seem to be, which provokes tension and struggles for prestige, for predominance, colonialism, selfishness; it is pride that disrupts brotherhood" (no. 4).

22:31–34. Jesus had previously told Peter that he was going to give him a specially important mission among the apostles—that of being the cornerstone, the foundation, of the Church he would found. " 'So you are Simon the son of John? You shall be called Cephas' (which means Peter)" (Jn 1:42), Jesus told him on the bank of the Jordan. Later, in Caesarea Philippi, after his profession of faith in the divinity of the Redeemer, Christ again referred to him as being a rock, as having a mission to strengthen the Church: "And I tell you, you are Peter, and on this rock I will build my church, and the powers of death shall not prevail against it" (Mt 16:18). Now, at this very solemn moment, when his death approaches and he has just instituted the Sacrifice of the New Testament, our Lord renews his promise to Peter to give him the primacy: Peter's faith, despite his fall, cannot fail because it is supported by the efficacious prayer of our Lord himself.

Jesus is giving Peter a privilege which is both personal and transferable. Peter will publicly deny his Lord in the high priest's house, but he will not lose his faith. As St John Chrysostom comments, it is as if our Lord were saying to Peter, "I have not prayed that you may not deny me but that your faith may not fail" (*Hom. on St Matthew*, 3). And Theophylact adds: "For, although St Peter would have to experience ups and downs he still had the hidden seed of faith, and he [Christ] adds, 'And when you have turned again, strengthen your brethren', as if to say, 'After you repent; confirm then your brethren, for I have made you the leader of the apostles; this is the task given you: you with me are the strength and the rock of my Church.' This should be taken not only as applying to the disciples who were present there, for them to be strengthened by Peter: it also refers to all the faithful who would follow, until the end of the world" (*Enarratio in Evangelium Lucae*, in loc.).

And, as it turned out, as a result of our Lord's prayer, Peter's faith did not fail and he recovered from his fall; he confirmed his brothers and was indeed the cornerstone of the Church.

Our Lord's prayer was effective in respect not only to Peter but also to his successors: their faith will not fail. This

k. The Greek word for *you* here is plural; in verse 32 it is singular

Appeal to the apostles

[35]And he said to them, "When I sent you out with no purse or bag Lk 9:3; 10:4
or sandals, did you lack anything?" They said, "Nothing." [36]He
said to them, "But now, let him who has a purse take it, and likewise a bag. And let him who has no sword sell his mantle and buy
one. [37]For I tell you that this scripture must be fulfilled in me, Is 53:12
'And he was reckoned with transgressors'; for what is written
about me has its fulfilment." [38]And they said, "Look, Lord, here
are two swords." And he said to them, "It is enough."

Jesus' prayer and agony in the garden

[39]And he came out, and went, as was his custom, to the Mount of Mt 26:30; 36–46
Olives; and the disciples followed him. [40]And when he came to Mk 14:26; 32–42

---

indefectibility of the faith of the bishop of Rome, the successor of St Peter, is to be seen as ensuring that he stay committed to the faith, a commitment guaranteed by the charism of infallibility: "This infallibility, with which the divine Redeemer wished to endow his Church in defining doctrine pertaining to faith and morals, is co-extensive with the deposit of revelation, which must be religiously guarded and loyally and courageously expounded. The Roman Pontiff, head of the college of bishops, enjoys this infallibility in virtue of his office, when, as supreme pastor and teacher of all the faithful—who confirms his brethren in the faith (cf. Lk 22:32)—he proclaims in an absolute decision a doctrine pertaining to faith or morals" (Vatican II, *Lumen gentium*, 25).

Therefore, when the Pope speaks *ex cathedra* (cf. Vatican I, *Pastor aeternus*, chap. 4) "he enjoys that infallibility with which the divine Redeemer wished to provide his Church … and therefore the definitions of the Roman Pontiff are irreformable by their very nature" (see also the note on Mt 16:13–20).

"The supreme power of the Roman Pontiff and his infallibility, when he speaks *ex cathedra*, are not a human invention: they are based on the explicit foundational will of Christ […]. No one in the Church enjoys absolute power by himself, as man. In the Church there is no leader other than but Christ. And Christ constituted a vicar of his—the Roman Pontiff—for his wayfaring spouse on earth […]. Love for the Pope must be in us a beautiful passion, because in him we see Christ" (St J. Escrivá, *In Love with the Church*, 13).

22:36–38. Jesus announces his passion by applying to himself the Isaiah prophecy about the Servant of Yahweh (Is 53:12)—"he was numbered with the transgressors"—and pointing out that all the other prophecies about the sufferings of the Redeemer will find fulfilment in him. The testing-time is imminent and our Lord is speaking symbolically when he talks about making provision and buying weapons to put up a fight. The apostles take him literally, and this leads him to express a certain indulgent understanding: "It is enough." "Just in the same way as we," Theophylact says, "when we are speaking to someone and see that he does not understand, say: 'Very well, leave it' " (*Enarratio in Evangelium Lucae*, in loc.).

22:39–71. Our Lord's passion is the out-

Lk 21:37 Jn 18:1 the place he said to them, "Pray that you may not enter into temptation." 41And he withdrew from them about a stone's throw, and
Mt 6:10 knelt down and prayed, 42"Father, if thou art willing, remove this
1 Kings 19:5–7 cup from me; nevertheless not my will, but thine, be done." 43And
Jn 12:29 there appeared to him an angel from heaven, strengthening him.

---

standing proof of God's love for men: "God so loved the world that he gave his only Son, that whoever believes in him should not perish but have eternal life" (Jn 3:16). It also proves beyond doubt that Christ, true God and true man, loves us, as he said himself: "Greater love has no man than this, that a man lay down his life for his friends" (Jn 15:13).

"Do you want to accompany Jesus closely, very closely? … Open the Holy Gospel and read the Passion of our Lord. But don't just read it: live it. There is a big difference. To read is to recall something that happened in the past; to live is to find oneself present at an event that is happening here and now, to be someone taking part in those scenes. Then, allow your heart to open wide; let it place itself next to our Lord. And when you notice it trying to slip away—when you see that you are a coward, like the others—ask forgiveness for your cowardice and mine" (St Josemaría Escrivá, *The Way of the Cross*, IX, 3).

22:39–40. It was Jesus' custom to retire to the garden of Gethsemane, on the Mount of Olives, in order to pray; this seems to be implied by both St John (Jn 18:1) and St Luke (21:37). This explains how Judas knew the place (Jn 18:1–2).

As soon as he reaches the garden our Lord prepares to face his agony. Before going aside to pray, he asks his disciples to pray as well because very soon they will be tempted to lose faith when they see him being arrested (cf. Mt 26:31). At the Last Supper Jesus had told them this would happen; now he warns them that if they are not watchful and prayerful they will not be able to resist the temptation. He also wants his apostles to keep him company when he suffers—which is why, when he comes back and finds them sleeping, he sorrowfully complains to Peter: "Could you not watch with me one hour?" (Mt 26:40).

We should stay close to our Lord and keep him company, even at times of difficulty and tribulation; the command Jesus gives here shows us how to go about this—by prayer and vigilance.

22:41. Jesus prays kneeling down. Many Gospel passages refer to our Lord's prayer but this is the only time his posture is described. It may well be that he knelt at other times also. Kneeling is an external expression of a humble attitude towards God.

22:42. Jesus Christ is perfect God and perfect man: as God he is equal to the Father, as man less than the Father. And therefore as man he could pray, he had to pray—as he did throughout his life. Now, when his spiritual suffering is so intense that he is in agony, our Lord addresses his Father with a prayer which shows both his trust and his anguish: he calls him, with immense affection, "Abba", Father, and asks him to remove this cup of bitterness. What causes our Lord his intense pain? Foreknowledge of all the sufferings involved in his passion, which he freely undergoes; and the weight of all the sins of mankind, the unfaithfulness of the chosen people and abandonment by his disciples. Christ's sensitive soul felt

44And being in an agony he prayed more earnestly; and his sweat
became like great drops of blood falling down upon the ground.[1]
45And when he rose from prayer, he came to the disciples and
found them sleeping for sorrow, 46and he said to them, "Why do
you sleep? Rise and pray that you may not enter into temptation."

---

the full impact of all this. So intense is our Redeemer's anguish that he actually sweats blood, an indication of the extent of his human capacity to suffer.

In this connexion St Thomas More comments: "The fear of death and torments carries no stigma of guilt but rather is an affliction of the sort Christ came to suffer, not to escape. We should not immediately consider it cowardice for someone to feel fear and horror at the thought of torments [...]. But to flee because of a fear of torture and death when the circumstances make it necessary to fight, or to give up all hope of victory and surrender to the enemy—that, to be sure, is a capital crime according to the military code. But otherwise, no matter how much the heart of the soldier is agitated and stricken by fear, if he still comes forward at the command of the general, goes on, fights and defeats the enemy, he has no reason to fear that his former fear might lessen his reward in any way. As a matter of fact, he ought to receive even more praise because of it, since he had to overcome not only the enemy but also his own fear, which is often harder to conquer than the enemy itself" (*De tristitia Christi*, in loc.).

Jesus perseveres in his prayer: "Not my will, but thine, be done"—which shows that he had a human will and that it was in total harmony with the divine will. This prayer of our Lord is also a perfect lesson in abandonment to and union with the Will of God—features which should be found in our own prayer, particularly in moments of difficulty. "Are things going against you? Are you going through a rough time? Say very slowly, as if relishing it, this powerful and manly prayer: 'May the most just and most lovable will of God be done, be fulfilled, be praised and eternally exalted above all things. Amen, Amen.' I assure you that you will find peace" (St Josemaría Escrivá, *The Way*, 691).

22:43. In the Gospel we often see angels play a part in our Lord's life. An angel announces the mystery of the Incarnation to the Blessed Virgin (Lk 1:26); choirs of angels sing God's praises when Jesus is born in Bethlehem (Lk 2:13); angels minister to him after he is tempted in the wilderness (Mt 4:11); and now the Father sends an angel to comfort him in his agony.

Our Lord, who is God, accepts this consolation. The Creator of all, who is never in need of the help of his creatures, is ready to accept, as man, consolation and help from those who can give it.

In addition to aiding Jesus in his work as Redeemer, angels also minister to the Church in a special way. We often see them act in the early days of the Church (cf. Acts 5:19; 7:30; 8:26; 12:7; 27:23; etc.). God has given angels the mission of accompanying men and helping them as they make their way on earth towards their heavenly goal. The angels, says Paul VI, "intercede for us and come to the aid of our weakness in brotherly care" (*Creed of the People of God*, 29). Their caring presence should move us to rely constantly on our guardian angels, to

l. Other ancient authorities omit verses 43 and 44

Arrest of Jesus

Mt 26:47–56 Mk 14:43–49 Jn 18:2–11 [47]While he was still speaking, there came a crowd, and the man
called Judas, one of the twelve, was leading them. He drew near
to Jesus to kiss him; [48]but Jesus said to him, "Judas, would you
betray the Son of man with a kiss?" [49]And when those who were
about him saw what would follow, they said, "Lord, shall we
strike with the sword?" [50]And one of them struck the slave of the
high priest and cut off his right ear. [51]But Jesus said, "No more of
this!" And he touched his ear and healed him. [52]Then Jesus said to
the chief priests and captains of the temple and elders, who had
come out against him,* "Have you come out as against a robber,
Jn 7:30; 18:20 with swords and clubs? [53]When I was with you day after day in
the temple, you did not lay hands on me. But this is your hour,
and the power of darkness."

---

have recourse to them in our needs and to show them reverence.

22:47–48. Judas now gives the prearranged sign (cf. Mt 26:48); he comes forward to kiss our Lord—a form of friendly greeting normal among the Jews. When greeting someone like this, one would say *Shalom*, "peace". In contemplating this sad betrayal by an apostle, Jesus treats Judas in a very gentle way and yet shows up the malice and ugliness of his treachery: for the last time he tries to win Judas back.

There is no limit to the goodness of a merciful God, and not even the greatest sinner should despair of obtaining forgiveness. "Even to Judas," St Thomas More comments, "God gave many opportunities of coming to his senses. He did not deny him his companionship. He did not take away from him the dignity of his apostleship. He did not even take the purse-strings from him, even though he was a thief. He admitted the traitor to the fellowship of his beloved disciples at the last supper. He deigned to stoop down at the feet of the betrayer and to wash with his most innocent and sacred hands Judas' dirty feet, a fit symbol of his filthy mind [...]. Finally when Judas, coming with his crew to seize him, offered him a kiss, a kiss that was in fact the terrible token of his treachery, Christ received him calmly and gently [...]. Therefore, since God showed his great mercy, in so many ways even toward Judas, an apostle turned traitor, since he invited him to forgiveness so often and did not allow him to perish except through despair alone, certainly there is no reason why, in this life, anyone should despair of any imitator of Judas. Rather, according to that holy advice of the apostle, 'Pray for one another, that you may be healed' (Jas 5:16), if we see anyone wandering wildly from the right road, let us hope that he will one day return to the path, and meanwhile let us pray humbly and incessantly that God will hold out to him chances to come to his senses, and likewise that with God's help he will eagerly seize them, and having seized them will hold fast and not throw them away out of malice or let them slip away from him through wretched sloth" (*De tristitia Christi*, in loc.).

22:51. St Luke, who was a physician (cf. Col 4:15), here by divine inspiration records the last miracle worked by Jesus before his death. Ever merciful, Jesus restores to Malchus the ear Peter cut off

Peter's denials

Mt 26:57f; 69–75 Mk 14:53f; 66–72 Jn 18:12–18, 25–27

[54]Then they seized him and led him away, bringing him into the
high priest's house. Peter followed at a distance; [55]and when they
had kindled a fire in the middle of the courtyard and sat down
together, Peter sat among them. [56]Then a maid, seeing him as he
sat in the light and gazing at him, said, "This man also was with
him." [57]But he denied it, saying, "Woman, I do not know him."
[58]And a little later some one else saw him and said, "You also are
one of them." But Peter said, "Man, I am not." [59]And after an
interval of about an hour still another insisted, saying, "Certainly
this man also was with him; for he is a Galilean." [60]But Peter
said, "Man, I do not know what you are saying." And immediately, while he was still speaking, the cock crowed. [61]And the
Lord turned and looked at Peter. And Peter remembered the word

---

(cf. Jn 18:10)—thereby showing that he is still in control of events, even in the present situation. Careless of his own safety he cures one of the people who have come to arrest him. Also, Jesus, who is giving himself up to death in obedience to his Father, refuses to have violence used in his defence. In fulfilment of the prophecies he offers no resistance, he goes like a sheep to the slaughter (cf. Is 53:7).

22:52–53. The "captains of the temple" were a military corps charged with policing the temple precincts; they reported to the high priest. To them, as well as to the priests and elders, our Lord addresses these words.

"This is your hour," that is, the time when you, the prince of darkness, can unleash all your hatred against me: our Lord shows that he knows his death is at hand. Previous attempts to arrest him had failed; but this one will succeed, because, as he explains, God allows it to happen. This is the hour the Father has fixed to accomplish the redemption of mankind; therefore, Jesus freely lets himself be taken prisoner.

22:55–62. Peter, who has been following the throng of people hustling our Lord, enters the house of the high priest. While Jesus is undergoing his first trial the saddest event in the apostle's life takes place. The evangelists give vivid accounts of the scene. Peter is in a state of shock and is all confused. Inevitably, that night, people would have spoken about Jesus and his disciples a number of times. In conversation Peter says three times that he does not know Jesus, that he is not a follower of his. He does want to continue to follow our Lord, but wanting is not enough: he has a duty not to disguise the fact that he is a disciple, even though it is obviously risky to do so; that is why his denial is a grave sin. No one is justified in denying or disguising his faith, the fact that he is a Christian, a follower of Christ.

After the cock crows Jesus' glance meets Peter's. The apostle is moved by this silent and tender gesture. Peter realizes the seriousness of his sin and the fact that it fulfils our Lord's prophecy about his betrayal. "He went out and wept bitterly." Tears like these are the natural reaction of a noble heart moved by God's grace; this lovesorrow, this contrition, when it is sincere, leads a person to make the firm resolution to do anything necessary to erase the least trace of the sin he has committed.

of the Lord, how he had said to him, "Before the cock crows
today, you will deny me three times." 62And he went out and wept
bitterly.

Jesus abused by the guards

Mt 26:67–68 63Now the men who were holding Jesus mocked him and beat
Mk 14:65 him; 64they also blindfolded him and asked him, "Prophesy! Who
is it that struck you?" 65And they spoke many other words against
him, reviling him.

Jesus before the chief priests

Mk 26:59–66 66When day came, the assembly of the elders of the people gath-
Mk 14:55–64 ered together, both chief priests and scribes; and they led him
Jn 8:45; 10:24 away to their council, and they said, 67"If you are the Christ, tell
Dan 7:13 us." But he said to them, "If I tell you, you will not believe; 68and
Ps 110:1 if I ask you, you will not answer. 69But from now on the Son of

---

22:66–71. Our Lord's first trial, which took place at night, was aimed at establishing the charges to be laid against him (Mt 26:59–66; Mk 14:53–64). Now, as day dawns, the Sanhedrin trial begins: this trial was required because Jewish custom forbade night trials on serious charges—which meant that any decisions taken at such trials had no legal validity. The authorities want to charge Jesus with a crime carrying the death penalty, and they decide to establish that he has committed blasphemy; but the evidence is so inconsistent that it fails to provide a pretext for condemning him. Therefore the Sanhedrin endeavours to get our Lord to say something which will compromise him. Although he knows that his reply provides the Pharisees with the pretext they are looking for, Jesus solemnly states, to the indignation of those present, not only that he is the Messiah but that he is the Son of God, equal to the Father; and he emphasizes that in him the ancient prophecies are being fulfilled (cf. Dan 7:13; Ps 110:1). The members of the Sanhedrin know exactly what our Lord's answer means and, tearing their garments to show their horror, they call for his death: he deserves death because he has committed the blasphemy of claiming to be on the same level as God.

Recognizing Jesus would involve their doing an about-turn in their attitude towards him—which they would have found very embarrassing. They are too proud to change, and they close the door on faith—a lesson to us all not to let pride blind us to our mistakes and sins.

23:1–2. Jesus underwent two trials—a religious one, following the Jewish system, and a civil one, following the Roman.

In the first trial, the Jewish authorities condemned Jesus to death on religious grounds for claiming to be the Son of God; but they could not carry out the sentence because the Romans reserved to themselves the exercise of the death penalty. The Sanhedrin now arranges a new trial before Pilate in order to get the Romans to execute the sentence they themselves have already passed. Events are moving to fulfil Jesus' prophecy that

man shall be seated at the right hand of the power of God." 70And
they all said, "Are you the Son of God, then?" And he said to
them, "You say that I am." 71And they said, "What further testimony do we need? We have heard it ourselves from his own
lips."

Jesus before Pilate

23 1Then the whole company of them arose, and brought him Mt 27:2, 11–31
before Pilate. 2And they began to accuse him, saying, "We Mk 15:1–20 Jn 18:28–19:6
found this man perverting our nation, and forbidding us to give Lk 20:25
tribute to Caesar, and saying that he himself is Christ a
king."* 3And Pilate asked him, "Are you the King of the Jews?" 1 Tim 6:13
And he answered him, "You have said so." 4And Pilate said to the
chief priests and the multitudes, "I find no crime in this man."
5But they were urgent, saying, "He stirs up the people, teaching
throughout all Judea, from Galilee even to this place."

---

he will die at the hands of the Gentiles (cf. Lk 18:32).

Due to the fact that the Romans were very tolerant of religious customs of subject peoples—and took no interest in them provided they did not lead to public unrest—the Jewish leaders alter the charges they bring against Jesus: from now on they accuse him of political crimes—of inciting rebellion against the Romans and of seeking to become king. And they present these charges in such a way that a verdict favourable to the accused might be interpreted in Rome as a treacherous act: "If you release this man, you are not Caesar's friend; every one who makes himself a king sets himself against Caesar" (Jn 19:12).

23:2. To give their charges a veneer of credibility, they produce half-truths, taken out of context and interpreted in the worst possible light. Jesus had taught: "Render therefore to Caesar the things that are Caesar's, and to God the things that are God's" (Mt 22:21; cf. the note on same), and in his preaching he stated that by virtue of being the Messiah he was King as well as Prophet and Priest; but he also preached that his was a spiritual kingship and therefore he energetically rejected all the people's attempts to proclaim him king (cf. Jn 6:15).

23:3–4. Jesus openly confesses that he is King, but from what he says he makes quite clear the spiritual nature of this kingship (Jn 18:33–38). Pilate becomes convinced that he is guilty of no crime (Jn 18:38; 19:4) and that all the charges brought against him are groundless (Mt 27:18). However, instead of efficiently delivering judgment in favour of the accused, he temporizes; he tries to gain popularity at Jesus' expense and settles for indicating that he is convinced of his innocence—as if inviting the accusers to back off; but this only encourages them to become vociferous and complicates the situation.

By behaving in this way Pilate becomes the classic example of a compromiser: "A man, a 'gentleman', ready to compromise would condemn Jesus to death again" (St Josemaría Escrivá, *The Way*, 393).

Jesus before Herod

Lk 3:1 6When Pilate heard this, he asked whether the man was a
Galilean. 7And when he learned that he belonged to Herod's jurisdiction, he sent him over to Herod, who was himself in Jerusalem
Lk 9:9 at that time. 8When Herod saw Jesus, he was very glad, for he had
long desired to see him, because he had heard about him, and he
was hoping to see some sign done by him. 9So he questioned him
Acts 25:7 at some length; but he made no answer. 10The chief priests and the
scribes stood by, vehemently accusing him. 11And Herod with his
soldiers treated him with contempt and mocked him; then, array-
ing him in gorgeous apparel, he sent him back to Pilate. 12And
Acts 4:27 Herod and Pilate became friends with each other that very day, for
before this they had been at enmity with each other.

Jesus is condemned to death

13Pilate then called together the chief priests and the rulers and the
Acts 28:18–19 people, 14and said to them, "You brought me this man as one who
was perverting the people; and after examining him before you,
behold, I did not find this man guilty of any of your charges

---

23:7. Herod Antipas normally went up to Jerusalem for the Passover, staying in his own palace in the centre of the city. By sending Jesus to Herod Pilate is trying to rid himself of a troublesome case and build up a friendship useful to his own political career.

23:8–11. Our Lord adopts a very different attitude to Herod Antipas compared with his attitude to Pilate. Herod was superstitious, sensual and adulterous. In spite of his regard for John the Baptist, he had him beheaded to keep his oath to Salome (cf. Mk 6:14–29). Now he tries to get Jesus to perform a miracle, as if Jesus were a magician putting on a show for Herod's entertainment. Jesus does not reply to his flattery. Our Lord's attitude is simple, stately and also severe. His eloquent silence is a perfect example of the way to deal with behaviour of this type. Herod reacts by dressing Jesus in a rich robe, to make fun of him.

23:12. Psalm 2 said this in prophecy of the Messiah: "The kings of the earth set themselves, and the rulers take counsel together, against the Lord and his anointed." These words are now fulfilled to the letter, as the Book of the Acts points out: "For truly in this city there were gathered together against thy holy servant Jesus, whom thou didst anoint, both Herod and Pontius Pilate, with the Gentiles and the people of Israel, to do whatever thy hand and thy plan had predestined to take place" (Acts 4:27f).

23:17. Verse 17—"Necesse autem habebat dimittere eis per diem festum, unum" (in the Old Vulgate)—has not been included in the New Vulgate because it is absent from most of the better Greek manuscripts.

23:24–25. Jesus condemned to death and made to carry the cross (cf. Jn 19:16–17) is devoutly contemplated by Christians in the first and second stations

against him;* [15]neither did Herod, for he sent him back to us.
Behold, nothing deserving death has been done by him; [16]I will
therefore chastise him and release him."[m]
[18]But they all cried out together, "Away with this man, and
release to us Barabbas"—[19]a man who had been thrown into
prison for an insurrection started in the city, and for murder.
[20]Pilate addressed them once more, desiring to release Jesus; [21]but
they shouted out, "Crucify, crucify him!" [22]A third time he said to
them, "Why, what evil has he done? I have found in him no crime
deserving death; I will therefore chastise him and release him."
[23]But they were urgent, demanding with loud cries that he should
be crucified. And their voices prevailed. [24]So Pilate gave sentence
that their demand should be granted. [25]He released the man who Mt 17:12
had been thrown into prison for insurrection and murder, whom
they asked for; but Jesus he delivered up to their will.

The crucifixion and death of Jesus

[26]And as they led him away, they seized one Simon of Cyrene, Mt 27:32
who was coming in from the country, and laid on him the cross, Mk 15:21

---

of the Way of the Cross. Pilate at last gives in to the Sanhedrin and condemns our Lord to the most ignominous form of punishment, death by crucifixion.

It was customary for people condemned to crucifixion to be made to carry the instrument of their own death. Our Lord fulfils in his own person the prophecies of Isaiah: "By oppression and judgment he was taken away; [...] he was cut off out of the land of the living, stricken for the transgression of my people? And they made his grave with the wicked" (Is 53:8–9).

23:26. Christian piety contemplates this episode of the Passion in the fifth station of the Way of the Cross. The soldiers force Simon to help Jesus carry the cross, not because they feel pity for our Lord, but because they realize that he is getting weaker and weaker and they are afraid he may die before reaching Calvary. According to tradition, preserved in the third, seventh and ninth stations, Jesus fell three times under the weight of the cross; but he got up again and lovingly embraced it once more in obedience to his heavenly Father's will, seeing in the cross the altar on which he would give his life as a propitiatory Victim for the salvation of mankind.

However, our Lord chose to be helped by Simon of Cyrene in order to show us that we—whom Simon represents—have to become co-redeemers with him. "Love for God invites us to take up the cross and feel on our own shoulders the weight of humanity. It leads us to fulfill the clear and loving plans of the Father's will in all the circumstances of our work and life" (St Josemaría Escrivá, *Christ Is Passing By*, 97). God the Father, in his providence,

m. Here, or after verse 19, other ancient authorities add verse 17, *Now he was obliged to release one man to them at the festival*

to carry it behind Jesus. [27]And there followed him a great multi-
tude of the people, and of women who bewailed and lamented
Rev 1:7 him. [28]But Jesus turning to them said, "Daughters of Jerusalem,
do not weep for me, but weep for yourselves and for your chil-
Lk 11:27; 21:23 dren. [29]For behold, the days are coming when they will say,
'Blessed are the barren, and the wombs that never bore, and the

---

gave his Son this small consolation in the midst of his terrible suffering—just as he sent an angel to comfort him in his agony in Gethsemane (Lk 22:43).

Other aspects of this scene of the Gospel are commented on in notes on Mt 27:32 and Mk 15:21.

23:27–31. The piety of these women shows that Jesus had friends as well as enemies. If we bear in mind that Jewish traditions, as recorded in the Talmud, forbade wailing for people condemned to death, we will appreciate the value of these women's gesture.

"Among the people watching our Lord as he passes by are a number of women who are unable to restrain their compassion and break into tears, perhaps recalling those glorious days spent with Jesus, when everyone exclaimed in amazement: *bene omnia fecit* (Mk 7:37), he has done all things well.

"But our Lord wishes to channel their weeping towards a more supernatural motive, and he invites them to weep for sins, which are the cause of the Passion and which will draw down the rigour of divine justice: 'Daughters of Jerusalem, do not weep for me, but weep for yourselves and for your children. ... For if they do this when the wood is green, what will happen when it is dry?' (Lk 23:28, 31).

"Your sins, my sins, the sins of all men, rise up. All the evil we have done and the good that we have neglected to do. The desolate panorama of the countless crimes and iniquities which we would have committed, if he, Jesus, had not strengthened us with the light of his most loving glance. How little a life is for making atonement!" (St Josemaría Escrivá, *The Way of the Cross*, VIII).

Christian devotion also includes in the Way of the Cross a pious tradition that a woman, called Veronica (Berenice), approached Jesus and wiped his face with a linen cloth—a brave action on her part, in view of the hostility of the crowd (*sixth station*). And another station, the *fourth*, venerates Jesus' meeting with his blessed Mother on the way to Calvary, a sorrowful meeting which fulfils Simeon's prophecy to the Blessed Virgin (cf. Lk 2:35).

On the way to Calvary the only people who give Jesus consolation are women—evidencing their bravery and religious sensitivity during this painful time in Jesus' life; whereas only one man—John—is to be seen.

In spite of his awful suffering, Jesus is mindful of the terrible times which are approaching. His words in response to the women's lament are a prophecy about the destruction of Jerusalem, which will come about within a few years.

The "green wood" refers to the just and innocent; the "dry wood", to the sinner, the guilty one. Jesus, the Son of God, is the only truly just and innocent man.

23:33. The crucifixion is contemplated in the eleventh station of the Way of the Cross. The soldiers nail Jesus' hands and feet to the beams. The purpose of this

breasts that never gave suck!' [30]Then they will begin to say to the Hos 10:8
mountains, 'Fall on us'; and to the hills, 'Cover us.' [31]For if they do Rev 6:16; 9:6
this when the wood is green, what will happen when it is dry?"* 1 Pet 4:17f
[32]Two others also, who were criminals, were led away to be put to
death with him. [33]And when they came to the place which is Mt 27:33–56
called The Skull, there they crucified him, and the criminals, Mk 15:22–41 Jn 19:17–30

---

punishment is to bring on a slow death, involving maximum suffering: "Now they are crucifying our Lord, and with him two thieves, one on his right and one on his left. Meanwhile, Jesus says: 'Father, forgive them; for they know not what they do' (Lk 23:34).

"It is Love that has brought Jesus to Calvary. And once on the Cross, all his gestures and all his words are of love, a love both calm and strong. With a gesture befitting an Eternal Priest, without father or mother, without lineage (cf. Heb 7:3), he opens his arms to the whole human race.

"With the hammerblows with which Jesus is being nailed, there resound the prophetic words of Holy Scripture: 'They have pierced my hands and my feet. I can count all my bones, and they stare and gloat over me' (Ps 22:17–18). 'My people, what have I done to you? In what have I wearied you? Answer me!' (Mic 6:3).

"And we, our soul rent with sorrow, say to Jesus in all sincerity: I am yours and I give my whole self to you; gladly do I nail myself to your Cross, ready to be in the crossroads of this world a soul dedicated to you, to your glory, to the work of Redemption, the co-redemption of the whole human race" (St Josemaría Escrivá, *The Way of the Cross*, XI).

"It is good for us to try to understand better the meaning of Christ's death. We must get beyond external appearances and clichés. […] Let us, above all, come close to Jesus in his death and to his cross which stands out in silhouette above the summit of Golgotha. But we must approach him sincerely and with the interior recollection that is a sign of Christian maturity. The divine and human events of the Passion will then pierce our soul as words spoken to us by God to uncover the secrets of our heart and show us what he expects of our lives" (St Josemaría Escrivá, *Christ Is Passing By*, 101).

Jesus' terrible suffering on the cross clearly shows the gravity of the sins of men, of my sin. This gravity is measured by the infinite greatness and honour of God, the offended one. God, who is infinitely merciful and at the same time infinitely just, exercised both these attributes: his infinite justice required an infinite reparation, of which mere man was incapable; his infinite mercy found the solution: the second person of the Trinity, taking on human nature, becoming truly man while not ceasing to be true God, suffered the punishment which was man's due. In this way, by being represented in Jesus' sacred humanity, men would be able to make sufficient atonement to God's justice. No words can express God's love for us as manifested on the cross. A living faith in the mystery of our redemption will lead us to respond with gratitude and love: "We believe that our Lord Jesus Christ redeemed us by the sacrifice on the Cross from original sin and from all those personal sins to which we confess, so that the truth of the apostle's words is vindicated that where sin increased, grace abounded all the more" (Paul VI, *Creed of the People of God*, 17).

Mt 5:44 one on the right and one on the left. 34 And Jesus said, "Father, for-
Is 53:12 Ps 22:18 give them; for they know not what they do."[n] And they cast lots
Ps 22:7 to divide his garments. 35 And the people stood by, watching; but
the rulers scoffed at him, saying, "He saved others; let him save
himself, if he is the Christ of God, his Chosen One!" 36 The sol-
Ps 69:21 diers also mocked him, coming up and offering him vinegar, 37 and
saying, "If you are the King of the Jews, save yourself!" 38 There
was also an inscription over him,[o] "This is the King of the Jews."

23:34. Jesus addresses the Father in a tone of supplication (cf. Heb 5:7). We can distinguish two parts in his prayer—his simple request: "Father, forgive them," and the excuse he offers, "for they know not what they do." We can see him as one who practises what he preaches (cf. Acts 1:1) and as a model whom we should imitate. He had taught us that we have a duty to forgive offences (cf. Mt 6:12–15; 18:21–35), and even to love our enemies (cf. Mt 5:44–45; Rom 12:14, 20), because he had come into the world to offer himself as a victim "for the forgiveness of sins" (Mt 26:28; cf. Eph 1:7) and to enable us to obtain pardon.

The excuse which Jesus offers may at first take us by surprise: "for they know not what they do." His love, his perfect mercy and justice make maximum allowance for factors rendering our sins less heinous. It is quite clear that the people directly responsible were perfectly aware that they were condemning an innocent person to death, that they were guilty of homicide; but they did not realize, in these moments of passion, that they were also committing deicide. This is what St Peter means when he tells the Jews, encouraging them to repent, that they acted "in ignorance" (Acts 3:17), and St Paul adds that if they had understood the hidden wisdom of God "they would not have crucified the Lord of glory" (1 Cor 2:8). Jesus in his mercy excuses them on the grounds of ignorance.

In any sinful action there are always areas of darkness, passion, blindness, which without taking away a person's freedom and responsibility do enable him to carry out an evil action through being attracted by apparently good aspects which that action involves; and this does lessen the evil that we do.

Christ teaches us to forgive those who offend us and to look for excuses for them, thereby leaving open the door to the hope of their pardon and repentance; only God can be the ultimate judge of men. This heroic charity was practised by Christians from the very beginning. Thus, the first martyr, St Stephen, dies begging God to pardon his executioners (cf. Acts 7:60). "Force yourself, if necessary, always to forgive those who offend you, from the very first moment. For the greatest injury or offence that you can suffer from them is as nothing compared with what God has pardoned you" (St Josemaría Escrivá, *The Way*, 452).

23:35–37. The Roman governor's soldiers join the Jewish people and their leaders in mocking Jesus; thus, everyone—Jews and Gentiles—contributed to making Christ's passion even more bitter.

n. Other ancient authorities omit the sentence *And Jesus ... what they do* **o.** Other ancient authorities add *in letters of Greek and Latin and Hebrew*

[39]One of the criminals who were hanged railed at him, saying,
"Are you not the Christ? Save yourself and us!" [40]But the other
rebuked him, saying, "Do you not fear God, since you are under
the same sentence of condemnation? [41]And we indeed justly; for
we are receiving the due reward of our deeds; but this man has
done nothing wrong." [42]And he said, "Jesus, remember me when Mt 16:28
you come in your kingly power."[p] [43]And he said to him, "Truly, I
say to you, today you will be with me in Paradise."

But we should not forget that we too make a mockery of our Lord every time we fall into sin or fail to respond sufficiently to grace. This is why St Paul says that those who sin "crucify the Son of God on their own account and hold him up to contempt" (Heb 6:6).

23:39–43. The episode of the two thieves invites us to admire the designs of divine providence, of grace and human freedom. Both thieves are in the same position—in the presence of the Eternal High Priest as he offers himself in sacrifice for them and for all mankind. One of them hardens his heart, despairs and blasphemes, while the other repents, prays with confidence to Christ and is promised immediate salvation. "The Lord," St Ambrose comments, "always grants more than one asks: the thief only asked him to remember him, but the Lord says to him, 'Truly, I say to you, today you will be with me in Paradise.' Life consists in dwelling with Jesus Christ, and where Jesus Christ is there is his Kingdom" (*Expositio Evangelii sec. Lucam*, in loc.). "It is one thing for man to judge someone he does not know; another, for God, who can see into a person's conscience. Among men, confession is followed by punishment; whereas confession to God is followed by salvation" (St John Chrysostom, *De Cruce et latrone*).

While we make our way through life, we all sin, but we can all repent also. God is always waiting for us with his arms wide open, ready to forgive us. Therefore, no one should despair: everyone should try to have a strong hope in God's mercy. But no one may presume that he will be saved, for none of us can be absolutely certain of our final perseverance (cf. Council of Trent, *De Iustificatione*, can. 16). This relative uncertainty is a spur God gives us to be ever vigilant; this vigilance in turn helps us progress in the work of our sanctification as Christians.

23:42. "Many times have I repeated that verse of the Eucharistic hymn: *Peto quod petivit latro poenitens*, and it always fills me with emotion: to ask like the penitent thief did! He recognized that he himself deserved that awful punishment.... And with a word he stole Christ's heart and 'opened up for himself' the gates of heaven" (St Josemaría Escrivá, *The Way of the Cross*, XII, 4).

23:43. In responding to the good thief, Jesus reveals that he is God, for he has power over man's eternal destiny; and he also shows that he is infinitely merciful and does not reject the soul who sincerely repents. Similarly by these words Jesus reveals to us a basic truth of faith: "We believe in eternal life. We believe

p. Greek *kingdom*

Amos 8:9 44It was now about the sixth hour, and there was darkness over
Ex 36:35 the whole land[q] until the ninth hour, 45while the sun's light failed;[r]
Ps 31:5 and the curtain of the temple was torn in two. 46Then Jesus, crying
Acts 7:59 with a loud voice, said, "Father, into thy hands I commit my
spirit!" And having said this he breathed his last. 47Now when the
Lk 7:16 centurion saw what had taken place, he praised God, and said,
"Certainly this man was innocent!" 48And all the multitudes who

---

that the souls of all those who die in the grace of Christ—whether they must still make expiation in the fire of purgatory, or whether from the moment they leave their bodies they are received by Jesus Christ into Paradise like the good thief—go to form that People of God which succeeds death, death which will be totally destroyed on the day of the Resurrection when these souls are reunited with their bodies" (Paul VI, *Creed of the People of God*, 28).

23:45. The darkening of the sun is a sign of the magnitude and gravity of the Lord's death (cf. the note on Mk 15:33). The tearing of the curtain of the temple shows the end of the Old Covenant and the beginning of the New Covenant, sealed in the blood of Christ (cf. the note on Mk 15:38).

23:46. The Way of the Cross contemplates Jesus' death as the twelfth station. Christ's life is totally influenced by the fact that he is the only Son of the Father: "I came from the Father and have come into the world; again, I am leaving the world and going to the Father" (Jn 16:28). All along, his only desire was to do the will of him who sent him (cf. Jn 4:34), who, as Christ himself says, "is with me; he has not left me alone, for I always do what is pleasing to him" (Jn 8:29).

At this, the climax of his life on earth, when he is apparently left totally on his own, Christ makes an act of supreme confidence, throws himself into his Father's arms, and freely gives up his life. He was not forced to die nor did he die against his will; he died because he wanted to die. "It was the peculiar privilege of Christ the Lord to have died when he himself decreed to die, and to have died not so much by external violence as by internal assent. Not only his death, but also its time and place, were ordained by him. For thus Isaiah wrote: 'He was offered because it was his own will' (Is 53:7). The Lord, before his Passion, declared the same of himself, 'I lay down my life, that I may take it again. No one takes it from me, but I lay it down of my own accord. I have power to lay it down, and I have power to take it again' (Jn 10:17f)" (St Pius V, *Catechism*, 1, 6, 7).

"We know", says St Paul, "that our old self was crucified with him so that the sinful body might be destroyed, and we might no longer be enslaved to sin.—The death he died he died to sin, once for all. … So you also must consider yourselves dead to sin and alive to God in Christ Jesus" (Rom 6:6, 10f). Therefore, Vatican II explains, "This work of redeeming mankind […] Christ the Lord achieved principally by the paschal mystery of his blessed Passion, Resurrection from the dead, and glorious Ascension, whereby 'dying, he destroyed our death, and rising, he restored our life.' For it was

q. Or *earth* **r.** Or *the sun was eclipsed*. Other ancient authorities read the *sun was darkened*

assembled to see the sight, when they saw what had taken place,
returned home beating their breasts. [49]And all his acquaintances Ps 88:8; 37:12
and the women who had followed him from Galilee stood at a dis- Lk 8:2–3
tance and saw these things.

The burial Mt 27:57–61

[50]Now there was a man named Joseph from the Jewish town of Mk 15:42–47 Jn 19:38–42
Arimathea. He was a member of the council, a good and righteous Lk 2:25, 38

---

from the side of Christ as he slept the sleep of death upon the Cross that there came forth 'the wondrous sacrament of the whole Church' " (*Sacrosanctum Concilium*, 5).

23:47. The three Synoptic Gospels all report the profound reaction of the centurion, the reaction of an upright man who, helped by grace, studies these events with an openness to the mystery of the supernatural. The parallel accounts in Matthew 27:54 and Mark 15:39 show more clearly that the centurion recognized the divinity of Jesus Christ. See the note on Mk 15:39.

23:48. Jesus' redemptive death on the cross immediately begins to draw people towards God by way of repentance: as he made his way to Calvary there was the probable conversion of Simon of Cyrene and the lamentations of the women of Jerusalem; at the cross, the repentance of the good thief, the effect of grace on the Roman centurion, and the compunction felt by the crowd reported in this verse. Jesus had prophesied, "When I am lifted up from the earth, I will draw all men to myself" (Jn 12:32). This prophecy begins to come true on Golgotha, and it will continue to be fulfilled until the end of time.

"On the Cross hangs our Lord's—now lifeless—body. The people, 'when they saw what had taken place, returned home beating their breasts' (Lk 23:48).

"Now that you have repented, promise Jesus that, with his help, you will not crucify him again. Say it with faith. Repeat, over and over again: I will love you, my God, because ever since you were born, ever since you were a child, you abandoned yourself in my arms, defenceless, trusting in my loyalty" (St Josemaría Escrivá, *The Way of the Cross*, XII, 5).

23:49. We should note here the presence of a number of women, some of whose names have been recorded by St Matthew (27:56) and St Mark (15:40–41)—Mary Magdalene, Mary the mother of James and Joseph, and Salome. The soldiers would not have allowed them to approach the cross while Jesus was alive; but the women would have waited, watching from a distance, and then come up close to it, and unashamedly stood there (cf. Jn 19:25), impelled by their deep love for Jesus. "Woman is stronger than man, and more faithful, in the hour of trial: Mary of Magdala and Mary Cleophas and Salome! With a group of valiant women like these, closely united to our Lady of Sorrows, what work for souls could be done in the world!" (St Josemaría Escrivá, *The Way*, 982).

23:50–54. St John's Gospel tells us that "Nicodemus also, who had at first come to him by night, came bringing a mixture of myrrh and aloes, about a hundred pounds' weight" (Jn 19:39). "Joseph of

man, [51]who had not consented to their purpose and deed, and he
was looking for the kingdom of God. [52]This man went to Pilate
and asked for the body of Jesus. [53]Then he took it down and
wrapped it in a linen shroud, and laid him in a rock-hewn tomb,
where no one had ever yet been laid. [54]It was the day of
Preparation, and the sabbath was beginning.[s] [55]The women who
had come with him from Galilee followed, and saw the tomb, and
Ex 12:16; 20:10 Lev 23:8 how his body was laid; [56]then they returned, and prepared spices
and ointments.

On the sabbath they rested according to the commandment.

Arimathea and Nicodemus visit Jesus secretly in ordinary times and in the time of triumph. But they are courageous in the face of authority, declaring their love for Christ *audacter*—boldly—in the time of cowardice. Learn from them" (*The Way*, 841).

"With them I too will go up to the foot of the Cross; I will press my arms tightly round the cold Body, the corpse of Christ, with the fire of my love …; I will unnail it, with my reparation and mortifications …; I will wrap it in the new winding-sheet of my clean life, and I will bury it in the living rock of my breast, where no one can tear it away from me, and there, Lord, take your rest!

"Were the whole world to abandon you and to scorn you …, *serviam!*, I will serve you, Lord" (St Josemaría Escrivá, *The Way of the Cross*, XIV, 1).

Joseph of Arimathea's and Nicodemus' love for our Lord leads them to ignore the dangers—the hatred of their colleagues in the Sanhedrin, possible reprisals from fanatics. They show the body of Jesus utmost reverence, doing everything required for its pious burial and thereby giving an example to every disciple of Christ who should be ready to risk honour, position and wealth for love for his Lord. In the thirteenth and fourteenth stations of the Cross Christian piety contemplates the descent from the cross, and the noble actions of these two men, whose respect God chose to reward by inscribing their names in the Gospel text (cf. the note on Mt 15:43–46).

23:55–56. These holy women—who were familiar with the material poverty of our Lord when he was born in Bethlehem, and in the course of his public ministry and on the cross—do not skimp in showing veneration for the body of the Lord. When the Christian people generously endow eucharistic worship they are simply showing that they have learned well the lesson taught by these first disciples.

24:1–4. The affection which led the holy women to make the necessary preparations for the embalming of Jesus' body was, perhaps, an intuition of faith which the Church would express more elaborately much later on: "We firmly believe that when his soul was dissociated from his body, his divinity continued always united both to his body in the sepulchre and to his soul in limbo" (St Pius V, *Catechism*, 1, 5, 6).

24:5–8. True faith concerning the resurrection of Jesus teaches that he truly died, that is, his soul was separated from his

s. Greek *was dawning*

The resurrection of Jesus. The empty tomb

24 [1]But on the first day of the week, at early dawn, they went Mt 28:1–8 Mk 16:1–8
to the tomb, taking the spices which they had prepared. Jn 20:1–13
[2]And they found the stone rolled away from the tomb, [3]but when Rom 1:4
they went in they did not find the body.[t] [4]While they were per- Acts 1:10
plexed about this, behold, two men stood by them in dazzling
apparel; [5]and as they were frightened and bowed their faces to the Rev 1:18
ground, the men said to them, "Why do you seek the living
among the dead? He is not here, but has risen.[u] [6]Remember how
he told you, while he was still in Galilee, [7]that the Son of man

---

body, and his body was in the grave for three days; and that then by his own power his body and soul were united once more, never again to be separated (cf. St Pius V, *Catechism*, 1, 6, 7).

Although this is a strictly supernatural mystery there are some elements in it which come within the category of sense experience—death, burial, the empty tomb, appearances, etc.—and in this sense it is a demonstrable fact and one which has been verified (cf. St Pius X, *Lamentabili*, 36–37).

Jesus Christ's resurrection completes the work of Redemption. "For just as by dying he endured all evil to deliver us from evil, so was he glorified in rising again to advance us towards good things, according to Romans 4:25 which says that 'he was put to death for our trespasses and raised for our justification' " (St Thomas Aquinas, *Summa theologiae*, 3, 53, 1, c.).

" 'Christ is alive.' This is the great truth which fills our faith with meaning. Jesus, who died on the cross, has risen. He has triumphed over death; he has overcome sorrow, anguish and the power of darkness. 'Do not be amazed' was how the angels greeted the women who came to the tomb. 'Do not be amazed. You seek Jesus of Nazareth, who was crucified. He has risen; he is not here' (Mk 16:6). 'This is the day which the Lord has made; let us rejoice and be glad in it' (Ps 118:24).

"Easter is a time of joy—a joy not confined to this period of the liturgical year, for it should always be present in the Christian's heart. For Christ is alive. He is not someone who has gone, someone who existed for a time and then passed on, leaving us a wonderful example and a great memory.

"No, Christ is alive, Jesus is the Emmanuel: God with us. His resurrection shows us that God does not abandon his own. He promised he would not: 'Can a woman forget her sucking child, that she should have no compassion on the son of her womb? Even these may forget, yet I will not forget you' (Is 49:15). And he has kept his promise. His delight is still to be with the children of men (cf. Prov 8:31)" (St Josemaría Escrivá, *Christ Is Passing By*, 102).

Through Baptism and the other sacraments, a Christian becomes part of the redemptive mystery of Christ, part of his death and resurrection: "You were buried with him in baptism, in which you were also raised with him through faith in the working of God, who raised him from the dead" (Col 2:12). "If then you have been raised with Christ, seek the things that are above, where Christ is, seated at

t. Other ancient authorities add *of the Lord Jesus* **u.** Other ancient authorities omit *He is not here, but has risen*

must be delivered into the hands of sinful men, and be crucified,
and on the third day rise." [8]And they remembered his words, [9]and
returning from the tomb they told all this to the eleven and to all
Lk 8:2–3 the rest. [10]Now it was Mary Magdalene and Joanna and Mary the
mother of James and the other women with them who told this to
the apostles; [11]but these words seemed to them an idle tale, and
they did not believe them. [12]But Peter rose and ran to the tomb;
stooping and looking in, he saw the linen cloths by themselves;
and he went home wondering at what had happened.[v]

The road to Emmaus

Mk 16:12–13 [13]That very day two of them were going to a village named
Emmaus, about seven miles[w] from Jerusalem, [14]and talking with

---

the right hand of God. Set your minds on things that are above, not on things that are on earth. For you have died, and your life is hid with Christ in God" (Col 3:1–3).

24:9–12. The first people to whom the angel announced the birth of Christ were the shepherds at Bethlehem; and the first to be told of his resurrection are these devout women: one further sign of God's preference for simple and sincere souls is the fact that he gives them this honour which the world would not appreciate (cf. Mt 11:25). But it is not only their simplicity and kindness and sincerity that attracts him: poor people (such as shepherds) and women were looked down on in those times, and Jesus loves anyone who is humbled by the pride of men. The women's very simplicity and goodness lead them to go immediately to Peter and the apostles to tell them everything they have seen and heard. Peter, whom Christ promised to make his vicar on earth (cf. Mt 16:18), feels he must take the initiative in checking out their story.

24:13–35. In the course of their conversation with Jesus, the disciples' mood changes from sadness to joy; they begin to hope again, and feel the need to share their joy with others, thus becoming heralds and witnesses of the risen Christ.

This is an episode exclusive to St Luke, who describes it in a masterly way. It shows our Lord's zeal for souls. "As he is walking along, Christ meets two men who have nearly lost all hope. They are beginning to feel that life has no meaning for them. Christ understands their sorrow; he sees into their heart and communicates to them some of the life he carries within himself. When they draw near the village, he makes as if he is going on, but the two disciples stop him and practically force him to stay with them. They recognize him later when he breaks the bread. The Lord, they exclaimed, has been with us! 'And they said to each other: "Did not our hearts burn within us while he talked to us on the road, while he opened to us the scriptures?"' (Lk 24:32). Every Christian should make Christ present among men. He ought to act in such a way that those who know him sense 'the aroma of Christ' (cf. 2 Cor 2:15). Men should be

---

v. Other ancient authorities omit verse 12 **w.** Greek *sixty stadia*; other ancient authorities read *a hundred and sixty stadia*

each other about all these things that had happened. [15]While they Mt 18:20
were talking and discussing together, Jesus himself drew near and
went with them. [16]But their eyes were kept from recognizing him. Lk 24:31
[17]And he said to them, "What is this conversation which you are
holding with each other as you walk?" And they stood still, looking sad. [18]Then one of them, named Cleopas, answered him, "Are
you the only visitor to Jerusalem who does not know the things
that have happened there in these days?" [19]And he said to them, Mt 21:11
"What things?" And they said to him, "Concerning Jesus of Acts 2:22
Nazareth, who was a prophet mighty in deed and word before God
and all the people, [20]and how our chief priests and rulers delivered
him up to be condemned to death, and crucified him. [21]But we had Lk 1:68; 2:38;
hoped that he was the one to redeem Israel. Yes, and besides all 19:11 Acts 1:6

---

able to recognize the Master in his disciples" (St Josemaría Escrivá, *Christ Is Passing By*, 105).

24:13–27. Jesus' conversation with the two disciples on the road to Emmaus gives us a very good idea of the disillusionment felt by his disciples after his apparent total failure. Cleopas' words summarize Christ's life and mission (v. 19), his passion and death (v. 20), the despair felt by his disciples (v. 21), and the events of that Sunday morning (v. 22).

Earlier, Jesus had said to the Jews: "You search the scriptures, because you think that in them you have eternal life; and it is they that bear witness to me" (Jn 5:39). In saying this he indicated the best way for us to get to know him. Pope Paul VI points out that today also frequent reading of and devotion to Holy Scripture is a clear inspiration of the Holy Spirit: "The progress made in biblical studies, the increasing dissemination of the Sacred Scriptures, and above all the example of tradition and the interior action of the Holy Spirit are tending to cause the modern Christian to use the Bible ever increasingly as the basic prayerbook and to draw from it genuine inspiration and unsurpassable examples" (*Marialis cultus*, 30).

Because the disciples are so downhearted, Jesus patiently opens for them the meaning of all the scriptural passages concerning the Messiah. "Was it not necessary that the Christ should suffer these things and enter into his glory?": with these words he disabuses them of the notion of an earthly and political Messiah and shows them that Christ's mission is a supernatural one—to save all mankind.

Holy Scripture contained the prophecy that God would bring about salvation through the redemptive passion and death of the Messiah. The Cross does not mean failure: it is the route chosen by God for Christ to achieve definitive victory over sin and death (cf. 1 Cor 1:23–24). Many of our Lord's contemporaries failed to understand his supernatural mission because they misinterpreted the Old Testament texts. No one knew the meaning of Sacred Scripture like Jesus. And, after him, only the Church has the mission and responsibility of conserving Scripture and interpreting it correctly: "all that has been said about the manner of interpreting Scripture is ultimately subject to the judgment of the Church which exercises the divinely conferred commission and ministry of watching over and interpreting the Word of God" (Vatican II, *Dei Verbum*, 12).

this, it is now the third day since this happened. [22]Moreover, some
women of our company amazed us. They were at the tomb early in
the morning [23]and did not find his body; and they came back
saying that they had even seen a vision of angels, who said that he
Jn 20:3–10 was alive. [24]Some of those who were with us went to the tomb, and
found it just as the women had said; but him they did not see."
[25]And he said to them, "O foolish men, and slow of heart to believe
all that the prophets have spoken! [26]Was it not necessary that the
Christ should suffer these things and enter into his glory?" [27]And
Deut 18:15 Ps 22 Is 53 beginning with Moses and all the prophets, he interpreted to them
in all the scriptures the things concerning himself.

[28]So they drew near to the village to which they were going.
He appeared to be going further, [29]but they constrained him,
saying, "Stay with us, for it is toward evening and the day is now

---

24:28–35. The Master's presence and words restore the disciples' spirits and give them new and lasting hope. "There were two disciples on their way to Emmaus. They were walking along at a normal pace, like so many other travellers on that road. And there, without any fuss, Jesus appears to them, and walks with them, his conversation helping to alleviate their tiredness. I can well imagine the scene, just as dusk is falling. A gentle breeze is blowing. All around are fields ripe with wheat, and venerable olive trees, their branches shimmering in the soft glowing light.

"Jesus joins them as they go along their way. Lord, how great you are, in everything! But you move me even more when you come down to our level, to follow us and to seek us in the hustle and bustle of each day. Lord, grant us a childlike spirit, pure eyes and a clear head so that we may recognize you when you come without any outward sign of your glory.

"The journey ends when they reach the village. The two disciples who, without realizing it, have been deeply stirred by the words and love shown by God made man, are sorry to see him leaving. For Jesus 'appeared to be going further' (Lk 24:28). This Lord of ours never forces himself on us. He wants us to turn to him freely, when we begin to grasp the purity of his Love which he has placed in our souls. We have to hold him back ('they constrained him') and beg him: 'Stay with us, for it is towards evening and the day is now far spent' (Lk 24:29).

"That's just like us—always short on daring, perhaps because we are insincere, or because we feel embarrassed. Deep down, what we are really thinking is: 'Stay with us, because our souls are shrouded in darkness and You alone are the light. You alone can satisfy this longing that consumes us.' For 'we know full well which among all things fair and honourable is the best—to possess God for ever' (St Gregory Nazianzen, *Epistolae*, 212).

"And Jesus stays. Our eyes are opened, as were those of Cleopas and his companion, when Christ breaks the bread; and, though he vanishes once more from sight, we too will find strength to start out once more—though night is falling—to tell the others about him, because so much joy cannot be kept in one heart alone.

"The road to Emmaus—our God has filled this name with sweetness. Now the

far spent." So he went in to stay with them. 30When he was at Lk 22:19
table with them, he took the bread and blessed, and broke it, and
gave it to them. 31And their eyes were opened and they recognized Lk 24:16
him; and he vanished out of their sight. 32They said to each other,
"Did not our hearts burn within us while he talked to us on the
road, while he opened to us the scriptures?" 33And they rose that
same hour and returned to Jerusalem; and they found the eleven
gathered together and those who were with them, 34who said, 1 Cor 15:4–5
"The Lord has risen indeed, and has appeared to Simon!" 35Then
they told what had happened on the road, and how he was known
to them in the breaking of the bread.

Jesus appears to the disciples in the upper room Mk 16:14–18 Jn 20:19–23
36As they were saying this, Jesus himself stood among them, and 1 Cor 15:5
said to them, "Peace to you!"[x] 37But they were startled and fright- Mt 14:26

entire world has become an Emmaus, for the Lord has opened up all the divine paths of the earth" (St Josemaría Escrivá, *Friends of God*, 313f).

24:32. "If you are an apostle, these words of the disciples of Emmaus should rise spontaneously to the lips of your professional companions when they meet you along the way of their lives" (St Josemaría Escrivá, *The Way*, 917).

24:33–35. The disciples now feel the need to return to Jerusalem immediately; there they find the apostles and some other disciples gathered together with Peter, to whom Jesus has appeared.

In sacred history, Jerusalem was the place where God chose to be praised in a very special way and where the prophets carried out their main ministry. God willed that Christ should suffer, die and rise again in Jerusalem, and from there the Kingdom of God begins to spread (cf. Lk 24:47; Acts 1:8). In the New Testament the Church of Christ is described as "the Jerusalem above" (Gal 4:26), "the heavenly Jerusalem" (Heb 12:22) and the "new Jerusalem" (Rev 21:2).

The Church began in the Holy City. Later on, St Peter, not without a special intervention of Providence, moved to Rome, thereby making that city the centre of the Church. Just as Peter strengthened these first disciples in the faith, so too Christians of all generations have recourse to the See of Peter to strengthen their faith and thereby build up the unity of the Church: "Take away the Pope and the Catholic Church would no longer be catholic. Moreover, without the supreme, effective and authoritative pastoral office of Peter the unity of Christ's Church would collapse. It would be vain to look for other principles of unity in place of the true one established by Christ himself [...]. We would add that this cardinal principle of holy Church is not a supremacy of spiritual pride and a desire to dominate mankind, but a primacy of service, ministration and love. It is no vapid rhetoric which confers on Christ's vicar the title: 'Servant of the servants of God'" (Paul VI, *Ecclesiam suam*, 83).

24:36–43. This appearance of the risen Jesus is reported by St Luke and St John

x. Other ancient authorities omit *and said to them, "Peace to you!"*

ened, and supposed that they saw a spirit. [38]And he said to them,
"Why are you troubled, and why do questionings rise in your
1 Jn 1:1 hearts?* [39]See my hands and my feet, that it is I myself; handle
me, and see; for a spirit has not flesh and bones as you see that I
have." [40]And when he had said this, he showed them his hands
and his feet.[y] [41]And while they still disbelieved for joy, and won-
Jn 21:5–10 dered, he said to them, "Have you anything here to eat?" [42]They
Acts 10:41 gave him a piece of broiled fish, [43]and he took it and ate before
them.
Lk 9:22–45; 18:31–33 [44]Then he said to them, "These are my words which I spoke to
Jn 5:46 you, while I was still with you, that everything written about me

---

(cf. Jn 20:19–23). St John reports the institution of the sacrament of Penance, whereas St Luke puts the stress on the disciples' difficulty in accepting the miracle of the resurrection, despite the angels' testimony to the women (cf. Mt 28:5–7; Mk 16:5–7; Lk 24:4–11) and despite the witness of those who had already seen the risen Lord (cf. Mt 28:9–10; Mk 16:9–13; Lk 24:13ff; Jn 20:11–18).

Jesus appears all of a sudden, when the doors are closed (cf. Jn 20:19), which explains their surprised reaction. St Ambrose comments that "he penetrated their closed retreat not because his nature was incorporeal, but because he had the quality of a resurrected body" (*Expositio Evangelii sec. Lucam*, in loc.). "Subtility", which is one of the qualities of a glorifed body, means that "the body is totally subject to the soul and ever ready to obey its wishes" (St Pius V, *Catechism*, 1, 12, 13), with the result that it can pass through material obstacles without any difficulty.

This scene showing Christ's condescension to confirm for them the truth of his resurrection has a charm all of its own.

24:41–43. Although his risen body is incapable of suffering, and therefore has no need of food to nourish it, our Lord confirms his disciples' faith in his resurrection by giving them these two proofs—inviting them to touch him and eating in their presence. "For myself, I know and believe that our Lord was in the flesh even after the Resurrection. And when he came to Peter and his companions, he said to them: 'Here, feel me and see that I am not a bodiless ghost.' They touched him and believed, and were convinced that he was flesh and spirit [...]. Moreover, after the Resurrection, he ate and drank with them like a man of flesh and blood, though spiritually one with the Father" (St Ignatius of Antioch, *Letter to the Christians at Smyrna*, 3, 1–3).

24:44–49. St Matthew stresses that the Old Testament prophecies are fulfilled in Christ, because his immediate audience was Jews, who would accept this as proof that Jesus was indeed the promised Messiah. St Luke does not usually argue along these lines because he is writing for Gentiles; however, in this epilogue he does report, in a summarized way, Christ's statement to the effect that everything foretold about him had come true. By doing so he shows the unity of Old

y. Other ancient authorities omit verse 40

in the law of Moses and the prophets and the psalms must be fulfilled." 45Then he opened their minds to understand the scriptures,
46and said to them, "Thus it is written, that the Christ should suffer 1 Tim 3:16
and on the third day rise from the dead, 47and that repentance and Acts 17:30
forgiveness of sins should be preached in his name to all nations,[z]
beginning from Jerusalem. 48You are witnesses of these things. Jn 15:26; 16:7
49And behold, I send the promise of my Father upon you; but stay Acts 1:4
in the city, until you are clothed with power from on high."

The ascension of our Lord

50Then he led them out as far as Bethany, and lifting up his hands Mk 16:19
he blessed them. 51While he blessed them, he parted from them, Acts 1:4–15

---

and New Testaments and that Jesus is truly the Messiah.

St Luke also refers to the promise of the Holy Spirit (cf. Jn 14:16–17, 26; 15:26; 16:7ff), whose fulfilment on the day of Pentecost he will narrate in detail in the Book of the Acts (cf. Acts 2:1–4).

24:46. From St Luke's account we have seen how slow the apostles were to grasp Jesus' prophecy of his death and resurrection (cf. 9:45; 18:34). Now that the prophecy is fulfilled Jesus reminds them that it was necessary for the Christ to suffer and to rise from the dead (cf. Acts 2:1–4).

The Cross is a mystery, in our own life as well as in Christ's: "Jesus suffers to carry out the will of the Father. And you, who also want to carry out the most holy will of God, following the steps of the Master, can you complain if you meet suffering on your way?" (St Josemaría Escrivá, *The Way*, 213).

24:49. "I send the promise of my Father upon you," that is, the Holy Spirit who, some days later, at Pentecost, would come down upon them in the cenacle (cf. Acts 2:1–4) as the Father's gift to them (cf. Lk 11:13).

24:50–53. St Luke, who will report our Lord's ascension in the Acts of the Apostles, here gives a summary account of this mystery which marks the end of Jesus' visible presence on earth. St Thomas Aquinas explains that it was inappropriate for Christ to remain on earth after the Resurrection, whereas it was appropriate that he should ascend into heaven, because, although his risen body was already a glorified one, it now receives an increase in glory due to the dignity of the place to which it ascends (cf. *Summa theologiae*, 3, 57, 1).

"Our Lord's Ascension also reminds us of another fact. The same Christ, who encourages us to carry out our task in the world, awaits us in heaven. In other words, our life on earth, which we love, is not definitive. 'Here we have no lasting city, but we seek the city which is to come' (Heb 13:14), a changeless home, where we may live forever. […] Christ awaits us. We are 'citizens of heaven' (Phil 3:20), and at the same time fully-fledged citizens of this earth, in the midst of difficulties, injustices and lack of understanding, but also in the midst of the joy and serenity that comes from knowing that we are children of God" (St J. Escrivá, *Christ Is Passing By*, 126).

z. Or *nations. Beginning from Jerusalem you are witnesses*

Jn 14:28; 16:22

and was carried up into heaven.[a] 52And they worshipped him, and[b]
returned to Jerusalem with great joy, 53and were continually in the
temple blessing God.

We have come to the end of St Luke's narrative. Words cannot express the gratitude and love we feel when we reflect on Christ's life among us. Let us offer God our desire to be ever more faithful children and disciples of his, as we savour this summary of Christ's life given us by the Magisterium: "We believe in our Lord Jesus Christ, who is the Son of God. He is the eternal Word born of the Father before time began [...]. He dwelt among us full of grace and truth. He announced and established the Kingdom of God, enabling us to know the Father. He gave us the commandment that we should love one another as he loved us. He taught us the way of the Gospel Beatitudes, according to which we were to be poor in spirit and humble, bearing suffering in patience, thirsting after justice, merciful, clean of heart, peaceful, enduring persecution for justice's sake. He suffered under Pontius Pilate, the Lamb of God taking to himself the sins of the world, and he died for us, nailed to the Cross, saving us by his redeeming blood. After he had been buried he rose from the dead of his own power, lifting us by his Resurrection to that sharing in the divine life which is grace. He ascended into heaven whence he will come again to judge the living and the dead, each according to his merits. Those who have responded to the love and compassion of God will go into eternal life. Those who have refused them to the end will be consigned to the fire that is never extinguished. And of his kingdom there will be no end" (Paul VI, *Creed of the People of God*, 11f).

a. Other ancient authorities omit *and was carried up into heaven* **b.** Other ancient authorities omit *worshipped him, and*

Introduction to the Gospel according to John

THE AUTHOR

Some New Testament texts contain the writer's name, but in the case of the Gospels and the Acts of the Apostles no name is explicitly given. This might not seem to be particularly important, for what really matters is the Church's acceptance of a text as canonical, that is, inspired by God. Yet it is interesting to know who wrote a particular inspired book, especially if the human author was an eyewitness of the events he reports, and even more so if the book deals with the life of Jesus Christ, his teaching and his death and resurrection—as is the case with the Fourth Gospel, which says that "he who saw it has borne witness—his testimony is true" (Jn 19:35); and "this is the disciple who is bearing witness to these things …; and we know that his testimony is true" (Jn 21:24).

To discover who wrote a New Testament book we must explore the very early tradition of the Church, which is contemporary with or almost contemporary with when it was written. The authenticity of these sacred writings was as much a matter of concern to the early Christians as to later generations. They were living very soon after Christ's time; they often spoke among themselves, in the way people discuss recent events, about the historical facts of the Master's life; and they believed in Jesus' divinity because these facts—the miracles, the prophecies and especially his glorious resurrection—clearly bore out that he was the Son of God. This explains why they defended Christian truth against sceptics; they were ready at any time to answer anyone who called on them to account for their hope (cf. 1 Pet 3:15), quoting for them the testimony given by those who had seen and heard Christ, for, as St Peter averred, "we did not follow cleverly devised myths when we made known to you the power and coming of our Lord Jesus Christ, but we were eyewitnesses of his majesty" (2 Pet 1:16).

The Gospel we are now discussing enjoyed great prestige from as early as the beginning of the second century, as evidenced by the fact that phrases taken from it or based on it are to be found in very early documents. Thus St Ignatius of Antioch (d. 107–115) speaks of the Spirit which knows where it comes from and where it is going to[1] and says that the Word, the Son of God,

1. *Letter to the Philadelphians*, 7, 1, referring to Jn 3:8.

always does what is pleasing to him who sent him (cf. Jn 1:1; 7:28; 8:29); St Polycarp in his letter to the Philippians (*c.*110) also echoes some phrases of the Fourth Gospel, as does St Justin (*c.*150) when he says it is necessary to be born again to enter the Kingdom of heaven (cf. Jn 3:5).

In addition to these references, there are explicit testimonies which clearly state that the apostle St John wrote the Fourth Gospel. The famous "Muratorian Canon" written in Rome around the year 180 contains a prologue against Marcion and his followers, in which it is said that "the Gospel of John was communicated and proclaimed to the churches by John himself, while he was still alive, according to Papias of Hierapolis." Papias lived around the year 135, and it is known that he was a disciple of John, so what he has to say is particularly valuable.

St Irenaeus, bishop of Lyons, also refers to the authenticity of this Gospel. Irenaeus was born around 130 in Smyrna (Asia Minor), where he knew St Polycarp, who according to Tertullian was made bishop of Smyrna by St John himself. St Irenaeus says that "John, the disciple of the Lord, who had even rested on his breast, himself published the Gospel, while he was living in Ephesus."[2] This testimony carries special weight, given Irenaeus' connexion with Polycarp.

Eusebius, in his *Ecclesiastical History* (6, 14, 5–7), refers to the testimony of Clement of Alexandria, who passes on a tradition which says that John wrote his Gospel after the other evangelists had written theirs. Victorinus of Pettau's witness is of a later date (*c.*305).[3] From the fourth century on there is a unanimous tradition that St John wrote the Gospel which bears his name. Internal analysis of the text confirms what tradition tells us. The developed form of doctrine we find in the Gospel indicates that, to produce it, God availed himself of a man who had for years meditated on and made his own everything which he reports to us concerning Jesus and his disciples. Besides, there are many little points in the Gospel which can be explained only if John is the author. For example, he refers to John as the Precursor of Christ, where the Synoptic Gospels call him John the Baptist: they have to call him that to avoid any possible confusion with John the apostle. But in the Fourth Gospel there is no danger of any such confusion since the name of John the evangelist is nowhere mentioned.

Also, we learn from the Gospel that its author is "the disciple whom Jesus loved" (Jn 21:20) and who was one of the twelve apostles, for he is present when the risen Lord appears among them by the Sea of Tiberias (cf. Jn 21:1). Now, the Synoptics tell us that Jesus loved three of his disciples in a special way, choosing them to see his glory on Tabor (cf. Mt 17:1–2) and his humiliation in Gethsemane (cf. Mk 14:33). These were Peter, James the Greater and John. And one of these is the "beloved disciple", who wrote the

2. *Against Heresies*, 3, 1, 1. **3.** Cf. *Commentary on the Apocalypse*, 11, 1.

Gospel. St Peter it cannot be, for on various occasions we see him accompanied by the beloved disciple (cf. Jn 20:2ff; 21:20). Nor can it be James the Greater, because he was martyred around the year 40 (cf. Acts 12:2) and the Fourth Gospel was written towards the end of the century—which leaves only St John the evangelist. Besides, many literary features of the Gospel confirm its authenticity. The writer is obviously Jewish, very familiar with Jewish customs and interested in Jewish feasts. He has an intimate knowledge of the geography of Palestine and gives many topographical references (cf. Jn 1:28; 3:23; 4:5–6; 10:22; 11:18). The style of writing is markedly Semitic.

The only ambiguous text in Tradition on this subject is a passage from Papias quoted by Eusebius, in which the name of John is mentioned twice. This text reads: "If someone came along who had heard the presbyters speak, I used to make a point of asking him what did the presbyters hear from the lips of Andrew or Peter or Philip or Thomas or James or John or Matthew or any other disciple of the Lord, and also what do Aristion and the presbyter John say."[4] Interpretation of this text presents two difficulties. First, was Papias referring on both occasions to the apostle St John—naming him twice simply because he lived so much longer after the death of the other disciples; or is his second reference to another John, a person of importance but not the apostle? Second, if the latter hypothesis is correct, which of the two is the author of the Gospel—"John the apostle" or "John the presbyter", both "disciples of the Lord"? Eusebius attributes the Gospel explicitly to John the apostle, and so does St Irenaeus, as we have seen.

Rationalist critics, however, on the basis of this text of Papias, argue that St Irenaeus confused this "John the presbyter" with the apostle John: they argue that it was John the presbyter who appointed St Polycarp bishop of Smyrna and who wrote the Fourth Gospel. But there is no basis for attributing this mistake to St Irenaeus, and besides, the great mass of the information that has come down to us from Christian antiquity, and the internal evidence, all argue in favour of St John the apostle as author of the Fourth Gospel. So it is not surprising that the Church has always held to the traditional attribution of the Fourth Gospel to St John.[5]

THE RELATIONSHIP BETWEEN THE GOSPEL OF ST JOHN AND THE SYNOPTIC GOSPELS

If we enter St John's Gospel after reading the Synoptics we sense that we are entering a different atmosphere. Even in the prologue the evangelist soars towards the heights of divinity. It is not surprising that St John is symbolized

4. *Ecclesiastical History*, 3, 39, 4. **5.** Cf. *EB*, 180–182, 200–202 and 475.

by an eagle. The evangelist "soars very high, mounts beyond the darkness of the earth and fixes his gaze on the light of truth ...".[6]

Even in the way it reports facts, the Fourth Gospel adopts an approach different from the Synoptics. For example, it centres Jesus' public ministry mainly in Judea; although the Gospel does mention his ministry in Galilee (cf. Jn 2; 6), which the Synoptics cover very well, St John concentrates mainly on Jesus' activity in Jerusalem. The first three Gospels only tell us of our Lord going up to the Holy City once during his public ministry, the occasion when he will die during the feast of the Passover, whereas John refers to at least three visits (cf. Jn 2:13, 23; 5:1; 6:4; 12:1). Of the twenty-nine miracles described in the Synoptics, St John refers to only two (cf. Jn 6:11, 19) and he tells us of five additional ones (cf. Jn 2:1–11; 4:46–54; 5:1–9; 9:1–41; 11:33–44). But he does not mention the Transfiguration; nor the institution of the Eucharist at the Last Supper—which is not to say that he is unaware of its importance, for he gives us very full and very clear accounts of Jesus' discourses about the Bread of Life (cf. Jn 6:32–58).

On the history of the passion, death and resurrection of Jesus Christ, the Fourth Gospel coincides with the Synoptics, but here also it has a perspective of its own: it describes everything very much in terms of the glorification of Christ: this is Jesus' "hour" (Jn 2:4; 7:30; 13:1; 17:1), when the Father glorifies the Son; when the Son, by dying, overcomes the devil, sin and death and is raised up above all things (cf. Jn 12:32–33). And so, when Jesus announces his passion in advance, the Synoptics focus on the appropriateness of the Son *suffering* (cf. Mt 16:21 and par.), whereas St John stresses how fitting it is that the Son of man should be "lifted up" (Jn 3:14–15; 8:28; 12:32–33).

Even Jesus' teaching contains different nuances in St John: for example, the Fourth Gospel only once mentions the "kingdom of God", whereas the Synoptics, especially St Matthew, refer to it often (Jn 3:5; cf. Mt 3:2; 4:23; 5:3; 11:12; 13:24; etc.). There are subjects not treated by St John which appear frequently in the Synoptics, such as the question of the sabbath, Pharisees' legislation, etc.; but he speaks about life, truth, light, glory—which are hardly mentioned in the first three Gospels.

Scholars have proposed various hypotheses to explain why St John wrote like this. Some say that he was not acquainted with the other Gospels and that he just wrote what he thought best fitted his purpose. This is very unlikely, given that the first three Gospels were written so much earlier: John must have known them. Besides, it does not explain why he omits important things like the Transfiguration and the institution of the Blessed Eucharist: he would only have done that if he knew they were covered in the other Gospels.

One coherent explanation is that John was mainly trying to fill out the Synoptics, focusing more light on certain episodes. His Gospel does not con-

6. St Augustine, *In Ioann. Evang.*, 15, 1.

tradict the Synoptics; what it does is give more detail. For example, he reports Jesus' triple commandment to St Peter to feed the sheep—which explains how Peter should approach the mission he has received to be the rock on which Christ will build his Church (cf. Mt 16:18).

St John himself gives us one reason why his Gospel is different. He says that it is a testimony to what he has seen and heard. Rather than speak of evangelizing or preaching, the Fourth Gospel prefers to use "testify" or "bear witness" or "teach". Thus, he presents the preaching of the Baptist as an instance of testimony to Christ (cf. Jn 1:7, 19, 32, 34; 3:26; 5:33). Our Lord is always the object of this testimony, which comes from different directions in the Fourth Gospel: first and foremost, it comes from the Father who has sent Jesus to bear witness to him (cf. Jn 5:37); then, Jesus bears witness to himself, because he knows where he has come from and where he is going to (cf. Jn 8:14) and he is attesting to what he has seen (cf. Jn 3:11); the Scriptures also bear witness to Jesus Christ (cf. Jn 5:39), as will the Holy Spirit whom he will send (cf. Jn 15:26); and, finally, our Lord says to the apostles: "You also are witnesses, because you have been with me from the beginning" (Jn 15:27).

This concept of bearing witness is also present in other inspired writers, though not as clearly as in St John—in Hebrews 12:1, for example. In the early centuries of the Church it was quite common for Christians to ratify in their blood the testimony of faith in Christ—martyrdom becoming, as it were, the climax of perfect commitment to the Lord. The word "martyr" comes from the Greek verb *martireo*, which means "bearing witness". Every Christian therefore, has to be a "martyr", a faithful witness, wherever he is, a living testimony of Christ to people around him.

Another unusual feature of St John's Gospel is that it is a "spiritual gospel", in the words of Clement of Alexandria (on account of which St John has been called "the theologian"). This refers to John's desire to explore and explain the deeper meaning of Jesus' words and actions. In St John's account our Lord usually begins his teachings with an intriguing remark or question, to awaken the curiosity of his listeners, and then moves on to explain some point of doctrine. For example, in the case of Nicodemus, when he speaks about being born again; or his conversation with the Samaritan woman about living water: what Jesus is saying obviously means much more than one would get from a first glance at the text. In fact, it is only when the Holy Spirit comes that the disciples grasp the full meaning of the Master's words (cf. Jn 14:26). And so, on a number of occasions, the Evangelist actually says that they did not understand what Jesus was trying to tell them but that after his resurrection they did understand its profound meaning (cf. Jn 2:17, 22; 12:16; 13:7; 16:4). The Master, when he sees they cannot grasp his meaning, consoles them by promising the "Spirit of truth", who will guide them into all the truth (Jn 16:13).

Also, events treated in the narrative have a deeper meaning than is at first obvious. This has led some to think that St John's narrative is not history, and that the miracles Jesus works, and even the people involved, are mere symbols, literary devices invented by the evangelist—like examples a catechist might devise to illustrate his teaching. This view means denying the inerrancy of an inspired text, and therefore, it is rejected by the Magisterium of the Church, which maintains the historicity of the text of the Fourth Gospel.[7] The Pontifical Biblical Commission teaches that it cannot be "said that the facts narrated in the Fourth Gospel were invented wholly or in part as allegories or doctrinal symbols", nor may it be affirmed that "the sermons of our Lord are not properly and truly discourses of the Lord himself, but instead theological compositions of the writer, placed on our Lord's lips."[8]

Besides, to say that St John invents facts is to fail to understand the whole character of the Fourth Gospel and the Semitic mind, which is so fond of the concrete and particular: quite often events themselves provide the starting point for explaining some matter of doctrine (cf. Hos 1:2–11; Jer 16:1–3; 18:1–5).

St John selects particular miracles of Jesus because he wants to use them to emphasize a teaching: at the wedding at Cana our Lord manifests his glory and at the same time reveals that the messianic age has begun, and light is thrown on the role of his mother, Mary, in the redemption of mankind (cf. Jn 2:1–11); the multiplication of the loaves and the fish, attested to also by the Synoptics, provides the historical prologue to Christ's words about the Bread of Life (cf. Jn 6); the curing of the man blind from birth provides the Evangelist with an opportunity to show how blind the Pharisees are to the light of the world, Christ (cf. Jn 9); by raising Lazarus, the Master shows that only he is the Resurrection and the Life (cf. Jn 11).

St John insists that he "has seen" all this; that he has "touched" it with his hands (Jn 1:14; 19:35; 1 Jn 1:2). After a lifetime of preaching and prayer, it is only logical that he should see it all from a deeper, clearer perspective. St Augustine is right when he says that St John "soared beyond the flesh, soared beyond the earth which he trod, beyond the seas which he saw, beyond the air where birds fly; soared beyond the sun, beyond the moon and the stars, beyond all spirits which are unseen, beyond his own intelligence and the very reason of his thinking soul. Soaring beyond all these, beyond his very self, where did he reach, what did he see? 'In the beginning was the Word, and the Word was with God, and the Word was God'."[9] Therefore, what he narrates, far from contradicting what we read in the Synoptics, takes it as read, and fills it out.

JOHN THE APOSTLE

Of all the Gospels, the Fourth most clearly reflects the personality of its human author. The other Gospels also tell us something about St John the

7. *EB*, 187. **8.** *EB*, 189. **9.** *In Ioann. Evang.*, 20, 13.

apostle, to which we can add further information—though not as much as we would like—from primitive Christian tradition. He was a native of Bethsaida, a town of Galilee on the northern shore of the Sea of Tiberias. His parents were Zebedee and Salome, and his brother James the Greater. They were fishing folk, fairly well off, a family which did not hesitate to put itself completely at Jesus' disposal. James and John, in response to Jesus' call, "left their father Zebedee in the boat with the hired servants, and followed him" (Mk 1:20 and par.). Salome, their mother, also followed Jesus, providing for him from her means, in Galilee and Jerusalem; she was with him right up to Calvary (cf. Mk 15:40–41 and par.)

Along with Andrew, Peter's brother, John had been with John the Baptist on the banks of the Jordan and had even become one of his disciples, until one day, on seeing Jesus, the Baptist exclaimed, "Behold, the Lamb of God!"; as soon as they heard him say this they followed Jesus and spent the whole day with him (Jn 1:35–39). They returned home to Bethsaida and went back to fishing; and a little later on, Jesus, who had been preparing them since that first meeting, called them, in a definitive way, to be among the Twelve. St John would not have been twenty at the time.

From then on St John follows Christ and never leaves him. The Gospels all list him among the Twelve alongside his brother James, after St Peter and, sometimes, after St Andrew (cf. Mk 3:17 and par.). The passionate love these two brothers had for the Lord led them on occasions to react energetically against people who rejected the Master. When certain Samaritans refused to receive him, the sons of Zebedee asked Jesus (Lk 9:54), "Lord, do you want us to bid fire come down from heaven and consume them?" (as happened to the messengers of King Ahaziah: 2 Kings 1:10–15). They had not yet fully understood Jesus' mission—to show men the Father's love. Gradually, taught by our Lord, they did come to understand it: so much so that it will be John who engraves on our mind the truth that "God is love" (1 Jn 4:8, 16). But, in those early days, James and John sometimes seem impatient to see the triumph of their Master and are ready to call for punishment from heaven. It is not surprising, then, that our Lord describes them as "Boanerges, that is, sons of thunder" (Mk 3:17). John's strong character and youthful spontaneity make him the disciples' mouthpiece when, on another occasion, they want to prevent someone not of their company from using Jesus' name to cast out demons (cf. Lk 9:49).

Our Lord showed the sons of Zebedee, and Peter, special signs of trust and friendship (cf. Mk 1:17; 5:37; 9:2ff; 14:32–42). St John discreetly refers to himself in the Gospel as the disciple whom Jesus loved (cf. Jn 13:23; 19:26; 20:2; 21:7, 20), meaning that our Lord had special affection for him. He puts it on record that, at that solemn point in the Last Supper when Jesus announces that one of them will betray him, he did not hesitate to ask our Lord, resting his head on his chest, who the traitor would be (cf. Jn 13:23). So much, in fact, did Jesus trust his beloved disciple that, from the cross, he gave into his charge the person he loved most in the world—his blessed Mother.

St John was very close to St Peter, whom he knew before either of them met Christ (both were fishermen from Bethsaida). They were the two to whom our Lord gave the job of preparing the paschal meal (cf. Lk 22:8), and, on the night of the Passion, it was probably John who managed to get Peter into the chief priest's house (cf. Jn 18:16). They ran together to the tomb on the morning of Easter Sunday. St John never forgot that empty sepulchre, which led him to believe in the Resurrection. In his Gospel he recalls how he ran faster than Peter and reached the tomb first but stayed outside—we must presume in deference to Peter, to whom our Lord had promised the primacy of the Church (cf. Jn 20:3–9). John was the first to recognize the risen Jesus when he appeared to a group of disciples on the lakeshore. He joyfully tells Peter, "It is the Lord!" (Jn 21:7). This was the occasion when Jesus, in reply to a question from Peter about what would happen to John, makes a reference to John's death (cf. Jn 21:20–23). The Fourth Gospel closes with this scene where the two most prominent apostles converse with Jesus.

After the Lord's ascension, St John stays close to St Peter. The Acts of the Apostles shows them going together to the temple to pray, and there, at the Beautiful Gate, through Jesus' power, they cure a man lame from birth (cf. Acts 3:1–9; 2:46). There and then, St Peter preaches the Gospel of Jesus Christ and the leading priests became "annoyed because they were teaching the people and proclaiming in Jesus the resurrection from the dead. And they arrested them and put them in custody until the morrow" (Acts 4:2–3). But this only encouraged the apostles to preach the Gospel more boldly, even to their judges (cf. Acts 4:13–22). They prayed and preached together, and they also shared the joy of being "counted worthy to suffer dishonour for the name" of Jesus (Acts 5:41). When they were set free by the Jewish authorities, they went back to their friends and all prayed the second Psalm (cf. Acts 4:25). In prayer they obtained the strength to preach boldly in the midst of adversity and persecution.

Peter and John are also seen together when they are sent by the apostolic college to administer the sacrament of Confirmation to people in Samaria already baptized by Philip (cf. Acts 8:14). Years later, around the year 50, at the first Council of the Church, held in Jerusalem, James and Peter and John appear as pillars of the Church (cf. Gal 2:9).

From this point forward, our information about St John's life comes from Church tradition. Reliable reports tell us that he left Palestine and went to Ephesus, where he looked after the churches of Asia Minor (so says St Polycarp of Smyrna, who died in 155 at the age of eighty-six and who, we are told, was a disciple of St John himself).[10] This piece of information agrees

10. Cf. *Against Heresies*, 2, 22, 5; 3, 1, 1.

with the testimony of Polycrates, bishop of Ephesus (died *c.*190)—which Eusebius of Caesarea quotes;[11] he says that John belonged to a Jewish priestly family and died in Ephesus, a tradition consistent with the fact that the Fourth Gospel mentions Jewish feasts so often and with the fact that John was known to the high priest (cf. Jn 18:16).

What is not so clear is when exactly he moved to Ephesus. We have already said that he was still in Jerusalem around the year 50. And it seems likely that he had not yet gone to Ephesus when St Paul wrote his Second Letter to Timothy, around the year 66 or 67, in which he gives him instructions on how to govern that church (cf. 2 Tim 4:1–2); all of which points to St John arriving in Ephesus after the death of St Paul, which took place in 67: for one thing, all the churches of the region would have been in need of his attention, and, also, the Jewish War, the war between Judea and Rome (which would end in the destruction of Jerusalem in the year 70), caused most Christians to flee both the Holy City and Palestine. We do not know with any certainty whether St John brought the Virgin Mary with him to Ephesus at that time or whether she had already been assumed into heaven; but we can be sure that the apostle took great care of her until the end of her life.

Tradition does not give us a clear picture of what happened to John in Ephesus. It does confirm the reports of St Irenaeus, Eusebius and other ecclesiastical writers that he was sent into exile on the island of Patmos, where he wrote the Apocalypse (cf. Rev 1:9); this took place in the fourteenth year of Domitian's reign, 95. After Domitian's death the following year, John returned to Ephesus where he had now to face not only external enemies of the Church but certain Christians who had become obstinate heretics. With fatherly solicitude the apostle tried to heal the divisions and, under the inspiration of the Holy Spirit, he wrote three letters to faithful Christians warning them of dangers. It would seem that the letter we know as 3 John was in fact the first.

This "third letter" is addressed to Gaius, a priest, who had remained loyal to John's authority and to the truth of the Gospel. The apostle's main concern at this time is to strengthen his children in the faith: "No greater joy can I have than this, to hear that my children follow the truth" (3 Jn 4); and he advises Gaius not to imitate evil people like Diotrephes who criticize the apostle out of jealousy.

The second letter is addressed to a particular church—which one, we cannot tell—whom St John calls "the elect lady", in the same way as St Peter (1 Pet 5:13) calls the church at Rome the one who is likewise "chosen". He is worried lest the truth become adulterated, and he warns the church against deceivers who deny the incarnation of our Lord Jesus Christ (cf. 2 Jn 9–11). Also, presumably because these heretics were deforming the true ideal of Christian love, he spells it out absolutely clearly: "And this is love, that we

11. *Ecclesiastical History*, 3, 31, 3; 5, 24, 3.

follow his commandments" (2 Jn 6). This and the previous letter are both very short.

St John ranges more widely in the "first letter", which is perhaps the last he wrote. It is addressed to the faithful in general, and may have been a kind of encyclical letter to the churches of Asia Minor. In it he keeps concentrating on two themes (the same as in 2 John)—Christian faith and love, which heretics are trying to undermine. He never tires of telling them, "Let what you heard from the beginning abide in you" (1 Jn 2:24; cf. 2:7, 25; 3:11). To strengthen their resolve to stand fast in faith and Christian living (cf. 5:13), he deals, one after the other, with various parallel themes—light (cf. 1:5ff), righteousness (cf. 2:29ff), love (cf. 4:7ff) and truth (cf. 5:6ff); but the same basic ideas underlie the whole letter: we are children of God, who is Love, and this means that we must live according to his commandments (cf. 3:23). St John's style and teaching in this letter are so reminiscent of the Fourth Gospel that we cannot doubt that they are written by the same hand. In fact, all the indicators are that St John wrote both these texts in the same period, but we cannot work out which came first.

We can take it therefore, that it was at Ephesus, between his exile on Patmos and his death at the start of Trajan's reign (98–117), that St John, in his solicitude for the Church, wrote the three letters and the Gospel. What little more tradition tells us about the last years of his life confirms his concern for purity of doctrine and faithfulness to the commandment of love. St Jerome tells how the disciples used to carry him to Christian meetings, his age preventing him from walking, and how he used to repeat all the time: "My little children, love one another." And when the disciples asked him why he was always saying the same thing, he replied, "It is the Lord's commandment, and if you keep it, that alone suffices."[12]

STRUCTURE AND CONTENT

The structure of St John's Gospel fits in with his aim in writing it, moved as he was by the Holy Spirit: he tells us himself that he wrote the Gospel "that you may believe that Jesus is the Christ, the Son of God, and that believing you may have life in his name" (Jn 20:31). In general, St John follows the same order as followed by the apostles in their oral preaching, and in so doing he coincides with the Synoptic Gospels: Jesus begins his public ministry after being baptized in the Jordan by John the Baptist; he preaches and works miracles in Galilee and Jerusalem; and his life on earth ends with his passion and glorious resurrection (cf. Acts 10:38–41).

Within this general framework, St John follows a plan of his own, different from that of the Synoptics. For this he uses certain basic ideas which he devel-

12. *Commentary on Galatians*, 3, chap. 6.

ops in the course of his Gospel—the succession of Jewish feasts which mark the different stages in his account; the treatment of certain concepts, like the New Testament taking the place of the Old; the themes of life, of the Bread of Life, of the light, truth, love, etc.; and the gradual and dramatic manifestation of Jesus as the Messiah and Son of God, contrasting with the growing blindness of those Jews who reject him, until the high point comes, the "hour" of Jesus and of the power of darkness. All these threads are woven together to form this Gospel, giving it a particular structure and thematic cohesion. Broadly, we might say that the structure of the Fourth Gospel is along these lines:

Prologue (1:1–18). This introduction is of great theological importance. Jesus Christ, the eternal word of God, with the Father, creator of the world, true Light, has become man in order to bring the world light, that is, definitive and saving revelation for all men. However, the Jews in general did not accept the Light even though John the Baptist bore witness to it; but those who do accept it and believe in him are raised to become children of God. This prologue contains, in essence, all the great themes which the Gospel will develop—Christ's revealing of himself, light, truth, life, glory, revelation of the Father, faith and unbelief.

PART ONE: JESUS IS MANIFESTED AS THE MESSIAH BY SIGNS AND WORDS

This part runs from the Baptist's testimony regarding Jesus (1:19) to the Last Supper (chap. 13). It can be divided into various sections:

1. *Introduction* and 2. *Jesus, the author of the new economy of salvation: first signs of faith in him* (1:19—4:54). Section 2 includes the Baptist's testimony (cf. 1:19–34), the calling of the first disciples (cf. 1:35–51), and our Lord's ministry in Galilee when he performed his first miracle at the wedding at Cana (cf. 2:1–12). These episodes cover the first weeks of Jesus' public life: the days are counted off, one by one. At the centre of this section we find the feast of the Passover, the first such feast in our Lord's public ministry. During his stay in Jerusalem he cleanses the temple (cf. 2:13–25) and converses with Nicodemus (cf. 3:1–21). The section ends with the Baptist's last testimony to Jesus (cf. 3:22–36) and Jesus' return from Jerusalem through Samaria, where he has the meeting with the Samaritan woman (cf. 4:1–42), and through Galilee, where he works the second miracle, curing the son of the royal official (cf. 4:46–54).

The whole section is given unity by the fact that our Lord is showing himself to be the founder of the new economy of grace, an economy superior to that of the temple and the Old Law. This is clearly reflected in the changing of the water into wine at Cana in Galilee (cf. 2:9); in St John's comment on the episode of the cleansing of the temple ("he spoke of the temple of his body": 2:21); in the revelation to Nicodemus about new birth through Baptism (cf. 3:5); and in our Lord's conversation with the Samaritan woman, where he lays down that true adoration should be "in spirit and truth" (4:24). This manifestation of the Lord causes his disciples (cf. 1:50; 2:11) and the people (cf. 2:23; 4:42–53) to begin to have faith in him, and also causes the first signs of rejection on the part of some Jews (cf. 2:24–25; 3:11, 18, etc.).

3. *Jesus reveals his divinity* (chap. 5). St John relates the curing of a paralyzed man at the pool of Bethzatha (cf. 5:1–18) and then goes on to give us one of our Lord's discourses, where he reveals that he acts in union with the Father because he is the Father's Son. All this happens on "a feast of the Jews" (5:1), which could be Passover or perhaps the feast of Pentecost, which falls fifty days after Passover. This new manifestation of our Lord, in which he clearly states his divinity, both through the miracle and through what he says in the discourse, provokes some Jews to open hatred : from then on they "sought all the more to kill him, because he not only broke the sabbath but also called God his Father, making him equal with God" (5:18).

4. *Jesus is the bread of life* (chap. 6). This has a structure very like that of the previous chapter: first, two miracles—the multiplication of the loaves and fish, and Jesus' walking on the water; and then a discourse—that of the synagogue of Capernaum, in which the Lord reveals himself as the Bread of Life, announcing the mystery of the Blessed Eucharist. St John points out that this occurred when "the Passover, the feast of the Jews, was at hand" (6:4), thereby hinting that the eucharistic banquet would in the future be the New Passover. Many of his followers were scandalized by these words of Jesus, so much so that those who chose not to believe left him, and those who believed grew more attached to him: "After this many of his disciples drew back and no longer went about with him" (6:66); whereas Simon Peter, speaking for the Twelve, confessed "we have believed, and have come to know that you are the Holy One of God" (6:69), that is, the Messiah, the Son of God.

From chapter 7 onwards it is not so easy to divide the narrative into such distinct sections. The five remaining chapters of the first part certainly have some basic cohesion in that Jerusalem or its environs provides the setting. Jesus reveals himself as Light and Life of the world, and opposition becomes more and more pronounced. However, we will divide these chapters into two sections, centering on two great miracles, in which Jesus reveals himself as Light and Life.

5. *Jesus is the light of the world* (chaps. 7–10). It opens with the observation that "Jesus went about in Galilee; he would not go about in Judea, because the Jews sought to kill him" (7:1). But, because it was the feast of Tabernacles, "about the middle of the feast Jesus went up into the temple and taught" (7:14). This visit to Jerusalem gives our Lord an opportunity to show himself more clearly to the Jewish authorities and to the people; everyone is talking

about him. Jesus teaches that he has been sent by the Father (cf. 7:28–29). The Jewish authorities want to arrest him, but they do not do so because, St John remarks, "his hour had not yet come" (7:30). On the last day of the feast Jesus reveals himself as the one the Holy Spirit is to send—which again leads to division among the people. For some he is the Messiah, "the Christ" (7:41); for others—the chief priests and Pharisees—he is not, and they want to arrest him for blasphemy, but they do not dare (cf. 7:44ff).

At dawn the next day Jesus returns to the temple to teach, and the episode of the adulterous woman occurs (cf. 8:1–11). Then Jesus reveals himself as "the light of the world" (8:12), sent by the Father (cf. 8:16), equal to God (cf. 8:19), greater than Abraham (cf. 8:58). People become so angry they want to stone him (cf. 8:59).

But Jesus also reveals he is the Light of the world by performing a miracle, a sign proving the truth of what he is saying—the miracle of curing a man born blind (cf. 9:1–38), which provides our Lord with an occasion to speak to us about God's judgment : "For judgment I came into this world, that those who do not see may see, and that those who see may become blind" (9:39). The man who has been cured, who now confesses his faith in Christ, is a model for all believers; whereas the Pharisees, who are full of pride, which they disguise with religiosity, become blind by rejecting Christ, the Light of the world.

Only through faith in Christ and by his grace can man attain salvation, for he is "the door of entry to eternal life" (10:7–10), "the Good shepherd" who guides us and has given his life for us (10:11–18). This revelation causes more arguments among the Jews, with some saying that he is possessed by a devil and others recognizing that he has worked a miracle (cf. 10:19–21).

6. *Jesus and the Father.* Then comes a further manifestation of our Lord, on the occasion of the feast of the Dedication of the Temple: it is wintertime and Jesus is walking in the portico of Solomon (cf. 10:22–23); the Jews ask him to tell them openly if he is the Christ, to which he replies that he is the Son of God, equal to the Father : "I and the Father are one" (10:30) and "the Father is in me and I am in the Father" (10:38). The Jews realize perfectly well that he is revealing himself as God; so they try once more to stone him (cf. 10:31) and arrest him (cf. 10:39); but he goes away across the Jordan, and many people follow him and believe in him (cf. 10:42).

7. *Jesus is the life of the world* (chaps. 11–12). The outstanding event here is the miracle of the raising of Lazarus. Jesus took occasion of this to reveal that he is "the resurrection and the life" for those who believe in him (11:25). Martha's reaction of faith also stands out: "I believe that you are the Christ, the Son of God, he who is coming into the world" (11:27), as does the Pharisees' reaction, which is one of hatred: they meet in council and formally decide to put him to death (cf. 11:45–53). St John observes that "the Passover of the

Jews was at hand" (11:55), which suggests that these events and those of chapter 12 are to herald Christ's redemptive death and glorious resurrection.

8. *Jesus is acclaimed as the messianic king.* Our Lord in fact links the anointing at Bethany, which takes place six days before the Passover, with the day of his burial (cf. 12:1, 7).

The triumphal entry into Jerusalem is an anticipation of Jesus' glorification in the Resurrection, which is why St John comments that "his disciples did not understand this at first; but when Jesus was glorified, then they remembered that this had been written of him and had been done to him" (12:16). Our Lord's own words, announcing that the hour has come for his glorification through death on the cross and resurrection (cf. 12:23ff, 33), are a last invitation to men to believe in him (cf. 12:35–36). Many people, even many prominent Jews, believe in him; others prefer the glory of men (12:42); but those who do not receive Jesus' words will be condemned by those very words on the last day (12:48).

This brings us to the end of the first part of the Gospel, in which Jesus progressively reveals himself as the Messiah, through his miracles (a sign of his divinity) and through his words, in which he declares that he is the Messiah, the Son of God and equal to the Father. All this moves in a dramatic crescendo to Jesus' "hour", culminating in his death and resurrection, which are the subject of the second part of the Gospel.

PART TWO: JESUS IS MANIFESTED AS THE MESSIAH, SON OF GOD, IN HIS PASSION, DEATH AND RESURRECTION

In this second part there are three sections dealing with the Last Supper, the passion and death of our Lord, and his resurrection. In each of the three we find Christ being revealed, and people reacting to him in different ways; the point of climax is imminent.

9. *The Last Supper* (chaps. 13–17). Jesus' revelation to his disciples in the intimacy of the Last Supper is given. It begins with St John informing us that it was the eve of the feast of the Passover "when Jesus knew that his hour had come to depart out of this world to the Father" (Jn 13:1). This section comprises, firstly, the account of the washing of feet and the prediction of Judas' betrayal. Christ's love contrasts with the Jews' hatred. Probably St John purposely points out that when Judas left the room "it was night" (13:30), for if one leaves the light of Christ one is submerged in the kingdom of darkness and unbelief. The Lord's discourses follow, running up to chapter 16. It is not easy to impose a pattern on them, but basically there are three main themes: first, love—*agape*—which has its root in Christ's love and becomes the commandment of the Lord (cf. 13:34–35; 15:11–17); second, the consolation Jesus gives

his disciples before he leaves them (cf. 13:33; 14:1–7), by saying he will return (cf. 14:1–3; 16:16–26) and by promising that he will send the Holy Spirit, who is called here the Paraclete (Counsellor) and who will lead them to all truth (14:15–17, 26; 16:5–15); thirdly, Christ's solidarity with his disciples, using the simile of the vine and the branches, a unity based on love and on keeping the commandments (cf. 15:1–11). Along with these subjects, there is Jesus' revelation that he is God (cf. 14:10) and also his prediction of the hatred the world will show his disciples (cf. 15:18—16:4). The section concludes with Christ's priestly prayer (chap. 17), which once again brings in the subjects of his glorification and his disciples' faith and unity, for which he prays to the Father.

10. *The passion and death of Jesus* (chaps. 18–19). It contains the account of our Lord's passion. The narrative follows the course of events of that night and of the morning of Good Friday: arrest, interrogation before Annas and Caiaphas, and Peter's denials (cf. 18:1–27); the trial before Pontius Pilate (cf. 18:28—19:26); crucifixion, death and burial (19:17–42). The sacred text gives lots of details which emphasize that the Passion is the supreme manifestation of Christ as Messiah-King and of his glory: when he says, "I am he", the people who have come to arrest him draw back and fall to the ground; to Pilate he declares that he is a king (cf. 18:33–37; 19:2–3, 19–22); and he shows that he has full knowledge and control of these events (cf. 18:4; 19:28) whereby his Father's will is being fulfilled (cf. 18:11; 19:30). Christ is the new passover lamb, by whose redemptive death the sin of the world is taken away (cf. 19:31; 1:29). From Jesus' side, water flows as well as blood, symbolizing Baptism and the promised Holy Spirit (cf. 7:37–39).

The Passion marks the climax of the Jews' and the world's hatred of Christ; it is the hour of the powers of darkness, affecting even his disciples, for they abandon him or deny him (cf. 18:25–27). But at the foot of the cross the supreme confession of faith in Jesus also takes place—the faith of the Blessed Virgin, whom our Lord makes Mother of mankind, mankind being represented by the beloved disciple, St John (cf. 19:25–27).

11. *Appearances of the risen Christ* (chaps. 20–21). This completes the glorious manifestation of Jesus as Messiah and Son of God, the story of which St John has told to strengthen our faith (cf. 20:31). This section contains the resurrection of the Lord as revealed in the empty tomb (cf. 20:1–10), and in his appearances to Mary Magdalene (cf. 20:11–18) and to the disciples (cf. 20:19–29). The resurrection, closely linked with the passion and death, is the climax of Christ's revelation. After the events of Holy Week, enlightened now by the Holy Spirit, the apostles grasp the meaning of the Old Testament prophecies about Christ, and also of what he himself said and did (cf. 20:8–9; 2:22; 12:16). The risen Christ gives the apostles the Holy Spirit and the power to forgive sins (cf. 20:22–23), and praises all those who, unlike St Thomas,

believe without having seen him (cf. 20:29). The account of the miraculous draught of fish at the Sea of Tiberias (cf. 21:1–14) prefigures the multitude of people whom the Church will bring to Christ; into this ecclesiological context fits the rest of chapter 21, which tells of St Peter being given the primacy of the Church (cf. 21:15–19). The Gospel concludes with a statement of the truthfulness of the testimony borne by the Evangelist, who has seen and heard the things he has recounted (cf. 21:24–25).

DOCTRINAL CONTENT

THE BLESSED TRINITY

St John's Gospel is the most explicit New Testament document as far as revelation of the mystery of the Blessed Trinity is concerned—as can be seen, for example, by the fact that St Augustine devotes a lot of space to the study of this mystery in his *Treatise on the Gospel of St John.*[13] The Evangelist enters deep into this unfathomable mystery, quoting the words of Christ, the Only-begotten Son who is in the bosom of the Father and who becomes man in order to tell us the secret of God's intimate inner life (cf. Jn 1:18). This is the reason why the Fourth Gospel particularly has been attacked by those who do not accept the divinity of Jesus Christ; whereas it is constantly quoted by the Magisterium of the Church when it is explaining and giving dogmatic formulation to the mystery of the Trinity or anything to do with the Incarnation of the Word.[14]

At the very beginning the Gospel asserts that the Word is God, and also that he is one in substance with the Father : when it says that "the Word was with God", the original Greek is very precise because it uses the word *Theos* with the article when it means the Person of the Father, and without the article when it refers to the divine essence. Later on, the Gospel speaks about the oneness of God and also about each of the three divine Persons. Of the One God it affirms that he has sent the Baptist (cf. 1:6), that we are born of him to the life of grace (cf. 1:12–13), that no one has ever seen him (cf. 1:18), and that in him are good deeds done (cf. 3:21); the oneness of God is proclaimed with tremendous force (cf. 5:44).[15] But also each of the three divine Persons is often referred to. The Gospel introduces the Word as the only Son of the Father (cf. 1:14), and throughout Jesus will speak again and again about his Father: for example, on the two occasions when he prays out loud he begins with the

13. Cf. *In Ioann. Evang.*, 15, 1. **14.** Cf. e.g., *Dz-Sch*, 178, 502, 803–806. **15.** The RSVCE gives "the glory that comes from the only God"; and the Navarre Spanish parallels that; however, the Navarre edition carries a note which reads: "in so translating we have followed the text accepted by the New Vulgate, but the oldest papyri (the Bodmer papyri) and codexes as important as the Vatican Codex do not use the word God and instead speak of the Only One—the glory that comes from the Only One—which reaffirms and emphasizes God's unicity".

word "Father" (11:41; 17:1). While making this distinction between himself and the Father, he also says that they share the same nature: "I and the Father are one" (10:30). On other occasions, he says that if they knew him, they "would know the Father also" (8:19; cf. 14:8–11), and that the Father is in him and he is in the Father (cf. 10:34–39). Jesus also teaches that God is his Father in a different way from which he is the Father of men: "I am ascending to my Father and your Father, to my God and your God ..." (20:17). This relationship of the Christian as son to his Father God, which is already taught in the prologue to the Gospel (cf. 1:12–13), is something which causes St John to exclaim: "See what love the Father has given us that we should be called children of God; and so we are" (1 Jn 3:1).

The Incarnate Word is the beginning, centre and end of the Fourth Gospel: it begins by telling us that the Word was God and was with God. We should remember that the tense used here expresses the idea of the timelessness of eternity.[16] The Word is the envoy of the Father (cf. 3:17–34; 5:36; 6:57; 7:33; etc.); the greatest possible expression of God's love for the world is the fact that God gave it his only Son (cf. 3:16). Jesus Christ, the Incarnate Word, is God's definitive rapprochement to mankind; in his most holy human nature the great God himself is made manifest (cf. Heb 1:1ff). This is why he complains when his disciples, after being with him for so long, ask him to show them the Father: when they see him they are seeing the Father also (cf. Jn 14:8–11); not only himself and his words, but his whole life, everything he does (cf. 9:4; 10:32–37; 14:12) and particularly his death and resurrection, reveal the Father. The Gospel of St John frequently tells us that Christ reveals the Father to us, and this saving revelation reaches its climax on the cross, where Christ is raised up, enthroned above the earth, which he embraces as its King. Jesus Christ crucified is thus the supreme expression of God's salvific love. Just as the bronze serpent was raised up in the wilderness to save those who had been bitten by the snakes, "so must the Son of man be lifted up, that whoever believes in him may have eternal life" (3:14–15). This is what Christ means also when he says (12:32): "I, when I am lifted up from the earth, will draw all men to myself."[17]

The Fourth Gospel also reveals the existence of the Holy Spirit as a distinct transcendent Person. In the Baptist's testimony of Jesus as "Son of God" (1:34), the unmistakable sign given is the descent of the Spirit over the Messiah in the form of a dove—the Messiah who will baptize in the Holy Spirit, whereas the Precursor's baptism is with water: "unless one is born of

16. This can be seen clearly in the very prologue of the Gospel when, speaking now of time past, it uses the second aorist (*egeneto*): Jesus is the Word made flesh who comes to dwell among men and who possesses the glory of the Only-begotten of the Father, full of grace and truth (1:14). **17.** And so in this way "his humanity united with the Person of the Word was the instrument of our salvation. Therefore, 'in Christ the perfect achievement of our reconciliation came forth ...'" (Vatican II, *Sacrosanctum Concilium*, 5).

water and the Spirit, he cannot enter the kingdom of God" (3:5). This relationship between water and the Spirit reappears in 7:37–39, where our Lord says that rivers of living water will flow out of him who believes in him, and the Evangelist explains that "this he said about the Spirit, which those who believed in him were to receive; for as yet the Spirit had not been given, because Jesus was not yet glorified" (7:39). This water/Spirit relationship is hinted at in the Old Testament (cf. Gen 1:2; Ezek 36:25–27), implying the power which water is given through the Spirit.

At the Last Supper, and after the Resurrection, the Evangelist gives us Jesus' words on the third Person of the Blessed Trinity and his sanctifying action: Jesus says that he will pray the Father to send them "another Counsellor", "the Spirit of truth" (14:16–17; 15:26; 16:13). The Father will listen to Christ's prayer and will send "the Holy Spirit" (14:26), who proceeds from the Father and the Son and says what the Son gives him to say (cf. 16:13–15). Thus, the Holy Spirit proceeds from the Father and the Son, who send him to their own who are still in the world.

The Holy Spirit, then, is the Counsellor who will always be with those who believe in Christ, making his home in them (cf. 14:16–17); he it is also who will remind them of all that Jesus has taught them and who will enlighten them to understand the true meaning of those words (cf. 14:26). He will bear witness to Christ for the apostles as they in their turn will do for other men (cf. 15:26–27). The Holy Spirit will also proclaim to them everything to do with the mystery of salvation (cf. 16:14–15). Under his sure guidance the disciples will reach all truth (cf. 16:13).

Then, after rising from the dead, Jesus breathes on his disciples and says: "Receive the Holy Spirit. If you forgive the sins of any, they are forgiven; if you retain the sins of any, they are retained" (20:22–23). This outpouring of the Holy Spirit for the forgiveness of sins is, as it were, a joyful anticipation of the definitive outpouring at Pentecost (cf. Acts 2:1ff), and, together with the regeneration worked by Baptism, the most moving expression of God's mercy whereby the sacrament of Penance is instituted to bring us God's forgiveness.

FAITH

St John actually says that he has written his Gospel "that you may believe that Jesus is the Christ, the Son of God, and that believing you may have life in his name" (Jn 20:31). Faith in Jesus Christ leads to eternal life, because through faith we become united to Jesus and share in his victory over sin and death: "This is the victory that overcomes the world, our faith" (1 Jn 5:4); and because by believing we fulfil *the commandment* of the Lord: "This is his commandment, that we should believe in the name of his Son Jesus Christ" (1 Jn 3:23). Faith is our loving response to God's love for us as manifested in Christ: "God so loved the world that he gave his only Son, that whoever believes in him should not perish but have eternal life" (Jn 3:16). Jesus showed us how important faith is when he worked his miracles; for example, before raising Lazarus from the dead he says to Martha: "whoever lives and believes in me shall never die" (11:26; cf. also 5:24; 6:40; 6:47; etc.).

People adopt one of two attitudes to Revelation. Some believe, and by doing so they already share in some way in eternal life: "he who believes in the Son has eternal life" (3:36; cf. 3:18; 5:24; etc.); others do not believe and therefore they are already condemned by God: "he who does not believe is condemned already, because he has not believed in the name of the only Son of God" (3:18; cf. 3:36; etc.).

The Fourth Gospel is a living testimony designed to strengthen our faith in eternal life (cf. 20:31). Faith in Jesus Christ has a reasonable basis in the witness borne by those who saw and heard Jesus (cf. Jn 21:24; Lk 1:1–4) and who faithfully pass on to us what Jesus did and taught.[18] So, believing means knowing revealed truth or, better, recognizing the authority of God revealing truth. In fact, in this Gospel we often find the verbs "to believe" and "to know" side by side in the one phrase; sometimes they seem to be interchangeable (cf. Jn 6:69; 17:8; etc.). The verb "to know" has the meaning not just of knowing intellectually, of grasping the truth; it takes on an Old Testament meaning, indicating unreserved adhesion to the Truth that is Jesus Christ. Therefore, faith includes the act of trusting commitment as well as the act of knowing. Recognizing supernatural truth through the testimony given us, we adhere to that truth and, by accepting it with our whole heart, we obtain deep knowledge of God's truth.

There are different degrees of faith. The Gospel shows us the apostles' faith growing. It tells us that our Lord was unable to trust some of those who had faith, because their faith was still weak (cf. 2:23ff). Growth in faith goes hand in hand with growth in knowledge of Jesus Christ.

Faith is at one and the same time a free gift of God and a free action on man's part: man reaches genuine freedom to believe when God gives him the grace which enables him to adhere to revealed truths; but as long as man is a wayfarer in this life, freedom means that he can ultimately reject God's gift. Jesus keeps on exhorting people to believe in him, because men, being free, can reject him (cf. 8:24; 3:36; 15:22; etc.), despite the good reasons they have for believing. But at the same time it is the Son of God himself who gives us understanding to believe (cf. 1 Jn 5:20), and no one can believe in him unless it is granted him by the Father (cf. Jn 6:65).

To sum up: faith is the result of God's action which attests to Christ by means of apostolic preaching; and it is also the result of man's freedom, whereby man recognizes the truth of the testimony God has given him and surrenders himself to Christ freely and joyfully.

18. Cf. Vatican II, *Dei Verbum*, 19.

CHARITY

Charity is the favourite theme of the beloved disciple of Jesus, "on whose breast he rested at the Supper, which means that he drank of the deepest secrets of (Jesus') heart."[19] He had experienced Christ's love in a special way and was therefore in a unique position to teach us how to be loved by Jesus and how to love him.[20]

It is God who takes the initiative in love (cf. Jn 1:11; 4:7; 15:16; 1 Jn 4:10), which shows that it is he who loves most. Love can be measured by the value of the gift that is given, and God gives us what he most values, what he most loves, his own Son: "God so loved the world that he gave his only Son" (Jn 3:16), him whom he most loved, who most pleased him (cf. Mt 3:17).

The supreme expression of this love occurred in the sacrifice of the cross. When Abraham was about to sacrifice his only son, God stayed his hand, but he does not prevent men from nailing his own Son to the Cross—which leads St Paul to exclaim, full of hope: "He who did not spare his own Son […], will he not also give us all things with him?" (Rom 8:32).

Seeing that God loves him so much, man feels obliged to respond, to practise the great truth that love can be repaid only with love. Man has been created "in the image of God" (Gen 1:27), and "God", St John tells us, "is love" (1 Jn 4:8). It follows that man's heart is made to love, and the more he loves, the more he becomes one with God: only when he loves can he be happy. God wants us to be happy, in this life as well as in the next. St John gives us deep insights into Jesus' teaching on charity, not only through what Jesus says, but particularly by his narrative of our Lord's life (cf. Acts 1:1).

The best proof of love is fidelity, an unswerving loyalty, total commitment to God's will: Jesus shows us his hunger to do the will of his Father and he tells us that his food is to do the will of him who sent him (cf. Jn 4:34). "I have kept my Father's commandments", our Lord says, "and abide in his love" (15:10). Jesus asserts that the world knows that he loves the Father and does what the Father has commanded him (cf. 14:31). This supreme love leads him also to love the world and man, for the lover cannot cease loving what he loves (cf. 3:16), nor can one love a father without loving his children also. All men are called to become children of God through the grace of Baptism (cf. 1:12–13; 3:3). If the Father loves the world and men, then Jesus also loves them. This love brought him even to die for them. After speaking about how right it was for the world to know that he loves the Father, he adds: "Rise, let us go hence" (14:31), showing us how eager he is to give himself, for he is on his way to Gethsemane to meet his passion and death. Jesus sacrifices himself totally, as a good shepherd who gives his life for his sheep (cf. 10:11). He

19. St Augustine, *In Ioann. Evang.*, 18, 1. **20.** Cf. St Thomas Aquinas, *Commentary on St John*, 21, 20.

rightly says that no one has greater love than he who gives up his life for the loved one (cf. 15:13): St John explains that having loved his own who were in the world, he loved them to the end (cf. 13:1; 19:28).

St John lays special emphasis on Jesus' love, in both its divine and its human dimensions. We are shown how much he loved his friend Lazarus, and Martha and Mary (cf. 11:5); when his friend dies he makes his way to the tomb and he cannot help crying—and the people realize how deeply he loved Lazarus (cf. 11:33, 35).

Jesus has given us an example to imitate (cf. 13:15). The apostles responded to the love he showed them: "the Father himself loves you," the Master assures them, "because you have loved me and have believed that I come from the Father" (16:27). They all protest their love when Jesus tells them he is going to be betrayed (cf. Mt 26:35; Mk 14:31): "I will lay down my life for you", St Peter says (Jn 13:37). They respond in their own way to Christ's love; but the Lord points out that only he who keeps the commandments really loves him (cf. 14:21); this is a constant in his teaching: they remain in his love by keeping his commandments (cf. 15:9–10).

There is also a second commandment, which is like the first: we should imitate Christ not only in his love for his Father but also in his love for the brethren (cf. 15:9). Three times in the Last Supper our Lord gives the commandment to love: "A new commandment I give to you, that you love one another, even as I have loved you, that you also love one another" (13:34; cf. 15:12, 17). This will be the special characteristic of his true disciple, the distinguishing mark of the Christian. "Only charity distinguishes the children of God from the children of the devil. Though all may mark themselves with the sign of the cross of Christ, though all may say Amen, though all sing alleluia, though they enter the Church, though they build basilicas, nothing will distinguish the children of God from the children of the devil unless it be charity. Those who have love are born of God, those who have not, are not [...]; charity is the precious pearl (Mt 13:46); if you have it, that alone suffices."[21] Love is the source of the unity which Jesus prays for in his last prayer on this unforgettable night: "I in them and them in me, that they may become perfectly one, so that the world may know that thou hast sent me and hast loved them even as thou hast loved me" (Jn 17:23). Only through charity will people recognize the sign of the Redemption (cf. 17:21).

God wants what is best for us, what makes for our happiness and joy—which is precisely why he lays down the law of charity. In the Last Supper, also, the Master teaches the meaning of joy: seeing how sad the apostles are because they sense that he is leaving them, he tells them that if they loved him, they would be in fact rejoicing, to see him so near his moment of triumph (cf. 14:28). After speaking to them about persevering in his love and keeping faith

21. *In Epist. Ioann. ad Parthos*, 5, 7.

with him, he assures them that he is telling them all this so that they can share his own joy: their joy, even in the midst of the difficulties of this life, will be full (cf. 15:11). He does not hide from them the difficulties that lie ahead; yet he assures them that their sorrow will turn into joy: "You have sorrow now, but I will see you again and your hearts will rejoice, and no one will take your joy from you" (16:22). And in fact the return of the risen Jesus did fill them with hope and joy; our Lord's words, which they could not understand when they heard them first, came completely true: the Acts of the Apostles tells us how they left the Sanhedrin after being beaten, happy that they had suffered for the Lord (cf. Acts 5:40): charity had given them perfect joy (cf. Jn 16:24)

THE SACRAMENTS

St John often mentions different Jewish feasts, especially the Passover. He refers to four occasions of this great festival (2:13, 23; 5:1; 6:4; 12:1), unlike the Synoptics, which only refer to the Passover at which Jesus died. John's Gospel also refers to the deep, mysterious link between our Lord's own body and the temple of Jerusalem: the temple was the symbol of God's presence among men, a presence which was realized perfectly in Christ's human nature (cf. 2:19). In the book of Revelation it says that there will be no temple in the heavenly Jerusalem, for the Lamb of God will be the temple, Jesus Christ, forever victorious (cf. Rev 21:22).

All these festivals are a prelude to Christian celebrations, and the old Passover yields to a new one in which Christ is the perfect victim who brings about our redemption (cf. 1 Cor 5:7). St John here hints at the importance of liturgy in the sanctification of men through Christ, our Pasch.

The Evangelist goes from the sphere of the senses to that of the spirit; he discloses to us that behind our Lord's actions lie certain supernatural, saving realities, and that through Christ's human nature the splendour of his divinity is made manifest. All this is closely connected with the basic principle of the sacramental system: material, visible, natural elements are instruments which God selects to signify and produce invisible grace, the sanctification of the soul.

In a broad sense it can be said that Christ is the Sacrament of the Father, and "the Church, in Christ, is in the nature of a sacrament—a sign and instrument, that is, of communion with God and of unity among all men."[22] Here Vatican II is speaking of a "sacrament" not in the strict sense in which the essence of the sacraments of the New Alliance is dogmatically defined (for Trent categorically states that, strictly speaking, there are only seven sacraments).[23] Of these seven sacraments St John refers explicitly to Baptism, Eucharist and Penance. We can say that he also speaks of Confirmation,

22. Vatican II, *Lumen gentium*, 1. **23.** Council of Trent, sess. VII, c. 1.

Marriage and priestly Order, though not in a direct way. As regards Confirmation he includes Jesus' promise to send the Holy Spirit to the apostles (cf. Jn 14:26; 16:13), who will confirm them in the mission entrusted to them and guide them into all truth. On Marriage there is a passage which is usually regarded as important—the wedding at Cana (cf. 2:1–11). "Our Lord, in coming to the wedding, to which he had been invited," St Augustine says, "wished to enhance it and to confirm again that he is the author of marriage."[24] It can also be said that in this event there is a clear echo of Christ's espousal of the Church, which the prophets had foretold (cf. Is 54:4–8; 62:4–5; Ezek 16; etc.) and which St Paul takes up when he speaks about marriage as *sacramentum magnum* (Eph 5:3), a great sacrament, and refers to Jesus Christ as spouse of the Church (cf. Eph 5:27). In the book of Revelation St John also speaks about the wedding between the Lamb and the new Bride, the new Jerusalem, "coming down out of heaven from God, prepared as a bride adorned for her husband" (Rev 21:2). As far as priestly Order is concerned, this sacrament is covered in what is called "the priestly prayer of Jesus" (cf. Jn 17), where our Lord intercedes as High Priest before the Eternal Father on behalf of his own and offers himself as a holy victim "that they also may be consecrated in truth" (17:19).

As regards Baptism, Jesus' conversation with Nicodemus (cf. Jn 3:1–21) can be seen as really a form of baptismal instruction: it is necessary to be born again of water and the Spirit to be able to enter the Kingdom of heaven. (In Romans 6, St Paul speaks about this new life which is infused by Baptism.) And the episode at the pool of Bethzatha (cf. Jn 5) prefigures the baptismal rite of the early Church: the neophytes, on leaving the water after the words of Baptism have been spoken over them, are cleared of all sin and reborn into the life of grace.

Chapter 6 of the Gospel deals almost entirely with the Blessed Eucharist. Our Lord uses the miracle of the multiplication of the loaves and the fish (also recounted in the Synoptics) to explain in detail his teaching about the Bread of Life, the Bread which has come down from heaven to give eternal life. His words are clear and final: "Truly, truly, I say to you, unless you eat the flesh of the Son of man and drink his blood, you have no life in you" (6:53). "My flesh," Jesus says, "is food indeed, and my blood is drink indeed. He who eats my flesh and drinks my blood abides in me, and I in him" (6:55–56). Our Lord could not have spoken in a more explicit, more realistic, way about his own sacrifice: by which, after dying in a bloody way on the cross, he gives himself to us in the Eucharist, in an unbloody way as nourishment for our soul and leads us to the closest intimacy with God.

In this chapter there is an allusion to the Old Testament: "It is written in the prophets, 'And they shall all be taught by God' " (6:45), the prophets being

24. *In Ioann. Evang.*, 9, 2.

Isaiah and Jeremiah (cf. Is 54:13 and Jer 31:33), who were referring to the messianic times, when the people of God would be given a New Law written on their hearts, times when God would seal a New Alliance by the sacrifice of the Messiah. By this reference to the Old Testament, our Lord is teaching that the messianic times have arrived, and that the New Alliance is ratified by the sacrifice of Christ, who brings "eternal life" through his death (6:54). The institution of the Eucharist reminds us of all this.[25]

The Gospel speaks about the sacrament of Penance when the risen Lord appears to the apostles in the Cenacle: " 'As the Father has sent me, even so I send you.' And when he had said this, he breathed on them, and said to them, 'Receive the Holy Spirit. If you forgive the sins of any, they are forgiven; if you retain the sins of any, they are retained' " (20:21–23). According to the interpretation authorized by the Magisterium of the Church,[26] this passage refers to the institution of the sacrament of Penance.

THE BLESSED VIRGIN MARY

The apostle St John also found himself in a privileged position in relation to our Lady, for Jesus entrusted his Mother to John just before he died on the cross. From then on she would always be close to him, and to him, as to none other, she could speak about everything she kept in her heart (cf. Lk 2:51).

In Mary, the Gospel says, the Word became flesh. The very Son of the Eternal Father became Son of man, to enable the sons of men to become sons of God. The Song of Consolation (cf. Is 40:1–11) had spoken of God coming to those who suffered: now God himself will personally guide his people in a new exodus to the Promised Land. Once she consents to the Word becoming flesh, the Mother of God retires into the background; this is to be her usual role in the Gospel—that of passing unnoticed, especially at Jesus' moments of glory. Later, as no other creature does, she will share in Christ's glorious triumph, and it will be John who describes her in all her splendour: "A great portent appeared in heaven, a woman clothed with the sun, with the moon under her feet, and on her head a crown of twelve stars" (Rev 12:1).

In John 2:1–11 the wedding at Cana is described, and in 19:25–27 we are told of Mary's presence on Calvary. The two accounts are quite in parallel: in both she is described as the Mother of Jesus and in both our Lord refers to her as "woman". At both Cana and Calvary Jesus' "hour" is referred to—in the first case as something which has not yet arrived, and in the second as a present fact. This "hour" of Jesus is something which marks his whole life until it culminates in the cross (cf. Jn 7:30; 8:20; 12:27; 13:1; 17:1). "When he had done everything which he judged it appropriate to do", St Augustine says, "that is when the appointed hour arrived—through his will and not of neces-

25. Cf. Roman Canon of the Mass (Eucharistic Prayer 1). **26.** Council of Trent, *De Paen.*, can. 3.

sity, through his power and no exigency of any kind."[27] And St Thomas Aquinas says, "the hour of the Passion is to be understood not as imposed by necessity but as determined by divine providence."[28]

The first thing one notices in the story of the wedding at Cana is Mary's exquisite charity and her absolute faith in Jesus' power. We can also see that here, as at Calvary, Mary has a role closely linked with the Messiah's role as Redeemer. When Jesus changes into wine the water set aside for Jewish ritual purification, he is implying that the messianic times have begun. For, in the prophecies wine symbolizes the times of the Messiah, when the vats will be full of good wine (cf. Amos 9:13ff; Joel 2:24; 4:18), and on Mount Zion a feast will be celebrated with succulent food and fine wines (cf. Is 25:6). Jesus himself speaks about the fruit of the vine which will be drunk in the Kingdom (cf. Mt 26:29), and contrasts the new wine with the old (Mk 2:22). The wedding feast also evokes the marriage banquet for Yahweh and the daughter of Zion, meaning the Old Alliance (cf. Is 54:4–8; 62:4–5; Ezek 16), just as Christ's espousal of the Church means the New Alliance (cf. Eph 5:25; Rev 21), which is also alluded to in certain parables (cf. Mt 22:1–14; 25:1–13). All of which implies that the figure of the Virgin Mary and the words which refer to her should be contemplated in the light of the messianic meaning of the whole passage.

The Fourth Gospel contemplates Mary's divine motherhood in all its fulness, aware that she is the Mother not only of the head but also of the members of Christ's mystical body. This is why, instead of referring to Mary by name, the Fourth Gospel uses the titles of "Mother of Jesus" and "woman", which have a special significance connected with her spiritual motherhood; this is why at Cana, Jesus calls his Mother "woman" (Jn 2:4). Similarly in 19:25–27, where the Gospel speaks of our Lady's presence on Calvary, our Lord's words have a deeper meaning than might at first appear. After entrusting his Mother to the care of John, Jesus announces that his mission is accomplished (cf. 19:28); only "now", not before. His announcement that Mary is the Mother of the beloved disciple, therefore, establishes her role in the work of salvation which has at that moment reached its climax: in addition to being a son's act of devotion it has a more transcendental meaning—Mary's spiritual maternity. This is the moment at which the Virgin Mary's co-redemption acquires its full force and meaning. Now we can indeed see how closely united Mary is to Jesus, now her divine motherhood attains its full measure, now she is made spiritual Mother of all believers. The beloved disciple stands for all those who will follow the Master and who in the apostle John receive Mary as their Mother.

The word "woman" also implies a certain solemnity and contains a special emphasis: most authors are inclined to see in this title given to Mary a clear

27. *In Ioann. Evang.*, 8, 12. **28.** *Commentary on St John*, 2, 3.

allusion to the "protoevangelium" (cf. Gen 3:15), which speaks of the triumph of the woman and her seed over the serpent. In addition to being endorsed by the text itself (the use of the word "woman"), this allusion is confirmed by interpretations given by the Fathers when they speak of the parallelism between Eve and Mary, a parallelism similar to that between Adam and Christ (cf. Rom 5:12–14). In Christ's death that triumph over the serpent takes place, because by dying Jesus redeems us from slavery to the devil. *Mors per Evam, vita per Mariam*, death came upon us through Eve, Mary brings us life.[29] "The first Eve," St Irenaeus teaches, "disobeyed God; but the second obeyed him; and so the Virgin Mary can be the advocate of the virgin Eve."[30] Our Lady "in a wholly singular way cooperated by her obedience, faith, hope and burning charity in the work of the Saviour in restoring supernatural life to souls. For this reason she is a Mother to us in the order of grace"[31] and "continues in heaven her maternal role towards the members of Christ, in that she cooperates with the birth and growth of divine life in the souls of the redeemed".[32]

Origen comments: "We dare to say that the Gospels are the flower of the Scriptures, and the flower of the Gospels is that of St John. But no one can penetrate its meaning who has not rested on Jesus' breast and taken Mary as his Mother. To be like John one needs to be able, like him, to be pointed out by Jesus as another Jesus. And so, if Mary had no other children but Jesus, and Jesus says to his Mother: 'Behold, your son' and not 'Behold, another son', then it is as if he were saying, 'Behold, Jesus, to whom you have given life.' And so it is: anyone who has identified with Christ, no longer lives for himself: Christ lives in him (cf. Gal 2:20), and given that Christ lives in him, Jesus says of him to Mary: 'Behold, your son—Christ'."[33]

We have received through Baptism, by sharing in the death and resurrection of Christ (cf. Rom 6:1–14), the gift of divine sonship (cf. Jn 1:12–13), but in order to become completely one with Jesus, "we have to join him through faith, letting his life show forth in ours to such an extent that each Christian is not simply *alter Christus*, another Christ, but also *ipse Christus*, Christ himself!"[34]

29. St Jerome, *Letter to Eustochium, PL* 22, 408. **30.** *Against Heresies*, 5, 19, 1. **31.** Vatican II, *Lumen gentium*, 61. **32.** Paul VI, *Creed to the People of God*, 15. **33.** *Comm. in Evang. Ioann.*, on Jn 19:26–27. **34.** St Josemaría Escrivá, *Christ Is Passing By*, 104.

PROLOGUE

1 [1]In the beginning was the Word, and the Word was with God, 1 Jn 1:1–2 Rev 19:13
and the Word was God.* [2]He was in the beginning with God; Gen 1:1–5 Prov 8:22–27

1:1–18. These verses form the introduction to the Fourth Gospel; they are a poem prefacing the account of Jesus Christ's life on earth, proclaiming and praising his divinity and eternity. Jesus is the uncreated Word, God the Only-begotten, who takes on our human condition and offers us the chance to become sons and daughters of God, that is, to share in God's own life in a real and supernatural way.

Right through his Gospel St John lays special emphasis on our Lord's divinity; his existence did not begin when he became man in Mary's virginal womb: before that he existed in divine eternity as the Word, one in substance with the Father and the Holy Spirit. This luminous truth helps us understand all that Jesus says and does as reported in this Gospel.

St John's personal experience with Jesus' public ministry and his appearances after the Resurrection were the material he drew on to contemplate God's divinity and express it as "the Word of God". By placing this poem as a prologue to his Gospel, the apostle is giving us a key to understand all that follows, in the same sort of way as the first chapters of the Gospels of St Matthew and St Luke initiate us into the contemplation of the life of Christ by telling us about the virgin birth and other episodes to do with his infancy; in structure and content, however, this passage is akin to the opening passages of other New Testament books, such as Col 1:15–20, Eph 1:13–14 and 1 Jn 1–4.

The prologue is a magnificent hymn in praise of Christ. We do not know whether St John composed it when writing his Gospel, or whether he based it on some existing liturgical hymn; but there is no trace of any such text in other early Christian documents.

The prologue is very reminiscent of the first chapter of Genesis, on a number of scores: 1) the opening words are the same: "In the beginning …"; in the Gospel they refer to absolute beginning, that is, eternity, whereas in Genesis they mean the beginning of creation and time; 2) there is a parallelism in the role of the Word: in Genesis, God creates things by his word ("And God said … "); in the Gospel, we are told that they were made through the Word of God; 3) in Genesis, God's work of creation reaches its peak when he creates man in his own image and likeness; in the Gospel, the work of the Incarnate Word culminates when man is raised (by a new creation, as it were) to the dignity of being a son of God.

The main teachings in the prologue are: 1) the divinity and eternity of the Word; 2) his incarnation and manifestation as man; 3) the part played by him in creation and in the salvation of mankind; 4) the ways in which people react to his coming—some accepting him with faith, others rejecting him; 5) finally, John the Baptist bears witness to the presence of the Word in the world.

The Church has always given special importance to this prologue; many Fathers and ancient Christian writers wrote commentaries on it, and for centuries it was always read at the end of Mass for instruction and meditation.

The prologue is poetic in style. Its teaching is given in verses, which combine to make up stanzas (vv. 1–5; 6–8;

Col 1:15–20
Heb 1:1–3

3all things were made through him, and without him was not anything made that was made. 4In him was life,[a] and the life was the

---

9–13; 14–18). Just as a stone dropped in a pool produces ever widening ripples, so the idea expressed in each stanza tends to be expanded in later verses. This kind of exposition was much favoured in olden times because it makes it easier to get the meaning across—and God used it to help us go deeper into the central mysteries of our faith.

1:1. The sacred text calls the Son of God "the Word". The following comparison may help us understand the notion of "Word": just as a person becoming conscious of himself forms an image of himself in his mind, in the same way God the Father on knowing himself begets the eternal Word. This Word of God is singular, unique; no other can exist because in him is expressed the entire essence of God. Therefore, the Gospel does not call him simply "Word", but "the Word". Three truths are affirmed regarding the Word—that he is eternal, that he is distinct from the Father, and that he is God. "Affirming that he existed in the beginning is equivalent to saying that he existed before all things" (St Augustine, *De Trinitate*, 6, 2). Also, the text says that he was with God, that is, with the Father, which means that the person of the Word is distinct from that of the Father and yet the Word is so intimately related to the Father that he even shares his divine nature: he is one in substance with the Father (cf. *Nicene Creed*).

To mark the Year of Faith (1967–1968) Pope Paul VI summed up this truth concerning the most Holy Trinity in what is called the *Creed of the People of God* (n. 11) in these words: "We believe in our Lord Jesus Christ, who is the Son of God. He is the eternal Word, born of the Father before time began, and one in substance with the Father, *homoousios to Patri*, and through him all things were made. He was incarnate of the Virgin Mary by the power of the Holy Spirit, and was made man: equal therefore to the Father according to his divinity, and inferior to the Father according to his humanity and himself one, not by some impossible confusion of his natures, but by the unity of his person."

"In the beginning": "what this means is that he always was, and that he is eternal. [...] For if he is God, as indeed he is, there is nothing prior to him; if he is creator of all things, then he is the First; if he is Lord of all, then everything comes after him—created things and time" (St John Chrysostom, *Hom. on St John*, 2, 4).

1:3. After showing that the Word is in the bosom of the Father, the prologue goes on to deal with his relationship to created things. Already in the Old Testament the Word of God is shown as a creative power (cf. Is 55:10–11), as Wisdom present at the creation of the world (cf. Prov 8:22–26). Now Revelation is extended: we are shown that creation was caused by the Word; this does not mean that the Word is an instrument subordinate and inferior to the Father: he is an active principle along with the Father and the Holy Spirit. The work of creation is an activity common to the three divine Persons of the Blessed Trinity: "the Father generating, the Son being born, the Holy Spirit proceeding; consubstantial, co-equal, co-

a. Or *was not anything made. That which has been made was life in him*

light of men. [5]The light shines in the darkness,* and the darkness has not overcome it.

Jn 3:19; 5:26; 12:35–36

omnipotent and co-eternal; one origin of all things: the creator of all things visible and invisible, spiritual and corporal" (Fourth Lateran Council, *De fide catholica*, *Dz-Sch*, 800). From this can be deduced, among other things, the hand of the Trinity in the work of creation and, therefore, the fact that all created things are basically good.

1:4. The prologue now goes on to expound two basic truths about the Word—that he is Life and that he is Light. The Life referred to here is divine life, the primary source of all life, natural and supernatural. And that Life is the light of men, for from God we receive the light of reason, the Light of truth and the light of glory, which are a participation in God's mind. Only a rational creature is capable of having knowledge of God in this world and of later contemplating him joyfully in heaven for all eternity. Also the Life (the Word) is the Light of men because he brings them out of the darkness of sin and error (cf. Is 9:1–2; Mt 4:15–16; Lk 1:79). Later on Jesus will say: "I am the light of the world; he who follows me will not walk in darkness, but will have the light of life" (Jn 8:12; cf. 12:46).

Verses 3 and 4 can be read with another punctuation, now generally abandoned but which had its supporters in ancient times: "All things were made through him, and without him nothing was made; in so far as anything was made in him, he was the life and the life was the light of men." This reading would suggest that everything that has been created is life in the Word, that is, that all things receive their being and activity, their life, through the Word: without him they cannot possibly exist.

1:5. "And the darkness has not overcome it": the original Greek verb, given in Latin as *comprehenderunt*, means to embrace or contain as if putting one's arms around it—an action which can be done with good dispositions (a friendly embrace) or with hostility (the action of smothering or crushing someone). So there are two possible translations: the former is that given in the Navarre Spanish, the latter that in the RSV. The RSV option would indicate that Christ and the Gospel continue to shine among men despite the world's opposition, indeed overcoming it, as Jesus later says: "Be of good cheer, I have overcome the world" (Jn 16:33; cf. 12:31; 1 Jn 5:4). Either way, the verse expresses the darkness' resistance to, repugnance for, the light. As his Gospel proceeds, St John explains further about the light and darkness: soon, in vv. 9–11, he refers to the struggle between them; later he will describe evil and the powers of the evil one, as a darkness enveloping man's mind and preventing him from knowing God (cf. Jn 12:15–46; 1 Jn 5:6).

St Augustine (*In Ioann. Evang.*, 1, 19) comments on this passage as follows: "But, it may be, the dull hearts of some cannot yet receive this light. Their sins weigh them down, and they cannot discern it. Let them not think, however, that, because they cannot discern it, therefore it is not present with them. For they themselves, because of their sins, are darkness. Just as if you place a blind person in the sunshine, although the sun is present to him, yet he is absent from the sun; in the same way, every foolish man, every unrighteous man, every ungodly man, is blind in heart. […] What course then ought such a one to take? Let him cleanse the eyes of his

Lk 1:3–17; 1:57–60 Mt 3:1 Mk 1:4 Jn 1:19–34 Lk 3:3

6 There was a man sent from God, whose name was John. 7 He came for testimony, to bear witness to the light, that all might believe through him. 8 He was not the light, but came to bear witness to the light.

---

heart, that he may be able to see God. He will see Wisdom, for God is Wisdom itself, and it is written: 'Blessed are the clean of heart, for they shall see God.'" There is no doubt that sin obscures man's spiritual vision, rendering him unable to see and enjoy the things of God.

1:6–8. After considering the divinity of the Lord, the text moves on to deal with his incarnation, and begins by speaking of John the Baptist, who makes his appearance at a precise point in history to bear direct witness before man to Jesus Christ (Jn 1:15, 19–36; 3:22ff). As St Augustine comments: "For as much as he [the Word Incarnate] was man and his Godhead was concealed, there was sent before him a great man, through whose testimony he might be found to be more than man" (*In Ioann. Evang.*, 2, 5).

All of the Old Testament was a preparation for the coming of Christ. Thus, the patriarchs and prophets announced, in different ways, the salvation the Messiah would bring. But John the Baptist, the greatest of those born of woman (cf. Mt 11:11), was actually able to point out the Messiah himself; his testimony marked the culmination of all the previous prophecies.

So important is John the Baptist's mission to bear witness to Jesus Christ that the Synoptic Gospels start their account of the public ministry with John's testimony. The discourses of St Peter and St Paul recorded in the Acts of the Apostles also refer to this testimony (Acts 1:22; 10:37; 12:24). The Fourth Gospel mentions it as many as seven times (1:6, 15, 19, 29, 36; 3:27; 5:33). We know, of course, that St John the apostle was a disciple of the Baptist before becoming a disciple of Jesus, and that it was in fact the Baptist who showed him the way to Christ (cf. 1:37ff).

The New Testament, then, shows us the importance of the Baptist's mission, as also his own awareness that he is merely the immediate Precursor of the Messiah, whose sandals he is unworthy to untie (cf. Mk 1:7): the Baptist stresses his role as witness to Christ and his mission as preparer of the way for the Messiah (cf. Lk 1:15–17; Mt 3:3–12). John the Baptist's testimony is undiminished by time: he invites people in every generation to have faith in Jesus, the true Light.

1:9. "The true light … ". The Spanish translation of this verse is along these lines: "It was the true light that enlightens every man who comes into the world." The Fathers, early translations and most modern commentators see "the Word" as being the subject of this sentence, which could therefore be translated as "the Word was the true light that enlightens every man who comes into the world … ". Another interpretation favoured by many modern scholars makes "the light" the subject, in which case it would read "the true light existed, which enlightens …". Either way, the meaning is much the same.

"Coming into the world": it is not clear in the Greek whether these words refer to "the light" or to "every man". In the first case it is the Light (the Word) that is coming into this world to enlighten all men; in the second it is the

[9]The true light that enlightens every man was coming into the Jn 3:19; 8:12; 12:46
world. [10]He was in the world, and the world was made through Jn 14:17
him, yet the world knew him not. [11]He came to his own home, and Mt 21:38–43

---

men who, on coming into this world, on being born, are enlightened by the Word; the RSV and the New Vulgate opt for the first interpretation. The Word is called "the true light" because he is the original light from which every other light or revelation of God derives. By the Word's coming, the world is fully lit up by the authentic Light. The prophets and all the other messengers of God, including John the Baptist, were not the true light but his reflection, attesting to the Light of the Word.

Apropos of the fulness of light which the Word is, St John Chrysostom asks: "If he enlightens every man who comes into the world, how is it that so many have remained unenlightened? For not all, to be sure, have recognized the high dignity of Christ. How, then, does he enlighten every man? As much as he is permitted to do so. But if some, deliberately closing the eyes of their minds, do not wish to receive the beams of this light, darkness is theirs. This is not because of the nature of the light, but is a result of the wickedness of men who deliberately deprive themselves of the gift of grace" (*Hom. on St John*, 8, 1).

1:10. The Word is in this world as the maker who controls what he has made (cf. St Augustine, *In Ioann. Evang*., 2, 10). In St John's Gospel the term "world" means "all creation, all created things (including all mankind)"; thus, Christ came to save all mankind: "For God so loved the world that he gave his only Son, that whoever believes in him should not perish but have eternal life. For God sent the Son into the world, not to condemn the world, but that the world might be saved through him" (Jn 3:16–17). But insofar as many people have rejected the Light, that is, rejected Christ, "world" also means everything opposed to God (cf. Jn 17:14–15). Blinded by their sins, men do not recognize in the world the hand of the Creator (cf. Rom 1:18–20; Wis 13:1–15): "they become attached to the world and relish only the things that are of the world" (St John Chrysostom, *Hom. on St John*, 7). But the Word, "the true light", comes to show us the truth about the world (cf. Jn 1:9; 18:37) and to save us.

1:11. "His own home, his own people": this means, in the first place, the Jewish people, who were chosen by God as his own personal "property", to be the people from whom Christ would be born. It can also mean all mankind, for mankind is also his: he created it and his work of redemption extends to everyone. So the reproach that they did not receive the Word made man should be understood as addressed not only to the Jews but to all those who rejected God despite his calling them to be his friends: "Christ came; but by a mysterious and terrible misfortune, not everyone accepted him. […] It is the picture of humanity before us today, after twenty centuries of Christianity. How did this happen? What shall we say? We do not claim to fathom a reality immersed in mysteries that transcend us—the mystery of good and evil. But we can recall that the economy of Christ, for its light to spread, requires a subordinate but necessary cooperation on the part of man—the cooperation of evangelization, of the apostolic and missionary Church. If there is still work to

Gal 3:26 Jn 10:35 1 Jn 3:2; 5:13 his own people received him not. 12But to all who received him,
who believed in his name, he gave power to become children of

be done, it is all the more necessary for everyone to help her" (Paul VI, General Audience, 4 December 1974).

1:12. Receiving the Word means accepting him through faith, for it is through faith that Christ dwells in our hearts (cf. Eph 3:17). Believing in his name means believing in his Person, in Jesus as the Christ, the Son of God. In other words, "those who believe in his name are those who fully hold the name of Christ, not in any way lessening his divinity or his humanity" (St Thomas Aquinas, *Comm. on St John*, in loc.).

"He gave power [to them]" is the same as saying "he gave them a free gift"—sanctifying grace—"because it is not in our power to make ourselves sons of God" (ibid.). This gift is extended through Baptism to everyone, whatever his race, age, education etc. (cf. Acts 10:45; Gal 3:28). The only condition is that we have faith.

"The Son of God became man", St Athanasius explains, "in order that the sons of men, the sons of Adam, might become sons of God. [...] He is the Son of God by nature; we, by grace" (*De incarnatione contra arrianos*). What is referred to here is birth to supernatural life: in which "Whether they be slaves or freemen, whether Greeks or barbarians or Scythians, foolish or wise, female or male, children or old men, honourable or without honour, rich or poor, rulers or private citizens, all, he meant, would merit the same honour. [...] Such is the power of faith in him; such the greatness of his grace" (St John Chrysostom, *Hom. on St John*, 10, 2).

"Christ's union with man is power and the source of power, as St John stated so incisively in the prologue of his Gospel: '(The Word) gave power to become children of God.' Man is transformed inwardly by this power as the source of a new life that does not disappear and pass away but lasts to eternal life (cf. Jn 4:14)" (John Paul II, *Redemptor hominis*, 18).

1:13. The birth spoken about here is a real, spiritual type of generation which is effected in Baptism (cf. 3:6ff). Instead of the plural adopted here, referring to the supernatural birth of men, some Fathers and early translations read it in the singular: "who was born, not of blood ... but of God", in which case the text would refer to the eternal generation of the Word and to Jesus' generation through the Holy Spirit in the pure womb of the Virgin Mary. Although the second reading is very attractive, the documents (Greek manuscripts, early translations, references in the works of ecclesiastical writers, etc.) show the plural text to be the more usual, and the one that prevailed from the fourth century forward. Besides, in St John's writings we frequently find reference to believers as being born of God (cf. Jn 3:3–6; 1 Jn 2:29; 3:9; 4:7; 5:1, 4, 18).

The contrast between man's natural birth (by blood and the will of man) and his supernatural birth (which comes from God) shows that those who believe in Jesus Christ are made children of God not only by their creation but above all by the free gift of faith and grace.

1:14. This is a text central to the mystery of Christ. It expresses in a very condensed form the unfathomable fact of the incarnation of the Son of God. "When the time had fully come, God sent forth his Son, born of woman" (Gal 4:4).

God; 13who were born, not of blood nor of the will of the flesh nor
of the will of man, but of God.
14And the Word became flesh and dwelt among us, full of grace
and truth; we have beheld his glory, glory as of the only Son from

Jn 3:3–6
Ex 25:8
Is 7:4; 60:1
1 Jn 4:2
2 Pet 1:16–17
Rev 21:3

The word "flesh" means man in his totality (cf. Jn 3:6; 17:2; Gen 6:3; Ps 56:4); so the sentence "the Word became flesh" means the same as "the Word became man." The theological term "incarnation" arose mainly out of this text. The noun "flesh" carries a great deal of force against heresies which deny that Christ is truly man. The word also accentuates that our Saviour, who dwelt among us and shared our nature, was capable of suffering and dying, and it evokes the "Book of the Consolation of Israel" (Is 40:1–11), where the fragility of the flesh is contrasted with the permanence of the Word of God: "The grass withers, the flower fades; but the word of our God will stand for ever" (Is 40:8). This does not mean that the Word's taking on human nature is something precarious and temporary.

"And dwelt among us": the Greek verb which St John uses originally means "to pitch one's tent", hence, to live in a place. The careful reader of Scripture will immediately think of the tabernacle, or tent, in the period of the exodus from Egypt, where God showed his presence before all the people of Israel through certain sights of his glory such as the cloud covering the tent (cf., for example, Ex 25:8; 40:34–35). In many passages of the Old Testament it is announced that God "will dwell in the midst of the people" (cf., for example, Jer 7:3; Ezek 43:9; Sir 24:8). These signs of God's presence, first in the pilgrim tent of the Ark in the desert and then in the temple of Jerusalem, are followed by the most wonderful form of God's presence among us—Jesus Christ, perfect God and perfect Man, in whom the ancient promise is fulfilled in a way that far exceeded men's greatest expectations. Also the promise made through Isaiah about the "Immanuel" or "God-with-us" (Is 7:14; cf. Mt 1:23) is completely fulfilled through this dwelling of the Incarnate Son of God among us. Therefore, when we devoutly read these words of the Gospel "and dwelt among us" or pray them during the Angelus, we have a good opportunity to make an act of deep faith and gratitude and to adore our Lord's most holy human nature.

"Remembering that 'the Word became flesh', that is, that the Son of God became man, we must become conscious of *how great* each man has become through this mystery, *through the Incarnation of the Son of God!* Christ, in fact, was conceived in the womb of Mary and became man to reveal the eternal love of the Creator and Father and to make known the dignity of each one of us" (John Paul II, Angelus Address at Jasna Gora Shrine, 5 June 1979).

Although the Word's self-emptying by assuming a human nature concealed in some way his divine nature, of which he never divested himself, the Apostles did see the glory of his divinity through his human nature: it was revealed in the transfiguration (Lk 9:32–35), in his miracles (Jn 2:11; 11:40), and especially in his resurrection (cf. Jn 3:11; 1 Jn 1:1). The glory of God, which shone out in the early tabernacle in the desert and in the temple at Jerusalem, was nothing but an imperfect anticipation of the reality of God's glory revealed through the holy human nature of the Only-begotten of the

Lk 9:28–35 the Father. 15(John bore witness to him, and cried, "This was he of
Jn 1:30 whom I said, 'He who comes after me ranks before me, for he was
Col 1:19; 2:9–10 before me.'") 16And from his fullness have we all received, grace

---

Father. St John the Apostle speaks in a very formal way in the first person plural: "we have beheld his glory", because he counts himself among the witnesses who lived with Christ and, in particular, were present at his transfiguration and saw the glory of his resurrection.

The words "only Son" ("Only-begotten") convey very well the eternal and unique generation of the Word by the Father. The first three Gospels stressed Christ's birth in time; St John complements this by emphasizing his eternal generation.

The words "grace and truth" are synonyms of "goodness and fidelity", two attributes which, in the Old Testament, are constantly applied to Yahweh (cf., e.g., Ex 34:6; Ps 118; Ps 136; Hos 2:16–20): so, grace is the expression of God's love for men, the way he expresses his goodness and mercy. Truth implies permanence, loyalty, constancy, fidelity. Jesus, who is the Word of God made man, that is, God himself, is therefore "the only Son of the Father, full of grace and truth"; he is the "merciful and faithful high priest" (Heb 2:17). These two qualities, being good and faithful, are a kind of compendium or summary of Christ's greatness. And they also parallel, though on an infinitely lower level, the quality essential to every Christian, as stated expressly by our Lord when he praised the "good and faithful servant" (Mt 25:21).

As Chrysostom explains: "Having declared that they who received him were 'born of God' and 'become sons of God,' he then set forth the cause and reason for this ineffable honour. It is that 'the Word became flesh' and the Master took on the form of a slave. He became the Son of Man, though he was the true Son of God, in order that he might make the sons of men children of God" (*Hom. on St John*, 11,1).

The profound mystery of Christ was solemnly defined by the Church's Magisterium in the famous text of the ecumenical Council of Chalcedon (in the year 451): "Following the holy Fathers, therefore, we all with one accord teach the profession of faith in the one identical Son, our Lord Jesus Christ. We declare that he is perfect both in his divinity and in his humanity, truly God and truly man, composed of body and rational soul; that he is consubstantial with the Father in his divinity, consubstantial with us in his humanity, like us in every respect except for sin (cf. Heb 4:15). We declare that in his divinity he was begotten in this last age of Mary the Virgin, the Mother of God, for us and for our salvation" (*Dz-Sch*, 301).

1:15. Further on (Jn 1:19–36) the Gospel tells us more about John the Baptist's mission as a witness to the messiahship and divinity of Jesus. Just as God planned that the apostles should bear witness to Jesus after the resurrection, so he planned that the Baptist would be the witness chosen to proclaim Jesus at the very outset of his public ministry (cf. the note on Jn 1:6–8).

1:16. "Grace upon grace": this can be understood, as it was by Chrysostom and other Fathers, as "grace for grace", the Old Testament economy of salvation giving way to the new economy of grace

upon grace. [17]For the law was given through Moses; grace and
truth came through Jesus Christ. [18]No one has ever seen God; the
only Son,[b] who is in the bosom of the Father, he has made him
known.

Ex 34:6
Rom 3:24; 6:14; 10:4
40:11; 85:11
Jn 6:46
Mt 11:27
Lk 10:22
1 Tim 6:16

---

brought by Christ. It can also mean (as the RSV suggests) that Jesus brings a superabundance of gifts, adding on, to existing graces, others—all of which pour out of the one inexhaustible source, Christ, who is for ever full of grace. "Not by sharing with us, says the Evangelist, does Christ possess the gift, but he himself is both fountain and root of all virtues. He himself is life, and light, and truth, not keeping within himself the wealth of these blessings, but pouring it forth upon all others, and even after the outpouring still remaining full. He suffers no loss by giving his wealth to others, but, while always pouring out and sharing these virtues with all men, he remains in the same state of perfection" (St John Chrysostom, *Hom. on St John*, 14, 1).

1:17. Here, for the first time in St John's Gospel, the name of Jesus Christ appears, identified with the Word of whom John has been speaking.

Whereas the Law given by Moses went no further than indicate the way man ought follow (cf. Rom 8:7–10), the grace brought by Jesus has the power to save those who receive it (cf. Rom 7:25). Through grace "we have become dear to God, no longer merely as servants, but as sons and friends" (St John Chrysostom, *Hom. on St John*, 14, 2).

On "grace and truth" see the note on Jn 1:14.

1:18. "No one has ever seen God": in this world men have never seen God other than indirectly: all that they could contemplate was God's "glory", that is, the aura of his greatness: for example, Moses saw the burning bush (Ex 3:2); Elijah felt the breeze on Mount Horeb—the "still small voice" (1 Kings 19:11–13). But in the fulness of time God comes much closer to man and reveals himself almost directly, for Jesus Christ is the visible image of the invisible God (cf. Col 1:15), the maximum revelation of God in this world, to such an extent that he assures us that "he who has seen me has seen the Father" (Jn 14:9). "The most intimate truth which this revelation gives us about God and the salvation of man shines forth in Christ, who is himself both the mediator and the sum total of Revelation" (Vatican II, *Dei Verbum*, 2).

There is no greater revelation God could make of himself than the incarnation of his eternal Word. As St John of the Cross puts it so well: "In giving to us, as he has done, his Son, who is his only Word, he has spoken to us once and for all by his own and only Word, and has nothing further to reveal" (*Ascent of Mount Carmel*, book II, chap. 22).

"The only Son": the RSV note says that "other ancient authorities read *God*" (for *Son*); the Navarre Spanish has "the Only-begotten God" and comments as follows: some Greek manuscripts and some translations give "the Only-begotten Son" or "the Only-begotten". "The Only-begotten God" is preferable because it finds best support in the codexes. Besides, although the meaning does not change substantially, this translation has a richer content because it again explicitly reveals Christ's divinity.

b. Other ancient authorities read *God*

PART ONE

Jesus is manifested as the Messiah by his signs and words

1. INTRODUCTION

Jn 5:33 **The witness of John the Baptist**
Lk 3:15–16 [19]And this is the testimony of John, when the Jews sent priests and
Acts 13:25 Levites from Jerusalem to ask him, "Who are you?" [20]He con-
Jn 6:14; 7:40 Mt 17:10 fessed, he did not deny, but confessed, "I am not the Christ."
Deut 18:15 [21]And they asked him, "What then? Are you Elijah?" He said, "I

1:19–34. This passage forms a unity, beginning and ending with reference to the Baptist's "testimony": it thereby emphasizes the mission given him by God to bear witness, by his life and preaching, to Jesus as the Messiah and Son of God. The Precursor exhorts people to do penance and he practises the austerity he preaches; he points Jesus out as the Lamb of God who takes away the sin of the world; and he proclaims him boldly in the face of the Jewish authorities. He is an example to us of the fortitude with which we should confess Christ: "All Christians by the example of their lives and the witness of the word, wherever they live, have an obligation to manifest the new man which they put on in Baptism" (Vatican II, *Ad gentes*, 11).

1:19–24. In this setting of intense expectation of the imminent coming of the Messiah, the Baptist is a personality with enormous prestige, as is shown by the fact that the Jewish authorities send qualified people (priests and Levites from Jerusalem) to ask him if he is the Messiah.

John's great humility should be noted: he is quick to tell his questioners: "I am not the Christ". He sees himself as someone insignificant compared with our Lord: "I am not worthy to untie [the thong of his sandal]" (v. 27). He places all his prestige at the service of his mission as precursor of the Messiah, and, leaving himself completely to one side, he asserts that "he must increase, but I must decrease" (Jn 3:30).

1:25–26. "Baptize": this originally meant to submerge in water, to bathe. For the Jews the rite of immersion meant legal purification of those who had contracted some impurity under the Law. Baptism was also used as a rite for the incorporation of Gentile proselytes into the Jewish people. In the Dead Sea scrolls there is mention of a baptism as a rite of initiation and purification into the Jewish Qumran community, which existed in our Lord's time.

John's baptism laid marked stress on interior conversion. His words of exhortation and the person's humble recognition of his sins prepared people to receive Christ's grace: it was a very efficacious rite of penance, preparing the people for the coming of the Messiah, and it fulfilled the prophecies that spoke precisely

am not." "Are you the prophet?" And he answered, "No." 22They
said to him then, "Who are you? Let us have an answer for those
who sent us. What do you say about yourself?" 23He said, "I am Is 40:3
the voice of one crying in the wilderness, 'Make straight the way Mt 3:3
of the Lord,' as the prophet Isaiah said."
24Now they had been sent from the Pharisees. 25They asked Mt 16:24;
him, "Then why are you baptizing, if you are neither the Christ, 21:25
nor Elijah, nor the prophet?" 26John answered them, "I baptize Mt 3:11
with water; but among you stands one whom you do not know, Mk 1:7ff
27even he who comes after me, the thong of whose sandal I am not Jn 3:26
worthy to untie." 28This took place in Bethany beyond the Jordan, Acts 3:25
where John was baptizing. Jn 10:40 Mt 3:6–13
29The next day he saw Jesus coming toward him, and said, Jn 1:36
"Behold, the Lamb of God, who takes away the sin of the world!* Is 53:7 Rev 5:6

---

of a cleansing by water prior to the coming of the Kingdom of God in the messianic times (cf. Zech 13:1; Ezek 36:25; 37:23; Jer 4:14). John's baptism, however, had no power to cleanse the soul of sins, as Christian Baptism does (cf. Mt 3:11; Mk 1:4)

"One whom you do not know": Jesus had not yet publicly revealed himself as Messiah and Son of God; although some people did know him as a man, St John the Baptist could assert that really they did not know him.

1:27. The Baptist declares Christ's importance by comparing himself to a slave undoing the laces of his master's sandals. If we want to approach Christ, whom St John heralds, we need to imitate the Baptist. As St Augustine says: "He who imitates the humility of the Precursor will understand these words. [...] John's greatest merit, my brethren, is this act of humility" (*In Ioann. Evang*., 4, 7).

1:28. This is a reference to the town of Bethany which was situated on the eastern bank of the Jordan, across from Jericho—different from the Bethany where Lazarus and his family lived, near Jerusalem (cf. Jn 11:18).

1:29. For the first time in the Gospel Christ is called the "Lamb of God". Isaiah had compared the sufferings of the Servant of Yahweh, the Messiah, with the sacrifice of a lamb (cf. Is 53:7); and the blood of the paschal lamb smeared on the doors of houses had served to protect the first-born of the Israelites in Egypt (cf. Ex 12:6–7): all this was a promise and prefiguring of the true Lamb, Christ, the victim in the sacrifice of Calvary on behalf of all mankind. This is why St Paul will say that "Christ, our paschal lamb, has been sacrificed" (1 Cor 5:7). The expression "Lamb of God" also suggests the spotless innocence of the Redeemer (cf. 1 Pet 1:18–20; 1 Jn 3:5).

The sacred text says "the sin of the world", in the singular, to make it absolutely clear that every kind of sin is taken away: Christ came to free us from original sin, which in Adam affected all men, and from all personal sins.

The book of Revelation reveals to us that Jesus is victorious and glorious in heaven as the slain lamb (cf. Rev 5:6–14), surrounded by saints, martyrs and virgins (Rev 7:9, 14; 14:1–5), who render him the praise and glory due him as God (Rev 7:10). Since Holy Com-

Jn 1:15–17 30 This is he of whom I said, 'After me comes a man who ranks
before me, for he was before me.' 31 I myself did not know him;
but for this I came baptizing with water, that he might be revealed
Mt 3:16 to Israel." 32 And John bore witness, "I saw the Spirit descend as a
Mk 1:10 Lk 3:22 dove from heaven, and it remained on him. 33 I myself did not
know him; but he who sent me to baptize with water said to me,
Mt 3:11–26 'He on whom you see the Spirit descend and remain, this is he
Mt 3:17 who baptizes with the Holy Spirit.' 34 And I have seen and borne
witness that this is the Son of God."

---

munion is a sharing in the sacrifice of Christ, priests say these words of the Baptist before administering it, to encourage the faithful to be grateful to our Lord for giving himself up to death to save us and for giving himself to us as nourishment for our souls.

1:30–31. John the Baptist here asserts Jesus' superiority by saying that he existed before him, even though he was born after him. Thereby he shows us the divinity of Christ, who was generated by the Father from all eternity and born of the Virgin Mary in time. It is as if the Baptist were saying: "Although I was born before him, he is not limited by the ties of his birth; for although he is born of his mother in time, he was generated by his Father outside of time" (St Gregory the Great, *In Evangelia homiliae*, 7).

By saying what he says in v. 31, the Precursor does not mean to deny his personal knowledge of Jesus (cf. Lk 1:36 and Mt 3:14), but to make it plain that God revealed to him the moment when he should publicly proclaim Jesus as Messiah and Son of God, and that he also understood that his own mission as precursor had no other purpose than to bear witness to Jesus Christ.

1:32–34. To emphasize the divinity of Jesus Christ, the evangelist includes here the Precursor's testimony regarding Jesus' Baptism (cf. the other Gospels, which describe in more detail what happened on this occasion: Mt 3:13–17 and par.). It is one of the key points in our Lord's life, in which the mystery of the Blessed Trinity is revealed (cf. the note on Mt 3:16).

The dove is a symbol of the Holy Spirit, of whom it is said in Genesis 1:2 that he was moving over the face of the waters. Through this sign of the dove, the Isaiah prophecies (11:2–5; 42:1–2) are fulfilled which say that the Messiah will be full of the power of the Holy Spirit. The Baptist points to the great difference between the baptism he confers and Christ's Baptism; in John 3, Jesus will speak about this new Baptism in water and in the Spirit (cf. Acts 1:5; Tit 3:5).

"The Son of God": it should be pointed out that in the original text this expression carries the definite article, which means that John the Baptist confesses before his listeners the supernatural and transcendent character of Christ's messiahship—very far removed from the politico-religious notion which Jewish leaders had forged.

1:35–39. Through these words of the Baptist, these two disciples are moved by grace to approach the Lord. John's testimony is an example of the special graces God distributes to attract people to himself. Sometimes he addresses a person

The calling of the first disciples

35The next day again John was standing with two of his disciples; Jn 1:29 Is 53:7
36and he looked at Jesus as he walked, and said, "Behold, the
Lamb of God!" 37The two disciples heard him say this, and they
followed Jesus. 38Jesus turned, and saw them following, and said
to them, "What do you seek?" And they said to him, "Rabbi"
(which means Teacher), "where are you staying?" 39He said to
them, "Come and see." They came and saw where he was staying;
and they stayed with him that day, for it was about the tenth hour.
40One of the two who heard John speak, and followed him, was Mt 4:18
Andrew, Simon Peter's brother. 41He first found his brother

---

directly by stirring his soul and inviting him to follow him; at other times, as in the present case, he chooses to use someone close to us who knows us, to bring us to meet Christ.

The two disciples already had a keen desire to see the Messiah; John's words move them to try to become friends of our Lord: it is not merely natural curiosity but Christ's personality which attracts them. They want to get to know him, to be taught by him and to enjoy his company. "Come and see" (1:39; cf. 11:34)—a tender invitation to begin that intimate friendship they were seeking. Time and personal contact with Christ will be needed to make them more secure in their vocation. The apostle St John, one of the protagonists in this scene, notes the exact time it took place: "it was about the tenth hour", roughly four in the afternoon.

Christian faith can never be just a matter of intellectual curiosity; it affects one's whole life: a person cannot understand it unless he really lives it; therefore, our Lord does not at this point tell them in detail about his way of life; he invites them to spend the day with him. St Thomas Aquinas comments on this passage saying that our Lord speaks in a lofty, mystical way because what God is (in himself or in grace) can only be understood through experience: words cannot describe it. We grow in this understanding by doing good works (they immediately accepted Christ's invitation and as a reward "they saw"), by recollection and by applying our mind to the contemplation of divine things, by desiring to taste the sweetness of God, by assiduous prayer. Our Lord invited everyone to do all this when he said, "Come and see", and the disciples discovered it all when, in obedience to our Lord, "they went" and were able to learn by personal experience, whereas they could not understand the words alone (cf. *Comm. on St John*, in loc.).

1:40–41. The evangelist now gives us the name of one of the two disciples involved in the previous scene; he will mention Andrew again in connexion with the multiplication of the loaves (cf. 6:8) and the last Passover (cf. 12:22).

We cannot be absolutely sure who the second disciple was; but since the very earliest centuries of the Christian era he has always been taken to be the Evangelist himself. The vividness of the account, the detail of giving the exact time, and even John's tendency to remain anonymous (cf. 19:26; 20:2; 21:7, 20) seem to confirm this.

"St John the Apostle, who pours into his narrative so much that is first-hand, tells of his first unforgettable conversation

Mt 16:18 Simon, and said to him, "We have found the Messiah" (which
Mk 3:16 means Christ). 42 He brought him to Jesus. Jesus looked at him,
Lk 6:14 and said, "So you are Simon the son of John? You shall be called
Mk 8:22 Cephas" (which means Peter[c]).
Lk 9:59; 9:9 43 The next day Jesus decided to go to Galilee. And he found
Deut 18:18 Philip and said to him, "Follow me." 44 Now Philip was from
Is 7:14; 53:2 Jer 23:5 Bethsaida, the city of Andrew and Peter. 45 Philip found Nathanael,
Ezek 34:23 and said to him, "We have found him of whom Moses in the law
Jn 7:41, 52 and also the prophets wrote, Jesus of Nazareth, the son of Joseph."
Mt 13:54ff 46 Nathanael said to him, "Can anything good come out of

---

with Christ. '"Master, where are you staying?" He said to them, "Come and see." They went and saw where he was staying; and they stayed with him that day, for it was about the tenth hour' (Jn 1:38–39).

"This divine and human dialogue completely changed the life of John and Andrew, and Peter and James and so many others. It prepared their hearts to listen to the authoritative teaching which Jesus gave them beside the Sea of Galilee" (St J. Escrivá, *Christ Is Passing By*, 108).

Those hours spent with our Lord soon produce the first results of apostolate. Andrew, unable to contain his joy, tells Simon Peter the news that he has found the Messiah, and brings him to him. Now, as then, there is a pressing need to bring others to know the Lord.

"Open your own hearts to Jesus and tell him your story. I don't want to generalize. But one day perhaps an ordinary Christian, just like you, opened your eyes to horizons both deep and new, yet as old as the Gospel. He suggested to you the prospect of following Christ earnestly, seriously, of becoming an apostle of apostles. Perhaps you lost your balance then and didn't recover it. Your complacency wasn't quite replaced by true peace until you freely said 'yes' to God, because you wanted to, which is the most supernatural of reasons. And in its wake came a strong, constant joy, which disappears only when you abandon him" (ibid., 1).

1:42. What was it like when Jesus looked at someone? From what he says here, he seems both imperious and tender. On other occasions his glance is enough to invite a person to leave everything and follow him, as in the case of Matthew (Mt 9:9); or he seems to be full of love, as in his meeting with the rich young man (Mk 10:21); or he seems angry or sad, because of the Pharisees' unbelief (Mk 2:5), or compassionate, towards the widow of Nain (Lk 7:13). He is able to move Zacchaeus' heart to conversion (Lk 19:5); and he himself is moved by the faith and generosity of the poor widow who gave in alms everything she had (Mk 12:41–44). His penetrating look seems to lay the soul bare to God and provoke one to self-examination and contrition—as happened to the adulterous woman (Jn 8:10) and to Peter who, after denying Christ (Lk 22:61) wept bitterly (Mk 14:72).

"You shall be called Cephas": naming something is the same as taking possession of the thing named (cf. Gen 17:5; 22:28; 32:28; Is 62:2). Thus, for example, Adam when he was made lord of creation, gave names to created things (Gen 2:20). "Cephas" is the Greek transcription of an Aramaic word meaning

c. From the word for *rock* in Aramaic and Greek respectively

Nazareth?" Philip said to him, "Come and see." 47 Jesus saw
Nathanael coming to him, and said to him, "Behold, an Israelite
indeed, in whom is no guile!" 48 Nathanael said to him, "How do Jn 21:2
you know me?" Jesus answered him, "Before Philip called you, Jn 6:69
when you were under the fig tree, I saw you." 49 Nathanael 2 Sam 7:14
answered him, "Rabbi, you are the Son of God! You are the King Ps 2:7
of Israel!" 50 Jesus answered him, "Because I said to you, I saw Mt 14:33; 16:16
you under the fig tree, do you believe? You shall see greater things
than these." 51 And he said to him, "Truly, truly, I say to you, you Gen 28:12
will see heaven opened, and the angels of God ascending and Mt 4:11 Mk 1:13
descending upon the Son of man." Mt 25:31

---

stone, rock: therefore, St John, writing in Greek, has to explain the meaning of the word Jesus used. Cephas was not a proper name, but our Lord put it on Peter to indicate his role as his vicar, which he will later on reveal (Mt 16:16–18): Simon was destined to be the stone, the rock, of the Church.

The first Christians regarded this new name as so significant that they used it without translating it (cf. Gal 2:9, 11, 14); later its translation "Peter" (Petros, Petrus) became current, pushing the Apostle's old name *Simon* into the background.

"Son of John": ancient manuscripts include variants, such as "son of Jona".

1:43. "Follow me" is what Jesus usually says to all his disciples (cf. Mt 4:19; 8:22; 9:9). During Jesus' lifetime, his invitation to follow him implied being with him in his public ministry, listening to his teaching, imitating his lifestyle, etc. Once the Lord ascended into heaven, following him obviously does not mean going with him along the roads of Palestine; it means that "a Christian should live as Christ lived, making the affections of Christ his own, so that he can exclaim with St Paul: 'It is now no longer I that live, but Christ lives in me (Gal 2:20)' " (St J. Escrivá, *Christ Is Passing By*, 103). In all cases our Lord's invitation involves setting out on a journey: that is, it requires one to lead a life of striving always to do God's will even if this involves generous self-sacrifice.

1:45–51. The apostle Philip is so moved that he cannot but tell his friend Nathanael (Bartholomew) about his wonderful discovery (v. 45). "Nathanael had heard from Scripture that Jesus must come from Bethlehem, from the people of David. This belief prevailed among the Jews and also the prophet had proclaimed it of old, saying: 'But you, O Bethlehem, who are little to be among the clans of Judah, from you shall come forth for me one who is to be ruler of Israel' (Mic 5:2). Therefore, when he heard that he was from Nazareth, he was troubled and in doubt, since he found that the announcement of Philip was not in agreement with the words of the prophecy" (St John Chysostom, *Hom. on St John*, 20, 1).

A Christian may find that, in trying to communicate his faith to others, they raise difficulties. What should he do? What Philip did—not trust his own explanation, but invite them to approach Jesus personally: "Come and see" (v. 46). In other words, a Christian should bring his fellowmen, his brothers into Jesus' presence through the means of grace which he has given them and which the Church ministers—frequent reception of the sacraments, and devout Christian practices.

2. JESUS, THE AUTHOR OF THE NEW ECONOMY OF SALVATION. FIRST SIGNS OF FAITH

The wedding at Cana—the first sign worked by Jesus

2 [1]On the third day there was a marriage at Cana in Galilee, and
the mother of Jesus was there; [2]Jesus also was invited to the

---

Nathanael, a sincere person (v. 47), goes along with Philip to see Jesus; he makes personal contact with our Lord (v. 48), and the outcome is that he receives faith (the result of his ready reception of grace, which reaches him through Christ's human nature: v. 49).

As far as we can deduce from the Gospels, Nathanael is the first apostle to make an explicit confession of faith in Jesus as Messiah and as Son of God. Later on St Peter, in a more formal way, will recognize our Lord's divinity (cf. Mt 16:16). Here (v. 51) Jesus evokes a text from Daniel (7:13) to confirm and give deeper meaning to the words spoken by his new disciple.

2:1. Cana in Galilee was probably what is now Kef Kenna, seven kilometres (four miles) north-east of Nazareth. The first guest to be mentioned is Mary: St Joseph is not mentioned, which cannot be put down to St John's forgetfulness: his silence here and on other occasions in his Gospel leads us to believe that Joseph had already died. Wedding celebrations lasted quite a while in the East (Gen 29:27; Judg 14:10, 12, 17; Job 9:12; 10:1). In the course of the celebrations, relatives and friends would come to greet the newly-weds; even people passing through could join in. Wine was regarded as an indispensable element in meals and also helped to create a festive atmosphere. The women looked after the catering: here our Lady would have lent a hand, which was how she realized they were running out of wine.

2:2. "To show that all states in life are good, […] Jesus deigned to be born in the pure womb of the Virgin Mary; soon after he was born he received praise from the prophetic lips of Anna, a widow, and, invited in his youth by the betrothed couple, he honoured the wedding with the power of his presence" (St Bede, *Hom.*, 13, for the 2nd Sunday after the Epiphany). Christ's presence at the wedding is a sign that he blesses love between man and woman joined in marriage: God instituted marriage at the beginning of creation (cf. Gen 1:27–28; 2:24); Jesus confirmed it and raised it to the dignity of a sacrament (cf. Mt 19:6).

2:3. In the Fourth Gospel the Mother of Jesus (this is the title St John gives her) appears only twice—here and on Calvary (Jn 19:25). This suggests Mary's involvement in the Redemption. A number of analogies can be drawn between Cana and Calvary. They are located at the beginning and at the end of Jesus' public life, as if to show that Mary was present in everything that Jesus did. Her title—Mother—carries very special tones: Mary acts as Jesus' true Mother at these two points in which his divinity is being revealed. Also, both episodes demonstrate Mary's special solicitude towards everyone: in one case she intercedes when "the hour" has not yet come; in the other she offers the Father the redeeming death of her Son, and accepts the mission Jesus confers on her to be the Mother of all believers, who are represented on Calvary by the beloved disciple.

marriage, with his disciples. [3]When the wine failed, the mother of
Jesus said to him, "They have no wine." [4]And Jesus said to her, Jn 19:26
"O woman, what have you to do with me?* My hour has not yet Mt 12:48 Mk 1:24
come." [5]His mother said to the servants, "Do whatever he tells Gen 41:55

"In the public life of Jesus Mary appears prominently; at the very beginning when at the marriage feast of Cana, moved with pity, she brought about by her intercession the beginning of the miracles of Jesus the Messiah (cf. John 2:1–11). In the course of her Son's preaching she received the words whereby, in extolling a kingdom beyond the concerns and ties of flesh and blood, he declared blessed those who heard and kept the word of God (cf. Mk 3:35; Lk 11:27–28) as she was faithfully doing (cf. Lk 2:19, 51). Thus the Blessed Virgin advanced in her pilgrimage of faith, and faithfully persevered in her union with her Son unto the cross, where she stood (cf. Jn 19:25), in line with the divine plan, enduring with her only-begotten Son the intensity of his passion, with his sacrifice, associating herself in her mother's heart, and lovingly consenting to the immolation of this victim who was born of her. Finally, she was given by the same Christ Jesus dying on the cross as a mother to his disciple, with these words: 'Woman, behold, thy son' (Jn 19:26–27)" (Vatican II, *Lumen gentium*, 58).

2:4. For the meaning of the words of this verse see the section on our Lady above (pp. 542ff). It should also be said that the Gospel account of this dialogue between Jesus and his Mother does not give us his gestures, tone of voice etc.: to us, for example, his answer sounds harsh, as if he were saying, "This is no concern of ours". But that was not the case.

"Woman" is a respectful title, rather like "lady" or "madam"; it is a formal way of speaking. On the cross Jesus will use the same word with great affection and veneration (Jn 19:26).

[The sentence rendered "What have you to do with me?" is the subject of a note in RSVCE which says "while this expression always implies a divergence of view, the precise meaning is to be determined by the context, which here shows that it is not an unqualified rebuttal, still less a rebuke." The Navarre Spanish is the equivalent of "What has it to do with you and me?"] The sentence "What has it to do with you and me?" is an Eastern way of speaking which can have different nuances. Jesus' reply seems to indicate that although in principle it was not part of God's plan for him to use his power to solve the problem the wedding feast had run into, our Lady's request moves him to do precisely that. Also, one could surmise that God's plan envisaged that Jesus should work the miracle at his Mother's request. In any event, God willed that the Revelation of the New Testament should include this important teaching: so influential is our Lady's intercession that God will listen to all petitions made through her; which is why Christian piety, with theological accuracy, has called our Lady "supplicant omnipotence".

"My hour has not yet come": the term "hour" is sometimes used by Jesus to designate the moment of his coming in glory (cf. Jn 5:28), but generally it refers to the time of his passion, death and resurrection (cf. Jn 7:30; 12:23; 13:1; 17:1).

2:5. Like a good mother, the Virgin Mary knows perfectly well what her son's reply means—though to us it is ambiguous ("What has it to do with you and me?"): she is confident that Jesus will do something to come to the family's

Mk 7:3–4 you." [6]Now six stone jars were standing there, for the Jewish rites
of purification, each holding twenty or thirty gallons. [7]Jesus said
to them, "Fill the jars with water." And they filled them up to the
brim. [8]He said to them, "Now draw some out, and take it to the
steward of the feast." So they took it. [9]When the steward of the
feast tasted the water now become wine, and did not know where
it came from (though the servants who had drawn the water
knew), the steward of the feast called the bridegroom [10]and said to
him, "Every man serves the good wine first; and when men have
drunk freely, then the poor wine; but you have kept the good wine

---

rescue. This is why she tells the servants so specifically to do what Jesus tells them. These words of our Lady can be seen as a permanent invitation to each of us: "in that all Christian holiness consists: for perfect holiness is obeying Christ in all things" (St Thomas Aquinas, *Comm. on St John*, in loc.).

We find the same attitude in Pope John Paul II's prayer at our Lady's shrine at Knock, when he consecrated the Irish people to God: "At this solemn moment *we listen* with particular attention to your words: 'Do whatever my Son tells you.' And *we wish* to respond to your words with all our heart. We wish to do what your Son tells us, what he commands us, for he has the words of eternal life. We wish to carry out and fulfil all that comes from him, all that is contained in the Good News, as our forefathers did for many centuries. [...] Today, therefore, [...] we entrust and consecrate to you, Mother of Christ and Mother of the Church, our hearts, our consciences, and our works, in order that they may be in keeping with the faith we profess. We entrust and consecrate to you each and every one of those who make up both the community of the Irish people and the community of the People of God living in this land" (Homily at Knock Shrine, 30 September 1979).

2:6. We are talking about 500–700 litres (100–150 gallons) of top quality wine. St John stresses the magnificence of the gift produced by the miracle—as he also does at the multiplication of the loaves (Jn 6:12–13). One of the signs of the arrival of the Messiah was abundance; here we have the fulfilment of the ancient prophecies: "the Lord will give what is good, and our land will yield its increase", as Psalm 85:12 proclaims; "the threshing floors shall be full of grain, the vats shall overflow with wine and oil" (Joel 2:24; cf. Amos 9:13–15). This abundance of material goods is a symbol of the supernatural gifts Christ obtains for us through the Redemption: later on St John highlights our Lord's words: "I came that they may have life, and have it abundantly" (Jn 10:10; cf. Rom 5:20).

2:7. "Up to the brim": the Evangelist gives us this further piece of information to emphasize the superabundance of the riches of Redemption and also to show how very precisely the servants did what they were told, as if hinting at the importance of docility in fulfilling the will of God, even in small details.

2:9–10. Jesus works miracles in a munificent way; for example, in the multiplication of the loaves and fish (cf. Jn 6:10–13) he feeds five thousand men—who eat as much as they want—and the left-overs fill twelve baskets. In this present miracle he does not change the water

till now." [11]This, the first of his signs, Jesus did at Cana in Galilee, Jn 1:14; 11:40
and manifested his glory; and his disciples believed in him.
[12]After this he went down to Capernaum, with his mother and Mt 4:13
his brethren* and his disciples; and there they stayed for a few
days.

Cleansing of the temple—Christ, God's new temple

[13]The Passover of the Jews was at hand, and Jesus went up to Jn 2:23; 6:4; 11:55; 12:1
Jerusalem. [14]In the temple he found those who were selling oxen Mt 21:12

---

into just any wine but into wine of excellent quality.

The Fathers see in this good wine, kept for the end of the celebrations, and in its abundance, a prefiguring of the crowning of the history of salvation: formerly God sent the patriarchs and prophets, but in the fullness of time he sent his own Son, whose teaching perfects the old revelation and whose grace far exceeds the expectations of the righteous in the Old Testament. They also have seen, in this good wine coming at the end, the reward and joy of eternal life which God grants to those who desire to follow Christ and who have suffered bitterness and contradiction in this life (cf. St Thomas Aquinas, *Comm. on St John*, in loc.).

2:11. Before he worked this miracle the disciples already believed that Jesus was the Messiah; but they had too earthbound a concept of his salvific mission. St John testifies here that this miracle was the beginning of a new dimension in their faith; it became much deeper. "At Cana, Mary appears once more as the Virgin in prayer: when she tactfully told her Son of a temporal need, she also obtained an effect of grace, namely, that Jesus, in working the first of his 'signs', confirmed his disciples' faith in him" (Paul VI, *Marialis cultus*, 18).

"Why are Mary's prayers so effective with God? The prayers of the saints are prayers of servants, whereas Mary's are a Mother's prayer, whence flows their efficacy and their authority; and since Jesus has immense love for his Mother, she cannot pray without being listened to. [...]

"To understand Mary's great goodness, let us remember what the Gospel says. [...] There was a shortage of wine, which naturally worried the married couple. No one asks the Blessed Virgin to intervene and request her Son to come to the rescue of the couple. But Mary's heart cannot but take pity on the unfortunate couple [...]; it stirs her to act as intercessor and ask her Son for the miracle, even though no one asks her to. [...] If our Lady acted like this without being asked, what would she not have done if they actually asked her to intervene?" (St Alphonsus, *Sunday Sermons*, 48).

2:12. Regarding the "brethren" of Jesus cf. the notes on Mt 12:46–47 and Mk 6:1–3.

2:13. "The Passover of the Jews": this is the most important religious feast for the people of the Old Testament, the prefiguring of the Christian Easter (cf. the note on Mt 26:2). The Jewish Passover was celebrated on the fourteenth day of the month of Nisan and was followed by the festival week of the Azymes (unleavened bread). According to the Law of Moses, on those days every male Israelite had to "appear before the Lord God" (Ex 34:23; Deut 16:16)—hence the pious custom of

Mk 11:15ff and sheep and pigeons, and the money-changers at their business.
Lk 19:45 [15]And making a whip of cords, he drove them all, with the sheep
and oxen, out of the temple; and he poured out the coins of the
Zech 14:21 money-changers and overturned their tables. [16]And he told those
Lk 2:49 who sold the pigeons, "Take these things away; you shall not
Ps 69:9 make my Father's house a house of trade." [17]His disciples remem-
bered that it was written, "Zeal for thy house will consume me."
Mt 21:23 [18]The Jews then said to him, "What sign have you to show us for
Mt 26:61; doing this?" [19]Jesus answered them, "Destroy this temple, and in
27:40 three days I will raise it up." [20]The Jews then said, "It has taken

---

making a pilgrimage to the temple of Jerusalem for these days, hence the crowd and all the vendors to supply the needs of the pilgrims; this trading gave rise to abuses.

"Jesus went up to Jerusalem": by doing this Jesus publicly shows that he observes the Law of God. But, as we shall soon see, he goes to the temple as the Only-begotten Son who must ensure that all due decorum is observed in the House of the Father: "And from thenceforth Jesus, the Anointed of God, always begins by reforming abuses and purifying from sin; both when he visits his Church, and when he visits the Christian soul" (Origen, *Hom. on St John*, 1).

2:14–15. Every Israelite had to offer as a passover sacrifice an ox or a sheep, if he was wealthy; or two turtledoves or two pigeons if he was not (Lev 5:7). In addition he had to pay a half shekel every year, if he was twenty or over. The half shekel, which was the equivalent of a day's pay of a worker, was a special coin also called temple money (cf. Ex 30:13); other coins in circulation (denarii, drachmas etc.) were considered impure because they bore the image of pagan rulers. During the Passover, because of the extra crowd, the outer courtyard of the temple, the court of the Gentiles, was full of traders, money-changers etc., and inevitably this meant noise, shouting, bellowing, manure etc. Prophets had already fulminated against these abuses, which grew up with the tacit permission of the temple authorities, who made money by permitting trading. Cf. the notes on Mt 21:12–13 and Mk 11:15–18.

2:16–17. "Zeal for thy house will consume me"—a quotation from Psalm 69:9. Jesus has just made a most significant assertion: "You shall not make my Father's house a house of trade." By calling God his Father and acting so energetically, he is proclaiming he is the Messiah, the Son of God. Jesus' zeal for his Father's glory did not escape the attention of his disciples who realized that what he did fulfilled the words of Psalm 69.

2:18–22. The temple of Jerusalem, which had replaced the previous sanctuary which the Israelites carried around in the wilderness, was the place selected by God during the Old Covenant to express his presence to the people in a special way. But this was only an imperfect anticipation or prefiguring of the full expression of his presence among men—the Word of God became man. Jesus, in whom "the whole fulness of deity dwells bodily" (Col 2:9), is the full presence of God here on earth and, therefore, the true

forty-six years to build this temple, and will you raise it up in
three days?" [21]But he spoke of the temple of his body. [22]When 1 Cor 3:17; 6:19
therefore he was raised from the dead, his disciples remembered
that he had said this; and they believed the scripture and the word
which Jesus had spoken.

[23]Now when he was in Jerusalem at the Passover feast, many
believed in his name when they saw the signs which he did; [24]but
Jesus did not trust himself to them, [25]because he knew all men and Lk 16:15
needed no one to bear witness of man; for he himself knew what
was in man.

---

temple of God. Jesus identifies the temple of Jerusalem with his own body, and by so doing refers to one of the most profound truths about himself—the Incarnation. After the ascension of the Lord into heaven this real and very special presence of God among men is continued in the sacrament of the Blessed Eucharist.

Christ's words and actions as he expels the traders from the temple clearly show that he is the Messiah foretold by the prophets. That is why some Jews approach him and ask him to give a sign of his power (cf. Mt 16:1; Mk 8:11; Lk 11:29). Jesus' reply (v. 19), whose meaning remains obscure until his resurrection, the Jewish authorities try to turn into an attack on the temple—which merits the death penalty (Mt 26:61; Mk 14:58; cf. Jer 26:4ff); later they will taunt him with it when he is suffering on the cross (Mt 27:40; Mk 15:29) and later still in their case against St Stephen before the Sanhedrin they will claim to have heard him repeat it (Acts 6:14).

There was nothing derogatory in what Jesus said, contrary to what false witnesses made out. The miracle he offers them, which he calls "the sign of Jonah" (cf. Mt 16:4), will be his own resurrection on the third day. Jesus is using a metaphor, as if to say: Do you see this temple? Well, imagine if it were destroyed, would it not be a great miracle to rebuild it in three days? That is what I will do for you as a sign. For you will destroy my body, which is the true temple, and I will rise again on the third day.

No one understood what he was saying. Jews and disciples alike thought he was speaking about rebuilding the temple which Herod the Great had begun to construct in 19–20 BC. Later on the disciples grasped what he really meant.

2:23–25. Jesus' miracles moved many to recognize that he had extraordinary, divine powers. But that falls short of perfect theological faith. Jesus knew their faith was limited, and that they were not very deeply attached to him: they were interested in him as a miracle-worker. This explains why he did not trust them (cf. Jn 6:15, 26). "Many people today are like that. They carry the name of faithful, but they are fickle and inconstant", comments Chrysostom (*Hom. on St John*, 23, 1).

Jesus' knowledge of men's hearts is another sign of his divinity; for example, Nathanael and the Samaritan woman recognized him as the Messiah because they were convinced by the evidence of supernatural power he showed by reading their hearts (cf. Jn 1:49; 4:29).

Nicodemus visits Jesus

Jn 7:50; 9:39 Mt 22:16 3 [1]Now there was a man of the Pharisees, named Nicodemus, a
ruler of the Jews. [2]This man came to Jesus[d] by night and said
to him, "Rabbi, we know that you are a teacher come from God;
for no one can do these signs that you do, unless God is with him."
Mt 18:3 Lk 17:21 1 Pet 1:23 [3]Jesus answered him, "Truly, truly, I say to you, unless one is born
anew,[e] he cannot see the kingdom of God." [4]Nicodemus said to
him, "How can a man be born when he is old? Can he enter a

3:1–21. Nicodemus was a member of the Sanhedrin of Jerusalem (cf. Jn 7:50). He must also have been an educated man, probably a scribe or teacher of the Law: Jesus addresses him as a "teacher of Israel". He would have been what is called an intellectual—a person who reasons things out, for whom the search for truth is a basic part of life. He was, naturally, much influenced by the Jewish intellectual climate of his time. However, if divine things are to be understood, reason is not enough: a person must be humble. The first thing Christ is going to do in his conversation with Nicodemus is to highlight the need for this virtue; that is why he does not immediately answer his questions: instead, he shows him how far he is from true wisdom: "Are you a teacher of Israel, and yet you do not understand this?" Nicodemus needs to recognize that, despite all his studies, he is still ignorant of the things of God. As St Thomas Aquinas comments: "The Lord does not reprove him to offend him but rather because Nicodemus still relies on his own learning; therefore he desired, by having him experience this humiliation, to make him a fit dwelling-place for the Holy Spirit" (*Comm. on St John*, in loc.). From the way the conversation develops Nicodemus obviously takes this step of humility and he sits before Jesus as a disciple before his master. Then our Lord reveals to him the mysteries of faith. From this moment onwards Nicodemus will be much wiser than all those colleagues of his who have not taken this step.

Human knowledge, on any scale, is something minute compared with the truths—simple to state but extremely profound—of the articles of faith (cf. Eph 3:15–19; 1 Cor 2:9). Divine truths need to be received with the simplicity of a child (without which we cannot enter the Kingdom of heaven); then they can be meditated on right through one's life and studied with a sense of awe, aware that divine things are always far above our heads.

3:1–2. Throughout this intimate dialogue, Nicodemus behaves with great refinement: he addresses Jesus with respect and calls him Rabbi, Master. He had probably been impressed by Christ's miracles and preaching and wanted to know more. The way he reacts to our Lord's teaching is not as yet very supernatural, but he is noble and upright. His visiting Jesus by night, for fear of the Jews (cf. Jn 19:39), is very understandable, given his position as a member of the Sanhedrin: but he takes the risk and goes to see Jesus.

When the Pharisees tried to arrest Jesus (Jn 7:32), failing to do so because he had such support among the people, Nicodemus energetically opposed the

d. Greek *him*

second time into his mother's womb and be born?" [5]Jesus | Ezek 36:25–27
answered, "Truly, truly, I say to you, unless one is born of water | Eph 5:26 Tit 3:5
and the Spirit, he cannot enter the kingdom of God. [6]That which is | 1 Jn 3:9; 5:1
born of the flesh is flesh, and that which is born of the Spirit is | Jn 1:13 Gen 6:3
spirit.[f] [7]Do not marvel that I said to you, 'You must be born anew.'[e]
[8]The wind[f] blows where it wills, and you hear the sound of it, but | Eccles 11:5
you do not know whence it comes or whither it goes; so it is with
every one who is born of the Spirit." [9]Nicodemus said to him, | Lk 1:34

---

injustice of condemning a man without giving him a hearing; he also showed no fear, at the most difficult time of all, by honouring the dead body of the Lord (Jn 19:40).

3:3–8. Nicodemus' first question shows that he still has doubts about Jesus (Is he a prophet? Is he the Messiah?); and our Lord replies to him in a completely unexpected way: Nicodemus presumed he would say something about his mission and, instead, he reveals to him an astonishing truth: one must be born again, in a spiritual birth, by water and the spirit; a whole new world opens up before Nicodemus.

Our Lord's words also paint a limitless horizon for the spiritual advancement of any Christian who willingly lets himself or herself be led by divine grace and the gifts of the Holy Spirit, which are infused at Baptism and enhanced by the sacraments. As well as opening his soul to God, the Christian also needs to keep at bay his selfish appetites and the inclinations of pride, if he is to understand what God is teaching him in his soul: "Therefore must the soul be stripped of all things created, and of its own actions and abilities—namely, of its understanding, perception and feelings—so that, when all that is unlike God and unconformed to him is cast out, the soul may receive the likeness of God; and nothing will then remain in it that is not the will of God and it will thus be transformed in God. Wherefore, although it is true that, as we have said, God is ever in the soul, giving it, and through his presence conserving within it, its natural being, yet he does not always communicate supernatural being to it. For this is communicated only by love and grace, which not all souls possess; and all those that possess it have it not in the same degree; for some have attained more degrees of love and others fewer. Wherefore God communicates himself most to that soul that has progressed farthest in love; namely, that has its will in closest conformity with the will of God. And the soul that has attained complete conformity and likeness of will is totally united and transformed in God supernaturally" (St John of the Cross, *Ascent of Mount Carmel*, book 2, chap. 5).

Jesus speaks very forcefully about man's new condition: it is no longer a question of being born of the flesh, of the line of Abraham (cf. Jn 1:13), but of being reborn through the action of the Holy Spirit, by means of water. This is our Lord's first reference to Christian Baptism, confirming John the Baptist's prophecy (cf. Mt 3:11; Jn 1:33) that he had come to institute a baptism with the Holy Spirit.

"Nicodemus had not yet savoured this spirit and this life. [...] He knew but

e. Or *from above* **f.** The same Greek word means both *wind* and spirit

"How can this be?" [10]Jesus answered him, "Are you a teacher of
Jn 7:16; 8:26ff; 12:49 Israel, and yet you do not understand this? [11]Truly, truly, I say to
you, we speak of what we know, and bear witness to what we have
Lk 22:67 Wis 9:16 seen; but you do not receive our testimony. [12]If I have told you
earthly things and you do not believe, how can you believe if I tell
Prov 30:4 Eph 4:9 you heavenly things? [13]No one has ascended into heaven but he
who descended from heaven, the Son of man.[g] [14]And as Moses
Jn 8:28; 12:32; 18:32 Num 21:8–9 lifted up the serpent in the wilderness, so must the Son of man be
lifted up, [15]that whoever believes in him may have eternal life."[h]
[16]For God so loved the world that he gave his only Son, that
Rom 5:8; 8:32 1 Jn 4:9 whoever believes in him should not perish but have eternal life.

---

one birth, which is from Adam and Eve; that which is from God and the Church, he did not yet know; he knew only the paternity which engenders to death; he did not yet know the paternity which engenders to life. […] Whereas there are two births, he knew only of one. One is of earth, the other of heaven; one of the flesh, the other of the Spirit; one of mortality, the other of eternity; one of male and female, the other of God and the Church. But the two are each unique; neither one nor the other can be repeated" (St Augustine, *In Ioann. Evang*., 11, 6).

Our Lord speaks of the wonderful effects the Holy Spirit produces in the soul of the baptized. Just as with the wind—when it blows we realize its presence, we hear it whistling, but we do not know where it came from, or where it will end up—so with the Holy Spirit, the divine "breath" (*pneuma*) given us in Baptism: we do not know how he comes to penetrate our heart but he makes his presence felt by the change in the conduct of whoever receives him.

3:10–12. Even though Nicodemus finds them puzzling, Jesus confirms that his words still stand, and he explains that he speaks about the things of heaven because that is where he comes from, and to make himself understood he uses earthly comparisons and images. Even so, this language will fail to convince those who adopt an attitude of disbelief.

Chrysostom comments: "It was with reason that he said not: 'You do not understand,' but: 'You do not believe.' When a person baulks and does not readily accept things which it is possible for the mind to receive, he may with reason be accused of stupidity; when he does not accept things which it is not possible to grasp by reason but only by faith, the charge is no longer that of stupidity, but of incredulity" (*Hom. on St John*, 27, 1).

3:13. This is a formal declaration of the divinity of Jesus. No one has gone up into heaven and, therefore, no one can have perfect knowledge of God's secrets, except God himself who became man and came down from heaven—Jesus, the second Person of the Blessed Trinity, the Son of man foretold in the Old Testament (cf. Dan 7:13), to whom has been given eternal lordship over all peoples.

The Word does not stop being God on becoming man: even when he is on earth as man, he is in heaven as God. It is

g. Other ancient authoritied add *who is in heaven* **h.** Some interpreters hold that the quotation continues through verse 21

17For God sent the Son into the world, not to condemn the world, Jn 5:22; 12:47
but that the world might be saved through him. 18He who believes Lk 19:10 Acts 17:31
in him is not condemned; he who does not believe is condemned Jn 3:36; 5:24
already, because he has not believed in the name of the only Son
of God. 19And this is the judgment, that the light has come into the Jn 1:5, 9–11;
world, and men loved darkness rather than light, because their 12:48
deeds were evil. 20For every one who does evil hates the light, and Eph 5:13
does not come to the light, lest his deeds should be exposed. 21But
he who does what is true comes to the light, that it may be clearly
seen that his deeds have been wrought in God.

---

only after the Resurrection and the Ascension that Jesus is in heaven as man also.

3:14–15. The bronze serpent which Moses set up on a pole was established by God to cure those who had been bitten by the poisonous serpents in the desert (cf. Num 21:8–9). Jesus compares this with his crucifixion, to show the value of his being raised up on the cross: those who look on him with faith can obtain salvation. We could say that the good thief was the first to experience the saving power of Christ on the cross: he saw the crucified Jesus, the King of Israel, the Messiah, and was immediately promised that he would be in Paradise that very day (cf. Lk 23:39–43).

The Son of God took on our human nature to make known the hidden mystery of God's own life (cf. Mk 4:11; Jn 1:18; 3:1–13; Eph 3:9) and to free from sin and death those who look at him with faith and love and who accept the cross of every day.

The faith of which our Lord speaks is not just intellectual acceptance of the truths he has taught: it involves recognizing him as Son of God (cf. 1 Jn 5:1), sharing his very life (cf. Jn 1:12) and surrendering ourselves out of love and therefore becoming like him (cf. Jn 10:27; 1 Jn 3:2). But this faith is a gift of God (cf. Jn 3:3, 5–8), and we should ask him to strengthen it and increase it as the Apostles did: Lord "increase our faith!" (Lk 17:5). While faith is a supernatural, free gift, it is also a virtue, a good habit, which a person can practise and thereby develop: so the Christian, who already has the divine gift of faith, needs with the help of grace to make explicit acts of faith in order to make this virtue grow.

3:16–21. These words, so charged with meaning, summarize how Christ's death is the supreme sign of God's love for men (cf. the section on charity, pp. 538ff above). "'For God so loved the world that he gave his only Son' for its salvation. All our religion is a revelation of God's kindness, mercy and love for us. 'God is love' (1 Jn 4:16), that is, love poured forth unsparingly. All is summed up in this supreme truth, which explains and illuminates everything. The story of Jesus must be seen in this light. '(He) loved me', St Paul writes. Each of us can and must repeat it for himself—'He loved me, and gave himself for me' (Gal 2:20)" (Paul VI, Homily on Corpus Christi, 13 June 1976).

Christ's self-surrender is a pressing call to respond to his great love for us: "If it is true that God has created us, that he has redeemed us, that he loves us so much that he has given up his only-begotten Son for us (cf. Jn 3:16), that he waits for us—every day!—as eagerly as

The Baptist again bears witness

Jn 2:12; 4:2; 5:1; 6:1; 7:1 22After this Jesus and his disciples went into the land of Judea;
there he remained with them and baptized.* 23John also was bap-
Mt 4:12 tizing at Aenon near Salim, because there was much water there;
Lk 3:20 and people came and were baptized. 24For John had not yet been
put in prison.*
25Now a discussion arose between John's disciples and a Jew
Jn 1:26–34 over purifying. 26And they came to John, and said to him, "Rabbi,

---

the father of the prodigal son did (cf. Lk 15:11–32), how can we doubt that he wants us to respond to him with all our love? The strange thing would be not to talk to God, to draw away and forget him, and busy ourselves in activities which are closed to the constant promptings of his grace" (St Josemaría Escrivá, *Friends of God*, 251).

"Man cannot live without love. He remains a being that is incomprehensible for himself, his life is senseless, if love is not revealed to him, if he does not encounter love, if he does not experience it and make it his own, if he does not participate intimately in it. This [...] is why Christ the Redeemer 'fully reveals man to himself'. If we may use the expression, this is the human dimension of the mystery of the Redemption. In this dimension man finds again the greatness, dignity and value that belong to his humanity. [...] The one who wishes to understand himself thoroughly [...] must, with his unrest and uncertainty and even his weakness and sinfulness, with his life and death, draw near to Christ. He must, so to speak, enter into him with all his own self, he must 'appropriate' and assimilate the whole of the reality of the Incarnation and Redemption in order to find himself. If this profound process takes place within him, he then bears fruit not only of adoration of God but also of deep wonder at himself. How precious must man be in the eyes of the Creator, if he 'gained so great a Redeemer' (*Roman Missal, Exultet* at Easter Vigil), and if God 'gave his only Son' in order that man 'should not perish but have eternal life'. [...]

"Increasingly contemplating the whole of Christ's mystery, the Church knows with all the certainty of faith that the Redemption that took place through the Cross has definitively restored his dignity to man and given back meaning to his life in the world, a meaning that was lost to a considerable extent because of sin. And for that reason, the Redemption was accomplished in the paschal mystery, leading through the Cross and death to Resurrection" (John Paul II, *Redemptor hominis*, 10).

Jesus demands that we have faith in him as a first prerequisite to sharing in his love. Faith brings us out of darkness into the light, and sets us on the road to salvation. "He who does not believe is condemned already" (v. 18). "The words of Christ are at once words of judgment and grace, of life and death. For it is only by putting to death that which is old that we can come to newness of life. Now, although this refers primarily to people, it is also true of various worldly goods which bear the mark both of man's sin and the blessing of God. [...] No one is freed from sin by himself or by his own efforts, no one is raised above himself or completely delivered from his own weakness, solitude or slavery; all have need of Christ, who is the model, master, liberator, saviour, and giver of life. Even in the

he who was with you beyond the Jordan, to whom you bore wit- Heb 5:4
ness, here he is, baptizing, and all are going to him." 27John 1 Cor 4:7
answered, "No one can receive anything except what is given him Jn 1:20, 23, 27
from heaven. 28You yourselves bear me witness, that I said, I am Mt 11:10 Mk 1:2
not the Christ, but I have been sent before him. 29He who has the
bride is the bridegroom; the friend of the bridegroom, who stands Mt 9:15; 22:2
and hears him, rejoices greatly at the bridegroom's voice; therefore this joy of mine is now full. 30He must increase, but I must 2 Sam 3:1
decrease."[i]

---

secular history of mankind the Gospel has acted as a leaven in the interests of liberty and progress, and it always offers itself as a leaven with regard to brotherhood, unity and peace" (Vatican II, *Ad gentes*, 8).

3:22–24. A little later on (Jn 4:2) the Evangelist makes it clear that it was not Jesus himself who baptized, but his disciples. Our Lord probably wanted them from the very beginning to get practice in exhorting people to conversion. The rite referred to here was not yet Christian Baptism—which only began after the resurrection of Christ (cf. Jn 7:39; 16:7; Mt 28:19)—but "both baptisms, that of St John the Baptist and that of our Lord's disciples [...], had a single purpose—to bring the baptized to Christ [...] and prepare the way for future faith" (St John Chrysostom, *Hom. on St John*, 29, 1).

The Gospel gives the exact time and place of this episode. Aenon is an Aramaic word meaning "wells". Salim was situated to the northeast of Samaria, south of the town of Scythopolis or Beisan, near the western bank of the Jordan, about twenty kilometres (thirteen miles) to the south of the Lake of Gennesaret.

The Gospel notes that "John had not yet been put in prison" (v. 24), thus rounding out the information given by the Synoptics (cf. Mt 4:12; Mk 1:14). We know, therefore, that Jesus' public ministry began when John the Baptist's mission was still going on, and, particularly, that there was no competition of any kind between them; on the contrary, the Baptist, who was preparing the way of the Lord, had the joy of actually seeing his own disciples follow Jesus (cf. Jn 1:37).

3:27–29. John the Baptist is speaking in a symbolic way here, after the style of the prophets; our Lord himself does the same thing. The bridegroom is Jesus Christ. From other passages in the New Testament we know that the Church is described as the Bride (cf. Eph 5:24–32; Rev 19:7–9). This symbol of the wedding expresses the way Christ unites the Church to himself, and the way the Church is hallowed and shaped in God's own life. The Baptist rejoices to see that the Messiah has already begun his public ministry, and he recognizes the infinite distance between his position and that of Christ: his joy is full because he sees Jesus calling people and them following him.

"The friend of the bridegroom", according to Jewish custom, refers to the man who used to accompany the bridegroom at the start of the wedding and play a formal part in the wedding celebration—the best man. Obviously,

i. Some interpreters hold that the quotation continues through verse 36

Jn 8:23 [31]He who comes from above is above all; he who is of the
earth belongs to the earth, and of the earth he speaks; he who
Jn 3:11 comes from heaven is above all. [32]He bears witness to what he has
seen and heard, yet no one receives his testimony; [33]he who
Jn 1:33–34 receives his testimony sets his seal to this, that God is true. [34]For
Jn 5:20; 17:2 he whom God has sent utters the words of God, for it is not by
Mt 11:27 measure that he gives the Spirit; [35]the Father loves the Son, and
Jn 1:18; 20:31 has given all things into his hand. [36]He who believes in the Son
has eternal life; he who does not obey the Son shall not see life,
but the wrath of God rests upon him.

---

as the Baptist says, there is a great difference between him and the bridegroom, who occupies the centre of the stage.

3:30. The Baptist knew his mission was one of preparing the way of the Lord; he was to fade into the background once the Messiah arrived, which he did faithfully and humbly. In the same way, a Christian, when engaged in apostolate, should try to keep out of the limelight and allow Christ to seek men out; he should be always emptying himself, to allow Christ to fill his life. “It is necessary for Christ to grow in you, for you to progress in your knowledge and love of him: for, the more you know him and love him, the more he grows in you. […] Therefore, people who advance in this way need to have less self-esteem, because the more a person discovers God’s greatness the less importance he gives to his own human condition” (St Thomas Aquinas, *Comm. on St John*, in loc.).

3:31–36. This paragraph shows us Christ’s divinity, his relationship with the Father and the Holy Spirit, and the share those have in God’s eternal life who believe in Jesus Christ. Outside of faith there is no life nor any room for hope.

4:3. This point marks the beginning of the Pharisees’ hostility towards Jesus. Because it was not yet time for him to suffer, the Lord retired to the north of Palestine, to Galilee, where the Pharisees had less influence, thereby avoiding their killing him before the time appointed by God the Father.

Divine providence does not exempt the believer from using his reason and will—as Christ did—to prudently discover what God wants him to do: “Such wisdom of the heart, such prudence will never become the prudence of the flesh that St Paul speaks of (cf. Rom 8:6), the prudence of those who are intelligent but try not to use their intelligence to seek and love our Lord. A truly prudent person is ever attentive to God’s promptings and, through this vigilant listening, he receives in his soul the promise and reality of salvation. […] Wisdom of the heart guides and governs many other virtues. Through prudence, a man learns to be daring without being rash. He will not make excuses (based on hidden motives of indolence) to avoid the effort involved in living wholeheartedly according to God’s plans” (St Josemaría Escrivá, *Friends of God*, 87).

4:4–5. There were two normal routes for going from Judea to Galilee. The shorter one went through the city of Samaria; the other, which followed the Jordan, was longer. Jesus took the Samaria route, per-

Jesus and the Samaritan woman

4 1Now when the Lord knew that the Pharisees had heard that Jn 3:22–26
Jesus was making and baptizing more disciples than John
2(although Jesus himself did not baptize, but only his disciples), 1 Cor 1:17
3he left Judea and departed again to Galilee. 4He had to pass Lk 9:52
through Samaria. 5So he came to a city of Samaria, called Sychar, Gen 48:22
near the field that Jacob gave to his son Joseph. 6Jacob's well was Josh 24:32
there, and so Jesus, wearied as he was with his journey, sat down
beside the well. It was about the sixth hour.

7There came a woman of Samaria to draw water. Jesus said to
her, "Give me a drink." 8For his disciples had gone away into the

---

haps not just because it was shorter and busier but also to have a chance of preaching to the Samaritans. When he was approaching Samaria, near Sychar, the present-day El 'Askar, at the foot of Mount Ebal, he met this Samaritan woman.

4:6. The Gospels, particularly St John's, sometimes give us little bits of information which seem irrelevant but really are not. Like us, Jesus did get tired, he needed to take regular rest, he felt hunger and thirst; but despite his tiredness he does not waste an opportunity to do good to souls.

"Recollect yourselves and go over the scene again slowly in your minds. Jesus Christ, *perfectus Deus, perfectus homo*, is tired out from his travels and his apostolic work. Perhaps there have been times when the same thing has happened to you and you have ended up worn out, because you have reached the limit of your resources. It is a touching sight to see our Master so exhausted. He is hungry too—his disciples have gone to a neighbouring village to look for food. And he is thirsty […].

"Whenever we get tired—in our work, in our studies, in our apostolic endeavours—when our horizon is darkened by lowering clouds, then let us turn our eyes to Jesus, to Jesus who is so good, and who also gets tired; to Jesus who is hungry and suffers thirst. Lord, how well you make yourself understood! How lovable you are! You show us that you are just like us, in everything but sin, so that we can feel utterly sure that, together with you, we can conquer all our evil inclinations, all our faults. For neither weariness nor hunger matters, nor thirst, nor tears … since Christ also grew weary, knew hunger, was thirsty, and wept. What is important is that we struggle to fulfil the will of our heavenly Father (cf. Jn 4:34), battling away goodheartedly, for our Lord is always at our side" (St Josemaría Escrivá, *Friends of God*, 176 and 201).

4:7. Jesus has come to save what was lost. He spares no effort in this mission. The hostility between Jews and Samaritans was proverbial; but Jesus embraced everyone, he loved all souls and he shed his blood for each and every person. He begins his conversation with this woman, by asking a favour of her—which indicates God's great respect for us: here we have Almighty God asking a mere creature to do him a favour. "Give me a drink": Jesus makes this request not just to slake his physical thirst but because his love made him thirst for the salvation of all men. When nailed to the cross he again said: "I thirst" (Jn 19:28).

Lk 9:53 city to buy food. 9The Samaritan woman said to him, "How is it
that you, a Jew, ask a drink of me, a woman of Samaria?" For
Jn 7:38–39 Jews have no dealings with Samaritans. 10Jesus answered her, "If
you knew the gift of God, and who it is that is saying to you,
'Give me a drink,' you would have asked him, and he would have
given you living water." 11The woman said to him, "Sir, you have
nothing to draw with, and the well is deep; where do you get that
Jn 8:53 living water? 12Are you greater than our father Jacob, who gave us
the well, and drank from it himself, and his sons, and his cattle?"
Jn 6:58 13Jesus said to her, "Every one who drinks of this water will thirst
Jn 6:27, 35; 7:37–39 again, 14but whoever drinks of the water that I shall give him will
Is 58:11 never thirst; the water that I shall give him will become in him a

---

4:9. The Samaritan woman's reply starts the dialogue and shows how well she is responding to the action of grace in her soul: her readiness to talk to Christ, who was a Jew, is the first stage in her change of heart. Later (v. 11), by taking a real interest in what Christ is saying, she opens up further to God's influence. Her religious feelings begin to revive ("our father Jacob": v. 12). Jesus rewards her and she replies truthfully: "I have no husband" (v. 17); and, seeing that Jesus has penetrated the intimacy of her conscience, she makes an act of faith: "I perceive that you are a prophet" (v. 19).

4:10. As in his dialogue with Nicodemus, Jesus makes use of common expressions to get across teachings of a much deeper nature. Everyone knows from experience that water is absolutely necessary for human life; similarly, the grace of Christ is absolutely necessary for supernatural life. The water which can truly quench man's thirst does not come from this or any other well: it is Christ's grace, the "living water" which provides eternal life.

Once again, taking occasion of human interests and preoccupations, Jesus awakens a desire for things supernatural; in the same way as he led St Peter and others away from their work as fishermen to involve them in the apostolic work of being fishers of men, he leads the Samaritan woman away from her chore of drawing water from the well to the point where she desires to find this better water which wells up to eternal life (v. 14).

4:13–14. Our Lord's reply is surprising and really captures the woman's attention. Here is someone greater than Jacob, someone offering her water that will quench her thirst once and for all. Christ is referring to the change worked in every person by sanctifying grace, a share in God's own life, the presence of the Holy Spirit in the soul, the great gift which those who believe in him will receive.

We worry about the future, we are full of desires to be happy and at peace; a person who receives our Lord and remains united to him as a branch to the vine (cf. Jn 15:4–5) will not only slake his thirst but become a well of living water (cf. Jn 7:37–39).

4:16–19. Although the woman cannot yet realize the deep meaning of what he is saying, Jesus uses her growing interest to reveal to her his divinity, little by little: he shows that he knows about her life, the secrets of her heart; he can read her conscience. In this way he gives her enough to motivate her to make her first

spring of water welling up to eternal life." 15The woman said to
him, "Sir, give me this water, that I may not thirst, nor come here
to draw."
16Jesus said to her, "Go, call your husband, and come here."
17The woman answered him, "I have no husband." Jesus said to
her, "You are right in saying, 'I have no husband'; 18for you have
had five husbands, and he whom you now have is not your hus-
band; this you said truly." 19The woman said to him, "Sir, I per- 1 Cor 14:24–25
ceive that you are a prophet. 20Our fathers worshipped on this
mountain;* and you say that in Jerusalem is the place where men
ought to worship." 21Jesus said to her, "Woman, believe me, the Deut 12:5
hour is coming when neither on this mountain nor in Jerusalem Ps 122

---

act of faith: "I perceive that you are a prophet." Her conversion has begun.

4:20. The origin of the Samaritan people goes back to the period of the conquest of Samaria by the Assyrians in the eighth century before Christ (cf. 2 Kings 13:24–31). They were foreigners who very quickly integrated with the Israelites in the region. After the Babylonian captivity they tried to ally themselves with the Jews for political reasons and to contribute to the rebuilding of the temple, but the Jews would have none of them. From that time onwards the Jews and the Samaritans were always hostile to each other (cf. Ezra 4:1ff; Jn 4:9).

On this occasion, the Samaritan woman, now fully aware that she is speaking to someone of authority, asks our Lord one of the key questions affecting the religious life of the two peoples: where was the right place to offer worship to God; the Jews held that only Jerusalem would do; whereas the Samaritans claimed that the shrine erected on Mount Gerizim was also legitimate (they based their claim on some passages in the Pentateuch: cf. Gen 12:7; 22:2; 33:20).

4:21–24. Jesus not only answers the question but takes advantage of it to confirm the value of the teachings of the prophets and thereby reaffirm revealed truth: the Samaritans are in the dark about many of God's plans because they do not accept any revelation not found in the first five books of Holy Scripture, that is, in the Law of Moses; the Jews, on the other hand, are much nearer the truth because they accept the whole of the Old Testament. But both Samaritans and Jews need to open themselves to the new revelation of Jesus Christ. With the coming of the Messiah, whom both peoples are awaiting, and who is the true dwelling-place of God among men (cf. Jn 2:19), the new, definitive Alliance has begun; and neither Gerizim nor Jerusalem count any more; what the Father wishes is for all to accept the Messiah, his Son, the new temple of God, by offering him a form of worship which comes right from the heart (cf. Jn 1:12; 2 Tim 2:22) and which the Spirit of God himself stirs people to render (cf. Rom 8:15).

This is why the Church's solemn Magisterium teaches that through Baptism we become true worshippers of God: "By Baptism men are grafted into the paschal mystery of Christ; they die with him, are buried with him, and rise with him. They receive the spirit of adoption as sons 'in which we cry, Abba, Father' (Rom 8:15) and thus become true adorers

2 Kings 17:29–41 will you worship the Father. 22 You worship what you do not
Is 2:3 know; we worship what we know, for salvation is from the Jews.
23 But the hour is coming, and now is, when the true worshippers
will worship the Father in spirit and truth, for such the Father
Rom 12:1 seeks to worship him. 24 God is spirit, and those who worship him
2 Cor 3:17 must worship in spirit and truth." 25 The woman said to him, "I
Jn 1:14 know that Messiah is coming (he who is called Christ); when he
comes, he will show us all things." 26 Jesus said to her, "I who
Jn 9:37; 10:25 speak to you am he."

27 Just then the disciples came. They marvelled that he was
talking with a woman, but none said, "What do you wish?" or,
"Why are you talking with her?" 28 So the woman left her water
jar, and went away into the city, and said to the people, 29 "Come,
see a man who told me all that I ever did. Can this be the Christ?"
30 They went out of the city and were coming to him.

---

such as the Father seeks" (Vatican II, *Sacrosanctum Concilium*, 6).

4:25–26. This is the last stage in the Samaritan woman's conversion: she has come from acknowledging her sins to accepting the true teaching about worshipping the Father in spirit and truth. But she still has to recognize Jesus as the Messiah; on this subject she simply confesses her ignorance. Seeing that she is favourably disposed, Jesus explictly reveals that he is the Messiah: "I who speak to you am he".

These words of our Lord are especially significant: he declares that he is the Messiah, and he uses words—"I … am he"—which evoke the words Yahweh used to reveal himself to Moses (cf. Ex 3:14) and which on Jesus' lips indicate a revelation not only of his messiahship but also of his divinity (cf. Jn 8:24, 28, 58; 18:6).

4:27. "During the course of his life on earth, Jesus our Lord had all manner of insults heaped upon him and was mistreated in every way possible. Remember the way it was rumoured that he was a trouble-maker and how he was said to be possessed (cf. Mt 11:18)? At other times, demonstrations of his infinite Love were deliberately misinterpreted, and he was accused of being a friend of sinners (cf. Mt 9:11).

"Later on he, who personified penance and moderation, was accused of haunting the tables of the rich (cf. Lk 19:7). He was also contemptuously referred to as *fabri filius* (Mt 13:55), the carpenter's son, the worker's son, as if this were an insult. He allowed himself to be denounced as a glutton and a drunkard … He let his enemies accuse him of everything, except that he was not chaste. On this point he sealed their lips, because he wanted us to keep a vivid memory of his immaculate example—a wonderful example of purity, of cleanliness, of light, of a love that can set the whole world on fire in order to purify it.

"For myself, I always like to consider holy purity in the light of our Lord's own behaviour. In practising this virtue, what refinement he showed! See what St John says about Jesus when *fatigatus ex itinere, sedebat sic super fontem* (Jn 4:6), wearied as he was from the journey, he was sitting by the well. […]

[31]Meanwhile the disciples besought him, saying, "Rabbi, eat."
[32]But he said to them, "I have food to eat of which you do not
know." [33]So the disciples said to one another, "Has any one
brought him food?" [34]Jesus said to them, "My food is to do the Jn 5:36; 17:4
will of him who sent me, and to accomplish his work. [35]Do you Mt 9:37
not say, 'There are yet four months, then comes the harvest'? I tell Lk 10:2
you, lift up your eyes, and see how the fields are already white for
harvest. [36]He who reaps receives wages, and gathers fruit for eternal life, so that sower and reaper may rejoice together. [37]For here Mic 6:15
the saying holds true, 'One sows and another reaps.' [38]I sent you
to reap that for which you did not labour; others have laboured,
and you have entered into their labour."

"But tired though his body is, his thirst for souls is even greater. So when the Samaritan woman, the sinner, arrives, Christ with his priestly heart turns eagerly to save the lost sheep, and he forgets his tiredness, his hunger and his thirst.

"Our Lord was busy with this great work of charity when the Apostles came back from the village, and they *mirabantur quia cum muliere loquebatur* (Jn 4:27), they were astonished to find him talking to a woman, alone. How careful he was! What love he had for the beautiful virtue of holy purity, that virtue which helps us to be stronger, more manly, more fruitful, better able to work for God, and more capable of undertaking great things!" (St Josemaría Escrivá, *Friends of God*, 176).

4:28–30. Grace brings about an amazing change in this woman. Now her whole thinking centres around Jesus; she forgets what brought her to the well; she leaves her pitcher behind her and goes off to the town to tell people about her discovery. "The Apostles, when they were called, left their nets; this woman leaves her water jar and proclaims the Gospel, calling not just one person but influencing the whole city" (St John Chrysostom, *Hom. on St John*, 33). Every genuine conversion is necessarily projected towards others, in a desire to have them share in the joy of encountering Jesus.

4:32–38. Our Lord uses the occasion to speak about a spiritual form of food—doing the will of God. He has just brought about the conversion of a sinful woman and his spirit feels replete. The conversion of souls must be the apostles' food also, and the food of all those who through priestly ordination are sacramentally associated with Christ's ministry (cf. 1 Cor 4:9–15; 2 Cor 4:7–12; 11:27–29). Apostolic work sometimes means sowing, with no apparent results, and sometimes reaping where others sowed. The apostles will reap what was generously sown by the patriarchs and prophets and especially by Christ. And they in their turn must prepare the ground, with the same generosity, so that others can later reap the harvest.

But it is not only ministers who have this apostolic role: all the faithful are called to take part in the work of apostolate: "Since Christians have different gifts they should collaborate in the work of the Gospel, each according to his opportunity, ability, charism and ministry; all who sow and reap, plant and water, should be one so that 'working

39Many Samaritans from that city believed in him because of
the woman's testimony, "He told me all that I ever did." 40So when
the Samaritans came to him, they asked him to stay with them;
and he stayed there two days. 41And many more believed because
1 Jn 4:14 of his word. 42They said to the woman, "It is no longer because of
1 Tim 4:10 your words that we believe, for we have heard for ourselves, and
we know that this is indeed the Saviour of the world."
Mt 4:12 43After the two days he departed to Galilee. 44For Jesus himself
Mt 13:57 testified that a prophet has no honour in his own country. 45So
Mk 6:4 when he came to Galilee, the Galileans welcomed him, having
Lk 4:24 seen all that he had done in Jerusalem at the feast, for they too had
Jn 2:23 gone to the feast.

Curing of a royal official's son—the second sign worked by Jesus

Jn 2:1–9 46So he came again to Cana in Galilee, where he had made the
Mt 8:5ff water wine. And at Capernaum there was an official whose son

---

together for the same end in a free and orderly manner' they might together devote their powers to the building up of the Church" (Vatican II, *Ad gentes*, 28).

4:39–42. This episode shows a whole evangelization process at work, beginning with the Samaritan woman's enthusiasm. "The same thing happens today with those who are outside, who are not Christians: they receive tidings of Christ through Christian friends; like that woman, they learn of Christ through the Church; then they come to Christ, that is, they believe in Christ through this report, and then Jesus stays two days among them and many more believe, and believe more firmly, that he indeed is the Saviour of the world" (St Augustine, *In Ioann. Evang*., 15, 33).

4:46. St John is speaking about a royal official, probably in the service of Herod Antipas who, although he was only tetrarch or governor of Galilee (cf. Lk 3:1), was also referred to as king (cf. Mk 6:14). The official, therefore, would have been someone of high rank (v. 51), who lived in Capernaum, a town with a customs post. This is why St Jerome thought he must have been a *palatinus*, a palace courtier, as the corresponding Greek word implies.

4:48. Jesus seems to be addressing not so much the official as the people of Galilee who flock to him to get him to perform miracles and work wonders. On another occasion our Lord reproaches the towns of Chorazin, Bethsaida and Capernaum for their disbelief (Mt 11:21–23), because the miracles he worked there would have been enough to move the Phoenician cities of Tyre and Sidon, and even Sodom itself, to do penance. The Galileans in general were more inclined to watch him perform miracles than listen to his preaching. Later on, after the miracle of the multiplication of the loaves, they will look for Jesus to make him king—but they are slower to believe when he tells them about the Eucharist (Jn 6:15, 53, 62). Jesus asks people to have a strong, committed faith which, though it may draw support from miracles, does not require them. Be that as it

was ill. [47]When he heard that Jesus had come from Judea to Galilee, he went and begged him to come down and heal his son, for he was at the point of death. [48]Jesus therefore said to him, "Unless you see signs and wonders you will not believe." [49]The official said to him, "Sir, come down before my child dies." [50]Jesus said to him, "Go, your son will live." The man believed the word that Jesus spoke to him and went his way. [51]As he was going down, his servants met him and told him that his son was living. [52]So he asked them the hour when he began to mend, and they said to him, "Yesterday at the seventh hour the fever left him." [53]The father knew that was the hour when Jesus had said to him, "Your son will live"; and he himself believed, and all his household. [54]This was now the second sign that Jesus did when he had come from Judea to Galilee.

Lk 7:2

Jn 2:18
1 Cor 1:22

Acts 16:15–31

Jn 2:11–23

---

may, in all ages God continues to work miracles, which help bolster our faith.

"I'm not one for miracles. I have told you that in the Holy Gospel I can find more than enough miracles to confirm my faith. But I can't help pitying those Christians—pious people, 'apostles' many of them—who smile at the idea of extraordinary ways, of supernatural events. I feel the urge to tell them: Yes, this is still the age of miracles. We too would work them if we had faith!" (St Josemaría Escrivá, *The Way*, 583).

4:49–50. In spite of Jesus' apparent coldness, the official keeps trying: "Sir, come down before my child dies". Although his faith is imperfect, it did bring him to travel the 33 kilometres (20 miles) between Capernaum and Cana, and despite his important position here he was, begging our Lord for help. Jesus likes the man's perseverance and humility; he rewards his faith: "'*Si habueritis fidem, sicut granum sinapis!* If your faith were the size of a mustard seed ... !' What promises are contained in this exclamation of the Master!" (*The Way*, 585).

The Fathers compare this miracle with that of the centurion's servant, contrasting the amazing faith of the centurion—from the start—with the initially imperfect faith of this official from Capernaum. St John Chrysostom comments: "Here was a robust faith [in the case of this official]; therefore, Jesus made him the promise, so that we might learn from this man's devotion; his faith was as yet imperfect, and he did not clearly realize that Jesus could effect the cure at a distance; thus, the Lord, by not agreeing to go down to the man's house, wished us to learn the need to have faith" (*Hom. on St John*, 35).

4:53. The miracle is so convincing that this man and all his family become believers. All parents should do what they can to bring their household to the faith. As St Paul says, "If anyone does not provide for his relatives, and especially for his own family, he has disowned the faith, and is worse than an unbeliever" (1 Tim 5:8). In Acts 16:14, we are told that Lydia brought her whole household along with her to be baptized; Acts 18:8 mentions Crispus, the ruler of the synagogue, doing the same thing, as does the prison warden (Acts 16:33).

3. JESUS REVEALS HIS DIVINITY

Curing of a paralyzed man

5 [1]After this there was a feast of the Jews, and Jesus went up to
Jerusalem. [2]Now there is in Jerusalem by the Sheep Gate a
pool, in Hebrew called Bethzatha,[j] which has five porticoes. [3]In
these lay a multitude of invalids, blind, lame, paralyzed.[k] [5]One
man was there, who had been ill for thirty-eight years. [6]When
Jesus saw him and knew that he had been lying there a long time,
he said to him, "Do you want to be healed?" [7]The sick man
answered him, "Sir, I have no man to put me into the pool when
the water is troubled, and while I am going another steps down
Mt 9:6 before me." [8]Jesus said to him, "Rise, take up your pallet, and

---

5:1. We cannot be certain what festival this was; it probably refers to the Passover, known the world over at the time as the national festival of the Jewish people. But it could refer to another festival, Pentecost perhaps.

5:2. This pool was also called the "Probatic" pool because it was located on the outskirts of Jerusalem, beside the Probatic Gate or Sheep Gate (cf. Neh 3:1–32; 12:39) through which came the livestock to be sacrificed in the temple. Around the end of the nineteenth century the remains of a pool were discovered: excavated out of rock, it was rectangular in shape and was surrounded by four galleries or porches, with a fifth porch dividing the pool into two.

5:3–4. The Fathers teach that this pool is a symbol of Christian Baptism; but that whereas the pool of Bethzatha cured physical ailments, Baptism cures those of the soul; in Bethzatha's case only one person was cured, now and again; Baptism is available to everyone, at all times; in both cases God's power is shown through the medium of water (cf. Chrysostom, *Hom. on St John*, 36, 1).

The Sixto-Clementine edition of the Vulgate includes here, as a second part of v. 3 and all v. 4: "*Exspectantium aquae motum. [4]Angelus autem Domini descendebat secundum tempus in piscinam et movebatur aqua. Et qui prior descendisset in piscinam post motionem aquae sanus fiebat a quacumque detinebatur infirmitate*" [which translates as the RSV note **k** below]. The New Vulgate, however, omits this passage, assigning it to a footnote, because it does not appear in important Greek codexes and papyri, nor in many ancient translations.

5:14. The man may have come to the temple to thank God for his cure. Jesus goes over to him and reminds him that the health of the soul is more important than physical health.

Our Lord uses holy fear of God as motivation in the struggle against sin: "Sin no more, that nothing worse befall you". This holy fear is born out of

---

j. Other ancient authorities read *Bethesda*, others *Bethsaida* **k.** Other ancient authorities insert, wholly or in part, *waiting for the moving of the water; [4]for an angel of the Lord went down at certain seasons into the pool, and troubled the water: whoever stepped in first after the troubling of the water was healed of whatever disease he had*

walk." 9And at once the man was healed, and he took up his pallet Jn 9:14
and walked.
Now that day was the sabbath. 10So the Jews said to the man Jer 17:21
who was cured, "It is the sabbath, it is not lawful for you to carry Lk 6:2
your pallet." 11But he answered them, "The man who healed me
said to me, 'Take up your pallet, and walk.'" 12They asked him, Lk 5:24
"Who is the man who said to you, 'Take up your pallet, and
walk'?" 13Now the man who had been healed did not know who it
was, for Jesus had withdrawn, as there was a crowd in the place.
14Afterward, Jesus found him in the temple, and said to him, "See, Jn 8:11
you are well! Sin no more, that nothing worse befall you." 15The
man went away and told the Jews that it was Jesus who had
healed him. 16And this was why the Jews persecuted Jesus, Mt 12:14

---

respect for God our Father; it is perfectly compatible with love. Just as children love and respect their parents and try to avoid annoying them partly because they are afraid of being punished, so we should fight against sin firstly because it is an offence against God, but also because we can be punished in this life and, above all, in the next.

5:16–18. The Law of Moses established the sabbath as a weekly day of rest. Through keeping the sabbath the Jews felt they were imitating God, who rested from the work of creation on the seventh day. St Thomas Aquinas observes that Jesus rejects this strict interpretation: "(The Jews), in their desire to imitate God, did nothing on the sabbath, as if God on that day had ceased absolutely to act. It is true that he rested on the sabbath from his work of creating new creatures, but he is always continually at work, maintaining them in existence. […] God is the cause of all things in the sense that he also maintains them in existence; for if for one moment he were to stop exercising his power, at that very moment everything that nature contains would cease to exist" (*Comm. on St John*, in loc.).

"My Father is working still, and I am working": we have already said that God is continually acting. Since the Son acts together with the Father, who with the Holy Spirit are the one and only God, our Lord Jesus Christ, the Son of God, can say that he is always working. These words of Jesus contain an implicit reference to his divinity: the Jews realize this and they want to kill him because they consider it blasphemous. "We all call God our Father, who is in heaven (Is 63:16; 64:8). Therefore, they were angry, not at this, that he said God was his Father, but that he said it in quite another way than men. Notice: the Jews understand what Arians do not understand. Arians affirm the Son to be not equal to the Father, and that was why their heresy was driven from the Church. Here, even the blind, even the slayers of Christ, understand the words of Christ" (St Augustine, *In Ioann. Evang.*, 17, 16). We call God our Father because through grace we are his adopted children; Jesus calls him his Father because he is his Son by nature. This is why he says after the Resurrection: "I am ascending to my Father and your Father" (Jn 20:17), making a clear distinction between the two ways of being a son of God.

Jn 9:4 because he did this on the sabbath. 17But Jesus answered them,
Jn 7:1, 19, 30; 10:33–36 "My Father is working still, and I am working." 18This was why
the Jews sought all the more to kill him, because he not only
broke the sabbath* but also called God his Father, making himself
equal with God.

The authority of the Son of God

Jn 3:11, 32; 5:30 19Jesus said to them, "Truly, truly, I say to you, the Son can do
nothing of his own accord, but only what he sees the Father doing;
Jn 3:35 for whatever he does, that the Son does likewise. 20For the Father

---

5:19. Jesus speaks of the equality and also the distinction between Father and Son. The two are equal: all the Son's power is the Father's, all the Son does the Father does; but they are two distinct persons: which is why the Son does what he has seen the Father do.

These words of our Lord should not be taken to mean that the Son sees what the Father does and then does it himself, like a disciple imitating his master; he says what he says to show that the Father's powers are communicated to the Son through generation. The word "see" is used because men come to know things through the senses, particularly through sight; to say that the Son sees what the Father does is a way of referring to all the powers which he receives from him for all eternity (cf. St Thomas Aquinas, *Comm. on St John,* in loc.).

5:20–21. When he says that the Father shows the Son "all that he himself is doing", this means that Christ can do the same as the Father. Thus, when Jesus does things which are proper to God, he is testifying to his divinity through them (cf. v. 36).

"Greater works": this may be a reference to the miracles Jesus will work during his lifetime and to his authority to execute judgment. But *the* miracle of Jesus was his own resurrection, the cause and pledge of our own (cf. 1 Cor 15:20ff), and our passport to supernatural life. Christ, like his Father, has unlimited power to communicate life. This teaching is developed in verses 22–29.

5:22–30. Authority to judge has also been given by the Father to the Incarnate Word. Whoever does not believe in Christ and in his word will be condemned (cf. 3:18). We must accept Jesus Christ's lordship; by doing so we honour the Father; if we do not know the Son we do not know the Father who sent him (v. 23). Through accepting Christ, through accepting his word, we gain eternal life and are freed from condemnation. He, who has taken on human nature which he will retain for ever, has been established as our judge, and his judgment is just, because he seeks to fulfil the will of the Father who sent him, and he does nothing on his own account: in other words, his human will is perfectly at one with his divine will; which is why Jesus can say that he does not do his own will but the will of him who sent him.

5:22. God, being Creator of the world, is the supreme Judge of all creation. He alone can know with absolute certainty whether the people and things he has created achieve the end he has envisaged for them. Jesus Christ, the Incarnate Word, has received divine authority (cf.

loves the Son, and shows him all that he himself is doing; and
greater works than these will he show him, that you may marvel. Deut 32:39
[21]For as the Father raises the dead and gives them life, so also the 1 Sam 2:6 2 Kings 5:7
Son gives life to whom he will. [22]The Father judges no one, but Dan 7, 10, 13, 14
has given all judgment to the Son, [23]that all may honour the Son, Acts 10:42
even as they honour the Father. He who does not honour the Son Lk 10:16
does not honour the Father who sent him. [24]Truly, truly, I say to Phil 2:10, 11 1 Jn 2:23
you, he who hears my word and believes him who sent me, has Jn 3:16, 18; 8:51
eternal life; he does not come into judgment, but has passed from 1 Jn 3:14
death to life.

Mt 11:27; 28:18; Dan 7:14), including authority to judge mankind. Now, it is God's will that everyone should be saved: Christ did not come to condemn the world but to save it (cf. Jn 12:47). Only someone who refuses to accept the divine mission of the Son puts himself outside the pale of salvation. As the Church's Magisterium teaches: "He claimed judicial power as received from his Father, when the Jews accused him of breaking the sabbath by the miraculous cure of a sick man. [...] In this power is included the right of rewarding and punishing all men, even in this life" (Pius XI, *Quas primas, Dz-Sch* 3677). Jesus Christ, therefore, is the Judge of the living and the dead, and will reward everyone according to his works (cf. 1 Pet 1:17).

"We have, I admit, a rigorous account to give of our sins; but who will be our judge? The Father [...] has given all judgment to the Son. Let us be comforted: the eternal Father has placed our cause in the hands of our Redeemer himself. St Paul encourages us, saying, Who is [the judge] who is to condemn us? It is Jesus Christ, who died [...] who indeed intercedes for us (Rom 8:34). It is the Saviour himself, who, in order that he should not condemn us to eternal death, has condemned himself to death for our sake, and who, not content with this, still continues to intercede for us in heaven with God his Father" (St Alphonsus Liguori, *The Love of Our Lord Jesus Christ*, chap. 3).

5:24. There is also a close connexion between hearing the word of Christ and believing in him who has sent him, that is, in the Father. Whatever Jesus Christ says is divine revelation; therefore, accepting Jesus' words is equivalent to believing in God the Father: "He who believes in me, believes not in me, but in him who sent me. [...] For I have not spoken on my own authority; the Father who sent me has himself given me commandment what to say and what to speak" (Jn 12:44, 49).

A person with faith is on the way to eternal life, because even in this earthly life he is sharing in divine life, which is eternal; but he has not yet attained eternal life in a definitive way (for he can lose it), nor in a full way: "Beloved, we are God's children now; it does not yet appear what we shall be, but we know that when he appears we shall be like him" (1 Jn 3:2). If a person stays firm in the faith and lives up to its demands, God's judgment will not condemn him but save him.

Therefore, it makes sense to strive, with the help of grace, to live a life consistent with the faith: "If men go to so much trouble and effort to live here a little longer, ought they not strive so much

Mt 8:22 Eph 2:5f; 5:14 Jn 1:1–4; 6:53, 57 25“Truly, truly, I say to you, the hour is coming, and now is,
when the dead will hear the voice of the Son of God, and those
who hear will live. 26For as the Father has life in himself, so he
Dan 7:13, 14, 22 has granted the Son also to have life in himself, 27and has given
him authority to execute judgment, because he is the Son of man.
28Do not marvel at this; for the hour is coming when all who are
Jn 6:40 Dan12:2 Mt 16:27 in the tombs will hear his voice 29and come forth, those who have
done good, to the resurrection of life, and those who have done
evil, to the resurrection of judgment.

Jn 5:19; 6:38 30“I can do nothing on my own authority; as I hear, I judge; and
my judgment is just, because I seek not my own will but the will
Jn 8:14 of him who sent me. 31If I bear witness to myself, my testimony is
not true; 32there is another who bears witness to me, and I know
Jn 5:36–37 1 Jn 5:9 that the testimony which he bears to me is true. 33You sent to John,

---

harder to live eternally?” (St Augustine, *De verb. Dom. serm.*, 64).

5:25–30. These verses bring the first part of our Lord’s discourse to a close (it runs from 5:19 to 5:47); its core is a revelation about his relationship with his Father. To understand the statement our Lord makes here we need to remember that, because he is a single (divine) person, a single subject of operations, a single I, he is expressing in human words not only his sentiments as a man but also the deepest dimension of his being: he is the Son of God, both in his generation in eternity by the Father, and in his generation in time through taking up human nature. Hence Jesus Christ has a profound awareness (so profound that we cannot even imagine it) of his Sonship, which leads him to treat his Father with a very special intimacy, with love and also with respect; he is aware also of his equality with the Father; therefore when he speaks about the Father having given him life (v. 26) or authority (v. 27), it is not that he has received part of the Father’s life or authority: he has received absolutely all of it, without the Father losing any.

“Do you perceive how their equality is shown and that they differ in one respect only, namely, that one is the Father, while the other is the Son? The expression ‘he has given’ implies this distinction only, and shows that all the other attributes are equal and without difference. From this it is clear that he does everything with as much authority and power as the Father and is not endowed with power from some outside source, for he has life as the Father has” (St John Chrysostom, *Hom. on St John*, 39, 3).

One of the amazing things about these passages of the Gospel is how Jesus manages to express the sentiments of God-Man despite the limitations of human language. Christ, true God, true man, is a mystery which the Christian should contemplate even though he cannot understand it: he feels bathed in a light so strong that it is beyond understanding, yet fills his soul with faith and with a desire to worship his Lord.

5:31–40. Because Jesus is Son of God, his own word is self-sufficient, it needs no corroboration (cf. 8:18); but, as on other occasions, he accommodates himself to human customs and to the mental outlook of his hearers: he anticipates a possible objection from the Jews to the effect that it is not enough for a person to

and he has borne witness to the truth. [34]Not that the testimony Jn 1:19–34
which I receive is from man; but I say this that you may be saved.
[35]He was a burning and shining lamp, and you were willing to Jn 1:8
rejoice for a while in his light. [36]But the testimony which I have is Lk 1:17
greater than that of John; for the works which the Father has Jn 1:33; 3:2 1 Jn 5:9
granted me to accomplish, these very works which I am doing,
bear me witness that the Father has sent me. [37]And the Father who Deut 4:12
sent me has himself borne witness to me. His voice you have never Mt 3:17
heard, his form you have never seen; [38]and you do not have his
word abiding in you, for you do not believe him whom he has sent.
[39]You search the scriptures, because you think that in them you Lk 24:27, 44
have eternal life; and it is they that bear witness to me; [40]yet you 2 Tim 3:15–17
refuse to come to me that you may have life. [41]I do not receive 1 Pet 1:11
glory from men. [42]But I know that you have not the love of God

---

testify in his own cause (cf. Deut 19:15) and he explains that what he is saying is endorsed by four witnesses—John the Baptist, his own miracles, the Father, and the Sacred Scriptures of the Old Testament.

John the Baptist bore witness that Jesus was the Son of God (1:34). Although Jesus had no need to have recourse to any man's testimony, not even that of a great prophet, John's testimony was given for the sake of the Jews, that they might recognize the Messiah. Jesus can also point to another testimony, better than that of the Baptist—the miracles he has worked, which are, for anyone who examines them honestly, unmistakable signs of his divine power, which comes from the Father; Jesus' miracles, then, are a form of witness the Father bears concerning his Son, whom he has sent into the world. The Father manifests the divinity of Jesus on other occasions—at his Baptism (cf. 1:31–34); at the Transfiguration (cf. Mt 17:1–8), and later, in the presence of the whole crowd (cf. Jn 12:28–30).

Jesus appeals to another divine testimony—that of the Sacred Scriptures. These speak of him, but the Jews fail to grasp the Scriptures' true meaning, because they read them without letting themselves be enlightened by him whom God has sent and in whom all the prophecies are fulfilled: "The economy of the Old Testament was deliberately so orientated that it should prepare for and declare in prophecy the coming of Christ, redeemer of all men, and of the messianic kingdom (cf. Lk 24:44; Jn 5:39; 1 Pet 1:10), and should indicate it by means of different types (cf. 1 Cor 10:11). [...] Christians should accept with veneration these writings which give expression to a lively sense of God, which are a storehouse of sublime teaching on God and of sound wisdom on human life, as well as a wonderful treasury of prayers; in them, too, the mystery of our salvation is present in a hidden way" (Vatican II, *Dei Verbum*, 15).

5:41–47. Jesus identifies three obstacles preventing his hearers from recognizing that he is the Messiah and Son of God—their lack of love of God, their striving after human glory and their prejudiced interpretation of sacred texts. His defence of his own actions and of his relationship with the Father might lead his adversaries to think that he was looking for human glory. But the testimonies he has adduced

Jn 7:18
Mt 24:5

within you. [43]I have come in my Father's name, and you do not
receive me; if another comes in his own name, him you will
receive. [44]How can you believe, who receive glory from one
another and do not seek the glory that comes from the only God?
[45]Do not think that I shall accuse you to the Father; it is Moses
who accuses you, on whom you set your hope. [46]If you believed
Moses, you would believe me, for he wrote of me. [47]But if you do
not believe his writings, how will you believe my words?"

Jn 12:43
Mt 23:5–7
Rom 2:29
Deut 31:26
Jn 7:19
Gen 3:15; 49:10
Deut 18:15
Lk 16:31

4. JESUS IS THE BREAD OF LIFE

Miracle of the loaves and fish

Mt 14:13–21
Mk 6:32–44
Lk 9:10–17

6 [1]After this Jesus went to the other side of the Sea of Galilee,
which is the Sea of Tiberias. [2]And a multitude followed him,

---

(the Baptist, the miracles, the Father and the Scriptures) show clearly that it is not he who is seeking his glory, and that the Jews oppose him not out of love of God or in defence of God's honour, but for unworthy reasons or because of their merely human outlook.

The Old Testament, therefore, leads a person towards recognizing who Jesus Christ is (cf. Jn 1:45; 2:17, 22; 5:39, 46; 12:16, 41); yet the Jews remain unbelievers because their attitude is wrong: they have reduced the messianic promises in the sacred books to the level of mere nationalistic aspirations. This outlook, which is in no way supernatural, closes their soul to Jesus' words and actions and prevents them from seeing that the ancient prophecies are coming true in him (cf. 2 Cor 3:14–16).

6:1. This is the second lake formed by the river Jordan. It is sometimes described in the Gospels as the "lake of Gennesaret" (Lk 5:1), because that is the name of the area on the north-eastern bank of the lake, and sometimes as the "Sea of Galilee" (Mt 4:18; 15:29; Mk 1:16; 7:31), after the region in which it is located. St John also calls it the "Sea of Tiberias" (cf. 21:1), after the city of that name which Herod Antipas founded and named after the Emperor Tiberius. In Jesus' time there were a number of towns on the shore of this lake—Tiberias, Magdala, Capernaum, Bethsaida, etc.—and the shore was often the setting for his preaching.

6:2. Although St John refers to only seven miracles and does not mention others which are reported in the Synoptics, in this verse and more expressly at the end of his Gospel (20:30; 21:25) he says that the Lord worked many miracles; the reason why the Evangelist, under God's inspiration, chose these seven must surely be because they best suited his purpose—to highlight certain facets of the mystery of Christ. He now goes on to recount the miracle of the multiplication of the loaves and the fish, a miracle directly connected with the discourses at Capernaum in which Jesus presents himself as "the bread of life" (6:35, 48).

6:4. St John's Gospel often mentions Jewish feasts when referring to events in

because they saw the signs which he did on those who were dis-
eased. 3Jesus went up into the hills, and there sat down with his Mt 5:1
disciples. 4Now the Passover, the feast of the Jews, was at hand. Jn 2:13 Jn 11:15
5Lifting up his eyes, then, and seeing that a multitude was coming
to him, Jesus said to Philip, "How are we to buy bread, so that Lk 22:1
these people may eat?" 6This he said to test them, for he himself
knew what he would do. 7Philip answered him, "Two hundred
denarii[1] would not buy enough bread for each of them to get a
little." 8One of his disciples, Andrew, Simon Peter's brother, said
to him, 9"There is a lad here who has five barley loaves and two 2 Kings
fish; but what are they among so many?" 10Jesus said, "Make the 4:42–44
people sit down." Now there was much grass in the place; so the
men sat down, in number about five thousand. 11Jesus then took
the loaves, and when he had given thanks, he distributed them to
those who were seated; so also the fish, as much as they wanted.

---

our Lord's public ministry—as is the case here (cf. pp. 530–532).

Shortly before this Passover Jesus works the miracle of the multiplication of the loaves and the fish, which prefigures the Christian Easter and the mystery of the Blessed Eucharist, as he himself explains in the discourse, beginning at v. 26 in which he promises himself as nourishment for our souls.

6:5–9. Jesus is sensitive to people's material and spiritual needs. Here we see him take the initiative to satisfy the hunger of the crowd of people who have been following him.

Through these conversations and the miracle he is going to work, Jesus also teaches his disciples to trust in him whenever they meet up with difficulties in their apostolic endeavours in the future: they should engage in them using whatever resources they have—even if they are plainly inadequate, as was the case with the five loaves and two fish. He will supply what is lacking. In the Christian life we must put what we have at the service of our Lord, even if we do not think it amounts to very much. He can make meagre resources productive.

"We must, then, have faith and not be dispirited. We must not be stopped by any kind of human calculation. To overcome the obstacles we have to throw ourselves into the task so that the very effort we make will open up new paths" (St J. Escrivá, *Christ Is Passing By*, 160).

6:10. The Evangelist gives us an apparently unimportant piece of information: "there was much grass in the place." This indicates that the miracle took place in the height of the Palestinian spring, very near the Passover, as mentioned in v. 4. There are very few big meadows in Palestine; even today there is one on the eastern bank of the lake of Gennesaret, called el-Batihah, where five thousand people could fit seated: it may have been the site of this miracle.

6:11. The account of the miracle begins with almost the very same words as those which the Synoptics and St Paul use to describe the institution of the Eucharist (cf. Mt 26:26; Mk 14:22; Lk 22:19; 1

1. The denarius was a day's wage for a labourer

12 And when they had eaten their fill, he told his disciples, "Gather
up the fragments left over, that nothing may be lost." 13 So they
gathered them up and filled twelve baskets with fragments from
Deut 18:15 the five barley loaves, left by those who had eaten. 14 When the
people saw the sign which he had done, they said, "This is indeed
the prophet who is to come into the world!"
Jn 12:13; 18:36 15 Perceiving then that they were about to come and take him
by force to make him king, Jesus withdrew again to the hills by
himself.

Jesus walks on water

Mt 14:22f
Mk 6:45–52 16 When evening came, his disciples went down to the sea, 17 got
into a boat, and started across the sea to Capernaum. It was now

---

Cor 11:25). This indicates that the miracle, in addition to being an expression of Jesus' mercy towards the needy, is a symbol of the Blessed Eucharist, about which our Lord will speak a little later on (cf. Jn 6:26–58).

6:12–13. The profusion of detail shows how accurate this narrative is—the names of the apostles who address our Lord (vv. 5, 8), the fact that they were barley loaves (v. 9), the boy who provided the wherewithal (v. 9) and, finally, Jesus telling them to gather up the left-overs.

This miracle shows Jesus' divine power over matter, and his largesse recalls the abundance of messianic benefits which the prophets had foretold (cf. Jer 31:14).

Christ's instruction to pick up the left-overs teaches us that material resources are gifts of God and should not be wasted: they should be used in a spirit of poverty (cf. the note on Mk 6:42). In this connexion Paul VI pointed out that "after liberally feeding the crowds, the Lord told his disciples to gather up what was left over, lest anything should be lost (cf. Jn 6:12). What an excellent lesson in thrift—in the finest and fullest meaning of the term—for our age, given as it is to wastefulness! It carries with it the condemnation of a whole concept of society wherein consumption tends to become an end in itself, with contempt for the needy, and to the detriment, ultimately, of those very people who believed themselves to be its beneficiaries, having become incapable of perceiving that man is called to a higher destiny" (Paul VI, Address to participants at the World Food Conference, 9 November 1974).

6:14–15. The faith which the miracle causes in the hearts of these people is still very imperfect: they recognize him as the Messiah promised in the Old Testament (cf. Deut 18:15), but they are thinking in terms of an earthly, political messianism; they want to make him king because they think the Messiah's function is to free them from Roman domination.

Our Lord, who later on (vv. 26–27) will explain the true meaning of the multiplication of the loaves and the fish, simply goes away, to avoid the people proclaiming him for what he is not. In his dialogue with Pilate (cf. Jn 18:36) he will explain that his kingship "is not of this world": "The Gospels clearly show that for Jesus anything that would alter his mission as the Servant of Yahweh was a temptation (cf. Mt 4:8; Lk 4:5). He does

dark, and Jesus had not yet come to them. [18]The sea rose because Mt 8:24
a strong wind was blowing. [19]When they had rowed about three or Ps 77:19
four miles,[m] they saw Jesus walking on the sea and drawing near
to the boat. They were frightened, [20]but he said to them, "It is I; do
not be afraid." [21]Then they were glad to take him into the boat,
and immediately the boat was at the land to which they were
going.

The people look for Jesus

[22]On the next day the people who remained on the other side of
the sea saw that there had been only one boat there, and that Jesus
had not entered the boat with his disciples, but that his disciples
had gone away alone. [23]However, boats from Tiberias came near Jn 6:11

---

not accept the position of those who mixed the things of God with merely political attitudes (cf. Mt 22:21; Mk 12:17; Jn 18:36). […] The perspective of his mission is much deeper. It consists in complete salvation through transforming, peacemaking, pardoning, and reconciling love. There is no doubt, moreover, that all this makes many demands on the Christian who wishes truly to serve his least brethren, the poor, the needy, the outcast; in a word, all those who in their lives reflect the sorrowing face of the Lord (cf. *Lumen gentium*, 8)" (John Paul II, Opening Address to the third general conference of Latin American Bishops, 28 January 1979).

Christianity, therefore, must not be confused with any social or political ideology, however excellent. "I do not approve of committed Christians in the world forming a political-religious movement. That would be madness, even if it were motivated by a desire to spread the spirit of Christ in all the activities of men. What we have to do is put God in the heart of every single person, no matter who he is. Let us try to speak then in such a way that every Christian is able to bear witness to the faith he professes by example and word in his own circumstances, which are determined alike by his place in the Church and in civil life, as well as by ongoing events.

"By the very fact of being a man, a Christian has a full right to live in the world. If he lets Christ live and reign in his heart, he will feel—quite noticeably—the saving effectiveness of our Lord in everything he does" (St Josemaría Escrivá, *Christ Is Passing By*, 183).

6:16–21. It seems the disciples were disconcerted because darkness had fallen, the sea was getting rough and Jesus had still not appeared. But our Lord does not abandon them; when they had been rowing for some five kilometres (three miles), he arrives unexpectedly, walking on the water—to strengthen their faith, which was still weak (cf. the notes on Mt 14:22–23 and Mk 6:48, 52).

In meditating on this episode Christian tradition has seen the boat as symbolizing the Church, which will have to cope with many difficulties and which our Lord has promised to help all through the centuries (cf. Mt 28:20); the Church, therefore, will always remain firm. St Thomas Aquinas comments: "The

m. Greek *twenty-five or thirty stadia*

the place where they ate the bread after the Lord had given thanks.
[24]So when the people saw that Jesus was not there, nor his disciples, they themselves got into the boats and went to Capernaum, seeking Jesus. [25]When they found him on the other side of the sea, they said to him, "Rabbi, when did you come here?"

The discourse on the Bread of Life

[26]Jesus answered them, "Truly, truly, I say to you, you seek me, not because you saw signs, but because you ate your fill of the loaves. [27]Do not labour for the food which perishes, but for the food which endures to eternal life, which the Son of man will give to you; for on him has God the Father set his seal." [28]Then

Jn 4:14; 5:36
Mt 16:12

wind symbolizes the temptations and persecution the Church will suffer due to lack of love. For, as St Augustine says, when love grows cold, the sea becomes rougher and the boat begins to founder. Yet the wind, the storm, the waves and the darkness will fail to put it off course and wreck it" (*Comm. on St John*, in loc.).

6:26. Our Lord begins by pointing out that their attitudes are wrong: if they have the right attitude they will be able to understand his teaching in the eucharistic discourse. "You seek me", St Augustine comments, "for the flesh, not for the spirit. How many seek Jesus for no other purpose than that he may do them good in this present life! […] Scarcely ever is Jesus sought for Jesus' sake" (*In Ioann. Evang*., 25, 10).

This verse marks the beginning of the discourse on the bread of life which goes up to v. 58. It opens with an introduction in the form of a dialogue between Jesus and the Jews (vv. 25–34), in which our Lord reveals himself as the bringer of the messianic gifts. Then comes the first part of the discourse (vv. 35–47), in which Jesus presents himself as the Bread of Life, in the sense that faith in him is food for eternal life. In the second part (vv. 48–58) Christ reveals the mystery of the Eucharist: he is the Bread of Life who gives himself sacramentally as genuine food.

6:27. Bodily food helps keep us alive in this world; spiritual food sustains and develops supernatural life, which will last forever in heaven. This food, which only God can give us, consists mainly in the gift of faith and sanctifying grace. Through God's infinite love we are given, in the Blessed Eucharist, the very author of these gifts, Jesus Christ, as nourishment for our souls.

"On him has God the Father set his seal": our Lord here refers to the authority by virtue of which he can give men the gifts he has referred to: for, being God and man, Jesus' human nature is the instrument by means of which the second Person of the Blessed Trinity acts. St Thomas Aquinas comments on this sentence as follows: "What the Son of Man will give he possesses through his superiority over all other men in his singular and outstanding fulness of grace … . When a seal is impressed on wax, the wax receives the complete form of the seal. So it is that the Son received the entire form of the Father. This occurred in two ways; eternally (eternal genera-

they said to him, “What must we do, to be doing the works of
God?” 29Jesus answered them, “This is the work of God, that you 1 Jn 3:23
believe in him whom he has sent.” 30So they said to him, “Then
what sign do you do, that we may see, and believe you? What Jn 2:18 Mk 8:11
work do you perform? 31Our fathers ate the manna in the wilder- Ex 16:13–14
ness; as it is written, ‘He gave them bread from heaven to eat.’” Ps 78:24f Wis 16:20
32Jesus then said to them, “Truly, truly, I say to you, it was not Jn 6:49
Moses who gave you the bread from heaven; my Father gives
you the true bread from heaven. 33For the bread of God is that
which comes down from heaven, and gives life to the world.” Jn 6:51
34They said to him, “Lord, give us this bread always.”

---

tion), which is not referred to here because the seal and the sealed are different in nature from one another; what is referred to here is the other manner, that is, the mystery of the Incarnation, whereby God the Father impressed on human nature the Word, who is the reflection and the very stamp of God’s nature, as Hebrews 1:3 says” (*Comm. on St John*, in loc.).

6:28–34. This dialogue between Jesus and his hearers is reminiscent of the episode of the Samaritan woman (cf. Jn 4:11–15). On that occasion Jesus was speaking about water springing up to eternal life; here, he speaks of bread coming down from heaven to give life to the world. There, the woman was asking Jesus if he was greater than Jacob; here the people want to know if he can compare with Moses (cf. Ex 16:13). “The Lord spoke of himself in a way that made him seem superior to Moses, for Moses never dared to say that he would give food which would never perish but would endure to eternal life. Jesus promises much more than Moses. Moses promised a kingdom, and a land flowing with milk and honey, good health and other temporal blessings […], plenty for the belly, but food which perishes; whereas Christ promised food which never perishes but which endures forever” (St Augustine, *In Ioann. Evang.*, 25:12).

These people know that the manna—food which the Jews collected every day during their journey through the wilderness (cf. Ex 16:13ff)—symbolized messianic blessings; which was why they asked our Lord for a dramatic sign like the manna. But there was no way they could suspect that the manna was a figure of a great supernatural messianic gift which Christ was bringing to mankind—the Blessed Eucharist. In this dialogue and in the first part of the discourse (vv. 35–47), the main thing Jesus is trying to do is bring them to make an act of faith in him, so that he can then openly reveal to them the mystery of the Blessed Eucharist—that he is the bread “which comes down from heaven, and gives life to the world” (v. 33). Also, St Paul explains that the manna and the other marvels which happened in the wilderness were a clear prefiguring of Jesus Christ (cf. 1 Cor 10:3–4). The disbelieving attitude of these Jews prevented them from accepting what Jesus revealed. To accept the mystery of the Eucharist, faith is required, as Paul VI stressed: “In the first place we want to remind you that the Eucharist is a very great mystery; strictly speaking, to use the words of sacred liturgy, it is ‘the mystery of faith’. This is

Jesus is the one who reveals the Father

Jn 4:14; 6:48; [35]Jesus said to them, "I am the bread of life; he who comes to me
7:37 shall not hunger, and he who believes in me shall never thirst. [36]But
Jn 6:26–29 I said to you that you have seen me and yet do not believe. [37]All
Jn 17:6–8 that the Father gives me will come to me; and him who comes to
Mt 11:28 me I will not cast out. [38]For I have come down from heaven, not to
Jn 4:34 do my own will, but the will of him who sent me; [39]and this is the
Mt 26:39 will of him who sent me, that I should lose nothing of all that he
Jn 10:28f; 17:12 has given me, but raise it up on the last day. [40]For this is the will of
Jn 5:29; 11:42 my Father, that every one who sees the Son and believes in him
should have eternal life; and I will raise him up at the last day."

---

something well known to you but it is essential to the purpose of rejecting any poisonous rationalism. Many martyrs have witnessed to it with their blood. Distinguished Fathers and Doctors of the Church in unbroken succession have taught and professed it. [...] We must, therefore, approach this mystery, above all, with humble reverence, not following human arguments, which ought to be hushed, but in steadfast adherence to divine revelation" (*Mysterium fidei*).

6:35. Going to Jesus means believing in him, for it is through faith that we approach our Lord. Jesus uses the metaphor of food and drink to show that he is the one who really meets all man's noblest aspirations: "How beautiful is our Catholic faith! It provides a solution for all our anxieties, calms our minds and fills our hearts with hope" (St Josemaría Escrivá, *The Way*, 582).

6:37–40. Jesus clearly reveals that he is the one sent by the Father. This is something St John the Baptist proclaimed earlier on (Jn 3:33–36), and Jesus himself stated it in his dialogue with Nicodemus (Jn 3:17–21) and announced publicly to the Jews in Jerusalem (Jn 5:20–30). Since Jesus is the one sent by the Father, the bread of life come down from heaven to give life to the world, everyone who believes in him has eternal life, for it is God's will that everyone should be saved through Jesus Christ. These words of Jesus contain three mysteries: 1) that of faith in Jesus Christ, which means "going to Jesus", accepting his miracles (signs) and his words; 2) the mystery of the resurrection of believers, something which begins in this life through faith and becomes fully true in heaven; 3) the mystery of predestination, the will of our Father in heaven that all men be saved. These solemn words of our Lord fill the believer with hope.

St Augustine, commenting on vv. 37 and 38, praises the humility of Jesus, the perfect model for the humility of the Christian: Jesus chose not to do his own will but that of the Father who sent him: "Humbly am I come, to teach humility am I come, as the master of humility am I come; he who comes to me is incorporated in me; he who comes to me, becomes humble; he who cleaves to me will be humble, for he does not his will but God's" (*In Ioann. Evang*., 25, 15 and 16).

6:42. This is the second and last time St John mentions St Joseph in his Gospel, putting on record the general, though mistaken, opinion of those who knew Jesus and regarded him as the son of Joseph (cf. Jn 1:45; Lk 3:23; 4:22; Mt 13:55). Conceived in the virginal womb

41The Jews then murmured at him, because he said, "I am the Jn 6:61
bread which came down from heaven." 42They said, "Is not this
Jesus, the son of Joseph, whose father and mother we know? How Lk 4:22
does he now say, 'I have come down from heaven'?" 43Jesus
answered them, "Do not murmur among yourselves. 44No one can Jn 6:65
come to me unless the Father who sent me draws him; and I will
raise him up on the last day. 45It is written in the prophets, 'And Is 54:13
they shall all be taught by God.' Every one who has heard and Jer 31:33f
learned from the Father comes to me. 46Not that any one has seen
the Father except him who is from God; he has seen the Father. Jn 1:18

---

of Mary by the action of the Holy Spirit, our Lord's only Father was God himself (cf. the note on Jn 5:18). However, St Joseph acted as Jesus' father on earth, as God had planned (cf. the notes on Mt 1:16, 18). Therefore, Joseph was called the father of Jesus and he certainly was extremely faithful in fulfilling his mission to look after Jesus. St Augustine explains St Joseph's fatherhood in this way: "Not only does Joseph deserve the name of father: he deserves it more than anyone else. In what way was he a father? As profoundly as his fatherhood was chaste. Some people thought that he was the father of our Lord Jesus Christ in the same way as others are fathers, begetting according to the flesh and not receiving their children as fruit of their spiritual affection. That is why St Luke says that they supposed he was the father of Jesus. Why does he say that they only supposed it? Because human thoughts and judgments are based on what normally happens. And our Lord was not born of the seed of Joseph. However, to the piety and charity of Joseph a son was born to him of the Virgin Mary, who was the Son of God" (*Sermons*, 51, 20).

In this verse, as elsewhere (cf. Jn 4:29; 7:42), St John put on record the people's ignorance, whereas he and his readers knew the truth about Jesus. The Jews' objection is not directly refuted; it is simply reported, on the assumption that it presents no difficulty to the Christian reader, to whom the Gospel is addressed.

6:44–45. Seeking Jesus until one finds him is a free gift which no one can obtain through his own efforts, although everyone should try to be well disposed to receiving it. The Magisterium of the Church has recalled this teaching in Vatican II: "Before this faith can be exercised, man must have the grace of God to move and assist him; he must have the interior help of the Holy Spirit, who moves the heart and converts it to God, who opens the eyes of the mind and makes it easy for all to accept and believe the truth" (*Dei Verbum*, 5).

When Jesus says "They shall all be taught by God", he is evoking Isaiah 54:13 and Jeremiah 31:33ff, where the prophets refer to the future Covenant which God will establish with his people when the Messiah comes, the Covenant which will be sealed forever with the blood of the Messiah and which God will write on their hearts (cf. Is 53:10–12; Jer 31:31–34).

The last sentence of v. 45 refers to God's revelation through the prophets and especially through Jesus Christ.

6:46. Men can know God the Father only through Jesus Christ, because only he has seen the Father, whom he has

Jn 3:16 Jn 6:35 47 Truly, truly, I say to you, he who believes has eternal life.

Jesus is the Bread of Life in the Eucharist

Jn 6:31f 48 I am the bread of life. 49 Your fathers ate the manna in the wilder-
1 Cor 10:3–5 ness, and they died. 50 This is the bread which comes down from
heaven, that a man may eat of it and not die. 51 I am the living
bread* which came down from heaven; if any one eats of this
Heb 10:5–10 bread, he will live for ever; and the bread which I shall give for
the life of the world is my flesh."

---

come to reveal to us. In his prologue St John has already said: "No one has ever seen God; the only Son, who is in the bosom of the Father, he has made him known" (Jn 1:18). Later on Jesus will say to Philip at the Last Supper: "He who has seen me has seen the Father" (Jn 14:9), for Christ is the Way, the Truth and the Life, and no one goes to the Father except through him (cf. Jn 14:6).

In other words, in Christ God's revelation to men reaches its climax: "For he sent his Son, the eternal Word who enlightens all men, to dwell among men and to tell them about the inner life of God (cf. Jn 1:1–18). Hence, Jesus Christ, sent as 'a man among men', 'utters the words of God' (Jn 3:34), and accomplishes the saving work which the Father gave him to do (cf. Jn 5:36; 17:4). To see Jesus is to see his Father (cf. Jn 14:9)" (Vatican II, *Dei Verbum*, 4).

6:48. With this solemn declaration, which he repeats because of his audience's doubts (cf. Jn 6:35, 41), Jesus begins the second part of his discourse, in which he explicitly reveals the great mystery of the Blessed Eucharist. Christ's words have such a tremendous realism about them that they cannot be interpreted in a figurative way: if Christ were not really present under the species of bread and wine, this discourse would make absolutely no sense. But if his real presence in the Eucharist is accepted on faith, then his meaning is quite clear and we can see how infinite and tender his love for us is.

This is so great a mystery that it has always acted as a touchstone for Christian faith: it is proclaimed as "the mystery of our faith" immediately after the Consecration of the Mass. Some of our Lord's hearers were scandalized by what he said on this occasion (cf. vv. 60–66). Down through history people have tried to dilute the obvious meaning of our Lord's words. In our own day the church Magisterium has explained this teaching in these words: "When transubstantiation has taken place, there is no doubt that the appearance of the bread and the appearance of the wine take on a new expressiveness and a new purpose since they are no longer common bread and common drink, but rather the sign of something sacred and the sign of spiritual food. But they take on a new expressiveness and a new purpose for the very reason that they contain a new 'reality' which we are right to call *ontological*. For beneath these appearances there is no longer what was there before but something quite different [...] since on the conversion of the bread and wine's substance, or nature, into the body and blood of Christ, nothing is left of the bread and the wine but the appearances alone. Beneath these appearances Christ is present whole and entire, bodily present too, in his physical 'reality', although not in the manner in which bodies are present in place.

"For this reason the Fathers have had to issue frequent warnings to the faithful, when they consider this august sacra-

[52]The Jews then disputed among themselves, saying, "How
can this man give us his flesh to eat?"* [53]So Jesus said to them, Jn 6:60
"Truly, truly, I say to you, unless you eat the flesh of the Son of Jn 5:26
man and drink his blood, you have no life in you; [54]he who eats
my flesh and drinks my blood has eternal life, and I will raise him
up on the last day. [55]For my flesh is food indeed, and my blood is

---

ment, not to be satisfied with the senses which announce the properties of bread and wine. They should rather assent to the words of Christ: these are of such power that they change, transform, 'transelement' the bread and the wine into his body and blood. The reason for this, as the same Fathers say more than once, is that the power which performs this action is the same power of almighty God that created the whole universe out of nothing at the beginning of time" (Paul VI, *Mysterium fidei*).

Concerning the Blessed Eucharist cf. also the notes on Mt 26:26–29; Mk 14:22, 24, 25; and Lk 22:16–20.

6:49–51. The manna during the Exodus was a figure of this bread—Christ himself—which nourishes Christians on their pilgrimage through this world. Communion is the wonderful banquet at which Christ gives himself to us: "the bread which I shall give for the life of the world is my flesh". These words promise the manifestation of the Eucharist at the Last Supper: "This is my body which is for you" (1 Cor 11:24). The words "for the life of the world" and "for you" refer to the redemptive value of the sacrifice of Christ on the cross. In some sacrifices of the Old Testament, which were a figure of the sacrifice of Christ, part of the animal offered up was later used for food, signifying participation in the sacred rite (cf. Ex 11:3–4). So, by receiving Holy Communion, we are sharing in the sacrifice of Christ: which is why the Church sings in the Divine Office on the feast of Corpus Christi: "O sacred feast in which we partake of Christ: his sufferings are remembered, our minds are filled with his grace and we receive a pledge of the glory that is to be ours" (*Magnificat* antiphon, evening prayer II).

6:52. Christ's hearers understand perfectly well that he means exactly what he says; but they cannot believe that what he says could be true. If they had understood him in a metaphorical, figurative or symbolic sense there would be no reason for them to be so surprised and nothing to cause an argument. Later, Jesus reaffirms what he has said—confirming what they have understood him to say (cf. vv. 54–56).

6:53. Once again Jesus stresses very forcefully that it is necessary to receive him in the Blessed Eucharist in order to share in divine life and develop the life of grace received in Baptism. No parent is content to bring children into the world: they have to be nourished and looked after to enable them to reach maturity. "We receive Jesus Christ in Holy Communion to nourish our souls and to give us an increase of grace and the gift of eternal life" (St Pius X, *Catechism*, 289).

6:54. Jesus clearly states that his body and blood are a pledge of eternal life and a guarantee of the resurrection of the body. St Thomas Aquinas gives this explanation: "The Word gives life to our souls, but the Word made flesh nourishes our bodies. In this sacrament is contained the Word not only in his divinity but also in

Jn 15:4; 17:21, 26 drink indeed. [56]He who eats my flesh and drinks my blood abides
1 Jn 2:24; 3:24 in me, and I in him. [57]As the living Father sent me, and I live
because of the Father, so he who eats me will live because of me.

---

his humanity; therefore, it is the cause not only of the glorification of our souls but also of that of our bodies" (*Comm. on St John*, in loc.).

Our Lord uses a stronger word than just "eating" (the original verb could be translated as "chewing") which shows that Communion is a real meal. There is no room for saying that he was speaking only symbolically, which would mean that Communion was only a metaphor and not really eating and drinking the body and the blood of Christ.

"All these invitations, promises and threats sprang from the great desire which (Jesus) had of giving us himself in the holy sacrament of the altar. But why should Jesus so ardently desire us to receive him in holy communion? It is because love always sighs for, and tends to a union with, the object beloved. True friends wish to be united in such a manner as to become only one. The love of God for us being immense, he destined us to possess him not only in heaven, but also here below, by the most intimate union, under the appearance of bread in the Eucharist. It is true we do not see him; but he beholds us, and is really present; yes, he is present in order that we may possess him and he conceals himself, that we may desire him, and until we reach our true homeland Jesus Christ wishes in this way to be entirely ours, and to be perfectly united to us" (St Alphonsus Liguori, *The Love of Our Lord Jesus Christ*, chap. 2).

6:55. In the same way as bodily food is necessary for life on earth, Holy Communion is necessary for maintaining the life of the soul, which is why the Church exhorts us to receive this sacrament frequently:

"Every day, as is desirable, and in the greatest possible numbers, the faithful must take an active part in the sacrifice of the Mass, avail themselves of the pure, holy refreshment of Holy Communion and make a suitable thanksgiving in return for this great gift of Christ the Lord. Here are words they should keep in mind: 'Jesus Christ and the Church desire all Christ's faithful to approach the sacred banquet every day. The basis of this desire is that they should be united to God by the sacrament and draw strength from it to restrain lust, to wash away the slight faults of daily occurrence and to take precautions against the more serious sins to which human frailty is liable' (Decree of the S.C. of the Council, 20 December 1905)" (Paul VI, *Mysterium fidei*).

"The Saviour has instituted the most august sacrament of the Eucharist, which truly contains his flesh and his blood, so that he who eats this bread may live forever; whosoever, therefore, makes use of it often with devotion so strengthens the health and the life of his soul, that it is almost impossible for him to be poisoned by any kind of evil affection. We cannot be nourished with this flesh of life, and live with the affections of death. [...] Christians who are damned will be unable to make any reply when the just Judge shows them how much they are to blame for dying spiritually, since it was so easy for them to maintain themselves in life and in health by eating his Body which he had left them for this purpose. Unhappy souls, he will say, why did you die, seeing that you had at your com-

[58]This is the bread which came from heaven, not such as the
fathers ate and died; he who eats this bread will live for ever."
[59]This he said in the synagogue, as he taught in Capernaum.

---

mand the fruit and the food of life?" (St Francis de Sales, *Introduction to the Devout Life*, 2, 20, 1).

6:56. The most important effect of the Blessed Eucharist is intimate union with Jesus Christ. The very word "communion" suggests sharing in the life of our Lord and becoming one with him; if our union with Jesus is promoted by all the sacraments through the grace which they give us, this happens more intensely in the Eucharist, for in it we receive not only grace but the very Author of grace: "Really sharing in the body of the Lord in the breaking of the eucharistic bread, we are taken up into communion with him and with one another. 'Because the bread is one, we, though many, are one body, all of us who partake of the one bread' (1 Cor 10:17)" (Vatican II, *Lumen gentium*, 7). Precisely because the Eucharist is the sacrament which best signifies and effects our union with Christ, it is there that the whole Church manifests and effects its unity: Jesus Christ "instituted in his Church the wonderful sacrament of the Eucharist, by which the unity of the Church is both signified and brought about" (Vatican II, *Unitatis redintegratio*, 2).

6:57. In Christ, the Incarnate Word sent to mankind, "the whole fullness of deity, dwells bodily" (Col 2:9) through the ineffable union of his human nature and his divine nature in the Person of the Word. By receiving in this sacrament the body and blood of Christ indissolubly united to his divinity, we share in the divine life of the second Person of the Blessed Trinity. We will never be able to appreciate enough the intimacy with God himself—Father, Son and Holy Spirit—that we are offered in the eucharistic banquet.

"We can therefore do nothing more agreeable to Jesus Christ than to go to Communion with the dispositions suitable to so great an action, since we are then united to Jesus Christ, according to the desire of this all-loving God. I have said with 'suitable' and not 'worthy' disposition, for who could communicate if it was necessary to be worthy of so great a Saviour? No one but a God would be worthy to receive a God. But by this word suitable, or convenient, I mean such a disposition as becomes a miserable creature, who is clothed with the unhappy flesh of Adam. Ordinarily speaking, it is sufficient that we communicate in a state of grace and with an anxious desire of advancing in the love of Jesus Christ" (St Alphonsus Liguori, *The Love of Our Lord Jesus Christ*, chap. 2).

6:58. For the third time (cf. 6:31–32 and 6:49) Jesus compares the true bread of life, his own body, with the manna God used to feed the Israelites every day during their forty years in the wilderness—thereby, inviting us to nourish our soul frequently with the food of his body.

"'Going to Communion every day for so many years! Anybody else would be a saint by now', you told me, 'and I … I'm always the same!' 'Son,' I replied, 'keep up your daily Communion, and think: what would I be if I had not gone'" (St Josemaría Escrivá, *The Way*, 534).

The disciples' reaction

[60]Many of his disciples, when they heard of it, said, "This is a
Jn 6:41 hard saying; who can listen to it?" [61]But Jesus, knowing in him-
self that his disciples murmured at it, said to them, "Do you take
Jn 3:13 offence at this? [62]Then what if you were to see the Son of man
2 Cor 3:6 ascending where he was before?* [63]It is the spirit that gives life,
the flesh is of no avail; the words that I have spoken to you are
Jn 13:11 spirit and life. [64]But there are some of you that do not believe."
For Jesus knew from the first who those were that did not believe,
Jn 6:44 and who it was that should betray him. [65]And he said, "This is
why I told you that no one can come to me unless it is granted
him by the Father."

6:60–62. Many of his listeners find the eucharistic mystery completely incomprehensible. Jesus Christ requires his disciples to accept his words because it is he who has spoken them. That is what the supernatural act of faith involves— that act "whereby, inspired and assisted by the grace of God, we believe that the things which he has revealed are true; not because of the intrinsic truth of the things, viewed by the natural light of reason, but because of the authority of God himself who reveals them, and who can neither be deceived nor deceive" (Vatican I, *Dei Filius*, chap. 3).

As on other occasions, Jesus speaks about future events to help his disciples believe: "I have told you before it takes place, so that when it does take place, you may believe" (Jn 14:29).

6:63. Jesus says that we cannot accept this mystery if we think of it in too human a way, in other words, by just seeking to indulge our senses or having too earthbound a view of things. Only someone who listens to his words and receives them as God's revelation, which is "spirit and life", is in a position to accept them.

6:66. The promise of the Eucharist, which caused arguments (v. 52) among Christ's hearers at Capernaum and scandalized some of them (v. 61), led many people to give up following him. Jesus had outlined a wonderful and salvific truth, but those disciples closed themselves to divine grace; they were not ready to accept anything which went beyond their very limited horizons. The mystery of the Eucharist does call for a special act of faith. St John Chrysostom therefore advised Christians: "Let us in everything believe God, and gainsay him in nothing, though what is said be contrary to our thoughts and senses. […] Let us act likewise in respect to the [eucharistic] mysteries, not looking at the things set before us, but keeping in mind his words. For his word cannot deceive" (St John Chrysostom, *Hom. on St Matthew*, 82).

6:67–71. This passage is similar to that at Capernaum where Peter again, in the name of the Twelve, takes the initiative in expressing his faith in Jesus as Messiah (cf. Mt 16:13–20; Mk 8:27–30). Other people present may have been unbelieving, but the apostles are not scandalized by our Lord's words: they say that they have already a deep-rooted confidence in him; they do not want to leave him. What St Peter says (v. 68) is not just a statement of human solidarity but an expres-

[66]After this many of his disciples drew back and no longer
went with him. [67]Jesus said to the twelve, "Will you also go Lk 2:28
away?" [68]Simon Peter answered him, "Lord, to whom shall we Jn 6:63
go? You have the words of eternal life; [69]and we have believed, Jn 1:49; 11:27
and have come to know, that you are the Holy One of God." Mt 14:33; 16:16
[70]Jesus answered them, "Did I not choose you, the twelve, and
one of you is a devil?" [71]He spoke of Judas the son of Simon Jn 6:64
Iscariot, for he, one of the twelve, was to betray him.

5. JESUS, SENT BY THE FATHER, IS THE LIGHT OF THE WORLD AND THE GOOD SHEPHERD

Jesus goes up to Jerusalem during the feast of Tabernacles

7 [1]After this Jesus went about in Galilee; he would not go about Jn 5:18
in Judea, because the Jews[n] sought to kill him. [2]Now the Jews' Mk 9:30

sion of genuine supernatural faith—as yet imperfect—which is the result of the influence of divine grace on his soul (cf. Mt 16:17).

Although the Twelve stay with him at this point, Judas will later betray the Master. Jesus' foreknowledge of this future infidelity throws a shadow over his joy at the loyalty of the Twelve. We Christians should be humble enough to realize that we are capable of betraying our Lord if we give up using the means he has left us to cleave to him. St Peter's words (v. 68) are a beautiful aspiration we can use whenever we feel tempted.

6:68. Simon Peter expresses the feelings of the apostles who, through staying loyal to Jesus, are getting to know him much better and becoming more closely involved with him: "Seek Jesus; endeavouring to acquire a deep personal faith that will inform and direct your whole life. But, above all, let it be your commitment and your programme to love Jesus, with a sincere, authentic and personal love. He must be your friend and your support along the path of life. He alone has words of eternal life" (John Paul II, Address to students in Guadalajara, 30 January 1979).

6:69. "The Holy One of God": this is what the original text must have said, according to most of the Greek codexes and the most important early translations. "The Holy One" is one of the expressions which designate the Messiah (cf. Mk 1:24; Lk 1:35; 4:34; Acts 2:27; Ps 16:10), or God himself (cf. Is 6:3; 43:15; 1 Pet 1:15; 1 Jn 2:20; etc.). The rendering "the Christ, the Son of God" found in some translations, including the Vulgate, is supported by less important Greek manuscripts, and would seem to be an explanation of the messianic significance of the original phrase.

7:1–3. The Jewish custom was for closer relatives to be called "brothers", brethren (cf. the notes on Mt 12:46–47 and Mk 6:1–3). These relatives of Jesus followed him without understanding his teaching or his mission (cf. Mk 3:31); but, because he worked such obvious miracles in Galilee (cf. Mt 15:32–39; Mk 8:1–10,

n. Or *Judeans*

Ex 23:15 Lev 23:34 feast of Tabernacles was at hand. 3 So his brethren* said to him,
Zech 14:16–19 “Leave here and go to Judea, that your disciples may see the
Jn 2:11–12 Mt 12:46 works you are doing. 4 For no man works in secret if he seeks to be
known openly. If you do these things, show yourself to the world.”
5 For even his brethren did not believe in him. 6 Jesus said to them,
Jn 2:4; 17:1 “My time has not yet come, but your time is always here. 7 The
Jn 3:19; 15:18 world cannot hate you, but it hates me because I testify of it that
its works are evil. 8 Go to the feast yourselves; I am not[o] going up
to this feast, for my time has not fully come.” 9 So saying, he
remained in Galilee.

10 But after his brethren had gone up to the feast, then he also
Mt 27:63 went up, not publicly but in private. 11 The Jews were looking for

---

22–26) they suggest to him that he show himself publicly in Jerusalem and throughout Judea. Perhaps they wanted him to be a big success, which would have indulged their family pride.

7:2. The name of the feast recalls the time the Israelites spent living under canvas in the wilderness (cf. Lev 23:34–36). During the eight days the feast lasted (cf. Neh 8:13–18), around the beginning of autumn, the Jews commemorated the protection God had given the Israelites over the forty years of the Exodus. Because it coincided with the end of the harvest, it was also called the feast of ingathering (cf. Ex 23:16).

7:6–8. When the Jews who lived far away went up to Jerusalem to celebrate the main religious festivals, they usually went in caravans. Jesus had joined such caravans on other occasions (cf. Lk 2:41–45); but this time he does not want to go up to the Holy City with the crowd. He knows that the time is not ripe for him to show himself publicly in Jerusalem, for the teachers of the Law, whom he had severely taken to task (cf. 5:42–47) wanted to discredit him before the people and get rid of him (cf. 7:1). Our Lord does not want to advance the time fixed by his Father, whose will he has come to do (cf. 4:34; 12:33; 13:1). However, his adherents could go up to Jerusalem because they had nothing to fear.

On the concept of “world” cf. the notes on Jn 1:10 and 15:18–19.

7:10. Because he had not arrived in advance of the feast (which was what people normally did), the first caravans would have reported that Jesus was not coming up, and therefore the members of the Sanhedrin would have stopped planning anything against him (cf. 7:1). By going up later, the religious authorities would not dare make any move against him for fear of hostile public reaction (cf. Mt 26:5). Jesus, possibly accompanied by his disciples, arrives unnoticed at Jerusalem, “in private”, almost in a hidden way. Half-way through the feast, on the fourth or fifth day, he begins to preach in the temple (cf. 7:14).

7:12. Once again Jesus appears as a sign of contradiction, in line with the prophecy of Simeon in the temple (cf. Lk 2:34). People are divided in their opinions of him, but no one is indifferent. A Christian

o. Other ancient authorities add *yet*

him at the feast, and saying, "Where is he?" [12]And there was
much muttering about him among the people. While some said, Jn 9:22; 12:42;
"He is a good man," others said, "No, he is leading the people 19:38
astray." [13]Yet for fear of the Jews no one spoke openly of him. Mt 13:54–57

Lk 2:47
Jn 3:11; 12:49

Jesus' teaching comes from God

[14]About the middle of the feast Jesus went up into the temple and
taught. [15]The Jews marvelled at it, saying, "How is it that this man
has learning,[p] when he has never studied?" [16]So Jesus answered
them, "My teaching is not mine, but his who sent me; [17]if any
man's will is to do his will, he shall know whether the teaching is
from God or whether I am speaking on my own authority. [18]He
who speaks on his own authority seeks his own glory; but he who Jn 5:41–44; 8:50
seeks the glory of him who sent him is true, and in him there is no

---

who takes his faith seriously may well have the same experience. "Of anyone in whom any grace shines," St Augustine comments, "some say that he is good; others that he is not, that he is deceiving the people. If this is said of God, it should console every Christian of whom the same is said" (*In Ioann. Evang*., 28, 12).

7:15–16. The Evangelist does not stop here to tell us what exactly Jesus was preaching about; but he does repeat how impressed the Jews were, teachers of the Law included. They marvelled at the teaching of this man, whom they had never seen attending the schools run by the teachers of the Law, and they asked him this question, which is really quite malicious: Is he not interpreting the Law for himself, without having regard to the official teaching of the "masters"? At this point our Lord uses the opportunity to give a brief outline of his messianic dignity (7:16–24): he has not invented anything; his teaching is divine; the Father has revealed it to him (cf. 5:30; 8:28; 12:49; 14:10, 24). Because he is true God and true Man, he can speak about the things of God with singular authority. (see 1:18).

7:17–18. An upright intention is needed if one is to discern that Jesus' doctrine comes from God. Jesus, for his part, suggests a criterion for recognizing that he is acting rightly: he should be judged not by the sublimity of his teaching and his works (cf. 8:54) but by the fact that he seeks the glorification of his Father, and is expounding the teaching that has been given him (cf. 7:16). Jesus worked spectacular miracles, the prophecies are being fulfilled in him and even his enemies can find nothing wrong with his doctrine or with his behaviour: why, then, do they not believe in him? The reason is that they are very prejudiced; they do not weigh the evidence calmly: that is the only explanation for their attributing to devils the things that Jesus has done (cf. v. 20). But if a person makes an effort to faithfully fulfil the will of God according to his lights, he will be well disposed to receive from God new light to allow him to discover Christ and his teaching.

Following Christ's example, the Church does not seek human success,

p. Or *this man knows his letters*

Rom 2:17–23 falsehood. 19Did not Moses give you the law? Yet none of you
keeps the law. Why do you seek to kill me?" 20The people
Jn 10:20 answered, "You have a demon! Who is seeking to kill you?"
Mk 3:22–27 21Jesus answered them, "I did one deed, and you all marvel at it.
Gen 17:10–12 22Moses gave you circumcision (not that it is from Moses, but
Lev 12:3 from the fathers), and you circumcise a man upon the sabbath. 23If
Jn 5:16 on the sabbath a man receives circumcision, so that the law of
Mt 12:1–5 Moses may not be broken, are you angry with me because on the
Jn 8:15 sabbath I made a man's whole body well? 24Do not judge by
Zech 7:9 appearances, but judge with right judgment."

Jesus comes from God

25Some of the people of Jerusalem therefore said, "Is not this the
Jn 5:18 man whom they seek to kill? 26And here he is, speaking openly,
and they say nothing to him! Can it be that the authorities really
know that this is the Christ? 27Yet we know where this man comes

---

but the good of souls and the glory of God. "God is fully glorified, when men fully and consciously accept the work of salvation which he accomplished in Christ. By means of it God's plan is realized, a plan to which Christ lovingly and obediently submitted for the glory of the Father who sent him in order that the whole human race might become one people of God, form one body of Christ, and be built up into one temple of the Holy Spirit" (Vatican II, *Ad gentes*, 7).

7:19–24. Jesus is justifying the cures he has worked on the sabbath. On that day, for example, he cured the paralyzed man at the pool of Bethzatha (Jn 5:1–18), the man with the withered hand (Mt 12:10–13 and par.), the woman who was bent over (Lk 13:10–17), and a man with dropsy (Lk 14:1–6). Our Lord compares his behaviour with keeping two apparently opposed precepts of the Law: the sabbath is a day of rest, and yet the obligation of circumcision on the eighth day applies even if that day falls on a sabbath. Clearly, if it is lawful to circumcise on the sabbath, it must be even more so to work a miraculous cure on the sabbath. That is why he asks them to judge rightly and recognize his saving power—to try to grasp the profound significance of the things that he is doing, even if they at first seem to go against the Law.

7:27. In this chapter we often see the Jews disconcerted, in two minds. They argue with one another over whether Jesus is the Messiah, or a prophet, or an imposter (v. 12); they do not know where he gets his wisdom from (v. 15); they are short-tempered (vv. 19–20); and they are surprised by the attitudes of the Sanhedrin (v. 26). Despite the signs they have seen (miracles, teaching) they do not want to believe that Jesus is the Messiah. Perhaps some, thinking that he came from Nazareth and was the son of Joseph and Mary, cannot see how this fits in with the notion usually taken from Isaiah's prophecy (Is 53:1–9) about the Messiah's origin being unknown—except for his coming from the line of David and being born in Bethlehem (cf. Mt 2:5 which quotes Mic 5:2; cf. Jn 7:42). In fact Jesus did fulfil those prophetic predictions, though most Jews did not know

from; and when the Christ appears, no one will know where he
comes from.” 28 So Jesus proclaimed, as he taught in the temple, Jn 8:19; 19:9
“You know me, and you know where I come from? But I have not
come of my own accord; he who sent me is true, and him you do Jn 1:1; 8:55
not know. 29 I know him, for I come from him, and he sent me.” Mt 11:27
30 So they sought to arrest him; but no one laid hands on him, Jn 7:44; 8:20 Lk 4:29; 22:53
because his hour had not yet come.

Jesus must return to the Father

31 Yet many of the people believed in him; they said, “When the Jn 8:30
Christ appears, will he do more signs than this man has done?”
32 The Pharisees heard the crowd thus muttering about him, and
the chief priests and Pharisees sent officers to arrest him. 33 Jesus
then said, “I shall be with you a little longer, and then I go to him Jn 13:33
who sent me; 34 you will seek me and you will not find me; where Jn 8:21; 17:24

---

it because they knew nothing about his virginal birth in Bethlehem or his descent from David. Others must have known that he was of the house of David and had been born in Bethlehem, but even so they did not want to accept his teaching because it demanded a mental and moral conversion.

7:28–29. Not without a certain irony, Jesus refers to the superficial knowledge these Jews had of him: however, he asserts that he comes from the Father who has sent him, whom only he knows, precisely because he is the Son of God (cf. Jn 1:18).

7:30. The Jews realized that Jesus was making himself God’s equal, which was regarded as blasphemy and, according to the Law, was something punishable by death by stoning (cf. Lev 24:15–16, 23).

This is not the first time St John refers to the Jews’ hostility (cf. Jn 5:10), nor will it be the last (8:59; 10:31–33). He stresses this hostility because it was a fact and perhaps also to show that Jesus acts freely when, to fulfil his Father’s will he gives himself over to his enemies when his “hour” arrives (cf. Jn 18:4–8). “He did not therefore mean an hour when he would be forced to die, but one when he would allow himself to be put to death. For he was waiting for the time in which he should die, even as he waited for the time in which he should be born” (St Augustine, *In Ioann. Evang.*, 31, 5).

7:31–32. In Jesus the prophecy of Simeon to the Virgin Mary is being fulfilled: he is a sign of contradiction for his own people (cf. Lk 2:34). Some believe in him (v. 31), others are in two minds (vv. 41–42), others violently reject him (vv. 44–48). The poor and the humble believe, says St Augustine,—those who recognize that they are ailing and are keen to have medicine; whereas the powerful and the proud are angry with him. Not only do they not recognize the physician, they want to kill him (cf. *In Ioann. Evang.*, 31, 7).

7:33–34. This prophecy refers to the death and ascension of Jesus. He says “where I am” to indicate the glorious state of his soul, which his body also will enjoy after its resurrection. The Jews who reject him have blocked their route to heaven. However, later on, Jesus, moved by infinite charity, will ask the Father to forgive them because they do not know

Is 55:6
Deut 4:29
Prov 1:28
Hos 5:6
Jn 4:10–14
Is 55:1–3
Ezek 47:1–12
Jn 19:34
Acts 2:1–13;
5:32

I am you cannot come." 35 The Jews said to one another, "Where
does this man intend to go that we shall not find him? Does he
intend to go to the Dispersion among the Greeks and teach the
Greeks? 36 What does he mean by saying, 'You will seek me and
you will not find me,' and, 'Where I am you cannot come'?"
37 On the last day of the feast, the great day, Jesus stood up and
proclaimed, "If any one thirst, let him come to me and drink. 38 He
who believes in me, as[q] the scripture has said, 'Out of his heart
shall flow rivers of living water.'" 39 Now this he said about the

---

what they are doing (Lk 23:34). And so, at Pentecost, many will repent of their sin and God will pardon them (cf. Acts 2:38) and the gates of heaven will be open to them again; but others will remain adamant in their unbelief.

7:37–39. On each of the eight days of the feast of Tabernacles the high priest went to the pool of Siloam and used a golden cup to bring water to the temple and sprinkle it on the altar, in remembrance of the water which sprang up miraculously in the desert, asking God to send rain in plenty (cf. Ex 17:1–7). Meanwhile, a passage from the prophet Isaiah was chanted (cf. Is 12:3) which told of the coming of the Saviour and of the outpouring of heavenly gifts that would accompany him; Ezekiel 47 was also read, in which it spoke of the torrents of water which would pour out of the temple. Jesus, who would have been at this ceremony, now proclaims—in the presence of a huge crowd, undoubtedly, because it was the most solemn day of the festival—that that time has come: "If any one thirst, let him come to me and drink …". This invitation recalls the words of divine wisdom: "Come to me, you who desire me, and eat your fill" (Sir 24:19; cf. Prov 9:4–5). Our Lord presents himself as him who can fill man's heart and bring him peace (cf. also Mt 11:28). In this connexion St Augustine exclaims: "You made us for yourself, Lord, and our hearts find no peace until they rest in you" (*Confessions*, 1, 1, 1).

Jesus' words as preserved in v. 37 led St Alphonsus to write this tender commentary full of love for our Saviour: "In Jesus Christ we have three fountains of grace. The first is the fountain of mercy, where we can be purified of all the stains of our sins. […] The second is that of love: no one who meditates on the suffering and shame that Jesus Christ undergoes out of love for us, from his birth to his death, can fail to be kindled by that happy fire which comes down on earth to set on fire the hearts of all men. […] The third is the fountain of peace: let him who seeks peace of heart come to me, who is the God of peace" (*Meditations for Advent*, med. 8).

Furthermore, when Jesus speaks of "rivers of living water" flowing out of his heart, he is probably referring to Ezekiel 36:25ff where it is announced that in messianic times the people will be sprinkled with clean water and will be given a new spirit and their heart of stone will be changed for a heart of flesh. In other words, Jesus, once he has been exalted as befits his position as Son of God, will send at Pentecost the Holy Spirit, who will change the hearts of those who believe in him. "For this reason, Christian tradition has summarized the attitude we should adopt

q. Or *let him come to me, and let him who believes in me drink. As*

Spirit, which those who believed in him were to receive; for as yet
the Spirit had not been given, because Jesus was not yet glorified.

1 Cor 10:4

Different opinions about Jesus 2 Cor 3:17
[40]When they heard these words, some of the people said, "This is Deut 18:15
really the prophet." [41]Others said, "This is the Christ." But some Jn 1:46 2 Sam 7:12
said, "Is the Christ to come from Galilee? [42]Has not the scripture Mic 5:2 Mt 2:6; 22:42
said that the Christ is descended from David, and comes from Lk 2:4–11
Bethlehem, the village where David was?" [43]So there was a division among the people over him. [44]Some of them wanted to arrest Jn 9:16
him, but no one laid hands on him. Jn 7:30
[45]The officers then went back to the chief priests and Mt 7:28;
Pharisees, who said to them, "Why did you not bring him?" [46]The 13:54–56

---

towards the Holy Spirit in just one idea—docility. That means we should be aware of the work of the Holy Spirit all around us, and in our own selves we should recognize the gifts he distributes, the movements and institutions he inspires, the affections and decisions he provokes in our hearts" (St J. Escrivá, *Christ Is Passing By*, 130).

To say that the Holy Spirit will come visibly at Pentecost does not mean that he has not been active before: when the Old Testament prophets speak they are inspired by the Holy Spirit (cf. 2 Pet 1:21) and there are countless passages in the New Testament where we are told that he is acting: for example, he overshadows the Blessed Virgin at the Annunciation; he moves Zechariah to prophesy the wonders of the Lord, and Simeon to proclaim that the Saviour of the world has come.

But, asks St Augustine, "how are the words of the Evangelist to be understood: 'The Spirit had not yet been given, since Jesus was not yet glorified', if not in the sense that, after the glorification of Christ, there would certainly be a giving or sending of the Holy Spirit of such a kind as there had never been before?" (*De Trinitate*, 4, 20). Our Lord was referring, therefore, to the coming of the Holy Spirit after his ascension into heaven, an outpouring which St John sees as symbolically anticipated when Christ's side is pierced by a lance and blood and water flow out (Jn 19:34). The Fathers saw in this the birth of the Church and the sanctifying power of the sacraments, especially those of Baptism and the Eucharist.

7:40–43. "The prophet" refers to Deuteronomy 18:18, which predicts the coming of a prophet during the last times, a prophet to whom all must listen (cf. Jn 1:21; 6:14); and "the Christ" ("the Messiah") was the title most used in the Old Testament to designate the future Saviour whom God would send. This passage shows us, once again, the range of people's attitudes towards Jesus. Many Jews—not taking the trouble to check—did not know that he had been born in Bethlehem, the city of David, where Micah (5:2) says the Lord will be born. It was their own fault that they used this ignorance as an excuse for not accepting Christ. Others, however, realized from his miracles that he must be the Messiah. The same pattern prevails throughout history: some people see him simply as an extraordinary man, not wanting to admit that his greatness comes precisely from the fact that he is the Son of God.

7:46. The truth begins to influence the straightforward souls of the servants of

officers answered, "No man ever spoke like this man!" [47]The
Jn 12:42 Pharisees answered them, "Are you led astray, you also? [48]Have
any of the authorities or of the Pharisees believed in him? [49]But
this crowd, who do not know the law, are accursed." [50]Nicodemus,
Jn 3:1–2 who had gone to him before, and who was one of them, said to
Deut 1:16–7 them, [51]"Does our law judge a man without first giving him a
hearing and learning what he does?" [52]They replied, "Are you
Jn 1:46; 7:41 from Galilee too? Search and you will see that no prophet is to
rise from Galilee." [53]They went each to his own house, [1]but Jesus
went to the Mount of Olives.

---

the Sanhedrin but it cannot make headway against the obstinacy of the Pharisees. "Notice that the Pharisees and scribes derive no benefit either from witnessing miracles or reading the Scriptures; whereas their servants, without these helps, were captivated by a single discourse, and those who set out to arrest Jesus went back under the influence of his authority. And they did not say, 'We cannot arrest him, the people will not let us'; instead they extolled Christ's wisdom. Not only is their prudence admirable, for they did not need signs; it is also impressive that they were won over by his teaching on its own; they did not say, in effect, 'No man has ever worked such miracles,' but 'No man ever spoke like this man.' Their conviction also is worthy of admiration: they go to the Pharisees, who were opposed to Christ, and address them in the way they do" (St John Chrysostom, *Hom. on St John*, 9).

8:1–11. This passage is absent from many ancient codexes, but it was in the Vulgate when the Magisterium, at the Council of Trent, defined the canon of Holy Scripture. Therefore, the Church regards it as canonical and inspired, and has used it and continues to use it in the liturgy. It is also included in the New Vulgate, in the same position as it occupied before.

St Augustine said that the reason doubts were raised about the passage was that it showed Jesus to be so merciful that some rigorists thought it would lead to a relaxation of moral rules—and therefore many copyists suppressed it from their manuscripts (cf. *De coniugiis adulterinis*, 2, 6).

In commenting on the episode of the woman caught in adultery Fray Luis de Granada gives these general considerations on the mercy of Christ: "Your feelings, your deeds and your words should be akin to these, if you desire to be a beautiful likeness of the Lord. And therefore the Apostle is not content with telling us to be merciful; he tells us, as God's sons, to put on 'the bowels of mercy' (cf. Col 3:12). Imagine, then, what the world would be like if everyone arrayed themselves in this way.

"All this is said to help us understand to some degree the great abundance of the goodness and compassion of our Saviour, which shine forth so clearly in these actions of his, for [...] in this life we cannot know God in himself; we can know him only through his actions. [...] But it should also be pointed out that we should never act in such a way in view of God's mercy, that we forget about his justice; nor should we attend to his justice forgetting about his mercy; for hope should have in it an element of fear, and fear an element of hope" (*Life of Jesus Christ*, 13, 4).

The adulterous woman—Jesus as judge

8 2Early in the morning he came again to the temple; all the Lk 21:37f
people came to him, and he sat down and taught them. 3The
scribes and the Pharisees brought a woman who had been caught
in adultery, and placing her in the midst 4they said to him,
"Teacher, this woman has been caught in the act of adultery. 5Now Lev 20:10
in the law Moses commanded us to stone such. What do you say Deut 22:22–24
about her?" 6This they said to test him, that they might have some Mt 22:15 Lk 20:20
charge to bring against him. Jesus bent down and wrote with his
finger on the ground. 7And as they continued to ask him, he stood Deut 17:7
up and said to them, "Let him who is without sin among you be Rom 2:1, 22
the first to throw a stone at her." 8And once more he bent down

---

8:1. We know that on a number of occasions our Lord withdrew to the Mount of Olives to pray (cf. Jn 18:1; Lk 22:39). This place was to the east of Jerusalem; the Kidron valley (cf. Jn 18:1) divided it from the hill on which the temple was built. It had from ancient times been a place of prayer: David went there to adore God during the difficult period when Absalom was in revolt (2 Sam 15:32), and there the prophet Ezekiel contemplated the glory of Yahweh entering the temple (Ezek 43:1–5). At the foot of the hill there was a garden, called Gethsemane or "the place of the oil-press", an enclosed plot containing a plantation of olive trees. Christian tradition has treated this place with great respect and has maintained it as a place of prayer. Towards the end of the fourth century a church was built there, on whose remains the present church was built. There are still some ancient olive trees growing there which could well derive from those of our Lord's time.

8:6. The question put by the scribes and Pharisees has a catch: our Lord had often shown understanding to people whom they considered sinners; they come to him now with this case to see if he will be equally indulgent—which will allow them to accuse him of infringing a very clear precept of the Law (cf. Lev 20:10).

8:7. Jesus' reply refers to the way stoning was carried out: those who witnessed the crime had to throw the first stones, and then others joined in, to erase the slur on the people which the crime implied (cf. Deut 17:7). The question put to Jesus was couched in legal terms; he raises it to the moral plane (the basis and justification of the legal plane), appealing to the people's conscience. He does not violate the law, St Augustine says, and at the same time he does not want to lose what he is seeking—for he has come to save that which was lost: "His answer is so full of justice, gentleness and truth. [...] O true answer of Wisdom. You have heard: Keep the Law, let the woman be stoned. But how can sinners keep the Law and punish this woman? Let each of them look inside himself and enter the tribunal of his heart and conscience; there he will discover that he is a sinner. Let this woman be punished, but not by sinners; let the Law be applied, but not by its transgressors" (St Augustine, *In Ioann. Evang.*, 33, 5).

and wrote with his finger on the ground. 9But when they heard it,
they went away, one by one, beginning with the eldest, and Jesus
was left alone with the woman standing before him. 10Jesus
looked up and said to her, "Woman, where are they? Has no one
Jn 5:14 condemned you?" 11She said, "No one, Lord." And Jesus said,
Ezek 33:11 "Neither do I condemn you; go, and do not sin again."[r]*

Jesus, the light of the world

Jn 1:5–9; 12:46 Is 49:6 12Again Jesus spoke to them, saying, "I am the light of the world;
Mt 5:14 he who follows me will not walk in darkness, but will have the

---

8:11. "The two of them were left on their own, the wretched woman and Mercy. But the Lord, having smitten them with the dart of justice, does not even deign to watch them go but turns his gaze away from them and once more writes on the ground with his finger. But when the woman was left alone and they had all gone, he lifted up his eyes to the woman. We have already heard the voice of justice; let us now hear the voice of gentleness. I think that woman was the more terrified when she heard the Lord say, 'Let him who is without sin among you be the first to throw a stone at her,' [...] fearing now that she would be punished by him, in whom no sin could be found. But he, who had driven away her adversaries with the tongue of justice, now looking at her with the eyes of gentleness asks her, 'Has no one condemned you?' She replies, 'No one, Lord.' And he says, 'Neither do I condemn you; I who perhaps you feared would punish you, because in me you have found no sin.' Lord, can it be that you favour sinners? Assuredly not. See what follows: 'Go and sin no more.' Therefore, the Lord also condemned sin, but not the woman" (St Augustine, *In Ioann. Evang.*, 33, 5–6).

Jesus, who is the Just One, does not condemn the woman; whereas these people are sinners, yet they pass sentence of death. God's infinite mercy should move us always to have compassion on those who commit sins, because we ourselves are sinners and in need of God's forgiveness.

8:12. This is the beginning of another dispute between Jesus and the Pharisees. The scene is the precincts of the temple —to be more precise, what was called the "court of the women"; this came before the court of the people, which in turn came before the court of the priests, which contained the altar of holocausts (cf. the note to Mk 1:21).

It is still the feast of Tabernacles (cf. Jn 7:2); and it was the custom on the first night to fill the court of the women with the bright light of huge lamps which lit up the sky. This brought to mind the bright cloud of God's presence which guided the Israelites through the wilderness during the Exodus. It was probably during this feast that Jesus spoke of himself as "the Light". In any event, the image of light is often found in the Old Testament to designate the Messiah: the prophet Isaiah predicted that a great light would shine for the people who walked in darkness, beginning with the tribes of the North (Is 9:1–6; cf. Mt 4:15–16), and

r. Some ancient authorities insert 7:53—8:11 either at the end of this gospel or after Lk 21:38, with variations of the text. Others omit it altogether

light of life." [13]The Pharisees then said to him, "You are bearing
witness to yourself; your testimony is not true." [14]Jesus answered, Is 5:31
"Even if I do bear witness to myself, my testimony is true, for I
know whence I have come and whither I am going, but you do not
know whence I have come or whither I am going. [15]You judge Jn 7:24; 12:47
according to the flesh, I judge no one. [16]Yet even if I do judge, my Jn 5:30; 8:29
judgment is true, for it is not I alone that judge, but I and he[s] who
sent me. [17]In your law it is written that the testimony of two men Deut 17:6; 19:15
is true; [18]I bear witness to myself, and the Father who sent me 1 Jn 5:9
bears witness to me." [19]They said to him therefore, "Where is your Jn 12:45; 14:7

---

that the Messiah would not only be the King of Israel but the light of the nations (Is 42:6; 49:6); and David spoke of God as a light enlightening the soul of the righteous man and giving him strength (Ps 27:1). This image, therefore, was well understood during Jesus' time: Zechariah uses it (Lk 1:78), as does Simeon (Lk 2:30–32), to show his joy on seeing the ancient prophecies fulfilled.

Our Lord applies this image to himself in two ways: he is the light which enlightens our minds, for he is the fulness of divine revelation (cf. Jn 1:9, 18); and he is also the light which enlightens our hearts to enable us to accept this Revelation and live according to it (cf. Jn 1:4–5). This is why Jesus asks them to follow him and "become sons of light" (Jn 12:36), although he knows that many will reject this light because they do not want their evil deeds to be uncovered (cf. Jn 3:20).

"See how the words of the Lord accord with the truth of the Psalm: 'With thee is the fountain of life; in thy light do we see light' (Ps 36:9). The psalmist connects light with the source of life, and the Lord speaks of a 'light of life'. When we are thirsty we look for a fountain; when we are in darkness we look for light. [...] Not so with God: he is light and fountain. He who shines for you to enable you to see, flows for you to enable you to drink" (St Augustine, *In. Ioann. Evang.*, 34, 6).

8:13–18. The Pharisees try to dilute the force of Jesus' arguments: they make out that he has only his own word to go on and no one can bear witness on his own behalf: so what he says has no validity.

In a similar situation (cf. Jn 5:31ff) Jesus had cited four witnesses to support him—John the Baptist's teaching, the miracles he himself performed, the words his Father spoke when he was baptized in the Jordan, and Holy Scripture. Here Jesus affirms the validity of his own testimony (v. 14) on the grounds that he is one with the Father. This is the same as saying that his is a more than human testimony. "He speaks to tell them that he comes from God, that he is God, and that he is the Son of God, but he does not say so openly, because he always connects humility with profundity. God deserves that we should believe in him" (St John Chrysostom, *Hom. on St John*, 51).

8:19. The Pharisees, who did not want to admit Jesus' divine origin, now ask him for proof that what he says is true. Their question is insidious and malicious, for they do not think he can show them the Father.

s. Other ancient authorities read *the Father*

Father?" Jesus answered, "You know neither me nor my Father; if
you knew me, you would know my Father also." 20These words he
Jn 13:1 Lk 22:53 spoke in the treasury, as he taught in the temple; but no one
arrested him, because his hour had not yet come.

Jesus says he has been sent by the Father

Jn 7:32–36; 13:33, 36 Prov 1:28 21Again he said to them, "I go away, and you will seek me and die
in your sin;* where I am going, you cannot come." 22Then said the
Jn 7:35 Jews, "Will he kill himself, since he says, 'Where I am going, you

---

Knowing Jesus, that is, believing in him and accepting the mystery of his divinity, means knowing the Father. John 12:44–45 repeats the same teaching in other words. And Jesus is saying the same when he reproaches Philip: "Have I been with you so long, and yet you do not know me, Philip? He who has seen me has seen the Father" (Jn 14:9). Jesus is the visible manifestation of the invisible God, the ultimate, definitive revelation of God to men (cf. Heb 1:1–3). Jesus Christ "by the total fact of his presence and self-manifestation—by words and works, signs and miracles, but above all by his death and glorious resurrection from the dead, and finally by sending the Spirit of truth [...] revealed that God was with us, to deliver us from the darkness of sin and death, and to raise us up to eternal life" (Vatican II, *Dei Verbum*, 4).

8:20. "The treasury", where money for the poor was collected, was located in the women's courtyard. For more information see the note on Lk 21:1–4.

8:21–24. At the outset of his public ministry, Jesus could be seen to have all the features of the promised Messiah; some people recognized him as such and became his followers (cf. Jn 1:12–13; 4:42; 6:69; 7:41); but the Jewish authorities, although they were expecting the Messiah (cf. Jn 1:19ff), persisted in their rejection of Jesus. Hence the warning to them: he is going where they cannot follow, that is, he is going to heaven, which is where he has come from (cf. Jn 6:41ff), and they will keep on looking out for the Messiah foretold by the prophets; but they will not find him because they look for him outside of Jesus, nor can they follow him, for they do not believe in him. You are of the world, our Lord is saying to them, not because you are on earth but because you are living under the influence of the prince of this world (cf. Jn 12:31; 14:30; 16:11); you are his vassals and you do his deeds (cf. 8:44); therefore, you will die in your sin. "We were all born with sin", St Augustine comments, "all by our living have added to what we were by nature, and have become more of this world than we then were, when we were born of our parents. Where would we be if he had not come, who had no sin at all, to loose all sin? The Jews, because they did not believe in him, deserved to have it said to them, You will die in your sin" (*In Ioann. Evang.*, 38, 6).

The salvation which Christ brings will be applied to those who believe in his divinity. Jesus declares his divinity when he says "I am he", for this expression, which he repeats on other occasions (cf. Jn 8:28; 13:19), is reserved to Yahweh in the Old Testament (cf. Deut

cannot come'?" [23]He said to them, "You are from below, I am Jn 3:31
from above; you are of this world, I am not of this world. [24]I told Ex 3:14
you that you would die in your sins, for you will die in your sins
unless you believe that I am he." [25]They said to him, "Who are
you?" Jesus said to them, "Even what I have told you from the
beginning.[t] [26]I have much to say about you and much to judge; but Jn 7:28; 12:48–50
he who sent me is true, and I declare to the world what I have
heard from him." [27]They did not understand that he spoke to them

---

32:39; Is 43:10–11), where God, in revealing his name and therefore his essence, says to Moses "I AM WHO I AM" (Ex 3:14). In this profound way God says that he is the Supreme Being in a full, absolute sense, that he is dependent on no other being, that all other things depend on him for their being and existence. Thus, when Jesus says of himself "I am he", he is revealing that he is God.

8:25. A little before this Jesus had spoken about his heavenly origin and his divine nature (cf. vv. 23–24); but the Jews do not want to accept this revelation; which is why they ask him for an even more explicit statement: "Who are you?" Our Lord's reply can be understood in different ways, because the Greek text has two meanings: 1) our Lord is confirming what he has just asserted (cf. vv. 23–24) and what he has been teaching throughout this visit to Jerusalem—in which case it may be translated "precisely what I am telling you" or else "in the first place what I am telling you". This is the interpretation given in the New Vulgate. 2) Jesus is indicating that he is the "Beginning", which is the word St John also uses in the Apocalypse to designate the Word, the cause of all creation (Rev 3:14; cf. Rev 1:8). In this way Jesus states his divine origin. This is the interpretation given in the Vulgate. Either way, Christ is once more revealing his divinity; he is reaffirming what he said earlier, but without saying it all over again.

"Many people in our own days ask the same question: 'Who are you?' [...] Who, then, was Jesus? Our faith exults and cries out: it is he, it is he, the Son of God made man. He is the Messiah we were expecting: he is the Saviour of the world, the Master of our lives; he is the Shepherd that guides men to their pastures in time, to their destinies beyond time. He is the joy of the world; he is the image of the invisible God; he is the way, the truth and the life; he is the interior friend; he is the One who knows us even from afar; he knows our thoughts; he is the One who can forgive us, console, cure, even raise from the dead; and he is the One who will return, the judge of one and all, in the fullness of his glory and our eternal happiness" (Paul VI, *General Audience*, 11 December 1974).

8:26–27. "He who sent me": an expression very often found in St John's Gospel, referring to God the Father (cf. 5:37; 6:44; 7:28; 8:16).

The Jews who were listening to Jesus did not understand whom he was referring to; but St John, in recounting this episode, explains that he meant his Father, from whom he came.

"He spoke to them of the Father": this is the reading in most of the Greek codexes, including the more important

t. Or *Why do I talk to you at all?*

Jn 3:14; 12:32 of the Father. [28]So Jesus said, "When you have lifted up the Son
of man, then you will know that I am he, and that I do nothing on
Jn 4:34; 16:32 my own authority but speak thus as the Father taught me. [29]And
he who sent me is with me; he has not left me alone, for I always

---

ones. Other Greek codexes and some translations, including the Vulgate, read "he was calling God his Father".

"What I have heard from him": Jesus had connatural knowledge of his Father, and it is from this knowledge that he speaks to men; he knows God not through revelation or inspiration as the prophets and sacred writers did, but in an infinitely higher way: which is why he can say that no one knows the Father but the Son and he to whom the Son chooses to reveal him (cf. Mt 11:27). On the type of knowledge Jesus had during his life on earth, see the note on Luke 2:52.

8:28. Our Lord is referring to his passion and death: (see Jn 12:32–33). Rounding out the Synoptics and the letters of St Paul, the Fourth Gospel presents the cross, above all, as a royal throne on which Christ is "lifted up" and from which he offers all men the fruits of salvation (cf. Jn 3:14–15; Num 21:9ff; Wis 16:6).

Jesus says that when that time comes, the Jews will know who he is and his intimate union with the Father, because many of them will discover, thanks to his death and resurrection, that he is the Messiah, the Son of God (cf. Mk 15:39; Lk 23:48). After the coming of the Holy Spirit many thousands will believe in him.

8:30–32. Of those Jews who do believe in him Jesus asks much more than a shallow faith resulting from superficial enthusiasm: they should be true disciples; Jesus' words should imbue their whole life. That kind of faith will bring them to know the truth and to become really free persons.

The knowledge of the truth which Christ is speaking about is not just intellectual knowledge; it is rather the maturing in the soul of the seed of divine revelation. That revelation's climax is to be found in Christ's teaching, and it constitutes a genuine communication of supernatural life (cf. Jn 5:24): he who believes in Jesus, and through him in the Father, receives the wonderful gift of eternal life. Knowing the truth is, in the last analysis, knowing Christ himself, God become man to save us; it means realizing that the inaccessible God has become man, our Friend, our Life.

This is the only kind of knowledge which really sets us free, because it removes us from a position of alienation from God—the state of sin and therefore of slavery to the devil and to all the attachments of our fallen nature—and puts us on the path of friendship with God, the path of grace, of the Kingdom of God. Therefore, the liberation we obtain is not just light which shows us the way; it is grace, which empowers us to keep to that way despite our limitations.

"Jesus Christ meets the man of every age, including our own, with the same words: 'You will know the truth, and the truth will make you free' (Jn 8:32). These words contain both a fundamental requirement and a warning: the requirement of an honest relationship with regard to truth as a condition for authentic freedom, and the warning to avoid every kind of illusory freedom, every superficial unilateral freedom, every freedom that fails to enter into the whole truth about man and the world. Today also, even after two thousand years, we see Christ as the one who brings man freedom based on truth, frees man from

do what is pleasing to him." [30]As he spoke thus, many believed in him.

"The truth will set you free"

[31]Jesus then said to the Jews who had believed in him, "If you Jn 15:14
continue in my word, you are truly my disciples, [32]and you will
know the truth, and the truth will make you free." [33]They

---

what curtails, diminishes and as it were breaks off this freedom at its root, in man's soul, his heart and his conscience. What a stupendous confirmation of this has been given and is still being given by those who, thanks to Christ and in Christ, have reached true freedom and have manifested it even in situations of external constraint!" (John Paul II, *Redemptor hominis*, 12).

"Christ himself links liberation particularly with knowledge of the truth; 'You will know the truth and the truth will make you free' (Jn 8:32). This sentence testifies above all to the intimate significance of the freedom for which Christ liberates us. Liberation means man's inner transformation, which is a consequence of the knowledge of truth. The transformation is, therefore, a spiritual process, in which man matures 'in true righteousness and holiness' (Eph 4:24). […] Truth is important not only for the growth of human knowledge, deepening man's interior life in this way; truth has also a prophetic significance and power. It constitutes the content of testimony and it calls for testimony. We find this prophetic power of truth in the teaching of Christ. As a prophet, as a witness to truth, Christ repeatedly opposes non-truth; he does so with great forcefulness and decision and often he does not hesitate to condemn falsehood" (John Paul II, General Audience, 21 February 1979).

St Thomas Aquinas says: "In this passage, being made free does not refer to being freed of every type of wrong […]; it means being freed in the proper sense of the word, in three ways: first, the truth of his teaching will free us from the error of untruth […]; second, the truth of grace will liberate us from the slavery of sin: 'the law of the Spirit of life in Christ Jesus has set me free from the law of sin and death' (Rom 8:2); third, the truth of eternity in Christ Jesus will free us from decay (cf. Rom 8:21)" (*Comm. on St John*, in loc.).

"The truth will set you free. How great a truth is this, which opens the way to freedom and gives it meaning throughout our lives. I will sum it up for you, with the joy and certainty which flow from knowing there is a close relationship between God and his creatures. It is the knowledge that we have come from the hands of God, that the Blessed Trinity looks upon us with predilection, that we are children of so wonderful a Father. I ask my Lord to help us decide to take this truth to heart, to dwell upon it day by day; only then will we be acting as free men. Do not forget: anyone who does not realize that he is a child of God is unaware of the deepest truth about himself. When he acts he lacks the dominion and self-mastery we find in those who love our Lord above all else" (St Josemaría Escrivá, *Friends of God*, 26).

8:33–34. For centuries the people of Israel were ruled by other nations (Egypt, Babylon, Persia …), and now they were

Mt 3:9 answered him, "We are descendants of Abraham, and have never
been in bondage to any one. How is it that you say, 'You will be
made free'?"

Rom 6:17–20 34Jesus answered them, "Truly, truly, I say to you, every one
Gen 21:10 who commits sin is a slave of sin. 35The slave does not continue in
Gal 4:30 the house for ever; the son continues for ever. 36So if the Son
Gal 5:1 makes you free, you will be free indeed. 37I know that you are
Jn 5:38
Mt 21:36–46 descendants of Abraham; yet you seek to kill me, because my
word finds no place in you. 38I speak of what I have seen with my
Father, and you do what you have heard from your father."

The true children of Abraham

39They answered him, "Abraham is our father." Jesus said to them,
"If you were Abraham's children, you would do what Abraham

---

under the dominion of Rome. The Jews think Jesus is referring to political bondage or dominion—which in fact they had experienced but never accepted. In addition, since they belong to the people chosen by God, they regard themselves as free of the moral errors and aberrations of Gentile nations.

They thought that true freedom was a matter of belonging to the chosen people. Our Lord replies that it is not enough to belong to the line of Abraham: true freedom consists in not being slaves of sin. Both Jews and Gentiles were subject to the slavery of original sin and personal sin (cf. Rom 5:12; 6:20 and 8:2). Only Christ, the Son of God, can liberate man from that sorry state (cf. Gal 4:21–31); but these Jews do not understand the redemptive work which Christ is doing and which will reach its climax in his death and resurrection.

"The Saviour", St Augustine comments, "is here explaining that we will not be freed from overlords, but from the devil; not from captivity of the body but from malice of soul" (*Sermons*, 48).

8:35–36. The words "slave" and "son" are reminiscent of the two sons of Abraham: Ishmael, born of the slave woman Hagar, who would be given no part in the inheritance; and Isaac, son of the free woman Sarah, who would be the heir to God's promises (cf. Gen 21:10–12; Gal 4:28–31). Physical descent from Abraham is not enough for inheriting God's promises and attaining salvation: by faith and charity one must identify oneself with Jesus Christ, the true and only Son of the Father, the only one who can make us sons of God and thereby bring us true freedom (cf. Rom 8:21; Gal 4:31). Christ gives "power to become children of God [to those] who were born, not of blood nor of the will of the flesh nor of the will of man, but of God" (Jn 1:12–13). Thus, a person who identifies himself with Christ becomes a son of God and obtains the freedom proper to sons.

"Freedom finds its true meaning when it is put to the service of the truth which redeems, when it is spent in seeking God's infinite Love which liberates us from all forms of slavery. Each passing day increases my yearning to proclaim to the four winds this inexhaustible treasure that belongs to Christianity: 'the glorious freedom of the children of God!' (Rom 8:21). […] Where does our free-

did, 40but now you seek to kill me, a man who has told you the
truth which I heard from God; this is not what Abraham did. Ex 4:22
41You do what your father did." They said to him, "We were not Deut 32:6
born of fornication; we have one Father, even God."* 42Jesus said 1 Jn 5:1
of them, "If God were your Father, you would love me, for I proceeded and came forth from God; I came not of my own account,
but he sent me. 43Why do you not understand what I say? It is Jn 12:39
because you cannot bear to hear my word. 44You are of your father Mt 12:34 1 Jn 3:8–15
the devil, and your will is to do your father's desires. He was a Gen 3:1–4
murderer from the beginning, and has nothing to do with the truth, Wis 2:24 2 Pet 2:4
because there is no truth in him. When he lies, he speaks accord-
ing to his own nature, for he is a liar and the father of lies.
45But, because I tell the truth, you do not believe me. 46Which of 2 Cor 5:21
you convicts me of sin? If I tell the truth, why do you not believe 1 Pet 2:22

---

dom come from? It comes from Christ our Lord. This is the freedom with which he has ransomed us (cf. Gal 4:31). That is why he teaches, 'if the Son makes you free, you will be free indeed' (Jn 8:36)" (St J. Escrivá, *Friends of God*, 27 and 35).

8:37–41. Our Lord replies to the Jews' objection: yes indeed, they are Abraham's children, but only in a natural sense, according to the flesh; that does not count any more; what matters now is acceptance of Jesus as the One sent by the Father. Jesus' questioners are spiritually very far away from being true children of Abraham: Abraham rejoiced to see the Messiah (cf. Jn 8:56); through his faith he was reckoned righteous (cf. Rom 4:1ff), and his faith led him to act consequentially (cf. Jas 2:21–24); this was how he attained the joy of eternal blessedness (cf. Mt 8:11; Lk 16:24). Although those Jews "derived from him the generation of the flesh, they had become degenerate, by not imitating the faith of him whose sons they were" (St Augustine, *In Ioann. Evang*., 42, 1). Those who live by faith are the true sons of Abraham and like him they will be blessed by God (cf. Gal 3:7–9). In fact, the people who are arguing with our Lord have not only rejected his teaching: their own deeds indicate that they have a radically different affiliation: "You do what your father did" is a veiled accusation that they are children of the devil (cf. v. 44).

The false security Jews felt in being descended from Abraham has its parallel in a Christian who is content with being baptized and with a few religious observances, but does not live up to the requirements of faith in Christ.

8:42–44. In claiming to be children of God, the Jews appeal to statements in the Old Testament (cf. Ex 4:22; Deut 32:6; Is 63:16; Jer 3:4; 31:9; Mal 1:6). However, the attitude they adopt towards Jesus is in contradiction with this condition of being children of God—for that should lead them to accept Jesus, since he is the One sent by the Father. Because they reject the Only-begotten Son they are acting like partisans or sons of God's enemy, the devil. The devil, because he opposes our Lord, who is the Truth, is the father of lies: by lying he seduced our first parents and he deceives all those who yield to his temptations.

Jn 8:37 1 Jn 4:6 me? [47]He who is of God hears the words of God; the reason why
you do not hear them is that you are not of God."
Jn 7:20 Mk 3:21ff [48]The Jews answered him, "Are we not right in saying that you
are a Samaritan and have a demon?" [49]Jesus answered, "I have not
a demon; but I honour my Father, and you dishonour me. [50]Yet I
Jn 5:41; 7:18 do not seek my own glory; there is One who seeks it and he will
Jn 5:24–28; 6:40, 47, 11:25 be the judge. [51]Truly, truly, I say to you, if any one keeps my
word, he will never see death."

"Before Abraham was, I am"

Jn 7:20 [52]The Jews said to him, "Now we know that you have a demon.
Abraham died, as did the prophets; and you say, 'If any one keeps
Jn 4:12 my word, he will never taste death.' [53]Are you greater than our

---

8:48. Instead of replying to Jesus' line of argument, the Jews attack him by insulting him. Before all this, they had spread the calumny that he was possessed by the devil, that he was out of his mind (cf. Mk 3:21) and that he cast out demons in the name of the prince of demons (cf. Mk 3:22; Mt 12:24). By calling him a Samaritan they accuse him of being a heretic, a violator of the Law, a semi-pagan: the Jews regarded the Samaritans as the prototypes of religious perversion. (On the origin of the Samaritan people and why there was such hostility between them and the Jews, cf. the notes on Lk 9:52–53 and Jn 4:20, 21–24).

8:50. Faced with these wild accusations, Jesus acts with great patience, while still firmly defending divine truth. "When it was necessary for him to teach", St John Chrysostom says, "and bend his enemies' pride, he acted very resolutely; whereas, when he had to bear an insult, he acted with great meekness, thus teaching us to defend God's rights and be forgetful of our own" (*Hom. on St John*, 54).

Jesus leaves this argument to the judgment of God, for he is not seeking human fame. St Paul will reiterate this teaching of our Lord, to underline his own upright intention and the kindness with which we should treat everyone (cf. Rom 12:19–20).

8:51–53. "He will never see death": our Lord promises eternal life to those who accept and remain faithful to his teaching.

Sin, as the Fourth Gospel teaches, is death of the soul; and sanctifying grace, life (cf. Jn 1:4, 13; 3:15, 16, 36; etc.). Through grace we enter eternal life, a pledge of the glory we shall attain beyond this earthly life and which is the true Life. Blinded by their hostility, the Jews do not want to listen to the Lord and therefore they fail to understand him.

8:55. The knowledge our Lord is speaking about is more than intellectual knowledge. The Old Testament speaks of this "knowing" in the sense of love, faithfulness, generous self-surrender. Love for God comes from the certain knowledge we have of him, and the more we love him, the better we get to know him.

Jesus, whose holy human nature was intimately united (though not mixed) with his divinity in the one Person of the Word, continues to assert his singular and ineffable knowledge of the Father. But this accurate language of Jesus is absol-

father Abraham, who died? And the prophets died! Who do you
claim to be?" [54]Jesus answered, "If I glorify myself, my glory is
nothing; it is my Father who glorifies me, of whom you say that
he is your God. [55]But you have not known him; I know him. If I Jn 7:28–29
said, I do not know him, I should be a liar like you; but I do know
him and I keep his word. [56]Your father Abraham rejoiced that he Gen 17:17
was to see my day; he saw it* and was glad." [57]The Jews then said Mt 13:17–18
to him, "You are not yet fifty years old, and have you seen
Abraham?"[u] [58]Jesus said to them, "Truly, truly, I say to you,
before Abraham was, I am."* [59]So they took up stones to throw at Jn 8:24
him; but Jesus hid himself, and went out of the temple. Jn 10:31 Lk 4:29ff

---

utely incomprehensible to those who close themselves to faith: they even think he is blaspheming (cf. v. 59).

8:56. Jesus presents himself as the fulfilment of the hopes of the Old Testament patriarchs. They had stayed faithful, eager to see the Day of Salvation. Referring to their faith, St Paul exclaims: "These all died in faith, not having received what was promised, but having seen it and greeted it from afar, and having acknowledged that they were strangers and exiles on the earth" (Heb 11:13). The most outstanding of those patriarchs was Abraham, our father in faith (cf. Gal 3:7), who received the promise of being father of an immense people, the chosen people from whom would be born the Messiah.

The future fulfilment of the messianic promises was a source of great joy for Abraham: "Abraham, our father, who was set apart for the future accomplishment of the Promise, and who hoped against hope, receives when his son Isaac is born the prophetic firstfruits of this joy. This joy becomes transfigured through a trial touching death, when this only son is restored to him alive, a prefiguring of the resurrection of the one who was to come: the only son of God, promised for the redeeming sacrifice. Abraham rejoiced at the thought of seeing the Day of Christ, the Day of Salvation: 'he saw it and was glad'" (Paul VI, *Gaudete in Domino*, 2).

Jesus moves on a plane superior to that of the patriarchs, for they only saw prophetically, from "afar", the Day of Christ, that is, the actual event of the Redemption, whereas it is Christ who brings it to pass.

8:58. Jesus' reply to the sceptical remarks of the Jews contains a revelation of his divinity. By saying "Before Abraham was, I am" our Lord is referring to his being eternal, because he is God. Therefore, St Augustine explains: "Acknowledge the Creator, discern the creature. He who was speaking was a descendant of Abraham, but that Abraham might be made, before Abraham he was" (*In Ioann. Evang.*, 43, 17). The Fathers recall, in connexion with the words of Christ, the solemn theophany of Sinai: "I AM WHO I AM" (Ex 3:14), and also St John's distinction, in the prologue to his Gospel, between the world which "was made" and the Word which "was" from all eternity (cf. Jn 1:1–3). The words "I

u. Other ancient authorities read *has Abraham seen you?*

Curing of the man born blind

Ex 20:5 **9** 1As he passed by, he saw a man blind from his birth. 2And his
Lk 13:2 disciples asked him, "Rabbi, who sinned, this man or his par-
Jn 11:4 ents, that he was born blind?" 3Jesus answered, "It was not that
this man sinned, or his parents, but that the works of God might
Jn 5:17–20; be made manifest in him. 4We must work the works of him who
11:9–10 sent me, while it is day; night comes, when no one can work.* 5As
Jn 8:12; 12:35 long as I am in the world, I am the light of the world." 6As he said
Mk 8:23 this, he spat on the ground and made clay of the spittle and

---

am", used by Jesus so absolutely, are the equivalent therefore, of his affirming his eternity and his divinity. Cf. the note on Jn 8:21–24.

9:2–3. The disciples' question echoes general Jewish views on the causes of illness and of misfortunes in general: they regarded them as punishment for personal sins (cf. Job 4:7–8; 2 Mac 7:18), or as the sins of parents being visited on their children (cf. Tob 3:3).

We know through Revelation (cf. Gen 3:16–19; Rom 5:12; etc.) that the origin of all the misfortunes which afflict mankind is sin—original sin and later personal sin. However, this does not mean that each misfortune or illness has its immediate cause in a personal sin, as if God inflicted or allowed evils to happen in direct proportion to every sin committed. Suffering, which is so often a factor in the life of the just man, can be a resource God sends him to cleanse him of his imperfections, to exercise him in virtue and to unite him to the sufferings of Christ the Redeemer who, although he was innocent, bore in himself the punishment our sins merited (cf. Is 53:4; 1 Pet 2:24; 1 Jn 3:5). For example, our Lady and St Joseph and all the saints have experienced intense suffering, thereby sharing in the redemptive suffering of Christ.

9:4–5. The "day" refers to Jesus' life on earth. Hence the urgency with which he approaches the task of doing the will of the Father until he reaches his death, which he compares with "night". This "night" can also be understood as referring to the end of the world; in this passage it means that the Redemption of men brought about by Christ needs to be continued by the Church throughout the centuries, and also that Christians should strive to spread the Kingdom of God.

"Time is precious, time passes, time is a phase of experiment with regard to our decisive and definitive fate. Our future and eternal destiny depends on the proof we give of faithfulness to our duties. Time is a gift from God; it is a question posed by God's love to our free and, it can be said, fateful answer. We must be sparing of time, in order to use it well, in the intense activity of our life of work, love and suffering. Idleness or boredom have no place in the life of a Christian! Rest, yes, when necessary (cf. Mk 6:31), but always with a view to vigilance, which only on the last day will open to a light on which the sun will never set" (Paul VI, Homily, 1 January 1976).

Jesus proclaims that he is the light of the world because his life among men has given us the ultimate meaning of the world, of the life of every man and every woman, and of mankind as a whole. Without Jesus all creation is in darkness, it does not understand itself, it does not know where it is going. "Only in the

anointed the man's eyes with the clay, 7saying to him, "Go, wash Is 8:6
in the pool of Siloam" (which means Sent). So he went and washed and came back seeing. 8The neighbours and those who had
seen him before as a beggar, said, "Is not this the man who used
to sit and beg?" 9Some said, "It is he"; others said, "No, but he is
like him." He said, "I am the man." 10They said to him, "Then how
were your eyes opened?" 11He answered, "The man called Jesus
made clay and anointed my eyes and said to me, 'Go to Siloam
and wash'; so I went and washed and received my sight." 12They
said to him, "Where is he?" He said, "I do not know."

---

mystery of the Incarnate Word does the mystery of man take on light. [...] Through Christ and in Christ, the riddles of sorrow and death grow meaningful; apart from his Gospel they overwhelm us" (Vatican II, *Gaudium et spes*, 22). Jesus warns us—as he will do more clearly in John 12:35–36—of the need to let ourselves be enlightened by the light, which is he himself (cf. Jn 1:9–12).

9:6–7. This cure is done in two stages—Jesus' action on the eyes of the blind man, and the man being told to go and wash in the pool of Siloam. Our Lord also used saliva to cure a man who was deaf and dumb (cf. Mk 7:33) and another blind man (cf. Mk 8:23). The pool of Siloam was a reservoir built by King Hezekiah, in the seventh century BC, to supply Jerusalem with water (cf. 2 Kings 20:20; 2 Chron 32:30); the prophets regarded these waters as a sign of divine favour (cf. Is 8:6; 22:11). St John, using the broader etymology of the word "Siloam", applies it to Jesus who is the "One sent" by the Father. Our Lord works through the medium of matter to produce effects which exceed anything matter can do. Something similar will occur with the sacraments: through his word he will confer on material media the power of spiritually regenerating man.

Our Lord's instruction to the blind man is reminiscent of the miracle of Naaman, the Syrian general who was cured of leprosy when, on the instruction of the prophet Elisha, he washed seven times in the waters of the Jordan (cf. 2 Kings 5:1ff). Naaman had hesitated before obeying, whereas the blind man obeys promptly without asking questions or raising objections.

"What an example of firm faith the blind man gives us! A living, operative faith. Do you behave like this when God commands, when so often you cannot see, when your soul is worried and the light is gone? What power could the water possibly contain that when the blind man's eyes were moistened with it they were cured? Surely some mysterious eye salve, or a precious medicine made up in the laboratory of some wise alchemist, would have done better? But the man believed; he acted upon the command of God, and he returned with eyes full of light" (St Josemaría Escrivá, *Friends of God*, 193).

9:8–34. After recounting the miracle, the Evangelist reports the doubts of the man's friends and neighbours (vv. 8–12) and the inquiry made by the Pharisees: they question the man (vv. 13–17), his parents (vv. 18–23), and then the man again, whom they end up condemning and expelling from their presence (vv. 24–34). This passage is so full of detail that it looks like an eyewitness account.

[13]They brought to the Pharisees the man who had formerly
Jn 5:9 been blind. [14]Now it was a sabbath day when Jesus made the clay
Mt 12:10–11 Lk 3:10ff and opened his eyes. [15]The Pharisees again asked him how he had
received his sight. And he said to them, "He put clay on my eyes,
Jn 3:2; 7:43; and I washed, and I see." [16]Some of the Pharisees said, "This man
9:31, 33 is not from God, for he does not keep the sabbath." But others
said, "How can a man who is a sinner do such signs?" There was
Jn 4:19 a division among them. [17]So they again said to the blind man,
Mt 16:14 "What do you say about him, since he has opened your eyes?" He
said, "He is a prophet."

[18]The Jews did not believe that he had been blind and had
received his sight, until they called the parents of the man who
had received his sight, [19]and asked them, "Is this your son, who
you say was born blind? How then does he now see?" [20]His par-

---

The Fathers and Doctors of the Church have seen this miracle as symbolizing the sacrament of Baptism in which, through the medium of water, the soul is cleansed and receives the light of faith: "He sent the man to the pool called the pool of Siloam, to be cleansed and to be enlightened, that is, to be baptized and receive in baptism full enlightenment" (St Thomas Aquinas, *Comm. on St John*, in loc.).

This episode also reflects the different attitudes of people to our Lord and his miracles. The blind man, a straightforward person, believes in Jesus as envoy, prophet (vv. 17, 33) and Son of God (vv. 17, 33, 38); whereas the Pharisees persist in not wanting to see or believe, despite the clear evidence before them (vv. 24–34).

In this miracle Jesus once again reveals himself as the light of the world. This bears out the statement in the prologue: "The true light that enlightens every man was coming into the world" (1:9). Not only does he give light to the eyes of the blind man: he enlightens his soul, leading him to make an act of faith in his divinity (v. 38). At the same time we can see the obvious drama of those whose blindness darkens their minds, as our Lord said in his dialogue with Nicodemus: "The light has come into the world, and men loved darkness rather than light, because their deeds were evil" (Jn 3:19).

9:14–16. The Pharisees bring up the same accusation as they did when the paralyzed man was cured beside the pool (Jn 5:10) and as on other occasions: Jesus has broken the Law because he cures the sick on the sabbath (cf. Lk 13:16; 14:5; etc.). Christ had often taught that observance of the law of sabbath rest (cf. Ex 20:8, 11; 21:13; Deut 5:14) was compatible with the duty to do good (cf. Mt 12:3–8; Mk 2:28; Lk 6:5). Charity, the good of others, takes precedence over all the other commandments (cf. the note on Mt 12:3–8). If rules are given precedence in a blind sort of way over the inescapable obligations of justice and charity, the result is fanaticism, which always goes against the Gospel and even against right reason—as happens in this instance with the Pharisees. Their minds are so closed that they do not want to see God's hand in something which simply could not be done without divine power. The dilemma

ents answered, "We know that this is our son, and that he was
born blind; [21]but how he now sees we do not know, nor do we
know who opened his eyes. Ask him; he is of age, he will speak
for himself." [22]His parents said this because they feared the Jews, Jn 7:13; 14:22; 16:2
for the Jews had already agreed that if any one should confess him
to be Christ, he was to be put out of the synagogue. [23]Therefore
his parents said, "He is of age, ask him."

The blindness of the Jews

[24]So for the second time they called the man who had been blind, Josh 7:19
and said to him, "Give God the praise; we know that this man is a
sinner." [25]He answered, "Whether he is a sinner, I do not know;
one thing I know, that though I was blind, now I see." [26]They said
to him, "What did he do to you? How did he open your eyes?"

---

they pose themselves—Is he a man of God, as his miracles imply; or a sinner, because he does not keep the sabbath (cf. Mk 3:23–30)?—can only arise in people whose outlook is that of religious fanatics. Their mistaken interpretation of how certain precepts should be kept leads them to forget the essence of the Law—love of God and love of neighbour.

To avoid accepting Jesus' divinity, the Pharisees reject the only possible correct interpretation of the miracle; whereas the blind man—like all unprejudiced people open to the truth— finds solid grounds in the miracle for confessing that Christ works through the power of God (Jn 9:33): "He supported and confirmed his preaching by miracles to arouse the faith of his hearers and give them assurance, but not to coerce them" (Vatican II, *Dignitatis humanae*, 11).

9:24. "Give God the praise": a solemn declaration, like an oath, exhorting a person to tell the truth. But the Pharisees are not looking for the truth: they want to intimidate the man to get him to withdraw his statement. They try to pressure him by warning him: "We know this man is a sinner." St Augustine comments: "What do they mean, Give God the praise? They mean, deny what you have received. Clearly, this is not to give God the praise, but rather to blaspheme against God" (*In Ioann. Evang*., 44, 11).

9:25–34. This interrogation shows that the miracle was so patent that not even his enemies could deny it. Our Lord worked many miracles during his public ministry, showing that he had complete power over everything, in other words that he was divine.

Rationalism, basing itself on an erroneous philosophical principle, refuses to accept that God can intervene in a supernatural way in this world; it therefore denies the possibility of miracles: but the Church has always taught that miracles do happen and that they serve a purpose: "If any one shall say that miracles are impossible, and that therefore all the accounts regarding them, even those contained in Holy Scripture, are to be dismissed as fabulous or mythical; or that miracles can never be known with certainty, and that the divine origin of Christianity cannot be proved by them—let him be *anathema*" (Vatican I, *Dei Filius*, chap. 3 and can. 4).

[27]He answered them, "I have told you already, and you would not
listen. Why do you want to hear it again? Do you too want to
become his disciples?" [28]And they reviled him, saying, "You are
his disciple, but we are disciples of Moses. [29]We know that God
has spoken to Moses, but as for this man, we do not know where
he comes from." [30]The man answered, "Why, this is a marvel! You
do not know where he comes from, and yet he opened my eyes.
Is 1:15 Prov 15:29 Acts 10:35 [31]We know that God does not listen to sinners, but if any one is a
worshipper of God and does his will, God listens to him. [32]Never
since the world began has it been heard that any one opened the
Jn 9:16 eyes of a man born blind. [33]If this man were not from God, he
Jn 9:2 could do nothing." [34]They answered him, "You were born in utter
sin, and would you teach us?" And they cast him out.
[35]Jesus heard that they had cast him out and having found him
he said, "Do you believe in the Son of man?"[v] [36]He answered,

9:29. Everyone saw the miracle, but the Pharisees are so stubborn that they will not accept the significance of the event, not even after questioning the man himself and his parents. "The sin of the Pharisees did not consist in not seeing God in Christ, but in voluntarily shutting themselves up within themselves, in not letting Jesus, who is the light, open their eyes (cf. Jn 9:39–41)" (St Josemaría Escrivá, *Christ Is Passing By*, 71). As this episode proceeds, the faith of the man himself deepens. He begins by recognizing Jesus as a prophet (v. 17) and he ends up acknowledging his divinity (v. 35); whereas over the same course of events the authorities become more and more obstinate—moving from doubt (v.16), through the blasphemous assertion that Jesus is a sinner, to eventually expelling the beggar (v. 34)—a useful warning about the danger of pride which can blind one to the obvious.

9:34. After the Babylonian exile (sixth century BC), a Jewish custom developed of expelling from the synagogue those who had committed certain crimes. This took two forms—temporary expulsion for thirty days as a disciplinary measure, and permanent expulsion, which later was often imposed on Jews who became Christians. What is being referred to here is probably permanent expulsion, which was what was planned (v. 22) and which is noted elsewhere in the Gospels (cf. Jn 12:42; 16:2; Lk 6:22).

9:35–38. This does not seem to have been an accidental meeting. The Pharisees have cast the man out of the synagogue; our Lord not only receives him but helps him make an act of faith in his divinity: "Now with the face of his heart washed and with his conscience cleansed, he acknowledges him to be not only Son of man but Son of God" (St Augustine, *In Ioann. Evang.*, 44, 15). This dialogue reminds us of Jesus' conversation with the Samaritan woman (cf. Jn 4:26).

9:39. This judgment which our Lord pronounces follows on the act of faith of the man who has been cured, and the persistent obstinacy of the Pharisees. He has not come to condemn the world but to

v. Other ancient authorities read *the Son of God*

“And who is he, sir, that I may believe in him?” 37Jesus said to
him, “You have seen him, and it is he who speaks to you.” 38He Jn 4:26
said, “Lord, I believe”; and he worshipped him. 39Jesus said, “For Jn 8:12
judgment I came into this world, that those who do not see may Mt 13:13
see, and that those who see may become blind.” 40Some of the Mt 15:14
Pharisees near him heard this, and they said to him, “Are we also
blind?” 41Jesus said to them, “If you were blind, you would have Jn 3:36
no guilt; but now that you say, ‘We see,’ your guilt remains.” Prov 26:12

The Good Shepherd

10 1“Truly, truly, I say to you, he who does not enter the Ezek 34:1–31
sheepfold by the door but climbs in by another way, that Jer 23:1–3
man is a thief and a robber; 2but he who enters by the door is the

---

save it (cf. Jn 3:17), but his presence among us already involves a judgment, because each of us has to take a stand on whether to reject or accept Jesus. Christ’s coming implies the fall of some and the salvation of others (cf. Lk 2:34). In this sense, we will fall into one of two categories (cf. Jn 3:18–21; 12:47–48): on the one hand, the humble of heart (cf. Mt 11:25), who recognize their failings and who go to Jesus in search of forgiveness (these will receive the light he is speaking of); on the other hand, those who are satisfied with themselves and think that they do not need Christ or his word (they say they see but they are blind). Thus we ourselves decide our ultimate fate, depending on whether we accept or reject Jesus.

9:40–41. Jesus’ words sting the Pharisees, who are always looking to catch him in something he says. They realize that he is referring to them and they ask him, “Are we also blind?” Jesus’ answer is quite clear: they can see but they do not want to: therefore they are unworthy. “If you realized you were blind, if you admitted you were blind and ran to the physician, you would have no sin, for I have come to take away sin; but because you say that you can see, you remain in your blindness” (St Augustine, *In Ioann. Evang.*, 45, 17).

10:1–18. The image of the Good Shepherd recalls a favourite theme of Old Testament prophetic literature: the chosen people is the flock, and Yahweh is their shepherd (cf. Ps 23). Kings and priests are also described as shepherds or pastors. Jeremiah inveighs against those pastors who had let their sheep go astray and in God’s name promises new pastors who will graze their flocks properly so that they will never again be harassed or anxious (cf. 23:1–6; also 2:8; 3:15; 10:21; Is 40:1–11). Ezekiel reproaches pastors for their misdeeds and sloth, their greed and neglect of their responsibility: Yahweh will take the flock away from them and he himself will look after their sheep; indeed, a unique shepherd will appear, descended from David, who will graze them and protect them (Ezek 34). Jesus presents himself as this shepherd who looks after his sheep, seeks out the strays, cures the crippled and carries the weak on his shoulders (cf. Mt 18:12–14; Lk 15:4–7), thereby fulfilling the ancient prophecies.

From earliest times, Christian art found its inspiration in this touching image of the Good Shepherd, thereby

shepherd of the sheep. [3]To him the gatekeeper opens; the sheep
hear his voice, and he calls his own sheep by name and leads them
Jn 10:27 out. [4]When he has brought out all his own, he goes before them,
and the sheep follow him, for they know his voice. [5]A stranger
they will not follow, but they will flee from him, for they do not
know the voice of strangers." [6]This figure Jesus used with them,
but they did not understand what he was saying to them.
Ps 118:20 [7]So Jesus again said to them, "Truly, truly, I say to you, I am
the door of the sheep. [8]All who came before me are thieves and
robbers; but the sheep did not heed them. [9]I am the door; if any

---

leaving us a representation of Christ's love for each of us.

In addition to the title of Good Shepherd, Christ applies to himself the image of the door into the sheepfold of the Church. "The Church," Vatican II teaches, "is a sheepfold, the sole and necessary gateway to which is Christ (cf. Jn 10:1–10). It is also a flock, of which God foretold that he himself would be the shepherd (cf. Is 40:11; Ezek 34:11ff), and whose sheep, although watched over by human shepherds, are nevertheless at all times led and brought to pasture by Christ himself, the Good Shepherd and prince of shepherds (cf. Jn 10:11; 1 Pet 5:4), who gave his life for his sheep (cf. Jn 10:11–15)" (*Lumen gentium*, 6).

10:1–2. The flock can be harmed in a subtle, hidden way, or in a blatant way through abuse of authority. The history of the Church shows that its enemies have used both methods: sometimes they enter the flock in a secretive way to harm it from within; sometimes they attack it from outside, openly and violently. "Who is the good shepherd? 'He who enters by the door' of faithfulness to the Church's doctrine and does not act like the hireling 'who sees the wolf coming and leaves the sheep and flees'; whereupon 'the wolf snatches them and scatters them (cf. Jn 10:1–21)'" (St Josemaría Escrivá, *Christ Is Passing By*, 34).

10:3–5. In those times it was usual at nightfall to bring a number of flocks together into one sheepfold, where they would be kept for the night with someone acting as lookout. Then at dawn the shepherds would come back and open the sheepfold and each would call his sheep which would gather round and follow him out of the pen (they were used to his voice because he used to call them to prevent them from going astray) and he would then lead them to pasture. Our Lord uses this image—one very familiar to his listeners—to teach them a divine truth: since there are strange voices around, we need to know the voice of Christ—which is continually addressing us through the Magisterium of the Church—and to follow it, if we are to get the nourishment our soul needs. "Christ has given his Church sureness in doctrine and a fountain of grace in the sacraments. He has arranged things so that there will always be people to guide and lead us, to remind us constantly of our way. There is an infinite treasure of knowledge available to us: the word of God kept safe by the Church, the grace of Christ administered in the sacraments and also the witness and example of those who live by our side and have known how to build with their good lives a road of faithfulness to God" (*Christ Is Passing By*, 34).

one enters by me, he will be saved, and will go in and out and find Jn 3:17
pasture. [10]The thief comes only to steal and kill and destroy; I Is 49:9–10
came that they may have life, and have it abundantly. [11]I am the
good shepherd. The good shepherd lays down his life for the Ps 23:1ff
sheep. [12]He who is a hireling and not a shepherd, whose own the Lk 15:4–7
sheep are not, sees the wolf coming and leaves the sheep and Acts 20:29
flees; and the wolf snatches them and scatters them. [13]He flees 1 Pet 2:25
because he is a hireling and cares nothing for the sheep. [14]I am the
good shepherd;* I know my own and my own know me, [15]as the 2 Tim 2:19
Father knows me and I know the Father; and I lay down my life Mt 11:25–27

10:6. Christ develops and interprets the image of the shepherd and the flock, to ensure that everyone who is well-disposed can understand his meaning. But the Jews fail to understand—as happened also when he promised the Eucharist (Jn 6:41–43) and spoke of the "living water" (Jn 7:40–43), or when he raised Lazarus from the dead (Jn 11:45–46).

10:7. After describing his future Church through the image of the flock, Christ extends the simile and calls himself the "door of the sheep". The shepherds and the sheep enter the sheepfold: both must enter through the door, which is Christ. "I", St Augustine preached, "seeking to enter in among you, that is, into your heart, preach Christ: if I were to preach other than that, I should be trying to enter by some other way. Through Christ I enter in, not to your houses but to your hearts. Through him I enter and you have willingly heard me speak of him. Why? Because you are Christ's sheep and you have been purchased with Christ's blood" (*In Ioann. Evang.*, 47, 2–3).

10:8. The severe reproach Jesus levels against those who came before him does not apply to Moses or the prophets (cf. Jn 5:39, 45; 8:56; 12:41), nor to the Baptist (cf. Jn 5:33), for they proclaimed the future Messiah and prepared the way for him. He is referring to the false prophets and deceivers of the people, among them some teachers of the Law—blind men and blind guides (cf. Mt 23:16–24) who block the people's way to Christ, as happened just a little before when the man born blind was cured (cf. Jn 9).

10:11–15. "The good shepherd lays down his life for the sheep": "Here," says St John Chrysostom, "he is speaking of his passion, making it clear this would take place for the salvation of the world and that he would go to it freely and willingly" (*Hom. on St John*, 59, 3). Our Lord spoke further about giving abundant pasture; now he speaks about giving his very life: "He did what he said he would do," St Gregory comments; "he gave his life for his sheep, and he gave his body and blood in the Sacrament to nourish with his flesh the sheep he had redeemed" (*In Evangelia homiliae*, 14, ad loc.). Hired men, on the other hand, run away if there is any danger, leaving the flock at risk. "Who is the hireling? He who sees the wolf coming and flees. The man who seeks his own glory, not the glory of Christ; the man who does not dare to reprove sinners. You are the hireling; you have seen the wolf coming and have fled [...] because you held your peace; and you held your peace, because you were afraid" (St Augustine, *In Ioann. Evang.*, 46, 8).

"Let them remember that their priestly ministry ... is—in a special way —'ordered' to the great solicitude of the

Jn 11:52 Ezek 37:24 Eph 4:4–5 for the sheep. [16]And I have other sheep, that are not of this fold; I
must bring them also, and they will heed my voice. So there shall
be one flock, one shepherd. [17]For this reason the Father loves me,
Phil 2:8–9 because I lay down my life, that I may take it again. [18]No one
Jn 5:26 takes it from me, but I lay it down of my own accord. I have
power to lay it down, and I have power to take it again; this charge
I have received from my Father."*
Jn 7:43; 9:16 [19]There was again a division among the Jews because of these
Jn 7:20; 8:48 words. [20]Many of them said, "He has a demon, and he is mad;

Good Shepherd, solicitude for the salvation of every human being. And this we must all remember: that it is not lawful for any one of us to deserve the name of 'hireling', that is to say, the name of one 'to whom the sheep do not belong', one who, 'since he is not the shepherd and the sheep do not belong to him, abandons the sheep and runs away as soon as he sees the wolf coming, and then the wolf attacks and scatters the sheep; this is because he is only a hired man and has no concern for the sheep.' The solicitude of every good shepherd is that all people 'may have life and have it to the full', so that none of them may be lost, but should have eternal life. Let us endeavour to make this solicitude penetrate deeply into our souls; let us strive to live it. May it characterize our personality, and be at the foundation of our priestly identity" (John Paul II, *Letter to priests*, 8 April 1979).

The Good Shepherd knows each of his sheep and calls it by name. This touching simile seems to be an exhortation to future pastors of the Church, as St Peter will later on explain: "Tend the flock of God that is your charge, not for shameful gain but eagerly, not as domineering over those in your charge but being examples to the flock" (1 Pet 5:2).

"The holiness of Christ's Spouse has always been shown—as it can be seen today—by the abundance of good shepherds. But our Christian faith, which teaches us to be simple, does not bid us be simple-minded. There are hirelings who keep silent, and there are hirelings who speak with words which are not those of Christ. That is why, if the Lord allows us to be left in the dark even in little things, if we feel that our faith is not firm, we should go to the good shepherd. He enters by the door as of right. He gives his life for others and wants to be in word and behaviour a soul in love. He may be a sinner too, but he trusts always in Christ's forgiveness and mercy" (St Josemaría Escrivá, *Christ Is Passing By*, 34).

10:16. "One flock, one shepherd." Christ's mission extends to everyone even though his own preaching is addressed, in the first instance, to the sheep of the house of Israel, as he himself revealed to the Canaanite woman (cf. Mt 15:24), and even though he sent the apostles on their first mission to preach to the people of Israel (cf. Mt 10:6). Now, however, foreseeing the fruits of his redemptive death (v. 15), he reveals that these will be applied to "other sheep, that are not of this fold", that is, Israel, and, after the resurrection, he does send the apostles to all nations (cf. Mt 28:19), to preach the Gospel to all creation (cf. Mk 16:15), beginning in Jerusalem and extending to all Judea, Samaria and the ends of the earth (cf. Acts 1:8). This fulfils the ancient promises about the rule of the Messiah covering the whole world (cf. Ps 2:8; Is 2:2–6; 66:17–19). The universal

why listen to him?" [21]Others said, "These are not the sayings of Mk 3:21
one who has a demon. Can a demon open the eyes of the blind?"

6. JESUS AND THE FATHER

Jesus and the Father are one

[22]It was the feast of the Dedication at Jerusalem; [23]it was winter, 1 Mac 4:36, 59
and Jesus was walking in the temple, in the portico of Solomon. Acts 3:11

---

scope of salvation caused St Paul to exclaim: "Remember that at one time you ... were ... separated from Christ, alienated from the commonwealth of Israel, and strangers to the covenants of promise, having no hope and without God in the world. But now in Christ Jesus you who once were far off have been brought near in the blood of Christ" (Eph 2:11–13; cf. Gal 3:27–28; Rom 3:22).

The unity of the Church is to be found under one visible head, for "it was to the Apostolic College alone, of which Peter is the head, that we believe that our Lord entrusted all the blessings of the New Covenant, in order to establish on earth the one Body of Christ into which all those should be fully incorporated who belong in any way to the people of God" (Vatican II, *Unitatis redintegratio*, 3). It is a Catholic's constant yearning that everyone should come to the true Church, "God's only flock, which like a standard lifted high for the nations to see, ministers the Gospel of peace to all mankind, as it makes its pilgrim way in hope towards its goal, the fatherland above" (ibid., 2).

10:17–18. Jesus shows that of his own free will he will give himself up to death for the sake of the flock (cf. Jn 6:51). Having been given supreme authority, Christ is free to offer himself as a sacrifice of expiation, and he voluntarily accepts his Father's commandment, in an act of perfect obedience. "We will never fully understand Jesus' freedom. It is immense, infinite, as is his love. But the priceless treasure of his generous holocaust should move us to ask, 'Why, Lord, have you granted me this privilege which I can use to follow in your footsteps, but also offend you?' Thus we come to appreciate that freedom is used properly when it is directed towards the good; and that it is misused when men are forgetful and turn away from the Love of loves" (St Josemaría Escrivá, *Friends of God*, 26).

10:19–21. The evangelist has reported a number of instances (cf. Jn 6:52; 7:12, 25–27, 31, 40–43) where people argued with each other about something our Lord said. On this occasion some people reject his teaching and repeat the calumny that he is possessed (Jn 7:20; 8:48) and does miracles through the power of the prince of demons (cf. Mt 9:34; 12:24; Mk 3:22; Lk 11:15); while others open their minds to the light and recognize that he must have divine powers if he can cure a blind man (cf. Jn 9).

The scene is forever being repeated. "Jesus: wherever you have passed no heart remains indifferent. You are either loved or hated. When an apostle follows you, carrying out his duty, is it surprising that—if he is another Christ—he should arouse similar murmurs of aversion or of love?" (St J. Escrivá, *The Way*, 687).

10:22. This feast commemorates an

Lk 22:67 [24]So the Jews gathered round him and said to him, "How long will
you keep us in suspense? If you are the Christ, tell us plainly."
Jn 5:36 [25]Jesus answered them, "I told you, and you do not believe. The
works that I do in my Father's name, they bear witness to me;
Jn 6:64; 8:45 [26]but you do not believe, because you do not belong to my sheep.
Jn 10:3–4:14 Prov 28:5 [27]My sheep hear my voice, and I know them, and they follow me;
1 Cor 2:14 [28]and I give them eternal life, and they shall never perish, and no
Jn 6:39; 10:10; 17:12 one shall snatch them out of my hand. [29]My Father, who has given
Rom 8:33–39 them to me,[w] is greater than all, and no one is able to snatch them
Deut 32–39 Is 43:13 out of the Father's hand. [30]I and the Father are one."
1 Jn 4:4
Jn 1:1; 14:10–11

---

episode in Jewish history (cf. 1 Mac 4:36–59; 2 Mac 1–2, 19; 10:1–8) when Judas Maccabeus, in the year 165 BC, after liberating Jerusalem from the control of the Seleucid kings of Syria, cleansed the temple of the profanations of Antiochus Epiphanes (1 Mac 1:54). From then onwards, on the twenty-fifth day of the month of Kisleu (November-December) and throughout the following week, all Judea celebrated the anniversary of the dedication of the new altar. It was also known as the "festival of lights" because it was customary to light lamps, a symbol of the Law, and put them in the windows of the houses (cf. 2 Mac 1:18).

10:24–25. When these Jews ask Jesus if he is the Messiah, "they speak in this way", St Augustine comments, "not because they desire truth, but to prepare the way for calumny" *(In Ioann. Evang.*, 48, 3). We have already seen Jesus reveal, by his words and deeds, that he is the only Son of God (5:19ff; 7:16ff; 8:25ff). In view of their good dispositions, he explicitly told the Samaritan woman (4:26) and the man born blind (9:37) that he was the Messiah and Saviour. Now he reproaches his listeners for refusing to recognize the works he does in his Father's name (cf. 5:36; 10:38). On other occasions he referred to works as a way to distinguish true prophets from false ones: "You will know them by their fruits" (Mt 7:16; cf. Mt 12:33).

10:26–29. Certainly faith and eternal life cannot be merited by man's own efforts: they are a gift of God. But the Lord does not deny anyone grace to believe and be saved, because he "desires all men to be saved and to come to the knowledge of the truth" (1 Tim 2:4). If someone tries to avoid receiving the gift of faith, his unbelief is blameworthy. On this point St Thomas Aquinas teaches: "I can see, thanks to the light of the sun; but if I close my eyes, I cannot see: this is no fault of the sun, it is my own fault, because by closing my eyes, I prevent the sunlight from reaching me" (*Comm. on St John,* ad loc.).

But those who do not oppose divine grace do come to believe in Jesus. They are known to and loved by him, enter under his protection and remain faithful with the help of his grace, which is a pledge of the eternal life which the Good Shepherd will eventually give them. It is true that in this world they will have to strive and in the course of striving they will sustain wounds; but if they stay united to the Good Shepherd nothing and no one will snatch Christ's sheep from

w. Other ancient authorities read *What my Father has given to me*

An attempt to stone Jesus

31The Jews took up stones again to stone him. 32Jesus answered Jer 8:59
them, "I have shown you many good works from the Father; for
which of these do you stone me?" 33The Jews answered him, "We Jn 5:18
stone you for no good work but for blasphemy; because you, Mt 26:65f
being a man, make yourself God." 34Jesus answered them, "Is it Ps 82:6

---

him, because our Father, God, is stronger than the Evil One. Our hope that God will grant us final perseverance is not based on our strength but on God's mercy: this hope should always motivate us to strive to respond to grace and to be ever more faithful to the demands of our faith.

10:30. Jesus reveals that he and the Father are one in substance. Earlier he proclaimed that God was his Father, "making himself equal with God"—which is why a number of times the Jewish authorities think of putting him to death (cf. 5:18; 8:59). Now he speaks about the mystery of God, which is something we can know about only through Revelation. Later on he will reveal more about this mystery, particularly at the Last Supper (14:10; 17:21–22). It is something the evangelist reflects on at the very beginning of the Gospel, in the prologue (cf. Jn 1:1 and note).

"Listen to the Son himself", St Augustine invites us. "'I and the Father are one.' He did not say, 'I am the Father' or 'I and the Father are one [Person].' But when he says 'I and the Father are one,' notice the two words '[we are]' and 'one' … For if they are one, then they are not diverse; if '[we] are', then there is both a Father and a Son" (*In Ioann. Evang.*, 36, 9). Jesus reveals that he is one in substance with the Father as far as divine essence or nature is concerned, but he also reveals that the Father and the Son are distinct Persons: "We believe then in the Father who eternally begets the Son; in the Son, the Word of God, who is eternally begotten; in the Holy Spirit, the uncreated Person who proceeds from the Father and the Son as their eternal Love. Thus in the three divine Persons, *coaeternae sibi et coaequales*, the life and beatitude of God perfectly One superabound and are consummated in the supreme excellence and glory proper to uncreated Being, and always 'there should be venerated Unity in the Trinity and Trinity in the Unity'" (Paul VI, *Creed of the People of God*, 10).

10:31–33. The Jews realize that Jesus is saying that he is God, but they interpret his words as blasphemy. He was called a blasphemer when he forgave the sins of the paralytic (Mt 9:1–8), and he will also be accused of blasphemy when he is condemned after solemnly confessing his divinity before the Sanhedrin (Mt 26:63–65). Our Lord, then, did reveal that he was God; but his hearers rejected this revelation of the mystery of the Incarnate God, refusing to examine the proof Jesus offered them; consequently, they accuse him, a man, of making himself God. Faith bases itself on reasonable evidence—miracles and prophecies—for believing that Jesus is really man and really God, even though our limited minds cannot work out how this can be so. Thus, our Lord, in order to affirm his divinity once more, uses two arguments which his adversaries cannot refute—the testimony of Holy Scripture (prophecies) and that of his own works (miracles).

10:34–36. On a number of occasions the Gospel has shown our Lord replying to the Jews' objections. Here he patiently

Mt 5:17 not written in your law, 'I said, you are gods'? [35]If he called them
gods to whom the word of God came (and scripture cannot be
Jer 1:5 broken), [36]do you say of him whom the Father consecrated and
sent into the world, 'You are blaspheming,' because I said, 'I am
the Son of God'? [37]If I am not doing the works of my Father, then
Jn 2:11 do not believe me; [38]but if I do them, even though you do not
believe me, believe the works, that you may know and understand
Jn 8:59 that the Father is in me and I am in the Father." [39]Again they tried
Lk 4:30 to arrest him, but he escaped from their hands.
Jn 1:28 [40]He went away again across the Jordan to the place where
Mt 19:1 John at first baptized, and there he remained. [41]And many came to

---

uses a form of argument which they regard as decisive—the authority of Holy Scripture. He quotes Psalm 82 in which God upbraids certain judges for acting unjustly despite his reminding them that "You are gods, sons of the Most High, all of you" (Ps 82:6). If this psalm calls the sons of Israel gods and sons of God, with how much more reason should he be called God who has been sanctified and sent by God? Christ's human nature, on being assumed by the Word, is sanctified completely and comes to the world to sanctify men. "The Fathers of the Church constantly proclaim that what was not assumed by Christ was not healed. Now Christ took a complete human nature just as it is found in us poor unfortunates, but one that was without sin, for Christ said of himself that he was the one 'whom the Father consecrated and sent into the world'" (Vatican II, *Ad gentes*, 3).

By using Sacred Scripture (cf. Mt 4:4, 7, 10; Lk 4:1) Jesus teaches us that Scripture comes from God. Therefore, the Church believes and affirms that "those divinely revealed realities which are contained and presented in Sacred Scripture have been committed to writing under the inspiration of the Holy Spirit. Holy Mother Church, relying on the belief of the Apostles, holds that the books of both the Old and New Testament in their entirety, with all their parts, are sacred and canonical because, having been written under the inspiration of the Holy Spirit (cf. Jn 20:31; 2 Tim 3:16; 2 Pet 1:19–21) they have God as their author and have been handed on as such to the Church. [...] Therefore, since everything is asserted by the Holy Spirit, it follows that the books of Scripture must be acknowledged as teaching firmly, faithfully, and without error that truth which God wanted to put into the sacred writings for the sake of our salvation" (Vatican II, *Dei Verbum*, 11).

10:37–38. The works which our Lord is referring to are his miracles, through which God's power is made manifest. Jesus presents his words and his works as forming a unity, with the miracles confirming his words and his words explaining the meaning of miracles. Therefore, when he asserts that he is the Son of God, this revelation is supported by the credentials of the miracles he works: hence, if no one can deny the fact of the miracles, it is only right for him to accept the truth of the words.

10:41–42. The opposition offered by some people (cf. Jn 10:20, 31, 39) contrasts with the way other people accept him and follow him to where he goes after this. St John the Baptist's preparatory work is still

him; and they said, "John did no sign, but everything that John
said about this man was true." [42]And many believed in him there. Jn 8:30

7. JESUS IS THE RESURRECTION AND THE LIFE

Jesus' reaction to the death of Lazarus

11 [1]Now a certain man was ill, Lazarus of Bethany, the village Lk 10:38
of Mary and her sister Martha. [2]It was Mary who anointed Jn 12:3
the Lord with ointment and wiped his feet with her hair, whose Lk 7:37
brother Lazarus was ill. [3]So the sisters sent to him, saying, "Lord,

---

producing results: those who accepted the Baptist's message now look for Christ and they believe when they see the truth of what the Precursor said: Jesus is the Messiah, the Son of God (cf. Jn 1:34).

Work done in the Lord's name is never useless: "Therefore, my beloved brethren, be steadfast, immovable, always abounding in the work of the Lord, knowing that in the Lord your labour is not in vain" (1 Cor 15:58). Just as the Baptist's word and example had the effect of helping many people later to believe in Jesus, the apostolic example given by Christians will never be in vain, even though the results may not come immediately. "To sow. The sower went out … Scatter your seed, apostolic soul. The wind of grace will bear it away if the furrow where it falls is not worthy … Sow, and be certain that the seed will take root and bear fruit" (St Josemaría Escrivá, *The Way*, 794).

11:1–45. This chapter deals with one of Jesus' most outstanding miracles. The Fourth Gospel, by including it, demonstrates Jesus' power over death, which the Synoptic Gospels showed by reporting the raising of the daughter of Jairus (Mt 9:255 and par.) and of the son of the widow of Nain (Lk 7:12).

The evangelist first sets the scene (vv. 1–16); then he gives Jesus' conversation with Lazarus' sisters (vv. 17–37); finally, he reports the raising of Lazarus four days after his death (vv. 38–45). Bethany was only about three kilometres (two miles) from Jerusalem (v. 18). On the days prior to his passion, Jesus often visited this family, to which he was very attached. St John records Jesus' affection (vv. 3, 5, 36) by describing his emotion and sorrow at the death of his friend.

By raising Lazarus our Lord shows his divine power over death and thereby gives proof of his divinity, in order to confirm his disciples' faith and reveal himself as the Resurrection and the Life. Most Jews, but not the Sadducees, believed in the resurrection of the body. Martha believed in it (cf. v. 24).

Apart from being a real, historical event, Lazarus' return to life is a sign of our future resurrection: we too will return to life. Christ, by his glorious resurrection through which he is the "first-born from the dead" (Col 1:18; 1 Cor 15:20; Rev 1:5), is also the cause and model of our resurrection. In this his resurrection is different from that of Lazarus, for "Christ being raised from the dead will never die again" (Rom 6:9), whereas Lazarus returned to earthly life, later to die again.

11:2. There are a number of women in the Gospels who are called Mary. The Mary here is Mary of Bethany, the sister

Jn 9:3 he whom you love is ill." [4]But when Jesus heard it he said, "This
illness is not unto death; it is for the glory of God, so that the Son
of God may be glorified by means of it."
[5]Now Jesus loved Martha and her sister and Lazarus. [6]So when
he heard that he was ill, he stayed two days longer* in the place
where he was. [7]Then after this he said to the disciples, "Let us go
Jn 8:59; 10:31 into Judea again." [8]The disciples said to him, "Rabbi, the Jews
were but now seeking to stone you, and are you going there
1 Jn 2:10f again?" [9]Jesus answered, "Are there not twelve hours in the day?
If any one walks in the day, he does not stumble, because he sees
Jn 12:35 the light of this world. [10]But if any one walks in the night, he
Mt 9:24 stumbles, because the light is not in him." [11]Thus he spoke, and
then he said to them, "Our friend Lazarus has fallen asleep, but I
go to awake him out of sleep." [12]The disciples said to him, "Lord,

---

of Lazarus (v. 2), the woman who later anointed our Lord, again in Bethany, at the house of Simon the leper (cf. Jn 12:1–8; Mk 14:3): the indefinite or aorist "(she) anointed" expresses an action which occurred prior to the time of writing, but the anointing took place after the resurrection of Lazarus.

Were Mary of Bethany, Mary Magdalene and the "sinful" woman who anointed Jesus' feet in Galilee (cf. Lk 7:37) one, two or three women? Although sometimes it is argued that they are one and the same, it seems more likely that they were all different people. Firstly, we must distinguish the Galilee anointing (Lk 7:38) by the "sinner" from the Bethany anointing done by Lazarus' sister (Jn 12:1): because of the time they took place and particular details reported, they are clearly distinct (cf. the note on Jn 12:1). Besides, the Gospels give us no positive indication that Mary of Bethany was the same person as the "sinner" of Galilee. Nor are there strong grounds for identifying Mary Magdalene and the "sinner", whose name is not given; Mary Magdalene appears among the women who follow Jesus in Galilee as the woman out of whom seven demons were cast (cf. Lk 8:2), and Luke presents her in his account as someone new: no information is given which could link her with either of the two other women.

Nor can Mary of Bethany and Mary Magdalene be identified, for John differentiates between the two: he never calls Lazarus' sister Mary Magdalene, nor does he in any way link the latter (who stays beside the cross—Jn 19:25—and who goes to the tomb and sees the risen Lord) with Mary of Bethany.

The reason why Mary of Bethany has sometimes been confused with Mary Magdalene is due (1) to the identification of the latter with the "sinner" of Galilee through connecting Magdalene's possession by the devil with the sinfulness of the woman who did the anointing in Galilee; and (2) to confusing the two anointings, which would make Lazarus' sister the "sinner" who does the first anointing. This was how the three women were made out to be one, but there are no grounds for that interpretation. The best-grounded and most common interpretation offered by exegetes is that they are three distinct women.

11:4. The glory which Christ speaks of

if he has fallen asleep, he will recover." [13]Now Jesus had spoken
of his death, but they thought that he meant taking rest in sleep.
[14]Then Jesus told them plainly, "Lazarus is dead; [15]and for your
sake I am glad that I was not there, so that you may believe. But
let us go to him." [16]Thomas, called the Twin, said to his fellow Jn 14:5;
disciples, "Let us also go, that we may die with him." 20:24–29 Mk 10:32

[17]Now when Jesus came, he found that Lazarus[x] had already
been in the tomb four days. [18]Bethany was near Jerusalem, about
two miles[y] off, [19]and many of the Jews had come to Martha and
Mary to console them concerning their brother. [20]When Martha Lk 10:39ff
heard that Jesus was coming, she went to meet him, while Mary
sat in the house. [21]Martha said to Jesus, "Lord, if you had been
here, my brother would not have died. [22]And even now I know Mt 11:43
that whatever you ask from God, God will give you." [23]Jesus said Mk 11:24

---

here, St Augustine says, "was no gain to Jesus; it was only for our good. Therefore, Jesus says that his illness is not unto death, because the particular death was not for death but rather for a miracle, which being wrought men should believe in Christ and thereby avoid the true death" (*In Ioann. Evang.*, 49, 6).

11:8–10. Stoning was the form of capital punishment applying to blasphemy (cf. Lev 24:16). We have seen that people tried to stone Jesus at least twice: first, when he proclaimed that he was the Son of God and that he existed from eternity (by saying that he "was" before Abraham lived)—Jn 8:58–59; second, when he revealed that he and the Father were one (cf. Jn 10:30–31).

These attempts by the Jewish authorities failed because Jesus "hour" had not yet arrived—that is, the time laid down by his Father for his death and resurrection. When the crucifixion comes, it will be the hour of his enemies and of "the power of darkness" (Lk 22:53). But until that moment it is daytime, and our Lord can walk without his life being in danger.

11:16. Thomas' words remind us of the apostles saying at the Last Supper that they would be ready to die for their Master (cf. Mt 2:31–35). We have seen how the apostles stayed loyal when many disciples left our Lord after his discourse on the Bread of Life (Jn 6:67–71), and how they remained faithful to him despite their personal weaknesses. But when, after Judas Iscariot's betrayal, Jesus lets himself be arrested without offering resistance—in fact, forbidding the use of weapons (cf. Jn 18:11)—they become disconcerted and run away. Only St. John will stay faithful in Jesus' hour of greatest need.

11:18. Fifteen stadia, in Greek measurement: three kilometres (two miles).

11:21–22. According to St Augustine, Martha's request is a good example of confident prayer, a prayer of abandonment into the hands of God, who knows better than we what we need. Therefore, "she did not say, But now I ask you to raise my brother to life again. [...] All she said was, I know that you can do it; if you will, do it; it is for you to judge

x. Greek *he* **y.** Greek *fifteen stadia*

Jn 5:25; 6:40 to her, "Your brother will rise again." [24]Martha said to him, "I
know that he will rise again in the resurrection at the last day."
Jn 5:25; 8:51 [25]Jesus said to her, "I am the resurrection and the life,[z] he who
believes in me, though he die, yet shall he live, [26]and whoever
Jn 6:69 lives and believes in me shall never die. Do you believe this?"
Mt 16:16 [27]She said to him, "Yes, Lord; I believe that you are the Christ, the
son of God, he who is coming into the world."

[28]When she had said this, she went and called her sister Mary,
saying quietly, "The Teacher is here and is calling for you." [29]And
when she heard it, she rose quickly and went to him. [30]Now Jesus
had not yet come to the village, but was still in the place where
Martha had met him. [31]When the Jews who were with her in the
house, consoling her, saw Mary rise quickly and go out, they followed her, supposing that she was going to the tomb to weep
Jn 11:21 there. [32]Then Mary, when she came to where Jesus was and saw

---

whether to do it, not for me to presume" (*In Ioann. Evang.*, 49, 13). The same can be said of Mary's words, which St John repeats at v. 32.

11:24–26. Here we have one of the most concise definitions Christ gives of himself, and which St John faithfully passes on to us (cf. Jn 10:9; 14:6; 15:1): Jesus is the Resurrection and the Life. He is the Resurrection because by his victory over death he is the cause of the resurrection of all men. The miracle he works in raising Lazarus is a sign of Christ's power to give life to people. And so, by faith in Jesus Christ, who arose first from among the dead, the Christian is sure that he too will rise one day, like Christ (cf. 1 Cor 15:23; Col 1:18). Therefore, for the believer death is not the end; it is simply the step to eternal life, a change of dwelling place, as one of the *Roman Missal*'s Prefaces of Christian Death puts it: "Lord, for your faithful people life is changed, not ended. When the body of our earthly dwelling lies in death, we gain an everlasting dwelling place in heaven".

By saying that he is Life, Jesus is referring not only to that life which begins beyond the grave, but also to the supernatural life which grace brings to the soul of man when he is still a wayfarer on this earth.

"This life, which the Father has promised and offered to each man in Jesus Christ, his eternal and only Son, who 'when the time had fully come' (Gal 4:4), became incarnate and was born of the Virgin Mary, is the final fulfilment of man's vocation. It is in a way the fulfilment of the 'destiny' that God has prepared for him from eternity. This 'divine destiny' is advancing, in spite of all the enigmas, the unsolved riddles, the twists and turns of 'human destiny' in the world of time. Indeed, while all this, in spite of all the riches of life in times, necessarily and inevitably leads to the frontiers of death and the goal of the destruction of the human body, beyond that goal we see Christ. 'I am the resurrection and the life, he who believes in me ... shall never die.' In Jesus Christ, who was crucified and laid in the tomb and then rose again, 'our hope of resurrection dawned ... the

z. Other ancient authorities omit *and the life*

him, fell at his feet, saying to him, "Lord, if you had been here,
my brother would not have died." [33]When Jesus saw her weeping, Jn 11:38; 13:21
and the Jews who came with her also weeping, he was deeply Mt 9:36
moved in spirit and troubled; [34]and he said, "Where have you laid Mk 6:34
him?" They said to him, "Lord, come and see." [35]Jesus wept. [36]So Lk 19:41
the Jews said, "See how he loved him!" [37]But some of them said,
"Could not he who opened the eyes of a blind man have kept this
man from dying?"

The raising of Lazarus

[38]Then Jesus, deeply moved again, came to the tomb; it was a
cave, and a stone lay upon it. [39]Jesus said, "Take away the stone."
Martha, the sister of the dead man, said to him, "Lord, by this
time there will be an odour, for he has been dead four days."
[40]Jesus said to her, "Did I not tell you that if you would believe
you would see the glory of God?" [41]So they took away the stone. Jn 17:1
And Jesus lifted his eyes and said, "Father, I thank thee that thou Mt 14:19

---

bright promise of immortality' (*Roman Missal*, Preface of Christian Death, I), on the way to which man, through the death of the body, shares with the whole of visible creation the necessity to which matter is subject" (John Paul II, *Redemptor hominis*, 18).

11:33–36. This passage gives us an opportunity to reflect on the depth and tenderness of Jesus' feelings. If the physical death of his friend can move him to tears, what will he not feel over the spiritual death of a sinner who has brought about his eternal condemnation? "Christ wept: let man also weep for himself. For why did Christ weep, but to teach men to weep" (St Augustine, *In Ioann. Evang.*, 49, 19). We also should weep—but for our sins, to help us return to the life of grace through conversion and repentance. We should appreciate our Lord's tears: he is praying for us, who are sinners: "Jesus is your friend. The Friend. With a human heart, like yours. With loving eyes that wept for Lazarus. And he loves you as much as he loved Lazarus" (St Josemaría Escrivá, *The Way*, 422).

11:41–42. Through his sacred humanity Jesus is expressing himself as the natural Son of God, that is, he is the metaphysical Son of God, not adopted like the rest of men. This is the source of Jesus' feelings, which helps us to understand that when he says "Father" he is speaking with a unique and indescribable intensity. When the Gospels let us see Jesus praying, they always show him beginning with the invocation "Father", which reflects his singular trust and love. These sentiments should also in some way find a place in our prayer, for through Baptism we are joined to Christ and in him we became children of God (cf. Jn 1:12; Rom 6:1–11; 8:14–17), and so we should always pray in a spirit of sonship and gratitude for the many good things our Father God has given us.

The miracle of the raising of Lazarus, which really is an extraordinary miracle, is a proof that Jesus is the Son of God, sent into the world by his Father. And so it is, that when Lazarus is brought back to life, people's faith in Jesus is increased—the disciples' (v. 15), Martha's and Mary's (vv. 26, 40) and that of the people at large (vv. 36, 45).

Jn 12:30 Mt 14:23 hast heard me. 42I knew that thou hearest me always, but I have
said this on account of the people standing by, that they may
Jn 5:27–29 believe that thou didst send me." 43When he had said this, he cried
with a loud voice, "Lazarus, come out." 44The dead man came out,
his hands and feet bound with bandages, and his face wrapped
with a cloth. Jesus said to them, "Unbind him, and let him go."

The Sanhedrin decides on the death of Jesus

45Many of the Jews therefore, who had come with Mary and had
Lk 16:31 seen what he did, believed in him; 46but some of them went to the
Mt 26:3–5 Pharisees and told them what Jesus had done. 47So the chief
priests and the Pharisees gathered the council, and said, "What are

---

11:43. Jesus calls Lazarus by name. Although he is really dead, he has not thereby lost his personal identity: dead people continue to exist, but they have a different mode of existence, because they have changed from mortal life to eternal life. This is why Jesus states that God "is not God of the dead, but of the living", for to him all are alive (cf. Mt 22:32; Lk 20:38).

This passage can be applied to the spiritual resurrection of the soul who has sinned and recovers grace. God wants us to be saved (cf. 1 Tim 2:4); therefore we should never lose heart; we should always desire and hope to reach this goal: "Never despair. Lazarus was dead and decaying: 'Iam foetet, quatriduanus enim est. By now he will smell; this is the fourth day,' says Martha to Jesus. If you hear God's inspiration and follow it—'Lazare, veni foras!: Lazarus, come out!'—you will return to Life" (St Josemaría Escrivá, *The Way*, 719).

11:44. The Jews prepared the body for burial by washing it and anointing it with aromatic ointments to delay decomposition and counteract offensive odours; they then wrapped the body in linen cloths and bandages, covering the head with a napkin—a method very like the Egyptians', but not entirely extending to full embalming, which involved removing certain internal organs.

Lazarus' tomb would have consisted of a subterranean chamber linked to the surface by steps, with the entrance blocked by a slab. Lazarus was moved out to the entrance by a supernatural force. As happened in the case of the raising of Jairus' daughter (Mk 5:42–43), due to their astonishment no one moved until our Lord's words broke the atmosphere of silence and terror which had been created. St Augustine sees in the raising of Lazarus a symbol of the sacrament of Penance: in the same way as Lazarus comes out of the tomb, "when you confess, you come forth. For what does 'come forth' mean if not emerging from what is hidden, to be made manifest. But for you to confess is God's doing; he calls you with an urgent voice, by an extraordinary grace. And just as the dead man came out still bound, so you go to confession still guilty. In order that his sins be loosed, the Lord said this to his ministers: 'Unbind him and let him go'. What you will loose on earth will be loosed also in heaven" (St Augustine, *In Ioann. Evang*., 49, 24). Christian art has used this comparison from very early on; in the catacombs we find some one hun-

we to do? For this man performs many signs. [48]If we let him go on
thus, every one will believe in him, and the Romans will come
and destroy our holy place[a] and our nation." [49]But one of them, Jn 18:31
Caiaphas, who was high priest that year, said to them, "You know Lk 3:2
nothing at all; [50]you do not understand that it is expedient for you
that one man should die for the people, and that the whole nation
should not perish."* [51]He did not say this of his own accord, but Num 27:21
being high priest that year he prophesied that Jesus should die for
the nation, [52]and not for the nation only, but to gather into one the Jn 10:6
children of God who are scattered abroad. [53]So from that day on 1 Jn 2:2
they took counsel how to put him to death. Jn 5:18 Mt 12:14

---

dred and fifty representations of the raising of Lazarus, symbolizing thereby the gift of the life of grace which comes through the priest, who in effect repeats these words to the sinner: "Lazarus, come out."

11:45–48. Once again, as Simeon had predicted, Jesus is a sign of contradiction (cf. Lk 2:34; Jn 7:12, 31, 40; 9:16; etc.): presented with the miracle of the raising of Lazarus some people believe in Jesus (cf. v. 45), and some denounce him to his enemies (cf. vv. 46–47)—confirming what is said in the parable of the rich man: "neither will they be convinced if someone should rise from the dead" (cf. Lk 16:31).

"Our (holy) place": this expression or similar expressions such as "the place", "this place", was used to designate the temple, the holy place par excellence and, by extension, all the Holy City of Jerusalem (cf. 2 Mac 5:19; Acts 6:14).

11:49–53. Caiaphas held the high priesthood from the year AD 18 to the year 36. Caiaphas was the instrument God used to prophesy the redemptive death of the Saviour, for it was one of the functions of the high priest to consult God on how to lead the people (cf. Ex 28:30; Num 27:21; 1 Sam 23:9; 30:7–8). Here Caiaphas' words have a dual meaning: one, Caiaphas' meaning, is that he wants to put Christ to death, on the pretext that that will ensure the political peace and survival of Israel; the other, the meaning intended by the Holy Spirit, is the announcement of the foundation of the new Israel, the Church, through the death of Christ on the cross (Caiaphas is unaware of this meaning). And so it happens that the last high priest of the Old Alliance prophesies the investiture of the High Priest of the New Alliance, which will be sealed with his own blood.

When the Evangelist states that Christ was going to die "to gather into one the children of God who are scattered abroad" (v. 52), he is referring to what our Lord had said regarding the salvific effects of his death (cf. Jn 10:14–15). The prophets had already announced the future assembly of Israelites faithful to God to form the new people of Israel (cf. Is 43:5; Jer 23:3–5; Ezek 34:23; 37:21–24). These prophecies are fulfilled by the death of Christ, who, on being raised up on the cross, draws and gathers together the true people of God, composed of all believers, whether Israelites or not. The Second Vatican Council uses this passage as a source

a. Greek *our place*

Jn 7:1 [54]Jesus therefore no longer went about openly among the Jews,
but went from there to the country near the wilderness, to a town
called Ephraim; and there he stayed with the disciples.
Jn 2:13; 6:4 2 Chron 30:17 [55]Now the Passover of the Jews was at hand, and many went
up from the country to Jerusalem before the Passover, to purify
themselves. [56]They were looking for Jesus and saying to one
Jn 7:11 another as they stood in the temple, "What do you think? That he
will not come to the feast?" [57]Now the chief priests and the
Pharisees had given orders that if any one knew where he was, he
should let them know, so that they might arrest him.

---

when speaking of the universality of the Church: "All men are called to belong to the new people of God. This people therefore, whilst remaining one and only one, is to be spread throughout the whole world and to all ages in order that the design of God's will may be fulfilled: he made human nature one in the beginning and has decreed that all his children who were scattered should be finally gathered together as one (cf. Jn 11:52). It was for this purpose that God sent his Son; whom he appointed heir of all things (cf. Heb 1:2), that he might be teacher, king and priest of all, the head of the new and universal people of God's sons" (*Lumen gentium*, 13).

In the fourth century, St John Chrysostom explained the catholicity of the Church using these words: "What is the meaning of 'to gather into one those who are scattered abroad'? He made them one body. He who dwells in Rome knows that the Christians of India are his members" (Hom. on St John, 65, 1).

11:54. The time for him to die has not yet arrived; therefore Jesus acts prudently, taking the steps anyone would take not to precipitate events.

11:55. Since the Passover was the most solemn Jewish feast, the people used to arrive in Jerusalem some days in advance to prepare for it by washings, fasts and offerings—practices established not by the Mosaic law but by popular piety; the rites of the Passover itself, with the sacrificing of the lamb, were a rite of purification and expiation for sins. The Passover of the Jews was a figure of the Christian Pasch or Easter, for, as St Paul the Apostle teaches us, our paschal lamb is Christ (cf. Cor 5:7), who offered himself once and for all to the eternal Father on the cross to atone for our sins. Paul VI recalled this happy truth of faith: "Gave himself for me? But does there still exist a religion which is expressed in sacrifices? No, the sacrifices of the ancient law and pagan religions have no longer any reason to exist; but the world always needs a sacrifice, a valid, unique and perennial one, for the redemption of human sin [...]; it is the sacrifice of Christ on the cross, which wipes out sin from the world; a sacrifice which the Eucharist actualizes in time and makes it possible for the men of this earth to take part in it" (*Homily on Corpus Christi*, 17 June 1976).

If the Jews prepared to celebrate the Passover with all these rites and ablutions, it is obvious what steps we should take to celebrate or participate in the Mass and to receive Christ—our Pasch—in the Eucharist. "On this earth, when we receive an important person, we bring out the best—lights, music, formal dress. How should we prepare to receive Christ

8. JESUS IS ACCLAIMED AS THE MESSIANIC KING

Mary anoints our Lord at Bethany

12 *[1]Six days before the Passover, Jesus came to Bethany, Jn 11:1ff Mt 26:6–13
where Lazarus was, whom Jesus had raised from the dead. Mk 14:3–9
[2]There they made him a supper; Martha served, and Lazarus was Lk 10:40
one of those at table with him. [3]Mary took a pound of costly oint- Lk 7:38
ment of pure nard and anointed the feet of Jesus and wiped his
feet with her hair; and the house was filled with the fragrance of
the ointment. [4]But Judas Iscariot, one of his disciples (he who was

---

into our soul? Have we ever thought about how we would behave if we could only receive him once in a lifetime?" (St J. Escrivá, *Christ Is Passing By*, 91).

12:1. Jesus pays another visit to his friends in Bethany. It is very touching to see this friendship, at once divine and human, expressed in the form of frequent contact. "It's true that I always call our tabernacle 'Bethany'. Become a friend of the Master's friends—Lazarus, Martha, Mary—and then you won't ask me any more why I call our tabernacle 'Bethany'" (St Josemaría Escrivá, *The Way*, 322).

12:2–3. Apparently, our Lord was anointed on two different occasions—first, at the start of his public ministry, in Galilee, as recounted by St Luke (7:36–50); and second, towards the end of his life, in Bethany, reported here by St John and undoubtedly the same incident as described by St Matthew (26:6–13) and St Mark (14:3–9). The two anointings are quite distinct: they occur at different times and the details of the accounts differ: the first is a demonstration of repentance followed by pardon; the second, a delicate expression of love, which Jesus further interprets as an anticipation of the anointing of his body in burial (v. 7).

Although these anointings of Jesus had a particular significance, they should be seen in the context of eastern hospitality; cf. the note on Mk 14:3–9.

The pound was a measure of weight equivalent to three hundred grams; a denarius, as we have indicated elsewhere, was a day's wage of an agricultural labourer; therefore, the cost of the flask of perfume would have amounted to a year's wage.

"What a shining proof of magnanimity is this 'extravagance' on Mary's part! Judas on the other hand laments this 'waste' of so valuable a perfume; in his greed he had been calculating the price: it would have fetched at least 'three hundred silver pieces'.

"True detachment leads us to be very generous with God and with our fellowmen. […] Don't be mean and grudging with people who, without counting the cost, have given of their all, everything they have, for your sake. Just ask yourselves, how much does it cost you—in financial terms as well—to be Christians? Above all, don't forget that 'God loves a cheerful giver' (2 Cor 9:7)" (St Josemaría Escrivá, *Friends of God*, 126).

12:4–6. From this passage and from John 13:29 we know that Judas was the person in charge of the money. His petty thefts—they could not have been any

to betray him), said, 5“Why was this ointment not sold for three
Jn 13:29 hundred denarii[b] and given to the poor?” 6This he said, not that he
Lk 8:3 cared for the poor, but because he was a thief, and as he had the
money box he used to take what was put into it. 7Jesus said, “Let
Deut 15:11 her alone, let her keep it for the day of my burial. 8The poor you
always have with you, but you do not always have me.”
Jn 11:56ff 9When the great crowd of the Jews learned that he was there,
they came, not only on account of Jesus but also to see Lazarus,
whom he had raised from the dead. 10So the chief priests planned
Jn 7:31 to put Lazarus also to death, 11because on account of him many of
the Jews were going away and believing in Jesus.

Mt 21:1–11
Mk 11:1–10
Lk 19:28–38
1 Mac 13:51

The Messiah’s entry into Jerusalem

12The next day a great crowd who had come to the feast heard that
Jesus was coming to Jerusalem. 13So they took branches of palm

---

more than that, given the meagre resources of Jesus and the Twelve—played their part in disposing him to commit his eventual sin of betraying Jesus; his complaint about the woman’s generosity was quite hypocritical. “Frequently the servants of Satan disguise themselves as servants of righteousness (cf. 2 Cor 11:14–15). Therefore, (Judas) hid his malice under a cloak of piety” (St Thomas Aquinas, *Comm. on St John*, ad loc.).

12:7–8. As well as praising Mary’s generous gesture, our Lord indirectly announces his death, even implying that it will happen so precipitously that there will hardly be time to prepare his body for burial in the normal way (cf. Lk 23:56; see also the note on Jn 11:44). He is not saying that almsgiving is not a good thing (he often recommended it: cf. Lk 11:41; 12:33); nor that people should have no concern for the poor (cf. Mt 25:40); what he is doing here is exposing the hypocrisy of people like Judas who deceitfully profess noble motives in order to avoid giving God the honour he is due (cf. also the notes on Mt 26:8–11; Mk 14:3–9).

12:9–11. The news of the raising of Lazarus has spread rapidly among the people of Judea and those travelling up to Jerusalem for the Passover; many believe in Jesus (cf. Jn 11:45); others look for him (cf. Jn 11:56) perhaps more out of curiosity (cf. Jn 12:9) than faith. Following Christ demands more of each of us than just superficial, short-lived enthusiasm. We should not forget those “who, when they hear the word, immediately receive it with joy; and they have no root in themselves, but endure for a while; then, when tribulation or persecution arises on account of the word, immediately they fall away” (Mk 4:16–17).

12:13. When the crowd uses the words “Blessed is he who comes in the name of the Lord”, taken from Psalm 118:26, they are acclaiming Jesus as the Messiah. The words “the king of Israel”, not included in the Synoptics, underline Christ’s royalty: the Messiah is the King of Israel *par excellence*. However, Jesus had previously fled from those who wanted to make him king because they had an

b. The denarius was a day’s wage for a labourer

trees and went out to meet him, crying, "Hosanna! Blessed is he Rev 7:9
who comes in the name of the Lord, even the King of Israel! Ps 118:26
14 And Jesus found a young ass and sat upon it; as it is written, Jn 1:49; 6:25

15 "Fear not, daughter of Zion; Zech 9:9
behold, your king is coming, Is 40:9
sitting on an ass's colt!"

16 His disciples did not understand this at first; but when Jesus was Jn 2:22; 7:39
glorified, then they remembered that this had been written of him
and had been done to him. 17 The crowd that had been with him
when he called Lazarus out of the tomb and raised him from the
dead bore witness. 18 The reason why the crowd went to meet him
was that they heard he had done this sign. 19 The Pharisees then Jn 11:47f
said to one another, "You see that you can do nothing; look, the
world has gone after him."

Jesus announces his glorification

20 Now among those who went up to worship at the feast were Jn 1:44; 7:34f;
some Greeks. 21 So these came to Philip, who was from Bethsaida 11:55

---

earth-bound view of his mission (Jn 6:14–15). Later on, before Pilate, he will explain that his kingship "is not of this world". "Christ", St Augustine teaches, "was not king of Israel for exacting tribute, or arming a host with the sword; but king of Israel to rule souls, to counsel them for eternal life, to bring to the Kingdom of heaven those that believe, hope and love" (*In Ioann. Evang.*, 51, 4).

"Christ should reign first and foremost in our soul. But how would we reply if he asks us: 'How do you go about letting me reign in you?' I would reply that I need lots of his grace. Only that way can my every heartbeat and breath, my least intense look, my most ordinary word, my most basic feeling be transformed into a hosanna to Christ my King" (St Josemaría Escrivá, *Christ Is Passing By*, 181).

12:14–16. After Jesus' resurrection, the apostles will grasp the meaning of many episodes in our Lord's life which they had not previously understood fully (cf. Jn 2:22). For example, in his triumphal entry into Jerusalem with all the people acclaiming him as Messiah, they will see the fulfilment of the Old Testament prophecies (cf., e.g., in addition to Zech 9:9, which the Gospel quotes, Gen 49:10–11). See the notes on Mt 21:1–5; Mk 11:1–11; and Lk 19:39–35.

12:17–19. The Gospel records the part played by the raising of Lazarus in bringing about Jesus' death. Those who witnessed the miracle see Jesus as the Messiah sent by God, and their faith influences many of the pilgrims who have come up for the Passover; but the Pharisees persist in their blindness, which leads them to seek Christ's death (cf. Jn 11:53).

12:20–23. These "Greeks" approach Philip because seemingly this Apostle, who has a Greek name, must have understood Greek and been able to act as interpreter. If that was the case, then this is a very important moment because it means

in Galilee, and said to him, "Sir, we wish to see Jesus." [23]Philip
went and told Andrew; Andrew went with Philip and they told
Jn 2:4 Jesus. [23]And Jesus answered them, "The hour has come for the
Is 53:10–12 Son of man to be glorified. [24]Truly, truly, I say to you, unless a
Rom 14:9 1 Cor 15:36 grain of wheat falls into the earth and dies, it remains alone; but if
it dies, it bears much fruit. [25]He who loves his life loses it, and he
Mt 16:25 Mk 8:35 who hates his life in this world will keep it for eternal life. [26]If any
Lk 9:24 one serves me, he must follow me; and where I am, there shall my
Jn 14:3; 17:24 servant be also; if any one serves me, the Father will honour him.

---

that people of a non-Jewish culture came in search of Christ: which would make them the first-fruits of the spread of the Christian faith in the hellenic world. This would make it easier to understand our Lord's exclamation in verse 23, about his own glorification, which has to do not only with his being raised up to the right hand of the Father (cf. Phil 2:6–11) but also with his attracting all men to himself (cf. Jn 12:32).

Jesus refers to "the hour" on other occasions also. Sometimes he means the end of the world (cf. Mk 13:32; Jn 5:25); sometimes, as is the case here, it means the moment of redemption through his death and glorification (cf. Mk 14:41; Jn 2:4; 4:23; 7:30; 8:20; 12:27; 13:1; 17:1).

12:24–25. There is an apparent paradox here between Christ's humiliation and his glorification. Thus, "it was appropriate that the loftiness of his glorification should be preceded by the lowliness of his passion" (St Augustine, *In Ioann. Evang.*, 51, 8). This is the same idea as we find in St Paul, when he says that Christ humbled himself and became obedient unto death, even death on a cross, and that therefore God the Father exalted him above all created things (cf. Phil 2:8–9). This is a lesson and an encouragement to the Christian, who should see every type of suffering and contradiction as a sharing in Christ's cross, which redeems us and exalts us. To be supernaturally effective, a person has to die to himself, forgetting his comfort and shedding his selfishness. "If the grain of wheat does not die, it remains unfruitful. Don't you want to be a grain of wheat, to die through mortification, and to yield a rich harvest? May Jesus bless your wheatfield!" (St J. Escrivá, *The Way*, 199).

12:26. Our Lord has spoken about his sacrifice being a condition of his entering his glory. And what holds good for the Master applies also to his disciples (cf. Mt 10:24; Lk 6:40). Jesus wants each of us to be of service to him. It is a mystery of God's plans that he—who is all, who has all and who needs nothing and nobody—should choose to need our help to ensure that his teaching and the salvation wrought by him reaches all men.

"To follow Christ: that is the secret. We must accompany him so closely that we come to live with him, like the first Twelve did; so closely, that we become identified with him. Soon we will be able to say, provided we have not put obstacles in the way of grace, that we have put on, have clothed ourselves with, our Lord Jesus Christ (cf. Rom 13:14). […]

"I have distinguished as it were four stages in our effort to identify ourselves with Christ—seeking him, finding him, getting to know him, loving him. It may seem clear to you that you are only at the first stage. Seek him then, hungrily; seek him within yourselves with all your

[27]"Now is my soul troubled. And what shall I say? 'Father, Jn 11:33
save me from this hour'? No, for this purpose I have come to this Ps 6:3 Mt 26:38
hour. [28]Father, glorify thy name." Then a voice came from heaven, Heb 5:7–8
"I have glorified it, and I will glorify it again." [29]The crowd stand- Jn 5:37 Mt 17:5
ing by heard it and said that it had thundered. Others said, "An Lk 22:43
angel has spoken to him." [30]Jesus answered, "This voice has come Jn 11:42
for your sake, not for mine. [31]Now is the judgment of this world, Jn 3:19; 14:30 Lk 10:18

---

strength. If you act with determination, I am ready to guarantee that you have already found him, and have begun to get to know him and to love him, and to hold your conversation in heaven (cf. Phil 3:20)" (St Josemaría Escrivá, *Friends of God*, 299–300).

12:27. The thought of the death that awaits him saddens Jesus, and he turns to the Father in a prayer very similar to that of Gethsemane (cf. Mt 26:39; Mk 14:36; Lk 22:42): our Lord, as man, seeks support in the love and power of his Father God to be strengthened to fulfil his mission. We find this very consoling, for we often feel weak in moments of trial: like Jesus we should seek support in God's strength, for "thou art my rock and my fortress" (Ps 31:3).

12:28. "Glory" in Holy Scripture implies God's holiness and power; the "glory of God" dwelt in the sanctuary in the desert and in the temple of Jerusalem (cf. Ex 40:35; 1 Kings 8:11). The voice of the Father saying "I have glorified it, and I will glorify it again" is a solemn ratification that the fullness of divinity dwells in Jesus (cf. Col 2:9; Jn 1:14) and that, through his passion, death and resurrection, it will be made patent, in his human nature itself, that Jesus is the Son of God (cf. Mk 15:39).

This episode evokes other occasions—at Christ's baptism (cf. Mt 3:13–17 and par.) and his transfiguration (Mt 17:1–5 and par.)—when God the Father bears witness to the divinity of Jesus.

12:31–33. Jesus tells them the results that will flow from his passion and death. "Now is the judgment of this world", that is, of those who persist in serving Satan, the "prince of this world". Although "world" means the totality of mankind whom Christ comes to save (cf. Jn 3:16–17), it also often means all that is opposed to God (cf. the note on Jn 1:10) which is the sense it has here. On being nailed to the cross, Jesus is the supreme sign of contradiction for all men: those who recognize him as Son of God will be saved (cf. Lk 23:39–43); those who reject him will be condemned. Christ crucified is the maximum expression of the Father's love for us (cf. Jn 3:14–16; Rom 8:32), the sign raised on high which was prefigured in the bronze serpent raised up by Moses in the wilderness (cf. Jn 3:14; Num 21:9).

Our Lord on the cross, then, is the Judge who will condemn the world (cf. Jn 3:17) and the devil (cf. Jn 16:11); in fact they have provoked their own condemnation by not accepting or believing in God's love. From the cross the Lord will attract all men to himself, for all will be able to see him there, crucified

"Christ our Lord was crucified; from the height of the cross he redeemed the world, thereby restoring peace between God and men. Jesus reminds all of us: '*Et ego, si exaltatus fuero a terra, omnia traham ad meipsum*, and I, when I am

Rev 12:9 now shall the ruler of this world be cast out; 32 and I, when I am
Jn 8:28 lifted up* from the earth, will draw all men to myself." 33 He said
Is 9:6f this to show by what death he was to die. 34 The crowd answered
Dan 7:14 him, "We have heard from the law that the Christ remains for
ever. How can you say that the Son of man must be lifted up?
Jn 8:12; 9:5; 11:10 Who is this Son of man?" 35 Jesus said to them, "The light is with
you for a little longer. Walk while you have the light, lest the dark-
ness overtake you; he who walks in the darkness does not know
Jer 13:16 where he goes. 36 While you have the light, believe in the light, that
Eph 5:8 you may become sons of light."

When Jesus had said this, he departed and hid himself from them.

---

lifted up from the earth, will draw all things to myself' (Jn 12:32). If you put me at the centre of all earthly activities, he is saying, by fulfilling the duty of each moment, in what appears important and what appears unimportant, I will draw everything to myself. My kingdom among you will be a reality!" (St Josemaría Escrivá, *Christ Is Passing By*, 183). Every Christian, following Christ, has to be a flag raised aloft, a light on a lampstand—through prayer and mortification, a sign of the saving love of God the Father.

"Through his incarnation, through his work at Nazareth and his preaching and miracles in the land of Judea and Galilee, through his death on the cross, and through his resurrection, Christ is the centre of the universe, the firstborn and Lord of all creation.

"Our task as Christians is to proclaim this kingship of Christ, announcing it through what we say and do. Our Lord wants men and women of his own in all walks of life. Some he calls away from society, asking them to give up involvement in the world, so that they can remind the rest of us by their example that God exists. To others he entrusts the priestly ministry. But he wants the vast majority to stay right where they are, in all earthly occupations in which they work—the factory, the laboratory, the farm, the trades, the streets of the big cities and the trails of the mountains" (ibid., 105).

12:32. "I will draw all men to myself." The Vulgate, following important Greek manuscripts, translates this as *omnia*, "all things"; the New Vulgate, using equally important and more numerous manuscripts, opts for *omnes*, "everyone". There is no compelling reason for adopting one or other reading: both are theologically correct and neither excludes the other, for Christ attracts all creation to himself, but especially mankind (cf. Rom 8:18–23).

12:34–36. The question posed here touches on the mystery of the Messiah. Jesus does not provide a direct explanation, perhaps because they would be able to understand it only after his resurrection. He limits himself to suggesting that his presence among them is light enough for them to glimpse the mystery of Christ.

"To deserve this light from God, we must love. We must be humble enough to realize we need to be saved, and we must say with Peter: 'Lord, to whom shall we go? You have the words of life everlasting, and we have believed and have come to know that you are the Christ, the Son of God' (Jn 6:68–69). If we really do this, if we allow God's word to enter our

Jesus appeals for faith in himself

37Though he had done so many signs before them, yet they did not
believe in him; 38it was that the word spoken by the prophet Isaiah Is 53:1
might be fulfilled: Rom 10:16

"Lord, who has believed our report,
and to whom has the arm of the Lord been revealed?"

39Therefore they could not believe. For Isaiah again said,

40"He has blinded their eyes and hardened their heart, Is 6:9–10
lest they should see with their eyes and perceive with their heart, Mt 13:14ff Acts 28:26f
and turn for me to heal them."

---

hearts, we can truly say that we do not walk in darkness, for the light of God will shine out over our weakness and our personal defects, as the sun shines above the storm" (St Josemaría Escrivá, *Christ Is Passing By*, 45).

12:37–40. The Evangelist here summarizes the rejection of Jesus by the Jews, giving the reason why many failed to believe in him despite witnessing his miracles and hearing him teach. He quotes two prophecies of Isaiah. From the first (Is 53:1) we can see that faith is a gift from God which we cannot merit by our works nor attain through reason, though this does not mean that the grounds on which it rests—miracles, prophecies etc.—are not evident, or that what faith teaches is opposed to reason. However, in addition to receiving this gift, we must cooperate with it freely and voluntarily; as the Magisterium of the Church teaches: "But though the assent of faith is by no means a blind action of the mind, still no man can 'assent to the Gospel teaching', as is necessary to obtain salvation 'without the illumination and inspiration of the Holy Spirit, who gives to all men sweetness in assenting to and believing in truth'. Wherefore, faith itself, even when it does not work by charity (cf. Gal 5:6), is in itself a gift of God, and the act of faith is a work appertaining to salvation, by which man yields voluntary obedience to God himself by assenting to and cooperating with his grace, which he is able to resist" (Vatican I, *Dei Filius*, chap. 3, *Dz-Sch*, 3010).

With the second prophecy (Is 6:910), to which other books of the New Testament also refer (cf. Mt 13:14; Mk 4:12; Lk 8:10; Acts 28:26; Rom 9:1–13; 11:18), St John explains that the unbelief of the Jews, which could have been a source of scandal to the early Christians, was in fact something foreseen and predicted: "Some, then, mutter in themselves and, when they can, now and then cry out, saying, What did the Jews do or what was their faith, for it to be necessary for the words of the prophet Isaiah to be fulfilled? To this we answer that the Lord, who knows the future, predicted by the prophet the unbelief of the Jews; he predicted it, but he was not its cause. Just as God compels no one to sin, though he knows already man's future sins. [...] Consequently, what the Jews did was sin; but they were not compelled to do so by him who hates sin; and it was only predicted that they would sin, by him from whom nothing is hidden. If they had wished to do not evil but good, they would not have been hindered; but then God would have foreseen this, for he

Is 6:1 41Isaiah said this because he saw his glory and spoke of him.
Jn 7:48; 9:22 42Nevertheless many even of the authorities believed in him, but
for fear of the Pharisees they did not confess it, lest they should be
Jn 5:44 put out of the synagogue: 43for they loved the praise of men more
than the praise of God.

Mt 10:40 44And Jesus cried out and said, "He who believes in me,
Jn 14:7–9 believes not in me, but in him who sent me. 45And he who sees me
Jn 8:12; 12:53 sees him who sent me. 46I have come as light into the world, that
Jn 3:17 whoever believes in me may not remain in darkness. 47If any one
Lk 8:21 hears my sayings and does not keep them, I do not judge him; for
I did not come to judge the world but to save the world. 48He who
Lk 20:16 rejects me and does not receive my sayings has a judge; the word
Heb 4:12 that I have spoken will be his judge on the last day. 49For I have
Deut 18:18f not spoken on my own authority; the Father who sent me has him-
self given me commandment what to say and what to speak.
Jn 8:26–28 50And I know that his commandment is eternal life. What I say,
therefore, I say as the Father has bidden me."

---

knows what each man will do, and what he will render him according to his works" (St Augustine, *In Ioann. Evang.*, 53, 4).

12:42–43. On a number of occasions our Lord praised individuals who confessed their faith in him, for example, the woman who had the flow of blood (Lk 8:43–48), the centurion (Mt 8:8–10), the Canaanite woman (Mt 15:21–28), St Peter (Mt 16:16–17). But now, in this very tense situation, these Jewish leaders are afraid to confess him publicly (cf. also Jn 7:13); they do not want to face being expelled from the Jewish community (cf. Jn 9:22) or compromise their social position (cf. Jn 5:44).

Christians can often experience contradiction because they act in a way consistent with the demands of their faith (cf. 1 Pet 5:9): "What does it matter if you have the whole world against you, with all its power? You … keep going! Repeat the words of the psalm: 'The Lord is my light and my salvation: whom need I fear? *Si consistant adversum me castra, non timebit cor meum.* Though an army pitched camp against me, my heart shall not be afraid'" (St Josemaría Escrivá, *The Way*, 482).

12:44–50. With these verses St John brings to an end his account of our Lord's public ministry. He brings together certain fundamental themes developed in previous chapters—the need for faith in Christ (v. 44); the Father and the Son are one yet distinct (v. 45); Jesus is Light and Life of the world (vv. 46, 50); men will be judged in accordance with whether they accept or reject the Son of God (vv. 47–49). The chapters which follow contain Jesus' teaching to his Apostles at the Last Supper, and the accounts of the Passion and Resurrection.

12:45. Christ, the Word Incarnate, is one with the Father (cf. Jn 10:30): "he reflects the glory of God" (Heb 1:3); "he is the image of the invisible God" (Col 1:15). In John 14:9 Jesus expresses himself in almost the same words: "He who has seen me has seen the Father". At the

PART TWO

Jesus is manifested as the Messiah Son of God in his passion, death and resurrection

9. THE LAST SUPPER

Jesus washes his disciples' feet

13 *[1]Now before the feast of the Passover, when Jesus knew that his hour had come to depart out of this world to the

Jn 2:4; 7:30; 8:20; 15:13
Gal 2:20
1 Jn 3:16

---

same time he speaks of his oneness with the Father, we are clearly shown the distinction of persons—the Father who sends, and the Son who is sent.

In Christ's holy human nature his divinity is, as it were, hidden, that divinity which he possesses with the Father in the unity of the Holy Spirit (cf. Jn 14:7–11). In theology "circumincession" is the word usually used for the fact that, by virtue of the unity among the three Persons of the Blessed Trinity, "the Father is wholly in the Son and wholly in the Holy Spirit; the Son wholly in the Father and wholly in the Holy Spirit; the Holy Spirit wholly in the Father and wholly in the Son" (Council of Florence, Decree *Pro Jacobitis*, *Dz-Sch*, 1331).

12:47. Christ has come to save the world by offering himself in sacrifice for our sins and bringing us supernatural life (cf. Jn 3:17). But he has also been made Judge of the living and the dead (cf. Acts 10:42): he passes sentence at the particular judgment which happens immediately after death, and at the end of the world, at his second coming or Parousia, at the universal judgment (cf. Jn 5:22; 8:15–16; and see the note on Jn 15:22–25).

13:1–38. St John devotes a large part of his Gospel (chaps. 13–17) to recounting Jesus' teaching to his apostles at the Last Supper. This section also tells us things which are not reported in the Synoptics—the washing of feet, for example; and it omits the institution of the Eucharist, which the other Gospels and St Paul had already passed on (cf. Mt 26:26–28 and par.; 1 Cor 11:23–27), and which St John himself dealt with in chapter 6. In chapters 13 to 17 the Evangelist extensively reports our Lord's words on this exceptionally important occasion. Chapter 13 begins by describing just how important the occasion was (vv. 1–3). It goes on to narrate the washing of feet (vv. 4–11) and Jesus' explanation of why he did it (vv. 12–17). It then mentions the denunciation of the betrayer (vv. 18–32) and ends with the teaching of the new commandment (vv. 33–35) and the prediction of Peter's denial (vv. 36–38).

13:1. Jewish families sacrificed a lamb on the eve of the Passover, in keeping with God's command at the time of the exodus when God liberated them from the slavery of the Pharaoh (cf. Ex 12:3–14; Deut 16:1–8). This liberation

Jn 11:27 Lk 22:3 | Jn 1:1; 3:35; 16:28; 17:2 | Mt 11:29; 20:28 Lk 12:37

Father, having loved his own who were in the world, he loved
them to the end. [2]And during supper, when the devil had already
put it into the heart of Judas Iscariot, Simon's son, to betray him,
[3]Jesus, knowing that the Father had given all things into his hands,
and that he had come from God and was going to God, [4]rose from
supper, laid aside his garments, and girded himself with a towel.
[5]Then he poured water into a basin, and began to wash the disciples' feet, and to wipe them with the towel with which he was
girded. [6]He came to Simon Peter, and Peter said to him, "Lord, do

---

prefigured that which Jesus Christ would bring about—the redemption of men from the slavery of sin by means of his sacrifice on the cross (cf. 1:29). This is why the celebration of the Jewish Passover was the ideal framework for the institution of the new Christian Passover.

Jesus knew everything that was going to happen; he knew his death and resurrection were imminent (cf. 18:4); this is why his words acquire a special tone of intimacy and love towards those whom he is leaving behind in the world. Surrounded by those whom he has chosen and who have believed in him, he gives them his final teachings and institutes the Eucharist, the source and centre of the life of the Church. "He himself wished to give that encounter such a fulness of meaning, such a richness of memories, such a moving image of words and thoughts, such a newness of acts and precepts, that we can never exhaust our reflection and exploration of it. It was a testamentary supper, infinitely affectionate and immensely sad, and at the same time a mysterious revelation of divine promises, of supreme visions. Death was imminent, with silent omens of betrayal, of abandonment, of immolation; the conversation dies down but Jesus continues to speak in words that are new and beautifully reflective, in almost supreme intimacy, almost hovering between life and death" (Paul VI, Homily on Holy Thursday, 27 March 1975).

What Christ did for his own may be summed up in this sentence: "He loved them to the end." It shows the intensity of his love—which brings him even to give up his life (cf. Jn 15:13); but this love does not stop with his death, for Christ lives on after his resurrection and he continues loving us infinitely: "It was not only thus far that he loved us, who always and forever loves us. Far be it from us to imagine that he made death the end of his loving, who did not make death the end of his living" (St Augustine, *In Ioann. Evang.*, 55, 2).

13:2. The Gospels show us the presence and activity of the devil running right through Jesus' life (cf. Mt 4:1–11; Lk 22:3; Jn 8:44; 12:31; etc.). Satan is "the enemy" (Mt 13:39), "the evil one" (1 Jn 2:13). St Thomas Aquinas (cf. *Comm. on St John*, in loc.) points out that, in this passage, on the one hand we clearly see the malice of Judas, who fails to respond to this demonstration of love, and on the other hand great emphasis is laid on the goodness of Christ, who reaches out beyond Judas' malice by washing his feet also and by treating him as a friend right up to the moment when he betrays him (cf. Lk 22:48).

13:3–6. Aware that he is the Son of God, Jesus voluntarily humbles himself to the point of performing a service appropriate to household servants. This passage recalls

you wash my feet?" 7Jesus answered him, "What I am doing you Jn 13:12ff; 14:26
do not know now, but afterward you will understand." 8Peter said
to him, "You shall never wash my feet." Jesus answered him, "If
I do not wash you, you have no part in me." 9Simon Peter said to
him, "Lord, not my feet only but also my hands and my head!"
10Jesus said to him, "He who has bathed does not need to wash, Jn 15:3
except for his feet,[c] but he is clean all over; and you are clean, but
not all of you." 11For he knew who was to betray him; that was Jn 6:64, 70f
why he said, "You are not all clean."

---

the Christological hymn in St Paul's Letter to the Philippians: "Christ Jesus, who, though he was in the form of God, did not count equality with God a thing to be grasped, but emptied himself, taking the form of a servant ..." (Phil 2:5–7).

Christ had said that he came to the world "not to be served but to serve" (Mk 10:45). In this scene he teaches us the same thing, through specific example, thereby exhorting us to serve each other in all humility and simplicity (cf. Gal 6:2; Phil 2:3). "Once again he preaches by example, by his deeds. In the presence of his disciples, who are arguing out of pride and vanity, Jesus bows down and gladly carries out the task of a servant [...] This tactfulness of our Lord moves me deeply. He does not say: 'If I do this, how much more ought you to do?' He puts himself at their level, and he lovingly chides those men for their lack of generosity.

"As he did with the first twelve, so also, with us, our Lord can and does whisper in our ear, time and again: *exemplum dedi vobis* (Jn 13:15), I have given you an example of humility. I have become a slave, so that you too may learn to serve all men with a meek and humble heart" (St Josemaría Escrivá, *Friends of God*, 103).

Peter understands particularly well how thoroughly our Lord has humbled himself, and he protests, in the same kind of way as he did on other occasions, that he will not hear of Christ suffering (cf. Mk 8:32 and par.). St Augustine comments: "Who would not shrink back in dismay from having his feet washed by the Son of God .... You? Me? Words to be pondered on rather than spoken about, lest words fail to express their true meaning" (*In Ioann. Evang.*, 56, 1).

13:7–14. Our Lord's gesture had a deeper significance than St Peter was able to grasp at this point; nor could he have suspected that God planned to save men through the sacrificing of Christ (cf. Mt 16:22ff). After the Resurrection the apostles understood the mystery of this service rendered by the Redeemer: by washing their feet, Jesus was stating in a simple and symbolic way that he had not come "to be served but to serve". His service, as he already told them, consists in giving "his life as a ransom for many" (Mt 20:28; Mk 10:45).

Our Lord tells the apostles that they are now clean, for they have accepted his words and have followed him (cf. 15:3)—all but Judas, who plans to betray him. St John Chrysostom comments as follows: "You are already clean because of the word that I have spoken to you. That is: You are clean only to that extent. You have already received the Light; you

c. Other ancient authorities omit *except for his feet*

12When he had washed their feet, and taken his garments, and
resumed his place, he said to them, "Do you know what I have
done to you? 13You call me Teacher and Lord; and you are right,
for so I am. 14If I then, your Lord and Teacher, have washed your
feet, you also ought to wash one another's feet. 15For I have given
you an example, that you also should do as I have done to you.
16Truly, truly, I say to you, a servant[d] is not greater than his
master; nor is he who is sent greater than he who sent him. 17If
you know these things, blessed are you if you do them. 18I am not
speaking of you all; I know whom I have chosen; it is that the
scripture may be fulfilled, 'He who ate my bread has lifted his

Mt 23:8, 10
Sir 32:1
Lk 22:27
1 Tim 5:10
Phil 2:5
Col 3:13
1 Pet 2:21; 5:3
Mt 10:24
Lk 6:40
Mt 7:24
Jas 1:25
Jn 6:70
Ps 41:9

---

have already got rid of the Jewish error. The Prophet asserted: 'Wash yourselves; make yourselves clean; remove the evil from your souls' (Is 1:16)… . Therefore, since they had rooted out all evil from their souls and were following him with complete sincerity, he declared, in accordance with the Prophet's words: 'He who has bathed is clean all over'" (St John Chrysostom, *Hom. on St John*, 70, 3).

Also, when our Lord speaks about the apostles being clean, now, just before the institution of the Blessed Eucharist, he is referring to the need for the soul to be free from sin if it is to receive this sacrament. St Paul repeats this teaching when he says: "Whoever eats the bread or drinks the cup of the lord in an unworthy manner will be guilty of profaning the body and blood of the Lord" (1 Cor 11:27). On the basis of these teachings of Jesus and the apostles, the Church lays down that anyone who is conscious of having committed a grave sin, or who has any positive doubt on that score, must go to confession before receiving Holy Communion.

13:15–17. Jesus' whole life was an example of service towards men, fulfilling his Father's will to the point of dying on the cross. Here our Lord promises us that if we imitate him, our Teacher, in disinterested service (which always implies sacrifice), we will find true happiness which no one can wrest from us (cf. 16:22; 17:13). "'I have given you an example', he tells his disciples after washing their feet, on the night of the Last Supper. Let us reject from our hearts any pride, any ambition, any desire to dominate; and peace and joy will reign around us and within us, as a consequence of our personal sacrifice" (St Josemaría Escrivá, *Christ Is Passing By*, 94).

13:18. Lifting one's heel against someone means hitting him brutally; metaphorically, therefore, it means violent enmity. Judas' treachery fulfils the words of Psalm 41:9 where the psalmist complains bitterly of a friend's treachery. Once again the Old Testament prefigures events which find their full expression in the New.

Through Baptism, the Christian has become a son of God and is called to share in God's good things, not only in heaven but also on earth: he has received grace, he shares in the eucharistic banquet, he shares with his brethren, other Christians, the friendship of Jesus. Therefore, if a person sins who has been born again through Baptism, in some

d. Or *slave*

heel against me.' [19]I tell you this now, before it takes place, that
when it does take place you may believe that I am he. [20]Truly,
truly, I say to you, he who receives any one whom I send receives
me; and he who receives me receives him who sent me."

Jn 14:29; 16:4; 8:24
Mt 10:40
Mk 9:37
Lk 9:48

The treachery of Judas foretold

[21]When Jesus had thus spoken, he was troubled in spirit, and testified, "Truly, truly, I say to you, one of you will betray me." [22]The
disciples looked at one another, uncertain of whom he spoke.
[23]One of his disciples, whom Jesus loved, was lying close to the
breast of Jesus; [24]so Simon Peter beckoned to him and said, "Tell

Mt 26:21–25
Mk 14:18, 21
Lk 22:21–23
Jn 12:27
Jn 19:26; 20:2; 21:7–20

---

sense his is a sort of treachery similar to that of Judas'. However, we have the recourse of repentance: if we trust in God's mercy we can set about recovering our friendship with God.

"Wake up! Listen to what the Holy Spirit tells you: '*Si inimicus meus maledixisset mihi, sustinuissem utique*— If it were an enemy who insulted me, I could put up with that.' But you … '*tu vero homo unanimis, dux meus, et notus meus, qui simul mecum dulces capiebas cibos*—you, my friend, my apostle, who sit at my table and take sweet food with me!'" (St J. Escrivá, *The Way*, 244).

13:19. Jesus tells the Apostles in advance about Judas' treachery, so that when they see Christ's predictions come true, they will realize he has divine knowledge and that in him are fullfilled the Scriptures of the Old Testament (cf. Jn 2:22). On the words "I am", cf. the note on Jn 8:21–24.

13:21. Christ's sadness is proportionate to the gravity of the offence. Judas was one of those whom Jesus chose to be an apostle: he had been on intimate terms with him for three years, he had followed him everywhere, had seen his miracles, had heard his divine teaching, and experienced the tenderness of his affection. And despite all that, when the moment of truth comes, Judas not only abandons the Master but betrays him and sells him. Betrayal by an intimate friend is something much more painful and cruel than betrayal by a stranger, for it involves a lack of loyalty. The spiritual life of the Christian is also true friendship with Jesus; this means it is based on loyalty and uprightness, and on being true to one's word.

Judas had already decided to hand Jesus over and had made arrangements with the chief priests (cf. Mt 26:14; Mk 14:10–11; Lk 22:3–6). Temptation had been burrowing its way into Judas' heart for some time back, as we saw at the anointing in Bethany when he protested against Mary's loving gesture; St John commented in that connexion that he did it not out of love for the poor but because he was a thief (cf. Jn 12:6).

13:23. In that period, on important occasions the customary thing was to eat reclining on a kind of divan called a *triclinium*. The diner rested on his left elbow and ate with his right hand. This meant it was easy to lean on the person on one's left and talk to him without people hearing. In this verse we can see the intimacy and trust which existed between the Master and his beloved disciple (cf. Jn 19:27; 20:2; 21:23), a model of Jesus' love for all his true disciples and of theirs for their Master.

us who it is of whom he speaks." 25So lying thus, close to the
breast of Jesus, he said to him, "Lord, who is it?" 26Jesus ans-
wered, "It is he whom I shall give this morsel when I have dipped
it." So when he had dipped the morsel, he gave it to Judas, the son
Jn 13:2 of Simon Iscariot. 27Then after the morsel, Satan entered into him.
Lk 22:3 Jesus said to him, "What you are going to do, do quickly," 28Now
no one at the table knew why he said this to him. 29Some thought
Jn 12:6 that, because Judas had the money box, Jesus was telling him,
"Buy what you need for the feast"; or, that he should give some-
Jn 8:12 thing to the poor. 30So, after receiving the morsel, he immediately
Lk 22:53 went out; and it was night.

13:26–27. The morsel which Jesus offers him is a sign of friendship and, therefore, an invitation to him to give up his evil plotting. But Judas rejects the chance he is offered. "What he received is good", St Augustine comments, "but he received it to his own perdition, because he, being evil, received in an evil manner what is good" (*In Ioann. Evang.*, 61, 6). Satan entering into him means that from that moment Judas gave in completely to the devil's temptation.

13:29. "These details have been recorded that we may not bear ill will against those who wrong us, but may reproach them and weep over them. Indeed, not those who are wronged, but those who do wrong deserve our tears. For the covetous man and the slanderer, and the man guilty of any other wrongdoing injure themselves most of all. [...] Christ repaid the man who was going to betray him with just the opposite. For example, he washed his feet, reproved him without bitterness, censured him in private, ministered to him, allowed him to share in his table and his kiss. Yet, though Judas did not become better because of these things, Jesus himself persevered in his course of action" (St John Chrysostom, *Hom. on St John*, 71, 4).

13:30. The indication that "it was night" is not just a reference to the time of day but to darkness as an image of sin, an image of the power of darkness whose hour was beginning at that very moment (cf. Lk 22:53). The contrast between light and darkness, the opposition of good and evil, is frequently met with in the Bible, especially in the Fourth Gospel: even in the prologue we are told that Christ is the true Light which the darkness has not overcome (cf. Jn 1:5).

13:31–32. This glorification refers above all to the glory which Christ will receive once he is raised up on the cross (Jn 3:14; 12:32). St John stresses that Christ's death is the beginning of his victory: his very crucifixion can be considered the first step in his ascension to his Father. At the same time it is glorification of the Father, because Christ, by voluntarily accepting death out of love, as a supreme act of obedience to the will of God, performs the greatest sacrifice man can offer for the glorification of God. The Father will respond to this glorification which Christ offers him by glorifying Christ as Son of man, that is, in his holy human nature, through his resurrection and ascension to God's right hand. Thus the glory which the Son gives the Father is at the same time glory for the Son. Christ's disciple will also find his highest motivation by identifying himself with Christ's obedience. St Paul teaches this very

The new commandment. The disciples' desertion foretold

31When he had gone out, Jesus said, "Now is the Son of man glorified, and in him God is glorified; 32if God is glorified in him, Jn 12:23;
God will also glorify him in himself, and glorify him at once. 17:1–5
33Little children, yet a little while I am with you. You will seek Jn 7:33; 8:21
me; and as I said to the Jews so now I say to you, 'Where I am Jn 15:12, 13, 17
going you cannot come.' 34A new commandment* I give to you, 1 Jn 2:8
that you love one another; even as I have loved you, that you also Lev 19:18
love one another. 35By this all men will know that you are my dis- Jn 17:23 Acts 4:32
ciples, if you have love for one another." Jn 21:18f
36Simon Peter said to him, "Lord, where are you going?" Jesus Mt 26:33–35 Mk 14:29, 31
answered, "Where I am going you cannot follow me now; but you Lk 22:31–34

---

clearly when he says: "Far be it from me to glory except in the cross of the Lord Jesus Christ" (Gal 6:14).

13:33. From this verse onward the Evangelist recounts what is usually called the discourse of the Last Supper; in it we can distinguish three parts. In the first, our Lord begins by proclaiming the New Commandment (vv. 33–35) and predicts Peter's denials (vv. 36–38); he tells them that his death means his going to his Father (chap. 14), with whom he is one because he is God (vv. 1–14); and he announces that after his resurrection he will send them the Holy Spirit, who will guide them by teaching them and reminding them of everything he told them (vv. 15–31).

The second part of the discourse is contained in chapters 15 and 16. Jesus promises to those who believe in him a new life of union with him, as intimate as that of a vine and its branches (15:1–8). To attain this union one must keep his New Commandment (vv. 9–17). He forewarns them about the contradictions they will suffer, and he encourages them by promising the Holy Spirit who will protect them and console them (vv. 18–27). The action of the Paraclete or Consoler will lead them to fulfil the mission Jesus has entrusted to them (16:1–15). The fruit of the presence of the Holy Spirit will be fullness of joy (vv. 16–33).

The third part (chap. 17) gives Jesus' priestly prayer, in which he asks the Father to glorify him through the cross (vv. 1–5). He prays also for his disciples (vv. 6–19) and for all those who through them will believe in him, so that, staying in the world without being in the world, the love of God should be in them and they should bear witness to Christ being the envoy of the Father (vv. 20–26).

13:34–35. After announcing that he is leaving them (v. 33). Christ summarizes his commandments in one—the New Commandment. He will repeat it a number of times during the discourse of the Supper (cf. Jn 15:12, 17), and St John in his First Letter will insist on the need to practise this commandment of the Lord and on the demands it implies (cf. 1 Jn 2:8; 3:7–21).

Love of neighbour was already commanded in the Old Testament (cf. Lev 19:18)—and Jesus ratified this when he specified that it was the second precept of the whole Law and similar to the first: Love God with all your heart and soul and mind (cf. Mt 22:37–40). But Jesus gives the precept of brotherly love new meaning and content by saying "even as I have loved you".

shall follow afterward." 37Peter said to him, "Lord, why cannot I
follow you now? I will lay down my life for you." 38Jesus
answered, "Will you lay down your life for me? Truly, truly, I say
to you, the cock will not crow, till you have denied me three
times.

The love of neighbour called for by the Old Law did also in some way extend to one's enemies (Ex 23:4–5); however, the love which Jesus preaches is much more demanding and includes returning good for evil (cf. Mt 5:43–44), because Christian love is measured not by man's heart but by the heart of Christ, who gives up his life on the cross to redeem all men (cf. 1 Jn 4:9–11). Here lies the novelty of Jesus' teaching, and our Lord can rightly say that it is his commandment, the principal clause of his last will and testament. Love of neighbour cannot be separated from love of God: "The greatest commandment of the law is to love God with one's whole heart and one's neighbour as oneself (cf. Mt 22:37–40). Christ has made this love of neighbour his personal commandment and has enriched it with a new meaning when he willed himself, along with his brothers, to be the object of this charity, saying: 'As you did it to one of the least of these my brethren, you did it to me' (Mt 25:40). In assuming human nature he has united to himself all humanity in a supernatural solidarity which makes of it one single family. He has made charity the distinguishing mark of his disciples, in the words: 'By this all men will know that you are my disciples, if you have love for one another'" (Vatican II, *Apostolicam actuositatem*, 8).

Even though Christ is purity itself, and temperance and humility, he does not, however, make any one of these virtues the distinguishing mark of his disciples: he makes charity that mark. "The Master's message and example are clear and precise. He confirmed his teaching with deeds. Yet I have often thought that, after twenty centuries, it is still a *new* commandment, for very few people have taken the trouble to practise it. The others, the majority of men, both in the past and still today, have chosen to ignore it. Their selfishness has led them to the conclusion: 'Why should I complicate my life? I have more than enough to do just looking after myself.'

"Such an attitude is not good enough for us Christians. If we profess the same faith and are really eager to follow in the clear footprints left by Christ when he walked on this earth, we cannot be content merely with avoiding doing unto others the evil that we would not have them do unto us. That is a lot, but it is still very little when we consider that our love is to be measured in terms of Jesus' own conduct. Besides, he does not give us this standard as a distant target, as a crowning point of a whole lifetime of struggle. It is—it ought to be, I repeat, so that you may turn it into specific resolutions—our starting point, for our Lord presents it as a sign of Christianity: 'By this shall all men know that you are my disciples'" (St Josemaría Escrivá, *Friends of God*, 223).

And this is what in fact happened among Christians in the early centuries in the midst of pagan society, so much so that Tertuallian, writing around the end of the second century, reported that people could indeed say, looking at the way these Christians lived: "See how they love one another" (*Apologeticum*, 39).

Jesus reveals the Father

14 [1]"Let not your hearts be troubled; believe[e] in God, believe Jn 14:27
also in me. [2]In my Father's house are many rooms; if it Mk 11:22
were not so, would I have told you that I go to prepare a place for
you? [3]And when I go and prepare a place for you, I will come Jn 12:26; 17:24
again and will take you to myself, that where I am you may be Heb 6:19f
also. [4]And you know the way where I am going."[f] [5]Thomas said to

13:36–38. Once again Peter in his simplicity and sincerity tells his Master that he is ready to follow him even to the point of dying for him. But he is not yet ready for that. Our Lord, St Augustine comments, "establishes here a delay; he does not destroy the hope, indeed he confirms it by saying, 'You shall follow afterwards! Why are you in haste, Peter? As yet the rock has not made you strong inwardly: do not be brought down by your presumption. Now you cannot follow me, but do not despair: later, you will'" (*In Ioann. Evang.*, 66, 1). Peter had certainly meant what he said, but his resolution was not very solid. Later on he would develop a fortitude based on humility; then, not considering himself worthy to die in the way his master did, he will die on a cross, head downwards, rooting in the soil of Rome that solid stone which endures in those who succeed him and forming the basis on which the Church, which is indefectible, is built.

Peter's denials, which are signs of his weakness, were amply compensated for by his profound repentance. "Let everyone draw from this example of contrition, and if he has fallen let him not despair, but always remember that he can become worthy of forgiveness" (St Bede, *In Ioann. Evang. expositio*, in loc.).

14:1–3. Apparently this prediction of Peter's denial has saddened the disciples. Jesus cheers them up by telling them that he is going away to prepare a place for them in heaven, for heaven they will eventually attain, despite their shortcomings and dragging their feet. The return which Jesus refers to includes his second coming (Parousia) at the end of the world (cf. 1 Cor 4:5; 11:36; 1 Thess 4:16–17; 1 Jn 2:28) and his meeting with each soul after death: Christ has prepared a heavenly dwelling place through his work of redemption. Therefore, his words can be regarded as being addressed not only to the Twelve but also to everyone who believes in him over the course of the centuries. The Lord will bring with him into his glory all those who have believed in him and have stayed faithful to him.

14:4–7. The Apostles did not really understand what Jesus was telling them: hence Thomas' question. The Lord explains that he is the way to the Father. "It was necessary for him to say 'I am the Way' to show them that they really knew what they thought they were ignorant of, because they knew him" (St Augustine, *In Ioann. Evang.*, 66, 2).

Jesus is the way to the Father—through what he teaches, for by keeping to his teaching we will reach heaven; through faith, which he inspires, because he came to this world so "that whoever believes in him may have eternal life" (Jn 3:15); through his example, since no one

e. Or *you believe* **f.** Other ancient authorities read *where I am going you know, and the way you know*

him, "Lord, we do not know where you are going; how can we
Jn 11:25 Mt 11:27 know the way?" [6]Jesus said to him, "I am the way, and the truth,
and the life; no one comes to the Father, but by me. [7]If you had
Rom 5:1ff Heb 10:20 known me, you would have known my Father also; henceforth
you know him and have seen him."

[8]Philip said to him, "Lord, show us the Father, and we shall be
Jn 12:45 satisfied." [9]Jesus said to him, "Have I been with you so long, and
Mt 17:17 Heb 1:3 yet you do not know me, Philip? He who has seen me has seen the
Father; how can you say, 'Show us the Father'? [10]Do you not
Jn 12:49 believe that I am in the Father and the Father in me? The words

---

can go to the Father without imitating the Son; through his merits, which make it possible for us to enter our heavenly home; and above all he is the way because he reveals the Father, with whom he is one because of his divine nature.

"Just as children by listening to their mothers, and prattling with them, learn to speak their language, so we, by keeping close to the Saviour in mediation, and observing his words, his actions, and his affections, shall learn, with the help of his grace, to speak, to act, and to will like him.

"We must pause here ... ; we can reach God the Father by no other route ...; the Divinity could not well be contemplated by us in this world below if it were not united to the sacred humanity of the Saviour, whose life and death are the most appropriate, sweet, delicious and profitable subject which we can choose for our ordinary meditations" (St Francis de Sales, *Introduction to the Devout Life*, part 2, chaps. 1, 2).

"I am the way": he is the only path linking heaven and earth. "He is speaking to all men, but in a special way he is thinking of people who, like you and me, are determined to take our Christian vocation seriously: he wants God to be forever in our thoughts, on our lips and in everything we do, including our most ordinary and routine actions.

"Jesus is the way. Behind him on this earth of ours he has left the clear outlines of his footprints. They are indelible signs which neither the erosion of time nor the treachery of the evil one have been able to erase" (St J. Escrivá, *Friends of God*, 127). Jesus' words do much more than provide an answer to Thomas' question; he tells us, "I am the way, and the truth, and the life". Being the Truth and the Life is something proper to the Son of God become man, who St John says in the prologue of his Gospel is "full of truth and grace" (1:14). He is the Truth because by coming to this world he shows that God is faithful to his promises, and because he teaches the truth about who God is and tells us that true worship must be "in spirit and truth" (Jn 4:23). He is the Life because from all eternity he has divine life with his Father (cf. Jn 1:4), and because he makes us, through grace, sharers in that divine life. This is why the Gospel says: "This is eternal life, that they know thee, the only true God, and Jesus Christ whom thou has sent" (Jn 17:3).

By his reply Jesus is, "as it were, saying, By which route do you want to go? I am the Way. To where do you want to go? I am the Truth. Where do you want to remain? I am the Life. Every man can attain an understanding of the Truth and the Life; but not all find the Way. The wise of this world realize that

that I say to you I do not speak on my own authority; but the
Father who dwells in me does his works. [11]Believe me that I am in Jn 10:25, 38; 14:20
the Father and the Father in me; or else believe me for the sake of
the works themselves.
[12]Truly, truly, I say to you, he who believes in me will also do Mk 16:19f
the works that I do; and greater works than these will he do; Jn 15:7–16
because I go to the Father. [13]Whatever you ask in my name, I will Mk 11:24 1 Jn 5:14
do it, that the Father may be glorified in the Son; [14]if you ask[g] any- Jn 15:10;
thing in my name, I will do it. 16:23f

God is eternal life and knowable truth; but the Word of God, who is Truth and Life joined to the Father, has become the Way by taking a human nature. Make your way contemplating his humility and you will reach God" (St Augustine, *De verbis Domini sermones*, 54).

14:8–11. The apostles still find our Lord's words very mysterious, because they cannot understand the oneness of Father and Son. Hence Philip's persistence. Then Jesus "upbraids the apostle for not yet knowing him, even though his works are proper to God—walking on the water, controlling the wind, forgiving sins, raising the dead. This is why he reproves him: for not recognizing his divine condition through his human nature" (St Augustine, *De Trinitate*, book 7).

Obviously the sight of the Father which Jesus refers to in this passage is a vision through faith, for no one has ever seen God as he is (cf. Jn 1:18; 6:46). All manifestations of God, or "theophanies", have been through some medium; they are only a reflexion of God's greatness. The highest expression which we have of God our Father is in Christ Jesus, the Son of God sent among men. "He did this by the total fact of his presence and self-manifestation—by words and works, signs and miracles, but above all by his death and glorious resurrection from the dead, and finally by sending the Spirit of truth. He revealed that God was with us, to deliver us from the darkness of sin and death, and to raise us up to eternal life" (Vatican II, *Dei Verbum*, 4).

14:12–14. Before leaving this world, the Lord promises his apostles to make them sharers in his power so that God's salvation may be manifested through them. These "works" are the miracles they will work in the name of Jesus Christ (cf. Acts 3:1–10; 5:15–16, etc.), and especially the conversion of people to the Christian faith and their sanctification by preaching and the ministry of the sacraments. They can be considered greater works than Jesus' own insofar as, by the apostles' ministry, the Gospel was not only preached in Palestine but was spread to the ends of the earth; but this extraordinary power of apostolic preaching proceeds from Christ, who has ascended to the Father: after undergoing the humiliation of the cross Jesus has been glorified and from heaven he manifests his power by acting through the apostles.

The apostles' power, therefore, derives from Christ glorified. Christ our Lord says as much: "Whatever you ask in my name, I will do it". "It is not that he who believes in me will be greater than me, but only that I shall then do greater works than

g. Other ancient authotities add *me*

Promise of the Holy Spirit

1 Jn 5:3; Deut 6:4–9; Jn 14:26; 15:26; 16:7; 1 Jn 2:1; Jn 7:35; 16:13; Mt 10:20; Rom 8:26; Jn 6:57; 16:16

15 “If you love me, you will keep my commandments. 16 And I will
pray the Father, and he will give you another Counsellor, to be
with you for ever, 17 even the Spirit of truth, whom the world
cannot receive, because it neither sees him nor knows him; you
know him, for he dwells with you, and will be in you.
18 “I will not leave you desolate; I will come to you. 19 Yet a
little while, and the world will see me no more, but you will see

---

now; greater, by him who believes in me, than I now do by myself without him” (St Augustine, *In Ioann. Evang.*, 72, 1).

Jesus Christ is our intercessor in heaven; therefore, he promises us that everything we ask for in his name, he will do. Asking in his name (cf. 15:7, 16; 16:23–24) means appealing to the power of the risen Christ, believing that he is all-powerful and merciful because he is true God; and it also means asking for what is conducive to our salvation, for Jesus is our Saviour. Thus, by “whatever you ask” we must understand what is for the good of the asker. When our Lord does not give what we ask for, the reason is that it would not make for our salvation. In this way we can see that he is our Saviour both when he refuses us what we ask and when he grants it.

14:15. Genuine love must express itself in deeds. “This indeed is love: obeying and believing in the loved one” (St John Chrysostom, *Hom. on St John*, 74). Therefore, Jesus wants us to understand that love of God, if it is to be authentic, must be reflected in a life of generous and faithful self-giving, obedient to the will of God: he who accepts God’s commandments and obeys them, he it is who loves him (cf. Jn 14:21). St John himself exhorts us in another passage not to “love in word or speech but in deed and in truth” (1 Jn 3:18), and he teaches us that “this is the love of God, that we keep his commandments” (1 Jn 5:3).

14:16–17. On a number of occasions the Lord promises the apostles that he will send them the Holy Spirit (cf. 14:26; 15:26; 16:7–14; Mt 10:20). Here he tells them that one result of his mediation with the Father will be the coming of the Paraclete. The Holy Spirit in fact does come down on the disciples after our Lord’s ascension (cf. Acts 2:1–13), sent by the Father and by the Son. In promising here that through him the Father will send them the Holy Spirit, Jesus is revealing the mystery of the Blessed Trinity.

“Counsellor”: the Greek word sometimes anglicized as “paraclete” means, etymologically, “called to be beside one” to accompany, console, protect, defend. Hence the word is translated as Counsellor, Advocate, etc. Jesus speaks of the Holy Spirit as “another Counsellor”, because he will be given them in Christ’s place as Advocate or Defender to help them, since Jesus is going to ascend to heaven. In 1 John 2:1 Jesus Christ is described as a Paraclete: “We have an advocate with the Father, Jesus Christ, the righteous”. Jesus Christ, then, also is our Advocate and Mediator in heaven where he is with the Father (cf. Heb 7:25). It is now the role of the Holy Spirit to guide, protect and vivify the Church, “for there are, as we know, two factors which Christ has promised and arranged in different ways to continue his mission […]: the apostolate and the Spirit. The apostolate is the external and objective

me; because I live, you will live also. 20 In that day you will know Jn 17:21–23
that I am in my Father, and you in me, and I in you. 21 He who has 2 Cor 3:18
my commandments and keeps them, he it is who loves me; and he 1 Jn 5:3
who loves me will be loved by my Father, and I will love him and
manifest myself to him. 22 Judas (not Iscariot) said to him, "Lord, Acts 10:41
how is it that you will manifest yourself to us, and not to the Jn 14:21; 13:34
world?" 23 Jesus answered him, "If a man loves me, he will keep Prov 8:17 Mt 10:20; 28:20
my word, and my Father will love him, and we will come to him Eph 3:17 2 Cor 6:16

---

factor, it forms the material body, so to speak, of the Church and is the source of her visible and social structures. The Holy Spirit acts internally within each person, as well as on the whole community, animating, vivifying, sanctifying" (Paul VI, Opening Address at the third session of Vatican II, 14 September 1964).

The Holy Spirit is Counsellor as we make our way in this world amid difficulties and the temptation to feel depressed. "In spite of our great limitations, we can look up to heaven with confidence and joy: God loves us and frees us from our sins. The presence and the action of the Holy Spirit in the Church are a foretaste of eternal happiness, of the joy and peace for which we are destined by God" (St Josemaría Escrivá, *Christ Is Passing By*, 128).

14:18–20. At various points in the Supper, we can see the apostles growing sad when the Lord bids them farewell (cf. Jn 15:16; 16:22). Jesus speaks to them with great tenderness, calling them "little children" (Jn 13:33) and "friends" (Jn 15:15), and he promises that he will not leave them alone, for he will send the Holy Spirit, and he himself will return to be with them again. And in fact he will see them again after the Resurrection when he appears to them over a period of forty days to tell them about the Kingdom of God (cf. Acts 1:3). When he ascends into heaven they will see him no longer; yet Jesus still continues to be in the midst of his disciples as he promised he would (cf. Mt 28:20), and we will see him face to face in heaven. "Then it shall be that we will be able to see that which we believe. For even now he is with us, and we in him […]; but now we know by believing, whereas then we shall know by beholding. As long as we are in the body, such as it is now, that is, corruptible, which weighs down the soul, we are making our way towards the Lord: for we walk by faith, not by sight. But then we shall see him directly, we shall see him as he is" (St Augustine, *In Ioann. Evang.*, 75, 4).

14:22–23. It was commonly held by the Jews that when the Messiah came he would be revealed to the whole world as King and Saviour. The apostles take Jesus' words as a revelation for themselves alone, and they are puzzled. Hence the question from Judas Thaddeus. It is interesting to note how easy the Apostles' relations with our Lord are: they simply ask him about things they do not know and get him to clear up any doubts they have. This is a good example of how we should approach Jesus, who is also our Teacher and Friend.

Jesus' reply may seem evasive but in fact, by referring to the form his manifestation takes, he explains why he does not reveal himself to the world: he makes himself known to him who loves him and keeps his commandments. God repeat-

Jn 7:16
1 Jn 2:5

and make our home with him. [24]He who does not love me does
not keep my words; and the word which you hear is not mine but
the Father's who sent me.

---

edly revealed himself in the Old Testament and promised to dwell in the midst of the people (cf. Ex 29:45; Ezek 37:26–27; etc.); but here Jesus speaks of a presence of God in each person. St Paul refers to this presence when he asserts that each of us is a temple of the Holy Spirit (cf. 2 Cor 6:16–17). St Augustine, in reflecting on God's ineffable nearness in the soul, exclaims: "Late have I loved you, O beauty so ancient and so new, late have I loved you! You were within me, and I was in the world outside myself. I searched for you in the world outside myself… . You were with me, but I was not with you. The beautiful things of this world kept me far from you and yet, if they had not been in you, they would have had no being at all. You called me; you cried aloud to me; you broke my barrier of deafness; you shone upon me; your radiance enveloped me; you cured my blindness" (*Confessions*, 10, 27, 38).

Jesus is referring to the indwelling of the Holy Spirit in the soul renewed by grace: "Our heart now needs to distinguish and adore each one of the divine Persons. The soul is, as it were, making a discovery in the supernatural life, like a little child opening his eyes to the world about him. The soul spends time lovingly with the Father and the Son and the Holy Spirit, and readily submits to the work of the lifegiving Paraclete, who gives himself to us with no merit on our part, bestowing his gifts and the supernatural virtues!" (St Josemaría Escrivá, *Friends of God*, 306).

14:25–26. Jesus has expounded his teaching very clearly, but the Apostles do not yet fully understand it; they will do so later on, when they receive the Holy Spirit who will guide them unto all truth (cf. Jn 16:13). "And so the Holy Spirit did teach them and remind them: he taught them what Christ had not said because they could not take it in, and he reminded them of what the Lord has taught and which, either because of the obscurity of the things or because of the dullness of their minds, they had not been able to retain" (Theophylact, *Enarratio in Evangelium Ioannis*, ad loc.).

The word translated here as "bring to your remembrance" also includes the idea of "suggesting": the Holy Spirit will recall to the apostles' memory what they have already heard Jesus say and he will give them light to enable them to discover the depth and richness of everything they have seen and heard. Thus, "the Apostles handed on to their hearers what he had said and done, but with that fuller understanding which they, instructed by the glorious events of Christ (cf. Jn 2:33) and enlightened by the Spirit of truth, now enjoyed" (Vatican II, *Dei Verbum*, 19).

"Christ has not left his followers without guidance in the task of understanding and living the Gospel. Before returning to his Father, he promised to send his Holy Spirit to the Church: 'But the Counsellor, the Holy Spirit, whom the Father will send in my name, he will teach you all things, and bring to your remembrance all I have said to you'" (Jn 14:26).

"This same Spirit guides the successors of the Apostles, your bishops, united with the Bishop of Rome, to whom it was entrusted to preserve the faith and to 'preach the gospel to the whole creation'

[25]"These things I have spoken to you, while I am still with Jn 14:16
you. [26]But the Counsellor, the Holy Spirit, whom the Father will Mt 10:19ff 1 Jn 2:27
send in my name, he will teach you all things,* and bring to your
remembrance all that I have said to you. [27]Peace I leave with you; Jn 14:1; 16:33 Eph 2:14, 18

(Mk 16:15). Listen to their voices, for they bring you the word of the Lord" (John Paul II, Homily at Knock Shrine, 30 September 1979).

In the Gospels is consigned to writing, under the charism of divine inspiration, the apostles' version of everything they had witnessed—and the understanding of it, which they obtained after Pentecost. So it is that these sacred writers "faithfully hand on what Jesus, the Son of God, while he lived among men, really did and taught for their eternal salvation, until the day when he was taken up (cf. Acts 1:1–2)" (Vatican II, *Dei Verbum*, 19). This is why the Church so earnestly recommends the reading of Holy Scripture, particularly the Gospels. "How I wish your bearing and conversation were such that, on seeing or hearing you, people would say: This man reads the life of Jesus Christ" (St Josemaría Escrivá, *The Way*, 2).

14:27. Wishing a person peace was, and still is, the usual form of greeting among Jews and Arabs. It is the greeting Jesus used, and which the apostles continued to use, as we can see from their letters (cf. 1 Pet 1–2; 3 Jn 15; Rom 1:7; etc.). The Church still uses it in the liturgy: for example, before Communion the celebrant wishes those present peace, a condition for worthily sharing in the holy sacrifice (cf. Mt 5:23–25) and also a fruit of that sacrifice. On our Lord's lips this common greeting acquires its deepest meaning; peace is one of the great messianic gifts (cf. Is 9:7; 48:18; Mic 5:5; Mt 10:22; Lk 2:14; 19:38). The peace which Jesus gives us completely transcends the peace of the world (cf. the note on Mt 10:34–37), which can be superficial and misleading and compatible with injustice. The peace of Christ is, above all, reconciliation with God and reconciliation of men with one another; it is one of the fruits of the Holy Spirit (cf. Gal 5:22–23); it is "serenity of mind, tranquillity of soul, simplicity of heart, a bond of love, a union of charity: no one can inherit God if he does not keep his testament of peace, or live in unity with Christ if he is separated from Christianity" (St Augustine, *De verbis Domini serm*, 58).

"'Christ is our peace' (Eph 2:14). And today and forever he repeats to us: 'My peace I give to you, my peace I leave with you'. [...] Never before in the history of mankind has peace been so much talked about and so ardently desired as in our day. [...] And yet again and again, one can see how peace is undermined and destroyed. [...] Peace is the result of many converging attitudes and realities; it is the product of moral concerns, of ethical principles based on the Gospel message and fortified by it. [...] In his message for the 1971 Day of Peace, my reverend predecessor, that pilgrim for peace, Paul VI, said: 'True peace must be founded upon justice, upon a sense of the untouchable dignity of man, upon the recognition of an indelible and happy equality between men, upon the basic principle of human brotherhood, that is, of the respect and true love due to each man, because he is man'. [...] Every human being has inalienable rights that must be respected. Each human community—ethnic, historical, cultural

Phil 4:7 my peace I give to you; not as the world gives do I give to you.
Jn 14:3, 6, 18 Let not your hearts be troubled, neither let them be afraid. [28]You
Lk 24:52 heard me say to you, 'I go away, and I will come to you.' If you
loved me, you would have rejoiced, because I go to the Father; for
Jn 13:19; 16:14 the Father is greater than I. [29]And now I have told you before it
Jn 12:31 takes place, so that when it does take place, you may believe. [30]I
Eph 2:2 will no longer talk much with you, for the ruler of this world is
Jn 10:18 coming. He has no power over me; [31]but I do as the Father has

---

or religious—has rights which must be respected. Peace is threatened every time one of these rights is violated. The moral law, guardian of human rights, protector of the dignity of man, cannot be set aside by any person or group, or by the State itself, for any cause, not even for security or in the interests of law and order. The law of God stands in judgment over all reasons of State. As long as injustices exist in any of the areas that touch upon the dignity of the human person, be it in the political, social or economic field, be it in the cultural or religious sphere, true peace will not exist. […] Peace cannot be established by violence, peace can never flourish in a climate of terror, intimidation and death. It is Jesus himself who said: 'All who take the sword will perish by the sword' (Mt 26:52). This is the word of God, and it commands this generation of violent men to desist from hatred and violence and to repent" (John Paul II, Homily at Drogheda, 29 September 1979). The peace and joy which Christ brings us should be typical of believers: "Get rid of those scruples that deprive you of peace. What takes away your peace of soul cannot come from God. When God comes to you, you will realize the truth of those greetings: My peace I give to you … , my peace I leave you … , my peace be with you … , and you will feel it even in the midst of troubles" (St Josemaría Escrivá, *The Way*, 258).

14:28. Jesus Christ, as Only-begotten Son of God, possesses divine glory for all eternity; but while he is on earth this glory is veiled and hidden behind his holy human nature (cf. 17:5; Phil 2:7). It only shows itself on a few occasions, such as when he performs miracles (cf. 2:11) or at the Transfiguration (cf. Mt 17:1–8 and par.). Now, through his death, resurrection and ascension into heaven Jesus will be glorified—in his body also—as he returns to the Father and enters into his glory. Therefore, his departure from this world should be a source of joy for his disciples; but they do not properly understand what he is saying, and they are saddened because they are more aware of the Master being physically separated from them than the glory which awaits him.

When Jesus says that the Father is greater than he, he is thinking about his human nature; as man Jesus is going to be glorified, ascending as he does to the right hand of the Father. Jesus Christ "is equal to the Father in his divinity, less than the Father in his humanity" (*Athanasian Creed*). St Augustine exhorts us to "acknowledge the twofold nature of Christ—the divine, by which he is equal to the Father; the human, by which he is less than the Father. But the one and the other are together not two, but one Christ" (*In Ioann. Evang.*, 78, 3). However, although the Father and the Son are equal in nature, eternity and dignity, our Lord's words can also be under-

commanded me, so that the world may know that I love the Mt 26:46
Father. Rise, let us go hence. Mk 14:42

The vine and the branches

15 [1]"I am the true vine, and my Father is the vinedresser. Is 5:1
[2]Every branch of mine that bears no fruit, he takes away, Jer 2:21
and every branch that does bear fruit he prunes that it may bear Ps 80:8–15 Sir 24:23

stood by taking "greater" to refer to his origin: only the Father is "beginning without beginning", whereas the Son proceeds eternally from the Father by way of a generation which is also eternal. Jesus Christ is God from God, Light from Light, True God from True God (cf. *Nicene Creed*).

14:30. Clearly the world is good, for it has been created by God, and God loved it so much that he sent his Only-begotten Son (Cf. Jn 3:16). However, in this passage "world" means all those who reject Christ; and "the ruler of this world" is the devil (cf. Jn 1:10; 7:7; 15:18–19). The devil opposed the work of Jesus right from the start of his public life when he tempted him in the desert (cf. Mt 4:1–11 and par.). Now, in the passion, he will apparently overcome Christ. This is the hour of the power of darkness when, availing of Judas' treachery (cf. Lk 22:53; Jn 13:27), the devil manages to have our Lord arrested and crucified.

15:1. The comparison of the chosen people with a vine was used in the Old Testament: Psalm 80 speaks of the uprooting of the vine in Egypt and its replanting in another land; and in Isaiah's Song of the Vineyard (5:1–7) God complains that despite the care and love he has lavished on it, his vineyard has yielded only wild grapes. Jesus previously used this imagery in his parable about the murderous tenants (Mt 21:33–43) to signify the Jews' rejection of the Son and the calling of the Gentiles. But here the comparison has a different, more personal meaning: Christ explains that he himself is the true vine, because the old vine, the original chosen people, has been succeeded by the new vine, the Church, whose head is Christ (cf. 1 Cor 3:9). To be fruitful one must be joined to the new, true vine, Christ: it is no longer a matter of simply belonging to a community but of living the life of Christ, the life of grace, which is the nourishment which passes life on to the believer and enables him to yield fruits of eternal life. This image of the vine also helps us understand the unity of the Church, Christ's mystical body, in which all the members are intimately united with the head and thereby are also united to one another (1 Cor 12:12–26; Rom 12:4–5; Eph 4:15–16).

15:2. Our Lord is describing two situations: that of those who, although they are still joined to the vine externally, yield no fruit; and that of those who do yield fruit but could yield still more. The Letter of St James carries the same message when it says that faith alone is not enough (cf. Jas 2:17). Although it is true that faith is the beginning of salvation and that without faith we cannot please God, it is also true that a living faith must yield fruit in the form of deeds. "For in Christ Jesus neither circumcision nor uncircumcision is of any avail, but faith working through love" (Gal 5:6). So, one can say

Mt 15:13; 21:33 more fruit. [3]You are already made clean by the word which I have
spoken to you. [4]Abide in me, and I in you. As the branch cannot
bear fruit by itself, unless it abides in the vine, neither can you,
1 Cor 12:12–27 2 Cor 3:5 unless you abide in me. [5]I am the vine, you are the branches. He
who abides in me, and I in him, he it is that bears much fruit, for
Mt 3:10; 13:6, 40 apart from me you can do nothing. [6]If a man does not abide in me,
Ezek 15:1–8 he is cast forth as a branch and withers; and the branches are gath-
Mt 11:24 ered, thrown into the fire and burned. [7]If you abide in me, and my
words abide in you, ask whatever you will, and it shall be done for
Mt 5:16 Rom 7:4 you. [8]By this my Father is glorified, that you bear much fruit, and
so prove to be my disciples.

---

that in order to produce fruit pleasing to God, it is not enough to have received Baptism and to profess the faith externally: a person has to share in Christ's life through grace and has to cooperate with him in his work of redemption.

Jesus uses the same verb to refer to the pruning of the branches as he uses to refer to the cleanness of the disciples in the next verse: literally the translation should run: "He cleanses him who bears fruit so that he bear more fruit". In other words, he is making it quite clear that God is not content with a half-hearted commitment, and therefore he purifies his own by means of contradictions and difficulties, which are a form of pruning, to produce more fruit. In this we can see an explanation of the purpose of suffering: "Have you not heard the Master himself tell the parable of the vine and the branches? Here we can find consolation. He demands much of you, for you are the branch that bears fruit. And he must prune you '*ut fructum plus afferas*—to make you bear more fruit'. Of course that cutting, that pruning, hurts. But, afterwards, what richness in your fruits, what maturity in your actions" (St Josemaría Escrivá, *The Way*, 701).

15:3. After washing Peter's feet Jesus had already said that his apostles were clean, though not all of them (cf. Jn 13:10). Here, once more, he refers to that inner cleansing which results from accepting his teachings. "For Christ's word in the first place cleanses us from errors, by instructing us (cf. Tit 1:9) […]; secondly, it purifies our hearts of earthly affections, filling them with desire for heavenly things […]; finally, his word purifies us with the strength of faith, for 'he cleansed their hearts by faith' (Acts 15:9)" (St Thomas Aquinas, *Comm. on St John*, in loc.).

15:4–5. Our Lord draws more conclusions from the image of the vine and the branches. Now he emphasizes that anyone who is separated from him is good for nothing, like a branch separated from the vine. "You see, the branches are full of fruit, because they share in the sap that come from the stem. Otherwise, from the tiny buds we knew just a few months back, they could not have produced the sweet ripe fruit that gladdens the eye and makes the heart rejoice (cf. Ps 103:15). Here and there on the ground we may find some dry twigs, lying half-buried in the soil. Once they too were branches of the vine; now they lie there withered and dead, a perfect image of barrenness: 'apart from me, you can do nothing'" (St Josemaría Escrivá, *Friends of God*, 245).

The life of union with Christ is necessarily something which goes far beyond

The law of love

[9]As the Father has loved me, so have I loved you; abide in my Jn 10:14, 15
love. [10]If you keep my commandments, you will abide in my Jn 14:15; 8:29
love, just as I have kept my Father's commandments and abide 1 Jn 2:4, 8
in his love. [11]These things I have spoken to you, that my joy may Jn 16:24; 17:13
be in you, and that your joy may be full. 1 Jn 1:4

[12]"This is my commandment, that you love one another as I Jn 13:34
have loved you. [13]Greater love has no man than this, that a man 1 Jn 3:11 Mk 12:31

---

one's private life: it has to be focused on the good of others; and if this happens, a fruitful apostolate is the result, for "apostolate, of whatever kind it be, must be an overflow of the interior life" (St Josemaría Escrivá, *Friends of God*, 239). The Second Vatican Council, quoting this page from St John, teaches what a Christian apostolate should be: "Christ, sent by the Father, is the source of the Church's whole apostolate. Clearly then, the fruitfulness of the apostolate of lay people depends on their living union with Christ; as the Lord himself said: 'He who abides in me, and I in him, he it is that bears much fruit, for apart from me you can do nothing'. This life of intimate union with Christ in the Church is maintained by the spiritual helps common to all the faithful, chiefly by active participation in the liturgy. Laymen should make such a use of these helps that, while meeting their human obligations in the ordinary conditions of life, they do not separate their union with Christ from their ordinary life; but through the very performance of their tasks, which are God's will for them, actually promote the growth of their union with him" (*Apostolicam actuositatem*, 4).

15:6. If a person is not united to Christ by means of grace he will ultimately meet the same fate as the dead branches—fire. There is a clear parallelism with other images our Lord uses—the parables of the sound tree and the bad tree (Mt 7:15–20), the dragnet (Mt 13:47–50), and the invitation to the wedding (Mt 22:11–14), etc. Here is how St Augustine comments on this passage: "The wood of the vine is the more contemptible if it does not abide in the vine, and the more glorious if it does abide … . For, being cut off it is profitable neither for the vinedresser nor for the carpenter. For one of these only is it useful—the vine or the fire. If it is not in the vine, it goes to the fire; to avoid going to the fire it must be joined to the vine" (*In Ioann. Evang.*, 81, 3).

15:9–11. Christ's love for Christians is a reflection of the love the three divine Persons have for one another and for all men: "We love, because he first loved us" (1 Jn 4:19).

The certainty that God loves us is the source of Christian joy (v. 11), but it is also something which calls for a fruitful response on our part, which should take the form of a fervent desire to do God's will in everything, that is, to keep his commandments, in imitation of Jesus Christ, who did the will of his Father (cf. Jn 4:34).

15:12–15. Jesus insists on the "new commandment", which he himself keeps by giving his life for us. See the note on Jn 13:34–35.

Christ's friendship with the Christian, which our Lord expresses in a very spe-

Jn 10:11 lay down his life for his friends. [14]You are my friends if you do
1 Jn 3:16 what I command you. [15]No longer do I call you servants,[h] for the
Jn 8:31 Mt 12:50; 28:10 servant[i] does not know what his master is doing; but I have called
you friends, for all that I have heard from my Father I have made
Jn 13:18 known to you. [16]You did not choose me, but I chose you and
Rom 6:20–23 appointed you that you should go and bear fruit and that your fruit
should abide; so that whatever you ask the Father in my name, he
may give it to you. [17]This I command you, to love one another.

Jn 7:7 **A hostile world**
1 Jn 3:13 Jn 17:14–16 [18]"If the world hates you, know that it has hated me before it hated
1 Jn 4:5 you.* [19]If you were of the world, the world would love its own;

---

cial way in this passage, is something very evident in St Josemaría Escrivá's preaching: "The life of the Christian who decides to behave in accordance with the greatness of his vocation is so to speak a prolonged echo of those words of our Lord, 'No longer do I call you my servants; a servant is one who does not understand what his master is about, whereas I have made known to you all that my Father has told me; and so I have called you my friends' (Jn 15:15). When we decide to be docile and follow the will of God, hitherto unimagined horizons open up before us [...]. There is nothing better than, recognizing that Love has made us slaves of God. From the moment we recognize this we cease being slaves and become friends, sons" (St Josemaría Escrivá, *Friends of God*, 35].

"Sons of God, *Friends of God*. [...] Jesus Christ is truly God and truly Man, he is our Brother and our Friend. If we make an effort to get to know him well, 'we will share in the joy of being God's friends' [ibid., 300]. If we do all we can to keep him company, from Bethlehem to Calvary, sharing his joys and sufferings, we will become worthy of entering into loving conversation with him. As the Liturgy of the Hours sings, *calicem Domini biberunt, et amici Dei facti sunt*, they drank the chalice of the Lord and so became friends of God.

"Being his children and being his friends are two inseparable realities for those who love God. We go to him as children, carrying on a trusting dialogue that should fill the whole of our lives; and we go to him as friends. [...] In the same way our divine sonship urges us to translate the overflow of our interior life into apostolic activity, just as our friendship with God leads us to place ourselves at 'the service of all men. We are called to use the gifts God has given us as instruments to help others discover Christ' [ibid., 258]" (Monsignor A. del Portillo in the foreword to Escrivá, *Friends of God*).

15:16. There are three ideas contained in these words of our Lord. One, that the calling which the apostles received and which every Christian also receives does not originate in the individual's good desires but in Christ's free choice. It was not the apostles who chose the Lord as Master, in the way someone would go

h. Or *slaves* **i.** Or *slave*

but because you are not of the world, but I chose you out of the
world, therefore the world hates you. [20]Remember the word that I Jn 13:16
said to you, 'A servant[i] is not greater than his master.' If they per- Mt 10:24
secuted me, they will persecute you; if they kept my word, they
will keep yours also. [21]But all this they will do to you on my Jn 10:22
account, because they do not know him who sent me. [22]If I had Mt 5:11 Mk 13:13
not come and spoken to them, they would not have sin; but now Acts 5:41
they have no excuse for their sin. [23]He who hates me hates my Jn 5:23
Father also. [24]If I had not done among them the works which no 1 Jn 2:23
one else did, they would not have sin; but now they have seen and Jn 9:41; 14:11
hated both me and my Father. [25]It is to fulfil the word that is writ- Ps 35:19; 69:4

---

about choosing a rabbi: it was Christ who chose them. The second idea is that the apostles' mission and the mission of every Christian is to follow Christ, to seek holiness and contribute to the spread of the Gospel. The third teaching refers to the effectiveness of prayer done in the name of Christ; which is why the Church usually ends the prayers of the liturgy with the invocation "Through Jesus Christ our Lord …".

The three ideas are all interconnected: prayer is necessary if the Christian life is to prove fruitful, for it is "God who gives the growth" (1 Cor 3:7); and the obligation to seek holiness and to be apostolic derives from the fact that it is Christ himself who has given us this mission. "Bear in mind, son, that you are not just a soul who has joined other souls in order to do a good thing. That is a lot, but it's still little. You are the apostle who is carrying out an imperative command from Christ" (St Josemaría Escrivá, *The Way*, 941–942).

15:18–19. Jesus states that there can be no compromise between him and the world, the kingdom of sin: anyone who lives in sin abhors the light (cf. Jn 3:19–20). This is why Christ is persecuted, and why the apostles will be in their turn. "The hostility of the perverse sounds like praise for our life", St Gregory says, "because it shows that we have at least some rectitude if we are an annoyance to those who do not love God; no one can be pleasing to God and to God's enemies at the same time. He who seeks to please those who oppose God is no friend of God; and he who submits himself to the truth will fight against those who strive against the truth" (*In Ezechielem homiliae*, 9).

15:22–25. Our Lord points out that those who deny him would not have sin had he not revealed himself, had the Light not shone; but it has shone and they have no excuse now (cf. Jn 9:41; Mt 12:31ff). "This is the sin", St Augustine comments, "that they did not believe in what Christ said and did. We are not to suppose that they had no sin before he spoke to them and worked miracles among them; but this sin, their not believing in him, is mentioned in this way, because in this sin of unbelief are all other sins rooted. For if they had believed in him, the rest would be forgiven" (*In Ioann. Evang.*, 91, 1).

Hatred of Christ, who "went about doing good" (Acts 10:38), cannot be explained except by men being deeply affected by the devil's hatred of God. The

i. Or *slave*

Jn 14:26 ten in their law, ‘They hated me without a cause.’ 26But when the
Lk 24:49 Counsellor comes, whom I shall send to you from the Father, even
the Spirit of truth, who proceeds from the Father, he will bear wit-
Lk 1:2 ness to me; 27and you also are witnesses, because you have been
Acts 1:8; 5:32 with me from the beginning.

The action of the Holy Spirit

Jn 14:29 **16** 1“I have said all this to you to keep you from falling away.
Jn 9:22 Mt 5:11; 24:9 2They will put you out of the synagogues; indeed, the hour
Lk 6:22 is coming when whoever kills you will think he is offering service
Acts 26:9–11 to God. 3And they will do this because they have not known the
Jn 15:21 Father, nor me. 4But I have said these things to you, that when
Jn 17:12 Lk 22:53 their hour comes you may remember that I told you of them.
“I did not say these things to you from the beginning, because
Jn 7:33; 13:36; 14:5 I was with you. 5But now I am going to him who sent me; yet

---

Old Testament foretold that he would be hated so viciously: “Let not those rejoice over me who are wrongfully my foes, and let not those wink the eye who hate me without cause” (Ps 35:19; cf. also Ps 2:1–2; 22:16–18).

15:26–27. Just before the ascension our Lord will again charge the apostles with the mission to bear witness to him (cf. Acts 1:8). They have been witnesses to the public ministry, death and resurrection of Christ, which is a condition for belonging to the apostolic college, as we see when Matthias is elected to take the place of Judas (cf. Acts 1:21–22). But the public preaching of the Twelve and the life of the Church will not start until the Holy Spirit comes. Every Christian should be a living witness to Jesus, and the Church as a whole is a permanent testimony to him: “The mission of the Church is carried out by means of that activity through which, in obedience to Christ’s command and moved by the grace and love of the Holy Spirit, the Church makes itself fully present to all men and peoples in order to lead them to the faith, freedom and peace of Christ by the example of its life and teaching, by the sacraments and other means of grace” (Vatican II, *Ad gentes*, 5).

16:2–3. Fanaticism can even bring a person to think that it is permissible to commit a crime in order to serve the cause of religion—as happened with those Jews who persecuted Jesus to the point of bringing about his death, and who later persecuted the Church. Paul of Tarsus was a typical example of misguided zeal (cf. Acts 22:3–16); but once Paul realized he was wrong he changed and became one of Christ’s most fervent apostles. As Jesus predicted, the Church has often experienced this sort of fanatical, diabolical hatred. At other times this false zeal, though not so obvious, takes the form of systematic and unjust opposition to the things of God. “In the moments of struggle and opposition, when perhaps ‘the good’ fill your way with obstacles, lift up your apostolic heart: listen to Jesus as he speaks of the grain of mustard-seed and of the leaven. And say to him ‘*Edissere nobis parabolam*: Explain the parable to me.’

“And you will feel the joy of contem-

none of you asks me, 'Where are you going?' 6But because I have
said these things to you, sorrow has filled your hearts. 7Never- Jn 14:16; 26:28
theless I tell you the truth: it is to your advantage that I go away,
for if I do not go away, the Counsellor will not come to you; but 1 Cor 14:24
if I go, I will send him to you. 8And when he comes, he will con- Heb 14:12 Acts 24:25
vince the world of sin and of righteousness and of judgment: 9of Jn 3:18
sin, because they do not believe in me; 10of righteousness, because Rom 1:18
I go to the Father, and you will see me no more;* 11of judgment, Acts 5:31 Rom 4:25
because the ruler of this world is judged. Jn 12:31; 14:30
12"I have yet many things to say to you, but you cannot bear 1 Cor 3:1
them now. 13When the Spirit of truth comes, he will guide you into Heb 5:11ff
all the truth; for he will not speak of his own authority, but what- Jn 14:26 Jm 2:27
ever he hears he will speak, and he will declare to you the things Acts 8:31

---

plating the victory to come: the birds of the air lodging in the branches of your apostolate, now only in its beginnings, and the whole of the meal leavened" (St Josemaría Escrivá, *The Way*, 695).

In these cases, as our Lord also pointed out, those who persecute God's true servants think they are serving him: they confuse God's interest with a deformed idea of religion.

16:4. Here Jesus prophesies not only his own death (cf. Mt 16:21–23) but also the persecution his disciples will suffer. He warns them of the contradictions they will experience so that they will not be scandalized or depressed when they do arise; in fact, difficulties will give them an opportunity to demonstrate their faith.

16:6–7. The thought that he is going to leave them saddens the apostles, and our Lord consoles them with the promise of the Paraclete, the Consoler. Later (vv. 20ff), he assures them that their sadness will turn into a joy which no one can take away from them.

Jesus speaks about the Holy Spirit three times during the discourse of the Last Supper. The first time (14:15ff), he says that another Paraclete (advocate, consoler) will come, sent by the Father, to be with them forever; secondly, he says (14:26) that he himself will send them, on behalf of the Father, the Spirit of truth who will teach them everything; and now he unfolds for them the complete plan of salvation and announces that the Holy Spirit will be sent once he ascends into heaven.

16:8–12. The word "world" here means all those who have not believed in Christ and have rejected him. These the Holy Spirit will accuse of sin because of their unbelief. He will accuse them of unrighteousness because he will show that Jesus was the Just One who was never guilty of sin (cf. Jn 8:46; Heb 4:15) and therefore is in glory beside his Father. And, finally, he will indict them by demonstrating that the devil, the prince of this world, has been overthrown through the death of Christ, which rescues man from the power of the Evil One and gives him grace to avoid the snares he lays.

16:13. It is the Holy Spirit who makes fully understood the truth revealed by Christ. As Vatican II teaches, our Lord "completed and perfected Revelation and confirmed it … finally by sending the

that are to come. [14]He will glorify me, for he will take what is mine
Jn 17:10 and declare it to you. [15]All that the Father has is mine; therefore I
said that he will take what is mine and declare it to you.

Fullness of joy

Jn 14:19 [16]"A little while, and you will see me no more; again a little while,
and you will see me." [17]Some of his disciples said to one another,
"What is this that he says to us, 'A little while, and you will not
see me, and again a little while, and you will see me'; and,
'because I go to the Father'?" [18]They said, "What does he mean
by 'a little while'? We do not know what he means." [19]Jesus knew
Lk 9:45 that they wanted to ask him; so he said to them, "Is this what you
are asking yourselves, what I meant by saying, 'A little while, and
you will not see me, and again a little while, and you will see
Rev 11:10 me'? [20]Truly, truly, I say to you, you will weep and lament, but the
world will rejoice; you will be sorrowful, but your sorrow will
Is 26:17–18; 66:14 turn into joy. [21]When a woman is in travail she has sorrow,
because her hour has come; but when she is delivered of the child,

---

Spirit of truth" (Vatican II, *Dei Verbum*, 4). Cf. the note on Jn 14:25–26.

16:14–15. Jesus Christ here reveals some aspects of the mystery of the Blessed Trinity. He teaches that the three divine Persons have the same nature when he says that everything that the Father has belongs to the Son, and everything the Son has belongs to the Father (cf. Jn 17:10) and that the Spirit also has what is common to the Father and the Son, that is, the divine essence. The activity specific to the Holy Spirit is that of glorifying Christ, reminding and clarifying for the disciples everything the Master taught them (cf. Jn 16:13). On being inspired by the Holy Spirit to recognize the Father through the Son, men render glory to Christ; and glorifying Christ is the same as giving glory to God (cf. Jn 17:1, 3–5, 10).

16:16–22. Earlier our Lord consoled the disciples by assuring them that he would send them the Holy Spirit after he went away (v. 7). Now he gives them further consolation: he is not leaving them permanently, he will come back to stay with them. However, the apostles fail to grasp what he means, and they ask each other what they make of it. Our Lord does not give them a direct explanation, perhaps because they would not understand what he meant (as happened before: cf. Mt 16:21–23 and par.). But he does emphasize that though they are sad now they will soon be rejoicing: after suffering tribulation they will be filled with a joy they will never lose (cf. Jn 17:13). This is a reference primarily to the Resurrection (cf. Lk 24:41), but also to their definitive encounter with Christ in heaven. This image of the woman giving birth (frequently used in the Old Testament to express intense pain) is also often used, particularly by the prophets, to mean the birth of the new messianic people (cf. Is 21:3; 26:17; 66:7; Jer 30:6; Hos 13:13; Mic 4:9–10). The words of Jesus reported here seem to be the fulfilment of those prophecies. The birth of the messianic

she no longer remembers the anguish, for joy that a child[j] is born
into the world. 22So you have sorrow now, but I will see you again Jn 20:20
and your hearts will rejoice, and no one will take your joy from
you. 23In that day you will ask nothing of me. Truly, truly, I say to Jn 14:13, 14, 20
you, if you ask anything of the Father, he will give it to you in my 1 Jn 5:14 Mt 7:7
name. 24Hitherto you have asked nothing in my name; ask, and Mk 11:24
you will receive, that your joy may be full. Jn 15:11; 17:3
25"I have said this to you in figures; the hour is coming when I 1 Jn 1:4
shall no longer speak to you in figures but tell you plainly of the Jn 10:6 Mt 13:34f
Father. 26In that day you will ask in my name; and I do not say to
you that I shall pray the Father for you; 27for the Father himself
loves you, because you have loved me and have believed that I Jn 14:21–23
came from the Father. 28I came from the Father and have come into
the world; again, I am leaving the world and going to the Father."
29His disciples said, "Ah, now you are speaking plainly, not in Jn 16:25
any figure! 30Now we know that you know all things, and need Jn 2:25
none to question you; by this we believe that you came from God."
31Jesus answered them, "Do you now believe? 32The hour is Zech 13:7 Mt 26:31, 45, 56

---

people—the Church of Christ—involves intense pain, not only for Jesus but also, to some degree, for the apostles. But this pain, like birthpains, will be made up for by the joy of the final coming of the Kingdom of Christ: "I consider," says St Paul, "that the sufferings of this present time are not worth comparing with the glory that is to be revealed to us" (Rom 8:18).

16:23–24. See the note on Jn 14:12–14.

16:25–30. As can be seen also from other passages in the Gospels, Jesus spent time explaining his doctrine in more detail to his apostles than to the crowd (cf. Mk 4:10–12 and par.)—to train them for their mission of preaching the Gospel to the whole world (cf. Mt 28:18–20). However, our Lord also used metaphors or parables when imparting instruction to the apostles, and he does so in this discourse of the Last Supper—the vine, the woman giving birth, etc.: he stimulates their curiosity and they, because they do not understand, ask him questions (cf. vv. 17–18). Jesus now tells them that the time is coming when he will speak to them in a completely clear way so that they will know exactly what he means. This he will do after the Resurrection (cf. Acts 1:3). But even now, since he knows their thoughts, he is making it even plainer to them that he is God, for only God can know what is happening inside someone (cf. Jn 2:25). Verse 28, "I came from the Father and have come into the world; again, I am leaving the world and going to the Father" summarizes the mystery of Christ's Person (cf. Jn 1:14; 20:31).

16:31–32. Jesus moderates the apostles' enthusiasm, which expresses itself in a spontaneous confession of faith; he does this by asking them a question which has two dimensions. On the one hand, it is a

j. Greek *a human being*

Mk 14:27, 50 coming, indeed it has come, when you will be scattered, every
Jn 8:29; 19:27 man to his home, and will leave me alone; yet I am not alone, for
Jn 14:27 the Father is with me. 33I have said this to you, that in me you may
Rom 5:1 have peace. In the world you have tribulation; but be of good
1 Jn 5:4 cheer, I have overcome the world."

The priestly prayer of Jesus

Jn 11:41; 13:31 17 1When Jesus had spoken these words, he lifted his eyes to
heaven and said,* "Father, the hour has come, glorify thy
Mt 11:27 Son that the Son may glorify thee, 2since thou hast given him
Wis 15:3 Jer 13:31–34 power over all flesh, to give eternal life to all whom thou hast
1 Jn 5:20 given him. 3And this is eternal life, that they know thee the only

---

kind of reproach for their having taken too long to believe in him: it is true that there were other occasions when they expressed faith in the Master (cf. Jn 6:68–69; etc.), but until now they have not fully realized that he is the One sent by the Father. The question also refers to the fragility of their faith: they believe, and yet very soon they will abandon him into the hands of his enemies. Jesus requires us to have a firm faith: it is not enough to show it in moments of enthusiasm, it has to stand the test of difficulties and opposition.

16:33. The Second Vatican Council teaches in connexion with this passage: "The Lord Jesus who said 'Be of good cheer, I have overcome the world' (Jn 16:33), did not by these words promise complete victory to his Church in this world. This sacred Council rejoices that the earth which has been sown with the seed of the Gospel is now bringing forth fruit in many places under the guidance of the Spirit of the Lord, who is filling the world" (*Presbyterorum ordinis*, 22).

17:1–26. At the end of the discourse of the Last Supper (chaps. 13–16) begins what is called the Priestly Prayer of Jesus, which takes up all of chapter 17. It is given that name because Jesus addresses his Father in a very moving dialogue in which, as Priest, he offers him the imminent sacrifice of his passion and death. It shows us the essential elements of his redemptive mission and provides us with teaching and a model for our own prayer. "The Lord, the Only-begotten and co-eternal with the Father, could have prayed in silence if necessary, but he desired to show himself to the Father in the attitude of a supplicant because he is our Teacher [...] Accordingly this prayer for his disciples was useful not only to those who heard it, but to all who would read it" (St Augustine, *In Ioann. Evang.*, 104, 2).

The Priestly Prayer consists of three parts: in the first (vv 1–5) Jesus asks for the glorification of his holy human nature and the acceptance, by the Father of his sacrifice on the cross. In the second part (vv. 6–19) he prays for his disciples, whom he is going to send out into the world to proclaim the redemption which he is now about to accomplish. And then (vv. 20–26) he prays for unity among all those who will believe in him over the course of the centuries, until they achieve full union with him in heaven.

17:1–5. The word "glory" here refers to the splendour, power and honour which

true God, and Jesus Christ whom thou hast sent. 4I glorified thee 1 Thess 1:9
on earth, having accomplished the work which thou gavest me to Jn 4:34
do; 5and now, Father, glorify thou me in thy own presence with Jn 17:24; 1:1
the glory which I had with thee before the world was made.* Phil 2:6–11
6"I have manifested thy name to the men whom thou gavest Jn 17:9
me out of the world; thine they were, and thou gavest them to me, Mt 6:9
and they have kept thy word. 7Now they know that everything that
thou hast given me is from thee; 8for I have given them the words Jn 16:30
which thou gavest me, and they have received them and know in
truth that I came from thee; and they have believed that thou didst
send me. 9I am praying for them; I am not praying for the world Jn 6:37, 44, 65
but for those whom thou hast given me, for they are thine; 10all

---

belong to God. The Son is God equal to the Father, and from the time of his incarnation and birth and especially through his death and resurrection his divinity has been made manifest. "We have beheld his glory, glory as of the only Son from the Father" (Jn 1:14). The glorification of Jesus has three dimensions to it. 1) It promotes the glory of the Father, because Christ, in obedience to God's redemptive decree (cf. Phil 2:6), makes the Father known and so brings God's saving work to completion. 2) Christ is glorified because his divinity, which he has voluntarily disguised, will eventually be manifested through his human nature which will be seen after the Resurrection invested with the very authority of God himself over all creation (vv. 2, 5). 3) Christ, through his glorification, gives man the opportunity to attain eternal life, to know God the Father and Jesus Christ, his only Son: this in turn redounds to the glorification of the Father and of Jesus while also involving man's participation in divine glory (v. 3).

"The Son glorifies you, making you known to all those you have given him. Furthermore, if the knowledge of God is life eternal, we the more tend to life, the more we advance in this knowledge. […] There shall the praise of God be without end, where there shall be full knowledge of God; and because in heaven this knowledge shall be full, there shall glorifying be of the highest" (St Augustine, *In Ioann. Evang.*, 105, 3).

17:6–8. Our Lord has prayed for himself; now he prays for his apostles, who will continue his redemptive work in the world. In praying for them, Jesus describes some of the prerogatives of those who will form part of the apostolic college.

First, there is the prerogative of being chosen by God: "thine they were …". God the Father chose them from all eternity (cf. Eph 1:3–4) and in due course Jesus revealed this to them: "The Lord Jesus, having prayed at length to the Father, called to himself those whom he willed and appointed twelve to be with him, whom he might send to preach the kingdom of God (cf. Mk 3:13–19; Mt 10:1–42). These apostles (cf. Lk 6:13) he constituted in the form of a college or permanent assembly, at the head of which he placed Peter, chosen from among them (cf. Jn 21:15–17)" (Vatican II, *Lumen gentium*, 19). Also, the Apostles enjoy the privilege of hearing God's teaching direct from Jesus. From this teaching, which they accept with docility,

Jn 16:15 mine are thine, and thine are mine, and I am glorified in them.
Lk 15:31 Jn 10:30 [11]And now I am no more in the world, but they are in the world,
Mt 6:13 and I am coming to thee. Holy Father, keep them in thy name,
which thou hast given me, that they may be one, even as we are
Jn 6:39 one. [12]While I was with them, I kept them in my name, which
2 Thess 2:3 thou hast given me; I have guarded them, and none of them is lost
but the son of perdition, that the scripture might be fulfilled. [13]But

---

they learn that Jesus came from the Father and that therefore he is God's envoy (v. 8): that is, they are given to know the relationships that exist between the Father and the Son.

The Christian, who also is a disciple of Jesus, gradually acquires knowledge of God and of divine things through living a life of faith and maintaining a personal relationship with Jesus Christ.

"Recalling this human refinement of Christ, who spent his life in the service of others, we are doing much more than describing a pattern of human behaviour; we are discovering God. Everything Christ did has a transcendental value. It shows us the nature of God and beckons us to believe in the love of God who created us and wants us to share his intimate life" (St Josemaría Escrivá, *Christ Is Passing By*, 109).

17:11–19. Jesus now asks the Father to give his disciples four things—unity, perseverance, joy and holiness. By praying him to keep them in his name (v. 11) he is asking for their perseverance in the teaching he has given them (cf. v. 6) and in communion with him. An immediate consequence of this perseverance is unity: "that they may be one, even as we are one"; this unity which he asks for his disciple is a reflection of the unity of the three divine Persons.

He also prays that none of them should be lost, that the Father should guard and protect them, just as he himself protected them while he was with them. Thirdly, as a result of their union with God and perseverance they will share in the joy of Christ (v. 13): in this life, the more we know God the more closely we are joined to him, the happier will we be; in eternal life our joy will be complete, because our knowledge and love of God will have reached its climax.

Finally, he prays for those who, though living in the world, are not of the world, that they may be truly holy and carry out the mission he has entrusted to them, just as he did the work his Father gave him to do.

17:12. "That the scripture might be fulfilled": this is an allusion to what he said to the apostles a little earlier (Jn 13:18) by directly quoting Holy Scripture: "He who ate my bread has lifted his heel against me" (Ps 41:9). Jesus makes these references to Judas' treachery in order to strengthen the apostles' faith by showing that he knew everything in advance and that the Scriptures had already foretold what would happen.

However, Judas went astray through his own fault and not because God arranged things that way; his treachery had been taking shape little by little, through his petty infidelities, and despite our Lord helping him to repent and get back on the right road (cf. the note on Jn 13:31–32); Judas did not respond to this grace and was responsible for his own downfall. God, who sees the future, predicted the treachery of Judas in the Scripture; Christ, being true God, knew

now I am coming to thee; and these things I speak in the world, Jn 15:11
that they may have my joy fulfilled in themselves. 14I have given Acts 1:16, 20 1 Jn 1:4
them thy word; and the world has hated them because they are not Jn 15:19
of the world, even as I am not of the world. 15I do not pray that
thou shouldst take them out of the world, but that thou shouldst 2 Thess 3:3
keep them from the evil one.[k] 16They are not of the world, even as 1 Jn 5:18 Mt 6:13
I am not of the world. 17Sanctify them in the truth; thy word is Lk 22:32 Jn 16:13

---

that Judas would betray him and it is with immense sorrow that he now tells the apostles.

17:14–16. In Scripture, "world" has a number of meanings. First, it means the whole of creation (Gen 1:1ff) and, within creation, mankind, which God loves most tenderly (Prov 8:31). This is the meaning intended here when our Lord says, "I do not pray that thou shouldst take them out of the world, but that thou shouldst keep them from the evil one" (v. 15). "I have taught this constantly using words from Holy Scripture. The world is not evil, because it has come from God's hands, because it is his creation, because Yahweh looked upon it and saw that it was good (cf. Gen 1:7ff). We ourselves, mankind, make it evil and ugly with our sins and infidelities. Have no doubt: any kind of evasion from the honest realities of daily life is for you, men and women of the world, something opposed to the will of God" (St J. Escrivá, *Conversations*, 114).

In the second place, "world" refers to the things of this world, which do not last and which can be at odds with the things of the spirit (cf. Mt 16:26).

Finally, because evil men have been enslaved by sin and by the devil, "the ruler of this world" (Jn 12:31; 16:11), the "world" sometimes means God's enemy, something opposed to Christ and his followers (cf. Jn 1:10). In this sense the "world" is evil, and therefore Jesus is not of the world, nor are his disciples (v. 16). It is also this pejorative meaning which is used by traditional teaching which describes the world, the flesh and the devil as enemies of the soul against which one has to be forever vigilant. "The world, the flesh and the devil are a band of adventurers who take advantage of the weakness of that savage you bear within you. In exchange for the glittering tinsel of a pleasure—which is worth nothing—they want you to hand over to them the pure gold and the pearls and the diamonds and rubies drenched in the living and redeeming blood of your God, which are the price and the treasure of your eternity" (St Josemaría Escrivá, *The Way*, 708).

17:17–19. Jesus prays for the holiness of his disciples. God alone is the Holy One; in his holiness people and things share. "Sanctifying" has to do with consecrating and dedicating something to God, excluding it from being used for profane purposes; thus God says to Jeremiah: "Before I formed you in the womb I knew you, and before you were born I consecrated you; I appointed you a prophet to the nations" (Jer 1:5). If something is to be consecrated to God it must be perfect, that is, holy. Hence, a consecrated person needs to have moral sanctity, needs to be practising the moral virtues. Our Lord here asks for both things for his disciples, because they

k. Or *from evil*

Jn 20:21 truth. 18 As thou didst send me into the world, so I have sent them
Heb 2:11; 10:20 into the world. 19 And for their sake I consecrate myself, that they
also may be consecrated in truth.

---

need them if they are to fulfil their supernatural mission in the world.

"For their sake I consecrate myself": these words mean that Jesus Christ, who has been burdened with the sins of men, consecrates himself to the Father through his sacrifice on the cross. By this are all Christians sanctified: "So Jesus also suffered outside the gate in order to sanctify the people through his own blood" (Heb 13:12). So, after Christ's death, men have been made sons of God by Baptism, sharers in the divine nature and enabled to attain the holiness to which they have been called (cf. Vatican II, *Lumen gentium*, 40).

17:20–23. Since it is Christ who is praying for the Church his prayer is infallibly effective, and therefore there will always be only one true Church of Jesus Christ. Unity is therefore an essential property of the Church. "We believe that the Church founded by Jesus Christ and for which he prayed is indefectibly one in faith, in worship and in the bond of hierarchical communion" (Paul VI, *Creed of the People of God*, 21). Moreover, Christ's prayer also indicates what the basis of the Church's unity will be and what effects will follow from it.

The source from which the unity of the Church flows is the intimate unity of the three divine Persons among whom there is mutual love and self-giving. "The Lord Jesus, when praying to the Father 'that they may all be one … even as we are one' (Jn 17:21–22), has opened up new horizons closed to human reason by implying that there is a certain parallel between the union existing among the divine persons and the union of the sons of God in truth and love. It follows, then, that if man is the only creature on earth that God has wanted for its own sake, man can fully discover his true self only in the sincere giving of himself" (Vatican II, *Gaudium et spes*, 24). The unity of the church is also grounded on the union of the faithful with Jesus Christ and through him with the Father (v. 23). Thus, the fullness of unity—*consummati in unum*—is attained through the supernatural grace which comes to us from Christ (cf. Jn 15:5).

The fruits of the unity of the Church are, on the one hand, the world believing in Christ and in his divine mission (vv. 21, 23); and, on the other, Christians themselves and all men recognizing God's special love for his faithful, a love which is a reflection of the love of the three divine Persons for each other. And so, Jesus' prayer embraces all mankind, for all are invited to be friends of God (cf. 1 Tim 2:4). "Thou hast loved them even as thou hast loved me": this, according to St Thomas Aquinas, "does not mean strict equality of love but similarity and like motivation. It is as if he were saying: the love with which you have loved me is the reason and the cause of your loving them, for, precisely because you love men do you love those who love me" (*Comm. on St John*, in loc.) Besides noting this theological explanation, we should also ponder on how expressively Christ describes his ardent love for men. The entire discourse of the Last Supper gives us a glimpse of the depth of Jesus' feelings—which infinitely exceeds anything we are capable of experiencing. Once again all we can do is bow down before the mystery of God made man.

[20]"I do not pray for these only, but also for those who believe Jn 17:9
in me through their word, [21]that they may all be one; even as thou,
Father, art in me, and I in thee, that they also may be in us, so that Gal 3:28

17:20. Christ prays for the Church, for all those who, over the course of centuries, will believe in him through the preaching of the apostles. "That divine mission, which was committed by Christ to the Apostles, is destined to last until the end of the world (cf. Mt 28:20), since the Gospel, which they were charged to hand on, is, for the Church, the principle of all its life for all time. For that very reason the Apostles were careful to appoint successors in this hierarchically constituted society" (*Lumen gentium*, 20).

The apostolic origin and basis of the Church is what is termed its "apostolicity", a special characteristic of the Church which we confess in the Creed. Apostolicity consists in the Pope and the bishops being successors of Peter and the apostles, holding the authority of the apostles and proclaiming the same teaching as they did. "The sacred synod teaches that the bishops have by divine institution taken the place of the apostles as pastors of the Church, in such wise that whoever listens to them is listening to Christ and whoever despises them despises Christ and him who sent Christ (cf. Lk 10:16)" (Vatican II, *Lumen gentium*, 20).

17:21. Union of Christians with Christ begets unity among themselves. This unity of the Church ultimately redounds to the benefit of all mankind, because since the Church is one and unique, she is seen as a sign raised up for the nations to see, inviting all to believe in Christ as sent by God come to save all men. The Church carries on this mission of salvation through its union with Christ, calling all mankind to join the Church and by so doing to share in union with Christ and the Father.

The Second Vatican Council, speaking of the principles of ecumenism, links the Church's unity with her universality: "Almost everyone, though in different ways, longs for the one visible Church of God, a Church truly universal and sent forth to the whole world that the world may be converted to the Gospel and so be saved, to the glory of God" (*Unitatis redintegratio*, 1). This universality is another characteristic of the Church, technically described as "catholicity". "For many centuries now the Church has been spread throughout the world, and it numbers persons of all races and walks of life. But the universality of the Church does not depend on its geographical distribution, even though this is a visible sign and a motive of credibility. The Church was catholic already at Pentecost: it was born catholic from the wounded heart of Jesus, as a fire which the Holy Spirit enkindled.

"In the second century the Christians called the Church catholic in order to distinguish it from sects which, using the name of Christ, were betraying its doctrine in one way or another. 'We call it catholic', writes St Cyril, 'not only because it is spread throughout the world, from one extreme to the other, but because in a universal way and without defect it teaches all the dogmas which men ought to know, of both the visible and the invisible, the celestial and the earthly. Likewise because it draws to true worship all types of men, governors and citizens, the learned and the ignorant. And finally, because it cures and heals all kinds of sins, whether of the soul or of

Acts 4:32 the world may believe that thou hast sent me. [22]The glory which
thou hast given me I have given to them, that they may be one
1 Cor 6:17 even as we are one, [23]I in them and thou in me, that they may
Gal 2:20 become perfectly one, so that the world may know that thou hast
Jn 10:29; sent me and hast loved them even as thou has loved me. [24]Father,
12:26, 32 I desire that they also, whom thou hast given me, may be with me
Eph 1:4 where I am, to behold my glory which thou has given me in thy
love for me before the foundation of the world. [25]O righteous

---

the body, possessing in addition—by whatever name it may be called—all the forms of virtue, in deeds and in words and in every kind of spiritual life' (*Cathechesis*, 18, 23)" (St Josemaría Escrivá, *In Love with the Church*, 9).

Every Christian should have the same desire for unity as Jesus Christ expresses in his prayer to the Father. "A privileged instrument for participation in pursuit of the unity of all Christians is prayer. Jesus Christ himself left us his final wish for unity through prayer to the Father: 'that they may all be one; even as thou, Father, art in me, and I in thee, that they also may be in us, so that the world may believe that thou hast sent me' (Jn 17:21).

"Also the Second Vatican Council strongly recommended to us prayer for the unity of Christians, defining it 'the soul of the whole ecumenical movement' (*Unitatis redintegratio*, 8). As the soul to the body, so prayer gives life, consistency, spirit, and finality to the ecumenical movement.

"Prayer puts us, first and foremost, before the Lord, purifies us in intentions, in sentiments, in our heart, and produces that 'interior conversion', without which there is no real ecumenism (cf. *Unitatis redintegratio*, 7).

"Prayer, furthermore, reminds us that unity, ultimately, is a gift from God, a gift for which we must ask and for which we must prepare in order that we may be granted it" (John Paul II, General Audience, 17 January 1979).

17:22–23. Jesus possesses glory, a manifestation of divinity, because he is God, equal to the Father (cf. the note on Jn 17:1–5). When he says that he is giving this glory to his disciples, he is indicating that through grace he makes us "partakers of the divine nature" (2 Pet 1:4). Glory and justification by grace are very closely united, as we can see from Sacred Scripture: "Those whom he predestines he also called, and those whom he called he also justified, and those whom he justified he also glorified" (Rom 8:30). The change grace works in Christians makes us ever more like Christ, who is the likeness of the Father (cf. 2 Cor 4:4; Heb 1:2–3): by communicating his glory Christ joins the faithful to God by giving them a share in supernatural life, which is the source of the holiness of Christians and of the Church: "Now we can understand better how […] one of the principal aspects of her holiness is that unity centred on the mystery of the one and triune God. 'There is one body and one Spirit, just as you were called to the one hope that belongs to your call, one Lord, one faith, one baptism; one God and Father of us all, who is above all and through all and in all' (Eph 4:4–6)" (St Josemaría Escrivá, *In Love with the Church*, 5).

17:24. Jesus concludes his prayer by asking that all Christians attain the blessedness of heaven. The word he uses, "I desire", not "I pray", indicates that he is asking for the most important thing of

Father, the world has not known thee, but I have known thee; and
these know that thou hast sent me. [26]I made known to them thy Ex 3:13
name, and I will make it known, that the love with which thou has Jn 17:6
loved me may be in them, and I in them."

10. THE PASSION AND DEATH OF JESUS

Arrest of Jesus

Mt 26:30, 36 Mk 14:26, 32 Lk 23:39 2 Sam 15:23

18 [1]When Jesus had spoken these words, he went forth with
his disciples across the Kidron valley, where there was a

---

all, for what his Father wants—that all may be saved and come to a knowledge of the truth (cf. 1 Tim 2:4): which is essentially the mission of the Church—the salvation of souls.

As long as we are on earth we share in God's life through knowledge (faith) and love (charity); but only in heaven will we attain the fulness of this supernatural life, the Church has her sights fixed on eternity, she is eschatological: that is, by having in this world all the resources necessary for teaching God's truth, for rendering him true worship and communicating the life of grace, she keeps alive people's hope of attaining the fulness of eternal life: "The Church, to which we are all called in Jesus Christ, and in which by the grace of God we acquire holiness, will receive its perfection only in the glory of heaven, when will come the time of the renewal of all things (Acts 3:21). At that time, together with the human race, the universe itself, which is so closely related to man and which attains its destiny through him, will be perfectly reestablished in Christ (cf. Eph 1:10; Col 1:20; 2 Pet 3:10–13)" (Vatican II, *Lumen gentium*, 48).

17:25–26. God's revelation of himself through Christ causes us to begin to share in the divine life, a sharing which will reach its climax in heaven: "God alone can give us the right and full knowledge of this reality by revealing himself as Father, Son and Holy Spirit, in whose eternal life we are by grace called to share, here below in the obscurity of faith and after death in eternal light" (Paul VI, *Creed of the People of God*).

Christ has revealed to us all we need to know in order to participate in the mutual love of the divine Persons—primarily, the mystery of who he is and what his mission is and, with that, the mystery of God himself ("I made known to them thy name"), thus fulfilling what he had announced: "No one knows the father except the Son and any one to whom the Son chooses to reveal him" (Mt 11:27). Christ continues to make known his Father's love, by means of the Church, in which he is always present: "I am with you always, to the close of the age" (Mt 28:20).

18:1. The previous chapter, dealing as it did with the glory of the Son of God (cf. Jn 17:1, 4, 10, 22, 24), is a magnificent prologue to our Lord's passion and death, which St John presents as part of Christ's glorification: he emphasizes that Jesus freely accepted his death (14:31) and freely allowed himself to be arrested (18:4, 11). The Gospel shows our Lord's superiority over his judges (18:20–21) and accusers (19:8, 12); and his majestic

Lk 21:37 garden, which he and his disciples entered. [2]Now Judas, who
betrayed him, also knew the place; for Jesus often met there with

---

serenity in the face of physical pain, which makes one more aware of the Redemption, the triumph of the cross, than of Jesus' actual sufferings.

Chapters 18 and 19 cover the passion and death of our Lord—events so important and decisive that all the books of the New Testament deal with them, in some way or other. Thus, the Synoptic Gospels give us extensive accounts of what happened; in the Acts of the Apostles these events, together with the resurrection, form the core of the apostles' preachings. St Paul explains the redemptive value of Jesus Christ's sacrifice, and the catholic epistles speak of his salvific death, as does the book of Revelation, where the Victor, enthroned in heaven, is the sacrificed Lamb, Jesus Christ. It should also be noted that whenever these sacred writings mention our Lord's death they go on to refer to his glorious resurrection.

St John's Gospel locates these events in five places. The first (18:1–12) is Gethsemane, where Jesus is arrested; after this (18:13–27) he is taken to the house of Annas, where the religious trial begins and Peter denies Jesus before the high priest's servants. The third scene is the praetorium (18:28—19:16), where Jesus is tried by the Roman procurator: St John gives an extensive account of his trial, highlighting the true character of Christ's kingship and his rejection by the Jews, who call for his crucifixion. He then goes on (19:17–37) to describe the events which occur after the procurator's unjust sentence; this scene centres on Calvary. St John then reports the burial of our Lord in the unused tomb near Calvary belonging to Joseph of Arimathea.

The climax of all these events is the glorification of Jesus, of which he himself has spoken (cf. Jn 17:1–5)—his resurrection and exaltation to his Father's side.

Here is Fray Luis de Granada's advice on how to meditate on the passion of our Lord: "There are five things we can reflect on when we think about the sacred passion. […] First, we can incline our hearts to sorrow and repentance for our sins; the passion of our Lord helps us do this because it is evident that everything he suffered he suffered on account of sins, so that if there were no sins in the world, there would have been no need for such painful reparation. Therefore, sins —yours and mine, like everyone else's—were the executioners who bound him and lashed him and crowned him with thorns and put him on the cross. So you can see how right it is for you to feel the enormity and malice of your sins, for it was these which really caused so much suffering, not because these sins required the Son of God to suffer but because divine justice chose to ask for such great atonement.

"We have here excellent motives, not only to abhor sin but also to love virtues: we have the example of this Lord's virtues, which so clearly shine out during his sacred passion: we can follow these virtues and learn to imitate them, especially his great humility, gentleness and silence, as well as the other virtues, for this is one of the best and most effective ways of meditating on the sacred passion—the way of imitation.

"At other times we should fix our attention on the great good the Lord does us here, reflecting on how much he loved us and how much he gave us and how much it cost him to do so. […] At other times it is good to focus our attention on knowledge of God, that is, to consider his

his disciples. [3]So Judas, procuring a band of soldiers and some Mt 26:47–56 Mk 14:43–52 Lk 22:47–53
officers from the chief priests and the Pharisees, went there with
lanterns and torches and weapons. [4]Then Jesus, knowing all that Jn 19:28

---

great goodness, his mercy, his justice, his kindness, and particularly his ardent charity, which shines forth in the sacred passion as nowhere else. For just as it is a greater proof of love to suffer evils on behalf of one's friend than to do good things for him, and God could do both [...], it pleased his divine nature to assume a nature which could suffer evils, very great evils, so that man could be quite convinced of God's love and thereby be moved to love him who so loved man.

"Finally, at other times one can reflect [...] on the wisdom of God in choosing this manner of atoning for mankind: that is, making satisfaction for our sins, inflaming our charity, curing our pride, our greed and our love of comfort, and inclining our souls to the virtue of humanity [...], abhorrence of sin and love for the Cross" (*Life of Jesus Christ*, 15).

18:1–2. "When Jesus had spoken these words": this is a formula often used in the Fourth Gospel to indicate a new episode linked with what has just been recounted (cf. Jn 2:12; 3:22; 5:1; 6:1; 13:21; etc.).

The Kidron (etymologically "turbid") was a brook which carried water only during rainy weather; it divided Jerusalem from the Mount of Olives, on the slopes of which lay the garden of Gethsemane (cf. Mt 26:30; Lk 21:37; 22:39). The distance from the Cenacle, where the Last Supper took place, to the garden of Gethsemane was little more than a kilometre.

18:3. Because Judea was occupied by Romans, there was a garrison stationed at Jerusalem—a cohort (600 men) quartered in the Antonia tower, under the authority of a tribune. In the Greek what is translated here as "a band of soldiers" is "the cohort", the name for the whole unit being used though only part is meant: it does not mean that 600 soldiers came out to arrest Jesus. Presumably the Jewish authorities, who had their own temple guard—referred to here as "officers from the chief priests and the Pharisees"—must have sought some assistance from the military. Judas' part consisted in leading the way to where Jesus was and identifying the man to be arrested.

18:4–9. Only the Fourth Gospel reports this episode prior to Jesus' arrest, recalling the words of the Psalm: "Then my enemies will be turned back in the day when I call" (Ps 56:9). Our Lord's majesty is apparent: he surrenders himself freely and voluntarily. This does not, however, mean that the Jews involved are free from blame. St Augustine comments on this passage: "The persecutors, who came with the traitor to lay hold of Jesus, found him whom they sought and heard him say, 'I am he'. Why did they not lay hold of him but fell back to the ground? Because that was what he wished, who could do whatever he wished. Had he not allowed himself to be taken by them, they would have been unable to effect their plan, but neither would he have done what he came to do. They in their rage sought him to put him to death; but he also sought us by dying for us. Therefore, after he displayed his power to those who had no power to hold him, they did lay hands on him and by means of them, all unwitting, he did what he wanted to do" (*In Ioann. Evang.*, 112, 3).

It is also moving to see how Jesus

was to befall him, came forward and said to them, “Whom do you
seek?” 5They answered him, “Jesus of Nazareth.” Jesus said to
them, “I am he.” Judas, who betrayed him, was standing with
Jn 8:24 them. 6When he said to them, “I am he,” they drew back and fell
to the ground. 7Again he asked them, “Whom do you seek?” And
they said, “Jesus of Nazareth,” 8Jesus answered, “I told you that I
Jn 17:12; 6:39 am he; so, if you seek me, let these men go.” 9This was to fulfil
the word which he had spoken, “Of those whom you gavest me I
lost not one.” 10Then Simon Peter, having a sword, drew it and
struck the high priest’s slave and cut off his right ear. The slave’s
Mt 26:29 name was Malchus. 11Jesus said to Peter, “Put your sword into its
sheath; shall I not drink the cup which the Father has given me?”

Mt 26:57–68 12So the band of soldiers and their captain and the officers of
Mk 14:53–72 Lk 22:54–71 the Jews seized Jesus and bound him.

Jesus before the chief priests. Peter’s denials

13First they led him to Annas; for he was the father-in-law of
Jn 11:49f Caiaphas, who was high priest that year.* 14It was Caiaphas who
had given counsel to the Jews that it was expedient that one man
should die for the people.

Jn 20:3 15Simon Peter followed Jesus, and so did another disciple. As
Acts 3:1 this disciple was known to the high priest, he entered the court of

---

takes care of his disciples, even though he himself is in danger. He had promised that none of his own should perish, except Judas Iscariot (cf. Jn 6:39; 17:12); although his promise referred to protecting them from eternal punishment, our Lord is also concerned about their immediate safety, for as yet they are not ready for martyrdom.

18:10–11. Once again we see Peter’s impetuosity and loyalty; he comes to our Lord’s defence, risking his own life, but he still does not understand God’s plan of salvation: he still cannot come to terms with the idea of Christ dying—just as he could not when Christ first foretold his passion (cf. Mt 16:21–22). Our Lord does not accept Peter’s violent defence: he refers back to what he said in his prayer in Gethsemane (cf. Mt 26:39), where he freely accepted his Father’s will, giving himself up to his captors in order to accomplish the Redemption.

We should show reverence to God’s will with the same docility and meekness as Jesus accepting his passion. “Stages: to be resigned to the will of God; to conform to the will of God; to want the will of God; to love the will of God” (St Josemaría Escrivá, *The Way*, 774).

18:13–18. Jesus is brought to the house of Annas, who, although he was no longer high priest, still exercised great religious and political influence (cf. the note on Lk 3:2). These two disciples, St Peter and the other disciple, probably John himself, are disconcerted; they do not know what to do, so they follow Jesus at a distance. Their attachment to him was not yet sufficiently supernatural; discouragement has displaced bravery and loyalty—and will soon lead to Peter’s triple denial. However noble his feelings, a Christian will be unable to live up to the demands

the high priest along with Jesus, [16]while Peter stood outside at the
door. So the other disciple, who was known to the high priest,
went out and spoke to the maid who kept the door, and brought
Peter in. [17]The maid who kept the door said to Peter, "Are not you
also one of this man's disciples?" He said, "I am not." [18]Now the
servants[l] and officers had made a charcoal fire, because it was
cold, and they were standing and warming themselves; Peter also
was with them, standing and warming himself.

[19]The high priest then questioned Jesus about his disciples and
his teaching. [20]Jesus answered him, "I have spoken openly to the Jn 7:14, 26
world; I have always taught in synagogues and in the temple, Mt 10:27 Is 45:19
where all Jews come together; I have said nothing secretly. [21]Why
do you ask me? Ask those who have heard me, what I said to
them; they know what I said." [22]When he had said this, one of the Jn 19:3
officers standing by struck Jesus with his hand, saying, "Is that Acts 23:2
how you answer the high priest?" [23]Jesus answered him, "If I have
spoken wrongly, bear witness to the wrong; but if I have spoken
rightly, why do you strike me?" [24]Annas then sent him bound to
Caiaphas the high priest.

[25]Now Simon Peter was standing and warming himself. They Jn 18:18
said to him, "Are not you also one of his disciples?" He denied it

---

of his faith unless his life has a basis of deep piety.

18:19–21. During his first interrogation—preliminary to his later examination by the Sanhedrin (Lk 22:66–71)—Jesus lays stress on the fact that he has always acted openly: everyone has had an opportunity to listen to him and to witness his miracles—so much so that at times he has been acclaimed as the Messiah (cf. Jn 12:12–19 and par.). The chief priests themselves have seen him in the temple and in the synagogues; but not wishing to see (cf. Jn 9:39–41), or believe (cf. Jn 10:37–38), they make out that his objectives are hidden and sinister.

18:22–23. Again, we see Jesus' serenity; he is master of the situation, as he is throughout his passion. To the unjust accusation made by this servant, our Lord replies meekly, but he does defend his conduct and points to the injustice with which he is being treated. This is how we should behave if people mistreat us in any way. Well-argued defence of one's rights is compatible with meekness and humility (cf. Acts 22:25).

18:25–27. Peter's denials are treated in less detail here than in the Synoptic Gospels, but here, as there, we can see the apostles' humility and sincerity, which lead them to tell about their own weaknesses. Peter's repentance is not referred to here, but is implied by the mention of the cock crowing: the very brevity of St John's account points to the fact that this episode is well known to the early Christians. After the Resurrection the full scope of Jesus' forgiveness will

l. Or *slaves*

and said, "I am not." [26]One of the servants[1] of the high priest, a
kinsman of the man whose ear Peter had cut off, asked, "Did I not
see you in the garden with him?" [27]Peter again denied it; and at
once the cock crowed.

Mt 27:1f **The trial before Pilate: Jesus is King**

Mk 15:1 Lk 23:1 [28]Then they led Jesus from the house of Caiaphas to the praeto-
Mt 23:11, 14 rium. It was early. They themselves did not enter the praetorium,
Mk 15:2, 5 so that they might not be defiled, but might eat the passover.* [29]So

---

be evidenced when he confirms Peter in his mission as leader of the apostles (cf. Jn 21:15–17). "In this adventure of love we should not be depressed by our falls, not even by serious falls, if we go to God in the sacrament of Penance contrite and resolved to improve. A Christian is not a neurotic collector of good behaviour reports. Jesus Christ our Lord was moved as much by Peter's repentance after his fall as by John's innocence and faithfulness. Jesus understands our weakness and draws us to himself on an inclined plane. He wants us to make an effort to climb a little each day" (St Josemaría Escrivá, *Christ Is Passing By*, 75).

18:28. The Synoptics also report the trial before Pilate, but St John gives a longer and more detailed account: John 18:28—19:16 is the centre of the five parts of his account of the Passion (cf. the note on 18:1). He describes the events that take place in the praetorium, highlighting the majesty of Christ as the messianic King, and also his rejection by the Jews.

There are seven stages here, marked by Pilate's entrances and exits. First (vv. 29–32) the Jews indict Jesus in a general way as an "evildoer". Then follows the dialogue between Pilate and Jesus (vv. 36–37) which culminates in Christ stating that he is a King, after which Pilate tries to save our Lord (vv. 38–40) by asking the people if they want him to release "the King of the Jews".

The centrepoint of the account (19:1–3) is the crowning with thorns, with the soldiers mockingly doing obeisance to Christ as "King of the Jews". After this our Lord is led out wearing the crown of thorns and draped in the purple robe (vv. 4–7)—the shameful scene of the *Ecce Homo*. The Jews' accusation now turns on Jesus' making himself the Son of God. Once again, Pilate, in the praetorium again, speaks with Jesus (vv. 8–12) and tries to probe further into his divine origin. The Jews then concentrate their hatred in a directly political accusation: "Everyone who makes himself a king sets himself against Caesar" (Jn 19:12). Finally (vv. 13–16), in a very formal way, stating time and place, St John narrates how Pilate points to Jesus and says: "Here is your King!" And the leaders of the Jews openly reject him who was and is the genuine King spoken of by the prophets.

"Praetorium": this was the Roman name for the official residence of the praetor or of other senior officials in the provinces of the Empire, such as the procurator or prefect in Palestine. Pilate's usual residence was on the coast, in Caesarea, but he normally moved to Jerusalem for the major festival periods, bringing additional troops to be used in the event of civil disorder. In Jerusalem, at this time and later, the procurator resided in Herod's palace (in the western part of the upper city) or else in the

Pilate went out to them and said, "What accusation do you bring Lk 23:2, 5
against this man?"* 30They answered him, "If this man were not
an evildoer, we would not have handed him over." 31Pilate said to Jn 19:6f
them, "Take him yourselves and judge him by your own law." The Acts 18:15
Jews said to him, "It is not lawful for us to put any man to
death."* 32This was to fulfil the word which Jesus had spoken to Jn 3:14; 12:32f
show by what death he was to die. Mt 20:19
33Pilate entered the praetorium again and called Jesus, and said
to him, "Are you the King of the Jews?" 34Jesus answered, "Do Mt 16:13

Antonia tower, a fortress backing onto the northeastern corner of the temple esplanade. It is not known for certain which of these two buildings was the praetorium mentioned in the Gospel; it was more likely the latter.

"So that they might not be defiled": Jewish tradition at the time (*Mishnah*; *Ohalot* treatise 7, 7) laid down that anyone who entered a Gentile or pagan house incurred seven days' legal defilement (cf. Acts 10:28); such defilement would have prevented them from celebrating the Passover. It is surprising that the chief priests had a scruple of this sort given their criminal inclinations against Jesus. Once more our Lord's accusation of them is seen to be well founded: "You blind guides, straining out a gnat and swallowing a camel" (Mt 23:24).

18:29–32. St John has omitted part of the interrogation which took place in the house of Caiaphas and which is reported in the Synoptics (Mt 26:57–66 and par.), which tell us that the meeting at Caiaphas' terminated with Jesus being declared deserving of death for the blasphemy of proclaiming himself the Son of God (cf. Mt 26:65–66). Under the Law of Moses blasphemy was punishable by stoning (cf. Lev 24:16); but they do not proceed to stone him—which they certainly could have done, even though the Romans were in control: they were ready to stone the adulterous woman (cf. Jn 8:1–11) and a short time later they did stone St Stephen (cf. Acts: 54–60)—because they wanted to bring the people along with them, and they knew that many of them regarded Jesus as Prophet and Messiah (cf. Mt 24:45–46; Mk 12:12; Lk 20:19). Not daring to stone him, they will shrewdly manage to turn a religious charge into a political question and have the authority of the Empire brought to bear on their side; they preferred to denounce Jesus to the procurator as a revolutionary who plotted against Caesar by declaring himself to be the Messiah and King of the Jews; by acting in this way they avoided risking the people's wrath and ensured that Jesus would be condemned by the Roman authorities to death by crucifixion.

Our Lord had foretold a number of times that he would die in this way (cf. Jn 3:14; 8:28; 12:32–33); as St Peter later put it, "Christ redeemed us from the curse of the law, having become a curse for us—for it is written, 'Cursed be every one who hangs on a tree'" (Gal 3:13; cf. Deut 21:23).

18:33–34. There is no onus on Pilate to interfere in religious questions, but because the accusation levelled against Jesus had to do with politics and public order, he begins his interrogation naturally by examining him on the main charge: "Are you the King of the Jews?"

By replying with another question,

you say this of your own accord, or did others say it to you about
Mt 20:19 me?" 35Pilate answered, "Am I a Jew? Your own nation and the
Mk 10:33 Lk 18:32 chief priests have handed you over to me; what have you done?"
36Jesus answered, "My kingship is not of this world; if my king-
Jn 8:47; 10:27 1 Tim 6:13 ship were of this world, my servants would fight, that I might not
be handed over to the Jews; but my kingship is not from the
world." 37Pilate said to him, "So you are a king?" Jesus answered,
"You say that I am a king. For this I was born, and for this I have

---

Jesus is not refusing to answer: he wishes to make quite clear, as he has always done, that his mission is a spiritual one. And really Pilate's was not an easy question to answer, because, to a Gentile, a king of the Jews meant simply a subverter of the Empire; whereas, to a Jewish nationalist, the King-Messiah was a politico-religious liberator who would obtain their freedom from Rome. The true character of Christ's messiahship completely transcends both these concepts—as Jesus explains to the procurator, although he realizes how enormously difficult it is for Pilate to understand what Christ's kingship really involves.

18:35–36. After the miracle of the multiplication of the loaves and the fish, Jesus refused to be proclaimed king because the people were thinking in terms of an earthly kingdom (cf. Jn 6:15). However, Jesus did enter Jerusalem in triumph, and he did accept acclamation as King-Messiah. Now, in the passion, he acknowledges before Pilate that he is truly a king, making it clear that his kingship is not an earthly one. Thus, "those who expected the Messiah to have visible temporal power were mistaken. 'The kingdom of God does not mean food and drink but righteousness and peace and joy in the Holy Spirit' (Rom 14:17). Truth and justice, peace and joy in the Holy Spirit. That is the kingdom of Christ: the divine activity which saves men and which will reach its culmination when history ends and the Lord comes from the heights of paradise finally to judge men" (St J. Escrivá, *Christ Is Passing By*, 180).

18:37. This is what his kingship really is: his kingdom is "the kingdom of Truth and Life, the kingdom of Holiness and Grace, the kingdom of Justice, Love and Peace" (*Roman Missal*, Preface of the Mass of Christ the King). Christ reigns over those who accept and practise the truth revealed by him—his Father's love for the world (Jn 3:16; 1 Jn 4:9). He became man to make this truth known and to enable men to accept it. And so, those who recognize Christ's kingship and sovereignty accept his authority, and he thus reigns over them in an eternal and universal kingdom.

For its part, "the Church, looking to Christ who bears witness to the truth, must always and everywhere ask herself, and in a certain sense also the contemporary 'world', how to make good emerge from man, how to liberate the dynamism of the good that is in man, in order that it may be stronger than evil, than any moral, social or other evil" (John Paul II, General Audience, 21 February 1979).

"If we [Christians] are trying to have Christ as our king we must be consistent. We must start by giving him our heart. Not to do that and still talk about the kingdom of Christ would be completely hollow. There would be no real Christian

come into the world, to bear witness to the truth. Every one who
is of the truth hears my voice." 38Pilate said to him, "What is
truth?"
After he had said this, he went out to the Jews again, and told
them, "I find no crime in him. 39But you have a custom that I
should release one man for you at the Passover; will you have me
release for you the King of the Jews?" 40They cried out again,
"Not this man, but Barabbas!" Now Barabbas was a robber.

Mt 27:15–23
Mk 15:6–14
Lk 23:17–23

---

substance in our behaviour. We would be making an outward show of a faith which simply did not exist. We would be misusing God's name to human advantage. [...] If we let Christ reign in our souls, we will not become authoritarian. Rather we will serve everyone. How I like that word: service! To serve my king, and through him, all those who have been redeemed by his blood. I really wish we Christians knew how to serve, for only by serving can we know and love Christ and make him known and loved" (St J. Escrivá, *Christ Is Passing By*, 181–182).

By his death and resurrection, Jesus shows that the accusations laid against him were based on lies: it was he who was telling the truth, not his judges and accusers, and God confirms the truth of Jesus—the truth of his words, of his deeds, of his revelation—by the singular miracle of his resurrection. To men Christ's kingship may seem paradoxical: he dies, yet he lives for ever; he is defeated and crucified, yet he is victorious. "When Jesus Christ himself appeared as a prisoner before Pilate's tribunal and was interrogated by him ... did he not answer: 'For this I was born, and for this I have come into the world, to bear witness to the truth'? It was as if with these words [...] he was once more confirming what he had said earlier: 'You will know the truth, and the truth will make you free'. In the course of so many centuries, of so many generations, from the time of the Apostles on, is it not often Jesus Christ himself that has made an appearance at the side of people judged for the sake of the truth? And has he not gone to death with people condemned for the sake of truth? Does he ever cease to be the continuous spokesman and advocate for the person who lives 'in spirit and truth' (cf. Jn 4:23)? Just as he does not cease to be it before the Father, he is it also with regard to the history of man" (John Paul II, *Redemptor hominis*, 12).

18:38–40. The outcome of the interrogation is that Pilate becomes convinced of Jesus' innocence (cf. Jn 19:4, 12). He probably realizes that the accusations made against Jesus were really an internal matter in which the Jews were trying to involve him; but the Jewish authorities are very irate. It is not easy for him to find a way out. He tries to do so by making concessions: first, he has recourse to a passover privilege, offering them the choice between a criminal and Jesus, but this does not work; so he looks for other ways to save him, and here also he fails. His cowardice and indecision cause him to yield to pressure and commit the injustice of condemning to death a man he knows to be innocent.

"The mystery of innocent suffering is one of the most obscure points on the entire horizon of human wisdom; and here it is affirmed in the most flagrant way. But before we uncover something of this problem, there already grows up

The scourging at the pillar and the crowning with thorns

Mt 27:26; 28:31 Mk 15:15, 17–20

19 [1]Then Pilate took Jesus and scourged him. [2]And the soldiers plaited a crown of thorns, and put it on his head, and
arrayed him in a purple robe; [3]they came up to him, saying, "Hail,
Is 50:6 King of the Jews!" and struck him with their hands. [4]Pilate went
out again, and said to them, "Behold, I am bringing him out to
you, that you may know that I find no crime in him." [5]So Jesus
came out, wearing the crown of thorns and the purple robe. Pilate
said to them, "Here is the man!" [6]When the chief priests and the
officers saw him, they cried out, "Crucify him, crucify him!"
Pilate said to them, "Take him yourselves and crucify him, for I
Jn 5:18; 10:33 Lev 24:16 find no crime in him." [7]The Jews answered him, "We have a law,
and by that law he ought to die, because he has made himself the

---

in us an unrestrained affection for the innocent one who suffers, for Jesus, [...] and for all innocent people—whether they be young or old—who are also suffering, and whose pain we cannot explain. The way of the cross leads us to meet the first person in a sorrowful procession of innocent people who suffer. And this first blameless and suffering person uncovers for us in the end the secret of his passion. It is a sacrifice" (Paul VI, Address on Good Friday, 12 April 1974).

19:1–3. Christ's prophecy is fulfilled to the letter: the Son of man "will be delivered to the Gentiles, and will be mocked and shamefully treated and spit upon; they will scourge him and kill him, and on the third day he will rise" (Lk 18:32f; cf. Mt 20:18f).

Scourging was one of the most severe punishments permitted under Roman law. The criminal was draped over a pillar or other form of support, his naked back exposed to the lash or *flagellum*.

Scourging was generally used as a preliminary to crucifixion to weaken the criminal and thereby hasten his death.

Crowning with thorns was not an official part of the punishment; it was an initiative of the soldiers themselves, a product of their cruelty and desire to mock Jesus. On the stone pavement in the Antonia tower some drawings have been found which must have been used in what was called the "king game": dice were thrown to pick out a mock king among those condemned, who was subjected to taunting before being led off for crucifixion.

St John locates this episode at the centre of his narrative of the events in the praetorium. He thereby highlights the crowning with thorns as the point at which Christ's kingship is at its most patent: the soldiers proclaim him as King of the Jews only in a sarcastic way (cf. Mk 15:15, 16–19), but the Evangelist gives us to understand that he is indeed the King.

19:5. Wearing the insignia of royalty, Christ, despite this tragic parody, still projects the majesty of the King of Kings. In Revelation 5:12 St John will say: "Worthy is the Lamb who was slain, to receive power and wealth and wisdom and might and honour and glory and blessing!"

"Imagine that divine face: swollen by blows, covered in spittle, torn by thorns, furrowed with blood, here fresh blood, there ugly dried blood. And, since the

Son of God."* [8]When Pilate heard these words, he was the more
afraid; [9]he entered the praetorium again and said to Jesus, "Where
are you from?"* But Jesus gave no answer. [10]Pilate therefore said
to him, "You will not speak to me? Do you not know that I have
the power to release you, and the power to crucify you?" [11]Jesus Jn 10:18
answered him, "You would have no power over me unless it had Acts 2:23
been given you from above; therefore he who delivered me to you
has the greater sin."

Pilate hands Jesus over

[12]Upon this Pilate sought to release him, but the Jews cried out, "If Acts 17:7
you release this man, you are not Caesar's friend; every one who
makes himself a king sets himself against Caesar." [13]When Pilate

---

sacred Lamb had his hands tied, he could not use them to wipe away the blood running into his eyes, and so those two luminaries of heaven were eclipsed and almost blinded and made mere pieces of flesh. Finally, so disfigured was he that one could not make out who he was; he scarcely seemed human; he had become an altarpiece depicting suffering, painted by those cruel artists and their evil president, producing this pitiful figure to plead his case before his enemies" (Fray Luis de Granada, *Life of Jesus Christ*, 24).

19:6–7. When Pilate hears the Jews accuse Jesus of claiming to be the Son of God, he grows still more alarmed: his wife has already unnerved him by sending him a message, after a dream, not to have anything to do with this "righteous man". But the shouting (v. 12) orchestrated by the Jewish authorities pressures him into agreeing to condemn Jesus.

Although technically Jesus is crucified for supposedly committing a political crime (cf. the note on Jn 18:29–32), in fact it is on clearly religious ground that he is sent to death.

19:8–11. Pilate is impressed by Jesus' silence, by his not defending himself, and when the procurator says that he has power to release him or to condemn him, our Lord then says something quite unexpected—that all power on earth comes from God. This means that in the last analysis even if people talk about the sovereignty of the king or of the people, such authority is never absolute; it is only relative, being subject to the absolute sovereignty of God: hence no human law can be just, and therefore binding in conscience, if it does not accord with divine law.

"He who delivered me"—a reference to all those who have contrived our Lord's death, that is, Judas, Caiaphas, the Jewish leaders, etc. (cf. 18:30–35). They are the ones who really sent Christ to the cross; but this does not exonerate Pontius Pilate from blame.

19:13. "The Pavement", in Greek *lithostrotos*, literally a "pavement", a "flagged expanse", therefore a yard or plaza paved with flags. The Hebrew word "Gabbatha" is not the equivalent of the Greek *lithostrotos*; it means a "height" or "eminence". But both words refer to the same place; however, its precise location is uncertain due to doubts about where the praetorium was located: cf. the note on Jn 18:28.

heard these words, he brought Jesus out and sat down on the judg-
ment seat at a place called The Pavement, and in Hebrew,
Jn 18:22–37 Gabbatha. 14Now it was the day of Preparation for the Passover; it
was about the sixth hour. He said to the Jews, "Here is your
Jn 19:6 King!" 15They cried out, "Away with him, away with him, crucify
Mt 27:31; 33:37f him!" Pilate said to them, "Shall I crucify your King?" The chief
Mk 15:20, 22, 25–27 priests answered, "We have no king but Caesar." 16Then he handed
Lk 23:33, 38 him over to them to be crucified.

Grammatically the Greek could be translated as follows: "Pilate … brought Jesus out and sat him down on the judgment seat": in which case the Evangelist implies that Pilate was ridiculing the Jewish leaders by a mock enthronement of the "King of the Jews". This would fit in with Pilate's attitude towards the Jewish leaders from this point onwards (vv. 14–22) and with the purpose of the inspired writer, who would see in this the enthronement of Christ as King.

19:14. "The day of Preparation", the *Parasceve*. The sixth hour began at midday. Around this time all leavened bread was removed from the houses and replaced by unleavened bread for the paschal meal (cf. Ex 12:15ff), and the lamb was officially sacrificed in the temple. St John notes that this was the time at which Jesus was condemned, thereby underlining the coincidence between the time of the death sentence and the time the lamb was sacrificed: Christ is the new Paschal Lamb; as St Paul says (1 Cor 5:7), "Christ, our paschal lamb, has been sacrificed."

There is some difficulty in reconciling what St John says about the sixth hour with the information given in Mark 15:25 about Jesus being crucified at the third hour. Various explanations are offered, the best being the Mark is referring to the end of the third hour and John to the beginning of the sixth hour: both would then be talking of around midday.

19:15. The history of the Jewish people helps us understand the tragic paradox of the attitude of the Jewish authorities at this point. The Jews were very conscious all along of being the people of God. For example, they proudly asserted that they had no Father but God (cf. Jn 8:4). In the Old Testament Yahweh is the true King of Israel (cf. Deut 33:5; Num 23:21; 1 Kings 22:19; Is 6:5); when they wanted to copy the neighbouring peoples and asked Samuel for a king (cf. 1 Sam 8:5, 20), Samuel resisted, because Israel had only one absolute sovereign, Yahweh (1 Sam 8:6–9). But eventually God gave in to their request and himself designated who should be king over his people. His first choice, Saul, was given a sacred anointing, as were David and his successors. This rite of anointing showed that the Israelite king was God's vicar. When the kings failed to meet the people's expectations, they increasingly yearned for the messianic king, the descendant or "Son" of David, the Anointed *par excellence* or Messiah, who would rule his people, liberate them from their enemies and lead them to rule the world (cf. 2 Sam 7:16; Ps 24:7; 44:4–5, etc.). For centuries they strove heroically for this ideal, rejecting foreign domination.

During Christ's time they also opposed Rome and Herod, whom, not being a Jew, they regarded as an illegitimate king. However, at this point in the Passion, they hypocritically accept the Roman emperor as their true and only

The crucifixion and death of Jesus

[17]So they took Jesus, and he went out, bearing his own cross, to
the place called the place of a skull, which is called in Hebrew
Golgotha. [18]There they crucified him, and with him two others, Gen 22:6

---

king. They also reject the "easy yoke" of Christ (cf. Mt 11:30) and bring the full weight of Rome down upon him.

"They themselves submitted to the punishment; therefore, the Lord handed them over. Thus, because they unanimously rejected God's government, the Lord let them be brought down through their own condemnation: for, rejecting the domination of Christ, they brought upon themselves that of Caesar" (St John Chrysostom, *Hom. on St John*, 83).

A similar kind of tragedy occurs when people who have been baptized and therefore have become part of the new people of God, throw off the "easy yoke" of Christ's sovereignty by their obstinacy in sin and submit to the terrible tyranny of the devil (cf. 2 Pet 2:21).

19:17. "The place of a skull" or Calvary seems to have got its name from the fact that it was shaped like a skull or head.

St Paul points to the parallelism that exists between Adam's disobedience and Christ's obedience (cf. Rom 5:12). On the feast of the Triumph of the Cross the Church sings "where life was lost, there life has been restored", to show how, just as the devil won victory by the tree of Paradise, so he was overpowered by Christ on the tree of the cross.

St John is the only Evangelist who clearly states that Jesus carried his own cross; the other three mention that Simon of Cyrene helped to carry it. See the notes on Mt 27:32 and Lk 23:26.

Christ's decisiveness in accepting the cross is an example which we should follow in our daily life: "You yourself must decide of your own free will to take up the cross; otherwise, your tongue may say that you are imitating Christ, but your actions will belie your words. That way, you will never get to know the Master intimately, or love him truly. It is really important that we Christians convince ourselves of this. We are not walking with our Lord unless we are spontaneously depriving ourselves of many things that our whims, vanity, pleasure or self-interest clamour for" (St Josemaría Escrivá, *Friends of God*, 129).

As Simeon had prophesied, Jesus would be a "sign that is spoken against" (Lk 2:34)—a standard raised on high which leaves no room for indifference, demanding that every man decide for or against him and his cross: "he was going therefore to the place where he was to be crucified, bearing his own Cross. An extraordinary spectacle: to impiety, something to jeer at; to piety, a great mystery. [...] Impiety looks on and laughs at a king bearing, instead of a sceptre, the wood of his punishment; piety looks on and sees the King bearing that cross for himself to be fixed on, a cross which would thereafter shine on the brows of kings; an object of contempt in the eyes of the impious, but something in which hereafter the hearts of the saints should glorify, as St Paul would later say, But God forbid that I should glory; save in the cross of our Lord Jesus Christ" (St Augustine, *In Ioann. Evang.*, 117, 3).

19:18. Knowing what crucifixion in ancient times entailed will help us understand better the extent of the humiliation and suffering Jesus bore for love of us. Crucifixion was a penalty reserved for

Is 53:12 one on either side, and Jesus between them. [19]Pilate also wrote a
title and put it on the cross; it read, "Jesus of Nazareth, the King of
Heb 13:12 the Jews." [20]Many of the Jews read this title, for the place where
Jesus was crucified was near the city; and it was written in Hebrew,
in Latin, and in Greek. [21]The chief priests of the Jews then said to
Pilate, "Do not write, 'The King of the Jews,' but 'This man said, I
am King of the Jews.'" [22]Pilate answered, "What I have written I
have written."

---

slaves, and applied to the most serious crimes; it was the most horrific and painful form of death possible; it was also an exemplary public punishment and therefore was carried out in a public place, with the body of the criminal being left exposed for days afterwards. These words of Cicero show how infamous a punishment it was: "That a Roman citizen should be bound is an abuse; that he be lashed is a crime; that he be put to death is virtually parricide; what, then, shall I say, if he be hung on a cross? There is no word fit to describe a deed so horrible" (*In Verrem*, 2, 5, 66).

A person undergoing crucifixion died after a painful agony involving loss of blood, fever caused by his wounds, thirst, and asphyxiation, etc. Sometimes the executioners hastened death by breaking the person's legs or piercing him with a lance, as in our Lord's case. This helps us understand better what St Paul says to the Philippians about Christ's humiliation on the cross: "[he] emptied himself, taking the form of a servant [or slave], being born in the likeness of men …; he humbled himself and became obedient unto death, even death on a cross" (Phil 2:7–8).

St John says little about the other two people being crucified, perhaps because the Synoptic Gospels had already spoken about them (see the notes on Lk 23:39–43).

19:19–22. The "title" was the technical term then used in Roman law to indicate the grounds on which the person was being punished. It was usually written on a board prominently displayed, summarizing the official document which was forwarded to the legal archives in Rome. This explains why, when the chief priests ask Pilate to change the wording of the inscription, the procurator firmly refuses to do so: the sentence, once dictated, was irrevocable; that is what he means when he says, "What I have written I have written." In the case of Christ, this title written in different languages proclaims his universal kingship, for it could be read by people from all over the world who had come to celebrate the Passover—thus confirming our Lord's words: "You say that I am a king. For this I was born, and for this I have come into the world" (Jn 18:37).

In establishing the feast of Christ the King, Pope Pius XI explained: "He is said to reign 'in the minds of men', both by reason of the keenness of his intellect and the extent of his knowledge, and also because he is Truth itself and it is from him that truth must be obediently received by all mankind. He reigns, too, in the wills of men, for in him the human will was perfectly and entirely obedient to the holy will of God, and further by his grace and inspiration he so subjects our free will as to incite us to the most noble endeavours. He is King of our hearts, too, by reason of his 'charity which surpasseth all knowledge', and his mercy and kindness which draw all men

[23]When the soldiers had crucified Jesus they took his garments Mt 27:35
and made four parts, one for each soldier; also his tunic. But the Mk 15:24 Lk 23:24
tunic was without seam, woven from top to bottom; [24]so they said
to one another, "Let us not tear it, but cast lots for it to see whose
it shall be." This was to fulfil the scripture,

> "They parted my garments among them, Ps 22:18
> and for my clothing they cast lots."

[25]So the soldiers did this. But standing by the cross of Jesus were Mt 27:55f
his mother, and his mother's sister, Mary the wife of Clopas, and Mk 15:40f Lk 23:49
Mary Magdalene. [26]When Jesus saw his mother, and the disciple Jn 2:4; 13:23

---

to him; for there never was, nor ever will be a man loved so much and so universally as Jesus Christ" (*Quas primas*).

19:23–24. And so the prophecy of Psalm 22 is fulfilled which describes so accurately the sufferings of the Messiah: "They divide my garments among them, and for my raiment they cast lots" (v. 18). The Fathers have seen in this seamless tunic a symbol of the unity of the Church (cf. St Augustine, *In Ioann. Evang.*, 118, 4).

19:25. Whereas the Apostles, with the exception of St John, abandon Jesus in the hour of his humiliation, these pious women, who had followed him during his public life (cf. Lk 8:2–3) now stay with their Master as he dies on the cross (cf. the note on Mt 27:55–56).

Pope John Paul II explains that our Lady's faithfulness was shown in four ways: first, in her generous desire to do all that God wanted of her (cf. Lk 1:34); second, in her total acceptance of God's will (cf. Lk 1:46f); third, in the consistency between her life and the commitment of faith which she made; and, finally, in her withstanding this test. "And only a consistency that lasts throughout the whole of life can be called faithfulness. Mary's 'fiat' in the Annunciation finds its fullness in the silent 'fiat' that she repeats at the foot of the Cross" (Homily in Mexico Cathedral, 26 January 1979).

The Church has always recognized the dignity of women and their important role in salvation history. It is enough to recall the veneration which from the earliest times the Christian people have had for the Mother of Christ, the Woman *par excellence* and the most sublime and most privileged creature ever to come from the hands of God. Addressing a special message to women, the Second Vatican Council said, among other things: "Women in trial, who stand upright at the foot of the cross like Mary, you who so often in history have given to men the strength to battle unto the very end and to give witness to the point of martyrdom, aid them now still once more to retain courage in their great undertakings, while at the same time maintaining patience and an esteem for humble beginnings" (Vatican II, *Message to women*, 8 December 1965).

19:26–27. "The spotless purity of John's whole life makes him strong before the cross. The other apostles fly from Golgotha; he, with the Mother of Christ, remains. Don't forget that purity strengthens and invigorates character" (St Josemaría Escrivá, *The Way*, 144).

Our Lord's gesture in entrusting his Blessed Mother to the disciple's care, has a dual meaning (see pp. 542ff). For one thing it expresses his filial love for the Virgin Mary. St Augustine sees it as

whom he loved standing near, he said to his mother, "Woman,
behold, your son!" 27Then he said to the disciple, "Behold, your
mother!" And from that hour the disciple took her to his own home.*
Mt 27:48–50 28After this Jesus, knowing that all was now finished, said (to
Mk 15:36f Lk 23:46 fulfil the scripture), "I thirst." 29A bowl full of vinegar stood there;
Ps 69:21 so they put a sponge full of vinegar on hyssop and held it to his

---

a lesson Jesus gives us on how to keep the fourth commandment: "Here is a lesson in morals. He is doing what he tells us to do and, like a good Teacher, he instructs his own by example, that it is the duty of good children to take care of their parents; as though the wood on which his dying members were fixed were also the chair of the teaching Master" (St Augustine, *In Ioann. Evang.*, 119, 2).

Our Lord's words also declare that Mary is our Mother: "The Blessed Virgin also advanced in her pilgrimage of faith, and faithfully persevered in her union with her Son unto the cross, where she stood, in keeping with the divine plan, enduring with her only begotten Son the intensity of his suffering, associating herself with his sacrifice in her mother's heart, and lovingly consenting to the immolation of this victim who was born of her. Finally, she was given by the same Christ Jesus dying on the cross as a mother to his disciple" (Vatican II, *Lumen Gentium*, 58).

All Christians, who are represented in the person of John, are children of Mary. By giving us his Mother to be our Mother, Christ demonstrates his love for his own to the end (cf. Jn 13:1). Our Lady's acceptance of John as her son shows her motherly care for us: "the son of God, and your Son, from the Cross indicated a man to you, Mary, and said: 'Behold, your son' (Jn 19:26). And in that man he entrusted to you every person, he entrusted everyone to you. And you, who at the moment of the Annunciation, concentrated the whole programme of your life in those simple words: 'Behold I am the handmaid of the Lord; let it be to me according to your word' (Lk 1:38): embrace everyone, draw close to everyone, seek everyone out with motherly care. Thus is accomplished what the last Council said about your presence in the mystery of Christ and the Church. In a wonderful way you are wherever men and women, his brother and sisters, are present, wherever the Church is present" (John Paul II, Homily in the Basilica of Guadalupe, 27 January 1979).

"John, the disciple whom Jesus loved, brought Mary into his home, into his life. Spiritual writers have seen these words of the Gospel as an invitation to all Christians to bring Mary into their lives. Mary certainly wants us to invoke her, to approach her confidently, to appeal to her as our mother, asking her to 'show that you are our mother'" (St Josemaría Escrivá, *Christ Is Passing By*, 140).

John Paul II constantly treats our Lady as his Mother. In bidding farewell to the Virgin of Czestochowa he prayed in this way: "Our Lady of the Bright Mountain, Mother of the Church! Once more I consecrate myself to you 'in your maternal slavery of love'. *Totus tuus!* I am all yours! I consecrate to you the whole Church—everywhere and to the ends of the earth! I consecrate to you humanity; I consecrate to you all men and women, my brothers and sisters. All peoples and all nations. I consecrate to you Europe and all the continents. I con-

mouth. 30When Jesus had received the vinegar, he said, "It is finished"; and he bowed his head and gave up his spirit.

Jesus' side is pierced. The burial
31Since it was the day of Preparation, in order to prevent the Deut 21:23
bodies from remaining on the cross on the sabbath (for that sab-

---

secrate to you Rome and Poland, united, through your servant, by a fresh bond of love. Mother, accept us! Mother, do not abandon us! Mother, be our guide!" (Farewell Address at Jasna Gora Shrine, 6 June 1979).

19:28–29. This was foretold in the Old Testament: "They gave me poison for food, and for my thirst they gave me vinegar to drink" (Ps 69:21). This does not mean that they gave Jesus vinegar to increase his suffering; it was customary to offer victims of crucifixion water mixed with vinegar to relieve their thirst. In addition to the natural dehydration Jesus was suffering, we can see in his thirst an expression of his burning desire to do his Father's will and to save all souls: "On the cross he cried out *Sitio!*, 'I thirst'. He thirsts for us, for our love, for our souls and for all the souls we ought to be bringing to him along the way of the Cross, which is the way to immortality and heavenly glory" (St Josemaría Escrivá, *Friends of God*, 202).

19:30. Jesus, nailed on the cross, dies to atone for all the sins and vileness of man. Despite his sufferings he dies serenely, majestically, bowing his head now that he has accomplished the mission entrusted to him. "Who can sleep when he wishes to, as Jesus died when he wished to? Who can lay aside his clothing when he wishes to, as he put off the flesh when he chose to? … What must we hope or fear to find his power when he comes in judgment, if it can be seen to be so great at the moment of his death!" (St Augustine, *In Ioann. Evang.*, 119, 6).

"Let us meditate on our Lord, wounded from head to foot out of love for us. Using a phrase which approaches the truth, although it does not express its full reality, we can repeat the words of an ancient writer: 'The body of Christ is a portrait in pain'. At the first sight of Christ bruised and broken—just a lifeless body taken down from the cross and given to his Mother—at the sight of Jesus destroyed in this way, we might have thought he had failed utterly. Where are the crowds that once followed him, where is the kingdom he foretold? But this is victory, not defeat. We are nearer the resurrection than ever before; we are going to see the glory which he has won with his obedience" (St Josemaría Escrivá, *Christ Is Passing By*, 95).

19:31–33. Jesus dies on the Preparation day of the Passover—the *Parasceve*—that is, the eve, when the paschal lambs were officially sacrificed in the temple. By stressing this, the Evangelist implies that Christ's sacrifice took the place of the sacrifices of the Old Law and inaugurated the New Alliance in his blood (cf. Heb 9:12).

The Law of Moses required that the bodies should be taken down before nightfall (cf. Deut 21:22–23); this is why Pilate is asked to have their legs broken, to bring on death and allow them to be buried before it gets dark, particularly since the next day is the feast of the Passover.

bath was a high day), the Jews asked Pilate that their legs might
be broken, and that they might be taken away. 32So the soldiers
came and broke the legs of the first, and of the other who had
been crucified with him; 33but when they came to Jesus and saw
that he was already dead, they did not break his legs. 34But one of
the soldiers pierced his side with a spear, and at once there came
out blood and water. 35He who saw it has borne witness—his testimony is true, and he knows that he tells the truth—that you also
Ex 12:46 may believe. 36For these things took place that the scripture might
Num 9:12 Ps 34:20 be fulfilled, "Not a bone of him shall be broken." 37And again
Zech 12:10 another scripture says, "They shall look on him whom they have
Rev 1:7 pierced."

19:34. The outflow of blood and water has a natural explanation. Probably the water was an accumulation of liquid in the lungs due to Jesus' intense sufferings. As on other occasions, the historical events narrated in the Fourth Gospel are laden with meaning. St Augustine and Christian tradition see the sacraments and the Church itself flowing from Jesus' open side: "Here was opened wide the door of life, from which the sacraments of the Church have flowed out, without which there is no entering in unto life which is true life. [...] Here the second Adam with bowed head slept upon the cross, that thence a wife might be formed of him, flowing from his side while he slept. O death, by which the dead come back to life!! Is there anything purer than this blood, any wound more healing!" (St Augustine, *In Ioann. Evang.*, 120, 2).

The Second Vatican Council, for its part, teaches: "The Church—that is, the kingdom of Christ—already present in mystery, grows visibly through the power of God in the world. The origin and growth of the Church are symbolized by the blood and water which flowed from the open side of the crucified Jesus" (Vatican II, *Lumen gentium*, 3).

"Jesus on the cross, with his heart overflowing with love for man, is such an eloquent commentary on the value of people and things that words only get in the way. People, their happiness and their life, are so important that the very Son of God gave himself to redeem and cleanse and raise them up" (St Josemaría Escrivá, *Christ Is Passing By*, 165).

19:35. St John's Gospel presents itself as a truthful witness of the events of our Lord's life and of their spiritual and doctrinal significance. From the words of John the Baptist at the outset of Jesus' public ministry (1:19) to the final paragraph of the Gospel (21:24–25), everything forms part of a testimony to the sublime phenomenon of the Word of Life made Man. Here the evangelist explicitly states that he was an eyewitness (cf. also Jn 20:30–31; 1 Jn 1:1–3).

19:36. This quotation refers to the precept of the Law that no bone of the paschal lamb should be broken (cf. Ex 12:46): again John's Gospel is telling us that Jesus is the true paschal Lamb who takes away the sins of the world (cf. Jn 1:29).

19:37. The account of the Passion concludes with a quotation from Zechariah (12:10) foretelling the salvation resulting from the mysterious suffering and death of a redeemer. The evangelist thereby evokes the salvation wrought by Christ,

[38]After this Joseph of Arimathea, who was a disciple of Jesus, Mt 27:57–60 Mk 15:42–46 Lk 23:50–54
but secretly, for fear of the Jews, asked Pilate that he might take
away the body of Jesus, and Pilate gave him leave. So he came
and took away his body. [39]Nicodemus also, who had at first come Jn 3:1 Mt 2:1
to him by night, came bringing a mixture of myrrh and aloes,
about a hundred pounds' weight. [40]They took the body of Jesus, Jn 11:44
and bound it in linen cloths with the spices, as is the burial custom
of the Jews. [41]Now in the place where he was crucified there was
a garden, and in the garden a new tomb where no one had ever
been laid. [42]So because of the Jewish day of Preparation, as the
tomb was close at hand, they laid Jesus there.

---

who, nailed to the cross, has fulfilled God's promise of redemption (cf. Jn 12:32). Everyone who looks upon him with faith receives the effects of his passion. Thus, the good thief, looking at Christ on the cross, recognized his kingship, placed his trust in him and received the promise of heaven (cf. Lk 23:42–43).

In the liturgy of Good Friday the Church invites us to contemplate and adore the cross: "Behold the wood of the Cross, on which was nailed the salvation of the world", and from the earliest time of the Church the crucifix has been the sign reminding Christians of the supreme point of Christ's love, when he died on the cross and freed us from eternal death.

"Your crucifix.—As a Christian, you should always carry your crucifix with you. And place it on your desk. And kiss it before going to bed and when you wake up: and when our poor body rebels against your soul, kiss it again" (St Josemaría Escrivá, *The Way*, 302).

19:38–39. Our Lord's sacrifice produces its firstfruits: people who were previously afraid now boldly confess themselves disciples of Christ and attend to his dead body with exquisite refinement and generosity. The evangelist mentions that Joseph of Arimathea and Nicodemus used a mixture of myrrh and aloes in lavish amount. Myrrh is a very expensive aromatic resin, and aloes a juice extracted from the leaves of certain plants. They were used as an expression of veneration for the dead.

19:40. The Fourth Gospel adds to the information on the burial given by the Synoptics. Sacred Scripture did not specify what form burial should take, with the result that the Jews followed the custom of the time. After piously taking our Lord's body down from the cross, they probably washed it carefully (cf. Acts 9:37), perfumed it and wrapped it in a linen cloth, covering the head with a sudarium or napkin (cf. Jn 20:5–6). But because of the imminence of the sabbath rest, they were unable to anoint the body with balsam, which the women planned to do once the sabbath was past (cf. Mk 16:1; Lk 24:1). Jesus himself, when he praised Mary for anointing him at Bethany, had foretold in a veiled way that his body would not be embalmed (cf. the note on Jn 12:7–8).

19:41. Many of the Fathers have probed the mystic meaning of the garden—usually to point out that Christ, who was arrested in the Garden of Olives and buried in another garden, has redeemed us superabundantly from that first sin which was committed also in a garden, the Garden of Paradise. They comment

11. APPEARANCES OF THE RISEN CHRIST

Mt 28:1–8 **The empty tomb**

Mk 16:1–8 20 1Now on the first day of the week Mary Magdalene came
Lk 24:1–11 to the tomb early, while it was still dark, and saw that the
Jn 13:23 stone had been taken away from the tomb. 2So she ran, and went
to Simon Peter and the other disciple, the one whom Jesus loved,
and said to them, "They have taken the Lord out of the tomb, and
we do not know where they have laid him." 3Peter then came out
with the other disciple, and they went toward the tomb. 4They

---

that because Jesus was the only one to be buried in this new tomb there would be no doubt that it was he and not someone else that rose from the dead. St Augustine also observes that "just as in the womb of the Virgin Mary none was conceived before him, none after him, so in this tomb none before him, none after was buried" (*In Ioann. Evang.*, 120, 5).

Among the truths of Christian doctrine to do with Christ's death and burial are these: "one, that the body of Christ was in no degree corrupted in the sepulchre, according to the prediction of the Prophet, 'Thou wilt not give thy holy one to see corruption' (Ps 16:10; Acts 2:31); the other … that burial, passion and death apply to Christ Jesus not as God but as man, yet they are also attributed to God, since, as is clear, they are predicted with propriety of that Person who is at once perfect God and perfect man" (St Pius V, *Catechism*, 1, 5, 9).

20:1–2. All four Gospels report the first testimonies of the holy women and the disciples regarding Christ's glorious resurrection, beginning with the fact of the empty tomb (cf. Mt 28:1–15; Mk 16:1ff; Lk 24:1–12) and then telling of the various appearances of the risen Jesus.

Mary Magdalene was one of the women who provided for our Lord during his journeys (Lk 8:1–3); along with the Virgin Mary she bravely stayed with him right up to his final moments (Jn 19:25), and she saw where his body was laid (Lk 23:55). Now, after the obligatory sabbath rest, she goes to visit the tomb. The Gospel points out that she went "early, while it was still dark": her love and veneration led her to go without delay, to be with our Lord's body.

20:4. The Fourth Gospel makes it clear that, although the women, and specifically Mary Magdalene, were the first to reach the tomb, the Apostles were the first to enter it and see the evidence that Christ had risen (the empty tomb, the linen clothes "lying" and the napkin in a place by itself). Bearing witness to this will be an essential factor in the mission which Christ will entrust to them: "You shall be my witnesses in Jerusalem … and to the end of the earth" (Acts 1:8; cf. Acts 2:32). John, who reached the tomb first (perhaps because he was the younger), did not go in, out of deference to Peter. This is an indication that Peter was already regarded as leader of the apostles.

20:5–7. The words the evangelist uses to describe what Peter and he saw in the empty tomb convey with vivid realism the impression it made on them, etching on their memory details which at first sight seem irrelevant.

both ran, but the other disciple outran Peter and reached the tomb
first; 5and stooping to look in, he saw the linen cloths lying there,
but he did not go in. 6Then Simon Peter came, following him, and Lk 24:12
went into the tomb; he saw the linen cloths lying, 7and the napkin, Jn 19:40
which had been on his head, not lying with the linen cloths but
rolled up in a place by itself. 8Then the other disciple, who Jn 2:22
reached the tomb first, also went in, and he saw and believed; 9for 1 Cor 15:4
as yet they did not know the scripture, that he must rise from the Acts 2:24–32
dead. 10Then the disciples went back to their homes.

The whole scene inside the tomb in some way caused them to intuit that the Lord had risen. Some of the words contained in the account need further explanation, so terse is the translation.

"The linen clothes lying there": the Greek participle translated as "lying there" seems to indicate that the clothes were flattened, deflated, as if they were emptied when the body of Jesus rose and disappeared—as if it had come out of the clothes and bandages without their being unrolled, passing right through them (just as later he entered the Cenacle when the doors were shut). This would explain the clothes being "fallen", "flat", "lying", which is how the Greek literally translates, after Jesus' body—which had filled them—left them. One can readily understand how this would amaze a witness, how unforgettable the scene would be.

"The napkin … rolled up in a place by itself": the first point to note is that the napkin, which had been wrapped round the head, was not on top of the clothes, but placed to one side. The second, even more surprising thing is that, like the clothes, it was still rolled up but, unlike the clothes, it still had a certain volume, like a container, possibly due to the stiffness given it by the ointments: this is what the Greek participle, here translated as "rolled", seems to indicate.

From these details concerning the empty tomb one deduces that Jesus' body must have risen in a heavenly manner, that is, in a way which transcended the laws of nature. It was not only a matter of the body being reanimated, as happened, for example, in the case of Lazarus, who had to be unbound before he could walk (cf. Jn 11:44).

20:8–10. As Mary Magdalene had told them, the Lord was not in the tomb; but the two apostles realized that there was no question of any robbery, which was what she thought had happened, because they saw the special way the clothes and napkin were; they now began to understand what the Master had so often told them about his death and resurrection (cf. Mt 16:21; Mk 8:31; Lk 9:22; etc.; cf. also the notes on Mt 12:39–40 and Lk 18:31–40).

The empty tomb and the other facts were perceptible to the senses; but the resurrection, even though it had effects that could be tested by experience, requires faith if it is to be accepted. Christ's resurrection is a real, historic fact: his body and soul were reunited. But since his was a glorious resurrection unlike Lazarus', far beyond our capacity in this life to understand what happened, and outside the scope of sense experience, a special gift of God is required—the gift of faith—to know and accept as a certainty this fact which, while it is historical, is also supernatural. Therefore, St Thomas Aquinas can say that "the indi-

The appearance to Mary Magdalene

Mt 28:9–10 Mk 16:9–11 11 But Mary stood weeping outside the tomb, and as she wept she
Jn 1:51 stooped to look into the tomb; 12 and she saw two angels in white,
Heb 1:14 sitting where the body of Jesus had lain, one at the head and one at
the feet. 13 They said to her, “Woman, why are you weeping?” She
said to them, “Because they have taken away my Lord, and I do
not know where they have laid him.” 14 Saying this, she turned
Jn 21:4 round and saw Jesus standing, but she did not know that it was
Jesus. 15 Jesus said to her, “Woman, why are you weeping? Whom
do you seek?” Supposing him to be the gardener, she said to him,
“Sir, if you have carried him away, tell me where you have laid him,
Mk 10:51 and I will take him away.” 16 Jesus said to her, “Mary.” She turned
and said to him in Hebrew, “Rabboni!” (which means Teacher).

---

vidual arguments taken alone are not sufficient proof of Christ’s resurrection, but taken together, in a cumulative way, they manifest it perfectly. Particularly important in this regard are the spiritual proofs (cf. specially Lk 24:25–27), the angelic testimony (cf. Lk 24:4–7) and Christ’s own post-resurrection word confirmed by miracles (cf. Jn 3:13; Mt 16:21; 17:22; 20:18)” (St Thomas Aquinas, *Summa theologiae*, 3, 55, 6 ad 1).

In addition to Christ’s predictions about his passion, death and resurrection (cf. Jn 2:19; Mt 16:21; Mk 9:31; Lk 9:22), the Old Testament also foretells the glorious victory of the Messiah and, in some way, his resurrection (cf. Ps 16:9; Is 52:13; Hos 6:2). The apostles begin to grasp the true meaning of Scripture after the resurrection, particularly once they receive the Holy Spirit, who fully enlightens their minds to understand the content of the Word of God. It is easy to imagine the surprise and elation they all feel when Peter and John tell them what they have seen in the tomb.

20:11–18. Mary’s affection and sensitivity lead her to be concerned about what has become of the dead body of Jesus. This woman out of whom seven demons were cast (cf. Lk 8:2) stayed faithful during his passion and even now her love is still ardent: our Lord has freed her from the Evil One and she responded to that grace humbly and generously.

After consoling Mary Magdalene, Jesus gives her a message for the Apostles, whom he tenderly calls his “brethren”. This message implies that he and they have the same Father, though each in an essentially different way: “I am ascending to my Father”—my own father by nature—“and to your Father”—for he is your father through the adoption I have won for you by my death. Jesus, the Good Shepherd, shows his great mercy and understanding by gathering together all his disciples who had abandoned him during his passion and were now in hiding for fear of the Jews (v. 19).

Mary Magdalene’s perseverance teaches us that anyone who sincerely keeps searching for Jesus Christ will eventually find him. Jesus’ gesture in calling his disciples his “brethren” despite their having run away should fill us with love in the midst of our own infidelities.

20:15. From Jesus’ dialogue with Mary Magdalene, we can see the frame of mind all his disciples must have been in: they were not expecting the resurrection.

17 Jesus said to her, "Do not hold me, for I have not yet ascended to Heb 2:11 Rom 8:29
the Father; but go to my brethren and say to them, I am ascending Ps 22:22
to my Father and your Father, to my God and your God."* 18 Mary
Magdalene went and said to the disciples, "I have seen the Lord";
and she told them that he had said these things to her.

Jesus' first appearance to the disciples

19 On the evening of that day, the first day of the week, the doors Mk 16:14–18
being shut where the disciples were, for fear of the Jews, Jesus Lk 24:36–49 Jn 14:27
came and stood among them and said to them, "Peace be with
you." 20 When he had said this, he showed them his hands and his Jn 16:22
side. Then the disciples were glad when they saw the Lord. 21 Jesus 1 Jn 1:1
said to them again, "Peace be with you. As the Father has sent me, Jn 17:18 Mt 28:18ff

---

20:17. "Do not hold me": the use of the negative imperative in the Greek, reflected in the New Vulgate ("noli me tenere") indicates that our Lord is telling Mary to release her hold on him, to let him go, since she will have another chance to see him before his ascension into heaven.

20:19–20. Jesus appears to the apostles on the evening of the day on which he rose. He presents himself without any need for the doors to be opened, by using the qualities of his glorified body; but in order to dispel any impression that he is only a spirit he shows them his hands and his side: there is no longer any doubt of its being Jesus himself, about his being truly risen from the dead. He greets them twice using the words of greeting customary among the Jews, with the same tenderness as he previously used put into this salutation. These friendly words dispel the fear and shame the apostles must have been feeling at behaving so disloyally during his passion: he has recreated the normal atmosphere of intimacy, and now he will endow them with transcendental powers.

20:21. Pope Leo XIII explained how Christ transferred his own mission to the apostles: "What did he wish in regard to the Church founded, or about to be founded? This: to transmit to it the same mission and the same mandate which he had received from the Father, that they should be perpetuated. This he clearly resolved to do: this he actually did. [Here the Pope cites John 20:21 and John 17:18.]. […] When about to ascend into heaven he sends his Apostles in virtue of the same power by which he had been sent from the Father; and he charges them to spread abroad and propagate his teachings (cf. Mt 21:19), so that those obeying the Apostles might be saved, and those disobeying should perish (cf. Mk 16:16). […] Hence he commands that the teaching of the Apostles should be religiously accepted and piously kept as if it were his own: 'He who hears you hears me, and he who rejects you rejects me' (Lk 10:16). Wherefore the Apostles are ambassadors of Christ as he is the ambassador of the Father" (*Satis cognitum*). In this mission the bishops are the successors of the apostles: "Christ sent the Apostles, as he himself had been sent by the Father, and then through the apostles made their successors, the bishops, sharers in his consecration and mission. The function of the bishops' ministry was handed over in a subordinate degree to priests so that they might be appointed

Jn 7:39 Gen 2:7 even so I send you." 22And when he had said this, he breathed on
1 Cor 15:45 them, and said to them, "Receive the Holy Spirit. 23If you forgive
Mt 16:19; 18:18 the sins of any, they are forgiven; if you retain the sins of any, they
are retained."

A second appearance with Thomas present

Jn 11:16; 14:5 24Now Thomas, one of the twelve, called the Twin, was not with
them when Jesus came. 25So the other disciples told him, "We
Jn 19:34 have seen the Lord." But he said to them, "Unless I see in his
1 Jn 1:1 hand the print of the nails, and place my finger in the mark of the
nails, and place my hand in his side, I will not believe."
Jn 20:19 26Eight days later, his disciples were again in the house, and
Thomas was with them. The doors were shut, but Jesus came and

---

in the order of the priesthood and be co-workers of the episcopal order for the proper fulfilment of the apostolic mission that had been entrusted to it by Christ" (Vatican II, *Presbyterorum ordinis*, 2).

20:22–23. The Church has always understood—and has in fact defined—that Jesus Christ here conferred on the Apostles authority to forgive sins, a power which is exercised in the sacrament of Penance. "The Lord then especially instituted the sacrament of Penance when, after being risen from the dead, he breathed upon his disciples and said: 'Receive the Holy Spirit …'. The consensus of all the Fathers has always acknowledged that by this action so sublime and words so clear the power of forgiving and retaining sins was given to the Apostles and their lawful successors for reconciling the faithful who have fallen after Baptism" (Council of Trent, *De Paenitentia*, chap. 1).

The sacrament of Penance is the most sublime expression of God's mercy, described so vividly in Jesus' parable of the prodigal son (cf. Lk 15:11–32). The Lord always awaits us, with his arms wide open, waiting for us to repent—and then he will forgive us and restore us to the dignity of being his sons.

The popes have consistently recommended Christians to have regular recourse to this sacrament: "For a constant and speedy advancement in the path of virtue we highly recommend the pious practice of frequent confession, introduced by the Church under the guidance of the Holy Spirit; for by this means we grow in a true knowledge of ourselves and in Christian humility, bad habits are uprooted, spiritual negligence and apathy are prevented, the conscience is purified and the will strengthened, salutary spiritual direction is obtained, and grace is increased by the efficacy of the sacrament itself" (Pius XII, *Mystici Corporis*).

20:24–28. Thomas' doubting moves our Lord to give him special proof that his risen body is quite real. By so doing he bolsters the faith of those who would later on find faith in him. "Surely you do not think", St Gregory the Great comments, "that it was a pure accident that that chosen disciple was missing; who on his return was told about the appearance and on hearing about it doubted; doubting, so that he might touch and believe by touching? It was not an accident; God arranged that it should happen. His clemency acted in this wonderful way so

stood among them, and said, "Peace be with you." 27Then he said Mk 16:44
to Thomas, "Put your finger here, and see my hands; and put out Lk 24:25
your hand, and place it in my side; do not be faithless, but believing." 28Thomas answered him, "My Lord and my God!" 29Jesus Jn 1:1
said to him, "Have you believed because you have seen me? Jn 1:50
Blessed are those who have not seen and yet believe." 1 Pet 1:8
30Now Jesus did many other signs in the presence of the disci- Jn 2:11; 21:25
ples, which are not written in this book; 31but these are written Jn 1:12
that you may believe that Jesus is the Christ, the Son of God, and 1 Jn 5:13 Rom 1:17
that believing you may have life in his name. Acts 3:16

---

that through the doubting disciple touching the wounds in his Master's body, our own wounds of incredulity might be healed. […] And so the disciple, doubting and touching, was changed into a witness of the truth and of the resurrection" (*In Evangelia homiliae*, 26, 7).

Thomas' reply is not simply an exclamation: it is an assertion, an admirable act of faith in the divinity of Christ: "My Lord and my God!" These words are an ejaculatory prayer often used by Christians, especially as an act of faith in the real presence of Christ in the Blessed Eucharist

20:29. St Gregory the Great explains these words of our Lord as follows: "By St Paul saying 'faith is the assurance of things hoped for, the conviction of things unseen' (Heb 11:1), it becomes clear that faith has to do with things which are not seen, for those which are seen are no longer the object of faith, but rather of experience. Well then, why is Thomas told, when he saw and touched, 'Because you have seen, you have believed'? Because he saw one thing, and believed another. It is certain that mortal man cannot see divinity; therefore, he saw the man and recognized him as God, saying, 'My Lord and my God.' In conclusion: seeing, he believed, because contemplating that real man he exclaimed that he was God, whom he could not see" (*In Evangelia homiliae*, 27, 8).

Like everyone else Thomas needed the grace of God to believe, but in addition to this grace he was given an exceptional proof; his faith would have more merit had he accepted the testimony of the other apostles. Revealed truths are normally transmitted by word, by the testimony of other people who, sent by Christ and aided by the Holy Spirit, preach the deposit of faith (cf. Mk 16:15–16). "So faith comes from what is heard, and what is heard comes from the preaching of Christ" (Rom 10:17). The preaching of the Gospel, therefore, carries with it sufficient guarantees of credibility, and by accepting that preaching man "offers the full submission of his intellect and will to God who reveals, willingly assenting to the revelation given" (Vatican II, *Dei Verbum*, 5).

"What follows pleases us greatly: 'Blessed are those who have not seen and yet believe.' For undoubtedly it is we who are meant, who confess with our soul him whom we have not seen in the flesh. It refers to us, provided we live in accordance with the faith, for only he truly believes who practises what he believes" (*In Evangelia homiliae*, 26, 9).

20:30–31. This is a kind of first epilogue or conclusion to the Gospel of St John. The most common opinion is that he added chapter 21 later, which covers such

The miraculous catch of fish

21 *[1]After this Jesus revealed himself again to the disciples by
the Sea of Tiberias; and he revealed himself in this way.
Jn 1:45–49; 11:16; 20:26–29 [2]Simon Peter, Thomas called the Twin, Nathanael of Cana in
Galilee, the sons of Zebedee, and two others of his disciples were
Lk 5:5 together. [3]Simon Peter said to them, "I am going fishing." They
said to him, "We will go with you." They went out and got into
the boat; but that night they caught nothing.
Jn 20:14 Lk 24:16 [4]Just as day was breaking, Jesus stood on the beach; yet the
disciples did not know that it was Jesus. [5]Jesus said to them,
Lk 24:41 "Children, have you any fish?" They answered him, "No." [6]He
Lk 5:4–7 said to them, "Cast the net on the right side of the boat, and you
will find some." So they cast it and now they were not able to haul
Jn 13:23 it in, for the quantity of fish. [7]That disciple whom Jesus loved*
said to Peter, "It is the Lord!" When Simon Peter heard that it was
the Lord, he put on his clothes, for he was stripped for work, and
sprang into the sea. [8]But the other disciples came in the boat,

---

important events as the triple confession of St Peter, confirmation of his primacy and our Lord's prophecy about the death of the beloved disciple. These verses sum up the inspired writer's whole purpose in writing his Gospel—to have men believe that Jesus was the Messiah, the Christ announced by the prophets in the Old Testament, the Son of God, so that by believing this saving truth, which is the core of Revelation, they might already begin to partake of eternal life (cf. Jn 1:12; 2:23; 3:18; 14:13; 15:16; 16:23–26).

21:1–3. There are some very significant things in this account: we find the disciples "by the sea of Tiberias", which means they have done what the risen Christ had told them to do (cf. Mt 28:7); they are together, which shows that there is a close fraternity among them; Peter takes the initiative, which in a way shows his authority; and they have gone back to their old jobs as fishermen, probably waiting for our Lord to give them new instructions.

This episode is reminiscent of the first miraculous draught of fish (cf. Lk 5:1–11), where our Lord promised Peter he would make him a fisher of men; now he is going to confirm him in his mission as visible head of the Church.

21:4–8. The risen Jesus goes in search of his disciples, to encourage them and tell them more about the great mission he had entrusted to them. This account describes a very moving scene, our Lord together with his own: "He passes by, close to the Apostles, close to those souls who have given themselves to him, and they do not realize he is there. How often Christ is not only near us, but in us; yet we still live in such a human way! [...] They, the disciples, recall what they have heard so often from their Master's lips: fishers of men, apostles. And they realize that all things are possible, because it is he who is directing their fishing.

"'Whereupon the disciple whom Jesus loved said to Peter, "It is the Lord!"' Love, love is farsighted. Love is the first to appreciate kindness. The adolescent

dragging the net full of fish, for they were not far from the land,
but about a hundred yards[m] off.
9When they got out on land, they saw a charcoal fire there, with
fish lying on it, and bread. 10Jesus said to them, "Bring some of the
fish that you have just caught." 11So Simon Peter went aboard and
hauled the net ashore, full of large fish, a hundred and fifty-three
of them; and although there were so many, the net was not torn.
12Jesus said to them, "Come and have breakfast." Now none of the
disciples dared ask him, "Who are you?" They knew it was the
Lord. 13Jesus came and took the bread and gave it to them, and so Jn 6:11
with the fish. 14This was now the third time that Jesus was revealed Jn 20:19, 26
to the disciples after he was raised from the dead.

Peter's primacy

15When they had finished breakfast, Jesus said to Simon Peter, Jn 1:42
"Simon, son of John, do you love me more than these?" He said Mt 16:17
to him, "Yes, Lord; you know that I love you." He said to him,

---

apostle, who felt a deep and firm affection for Jesus, because he loved Christ with all the purity and tenderness of a heart that had never been corrupted, exclaimed: 'It is the Lord!'

"'When Simon Peter heard that it was the Lord, he put on his clothes and sprang into the sea.' Peter personifies faith. Full of marvellous daring, he leaps into the sea. With a love like John's and a faith like Peter's, what is there that can stop us?" (St J. Escrivá, *Friends of God*, 265–266).

21:9–14. We can sense here the deep impression this appearance of the risen Jesus must have made on the apostles, and how sweet a memory St John kept of it. After the resurrection Jesus showed the same tenderness as characterized his public ministry. He makes use of natural things—the fire, the fish, etc.—to show that he really is there, and he maintains the familiar tone typical of when he lived with the disciples.

The Fathers and Doctors of the Church have often dwelt on the mystical meaning of this episode: the boat is the Church, whose unity is symbolized by the net which is not torn; the sea is the world, Peter in the boat stands for supreme authority in the Church, and the number of fish signifies the number of the elect (cf. St Thomas Aquinas, *Comm. on St John*, in loc.).

21:15–17. Jesus Christ had promised Peter that he would be the primate of the Church (cf. Mt 16:16–19 and the note on same). Despite his three denials during our Lord's passion, Christ now confers on him the primacy he promised.

"Jesus questions Peter, three times, as if to give him a triple chance to atone for his triple denial. Peter has learned his lesson from the bitter experience of his wretchedness. Aware of his weakness, he is deeply convinced that rash claims are pointless. Instead he puts everything in Christ's hands. 'Lord, you know well that I love you'" (St J. Escrivá, *Friends of God*, 267). The primacy was given to Peter directly and immediately. So the

m. Greek *two hundred cubits*

1 Pet 5:2, 4 "Feed my lambs." 16A second time he said to him, "Simon, son of
John, do you love me?" He said to him, "Yes, Lord; you know I
Jn 13:38; 16:30 love you." He said to him, "Tend my sheep." 17He said to him the
third time, "Simon, son of John, do you love me?" Peter was
grieved because he said to him the third time, "Do you love me?"
And he said to him, "Lord, you know everything; you know that I
love you." Jesus said to him, "Feed my sheep.* 18Truly, truly, I say
Mt 16:22 to you, when you were young, you girded yourself and walked
where you would; but when you are old, you will stretch out your
hands, and another will gird you and carry you where you do not
Jn 13:36 wish to go." 19(This he said to show by what death he was to glorify God.) And after this he said to him, "Follow me."

Jn 13:23; 18:15 20Peter turned and saw following them the disciple whom
Jesus loved, who had lain close to his breast at the supper and had
said, "Lord, who is it that is going to betray you?" 21When Peter

---

Church has always understood—and so Vatican I defined: "We therefore teach and declare that, according to the testimony of the Gospel, the primacy of jurisdiction over the universal Church of God was immediately and directly promised and given to Blessed Peter the Apostle by Christ our Lord. [...] And it was upon Simon Peter alone that Jesus after his resurrection bestowed the jurisdiction of chief pastor and ruler over all his fold in the words: 'Feed my lambs; feed my sheep'" (*Pastor aeternus*, chap. 1).

The primacy is a grace conferred on Peter and his successors, the popes; it is one of the basic elements in the Church, designed to guard and protect its unity: "In order that the episcopate also might be one and undivided, and that [...] the multitude of the faithful might be kept secure in the oneness of faith and communion, he set Blessed Peter over the rest of the Apostles, and fixed in him the abiding principle of this twofold unity, and its visible foundation" (*Pastor aeternus, Dz-Sch* 3051; cf. Vatican II, *Lumen gentium*, 18). Therefore, the primacy of Peter is perpetuated in each of his successors: this is something which Christ disposed; it is not based on human legislation or custom.

By virtue of the primacy, Peter, and each of his successors, is the shepherd of the whole Church and vicar of Christ on earth, because he exercises vicariously Christ's own authority. Love for the Pope, whom St Catherine of Siena used to call "the sweet Christ on earth", should express itself in prayer, sacrifice and obedience.

21:18–19. According to Tradition, St Peter followed his Master to the point of dying by crucifixion, head downwards, "Peter and Paul suffered martyrdom in Rome during Nero's persecution of Christians, which took place between the years 64 and 68. St Clement, the successor of the same Peter in the see of the Church of Rome, recalls this when, writing to the Corinthians, he puts before them 'the generous example of these two athletes': 'due to jealousy and envy, those who were the principal and holiest columns suffered persecution and fought the fight unto death'" (Paul VI, *Petrum et Paulum*).

"Follow me!": these words would have reminded the apostle of the first call

saw him, he said to Jesus, "Lord, what about this man?" [22]Jesus
said to him, "If it is my will that he remain until I come, what is
that to you? Follow me!" [23]The saying spread abroad among the
brethren that this disciple was not to die; yet Jesus did not say to
him that he was not to die, but, "If it is my will that he remain
until I come, what is that to you?"

Conclusion

[24]This is the disciple who is bearing witness to these things, and who Jn 15:27; 19:35
has written these things; and we know that his testimony is true. 3 Jn 12

[25]But there are also many other things which Jesus did; were
every one of them to be written, I suppose that the world itself Jn 20:30
could not contain the books that would be written.

---

he received (cf. Mt 4:19) and of the fact that Christ requires of his disciples complete self-surrender: "If any man would come after me, let him deny himself and take up the cross daily and follow me" (Lk 9:23). St Peter himself, in one of his letters, also testifies to the cross being something all Christians must carry: "For to this you have been called, because Christ also suffered for you, leaving you an example, that you should follow in his steps" (1 Pet 2:21).

21:20–23. According to St Irenaeus (*Against Heresies*, 2, 22, 5; 3, 3, 4), St John outlived all the other apostles, into the reign of Trajan AD 89–117). Possibly the evangelist wrote these verses to dispel the idea that he would not die. The important thing is not to be curious about what the future will bring but to serve the Lord faithfully, keeping to the way he has marked out for one.

21:24. This is an appeal to the testimony of the disciple "whom Jesus loved" as a guarantee of the veracity of everything contained in the book: everything which this Gospel says should be accepted by its readers as being absolutely true.

Many modern commentators think that vv. 24 and 25 were added by disciples of the apostle, as a conclusion to the Gospel, when it began to be circulated, a short time after St John completed it. Be that as it may, the fact is that both verses are to be found in all extant manuscripts of the Fouth Gospel.

21:25. St John's account, written under the inspiration of the Holy Spirit, has as its purpose the strengthening of our faith in Jesus Christ through reflecting on what our Lord said and did. Like the Fourth Gospel, we shall never be able to capture the full richness and depth of our Lord's personality. "Once we begin to be interested in Christ, one's interest can never cease. There is always something more to be known, to be said—infinitely more. St John the evangelist ends his Gospel making this very point (Jn 21:25). Everything to do with Christ is so rich, there are such depths for us to explore; such light, strength, joy, desire have their source in him. [...] His coming to the world, his presence in history and culture and [...] his vital relationship with our conscience: everything suggests that it is unseemly, unscientific and irreverent ever to think that we need not and cannot advance further in contemplation of Jesus Christ" (Paul VI, General Audience, 20 February 1974).

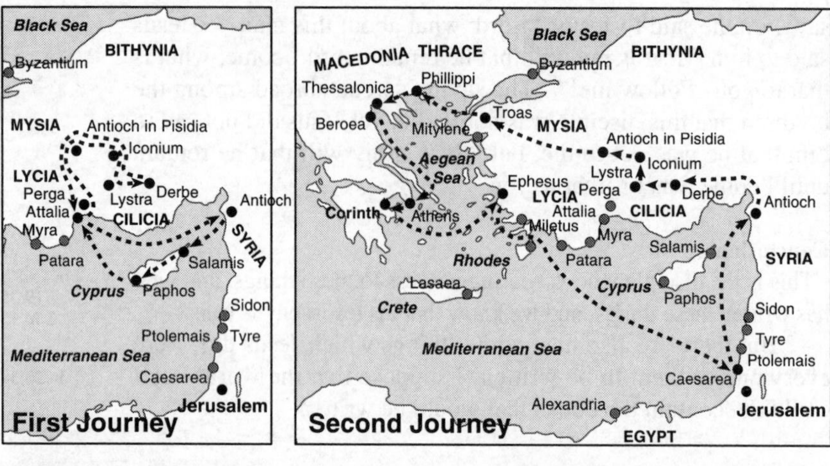

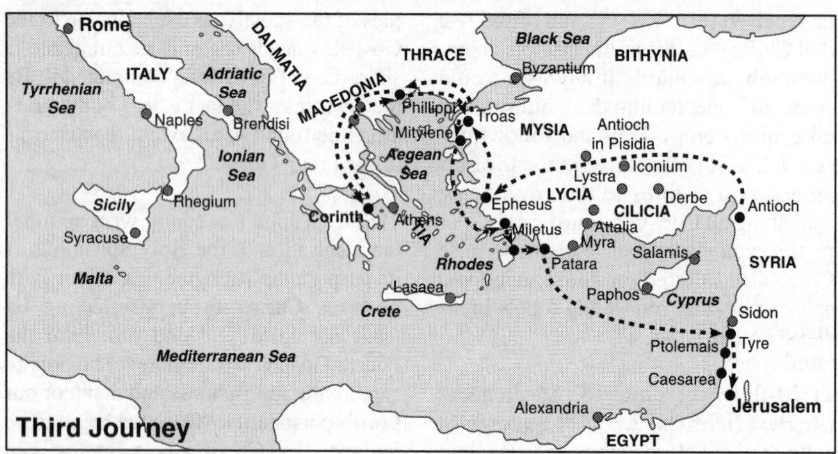

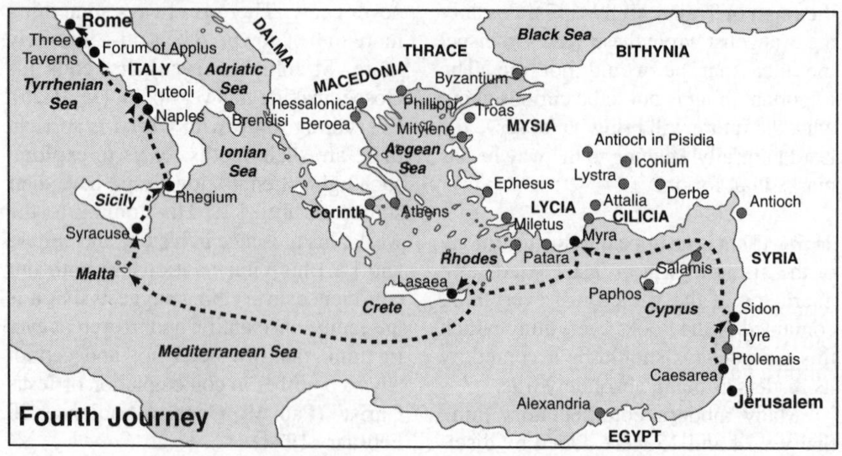

Missionary journeys of St Paul

Introduction to the Acts of the Apostles

TITLE AND LITERARY GENRE

The usual English title—"Acts of the Apostles"—corresponds to the Latin "Actus" or "Acta Apostolorum" and the Greek "Práxeis Apostolicón". This is the title invariably given the book from the middle of the second century onwards in all Greek manuscripts, in early translations and in references in the works of the Fathers and ecclesiastical writers. It seems likely, however, that the author did not give it this title but that it received it some time after it was written. It is not really an account of the activity of the apostles but rather a description of the early years of Christianity linked to the missionary work of the two most prominent apostles, Peter and Paul.

The Acts of the Apostles seeks to give an account of how the Church was originally established and of the first stage of the spread of the Gospel, after our Lord's ascension. It is a type of history book, the first history of Christianity. However, it does not belong only or primarily to the category of history; it is not a mere chronicle of events; it cannot and should not be separated from the Third Gospel, with which it is in total continuity as history and as theology. It is a book dominated by a religious purpose—to report events which, under the impulse of the Holy Spirit, reveal God's saving plan for mankind.

The sacred author has managed to combine history and theology remarkably well. He does not limit himself to producing a narrative similar in style to profane history; yet neither has he written a sacred book which is totally detached from the cultural environment in which he is living. He is well aware that any proclamation of the Gospel must also be to some degree an account of historical events which truly happened.

The Acts of the Apostles, in relating the beginnings of the Church, aims primarily at strengthening the faith of Christians, assuring them as to the origin and basis of that faith. Secondarily, it discreetly anticipates the kind of writing typical of the apologists of the second and third centuries, by arguing that Christ's disciples had a right to the same freedom and the same respect as the Empire gave to what were called "lawful religions" (particularly Judaism).

Acts portrays Christianity as an outstanding faith, trusting in God and self-assured, which has no time for obscurantism or the kind of secrecy typical of sects, and which is not afraid to debate its principles and convictions with all comers.

The entire narrative is imbued with an extraordinary spiritual joy—a joy which comes from the Holy Spirit, from certainty about the supernatural origin of the Church, from contemplation of the prodigies which God works in support of the preachers of his Gospel, from—essentially—the protection God gives his disciples despite the persecution they undergo.

THEME AND STRUCTURE

The book describes the way Jesus' prediction to his disciples prior to his ascension was fulfilled: "You shall be my witnesses in Jerusalem and in all Judea and Samaria and to the end of the earth" (1:8). Following a fairly precise and detailed chronological order, it covers events over a period of about thirty years—from the death, resurrection and ascension of our Lord until the end of St Paul's imprisonment in Rome about the year 63.

Commentators have suggested different ways of dividing the book up as a guide to understanding it better. From the point of view of God's plans of salvation, which the book reflects, it divides into two sections—before and after the Council of Jerusalem (15:6–29). This assembly at Jerusalem is certainly the theological centre of the book, due to the unique role it played in explaining God's will about the catholic nature of the Church and the primacy of grace over the Mosaic Law, and the impetus it gave to the universal spread of the Gospel.

If we look at the book in terms of the episodes it contains—stages as it were in the history of the preaching of the Gospel—the Acts of the Apostles can be divided into four parts:

Part 1. *Chapters 1–7.* These tell of the life of the early community in Jerusalem. They begin with our Lord's ascension, the sending of the Holy Spirit on Pentecost and the revealing of the supernatural character of the Church that followed on from that. Then comes the account of the growth of the first community around the apostle Peter. Miracles and prodigies accompany the spread of the Gospel. This is followed by persecution by the Jewish establishment, culminating in the martyrdom of Stephen.

Part 2. *Chapters 8–12.* These report the dispersion of the Christians: with the exception of the Twelve, this scattering is the result of persecution and it in turn leads to the Gospel being preached in Judea, Samaria and Syria. The Church begins to open its doors to the Gentiles. We are told of the conversion of the Ethiopian, an official of the court of the queen of that country, and learn that many Samaritans received Baptism. The conversion of Cornelius, a

Gentile—an event of extraordinary significance, with the Gospel breaking down ethnic barriers—is described in great detail. This section ends with the death of James, the brother of John, and the arrest and miraculous release of St Peter.

Part 3. *Chapters 13–20.* This section focuses on the missionary endeavours of Paul, who on his first journey with Barnabas prior to the Council of Jerusalem, and on two other subsequent journeys, brings the Gospel to the pagan world, in keeping with his special vocation as apostle of the Gentiles.

Part 4. *Chapters 21–28.* This section begins in Jerusalem with the imprisonment of Paul, who from this point onwards will, in chains, bear witness to the Gospel up to the time of his stay in Rome. From that city of cities the way lies open for the Gospel to be spread all over the world.

AUTHOR AND DATE OF COMPOSITION

Christian tradition and almost all commentators assert that the book of the Acts of the Apostles was written by the author of the Third Gospel and that that author was St Luke, the companion of St Paul on his second journey and his loyal aide (cf. Acts 16:10ff; Col 4:14; Philem 24). St Luke was also with the apostle from Troas to Jerusalem (cf. Acts 20:5ff) and, later on, from Caesarea to Rome (cf. 27:1ff). He was probably not Jewish by birth. An early tradition, attested by Eusebius of Caesarea, the historian,[1] and by St Jerome,[2] gave Antioch as his birthplace.

There are a number of good reasons for identifying St Luke as the author of Acts. The best internal evidence is found in the passages of the book written in the first person plural (cf. Acts 16:10–17; 20:5–15; 21:1–18; 27:1—28:16). The most obvious interpretation is that these passages were written by a companion of Paul and incorporated into the book without any change in style for the simple reason that the author of this source—which is possibly a travel diary—and the author of the rest of the book were one and the same person. By eliminating everyone mentioned in Acts by name, we are left with St Luke as the only one who could have been Paul's companion in Caesarea and Rome.

The external arguments are mainly the testimony of Christian writers, especially St Irenaeus of Lyons (d. 180), who refers to St Luke as author of the Third Gospel and of the Acts of the Apostles. This is also stated in the Muratorian Canon (end of the second century).

The date of the book can be established by reference to certain factors which place it within a period and help to pin it down more specifically. The

1. *Ecclesiastical History*, 3, 4, 6. **2.** Cf. *Comm. on Matthew*, preface.

main factors in question are Paul's Roman imprisonment and the destruction of Jerusalem. Clearly St Luke could not have written his work earlier than the year 62 or 63, the date of the apostle's confinement in Rome. Whether it was written before or after Paul's martyrdom is disputed, but that does not affect the choice of the earlier limit. On the other hand, it is virtually certain that Acts was written before the destruction of Jerusalem, that is, before the year 70. It is difficult to conceive how Luke could have written after that date and yet made no reference of any kind to such a tremendous event and one so relevant to the relationship between the nascent Church and Judaism and the temple. The reader of the book has the impression all along that the Holy City is still standing and that the temple is still the centre of Jewish worship. Some authors reach the same conclusion by arguing from the book's silence on the martyrdom of James, and of Peter, who fell victim to Nero's persecution.

We can conclude, then, that the Third Gospel and the Acts of the Apostles, which are two parts of a single work, could have been written over quite a short period of time and were completed prior to the year 70.

The book's dedication to Theophilus tells us—as does every such dedication in ancient writings—that the author has completed his work and made it available to the Christian readership for which he intended it, and indeed to Jewish readership also.

HISTORICAL ACCURACY

The Church has always maintained that the Acts of the Apostles is a true history of events. Luke's evangelizing and theological purpose did not prevent him from collecting, evaluating and interpreting facts with a skill that demonstrates he was an excellent historian. We have to put down to theological prejudice that scepticism expressed by some non-Catholic scholars about the historical value of Acts. These exegetes quite arbitrarily claim that the supernatural events reported in the book are later additions included into the text by an anonymous imaginative writer interested in projecting a particular image of Paul. Nowadays, there is a growing acceptance of the historicity of Acts: many non-Catholic scholars have come to this view through detailed study of the text, and their conviction has led others to tend in the same direction.

Few ancient texts provide such scope for checking their accuracy as Acts does. It is full of references to contemporary Jewish, Greek and Roman history, culture and topography. Everything it recounts is carefully set into an historical framework. Details of time and place are invariably found to be accurate, and the atmosphere of the period imbues the entire book. The writer leads his reader on a tour of the streets, markets, theatres and assemblies of the Ephesus, Thessalonica, Corinth and Philippi of the first century of the Christian era.

The events narrated in Acts invite and permit the scholar to check them for historical accuracy against the letters of St Paul, which deal with the same material, to some degree.

Like all writers of antiquity, the author of Acts focuses his attention on his principal characters and builds the narrative around them. He presents Paul as a fully mature Christian personality from the day of his conversion forward. This understandable simplification does not prevent us, however, from recognizing the Paul of Acts and the Paul of the Letters as being the same person. The Paul of Acts is the real Paul as seen retrospectively by a disciple who is also a friend.

The connexions between Acts and the Letters point to one and the same Paul. His activity as persecutor of the Church is recorded in similar language in Acts (8:3; 9:1) as in Galatians 1:13 and 1 Corinthians 15:9. Galatians 1:17 confirms what Acts says (9:3) about his conversion taking place in Damascus. In Acts 9:23–27 and Galatians 1:18 we are told that Paul made his first journey after his conversion from Damascus to Jerusalem. In Acts 9:30 and Galatians 1:21 we are told about Paul being sent to Tarsus after his stay in Jerusalem. His missionary companions after the split with Barnabas—that is, Silas and Timothy (cf. Acts 15:22, 40; 16:1)—are to be found in the letters written during this period. The itinerary in Acts 16–19 (Philippi – Thessalonica – Athens – Corinth – Ephesus – Macedonia – Achaia) is confirmed by 1 Thess 2:2; 3:1; 1 Cor 2:1; 16:5–9; 2 Cor 12:14ff, Rom 16:1, 23). Only the Letters tell us that Paul was of the tribe of Benjamin (cf. Rom 11:1; Phil 3:5). Acts merely says that his Jewish name was Saul (cf. Acts 7:58; 9:1; 13:9): this ties in, because it would be quite reasonable for parents from that tribe to call a child after the first king of Israel, its most outstanding member (cf. 1 Sam 9:1ff). Many more examples could be given in support of the historical accuracy of the book.

Another source which throws a great deal of light on Luke's narrative is Flavius Josephus' *Jewish Antiquities*, written some twenty years after Acts. Josephus helps us establish the dates of Herod Agrippa I's reign (from the year 41 to 10 March 44), and we can see the agreement between Acts 12 and *Antiquities*, 19, 274–363 on the circumstances of the king's death. Josephus' account also helps explain Luke's references (cf. Acts 5:36–37; *Antiquities*, 20, 169–172) to the Jewish rebels Judas of Galilee and Theudas. Luke's profile of the two governors Felix and Festus and of King Herod Agrippa II is confirmed and developed by Josephus. Another instance of corroboration is that Acts 18:12 describes Gallio as being proconsul of Achaia and this has been confirmed by an inscription found at Delphi, near Corinth.

This historical reliability of Acts only serves to reinforce its validity as a testimony to the faith of that early Church governed by the apostles and guided at every step by the invisible and often visible power of the Holy Spirit: Acts sets an example of faith and doctrine for the Church in every era.

The speeches which the book contains, especially the more important ones of Peter (cf. 2:14ff; 3:12ff; 10:34ff; 11:5ff), Stephen (cf. 7:2ff) and Paul (cf.

13:16ff; 17:22ff; 20:18ff; 22:1ff; 24:10ff; 26:2ff) have been the subject of many detailed studies. Naturally, the actual address in each case would have been longer than the version given in the book, and Luke would have had more to draw on for some than for others. However, the accounts which Luke gives are to be taken as accurate. The addresses can be seen to reflect traditional Jewish styles of quoting and interpreting Holy Scripture and, although similar in structure, there is also quite a variety in them. They obviously reflect the different speakers, locations and audiences, and they give a good idea of the Church's earliest form of preaching.

SOURCES

In line with the style of Jewish and Hellenist writers, St Luke made use of written sources to produce his book. He had not been an eyewitness of everything he reported and he would not have settled for simply word-of-mouth information: he would have used documents of different kinds, such as short narrative accounts, summaries of speeches, notes, travel diaries etc. It is quite likely that for the earlier part of the book he used material collected from the various churches or from the main people involved.

However, the book is so all-of-a-piece that it is difficult to reconstruct, with any accuracy, the sources he would have used. Some commentators suggest that Acts is based on two main groups of documents—a) an Antiochene source, containing information about Stephen, Philip, Barnabas and the early years of St Paul; and b) a collection of accounts of St Peter's activity. But this is only a hypothesis.

Nor is it possible to say whether Luke included all the material available to him or instead operated selectively. He certainly seems to have used his own judgment as to what material to incorporate and what not to, and when to edit, re-use, combine or divide up material made available to him. Whatever his method, he did manage to impose remarkable unity on his work, every page of which evidences the supernatural action of the Spirit of God.

DOCTRINAL CONTENT

Acts is a sort of compendium of the Christian faith in action. St Luke's purpose, which is one of instruction, leads him to put forward all the main truths of the Christian religion and to show the main outlines of the liturgical and sacramental life of the infant Church. His book also gives us accurate insights into the way the Church was structured and managed, and into the attitudes of Christians towards political and social questions of their time.

Its teachings on Christ, the Holy Spirit and the Church merit special attention.

Christology. Teaching on Christ in Acts is based on the Synoptic Gospels, on Jesus' life on earth and his glorification, which are the core of the Gospel message. All aspects of the paschal mystery—Passion, Death, Resurrection and Ascension—are given prominence, and that mystery is shown to fulfil the plans revealed by God in the Old Testament prophecies. Various Christological titles are applied to Jesus which show his divinity and his redemptive mission—titles such as Lord (2:36), Saviour (5:31), Servant of Yahweh (3:13, 16), the Righteous One (7:52), the Holy One (3:14) and especially Christ—the Messiah—which becomes his proper name.

Theology of the Holy Spirit. St Luke stresses the key role of the Holy Spirit in all aspects of the life of the Church. At one and the same time the Spirit of God and the Spirit of Jesus Christ, the Holy Spirit, at Pentecost causes the Church to be made manifest to all the people and enables it to begin its salvific activity. The Spirit is the personal possession and the common inheritance of Christians, and also the source of their joy and spiritual vitality. He endows and supports in a special way those Christians who are ordained to carry out the various sacred ministries; and it is he who guides the Church in its choice of rulers and missionaries and encourages it and protects it in its work of evangelization. This second book by St Luke has rightly been called "the Gospel of the Holy Spirit".

Ecclesiology. Acts is an indispensable source of documentation on the life of the Church in its very earliest period. In it we are shown the Church as the instrument God uses to fulfil the Old Testament promises. The Church is, then, the true Israel, a new people, a worldwide community of people joined by spiritual links, a people which is essentially missionary.

The Church is the outcome of the invisible but real presence of the risen Christ, who is the focus of Christian worship and the only Name by which men can be saved. Jesus' presence is really and truly effected in the "breaking of the bread", that is, in the eucharistic sacrifice, which his disciples already celebrate on Sunday, the first day of the week.

Acts describes the lifestyle of the early Christians in a very direct and moving way. Their life centres on prayer, the Eucharist and the apostles' teaching, and it expresses itself in attitudes and actions of detachment, concord and love. St Luke offers this lifestyle as a kind of model and heritage for future generations of Christians.

Two aspects of Christianity are combined extremely well in this book—expectation of our Lord's second coming (which runs right through the New Testament) and the need to commit oneself, through prayer, work and cheerful sacrifice, to the building up of the Kingdom of God on earth.

Acts also tells us a good deal about the structure of the Church in earliest times and provides us with a most valuable account of the first council of the Church (cf. 15:6ff).

Prologue

1 [1]In the first book,* O Theophilus, I have dealt with all that Lk 1:3
Jesus began to do and teach, [2]until the day when he was taken Mk 28:30 Lk 6:13

1:1–5. St Luke is the only New Testament author to begin his book with a prologue, in the style of secular historians. The main aim of this preface is to convey to the reader the profoundly religious character of the book which he is holding in his hands. It is a work which will give an account of events marking the fulfilment of the promises made by the God of Israel, the Creator and Saviour of the world. Under the inspiration of the Holy Spirit, into his book St Luke weaves quotations from the Psalms, Isaiah, Amos and Joel; it both reflects the Old Testament and interprets it in the light of its fulfilment in Jesus Christ.

The prologue refers to St Luke's Gospel as a "first book". It mentions the last events of our Lord's life on earth—the appearances of the risen Christ and his ascension into heaven—and links them up with the account which is now beginning.

St Luke's aim is to describe the origins and the early growth of Christianity, of which the main protagonist of this book, the Holy Spirit, has been the cause. Yet this is not simply an historical record: the Acts of the Apostles, St Jerome explains, "seems to be a straightforward historical account of the early years of the nascent Church. But if we bear in mind it is written by Luke the physician, who is praised in the Gospel (cf. 2 Cor 8:18), we will realize that everything he says is medicine for the ailing soul" (*Epistle* 53, 9).

The spiritual dimension of this book, which is one of a piece with the Third Gospel, nourished the soul of the first generations of Christians, providing them with a chronicle of God's faithful and loving support of the new Israel.

"This book", St John Chrysostom writes at the start of his great commentary, "will profit us no less than the Gospels, so replete is it with Christian wisdom and sound doctrine. It offers an account of the numerous miracles worked by the Holy Spirit. It contains the fulfilment of the prophecies of Jesus Christ recorded in the Gospel; we can observe in the very facts the bright evidence of Truth which shines in them, and the mighty change which is taking place in the apostles: they become perfect men, extraordinary men, now that the Holy Spirit has come upon them. All Christ's promises and predictions—He who believes in me will do these and even greater works, you will be dragged before tribunals and kings and beaten in the synagogues, and will suffer grievous things, and yet you will overcome your persecutors and executioners and will bring the Gospel to the ends of the earth—all this, how it came to pass, may be seen in this admirable book. Here you will see the apostles speeding their way over land and sea as if on wings. These Galileans, once so timorous and obtuse, we find suddenly changed into new men, despising wealth and honour, raised above passion and concupiscence" (*Hom. on Acts*, 1).

St Luke dedicates this book to Theophilus—as he did his Gospel. The dedication suggests that Theophilus was an educated Christian, of an upper-class background, but he may be a fictitious person symbolizing "the beloved of God", which is what the name means. It also may imply that Acts was written quite soon after the Third Gospel.

1:1. "To do and teach": these words very concisely sum up the work of Jesus

Jn 20:22 / 1 Tim 3:16 up, after he had given commandment through the Holy Spirit to
Acts 13:31 the apostles whom he had chosen. [3]To them he presented himself
alive after his passion by many proofs, appearing to them during
Lk 24:49 forty days, and speaking of the kingdom of God. [4]And while
Acts 10:41 staying[a] with them he charged them not to depart from Jerusalem,
but to wait for the promise of the Father, which, he said, "you
Mt 3:11 / Lk 3:16 heard from me, [5]for John baptized with water, but before many
Acts 11:16 days you shall be baptized with the Holy Spirit."

Christ, reported in the Gospels. They describe the way in which God's saving revelation operates: God lovingly announces and reveals himself in the course of human history through his actions and through his words. "The economy of revelation is realized by deeds and words, which are intrinsically bound up with each other", Vatican II teaches. "As a result, the works performed by God in the history of salvation show forth and bear out the doctrine and realities signified by the words; the words, for their part, proclaim the works, and bring to light the mystery they contain. The most intimate truth which this revelation gives us about God and the salvation of man shines forth in Christ, who is himself both the mediator and the sum total of Revelation" (*Dei Verbum*, 2).

The Lord "proclaimed the kingdom of the Father both by the testimony of his life and by the power of his word" (Vatican II, *Lumen gentium*, 35). He did not limit himself to speech, to being simply the Teacher whose words opened man's minds to the truth. He was, above all, the Redeemer, able to save fallen man through the divine efficacy of each and every moment of his life on earth.

"Our Lord took on all our weaknesses, which proceed from sin—with the exception of sin itself. He experienced hunger and thirst, sleep and fatigue, sadness and tears. He suffered in every possible way, even the supreme suffering of death. No one could be freed from the bonds of sinfulness had he who alone was totally innocent not been ready to die at the hands of impious men. Therefore, our Saviour, the Son of God, has left all those who believe in him an effective source of aid, and also an example. The first they obtain by being reborn through grace, the second by imitating his life" (St Leo the Great, *Twelfth homily on the Passion*).

Jesus' redemptive action—his miracles, his life of work, and the mystery of his death, resurrection and ascension, whose depth and meaning only faith can plumb—also constitute a simple and powerful stimulus for our everyday conduct. Faith should always be accompanied by words, by deeds, that is, our humble and necessary cooperation with God's saving plans.

"Don't forget that doing must come before teaching. '*Coepit facere et docere*', the holy Scripture says of Jesus Christ: 'He began to do and to teach.'

"First deeds: so that you and I might learn" (St J. Escrivá, *The Way*, 342).

1:3. This verse recalls the account in Luke 24:13–43 of the appearances of the risen Jesus to the disciples of Emmaus and to the apostles in the Cenacle.

It stresses the figure of *forty* days. This number may have a literal meaning and also a deeper meaning. In Holy Scripture periods of forty days or forty

a. Or *eating*

The Ascension

6So when they had come together, they asked him, "Lord, will you Lk 19:11
at this time restore the kingdom of Israel?" 7He said to them, "It Dan 2:22
is not for you to know times or seasons which the Father has fixed Mt 24:36 1 Thess 5:1–2
by his own authority. 8But you shall receive power when the Holy
Spirit has come upon you; and you shall be my witnesses in Mt 28:19 Lk 24:47–48
Jerusalem and in all Judea and Samaria and to the end of the Acts 2:32; 10:39

---

years have a clearly salvific meaning: they are periods during which God prepares or effects important stages in his plans. The great flood lasted forty days (Gen 7:17); the Israelites journeyed in the wilderness for forty years on their way to the promised land (Ps 95:10); Moses spent forty days on Mount Sinai to receive God's revelation of the Covenant (Ex 24:18); on the strength of the bread sent by God Elijah walked forty days and forty nights to reach his destination (1 Kings 19:8); and our Lord fasted in the wilderness for forty days in preparation for his public life (Mt 4:2).

1:5. "You shall be baptized with the Holy Spirit": this book has been well described as the "Gospel of the Holy Spirit". "There is hardly a page in the Acts of the Apostles where we fail to read about the Spirit and the action by which he guides, directs and enlivens the life and work of the early Christian community. It is he who inspires the preaching of St Peter (cf. Acts 4:8), who strengthens the faith of the disciples (cf. Acts 4:31), who confirms with his presence the calling of the Gentiles (cf. Acts 10:44–47), who sends Saul and Barnabas to distant lands, where they will open new paths for the teaching of Jesus (cf. Acts 13:2–4). In a word, his presence and doctrine are everywhere" (St Josemaría Escrivá, *Christ Is Passing By*, 127).

1:6–8. The apostles' question shows that they are still thinking in terms of earthly restoration of the Davidic dynasty. It would seem that for them—as for many Jews of their time—eschatological hope in the Kingdom extended no further than expectation of world-embracing Jewish hegemony.

"It seems to me", St John Chrysostom comments, "that they had not any clear notion of the nature of the Kingdom, for the Spirit had not yet instructed them. Notice that they do not ask when it shall come but 'Will you at this time restore the Kingdom to Israel?', as if the Kingdom were something that lay in the past. This question shows that they were still attracted by earthly things, though less than they had been" (*Hom. on Acts*, 2).

Our Lord gives an excellent and encouraging reply, patiently telling them that the Kingdom is mysterious in character, that it comes when one least expects, and that they need the help of the Holy Spirit to be able to grasp the teaching they have received. Jesus does not complain about their obtuseness; he simply corrects their ideas and instructs them.

1:8. The outline of Acts is given here: the author plans to tell the story of the growth of the Church, beginning in Jerusalem and spreading through Judea and Samaria to the ends of the earth. This is the geographical structure of St Luke's account. In the Third Gospel Jerusalem was the destination point of Jesus' public life (which began in Galilee); here it is the departure point.

Mk 16:19
Lk 24:50–51
Jn 6:62
Eph 4:8–10
1 Pet 3:22
Lk 24:4

Mt 24:30;
25:31; 26:64
Rev 1:7

earth." 9And when he had said this, as they were looking on, he
was lifted up, and a cloud took him out of their sight. 10And while
they were gazing into heaven as he went, behold, two men stood
by them in white robes, 11and said, "Men of Galilee, why do you
stand looking into heaven? This Jesus, who was taken up from
you into heaven, will come in the same way as you saw him go
into heaven."

The apostles' mission extends to the whole world. Underlying this verse we can see not so much a "geographical" dimension as the universalist aspirations of the Old Testament, articulated by Isaiah: "It shall come to pass in the latter days that the mountain of the house of the Lord shall be established as the highest of the mountains, and shall be raised above the hills; and all the nations shall flow to it, and many peoples shall come, and say: 'Come, let us go up to the mountain of the Lord, to the house of the God of Jacob; that he may teach us his ways and that we may walk in his paths.' For out of Zion shall go forth the law, and the word of the Lord from Jerusalem" (Is 2:2–3).

1:9. Jesus' life on earth did not end with his death on the cross but with his ascension into heaven. The ascension, reported here, is the last event, the last mystery of our Lord's life on earth (cf. also Lk 24:50–53)—and also it concerns the origins of the Church. The ascension scene takes place, so to speak, between heaven and earth. "Why did a cloud take him out of the apostles' sight?", St John Chrysostom asks. "The cloud was a sure sign that Jesus had already entered heaven; it was not a whirlwind or a chariot of fire, as in the case of the prophet Elijah (cf. 2 Kings 2:11), but a cloud, which was a symbol of heaven itself" (*Hom. on Acts*, 2). A cloud features in theophanies—manifestations of God—in both the Old Testament (cf. Ex 13:22) and the New (cf. Lk 9:34f).

Our Lord's ascension is one of the actions by which Jesus redeems us from sin and gives us the new life of grace. It is a redemptive mystery. "What we have already taught of the mystery of his death and resurrection the faithful should deem not less true of his ascension. For although we owe our redemption and salvation to the passion of Christ, whose merits opened heaven to the just, yet his ascension is not only proposed to us as a model, which teaches us to look on high and ascend in spirit into heaven, but it also imparts to us a divine virtue which enables us to accomplish what it teaches" (St Pius V, *Catechism*, 1, 7, 9).

Our Lord's going up into heaven is not simply something which stirs us to lift up our hearts—as we are invited to do at the preface of the Mass, to seek and love the "things that are above" (cf. Col 3:1–2); along with the other mysteries of his life, death and resurrection, Christ's ascension *saves* us. "Today we are not only made possessors of paradise", St Leo says, "but we have ascended with Christ, mystically but really, into the highest heaven, and through Christ we have obtained a more ineffable grace than that which we lost through the devil's envy" (*First homily on the Ascension*).

The ascension is the climax of Christ's exaltation, which was achieved in the first instance by his resurrection and which—along with his passion and death—constitutes the paschal mystery. The Second Vatican Council expresses

PART ONE

The Church in Jerusalem

1. THE DISCIPLES IN JERUSALEM

The apostolic college

12Then they returned to Jerusalem from the mount called Olivet,
which is near Jerusalem, a sabbath day's journey away; 13and

---

this as follows: "Christ our Lord redeemed mankind and gave perfect glory to God [...] principally by the paschal mystery of his blessed passion, resurrection from the dead, and glorious ascension" (*Sacrosanctum Concilium*, 5; cf. *Dei Verbum*, 19).

Theology has suggested reasons why it was very appropriate for the glorified Lord to go up into heaven to be "seated at the right hand of the Father". "First of all, he ascended because the glorious kingdom of the highest heavens, not the obscure abode of this earth, presented a suitable dwelling place for him whose body, rising from the tomb, was clothed with the glory of immortality. He ascended, however, not only to possess the throne of glory and the kingdom which he had merited by his blood, but also to attend to whatever regards our salvation. Again, he ascended to prove thereby that his kingdom is not of this world" (St Pius V, *Catechism*, 1, 7, 5; cf. *Summa theologiae*, 3, 57, 6).

The ascension marks the point when the celestial world celebrates the victory and glorification of Christ: "It is fitting that the sacred humanity of Christ should receive the homage, praise and adoration of all the hierarchies of the Angels and of all the legions of the blessed in heaven" (St Josemaría Escrivá, *Holy Rosary*, second glorious mystery).

1:11. The angels are referring to the Parousia—our Lord's second coming, when he will judge the living and the dead. "They said to them, 'What are you doing here, looking into heaven?' These words are full of solicitude, but they do not proclaim the second coming of the Saviour as imminent. The angels simply assert what is most important, that is, that Jesus Christ will come again and the confidence with which we should await his return" (St John Chrysostom, *Hom. on Acts*, 2).

We know for a certainty that Christ will come again at the end of time. We confess this in the Creed as part of our faith. However, we know "neither the day nor the hour" (Mt 25:13) of his coming. We do not need to know it. Christ is always imminent. We must always be on the watch, that is, we should busy ourselves in the service of God and of others, which is where our sanctification lies.

1:13–14. St Luke mentions the twelve apostles by name, with the exception of Judas Iscariot.

This is the first passage which tells of the spiritual life and devout practices of the disciples. Significantly it places the emphasis on prayer, in keeping with our Lord's own practice and with his constant recommendation to his followers (cf. Mt 6:5; 14:23; etc.).

Mt 10:2–4 Lk 6:14–16 when they had entered, they went up to the upper room, where
they were staying, Peter and John and James and Andrew, Philip
and Thomas, Bartholomew and Matthew, James the son of
Mt 13:55 Alphaeus and Simon the Zealot and Judas the son of James. 14 All
Lk 8:2–3; 24:10 these with one accord devoted themselves to prayer, together with
Acts 12:12 the women and Mary the mother of Jesus, and with his brethren.*

The election of Matthias

15 In those days Peter stood up among the brethren (the company
of persons was in all about a hundred and twenty), and said,
16 "Brethren, the scripture had to be fulfilled, which the Holy Spirit

---

"Prayer is the foundation of the spiritual edifice. Prayer is all-powerful" (St J. Escrivá, *The Way*, 83). It can truly be said that prayer is the bedrock of the Church, which will be made manifest with the coming of the Holy Spirit. The prayer of the disciples, including the women, in the company of Mary would have been a supplication of entreaty and praise and thanksgiving to God. This union of hearts and feelings produced by prayer is a kind of anticipation of the gifts the Holy Spirit will bring.

"We are told this time and again in the passage narrating the lives of the first followers of Christ. 'All these with one accord devoted themselves to prayer' (Acts 1:14). […] Prayer was then, as it is today, the only weapon, the most powerful means, for winning the battles of our interior struggle" (St Josemaría Escrivá, *Friends of God*, 242).

Here we see Mary as the spiritual centre round which Jesus' intimate friends gather: tradition has meditated on this "tableau", and found it to depict our Lady's motherhood over the whole Church, both at its beginning and over the course of the centuries.

On 21 November 1964, at the closing of the third session of Vatican II, Paul VI solemnly proclaimed Mary Mother of the Church: "Our vision of the Church must include loving contemplation of the marvels which God worked in his holy Mother. And knowledge of the true Catholic doctrine about Mary will always be the key to correct understanding of the mystery of Christ and of the Church.

"Reflection on the close ties linking Mary and the Church, so clearly indicated by the present constitution [*Lumen gentium*], allows us to think this is the most appropriate moment to satisfy a desire which, as we pointed out at the end of the last session, many council Fathers have made their own, calling insistently for an explicit declaration during this council of the maternal role which the Blessed Virgin exercises towards the Christian people. To this end we have considered it opportune to dedicate a title in honour of the Virgin which has been proposed in different parts of the Catholic world and which we find particularly touching, for it sums up in a wonderfully succinct way the privileged position which this council has recognized the Blessed Virgin to have in the Church.

"And so, for the glory of the Virgin and for our consolation, we proclaim Mary Most Holy to be the Mother of the Church, that is, Mother of the entire people of God, faithful as well as pastors, who call her loving Mother, and we desire that from now on she be honoured and invoked by the entire people of God under this most pleasing title."

spoke beforehand by the mouth of David, concerning Judas who Lk 22:47
was guide to those who arrested Jesus. 17For he was numbered Jn 13:18 Acts 1:20
among us, and was allotted his share in this ministry. 18(Now this Mt 27:3–10
man bought a field with the reward of his wickedness; and falling
headlong[b] he burst open in the middle and all his bowels gushed
out. 19And it became known to all the inhabitants of Jerusalem, so
that the field was called in their language Akeldama, that is, Field
of Blood.) 20For it is written in the Book of Psalms, Ps 69:25

'Let his habitation become desolate,
and let there be no one to live in it';

and

The text makes reference to Jesus' "brethren", an expression which also appears in the Gospels. Given that the Christian faith teaches us that the Virgin Mary had no children other than Jesus, whom she conceived by the action of the Holy Spirit and without intervention of man, this expression cannot mean that Jesus had blood brothers or sisters.

The explanation lies in the peculiarities of Semitic languages. The word used in the New Testament translates a Hebrew term which applied to all the members of a family group and was used for even distant cousins (cf. Lev 10:4) and for nephews (Gen 13:8). See the note on Mt 12:46–47. In the New Testament then, the word "brethren" has a very wide meaning—as happens, also, for example, with the word "apostle".

At one point Jesus describes those who hear and keep his word as his "brethren" (Lk 8:21), which seems to imply that, in addition to meaning belonging to the same family group, the word "brother" in the New Testament may be a designation for certain disciples who were particularly loyal to our Lord. St Paul, for his part, uses this term for all Christians (cf., e.g., 1 Cor 1:10; etc.), as does St Peter, according to Acts 12:17.

1:15–23. "Peter is the ardent and impetuous apostle to whom Christ entrusted the care of his flock; and since he is first in dignity, he is the first to speak" (St John Chrysostom, *Hom. on Acts*, 3).

Here we see Peter performing his ministry. Events will make for the gradual manifestation of the supreme role of government which Christ entrusted to him. His is a ministry of service—he is the *servus servorum Dei*, the servant of the servants of God—a ministry given to none other, different from all other ministries in the Church. Peter will carry it out in solidarity with his brothers in the Apostolate and in close contact with the whole Church represented here in the one hundred and twenty brethren around him.

This account of Peter with the other apostles and disciples all brought together is described by St John Chrysostom in these words: "Observe the admirable prudence of St Peter. He begins by quoting the authority of a prophet and does not say, 'My own word suffices,' so far is he from any thought of pride. But he seeks nothing less than the election of a twelfth apostle and he presses for this. His entire behaviour shows the degree of his authority and that he understood the apostolic office of government not as a position of honour but as a commitment

b. Or *swelling up*

Ps 109:8 ‘His office let another take.’
Jn 15:27 [21]So one of the men who have accompanied us during all the time
Acts 3:15 that the Lord Jesus went in and out among us, [22]beginning from
the baptism of John until the day when he was taken up from us—
Jer 11:20 one of these men must become with us a witness to his resurrec-
Lk 16:15 Acts 15:8 tion.”* [23]And they put forward two, Joseph called Barsabbas, who
Rev 2:23 was surnamed Justus, and Matthias. [24]And they prayed and said,

---

to watch over the spiritual health of those under him.

“The disciples were one hundred and twenty, and Peter asks for one of these. But he it is who proposes the election and exercises the principal authority because he has been entrusted with the care of all” (*Hom. on Acts*, 3).

1:21–22. The apostles are the witnesses *par excellence* of Jesus’ public life. The Church is “apostolic” because it relies on the solid testimony of people specially chosen to live with our Lord, witnessing his works and listening to his words. The twelve apostles certify that Jesus of Nazareth and the risen Lord are one and the same person and that the words and actions of Jesus preserved and passed on by the Church are indeed truly reported.

Everyone who maintains unity with the Pope and the bishops in communion with him maintains unity with the apostles and, through them, with Jesus Christ himself. “Orthodox teaching has been conserved by being passed on successively since the time of the apostles and so it has remained up to the present in all the churches. Therefore, only that teaching can be considered true which offers no discord with ecclesiastical and apostolic tradition” (Origen, *De principiis*, Preface, 2). See the note on Acts 1:26.

1:24–26. Verses 24–25 record the first prayer of the Church, which is linked with what we were told in v. 14—“all these with one accord devoted themselves to prayer”—and shows the disciples’ firm belief that God rules over all things and all events and looks after the Church in a very special way.

The Christian community leaves in God’s hands the choice as to who will fill the empty place in the Twelve. It does this by using the traditional Hebrew method of casting lots, the outcome of which will reveal God’s will. This method of divining God’s will is to be found quite a number of times in the Old Testament (cf. 1 Sam 14:41f); its use was restricted to Levites, to prevent it degenerating into a superstitious practice. In casting lots the Jews used dice, sticks, pieces of paper etc. each bearing the name of a candidate for an office, or of people suspected of having committed some crime etc. Lots were cast as often as necessary to fill the number of places to be filled or the suspected number of criminals.

In this instance they decide to cast lots because they consider that God has already made his choice and all that remains is for him to make his will known: his decision can be ascertained unerringly by using this simple human device. This method of appointing people, borrowed from Judaism, did not continue to be used in the Church for very long.

Now that Matthias has been appointed, the Twelve is complete again. The apostolic college is now ready to receive the Holy Spirit whom Jesus promised to send, and to go on to bear universal witness to the Good News.

"Lord, who knowest the hearts of all men, show which one of
these two thou hast chosen [25]to take the place in this ministry and
apostleship from which Judas turned aside, to go to his own
place." [26]And they cast lots for them, and the lot fell on Matthias; 1 Sam 14:41
and he was enrolled with the eleven apostles. Prov 16:33

1:26. St Luke usually applies the term "apostles" only to the Twelve (cf., for example, Acts 6:6), or the Eleven plus Peter, who appears as head of the apostolic college (cf. 2:14). Except in Acts 14:14, Luke never describes St Paul as an apostle—not because he minimizes Paul's role (indeed, half the chapters of Acts deal with Paul) but because he reserves to the Twelve the specific function of being witnesses to our Lord's life on earth.

This apostolic character or apostolicity is one of the marks of the true Church of Christ—a Church built, by the express wish of its Founder, on the solid basis of the Twelve.

The *St Pius V Catechism* (1, 10, 17) teaches that "the true Church is also to be recognized from her origin, which can be traced back under the law of grace to the apostles; for her doctrine is the truth not recently given, nor now first heard of, but delivered of old by the apostles, and disseminated throughout the entire world. [...] That all, therefore, might know which was the Catholic Church, the Fathers, guided by the Spirit of God, added to the Creed the word 'apostolic'. For the Holy Spirit, who presides over the Church, governs her by no other ministers than those of apostolic succession. This Spirit, first imparted to the apostles, has by the infinite goodness of God always continued in the Church."

The principal role of the apostles is to be witnesses to the resurrection of Jesus (cf. 1:22). They perform it through the ministry of the word (6:4), which takes various forms, such as preaching to the people (cf. 2:14–40; 3:12–26; 4:2, 33; 5:20–21), teaching the disciples within the Christian community itself (2:42), and declarations uttered fearlessly against the enemies and persecutors of the Gospel of Jesus (4:5–31; 5:27–41). Like the word of the Lord, that of the apostles is supported by signs and wonders, which render visible the salvation which they proclaim (2:14–21, 43; 3:1–11, 16; 4:8–12, 30; 5:12, 15–16; 9:31–43).

The Twelve also perform a role of government in the Church. When the members of the community at Jerusalem give up their property to help their brothers in need, they lay the money "at the apostles' feet" (4:35). When the Hellenist Christians need to be reassured, the Twelve summon the assembly to establish the ministry of the diaconate (6:2). When Saul goes up to Jerusalem after his conversion, he is introduced to the apostles by Barnabas (9:26–28). The apostles quite evidently exercise an authority given them by our Lord who invested them with untransferable responsibilities and duties connected with service to the entire Church.

The apostles also intervene outside Jerusalem as guarantors of internal and external unity, which also is an essential distinguishing mark of the Church. After Philip baptizes some Samaritans, the apostles Peter and John travel from Jerusalem to give them the Holy Spirit by the laying on of hands (8:14–17).

After the baptism of the pagan Cornelius, the apostles study the situation with Peter, to ascertain more exactly the designs of God and the details of the new

2. PENTECOST

The coming of the Holy Spirit

Lev 23:15–21 2 [1]When the day of Pentecost had come, they were all together
Jn 3:8 in one place. [2]And suddenly a sound came from heaven like
Acts 4:31 the rush of a mighty wind, and it filled all the house where they

---

economy of salvation (11:1–18). Apropos of the debate in Antioch about the circumcision of baptized pagans, the community decides to consult the apostles (15:2) to obtain a final decision on this delicate matter.

Most of St Luke's attention is concentrated on the figure of Peter, whom he mentions 56 times in Acts. Peter is always the centre of those scenes or episodes in which he appears with other apostles or disciples. In matters to do with the community at Jerusalem Peter acts as the spokesman of the Twelve (2:14, 37; 5:29) and plays a key role in the opening up of the Gospel to pagans.

The college of the twelve apostles, whose head is Peter, endures in the episcopacy of the Church, whose head is the Pope, the bishop of Rome, successor of Peter and vicar of Jesus Christ. The Second Vatican Council proposes this once again when it teaches that the "Lord Jesus, having prayed at length to the Father, called to himself those whom he willed and appointed twelve to be with him, whom he might send to preach the Kingdom of God (cf. Mk 3:13–19; Mt 10:1–42). These apostles (cf. Lk 6:13) he constituted in the form of a college or permanent assembly, at the head of which he placed Peter, chosen from among them (cf. Jn 21:15–17)" (*Lumen gentium*, 19).

"Just as, in accordance with the Lord's decree, St Peter and the rest of the apostles constitute a unique apostolic college, so in like fashion the Roman Pontiff, Peter's successor, and the bishops, the successors of the apostles, are related and united to one another. [...]

"In it the bishops, whilst loyally respecting the primacy and pre-eminence of their head, exercise their own proper authority for the good of their faithful, indeed even for the good of the whole Church, the organic structure and harmony of which are strengthened by the continued influence of the Holy Spirit. The supreme authority over the whole Church, which this college possesses, is exercised in a solemn way in an ecumenical council. [...] And it is the prerogative of the Roman Pontiff to convoke such councils, to preside over them and to confirm them" (ibid., 22).

2:1–13. This account of the Holy Spirit visibly coming down on the disciples who, in keeping with Jesus' instructions, had stayed together in Jerusalem, gives limited information as to the time and place of the event, yet it is full of content. Pentecost was one of the three great Jewish feasts for which many Israelites went on pilgrimage to the Holy City to worship God in the temple. It originated as a harvest thanksgiving, with an offering of first-fruits. Later it was given the additional dimension of commemorating the promulgation of the Law given by God to Moses on Sinai. The Pentecost celebration was held fifty days after the Passover, that is, after seven weeks had passed. The material harvest which the Jews celebrated so joyously became, through God's providence, the symbol of the spiritual harvest which the apostles began to reap on this day.

were sitting. [3]And there appeared to them tongues as of fire, dis- Ps 104:30
tributed and resting on each one of them. [4]And they were all filled Mt 3:11 Acts 10:44–46;
with the Holy Spirit and began to speak in other tongues, as the 19:6
Spirit gave them utterance. Mk 16:17

2:2–3. Wind and fire were elements which typically accompanied manifestations of God in the Old Testament (cf. Ex 3:2; 13:21–22; 2 Kings 5:24; Ps 104:3). In this instance, as Chrysostom explains, it would seem that separate tongues of fire came down on each of them: they were "separated, which means they came from one and the same source, to show that the Power all comes from the Paraclete" (*Hom. on Acts*, 4). The wind and the noise must have been so intense that they caused people to flock to the place. The fire symbolizes the action of the Holy Spirit who, by enlightening the minds of the disciples, enables them to understand Jesus' teachings—as Jesus promised at the Last Supper (cf. Jn 16:4–14); by inflaming their hearts with love he dispels their fear and moves them to preach boldly. Fire also has a purifying effect, God's action cleansing the soul of all trace of sin.

2:4. Pentecost was not an isolated event in the life of the Church, something over and done with. "We have the right, the duty and the joy to tell you that Pentecost is still happening. We can legitimately speak of the 'lasting value' of Pentecost. We know that fifty days after Easter, the apostles, gathered together in the same Cenacle as had been used for the first Eucharist and from which they had gone out to meet the Risen One for the first time, *discover* in themselves the power of the Holy Spirit who descended upon them, the strength of Him whom the Lord had promised so often as the outcome of his suffering on the Cross; and strengthened in this way, they began to act, that is, to perform their role. […] Thus is born the *apostolic Church*. But even today—and herein the continuity lies—the Basilica of St Peter in Rome and every Temple, every Oratory, every place where the disciples of the Lord gather, is an extension of that original Cenacle" (John Paul II, Homily, 25 May 1980).

Vatican II (cf. *Ad gentes*, 4) quotes St Augustine's description of the Holy Spirit as the soul, the source of life, of the Church, which was born on the cross on Good Friday and whose birth was announced publicly on the day of Pentecost: "Today, as you know, the Church was fully born, through the breath of Christ, the Holy Spirit; and in the Church was born the Word, the witness to and promulgation of salvation in the risen Jesus; and in him who listens to this promulgation is born faith, and with faith a new life, an awareness of the Christian vocation and the ability to hear that calling and to follow it by living a genuinely human life, indeed a life which is not only human but holy. And to make this divine intervention effective, today was born the apostolate, the priesthood, the ministry of the Spirit, the calling to unity, fraternity and peace" (Paul VI, Address, 25 May 1969).

"Mary, who conceived Christ by the work of the Holy Spirit, the Love of the living God, presides over the birth of the Church, on the day of Pentecost, when the same Holy Spirit comes down on the disciples and gives life to the mystical body of Christians in unity and charity" (Paul VI, Address, 25 October 1969).

[5]Now there were dwelling in Jerusalem Jews, devout men
Gen 11:1–9 from every nation under heaven. [6]And at this sound the multitude
came together, and they were bewildered, because each one heard
them speaking in his own language. [7]And they were amazed and
wondered, saying, "Are not all these who are speaking Galileans?
[8]And how is it that we hear, each of us in his own native language? [9]Parthians and Medes and Elamites and residents of Mesopotamia, Judea and Cappadocia, Pontus and Asia, [10]Phrygia and
Pamphylia, Egypt and the parts of Libya belonging to Cyrene, and

---

2:5–11. In his account of the events of Pentecost St Luke distinguishes "devout men" (v. 5), Jews and proselytes (v. 11). The first-mentioned were people who were residing in Jerusalem for reasons of study or piety, to be near the only temple the Jews had. They were Jews—not to be confused with "God-fearing men", that is, pagans sympathetic to Judaism, who worshipped the God of the Bible and who, if they became converts and members of the Jewish religion by being circumcised and by observing the Mosaic Law, were what were called "proselytes", whom Luke distinguishes from the "Jews", that is, those of Jewish race.

People of different races and tongues understand Peter, each in his or her own language. They can do so thanks to a special grace from the Holy Spirit given them for the occasion; this is not the same as the gift of "speaking with tongues" which some of the early Christians had (cf. 1 Cor 14), which allowed them to praise God and speak to him in a language which they themselves did not understand.

2:11. When the Fathers of the Church comment on this passage they frequently point to the contrast between the confusion of languages that came about at Babel (cf. Gen 11:1–9)—God's punishment for man's pride and infidelity—and the reversal of this confusion on the day of Pentecost, thanks to the grace of the Holy Spirit. The Second Vatican Council stresses the same idea: "Without doubt, the Holy Spirit was at work in the world before Christ was glorified. On the day of Pentecost, however, he came down on the disciples that he might remain with them forever (cf. Jn 14:16); on that day the Church was openly displayed to the crowds and the spread of the Gospel among the nations, through preaching, was begun. Finally, on that day was foreshadowed the union of all peoples in the catholicity of the faith by means of the Church of the New Alliance, a Church which speaks every language, understands and embraces all tongues in charity, and thus overcomes the dispersion of Babel" (*Ad gentes*, 4).

Christians need this gift for their apostolic activity and should ask the Holy Spirit to give it to them to help them express themselves in such a way that others can understand their message; to be able so to adapt what they say to suit the outlook and capacity of their hearers, that they pass Christ's truth on: "Every generation of Christians needs to redeem, to sanctify, its own time. To do this, it must understand and share the desires of other men—their equals—in order to make known to them, with a 'gift of tongues', how they are to respond to the action of the Holy Spirit, to that permanent outflow of rich treasures that comes from our Lord's heart. We Christians are called upon to announce, in our

visitors from Rome, both Jews and proselytes, [11]Cretans and
Arabians, we hear them telling in our own tongues the mighty
works of God." [12]And all were amazed and perplexed, saying to 1 Cor 14:22–25
one another, "What does this mean?" [13]But others mocking said,
"They are filled with new wine."

Peter's address

[14]But Peter,* standing with the eleven, lifted up his voice and Acts 1:15; 15:17
addressed them, "Men of Judea and all who dwell in Jerusalem,

---

own time, to this world to which we belong and in which we live, the message—old and at the same time new—of the Gospel" (St Josemaría Escrivá, *Christ Is Passing By*, 132).

2:12. The action of the Holy Spirit must have caused such amazement, in both the disciples and those who heard them, that everyone was "beside himself". The apostles were so filled with the Holy Spirit that they seemed to be drunk (cf. Acts 2:13).

"Then Peter stood up with the Eleven and addressed the people in a loud voice. We, people from a hundred nations, hear him. Each of us hears him in his own language—you and I in ours. He speaks to us of Christ Jesus and of the Holy Spirit and of the Father.

"He is not stoned nor thrown into prison; of those who have heard him, three thousand are converted and baptized.

"You and I, after helping the apostles administer baptism, bless God the Father, for his Son Jesus, and we too feel drunk with the Holy Spirit" (St J. Escrivá, *Holy Rosary*, third glorious mystery).

2:13. These devout Jews, from different countries, who happened to be in Jerusalem on the day of Pentecost—many of them living there, for reasons of study or piety, and others who had come up on pilgrimage for these days—listen to the apostles' preaching because they are impressed by the amazing things they can see actually happening. The same Holy Spirit who acted in our Lord's disciples also moved their listeners' hearts and led them to believe. There were others, however, who resisted the action of grace and looked for an excuse to justify their behaviour.

2:14–36. Even as the Church takes its first steps St Peter can be seen to occupy the position of main spokesman. In his address we can distinguish an introduction and two parts: in the first part (vv. 16–21) he is explaining that the messianic times foretold by Joel have now arrived; in the second (vv. 22–36) he proclaims that Jesus of Nazareth, whom the Jews crucified, is the Messiah promised by God and eagerly awaited by the righteous of the Old Testament; it is he who has effected God's saving plan for mankind.

2:14. In his commentaries St John Chrysostom draws attention to the change worked in Peter by the Holy Spirit: "Listen to him preach and argue so boldly, who shortly before had trembled at the word of a servant girl! This boldness is a significant proof of the resurrection of his Master: Peter preaches to men who mock and laugh at his enthusiasm. [...] Calumny ('they are filled with new wine') does not deter the apostles; sarcasm does not undermine their

let this be known to you, and give ear to my words. [15]For these
men are not drunk, as you suppose, since it is only the third hour
of the day; [16]but this is what was spoken by the prophet Joel:

Joel 2:28 [17]'And in the last days it shall be, God declares,
that I will pour out my Spirit upon all flesh,
and your sons and your daughters shall prophesy,
and your young men shall see visions,
and your old men shall dream dreams;

Rom 5:5 [18]yea, and on my menservants and my maidservants in
those days
I will pour out my Spirit; and they shall prophesy.

Acts 5:12 [19]And I will show wonders in the heaven above
and signs on the earth beneath,
blood, and fire, and vapour of smoke;

Rev 6:12 [20]the sun shall be turned into darkness
and the moon into blood,
before the day of the Lord comes,
the great and manifest day.

Rom 10:9–13 [21]And it shall be that whoever calls on the name of the Lord
shall be saved.'

Mt 2:23; Jn 3:2; 5:36 [22]"Men of Israel, hear these words: Jesus of Nazareth a man
attested to you by God with mighty works and wonders and signs
which God did through him in your midst, as you yourselves
Jn 19:6–11; Acts 3:15 know—[23]this Jesus, delivered up according to the definite plan
and foreknowledge of God, you crucified and killed by the hands

---

courage, for the coming of the Holy Spirit has made new men of them, men who can put up with every kind of human test. When the Holy Spirit enters into hearts he does so to elevate their affections and to change earthly souls, souls of clay, into chosen souls, people of real courage […]. Look at the harmony that exists among the apostles. See how they allow Peter to speak on behalf of them all. Peter raises his voice and speaks to the people with full assurance. That is the kind of courage a man has when he is the instrument of the Holy Spirit. […] Just as a burning coal does not lose its heat when it falls on a haystack but instead is enabled to release its heat, so Peter, now that he is in contact with the life-giving Spirit, spreads his inner fire to those around him" (*Hom. on Acts*, 4).

2:17. "In the last days": a reference to the coming of Christ and the era of salvation which follows; and also to the fact that the Holy Spirit, whom God would pour out on men of every nation and era when the Kingdom of the Messiah arrived, would continue to aid his Church until the day of the Last Judgment, which will be heralded by amazing events.

2:22–36. To demonstrate that Jesus of Nazareth is the Messiah foretold by the prophets, St Peter reminds his listeners of our Lord's miracles (v. 22), as well as of

of lawless men. 24 But God raised him up, having loosed the pangs Ps 18:4–5
of death, because it was not possible for him to be held by it. 25 For Acts 13:34
David says concerning him, Ps 16:8–11

> 'I saw the Lord always before me,
> for he is at my right hand that I may not be shaken;
> 26 therefore my heart was glad, and my tongue rejoiced;
> moreover my flesh will dwell in hope.
> 27 For thou wilt not abandon my soul to Hades,
> nor let thy Holy One see corruption.
> 28 Thou hast made known to me the ways of life;
> thou wilt make me full of gladness with thy presence.'

29 "Brethren, I may say to you confidently of the patriarch 1 Kings 2:10
David that he both died and was buried, and his tomb is with us to
this day. 30 Being therefore a prophet, and knowing that God had 2 Sam 7:12
sworn with an oath to him that he would set one of his descen- Ps 132:11
dants upon his throne, 31 he foresaw and spoke of the resurrection Ps 16:10
of the Christ, that he was not abandoned to Hades, nor did his
flesh see corruption. 32 This Jesus God raised up, and of that we all
are witnesses. 33 Being therefore exalted at the right hand of God, Acts 5:31
and having received from the Father the promise of the Holy Phil 2:9
Spirit, he has poured out this which you see and hear. 34 For David
did not ascend into the heavens; but he himself says, Ps 110:1

> 'The Lord said to my Lord, Sit at my right hand, Mt 22:44
> 35 till I make thy enemies a stool for thy feet.'

36 Let all the house of Israel therefore know assuredly that God has
made him both Lord and Christ, this Jesus whom you crucified."

---

his death (v. 23), resurrection (v. 24–32) and glorious ascension (vv. 33–35). His address ends with a brief summing-up (v. 36).

2:32. To proofs from prophecy, very important to the Jews, St Peter adds his own testimony on the resurrection of Jesus, and that of his brothers in the Apostolate.

2:36. During his life on earth Jesus had often presented himself as the Messiah and Son of God. His resurrection and ascension into heaven reveal him as such to the people at large.

In Peter's address we can see an outline of the content of the apostolic proclamation (*kerygma*), the content of Christian preaching, the object of faith. This proclamation bears witness to Christ's death and resurrection and subsequent exaltation; it recalls the main points of Jesus' mission, announced by John the Baptist, confirmed by miracles and brought to fulfilment by the appearances of the risen Lord and the outpouring of the Holy Spirit; it declares that the messianic time predicted by the prophets has arrived, and calls all men to conversion, in preparation for the Parousia, or second coming of Christ in glory.

Many baptisms

[37]Now when they heard this they were cut to the heart, and said to
Peter and the rest of the apostles, "Brethren, what shall we do?"
Mt 3:2 Lk 13:3 [38]And Peter said to them, "Repent, and be baptized every one of
Acts 3:19; 8:16 you in the name of Jesus Christ for the forgiveness of your sins;
Is 57:19 and you shall receive the gift of the Holy Spirit. [39]For the promise

---

2:37. St Peter's words were the instrument used by God's grace to move the hearts of his listeners: they are so impressed that they ask in all simplicity what they should do. Peter exhorts them to be converted, to repent (cf. the note on 3:19). The *St Pius V Catechism* explains that in order to receive Baptism adults "need to repent the sins they have committed and their evil past life and to be resolved not to commit sin henceforth […], for nothing is more opposed to the grace and power of Baptism than the outlook and disposition of those who never decide to abjure sin" (2, 2, 4).

2:38. "Be baptized in the name of Jesus Christ": this does not necessarily mean that this was the form of words the apostles normally used in the liturgy, rather than the Trinitarian formula prescribed by Jesus. In the *Didache* (written around the year 100) it is stated that Baptism should be given in the name of the Father and of the Son and of the Holy Spirit, but this does not prevent it, in other passages, from referring to "those baptized in the name of the Lord." The expression "baptized in the name of Christ" means, therefore, becoming a member of Christ, becoming a Christian (cf. *Didaché*, 7, 1; 9, 5).

"Like the men and women who came up to Peter on Pentecost, we too have been baptized. In baptism, our Father God has taken possession of our lives, has made us share in the life of Christ, and has given us the Holy Spirit" (St J. Escrivá, *Christ Is Passing By*, 128). From this point onwards, the Trinity begins to act in the soul of the baptized person. "In the same way as transparent bodies, when light shines on them, become resplendent and bright, souls elevated and enlightened by the Holy Spirit become spiritual too and lead others to the light of grace. From the Holy Spirit comes knowledge of future events, understanding of mysteries and of hidden truths, an outpouring of gifts, heavenly citizenship, conversation with angels. From him comes never-ending joy, perseverance in good, likeness to God and—the most sublime thing imaginable—becoming God" (St Basil, *On the Holy Spirit*, 9, 23).

This divinization which occurs in the baptized person shows how important it is for Christians to cultivate the Holy Spirit who has been infused into their souls, where he dwells as long as he is not driven out by sin. "Love the third Person of the most Blessed Trinity. Listen in the intimacy of your being to the divine motions of encouragement or reproach you receive from him. Walk through the earth in the light that is poured out in your soul. […] We can apply to ourselves the question asked by the apostle: 'Do you not know that you are God's temple and that God's Spirit dwells in you?' (1 Cor 3:16). And we can understand it as an invitation to deal with God in a more personal and direct manner. For some, unfortunately, the Paraclete is the Great Stranger. He is merely a name that is mentioned, but not Someone—not one of the three Persons

is to you and to your children and to all that are far off, every one Acts 3:26; 13:46
whom the Lord our God calls to him." [40]And he testified with Eph 2:13–17
many other words and exhorted them, saying, "Save yourselves Deut 32:5
from this crooked generation." [41]So those who received his word Mt 17:17
were baptized, and there were added that day about three thou- Lk 9:41 Acts 5:14; 6:7
sand souls.

---

in the one God—with whom we can talk and with whose life we can live. We have to deal with him simply and trustingly, as we are taught by the Church in its liturgy. Then we will come to know our Lord better, and at the same time, we will realize more fully the great favour that was granted us when we became Christians. We will see all the greatness and truth of this divinization, which is a sharing in God's own life" (St Josemaría Escrivá, *Christ Is Passing By*, 133–134).

2:39. The "promise" of the Holy Spirit applies to both Jews and Gentiles, but in the first instance it concerns the Jews: it is they to whom God entrusted his oracles; theirs was the privilege to receive the Old Testament and to be preached to directly by Jesus himself. St Peter makes it clear that this promise is also made "to all that are far off"—a reference to the Gentiles, as St Paul explains (cf. Eph 2:13–17) and in line with Isaiah's announcement, "Peace, peace, to the far and to the near" (Is 57:19). Cf. Acts 22:21.

2:40. "This crooked generation" is not only that part of the Jewish people who rejected Christ and his teaching, but everyone who is estranged from God (cf. Deut 32:5; Phil 2:15).

2:41. St Luke here concludes his Pentecost account and prepares to move on to a new topic. Before he does so he adds a note, as it were, to say that "about three thousand souls" became Christians as a result of Peter's address.

St Luke often makes reference to the numerical growth of the Church (2:47; 4:4; 5:14; 6:1, 7; 9:31; 11:21, 24; 16:5). Interesting in itself, this growth clearly shows the effectiveness of the Gospel message boldly proclaimed by the apostles. It proves that if the Gospel is preached with constancy and clarity it can take root in any setting and will always find men and women ready to receive it and put it into practice.

"It is not true that everyone today—in general—is closed or indifferent to what our Christian faith teaches about man's being and destiny. It is not true that men in our time are turned only toward the things of this earth and have forgotten to look up to heaven. There is no lack of narrow ideologies, it is true, or of persons who maintain them. But in our time we find both great desires and base attitudes, heroism and cowardice, zeal and disenchantment—people who dream of a new world, more just and more human, and others who, discouraged perhaps by the failure of their youthful idealism, take refuge in the selfishness of seeking only their own security or remaining immersed in their errors.

"To all those men and women, wherever they may be, in their more exalted moments or in their crises and defeats, we have to bring the solemn and unequivocal message of St Peter in the days that followed Pentecost: Jesus is the cornerstone, the Redeemer, the hope of our lives. 'For there is no other name under heaven given among men by which we must be saved' (Acts 4:12)" (*Christ Is Passing By*, 132).

The early Christians

42And they devoted themselves to the apostles' teaching and fellowship, to the breaking of bread and the prayers.

2:42–47. This is the first of the three summaries contained in the early chapters of Acts (cf. 4:32–35 and 5:12–16). In simple words it describes the key elements in the ascetical and liturgical-sacramental life of the first Christians. It gives a vivid spiritual profile of the community which now—after Pentecost extends beyond the Cenacle, a contemplative community, more and more involved in the world around it.

2:42. "The sacred writer", St John Chrysostom observes, "draws attention to two virtues in particular—perseverance and fellowship and tells us that the apostles spent a long period instructing the disciples" (*Hom. on Acts*, 7).

"The apostles' teaching": the instruction normally given new converts. This is not the proclamation of the Gospel to non-Christians but a type of *catechesis* (which became more structured and systematic as time went on) aimed at explaining to the disciples the Christian meaning of Sacred Scripture and the basic truths of faith (out of this grew the credal statements of the Church) which they had to believe and practise in order to attain salvation.

Catechesis—an ongoing preaching and explanation of the Gospel *within* the Church—is a phenomenon to be found even in the very early days of Christianity. "An evangelizer, the Church begins by evangelizing itself. A community of believers, a community of hope practised and transmitted, a community of fraternal love, it has a need to listen unceasingly to what it must believe, to the reasons for its hope, to the new commandment of love" (Paul VI, *Evangelii nuntiandi*, 15).

If catechesis is something which converts and in general all Christians *need*, obviously pastors have a grave duty to provide it. "The whole of the book of the Acts of the Apostles is a witness that they were faithful to their vocation and to the mission they had received. The members of the first Christian community are seen in it as 'devoted to the apostles' teaching and fellowship, to the breaking of bread and the prayers'. Without any doubt we find in that a lasting image of the Church being born of and continually nourished by the word of the Lord, thanks to the teaching of the apostles, celebrating that word in the eucharistic Sacrifice and bearing witness to it before the world in the sign of charity" (John Paul II, *Catechesi tradendae*, 10).

The "fellowship" referred to in this verse is that union of hearts brought about by the Holy Spirit. This profound solidarity among the disciples resulted from their practice of the faith and their appreciation of it as a peerless treasure which they all shared, a gift to them from God the Father through Jesus Christ. Their mutual affection enabled them to be detached from material things and to give up their possessions to help those in need.

The "breaking of bread" refers to the Blessed Eucharist and not just to an ordinary meal. This was a special way the early Christians had of referring to the making and distribution of the sacrament containing the Lord's body. This expression, connected with the idea of a banquet, was soon replaced by that of "Eucharist", which emphasizes the idea of thanksgiving (cf. *Didaché*, 9, 1). From Pentecost onwards the Mass and eucharistic communion form the centre of Christian worship. "From that time on-

[43]And fear came upon every soul; and many wonders and signs were done through the apostles. [44]And all who believed were

Acts 5:11–12
Acts 4:32, 34–35

wards the Church has never failed to come together to celebrate the paschal mystery, reading those things 'which were in all the scriptures concerning him' (Lk 24:27), celebrating the Eucharist in which 'the victory and triumph of his death are again made present' (Council of Trent, *De SS. Eucharistia*, chap. 5), and at the same time giving thanks to God" (Vatican II, *Sacrosanctum Concilium*, 6).

By receiving the Eucharist with a pure heart and clear conscience the disciples obtain the nourishment needed to follow the new life of the Gospel and to be in the world without being worldly. This connexion between the Eucharist and Christian living was something Pope John Paul II vigorously reminded Catholics about when he said in Dublin, "It is from the Eucharist that all of us receive the grace and strength for daily living—to live real Christian lives, in the joy of knowing that God loves us, that Christ died for us, and that the Holy Spirit lives in us.

"Our full participation in the Eucharist is the real source of the Christian spirit that we wish to see in our personal lives and in all aspects of society. Whether we serve in politics, in the economic, cultural, social or scientific fields—no matter what our occupation is—the Eucharist is a challenge to our daily lives.

"Our union with Christ in the Eucharist must be expressed in the truth of our lives today—in our actions, in our behaviour, in our lifestyle, and in our relationships with others. For each one of us the Eucharist is a call to ever greater effort, so that we may live as true followers of Jesus: truthful in our speech, generous in our deeds, concerned, respectful of the dignity and rights of all persons, whatever their rank or income, self-sacrificing, fair and just, kind, considerate, compassionate and self-controlled. [...] The truth of our union with Jesus Christ in the Eucharist is tested by whether or not we really love our fellow men and women; it is tested by how we treat others, especially our families. [...] It is tested by whether or not we try to be reconciled with our enemies, on whether or not we forgive those who hurt us or offend us" (Homily in Phoenix Park, 29 September 1979).

2:43. The fear referred to here is the religious awe the disciples felt when they saw the miracles and other supernatural signs which the Lord worked through his apostles. A healthy type of fear, denoting respect and reverence for holy things, it can cause a great change of attitude and behaviour in those who experience it.

An outstanding example of this sense of awe is St Peter's reaction at the miraculous catch of fish: "Depart from me, for I am a sinful man, O Lord": as St Luke explains, "he was astonished, and all that were with him, at the catch of fish they had taken" (Lk 5:8–9).

2:44. Charity and union of hearts lead the disciples to sacrifice their own interests to meet the material needs of their poorer brothers and sisters. The sharing of possessions referred to here was not a permanent, "communistic" kind of system. The more well-to-do Christians freely provided for those in need. Each of the disciples retained ownership of such property as he or she had: by handing it over to the community they showed their charity.

"This voluntary poverty and detachment", Chrysostom comments, "cut at

Acts 6:1 together and had all things in common; 45and they sold their pos-
sessions and goods and distributed them to all, as any had need.
Lk 24:53 46And day by day, attending the temple together and breaking bread
Acts 8:8; 16:34 in their homes, they partook of food with glad and generous hearts,
Acts 2:21; 13:48 47praising God and having favour with all the people. And the Lord
added to their number day by day those who were being saved.

---

the selfish root of many evils, and the new disciples showed that they had understood the Gospel teaching.

"This was not recklessness of the kind shown by certain philosophers, of whom some gave up their inheritance and others cast their gold into the sea: that was no contempt of riches, but folly and madness. For the devil has always made it his endeavour to disparage the things God has created, as if it were impossible to make good use of riches" (*Hom. on Acts*, 7).

A spendthrift who wastes his resources does not have the virtue of detachment; nor can someone be called selfish because he retains his property, provided that he uses it generously when the need arises. "Rather than in not having, true poverty consists in being detached, in voluntarily renouncing one's dominion over things.

"That is why there are poor who are really rich. And vice-versa" (St Josemaría Escrivá, *The Way*, 632).

2:46. In the early days of the Church the temple was a centre of Christian prayer and liturgy. The first Christians regarded it as God's house, the House of the Father of Jesus Christ. Although Christianity involved obvious differences from Judaism, they also realized that Christ's message was an extension of Judaism; for a while, it was quite natural for them to maintain certain external aspects of the religion of their forefathers.

In addition to this legitimate religious instinct to venerate the one, true, loving God, whom Jews and Christians adore, St Jerome suggests that prudence may have dictated this practice: "Because the early Church was made up of Jews," he says, "the apostles were very careful not to introduce any innovations, in order to avoid any possible scandal to believers" (*Epistles*, 26, 2).

However, the temple was not the only place in the Holy City where Christians met for prayer and worship. The reference to "breaking bread in their homes" reminds us that the Christian community in Jerusalem, as also the communities later founded by St Paul, did not yet have a building specially reserved for liturgical functions. They met in private houses—presumably in suitable rooms specially prepared. For financial as well as policy reasons (persecutions etc.), it was not until the third century that buildings designed solely for liturgical purposes began to be erected.

3:1. This was the hour of the evening sacrifice, which began around three o'clock and was attended by a large number of devout Jews. The ritual, which went on until dusk, was the second sacrifice of the day. The earlier one, on similar lines, began at dawn and lasted until nine in the morning.

3:2. None of the documents that have come down to us which describe the temple mentions a gate of this name. It was probably the Gate of Nicanor (or Corinthian Gate), which linked the court of the Gentiles with the court of the women

3. THE APOSTLES' WORK IN JERUSALEM

Curing of a man lame from birth

3 [1]Now Peter and John were going up to the temple at the hour Acts 10:3–30
of prayer, the ninth hour.* [2]And a man lame from birth was Jn 9:1
being carried, whom they laid daily at the gate of the temple Acts 14:8–10
which is called Beautiful to ask alms of those who entered the
temple. [3]Seeing Peter and John about to go into the temple, he

---

which led on to the court of the Israelites. It was architecturally a very fine structure and because of its location it was a very busy place, which would have made it a very good place for begging.

3:3–8. The cure of this cripple was the first miracle worked by the apostles. "This cure", says St John Chrysostom, "testifies to the resurrection of Christ, of which it is an image. […] Observe that they do not go up to the temple with the intention of performing a miracle, so clear were they of ambition, so closely did they imitate their Master" (*Hom. on Acts*, 8).

However, the apostles decide that the time has come to use the supernatural power given them by God. What Christ did in the Gospel using his own divine power, the apostles now do in his name, using his power. "The blind receive their sight, the lame walk, lepers are cleansed, and the deaf hear, the dead are raised up" (Lk 7:22). Our Lord now keeps his promise to empower his disciples to work miracles—visible signs of the coming of the Kingdom of God. These miracles are not extraordinary actions done casually or suddenly, without his disciples' involvement: they occur because our Lord is moved to perform them by the apostles' faith (faith is an essential precondition). The disciples are conscious of having received a gift and they act on foot of it.

These miracles in the New Testament obviously occur in situations where grace is intensely concentrated. However, that is not to say that miracles do not continue to occur in the Christian economy of salvation—miracles of different kinds, performed because God is attracted to men and women of faith. "The same is true of us. If we struggle daily to become saints, each of us in his own situation in the world and through his own job or profession, in our ordinary lives, then I assure you that God will make us into instruments that can work miracles and, if necessary, miracles of the most extraordinary kind. We will give sight to the blind. Who could not relate thousands of cases of people, blind almost from the day they were born, recovering their sight and receiving all the splendour of Christ's light? And others who were deaf, or dumb, who could not hear or pronounce words fitting to God's children … Their senses have been purified and now they hear and speak as men, not animals. *In nomine Iesu!* In the name of Jesus his apostles enable the cripple to move and walk, when previously he had been incapable of doing anything useful; and that other lazy character, who knew his duties but didn't fulfil them. … In the Lord's name, *surge et ambula!*, rise up and walk.

"Another man was dead, rotting, smelling like a corpse: he hears God's voice, as in the miracle of the son of the

asked for alms. 4And Peter directed his gaze at him, with John,
and said, "Look at us." 5And he fixed his attention upon them,
Acts 3:16 expecting to receive something from them. 6But Peter said, "I
have no silver and gold, but I give you what I have; in the name of
Is 35:6 Jesus Christ of Nazareth, walk." 7And he took him by the right
Lk 7:22 hand and raised him up; and immediately his feet and ankles were
made strong. 8And leaping up he stood and walked and entered
the temple with them, walking and leaping and praising God.
9And all the people saw him walking and praising God, 10and recognized him as the one who sat for alms at the Beautiful Gate of
the temple; and they were filled with wonder and amazement at
what had happened to him.

Jn 10:23
Acts 5:12
Ex 3:6, 15
Is 52:13
Lk 23:22
Jn 18:38; 19:4

Peter's address in the temple

11While he clung to Peter and John, all the people ran together to
them in the portico called Solomon's, astounded. 12And when

---

widow at Naim: 'Young man, I say to you, rise up' (Lk 7:14). We will work miracles like Christ did, like the first apostles did" (St Josemaría Escrivá, *Friends of God*, 262).

Miracles call for cooperation—*faith*—on the part of those who wish to be cured. The lame man does his bit, even if it is only the simple gesture of obeying Peter and looking at the apostles.

3:11–26. This second address by St Peter contains two parts: in the first (vv. 12–16) the apostle explains that the miracle has been worked in the name of Jesus and through faith in his name; in the second (vv. 17–26) he moves his listeners to repentance—people who were responsible in some degree for Jesus' death.

This discourse has the same purpose as that of Pentecost—to show the power of God made manifest in Jesus Christ and to make the Jews see the seriousness of their crime and have them repent. In both discourses there is reference to the second coming of the Lord and we can clearly see the special importance of testifying to the resurrection of Jesus; the apostolic college is presented as a witness to that unique event.

3:13. "Servant": the original Greek word (*pais*) is the equivalent of the Latin *puer* (slave, servant) and *filius* (son). By using this word St Peter must have in mind Isaiah's prophecy about the Servant of Yahweh: "Behold, my servant shall prosper, he shall be exalted and lifted up, and shall be very high. As many were astonished at him—his appearance was so marred, beyond human semblance, and his form beyond that of the sons of men—so shall he startle many nations" (52:13–15).

Peter identifies Jesus with the Servant of Yahweh, who, because he was a man of suffering and sorrow, the Jews did not identify with the future Messiah. That Messiah, Jesus Christ, combines in his person suffering and victory.

3:14. St Peter, referring to Jesus, uses terms which Jews can readily understand in a messianic sense. The expression "the Holy One of God" was already used by

Peter saw it he addressed the people, "Men of Israel, why do you
wonder at this, or why do you stare at us, as though by our own
power or piety we had made him walk? 13The God of Abraham
and of Isaac and of Jacob, the God of our fathers, glorified his servant[c] Jesus, whom you delivered up and denied in the presence of
Pilate, when he had decided to release him. 14But you denied the
Holy and Righteous One, and asked for a murderer to be granted
to you, 15and killed the Author of life, whom God raised from the
dead. To this we are witnesses. 16And his name, by faith in his
name, has made this man strong whom you see and know; and the
faith which is through Jesus[d] has given the man this perfect health
in the presence of you all.
17"And now, brethren, I know that you acted in ignorance, as
did also your rulers. 18But what God foretold by the mouth of all
the prophets, that his Christ should suffer, he thus fulfilled.

Rom 4:25
Eph 5:2
Mk 1:24
Lk 1:35; 23:25
Jn 6:69; 18:40
Acts 7:52
Rev 3:7
Acts 1:8; 13:31
Heb 2:10
Acts 4:10;
16:18; 19:13–17
Lk 23:34
Acts 13:27
1 Cor 2:8
I Tim 1:13
Lk 18:31;
24:27

Jesus as referring to the Messiah in Mark 1:24 and Luke 4:34. It is reminiscent of Old Testament language (cf. Ps 16:10).

The "Righteous One" also refers to the Messiah, whom the prophets described as a model and achiever of righteousness (cf. Acts 7:52). "Holy", "righteous" and "just" all have similar meaning.

3:15. When St Peter reminds his listeners about their choice of a murderer (Barabbas) in place of Jesus, the Author of Life, we might usefully consider that he was referring not only to physical life but also to spiritual life, the life of grace. Every time a person sins—sin means the death of the soul—this same choice is being made again. "It was he who created man in the beginning, and he left him in the power of his own inclination. If you will, you can keep the commandments, and to act faithfully is a matter of your own choice. He has placed before you fire and water: stretch out your hand for whichever you wish. Before a man are life and death, and whichever he chooses will be given to him" (Sir 15:14–17).

3:16. The original text, structured in a very Jewish way, is difficult to understand. One reason for this is the use of the word "name" instead of simply identifying who the person is. In this passage "name" means the same as "Jesus". Thus the verse can be interpreted in this way: through faith in Jesus, the man lame from birth, whom they know and have seen, has been cured; it is Jesus himself who has worked this complete and instantaneous cure.

3:17–18. The Jewish people acted in ignorance, St Peter says. Indeed, when he was on the cross Jesus had prayed, "Father, forgive them; for they know not what they do" (Lk 23:34). The people did not know that Jesus was the Christ, the Son of God. They let themselves be influenced by their priests. These, who were familiar with the Scriptures, should have recognized him.

God's pardon is offered to one and all. St Peter "tells them that Christ's death was a consequence of God's will and decree. [...] You can see how incomprehensible and profound God's design

c. Or *child* **d.** Greek *him*

Acts 2:38 [19]Repent therefore, and turn again, that your sins may be blotted
out, that times of refreshing may come from the presence of the
2 Pet 3:11–13 Lord, [20]and that he may send the Christ appointed for you, Jesus,
Acts 1:11 [21]whom heaven must receive until the time for establishing all that
Rev 10:7 God spoke by the mouth of his holy prophets from of old. [22]Moses
Deut 18:15, 19 said, 'The Lord God will raise up for you a prophet from your
Acts 7:37 brethren as he raised me up. You shall listen to him in whatever he
Lev 23:29 tells you. [23]And it shall be that every soul that does not listen to
Acts 10:43 that prophet shall be destroyed from the people.' [24]And all the
prophets who have spoken, from Samuel and those who came
Gen 12:3; 22:18 afterwards, also proclaimed these days. [25]You are the sons of the
Acts 13:32–34; 26:6–8 prophets and of the covenant which God gave to your fathers,

---

is. It was not just one but all the prophets who foretold this mystery. Yet although the Jews had been, without knowing it, the cause of Jesus' death, that death had been determined by the wisdom and will of God, who used the malice of the Jews to fulfil his designs. The apostle does not say, Although the prophets foretold this death and you acted out of ignorance, do not think you are entirely free from blame; Peter speaks to them gently: 'Repent and turn again.' To what end? 'That your sins may be blotted out'. Not only your murder but all the stains on your souls" (St John Chrysostom, *Hom. on Acts*, 9).

The Second Vatican Council tells us how Christians should treat Jewish people and those who follow other non-Christian religions—with respect and also a prudent zeal to attract them to the faith. "Even though the Jewish authorities and those who followed their lead pressed for the death of Christ (cf. Jn 19:6), neither all Jews indiscriminately at that time, nor Jews today, can be charged with the crimes committed during his passion. It is true that the Church is the new people of God, yet the Jews should not be spoken of as rejected or accursed. [...] Jews for the most part did not accept the Gospel; on the contrary, many opposed the spreading of it (cf. Rom 11:28–29). Even so, the apostle Paul maintains that the Jews remain very dear to God, for the sake of the patriarchs, since God does not take back the gifts he bestowed or the choice he made" (Vatican II, *Nostra aetate*, 4). We must not forget this special position of the Jewish people (cf. Rom 9:4–5) and the fact that from them came Jesus as far as his human lineage was concerned, and his Mother, the Blessed Virgin Mary, and the apostles—the foundation, the pillars of the Church—and many of the first disciples who proclaimed Christ's Gospel to the world.

Moved by charity, the Church prays to our Lord for the spiritual conversion of the Jewish people: "Christ, God and man, who is the Lord of David and his children, we beseech you that in keeping with the prophecies and promises, Israel recognize you as Messiah" (*Divine Office*, Morning Prayer, 31 December).

3:19. One result of sorrow for sin is a desire to make up for the damage done. On the day of Pentecost many Jews were moved by grace to ask the apostles what they should do to make atonement. Here also St Peter encourages them to change their lives and turn to God. This repentance or conversion which Peter preaches

saying to Abraham, 'And in your posterity shall all the families of
the earth be blessed.' [26]God having raised up his servant,[c] sent him Gal 3:8
to you first, to bless you in turning every one of you from your
wickedness."

Peter and John are arrested

4 [1]And as they were speaking to the people, the priests and the Lk 22:4–52
captain of the temple and the Sadducees came upon them, Acts 5:24
[2]annoyed because they were teaching the people and proclaiming Acts 23:6–8
in Jesus the resurrection from the dead.* [3]And they arrested them 1 Cor 15:20–23
and put them in custody until the morrow, for it was already
evening. [4]But many of those who heard the word believed; and the Acts 2:47
number of the men came to about five thousand.

---

is the same message as marked the initial proclamation of the Kingdom (cf. Mk 1:15; 13:1–4). "This means a change of outlook, and it applies to the state of sinful man, who needs to change his ways and turn to God, desirous of breaking away from his sins and repenting and calling on God's mercy" (Paul VI, Homily, 24 February 1971).

On another occasion Paul VI explained that the word "conversion" can be translated normally as "change of heart". "We are called to this change and it will make us see many things. The first has to do with interior analysis of our soul [...]: we should examine ourselves as to what is the main direction our life is taking, what attitude is usually to the fore in the way we think and act, what is our reason of being. [...] Is our rudder fixed so as to bring us exactly to our goal or does its direction need perhaps to be changed? [...] By examining ourselves in this way [...] we will discover sins, or at least weaknesses, which call for penance and profound reform" (Paul VI, General Audience, 21 March 1973).

3:20. A reference to the Parousia or second coming of Christ as Judge of the living and the dead (cf. the note on 1:11).

3:22–24. St Peter wants to show that the Old Testament prophecies are fulfilled in Jesus: he is descended from David (2:30), a prophet (cf. Deut 18:15), who suffered (2:23), who is the cornerstone (4:11) and who rose from the dead and sits in glory at the right hand of the Father (2:25–34).

4:1–4. On the Sadducee sect see the note on Mt 3:7.

In this chapter St Luke reports on the first conflict between the apostles and the Jerusalem authorities. Despite the incident at the end of Peter's address, his words are still an instrument of grace, stirring his listeners to believe and moving them to love.

A large crowd has gathered round Peter after the curing of the cripple, which brings on the scene the "captain of the temple", a priest second in line to the high priest whose function it was to maintain order. The priests St Luke refers to here would have been those who were on for this particular week and were responsible for the day-to-day affairs of the temple.

c. Or *child*

Address to the Sanhedrin

Acts 5:21 5 On the morrow their rulers and elders and scribes were gathered
Lk 3:2 together in Jerusalem, 6 with Annas the high priest and Caiaphas
and John and Alexander, and all who were of the high-priestly
Mt 21:23 family. 7 And when they had set them in the midst, they inquired,
Lk 20:2 "By what power or by what name did you do this?" 8 Then Peter,
Mt 10:19–20 filled with the Holy Spirit, said to them, "Rulers of the people and
elders, 9 if we are being examined today concerning a good deed

---

4:5–7. These three groups—rulers, elders, scribes—made up the Sanhedrin, the same tribunal as had recently judged and condemned our Lord (cf. the note on Mt 2:4). Jesus' words are already being fulfilled: "'A servant is not greater than his master.' If they persecuted me, they will persecute you" (Jn 15:20).

Annas was not in fact the high priest at this time, but the title was applied to him along with Caiaphas because of the authority he still wielded: he had been high priest and five of his sons succeeded him in the office, as well as Caiaphas, his son-in-law (cf. Flavius Josephus, *Jewish Antiquities*, 20, 198f).

4:8–12. The apostles' confidence and joy is quite remarkable, as is their outspokenness in asserting that "we cannot but speak of what we have seen and heard" (v. 20). "This is the glorious freedom of the children of God. Christians who let themselves be browbeaten or become inhibited or envious in the face of the licentious behaviour of those who do not accept the Word of God, show that they have a very poor idea of the faith. If we truly fulfil the law of Christ—that is, if we make the effort to do so, for we will not always fully succeed—we will find ourselves endowed with a wonderful gallantry of spirit" (St Josemaría Escrivá, *Friends of God*, 38).

Christians have a duty to confess their faith where silence would mean its implicit denial, disrespect for religion, an offence against God or scandal to their neighbour. Thus Vatican II: "Christians should approach those who are outside wisely, 'in the Holy Spirit, genuine love, truthful speech' (2 Cor 6:6–7), and should strive, even to the shedding of their blood, to spread the light of life with all confidence (cf. Acts 4:29) and apostolic courage. The disciple has a grave obligation to Christ, his Master, to grow daily in his knowledge of the truth he has received from him, to be faithful in announcing it and vigorous in defending it" (*Dignitatis humanae*, 14).

Pope Paul VI asked Catholics to check on any weak points in their faith, including ignorance and human respect, "that is, shame or timidness in professing their faith. We are not speaking of that discretion or reserve which in a pluralist and profane society like ours avoids certain signs of religion when with others. We are referring to weakness, to failure to profess one's own religious ideas for fear of ridicule, criticism or others' reactions […] and which is a cause—perhaps the main cause—of the abandonment of faith by people who simply conform to whatever new environment they find themselves in" (General Audience, 19 June 1968).

4:8. Even in the very early days of Christianity Jesus' prediction is borne out: "Beware of men; for they will deliver you up to councils […]. When

done to a cripple, by what means this man has been healed, [10]be it Acts 3:16
known to you all, and to all the people of Israel, that by the name
of Jesus Christ of Nazareth, whom you crucified, whom God Ps 118:22
raised from the dead, by him this man is standing before you well. Mt 21:42 1 Pet 2:4–7
[11]This is the stone which was rejected by you builders, but which Mt 1:21
has become the head of the corner. [12]And there is salvation in no Jn 1:12 Acts 2:21
one else, for there is no other name under heaven given among Lk 21:12–15
men by which we must be saved." Jn 7:15

---

they deliver you up, do not be anxious how you are to speak or what you are to say; for what you are to say will be given to you in that hour; for it is not you who speak, but the Spirit of your Father speaking through you" (Mt 10:17–20).

4:10. "Whom God raised from the dead": St Peter once again bears witness to the resurrection of Jesus, the central truth of apostolic preaching; he uses here the same words as he did at Pentecost. These are compatible with our holding that Jesus "rose by his own power on the third day" (Paul VI, *Creed of the People of God*, 12). The power by which Christ rose was that of his divine Person, to which both his soul and his body remained joined even after death separated them. "The divine power and operation of the Father and of the Son is one and the same; hence it follows that Christ rose by the power of the Father and by his own power" (St Thomas Aquinas, *Summa theologiae*, 3, 53, 4).

"By the word 'Resurrection'," the *Pius V Catechism* explains, "we are not merely to understand that Christ was raised from the dead, which happened to many others, but that he rose by his own power and virtue, a singular prerogative peculiar to him alone. For it is incompatible with nature and was never given to man to raise himself by his own power, from death to life. This was reserved for the almighty power of God [...]. We sometimes, it is true, read in Scripture that he was raised by the Father; but this refers to him as man, just as those passages on the other hand, which say that he rose by his own power, relate to him as God" (1, 6, 8).

4:11. St Peter applies the words of Psalm 118:22 to Jesus, conscious no doubt that our Lord had referred to himself as the stone rejected by the builders which had become the cornerstone, the stone which keeps the whole structure together (cf. Mt 21:42 and par.).

4:12. Invocation of the name of Jesus is all-powerful because this is our Saviour's own name (cf. the note on Mt 1:21). Our Lord himself told his apostles this: "If you ask anything of the Father, he will give it to you in my name" (Jn 16:23), and they, trusting in this promise, work miracles and obtain conversions "in the name of Jesus." Today—as ever—the power of this name will work wonders in the souls of those who call upon him. Blessed Escrivá gives this advice: "Don't be afraid to call our Lord by his name—Jesus—and to tell him that you love him" (*The Way*, 303); and the Divine Office invites us to pray: "God our Father, you are calling us to prayer, at the same hour as the apostles went up to the Temple. Grant that the prayer we offer with sincere hearts in the name of Jesus may bring salvation to all who call upon that holy name" (Week 1, Monday afternoon).

[13]Now when they saw the boldness of Peter and John, and perceived that they were uneducated, common men, they wondered;
and they recognized that they had been with Jesus. [14]But seeing
the man that had been healed standing beside them, they had
nothing to say in opposition. [15]But when they had commanded
them to go aside out of the council, they conferred with one
Jn 11:47 another, [16]saying, "What shall we do with these men? For that a
notable sign has been performed through them is manifest to all
the inhabitants of Jerusalem, and we cannot deny it. [17]But in order
that it may spread no further among the people, let us warn them
to speak no more to any one in this name." [18]So they called them
and charged them not to speak or teach at all in the name of Jesus.
Acts 5:29 [19]But Peter and John answered them, "Whether it is right in the
sight of God to listen to you rather than to God, you must judge;

4:13. The members of the Sanhedrin are surprised by Peter's confidence and by the way these men, who are not well versed in the Law, are able to use Holy Scripture. "Did not the apostles," Chrysostom asks in admiration, "poor and without earthly weapons, enter into battle against enemies who were fully armed …? Without experience, without skill of the tongue, they fought against experts in rhetoric and the language of the academies" (*Hom. on Acts*, 4).

4:18–20. In one of his homilies John Paul II gives us a practical commentary on this passage, which helps us see the right order of priorities and give pride of place to the things of God: "Whereas the elders of Israel charge the apostles not to speak about Christ, God, on the other hand, does not allow them to remain silent. […] In Peter's few sentences we find a full testimony to the Resurrection of the Lord. […] The word of the living God addressed to men obliges us more than any other human commandment or purpose. This word carries with it the supreme eloquence of truth, it carries the authority of God himself. […]

"Peter and the apostles are before the Sanhedrin. They are completely and absolutely certain that God himself has spoken in Christ, and has spoken definitively through his Cross and Resurrection. Peter and the apostles to whom this truth was directly given—as also those who in their time received the Holy Spirit—must bear witness *to it*.

"*Believing* means accepting with complete conviction the truth that comes from God, drawing support from the grace of the Holy Spirit 'whom God has given to those who obey him' (Acts 5:32) to accept what God has revealed and what comes to us through the Church in its living transmission, that is, in tradition. The organ of this tradition is the teaching of Peter and of the apostles and of their successors.

"Believing means accepting their testimony in the Church, who guards this deposit from generation to generation, and then—basing oneself upon it—expounding this same truth, with identical certainty and interior conviction.

"Over the centuries the sanhedrins change which seek to impose silence, abandonment or distortion of this truth. The *sanhedrins of the contemporary world* are many and of all types. These

20for we cannot but speak of what we have seen and heard." 21And 1 Cor 9:16
when they had further threatened them, they let them go, finding 2 Tim 1:7–8
no way to punish them, because of the people; for all men praised
God for what had happened. 22For the man on whom this sign of
healing was performed was more than forty years old.

The Church's thanksgiving prayer

23When they were released they went to their friends and reported Ex 20:11
what the chief priests and the elders had said to them. 24And when Ps 146:6
they heard it, they lifted their voices together to God and said, Is 37:16
"Sovereign Lord, who didst make the heaven and the earth and Jer 32:17
the sea and everything in them, 25who by the mouth of our father Rev 10:6
David, thy servant,[c] didst say by the Holy Spirit,

---

sanhedrins are each and every person who rejects divine truth; they are systems of human thought, of human knowledge; they are the various *conceptions of the world* and also the various programmes of human behaviour; they are also the different *forms of pressure* used by so-called public opinion, mass civilization, media of social communication, which are materialist or secular agnostic or anti-religious; they are, finally, certain contemporary *systems of government* which— if they do not totally deprive citizens of scope to profess the faith—at least limit that scope in different ways, marginalize believers and turn them into second-class citizens … and against all these modern types of the sanhedrin of that time, the response of faith is always the same: 'We must obey God rather than men' (Acts 5:29)" (Homily, 20 April 1980).

4:24–30. This prayer of the apostles and the community provides Christians with a model of reliance on God's help. They ask God to give them the strength they need to continue to proclaim the Word boldly and not be intimidated by persecution, and they also entreat him to accredit their preaching by enabling them to work signs and wonders.

The prayer includes some prophetic verses of Psalm 2 which find their fulfilment in Jesus Christ. The Psalm begins by referring to earthly rulers plotting against God and his Anointed. Jesus himself experienced this opposition, as the apostles do now and as the Church does throughout history. When we hear the clamour of the forces of evil, still striving to "burst their bonds asunder, and cast their cords from us" (v. 3), we should put our trust in the Lord, who "has them in derision. […] He will speak to them in his wrath, and terrify them in his fury" (vv. 4–5); in this way we make it possible for God's message to be heard by everyone: "Now, therefore, O kings, be wise; be warned, O rulers of the earth. Serve the Lord with fear, with trembling kiss his feet … Blessed are all who take refuge in him" (vv. 10–12).

Meditation on this psalm has been a source of comfort to Christians in all ages, filling them with confidence in the Lord's help: "Ask of me, and I will make the nations your heritage, and the ends of the earth your possession" (v. 8).

c. Or *child*

Ps 2:1–2 'Why did the Gentiles rage,
and the peoples imagine vain things?
26 The kings of the earth set themselves in array,
and the rulers were gathered together,
against the Lord and against his Anointed'—[e]
Lk 23:12 27 for truly in this city there were gathered together against thy
Mt 3:16 Acts 10:38 holy servant[c] Jesus, whom thou didst anoint, both Herod and
Acts 2:23 Pontius Pilate, with the Gentiles, and the peoples of Israel, 28 to do
whatever thy hand and thy plan had predestined to take place.
Eph 6:19 29 And now, Lord, look upon their threats, and grant to thy servants[f] to speak thy word with all boldness, 30 while thou stretchest
out thy hand to heal, and signs and wonders are performed

4:31. The Holy Spirit chose to demonstrate his presence visibly in order to encourage the nascent Church. The shaking that happens here was, St John Chrysostom comments, "a sign of approval. It is an action of God to instil a holy fear in the souls of the apostles, to strengthen them against the threats of senators and priests, and to inspire them with boldness to preach the Gospel. The Church was just beginning and it was necessary to support preaching with wonders, in order the better to win men over. It was a need then but later on it does not occur. … When the earth is shaken, this sometimes is a sign of heaven's wrath, sometimes of favour and providence. At the death of our Saviour the earth shook in protest against the death of its author. … But the shaking where the apostles were gathered together was a sign of God's goodness, for the result was that they were filled with the Holy Spirit" (*Hom. on Acts*, 11).

4:32–37. Here we are given a second summary of the life of the first Christian community—which, presided over by Peter and the other apostles, was *the Church*, the entire Church of Jesus Christ.

The Church of God on earth was only beginning, all contained within the Jerusalem foundation. Now every Christian community—no matter how small it be—which is in communion of faith and obedience with the Church of Rome is the Church.

"The Church of Christ", Vatican II teaches, "is really present in all legitimately organized local groups of the faithful, which, in so far as they are united to their pastors, are also quite appropriately called churches in the New Testament. … In them the faithful are gathered together through the preaching of the Gospel of Christ, and the mystery of the Lord's Supper is celebrated. … In each altar community, under the sacred ministry of the bishop, a manifest symbol is to be seen of that charity and 'unity of the mystical body, without which there can be no salvation' (*Summa theologiae*, 3, 73, 3). In these communities, though they may often be small and poor, or existing in the diaspora, Christ is present through whose power and influence the one, holy, catholic and apostolic Church is constituted" (*Lumen gentium*, 26).

4:32. The text stresses the importance of "being one": solidarity, unity, is a virtue of good Christians and one of the marks

e. Or *Christ* **f.** Or *slaves*

through the name of thy holy servant[c] Jesus." 31And when they
had prayed, the place in which they were gathered together was
shaken; and they were all filled with the Holy Spirit and spoke the
word of God with boldness.

The way of life of the early Christians

32Now the company of those who believed were of one heart and Jn 17:11–21
soul, and no one said that any of the things which he possessed Phil 1:27 Acts 2:44
was his own, but they had everything in common.* 33And with Acts 1:8, 22
great power the apostles gave their testimony to the resurrection
of the Lord Jesus, and great grace was upon them all. 34There was Deut 15:7–8
not a needy person among them, for as many as were possessors Lk 12:33 Acts 9:27

---

of the Church: "The apostles bore witness to the Resurrection not only by word but also by their virtues" (St John Chrysostom, *Hom. on Acts*, 11). The disciples obviously were joyful and self-sacrificed. This disposition, which results from charity, strives to promote forgiveness and harmony among the brethren, all sons and daughters of the same Father. The Church realizes that this harmony is often threatened by rancour, envy, misunderstanding and self-assertion. By asking, in prayers and hymns like *Ubi caritas*, for evil disputes and conflicts to cease, "so that Christ our God may dwell among us", it is drawing its inspiration from the example of unity and charity left it by the first Christian community in Jerusalem.

Harmony and mutual understanding among the disciples both reflects the internal and external unity of the Church itself and helps its practical implementation.

There is only one Church of Jesus Christ because it has only "one Lord, one faith, one baptism" (Eph 4:5), and only one visible head—the Pope—who represents Christ on earth. The model and ultimate source of this unity is the Trinity of divine Persons, that is, "the unity of one God, the Father and the Son in the Holy Spirit" (Vatican II, *Unitatis redintegratio*, 2). This characteristic work of the Church is visibly expressed: in confession of one and the same faith, in one system of government, in the celebration of the same form of divine worship, and in fraternal concord among all God's family (cf. ibid.).

The Church derives its life from the Holy Spirit; a main factor in nourishing this life and thereby reinforcing the Church's unity is the Blessed Eucharist: it acts in a mysterious but real way, incessantly, to build up the mystical body of the Lord.

God desires all Christians separated from the Church (they have Baptism, and the Gospel truths in varying degrees) to find their way to the flock of Christ—which they can do by spiritual renewal, and prayer, dialogue and study.

4:34–35. St Luke comes back again to the subject of renunciation of possessions, repeating what he says in 2:44 and going on to give two different kinds of example—that of Barnabas (4:36f) and that of Ananias and Sapphira (5:1f).

The disciples' detachment from material things does not only mean that they

c. Or *child*

Acts 11:22–30; 12:25; 13:1—15:39 1 Cor 9:6 Gal 2:1–13 Col 4:10

of lands or houses sold them, and brought the proceeds of what
was sold 35 and laid it at the apostles' feet; and distribution was
made to each as any had need. 36 Thus Joseph who was surnamed
by the apostles Barnabas (which means, Son of encouragement),
a Levite, a native of Cyprus, 37 sold a field which belonged to him,
and brought the money and laid it at the apostles' feet.

Deception by Ananias and Sapphira

5 1 But a man named Ananias with his wife Sapphira sold a piece
Acts 4:35, 37 of property, 2 and with his wife's knowledge he kept back some
of the proceeds, and brought only a part and laid it at the apostles'
Lk 22:3 feet. 3 But Peter said, "Ananias, why has Satan filled your heart to
lie to the Holy Spirit and to keep back part of the proceeds of the
land? 4 While it remained unsold, did it not remain your own? And
after it was sold, was it not at your disposal? How is it that you
have contrived this deed in your heart? You have not lied to men
Acts 5:11; 19:17 but to God." 5 When Ananias heard these words, he fell down and

---

have a caring attitude to those in need. It also shows their simplicity of heart, their desire to pass unnoticed and the full confidence they place in the Twelve. "They gave up their possessions and in doing so demonstrated their respect for the apostles. For they did not presume to give it into their hands, that is, they did not present it ostentatiously, but left it at their feet and made the apostles its owners and dispensers" (St John Chrysostom, *Hom. on Acts*, 11).

The text suggests that the Christians in Jerusalem had an organized system for the relief of the poor in the community. Judaism had social welfare institutions and probably the early Church used one of these as a model. However, the Christian system of helping each according to his need would have had characteristics of its own, deriving from the charity from which it sprang and as a result of gradual differentiation from the Jewish way of doing things.

4:36–37. Barnabas is mentioned because of his generosity and also in view of his important future role in the spreading of the Gospel. It will be he who introduces the new convert Saul to the apostles (9:27). Later, the apostles will send him to Antioch when the Christian church begins to develop there (11:22). He will be Paul's companion on his first journey (13:2) and will go up to Jerusalem with him in connexion with the controversy about circumcising Gentile converts (15:2). St Paul praises Barnabas' zeal and selflessness in the cause of the Gospel (cf. 1 Cor 9:6).

5:1–11. Ananias hypocritically pretended that he had given all the money from the sale of the land to the community welfare fund, whereas in fact he kept part of it, and his wife went along with him on that. No one was obliged to sell his property or give it to the apostles: people who did so acted with complete freedom. Ananias was free to sell the land or not, and to give all or part of the proceeds to help needy brethren. But he had no right to disguise his greed as charity and try to deceive God and the Church.

died. And great fear came upon all who heard of it. 6The young
men rose and wrapped him up and carried him out and buried
him.
7After an interval of about three hours his wife came in, not
knowing what had happened. 8And Peter said to her, "Tell me
whether you sold the land for so much." And she said, "Yes, for so
much." 9But Peter said to her, "How is it that you have agreed 1 Cor 10:9;
together to tempt the Spirit of the Lord? Hark, the feet of those 11:30–32
that have buried your husband are at the door, and they will carry
you out." 10Immediately she fell down at his feet and died. When
the young men came in they found her dead, and they carried her
out and buried her beside her husband. 11And great fear came Lk 1:12
upon the whole church,* and upon all who heard of these things.

Growth of the Church

12Now many signs and wonders were done among the people by Acts 2:19, 46
the hands of the apostles. And they were all together in Solomon's

---

God punished Ananias and Sapphira, St Ephrem says, "not only because they stole something and concealed it, but because they did not fear and sought to deceive those in whom dwelt the Holy Spirit who knows everything" (*Armenian Commentary on Acts*, ad loc.). By their hypocritical attitude Ananias and Sapphira show their greed and particularly their vainglory. The severe punishment they receive befits the circumstances: the Church was in a foundational period, when people had a special responsibility to be faithful and God was specially supportive.

"This fault could not have been treated lightly", St John Chrysostom explains; "like a gangrene it had to be cut out, before it infected the rest of the body. As it is, both the man himself benefits in that he is not left to advance further in wickedness, and the rest of the disciples, in that they were made more vigilant" (*Hom. on Acts*, 12). Some Fathers (cf. St Augustine, *Sermons*, 148, 1) think that God's punishment was that of physical death, not eternal reprobation.

This episode shows once again how much God detests hypocrisy; and from it we can appreciate the virtue of truthfulness. Veracity inclines people to bring what they say and what they do into line with their knowledge and convictions and to be people of their word. It is closely connected to the virtue of fidelity, which helps one to stay true to promises made (cf. *Summa theologiae*, 2–2, 80, 1). Only the truthful person, the faithful person, can keep the Lord's commandment: "Let what you say be simply 'Yes' or 'No'" (Mt 5:37).

5:12–16. In this third summary (cf. 2:42–47 and 4:32–37) of the lifestyle of the first community St Luke refers particularly to the apostles' power to work miracles. These miracles confirm to the people that the Kingdom of God has in fact come among them. Grace abounds and it shows its presence by spiritual conversions and physical cures. These "signs and wonders" are not done to amaze people or provoke curiosity but to awaken faith.

Portico. [13]None of the rest dared join them, but the people held
them in high honour. [14]And more than ever believers were added
Mk 6:56 to the Lord, multitudes both of men and women, [15]so that they
Acts 19:11–12 even carried out the sick into the streets, and laid them on beds
and pallets, that as Peter came by at least his shadow might fall on
Acts 8:6–7 some of them. [16]The people also gathered from the towns around
Jerusalem, bringing the sick and those afflicted with unclean spir-
its, and they were all healed.

The apostles are arrested and miraculously freed

Acts 4:1–6; 13:45 [17]But the high priest rose up and all who were with him, that is,
the party of the Sadducees, and filled with jealousy [18]they arrested
Acts 12:7 the apostles and put them in the common prison. [19]But at night an
angel of the Lord opened the prison doors and brought them out
Acts 7:38; 13:26 and said, [20]"Go and stand in the temple and speak to the people all
Phil 2:16 1 Jn 1:1 the words of this Life."* [21]And when they heard this, they entered
Acts 4:5 the temple at daybreak and taught.

Now the high priest came and those who were with him and
called together the council and all the senate of Israel, and sent to

---

Miracles always accompany God's revelation to men; they are part of that revelation. They are not simply a bending of the laws of nature: they are a kind of advance sign of the glorious transformation which the world will undergo at the end of time. Thus, just as a sinner, when he repents, obeys God without ceasing to be free, so matter can be changed if its Creator so ordains, without undermining or destroying its own laws.

Miracles are a form of accreditation God gives to the Gospel message: they are actions of God in support of the truth of his messengers' preaching. "If they had not worked miracles and wonders," Origen says, "Jesus' disciples could not have moved their hearers to give up their traditional religion for new teachings and truths, and to embrace, at the risk of their lives, the teachings which were being proclaimed to them" (*Against Celsus*, 1, 46). And St Ephraem comments: "The apostles' miracles made the resurrection and ascension of the Lord credible" (*Armenian Commentary*, ad loc.).

Through miracles God speaks to the minds and hearts of those who witness them, inviting them to believe but not forcing their freedom or lessening the merit of their faith. The apostles follow in the footsteps of our Lord, who "supported and confirmed his preaching by miracles to arouse the faith of his hearers and give them assurance, not to coerce them" (Vatican II, *Dignitatis humanae*, 11). If people have the right dispositions they will generally have no difficulty in recognizing and accepting miracles. Common sense and religious instinct tell them that miracles are possible, because all things are subject to God; however, prejudice and resistance to conversion and its implications can blind a person and make him deny something which is quite obvious to a man of good will.

"Since the apostles were all together, the people brought them their sick on beds and pallets. From every quarter fresh tribute of wonder accrued to

the prison to have them brought. [22]But when the officers came,
they did not find them in the prison, and they returned and reported, [23]"We found the prison securely locked and the sentries
standing at the doors, but when we opened it we found no one inside." [24]Now when the captain of the temple and the chief priests
heard these words, they were much perplexed about them, wondering what this would come to. [25]And some one came and told
them, "The men whom you put in prison are standing in the
temple and teaching the people."

The apostles before the Sanhedrin

[26]Then the captain with the officers went and brought them, but Lk 20:19; 22:2
without violence, for they were afraid of being stoned by the
people.
[27]And when they had brought them, they set them before the
council. And the high priest questioned them, [28]saying, "We Mt 27:25
strictly charged you not to teach in this name, yet here you have Acts 4:18
filled Jerusalem with your teaching and you intend to bring this
man's blood upon us." [29]But Peter and the apostles answered, "We Acts 4:19

---

them—from them that believed, from them that were healed, such was the apostles' boldness of speech and the virtuous behaviour of the believers. Although the apostles modestly ascribe these things to Christ, in whose name they acted, their own life and noble conduct also helped to produce this effect" (St John Chrysostom, *Hom. on Acts*, 12).

5:19. In Holy Scripture we meet angels as messengers of God and also as mediators, guardians and ministers of divine justice. Abraham sent his servant on a mission to his kindred and told him, "The Lord will send his angel before you and prosper your way" (Gen 24:7, 40). Tobit, Lot and his family, Daniel and his companions, Judith etc. also experienced the help of angels. The Psalms refer to trust in the angels (cf. Ps 34:7; 91:11–13) and the continuous help they render men in obedience to God's command.

This episode of the freeing of the apostles is one of the examples the *St Pius V Catechism* gives to illustrate "the countless benefits which the Lord distributes among men through angels, his interpreters and ministers, sent not only in isolated cases but appointed from our birth to watch over us, and constituted for the salvation of every individual person" (4, 9, 6).

This means, therefore, that the angels should have a place in a Christian's personal piety: "I ask our Lord that, during our stay on this earth of ours, we may never be parted from our divine travelling companion. To ensure this, let us also become firmer friends of the Holy Guardian Angels. We all need a lot of company, company from heaven and company on earth. Have great devotion to the Holy Angels" (St Josemaría Escrivá, *Friends of God*, 315).

5:29. The apostles' failure to obey the Sanhedrin is obviously not due to pride or to their not knowing their place (as citizens they are subject to the Sanhedrin's

Acts 2:23 Gal 3:13 Acts 2:33; 10:43; 13:38

must obey God rather than men. 30The God of our fathers raised
Jesus whom you killed by hanging him on a tree. 31God exalted
him at his right hand as Leader and Saviour, to give repentance to

---

authority); the Sanhedrin is imposing a ruling which would have them go against God's law and their own conscience.

The apostles humbly and boldly remind their judges that obedience to God comes first. They know that many members of the Sanhedrin are religious men, good Jews who can understand their message; they try not so much to justify themselves as to get the Sanhedrin to react: they are more concerned about their judges' spiritual health than about their own safety. St John Chrysostom comments: "God allowed the apostles to be brought to trial so that their adversaries might be instructed, if they so desired. [...] The apostles are not irritated by the judges; they plead with them compassionately, with tears in their eyes, and their only aim is to free them from error and from divine wrath" (*Hom. on Acts*, 13). They are convinced that "those who fear God are in no danger, only those who do not fear him" (ibid.) and that it is worse to commit injustice than to suffer it. We can see from the apostles' behaviour how deep their convictions run; grace and faith in Jesus Christ have given them high regard for the honour of God. They have begun at last to love and serve God without counting the cost. This is true Christian maturity. "In that cry *Serviam!* [I will serve!] you express your determination to 'serve' the Church of God most faithfully, even at the cost of fortune, of reputation and of life" (St Josemaría Escrivá, *The Way*, 519).

The Church often prays to God to give its children this resilience: they need it because there is always the danger of growing indifferent and of abandoning the faith to some extent. "Lord, fill us with that spirit of courage which gave your martyr Sebastian," his feast's liturgy says, "strength to offer his life in faithful witness. Help us to learn from him to cherish your law and to obey you rather than men" (*Roman Missal*).

A Christian should conform his behaviour to God's law: that law should be his very life. He should obey and love God's commandments as taught by the Church, if he wishes to live a truly human life. The law of God is not something burdensome: it is a way of freedom, as Sacred Scripture is at pains to point out: "The Lord is my portion, I promise to keep thy words. I entreat thy favour with all my heart; be gracious to me according to thy promise. When I think of thy ways, I turn my feet to thy testimonies; I hasten and do not delay to keep thy commandments. Though the cords of the wicked ensnare me, I do not forget thy law. At midnight I rise to praise thee, because of thy righteous ordinances. I am a companion of all who fear thee, of those who keep thy precepts. The earth, O Lord, is full of thy steadfast love; teach me thy statutes" (Ps 119:57–64).

Conscience, which teaches man in the depths of his heart, gradually shows him what the law of God involves: "Man has in his heart a law inscribed by God. His dignity lies in observing this law, and by it he will be judged (cf. Rom 2:15–16). His conscience is man's most secret core, and his sanctuary. There he is alone with God, whose voice echoes in his depths. By conscience, in a wonderful way, that law is made known. [...] The more a correct conscience prevails, the more do persons and groups turn aside from blind choice and try to be guided by the objective standards of moral conduct" (Vatican II, *Gaudium et spes*, 16).

Israel and forgiveness of sins. 32And we are witnesses to these things, and so is the Holy Spirit whom God has given to those who obey him." Lk 24:48 Jn 7:39; 15:26–27

Good and evil are facts of life. A person can identify them. There are such things as good actions—and there are evil actions, which should always be avoided. The goodness or badness of human actions is not essentially dependent on the circumstances, although sometimes these can affect it to some extent.

Like the eye, conscience is designed to enable a person to see, but it needs light from outside (God's law and the Church's guidance) to discover religious and moral truths and properly appreciate them. Without that help man simply tires himself out in his search; he seeks only himself and forgets about good and evil, and his conscience becomes darkened by sin and moral opportunism.

"With respect to conscience," Paul VI teaches, "an objection can arise: Is conscience not enough on its own as the norm of our conduct? Do the decalogues, the codes, imposed on us from outside, not undermine conscience [...]? This is a delicate and very current problem. Here all we will say is that subjective conscience is the first and immediate norm of our conduct, but it needs light, it needs to see which standard it should follow, especially when the action in question does not evidence its own moral exigencies. Conscience needs to be instructed and trained about what is the best choice to make, by the authority of a law" (General Audience, 28 March 1973).

A right conscience, which always goes hand in hand with moral prudence, will help a Christian to obey the law like a good citizen and also to take a stand, personally or in association with others, against any unjust laws which may be proposed or enacted. The State is not almighty in the sphere of law. It may not order or permit anything it likes; therefore not everything legal is morally lawful or just. Respect due to civil authority—which is part of the Gospel message and has always been taught by the Church—should not prevent Christians and people of good will from opposing legislators and rulers when they legislate and govern in a way that is contrary of the law of God and therefore to the common good. Obviously, this legitimate kind of resistance to authority should always involve the use of lawful methods.

It is not enough for good Christians to profess *privately* the teaching of the Gospel and the Church regarding human life, the family, education, freedom etc. They should realize that these are subjects of crucial importance for the welfare of their country, and they should strive, using all the usual means at their disposal, to see that the laws of the State are supportive of the common good. Passivity towards ideologies and stances that run counter to Christian values is quite deplorable.

5:30. "Hanging him on a tree": this is reminiscent of Deuteronomy 21:23: if a criminal is put to death "and you hang him on a tree, his body shall not remain all night upon the tree, but you shall bury him the same day, for a hanged man is accursed by God." This is a reference to crucifixion, a form of capital punishment which originated in Persia; it was common throughout the East and was later adopted by the Romans.

5:32. God sends the Holy Spirit to those who obey him, and, in turn, the apostles

33When they heard this they were enraged and wanted to kill
them.

Gamaliel's intervention

Acts 22:3 34But a Pharisee in the council named Gamaliel,* a teacher of the
law, held in honour by all the people, stood up and ordered the
men to be put outside for a while. 35And he said to them, "Men of
Israel, take care what you do with these men. 36For before these
days Theudas arose, giving himself out to be somebody, and a
number of men, about four hundred, joined him; but he was slain
and all who followed him were dispersed and came to nothing.
Lk 2:2 37After him Judas the Galilean arose in the days of the census and
drew away some of the people after him; he also perished, and all
who followed him were scattered. 38So in the present case I tell
2 Mac 7:19 you, keep away from these men and let them alone; for if this plan
Mt 15:13 or this undertaking is of men, it will fail; 39but if it is of God, you

---

obey the indications of the Spirit with complete docility.

If we are to obey the Holy Spirit and do what he asks us, we need to cultivate him and listen to what he says. "Get to know the Holy Spirit, the Great Stranger, on whom depends your sanctification.

"Don't forget that you are God's temple. The Advocate is in the centre of your soul: listen to him and be docile to his inspirations" (St Josemaría Escrivá, *The Way*, 57).

5:34–39. Gamaliel had been St Paul's teacher (cf. 22:3). He belonged to a moderate grouping among the Pharisees. He was a prudent man, impartial and religiously minded. The Fathers of the Church often propose him as an example of an upright man who is awaiting the Kingdom of God and dares to defend the apostles.

"Gamaliel does not say that the undertaking is of man or of God; he recommends that they let time decide. […] By speaking in the absence of the apostles he was better able to win over the judges. The gentleness of his word and arguments, based on justice, convinced them. He was almost preaching the Gospel. Indeed, his language is so correct that he seemed to be saying: Be convinced of it: you cannot destroy this undertaking. How is it that you do not believe? The Christian message is so impressive that even its adversaries bear witness to it" (St John Chrysostom, *Hom. on Acts*, 14).

This commentary seems to be recalling our Lord's words, "He that is not against us is for us" (Mk 9:40). Certainly, Gamaliel's intervention shows that a person with good will can discern God's action in events or at least investigate objectively without prejudging the issue.

The revolts of Theudas and Judas are referred to by Flavius Josephus (cf. *Jewish Antiquities*, 18, 4–10; 20, 169–172), but the dates he gives are vague; apparently these events occurred around the time of Jesus' birth. Both Theudas and Judas had considerable following; they revolted against the chosen people having to pay tribute to foreigners such as Herod and Imperial Rome.

will not be able to overthrow them. You might even be found opposing God!"

The apostles are flogged

[40]So they took his advice, and when they had called in the apos- Mt 10:17
tles, they beat them and charged them not to speak in the name of Acts 22:19
Jesus, and let them go. [41]Then they left the presence of the coun- Mt 5:10–12
cil, rejoicing that they were counted worthy to suffer dishonour 1 Pet 4:13–14
for the name. [42]And every day in the temple and at home they did Acts 18:5
not cease teaching and preaching Jesus as the Christ.

4. THE "DEACONS". ST STEPHEN

Appointment of the seven deacons

6 [1]Now in these days when the disciples were increasing in number, the Hellenists* murmured against the Hebrews

---

5:40–41. Most members of the Sanhedrin are unimpressed by Gamaliel's arguments; they simply decide to go as far as they safely can: they do not dare to condemn the apostles to death; but, in their stubborn opposition to the Gospel message, they decree that they be put under the lash in the hope that this will keep them quiet. However, it has just the opposite effect.

"It is true that Jeremiah was scourged for the word of God, and that Elijah and and other prophets were also threatened, but in this case the apostles, as they did earlier by their miracles, showed forth the power of God. He does not say that they did not suffer, but that they rejoiced over having to suffer. This we can see from their boldness afterwards: immediately after being beaten they went back to preaching" (St John Chrysostom, *Hom. on Acts*, 14).

The apostles must have remembered our Lord's words, "Blessed are you when men revile you and persecute you and utter all kinds of evil against you falsely on my account. Rejoice and be glad, for your reward is great in heaven, for so men persecuted the prophets who were before you" (Mt 5:11–12).

5:42. The apostles and the first disciples of Jesus were forever preaching, with the result that very soon all Jerusalem was filled with their teaching (cf. v. 28). These early brethren are an example to Christians in every age: zeal to attract others to the faith is a characteristic of every true disciple of Jesus and a consequence of love of God and love for others: "You have but little love if you are not zealous for the salvation of all souls. You have but poor love if you are not eager to inspire other apostles with your craziness" (St Josemaría Escrivá, *The Way*, 796).

6:1–6. A new section of the book begins at this point. It is introduced by reference to two groups in the early community, identified by their background prior to their conversion—the Hellenists and the Hebrews. From this chapter onwards, Christians are referred to as "disciples";

because their widows were neglected in the daily distribution.
Ex 18:17–23 2And the twelve summoned the body of the disciples and said, "It
is not right that we should give up preaching the word of God to

---

in other words this term is no longer applied only to the apostles and to those who were adherents of Jesus during his life on earth: all the baptized are "disciples". Jesus is the Lord of his Church and the Teacher of all: after his ascension into heaven he teaches, sanctifies and governs Christians through the ministry of the apostles, initially, and after the apostles' death, through the ministry of their successors, the Pope and the Bishops, who are aided by priests.

Hellenists were Jews who had been born and lived for a time outside Palestine. They spoke Greek and had synagogues of their own where the Greek translation of Scripture was used. They had a certain amount of Greek culture; the Hebrews would have also had some, but not as much. The Hebrews were Jews born in Palestine; they spoke Aramaic and used the Hebrew Bible in their synagogues. This difference of backgrounds naturally carried over into the Christian community during its early years, but it would be wrong to see it as divisive or to imagine that there were two opposed factions in early Christianity. Before the Church was founded there existed in Jerusalem a well-established Hellenist-Jewish community—an influential and sizeable grouping.

This chapter relates the establishment by the apostles of "the seven": this is the second, identifiable group of disciples entrusted with a ministry in the Church, the first being "the twelve".

Although St Luke does not clearly present this group as constituting a holy "order", it is quite clear that the seven have been given a public role in the community, a role which extends beyond distribution of relief. We shall now see Philip and Stephen preaching and baptizing—sharing in some ways in ministry of the apostles, involved in "care of souls".

St Luke uses the term *diakonia* (service), but he does not call the seven "deacons". Nor do later ancient writers imply that these seven were deacons (in the later technical sense of the word)—constituting with priests and Bishops the hierarchy of the Church. Therefore, we do not know for certain whether the diaconate as we know it derives directly from the seven. St John Chrysostom, for example, has doubts about this (cf. *Hom. on Acts*, 14). However, it is at least possible that the ministry described here played a part in the instituting of the diaconate proper.

In any event, the diaconate is a form of sacred office of apostolic origin. At ordination deacons take on an obligation to perform—under the direction of the diocesan bishop—certain duties to do with evangelization, catechesis, organization of liturgical ceremonies, Christian initiation of catechumens and neophytes, and Church charitable and social welfare work.

The Second Vatican Council teaches that "at a lower level of the hierarchy are to be found deacons, who receive the imposition of hands 'not unto the priesthood, but unto the ministry'. For, strengthened by sacramental grace they are dedicated to the people of God, in conjunction with the bishop and his body of priests, in the service of the liturgy, of the Gospel and of works of charity. It pertains to the office of a deacon, in so far as it may be assigned to him by the competent authority, to administer Bapt-

serve tables. [3]Therefore, brethren, pick out from among you seven 1 Tim 3:8–10
men of good repute, full of the Spirit and of wisdom, whom we
may appoint to this duty. [4]But we will devote ourselves to prayer

---

ism solemnly, to be custodian and distributor of the Eucharist, in the name of the Church to assist at and to bless marriages, to bring Viaticum to the dying, to read the Sacred Scripture to the faithful, to instruct and exhort the people, to preside over the worship and the prayer of the faithful, to administer sacramentals, and to officiate at funeral and burial services" (*Lumen gentium*, 29).

6:2–4. The Twelve establish a principle which they consider basic: their apostolic ministry is so absorbing that they have no time to do other things. In this particular case an honorable and useful function—distribution of food—cannot be allowed to get in the way of another even more important task essential to the life of the Church and of each of its members. "They speak of it 'not being right' in order to show that the two duties cannot in this case be made compatible" (St John Chrysostom, *Hom. on Acts*, 14).

The main responsibility of the pastors of the Church is the preaching of the word of God, the administration of the sacraments and the government of the people of God. Any other commitment they take on should be compatible with their pastoral work and supportive of it, in keeping with the example given by Christ: he cured people's physical ailments in order to reach their souls, and he preached justice and peace as signs of the Kingdom of God.

"A mark of our identity which no doubt ought to encroach upon and no objection eclipse is this: as pastors, we have been chosen by the mercy of the Supreme Pastor (cf. 1 Pet 5:4), in spite of our inadequacy, to proclaim with authority the Word of God, to assemble the scattered people of God, to nourish this people on the road to salvation, to maintain it in that unity of which we are, at different levels, active and living instruments, and increasingly to keep this community gathered around Christ faithful to its deepest vocation" (Paul VI, *Evangelii nuntiandi*, 68).

A priest should be avid for the word of God, John Paul II emphasizes; he should embrace it in its entirety, meditate on it, study it assiduously and spread it through his example and preaching (cf., e.g., addresses in Ireland and the United States, 1 October and 3 October 1979 respectively). His whole life should be a generous proclamation of Christ. Therefore, he should avoid the temptation to "temporal leadership: that can easily be a source of division, whereas he should be a sign and promoter of unity and fraternity" (To the priests of Mexico, 27 January 1979).

This passage allows us to see the difference between election and appointment to a ministry in the Church. A person can be elected or designated by the faithful; but power to carry out that ministry (which implies a calling from God) is something he must receive through ordination, which the apostles confer. "The apostles leave it to the body of the disciples to select the [seven], in order that it should not seem that they favour some in preference to others" (St John Chrysostom, *Hom. on Acts*, 14). However, those designated for ordination are not representatives or delegates of the Christian community; they are ministers of God. They have received a calling and, by the imposition of hands, God—not

Acts 8:5; 21:8 and to the ministry of the word." 5And what they said pleased the
whole multitude, and they chose Stephen, a man full of faith and
of the Holy Spirit, and Philip, and Prochorus, and Nicanor, and
Timon, and Parmenas, and Nicolaus, a proselyte of Antioch.
Acts 13:3 6These they set before the apostles, and they prayed and laid their
1 Tim 4:14 2 Tim 1:6 hands upon them.
Acts 12:24; 7And the word of God increased; and the number of the disci-
19:20 ples multiplied greatly in Jerusalem, and a great many of the
priests were obedient to the faith.

Stephen's arrest

8And Stephen, full of grace and power, did great wonders and
signs among the people. 9Then some of those who belonged to the
synagogue of the Freedmen (as it was called), and of the
Lk 21:15 Cyrenians, and of the Alexandrians, and of those from Cilicia and
Acts 1:8 Asia, arose and disputed with Stephen. 10But they could not with-

---

men—gives them a spiritual power which equips them to govern the Christian community, make and administer the sacraments and preach the Word.

Christian pastoral office, that is, the priesthood of the New Testament in its various degrees, does not derive from family relationship, as was the case with the Levitical priesthood in the Old Testament; nor is it a type of commissioning by the community. The initiative lies with the grace of God, who calls whom he chooses.

6:5. All the people chosen have Greek names. One of them is a "proselyte", that is, a pagan who became a Jew through circumcision and observance of the Law of Moses.

6:6. The apostles establish the seven in their office or ministry through prayer and the laying on of hands. This latter gesture is found sometimes in the Old Testament, principally as a rite of ordination of Levites (cf. Num 8:10) and as a way of conferring power and wisdom on Joshua, Moses' successor as leader of Israel (cf. Num 27:20).

Christians have retained this rite, as can be seen quite often in Acts. Sometimes it symbolizes curing (9:12, 17; 28:8), in line with the example given by our Lord in Luke 4:40. It is also a rite of blessing, as when Paul and Barnabas are sent out on their first apostolic journey (13:3); and it is used as a post-baptismal rite for bringing down the Holy Spirit (8:17; 19:6).

In this case it is a rite for the ordination of ministers of the Church—the first instance of sacred ordination reported by Acts (cf. 1 Tim 4:14; 5:22; 2 Tim 5:22). "St Luke is brief. He does not say how they were ordained, but simply that it was done with prayer, because it was an ordination. The hand of a man is laid [upon the person], but the whole work is of God and it is his hand which touches the head of the one ordained" (St John Chrysostom, *Hom. on Acts*, 14).

The essential part of the rite of ordination of deacons is the laying on of hands; this is done in silence, on the candidate's head, and then a prayer is said to God asking him to send the Holy Spirit to the person being ordained.

stand the wisdom and the Spirit with which he spoke. [11]Then they Mt 26:59–66
secretly instigated men, who said, "We have heard him speak
blasphemous words against Moses and God." [12]And they stirred Mt 10:17
up the people and the elders and the scribes, and they came upon
him and seized him, and brought him before the council, [13]and set Jer 26:11
up false witnesses who said, "This man never ceases to speak Acts 21:28
words against this holy place and the law; [14]for we have heard him Mk 14:58
say that this Jesus of Nazareth will destroy this place, and will
change the customs which Moses delivered to us." [15]And gazing
at him, all who sat in the council saw that his face was like the
face of an angel.

Stephen's address to the Sanhedrin

7 [1]And the high priest said, "Is this so?" [2]And Stephen said: Acts 24:9
"Brethren and fathers, hear me. The God of glory appeared to Ps 29:3
our father Abraham, when he was in Mesopotamia, before he

6:7. As in earlier chapters, St Luke here refers to the spread of the Church—this time reporting the conversion of "a great many of the priests." Many scholars think that these would have come from the lower ranks of the priesthood (like Zechariah: cf. Lk 1:5) and not from the great priestly families, which were Sadducees and enemies of the new-born Church (cf. 4:1; 5:17). Some have suggested that these priests may have included members of the Qumran sect. However, the only evidence we have to go on is what St Luke says here.

6:8–14. From the text it would appear that Stephen preached mainly among Hellenist Jews; this was his own background. Reference is made to synagogues of Jews of the Dispersion (Diaspora). These synagogues were used for worship and as meeting places. The very fact that these Hellenist Jews were living in the Holy City shows what devotion they had to the Law of their forebears.

No longer is it only the Sanhedrin who are opposed to the Gospel; other Jews have been affected by misunderstanding and by misrepresentation of the Christian message.

The charge of blasphemy—also made against our Lord—was the most serious that could be made against a Jew. As happened in Jesus' case, the accusers here resort to producing false witnesses, who twist Stephen's words and accuse him of a crime the penalty for which is death.

6:15. St John Chrysostom, commenting on this verse, recalls that the face of Moses, when he comes down from Sinai (cf. Ex 34:29–35), reflected the glory of God and likewise made the people afraid: "It was grace, it was the glory of Moses. I think that God clothed him in this splendour because perhaps he had something to say, and in order that his very appearance would strike terror into them. For it is possible, very possible, for figures full of heavenly grace to be attractive to friendly eyes and terrifying to the eyes of enemies" (*Hom. on Acts*, 15).

7:1–53. Stephen's discourse is the longest one given in Acts. It is a summary of the

Gen 12:1 lived in Haran, [3]and said to him, 'Depart from your land and from
Gen 11:32; 12:5 your kindred and go into the land which I will show you.' [4]Then
he departed from the land of the Chaldeans, and lived in Haran.
And after his father died, God removed him from there into this
Gen 12:7; 13:15; 17:8 Gal 3:16 land in which you are now living; [5]yet he gave him no inheritance
in it, not even a foot's length, but promised to give it to him in
possession and to his posterity after him, though he had no child.
Gen 15:13–14 Ex 12:40 [6]And God spoke to this effect, that his posterity would be aliens in
a land belonging to others, who would enslave them and ill-treat
Ex 3:12 them four hundred years. [7]'But I will judge the nation which they
serve,' said God, 'and after that they shall come out and worship
Gen 17:10; 21:4 me in this place.' [8]And he gave him the covenant of circumcision.
And so Abraham became the father of Isaac, and circumcised him
on the eighth day; and Isaac became the father of Jacob, and
Jacob of the twelve patriarchs.

Gen 37:11, 28 Wis 10:13 [9]"And the patriarchs, jealous of Joseph, sold him into Egypt;
but God was with him, [10]and rescued him out of all his afflictions,
Gen 39:21; 41:40–41 and gave him favour and wisdom before Pharaoh, king of Egypt,
who made him governor over Egypt and over all his household.
Gen 41:54 [11]Now there came a famine throughout all Egypt and Canaan, and
Gen 42:2 great affliction, and our fathers could find no food. [12]But when
Jacob heard that there was grain in Egypt, he sent forth our fathers
Gen 45:3–16 the first time. [13]And at the second visit Joseph made himself
known to his brothers, and Joseph's family became known to
Gen 46:27 Pharaoh. [14]And Joseph sent and called to him Jacob his father and
Gen 46:6; 49:33 all his kindred, seventy-five souls; [15]and Jacob went down into
Egypt. And he died, himself and our fathers, [16]and they were car-

---

history of Israel, divided into three periods—of the Patriarchs (vv. 1–16), of Moses (vv. 17–43) and of the building of the temple (vv. 44–50). It ends with a short section (vv. 51–53) where he brings his argument together.

One thing that stands out is that Stephen does not defend himself directly. He answers his accusers with a Christian vision of salvation history, in which the temple and the Law have already fulfilled their purpose. He tells them that he continues to respect the Mosaic Law and the temple, but that as a Christian his idea of God's law is more universal and more profound, his concept of the temple more spiritual (for God can be worshipped anywhere in the world). This approach, which respects and perfects the religious values of Judaism (because it probes their true meaning and brings them to fulfilment), is reinforced by the way he presents the figure of Moses. Stephen shows Moses as a "type" of Christ: Christ is the new Moses. Small elucidations of the Greek text of the Old Testament help in this direction: expressions like "they refused" or "deliverer" (v. 35) are not applied to Moses in the books of the Old Testament, but they are used here to suggest Christ. The Israelites' rebellious and aggressive treatment of Moses, who had

ried back to Shechem and laid in the tomb that Abraham had 1 Gen 50:13
bought for a sum of silver from the sons of Hamor in Shechem.
17“But as the time of the promise drew near, which God had Ex 1:7
granted to Abraham, the people grew and multiplied in Egypt 18till
there arose over Egypt another king who had not known Joseph.
19He dealt craftily with our race and forced our fathers to expose Ex 1:10–22
their infants, that they might not be kept alive. 20At this time Ex 2:2
Moses was born, and was beautiful before God. And he was Heb 11:23
brought up for three months in his father’s house; 21and when he Ex 2:5, 10
was exposed, Pharaoh’s daughter adopted him and brought him
up as her own son. 22And Moses was instructed in all the wisdom Lk 24:19
of the Egyptians, and he was mighty in his words and deeds.
23“When he was forty years old, it came into his heart to visit Ex 2:11
his brethren, the sons of Israel. 24And seeing one of them being Ex 2:12
wronged, he defended the oppressed man and avenged him by
striking the Egyptian. 25He supposed that his brethren understood
that God was giving them deliverance by his hand, but they did
not understand. 26And on the following day he appeared to them Ex 2:13
as they were quarrelling and would have reconciled them, saying,
‘Men, you are brethren, why do you wrong each other?’ 27But the Ex 2:14
man who was wronging his neighbour thrust him aside, saying, Lk 12:14
‘Who made you a ruler and a judge over us? 28Do you want to kill
me as you killed the Egyptian yesterday?’ 29At this retort Moses Ex 2:15, 22;
fled, and became an exile in the land of Midian, where he became 18:3
the father of two sons.
30“Now when forty years had passed, an angel appeared to him Ex 3:1–2
in the wilderness of Mount Sinai, in a flame of fire in a bush. Deut 33:16

---

a mission from God, is being repeated—much more seriously—in their rejection of the Gospel.

St John Chrysostom expands on the last words of the discourse in this way: “Is it to be wondered that you do not know Christ, seeing that you did not know Moses, and God himself, who was manifested by such wonders? […] ‘You always resist the Holy Spirit’. […] When you received commandments, you neglected them; when the temple already stood, you worshipped idols” (*Hom. on Acts*, 17). Despite the vigour of his reproaches, Chrysostom has to point out Stephen’s meekness: “he did not abuse them; all he did was remind them of the words of the Prophets” (ibid.).

St Ephrem, however, stresses other aspects of Stephen’s prayer: “Since he knew that the Jews were not going to take his words to heart and were only interested in killing him, full of joy in his soul […] he censured their hardness of heart. […] He discussed circumcision of the flesh, to exalt instead circumcision of the heart which sincerely seeks God, against whom they were in rebellion. In this way he added his own accusations to those of the prophet” (*Armenian Commentary*, ad loc.).

Ex 3:4 31 When Moses saw it he wondered at the sight; and as he drew
Ex 3:6 near to look, the voice of the Lord came, 32 'I am the God of your
Mt 22:32 fathers, the God of Abraham and of Isaac and of Jacob.' And
Ex 2:5 Moses trembled and did not dare to look. 33 And the Lord said to
him, 'Take off the shoes from your feet, for the place where you
Ex 3:7–10 are standing is holy ground. 34 I have surely seen the ill-treatment
of my people that are in Egypt and heard their groaning, and I
have come down to deliver them. And now come, I will send you
to Egypt.'

Ex 2:14 35 "This Moses whom they refused, saying, 'Who made you a
ruler and a judge?' God sent as both ruler and deliverer by the
Ex 7:3; 14:21 hand of the angel that appeared to him in the bush. 36 He led them
Num 14:33 out, having performed wonders and signs in Egypt and at the Red
Deut 18:15 Sea, and in the wilderness for forty years. 37 This is the Moses who
Acts 3:22 said to the Israelites, 'God will raise up for you a prophet from
Ex 19:3 your brethren as he raised me up.' 38 This is he who was in the con-
Deut 4:10; 9:10 Gal 3:19 gregation in the wilderness with the angel who spoke to him at
Heb 2:2 Mount Sinai, and with our fathers; and he received living oracles
Num 14:3 to give to us. 39 Our fathers refused to obey him, but thrust him
Ex 32:1, 23 aside, and in their hearts they turned to Egypt, 40 saying to Aaron,
'Make for us gods to go before us; as for this Moses who led us
out from the land of Egypt, we do not know what has become of
Ex 32:4–6 him.' 41 And they made a calf in those days, and offered a sacrifice
to the idol and rejoiced in the works of their hands. 42 But God
Jer 19:13 turned and gave them over to worship the host of heaven, as it is
Amos 5:25–27 written in the book of the prophets:

'Did you offer to me slain beasts and sacrifices,
forty years in the wilderness, O house of Israel?
43 And you took up the tent of Moloch,
and the star of the god Rephan,

7:42–43. "The host of heaven": Scripture normally uses this expression to refer to the stars, which were worshipped in some ancient religions. God sometimes allowed the Israelites to forget him and worship false gods.

The quotation from "the book of the prophets" to which Stephen refers is from Amos 5:25–27 (which in Acts is taken from the Septuagint Greek). It is not easy to work out what Amos means. We know from the Pentateuch that the Israelites a number of times offered sacrifices to Yahweh when they were in Sinai during the Exodus (cf. Ex 24:4–5; chap. 29; Lev chaps. 8–9; Num chap. 7), but all these sacrifices were offered at the foot of Mount Sinai, before they started out on their long pilgrimage through the wilderness, before they reached the promised land. Perhaps St Stephen is referring to those long years (about forty years) during which nothing is said in the Old Testament about their offering sacrifice to Yahweh. Even during the Exodus—a period when God frequently

the figures which you made to worship;
and I will remove you beyond Babylon.’
44“Our fathers had the tent of witness in the wilderness, even as Ex 25:40
he who spoke to Moses directed him to make it, according to the Heb 8:5
pattern that he had seen. 45Our fathers in turn brought it in with Josh 3:14; 18:1
Joshua when they dispossessed the nations which God thrust out
before our fathers. So it was until the days of David, 46who found 2 Sam 7:2
favour in the sight of God and asked leave to find a habitation for Ps 132:5
the God of Jacob. 47But it was Solomon who built a house for him. 1 Kings 6:1
48Yet the Most High does not dwell in houses made with hands; as Is 66:1
the prophet says, Acts 17:24
49‘Heaven is my throne, Heb 9:11, 24
and earth my footstool.
What house will you build for me, says the Lord,
or what is the place of my rest?
50Did not my hand make all these things?’
51“You stiff-necked people, uncircumcised in heart and ears, Ex 33:3 Is 63:10
you always resist the Holy Spirit. As your fathers did, so do you. Jer 4:4; 6:10;
52Which of the prophets did not your fathers persecute? And they 9:26 Mt 23:31
killed those who announced beforehand the coming of the
Righteous One, whom you have now betrayed and murdered, Acts 3:14
53you who received the law as delivered by angels and did not Acts 7:38
keep it.”

Martyrdom of St Stephen

54Now when they heard these things they were enraged, and they
ground their teeth against him. 55But he, full of the Holy Spirit,
gazed into heaven and saw the glory of God, and Jesus standing at
the right hand of God; 56and he said, “Behold, I see the heavens Dan 7:13
opened, and the Son of man standing at the right hand of God.” Lk 22:69

---

showed his special favour—the Israelites strayed from Yahweh.

7:55–56. “It is clear”, St Ephrem comments, “that those who suffer for Christ enjoy the glory of the whole Trinity. Stephen saw the Father and Jesus at his side, because Jesus appears only to his own, as was the case with the apostles after the Resurrection. While the champion of the faith stood there helpless in the midst of those who had killed the Lord, just at the point when the first martyr was to be crowned, he saw the Lord, holding a crown in his right hand, as if to encourage him to conquer death and to show that he inwardly helps those who are about to die on his account. He therefore reveals what he sees, that is, the heavens opened, which were closed to Adam and only opened to Christ at the Jordan, but open now after the Cross to all those who share Christ’s sufferings, and in the first instance open to this man. See how Stephen reveals why his face was lit up: it was because he was on the

[57]But they cried out with a loud voice and stopped their ears and
Acts 22:20 rushed together upon him. [58]Then they cast him out of the city and
stoned him; and the witnesses laid down their garments at the feet
Ps 31:5 of a young man named Saul. [59]And as they were stoning Stephen,
Lk 23:46 he prayed, "Lord Jesus, receive my spirit." [60]And he knelt down
Lk 23:34 and cried with a loud voice, "Lord, do not hold this sin against
them." And when he had said this, he fell asleep. [1a]And Saul was
consenting to his death.

---

point of contemplating this wondrous mission. That is why he took on the appearance of an angel—so that his testimony might be more reliable" (*Armenian Commentary*, ad loc.).

7:57–59. The cursory trial of Stephen ends without any formal sentence of death: this Jewish tribunal was unable to pass such sentences because the Romans restricted its competence. In any event no sentence proves necessary: the crowd becomes a lynching party; it takes over and proceeds to stone Stephen, with the tacit approval of the Sanhedrin.

Tradition regards Stephen as the first Christian martyr, an example of fortitude and suffering for love of Christ. "Could you keep all God's commandments," St Cyprian asks, "were it not for the strength of patience? That was what enabled Stephen to hold out: in spite of being stoned he did not call down vengeance on his executioners, but rather forgiveness. … How fitting it was for him to be Christ's first martyr, so that by being, through his glorious death, the model of all the martyrs that would come after him, he should not only be a preacher of the Lord's Passion, but should also imitate it in his meekness and immense patience" (*De bono patientiae*, 16).

Martyrdom is a supreme act of bravery and of true prudence, but to the world it makes no sense. It is also an expression of humility, because a martyr does not act out of bravado or overweening self-confidence; he is a weak man like anyone else, but God's grace gives him the strength he needs. Although martyrdom is something which happens rarely, it does show Christians what human nature can rise to if God gives it strength, and it establishes a standard, both real and symbolic, for the behaviour of every disciple of Christ.

"Since all the virtues and the perfection of all righteousness are born of love of God and one's neighbour," St Leo says, "in no one is this love more worthily found than in the blessed martyrs, who are nearest to our Lord in terms of imitation of both his charity and his Passion.

"The martyrs have been of great help to others, because the Lord has availed of the very strength as he granted them to ensure that the pain of death and the cruelty of the Cross do not frighten any of his own, but are seen as things in which man can imitate him ….

"No example is more useful for the instruction of the people of God than that of the martyrs. Eloquence is effective for entreating, argument for convincing; but examples are worth more than words, and it is better to teach by deeds than by speech" (*Hom. on the feast of St Laurence*).

The Second Vatican Council has reminded us of the excellence of martyrdom as a form of witness to the faith. Although there are heroic ways of imitat-

PART TWO

The Church spreads beyond Jerusalem

5. THE CHURCH IN SAMARIA

Persecution of the Church

8 [1b]And on that day a great persecution arose against the church in Jerusalem; and they were all scattered throughout the Jn 16:2 Acts 7:58; 11:19; 26:10

---

ing and following our Lord which do not involve the drama of bloodshed and death, all Christians should realize that confession of the faith in this way is not a thing of the past and is sometimes necessary.

"Since Jesus, the Son of God, showed his love by laying down his life for us, no one has greater love than he who lays down his life for him and for his brothers (cf. 1 Jn 3:16; Jn 15:13). Some Christians have been called from the beginning, and will always be called, to give this greatest testimony of love to all, especially to persecutors. Martyrdom makes the disciple like his Master. [...] Therefore, the Church considers it the highest gift and supreme test of love. And although it is given to few, all must be prepared to confess Christ before men and to follow him along the way of the Cross amidst the persecutions which the Church never lacks. Likewise the Church's holiness is fostered [...] by the manifold counsels which the Lord proposes to his disciples in the Gospel" (Vatican II, *Lumen gentium*, 42).

The Liturgy of the Church sums up the asceticism and theology of martyrdom in the preface for Christian martyrs: "Your holy martyr followed the example of Christ, and gave his life for the glory of your name. His death reveals your power shining through our human weakness. You choose the weak and make them strong in bearing witness to you."

Like Jesus, Stephen dies commending his soul to God and praying for his persecutors. At this point St Luke brings in Saul, who cooperates in the proceedings by watching the executioners' clothes; Saul will soon experience the benefit of Stephen's intercession. "If Stephen had not prayed to God, the Church would not have had Paul" (St Augustine, *Sermons*, 315, 7).

Stephen has died, but his example and teaching continue to speak across the world.

8:1. Stephen's death signals the start of a violent persecution of the Christian community and Hellenist members in particular.

A new situation has been created. "Far from diminishing the boldness of the disciples, Stephen's death increased it. Christians were scattered precisely in order to spread the word further afield" (St John Chrysostom, *Hom. on Acts*, 18). This scattering of the disciples is not simply flight from danger. It originates in danger, but they avail of it to serve God and the Gospel. "Flight, so far from implying cowardice, requires often greater courage than not to flee. It is a great

region of Judea and Samaria, except the apostles. [2]Devout men
Acts 9:1; 22:4 buried Stephen, and made great lamentation over him. [3]But Saul
Gal 1:13 laid waste the church, and entering house after house, he dragged
1 Cor 15:9
1 Tim 1:13 off men and women and committed them to prison.
[4]Now those who were scattered went about preaching the word.

Philip's preaching in Samaria

Acts 6:5 [5]Philip went down to a city of Samaria, and proclaimed to them

---

trial of heart. Death is an end of all trouble; he who flees is ever expecting death, and dies daily. [...] Exile is full of miseries. The afterconduct of the saints showed they had not fled for fear. [...] How would the Gospel ever have been preached throughout the world, if the apostles had not fled? And, since their time, those, too, who have become martyrs, at first fled; or, if they advanced to meet their persecutors, it was by some secret suggestion of the Divine Spirit. But, above all, while these instances abundantly illustrate the rule of duty in persecution, and the temper of mind necessary in those who observe it, we have that duty itself declared in a plain precept by no other than our Lord: 'When they shall persecute you in this city,' He says, 'flee into another'" (Ven. John Henry Newman, *Historical Sketches*, 2, 7).

8:4. "Observe how, in the middle of misfortune, the Christians keep up their preaching instead of neglecting it" (St John Chrysostom, *Hom. on Acts*, 18). Misfortune plays its part in the spread of the Gospel. God's plans always exceed man's calculations and expectations. An apparently mortal blow for the Gospel in fact plays a decisive role in its spread. What comes from God cannot be destroyed; its adversaries in fact contribute to its consolidation and progress. "The religion founded by the mystery of the cross of Christ cannot be destroyed by any form of cruelty. The Church is not diminished by persecutions; on the contrary, they make for its increase. The field of the Lord is clothed in a richer harvest. When the grain which falls dies, it is reborn and multiplied" (St Leo the Great, *Hom. on the feast of St Peter and St Paul*).

The disciples are disconcerted to begin with, but then they begin to have a better understanding of God's providence. They may well have been reminded of Isaiah's words: "My thoughts are not your thoughts, neither are your ways my ways" (55:8), and of the promises of a heavenly Father, who arranges all events to the benefit of his elect.

The different periods of Church history show certain similarities, and difficulties caused by hidden or overt enemies never create totally new situations. Christians always have good reason to be optimistic—with an optimism based on faith, self-sacrifice and prayer. "Christianity has been too often in what seemed deadly peril that we should fear for it any new trial now. So far is certain; on the other hand, what is uncertain [...] is the particular mode by which, in the event, Providence rescues and saves His elect inheritance. Sometimes our enemy is turned into a friend; sometimes he is despoiled of that special virulence of evil which was so threatening; sometimes he falls to pieces himself; sometimes he does just so much as is beneficial, and then is removed. Commonly the Church has nothing more to do than to go on in

the Christ. 6And the multitudes with one accord gave heed to what
was said by Philip, when they heard him and saw the signs which
he did. 7For unclean spirits came out of many who were pos- Mt 8:29
sessed, crying with a loud voice; and many who were paralyzed Mk 16:17
or lame were healed. 8So there was much joy in that city. Jn 4:38–41

Simon the magician

9But there was a man named Simon who had previously practised
magic in the city and amazed the nation of Samaria, saying that he

---

her own proper duties, in confidence and peace; to stand still and to see the salvation of God" (Ven. J.H. Newman, *Biglietto Speech*, 1879).

Those who do not know Christ may resist the Gospel, but that resistance makes good Christians spiritually stronger and helps to purify the Church. "The storm of persecution is good. What is the loss? What is already lost cannot be lost. When the tree is not torn up by the roots—and there is no wind or hurricane that can uproot the tree of the Church—only the dry branches fall. And they … are well fallen" (St Josemaría Escrivá, *The Way*, 685).

8:5. This is not Philip the apostle (1:13) but one of the seven deacons appointed to look after Christians in need (6:5). The Gospel is proclaimed to the Samaritans—who also were awaiting the Messiah. This means that it now spreads beyond the borders of Judea once and for all, and our Lord's promise (Acts 1:8) is fulfilled: "you shall be my witnesses in Jerusalem and in all Judea and Samaria."

The despised Samaritans became the first to benefit from the Gospel's determination to spread all over the world. We can sense St Luke's pleasure in reporting its proclamation to the Samaritans; earlier he already showed them in a favourable light: he is the only Evangelist to recount the parable of the Good Samaritan (cf. Lk 10:30–37) and to mention that the leper who came back to thank Jesus after being cured was a Samaritan (cf. Lk 17:16). On the Samaritans in general, see the note on Jn 4:20.

8:9–13. Simon the magician is an imposter who pretends to have spiritual powers and who trades on the credulity and superstition of his audience.

St Luke uses this episode to show the difference between the genuine miracles performed by the apostles in the name of Jesus and using Jesus' authority, and the real or apparent wonders worked by a charlatan: "As in the time of Moses, so now the distinction is made between different kinds of prodigies. Magic was practised, but it was easy to see the difference between it and genuine miracles. […] Unclean spirits, in great numbers, went out of possessed people, protesting as they went. This showed that they were being expelled. Those who practised magic did just the opposite: they reinforced the bonds that bound the possessed" (St John Chrysostom, *Hom. on Acts*, 18).

The power which Peter and John have is different from Simon Magus'. Further on (vv. 15–17), St Luke contrasts the magician and his desire to make money, and the apostles who are themselves poor but who enrich others with the Spirit. The apostles do not perform miracles through powers which they have

himself was somebody great. 10They all gave heed to him, from
the least to the greatest, saying, "This man is that power of God
which is called Great." 11And they gave heed to him, because for
a long time he had amazed them with his magic. 12But when they
Mt 28:19 believed Philip as he preached good news about the kingdom of
God and the name of Jesus Christ, they were baptized, both men
and women. 13Even Simon himself believed, and after being baptized he continued with Philip. And seeing signs and great miracles performed, he was amazed.

Peter and John in Samaria

Acts 11:1–22 14Now when the apostles at Jerusalem heard that Samaria had
received the word of God, they sent to them Peter and John, 15who

---

in their personal control; they always perform them by virtue of God's power, which they obtain by means of prayer. The miracles which Christians work are accompanied by prayer and never involve conjuring or spells. Luke makes the same point when recounting the episodes of Elymas (13:6ff), the diviner in Philippi (16:16ff) and the sons of Sceva (19:13ff).

Magic (occultism) and superstition (attempting to obtain supernatural effects using methods which cannot produce them) are a symptom of debased religion. Man has a natural obligation to be religious—to seek God, worship him and atone to him for sin. However, natural religion needs to be corrected, purified and filled out by supernatural revelation, whereby God seeks man out, raises him up and guides him on his way. Left to its own devices, natural religion can easily deviate and become useless or even harmful.

8:10. "That power of God which is called Great": it is not very clear what this means. It may mean that the Samaritans called that divine power "the Great" which they regarded as being the strongest. Another interpretation is that the Greek adjective *megale*, great, is not a Greek word, but a transcription of an Aramaic word meaning "Revealing". Whichever interpretation is correct, Simon Magus claimed to have this divine power.

8:14–17. Here we see the apostles exercising through Peter and John the authority they have over the entire Church. The two apostles proceed to confirm the disciples recently baptized by Philip: we may presume that in addition to laying their hands on them to communicate the Holy Spirit, the apostles made sure that they had a correct grasp of the central points of the Gospel message. At this time the apostles constituted the spiritual centre of the Church and took an active interest in ensuring that the new communities were conscious of the links—doctrinal and affective—that united them to the mother community in Jerusalem.

This passage bears witness to the existence of Baptism and the gift of the Holy Spirit (or Confirmation) as two distinct sacramental rites. The most important effects Christian Baptism has are the infusion of initial grace and the remission of original sin and any personal sin; it is the first sacrament a person receives,

came down and prayed for them that they might receive the Holy Acts 2:38
Spirit; [16]for it had not yet fallen on any of them, but they had only Acts 19:2–6
been baptized in the name of the Lord Jesus. [17]Then they laid their 1 Tim 4:14
hands on them and they received the Holy Spirit.

The sin of simony

[18]Now when Simon saw that the Spirit was given through the
laying on of the apostles' hands, he offered them money, [19]saying,
"Give me also this power, that any one on whom I lay my hands
may receive the Holy Spirit." [20]But Peter said to him, "Your silver Mt 10:8
perish with you, because you thought you could obtain the gift of
God with money!* [21]You have neither part nor lot in this matter,
for your heart is not right before God. [22]Repent therefore of this Heb 12:15

---

which is why it is called the "door of the Church".

There is a close connexion between Baptism and Confirmation, so much so that in the early centuries of Christianity, Confirmation was administered immediately after Baptism. There is a clear distinction between these two sacraments of Christian initiation, which helps us understand the different effects they have. A useful comparison is the difference, in natural life, between conception and later growth (cf. St Pius V, *Catechism*, 2, 3, 5). "As nature intends that all her children should grow up and attain full maturity […], so the Catholic Church, the common mother of all, earnestly wishes that, in those whom she has regenerated by Baptism, the perfection of Christian manhood be completed" (ibid., 2, 3, 17).

"The nature of the sacrament of Confirmation," John Paul II explains, "grows out of this endowment of strength which the Holy Spirit communicates to each baptized person, to make him or her—as the well-known language of the Catechism puts it—a perfect Christian and soldier of Christ, ready to witness boldly to his resurrection and its redemptive power: 'You shall be my witnesses' (Acts 1:8)" (Homily, 25 May 1980). "All Christians, incorporated into Christ and his Church by Baptism, are consecrated to God. They are called to profess the faith which they have received. By the sacrament of Confirmation they are further endowed by the Holy Spirit with special strength to be witnesses of Christ and sharers in his mission of salvation" (Homily in Limerick, 1 October 1979). "This is a sacrament which in a special way associates us with the mission of the apostles, in that it inserts each baptized person into the apostolate of the Church" (Homily in Cracow, 10 June 1979). In the sacrament of Confirmation divine grace anticipates the aggressive and demoralizing temptations a young Christian man or woman is likely to experience, and reminds them of the fact that they have a vocation to holiness; it makes them feel more identified with the Church, their Mother, and helps them live in accordance with their Catholic beliefs and convictions. From their formative years Christ makes them defenders of the faith.

8:18–24. Simon's disgraceful proposition—offering the apostles money in exchange for the power to transmit the Holy Spirit—gave rise to the term "simony", that is, trading in sacred

wickedness of yours, and pray to the Lord that, if possible, the
Deut 29:18 intent of your heart may be forgiven you. [23]For I see that you are
in the gall of bitterness and in the bond of iniquity." [24]And Simon
answered, "Pray for me to the Lord, that nothing of what you have
said may come upon me."

Jn 4:35 Acts 1:8 [25]Now when they had testified and spoken the word of the
Lord, they returned to Jerusalem, preaching the gospel to many
villages of the Samaritans.

---

things. Simony is the sin of buying or selling, in exchange for money or some other temporal thing, something spiritual—a sacrament, an indulgence, an ecclesiastical office etc. It is sinful because it degrades something supernatural, which is essentially a free gift, by using it unlawfully to obtain material benefit.

However, there is no simony involved in ministers of sacred worship accepting reasonable alms, in cash or kind, for their maintenance. Jesus teaches that the apostle deserves to receive wages (cf. Lk 10:7), and St Paul says that those who proclaim the Gospel should get their living from it (cf. 1 Cor 9:14). An example of valid earnings is the alms or stipend given to a minister to say Mass for one's intention: it is not given as payment for spiritual benefit, but as a contribution to the priest's keep.

The Church has striven and warned against its ministers falling into the sin of simony (cf. 1 Pet 5:2; 2 Pet 2:3), often recalling what our Lord said to his disciples in this connexion: "Heal the sick, raise the dead, cleanse lepers, cast out demons. You have received without pay, give without pay" (Mt 10:8), and particularly setting before them the wonderful example Jesus himself gave, in the way he lived and in the manner of his death.

Our Lord has left us a supreme example of disinterest and uprightness of intention in the service of men—by living and dying on our behalf, asking nothing in exchange except the just response his love merits.

A pastor of souls would be guilty of a serious sin if through his ministry he sought financial gain, social prestige, esteem, honours or political leadership. Instead of being a pastor he would be a mercenary, a hireling, who in time of real danger would only think of himself, leaving the faithful to fend for themselves (cf. Jn 10:12).

8:26–40. The baptism of the Ethiopian official marks an important step in the spread of Christianity. St Luke's account underlines the importance of Sacred Scripture, and its correct interpretation, in the work of evangelization. This episode encapsulates the various stages in apostolate: Christ's disciple is moved by the Spirit (v. 29) and readily obeys his instruction; he bases his preaching on Sacred Scripture—as Jesus did in the case of the disciples of Emmaus—and then administers Baptism.

8:27. Ethiopia: the kingdom of Nubia, whose capital was Meroe, to the south of Egypt, below Aswan, the first cataract on the Nile (part of modern Sudan). Candace, or Kandake, is not the name of an individual; it was the dynastic name of the queens of that country, a country at that time ruled by women (cf. Eusebius, *Ecclesiastical History*, 2, 1, 13).

The term "eunuch", like its equivalent in Hebrew, was often used indepen-

Philip baptizes an Ethiopian official

[26]But an angel of the Lord said to Philip, "Rise and go toward the
south[g] to the road that goes down from Jerusalem to Gaza." This
is a desert road. [27]And he rose and went. And behold, an Ethio- Ps 68:31
pian, a eunuch, a minister of Candace the queen of the Ethiopians, Is 56:3–7
in charge of all her treasure, had come to Jerusalem to worship
[28]and was returning; seated in his chariot, he was reading the
prophet Isaiah. [29]And the Spirit said to Philip, "Go up and join this
chariot." [30]So Philip ran to him, and heard him reading Isaiah the
prophet, and asked, "Do you understand what you are reading?"
[31]And he said, "How can I, unless some one guides me?" And he Rom 10:14

---

dently of its original physiological meaning and could refer to any court official (cf., e.g., Gen 39:1; 2 Kings 25:19). This particular man was an important official, the equivalent of a minister of finance. We do not know if he was a member of the Jewish race, a proselyte (a Jew not by race but by religion) or—perhaps—a God-fearer (cf. the note on Acts 2:5–11).

8:28. "Consider," St John Chrysostom says, "what a good thing it is not to neglect reading Scripture even when one is on a journey. … Let those reflect on this who do not even read the Scriptures at home, and, because they are with their wife, or are fighting in the army, or are very involved in family or other affairs, think that there is no particular need for them to make the effort to read the divine Scriptures. […] This Ethiopian has something to teach us all—those who have a family life, members of the army, officials, in a word, all men, and women too (particularly those women who are always at home), and all those who have chosen the monastic way of life. Let all learn that no situation is an obstacle to reading the word of God: this is something one can do not only when one is alone at home but also in the public square, on a journey, in the company of others, or when engaged in one's occupation. Let us not, I beg you, neglect to read the Scriptures" (*Hom. on Acts*, 35).

8:29–30. The fact that they are alone, that the road is empty, makes it easier for them to have a deep conversation and easier for Philip to explain Christian teaching. "I think so highly of your devotion to the early Christians that I will do all I can to encourage it, so that you—like them—will put more enthusiasm each day into that effective apostolate of discretion and friendship" (St J. Escrivá, *The Way*, 971). This was in fact one of the characteristic features of the kind of apostolate carried out by our first brothers and sisters in the faith as they spread gradually all over the Roman empire. They brought the Christian message to the people around them—the sailor to the rest of the crew, the slave to his fellow slaves, soldiers, traders, housewives. … This eager desire of theirs to spread the Gospel showed their genuine conviction and was an additional proof of the truth of the Christian message.

8:31. "How can I understand it, unless some one guides me?": to a Jew of this period the very idea of a Messiah who suffers and dies at the hands of his ene-

g. Or *at noon*

Is 53:7–8
Lk 18:31

invited Philip to come up and sit with him. [32]Now the passage of
the scripture which he was reading was this:

"As a sheep led to the slaughter
or a lamb before its shearer is dumb,
so he opens not his mouth.
[33]In his humiliation justice was denied him.
Who can describe his generation?
For his life is taken up from the earth."

---

mies was quite repugnant. This explains why the Ethiopian has difficulty in understanding this passage—and, indeed, the entire song of the Servant of Yahweh, from which it comes (cf. Is 53).

Sometimes it is difficult to understand a passage of Scripture; as St Jerome comments: "I am not (to speak in passing of myself) more learned or more holy than that eunuch who travelled to the temple from Ethiopia, that is, from the end of the earth: he left the royal palace and such was his desire for divine knowledge that he was even reading the sacred words in his chariot. And yet ... he did not realize whom he was venerating in that book. Philip comes along, he reveals to him Jesus hidden and as it were imprisoned in the text [...], and in that very moment he believes, is baptized, is faithful and holy. [...] I tell you this to show you that, unless you have a guide who goes ahead of you to show you the way, you cannot enter the holy Scriptures" (*Letters*, 53, 5–6).

This guide is the Church; God, who inspired the sacred books, has entrusted their interpretation to the Church. Therefore, the Second Vatican Council teaches that "If we are to derive their true meaning from the sacred texts," attention must be devoted "not only to their content but to the unity of the whole of Scripture, the living tradition of the entire Church, and the analogy of faith. [...] Everything to do with the interpretation of Scripture is ultimately subject to the judgment of the Church, which exercises the divinely conferred communion and ministry of watching over and interpreting the Word of God" (Vatican II, *Dei Verbum*, 12).

8:35. "The eunuch deserves our admiration for his readiness to believe," St John Chrysostom comments. "He has not seen Jesus Christ nor has he witnessed any miracle; what then is the reason for his change? It is because, being observant in matters of religion, he applies himself to the study of the sacred books and makes them his book of meditation and reading" (*Hom. on Acts*, 19).

8:36. "What is to prevent my being baptized?": the Ethiopian's question reminds us of the conditions necessary for receiving Baptism. Adults should be instructed in the faith before receiving this sacrament; however, a period of "Christian initiation" is not required if there is a good reason, such as danger of death.

The Church's Magisterium stresses the obligation to baptize children without delay. "The fact that children are incapable of making a personal profession of faith does not deter the Church from conferring this sacrament on them; what it does is baptize them in its own faith. This teaching was already clearly expressed by St Augustine: 'Children are presented for the reception of spiritual grace, not so much by those who carry them in their arms—although also by them, if they are

[34]And the eunuch said to Philip, "About whom, pray, does the
prophet say this, about himself or about some one else?" [35]Then Lk 24:27
Philip opened his mouth, and beginning with this scripture he told
him the good news of Jesus. [36]And as they went along the road Acts 10:47; 11:17
they came to some water, and the eunuch said, "See, here is
water! What is to prevent my being baptized?"[h] [38]And he commanded the chariot to stop, and they both went down into the
water, Philip and the eunuch, and he baptized him. [39]And when

---

good members of the Church—as by the universal society of saints and faithful. [...] It is Mother Church herself who acts in her saints, because the whole Church begets each and all' (*Letters*, 98, 5; cf. *Sermons*, 176, 2). St Thomas Aquinas, and after him most theologians, take up the same teaching: the child who is baptized does not believe for itself, by a personal act of faith, but rather through others 'by the faith of the Church which is communicated to the child' (*Summa theologiae*, 3, 69, 6, ad 3; cf. 68, 9, ad 3). This same teaching is expressed in the new rite of Baptism, when the celebrant asks the parents and godparents to profess the faith of the Church 'in which the children are being baptized' " (*Instruction on Infant Baptism*, 20 October 1980).

The Instruction goes on to say that "it is true that apostolic preaching is normally addressed to adults, and that the first to be baptized were adults who had been converted to the Christian faith. From what we read in the New Testament we might be led to think that it deals only with adults' faith. However, the practice of Baptism of infants is based on an ancient tradition of apostolic origin, whose value must not be underestimated; furthermore, Baptism has never been administered without faith: in the case of infants the faith that intervenes is the Church's own faith. Besides, according to the Council of Trent's teaching on the sacraments, Baptism is not only a sign of faith: it is also the cause of faith" (ibid).

Christian parents have a duty to see that their children are baptized quickly. The *Code of Canon Law* specifies that "parents are obliged to see that their infants are baptized within the first few weeks. As soon as possible after the birth, indeed often before it, they are to approach the parish priest to ask for the sacrament for their child, and to be themselves duly prepared for it" (can. 867).

8:37. This verse, not to be found in some Greek codexes or in the better translations, was probably a gloss which later found its way into the text. In the Vulgate it is given in this way: "*Dixit autem Philippus: Si credis ex toto corde, licet. Et respondens ait: Credo, Filium Dei esse Jesum Christum*" (see RSV note below) This very ancient gloss, inspired by baptismal liturgy, helps to demonstrate that faith in Christ's divine worship was the nucleus of the creed a person had to subscribe to in order to be baptized. On this occasion Philip, guided by the Holy Spirit, lays down no further condition and he immediately proceeds to baptize the Ethiopian.

8:39. St John Chrysostom pauses to note that the Spirit takes Philip away without

h. Other ancient authorities add all or most of verse 37, *And Philip said, "If you believe with all your heart, you may." And he replied, "I believe that Jesus Christ is the Son of God."*

1 Kings 18:12 they came up out of the water, the Spirit of the Lord caught up
Lk 24:31–32 Philip; and the eunuch saw him no more, and went on his way
Acts 21:8 rejoicing. 40But Philip was found at Azotus, and passing on he
preached the gospel to all the towns till he came to Caesarea.

---

giving him time to rejoice with the man he has just baptized: "Why did the Spirit of the Lord bear him away? Because he had to go on to preach in other cities. We should not be surprised that this happened in a divine rather than a human way" (*Hom. on Acts*, 19).

The official "went on his way rejoicing" that God had made him his son through Baptism. He had received the gift of faith, and with the help of divine grace he was ready to live up to all the demands of that faith, even in adverse circumstances: quite probably he would be the only Christian in all Ethiopia.

Faith is a gift of God and is received as such at Baptism; but man's response is necessary if this gift is not to prove fruitless.

Baptism is one of the sacraments which imprints an indelible mark on the soul and which can be received only once. However, a baptized person needs to be continually renewing his commitment; this is not something to be done only during the Easter liturgy: in his everyday activity he should be striving to act like a son of God.

It is natural and logical for the Ethiopian to be so happy, for Baptism brings with it many graces. These St John Chrysostom lists, using quotations from the Gospels and from the letters of St Paul: "The newly baptized are free, holy, righteous, sons of God, heirs of heaven, brothers and co-heirs of Christ, members of his body, temples of God, instruments of the Holy Spirit. … Those who yesterday were captives are today free men and citizens of the Church. Those who yesterday were in the shame of sin are now safe in righteousness; not alone are they free, they are holy" (*Baptismal Catechesis*, 3, 5).

9:1–3. The Roman authorities recognized the moral authority of the Sanhedrin and even permitted it to exercise a certain jurisdiction over members of Jewish communities outside Palestine—as was the case with Damascus. The Sanhedrin even had the right to extradite Jews to Palestine (cf. 1 Mac 15:21).

Damascus was about 230–250 kilometres (150 miles) from Jerusalem, depending on which route one took. Saul and his associates, who would probably have been mounted, would have had no difficulty in doing the journey in under a week. This apparition took place towards the end of the journey, when they were near Damascus.

9:2. "The Way": the corresponding word in Hebrew also means religious behaviour. Here it refers to both Christian lifestyle and the Gospel itself; indirectly it means all the early followers of Jesus (cf. Acts 18:25f; 19:9, 23; 22:4) and all those who come after them and are on the way to heaven; it reminds us of Jesus' words, "The gate is narrow and the way is hard, that leads to life, and those who find it are few" (Mt 7:14).

9:3–19. This is the first of the three accounts of the calling of Saul—occurring probably between the years 34 and 36—that are given in the Acts of the Apostles (cf. Acts 22:5–16; 26:10–18); where important events are concerned, St Luke does not mind repeating himself.

6. THE CONVERSION OF ST PAUL

Saul on his way to Damascus

9 [1]But Saul, still breathing threats and murder against the disci- Acts 22:5–16; 26:10–18
ples of the Lord, went to the high priest [2]and asked him for Gal 1:12–17
letters to the synagogues at Damascus, so that if he found any Acts 8:3
belonging to the Way, men or women, he might bring them bound
to Jerusalem. [3]Now as he journeyed he approached Damascus,

Once again the Light shines in the darkness (cf. Jn 1:5). It does so here in a spectacular way and, as in every conversion, it makes the convert see God, himself and others in a new way.

However, the episode on the road to Damascus is not only a conversion. It marks the beginning of St Paul's vocation: "What amazes you seems natural to me: that God has sought you out in the practice of your profession!

"This is how he sought the first, Peter and Andrew, James and John, beside their nets, and Matthew, sitting in the custom-house.

"And—wonder of wonders!—Paul, in his eagnerness to destroy the seed of Christianity" (St Josemaría Escrivá, *The Way*, 799).

The background to St Luke's concise account is easy to fill in. There would have been no Hellenist Christians left in Jerusalem: they had fled the city, some going as far afield as Phoenicia, Cyprus and Antioch. Many had sought refuge in Damascus, and Saul must have realized that their evangelizing zeal would win many converts among faithful Jews in that city. Saul genuinely wanted to serve God, which explains his readiness to respond to grace. Like most Jews of his time, he saw the Messiah as a political liberator, a warrior-king, a half-heavenly, half-earthly figure such as described in the apocryphal *Book of Enoch*, 46: "It is impossible to imagine how even his glance terrifies his enemies. Wherever he turns, everything trembles; wherever his voice reaches everything is overwhelmed and those who hear it are dissolved as wax in fire." A hero of this type does not fall into the power of his enemies, much less let them crucify him; on the contrary, he is a victor, he annihilates his enemies and establishes an everlasting kingdom of peace and justice. For Saul, Jesus' death on a cross was clear proof that he was a false messiah; and the whole notion of a brotherhood of Jews and Gentiles was inconceivable.

He has almost reached Damascus when a light flashes; he is thrown onto the ground and hears a voice from heaven calling his name twice, in a tone of sad complaint.

Saul surrenders unconditionally and places himself at the Lord's service. He does not bemoan his past life; he is ready to start anew. No longer is the Cross a "scandal": it has become for him a sign of salvation, the "power of God", a throne of victory, whose praises he will sing in his epistles. Soon St Paul will learn more about this Way and about all that Jesus did and taught, but from this moment onwards, the moment of his calling, he realizes that Jesus is the risen Messiah, in whom the prophecies find fulfilment; he believes in the divinity of Christ: he sees how different his idea of the Messiah was from the glorified, pre-existing and eternal Son of God; he understands Christ's mystical presence in his followers: "Why do you persecute

and suddenly a light from heaven flashed about him. [4]And he fell
1 Cor 15:8 to the ground and heard a voice saying to him, "Saul, Saul, why
do you persecute me?" [5]And he said, "Who are you, Lord?" And
he said, "I am Jesus, whom you are persecuting;* [6]but rise and
enter the city, and you will be told what you are to do." [7]The men
Dan 10:7 who were travelling with him stood speechless, hearing the voice
but seeing no one. [8]Saul arose from the ground; and when his eyes
were opened, he could see nothing; so they led him by the hand
and brought him into Damascus. [9]And for three days he was without sight, and neither ate nor drank.

Ananias baptizes Saul

1 Sam 3:4 [10]Now there was a disciple at Damascus called Ananias. The Lord
said to him in a vision, "Ananias." And he said, "Here I am,

---

me?" In other words, he realizes that he has been chosen by God, called by God, and he immediately places himself at his service.

9:4. This identification of Christ and Christians is something which the apostle will later elaborate on when he speaks of the mystical body of Christ (cf. Col 1:18; Eph 1:22f).

St Bede comments as follows: "Jesus does not say, 'Why do you persecute my members?', but, 'Why do you persecute me?', because he himself still suffers affronts in his body, which is the Church. Similarly Christ will take account of the good actions done to his members, for he said, 'I was hungry and you gave me food …' (Mt 25:35), and explaining these words he added, 'As you did it to one of the least of these my brethren, you did it to me' (Mt 25:40)" (*Super Act. expositio*, ad loc.).

9:5–6. In the Vulgate and in many other translations these words are added between the end of v. 5 and the start of v. 6: "It is hard for thee to kick against the goad. And he, trembling and astonished, said: Lord, what wilt thou have me to do? And the Lord said to him". These words do not seem to be part of the original sacred text but rather a later explanatory gloss; for this reason the New Vulgate omits them. (The first part of the addition comes from Paul's address in Acts 26:14.)

9:6. The calling of Saul was exceptional as regards the manner in which God called him; but the effect it had on him was the same as what happens when God gives a specific calling to the apostolate to certain individual Christians, inviting them to follow him more closely. Paul's immediate response is a model of how those who receive these specific callings should act (all Christians, of course, have a common calling to holiness and apostolate that comes with Baptism).

Paul VI describes in this way the effects of this specific kind of vocation in a person's soul: "The apostolate is […] an inner voice, which makes one both restless and serene, a voice that is both gentle and imperious, troublesome and affectionate, a voice which comes unexpectedly and with great events and then, at a particular point, exercises a strong attraction, as it were revealing to us our

Lord." 11And the Lord said to him, "Rise and go to the street
called Straight, and inquire in the house of Judas for a man of
Tarsus named Saul; for behold, he is praying, 12and he has seen a
man named Ananias come in and lay his hands on him so that he
might regain his sight." 13But Ananias answered, "Lord, I have
heard from many about this man, how much evil he has done to
thy saints* at Jerusalem; 14and here he has authority from the 1 Cor 1:2
chief priests to bind all who call upon thy name." 15But the Lord
said to him, "Go, for he is a chosen instrument of mine to carry
my name before the Gentiles and kings and the sons of Israel; 1 Cor 4:9–13 2 Cor 11:23–28
16for I will show him how much he must suffer for the sake of my 2 Tim 2:11–12
name." 17So Ananias departed and entered the house. And laying
his hands on him he said, "Brother Saul, the Lord Jesus who Acts 15:8; 22:14–16

---

life and our destiny. It speaks prophetically and almost in a tone of victory, which eventually dispels all uncertainty, all timidity and all fear, and which facilitates—making it easy, desirable and pleasant—the response of our whole personality, when we pronounce that word which reveals the supreme secret of love: Yes; Yes, Lord, tell me what I must do and I will try to do it, I will do it. Like St Paul, thrown to the ground at the gates of Damascus: What would you have me do?

"The roots of the apostolate run deep: the apostolate is vocation, election, interior encounter with Christ, abandonment of one's personal autonomy to his will, to his invisible presence; it is a kind of substitution of our poor, restless heart, inconstant and at times unfaithful yet hungry for love, for his heart, the heart of Christ which is beginning to pulsate in the one who has been chosen. And then comes the second act in the psychological drama of the apostolate: the need to spread, to do, to give, to speak, to pass on to others one's own treasure, one's own fire. [...]

"The apostolate becomes a continuous expansion of one's soul, the exuberance of a personality taken over by Christ and animated by his Spirit; it becomes a need to hasten, to work, to do everything one can to spread the Kingdom of God, to save other souls, to save all souls" (Homily, 14 October 1968).

9:8–11. Straight Street runs through Damascus from east to west and can still be identified today.

9:13. Ananias refers to Christ's followers as "saints"; this was the word normally used to describe the disciples, first in Palestine and then in the world at large. God is *the* Holy One (cf. Is 6:3); as the Old Testament repeatedly says, those who approach God and keep his commandments share in this holiness: "The Lord said to Moses, 'Say to all the congregation of the people of Israel, You shall be holy; for I the Lord your God am holy'" (Lev 19:1–2).

The use of this term is an example of the spiritual sensitivity of our first brothers and sisters in the faith: "What a moving name—saints!—the early Christians used to address each other! ...

"Learn to be a brother to your brothers" (St J. Escrivá, *The Way*, 469).

9:15–16. Our Lord calls St Paul his "vessel of election", which is a Hebraic-

appeared to you on the road by which you came, has sent me that
you may regain your sight and be filled with the Holy Spirit."
Tob 11:10–15 18And immediately something like scales fell from his eyes and he
regained his sight. Then he rose and was baptized, 19and took food
and was strengthened.

Paul begins his apostolate

Gal 1:16 For several days he was with the disciples at Damascus. 20And in
the synagogues immediately he proclaimed Jesus, saying, "He is
the Son of God." 21And all who heard him were amazed, and said,
"Is not this the man who made havoc in Jerusalem of those who
called on this name? And he has come here for this purpose, to
Acts 18:5, 28 bring them bound before the chief priests." 22But Saul increased
all the more in strength, and confounded the Jews who lived in
Damascus by proving that Jesus was the Christ.

---

ism equivalent to "chosen instrument", and he tells Ananias how much the apostle will have to suffer on his account. A Christian called to the apostolate is also, by virtue of this divine vocation, an instrument in the hands of God; to be effective he must be docile: he must let God use him and must do what God tells him.

The task God has given him is far beyond Paul's ability—"to carry my name before the Gentiles and kings and the sons of Israel". In Acts we will see how Paul fulfils his mission, with the help of God's grace and suffering a great deal on account of his name. Down through the centuries, in diverse circumstances, those whom the Lord elects to carry out specific missions will also be able to perform them if they are good instruments who allow grace to act in them and who are ready to suffer for their ideals.

9:19. In spite of the exceptional manner in which God called St Paul, he desired him to mature in the normal way—to be instructed by others and learn God's will through them. In this case he chose Ananias to confer Baptism on Paul and teach him the basics of the Christian faith.

In Ananias we can see a trace of the role of the spiritual director or guide in Christian asceticism. There is a principle which states that "no one can be a good judge in his own case, because everyone judges according to his own inclinations" (cf. Cassian, *Collationes*, 16, 11). A person guiding a soul has a special "grace of state" to make God's will known to him; and even if the guide makes a mistake, the person who is being guided will—if obedient—always do the right thing, always do God's will. In this connexion St Vincent Ferrer says: "Our Lord Jesus Christ, without whom we can do nothing, will not give his grace to him who, though he has access to an expert guide, rejects this precious means of sanctification, thinking that he can look after on his own everything that touches on his salvation. He who has a director, whom he obeys in everything, will reach his goal more easily and more quickly than if he acted as his own guide, even if he be

Paul flees from Damascus

23When many days had passed, the Jews plotted to kill him, 24but
their plot became known to Saul. They were watching the gates 2 Cor 11:32–33
day and night, to kill him; 25but his disciples took him by night
and let him down over the wall, lowering him in a basket.

Barnabas and Paul in Jerusalem

26And when he had come to Jerusalem he attempted to join the Gal 1:18f
disciples; and they were all afraid of him, for they did not believe
that he was a disciple. 27But Barnabas took him, and brought him
to the apostles, and declared to them how on the road he had seen
the Lord, who spoke to him, and how at Damascus he had
preached boldly in the name of Jesus. 28So he went in and out
among them at Jerusalem, 29preaching boldly in the name of the
Lord. And he spoke and disputed against the Hellenists; but they
were seeking to kill him. 30And when the brethren knew it, they Acts 11:25
brought him down to Caesarea, and sent him off to Tarsus. Gal 1:21

---

very intelligent and have the very best of spiritual books" (*Treatise on the Spiritual Life*, 2,1).

On the spiritual guidance of ordinary Christians, who seek holiness and carry out apostolate in the context of everyday life, St Escrivá, writes: "A director—you need one, so that you can give yourself to God, and give yourself fully … by obedience. You need a director who understands your apostolate, who knows what God wants: that way he will second the work of the Holy Spirit in your soul, without taking you from your place, filling you with peace, and teaching you how to make your work fruitful" (*The Way*, 62).

9:20–23. In his letter to the Galatians (cf. Gal 1:16f) St Paul tells of how he went into Arabia after his conversion and then returned to Damascus. He spent almost three years away, and it was on his return that he preached the divinity of Jesus, using all his energy and learning, now placed at the service of Christ. This surprised and confounded the Jews, who immediately began to take action against him.

9:25. In 2 Corinthians 11:32f St Paul tells of how he fled, after King Aretas tried to seize him at the instigation of the Jews of Damascus.

9:26. This is the first time Paul presents himself in Jerusalem after his conversion. He went up to see Peter, with whom he spent fifteen days (cf. Gal 1:18), and put himself at Peter's disposal; and to check that his teaching was in line with that of the apostles.

Barnabas (see the note on 4:36–37) dispelled the Jerusalem community's initial understandable suspicion of their one-time persecutor. They had been only too well aware of his determination to suppress the Church and had not yet heard about his preaching in Damascus.

During his short stay in Jerusalem Paul preached boldly his faith in the divinity of Jesus and met the same kind of opposition as he did in Damascus.

9:30. For the second time St Paul has to flee for his life. Commenting on this episode, St John Chrysostom explains

Growth of the Church

Acts 2:46 31So the church throughout all Judea and Galilee and Samaria had
peace and was built up; and walking in the fear of the Lord and in
the comfort of the Holy Spirit it was multiplied.

7. ST PETER'S ACTIVITY

Curing of a paralyzed man at Lydda

Acts 8:4 32Now as Peter went here and there among them all, he came
down also to the saints that lived at Lydda. 33There he found a
man named Aeneas, who had been bedridden for eight years and

---

that, in addition to grace, human resourcefulness has a part to play in apostolic activity. "The disciples were afraid that the Jews would do to Saul what they had done to St Stephen. This may be why they sent him to preach the Gospel in his homeland, where he would be safer. In this action of the apostles you can see that God does not do everything directly, by means of his grace, and that he frequently lets his disciples act in line with the rule of prudence" (*Hom. on Acts*, 20).

Chrysostom also sees in Paul's earlier flight from Damascus an example of prudent conduct: "Despite his great desire to be with God, he first had to carry out his mission for the salvation of souls. [...] Jesus Christ does not preserve his apostles from dangers: he lets them confront them, because he wants men to use the resources of prudence to escape from them. Why does he arrange things in this way? In order to have us understand that the apostles are also men and that grace does not do everything in its servants. Otherwise, would people not have seen them as inert and lifeless things? That is why the apostles did many things by following the dictates of prudence. Let us follow their example and use all our natural abilities to work with grace for the salvation of our brethren" (ibid.).

9:31. St Luke breaks his narrative to give an over-view of the steady progress of the Church as a whole and of the various communities that have grown up as a result of the Christians' flight from Jerusalem (cf. Acts 2:41, 47; 4:4; 5:14; 6:1, 7; 11:21, 24; 16:5). He emphasizes the peace and consolation the Holy Spirit has brought them. This note of justified optimism and trust in God confirms that God is with his Church and that no human force can destroy it (cf. 5:39).

9:32. Acts now turns to St Peter's apostolic activity in Palestine. Lydda (cf. 9:32–35), Joppa (cf. 9:36–43) and Maritime Caesarea (cf. 10:24–28; 12:19) were some of the cities in which the head of the apostles preached the Good News.

"St Luke goes on to speak about Peter and his visits to the faithful. He does not want to give the impression that fear is the reason for Peter's leaving Jerusalem, and so he first gives an account of the situation of the Church, after indicating, previously, that Peter had stayed in Jerusalem during the persecution. [...] Peter acts like a general reviewing his troops to see that they are properly trained and in good order, and to discover where his presence is most needed. We see him going in all direc-

was paralyzed. [34]And Peter said to him, "Aeneas, Jesus Christ Acts 3:7
heals you; rise and make your bed." And immediately he rose.
[35]And all the residents of Lydda and Sharon saw him, and they
turned to the Lord.

Peter raises Tabitha to life

[36]Now there was at Joppa a disciple named Tabitha, which means Lk 12:33
Dorcas or Gazelle. She was full of good works and acts of charity. [37]In those days she fell sick and died; and when they had
washed her, they laid her in an upper room. [38]Since Lydda was
near Joppa, the disciples, hearing that Peter was there, sent two
men to him entreating him, "Please come to us without delay."

---

tions and we find him in all parts. If he makes this present journey it is because he thinks that the faithful are in need of his teaching and encouragement" (St John Chrysostom, *Hom. on Acts*, 21).

The last report Acts gives of St Peter deals with his intervention at the Council of Jerusalem (chap. 15).

9:33–35. St Peter takes the initiative; he does not wait for the paralyzed man to seek his help. We are told about the man being sick for eight years, to show how difficult he was to cure—and yet through the power of Jesus Christ he is cured "immediately". "Why did Peter not wait for the man to show his faith? Why did he not first ask him if he wanted to be cured? Surely because it was necessary to impress the people by means of this miracle" (St John Chrysostom, *Hom. on Acts*, 21). However, the conversion of the people of Lydda and Sharon was also the result of Peter's work: miracles are not designed to make life easier for the apostles; their tireless preaching is by no means secondary or superfluous.

9:36–43. Joppa (Jaffa, today virtually part of Tel Aviv) is mentioned in the writings of Tell-el-Amarna where it is called Iapu. Its people were converted to Judaism in the time of Simon Maccabeus (*c*.140 BC).

The miracle of the raising of Tabitha by Peter is the first one of its kind reported in Acts. Here, as in the Gospel, miracles are performed to awaken faith in those who witness them with good dispositions and a readiness to believe. In this case the miracle is a kindness God shows Tabitha to reward her virtues, and an encouragement to the Christians of Joppa.

"In the Acts of the Apostles," St Cyprian writes, "it is clear that alms not only free us from spiritual death, but also from temporal death. Tabitha, a woman who did many 'good works and acts of charity,' had taken ill and died: and Peter was sent for. No sooner had he arrived, with all the diligence of his apostolic charity, than he was surrounded by widows in tears …, praying for the dead woman more by gestures than by words. Peter believed that he could obtain what they were asking for so insistently and that Christ's help would be available in answer to the prayers of the poor in whose persons he himself had been clothed. […] And so it was: he did come to Peter's aid, to whom he had said in the Gospel that he would grant everything asked for in his name. For this reason he

39So Peter rose and went with them. And when he had come, they
took him to the upper room. All the widows stood beside him
weeping, and showing coats and garments which Dorcas made
Mk 5:40 while she was with them. 40But Peter put them all outside and
knelt down and prayed; then turning to the body he said, "Tabitha,
rise." And she opened her eyes, and when she saw Peter she sat
Lk 7:15 up. 41And he gave her his hand and lifted her up. Then calling the
Acts 3:7 saints and widows he presented her alive. 42And it became known
throughout all Joppa, and many believed in the Lord. 43And he
Acts 10:6 stayed in Joppa for many days with one Simon, a tanner.

---

stops the course of death and the woman returns to life, and to the amazement of all she revives, restoring her risen body to the light of day. Such was the power of works of mercy, of good deeds" (*De opere et eleemosynis*, 6).

9:43. Tanning was a permitted trade, but observant Jews regarded it as unclean because it involved contact with dead animals (cf. Lev 11:39: "If any animal of which you may eat dies, he who touches its carcass shall be unclean until the evening").

By staying with Simon the tanner, St Peter shows that these Jewish prohibitions and standards no longer oblige in conscience. The freedom of the Gospel takes over and the only reason why one might sometimes observe them would be out of charity, to avoid giving scandal.

10:1–48. The conversion of the pagan Cornelius is one of the high points of Acts. It is an extremely important event because it demonstrates the fact that the Gospel is addressed to all men and shows that the power of the Holy Spirit knows no limits.

Up to this point the Gospel has been preached only to Jews. Its extension to the Samaritans was seen as an announcement of salvation to people who had at one time formed part of the chosen people. By preaching only to Jews, the disciples were having regard to the fact that the people of Israel were the only people chosen by God to be bearers of the divine promises: as such, they had a right to be the first to receive the definitive message of salvation. Our Lord himself had acted on this principle, and he had told his disciples to preach only "to the lost sheep of the house of Israel" (Mt 10:6; cf. 15:24).

The apostles had not yet asked themselves whether this preferential right of the Jewish people to receive the Gospel proclamation implied a certain exclusive right. Now God steps in to make Peter realize that the Good News is meant for all: it is his desire that all men be saved and therefore the Christians need to shed the narrow ideas of Judaism as regards the scope of salvation.

Peter is surprised to learn this, but he is completely docile to the voice of God and now begins to play an active part in the fulfilment of the divine promises. "God had previously foretold", St Cyprian writes, "that in the fulness of time many more faithful worshippers would adhere to him, people from every nation, race and city; that they would receive mercy through the divine gifts which the Jews had lost through not appreciating their own religion" (*Quod idola dii non sint*, 11).

St Luke describes the conversion of Cornelius at great length and in great

The vision of the centurion Cornelius

10 [1]At Caesarea there was a man named Cornelius, a centurion of what was known as the Italian Cohort, [2]a devout Lk 7:5
man who feared God with all his household, gave alms liberally
to the people, and prayed constantly to God. [3]About the ninth
hour of the day he saw clearly in a vision an angel of God coming Acts 9:10
in and saying to him, "Cornelius." [4]And he stared at him in terror, Tob 12:12
and said, "What is it, Lord?" And he said to him, "Your prayers Lk 1:12 Rev 8:3–4
and your alms have ascended as a memorial before God. [5]And
now send men to Joppa, and bring one Simon who is called Peter;

---

detail, deliberately repeating parts of the story to make sure that its key features are fully grasped. His whole account shows how important it is that pagans can and in fact do enter the Church without first being Jews.

Cornelius is regarded as the first pagan convert to Christianity. We do not know if the baptism of the Ethiopian, narrated in chapter 8, occurred after that of Cornelius or if the Ethiopian was in fact a pagan (cf. the note on Acts 8:27); but in any case that was an isolated, marginal event which does not affect the solemn character of the Roman centurion's conversion, which affects the core of the economy of salvation.

10:1. Maritime Caesarea, where Cornelius was living, should not be confused with Caesarea Philippi, where our Lord promised the primacy to Peter (cf. Mt 16:13–20). Maritime Caesarea was the seat of the Roman governor and was situated on the coast, about 100 kilometres (60 miles) from Jerusalem. It had a Roman garrison made up of auxiliaries, that is, not of legionaries.

10:2. Cornelius was a religious man, one who "feared God". "God-fearing men" or "God-fearers" was a special expression used to describe people who worshipped the God of the Bible and practised the Law of Israel without being formal converts to Judaism (cf. the note on Acts 2:5–11).

He was not a proselyte and therefore had not been circumcised (cf. Acts 11:3). "Do not imagine that grace was given them [Cornelius and the Ethiopian] because of their high rank: God forbid! It was because of their piety. Scripture mentions their distinguished stations to show the greatness of their piety; for it is more remarkable when a person in a position of wealth and power is such as these were" (St John Chrysostom, *Hom. on Acts*, 22).

In religious terms Cornelius was rather like the centurion in Capernaum, whose faith Jesus praises in St Luke's Gospel (7:1ff). Some authors think that Cornelius was a member of the Roman *gens* of that name and that St Luke, who, in writing Acts, had Roman readers in mind, takes special pleasure in recounting the story of Cornelius.

10:4. "Prayers and alms" were regarded by Jews and Christians as works pleasing to God and an expression of genuine piety. Cornelius' true devotion brings God's grace and mercy upon himself and his household. "Do you see how the work of the Gospel begins among the Gentiles? Through a devout man, whose deeds have made him worthy of this favour" (*Hom. on Acts*, 22).

The habitual practice of almsgiving—the epitome of many virtues—is

[6]he is lodging with Simon, a tanner, whose house is by the seaside." [7]When the angel who spoke to him had departed, he called
two of his servants and a devout soldier from among those that
waited on him, [8]and having related everything to them, he sent
them to Joppa.

Peter's vision

[9]The next day, as they were on their journey and coming near the
city, Peter went up on the housetop to pray, about the sixth hour.
[10]And he became hungry and desired something to eat; but while
they were preparing it, he fell into a trance [11]and saw the heaven
opened, and something descending, like a great sheet, let down by
four corners upon the earth. [12]In it were all kinds of animals and
reptiles and birds of the air. [13]And there came a voice to him,
Ezek 4:14 "Rise, Peter; kill and eat." [14]But Peter said, "No, Lord; for I have

---

highly praised in the Old Testament. "Give alms from your possessions," says the Book of Tobit, " … so you will be laying up a good treasure for yourself against the day of necessity. For charity delivers from death and keeps you from entering the darkness; and for all who practise it charity is an excellent offering in the presence of the Most High" (4:7, 9–11; cf. 12:9). Almsgiving is an excellent work of mercy which sanctifies the giver and denotes God's preferential love for him.

"Give, and it will be given to you" (Lk 6:38): these words of Christ, which his disciples should keep before their minds, are echoed in Christian writings down the ages. "Give to everyone what he asks you for, and do not claim it back, for it is the Father's wish that you give to all from the gifts you yourself have received. Blessed is he who, in accord with God's command, gives alms to the needy" (*Didache*, 1, 5)

Generous alms to help those in need, and contributions to the upkeep of the Church, its ministers and its works of zeal, are the responsibility of all Christians. It is not a matter of giving whatever one has left over. Obviously, people to whom God has given wealth and resources in plenty have to give more alms. The fact that they are well-to-do is a sign of the will of God, and he expects them to be ready to meet the reasonable needs of their neighbours.

A Christian who does not understand this obligation or is reluctant to meet it runs the risk of becoming like that rich man (cf. Lk 16:19ff) who was so selfish and so attached to his wealth that he failed to realize that the Lord had placed Lazarus at his gate for him to help him.

"'*Divitiae, si affluant, nolite cor apponere*. Though riches may increase keep your heart detached.' Strive, rather, to use them generously. And, if necessary, heroically. Be poor of spirit" (St Josemaría Escrivá, *The Way*, 636).

"True detachment leads us to be very generous with God and with our fellow men. It makes us actively resourceful and ready to spend ourselves in helping the needy. A Christian cannot be content with a job that only allows him to earn enough for himself and his family. He will be big-hearted enough to give others a helping hand both out of charity and as

never eaten anything that is common or unclean." 15And the voice Mt 15:11
came to him again a second time, "What God has cleansed, you Rom 14:14
must not call common." 16This happened three times, and the 1 Tim 4:4
thing was taken up at once to heaven.*
17Now while Peter was inwardly perplexed as to what the
vision which he had seen might mean, behold, the men that were
sent by Cornelius, having made inquiry for Simon's house, stood
before the gate 18and called out to ask whether Simon who was
called Peter was lodging there. 19And while Peter was pondering Acts 13:2
the vision, the Spirit said to him, "Behold, three men are looking
for you. 20Rise and go down, and accompany them without hesit-
ation; for I have sent them." 21And Peter went down to the men
and said, "I am the one you are looking for; what is the reason for
your coming?" 22And they said, "Cornelius, a centurion, an upright and God-fearing man, who is well spoken of by the whole

---

a matter of justice" (St Josemaría Escrivá, *Friends of God*, 126).

"As a memorial": in the Old Testament certain sacrifices are described as "memorial"—that is, offered to remind God, to have him be considerate towards the offerer (cf. Lev 2:1–3; Tob 12:12).

10:14. This imperious commandment to eat unclean food is something the apostle initially cannot understand. He reacts like a good Jew who loves and observes the divine law he has learned from his youth, including the regulations referring to food and the distinction between clean and unclean. But now he is invited to rise above so-called legal uncleanness.

Peter's humble attitude to what he is told during the vision enables him to take in God's will and realize that Jewish ritual precepts are not necessary for Christians. He does not arrive at this insight by a process of reasoning: rather, he obeys the voice of God; virtuous obedience, not simple human logic, causes him to change his attitude.

Peter's docility to the Holy Spirit gradually leads him to realize, first, that the regulations forbidding Jews to eat certain kinds of meat do not apply to Christians.

This simple and very important discovery, which he could not have made without special divine intervention, leads him to another even more important one: he now sees the full significance of all Jesus' teaching and realizes that in God's salvific plans Jews and pagans are equals.

Restrictions concerning food had led observant Jews to avoid sitting down to table with pagans. Food regulations and contact with Gentiles were very closely connected with one another and were subject to rigorous prohibition. Once the distinction between clean and unclean food was done away with, there would be no obstacle to communication with pagans: it would become quite clear what it meant in practice to say that the Lord "is not partial" (Deut 10:17), is no respecter of persons, and that having a clean heart is what really matters.

10:20. "Notice that the Holy Spirit does not say, 'Here is the explanation of the vision you have received' but 'I have sent them', to show thereby that obedience is called for and that it is not a

Jewish nation, was directed by a holy angel to send for you to
come to his house, and to hear what you have to say." 23So he
called them in to be his guests.

Peter in the house of Cornelius

The next day he rose and went off with them, and some of the
brethren from Joppa accompanied him. 24And on the following
day they entered Caesarea. Cornelius was expecting them and had
Mt 8:8 called together his kinsmen and close friends. 25When Peter
entered, Cornelius met him and fell down at his feet and wor-
Acts 14:15 shipped him. 26But Peter lifted him up, saying, "Stand up; I too
Rev 19:10 am a man." 27And as he talked with him, he went in and found

---

matter of asking questions. This sufficed for Peter to realize he had to listen to the Holy Spirit" (St John Chrysostom, *Hom. on Acts*, 22).

10:24. Cornelius, in his zeal, calls in his family and friends to listen to the saving word of God. The group he assembles represents the pagan world which has for centuries been waiting for Christ without knowing it. "I was ready to be sought by those who did not ask for me; I was ready to be found by those who did not seek me" (Is 65:1).

This episode, in which Cornelius the Roman officer plays the leading role, has a much wider significance. His conversion means that the Jews are not the only heirs of the promises: it shows that the Gospel brings a universal remedy to solve a universal need. "Cornelius was such a servant of God that an angel was sent to him, and to his merits must be attributed the mysterious event through which Peter was to rise above the restrictions of circumcision. … Once the apostle baptized him, the salvation of the Gentiles had begun" (St Jerome, *Epistles*, 79, 2).

10:25–26. It is difficult at first for pagans to realize what is happening when God manifests himself to them, makes his will known and confers his gifts upon them through the medium of other men: their first reaction is to think that these must be celestial beings or gods in human form (cf. 14:11), until it is quite clear that they are men of flesh and blood. That is how it is: men and women are the defective but essential instruments whom God normally uses to make known his plans of salvation. God in his providence acts in this way, first in the Old Testament and particularly in the New Testament; a prime example is to be seen in the Christian priesthood.

"Every high priest [is] chosen from among men" (Heb 5:1) to be sent back to his brethren as a minister of intercession and forgiveness. "He must therefore be a member of the human race, for it is God's desire that man have one of his like to come to his aid" (St Thomas Aquinas, *Commentary on Heb*, 5, 1).

It has been said that everything about the Gospel of Jesus Christ is quite excellent, except the persons of his ministers—because these priests, who have been consecrated by a special sacrament, are also sons of Adam, and they still have the weak nature of sons of Adam even after being ordained.

"Most strange is this in itself […] but not strange, when you consider it is the appointment of an all-merciful God; not

many persons gathered; [28]and he said to them, "You yourselves Gal 2:12
know how unlawful it is for a Jew to associate with or to visit any
one of another nation; but God has shown me that I should not
call any man common or unclean. [29]So when I was sent for, I
came without objection. I ask then why you sent for me."
[30]And Cornelius said, "Four days ago, about this hour, I was
keeping the ninth hour of prayer in my house; and behold, a man
stood before me in bright apparel, [31]saying, 'Cornelius, your
prayer has been heard and your alms have been remembered
before God. [32]Send therefore to Joppa and ask for Simon who is
called Peter; he is lodging in the house of Simon, a tanner, by the
seaside.' [33]So I sent for you at once, and you have been kind

---

strange in him. […] The priests of the New Law are men, in order that they may 'condole with those who are in ignorance and error, because they too are encompassed with infirmity' (Heb 5:2)" (St J. H. Newman, *Discourses addressed to Mixed Congregations*).

If priests were not men of flesh and blood, they would not feel for others, who are made of the same stuff; they would not understand their weakness. But in fact they do share the human condition and do experience the same temptations.

10:28. "The apostle did not wish it to appear that he was doing something prohibited out of consideration for Cornelius. Peter desires to make it plain that the Lord is the only reason for his action. That is why he reminds them that contact with pagans and even entering their houses is forbidden" (St John Chrysostom, *Hom. on Acts*, 23).

Peter justifies his actions, which are not in line with the way a strict Jew would act, by saying that he is obeying God's will, made known to him only a short while before. The Gospel no longer recognizes any distinction between clean and unclean people. All are equal in the sight of God if they listen to his word with a pure heart and repent their sins.

10:33. Grace disposes Cornelius to accept Peter's words as coming from God. The centurion was a man of good will and upright conscience, who worshipped God according to his lights. Prior to meeting Peter, he is an example of the religious person who sincerely seeks the truth and is therefore on the way to ensuring his eternal destiny. The Second Vatican Council teaches that "those who, through no fault of their own, do not know the Gospel of Christ or his Church, but who nevertheless seek God with a sincere heart, and, moved by grace, try in their actions to do his will as they know it through the dictates of their conscience—those too may achieve eternal salvation" (*Lumen gentium*, 16).

However, the spiritual blessings given to Cornelius and those with him go further than this: they actually prepare them to enter the Church. When God gives initial graces to people who are not yet Christians, he wishes them to attain the fullness of grace, which they will find in the Catholic Church. "This is God's intention, this is what he does. If he did not despise the Magi, the Ethiopian, the thief or the courtesan, how much less will he despise those who practise righteousness and desire it" (St John Chrysostom, *Hom. on Acts*, 23).

enough to come. Now therefore we are all here present in the
sight of God, to hear all that you have been commanded by the
Lord."

Peter preaches to Cornelius

Deut 0:17 34 And Peter opened his mouth and said: "Truly I perceive that
Rom 2:11 Gal 2:6 God shows no partiality, 35 but in every nation any one who fears
1 Pet 1:17 him and does what is right is acceptable to him. 36 You know the
Is 56:7 word which he sent to Israel, preaching good news of peace by
Rom 15:16 Jesus Christ (he is Lord of all), 37 the word which was proclaimed
Is 52:7 throughout all Judea, beginning from Galilee after the baptism
which John preached: 38 how God anointed Jesus of Nazareth with
Is 61:1 Mt 3:16 the Holy Spirit and with power; how he went about doing good
Acts 4:27 and healing all that were oppressed by the devil, for God was with
Acts 1:8 him. 39 And we are witnesses to all that he did both in the country
of the Jews and in Jerusalem. They put him to death by hanging
1 Cor 15:4 him on a tree; 40 but God raised him on the third day and made him
Lk 24:43 Jn 14:22 manifest; 41 not to all the people but to us who were chosen by
Acts 17:31 God as witnesses, who ate and drank with him after he rose from
2 Tim 4:1 1 Pet 4:5 the dead. 42 And he commanded us to preach to the people, and to

---

10:34–43. Peter's short address is his first to non-Jews. It begins with the central idea that God is impartial: he wants all men to be saved through the proclamation of the Gospel (vv. 34–36). This is followed by a summary of Jesus' public life (vv. 37–41) and, finally, the statement (the first time it appears in Acts) that Jesus Christ has been made Judge of the living and the dead (v. 42). As in all Christian preaching to Gentiles, proofs from Scripture take a secondary place (v. 43).

10:34. This verse refers to 1 Samuel 16:7, where the Lord, in connexion with the anointing of David as king of Israel, tells the prophet, "Do not look on his appearance or on the height of his stature, because I have rejected him; for the Lord sees not as man sees; man looks on the outward appearance, but the Lord looks on the heart." When God calls and offers salvation to his elect, he does not judge as men do. With him distinctions regarding social class, race, sex or education do not count.

Here St Peter proclaims that the Old Testament prophecies about the Jews and the Gentiles forming one single nation (Is 2:2–4; Joel 2:28; Amos 9:12; Mich 4:1) and Jesus' words calling everyone to enter his Kingdom (cf. Mt 8:11; Mk 16:15–16; Jn 10:16) should be interpreted literally.

10:40. Peter's summary of the Gospel of Jesus (vv. 37–41) reaches its climax with his statement that "God raised him on the third day." This had become the usual way of referring to our Lord's resurrection (cf. 1 Cor 15:4); see the note on Acts 4:10.

10:42. This verse refers to Christ's role as Judge: he has been made supreme Judge over all mankind and will deliver his judgment at his second coming

testify that he is the one ordained by God to be judge of the living
and the dead. 43 To him all the prophets bear witness that every one Is 33:24
who believes in him receives forgiveness of sins through his Jer 31:34
name."

The baptism of Cornelius and his household

44 While Peter was still saying this, the Holy Spirit fell on all who Acts 11:15; 15:8
heard the word. 45 And the believers from among the circumcised
who came with Peter were amazed, because the gift of the Holy
Spirit had been poured out even on the Gentiles. 46 For they heard Acts 2:4–11; 19:6
them speaking in tongues and extolling God. Then Peter declared,
47 "Can any one forbid water for baptizing these people who have Acts 8:36; 11:17
received the Holy Spirit just as we have?" 48 And he commanded
them to be baptized in the name of Jesus Christ. Then they asked
him to remain for some days.

In Jerusalem Peter justifies his conduct

11 1 Now the apostles and the brethren who were in Judea
heard that the Gentiles also had received the word of God.
2 So when Peter went up to Jerusalem, the circumcision party crit-

---

(Parousia). "The Sacred Scriptures inform us that there are two comings of the Son of God: the one when he assumed human flesh for our salvation in the womb of a virgin; the other when he shall come at the end of the world to judge all mankind" (*St Pius V Catechism*, 1, 8, 2).

Christ's coming as Judge means that men will appear before him twice, to render an account of their lives—of their thoughts, words, deeds and omissions. The first judgment will take place "when each of us departs this life; for then he is instantly placed before the judgment-seat of God, where all that he has ever done or spoken or thought during his life shall be subjected to the most rigid scrutiny. This is called the particular judgment. The second occurs when on the same day and in the same place all men shall stand together before the tribunal of their Judge [...], and this is called the general judgment" (ibid., 1, 8, 3).

10:44–48. This scene is reminiscent of Pentecost. There the Holy Spirit came down on the first disciples, Jews all of them. Now he is given to Gentiles, unexpectedly and irresistibly. It is as if the Lord wanted to confirm to Peter everything he had so far revealed to him about the admission of Cornelius to the Church. The centurion and his family are baptized on Peter's instructions, without first becoming Jews through circumcision.

11:1–18. Some members of the Jerusalem community are shocked to learn that Peter has eaten with people who are legally unclean and has allowed them to be baptized without first being circumcised.

"The circumcision party" refers, therefore, to those Christians who are scandalized by the Gospel's attitude to the ritual prohibitions and ethnic exclusiveness of the Mosaic Law.

The apostle's address has a positive effect and sets their minds at ease. This

Acts 10:28, 48 Eph 2:11 icized him, 3saying, "Why did you go to uncircumcised men and
eat with them?" 4But Peter began and explained to them in order:
Acts 10:9–48 5"I was in the city of Joppa praying; and in a trance I saw a vision,
something descending, like a great sheet, let down from heaven by
four corners; and it came down to me. 6Looking at it closely I
observed animals and beasts of prey and reptiles and birds of the
air. 7And I heard a voice saying to me, 'Rise, Peter; kill and eat.'
8But I said, 'No, Lord; for nothing common or unclean has ever
entered my mouth.' 9But the voice answered a second time from
heaven, 'What God has cleansed you must not call common.'
10This happened three times, and all was drawn up again into
heaven. 11And that very moment three men arrived at the house in
which we were, sent to me from Caesarea. 12And the Spirit told
me to go with them, making no distinction. These six brethren
also accompanied me, and we entered the man's house. 13And he
told us how he had seen the angel standing in this house and
saying, 'Send to Joppa and bring Simon called Peter; 14he will
declare to you a message by which you will be saved, you and all

---

attitude of the disciples, who are interested only in the will of God and the spread of the Gospel, shows how ready they are to accept instruction: their initial reserve was quite conscientious. Peter once again describes the vision he received (10:9–23), to show that if he had not baptized Cornelius he would have been disobeying God.

This account of the vision differs slightly from his earlier one, the main addition being in vv. 15–16, which connect the coming of the Holy Spirit at Pentecost (2:1ff) with his descent on the Gentile converts in Caesarea (10:44).

Unfortunately the stubborn Judaizing tendencies exhibited by some members of the infant Church took a long time to disappear, as is dramatically borne out in some of St Paul's letters: he refers to "false brethren secretly brought in, who slipped in to spy on our freedom which we have in Jesus Christ, that they might bring us into bondage" (Gal 2:4) and warns Christians to be on their guard against fanatics of the Law of Moses who are self-serving and "want to pervert the gospel of Christ" (Gal 1:7).

11:19–30. This account links up with Acts 8:1–4, which describes the flight of Christians from Jerusalem due to the first persecution following on the martyrdom of St Stephen. We are now told about the spread of the Gospel to Antioch on the Orontes, the capital of the Roman province of Syria. Antioch was the first major city of the ancient world where the word of Jesus Christ was preached. It was the third city of the empire, after Rome and Alexandria, with a population of about half a million and a sizeable Jewish colony, and was a very important cultural, economic and religious centre.

In Antioch the Gospel is proclaimed not only to Jews and proselytes. These Hellenist Jews from Jerusalem preach the Gospel to all and sundry as part of their ordinary everyday activity. St Luke does not give us any names: the preachers are ordinary Christians. "Notice", says St John Chrysostom, "that it is grace which

your household.' 15As I began to speak, the Holy Spirit fell on
them just as on us at the beginning. 16And I remembered the word Acts 1:5
of the Lord, how he said, 'John baptized with water, but you shall
be baptized with the Holy Spirit.' 17If then God gave the same gift Acts 15:8–9;
to them as he gave to us when we believed in the Lord Jesus 10:47
Christ, who was I that I could withstand God?" 18When they heard
this they were silenced. And they glorified God, saying, "Then to Acts 14:27
the Gentiles also God has granted repentance unto life."

Beginning of the Church in Antioch

19Now those who were scattered because of the persecution that Acts 8:1–4
arose over Stephen travelled as far as Phoenicia and Cyprus and
Antioch, speaking the word to none except Jews. 20But there were
some of them, men of Cyprus and Cyrene, who on coming to
Antioch spoke to the Greeks[i] also, preaching the Lord Jesus.
21And the hand of the Lord was with them, and a great number Acts 2:47
that believed turned to the Lord. 22News of this came to the ears Acts 4:36; 8:14
of the church in Jerusalem, and they sent Barnabas to Antioch.

---

does everything. And also reflect on the fact that this work is begun by unknown workers and only when it begins to prosper do the apostles send Barnabas" (*Hom. on Acts*, 25).

The Christian mission at Antioch played a key part in the spread of Christianity. Evangelization of non-Jews becomes the norm; it is not just something which happens in a few isolated cases. Nor is it limited to "God-fearers"; it extends to all the Gentiles. The centre of gravity of the Christian Church begins to move from Jerusalem to Antioch, which will become the springboard for the evangelization of the pagan world.

11:20. The title "Lord", often applied to Jesus in the New Testament and in the early Church, is a confession of faith in his divinity. To say "Jesus is Lord" (1 Cor 12:3; Rom 10:9) is the same as saying that Jesus Christ is God. It means that he is worshipped as the only Son of the Father and as sovereign of the Church, and receives the cult of *latria* which is rendered to God alone.

This acclamation of Jesus as Lord shows that from the very beginning the young Christian communities knew that he had dominion over all mankind and was not just the Messiah of one nation.

11:22–26. The community at Jerusalem, where the apostles were based, felt responsible for everything that happened in the Christian mission-field. This was why they sent Barnabas to oversee developments in Antioch. He was a man whom the apostles trusted, noted for his virtue (he was mentioned in Acts 4:36).

No doubt it was because of all the work opening before the preachers of the Gospel that Barnabas sought out Paul, who had returned to Tarsus after his conversion and his visit to Jerusalem (9:30). Barnabas probably knew that the future apostle was the very man he needed to join him in the work of evangelization about to be undertaken by the Antiochene

i. Other ancient authorities read *Hellenists*

Acts 13:43; 14:22 23 When he came and saw the grace of God, he was glad; and he
exhorted them all to remain faithful to the Lord with steadfast pur-
Acts 6:5 pose; 24 for he was a good man, full of the Holy Spirit and of faith.
Acts 9:30 And a large company was added to the Lord. 25 So Barnabas went
Acts 26:28 to Tarsus to look for Saul; 26 and when he had found him, he
1 Pet 4:16 brought him to Antioch. For a whole year they met with[j] the
church, and taught a large company of people; and in Antioch the
disciples were for the first time called Christians.

---

church. Barnabas' sense of responsibility and his zeal to find labourers for the Lord's harvest (cf. Mt 9:38) lead to the first of the great missionary journeys, in which Paul's vocation finds full scope.

11:26. We do not exactly know who first began to describe the disciples as "Christians". In any event the fact that they were given a name shows that everyone recognized them as an identifiable group. The name also suggests that the term *Christos*—Messiah, Anointed—is no longer regarded simply as a messianic title but also as a proper name.

Some Fathers of the Church see this name as further indication that people do not become disciples of the Lord through human causes. "Although the holy apostles were our teachers and have given us the Gospel of the Saviour, it is not from them that we have taken our name: we are *Christians* through Christ and it is for him that we are called in this way" (St Athanasius, *Oratio I contra arianos*, 2).

11:27. This is the first reference to prophets in the first Christian communities (cf. 13:1). As was the case with the Old Testament prophets, these prophets of the early Church receive special illumination from God—charisms—to speak in his name under the inspiration of the Holy Spirit. Their function is not only to predict future events (cf. 11:28; 21:11) but to show the way the divine promises and plans contained in Sacred Scripture have been fulfilled.

Acts refers to prophets a number of times. In addition to Agabus, it describes as prophets Judas and Silas (15:32) and the daughters of Philip the deacon (21:9). We also know that Paul had the gift of prophecy (cf. 1 Cor 12–14). In the infant Church the prophetic office was subordinate to the apostolic ministry and was exercised under the control of the apostles in the service and building up of the Christian community. "And God has appointed in the church first apostles, second prophets, third teachers" (1 Cor 12:28).

The gift of prophecy in the sense of a special charism as found in the early years of the Church is not to be found in later times. But the gifts of the Holy Spirit are still to be found in all the members of the mystical body of Christ, varying with the ecclesial role which each person has.

The hierarchy of the Church, with the Pope as its head, has the prophetic mission of unerringly proclaiming true teaching within and without the Church.

"The holy People of God", Vatican II teaches, "shares also in Christ's prophetic office: it spreads abroad a living witness to him, especially by a life of faith and love. […] The whole body of the faithful, who have an anointing that comes from

j. Or *were guests of*

Antioch helps the Church in Judea

27Now in these days prophets came down from Jerusalem to Antioch. 28And one of them named Agabus stood up and foretold by the Spirit that there would be a great famine over all the world; and this took place in the days of Claudius. 29And the disciples determined, every one according to his ability, to send relief to the brethren who lived in Judea; 30and they did so, sending it to the elders by the hand of Barnabas and Saul.

Acts 13:1; 15:32
Acts 21:10
Gal 2:10
Acts 12:25

---

the holy one (cf. 1 Jn 2:20, 27) cannot err in matters of belief. This characteristic is shown in the supernatural appreciation of the faith [*sensus fidei*] of the whole people, when, 'from the bishops to the last of the faithful' (St Augustine, *De praed. sanct.*, 14, 27) they manifest a universal consent in matters of faith and morals. By this appreciation of the faith, aroused and sustained by the Spirit of truth, the People of God, guided by the sacred teaching authority [*magisterium*], and obeying it, receives not the mere word of men, but truly the word of God (cf. 1 Thess 2:13), the faith once for all delivered to the saints (cf. Jude 3). The People unfailingly adheres to this faith, penetrates it more deeply with right judgment, and applies it more fully in daily life.

"It is not only through the sacraments and the ministrations of the Church that the Holy Spirit makes holy the People, leads them and enriches them with his virtues. Allotting his gifts according as he wills (cf. 1 Cor 12:11), he also distributes special graces among the faithful of every rank. By these gifts he makes them fit and ready to undertake various tasks and offices for the renewing and building up of the Church" (*Lumen gentium*, 12).

11:28–29. During the reign of Claudius (41–54), the empire suffered a severe food crisis. This famine, which afflicted Greece, Syria and Palestine as well as Rome during the years AD 47–49, would have been the one which Agabus foretold.

This imminent food shortage is what leads the prosperous Antiochene community to send aid to the mother community in Jerusalem. Like their first brothers in the faith (cf. 4:34), the disciples in Antioch show their charity and concern for their fellow-Christians and prove that they have the true Christian spirit.

11:30. This journey may be the same one as mentioned in 15:2 (cf. Gal 2:1–10). The money which Paul and Barnabas bring to Jerusalem on this occasion should not be confused with the results of the big collection organized later (cf. 24:17).

It is the elders of the community who receive and organize the distribution of the collection. These "elders" or presbyters—the traditional Jewish name for those in charge of the community—seem to have been aides of the apostles. We are not told about how they were instituted, but they appear a number of times in Acts (15:2—16:4; 21:18), they perform functions which are somewhat different from those of the Twelve, and they take part in the Council of Jerusalem.

Paul and Barnabas appoint elders and put them in charge of the churches they found during their first great missionary journey (cf. 14:23), and in the epistles to Timothy (5:17–19) and Titus (1:5) those entrusted with an established ministry in each community are described as elders.

Apparently, at the start the terms "bishop" and "elder" (cf. 10:17, 28; 1 Tim 3:2; Tit 1:7) were used interchange-

Persecution by Herod. Peter's arrest and miraculous deliverance

12 1About that time Herod the king laid violent hands upon
some who belonged to the church.* 2He killed James the
Mt 20:22–23 brother of John with the sword; 3and when he saw that it pleased
the Jews, he proceeded to arrest Peter also. This was during the
days of Unleavened Bread. 4And when he had seized him, he put
him in prison, and delivered him to four squads of soldiers to
guard him, intending after the Passover to bring him out to the
people. 5So Peter was kept in prison; but earnest prayer for him
Jas 5:16 was made to God by the church.
6The very night when Herod was about to bring him out, Peter
Acts 5:18–23; 16:25–40 was sleeping between two soldiers, bound with two chains, and

---

ably and then later on came to refer to the two highest levels of the hierarchy. By the second century the meaning of each term was clearly fixed. The difference consists in this: bishops have the fullness of the sacrament of Order (cf. Vatican II, *Lumen gentium*, 11), and presbyters, "true priests of the New Testament [...] after the image of Christ" (ibid., 28), carry out pastoral ministry as co-workers of their bishops and in communion with them.

The New Testament texts use the term "priest" only to refer to the ministers of the Old Law (cf. Mt 8:4; 20:18; Heb 7:23) and as a title belonging to Jesus Christ, the only true Priest (cf. Heb 4:15; 5:5; 8:1; 9:11), from whom all lawful priesthood derives. In general, the early Church avoids, where possible, the use of terminology which might imply that it was simply one more among the many religions in the Greco-Roman world.

12:1–19. This is an account of persecution of the Church by Herod Agrippa (37–44), which took place before the visit of Paul and Barnabas to the Holy City (cf. 11:30).

The information given in this chapter about the latest persecution of the Jerusalem community—more severe and more general than the earlier crises (cf. 5:17f; 8:1)—gives an accurate picture of the situation in Palestine and describes events in chronological sequence. Prior to this the Roman governors more or less protected the rights of the Jerusalem Christians. Now Agrippa, in his desire to ingratiate himself with the Pharisees, abandons the Christians to the growing resentment and hatred the Jewish authorities and people feel towards them.

This chapter brings to an end, so to speak, the story of the first Christian community in Jerusalem. From now on, attention is concentrated on the church of Antioch. The last stage of the Palestinian Judeo-Christian church, under the direction of James "the brother of the Lord", will not experience the expansion enjoyed by other churches, due to the grave turn which events take in the Holy Land.

12:1. This Herod is the third prince of that name to appear in the New Testament. He was a grandson of Herod the Great, who built the new temple of Jerusalem and was responsible for the massacre of the Holy Innocents (cf. Mt 2:16); he was also a nephew of Herod Antipas, the tetrarch of Galilee at the time of our Lord's death. Herod Agrippa I was a favourite of

sentries before the door were guarding the prison; [7]and behold, an 1 Kings 19:5
angel of the Lord appeared, and a light shone in the cell; and he
struck Peter on the side and woke him, saying, "Get up quickly."
And the chains fell off his hands. [8]And the angel said to him,
"Dress yourself and put on your sandals." And he did so. And he
said to him, "Wrap your mantle around you and follow me." [9]And
he went out and followed him; he did not know that what was Acts 10:17
done by the angel was real, but thought he was seeing a vision.
[10]When they had passed the first and the second guard, they came
to the iron gate leading into the city. It opened to them of its own
accord, and they went out and passed on through one street; and
immediately the angel left him. [11]And Peter came to himself, and
said, "Now I am sure that the Lord has sent his angel and rescued

---

the emperor Caligula, who gradually gave him more territory and allowed him to use the title of king. Agrippa I managed to extend his authority over all the territory his grandfather had ruled: Roman governors had ruled Judea up to the year 41, but in that year it was given over to Herod. He was a sophisticated type of person, a diplomat, so bent on consolidating his power that he had become a master of intrigue and a total opportunist. For largely political motives he practised Judaism with a certain rigour.

12:2. James the Greater would have been martyred in the year 42 or 43. He was the first apostle to die for the faith and the only one whose death is mentioned in the New Testament. The Liturgy of the Hours says of him: "The son of Zebedee and the brother of John, he was born in Bethsaida. He witnessed the principal miracles performed by our Lord and was put to death by Herod around the year 42. He is held in special veneration in the city of Compostela, where a famous church is dedicated to his name."

"The Lord permits this death," St John Chrysostom observes, "to show his murderers that these events do not cause the Christians to retreat or desist" (*Hom. on Acts*, 26).

12:5. "Notice the feelings of the faithful towards their pastors. They do not riot or rebel; they have recourse to prayer, which can solve all problems. They do not say to themselves: We do not count, there is no point in our praying for him. Their love led them to pray and they did not think along those lines. Have you noticed what these persecutors did without intending to? They made (their victims) more determined to stand the test, and (the faithful) more zealous and loving" (*Hom. on Acts*, 26).

St Luke, whose Gospel reports our Lord's words on perseverance in prayer (cf. 11:11–13; 18:1–8), here stresses that God listens to the whole community's prayer for Peter. He plans in his providence to save the apostle for the benefit of the Church, but he wants the outcome to be seen as an answer to the Church's fervent prayer.

12:7–10. The Lord comes to Peter's help by sending an angel, who opens the prison and leads him out. This miraculous freeing of the apostle is similar to what happened at the time of Peter and John's detention (5:19f) and when Paul and Silas are imprisoned in Philippi (16:19ff).

This extraordinary event, which must be understood exactly as it is described,

me from the hand of Herod and from all that the Jewish people
were expecting."

Acts 12:25; 13:5, 13; 15:37
Col 4:10
Philem 24
2 Tim 4:11
1 Pet 5:13

12When he realized this, he went to the house of Mary, the
mother of John whose other name was Mark, where many were
gathered together and were praying. 13And when he knocked at
the door of the gateway, a maid named Rhoda came to answer.
14Recognizing Peter's voice, in her joy she did not open the gate
but ran in and told that Peter was standing at the gate. 15They said
to her, "You are mad." But she insisted that it was so. They said,
"It is his angel!" 16But Peter continued knocking; and when they
opened, they saw him and were amazed. 17But motioning to them
with his hand to be silent, he described to them how the Lord had

Acts 15:13; 21:18
Gal 1:19

---

shows the loving care God takes of those whom he entrusts with a mission. They must strive to fulfil it, but they will "see" for themselves that he guides their steps and watches over them.

12:12. John Mark was Barnabas' cousin (cf. Col 4:10). He will accompany Barnabas and Paul on the first missionary journey (cf. 13:5) up to when they enter the province of Asia (cf. 13:13). Despite Paul's not wanting to have him on the second journey (cf. 15:37–39), we find him later again as a co-worker of the Apostle (cf. Col 4:10; 2 Tim 4:11) and also as a disciple and helper of Simon Peter (1 Pet 5:13). Church tradition credits him with the authorship of the Second Gospel.

"The house of Mary": this may have been the same house as the Cenacle, where Jesus celebrated his Last Supper with his disciples. See Introduction to St Mark, pp. 215–216 above.

12:15. The first Christians had a very lively faith in the guardian angels and their God-given role of assisting men. In the Old Testament God reveals the existence of angels; on various occasions we see them playing an active part (cf., for example, Gen 48:16; Tob 5:21; etc.). In the apocryphal books of the Old Testament and in writings composed between the two Testaments (which flourished around the time of Christ's life on earth) there are many references to angels. Our Lord spoke about them often, as we can see from the Gospels.

"In many parts of Sacred Scripture it is said that each of us has an angel. Our Lord affirms this when he speaks about children: 'in heaven their angels always behold the face of my Father' (Mt 18:10). And Jacob refers to the angel 'who freed him from all evil'. On this occasion the disciples thought that the angel of the apostle Peter was approaching" (St Bede, *Super Act. expositio,* ad loc.).

The first Christians' behaviour in adversity and their trust in God's help are an enduring example. "Drink at the clear fountain of the Acts of the Apostles. In the twelfth chapter, Peter, freed from prison by the ministry of angels, comes to the house of the mother of Mark. Those inside will not believe the servant girl, who says that Peter is at the door. '*Angelus ejus est!* It must be his angel!' they said. See on what intimate terms the early Christians were with their guardian angels. And what about you?" (St Josemaría Escrivá, *The Way*, 570).

12:17. After Peter and the other apostles leave Jerusalem, the community in that city is governed by James the Less, the

brought him out of the prison. And he said, "Tell this to James and
to the brethren." Then he departed and went to another place.
[18]Now when day came, there was no small stir among the soldiers over what had become of Peter. [19]And when Herod had
sought for him and could not find him, he examined the sentries
and ordered that they should be put to death. Then he went down
from Judea to Caesarea, and remained there.

Death of Herod

[20]Now Herod was angry with the people of Tyre and Sidon; and
they came to him in a body, and having persuaded Blastus, the
king's chamberlain, they asked for peace, because their country

---

"brother" of the Lord; even before that he was a prominent figure in the Jerusalem church. According to Flavius Josephus, this James was stoned to death by order of the Sanhedrin (cf. *Jewish Antiquities*, 20, 200).

We do not know where Peter went after leaving Jerusalem—probably to Antioch or Rome. He was certainly in Antioch at one stage (cf. Gal 2:11), but it may not have been at this point. Tradition does state that Peter had his see in Antioch for a period. We do know that he was present at the Council of Jerusalem. In any event he ultimately settled in Rome.

According to St Jerome, Peter arrived in Rome in the second year of Claudius' reign (43) and had his see there for twenty-five years, up to the fourteenth year of Nero's reign, that is, 68 (cf. *On Famous Men*, 1).

12:20–23. Herod Agrippa I must have died in Caesarea in the year 44 during the games in honour of Claudius. St Luke's brief account agrees with that of Josephus. "When at daybreak of the second day he made his way to the theatre", the Jewish historian writes, "and the rays of the sun made his garments look like silver and made him look splendid, his sycophants acclaimed him as a god and said, 'Up to this we regarded you as a man, but from now on we shall revere you as one who is more than mortal.' The king accepted this blasphemous flattery: he made no comment. But immediately he began to feel terrible stomach pains and he was dead within five days" (*Jewish Antiquities*, 19, 344–346).

The painful and unexpected death of this king who had persecuted the Church recalls the death of King Antiochus Epiphanes (cf. 2 Mac 9:5ff), another declared enemy of God's elect and of divine Law: "The all-seeing God of Israel struck him with an incurable and unseen blow."

Not content with persecuting the Church, Agrippa attributes to himself glory which belongs only to God; his evil life eventually provokes God to judge him in this way. "The hour of judgment has not yet come, but God wounds the most blameworthy of all, as an object lesson for others" (St John Chrysostom, *Hom. on Acts*, 27).

Agrippa's persecution of the Church and of Christians was the logical result of his failure to acknowledge God as lord of all: Agrippa sees him as a kind of rival. In his pride, he refuses to admit his human limitations and dependence on God; and he goes further and attacks God's work and God's servants. Human

depended on the king's country for food. [21]On an appointed day
Herod put on his royal robes, took his seat upon the throne, and
Ezek 28:2 made an oration to them. [22]And the people shouted, "The voice of
Dan 5:20 a god, and not of man!" [23]Immediately an angel of the Lord smote
2 Mac 9:5, 28 him, because he did not give God the glory; and he was eaten by
worms and died.

Barnabas and Paul return

Acts 6:7 [24]But the word of God grew and multiplied. [25]And Barnabas and
Acts 11:29; 12:12 Saul returned from[k] Jerusalem when they had fulfilled their mission, bringing with them John whose other name was Mark.

---

dignity is only possible if God's majesty is positively asserted and adored: in that recognition and service man's true wisdom lies.

"'*Deo omnis gloria*. All glory to God.' It is an emphatic confession of our nothingness. He, Jesus, is everything. We, without him, are worth nothing: nothing.

"Our vainglory would be just that: vain glory; it would be sacrilegious robbery. There should be no room for that 'I' anywhere" (St Josemaría Escrivá, *The Way*, 780).

12:24. St Luke contrasts the failure and downfall of the Church's persecutors with the irresistible progress of the Word of God.

12:25. They "returned from Jerusalem": following the best Greek manuscripts, the reading accepted by the New Vulgate is "returned to Jerusalem" (cf. RSV note). However, it does not seem to fit in with the end of chapter 11 and the beginning of chapter 13. Therefore, from very early on many Greek manuscripts and translations (including the Sixto-Clementine edition of the Vulgate) read "returned from Jerusalem". It is not clear which is correct; the Navarre Spanish follows the New Vulgate.

13:1. From this point onwards Luke's account centres on the church of Antioch. This was a flourishing community, with members drawn from all sectors of society. In some respects its organization structure was like that of the Jerusalem church; in others, not. It clearly had ordained ministers who were responsible for its government, who preached and administered the sacraments; alongside these we find prophets (cf. 11:27) and teachers, specially trained members of the community.

In the early Church "teachers" were disciples well versed in Sacred Scripture who were given charge of catechesis. They instructed the catechumens and other Christians in the basic teaching of the Gospel as passed on by the apostles, and some of them had a capacity for acquiring and communicating to others an extensive and profound knowledge of the faith.

Teachers do not necessarily have to be priests or preachers. Preaching was usually reserved to ordained ministers; teachers had an important position in the Church: they were responsible for on-

k. Other ancient authorities read *to*

PART THREE

The spread of the Church among the Gentiles. Missionary journeys of St Paul

8. ST PAUL'S FIRST APOSTOLIC JOURNEY

Paul and Barnabas are sent on a mission

13 [1]Now in the church at Antioch there were prophets and Acts 4:36; 11:20, 27
teachers, Barnabas, Symeon who was called Niger, Lucius
of Cyrene, Manaen a member of the court of Herod the tetrarch,
and Saul. [2]While they were worshipping the Lord and fasting, the Gal 1:15

---

going doctrinal and moral education and were expected faithfully to hand on the same teaching as they themselves had received. A virtuous life and due learning would have protected them against any temptation to invent new teachings or go in for mere speculation not based on the Gospel (cf. 1 Tim 4:7; 6:20; Tit 2:1).

The *Letter to Diognetus* describes the ideal Christian teacher: "I do not speak of passing things nor do I go in search of new things, but, like the disciple of the apostles that I am, I become a teacher of peoples. I do nothing but hand on what was given me by those who made themselves worthy disciples of the truth" (11, 1).

13:2–3. "Worship" of the Lord includes prayer, but it refers primarily to the celebration of the Blessed Eucharist, which is at the centre of all Christian ritual. This text indirectly establishes a parallel between the Mass and the sacrificial rite of the Mosaic Law. The Eucharist provides a Christian with the nourishment he needs, and its celebration "causes the Church of God to be built up and grow in stature" (Vatican II, *Unitatis redintegratio*, 15). Significantly, the Eucharist is associated with the start of this new stage in the expansion of the Church.

Paul and Barnabas receive a missionary task directly from the Holy Spirit, and by an external sign—the laying on of hands—the Antiochene community prays God to go with them and bless them. In his promotion of the spread of the Church the Holy Spirit does not act at a distance, so to speak. Every step in the progress of the Church in the world is rightly attributed to the initiative of the Paraclete. It is as if God were repeatedly ratifying his salvific plans to make it perfectly plain that he is ever-faithful to his promises. "The mission of the Church is carried out by means of that activity through which, in obedience to Christ's command and moved by the grace and love of the Holy Spirit, the Church makes itself fully present to all men and people" (Vatican II, *Ad gentes*, 5).

The dispatch of Paul and Barnabas is inspired by the Holy Spirit, but it is also an ecclesial act: the Church gives them this charge, specifying God's plans and activating the personal vocation of the two envoys.

The Lord, "who had set me apart before I was born, and had called me by

Holy Spirit said, "Set apart for me Barnabas and Saul for the work
Acts 6:6 to which I have called them." 3Then after fasting and praying they
laid their hands on them and sent them off.

Paul and Barnabas in Cyprus

4So, being sent out by the Holy Spirit, they went down to Seleu-
Acts 12:12 cia; and from there they sailed to Cyprus. 5When they arrived at

---

his grace [sent me] in order that I might preach him among the Gentiles" (Gal 1:15–16), now arranges, through the Church, for this mission to begin.

Fasting and prayer are the best preparation for the spiritual enterprise on which Paul and Barnabas are about to embark. "First, prayer; then, atonement; in the third place, very much 'in the third place', action" (St Josemaría Escrivá, *The Way*, 82). They know very well that their mission is not man-made and that it will produce results only with God's help. The prayer and penance which accompany apostolate are not just aimed at obtaining graces from God for others: the purpose of this prayer and fasting is to purify hearts and lips, so that the Lord will be at their side and ensure that none of their words "fall to the ground" (1 Sam 3:19).

13:4—14:28. This first missionary journey took Paul, accompanied by Barnabas, to Cyprus and central Galatia, in Asia Minor. He left Antioch in the spring of 45 and returned almost four years later, after preaching Christ to both Jews and Gentiles wherever he went.

St Luke's account, which covers chapters 13 and 14, is sketchy but accurate. At Seleucia (the port of Antioch, about 35 kilometres or 22 miles from the city) they embarked for Cyprus, the largest island in the eastern Mediterranean, where Barnabas came from. They disembarked at Salamis, the island's main city and port. There they went to the Jewish synagogues on a series of sabbaths.

In v. 6 it says that they crossed the island to Paphos, which is on the extreme west. This would have taken them several months because, although it is only 150 kilometres as the crow flies, there were many towns with Jewish communities, and since they had to stay in each for a number of sabbaths their progress would have been slow. We are told nothing about the result of this work of evangelizing en route from Salamis to Paphos, but the indications are that it was fruitful, because Barnabas will later go back to Cyprus, accompanied by Mark (cf. 15:39), to consolidate the work done on this first mission. New Paphos was where the proconsul resided.

From there they went on board ship again and travelled north, probably disembarking, after a short crossing, at Attalia. After a few miles they reached Perga in Pamphylia, a barren, inhospitable region at the base of the Taurus mountains, where Mark took leave of his companions.

Going from Perga to Pisidian Antioch (v. 14) meant a difficult journey of about 160 kilometres over mountain roads. This other Antioch was 1,200 metres above sea level and would have had a sizeable Jewish community, connected with the trade in hides. The busy commercial life of the region helped the spread of the Christian message (v. 49). Paul addressed his preaching to the Gentiles because of the hostility of many Jews.

Salamis, they proclaimed the word of God in the synagogues of
the Jews. And they had John to assist them. 6When they had gone
through the whole island as far as Paphos, they came upon a certain magician, a Jewish false prophet, named Bar-Jesus. 7He was
with the proconsul, Sergius Paulus, a man of intelligence, who
summoned Barnabas and Saul and sought to hear the word of
God. 8But Elymas the magician (for that is the meaning of his 2 Tim 3:8

The apostles were expelled and they headed for Iconium, about 130 kilometres south east, where they stayed some months and then left because of disturbances created by both Gentiles and Jews: they had to flee to the region of Lycaonia, to two minor cities, Lystra and Derbe. There were very few Jews in Lystra, and no synagogue, and therefore Paul preached to the local people, in the open air; but some Jews, who had arrived from Antioch and Iconium, stoned him and left him for dead. Possibly with the help of Timothy (cf. 16:1) they managed to reach Derbe, where they made many disciples, and then set out on the journey home, retracing their steps through Lystra, Iconium and Pisidian Antioch. Things had quieted down, the local magistrates were new, and with a little prudence everything worked out quite well. The new disciples were confirmed in the faith, and priests, elders, were appointed to each local church. Paul and Barnabas then went back to Pamphylia and Attalia, where they took a ship for Antioch, arriving probably well into the year 49.

13:5. In each city he visits, Paul usually begins his preaching of the Gospel in the local synagogue. This is not simply a tactic: it is in line with what he knows is God's plan of salvation. Like Jesus, he feels obliged to proclaim the Kingdom first to "Israelites [for] to them belong the sonship, the glory, the covenants, the giving of the law, the worship, and the promises; to them belong the patriarchs, and of their race, according to the flesh, is the Christ" (Rom 9:4–5). The Jews have a right to be the first to have the Gospel preached to them, for they were the first to receive the divine promises (cf. 13:46).

Although many Jews choose not to listen to or understand the word of God, there are many who do accept the Gospel for what it is—the fulness of the Old Testament. All over the Diaspora thousands of men and women like Simeon and Anna, who were awaiting the Kingdom and serving the God of their forefathers with fasting and prayer (cf. Lk 2:25, 37), will receive the light of the Holy Spirit enabling them to recognize and accept Paul's preaching as coming from God.

It is true that the many Jewish communities established in the main cities of the Roman empire often hindered the spread of the Gospel; yet their very existence played a providential part in its progress.

13:6–7. Since the year 22 Cyprus had been a senatorial province and, as such, was governed by a proconsul. Sergius Paulus was the brother of the philosopher Seneca, Nero's tutor. He is described here as "a man of intelligence", in other words, he was a man of upright conscience and with the right disposition to listen to the word of God. The proconsul's discernment helps him resist and reject the evil influence of the false prophet Bar-Jesus.

name) withstood them, seeking to turn away the proconsul from
the faith. [9]But Saul, who is also called Paul, filled with the Holy
Spirit, looked intently at him [10]and said, "You son of the devil,
Jn 8:44 you enemy of all righteousness, full of all deceit and villainy, will
you not stop making crooked the straight paths of the Lord? [11]And
Jn 9:39 now, behold, the hand of the Lord is upon you, and you shall be
blind and unable to see the sun for a time." Immediately mist and
darkness fell upon him and he went about seeking people to lead
Lk 4:32 him by the hand. [12]Then the proconsul believed, when he saw
what had occurred, for he was astonished at the teaching of the
Lord.

Acts 15:38 **Paul and Barnabas cross into Asia Minor**

[13]Now Paul and his company set sail from Paphos, and came to
Perga in Pamphylia. And John left them and returned to Jeru-
salem; [14]but they passed on from Perga and came to Antioch of
Pisidia.

13:9. Here we learn, in an aside, that Saul has changed his name and now calls himself Paul. He did not do this at God's bidding, as in the case of Abraham (cf. Gen 17:5) or that of Peter (cf. Mt 16:18), to show that God had given him a new charge or mission. He was simply following the eastern custom of using a Roman name when it suited. Paul is the Roman name for Saul, and from now on he uses it instead of Saul.

13:11. Paul's punishment of Bar-Jesus, Elymas, is one of the few punitive miracles in the New Testament; in fact his purpose is not so much to punish the false prophet as to convert him. "Paul chooses to convert him by means of a miracle similar to that by which he himself was converted. The words 'for a time' is not the word of one who punishes but of one who converts. If it had been the word of one who punishes it would have left him blind for ever. He punishes him only for a time, and also to win over the proconsul" (St John Chrysostom, *Hom. on Acts*, 28).

"From his own experience," St Bede says, "the apostle knew that the mind can raise itself to the light from the darkness of the eyes" (*Super Act. expositio*, ad loc.).

The punishment of Elymas does influence Sergius Paulus' conversion, but it is not crucial to it. What convinces the proconsul is the consistency and sublimity of Christian teaching, which speaks for itself to people of good will.

13:15. Sabbath services in synagogues went right back to the post-exilic period (after the Babylonian captivity, which lasted from 586 to 539 BC), and by now they had a very settled form. They consisted of readings from Sacred Scripture, preaching and public prayers. No one was especially appointed to preside over these services; the president or ruler of the synagogue could ask any member of the community to take the ceremony (cf. 18:8); he supervised the preparations and made sure that everything was done properly.

Preaching in the synagogue of Antioch of Pisidia

And on the sabbath day they went into the synagogue and sat
down. 15After the reading of the law and the prophets, the rulers Acts 15:21
of the synagogue sent to them, saying, "Brethren, if you have any
word of exhortation for the people, say it." 16So Paul stood up, and
motioning with his hand said:*

"Men of Israel, and you that fear God, listen. 17The God of this Ex 3–15
people Israel chose our fathers and made the people great during Is 1:2
their stay in the land of Egypt, and with uplifted arm he led them
out of it. 18And for about forty years he bore with[m] them in the Deut 1:31
wilderness. 19And when he had destroyed seven nations in the Deut 7:1
land of Canaan, he gave them their land as an inheritance, for Josh 14:2
about four hundred and fifty years. 20And after that he gave them Gen 15:13
judges until Samuel the prophet. 21Then they asked for a king; and Ex 12:40 Judg 2:16
God gave them Saul the son of Kish, a man of the tribe of 1 Sam 3:20
Benjamin, for forty years. 22And when he had removed him, he 1 Sam 8:10 Ps 89:20
raised up David to be their king; of whom he testified and said, 'I Is 44:28

13:16–41. Paul's address here is an excellent example of the way he used to present the Gospel to a mixed congregation of Jews and proselytes. He lists the benefits conferred by God on the chosen people from Abraham down to John the Baptist (vv. 16–25); he then shows how all the messianic prophecies were fulfilled in Jesus (vv. 26–37), and, by way of conclusion, states that justification comes about through faith in Jesus, who died and then rose from the dead (vv. 38–41).

This address contains all the main themes of apostolic preaching, that is, God's saving initiative in the history of Israel (vv. 17–22); reference to the Precursor (vv. 24–25); the proclamation of the Gospel or *kerygma* in the proper sense (vv. 26b–31a); mention of Jerusalem (v. 31b); arguments from Sacred Scripture (vv. 33–37) complementing apostolic teaching and tradition (vv. 38–39); and a final exhortation, eschatological in character, announcing the future (vv. 40–41). In many respects this address is like those of St Peter (cf. 2:14ff; 3:12ff), especially where it proclaims Jesus as Messiah and in its many quotations from Sacred Scripture, chosen to show that the decisive event of the resurrection confirms Christ's divinity.

Paul gives a general outline of salvation history and then locates Jesus in it as the expected Messiah, the point at which all the various strands in that history meet and all God's promises are fulfilled. He shows that all the steps which lead up to Jesus Christ, even the stage of John the Baptist, are just points on a route. Earlier, provisional, elements must now, in Christ, give way to a new, definitive situation.

"You that fear God" (v. 26): see the notes on Acts 2:5–11 and 10:2.

13:28. Paul does not back off from telling his Jewish listeners about the cross, the painful death freely undergone by the innocent Jesus. They naturally find

m. Other ancient authorities read *cared for* (Deut 1:31)

have found in David the son of Jesse a man after my heart, who
2 Sam 7:12 will do all my will.' [23]Of this man's posterity God has brought to
Lk 3:3 Israel a Saviour, Jesus, as he promised. [24]Before his coming John
had preached a baptism of repentance to all the people of Israel.
Mt 3:11 [25]And as John was finishing his course, he said, 'What do you
Jn 1:20–27 suppose that I am? I am not he. No, but after me one is coming,
the sandals of whose feet I am not worthy to untie.'

[26]"Brethren, sons of the family of Abraham, and those among
you that fear God, to us has been sent the message of this salva-
Acts 3:17 tion. [27]For those who live in Jerusalem and their rulers, because
they did not recognize him nor understand the utterances of the
prophets which are read every sabbath, fulfilled these by con-
Mt 27:22–23 demning him. [28]Though they could charge him with nothing
Mt 27:59–60 deserving death, yet they asked Pilate to have him killed. [29]And
Acts 5:30 when they had fulfilled all that was written of him, they took him
Acts 1:3; 3:15; down from the tree, and laid him in a tomb. [30]But God raised him
10:40 from the dead; [31]and for many days he appeared to those who
came up with him from Galilee to Jerusalem, who are now his

---

it shocking and hurtful, but it is true and it is what brings salvation. "When I came to you, brethren," he says on another occasion, "I did not come proclaiming to you the testimony of God in lofty words or wisdom. For I decided to know nothing among you except Jesus Christ and him crucified" (1 Cor 2:1f).

Sometimes human logic cannot understand how Jesus could have died in this way. But the very fact that he did is evidence of the divine character of the Gospel and supports belief in the Christian faith. With the help of grace man can in some way understand the Lord making himself "obedient unto death, even death on a cross" (Phil 2:8). He can discover some of the reasons why God decided on this superabundant way of redeeming man. "It was very fitting," St Thomas Aquinas writes, "that Christ should die on a cross. First, to give an example of virtue. [...] Also, because this kind of death was the one most suited to atoning for the sin of the first man. ... It was fitting for Christ, in order to make up for that fault, to allow himself be nailed to the wood, as if to restore what Adam had snatched away. [...] Also, because by dying on the cross Jesus prepares us for our ascent into heaven. [...] And because it also was fitting for the universal salvation of the entire world" (*Summa theologiae*, 3, 46, 4).

Through Jesus' death on the cross we can see how much God loved us and consequently we can feel moved to love him with our whole heart and with all our strength. Only the cross of our Lord, an inexhaustible source of grace, can make us holy.

13:29–31. The empty tomb and the appearances of the risen Jesus to his disciples are the basis of the Church's testimony to the resurrection of the Lord, and they demonstrate that he did truly rise. Jesus predicted that he would rise on the third day after his death (cf. Mt 12:40; 16:21; 17:22; Jn 2:19). Faith in the Resurrection is supported by the fact of

witnesses to the people. [32]And we bring you the good news that Acts 13:23
what God promised to the fathers, [33]this he has fulfilled to us their
children by raising Jesus; as also it is written in the second psalm,

> 'Thou art my Son, Ps 2:7
> today I have begotten thee.'

[34]And as for the fact that he raised him from the dead, no more to
return to corruption, he spoke in this way, Is 55:3

> 'I will give you the holy and sure blessings of David.'

[35]Therefore he says also in another psalm, Ps 16:10

> 'Thou wilt not let thy Holy One see corruption.'

[36]For David, after he had served the counsel of God in his own 1 Kings 2:10
generation, fell asleep, and was laid with his fathers, and saw cor- Acts 2:29
ruption; [37]but he whom God raised up saw no corruption. [38]Let it
be known to you therefore, brethren, that through this man for- Rom 3:20
giveness of sins is proclaimed to you, [39]and by him every one that Acts 15:11
believes is freed from everything from which you could not be Rom 10:4 Heb 10:1–4
freed by the law of Moses. [40]Beware, therefore, lest there come
upon you what is said in the prophets:

---

the empty tomb (because it was impossible for our Lord's body to have been stolen) and by his many appearances, during which he conversed with his disciples, allowed them to touch him, and ate with them (cf. Mt 28; Mk 16; Lk 24; Jn 20–21). In his First Letter to the Corinthians (15:3–6) Paul says that "[what I preached was] that Christ died for our sins in accordance with the scriptures, that he was buried, that he was raised on the third day in accordance with the scriptures, and that he appeared to Cephas, then to the twelve. Then he appeared to more than five hundred brethren."

13:32–37. Paul gives three pertinent quotations from Scripture—Ps 2:7 ("Thou art my Son"), Is 55:3 ("I will give you the holy and sure blessings of David") and Ps 16:10 ("thy Holy One"). All refer to aspects of the Lord's resurrection. Taken together, they help support and interpret one another, and to someone familiar with the Bible and with ways of interpreting it then current they reveal the full meaning of the main texts concerning the promises made to David. Paul's interpretation of Psalms 2 and 16 gets beneath the surface meaning of the texts and shows them to refer to the messianic king who, since he is born of God, will never experience the corruption of the grave.

13:38–39. This passage is reminiscent of Paul's teaching on justification as given in his Letter to the Romans. There we read that God "justifies him who has faith in Jesus" (3:26). The Council of Trent explains that "when the apostle says that man is justified by faith …, these words must be taken in the sense that […] 'faith is the beginning of salvation' (St Fulgentius, *De fide ad Petrum*, 1), the basis and root of all justification, without which 'it is impossible to please God' (Heb 11:6)" (*De Iustificatione*, chap. 8).

Once he has received faith, man with the help of grace can address God freely, can accept as true everything that God has revealed, can recognize that he is a

Hab 1:5 [41] 'Behold, you scoffers, and wonder, and perish;
for I do a deed in your days,
a deed you will never believe, if one declares it to you.'"
[42] As they went out, the people begged that these things might
Acts 11:23 be told them the next sabbath. [43] And when the meeting of the synagogue broke up, many Jews and devout converts to Judaism followed Paul and Barnabas, who spoke to them and urged them to
continue in the grace of God.

Paul and Barnabas preach to the pagans

[44] The next sabbath almost the whole city gathered together to hear
the word of God. [45] But when the Jews saw the multitudes, they
were filled with jealousy, and contradicted what was spoken by
Mt 10:6 Paul, and reviled him. [46] And Paul and Barnabas spoke out boldly,
saying, "It was necessary that the word of God should be spoken
first to you. Since you thrust it from you, and judge yourselves
unworthy of eternal life, behold, we turn to the Gentiles. [47] For so
Is 49:6 the Lord has commanded us, saying,
'I have set you to be a light for the Gentiles,
that you may bring salvation to the uttermost parts
of the earth.'"

---

sinner, can trust in God's mercy and—ready at last to receive Baptism—can decide to keep the commandments and begin to live a new life (cf. ibid., chap. 6).

However, what brings about justification—by eliminating sin and sanctifying the person—is sanctifying grace, with the virtues and gifts that come in its train.

13:45. The opposition of these Jews, who in their jealousy contradict what Paul says, will from now be the typical attitude of the synagogue to the Gospel. It emerges everywhere the apostle goes, with the exception of Beroea (cf. 17:10–12).

13:46. Paul may have been hoping that Christianity would flourish on the soil of Judaism, that the Jews would peacefully and religiously accept the Gospel as the natural development of God's plans. His experience proved otherwise: he encountered the terrible mystery of the infidelity of most of the chosen people, his own people.

Even if Israel had been faithful to God's promises, it would still have been necessary to preach the Gospel to the Gentiles. The evangelization of the pagan world is not a consequence of Jewish rejection of the Word; it is required by the universal character of Christianity. To all men Christianity is the only channel of saving grace; it perfects the Law of Moses and reaches out beyond the ethnic and geographical frontiers of Judaism.

13:47. Paul and Barnabas quote Isaiah 49:6 in support of their decision to preach to the Gentiles. The text referred to Christ, as Luke 2:32 confirms. But now Paul and Barnabas apply it to themselves because the Messiah is "light for the Gentiles" through the preaching of the apostles, for they are conscious of speaking in Christ's

48And when the Gentiles heard this, they were glad and glori- Rom 8:28–30
fied the word of God; and as many as were ordained to eternal life
believed. 49And the word of the Lord spread throughout all the
region. 50But the Jews incited the devout women of high standing
and the leading men of the city, and stirred up persecution against
Paul and Barnabas, and drove them out of their district. 51But they Mt 10:14
shook off the dust from their feet against them, and went to Icon- Acts 18:6
ium. 52And the disciples were filled with joy and with the Holy
Spirit.

Iconium evangelized. Persecution

14 1Now at Iconium they entered together into the Jewish syn- Acts 13:14, 44
agogue, and so spoke that a great company believed, both
of Jews and of Greeks. 2But the unbelieving Jews stirred up the 1 Thess 2:14
Gentiles and poisoned their minds against the brethren. 3So they Mk 16:17–20
remained for a long time, speaking boldly for the Lord, who bore Heb 2:4
witness to the word of his grace, granting signs and wonders to be
done by their hands. 4But the people of the city were divided;
some sided with the Jews, and some with the apostles. 5When an
attempt was made by both Gentiles and Jews, with their rulers, to 2 Tim 3:11
molest them and to stone them, 6they learned of it and fled to

---

name and on his authority. Therefore, probably here "the Lord" refers not to God the Father but to Christ.

13:51. "They shook the dust from their feet": a traditional expression; the Jews regarded as unclean the dust of anywhere other than the holy land of Palestine. Our Lord extended the meaning of the phrase when he told the disciples he was sending them out to preach, "If any one will not receive you or listen to your words, shake off the dust from your feet" (Mt 10:14; cf. Lk 9:5). This gesture of Paul and Barnabas echoes what Jesus said and amounted to "closing the case" or putting on record the unbelief of the Jews.

14:4. "He who is not with me is against me," our Lord says in the Gospel (Mt 12:30). The Word of God is a direct, personal call to which man cannot adopt an indifferent or passive attitude. He has to take sides, whether he likes it or not; and in fact he does take sides. Many people who persecute or criticize the Church and Christians are often trying to justify their own personal infidelity and resistance to God's grace.

St Luke here describes Paul and Barnabas as "apostles" (cf. 14:14). Even though Paul is not one of the group of "the Twelve", for whom Luke usually reserves the name of apostles, he is regarded as and regarded himself as an apostle by virtue of his unique vocation (cf. 1 Cor 15:9; 2 Cor 11:5) and was tireless in preaching to the Gentiles. When the writings of the Fathers mention "the apostle" without being any more specific than that, they mean St Paul, because he is the apostle most quoted and commented on, due to his many letters.

14:6. Lystra was a Roman colony; Timothy grew up there (cf. 16:1–2).

Mt 10:23 Acts 11:19–20 Lystra and Derbe, cities of Lycaonia, and to the surrounding country; 7and there they preached the gospel.

Curing of a cripple at Lystra

Acts 3:2; 9:33 8Now at Lystra there was a man sitting, who could not use his
feet; he was a cripple from birth, who had never walked. 9He lis-
Mt 9:28 tened to Paul speaking; and Paul, looking intently at him and
seeing that he had faith to be made well, 10said in a loud voice,
"Stand upright on your feet." And he sprang up and walked. 11And
Acts 28:6 when the crowds saw what Paul had done, they lifted up their
voices, saying in Lycaonian, "The gods have come down to us in
the likeness of men!" 12Barnabas they called Zeus, and Paul,
because he was the chief speaker, they called Hermes. 13And the
priest of Zeus, whose temple was in front of the city, brought oxen
and garlands to the gates and wanted to offer sacrifice with the
people. 14But when the apostles Barnabas and Paul heard of it,

---

14:8–10. "Just as the lame man whom Peter and John cured at the gate of the temple prefigured the salvation of the Jews, so too this cripple represents the Gentile peoples distanced from the religion of the Law and the temple, but now brought in through the preaching of the apostle Paul" (St Bede, *Super Act. expositio*, ad loc.).

We are told that Paul realized the man "had faith to be made well". The man is sure that he is going to be cured of his infirmity and he seems to be hoping also that Paul will cure his soul. Paul responds to the man's faith and, as our Lord did in the case of the paralytic in Capernaum (cf. Mk 2:1ff), he enables him to walk and cleanses his soul of sin.

14:11–13. Astonished by the miracle, the pagans of Lystra are reminded of an ancient Phrygian legend according to which Zeus and Hermes (Mercury) once visited the area in the guise of travellers and worked wonders for those who gave them hospitality. They think this is a repeat and therefore prepare to give Paul and Barnabas honours, thinking they are gods in human form (cf. 10:26).

14:14. Jews rent their garments to symbolize their feelings of shock at something they heard and to reject it out of hand. However, sometimes they did it only as a matter of form and not for genuine religious reasons (cf. Mt 26:65). By rending their garments Paul and Barnabas dramatically display their deepest convictions and religious feelings against the slightest sign of idolatry.

14:15–18. The apostles not only prevent any idolatry being offered them: they try to explain why they act in this way; they tell the Lystrans about the living God, the Creator of all things, who in his providence watches over mankind.

"Throughout history even to the present day, there is found among peoples a certain awareness of a hidden power, which lies behind the course of nature and the events of human life. At times there is even a recognition of a supreme being, or even a Father. This awareness and recognition results in a way of life that is imbued with a deep religious sense" (Vatican II, *Nostra aetate*, 2).

In this short exhortation (which antic-

they tore their garments and rushed out among the multitude,
crying, [15]"Men, why are you doing this? We also are men, of like
nature with you, and bring you good news, that you should turn Acts 10:26; 17:22–30
from these vain things to a living God who made the heaven and
the earth and the sea and all that is in them. [16]In past generations
he allowed all the nations to walk in their own ways; [17]yet he did
not leave himself without witness, for he did good and gave you Jer 5:24 Ps 147:8
from heaven rains and fruitful seasons, satisfying your hearts with
food and gladness." [18]With these words they scarcely restrained
the people from offering sacrifice to them.

Paul is stoned

[19]But Jews came there from Antioch and Iconium; and having persuaded the people, they stoned Paul and dragged him out of the 2 Cor 11:25
city, supposing that he was dead. [20]But when the disciples gathered about him, he rose up and entered the city; and on the next
day he went on with Barnabas to Derbe.

---

ipates some of the themes of Paul's address in Athens: cf. 17:22–31), the apostles use religious concepts accepted by pagans, trying to bring out their full meaning. They invite their listeners to give up idolatry and turn to the living God, of whom they have a vague knowledge. They speak to them, therefore, about a true God, who transcends man but is ever concerned about him. Everyday experience—the course of history, the changing seasons, and the fulfilment of noble human yearnings— demonstrates the providence of a God who invites people to find him in his works.

This first "natural" encounter with God, presaging future and greater revelations, stirs their consciences to interior conversion, that is, to change their lives and turn away from any action which deprives them of spiritual peace and prevents them from knowing God.

Acknowledging that God exists involves all kinds of practical consequences and is the foundation of the new type of life which the Gospel proposes and makes possible. When a person truly and sincerely recognizes his Creator as speaking to him through external things and in the intimacy of his conscience, he has taken a huge step in his spiritual life: he has controlled his tendency to assert moral autonomy and false independence and has taken the path of obedience and humility. It becomes easier for him to recognize and accept supernatural revelation under the inspiration of grace.

14:19. Paul mentions this stoning in his Second Letter to the Corinthians. "Five times I have received at the hands of the Jews the forty lashes less one. Three times I have been beaten with rods; once I was stoned" (11:24f).

14:20–22. "If you accept difficulties with a faint heart, you lose your joy and your peace, and you run the risk of not deriving any spiritual profit from the trial" (St J. Escrivá, *The Way*, 696).

St Paul is not cowed by persecution and physical suffering. He knows that this crisis is the prelude to abundant spiritual fruit, and in fact many people in this region do embrace the Gospel.

Even though St Luke records the

Return journey to Antioch

Mt 28:19 [21]When they had preached the gospel to that city and had made
many disciples, they returned to Lystra and to Iconium and to
Mt 10:22 Antioch, [22]strengthening the souls of the disciples, exhorting them
Acts 11:23 to continue in the faith, and saying that through many tribulations
1 Thess 3:3 Heb 10:36 we must enter the kingdom of God. [23]And when they had
Acts 13:3 appointed elders for them in every church, with prayer and fasting, they committed them to the Lord in whom they believed.
[24]Then they passed through Pisidia, and came to Pamphylia.
[25]And when they had spoken the word in Perga, they went down
Acts 13:1 to Attalia; [26]and from there they sailed to Antioch, where they had
been commended to the grace of God for the work which they had

---

progress and success of the word of God, he also shows that its preachers certainly encounter the cross (cf. 13:14, 50). The Gospel meets with acceptance everywhere—and also with opposition. "Where there are many laurels", St Ambrose says, "there is fierce combat. It is good for you to have persecutors: that way you attain more rapid success in your enterprises" (*Expositio in Ps 118*, 20, 43).

The apostles have no difficulty in pointing to events to show the disciples that suffering and difficulties form part of Christian living.

"Cross, toil, anguish: such will be your lot as long as you live. That was the way Christ went, and the disciple is not above his master" (St J. Escrivá, *The Way*, 699). "Each one of us has at some time or other experienced that serving Christ our Lord involves suffering and hardship; to deny this would imply that we had not yet found God. [...] Far from discouraging us, the difficulties we meet have to spur us on to mature as Christians. This fight sanctifies us and gives effectiveness to our apostolic endeavours" (St Josemaría Escrivá, *Friends of God,* 28 and 216).

14:23. The appointment of elders in each church means that certain Christians were invested with a ministry of government and religious worship, by a liturgical rite of ordination. These have a share in the hierarchical and priestly ministry of the apostles, from whom their own ministry derives.

"The ministry of priests [...]", Vatican II teaches, "shares in the authority by which Christ himself builds up and sanctifies and rules his Body" (*Presbyterorum ordinis*, 2). The ministerial office of priests is essential to the life of every Christian community, which draws its strength from the word of God and the sacraments. Their priesthood, derived from our Lord, is essentially different from what is called the "priesthood common to all the faithful".

A man becomes a priest of the New Testament through a special calling from God. "Our vocation," John Paul II told a huge gathering of priests in Philadelphia, "is a gift from the Lord Jesus himself. It is a personal, individual calling: we have been called by our name, just as Jeremiah was" (Homily, 4 October 1979).

The priestly life is a sublime vocation which cannot be delegated or transferred to anyone else. It is a lifelong vocation and means that one has to give himself entirely to God—and this he can do, with the help of grace, because "we do not claim back our gift once given. It cannot be that God, who gave us the impulse to say Yes, should now desire to hear us say No. ...

fulfilled. 27And when they arrived, they gathered the church Acts 14:3; 15:4
together and declared all that God had done with them, and how
he had opened a door of faith to the Gentiles. 28And they remained
no little time with the disciples.

9. THE COUNCIL OF JERUSALEM

Dissension at Antioch; Judaizers

15 1But some men came down from Judea and were teaching Gen 17:10
the brethren, "Unless you are circumcised according to the Gal 2:12

"It should not surprise the world that God's calling through the Church should continue, offering us a celibate ministry of love and service according to our Lord Jesus Christ's example. This calling from God touched the very depths of our being. And after centuries of experience the Church knows how appropriate it is that priests should respond in this specific way in their lives, to demonstrate the totality of the Yes they have said to our Lord" (ibid.).

"Since he wishes that no one be saved who has not first believed (cf. Mk 16:16), priests, like the co-workers of the bishops that they are, have as their first duty to proclaim to all men the Gospel of God" (Vatican II, *Presbyterorum ordinis*, 4). To carry out his mission well, a priest needs to be in contact with our Lord all the time—"a personal, living encounter—with eyes wide open and a heart beating fast—with the risen Christ" (John Paul II, Homily in Santo Domingo Cathedral, 26 January 1979).

Reminding priests of their special duty to be witnesses to God in the modern world, John Paul II invites them not only to bear in mind the Christian people, from whom they come and whom they must serve, but also people at large; they should not hide the fact that they are priests: "Do not help the trends towards 'taking God off the streets' by yourselves adopting secular modes of dress and behaviour" (Address at Maynooth University, 1 October 1979).

14:24–26. Paul and Barnabas return to Syrian Antioch, taking in the cities they have visited—in reverse order: Derbe, Lystra, Icononium, Pisidian Antioch and Perga. At the port of Attalia they take a ship for Syria and arrive shortly afterwards in Antioch. Their journey, which began around the year 45, has taken four years.

Despite the animosity and persecution they experienced in these cities, the two missionaries do not avoid returning. They want to complete arrangements for the government of the new churches and to consolidate the faith of the disciples. The possible risks involved do not cause them any concern.

"Whosoever would save his life will lose it; and whoever loses his life for my sake and the gospel's will save it" (Mk 8:35). "These are mysterious and paradoxical words," John Paul II writes. "But they cease to be mysterious if we strive to put them into practice. Then the paradox disappears and we can plainly see the deep simplicity of their meaning. To all of us this grace is granted in our priestly life and in our zealous service" (*Letter to all priests*, 8 April 1979, 5).

15:1–35. This chapter is the centre of Acts, not just because it comes right in

Gal 2:1–2 custom of Moses, you cannot be saved." [2]And when Paul and
Barnabas had no small dissension and debate with them, Paul and
Barnabas and some of the others were appointed to go up to
Jerusalem to the apostles and the elders about this question.

Paul and Barnabas go to Jerusalem

[3]So, being sent on their way by the church, they passed through
both Phoenicia and Samaria, reporting the conversion of the
Acts 14:27 Gentiles, and they gave great joy to all the brethren. [4]When they
came to Jerusalem, they were welcomed by the church and the
apostles and the elders, and they declared all that God had done
with them. [5]But some believers who belonged to the party of the

---

the middle of the book but also because it covers the key event as far as concerns the universality of the Gospel and its unrestricted spread among the Gentiles. It is directly linked to the conversion of the pagan Cornelius; here, with the help of the Holy Spirit, all the consequences of that event are drawn out. Christians with a Pharisee background—"certain men [who] came from James" (Gal 2:12)—arriving in Antioch, assert categorically that salvation is impossible unless a person is circumcised and practises the Law of Moses. They accept (cf. 11:18) that Gentile converts can be baptized and become part of the Church; but they do not properly understand the economy of the Gospel, that it is the *new* way; they think that the Mosaic rites and precepts are all still necessary for attaining salvation. The need arises, therefore, for the whole question to be brought to the apostles and elders in Jerusalem, who form the government of the Church.

15:2. Paul and Barnabas are once again commissioned by the Antiochene community to go to Jerusalem (cf.11:30). Paul says in Galatians 2:2 that this journey to the Holy City was due to a special revelation. Possibly the Holy Spirit inspired him to volunteer for it. "Paul," St Ephrem writes, "so as not to change without the apostles' accord anything which they would allow to be done perhaps because of the weakness of the Jews, makes his way to Jerusalem to see to the setting aside of the Law and of circumcision in the presence of the disciples: without the apostles' support they [Paul and Barnabas] do not want to set them aside" (*Armenian Commentary on Acts*, ad loc.).

15:4. This does not mean that all the members of the Church were present to receive Paul: the whole Church was morally present in those brethren who attended the gathering and particularly in the apostles and elders.

15:5. "Party": the Greek and the New Vulgate both literally say "heresy". However, in this context the word is not pejorative. It is a correct use of language in view of the religious exclusivity and separateness practised by the Pharisees: they saw themselves as, and in fact were, the rightful representatives of post-exilic Judaism (cf. the note on Acts 13:15). The Pharisees mentioned here were Christians who in practice still lived like Jews.

15:6–21. The hierarchical Church, consisting of the apostles and elders or priests, now meets to study and decide whether

Pharisees rose up, and said, "It is necessary to circumcise them, and to charge them to keep the law of Moses."

Peter's address to the council

6The apostles and the elders were gathered together to consider
this matter. 7And after there had been much debate, Peter rose and Acts 2:14
said to them, "Brethren, you know that in the early days God
made choice among you, that by my mouth the Gentiles should
hear the word of the gospel and believe.8And God who knows the Acts 10:44; 11:15
heart bore witness to them, giving them the Holy Spirit just as he
did to us; 9and he made no distinction between us and them, but Mt 11:30; 23:4
cleansed their hearts by faith. 10Now therefore why do you make Gal 5:1

---

baptized Gentiles are obliged or not to be circumcised and to keep the Old Law. This is a question of the utmost importance to the young Christian Church and the answer to it has to be absolutely correct. Under the leadership of St Peter, the meeting deliberates at length, but it is not going to devise a new truth or new principles: all it does is, with the aid of the Holy Spirit, to provide a correct interpretation of God's promises and commandments regarding the salvation of men and the way in which Gentiles can enter the New Israel.

This meeting is seen as the first general council of the Church, that is, the prototype of the series of councils of which the Second Vatican Council is the most recent. Thus, the Council of Jerusalem displays the same features as the later ecumenical councils in the history of the Church: a) it is a meeting of the rulers of the entire Church, not of ministers of one particular place; b) it promulgates rules which have binding force for all Christians; c) the content of its decrees deals with faith and morals; d) its decisions are recorded in a written document—a formal proclamation to the whole Church; e) Peter presides over the assembly.

According to the *Code of Canon Law* (can. 338–341) ecumenical councils are assemblies—summoned and presided over by the Pope—or bishops and some others endowed with jurisiction; decisions of these councils do not oblige unless they are confirmed and promulgated by the Pope. This assembly at Jerusalem probably took place in the year 49 or 50.

15:7–11. Peter's brief but decisive contribution follows on a lengthy discussion which would have covered the arguments for and against the need for circumcision to apply to Gentile Christians. St Luke does not give the arguments used by the Judaizing Christians (these undoubtedly were based on a literal interpretation of the compact God made with Abraham—cf. Gen 17—and on the notion that the Law was perennial).

Once again, Peter is a decisive factor in Church unity. Not only does he draw together all the various legitimate views of those trying to reach the truth on this occasion: he points out where the truth lies. Relying on his personal experience (what God directed him to do in connexion with the baptism of Cornelius: cf. chap. 10), Peter sums up the discussion and offers a solution which coincides with St Paul's view of the matter: it is grace and not the Law that saves, and therefore circumcision and the Law itself have been superseded by faith in Jesus Christ. Peter's argument is not based on

trial of God by putting a yoke upon the neck of the disciples
Gal 2:15–21; 3:22–26 which neither our fathers nor we have been able to bear? 11But we
Eph 2:1–10 believe that we shall be saved through the grace of the Lord Jesus,
just as they will."

James' speech

12And all the assembly kept silence; and they listened to Barnabas
and Paul as they related what signs and wonders God had done
Acts 12:17 Gal 2:9 through them among the Gentiles. 13After they finished speaking,
James replied, "Brethren, listen to me. 14Symeon has related how
God first visited the Gentiles, to take out of them a people for his
name. 15And with this the words of the prophets agree, as it is
written,

Amos 9:11–12 16'After this I will return,
And I will rebuild the dwelling of David, which has fallen;

---

the severity of the Old Law or the practical difficulties Jews experience in keeping it; his key point is that the Law of Moses has become irrelevant; now that the Gospel has been proclaimed the Law is not necessary for salvation: he does not accept that it is necessary to obey the Law in order to be saved. Whether one can or should keep the Law for other reasons is a different and secondary matter.

As a gloss on what Peter says, St Ephrem writes that "everything which God has given us through faith and the Law has been given by Christ to the Gentiles through faith and without observance of the Law" (*Armenian Commentary on Acts,* ad loc.).

15:11. St Paul makes the same point to the Galatians: "We ourselves, who are Jews by birth and not Gentile sinners, yet who know that a man is not justified by works of the law but through faith in Jesus Christ, even we have believed in Christ Jesus, in order to be justified by faith in Christ, and not by works of the law, because by works of the law shall no one be justified" (2:15f)."No one can be sanctified after sin," St Thomas Aquinas, says, "unless it be through Christ. [...] Just as the ancient fathers were saved by faith in the Christ to come, so we are saved by faith in the Christ who was born and suffered" (*Summa theologiae*, 3, 61, 3 and 4).

"That thing is absolutely necessary without which no one can attain salvation: this is the case with the grace of Christ and with the sacrament of Baptism, by which a person is reborn in Christ" (ibid., 84, 5).

15:13–21. James the Less, to whose authority the Judaizers had appealed, follows what Peter says. He refers to the apostle by his Semitic name—Symeon—and accepts that he has given a correct interpretation of what God announced through the prophets. In saying that God had "visited the Gentiles, to take out of them a people for his name" he seems to be giving up the Jewish practice of using "people" to refer to the Israelites (Ex 19:9; Deut 7:6; 14:2) as distinct from the Gentiles. Again the central message of Paul, that baptized pagans also belong to the people of the promise: "You are no longer strangers and sojourners, but you

I will rebuild its ruins,
and I will set it up,
17 that the rest of men may seek the Lord,
and all the Gentiles who are called by my name,
18 says the Lord, who has made these things known from of old.'
19 Therefore my judgment is that we should not trouble those of
the Gentiles who turn to God, 20 but should write to them to Gen 9:4 Lev 17:11
abstain from the pollutions of idols and from unchastity and from 1 Cor 8:10
what is strangled[n] and from blood. 21 For from early generations Acts 13:27
Moses has had in every city those who preach him, for he is read
every sabbath in the synagogues."

The council's decision

22 Then it seemed good to the apostles and the elders, with the
whole church, to choose men from among them and send them to

---

are fellow citizens with the saints and members of the household of God" (Eph 2:19).

James' concurrence with what Peter says and the fact that both are in agreement with the basic principles of Paul's preaching indicate that the Holy Spirit is at work, giving light to all to understand the true meaning of the promise contained in Scripture. "As I see it, the richness of these great events cannot be explained unless it be with help from the same Holy Spirit who was their author" (Origen, *In Ex hom.*, 4, 5).

James immediately goes on to propose that the meeting issue a solemn, formal statement which proclaims the secondary character of the Law and at the same time makes allowance for the religious sensitivity of Jewish Christians by prohibiting four things—1) the eating of meat from animals used in sacrifices to idols; 2) avoidance of fornication, which goes against the natural moral order; 3) eating meat which has blood in it; and 4) eating food made with the blood of animals.

These prohibitions are laid down in Leviticus and to be understood properly they must be read in the light of Leviticus. The Jews considered that if they ate meat offered to idols this implied in some way taking part in sacrilegious worship (Lev 17:7–9). Although St Paul makes it clear that Christians were free to act as they pleased in this regard (cf. 1 Cor 8–10), he will also ask them not to scandalize "the weak".

Irregular unions and transgressions in the area of sexual morality are mentioned in Leviticus 18:6ff; some of the impediments will later be included in Church marriage law.

Abstention from blood and from the meat of strangled animals (cf. Lev 17:10ff) was based on the idea that blood was the container of life and as such belonged to God alone. A Jew would find it almost impossible to overcome his religious and cultural repugnance at the consumption of blood.

15:22–29. The decree containing the decisions of the Council of Jerusalem incorporating St James' suggestions makes it clear that the participants at the Council are conscious of being guided in their conclusions by the Holy Spirit and that in the last analysis it is God who has decided the matter.

Antioch with Paul and Barnabas. They sent Judas called
Barsabbas, and Silas, leading men among the brethren, [23]with the
following letter: "The brethren, both the apostles and the elders,
to the brethren who are of the Gentiles in Antioch and Syria and
Acts 15:1 Cilicia, greeting. [24]Since we have heard that some persons from us
have troubled you with words, unsettling your minds, although we
gave them no instructions, [25]it has seemed good to us in assembly
to choose men and send them to you with our beloved Barnabas
Acts 21:13 and Paul, [26]men who have risked their lives for the sake of our
Lord Jesus Christ. [27]We have therefore sent Judas and Silas, who
themselves will tell you the same things by word of mouth. [28]For
it has seemed good to the Holy Spirit and to us to lay upon you no
greater burden than these necessary things: [29]that you abstain from
what has been sacrificed to idols and from blood and from what is
strangled[n] and from unchastity. If you keep yourselves from these,
you will do well. Farewell."

"We should take," Melchor Cano writes in the sixteenth century, "the same road as the apostle Paul considered to be the one best suited to solving all matters to do with the doctrine of the faith. [...] The Gentiles might have sought satisfaction from the Council because it seemed to take from the freedom granted them by Jesus Christ, and because it imposed on the disciples certain ceremonies as necessary, when in fact they were not, since faith is the key to salvation. Nor did the Jews object by invoking Sacred Scripture against the Council's decision on the grounds that Scripture seems to support their view that circumcision is necessary for salvation. So, by respecting the Council they gave us all the criteria which should be observed in all later times that is, to place full faith in the authority of synods confirmed by Peter and his legitimate successors. They say, It has seemed good to the Holy Spirit and to us; thus, the Council's decision is the decision of the Holy Spirit himself" (*De locis*, 5, 4).

It is the apostles and the elders, with the whole Church, who designate the people who are to publish the Council's decree, but it is the hierarchy which formulates and promulgates it. The text contains two parts—one dogmatic and moral (v. 28) and the other disciplinary (v. 29). The dogmatic part speaks on imposing no burden other than what is essential and therefore declares that pagan converts are free of the obligation of circumcision and of the Mosaic Law but are subject to the Gospel's perennial moral teaching on matters to do with chastity. This part is permanent: because it has to do with a necessary part of God's salvific will it cannot change.The disciplinary part of the decree lays down rules of prudence which can change, which are temporary. It asks Christians of Gentile background to abstain—out of charity towards Jewish Christians—from what has been sacrificed to idols, from blood and from meat of animals killed by strangulation.The effect on the decree means that the disciplinary rules contained in it, although they derive from the Mosaic

n. Other early authorities omit *and from what is strangled*

Reception of the council's decree

30So when they were sent off, they went down to Antioch; and
having gathered the congregation together, they delivered the
letter. 31And when they read it, they rejoiced at the exhortation.
32And Judas and Silas, who were themselves prophets, exhorted Acts 11:27
the brethren with many words and strengthened them. 33And after
they had spent some time, they were sent off in peace by the
brethren to those who had sent them.[o] 35But Paul and Barnabas Acts 14:28
remained in Antioch, teaching and preaching the word of the
Lord, with many others also.

10. ST PAUL'S SECOND APOSTOLIC JOURNEY

Silas, Paul's new companion

36And after some days Paul said to Barnabas, "Come, let us return
and visit the brethren in every city where we proclaimed the word

Law, no longer oblige by virtue of that law but rather by virtue of the authority of the Church, which has decided to apply them for the time being. What matters is not what Moses says but what Christ says through the Church. The Council "seems to maintain the Law in force", writes St John Chrysostom, "because it selects various prescriptions from it, but in fact it suppresses it, because it does not accept *all* its prescriptions. It had often spoken about these points, it sought to respect the Law and yet establish these regulations as coming not from Moses but from the apostles" (*Hom. on Acts*, 33).

15:34. This verse is not to be found in the more important manuscripts and is not in the New Vulgate. It did appear in the Sixto-Clementine edition of the Vulgate. It was probably a gloss added for clarification and not a part of the authentic text of Acts.

15:35. It was probably during this period that the incident took place in Antioch when St Paul publicly taxed St Peter with drawing back and separating himself from Gentile Christians, "fearing the circumcision party" (cf. Gal 2:11–14).

15:36–39. Paul and Barnabas part company because of a disagreement over Mark. "Paul sterner, Barnabas kinder, each holds on to his point of view. The argument shows human weakness at work" (St Jerome, *Dialogus adversus pelagianos*, 2, 17). At any event, both apostles are acting in good conscience and God amply blesses their new missionary journeys. "The gifts of the two men differ," Chrysostom comments, "and clearly this difference is itself a gift. [...] Now and then one hears an argument, but even that is part of God's providence, and all that happens is that each is put in the place which suits him best. ...

"Observe that there is nothing wrong in their separating if this means that they can evangelize all the Gentiles. If they go different ways, in order to teach and con-

o. Other ancient authorities insert verse 34, *But it seemed good to Silas to remain there*

Acts 12:12 of the Lord, and see how they are." [37]And Barnabas wanted to take
Acts 13:13 Col 4:10 2 Tim 4:11 with them John called Mark. [38]But Paul thought best not to take
with them one who had withdrawn from them in Pamphylia, and
had not gone with them to the work. [39]And there arose a sharp
contention, so that they separated from each other; Barnabas took
Mark with him and sailed away to Cyprus, [40]but Paul chose Silas
and departed, being commended by the brethren to the grace of
the Lord. [41]And he went through Syria and Cilicia, strengthening
the churches.

---

vert people, there is nothing wrong about that. What should be emphasized is not their difficulties but what unites them. [...] If only all our divisions were motivated by zeal for preaching!" (*Hom. on Acts*, 34).

This disagreement does not mean that the two disciples have become estranged. Paul always praised Barnabas and Mark for their zeal (cf. 1 Cor 9:6; Gal 2:9) and later on he was happy to have Mark work with him (cf. Col 4:10).

15:40—18:23. The original purpose of this second apostolic journey is to re-visit the brethren in the cities evangelized during the first journey and to confirm them in the faith. Once again the journey begins at Antioch and it will end there in the spring of 53.

St Paul is now acting on his own initiative: he has not been commissioned by any community to undertake this journey. He takes with him Silas, a Christian from Jerusalem and a Roman citizen, who like Paul has two names—Silas and Silvanus. This is the same Silvanus as mentioned in 2 Cor 1:19; 1 Thess 1:1; 2 Thess 1:1; and 1 Pet 5:12.

The account takes up almost three chapters of Acts, up to 18:23, at which point St Luke moves directly into his account of the apostle's third journey.

Paul sets out early in the year 50, with no fixed itinerary, heading for the as yet unevangelized cities which he aims to visit. The two apostles go to Derbe from Cilicia, Paul's native region, following the line of the Taurus mountains and the plain of Lycaonia. They then go on to Lystra, where Timothy lives, and he joins them as they make their way to Iconium and Pisidian Antioch. The Holy Spirit then instructs them to go north into Phrygia and Galatia, where Paul is taken ill: this illness must have held them up for some months; after evangelizing the Galatians the Spirit directs them to Macedonia and they make for Troas to take ship. St Luke, whom the apostle will later call "the beloved physician" (Col 4:14), must have joined them at this point.The sea journey from Troas to Neapolis is 230 kilometres (150 miles) and half-way across lay the island of Samothrace, where they briefly stopped. About 15 kilometres north of Neapolis lay Philippi, a Roman colony where the events described in chapter 16 take place. From there they went to Thessalonica, the seat of government of the Roman province of Macedonia. Due to disturbances they had to leave there and go to Beroea, and some of the disciples brought the apostle as far as Athens. The last part of chapter 17 describes what happenes in Athens.

The next city to be evangelized was Corinth, where St Paul stayed over a year and a half; at the end of his stay he decided to go to Jerusalem before returning to Antioch. On his way there he made a short stop at Ephesus, where he left

Timothy joins Paul

16 [1]And he came also to Derbe and to Lystra. A disciple was there, named Timothy, the son of a Jewish woman who was a believer; but his father was a Greek. [2]He was well spoken of by the brethren at Lystra and Iconium. [3]Paul wanted Timothy to accompany him; and he took him and circumcised him because of the Jews that were in those places, for they all knew that his father was a Greek.

Phil 2:19–22
2 Tim 1:5

Tour of the churches of Asia Minor

[4]As they went on their way through the cities, they delivered to them for observance the decisions which had been reached by the

Acts 15:23–29

Priscilla and Aquila, who had travelled with him from Corinth.

The whole journey lasted three years, in the course of which St Paul suffered illnesses, the lash, imprisonment and persecution, and won for Christ disciples in more than ten cities of Asia Minor and Europe and numerous other places on his route.

16:1–3. At Lystra, a city which he evangelized during his first journey (cf. 14:6), Paul meets a young Christian, Timothy, of whom he had received good reports. His Jewish mother Eunice and his grandmother Lois were Christians, and Timothy had received the faith from them.

Paul's apostolic plans for Timothy, and the fact that, despite being Jewish through his mother, he had not been circumcised, lead him to circumcise him: everyone in the city knew he was a Jew and those who practised the Mosaic Law might easily have regarded him as an apostate from Judaism, in which case he would be unlikely to be an effective preacher of the Gospel to Jews.

"He took Timothy," St Ephraem comments, "and circumcised him. Paul did not do this without deliberation: he always acted prudently; but given that Timothy was being trained to preach the Gospel to Jews everywhere, and to avoid their not giving him a good hearing because he was not circumcised, he decided to circumcise him. In doing this he was not aiming to show that circumcision was necessary—he had been the one most instrumental in eliminating it—but to avoid putting the Gospel at risk" (*Armenian Commentary on Acts*, ad loc.).

In the case of Titus, St Paul did not have him circumcised (cf. Gal 2:3–5), which showed that he did not consider circumcision to be a matter of principle; it is simply for reasons of pastoral prudence and common sense that he has Timothy circumcised. Titus was the son of Gentile parents; to have circumcised him—at a point when Paul was fighting against Judaizers—would have meant Paul giving up his principles. However, the circumcision of Timothy, which takes place later, is in itself something that has no relevance from the Christian point of view (cf. Gal 5:6, 15).

Timothy became one of Paul's most faithful disciples, a most valuable associate in his missionary work (cf. 17:14ff; 18:5; 19:22; 20:4; 1 Thess 3:2; Rom 16:21) and the recipient of two of the apostle's letters.

16:4. The text suggests that all Christians accepted the decisions of the Council of

Acts 2:41 apostles and elders who were at Jerusalem. 5So the churches were
strengthened in the faith, and they increased in numbers daily.
Acts 18:23 6And they went through the region of Phrygia and Galatia,
Gal 4:13–15 having been forbidden by the Holy Spirit to speak the word in
Asia. 7And when they had come opposite Mysia, they attempted
to go into Bithynia, but the Spirit of Jesus did not allow them; 8so,
passing by Mysia, they went down to Troas. 9And a vision
appeared to Paul in the night: a man of Macedonia was standing
beseeching him and saying, "Come over to Macedonia and help
us." 10And when he had seen the vision, immediately we sought to
go on into Macedonia, concluding that God had called us to
preach the gospel to them.*

Jerusalem in a spirit of obedience and joy. They saw them as being handed down by the Church through the apostles and as providing a satisfactory solution to a delicate problem. The disciples accept these commandments with internal and external assent: by putting them into practice they showed their docility. Everything which a lawful council lays down merits and demands acceptance by Christians, because it reflects, as the Council of Trent teaches, "the true and saving doctrine which Christ taught, the apostles then handed on, and the Catholic Church, under the inspiration of the Holy Spirit, ever maintains; therefore, no one should subsequently dare to believe, preach or teach anything different"(*De iustificatione*, preface).

John Paul II called on Christians to adhere sincerely to conciliar directives when he exhorted them in Mexico City to keep to the letter and the spirit of Vatican II: "Take in your hands the documents of the Council. Study them with loving attention, in a spirit of prayer, to discover what the Spirit wished to say about the Church" (Homily in Mexico Cathedral, 26 January 1979).

16:6. In Galatia Paul had the illness which he refers to in Galatians 4:13: "You know it was because of a bodily ailment that I preached the gospel to you at first"; his apostolic zeal makes him turn his illness, which prevented him from moving on, to good purpose.

16:7. We are not told how the Holy Spirit prevented Paul from going to Bithynia. It could have been through an interior voice or through some person sent by God.

Some Greek codexes and a few translations say simply "Spirit" instead of "Spirit of Jesus", but really the two mean the same: cf. Phil 1:19; Rom 8:9; 1 Pet 1:11.

16:9. This vision probably took place in a dream: Acts tells us of a number of instances where God made his will known in that way (cf. 9:10,12; 10:3, 17; 18:9; 22:17). Paul and his companions were convinced he had received a message from God.

The vision is quite right to describe the preaching of the Gospel as help for Macedonia: it is the greatest help, the greatest benefit, a person or a country could be given, an immense grace from God and a great act of charity on the part of the preacher, preparing his listeners, as he does, for the wonderful gift of faith.

16:10. The conviction that Paul and his companions have about what they must

Macedonia

[11]Setting sail therefore from Troas we made a direct voyage to
Samothrace, and the following day to Neapolis, [12]and from there
to Philippi, which is the leading city of the district[x] of Macedonia,
and a Roman colony.

The conversion of Lydia

We remained in this city some days; [13]and on the sabbath day we Acts 13:5–14
went outside the gate to the riverside, where we supposed there
was a place of prayer;* and we sat down and spoke to the women
who had come together. [14]One who heard us was a woman named
Lydia, from the city of Thyatira, a seller of purple goods, who was

---

do is the way every Christian, called as he is at Baptism, should feel about his vocation to imitate Christ and therefore be apostolic.

"All Christians", John Paul II teaches, "incorporated into Christ and his Church by baptism, are consecrated to God. They are called to profess the faith which they have received. By the sacrament of confirmation, they are further endowed by the Holy Spirit with special strength to be witnesses of Christ and sharers in his mission of salvation. Every lay Christian is therefore an extraordinary work of God's grace and is called to the heights of holiness. Sometimes, lay men and women do not seem to appreciate to the full the dignity and the vocation that is theirs as lay people. No, there is no such thing as an 'ordinary layman', for all of you have been called to conversion through the death and resurrection of Jesus Christ. As God's holy people you are called to fulfil your role in the evangelization of the world. Yes, the laity are 'a chosen race, a holy priesthood', also called to be 'the salt of the earth' and 'the light of the world'. It is their specific vocation and mission to express the Gospel in their lives and thereby to insert the Gospel as a leaven into the reality of the world in which they live and work" (Homily in Limerick, 1 October 1979).

Now the narrative moves into the first person plural (16:10–17; 20:5–8; 13–15; 21:1–18; 27:1—28:16). The author includes himself among St Paul's companions, as an eyewitness of what he reports. Luke must have joined the missionaries at Troas and then stayed behind in Philippi.

16:12. Philippi was a prosperous city, founded by the father of Alexander the Great (in the fourth century BC). Nearby, in 42 BC, there took place the battle in which those who assassinated Julius Caesar were defeated. Octavius raised Philippi to the status of a *colonia* and endowed it with many privileges.

Very few Jews lived in the city, as can be seen from the fact that it had no synagogue (for there to be a synagogue there had to be at least ten Jewish men living in a place). The text refers only to a group of women who met on the riverside to pray—a location probably chosen for the purpose of ritual purification.

16:14. Lydia was probably a surname taken from the region this woman came from. She was not a Jew by birth but a

x. The Greek text is uncertain

a worshipper of God. The Lord opened her heart to give heed to
Acts 10:44–48 what was said by Paul. 15And when she was baptized, with her
household, she besought us, saying, "If you have judged me to be
faithful to the Lord, come to my house and stay." And she prevailed upon us.

Curing of a possessed girl. Imprisonment of Paul

Acts 19:15–24 16As we were going to the place of prayer, we were met by a slave
girl who had a spirit of divination and brought her owners much
Mt 8:29 gain by soothsaying. 17She followed Paul and us, crying, "These
men are servants of the Most High God, who proclaim to you the
Mk 16:17 way of salvation." 18And this she did for many days. But Paul was

---

"God-fearer" (cf. the note on Acts 2:5–11). God chose her from this group of women to enlighten her with the light of faith, opening her heart to understand the words of the apostle. Origen explains that "God opens our mouth, our ears and our eyes to make us say, hear and see divine things" (*In Ex hom.*, III, 2). This shows that we can and ought to address God using the words of the Church's liturgy: "Open my lips, Lord, to bless your holy name; clean my heart of all evil thoughts; enlighten my understanding and inflame my will … so that I merit to be admitted to your presence" (*Divine Office*, introductory prayer).

When Christians address God, they ask him for the grace to pray well—not only at times of prayer but also in the course of everyday activities: "Lord, be the beginning and end of all that we do and say. Prompt our actions with your grace, and complete them with your all-powerful help" (ibid., morning prayer, Monday, first week).

This episode shows faith to be a gift from God, stemming from his goodness and wisdom: for "no one can give his assent to the Gospel message in a truly salvific way except it be by the light and inspiration of the Holy Spirit: he it is who gives to all the power necessary for affirming and believing the truth" (Vatican I, *Dei Filius*, chap. 3).

16:15. St Luke's succinct account shows that Lydia's good dispositions allow St Paul's preaching to bear fruit very quickly. Her whole family receives Baptism and she insists on the apostles' staying in her house. "Look at her wisdom, how full of humility her words are: 'If you have judged me to be faithful to the Lord.' Nothing could be more persuasive. Who would not have been softened by these words. She did not simply request or entreat: she left them free to decide and yet by her insistence obliged them to stay at her house. See how she straightaway bears fruit and accounts her calling a great gain" (St John Chrysostom, *Hom. on Acts*, 35).

It is worth reflecting on the fact that Christianity began in Europe through this lady's response to God's calling. Lydia set about her mission to Christianize the whole world from within, starting with her own family. Commenting on the role of women in the spread of Christianity, St Josemaría Escrivá says: "The main thing is that like Mary, who was a woman, a virgin and a mother, they live with their eyes on God, repeating her words *'fiat mihi secundum verbum tuum'* (Lk 1:38), 'let it be done to me according to your word'. On these words depends the faithfulness to one's personal vocation—which is always

annoyed, and turned and said to the spirit, "I charge you in the
name of Jesus Christ to come out of her." And it came out that
very hour.
[19]But when her owners saw that their hope of gain was gone,
they seized Paul and Silas and dragged them into the market place
before the rulers; [20]and when they had brought them to the magistrates they said, "These men are Jews and they are disturbing our
city. [21]They advocate customs which it is not lawful for us
Romans to accept or practise." [22]The crowd joined in attacking 2 Cor 11:25
them; and the magistrates tore the garments off them and gave Phil 1:30
orders to beat them with rods. [23]And when they had inflicted 1 Thess 2:2

---

unique and non-transferable—which will make us all cooperators in the work of salvation which God carries out in us and in the entire world" (*Conversations*, 112).

16:16–18. This slave girl must have been possessed by the devil; the devil knows the present and the past and he is so intelligent that he is good at divining the future (cf. St Thomas, *Summa theologiae*, 1, 57, 3). In Greek mythology Python was a serpent which uttered the Delphic oracles (hence *spiritus pythonis*, "a spirit of divination").

St Paul did not believe in Python but he did believe in the devil. "An unclean spirit is unworthy to proclaim the word of the Gospel; that is why (Paul) commands him to desist and to come out of the girl, for demons ought to confess God in fear and trembling, and not praise him with joy" (St Bede, *Super Act. expositio*, ad loc.).

Jesus addressed demons in the same kind of way (cf. Mk 1:24–27). St Ephrem comments: "The apostles were displeased to be honoured and praised by the evil spirit, just as our Lord rejected the devil who proclaimed him to the Jews. In like manner St Paul upbraids him, because he was motivated by deception and malice" (*Armenian Commentary on Acts*, ad loc.).

16:19–40. This is the first time St Paul comes into conflict with Gentiles. As might be expected, the incident does not take the form of a riot, as happened in cities of Asia Minor (13:50; 14:5, 19), but of a civil suit before local magistrates. The people who bring the charge say nothing about their real reason—loss of profit. They accuse Paul of two things. Their first charge is disturbance of the peace. The second seems to be based on regulations forbidding Roman citizens to practise alien cults, especially where these conflict with Roman custom. They see Paul's exorcism and his preaching as an attempt to propagate what they see as an unacceptable religion. It may well be that the charge also had to do with specific prohibitions on the propagation of Judaism to non-Jews. However, there is no hard evidence that any such prohibition existed; therefore, the charge against Paul must have been based on regulations in the colony separating Roman from alien religious practices.

16:21. For St Luke "Roman" means the same as "Roman citizen" (cf. 16:37–38; 22:25–29; 23:27–28): he is using legal terminology of the time.

16:23. St Paul refers specifically to this punishment in 1 Thessalonians 2:2. It was one of the three beatings mentioned in 2 Corinthians 11:25.

many blows upon them, they threw them into prison, charging the
jailer to keep them safely. 24Having received this charge, he put
them into the inner prison and fastened their feet in the stocks.

Baptism of the jailer

Col 3:16 25But about midnight Paul and Silas were praying and singing
hymns to God, and the prisoners were listening to them, 26and
Acts 12:6–11 suddenly there was a great earthquake, so that the foundations of
the prison were shaken; and immediately all the doors were
opened and every one's fetters were unfastened. 27When the jailer
Acts 12:19 woke and saw that the prison doors were open, he drew his sword
and was about to kill himself, supposing that the prisoners had
escaped. 28But Paul cried with a loud voice, "Do not harm yourself, for we are all here." 29And he called for lights and rushed in,
and trembling with fear he fell down before Paul and Silas, 30and

---

16:24. St John Chrysostom, reflecting on the punishment Paul and Silas underwent, sees them as sitting or lying on the ground, covered with wounds caused by the beating. He contrasts this suffering with the way many people avoid anything which involves effort, discomfort or suffering: "How we should weep over the disorders of our time! The apostles were subjected to the worst kinds of tribulation, and here we are, spending our time in search of pleasure and diversion. This pursuit of leisure and pleasure is the cause of our ruin. We do not see the value of suffering even the least injury or insult for love of Jesus Christ.

"Let us remember the tribulations the saints experienced; nothing alarmed them or scared them. Severe humiliations made them tough, enabled them to do God's work. They did not say, If we are preaching Jesus Christ, why does he not come to our rescue?" (*Hom. on Acts*, 35).

16:25. Paul and Silas spend the night praying and singing hymns. Commenting on this passage St John Chrysostom exhorts Christians to do the same and to sanctify night-time rest: "Show by your example that the night-time is not just for recovering the strength of your body: it is also a help in sanctifying your soul. [...] You do not have to say long prayers; one prayer, said well, is enough. [...] Offer God this sacrifice of a moment of prayer and he will reward you" (*Hom. on Acts*, 36).

St Bede notes the example Paul and Silas give Christians who are experiencing trials or temptations: "The piety and energy which fires the heart of the apostles expresses itself in prayer and brings them to sing hymns even in prison. Their praise causes the earth to move, the foundations to quake, the doors to open and even their fetters to break. Similarly, that Christian who rejoices when he is happy, let him rejoice also in his weakness, when he is tempted, so that Christ's strength comes to his aid. And then let him praise the Lord with hymns, as Paul and Silas did in the darkness of their prison, and sing with the psalmist, 'Thou does encompass me with deliverance' (Ps 32:7)" (*Super Act. expositio*, ad loc.).

16:30–34. This incident so affects the jailer with religious awe that he comes to

brought them out and said, "Men, what must I do to be saved?"
[31]And they said, "Believe in the Lord Jesus, and you will be saved,
you and your household." [32]And they spoke the word of the Lord
to him and to all that were in his house. [33]And he took them the
same hour of the night, and washed their wounds, and he was Acts 8:38
baptized at once with all his family. [34]Then he brought them up Acts 8:39
into his house, and set food before them; and he rejoiced with all
his household that he had believed in God.

Release from jail and departure from Philippi

[35]But when it was day, the magistrates sent the police, saying,
"Let those men go." [36]And the jailer reported the words to Paul,
saying, "The magistrates have sent to let you go; now therefore
come out and go in peace." [37]But Paul said to them, "They have Acts 22:35
beaten us publicly, uncondemned, men who are Roman citizens,

---

be converted. He has been helped to react in this way as a result of listening to the prayers and hymns of the apostles: "Notice how the jailer reveres the apostles. He opens his heart to them, when he sees the doors of the prison open. He lights the way further with his torch, but it is another kind of torch that lights up his soul. [...] Then he cleans their wounds, and his soul is cleansed from the filth of sin. On offering them material food, he receives in return a heavenly one. [...] His docility shows that he sincerely believed that all his sins had been forgiven" (St John Chrysostom, *Hom. on Acts*, 36).

A person can meet up with God in all kinds of unexpected situations—in which case he or she needs to have the same kind of docility as the jailer in order to receive the grace of God through the channels which God has established, normally the sacraments.

16:33. As happened with Lydia and her family, the jailer's household is baptized along with him. Noting that these families probably included children and infants, the Magisterium finds support here for its teaching that baptism of children is a practice which goes right back to apostolic times and is, as St Augustine says, "a tradition received from the apostles" (cf. *Instruction on Infant Baptism*, 20 October 1980, 4).

16:35. "Magistrates": in the Roman empire a *praetor* was a magistrate with jurisdiction either in Rome or in the provinces. The "police" (*lictores*) were officials who walked in front of higher magistrates bearing the insignia of Roman justice.

16:37–39. St Paul decides to let it be known that he is a Roman citizen. He probably said nothing about this earlier to avoid giving his fellow Jews the impression that he was not proud to be a Jew or gave more importance to his Roman citizenship.

Ancient Roman law forbade beating of Roman citizens; from the beginning of the Empire it was allowed—once a person had been tried and found guilty.

The magistrates' fear was very much in line with attitudes at the time: very few people had the privilege of Roman citizenship, and the provincial authorities

and have thrown us into prison; and do they now cast us out
secretly? No! let them come themselves and take us out." 38The
Acts 22:29 police reported these words to the magistrates, and they were
afraid when they heard that they were Roman citizens; 39so they
came and apologized to them. And they took them out and asked
them to leave the city. 40So they went out of the prison, and visited
Lydia; and when they had seen the brethren, they exhorted them
and departed.

---

were responsible for the protection of the rights of Romans.

St Paul chooses what he considers to be the appropriate time to claim his rights as a citizen, doing so to protect the cause of the Gospel. Some might consider his action haughty or self-assertive; but in fact he is only doing what duty dictates, uncomfortable though it makes him. In this particular situation the dignity of the word of God requires that he claim his rights. Paul sets an example to every Christian by showing him or her the line that should be taken in the interest of the common good. Sometimes charity requires that we do not exercise our rights; but at other times that would mean one was being irresponsible and unjust.

"That false humility is laziness. Such 'humbleness' is a handy way of giving up rights that are really duties" (St Josemaría Escrivá, *The Way*, 603).

In the ecclesial sphere every Christian has a right—which he or she may not renounce—to receive the help necessary for salvation, particularly Christian doctrine and the sacraments. He has a right to follow the spirituality of his choice and to do apostolate, that is, to make the Gospel known without let or hindrance. He is free to associate with others, in keeping with whatever Church law lays down; and others have a duty to respect his right to freely choose his state, his right to his good name and his right to follow his own liturgical rite (Latin, Maronite, etc.).

In the civil sphere citizens have rights which the State should recognize: for example, a right not to be discriminated against on religious grounds, a right to education in line with their legitimate beliefs and to be protected in their married and family life. They also have a right to engage in public affairs, that is, to vote, to occupy public office and to have some influence on legislation. These political rights can easily become serious obligations.

"Lay people", Vatican II teaches, "ought to take on themselves as their distinctive task this renewal of the temporal order. Guided by the light of the Gospel and the mind of the Church, prompted by Christian love, they should act in this domain in a direct way and in their own specific manner. As citizens among citizens they must bring to their cooperation with others their own special competence, and act on their own responsibility; everywhere and always they have to seek the justice of the Kingdom of God. The temporal order is to be renewed in such a way that, while its own principles are fully respected, it is harmonized with the principles of the Christian life and adapted to the various conditions of times, places and peoples" (*Apostolicam actuositatem*, 7).

"It is their duty to cultivate a properly informed conscience and to impress the divine law on the affairs of the earthly city" (*Gaudium et spes*, 43).

Difficulties with Jews in Thessalonica

17 [1]Now when they had passed through Amphipolis and Apollonia, they came to Thessalonica, where there was a synagogue of the Jews. [2]And Paul went in, as was his custom, and for three weeks[p] he argued with them from the scriptures, [3]explain-

1 Thess 2:2

Lk 4:16
Acts 16:13

16:40. The last verb seems to imply that St Luke stayed behind in Philippi. Before leaving, Paul and Silas go to Lydia's house to encourage the Christians of Philippi: the treatment they have received and now the fact that they are to leave the city have not weakened their hope in God. When things go wrong, either for himself or others, and a Christian feels disconcerted, he should try to see the situation in a supernatural light and should realize that God's strength more than makes up for human weakness.

"The experience of our weakness and of our failings, the painful realization of the smallness and meanness of some who call themselves Christians, the apparent failure or aimlessness of some works of apostolate, all these things, which bring home to us the reality of sin and human limitation, can still be a trial of our faith. Temptation and doubt can lead us to ask: Where are the strength and power of God? When that happens we have to react by practising the virtue of hope with greater purity and forcefulness, and by striving to be more faithful" (St J. Escrivá, *Christ Is Passing By*, 128).

17:1. Thessalonica was the seat of the Roman governor of the province of Macedonia; it was about 150 kilometres (90 miles) from Philippi. It had been founded in the fourth century BC and declared a "free city" by Augustus in 42 BC. It had a Jewish community, as can be seen from the fact that there was a synagogue.

In all, Paul must have stayed many weeks in this city, in the course of which he received donations from the Christians of Philippi (cf. Phil 4:16) and had to work to keep himself (cf. 1 Thess 2:9). It was a period of difficulties and joys, as he recalled later: "You yourselves know how you ought to imitate us; we were not idle when we were with you, we did not eat any one's bread without paying, but with toil and labour we worked night and day, that we might not burden any of you" (2 Thess 3:7–8).

Paul seems to have stayed with a prominent citizen called Jason (v. 5). It is not known whether Jason was a Jew or a Gentile; he probably had been converted to Christianity by Paul's teaching.

17:2. Chrysostom draws our attention to the ordinary everyday work of the preacher who, trusting in the power of God's word, engages in a peaceful war of words in which he patiently strives to persuade others of the truth: "His preaching was based on the Scriptures. That was the way Christ preached: wherever he went he explained the Scriptures. When people oppose Paul and call him an imposter, he speaks to them about the Scriptures. For a person who tries to convince others by miracles quite rightly becomes the object of suspicion, whereas he who uses the Scriptures to win people over is not treated with suspicion. St Paul often converted people simply through his preaching. [...] God did not allow them to work too many miracles, for to win without miracles is more wonderful than all possible miracles. God rules without resorting to miracles: that is his

p. Or *sabbaths*

Lk 24:25–27; 46–47 ing and proving that it was necessary for the Christ to suffer and to
Acts 18:5 rise from the dead, and saying, "This Jesus, whom I proclaim to
Acts 17:12 you, is the Christ." 4And some of them were persuaded, and joined
Paul and Silas; as did a great many of the devout Greeks and not a
1 Thess 2:14 few of the leading women. 5But the Jews were jealous, and taking
some wicked fellows of the rabble, they gathered a crowd, set the
city in an uproar, and attacked the house of Jason, seeking to bring
Acts 24:5 them out to the people. 6And when they could not find them, they
dragged Jason and some of the brethren before the city authorities,
crying, "These men who have turned the world upside down have
Lk 23:2 come here also, 7and Jason has received them; and they are all
Jn 19:12–15 acting against the decrees of Caesar, saying that there is another
king, Jesus." 8And the people and the city authorities were disturbed when they heard this. 9And when they had taken security
from Jason and the rest, they let them go.

---

usual policy. And so the apostles did not devote much energy to working miracles, and Paul himself says, 'We preach Christ crucified [rather than provide wisdom or signs]' (1 Cor 1:23)" (*Hom. on Acts*, 37).

17:3. St Luke, who has already reported at length one discourse of Paul to Jews (cf. 13:16ff), limits himself here to giving a very short summary of his preaching in the synagogue of Thessalonica. Paul develops his argument by using quotations from Scripture (probably Ps 2; 16; 110; Is 53) whose meaning he reveals to his listeners: Jesus must be the Messiah expected by Israel; the Messiah had to suffer and then rise from the dead.

What Paul proclaims here is essentially the same as what he says in 1 Corinthians 15:3–5, which is a passage based on very ancient traditions: it is very reasonable to suppose that the apostle is reiterating accepted Christian teaching that Jesus was the Messiah and the Redeemer of man.

17:5–9. Once again Paul's preaching provokes the Jews to jealousy. They see many Gentiles following him who otherwise might have become converts to Judaism. However, the main motive for their opposition is not religious zeal. There is an element of malice here; their sense of guilt over resisting the grace of the Gospel plays a part in their behaviour. "God opens the lips of those who utter divine words," Origen writes, "and I fear that it is the devil who opens other people's" (*In Ex hom.*, 3, 2).

St Luke calls the city magistrates "politarchs". This was unknown as a term for civic officials in non-Roman cities of Macedonia; but recently discovered inscriptions have shown it to be correct. As a "free city", Thessalonica had a popular assembly empowered to investigate charges.

The Jews bring a religious charge against Paul, but they disguise it in the form of two secular charges. They accuse him of causing a civil disturbance and, by saying that he is proposing "another king", they accuse him also of high treason. These are exactly the same crimes as were alleged against our Lord (cf. Lk 23:2; Jn 19:12).

His accusers have clearly twisted Paul's teaching: he would certainly have

Reception in Beroea

10The brethren immediately sent Paul and Silas away by night to
Beroea; and when they arrived they went into the Jewish synagogue. 11Now these Jews were more noble than those in Thess- Jn 5:39
alonica, for they received the word with all eagerness, examining
the scriptures daily to see if these things were so. 12Many of them
therefore believed, with not a few Greek women of high standing
as well as men. 13But when the Jews of Thessalonica learned that
the word of God was proclaimed by Paul at Beroea also, they
came there too, stirring up and inciting the crowds. 14Then the
brethren immediately sent Paul off on his way to the sea, but Silas
and Timothy remained there. 15Those who conducted Paul brought
him as far as Athens; and receiving a command for Silas and
Timothy to come to him as soon as possible, they departed.

Paul in Athens

16Now while Paul was waiting for them at Athens, his spirit was
provoked within him as he saw that the city was full of idols. 17So

---

spoken of Jesus as Lord, but not in the sense of predicting the establishment of an earthly religion.

The magistrates listen to the charges but they accept Jason's security and the charges fail to lead to a conviction.

17:11. The Jews of Beroea were the only ones not to reject Paul's teaching. They immediately began a search of the Scriptures, which led them to discover the truth of the Gospel. They were clearly very upright people who practised both the letter and the spirit of the law of God. "In order to study and understand the Scriptures," St Athanasius says, "one needs to be live a clean life and have a pure soul" (*De incarnatione contra arianos*, 57).

The same preaching has different effects on different people. "It is a fact that the teaching of the truth is differently received depending on the listeners' dispositions. The Word shows everyone what is good and what is bad; if a person is predisposed to do what is proclaimed to him, his soul is in the light; if he is not and he has not decided to fix his soul's gaze on the light of truth, then he will remain in the darkness of ignorance" (St Gregory of Nyssa, *On the Life of Moses*, 2, 65).

As St John of the Cross says, "to seek God one needs to have a heart which is naked and strong, free from all good and evil things that are not simply God" (*Spiritual Canticle*, stanza 3).

17:16–21. St Paul's missionary activity in Athens shows us the Gospel's first encounter with Hellenist paganism, both popular and intellectual. This is an important episode in the spread of the Christian message because it shows us the capacity of Gospel preaching to adapt itself to different outlooks, different cultures, while still remaining completely faithful to itself.

The Athens visited by St Paul was no longer the brilliant intellectual capital it had been in the time of Plato and Aristotle. It was in decline, culturally and

Acts 14:7–17

he argued in the synagogue with the Jews and the devout persons,
and in the market place every day with those who chanced to be
there. 18Some also of the Epicurean and Stoic philosophers met
him. And some said, "What would this babbler say?" Others said,
"He seems to be a preacher of foreign divinities"—because he
preached Jesus and the resurrection. 19And they took hold of him
and brought him to the Areopagus, saying, "May we know what
this new teaching is which you present? 20For you bring some

---

politically, but it still retained traces of its former glory. Here the philosophical currents of the day still had their spokesmen, and intellectual debate was always welcomed.

St Paul presents the Gospel to these pagan philosophers as "true philosophy" without in any sense taking from its transcendental, supernatural character. The point at which they coincide is this: philosophy is the science of life; it is a legitimate search for the answer to profound questions about human existence. Paul tries to lead them beyond mere intellectual curiosity, in a genuine search for perennial truth, which is religious in character. He supports the philosophers in their criticism of superstition, but points out that they have to go farther than just censuring aberrations of that kind.

Paul is well aware that preaching Christ crucified is "a stumbling block to Jews and folly to Gentiles" (1 Cor 1:23). However, this conviction does not prevent his feeling and expressing respect for pagan thought and religion, which he sees as providing a groundwork for the Gospel. In Paul's address we can see the first signs of the Church's and Christians' ongoing recognition of the value, albeit limited, of secular culture. "There are in profane culture", St Gregory of Nyssa writes, "aspects which should not be rejected when the time comes to grow in virtue. Natural moral philosophy can, in fact, be the companion of one who wants to lead a higher life [...], provided that its fruit does not carry any alien contamination" (*On the Life of Moses*, 2, 37).

Two centuries before Gregory, St Justin Martyr wrote about the merits and defects of pagan philosphy and the relative truth it contains: "I declare that I prayed and strove with all my might to be known as a Christian, not because the teachings of Plato are completely different from those of Christ, but because they are not in all respects the same; neither are those of other writers, Stoics, the poets and the historians. For each discoursed rightly, seeing through his participation in the seminal divine Word what related to it. But they that have uttered contrary opinions clearly do not have sound knowledge and irrefutable wisdom. Whatever has been uttered aright by any man in any place belongs to Christians; for, next to God, we worship and love the Word which is from the unbegotten and ineffable God. [...] All the profane authors were able to see the truth clearly, through the seed of reason [*logos*, word], implanted in them" (*Apology*, 2, 13, 2–3).

17:16. Paul's religious zeal makes him indignant at the failure to recognize the truth, the depraved forms of religious worship and the wretched spiritual situation of people who do not know God.

His devout, serene reaction brings him immediately to tell them about the true God and enlighten their darkened minds.

strange things to our ears; we wish to know therefore what these
things mean." 21Now all the Athenians and the foreigners who
lived there spent their time in nothing except telling or hearing
something new.

Paul's speech in the Areopagus
22So Paul, standing in the middle of the Areopagus, said: "Men of
Athens, I perceive that in every way you are very religious. 23For

---

17:17. As usual Paul preaches in the synagogue, but he also addresses anyone in the market place who is ready to listen to what he has to say. The verb St Luke uses really means "preach", not "argue" (cf. 20:7, 9).

"Market place": *Agora* was the Greek name for the main city square. The people used to foregather in the Agora to debate the political questions of the day; it was also used for other activities, including trading. The Agora in Athens was particularly famous from very early on: it was the centre of Athenian democracy, but it was also used for informal, everyday affairs.

17:18. Epicurean philosophers followed the teachings of Epicurus (341–270 BC), which tended to be rather materialistic. They spoke of there being no gods, or at least they regarded the gods as taking no interest in the doings of men. Epicurean ethics stressed the importance of pleasure and a life of ease and tranquillity.

The Stoics, who followed Zeno of Citium (340–265 BC), saw the *logos* as the cause which shapes, orders and directs the entire universe and the lives of those who inhabit it. The *logos* is the Reason for everything that exists, the ultimate principle, immanent in things; this is a pantheistic concept of the world. Stoic ethics stress individual responsibility and self-sufficiency; but although this philosophy speaks a great deal about freedom it sees Fate as playing a decisive role.

"Babbler": the Greek word does have a rather derogatory meaning and is used mainly to refer to people who never open their mouths without uttering clichés.

These people seem to take "Resurrection" as a proper name of some god accompanying Jesus.

17:19. The word "areopagus" can refer to a hill where the Athenians used to meet and also to a session of a tribunal or city council gathered together to listen to Paul's teaching. It is not clear from the text which meaning applies.

17:22–33. Of all Paul's addresses reported in Acts, this address in the Areopagus is his longest to a pagan audience (cf. 14:15ff). It is a highly significant one, paralleling in importance his address to the Jews of Pisidian Antioch (cf. 13:16ff). It is the first model we have of Christian apologetic method, which tends to stress the reasonableness of Christianity and the fact that it has no difficulty in holding its own with the best in human thought.

The speaker is clearly the same person as wrote the first three chapters of the Epistle to the Romans, someone with a lot of experience of preaching the Gospel; his method consists in first talking about the one, true, living God and then proclaiming Jesus Christ, the divine Saviour of all men (cf. 2 Tim 1:9–10).

After an introduction designed to catch the attention of listeners and highlight the central theme (vv. 22ff), the

as I passed along, and observed the objects of your worship, I
found also an altar with this inscription, 'To an unknown god.'
What therefore you worship as unknown, this I proclaim to you.
Is 42:5 Acts 14:15 [24]The God who made the world and everything in it, being Lord

---

address can be divided into three parts: 1) God is the Lord of the world; he does not need to live in temples built by men (vv. 24f); 2) man has been created by God and is dependent on him for everything (vv. 26f); 3) there is a special relationship between God and man; therefore, idolatry is a grave sin (vv. 28f). Then, in his conclusion, Paul exhorts his listeners to accept the truth about God, and to repent, bearing in mind the Last Judgment (vv. 30f).

The terminology Paul uses comes mainly from the Greek translation of the Old Testament—the Septuagint. Biblical beliefs are expressed in the language of the Hellenistic culture of the people.

17:22–24. "To an unknown God": St Paul praises the religious feelings of the Athenians, which lead them to offer worship to God. But he goes on to point out that their form of religion is very imperfect because they do not know enough about God and about the right way to worship him; nor does their religion free them from their sins or help them live in a way worthy of human dignity. Religious Athenians, he seems to say somewhat ironically, are in fact superstitious, and they do not know the one true God and his ways of salvation.

Paul criticizes pagan religion and points out its limitations, but he does not totally condemn it. He regards it as a basis to work on: at least it means that his listeners accept the possibility of the existence of a true God as yet unknown to them. They are predisposed to receive and accept the supernatural revelation of God in Christ. Revelation does not destroy natural religion: rather, it purifies it, completes it and raises it up, enabling a naturally religious person to know the mystery of God, One and Triune, to change his life with the help of the grace of Christ and to attain the salvation he needs and yearns for.

17:23. "Those who acted in accordance with what is universally, naturally and eternally good were pleasing to God and will be saved by Christ [...], just like the righteous who preceded them" (St Justin, *Dialogue with Tryphon*, 45). The Church's esteem for the positive elements in pagan religions leads her to preach to all men the fulness of truth and salvation which is to be found only in Jesus Christ. "The Catholic Church rejects nothing of what is true and holy in these religions. She has a high regard for the manner of life and conduct, the precepts and doctrines which, although differing in many ways from her own teaching, nevertheless often reflect a ray of that truth which enlightens all men. Yet she proclaims, and is in duty bound to proclaim without fail, Christ who is 'the way, and the truth, and the life' (Jn 14:6). In him, in whom God reconciled all things to himself, men find the fulness of their religious life" (Vatican II, *Nostra aetate*, 2).

17:24. Paul's language is in line with the way God is described in the Old Testament as being Lord of heaven and earth (cf. Is 42:5; Ex 20:21). The apostle speaks of God's infinite majesty: God is greater than the universe, of which he is the creator. However, Paul does not mean

of heaven and earth, does not live in shrines made by man, 25nor
is he served by human hands, as though he needed anything, since Ps 50:8–11

---

to imply that it is not desirable for God to be worshipped in sacred places designed for that purpose.

His words seem to echo those of Solomon at the dedication of the first temple: "Behold, heaven and the highest heaven cannot contain thee; how much less this house which I have built!" (1 Kings 8:27).

Any worship rendered to God should be "in spirit and truth" (Jn 4:24). But the Lord has desired to dwell in a special way and to receive homage in temples built by men. "The worship of God", St Thomas Aquinas writes, "regards both God who is worshipped and men who perform the worship. God is not confined to any place, and therefore it is not on his account that a tabernacle or temple has to be made. Worshippers, as corporeal beings, need a special tabernacle or temple set up for the worship of God; and this for two reasons. First, that the thought of its being appointed to the worship of God might instil a greater sense of reverence; second, that the way it is arranged and furnished might signify in various respects the excellence of Christ's divine or human nature. [...] From this it is clear that the house of the sanctuary was not set up to receive God as if dwelling there, but that his name might dwell there, that is, in order that the knowledge of God might be exhibited there" (*Summa theologiae*, 1–2, 102, 4, ad 1).

17:25. The idea that God does not need man's service and does not depend on man for his well-being and happiness is to be often found in the prophetical books. "Now in Babylon you will see", Jeremiah proclaims, "gods made of silver and gold and wood, which are carried on men's shoulders and inspire fear in the heathen. [...] Their tongues are smoothed by the craftsmen, and they themselves are overlaid with gold and silver; but they are false and cannot speak. [...] When they have been dressed in purple robes, their faces are wiped because of the dust from the temple, which is thick upon them. Like a local ruler the god holds a sceptre, though unable to destroy any one who offends it. [...] Having no feet, they are carried on men's shoulders, revealing to mankind their worthlessness. And those who serve them are ashamed because through them these gods are made to stand, lest they fall to the ground" (Bar 6:4, 8, 12–14, 26–27).

This does not mean that the Lord does not want men to respond to the love-offering which he makes them. "Hear, O heavens," Isaiah prophesies, "and give ear, O earth; for the Lord has spoken: 'Sons have I reared and brought up, but they have rebelled against me. The ox knows its owner, and the ass its master's crib; but Israel does not know, my people does not understand' " (1:2–3).

In addition to being offensive and senseless, sin implies indifference and ingratitude towards God, who, in an excess of love, is tireless in seeking man's friendship. "When Israel was a child, I loved him, and out of Egypt I called my son," we read in the prophet Hosea. "The more I called them, the more they went from me. [...] Yet it was I who taught Ephraim to walk, I took them up in my arms; but they did not know that I healed them. I led them with cords of compassion, with the bands of love" (11:1–4).

he himself gives to all men life and breath and everything. [26]And
Deut 32:8 2 Mac 7:23 he made from one every nation of men to live on all the face of
the earth, having determined allotted periods and the boundaries
Deut 4:29 of their habitation, [27]that they should seek God, in the hope that
Is 55:6 Rom 1:19 they might feel after him and find him. Yet he is not far from each
one of us, [28]for

By far the greatest sign of God's love for men is the Redemption, and the sacraments of the Church, through which the fruits of the Redemption reach us. His love is expressed in a special way in the Blessed Eucharist, which provides the Christian with nourishment and is where Jesus wishes us to adore him and keep him company.

17:26. "From one": St Paul is referring to the text of Genesis 2:7: "then the Lord God formed man of dust from the ground, and breathed into his nostrils the breath of life"; in other words, he is speaking of the first progenitor of the human race. The expression "from one" should not be interpreted as meaning from *one principle* but from *one man*.

17:27–28. St Paul is speaking about the absolute nearness of God and his mysterious but real presence in every man and woman. St Augustine echoes this teaching when he exclaims, "Yet all the time you were within me, more inward than the most inward place of my heart, and loftier than the highest" (*Confessions*, 3, 6, 11).

Merely to exist, man needs God, his Creator. He also needs him if he is to continue in existence, to live and act. He needs him if he is to think and love. And in particular he needs him in order to love goodness and be good. It is correct to say that God is in us. This intimate union of God and man does not in any way take from the fact that there is a perfect distinction and radical difference between God, who is infinite, and man, who is finite and limited.

"Men, who are incapable of existing of themselves," St Athanasius writes, "are to be found confined by place and dependent on the Word of God. But God exists of himself, he contains all things and is contained by none. He is to be found within everything as far as his goodness and power is concerned, and he is outside of everything as far as his own divine nature is concerned" (*De decretis nicaenae synodi*, 11).

Christian spirituality has traditionally seen in these ideas an invitation to seek God in the depth of one's soul and to always feel dependent upon him.

"Consider God", says St John of Avila, "who is the existence of everything that exists, and without whom there is nothing: and who is the life of all that lives, and without whom there is death; and who is the strength of all that has capacity to act, and without whom there is weakness; and who is the entire good of everything that is good, without whom nothing can have the least little bit of good in it" (*Audi, filia*, chap. 64).

St Francis de Sales writes: "Not only is God in the place where you are, but he is in a very special manner in your heart and in the depth of your soul, which he quickens and animates with his divine presence, since he is there as the heart of your heart, and the spirit of your soul; for, as the soul, being spread throughout the body, is present in every part of it, and yet resides in a special manner in the heart, so God, being present in all things,

'In him we live and move and have our being';
as even some of your poets have said,
'For we are indeed his offspring.'
29Being then God's offspring, we ought not to think that the Deity Acts 19:26
is like gold, or silver, or stone, a representation by the art and Rom 1:22–23
imagination of man. 30The times of ignorance God overlooked, Rom 3:25–26

---

is present nevertheless in a special manner in our spirit and therefore David called God 'the rock of his heart' (Ps 73:26); and Paul said that 'we live and move and have our being in God' (Acts 17:28). By reflecting on this truth, you will stir up in your heart a great reverence for God, who is so intimately present there" (*Introduction to the Devout Life*, 2, chap. 2).

This quotation—in the singular—is from the Stoic poet Aratus (3rd century BC). The plural in the quotation may refer to a similar verse in the hymn to Zeus written by Cleanthes (also 3rd century).

"The devil spoke words of Scripture but our Saviour reduced him to silence", St Athanasius comments. "Paul cites secular authors, but, saint that he is, he gives them a spiritual meaning" (*De synodis*, 39). "We are rightly called 'God's offspring', not the offspring of his divinity but created freely by his spirit and re-created through adoption as sons" (St Bede, *Super Act. expositio*, ad loc.).

17:29. If men are God's offspring, and are in some way like him, clearly an inanimate representation cannot contain the living God. Men have God's spirit and therefore they should recognize that God is spiritual. However, material representations of God do serve a useful purpose, due to the fact that human knowledge begins from sense experience. Visual images help us to realize that God is present and they help us to adore him. Veneration of images—as encouraged by the Church—is, therefore, quite different from idolatry: an idolator thinks that God dwells in the idol, that he acts only through the idol, and in some cases he actually thinks that the idol is God.

17:30. St Paul now moves on from speaking about natural knowledge of God to explaining the knowledge of God that comes from faith.

Although man can know God by using his reason, the Lord has chosen to make known the mysteries of his divine life in a supernatural way, in order to make it easier for man to attain salvation. "The Church maintains and teaches that God, the beginning and end of all things, can be known with certainty, by the natural light of human reason, from created things. [...] However, it pleased him in his wisdom and goodness to reveal himself to mankind and to make known the eternal decrees of his will in another, supernatural way" (Vatican I, *Dei Filius*, chap. 2).

"It was also necessary for man to be instructed by divine revelation concerning those truths concerning God, which human reason is able to discover, for these truths, attained by human reason, would reach man through the work of a few, after much effort and mixed in with many errors; yet the entire salvation of man, which lies in God, depends on knowledge of these truths. So, for salvation to reach men more rapidly and more surely, it was necessary for them to be instructed by divine revelation concerning the things of God" (St Thomas Aquinas, *Summa theologiae*, 1, 1, 1).

Lk 24:47 Acts 10:42 1 Pet 4:5

but now he commands all men everywhere to repent, [31]because he
has fixed a day on which he will judge the world in righteousness
by a man whom he has appointed, and of this he has given ass-
surance to all men by raising him from the dead."

Supernatural revelation assures man of easily attained, certain knowledge of divine mysteries; it also includes some truths—such as the existence of God—which unaided human reason can discover (cf. Rom 1:20).

"It pleased God, in his goodness and wisdom", Vatican II teaches, "to reveal himself and to make known the mystery of his will (cf. Eph 1:9). His will was that men should have access to the Father, through Christ, the Word made flesh, in the Holy Spirit, and thus become sharers in the divine nature (cf. Eph 2:18; 2 Pet 1:4). By this revelation, then, the invisible God (cf. Col 1:15; 1 Tim 1:17), from the fulness of his love, addresses men as his friends (cf. Ex 33:11; Jn 15:14–15), and moves among them in order to invite and receive them into his own company" (*Dei Verbum*, 2).

The knowledge of the triune God and his saving will which supernatural revelation offers men is not just theoretical or intellectual knowledge: it has the aim of converting man and leading him to repent and to change his life. It is, therefore, a calling from God; and God expects man to make a personal response to that call. " 'The obedience of faith' (Rom 16:26; cf. Rom 1:5; 2 Cor 10:5–6) must be given to God as he reveals himself. By faith man freely commits his entire self to God, making 'the full submission of his intellect and will to God who reveals' (Vatican I, *Dei Filius*, chap. 3), and willingly assenting to the Revelation given by him. Before this faith can be exercised, man must have the grace of God to move and assist him; he must have the interior helps of the Holy Spirit, who moves the heart and converts it to God" (Vatican II, *Dei Verbum*, 5).

This practical knowledge of the living and true God revealed in Christ is in fact the only way for man to know himself, despise his faults and sins, and find hope in divine mercy. It is a self-knowledge—given by God—which enables the repentant sinner to begin a new life and work freely with God at his own sanctification: "As I see it, we shall never succeed in knowing ourselves unless we seek to know God," St Teresa writes. "Let us think of his greatness and then come back to our own baseness; by looking at his purity we shall see our foulness; by meditating on his humility, we shall see how far we are from being humble" (*Interior Castle*, 1, 2, 9).

17:31. On Jesus Christ as Judge of all, see the note on Acts 10:42.

17:32. When St Paul begins to tell the Athenians about Jesus' resurrection from the dead, they actually begin to jeer. For pagans, the notion of resurrection from the dead was absurd, something they were not prepared to believe. If the apostle speaks in this way, the reason is that the truths of the Christian faith all lead into the mystery of the Resurrection; even though he may have anticipated his listeners' reaction, he does not avoid telling them about this truth, which forms the bedrock of our faith. "See how he leads them," Chrysostom points out,"to the God who takes care of the world, who is kind, merciful, powerful and wise: all these attributes of the Creator

[32]Now when they heard of the resurrection of the dead, some
mocked; but others said, "We will hear you again about this." [33]So
Paul went out from among them. [34]But some men joined him and
believed, among them Dionysius the Areopagite and a woman
named Damaris and others with them.

---

are confirmed in the Resurrection" (*Hom. on Acts*, 38).

The apostle fails to overcome the rationalist prejudices of most of his audience. Here we have, as it were, an application of what he wrote later to the Corinthians: "The Greeks seek wisdom, but we preach Christ crucified …, folly to the Gentiles" (1 Cor 1:22f), the reason being that if people do not have an attitude and disposition of faith, then reason goes out of control and haughtily rejects mysteries. If the human mind is made the measure of all things, it will despise and reject anything it does not understand—including things which are beyond human understanding. The mysteries God has revealed to man cannot be grasped by unaided human reason; they have to be accepted on faith. What moves the mind to accept these mysteries is not the evidence they contain but the authority of God, who is infallible truth and cannot deceive or be deceived. The act of faith, although strictly speaking an act of the assenting mind, is influenced by the will; the desire to believe presupposes that one loves him who is proposing the truth to be believed.

17:34. "Those careful to live an upright life do not take long to understand the word; but the same does not go for others" (*Hom. on Acts*, 39).

Among the few converts in Athens St Luke mentions Damaris. She is one of the many women who appear in Acts—which clearly shows that the preaching of the Gospel was addressed to everyone without distinction. In all that they did the apostles followed their Master's example, who in spite of the prejudices of his age proclaimed the Kingdom to women as well as men.

St Luke told us about the first convert in Europe being a woman (cf. 16:14ff). Something similar happened in the case of the Samaritans: it was a woman who first spoke to them about the Saviour (cf. Jn 4). In the Gospels we see how attentive women are to our Lord—standing at the foot of the cross or being the first to visit the tomb on Easter Sunday. And there is no record of women being hypocritical or hating Christ or abandoning him out of cowardice.

St Paul has a deep appreciation of the role of the Christian woman—as mother, wife and sister—in the spreading of Christianity, as can be seen from his letters and preaching. Lydia in Philippi, Priscilla and Chloe in Corinth, Phoebe in Cenchrae, the mother of Rufus—who was also a mother to him—and the daughters of Philip (Acts 21:9): these are some of the women to whom Paul was ever-grateful for their help and prayers.

"Women are called to bring to the family, to society and to the Church, characteristics which are their own and which they alone can give—their gentle warmth and untiring generosity, their love for detail, their quick-wittedness and intuition, their simple and deep piety, their constancy…" (St J. Escrivá, *Conversations*, 87). The Church looks to women to commit themselves and bear witness to human values and to where human happiness lies: "Women have received from God", John Paul II says, "a

Paul in Corinth, with Aquila and Priscilla

Rom 16:3 1 Cor 16:19 2 Tim 4:19

18 1After this he left Athens and went to Corinth. 2And he
found a Jew named Aquila, a native of Pontus, lately come
from Italy with his wife Priscilla, because Claudius had com-

---

natural charism of their own, which features great sensitivity, a fine sense of balance, a gift for detail and a providential love for life-in-the-making, life in need of loving attention. These are qualities which make for human maturity" (Address, 7 December 1979).

When these qualities, with which God has endowed feminine personality, are developed and brought into play, woman's "life and work will be really constructive, fruitful and full of meaning, whether she spends the day dedicated to her husband and children or whether, having given up the idea of marriage for a noble reason, she has given herself fully to other tasks.

"Each woman in her own sphere of life, if she is faithful to her divine and human vocation, can and, in fact, does achieve the fulness of her feminine personality. Let us remember that Mary, Mother of God and Mother of men, is not only a model but also a proof of the transcendental value of an apparently unimportant life" (*Conversations*, 87).

18:1–11. St Paul must have arrived in Corinth very discouraged by what happened in Athens, and very short of money. Some time later he wrote: "And I was with you in weakness and in much fear and trembling; and my speech and my message were not in plausible words of wisdom, but in demonstration of the Spirit and power, that your faith might not rest in the wisdom of men but in the power of God." (1 Cor 2:3–5). He would never forget his experience in the Areopagus before the Athenians, who "were friends of new speeches, yet who paid no heed to them or what they said; all they wanted was to have something new to talk about" (St John Chrysostom, *Hom. on Acts*, 39).

Corinth was a very commercial cosmopolitan city located on an isthmus between two gulfs (which are now joined). Ships came to Corinth from all over the world. Low moral standards, concentration on money-making and voluptuous worship of Aphrodite meant that Corinth did not seem the best ground for sowing the word of God; but the Lord can change people's hearts, especially if he has people as obedient and zealous as Paul, Silvanus, Timothy and the early Christians in general. The Athenians' intellectual pride proved to be a more formidable obstacle than the Corinthians' libertarian lifestyle.

Christians should not soft-pedal if they find themselves in situations where paganism and loose living seem to be the order of the day: indeed this should only spur them on. When addressing his Father at the Last Supper Jesus prayed "I do not pray that thou shouldst take them out of the world, but that thou shouldst keep them from the evil one" (Jn 17:15).

18:2. This married couple were probably already Christians when they arrived in Corinth. Since they came from Rome, the indications are that there was a community of Christians in the capital from very early on. Aquila and Priscilla (the diminutive of Prisca) proved to be of great help to Paul from the very beginning of his work in Corinth.

Later on they both must have returned to Rome (cf. Rom 16:3); and it may

manded all the Jews to leave Rome. And he went to see them;
3and because he was of the same trade he stayed with them, and Acts 20:34 1 Cor 4:12

well be that apostolic considerations dictated their movements, as would be the case with countless Christians after them. "The Christian family's faith and evangelizing mission also possesses this Catholic missionary inspiration. The sacrament of marriage takes up and re-proposes the task of defending and spreading the faith, a task which has its roots in Baptism and Confirmation and makes Christian married couples and parents witnesses of Christ 'to the end of the earth' (Acts 1:8) […]

"Just as at the dawn of Christianity Aquila and Priscilla were presented as a missionary couple (cf. Acts 18; Rom 16:3f), so today the Church shows forth her perennial newness and fruitfulness by the presence of Christian couples who […] work in missionary territories, proclaiming the Gospel and doing service to their fellowmen for the love of Jesus Christ" (John Paul II, *Familiaris consortio*, 54).

The edict of Claudius (41–54) expelling the Jews from Rome was issued before the year 50. It is referred to by Suetonius, the Roman historian, but the details of the decree are not known. We do know that Claudius had protected Jews on a number of occasions. He gave them the right to appoint the high priest and to have charge of the temple. Apparently, conflict between Jews and Christians in Rome led him to expel some Jews from the city, on a temporary basis, or at least to advise them to leave.

18:3. St Paul earns his living and manages to combine this with all his preaching of the Gospel. "This teaching of Christ on work," John Paul II writes, "based on the example of his life during his years in Nazareth, finds a particularly lively echo in the teaching of the apostle Paul. Paul boasts of working at his trade (he was probably a tentmaker: cf. Acts 18:3), and thanks to that work he was able even as an apostle to earn his own bread" (*Laborem exercens*, 26).

During this stay of a year and a half in Corinth St Paul wrote some rather severe letters to the Thessalonians, pointing out to them the need to work: "If any one will not work, let him not eat. […] We command and exhort [idlers] in the Lord Jesus Christ to do their work in quietness and to earn their own living" (2 Thess 3:10, 12). St John Chrysostom, commenting on this passage of Acts, says that "Work is man's natural state. Idleness is *against his nature*. God has placed man in this world to work, and the natural thing for the soul is to be active and not passive" (*Hom. on Acts*, 35).

Taking Christ's own example, St J. Escrivá points out that "Work is one of the highest human values and the way in which men contribute to the progress of society. But even more, it is a way to holiness" (*Conversations*, 24). In Jesus' hands, "a professional occupation, similar to that carried out by millions of people all over the world, was turned into a divine task. It became a part of our redemption, a way to salvation" (ibid., 55).

In fact, it is in work, in the middle of ordinary activity, that most people can and should find Christ. "God is calling you to serve him in and from the ordinary, material and secular activities of human life. He waits for us everyday […] in all the immense panorama of work" (ibid., 114). Man thereby finds God in the most visible, material things,

they worked, for by trade they were tentmakers. 4And he argued
in the synagogue every sabbath, and persuaded Jews and Greeks.

Preaching to Jews and Gentiles

Acts 17:14–15 5When Silas and Timothy arrived from Macedonia, Paul was
occupied with preaching, testifying to the Jews that the Christ was
Acts 13:46–51; 20:26; 28:28 Jesus. 6And when they opposed and reviled him, he shook out his
garments and said to them, "Your blood be upon your heads! I am

---

and Christians can avoid the danger of what might be called "a double life: on one side, an interior life, a life of relation with God; and on the other, a separate and distinct professional, social and family life, full of small earthly realities" (ibid.).

Like most people Paul spent part of his day working to earn his living. When engaged in work he was still the apostle of the Gentiles chosen by God, and his very work spoke to his companions and friends. We should not think that there was any split between his on-going personal relationship with God, and his apostolic activity or his work—or that he did not work in a concentrated or exemplary manner.

18:4. It is easy to imagine the hope and eagerness Paul felt when preaching the Gospel to his fellow Jews. He knew from experience the difficulties they had about recognizing Jesus as the Messiah and accepting the Good News. Paul feels both joy and sorrow: he is happy because the moment has arrived for the sons of Abraham to receive the Gospel as is their right by inheritance; but he also realizes that although it brings salvation to some, it spells rejection for those who refuse to accept it.

Origen spoke in similar terms: "I experience anxiety to speak and anxiety not to speak. I wish to speak for the benefit of those who are worthy, so that I may not be taken to task for refusing the word of truth to those who have the ability to grasp it. But I am afraid to speak in case I address those who are unworthy, because it means I am giving holy things to dogs and casting pearls before swine. Only Jesus was capable of distinguishing, among his listeners, those who were without from those who were within: he spoke in parables to the outsiders and explained the parables to those who entered with him into the house" (*Dialogue with Heraclides*, 15).

18:6. The blindness of the Jews once again causes Paul great sadness; here is further evidence of the mysterious resistance to faith of so many of the chosen people. As he did in Pisidian Antioch (cf. 13:51), the apostle shakes the dust from his clothes to show his break from the Jews of Corinth: their apparent fidelity to the religion of their forefathers disguises their proud rejection of God's promises.

He finds himself confronted by the great enigma of salvation history, in which God dialogues with human freedom. As St Justin writes, "The Jews, in truth, who had the prophecies and always looked for the coming of Christ, not only did not recognize him, but, far beyond that, even mistreated him. But the Gentiles, who had never even heard anything of Christ until his apostles went from Jerusalem and preached about him and gave them the prophecies, were filled with joy and faith, and turned away from their idols, and dedicated themselves to

innocent. From now on I will go to the Gentiles." [7]And he left
there and went to the house of a man named Titius[q] Justus, a worshipper of God; his house was next door to the synagogue.
[8]Crispus, the ruler of the synagogue, believed in the Lord, 1 Cor 1:14
together with all his household; and many of the Corinthians hearing Paul believed and were baptized. [9]And the Lord said to Paul 1 Cor 2:3
one night in a vision, "Do not be afraid, but speak and do not be

---

the Unbegotten God through Christ" (*Apology*, 1, 49, 5).

Paul's words on this occasion are addressed to the Jews of Corinth, not to Jews elsewhere. For a long time past he has directed his preaching to Gentiles as well as Jews. The phrase "From now on I will go to the Gentiles" does not mean that he will no longer address Jews, for in the course of his apostolic work he continues to evangelize Jews as well as Gentiles (cf. Acts 18:19; 28:17).

18:7. Titus Justus had a Roman name and was a Gentile, but the fact that he lived next door to the synagogue and, in particular, the Greek term used to identify him as a "worshipper" of God, indicates that he was a convert to Judaism. Cf. the note on Acts 2:5–11.

18:9. In this vision, given him to strengthen his resolve, Paul sees the Lord, that is, Jesus. The brief message he receives is reminiscent of the language God uses when he addresses the prophets and just men of the Old Testament (cf. Ex 3:12; Josh 1:5; Is 41:10). The words "Do not be afraid" occur often in divine visions and are designed to allay the impact of God's overpowering presence (cf. Lk 1:30).

In this case, the words are meant to allay Paul's premonitions about the severe treatment his opponents will hand out to him in Corinth. The vision once again indicates the graces which the Lord is bestowing on him to support his intense contemplative life, which is also a life of action in the service of Jesus and the Gospel.

"I tell you," St Teresa of Avila writes, "those of you whom God is not leading by this road [of contemplation], that, as I know from what I have seen and been told by those who are following this road, they are not bearing a lighter cross than you; you would be amazed at all the ways and manners in which God sends them crosses. I know about both types of life and I am well aware that the trials given by God to contemplatives are intolerable; and they of such a kind that, were he not to feed them with consolations, they could not be borne. It is clear that, since God leads those whom he most loves by the way of trials, the more he loves them, the greater will be their trials; and there is no reason to suppose that he hates contemplatives, since with his own mouth he praises them and calls them his friends.

"To suppose that he would admit to his close friendship people who are free from all trials is ridiculous. [...] I think, when those who lead an active life occasionally see contemplatives receiving consolations, they suppose that they never experience anything else. But I can assure you that you might not be able to endure their sufferings for as long as a day" (*Way of Perfection*, chap. 18).

q. Other early authorities read *Titus*

Is 41:10; 43:5 Jer 1:8 Jn 10:16 silent; [10]for I am with you, and no man shall attack you to harm
you; for I have many people in this city." [11]And he stayed a year
and six months, teaching the word of God among them.

Paul before Gallio

[12]But when Gallio was proconsul of Achaia, the Jews made a
united attack upon Paul and brought him before the tribunal,
[13]saying, "This man is persuading men to worship God contrary to
Acts 25:18–19 the law." [14]But when Paul was about to open his mouth, Gallio
said to the Jews, "If it were a matter of wrongdoing or vicious
crime, I should have reason to bear with you, O Jews; [15]but since
Jn 18:21 Acts 23:29 it is a matter of questions about words and names and your own
law, see to it yourselves; I refuse to be a judge of these things."
[16]And he drove them from the tribunal. [17]And they all seized
Sosthenes, the ruler of the synagogue, and beat him in front of the
tribunal. But Gallio paid no attention to this.

18:10. God has foreseen the people who are going to follow the call of grace. From this it follows that the Christian has a serious obligation to preach the Gospel to as many people as he can. This preaching has a guaranteed effectiveness, as can be seen from its capacity to convert men and women of every race, age, social condition etc. The Gospel is for all. God offers it, through Christians, to the rich and the poor, to the educated and the uneducated. Any person can accept this invitation to grace: "Not only philosophers and scholars believed in Christ […], but also workmen and people wholly uneducated, who all scorned glory, and fear, and death" (St Justin, *Apology*, 1, 10, 8).

18:12. Gallio was a brother of the Stoic philosopher Seneca. He had been adopted in Rome by Lucius Iunius Gallio, whose name he took. From an inscription at Delphi (reported in 1905) we learn that Gallio began his proconsulship of Achaia, of which Corinth was the capital, in July 51. Paul must have appeared before Gallio around the end of 52. This is one of the best-established dates we have for the apostle.

18:17. It is not quite clear what happened. Sosthenes may have been assaulted by the citizens of Corinth who were using the incident to vent their anti-Jewish feelings. But it is more likely that Sosthenes was in sympathy with the Christians and that the Jews were venting their frustration on him. In 1 Corinthians 1:1 a Christian called Sosthenes appears as co-author (amanuensis) of the letter; some commentators identify him with the ruler of the synagogue in this episode.

18:18. The vow taken by a "Nazirite" (one "consecrated to God") is described in the sixth chapter of the Book of Numbers. Among other things it involved not cutting one's hair (to symbolize that one was allowing God to act in one) and not drinking fermented drinks (meaning a resolution to practise self-denial). It is not clear whether it was Paul or Aquila who had taken the vow; apparently the vow ended at Cenchreae,

Return to Antioch via Ephesus

[18]After this Paul stayed many days longer and then took leave of Acts 21:24
the brethren and sailed for Syria, and with him Priscilla and
Aquila. At Cenchreae he cut his hair, for he had a vow. [19]And they Acts 19:8
came to Ephesus, and he left them there; but he himself went into
the synagogue and argued with the Jews. [20]When they asked him
to stay for a longer period, he declined; [21]but on taking leave of
them he said, "I will return to you if God wills," and he set sail
from Ephesus.
[22]When he had landed at Caesarea, he went up and greeted the Acts 21:15
church, and then went down to Antioch.

11. ST PAUL'S THIRD APOSTOLIC JOURNEY

Galatia and Phrygia

[23]After spending some time there he departed and went from place 1 Cor 3:6
to place through the region of Galatia and Phrygia, strengthening Tit 3:13
all the disciples.

---

for the devotee's hair was cut there. For more information, see the note on Acts 21:23–24.

18:19. Ephesus was the capital of proconsular Asia and one of the most flourishing cities of the empire. Its most famous building, the Artemision, or temple of Diana Artemis, was one of the wonders of the ancient world. The city's huge theatre had a capacity for 23,000 spectators. On this journey St Paul did not stay long in Ephesus—perhaps only long enough for the ship to unload and load. However, Ephesus will be the centre of his next missionary journey.

18:23—21:26. Paul's third apostolic journey starts, like the earlier ones, from Antioch, but it ends with his imprisonment in Jerusalem (Acts 21:27ff). It was a long journey, but Luke devotes most attention to events in Ephesus.

To begin with Paul tours the cities he already evangelized in Galatia and Phrygia: this would have taken him from the last months of 53 to early 54. Then he goes to Ephesus, where he stays for almost three years and meets up with all kinds of contradictions (cf. 2 Cor 1:8), as he describes it in his letter to the Corinthians in spring 57: "To the present hour we hunger and thirst, we are ill-clad and buffeted and homeless. … We have become, and are now, as the refuse of the world, the offscouring of all things" (1 Cor 4:11, 13). Despite this, or perhaps because of it, his apostolate was very fruitful and the Christian message spread through all proconsular Asia, to important cities like Colossae, Laodicae, Hierapolis etc. and to countless towns; as he put it in a letter to the Corinthians (1 Cor 16:9), "a wide door for effective work has opened to me".

The apostle had to leave Ephesus on account of the revolt of the silversmiths, moving on towards Macedonia and Achaia to visit the churches he founded

Apollos in Ephesus and Corinth

24Now a Jew named Apollos, a native of Alexandria, came to
Ephesus. He was an eloquent man, well versed in the scriptures.
Acts 19:3 25He had been instructed in the way of the Lord; and being fervent
in spirit, he spoke and taught accurately the things concerning
Jesus, though he knew only the baptism of John. 26He began to
speak boldly in the synagogue; but when Priscilla and Aquila
heard him, they took him and expounded to him the way of God
2 Cor 3:1 more accurately. 27And when he wished to cross to Achaia, the
Col 4:10 brethren encouraged him, and wrote to the disciples to receive
him. When he arrived, he greatly helped those who through grace

---

on his second journey—Philippi, Thessalonica and Corinth. He stayed there the three months of the winter of 57/58. On his return journey (to Jerusalem, to bring money collected) he went via Macedonia to avoid a Jewish plot. He embarked at Neapolis (the port near Philippi), stopping off at Troas, Miletus (where he met with the elders from Ephesus whom he had called to come to him), Tyre and Caesarea, and managing to reach Jerusalem in time for the Passover.

18:24. Priscilla and Aquila knew how valuable a man with Apollos' qualities would be if he were to dedicate himself to the Lord's service; so they took the initiative and spoke to him. St J. Escrivá sees this episode as a good lesson about boldness in speaking about God, as "an event that demonstrates the wonderful apostolic zeal of the early Christians. Scarcely a quarter of a century had passed since Jesus had gone up to heaven and already his fame had spread to many towns and villages. In the city of Ephesus a man arrived, Apollos by name, 'an eloquent man, well versed in the scriptures'. ... A glimmer of Christ's light had already filtered into the mind of this man. He had heard about our Lord and he passed the news on to others. But he still had some way to go. He needed to know more if he was to acquire the fulness of the faith and so come to love our Lord truly. A Christian couple, Aquila and Priscilla, hear him speaking; they are not inactive or indifferent. They do not think: 'This man already knows enough; it's not our business to teach him.' They were souls who were really eager to do apostolate and so they approached Apollos and 'took him and expounded to him the way of God more accurately'" (*Friends of God*, 270).

This was the kind of zeal the first Christians had; a little later on St Justin wrote: "We do our very best to warn them [Jews and heretics], as we do you, not to be deluded, for we know full well that whoever can speak out the truth and fails to do so shall be condemned by God" (*Dialogue with Tryphon*, 82, 3).

18:27. God uses people, in this case Apollos, to channel his grace to the faithful. They are instruments of his; they preach his word and reap an apostolic harvest, but it is God himself who makes the harvest grow, by providing his grace. "It depends not upon man's will or exertion, but upon God's mercy" (Rom 9:16). "It is not we who save souls and move them to do good. We are quite simply instruments, some more, some less worthy, for fulfilling God's plans for salvation. If at any time we were to think that we ourselves were the authors of the

had believed, [28]for he powerfully confuted the Jews in public, Acts 9:22
showing by the scriptures that the Christ was Jesus.

Disciples of John the Baptist at Ephesus

19 [1]While Apollos was at Corinth, Paul passed through the
upper country and came to Ephesus. There he found some
disciples. [2]And he said to them, "Did you receive the Holy Spirit Jn 7:39
when you believed?" And they said, "No, we have never even Acts 8:15–17
heard that there is a Holy Spirit." [3]And he said, "Into what then
were you baptized?" They said, "Into John's baptism." [4]And Paul
said, "John baptized with the baptism of repentance, telling the Mt 3:6–11
people to believe in the one who was to come after him, that is, Acts 13:24

---

good we do, then our pride would return, more twisted than ever. The salt would lose its flavour, the leaven would rot and the light would turn to darkness" (*Friends of God*, 250).

Hence the importance of supernatural resources in apostolic activity: building is in vain if God does not support it (cf. Ps 127:1). "It's useless to busy yourself in as many external works if you lack Love. It's like sewing with a needle and no thread" (St J. Escrivá, *The Way*, 967).

19:1–7. This presence in Ephesus of a group of disciples who had received only John's baptism is open to various interpretations. The text seems to imply that they were not, properly speaking, Christians but people who followed the Baptist's teaching and whom Paul regarded as incipient Christians, to the point of calling them disciples. We say this because in the New Testament being a Christian is always connected with receiving Baptism and having the Holy Spirit (cf. Jn 3:5; Rom 8:9; 1 Cor 12:3; Gal 3:2; Acts 11:16; etc.).

19:2. Leaving aside questions as to the origin and composition of this group of disciples, their simple statement about knowing nothing about the Holy Spirit and his part in fulfilling the messianic promises points to the need to preach Christian doctrine in a systematic, gradual and complete way.

Christian catechesis, John Paul II reminds us, "must be systematic, not improvised but programmed to reach a precise goal; it must deal with essentials, without any claim to tackle all disputed questions or to transform itself into theological research or scientific exegesis; it must nevertheless be sufficiently complete, not stopping short at the initial proclamation of the Christian mystery such as we have in the *kerygma*; it must be an integral Christian initiation, open to all the other factors of Christian life" (*Catechesi tradendae*, 21).

19:3–4. "The whole teaching and work of John," St Thomas Aquinas writes, "was in preparation for Christ, as the helper and under-craftsman are responsible for preparing the materials for the form which the head-craftsman produces. Grace was to be conferred on men through Christ: 'Grace and truth have come through Jesus Christ' (Jn 1:17). And therefore, the baptism of John did not confer grace, but only prepared the way for grace in a threefold way—in one way, by John's teaching, which led men

Jesus." 5On hearing this, they were baptized in the name of the
Acts 8:15–17; 11:15–16 Lord Jesus. 6And when Paul had laid his hands upon them, the
Holy Spirit came on them; and they spoke with tongues and
prophesied. 7There were about twelve of them in all.

Paul's preaching and miracles at Ephesus

8And he entered the synagogue and for three months spoke boldly,
arguing and pleading about the kingdom of God; 9but when some

---

to faith in Christ; in another way, by accustoming men to the rite of Christ's Baptism; and in a third way, through penance, which prepared men to receive the effect of Christ's Baptism" (*Summa theologiae*, 3, 38, 3).

19:5. "They were baptized in the name of the Lord Jesus": the view of most commentators is that this does not mean that the Trinitarian formula which appears in Matthew 28:19 (cf. the note on Acts 2:38) ("in the name of the Father and of the Son and of the Holy Spirit") was not used. The reference here may simply be a way of distinguishing Christian Baptism from other baptismal rites which were features of Judaism in apostolic times—particularly John the Baptist's rite. Besides, Christian Baptism was administered on Jesus Christ's instructions (cf. Mt 28:19), in union with him and using his power: Jesus' redemptive action is initiated by the Father and expresses itself in the full outpouring of the Holy Spirit.

19:6. This passage speaks of the laying on of hands, something distinct from Baptism, as seen already in Acts 8:14–17, whereby the Holy Spirit is received. This is the sacrament which will come to be called Confirmation and which has been conferred, from the beginnings of the Church, as one of the sacraments of Christian initiation.

Referring to Confirmation, John Paul II has said: "Christ's gift of the Holy Spirit is going to be poured out upon you in a particular way. You will hear the words of the Church spoken over you, calling upon the Holy Spirit to confirm your faith, to seal you in his love, to strengthen you for his service. You will then take your place among fellow-Christians throughout the world, full citizens now of the People of God. You will witness to the truth of the Gospel in the name of Jesus Christ. You will live your lives in such a way as to make holy all human life. Together with all the confirmed, you will become living stones in the cathedral of peace. Indeed you are called by God to be instruments of his peace […].

"You, too, are strengthened inwardly today by the gift of the Holy Spirit, so that each of you in your own way can carry the Good News to your companions and friends. […] The same Holy Spirit comes to you today in the sacrament of Confirmation, to involve you more completely in the Church's fight against sin and in her mission of fostering holiness. He comes to dwell more fully in your hearts and to strengthen you for the struggle with evil. […] The world of today needs you, for it needs men and women who are filled with the Holy Spirit. It needs your courage and hopefulness, your faith and your perseverance. The world of tomorrow will be built by you. Today you receive the gift of the Holy Spirit so that you may work with deep faith and with abiding charity, so

were stubborn and disbelieved, speaking evil of the Way before
the congregation, he withdrew from them, taking the disciples
with him, and argued daily in the hall of Tyrannus.[r] 10This continued for two years, so that all the residents of Asia heard the word
of the Lord, both Jews and Greeks.
11And God did extraordinary miracles by the hands of Paul, Acts 14:3

that you may help to bring to the world the fruits of reconciliation and peace. Strengthened by the Holy Spirit and his manifold gifts [...], strive to be unselfish try not to be obsessed with material things" (Homily at Coventry Airport, 30 May 1982).

As is the case with Baptism and Holy Orders, Confirmation imprints an indelible mark or character on the soul.

19:8–10. This summarized account of Paul's activity in Ephesus is filled out by the account we are given of the apostle's farewell to the elders of that city (cf. 20:18–35) and by information contained in his letters to the Corinthians. Paul made Ephesus the base for his missionary work in the surrounding region, for which he counted on help from Timothy, Erastus, Gaius, Titus and Epaphras of Colossae.

During his stay in Ephesus he wrote 1 Corinthians and the Letter to the Galatians.

19:8. Paul returns to the synagogue where he taught previously (cf. 18:19–21); the Jews' resistance and lack of understanding do not lessen his zeal.

19:9. The obstinacy of some of the Jews eventually obliges Paul to leave the synagogue. He now moves to the school of Tyrannus—who must have been a Christian or at least someone sympathetic to the Gospel. Paul may well have presented himself to the inhabitants of the city as a teacher of "philosophy," in the meaning of that word then current—the science of living.

The text also shows that Christians already had developed the practice of meeting in private houses to hear the word of God, thus avoiding any need to go to the synagogue.

19:10. To these "two years" should be added the three months Paul spent preaching in the synagogue (cf. v. 8), which means that he spent about two and a quarter years in Ephesus altogether. This ties in with what he says in his farewell remarks (20:31): "For three years ...": at that time parts of years were regarded as full years.

The region evangelized by Paul and his helpers was not the whole province of proconsular Asia but the cities of Smyrna, Pergamon, Thyatira, Sardis, Philadelphia, Laodicea, Colossae and Hierapolis, all of which looked to Ephesus as their centre.

19:11–16. Here we have another reference to miracles worked by Paul (cf. 13:11; 14:10)—the signs which he himself tells us accompanied his preaching (cf. 2 Cor 12:12; Rom 15:19).

St Luke here contrasts the spiritual vitality and the divine character of Paul's message with the falsity and uselessness of magic. Genuine Christian preaching is on a completely different plane from that of opponents or imitators of the Gospel. The author of Acts seems to be anticipating the objections of people who will

r. Other ancient authorities add *from the fifth hour to the tenth*

Mk 6:56 Lk 8:44–47 Acts 5:15 | [12]so that handkerchiefs or aprons were carried away from his body
to the sick, and diseases left them and the evil spirits came out of
them. [13]Then some of the itinerant Jewish exorcists undertook to
Mk 9:38 | pronounce the name of the Lord Jesus over those who had evil
spirits, saying, "I adjure you by the Jesus whom Paul preaches."
[14]Seven sons of a Jewish high priest named Sceva were doing this.
[15]But the evil spirit answered them, "Jesus I know, and Paul I
Lk 4:41 Acts 16:17 | know; but who are you?" [16]And the man in whom the evil spirit
was leaped on them, mastered all of them, and overpowered them,
so that they fled out of that house naked and wounded.

Books of magic burned

Lk 5:26 Acts 3:10 | [17]And this became known to all residents of Ephesus, both Jews
and Greeks; and fear fell upon them all; and the name of the Lord
Jesus was extolled. [18]Many also of those who were now believers
came, confessing and divulging their practices. [19]And a number of

---

argue that there was a certain amount of magic in the apostles' miracles. Origen dealt with similar objections in his reply to the pagan Celsus: "Did the disciples of Jesus learn to do miracles and thereby convince their hearers, or did they not do any. It is quite absurd to say that they did not do any miracles of any kind, and that, in blind faith … they went off everywhere to propagate a new teaching; for what would have kept their spirits up when they had to teach something which was so completely new. But if they did also work miracles, how on earth could these magicians have faced so many dangers to spread a teaching which explicitly forbade the use of magic?" (*Against Celsus*, 1, 38).

In religions of ancient times there were lots of exorcists like the sons of Sceva. This man, probably a member of an important priestly family, gave himself the title of high priest to help promote and gain credence for the magic-making his family went in for. Many magicians, fortune-tellers and exorcists were ready to invoke any and every God. For example, there were pagans who used the different names of Yahweh, and we have evidence in the form of a magician's papyrus which reads, "I abjure you by Jesus, the God of the Jews."

In this instance the evil spirit turns on the seven brothers, showing that "the Name does nothing unless it be spoken with faith" (St John Chrysostom, *Hom. on Acts*, 41).

"For the preacher's instruction to exercise its full force", writes St John of the Cross, "there must be two kinds of preparation—that of the preacher and that of the hearer; for, as a rule, the benefit derived from instruction depends on the preparation of the teacher. For this reason it is said, Like master, like pupil. For, when in the Acts of the Apostles those seven sons of that chief priest of the Jews used to cast out devils in the same way as St Paul did, the devil rose up against them […] and then, attacking them, stripped and wounded them. This was only because they had not the proper preparation" (*Ascent of Mount Carmel*, 3, chap. 45).

Paul's actions and their good effects, in contrast with the signs the agents of

those who practised magic arts brought their books together and
burned them in the sight of all; and they counted the value of them
and found it came to fifty thousand pieces of silver. 20So the word Acts 6:7
of the Lord grew and prevailed mightily.

Paul's plans for further journeys

21Now after these events Paul resolved in the Spirit to pass Acts 23:11
through Macedonia and Achaia and go to Jerusalem, saying, Rom 15:22–23
"After I have been there, I must also see Rome." 22And having 1 Cor 4:17
sent into Macedonia two of his helpers, Timothy and Erastus, he
himself stayed in Asia for a while.

---

superstition try to perform, fill many of the Ephesians with holy fear and bring about their conversion. "The sight of events like this can indeed cause conviction and faith in those who love the truth, who are not swayed by opinions and who do not let their evil passions gain the upper hand" (St Justin, *Apology*, 1, 53, 12).

19:12. From the very beginning Christians had great respect for and devotion to relics—not only the mortal remains of the saints but also their clothes or things they had used or things which had touched their tombs.

19:17–19. This fear which overtook the believers marked the start of their spiritual recovery. Fear of the Lord is a gift of the Holy Spirit, which inspires reverence towards God and fear of offending him, and helps us avoid evil and do good. It inspires the respect, admiration, obedience and love of one who wishes to please his Father.

Fear of offending God leads the people of Ephesus to be done with anything that distances them from him, in particular magical arts. Books on magic—each often only a few pages of manuscript—were common in ancient times; they were also worth a lot of money: firstly because of the much sought-after magical formulae they contained, and secondly because they were often very ornately produced.

The attitude of these Christians—inspired by the Holy Spirit—towards things which might lead them to offend God is to avoid them completely. "We Christians have a commitment of love to the call of divine grace, which we have freely accepted, an obligation which urges us to fight tenaciously. We know that we are as weak as other people, but we cannot forget that if we use the resources available to us, we will become salt and light and leaven of the world; we will be the consolation of God" (St Josemaría Escrivá, *Christ Is Passing By*, 74).

19:21–22. Paul's decision to go back to Macedonia and Achaia is another example of the way God encourages the apostle to build up the churches he earlier established in these regions. Paul will also use this visit to collect the donations set aside for the Jerusalem community.

His planned visit to Rome should not be seen in terms of a vague desire to go there some time, but as something he feels he really needs to do, something God wants him to do.

The silversmiths' riot in Ephesus

23About that time there arose no little stir concerning the Way.
Acts 16:16 24For a man named Demetrius, a silversmith, who made silver
shrines of Artemis, brought no little business to the craftsmen.
25These he gathered together, with the workmen of like occupation, and said, "Men, you know that from this business we have
Acts 17:29 our wealth. 26And you see and hear that not only at Ephesus but
almost throughout all Asia this Paul has persuaded and turned
away a considerable company of people, saying that gods made
with hands are not gods. 27And there is danger not only that this
trade of ours may come into disrepute but also that the temple of
the great goddess Artemis may count for nothing, and that she
may even be deposed from her magnificence, she whom all Asia
and the world worship."

28When they heard this they were enraged, and cried out,
Acts 20:4; 27:2 "Great is Artemis of the Ephesians!" 29So the city was filled with
the confusion; and they rushed together into the theatre, dragging
with them Gaius and Aristarchus, Macedonians who were Paul's
companions in travel. 30Paul wished to go in among the crowd, but
the disciples would not let him; 31some of the Asiarchs also, who

---

19:23. St Luke describes Christianity and the Church as the "Way" (cf. Acts 9:2; 22:4; 24:14, 22). This term was probably fairly widely used, with this meaning, by Christians of the period. It has Jewish roots and refers to a moral and religious lifestyle and even a set of moral criteria. In the Book of Acts (and among the first Christians) the word "way", then, often implies that "following Christ", embracing his religion, is not just one way of salvation among many, but the only way that God offers man; in certain passages of Acts it is referred to as *the* Way (cf. 9:2). Sometimes *the* Way is equivalent to *the* Church of Christ, outside of which there is no redemption.

"The preaching of the Gospel is rightly called 'way', for it is the route that truly leads to the Kingdom of heaven" (St John Chrysostom, *Hom. on Acts*, 41).

19:24. Artemis was the Greek name of the goddess the Romans called Diana, but through syncretism it was identified with an oriental goddess of fertility. A statue of Diana was worshipped in the *Artemision*. Feast-days of Artemis were celebrated with disgraceful orgies, for which people flocked into Ephesus from the surrounding region. Demetrius and his fellow-craftsmen did good business selling little statuettes of Diana which many visitors took home as souvenirs and cult objects.

19:26. Demetrius fairly accurately gives the gist of a central point of Paul's preaching against idolatry (cf. 17:29). Christians spoke out against the false gods of paganism, using arguments and passages from the Old Testament in the same way as Jewish apologists did (cf. Is 44:9–20; 46:1–7; Wis 13:10–19).

19:29. What started off as a meeting of craftsmen to discuss a threat to their business has become a huge popular gather-

were friends of his, sent to him and begged him not to venture
into the theatre. [32]Now some cried one thing, some another; for
the assembly was in confusion, and most of them did not know
why they had come together. [33]Some of the crowd prompted
Alexander, whom the Jews had put forward. And Alexander
motioned with his hand, wishing to make a defence to the people.
[34]But when they recognized that he was a Jew, for about two hours Acts 16:20
they all with one voice cried out, "Great is Artemis of the
Ephesians!" [35]And when the town clerk had quieted the crowd, he
said, "Men of Ephesus, what man is there who does not know that
the city of the Ephesians is temple keeper of the great Artemis,
and of the sacred stone* that fell from the sky?[s] [36]Seeing then that
these things cannot be contradicted, you ought to be quiet and do
nothing rash. [37]For you have brought these men here who are neither sacrilegious nor blasphemers of our goddess. [38]If therefore Acts 18:12
Demetrius and the craftsmen with him have a complaint against
any one, the courts are open, and there are proconsuls; let them
bring charges against one another. [39]But if you seek anything further,[t] it shall be settled in the regular assembly. [40]For we are in
danger of being charged with rioting today, there being no cause

---

ing. The Ephesians flock into the city's theatre, which was where all huge meetings usually took place. They do not really seem to know very much about what is going on; but we can detect a certain amount of anti-Jewish feeling. They were more familiar with Judaism than with the new Christian religion, and this may have led them to blame the Jews for the threat to their pagan practices and beliefs.

Aristarchus was from Thessalonica (cf. Acts 20:4). He accompanied St Paul on his journey to Rome and during his imprisonment there (cf. Acts 27:2 and Col 4:10). Gaius may have been the same Christian as is referred to in Acts 20:4.

19:30–31. As in other similar situations, Paul wants to use the opportunity to justify his actions and speak to the people about the faith he preaches and is proud to acknowledge. However, he goes along with the disciples' advice and decides that it would be imprudent to enter the theatre. Given the hysteria of the crowd he probably realizes that it would be counterproductive to appear before them.

The Asiarchs, as the magistrates of Ephesus were called, presided over meetings of the provincial assembly of Asia. Paul was apparently on friendly terms with them.

19:33–34. Alexander, a Jew, feels called to explain to those present that the Jews and their religion were not responsible for the events which led the people to assemble; but in fact this only causes further provocation.

19:35–40. The town clerk's sober remarks, especially his reference to legal channels, show him to be admirably impartial. He probably has some impression of the merits of the Christian mes-

s. The meaning of the Greek is uncertain **t.** Other ancient authorities read *about their own matters*

that we can give to justify this commotion." 41And when he had
said this, he dismissed the assembly.

Paul goes into Macedonia and begins his return journey

Acts 14:22; 16:40 20 1After the uproar ceased, Paul sent for the disciples and
having exhorted them took leave of them and departed for
Macedonia. 2When he had gone through these parts and had given
1 Cor 16:5–6 them much encouragement, he came to Greece. 3There he spent
three months, and when a plot was made against him by the Jews
as he was about to set sail for Syria, he determined to return
through Macedonia. 4Sopater of Beroea, the son of Pyrrhus,
accompanied him; and of the Thessalonians, Aristarchus and
Secundus; and Gaius of Derbe, and Timothy; and the Asians,
Tychicus and Trophimus. 5These went on and were waiting for us
at Troas, 6but we sailed away from Philippi after the days of
Unleavened Bread, and in five days we came to them at Troas,
where we stayed for seven days.

---

sage; anyone, indeed, who looks at Christianity calmly and closely cannot fail to be impressed by it.

20:1. This verse connects up with 19:22, at which point the narrative branched off to deal with the riot of the silversmiths. Paul's exhortations to the disciples of Ephesus must have been on the same lines as his address in vv. 18–35.

This journey to Macedonia is probably the same one as mentioned in 2 Corinthians 2:12–13: "When I came to Troas to preach the gospel of Christ, a door was opened for me in the Lord; but my mind could not rest because I did not find my brother Titus there. So I took leave of them and went on to Macedonia."

20:2. From here Paul wrote 2 Corinthians, which was delivered by Titus.

20:3. During his stay in Corinth Paul wrote and despatched his letter to the Romans.

We know nothing else about this Jewish plot which caused Paul to change his plans. Possibly some Jews, pilgrims to Jerusalem on the same boat as Paul, were planning to deal with him during the sea journey.

20:4. Paul has now set out on his last journey to Jerusalem. The seven brethren who travelled with him were presumably delegates of the churches appointed to help him bring the monies collected for the support of the Christians in Jerusalem.

20:5. The narrative changes again into the first person plural. Luke joined Paul at Philippi and will stay with him from now on. "We" means "Paul and I"; we have no reason to think that it includes other people.

20:6. The Azymes or days of the Unleavened Bread are the week when the Passover is celebrated. The Christian Easter and the Jewish Passover fell on the same days. See also the notes on Mt 26:2 and 26:17.

20:7. This is the first reference in Acts to the Christian custom of meeting on the first day of the week to celebrate the Eucharist

Celebration of the Eucharist. Eutychus' fall and recovery

[7]On the first day of the week, when we were gathered together to Acts 2:42
break bread,* Paul talked with them, intending to depart on the
morrow; and he prolonged his speech until midnight. [8]There were
many lights in the upper chamber where we were gathered. [9]And
a young man named Eutychus was sitting in the window. He sank
into a deep sleep as Paul talked still longer; and being overcome
by sleep, he fell down from the third storey and was taken up
dead. [10]But Paul went down and bent over him, and embracing 1 Kings
him said, "Do not be alarmed, for his life is in him." [11]And when 17:17–24
Paul had gone up and had broken bread and eaten, he conversed
with them a long time, until daybreak, and so departed. [12]And they
took the lad away alive, and were not a little comforted.

From Troas to Miletus

[13]But going ahead to the ship, we set sail for Assos, intending to
take Paul aboard there; for so he had arranged, intending himself

---

(cf. 2:42; 1 Cor 10:16). "In una autem sabbatorum: that is," St Bede comments, "on the Lord's Day, the first day after the sabbath, when we gather to celebrate our mysteries" (*Super Act. expositio*, ad loc.).

"We call this food," St Justin explains, "the Eucharist, of which only he can partake who has acknowledged the truth of our teachings, who has been cleansed by baptism for the remission of his sins and for his regeneration, and who regulates his life upon the principles laid down by Christ" (*Apology*, 1, 66, 1).

Christian writers have pointed to the profound connexion between the Eucharist and that true brotherhood which God lays as a duty on, and grants as a gift to, Christ's disciples. St Francis de Sales writes: "How the greatness of God has lowered itself on behalf of each and every one of us—and how high he desires to raise us! He desires us to be so perfectly united to him as to make us one with him. He has desired this in order to teach us that, since we have been loved with an equal love whereby he embraces us all in the most blessed Sacrament, he desires that we love one another with that love which tends towards union, and to the greatest and most perfect form of union. We are all nourished by the same bread, that heavenly bread of the divine Eucharist, the reception of which is called communion, and which symbolizes that unity that we should have one with another, without which we could not be called children of God" (*Sermon on the third Sunday of Lent*).

20:8–12. This is the only miracle recounted in Acts where Paul raises someone from the dead. St Bede sees in it a certain spiritual symbolism: "The restoring of this young man to life is brought about in the course of preaching. Thereby Paul's preaching is confirmed by the kindness of the miracle and the teaching; the effort involved in the long vigil is repaid with interest; and all those present are reminded vividly of their departed Master" (*Super Act. expositio*, ad loc.).

20:13–16. The various little details given by Luke suggest that he very likely kept

to go by land. 14And when he met us at Assos, we took him on
board and came to Mitylene. 15And sailing from there we came
the following day opposite Chios; the next day we touched at
Acts 18:21 Samos; and[u] the day after that we came to Miletus. 16For Paul had
decided to sail past Ephesus, so that he might not have to spend
time in Asia; for he was hastening to be at Jerusalem, if possible,
on the day of Pentecost.

Farewell address to the elders of Ephesus

17And from Miletus he sent to Ephesus and called to him the eld-
1 Thess 1:5 ers of the church. 18And when they came to him he said to them:

---

a diary which he later used when writing his book.

20:16. The Law laid down that all Jews should go up to Jerusalem three times a year, for the feasts of the Passover, Pentecost and Tabernacles (cf. Deut 16:16). St Paul's desire is to press on to Jerusalem to hand over the collection and to establish contact with the many Jews who would gather in the city for the festival.

20:18–35. Paul's address to the elders of Ephesus is his third great discourse related in Acts (the others being his address to Jews in Pisidian Antioch—13:16ff—and to pagans at Athens—17:22ff). It is, as it were, an emotional farewell to the churches which he had founded.

The address divides into two parts. The first (vv. 18–27) is a brief resume of Paul's life of dedication to the church of Ephesus, which he founded and directed, with hints of the difficulties which he expects to meet in the immediate future. Two parallel sections (vv. 18–21 and 26–27) frame the central passage of this section (vv. 22–25).

In the second section the apostle speaks movingly about the mission and role of elders. Two series of recommendations (vv. 28–31 and 33–35) hinge on the central verse (v. 32).

The pathos, vigour and spiritual depth of the discourse clearly show that it is Paul who is speaking. Here we have the Paul of the letters addressing a community which has already been evangelized, and inviting them to get to know their faith better and practise it better.

20:18–20. Paul is not embarrassed to set himself as an example of how to serve God and the disciples in the cause of the Gospel (cf. 1 Cor 11:1). He has worked diligently, out of love for Jesus Christ and the brethren, doing his duty, conscious that this kind of patient, persevering work is the way of perfection and holiness that God expects him to follow.

The Apostle has learned to imitate Christ both in his public life and in the long years of his hidden life, ever deepening in his love. In this connexion, St Francis de Sales writes: "Those are spiritually greedy who never have enough of exercises of devotion, so keen are they, they say, to attain perfection; as if perfection consisted in the amount of things we do and not in the perfection with which we do them. […] God has not made perfection to lie in the number of acts we do to please him, but in the way in which we

u. Other ancient authorities add *after remaining at Trogyllium*

"You yourselves know how I lived among you all the time
from the first day that I set foot in Asia, [19]serving the Lord with all 2 Cor 11:23–31
humility and with tears and with trials which befell me through Phil 2:3
the plots of the Jews; [20]how I did not shrink from declaring to you 2 Tim 4:2
anything that was profitable, and teaching you in public and from
house to house, [21]testifying both to Jews and to Greeks of repentance to God and of faith in our Lord Jesus Christ. [22]And now,
behold, I am going to Jerusalem, bound in the Spirit, not knowing

---

do them: that way is to do the little we have to do according to our calling, that is, to do it in love, through love and for love" (*Sermon on the first Sunday of Lent*).

St Catherine of Siena understood our Lord to say to her something along the same lines: "I reward every good which is done, great or small, according to the measure of the love of him who receives the reward" (*Dialogue*, chap. 68).

As in his letters, Paul associates the idea of service with humility (cf. 2 Cor 10:1; 1 Thess 2:6), tears (cf. Rom 9:2; Phil 3:18) and fortitude to keep on working despite persecution (cf. 2 Cor 11:24; 1 Thess 2:14–16). The apostle's true treasure is humility, for it allows him to discover his shortcomings and at the same time teaches him to rely on God's strength. As St Teresa says, "The truly humble person will have a genuine desire to be thought little of, and condemned unjustly, even in serious matters. For, if she desires to imitate the Lord, how can she do so better than in this? And no bodily strength is necessary here, nor the aid of anyone but God" (*Way of Perfection*, 15, 2).

20:21. This very brief summary of Paul's preaching to Jews and pagans mentions repentance and faith as inseparable elements in the new life Jesus confers on Christians. "It is good to know", Origen writes, "that we will be judged at the divine judgment seat not on our faith alone, as if we had not to answer for our conduct; nor on our conduct alone, as if our faith were not to be scrutinized. What justifies is our uprightness on both scores, and if we are short on either we shall deserve punishment" (*Dialogue with Heraclides*, 8).

The presence of grace and faith in the soul equips it to fight the Christian fight, which ultimately leads to rooting out sins and defects. "From the very day faith enters your soul," Origen also says, "battle must be joined between virtues and vices. Prior to the onslaught of the Word, vices were at peace within you, but from the moment the Word begins to judge them one by one, a great turmoil arises and a merciless war begins. 'For what partnership have righteousness and iniquity?' (2 Cor 6:14)" (*In Ex hom.*, 3, 3).

20:22. The apostle is convinced that God is guiding his steps and watching over him like a father; but he is also unsure about what lies ahead: this uncertainty about the future is part of the human condition. "Grace does not work on its own. It respects men in the actions they take, it influences them, it awakens and does not entirely dispel their restlessness" (St John Chrysostom, *Hom. on Acts*, 37).

"The true minister of Christ is concious of his own weakness and labours in humility. He searches to see what is well-pleasing to God (cf. Eph 5:10) and, bound as it were in the Spirit (cf. Acts

Acts 21:4–11 what shall befall me there; 23except that the Holy Spirit testifies to
Acts 26:16–18 me in every city that imprisonment and inflictions await me. 24But
2 Tim 4:7 I do not account my life of any value nor as precious to myself, if
only I may accomplish my course and the ministry which I
received from the Lord Jesus, to testify to the gospel of the grace
of God. 25And now, behold, I know that all you among whom I
have gone about preaching the kingdom will see my face no more.
Acts 18:6 26Therefore I testify to you this day that I am innocent of the

---

20:22), he is guided in all things by the will of him who wishes all men to be saved. He is able to discover and carry out that will in the course of his daily routine" (Vatican II, *Presbyterorum ordinis*, 15).

20:23. "No man, whether he be a Christian or not, has an easy life. To be sure, at certain times it seems as though everything goes as we planned. But this generally lasts for only a short time. Life is a matter of facing up to difficulties and of experiencing in our hearts both joy and sorrow. It is in this forge that a person can acquire fortitude, patience, magnanimity and composure [...].

"Naturally, the difficulties we meet in our daily lives will not be as great or as numerous as St Paul encountered. We will, however, discover our own meanness and selfishness, the sting of sensuality, the useless, ridiculous smack of pride, and many other failings besides: so very many weaknesses. But are we to give in to discouragement? Not at all. Together with St Paul, let us tell our Lord, 'For the sake of Christ, I am content with weakness, insults, hardships, persecutions and calamities; for when I am weak, then I am strong' (2 Cor 12:10)" (St Josemaría Escrivá, *Friends of God*, 77 and 212).

20:24. Paul has come to love Jesus Christ so much that he gives himself no importance: he sees his life as having no meaning other than that of doing what God wants him to do (cf. 2 Cor 4:7; Phil 1:19–26; Col 1:24). He sees holiness as a constant, uninterrupted striving towards his encounter with the Lord; and all the great Fathers of the Church have followed him in this: "On the subject of virtue," St Gregory of Nyssa, for example, writes, "we have learned from the apostle himself that the only limit to perfection of virtue is that there is no limit. This fine, noble man, this divine apostle, never ceases, when running on the course of virtue, to 'strain forward to what lies ahead' (Phil 3:13). He realizes it is dangerous to stop. Why? Because all good, by its very nature, is unlimited: its only limit is where it meets its opposite: thus, the limit of life is death, of light darkness, and in general of every good its opposite. Just as the end of life is the beginning of death, so too if one ceases to follow the path of virtue one is beginning to follow the path of vice" (*On the Life of Moses*, 1, 5).

20:26. "He considers himself innocent of the blood of the disciples because he has not neglected to point out to them their defects" (St Bede, *Super Act. expositio*, ad loc.) Paul not only preached the Gospel to them and educated them in the faith: he also corrected their faults, putting into practice the advice he gave to the Galatians: "if a man is overtaken in any trespass, you who are spiritual should restore him in a spirit of gentleness. Look

blood of all of you, [27]for I did not shrink from declaring to you the
whole counsel of God. [28]Take heed to yourselves and to all the 1 Tim 4:16
flock, in which the Holy Spirit has made you guardians, to feed 1 Pet 2:9; 5:2
the church of the Lord[v] which he obtained with his own blood.[w]
[29]I know that after my departure fierce wolves will come in among Mt 7:15 Jn 10:12
you, not sparing the flock; [30]and from among your own selves will 2 Pet 2:1–2
arise men speaking perverse things, to draw away the disciples 1 Jn 2:19
after them. [31]Therefore be alert, remembering that for three years 1 Thess 2:11 1 Pet 5:8–9

---

to yourself, lest you too be tempted" (Gal 6:1). "A disciple of Christ will never treat anyone badly. Error he will call error, but the person in error he will correct with kindness. Otherwise he will not be able to help him, to sanctify him" (St J. Escrivá, *Friends of God*, 9).

20:28. Using a metaphor often found in the New Testament to describe the people of God (Ps 100:3; Is 40:11; Jer 13:17), Paul describes the Church as a flock and its guardians or bishops (*episcopos*) as shepherds. "The Church is a sheepfold, the sole and necessary gateway to which is Christ (Jn 10:1–10). It is also a flock, of which God foretold that he would himself be the shepherd (cf. Is 40:11; Ezek 34:11f), and whose sheep, although watched over by human shepherds, are nevertheless at all times led and brought to pasture by Christ himself, the Good Shepherd and prince of shepherds (cf. Jn 10:11; 1 Pet 5:4), who gave his life for his sheep (cf. Jn 10:11–16)" (Vatican II, *Lumen gentium*, 6).

In the early days of the Church the terms "priest" and "bishop" had not yet become defined: they both refer to sacred ministers who have received the sacrament of priestly Order.

The last part of the verse refers to Christ's sacrifice: through his redeeming action, the Church has become God's special property. The price of redemption was the blood of Christ. Paul VI says that Christ, the Lamb of God, took to "himself the sins of the world, and he died for us, nailed to the Cross, saving us by his redeeming blood" (*Creed of the People of God*, 12).

The Council of Trent speaks of this when it presents the Redemption as an act of "his beloved Only-begotten, our Lord Jesus Christ, who … merited justification for us by his most holy Passion on the wood of the Cross and made satisfaction for us to God the Father" (*De Iustificatione*, 7).

20:30. Errors derive not only from outsiders: they are also the product of members of the Church who abuse their position as brethren and even as pastors, leading the people astray by taking advantage of their good will. "It is of this that John writes, 'They went out from us, but they were not of us' [1 Jn 2:19]" (St Bede, *Super Act. expositio*, ad loc.).

20:31. "Here he shows that he actually taught them and did not proclaim the teaching once only, just to ease his conscience" (St John Chrysostom, *Hom. on Acts*, 44). Paul did not avoid the pastoral work which fell to him; he set an example of what a bishop should be. "Those who rule the community must perform worthily the tasks of government. […] There is a danger that some who concern

v. Other ancient authorities read *of God* **w.** Or *with the blood of his Own*

I did not cease night or day to admonish every one with tears.
Deut 33:3 [32]And now I commend you to God and to the word of his grace,
Eph 2:20–22 which is able to build you up and to give you the inheritance
Mt 10:8 among all those who are sanctified. [33]I coveted no one's silver or
Acts 18:3 gold or apparel. [34]You yourselves know that these hands minis-
1 Cor 4:12 tered to my necessities, and to those who were with me.* [35]In all
1 Thess 2:9 things I have shown you that by so toiling one must help the
weak, remembering the words of the Lord Jesus, how he said, 'It
is more blessed to give than to receive.'"

Acts 21:5 [36]And when he had spoken thus, he knelt down and prayed
Rom 16:16 with them all. [37]And they all wept and embraced Paul and kissed
1 Pet 5:14 him, [38]sorrowing most of all because of the word he had spoken,
Acts 20:25 that they should see his face no more. And they brought him to the
ship.

PART FOUR

St Paul, in imprisonment, bears witness to Christ

12. ST PAUL IN JERUSALEM

From Miletus to Caesarea

21 [1]And when we had parted from them and set sail, we came
by a straight course to Cos, and the next day to Rhodes,

---

themselves with others and guide them towards eternal life may ruin themselves without realizing it. Those who are in charge must work harder than others, must be humbler than those under them, must in their own lives give an example of service, and must regard their subjects as a deposit which God has given them in trust" (St Gregory of Nyssa, *De instituto christiano*).

20:32. "It is not right for Christians to give such importance to human action that they think all the laurels depend on their efforts: their expectation of reward should be subject to the will of God" (ibid.).

20:33–35. "The teachings of the apostle of the Gentiles [...] have key importance for the morality and spirituality of human work. They are an important complement to the great though discreet gospel of work that we find in the life and parables of Christ, in what Jesus 'did and taught'" (John Paul II, *Laborem exercens*, 26).

and from there to Patara.[x] 2And having found a ship crossing to
Phoenicia, we went aboard, and set sail. 3When we had come in
sight of Cyprus, leaving it on the left we sailed to Syria, and
landed at Tyre; for there the ship was to unload its cargo. 4And Acts 20:23; 21:11
having sought out the disciples, we stayed there for seven days.
Through the Spirit they told Paul not to go* on to Jerusalem. 5And
when our days there were ended, we departed and went on our Acts 20:36
journey; and they all, with wives and children, brought us on our
way till we were outside the city; and kneeling down on the beach
we prayed and bade one another farewell. 6Then we went on
board the ship, and they returned home.
7When we had finished the voyage from Tyre, we arrived at
Ptolemais; and we greeted the brethren and stayed with them for
one day. 8On the morrow we departed and came to Caesarea; and Acts 6:5; 8:40

This saying of our Lord (v. 35) is not recorded in the Gospels.

20:36. For Christians every situation is suitable for prayer: "The Christian prays everywhere", Clement of Alexandria writes, "and in every situation, whether it be when taking a walk or in the company of friends, or while he is resting, or at the start of some spiritual work. And when he reflects in the interior of his soul and invokes the Father with unspeakable groanings" (*Stromata*, 7, 7).

20:37. They kiss Paul to show their affection for him and how moved they are. This is not the liturgical "kiss of peace". In the East kisses are a common expression of friendship and good manners—like handshaking in the West.

21:4. These Christians of Tyre were the fruit of earlier evangelization (cf. 11:19). The Spirit gave them foreknowledge of the "imprisonment and afflictions" (20:23) awaiting Paul in Jerusalem. It was only natural for them to try to dissuade him from going—a sign of Christian fraternity and mutual affection. Without losing our serenity we too should be concerned about our brothers' and sisters' physical and spiritual health: "I am glad that you feel concern for your brothers: there is no better proof of your mutual love. Take care, however, that your concern does not degenerate into anxiety" (St J. Escrivá, *The Way*, 465).

21:5. "Kneeling down on the beach we prayed": every place is suitable for raising one's heart to God and speaking to him. "Each day without fail we should devote some time especially to God, raising our minds to him, without any need for the words to come to our lips, for they are being sung in our heart. Let us give enough time to this devout practice; at a fixed hour, if possible. Before the Tabernacle, close to him who has remained there out of Love. If this is not possible, we can pray anywhere because our God is ineffably present in the heart of every soul in grace" (St Josemaría Escrivá, *Friends of God*, 249).

21:8. Philip was one of the seven Christians ordained deacons to serve the needy, as described in 6:5. He played an

x. Other ancient authorities add *and Myra*

we entered the house of Philip the evangelist, who was one of the
Acts 2:17 seven, and stayed with him. 9And he had four unmarried daughters, who prophesied.

The prophet Agabus

Acts 11:27–28 10While we were staying for some days, a prophet named Agabus
Acts 21:31–33 came down from Judea. 11And coming to us he took Paul's girdle
and bound his own feet and hands, and said, "Thus says the Holy
Spirit, 'So shall the Jews at Jerusalem bind the man who owns this
girdle and deliver him into the hands of the Gentiles.'" 12When we
heard this, we and the people there begged him not to go up to
Jerusalem. 13Then Paul answered, "What are you doing, weeping
and breaking my heart? For I am ready not only to be imprisoned
but even to die at Jerusalem for the name of the Lord Jesus."

---

important part in the evangelization of Samaria (cf. 8:5ff), opposed Simon the magician (cf. 8:9ff) and baptized the Ethiopian courtier (cf. 8:26ff).

21:9. Virginity is a gift of God which Paul discusses in his letters (cf. 1 Cor 7:25–40). In his apostolic exhortation on the family, John Paul II devotes a section to this form of self-dedication to God: "Virginity or celibacy for the sake of the Kingdom of God not only does not contradict the dignity of marriage but presupposes it and confirms it. Marriage and virginity or celibacy are two ways of expressing and living the one mystery of the covenant of God with his people [...].

"Virginity or celibacy, by liberating the human heart in a unique way (1 Cor 7:32–35), bears witness that the Kingdom of God and his justice is that pearl of great price which is preferred to every other value no matter how great, and hence must be sought as the only definitive value. It is for this reason that the Church, throughout her history, has always defended the superiority of this charism to that of marriage, by reason of the wholly singular link which it has with the Kingdom of God (cf. *Sacra virginitas*, 2).

"In spite of having renounced physical fecundity, the celibate person becomes spiritually fruitful, the father and mother of many, cooperating in the realization of the family according to God's plan" (*Familiaris consortio*, 16).

21:10–11. Agabus was the Christian prophet who, years earlier, warned of forthcoming famine and privation (cf. 11:27–28). In his present prophecy he uses symbolic gestures—like Old Testament prophets, particularly Jeremiah (cf. Jer 18:3ff; 19:1ff; 27:2ff). His action is somewhat reminiscent of our Lord's prophecy about St Peter in John 21:18: "Truly, truly, I say to you, when you were young, you girded yourself and walked where you would; but when you are old, you will stretch out your hands, and another will gird you and carry you where you do not wish to go."

21:12–14. The Spirit's words and warnings (cf. 20:23; 21:4) confirm Paul's readiness to accept the will of God and bear the trials which they foretell (cf. 20:25, 27ff). His serenity contrasts with

[14]And when he would not be persuaded, we ceased and said, "The Mt 6:10; 26:42
will of the Lord be done."

Paul arrives in Jerusalem and meets the Christians
[15]After these days we made ready and went up to Jerusalem.
[16]And some of the disciples from Caesarea went with us, bringing
us to the house of Mnason of Cyprus, an early disciple, with
whom we should lodge.
[17]When we had come to Jerusalem, the brethren received us
gladly. [18]On the following day Paul went in with us to James; and Acts 12:17
all the elders were present. [19]After greeting them, he related one Acts 15:4
by one the things that God had done among the Gentiles through
his ministry. [20]And when they heard it, they glorified God. And Acts 15:1

---

the concern felt by those around him, which stems from their affection for him. His long life of self-surrender and self-forgetfulness explains why he takes things so calmly at this time: "This consists mainly or entirely in our ceasing to care about ourselves and our own pleasures, for the least that anyone who is beginning to serve the Lord can truly offer him is his life. Once he has surrendered his will to him, what has he to fear?" (St Teresa, *Way of Perfection*, 12).

"Accepting the will of God wholeheartedly is a sure way of finding joy and peace: happiness in the cross. Then we realize that Christ's yoke is sweet and that his burden is not heavy" (St Josemaría Escrivá, *The Way*, 758).

Paul's example impresses the disciples and moves them to accept what God has disposed, in words reminiscent of Jesus' in the garden of Gethsemane (cf. Lk 22:42).

21:18. Paul and his companions are received by James the Less, who was probably the head of the church of Jerusalem during these years (cf. 12:17; 15:13; Gal 1:19; 1 Cor 15:7), and by the elders who aided him in the government and spiritual care of the community. St Luke usually distinguishes elders from apostles. Apparently the apostles, including Peter, were no longer resident in the city.

The narrative here ceases to use the first person plural and does not use it again until the account of the journey to Rome (cf. Acts 27:1). This indicates that Luke accompanied Paul as far as Jerusalem, and then was with him from Caesarea to Rome.

21:19. Paul's apostolic ministry among the Gentiles is readily accepted by the Christians of the mother church of Jerusalem because God has demonstrated its legitimacy by blessing it with great fruitfulness: God guides and plans the mission to the Gentiles.

Paul in fact attributes all his success to the Lord: "Neither he who plants nor he who waters is anything, but only God who gives the growth" (1 Cor 3:7). This conviction has guided every step he has taken. "Everyone who prudently and intelligently looks at the history of the apostles of Jesus will clearly see", Origen writes, "that they preached Christianity with God-given strength and thereby were able to attract men to the Word of God" (*Against Celsus*, 1, 62).

21:20. The "zealous" Jews referred to by St James should not be confused with

they said to him, "You see, brother, how many thousands there are
among the Jews of those who have believed; they are all zealous
Rom 2:25–29 for the law, 21and they have been told about you that you teach all
1 Cor 7:17–20 the Jews who are among the Gentiles to forsake Moses, telling
them not to circumcise their children or observe the customs.
22What then is to be done? They will certainly hear that you have
Acts 18:18 come. 23Do therefore what we tell you. We have four men who are
under a vow; 24take these men and purify yourself along with
them and pay their expenses, so that they may shave their heads.
Thus all will know that there is nothing in what they have been
told about you but that you yourself live in observance of the law.
Acts 15:28–29 25But as for the Gentiles who have believed, we have sent a letter
with our judgment that they should abstain from what has been
sacrificed to idols and from blood and from what is strangled[y] and
Num 6:1–20 from unchastity." 26Then Paul took the men, and the next day he
1 Cor 9:20 purified himself with them and went into the temple, to give

---

"Zealots". Ardent attachment to the traditions of the fathers and hatred of the Romans had led to the development of a sect of Zealots, men of violence who played a key role in the rebellion of 66. This anti-Roman revolt, described in detail by Flavius Josephus in his book *The Jewish War* (written between 75 and 79) ended with the total destruction of the temple and of Jerusalem by the armies of Vespasian and Titus.

21:21. The rumours which observant Jews had heard about Paul's preaching were not without foundation, because the apostle regarded the Mosaic Law as something secondary as far as salvation was concerned: he did not accept circumcision as absolutely necessary (cf. Gal 4:9; 5:11; Rom 2:25–29). But the accusation was unjust. Paul never exhorted Christians of Jewish background not to circumcise their sons, and he himself ensured that Timothy was circumcised (cf. 16:3). In Corinth he came out in support of women following the Jewish custom of wearing the veil at liturgical ceremonies (cf. 1 Cor 11:2–16); and he himself had no difficulty about taking a Nazirite vow (cf. 18:18).

"Paul was calumniated by those who did not understand the Spirit with which these customs should be kept by Jewish Christians, that is, in a spirit of homage to the divine authority and prophetic holiness of these signs—and not in order to attain salvation, which had been revealed with Christ and applied through the sacrament of Baptism. Those who calumniated were people who wanted to observe these customs as if believers in the Gospel could not attain salvation without them" (St Bede, *Super Act. expositio*, ad loc.).

21:23–24. This was a Nazirite vow (cf. Num 6). A Nazirite committed himself to abstaining from certain kinds of food and drink and not cutting his hair during the period of the vow (cf. the note on Acts 18:18). To end the vow the person arranged a sacrificial offering in the temple. St James suggests that Paul bear the expenses of this sacrifice—a common

y. Other early authorities omit *and from what is strangled*

notice when the days of purification would be fulfilled and the
offering presented for every one of them.

Paul is arrested in the temple

[27]When the seven days were almost completed, the Jews from
Asia, who had seen him in the temple, stirred up all the crowd,
and laid hands on him, [28]crying out, "Men of Israel, help! This is Ezek 44:9
the man who is teaching men everywhere against the people and Acts 6:13
the law and this place; moreover he also brought Greeks into the
temple, and he has defiled this holy place." [29]For they had previously seen Trophimus the Ephesian with him in the city, and they Acts 20:4
supposed that Paul had brought him into the temple. [30]Then all the
city was aroused, and the people ran together; they seized Paul
and dragged him out of the temple, and at once the gates were
shut. [31]And as they were trying to kill him, word came to the tri-

---

type of pious act. This will show to all who know him his respect for the Law and the temple. Paul is putting into practice here the advice he gave to Christians in Corinth: "To the Jews I became as a Jew, in order to win Jews; to those under the law I became as one under the law—though not being myself under the law—that I might win those under the law" (1 Cor 9:20).

21:25. St James quotes the decisions of the Council of Jerusalem, with which Paul was very familiar. Presumably he does this for the benefit of the apostle's companions, who were not required, naturally, to go with Paul to the temple.

21:27–29. Paul's action, which should have reassured these Jews, has in fact the contrary effect and leads to the kind of violent reaction typical of the fanatic. Jews come as pilgrims to Jerusalem for the Jewish feast of Pentecost and attack Paul as a loathsome man: everywhere he goes, they say, he speaks against the Jewish people, the Law and the temple, and now he has the effrontery to profane the sacred precincts.

These accusations are similar to those laid against our Lord in his time (cf. Mt 26:61; 27:40) and against Stephen (cf. Acts 6:11–14). They start shouting and soon bring everyone along with them—the crowd only too ready to indulge their prejudices by believing anything said against Paul. The (groundless) accusation that he has brought Gentiles into the inner courtyards of the temple was a very serious charge because that type of offence was punishable by death under Jewish law, and usually the Roman authorities did execute those found guilty of it. Archaeologists have unearthed one of the temple's stone plaques warning Gentiles, under pain of death, not to cross over the low wall marking off the courtyard of the Gentiles; the notice is in Greek and Latin.

21:30. It was probably not the main gates that were closed, but those between the court of the Gentiles and the other courtyards.

21:31–36. Paul would certainly have been killed if the Roman soldiers had not intervened. They were able to arrive on the scene so quickly because the Antonia Tower, where the Jerusalem garrison was

bune of the cohort that all Jerusalem was in confusion. [32]He at
once took soldiers and centurions, and ran down to them; and
when they saw the tribune and the soldiers, they stopped beating
Acts 21:11 Paul. [33]Then the tribune came up and arrested him, and ordered
him to be bound with two chains. He inquired who he was and
what he had done. [34]Some in the crowd shouted one thing, some
another; and as he could not learn the facts because of the uproar,
he ordered him to be brought into the barracks. [35]And when he
came to the steps, he was actually carried by the soldiers because
Lk 23:28 of the violence of the crowd; [36]for the mob of the people followed,
Acts 22:22 crying, "Away with him!"

[37]As Paul was about to be brought into the barracks, he said to
the tribune, "May I say something to you?" And he said, "Do you
know Greek? [38]Are you not the Egyptian, then, who recently
stirred up a revolt and led the four thousand men of the Assassins
out into the wilderness?" [39]Paul replied, "I am a Jew, from Tarsus

---

based, was located at one corner of the temple, only two flights of steps from the court of the Gentiles.

Having arrested Paul, whom the Romans take to be the cause of the uproar, the tribune prudently decides to transfer him to the fortress. A new section of the book now begins, in which St Luke will describe in detail the apostle's imprisonment (cf. Acts 21:33—22:29), his trial at Jerusalem and Caesarea (cf. chaps. 23–26) and his journey to Rome (cf. Acts 27:1—28:16) to appear before an imperial tribunal. From this point onwards Paul is not so much a tireless missionary and founder of churches as an imprisoned witness to the Gospel: even in these new circumstances he will manage to proclaim Christ.

21:38. This Egyptian outlaw is also mentioned by Flavius Josephus as a leader of a group of bandits who tried to capture Jerusalem and were put to flight by Felix, the governor (cf. *The Jewish War*, 2, 261–263).

The "Assassins" referred to were *sicarii*, so named because they always carried a dagger (Latin: *sica*). Together with the Zealots, they played a prominent and inglorious part in the Jewish rebellion against Rome.

21:39. Paul continues to say nothing about his Roman citizenship. He simply states that he comes from Tarsus, a city which enjoyed self-government and to which he was proud to belong. It would seem that from the time of Claudius onwards it was possible to hold dual citizenship—to be a Roman citizen and the citizen of a particular city.

In keeping with his courage and sense of mission, the apostle decides to address the threatening crowd. He is more interested in winning over his adversaries than in escaping from them; in taking them on he is supported by the Gospel's inner strength and his own firm dedication to the service of Christ. "There is nothing weaker in fact", comments Chrysostom, "than many sinners—and nothing stronger than a man who keeps the law of God" (*Hom. on Acts*, 26). "The soldiers of Christ, that is, those who pray," St Teresa writes, "do not think of the time

in Cilicia, a citizen of no mean city; I beg you, let me speak to the
people." [40]And when he had given him leave, Paul, standing on
the steps, motioned with his hand to the people; and when there
was a great hush, he spoke to them in the Hebrew language,
saying:

Paul defends himself before the crowd

22 [1]"Brethren and fathers, hear the defence which I now make Acts 7:2
before you."

[2]And when they heard that he addressed them in the Hebrew
language, they were the more quiet. And he said:
[3]"I am a Jew, born at Tarsus in Cilicia, but brought up in this Acts 26:4–5
city at the feet of Gamaliel, educated according to the strict 2 Cor 11:22 Gal 1:14
manner of the law of our fathers, being zealous for God as you all Phil 3:5–6
are this day. [4]I persecuted this Way to the death, binding and Acts 8:3

when they will have to fight, they never fear public enemies; for they already know them and they realize that nothing can withstand the strength the Lord has given them, and that they will always be victors and heaped with gain" (*Way of Perfection*, 38, 2).

Once again, Paul relies on God giving him the right things to say; he does not settle for simply reproaching them for their behaviour: he knows that "truth is not preached with swords and lances, or the aid of soldiers, but rather by means of persuasion and counsel" (St Athanasius, *Historia arianorum*, 33).

21:40. "In the Hebrew language": this must mean Aramaic, the language which, after the return of the Jews from the Babylonian captivity, gradually came into general use, due to the influence of the Persian empire.

22:1–21. St Luke gives us Paul's address to the Jews of Jerusalem, the first of three speeches in his own defence (cf. 24:10–21; 26:1–23) in which he tries to show that there is no reason why Christianity should be opposed by Jew or by Roman. Here he presents himself as a pious Jew, full of respect for his people and their sacred traditions. He earnestly desires his brethren to realize that there are compelling reasons for his commitment to Jesus. He is convinced that they can experience in their souls the same kind of spiritual change as he did. However, this speech is not a closely-argued apologia. His main intention is not so much to answer the accusations levelled against him as to use this opportunity to bear witness to Jesus Christ, whose commandments validate Paul's actions. What he is really trying to do is to get his hearers to obey the voice of the Lord.

22:1. "Brethren and fathers": the "fathers" may refer to members of the Sanhedrin present in the crowd.

22:3. Gamaliel (cf. 5:34) belonged to the school of the rabbi Hillel, which was noted for a less rigorous interpretation of the Law than that of Shammai and his disciples.

22:4. The situation described by Paul is confirmed by 1 Corinthians 15:9: "I am

delivering to prison both men and women, [5]as the high priest and
Acts 9:1–18; 26:9–18 the whole council of elders bear me witness. From them I
received letters to the brethren, and I journeyed to Damascus to
take those also who were there and bring them in bonds to
Jerusalem to be punished.

[6]"As I made my journey and drew near to Damascus, about
noon a great light from heaven suddenly shone about me. [7]And I
fell to the ground and heard a voice saying to me, 'Saul, Saul, why
Mt 2:23 do you persecute me?' [8]And I answered, 'Who are you, Lord?' And
he said to me, 'I am Jesus of Nazareth whom you are persecuting.'
Wis 18:1 [9]Now those who were with me saw the light but did not hear the
voice of the one who was speaking to me. [10]And I said, 'What
shall I do, Lord?' And the Lord said to me, 'Rise, and go into
Damascus, and there you will be told all that is appointed for you
to do.' [11]And when I could not see because of the brightness of
that light, I was led by the hand by those who were with me, and
came into Damascus.

[12]"And one Ananias, a devout man according to the law, well
spoken of by all the Jews who lived there, [13]came to me, and

---

the least of the apostles, unfit to be called an apostle, because I persecuted the church of God"; Galatians 1:13: "You have heard of my former life in Judaism, how I persecuted the church of God violently and tried to destroy it"; Philippians 3:5–6: "as to the law a Pharisee, as to zeal a persecutor of the church"; and 1 Timothy 1:13: "I formerly blasphemed and persecuted and insulted him [Christ]".

22:6–11. Paul describes in his own words what happened on the way to Damascus (cf. 9:3–9; 26:6–16). This account differs in some ways from—but does not contradict—the two other versions of the episode, especially that of chapter 9, which is told in St Luke's words.

Paul adds that the whole thing happened at midday (cf. 26:13), and he says that Jesus referred to himself as "Jesus of Nazareth". He also includes the question "What shall I do, Lord?", which is not given in chapter 9.

As far as Paul's companions were concerned, we know that they saw the light (cf. 22:9) but did not see anyone (cf. 9:7): they did not see the glorified Jesus; they heard a voice (cf. 9:7) but did not hear the voice of the one who was speaking to Paul (cf. 22:9), that is, did not understand what the voice said.

22:10. Paul addresses Jesus as "Lord", which shows that the vision has revealed to him the divinity of the One he was persecuting.

The divine voice orders him to get up from the ground and the future apostle of the Gentiles obeys immediately. The physical movement of getting up is a kind of symbol of the spiritual uplift his soul is given by God's call. "This was the first grace, that was given to the first Adam; but more powerful than it is the grace in the second Adam. The effect of the first grace was that a man might have justice, if he willed; the second grace, therefore, is more powerful, because it affects the will itself; it makes for a

standing by me said to me, 'Brother Saul, receive your sight.' And
in that very hour I received my sight and saw him. 14And he said,
'The God of our fathers appointed you to know his will, to see the Acts 3:14
Just One and to hear a voice from his mouth; 15for you will be a
witness for him to all men of what you have seen and heard.16And 1 Jn 1:1–3
now why do you wait? Rise and be baptized, and wash away your
sins, calling on his name.'

17"When I had returned to Jerusalem and was praying in the Acts 9:26
temple, I fell into a trance 18and saw him saying to me, 'Make Gal 1:18
haste and get quickly out of Jerusalem, because they will not Acts 13:46–48; 18:6; 28:25–28
accept your testimony about me.' 19And I said, 'Lord, they them-
selves know that in every synagogue I imprisoned and beat those
who believed in thee. 20And when the blood of Stephen thy wit- Acts 7:58; 8:1
ness* was shed, I also was standing by and approving, and keeping the garments of those who killed him.' 21And he said to me, Acts 9:15
'Depart; for I will send you far away to the Gentiles.'"

---

strong will, a burning charity, so that by a contrary will the spirit overcomes the conflicting will of the flesh" (St Augustine, *De correptione et gratia*, 11, 31).

"Many have come to Christianity", Origen says, "as if against their will, for a certain spirit, appearing to them, in sleep or when they are awake, suddenly silences their mind, and they change from hating the Word to dying for him" (*Against Celsus*, I, 46).

Paul's conversion is an outstanding example of what divine grace and divine assistance in general can effect in a person's heart.

22:12–16. This account of Ananias and his role in Paul's conversion is much shorter than that given in chapter 9 (cf. vv. 10–19). St Paul adapts it here to suit his audience (who are all Jews). He presents Jesus as the one in whom the Old Testament prophecies are fulfilled. Like Peter (cf. 3:13ff) and Stephen (cf. 7:52) he speaks of the "God of our fathers" and the "Just One" when referring to God and to Jesus respectively.

22:17–18. Paul's return to Jerusalem took place three years after his conversion. Paul deliberately mentiond his custom of going to pray in the temple, which at that time was a normal place of prayer for Christians. He refers to an ecstasy not mentioned anywhere else and to a vision of Jesus Christ reminiscent of that described in Revelation 1:10.

22:19. Synagogues were also used for non-liturgical purposes, they usually had additional rooms for meeting (cf. Mt 10:17; 23:34; Mk 13:9).

22:20. The word "witness" is beginning to acquire the meaning of "martyr" as now used in the Church: martyrdom is the supreme form of bearing witness to the Christian faith.

St Paul refers to his presence at the martyrdom of St Stephen to emphasize the miraculous nature of his own conversion.

22:21. By promising that he will "send" him to the Gentiles, our Lord makes him an "apostle", on a par with the Twelve.

Paul, the Roman citizen

Acts 25:24 [22]Up to this word they listened to him; then they lifted up their
voices and said, "Away with such a fellow from the earth! For he
ought not to live." [23]And as they cried out and waved their garments and threw dust into the air, [24]the tribune commanded him to
be brought into the barracks, and ordered him to be examined by
scourging, to find out why they shouted thus against him. [25]But
Acts 16:22–37 when they had tied him up with the thongs, Paul said to the centurion who was standing by, "Is it lawful for you to scourge a man
who is a Roman citizen, and uncondemned?" [26]When the centurion heard that, he went to the tribune and said to him, "What are
you about to do? For this man is a Roman citizen." [27]So the tribune came and said to him, "Tell me, are you a Roman citizen?"
And he said, "Yes." [28]The tribune answered, "I bought this citizenship for a large sum." Paul said, "But I was born a citizen."
Acts 16:38–39 [29]So those who were about to examine him withdrew from him
instantly; and the tribune also was afraid, for he realized that Paul
was a Roman citizen and that he had bound him.

Speech before the Sanhedrin

[30]But on the morrow, desiring to know the real reason why the
Jews accused him, he unbound him, and commanded the chief

22:22. The mere mention of preaching to the Gentiles leads to interruption: his listeners are so bigoted, their fear is so irrational, that they cannot listen calmly to what Paul has to say, never mind take it all in.

22:24. Roman law allowed suspects and slaves to be put under the lash in order to extract confessions.

22:25. As at Philippi (cf. 16:37), Paul stands on his rights as a Roman citizen; but this time he does so at an earlier stage and avoids being scourged.

22:30. This does not seem to have been a regular session of the Sanhedrin; it is an informal one arranged by Lysias (Acts 23:26) to enable documentation to be prepared, now that "evidence" cannot be extracted from Paul by torture.

23:1. In response to the Jews' accusations, which St Luke here takes as read, Paul sums up his defence with this key statement. Having an upright conscience is a central point in Pauline spirituality. It comes up all the time in his letters (cf. 1 Cor 4:4; 2 Cor 1:12; 1 Tim 1:5, 19; 2 Tim 1:3) and is borne out by his own conduct: even when he was a persecutor of the Church he was always trying to do his best to serve God; his sincerity was never in question, even if his zeal was misdirected. In this terse remark he rejects any suggestion that he was disrespectful to the Law.

23:2. This Ananias should not be confused with Annas (cf. 4:6). He was appointed high priest in 47 and deposed around the year 58. In 66 he was assassinated by Jews in revolt against Rome. He orders that Paul be struck, undoubtedly

priests and all the council to meet, and he brought Paul down and
set him before them.

23 1And Paul, looking intently at the council, said, "Brethren, Acts 24:16
I have lived before God in all good conscience up to this Heb 13:18
day." 2And the high priest Ananias commanded those who stood Jn 18:22
by him to strike him on the mouth. 3Then Paul said to him, "God Ezek 13:10–15
shall strike you, you whitewashed wall! Are you sitting to judge Mk 23:27
me according to the law, and yet contrary to the law you order me
to be struck?" 4Those who stood by said, "Would you revile God's
high priest?" 5And Paul said, "I did not know, brethren, that he Ex 22:28
was the high priest; for it is written, 'You shall not speak evil of a
ruler of your people.'"
6But when Paul perceived that one part were Sadducees and Acts 26:5
the other Pharisees, he cried out in the council, "Brethren, I am a
Pharisee, a son of Pharisees; with respect to the hope and the resurrection of the dead I am on trial." 7And when he had said this, a
dissension arose between the Pharisees and the Sadducees; and
the assembly was divided. 8For the Sadducees say that there is no Mt 22:23
resurrection, nor angel, nor spirit; but the Pharisees acknowledge

---

because he cannot answer what Paul says or because he feels personally offended. Josephus tells us that Ananias was an arrogant and hot-tempered man (cf. *Jewish Antiquities*, 20, 199).

23:3. Paul's harsh words are not due to his annoyance at being unjustly treated. We might have expected him, in imitation of Jesus (cf. Mt 27:12), to remain silent. However, Paul thinks that the right thing to do here is to speak out. His words are a deliberate prophecy of the fate that awaits Ananias.

23:5. Many scholars think that Paul is being sarcastic here, as if to say, "I would never have thought that anyone who gave an order against the Law like that could be the high priest." Others think that the apostle realizes that his words may have scandalized some of those present, and therefore he wants to make it clear that he respects Jewish institutions and the Law.

23:6–9. From St Luke's Gospel (cf. 20:27) we know that the Sadducees, unlike the Pharisees, did not believe in a future resurrection of the dead. This is the only place in the New Testament where it says that they also denied the existence of angels and spirits; however, this is confirmed by Jewish and secular sources.

In the course of his trial, Paul brings up a subject which sets his judges at each other. Personal advantage is not his main reason for doing this. He is obviously very shrewd, but he really does not expect to get an impartial hearing from the Sanhedrin. Therefore he tries to stir their consciences and awaken their love for the truth and thereby elicit some sympathy for Christians. Although Christian belief in the Resurrection was not the same thing as the Pharisees' belief, the two had this in common: they believed in the resurrection of the dead.

them all. [9]Then a great clamour arose; and some of the scribes of
the Pharisees' party stood up and contended, "We find nothing
wrong in this man. What if a spirit or an angel spoke to him?"
[10]And when the dissension became violent, the tribune, afraid that
Paul would be torn in pieces by them, commanded the soldiers to
go down and take him by force from among them and bring him
into the barracks.

Acts 18:9–10; 27:24 [11]The following night the Lord stood by him and said, "Take
courage, for as you have testified about me at Jerusalem, so you
must bear witness also at Rome."

A Jewish plot against Paul

Acts 9:23; 20:3 [12]When it was day, the Jews made a plot and bound themselves by
an oath neither to eat nor drink till they had killed Paul. [13]There
were more than forty who made this conspiracy. [14]And they went
to the chief priests and elders, and said, "We have strictly bound
ourselves by an oath to taste no food till we have killed Paul.
[15]You therefore, along with the council, give notice now to the tribune to bring him down to you, as though you were going to
determine his case more exactly. And we are ready to kill him
before he comes near."

[16]Now the son of Paul's sister heard of their ambush; so he
went and entered the barracks and told Paul. [17]And Paul called
one of the centurions and said, "Bring this young man to the tri-

---

23:9. They are referring to his vision on the road to Damascus. They are not going as far as to say that it was Jesus who spoke to Paul, but they do not rule out the possibility that he had a genuine spiritual experience.

23:11. The Lord is Jesus. These words of consolation to Paul show him that God will guide him all along, right up to his court appearance in Rome. From this point onwards the prisoner is seeking primarily to bear witness to the Gospel and not just to defend himself. In imprisonment he will continue to do the same work as he did when free. "Keep alert with all perseverance," he tells the Ephesians, "making supplication for all the saints, and also for me, that utterance may be given me in opening my mouth boldly to proclaim the mystery of the gospel, for which I am an ambassador in chains; that I may declare it boldly, as I ought to speak" (6:18–20).

23:12–22. Blinded by fanaticism, a small group of Jews take an oath to do away with Paul. Their promise not to eat or drink until they fulfil their intention is in line with similar vows taken in the service of better causes (cf. 1 Sam 14:24). Hatred has misdirected their piety, and what was originally religious conviction has changed into resistance to the Holy Spirit. "The Lord says, 'Blessed are those who hunger and thirst after justice'. These Jews, on the contrary, hunger after iniquity and thirst after blood. […] But there is no wisdom or

bune; for he has something to tell him." [18]So he took him and
brought him to the tribune and said, "Paul the prisoner called me
and asked me to bring this young man to you, as he has something
to say to you." [19]The tribune took him by the hand, and going
aside asked him privately, "What is it that you have to tell me?"
[20]And he said, "The Jews have agreed to ask you to bring Paul
down to the council tomorrow, as though they were going to
inquire somewhat more closely about him. [21]But do not yield to
them; for more than forty of their men lie in ambush for him,
having bound themselves by an oath neither to eat nor drink till
they have killed him; and now they are ready, waiting for the
promise from you."

13. FROM JERUSALEM TO ROME

Paul is moved to Caesarea

[22]So the tribune dismissed the young man, charging him, "Tell no
one that you have informed me of this."

[23]Then he called two of the centurions and said, "At the third
hour of the night get ready two hundred soldiers with seventy
horsemen and two hundred spearmen to go as far as Caesarea.
[24]Also provide mounts for Paul to ride, and bring him safely to
Felix the governor." [25]And he wrote a letter to this effect:

---

prudence or counsel that can prevent God's will. For, although Paul, a Jew with the Jews, offered sacrifices, shaving his head and going barefoot, he did not escape the chains which had been foretold. And although these men make plans and swear an oath and prepare an ambush, the apostle will receive protection to enable him, as he had already been told, to bear witness to Christ in Rome" (St Bede, *Super Act. expositio*, ad loc.).

23:16. This is the only reference in this book or the letters (with the exception of Rom 16:7–11) to Paul's relatives.

23:23–24. The information brought by Paul's nephew must have led Lysias to advance his plans for the transfer of the prisoner to the governor; besides, the Sanhedrin had only limited powers to detain a prisoner pending trial.

Felix had been governor or procurator of Judea since the year 52. He was a freedman who had risen remarkably high, but according to Tacitus he "exerted royal power with the mind of a slave". Felix was successful in repressing various riots which heralded the great Jewish uprising in the year 66, but he was recalled in 60 on account of his harsh and cruel rule (cf. 24:27).

23:25–30. This letter from Claudius Lysias is the only secular letter recorded in the New Testament. Lysias gives the governor a brief report on the detainee. He bends the facts a little in that he does not mention that at an early stage he planned

26“Claudius Lysias to his Excellency the governor Felix, greeting. 27This man was seized by the Jews, and was about to be killed
Act 22:25–29 by them, when I came upon them with the soldiers and rescued
him, having learned that he was a Roman citizen. 28And desiring
to know the charge on which they accused him, I brought him
down to their council. 29I found that he was accused about ques-
Acts 25:18–19; 26:31 tions of their law, but charged with nothing deserving death or
imprisonment. 30And when it was disclosed to me that there
would be a plot against the man, I sent him to you at once, ordering his accusers also to state before you what they have against
him.”

31So the soldiers, according to their instructions, took Paul and
brought him by night to Antipatris. 32And on the morrow they
returned to the barracks, leaving the horsemen to go on with him.
33When they came to Caesarea and delivered the letter to the governor, they presented Paul also before him. 34On reading the
letter, he asked to what province he belonged. When he learned
that he was from Cilicia 35he said, “I will hear you when your
accusers arrive.” And he commanded him to be guarded in
Herod’s praetorium.

---

to have Paul scourged: significantly the letter only mentions the Jews’ religious accusation to the effect that Paul was speaking against the Law (cf. 21:28) and does not give weight to the charge that he brought Gentiles into the temple (cf. 21:28b).

23:31. Antipatris was 60 kilometres (40 miles) from Jerusalem and 40 kilometres from Caesarea. It had been founded by Herod the Great in honour of his father, Antipater.

23:33–35. Felix acts in line with what the law lays down. He acquaints himself firsthand with Paul’s case and decides to try him as soon as his accusers arrive. The governor could have remitted the case to the legate of the province of Syria, which at that time included Cilicia, but he prefers to deal with the matter himself.

Herod’s praetorium was a palace built by Herod the Great, which later became the residence of the Roman governor.

24:1–21. By being sent to Caesarea by the tribune, Paul has entered the jurisdiction of Roman law. The Jews fail to change things so that he can be tried by the Sanhedrin. The judicial hearing now begins. Here we have an instance of the Roman judicial process known as *cognitio extra ordinem*, or extraordinary procedure, to distinguish it from the *cognitio ordinaria*, the normal kind of trial. The former was marked by more flexible procedures. In the *cognitio ordinaria* the magistrate allowed charges to be brought against the accused according to established legal procedures which did not allow much flexibility in the way the trial was conducted or in the type of sentence that could be passed. The *cognitio extra ordinem* allowed a judge more initiative; it had five stages: 1) private accusation; 2) a formal *pro tribunali* hearing; 3) use by the judge of expert legal advice; 4) hearing of evidence from the parties concerned; and 5) assessment of this evidence by the judge.

The trial before Felix

24 1And after five days the high priest Ananias came down Acts 23:2
with some elders and a spokesman, one Tertullus. They
laid before the governor their case against Paul; 2and when he was
called, Tertullus began to accuse him, saying:
"Since through you we enjoy much peace, and since by your
provision, most excellent Felix, reforms are introduced on behalf
of this nation, 3in every way and everywhere we accept this with
all gratitude. 4But, to detain you no further, I beg you in your
kindness to hear us briefly. 5For we have found this man a pesti- Acts 17:6
lent fellow, an agitator among all the Jews throughout the world,
and a ringleader of the sect of the Nazarenes. 6He even tried to Acts 21:28
profane the temple, but we seized him.[z] 8By examining him yourself you will be able to learn from him about everything of which
we accuse him."
9The Jews also joined in the charge, affirming that all this was so.
10And when the governor had motioned to him to speak, Paul
replied:

Chapters 24 and 25 of Acts are in fact an important source of information about the use of extraordinary procedures in criminal cases. The narrative tells us about Paul's being accused privately by Jews (cf. 23:35; 24:1). It uses the correct legal terminology when referring to hearings by the judge (cf. 25:6, 17). It mentions the committee of experts who assist the judge (cf. 25:9, 12). It describes the charges in some detail and shows the kind of discretion the magistrates (Felix and Festus) had in the way they handled the case and approached the evidence.

24:1. The charge had to be presented by a professional lawyer. Tertullus may have been a Jew skilled in Hebrew and Roman law. His language, at any rate, shows that he shares his clients' point of view.

24:2–4. Tertullus' opening words are sheer flattery. Felix's administration was in fact notoriously inefficient and had disastrous effects.

24:5–9. The Jews make a timid effort to have Paul transferred back into their own jurisdiction. They see him as a kind of Jewish heretic, and Christianity as just a Jewish sect. They level four charges against the apostle: Paul is a social undesirable, an agitator and a leader of a dangerous sect. These three vague charges frame a fourth charge, which is much more specific: he has tried to profane the temple, the symbol of the Jewish nation. Even though the charge is basically religious in character, Tertullus tries to present Paul as a politically dangerous type.

24:10–21. In his defence Paul points out that the Jews, by failing to recognize Jesus, have failed to understand the true religious tradition of Israel, and also that their charges about creating a disturbance

z. Other ancient authorities add *and we would have judged him according to our law. 7But the chief captain Lysias came and with great violence took him out of our hands, 8commanding his accusers to come before you*

"Realizing that for many years you have been judge over this
nation, I cheerfully make my defence. 11As you may ascertain, it
Acts 20:16 is not more than twelve days since I went up to worship at
Jerusalem; 12and they did not find me disputing with any one or
stirring up a crowd, either in the temple or in the synagogues, or
in the city. 13Neither can they prove to you what they now bring
Mt 5:17 up against me. 14But this I admit to you, that according to the Way,
Rom 3:31; 16:26 which they call a sect, I worship the God of our fathers, believing
everything laid down by the law or written in the prophets,
Jn 15:29 15having a hope in God which these themselves accept, that there
will be a resurrection of both the just and the unjust. 16So I always
Acts 23:1 take pains to have a clear conscience toward God and toward men.
Rom 15:25 17Now after some years I came to bring to my nation alms and
Acts 21:27 offerings. 18As I was doing this, they found me purified in the
temple, without any crowd or tumult. But some Jews from Asia—
19they ought to be here before you and to make an accusation, if

---

and profaning the temple are groundless and they have no proof for them.

The tone of the address is serious and sober, as befits the authority by which he is being judged. This is in keeping with what the Gospel teaches us about the respect due to civil authorities: they should be obeyed by all citizens because they are designed to protect the common good. "A Christian", Tertullian will write, "is an enemy of no one, least of all the emperor. Since he knows him to be appointed by his own God, he must love, reverence, honour, and wish him well, together with the whole Roman Empire, as long as the world shall last. [...] In this way, then, do we honour the emperor, as is both lawful for us and expedient for him, as a man next to God: who has received whatever he is from God; who is inferior to God alone" (*To Scapula*, 2).

"The political community and public authority", Vatican II teaches, "are based on human nature, and therefore they belong to an order established by God; nevertheless, the choice of political regime and the appointment of rulers are left to the free decision of the citizens (cf. Rom 13:1–5).

"It follows that political authority, either within the political community as such or through organizations representing the State, must be exercised within the limits of the moral order and directed toward the common good (understood in the dynamic sense of the term) according to the juridical order legitimately established or due to be established. Citizens, then, are bound in conscience to obey (cf. Rom 13:5). Accordingly, the responsibilty, the dignity, and the importance of State rulers is clear" (*Gaudium et spes*, 74).

24:11–12. Paul did not go up to Jerusalem to preach but rather to worship God in the temple.

24:14–16. The apostle rejects the charge that Christianity is a Jewish sect. It is something much more than that. For St Paul the Old Testament finds its fulfilment in the Gospel, and without the Gospel Judaism is incomplete. The central beliefs of the Jewish religion can be summed up as belief in God and in a

they have anything against me. [20]Or else let these men themselves
say what wrongdoing they found when I stood before the council,
[21]except this one thing which I cried out while standing among
them, 'With respect to the resurrection of the dead I am on trial
before you this day.'"
[22]But Felix, having a rather accurate knowledge of the Way,
put them off, saying, "When Lysias the tribune comes down, I
will decide your case." [23]Then he gave orders to the centurion that
he should be kept in custody but should have some liberty, and
that none of his friends should be prevented from attending to his
needs.

A further appearance before Felix

[24]After some days Felix came with his wife Drusilla, who was a
Jewess; and he sent for Paul and heard him speak upon faith in
Christ Jesus. [25]And as he argued about justice and self-control and Mk 6:17–20 Jn 16:8

---

future life and also upright conduct in line with the dictates of conscience; all this, Paul says, is also at the centre of Christian preaching.

The apostle establishes a direct connexion between hope in the resurrection and good deeds in this present life. The *St Pius V Catechism* will say, many centuries later, that the thought of a future resurrection "must also prove a powerful incentive to the faithful to use every exertion to lead lives of rectitude and integrity, unsullied by the defilement of sin. For if they reflect that those boundless riches which will follow after the resurrection are now offered to them as rewards, they will be easily attracted to the pursuit of virtue and piety.

"On the other hand, nothing will have greater effect in subduing the passions and withdrawing souls from sin, than frequently to remind the sinner of the miseries and torments with which the reprobate will be visited, who on the last day will come forth unto the resurrection of judgment.

"An ardent desire of the promised rewards of eternal life will always be one of the most effective encouragements in our Christian life. However sorely fidelity to our faith as Christians may be tried in certain circumstances, hope of this reward will lighten our burden and revive our spirit, and God will always find us prompt and cheerful in his divine service" (I, 12, 14; 13, 1).

St Paul says that both the just and the unjust will experience the resurrection of the body.

24:17. This is the only reference in Acts to the collection in aid of the Jerusalem community (cf. Rom 15:25).

24:19. Paul's objection carries great legal weight because Roman law laid down that those who brought charges had to appear before the tribunal.

24:24. Drusilla was a daughter of Herod Agrippa (cf. 12:1ff). She had left her lawful husband to marry the Roman governor.

24:25. It is very daring of Paul to speak about chastity to this couple living in

future judgment, Felix was alarmed and said, "Go away for the
present; when I have an opportunity I will summon you." 26At the
same time he hoped that money would be given him by Paul. So
Acts 25:9 he sent for him often and conversed with him. 27But when two
years had elapsed, Felix was succeeded by Porcius Festus; and
desiring to do the Jews a favour, Felix left Paul in prison.

Festus resumes the trial. Paul appeals to Caesar

25 1Now when Festus had come into his province, after three
days he went up to Jerusalem from Caesarea. 2And the
chief priests and the principal men of the Jews informed him
Acts 23:15 against Paul; and they urged him, 3asking as a favour to have the
man sent to Jerusalem, planning an ambush to kill him on the
way. 4Festus replied that Paul was being kept at Caesarea, and that
he himself intended to go there shortly. 5"So," said he, "let the
men of authority among you go down with me, and if there is anything wrong about the man, let them accuse him."

---

concubinage. "Observe", says St John Chrysostom, "that, when he has the opportunity to converse with the governor, Paul does not say anything which might influence his decision or flatter him: he says things which shock him and disturb his conscience" (*Hom. on Acts*, 51).

Felix's fear of future judgment has little to do with true fear of God, which is the beginning of wisdom and therefore of conversion. The governor's attitude shows that he does have remorse of conscience—but it does not make him change his lifestyle.

24:26. Felix may well have wanted to get some of the money Paul brought to Jerusalem, funds which Paul in fact has referred to (v. 17). Venal officials were common enough during this period.

24:27. "Two years": a biennium, a technical word used in Roman law for the maximum length a person could be detained without a trial (cf. 28:30).

It was normal practice for an outgoing governor to leave to his successor the resolution of important cases pending.

25:1–12. Paul's case is now re-heard before Festus, following the same procedure as described in the previous chapter. The new governor wants to examine the matter for himself before making a definitive judgment. He probably realizes or suspects that Paul is innocent, but he will soon be as perplexed as Felix his predecessor and as subject to the same pressures from the Jews.

Porcius Festus seems to have been a good governor. He held this position for two or three years, until the year 62, when he died.

25:1–2. Festus' courtesy visit to Jerusalem would enable him to be briefed on all matters awaiting decision, including Paul's case.

25:9. The governor is not thinking of handing the prisoner over to the Jewish courts. But his political prudence leads him to take Paul's accusers' requests

[6]When he had stayed among them not more than eight or ten
days, he went down to Caesarea; and the next day he took his seat
on the tribunal and ordered Paul to be brought. [7]And when he had Mt 26:59–60 Lk 23:14–15
come, the Jews who had gone down from Jerusalem stood about
him, bringing against him many serious charges which they could
not prove. [8]Paul said in his defence, "Neither against the law of Acts 24:14
the Jews, nor against the temple, nor against Caesar have I
offended at all." [9]But Festus, wishing to do the Jews a favour, said Acts 24:27
to Paul, "Do you wish to go up to Jerusalem, and there be tried on
these charges before me?" [10]But Paul said, "I am standing before
Caesar's tribunal, where I ought to be tried; to the Jews I have
done no wrong, as you know very well. [11]If then I am a wrong-
doer, and have committed anything for which I deserve to die, I
do not seek to escape death; but if there is nothing in their charges
against me, no one can give me up to them. I appeal to Caesar."
[12]Then Festus, when he had conferred with his council, answered,
"You have appealed to Caesar; to Caesar you shall go."

---

partly into account and give the Sanhedrin a say in the trial. Festus can also use the Sanhedrin as a *consilium*, a source of expert advice. It is in this sense that he invites Paul to agree to be tried in Jerusalem. The governor's question is in fact a rhetorical one: he is simply notifying Paul of a decision he has already made.

25:10–11. Paul realizes what Festus intends to do, and he appeals to Caesar in order to avoid being tried in unfavourable circumstances. From a strictly judicial point of view, Paul's action is not an "appeal" but what is termed in Roman law a *provocatio*. An appeal only operated once a lower court had passed sentence. A *provocatio* meant insisting that the case be brought to a higher court, for that court to decide whether the accused was guilty or not.

Only Roman citizens could ask for their cases to be examined by the imperial tribunal in Rome.

These various legal proceedings, ordained and used by Providence, help ensure that Paul fulfil the task God has marked out for him and foretold (cf. Acts 23:11). "He appeals to Caesar and hastens to Rome to persist still longer in preaching, and thereby go to Christ crowned with the many who thereby will come to believe, as well as those who already believe [through him]" (St Bede, *Super Act. expositio*, ad loc.).

Paul's characteristic generosity once again brings him to contemplate and accept the prospect of having to die. For him death would in the last analysis be God's will for him and not just the decision of a human court. But his sense of justice obliges him to ask that his actions be judged on the basis of his merits and demerits in the eyes of the law. "These are not the words of a man who condemns himself to death, but of a man who firmly believes in his own innocence" (St John Chrysostom, *Hom. on Acts*, 51).

25:12. Possibly Paul's appeal did not take automatic effect: the governor may not necessarily have been obliged by law

Festus briefs Agrippa

[13]Now when some days had passed, Agrippa the king and Bernice
arrived at Caesarea to welcome Festus. [14]And as they stayed there
many days, Festus laid Paul's case before the king, saying, "There
is a man left prisoner by Felix; [15]and when I was at Jerusalem, the
Acts 24:1; 25:2 chief priests and the elders of the Jews gave information about
him, asking for sentence against him. [16]I answered them that it
was not the custom of the Romans to give up any one before the
accused met the accusers face to face, and had opportunity to
make his defence concerning the charge laid against him. [17]When
therefore they came together here, I made no delay, but on the
next day took my seat on the tribunal and ordered the man to be
brought in. [18]When the accusers stood up, they brought no charge
Acts 18:5; 23:29 in his case of such evils as I supposed; [19]but they had certain
1 Cor 15:14 points of dispute with him about their own superstition and about
one Jesus, who was dead, but whom Paul asserted to be alive.
[20]Being at a loss how to investigate these questions, I asked
whether he wished to go to Jerusalem and be tried there regarding
them. [21]But when Paul had appealed to be kept in custody for the
decision of the emperor, I commanded him to be held until I send
Lk 23:8 him to Caesar." [22]And Agrippa said to Festus, "I should like to
hear the man myself." "Tomorrow," said he, "you shall hear him."

---

to send the detainee to Rome. But once the latter invoked his right of appeal, Festus would be able to escape the dilemma he faced, by sending Paul to Rome. If he did not transfer the case to Rome, this might have been taken as an insult to Caesar—involving political risk (cf. 26:32)—and if he set Paul free he would be needlessly offending the Jews.

25:13. Herod Agrippa II was a son of Herod Agrippa I. He was born in the year 27. Like his father he had won favour with Rome and had been given various territories in northern Palestine, which he was allowed to rule with the title of king. Bernice was his sister.

25:19. Festus' words show his indifference towards Paul's beliefs and his religious controversy with the Jews. The conversation between the two politicians reveals a typical attitude of worldly men to matters which they consider far-fetched and irrelevant as far as everyday affairs are concerned. This passage also shows us that in the course of his trial Paul must have had an opportunity to speak about Jesus and confess his faith in the Resurrection.

Jesus Christ is alive; he is the centre of history and the centre of each and every person's existence. "The Church believes that Christ, who died and was raised for the sake of all (cf. 2 Cor 5:15) can show man the way and strengthen him through the Spirit in order to be worthy of his destiny: nor is there any other name under heaven given among men by which they can be saved (cf. Acts 4:12). The Church likewise maintains that the key, the centre and the purpose of the whole of man's history is to be found in its Lord and Master. She also maintains that beneath all that changes there is

Paul before Agrippa

[23]So on the morrow Agrippa and Bernice came with great pomp,
and they entered the audience hall with the military tribunes and the
prominent men of the city. Then by command of Festus Paul was
brought in. [24]And Festus said, "King Agrippa and all who are present with us, you see this man about whom the whole Jewish people
petitioned me, both at Jerusalem and here, shouting that he ought
not to live any longer. [25]But I found that he had done nothing
deserving death; and as he himself appealed to the emperor, I
decided to send him. [26]But I have nothing definite to write to my
lord about him. Therefore I have brought him before you, and, especially before you, King Agrippa, that, after we have examined him,
I may have something to write. [27]For it seems to me unreasonable,
in sending a prisoner, not to indicate the charges against him."

Paul's speech in the presence of Agrippa

26 [1]Agrippa said to Paul, "You have permission to speak for
yourself." Then Paul stretched out his hand and made his
defence:

[2]"I think myself fortunate that it is before you, King Agrippa,
I am to make my defence today against all the accusations of the
Jews, [3]because you are especially familiar with all customs and

---

much that is unchanging, much that has its ultimate foundation in Christ, who is the same yesterday, and today, and for-ever (cf. Heb 13:8)" (Vatican II, *Gaudium et spes*, 10).

"Stir up that fire of faith. Christ is not a figure of the past. He is not a memory that is lost in history.

"He lives! '*Iesus Christus heri et hodie, ipse et in saecula*', says Saint Paul, 'Jesus Christ is the same today as he was yesterday and as he will be for ever'" (St Josemaría Escrivá, *The Way*, 584).

25:21. "Caesar" and "Augustus" were titles of the Roman emperor. At this time the emperor was Nero (54–68).

25:22. Agrippa's reply is reminiscent of a similar scene when his grand-uncle Herod Antipas expressed a desire to see Jesus (cf. Lk 9:9; 23:8). "His conversation with the governor awakens in Agrippa a strong desire to hear Paul. Festus meets his wish, and thereby Paul's glory is further enhanced. This is the outcome of the machinations against him: without them no judge would have deigned to listen to such things, nor would anyone have heard them with such rapt attention" (St John Chrysostom, *Hom. on Acts*, 51).

26:1–30. Paul has already defended himself before Festus, and his words (cf. 25:8ff) make it clear that he is innocent of any offence against Roman law. Now he will speak before Agrippa, in an address aimed mainly at Jews rather than Romans. He bears witness to the Gospel before a king—fulfilling the prophecy of Acts 9:15 and Luke 21:12.

26:2–3. "Observe", comments St John

controversies of the Jews; therefore I beg you to listen to me
patiently.
Acts 22:3 4“My manner of life from my youth, spent from the beginning
among my own nation and at Jerusalem, is known by all the Jews.
Gal 1:14; Phil 3:5 5They have known for a long time, if they are willing to testify,
that according to the strictest party of our religion I have lived as
Acts 23:6 a Pharisee. 6And now I stand here on trial for hope in the promise
Dan 12:1–3; 2 Mac 7 made by God to our fathers, 7to which our twelve tribes hope to
attain, as they earnestly worship night and day. And for this hope
I am accused by Jews, O king! 8Why is it thought incredible by
any of you that God raises the dead?

9“I myself was convinced that I ought to do many things in
opposing the name of Jesus of Nazareth. 10And I did so in
Jn 16:2; Acts 9:13; 22:20 Jerusalem; I not only shut up many of the saints in prison, by
authority from the chief priests, but when they were put to death I
cast my vote against them. 11And I punished them often in all the
synagogues and tried to make them blaspheme; and in raging fury
against them, I persecuted them even to foreign cities.

Chrysostom, “how Paul begins this exposition of his teaching not only about faith in the forgiveness of sin but also about the rules of human conduct. If his conscience had been heavy with any fault he would have been concerned about the idea of being judged by one who was in a position to know all the facts; but it is proper to a clear conscience not only not to reject as judge one who knows the facts but actually to rejoice at being judged by him” (*Hom. on Acts*, 52).

Paul wants to convince Agrippa, whom he regards as well versed in Jewish beliefs, that the Gospel is simply the fulfilment of the Holy Scriptures.

26:5. Paul uses the word “Pharisee” here to indicate his strict observance of the Law prior to becoming a Christian (cf. Phil 3:5).

25:6–8. In his addresses Paul frequently defends himself by referring to the fulfilment of the Old Testament prophecies and promises (cf. 23:6; 24:25; 28:20). In addition to revealing his own attitudes and convictions, he is saying that the fundamental question at issue is whether the Jews really believe in these prophecies or not.

Although he is speaking about resurrection in general terms, Paul’s words obviously refer to the resurrection of Jesus, which legitimates him as the Messiah. “Paul offers two proofs of resurrection. One is taken from the prophets. He does not quote any particular prophet; he simply says that this is what Jews believe. His second proof the apostle takes from the facts themselves. And what is it? That Christ, after rising from the dead, conversed with him” (*Hom. on Acts*, 52).

26:9–18. Paul once more gives an account of the circumstances of his conversion (cf. 9:3–9 and 22:6–11).

26:10. It is possible that Paul was involved in some way in Sanhedrin decisions to persecute the Church; or he may

12“Thus I journeyed to Damascus with the authority and commission of the chief priests. 13At midday, O king, I saw on the way
a light from heaven, brighter than the sun, shining round me and
those who journeyed with me. 14And when we had all fallen to the
ground, I heard a voice saying to me in the Hebrew language,
‘Saul, Saul, why do you persecute me? It hurts you to kick against
the goads.’ 15And I said, ‘Who are you, Lord?’ And the Lord said,
‘I am Jesus whom you are persecuting. 16But rise and stand upon — Ezek 2:1
your feet; for I have appeared to you for this purpose, to appoint
you to serve and bear witness to the things in which you have seen
me and to those in which I will appear to you, 17delivering you
from the people and from the Gentiles—to whom I send you 18to — Jer 1:7
open their eyes, that they may turn from darkness to light and — Is 42:7, 16
from the power of Satan to God, that they may receive forgiveness — Jn 8:12; Acts 9:17–18
of sins and a place among those who are sanctified by faith in — Col 1:12–14
me.’

19“Wherefore, O King Agrippa, I was not disobedient to the
heavenly vision, 20but declared first to those at Damascus, then at — Mt 3:8; Gal 1:16

---

be referring to the part he played in the martyrdom of Stephen (cf. 8:1).

26:14. The final sentence in this verse is not given in Paul’s two previous accounts of his conversion on the road to Damascus (cf. 9:4; 22:7). It is a Greek turn of phrase to describe useless resistance, but it was also known and used by Jews as a proverb (cf. *The Psalms of Solomon*, 16, 4).

26:16–18. Paul’s calling and mission are described in terms similar to that of the calling of the prophets of Israel (cf. Ezek 2:1; Is 42:6f). God makes known his design in an imperious command which radically changes the whole life of his chosen one. He addresses the man’s free will to get him to do what God wills simply because God wills it. But he also enlightens his mind to show him what his vocation means, so that he accept it in the conviction of being the recipient of a special grace to perform an important task.

26:19–23. This section is a summary of Paul’s preaching, presenting Christianity as the fulfilment of the ancient prophecies.

26:19. The apostle asserts that he has not embraced Christianity blindly: he is totally convinced of its truth. He explains his change of heart in terms of docility and obedience to the divine voice he heard. Paul’s experience is repeated in different (usually less dramatic) ways in the lives of every man and woman. At particular moments in life the Lord calls us and invites us to a new conversion which draws us out of sin or lukewarmness. What we have to do is to listen carefully to that calling and obey it. “We should let our Lord get involved in our lives, admitting him trustingly, removing from his way any obstacles or excuses. We tend to be on the defensive, to be attached to our selfishness. We always want to be in charge, even if it’s only to be in charge of our wretchedness. That is why we must go to Jesus, so to have him

Jerusalem and throughout all the country of Judea, and also to the
Gentiles, that they should repent and turn to God and perform
Acts 21:30–31 deeds worthy of their repentance. 21For this reason the Jews seized
me in the temple and tried to kill me. 22To this day I have had the
help that comes from God, and so I stand here testifying both to
small and great, saying nothing but what the prophets and Moses
Acts 13:47; 17:3 1 Cor 15:20–23 Col 1:18 said would come to pass: 23that the Christ must suffer, and that, by
being the first to rise from the dead, he would proclaim light both
to the people and to the Gentiles."

---

make us truly free. Only then will we be able to serve God and all men" (St J. Escrivá, *Christ Is Passing By*, 17).

Response to God's grace is a necessary pre-condition for being helped by God in the future. Accepting one grace is important for equipping us to accept the following one, a process which continues right through our life. "In this true perfection lies," St Gregory of Nyssa writes, "never stopping on the path towards the best and never putting limits on perfection" (*De perfecta christiani forma*).

"The grace of the Holy Spirit," Gregory says elsewhere, "is granted to every man with the idea that he ought to increase what he receives" (*De instituto christiano*). The same idea is expressed by St Teresa of Avila when she writes that "we must seek new strength with which to serve him, and endeavour not to be ungrateful, for that is the condition on which the Lord bestows his jewels. Unless we made good use of his treasures, and of the high estate to which he brings us, he will take those treasures back from us, and we shall be poorer than before, and His Majesty will give the jewels to some other person who can display them to advantage and to his own profit and that of others" (*Life*, 10, 6).

26:23. Paul identifies the Messiah with the suffering Servant of Yahweh (cf. Is 42:1ff; 49:1ff), and asserts that Jesus is the fulfilment of both these prophecies.

26:24. Festus cannot understand what Paul is saying; he thinks his mind is gone. He seems to have a certain sympathy for the apostle, but he cannot make him out. The fact is that divine wisdom does seem to make no sense humanly speaking. "He regarded it as madness for a man in chains not to deal with the calumnies that threatened him but, instead, to be speaking about the convictions which enlightened him from within" (St Bede, *Super Act. expositio*, in loc.).

26:27. Paul's only interest is in upholding the Gospel and bringing salvation to his hearers. He is trying to get Agrippa, who is presiding over this session and is Paul's main questioner, to react interiorly and allow grace to move his heart. "How admirably he behaves! Imprisoned for spreading the teachings of Christ, he misses no opportunity to preach the Gospel. Brought before Festus and Agrippa, he declares unflinchingly: 'To this day I have had the help that comes from God and so I stand here testifying to small and great …' (Acts 26:22).

"The apostle does not silence or hide his faith, or his apostolic preaching that had brought down on him the hatred of his persecutors. He continues preaching salvation to everyone he meets. And, with marvellous daring, he boldly faces Agrippa […]. Where did St Paul get all his strength from? *Omnia possum in eo qui me confortat!* (Phil 4:13). I can do all

Reactions to Paul's speech

24And as he thus made his defence, Festus said with a loud voice, Jn 10:20
"Paul, you are mad; your great learning is turning you mad." 25But
Paul said, "I am not mad, most excellent Festus, but I am speak- Jn 18:37
ing the sober truth. 26For the king knows about these things, and Jn 18:20
to him I speak freely; for I am persuaded that none of these things
has escaped his notice, for this was not done in a corner. 27King
Agrippa, do you believe the prophets? I know that you believe."
28And Agrippa said to Paul, "In a short time you think to make me Acts 11:26
a Christian!" 29And Paul said, "Whether short or long, I would to 1 Pet 4:16
God that not only you but also all who hear me this day might
become such as I am—except for these chains."

---

things in him who strengthens me. I can do all things, because God alone gives me this faith, this hope, this charity" (St Josemaría Escrivá, *Friends of God*, 270f).

Apostolate is a responsibility and a duty with which Christ charges every Christian at all times. "Nothing is more useless than a Christian who is not dedicated to saving his brethren. Do not appeal to your poverty: he whose alms amounted to only two little coins would rise up to accuse you, if you did; and so would Peter, who says, Silver and gold I have none; and Paul, who was so poor that he often went hungry. Do not appeal to your humble circumstances, because they too were humble people, of modest condition. Do not appeal to your lack of knowledge, for they too were unlettered. Are you a slave or a runaway? Onesimus was one also. [...] Are you unwell? So was Timothy" (St John Chrysostom, *Hom. on Acts*, 20).

26:28. The king's remark, which is angry yet serious, shows that Paul's words have touched him. He feels he cannot respond to the apostle's call, but his conscience and his position as a Jewish prince prevent him from denying that he has any faith in the prophecies God has given his people.

However, he resists the divine grace extended to him by what Paul has been saying and now by Paul's question. He lacks the inner dispositions which faith calls for—that is, the moral predisposition and attitude which allows someone to accept God's word and decide to give his life a new direction. He is not genuinely interested in seeking God. "If any man's will is to do his will, he shall know whether the teaching is from God or whether I am speaking on my own authority" (Jn 7:17).

26:29. Once again Paul shows his practical zeal for all souls; he is not overawed by the circumstances in which he finds himself.

"Charity with everyone means ... apostolate with everyone. It means we, for our part, must really translate into deeds the great desire of God 'who desires all men to be saved and to come to the knowledge of the truth' (1 Tim 2:4). [...] For Christians, loving means 'wanting to want', 'wanting to love', making up one's mind in Christ to work for the good of souls, without discrimination of any kind; trying to obtain for them, before any other good, the greatest good of all, that of knowing Christ and falling in love with him" (*Friends of God*, 230f).

30Then the king rose, and the governor and Bernice and those
who were sitting with them; 31and when they had withdrawn, they
said to one another, "This man is doing nothing to deserve death
or imprisonment." 32And Agrippa said to Festus, "This man could
have been set free if he had not appealed to Caesar."

Departure for Rome. Voyage to Crete

27 1And when it was decided that we should sail for Italy,
they delivered Paul and some other prisoners to a centu-
Acts 19:29 rion of the Augustan Cohort, named Julius. 2And embarking in a
ship of Adramyttium, which was about to sail to the ports along
the coast of Asia, we put to sea, accompanied by Aristarchus, a
Acts 24:23; 28:16 Macedonian from Thessalonica. 3The next day we put in at Sidon;
and Julius treated Paul kindly, and gave him leave to go to his
friends and be cared for. 4And putting to sea from there we sailed
under the lee of Cyprus, because the winds were against us. 5And
when we had sailed across the sea which is off Cilicia and
Pamphylia, we came to Myra in Lycia. 6There the centurion found
a ship of Alexandria sailing for Italy, and put us on board. 7We
sailed slowly for a number of days, and arrived with difficulty off
Cnidus, and as the wind did not allow us to go on, we sailed under
the lee of Crete off Salmone. 8Coasting along it with difficulty, we

---

26:32. To declare Paul innocent and set him free in spite of his appeal to Rome would have caused offence both to the emperor and to the Jews.

27:1—28:15. This account of St Paul's sea journey is so exact in its terminology that it is regarded as an important source of information on seafaring in ancient times. It gives a great deal of detail and describes things so vividly that it obviously is what it is—an account of an eyewitness, St Luke, who may even have made notes during the journey.

The narrative also shows how St Paul maintains supernatural outlook despite new difficulties; and how he keeps up his apostolic work and entrusts himself entirely to God's loving providence.

27:2. Prisoners were not sent on a special ship; instead, places were negotiated for them on merchant ships. The centurion finds places for these prisoners on a ship which has to call into various ports on the coast of Asia Minor, in the hope of eventually finding a ship bound for Italy.

27:3. The centurion Julius sees the Christians of Sidon as "friends" of Paul. St Luke uses the word "friend" here, but it was not the normal thing for Christians to call each other "friend"; however, they are friends of God—"you are my friends" (Jn 15:14)—and from this friendship is born the loving friendship which binds them together. So it is quite understandable that pagans should see Christians as good friends of one another.

27:6. The ship of Alexandria on which they embark must have been a grain ship, one of many used to transport grain from Egypt to Rome. These broad, heavy

came to a place called Fair Havens, near which was the city of
Lasaea.

The voyage is resumed against Paul's advice

9As much time had been lost, and the voyage was already dangerous Lev 16:29–31
because the fast had already gone by, Paul advised them, 10saying,
"Sirs, I perceive that the voyage will be with injury and much loss,
not only of the cargo and the ship, but also of our lives." 11But the
centurion paid more attention to the captain and to the owner of the
ship than to what Paul said. 12And because the harbour was not suitable to winter in, the majority advised to put to sea from there, on
the chance that somehow they could reach Phoenix, a harbour of
Crete, looking northeast and southeast,[a] and winter there.

A storm

13And when the south wind blew gently, supposing that they had
obtained their purpose, they weighed anchor and sailed along
Crete, close inshore. 14But soon a tempestuous wind, called the
northeaster, struck down from the land; 15and when the ship was
caught and could not face the wind, we gave way to it and were
driven. 16And running under the lee of a small island called
Cauda,[b] we managed with difficulty to secure the boat; 17after

---

boats had one mast amidship and another forward; the hull was covered by a deck which had openings or movable timbers which gave access to the hold, where the cargo was stored and where passengers took shelter in bad weather.

27:9. By the time they reach Fair Havens Paul and his companions have been travelling for almost forty days. At that time travel on the high seas was considered unsafe from the middle of September onwards, and out of the question from early November until March. The fast was that prescribed for all Jews on the Day of Atonement (cf. Lev 16:29–31). In the year 60 it fell at the end of October.

27:10–13. Prior to this, Paul had suffered shipwreck three times (cf. 2 Cor 11:25), and he knew very well how risky the voyage would be, but most of the people on board were hoping to reach Sicily or at least some port more suitable for wintering in. As soon as they got a suitable wind they weighed anchor and went along the coast in an easterly direction, using a skiff (which doubled as a sort of lifeboat) to take the ship out of harbour.

St John Chrysostom draws this lesson from the passage: "Let us stay firm in the faith, which is the safe port. Let us listen to it rather than to the pilot we have within, that is, our reason. Let us pay attention to Paul rather than to the pilot or the captain. If we do listen to experience we will not be injured or disdained" (*Hom. on Acts*, 53).

27:17–18. They managed to haul up the skiff, but due to the dark they were afraid of going on to the dangerous Syrtis sand-

a. Or *southwest and northwest* **b.** Other ancient authorities read *Clauda*

hoisting it up, they took measures[c] to undergird the ship; then,
fearing that they should run on the Syrtis, they lowered the gear,
and so were driven. 18As we were violently storm-tossed, they
began next day to throw the cargo overboard; 19and the third day
Jon 1:5 they cast out with their own hands the tackle of the ship. 20And
when neither sun nor stars appeared for many a day, and no small
tempest lay on us, all hope of our being saved was at last abandoned.

Paul's vision. He rallies his companions

Acts 27:33 21As they had been long without food, Paul then came forward
among them and said, "Men, you should have listened to me, and
should not have set sail from Crete and incurred this injury and
loss. 22I now bid you to take heart; for there will be no loss of life
among you, but only of the ship. 23For this very night there stood
by me an angel of the God to whom I belong and whom I wor-
Acts 23:11 ship, 24and he said, 'Do not be afraid, Paul; you must stand before
Caesar; and lo, God has granted you all those who sail with you.'
25So take heart, men, for I have faith in God that it will be exactly
as I have been told. 26But we shall have to run on some island."

27When the fourteenth night had come, as we were drifting
across the sea of Adria, about midnight the sailors suspected that
they were nearing land. 28So they sounded and found twenty fath-

---

banks off the coast of Africa. To prevent this they put out a sea anchor to brake the progress of the ship. They also go to drastic lengths to lighten the vessel.

27:19–20. These perils at sea remind us of the difficulties a person can come up against in the course of his life as he makes his way towards eternity. If we are in danger of being shipwrecked, of losing supernatural life, we need to throw out everything which is in the way, even things which up to then were necessary, such as the tackle and the cargo, in order to save our life.

In moments of disorientation and darkness, which the Lord permits souls to experience, when we cannot see the stars to work out which way to go, we need to use the resources God gives us for solving problems: "Christ has given his Church sureness in doctrine and a flow of grace in the sacraments. He has arranged things so that there will always be people to guide and lead us, to remind us constantly of our way" (St Josemaría Escrivá, *Christ Is Passing By*, 34). In particular, we have Mary, the Star of the Sea and the Morning Star, who has protected and will continue to protect and guide seafarers to their destination.

27:24. Paul prays to God for his own safety and that of his companions, and is made to understand that this prayer will definitely be granted. St John Chrysostom is very conscious of how apostolic Paul would have been in these circumstances

c. Greek *helps*

oms; a little farther on they sounded again and found fifteen fath-
oms. 29And fearing that we might run on the rocks, they let out
four anchors from the stern, and prayed for day to come. 30And as
the sailors were seeking to escape from the ship, and had lowered
the boat into the sea, under pretence of laying out anchors from
the bow, 31Paul said to the centurion and the soldiers, "Unless
these men stay in the ship, you cannot be saved." 32Then the soldiers cut away the ropes of the boat, and let it go.

33As day was about to dawn, Paul urged them all to take some
food, saying, "Today is the fourteenth day that you have continued in suspense and without food, having taken nothing.
34Therefore I urge you to take some food; it will give you strength, Mt 10:30
since not a hair is to perish from the head of any of you." 35And
when he had said this, he took bread, and giving thanks to God in Rom 14:5
the presence of all he broke it and began to eat. 36Then they all 1 Tim 4:4
were encouraged and ate some food themselves. 37(We were in all
two hundred and seventy-six[d] persons in the ship.) 38And when
they had eaten enough, they lightened the ship, throwing out the
wheat into the sea.

Shipwreck and rescue

39Now when it was day, they did not recognize the land, but they
noticed a bay with a beach, on which they planned if possible to

---

and, referring to his predictions about the fate of the ship, he says that "the apostle does not make them out of boasting; he wants to bring the seafarers to the faith and make them more receptive to what he has to teach" (*Hom. on Acts*, 53).

27:30–32. The sailors were trying to escape, but their skill was needed if everyone was to be saved. By letting the boat go, the centurion sees to it that all will contribute to ensuring that everyone on board reaches safety. This solidarity produces the desired result. In this we can see a symbol of what should happen in the ship of the Church: no one should leave the ship in an effort just to save himself, abandoning the others to their fate.

27:33. St John Chrysostom explains that "this long fast was not a miracle; it was that fear and danger took away their appetite completely. The miracle was that they escaped from the shipwreck. Despite all the misfortunes of the voyage, it gave Paul the chance to instruct the soldiers and crew, and how happy he would have been if all had embraced the faith" (*Hom. on Acts*, 53).

St Paul inspires the other seafarers with his own confidence; his serenity and initiative are in contrast with the despair felt by the others, who have no supernatural outlook of any kind.

27:35. This food which they eat is ordinary food, not the Eucharist or Christian *agape*; before the meal he gives thanks in

d. Other ancient authorities read *seventy-six* or *about seventy-six*

bring the ship ashore. 40So they cast off the anchors and left them
in the sea, at the same time loosening the ropes that tied the rud-
ders; then hoisting the foresail to the wind they made for the
beach. 41But striking a shoal[e] they ran the vessel aground; the bow
struck and remained immovable, and the stern was broken up by
the surf. 42The soldiers' plan was to kill the prisoners, lest any
should swim away and escape; 43but the centurion, wishing to
save Paul, kept them from carrying out their purpose. He ordered
those who could swim to throw themselves overboard first and
make for the land, 44and the rest on planks or on pieces of the
ship. And so it was that all escaped to land.

Waiting in Malta

28 1After we had escaped, we then learned that the island was
called Malta. 2And the natives showed us unusual kindness,
for they kindled a fire and welcomed us all, because it had begun
to rain and was cold. 3Paul had gathered a bundle of sticks and put
them on the fire, when a viper came out because of the heat and
fastened on his hand. 4When the natives saw the creature hanging
from his hand, they said to one another, "No doubt this man is a

---

accordance with Jewish custom. Commenting on this, St Bede draws a lesson about our need of the bread of life to save us from the danger of this world: "Paul encourages those whom he has promised will come safe out of the shipwreck, to take some food. If four anchors had kept them afloat during the night, when the sun came up they were going to reach *terra firma*. But only he who eats the bread of life can avoid the storms of this world" (*Super Act. expositio*, ad loc.).

27:41. The present-day "St Paul's Bay" on the island of Malta exactly fits the description St Luke gives here. The sailors tried to steer the ship into the small inlet, but it ran aground on a sandbank before they could get there. Although they were within striking distance of the beach, the sea was so rough that it broke up the ship, whose prow was trapped. "This is what happens to souls given to this world who do not strive to despise worldly things: the prow of their intentions is completely locked into the earth and the force of the waves completely demolishes all the work they have accomplished" (St Bede, *Super Act. expositio*, ad loc.).

"Why did God not save the boat from shipwreck? So that the travellers would realize the scale of the danger and that they were saved from it not by any human help but by God, who saved their lives after the boat broke up. In like manner the just are well off even in storms and tempests, on the high seas or in a rough bay, because they are protected from everything and even come to the rescue of others.

"Aboard a ship in danger of being engulfed by the waves, the enchained prisoners and the whole crew owe their

e. Greek *place of two seas*

murderer. Though he has escaped from the sea, justice has not
allowed him to live." 5He, however, shook off the creature into the Mk 16:18
fire and suffered no harm. 6They waited, expecting him to swell Lk 10:19
up or suddenly fall down dead; but when they had waited a long Acts 14:11
time and saw no misfortune come to him, they changed their
minds and said that he was a god.

7Now in the neighbourhood of that place were lands belonging
to the chief man of the island, named Publius, who received us
and entertained us hospitably for three days. 8It happened that the
father of Publius lay sick with fever and dysentery; and Paul vis- Lk 4:38–40;
ited him and prayed, and putting his hands on him healed him. 10:9
9And when this had taken place, the rest of the people on the
island who had diseases also came and were cured. 10They presented many gifts to us;[f] and when we sailed, they put on board
whatever we needed.

Arrival in Rome

11After three months we set sail in a ship which had wintered in
the island, a ship of Alexandria, with the Twin Brothers as figure-
heads. 12Putting in at Syracuse, we stayed there for three days.

---

safety to the presence of Paul. See how useful it is to live in the company of a devout and saintly person. Frequent and terrible storms buffet our souls. God can free us from them if we are as sensible as those sailors and pay attention to the saints' advice. [...] Not only were they saved from shipwreck but they embraced the faith.

"Let us believe St Paul. Even if we be in the midst of storms we shall be set free from dangers; even if we be fasting for forty days, we shall stay alive; even if we fall into darkness and obscurity, if we believe in him we shall be freed" (St John Chrysostom, *Hom. on Acts*, 53).

28:2. "Natives": literally "barbarians". The Maltese were Phoenicians by race and did not speak Greek—which is why Luke describes them in this way.

28:4. "Justice", here, is a proper name. The notion of justice was personified in a goddess of vengeance or vindictive justice.

28:5. This is a fulfilment of a promise made by our Lord: "These signs will accompany those who believe: in my name they will cast out demons; they will speak in new tongues; they will pick up serpents, and if they drink any deadly thing, it will not hurt them" (Mk 16:17–18).

28:12–14. Syracuse was then the main city of Sicily. From there they went along the eastern coast of the island and crossed the straits of Messina to reach Rhegium, where they stopped for a day. Finally, they disembarked at Pozzuoli, which was the principal port in the gulf of Naples. There Paul found a Christian community and stayed with them for a week, and they

f. Or *honoured us with many honours*

13 And from there we made a circuit and arrived at Rhegium; and
after one day a south wind sprang up, and on the second day we
came to Puteoli. 14 There we found brethren, and were invited to
stay with them for seven days. And so we came to Rome. 15 And
the brethren there, when they heard of us, came as far as the
Forum of Appius and Three Taverns to meet us. On seeing them
Paul thanked God and took courage. 16 And when we came into
Rome, Paul was allowed to stay by himself, with the soldier that
guarded him.

Paul and the Roman Jews

17 After three days he called together the local leaders of the Jews;
and when they had gathered, he said to them, "Brethren, though I
had done nothing against the people or the customs of our fathers,
yet I was delivered prisoner from Jerusalem into the hands of the
Acts 23:29 Romans. 18 When they had examined me, they wished to set me at
liberty, because there was no reason for the death penalty in my
Acts 25:11; 26:32 case. 19 But when the Jews objected, I was compelled to appeal to
Caesar—though I had no charge to bring against my nation. 20 For

---

would have sent word on to the Christians at Rome to tell them that Paul would soon be with them.

28:14. The text conveys the atmosphere of human and supernatural brotherhood that existed among the Christians. Paul would have been extremely happy to be received so affectionately by the brethren. Now at least he would have a chance to rest after his long journey.

"How well the early Christians practised this ardent charity which went beyond the limits of mere human solidarity or natural kindness. They love one another, through the heart of Christ, with a love both tender and strong. [...] The principal apostolate we Christians must carry out in the world, and the best witness we can give of our faith, is to help bring about a climate of genuine charity within the Church. For who indeed could feel attracted to the Gospel if those who say they preach the Good News do not really love one another, but spend their time attacking one another, spreading slander and rancour" (St Josemaría Escrivá, *Friends of God*, 225f).

28:15. The Forum of Appius and Three Taverns were 69 kilometres (about 40 miles) and 53 kilometres from Rome, respectively, on the Via Appia, which ran south from Rome to the port of Puteoli (modern Pozzuoli). We do not know anything about the Christian community in Rome at this time or how it came to be founded. The tradition is that it was founded by St Peter, which does not necessarily mean that no other Christians arrived there before him, or that there had not been conversions there of pagans or of Jewish residents. In fact, St Augustine (cf. *Letters*, 102, 8) quotes the philosopher Porphyry as saying that there were Jews in Rome shortly after the reign of Caligula (AD March 37 to January 41).

28:16. Paul must have arrived in Rome around the year 61. He was allowed to

this reason therefore I have asked to see you and speak with you,
since it is because of the hope of Israel that I am bound with this
chain." 21And they said to him, "We have received no letters from
Judea about you, and none of the brethren coming here has
reported or spoken any evil about you. 22But we desire to hear Acts 17:19
from you what your views are; for with regard to this sect we
know that everywhere it is spoken against."

23When they had appointed a day for him, they came to him at Acts 13:15–41
his lodging in great numbers. And he expounded the matter to
them from morning till evening, testifying to the kingdom of God
and trying to convince them about Jesus both from the law of
Moses and from the prophets. 24And some were convinced by Acts 13:46–47
what he said, while others disbelieved. 25So, as they disagreed
among themselves, they departed, after Paul had made one statement: "The Holy Spirit was right in saying to your fathers through
Isaiah the prophet:

26'Go to this people, and say, Is 6:9–10
You shall indeed hear but never understand, Mt 13:14
and you shall indeed see but never perceive.

---

stay in a private house; in other words, he was under *custodia militaris*, which meant that the only restriction was that he was guarded by a soldier at all times. This is the last verse where St Luke uses the first person plural.

28:17. In keeping with his missionary custom, Paul immediately addresses the Jews of Rome; in fact there is no further mention of his contact with the Christians in the city. The apostle wants to give his fellow Jews a kind of last opportunity to hear and understand the Gospel. He presents himself as a member of the Jewish community who wants to take a normal part in the life of that community and feels he has to explain his own position.

28:19. The use of Roman privileges by a Jew might have been regarded by Jews as a sign of disrespect towards their own beliefs and customs. Therefore, Paul tries to explain why he took the exceptional step of invoking his Roman citizenship and appealing to Caesar.

28:23. Paul speaks now not about his own salvation but about the Gospel, and, as he usually did in synagogues, he proclaims to his Jewish listeners that Jesus is the Messiah foretold by the prophets and promised to the people of Israel.

28:25–28. Since now, in Rome also, many Jews have rejected the Gospel, Paul announces that he is free of his self-imposed obligation to proclaim the Gospel first to the Jews. His words suggest that it is the Christians who have understood the meaning of the promises made by God to the chosen people, and that it is they who are really the true Israel. Christ's disciples have not abandoned the Law. It is, rather, the Jews who have renounced their position as the chosen people. "We are the true, spiritual people of Israel," St Justin writes, "the race of Judah, and of Jacob, and of Isaac and of

Jn 12:39
2 Cor 3:14

[27]For this people's heart has grown dull,
and their ears are heavy of hearing,
and their eyes they have closed;
lest they should perceive with their eyes,
and hear with their ears,
and understand with their heart,
and turn for me to heal them.'
[28]Let it be known to you then that this salvation of God has been
sent to the Gentiles; they will listen."[g]

Paul's ministry in Rome

[30]And he lived there two whole years at his own expense,[h] and
welcomed all who came to him, [31]preaching the kingdom of God
and teaching about the Lord Jesus Christ quite openly and unhin-
dered.

Phil 1:14
2 Tim 2:9

Abraham, he who was testified to by God even while he was still uncircumcised, he who was blessed and named the father of many nations" (*Dialogue with Tryphon*, 11, 5).

28:30–31. "Not only was he not forbidden to preach in Rome", St Bede writes, "but despite the enormous power of Nero and all his crimes which history reports, he remained free to proclaim the Gospel of Christ to the furthest parts of the West, as he himself writes to the Romans: 'At present, however, I am going to Jerusalem with aid for the saints' (Rom 15:25); and a little later: 'When therefore I have completed this, and have delivered to them what has been raised, I shall go on by way of you to Spain' (v. 28). Finally he was crowned with martyrdom in the last years of Nero" (*Super Act. expositio*, ad loc.).

We do not know exactly what happened at the end of the two years. It may be that Paul's Jewish accusers did not appear, or they may have argued their case before the imperial tribunal and Paul was found not guilty. At any event, he was set free and Luke considers his task done—the work God gave him to do when he inspired him to write his book.

"If you ask me", St John Chrysostom observes, "why St Luke, who stayed with the apostle up to his martyrdom, did not bring his narrative up to that point, I will reply that the Book of the Acts, in the form that has come down to us, perfectly fulfils its author's purpose. For the evangelists' only aim was to write down the most essential things" (*Hom. on Acts*, 1).

The kind of conventional way the book concludes has led many commentators (from early times up to the present day) to think that it had already been finished before the end of Paul's first imprisonment in Rome. Christian tradition has nothing very concrete to say about exactly when the Acts of the Apostles was written.

g. Other ancient authorities add verse 29, *And when he had said these words, the Jews departed, holding much dispute among themselves* **h.** Or *in his own hired dwelling*

New Vulgate Text

EVANGELIUM SECUNDUM MATTHAEUM

[1] 1 Liber generationis Iesu Christi filii David filii Abraham. 2 Abraham genuit Isaac, Isaac autem genuit Iacob, Iacob autem genuit Iudam et fratres eius, 3 Iudas autem genuit Phares et Zara de Thamar, Phares autem genuit Esrom, Esrom autem genuit Aram, 4 Aram autem genuit Aminadab, Aminadab autem genuit Naasson, Naasson autem genuit Salmon, 5 Salmon autem genuit Booz de Rahab, Booz autem genuit Obed ex Ruth, Obed autem genuit Iesse, 6 Iesse autem genuit David regem. David autem genuit Salomonem ex ea, quae fuit Uriae, 7 Salomon autem genuit Roboam, Roboam autem genuit Abiam, Abia autem genuit Asa, 8 Asa autem genuit Iosaphat, Iosaphat autem genuit Ioram, Ioram autem genuit Oziam, 9 Ozias autem genuit Ioatham, Ioatham autem genuit Achaz, Achaz autem genuit Ezechiam, 10 Ezechias autem genuit Manassen, Manasses autem genuit Amon, Amon autem genuit Iosiam, 11 Iosias autem genuit Iechoniam et fratres eius in transmigratione Babylonis. 12 Et post transmigrationem Babylonis Iechonias genuit Salathiel, Salathiel autem genuit Zorobabel, 13 Zorobabel autem genuit Abiud, Abiud autem genuit Eliachim, Eliachim autem genuit Azor, 14 Azor autem genuit Sadoc, Sadoc autem genuit Achim, Achim autem genuit Eliud, 15 Eliud autem genuit Eleazar, Eleazar autem genuit Matthan, Matthan autem genuit Iacob, 16 Iacob autem genuit Ioseph virum Mariae, de qua natus est Iesus, qui vocatur Christus. 17 Omnes ergo generationes ab Abraham usque ad David generationes quattuordecim; et a David usque ad transmigrationem Babylonis generationes quattuordecim; et a transmigratione Babylonis usque ad Christum generationes quattuordecim. 18 Iesu Christi autem generatio sic erat. Cum esset desponsata mater eius Maria Ioseph, antequam convenirent inventa est in utero habens de Spiritu Sancto. 19 Ioseph autem vir eius, cum esset iustus et nollet eam traducere, voluit occulte dimittere eam. 20 Haec autem eo cogitante, ecce angelus Domini in somnis apparuit ei dicens: «Ioseph fili David, noli timere accipere Mariam coniugem tuam. Quod enim in ea natum est, de Spiritu Sancto est; 21 pariet autem filium, et vocabis nomen eius Iesum: ipse enim salvum faciet populum suum a peccatis eorum». 22 Hoc autem totum factum est, ut adimpleretur id, quod dictum est a Domino per prophetam dicentem: 23 «*Ecce, virgo in utero habebit et pariet filium, et vocabunt nomen eius Emmanuel*», quod est interpretatum *Nobiscum Deus*. 24 Exsurgens autem Ioseph a somno fecit, sicut praecepit ei angelus Domini, et accepit coniugem suam; 25 et non cognoscebat eam, donec peperit filium, et vocavit nomen eius Iesum. **[2]** 1 Cum autem natus esset Iesus in Bethlehem Iudaeae in diebus Herodis regis, ecce Magi ab oriente venerunt Hierosolymam, 2 dicentes: «Ubi est, qui natus est, rex Iudaeorum? Vidimus enim stellam eius in oriente et venimus adorare eum». 3 Audiens autem Herodes rex turbatus est et omnis Hierosolyma cum illo; 4 et congregans omnes principes sacerdotum et scribas populi, sciscitabatur ab eis ubi Christus nasceretur. 5 At illi dixerunt ei: «In Bethlehem Iudaeae. Sic enim scriptum est per prophetam: 6 "*Et tu, Bethlehem* terra Iudae, / nequaquam *minima es in principibus Iudae*; / *ex te enim exiet dux, / qui reget populum meum Israel*"». 7 Tunc Herodes, clam vocatis Magis, diligenter didicit ab eis tempus stellae, quae apparuit eis, 8 et mittens illos in Bethlehem dixit: «Ite et interrogate diligenter de puero; et cum inveneritis renuntiate mihi, ut et ego veniens adorem eum». 9 Qui cum audissent regem, abierunt. Et ecce stella, quam viderant in oriente, antecedebat eos, usque dum veniens staret supra, ubi erat puer. 10 Videntes autem stellam gavisi sunt gaudio magno valde. 11 Et intrantes domum viderunt puerum cum Maria matre eius, et procidentes adoraverunt eum; et apertis thesauris suis, obtulerunt ei munera, aurum et tus et myrrham. 12 Et responso accepto in somnis, ne redirent ad Herodem, per aliam viam reversi sunt in regionem suam. 13 Qui cum recessissent, ecce angelus Domini apparet in somnis Ioseph dicens: «Surge et accipe puerum et matrem eius et fuge in Aegyptum et esto ibi, usque dum dicam tibi; futurum est enim ut Herodes quaerat puerum ad perdendum eum». 14 Qui consurgens accepit puerum et matrem eius nocte et recessit in Aegyptum 15 et erat ibi usque ad obitum Herodis, ut adimpleretur, quod dictum est a Domino per prophetam dicentem: «*Ex Aegypto vocavi filium meum*». 16 Tunc Herodes videns quoniam illusus esset a Magis, iratus est valde et mittens occidit omnes pueros, qui erant in Bethlehem et in omnibus finibus eius, a bimatu et infra, secundum tempus, quod exquisierat a Magis. [17]Tunc adimpletum est, quod dictum est per Ieremiam prophetam dicentem: [18]«*Vox in Rama audita est, / ploratus et ululatus multus: / Rachel plorans filios suos, / et noluit consolari, quia non sunt*». [19]Defuncto autem Herode, ecce apparet angelus Domini in somnis Ioseph in Aegypto [20]dicens: «Surge et accipe puerum et matrem eius et vade in terram Israel; defuncti sunt enim, qui quaerebant animam pueri». [21]Qui surgens accepit puerum et matrem eius et venit in terram Israel. [22]Audiens autem quia Archelaus regnaret in Iudaea pro Herode patre suo, timuit illuc ire; et admonitus in somnis, secessit in partes Galilaeae [23]et veniens habitavit in civitate, quae vocatur Nazareth, ut adimpleretur, quod dictum est per Prophetas: «Nazaraeus vocabitur». **[3]** [1]In diebus autem illis venit Ioannes Baptista praedicans in deserto Iudaeae [2]et dicens: «Paenitentiam agite; appropinquavit enim regnum caelorum». [3]Hic est enim, qui dictus est per Isaiam prophetam dicentem: «*Vox clamantis in deserto: / "Parate viam Domini, / rectas facite semitas eius!*"». [4]Ipse autem Ioannes habebat vestimentum de pilis cameli et zonam pelliceam circa lumbos suos; esca autem eius erat locustae et mel silvestre. [5]Tunc exibat ad eum Hierosolyma et omnis Iudaea et omnis regio circa Iordanem, [6]et baptizabantur in Iordane flumine ab eo, confitentes peccata sua. [7]Videns autem multos pharisaeorum et sadducaeorum venientes ad baptismum suum, dixit eis: «Progenies viperarum, quis demonstravit vobis fugere a futura ira? [8]Facite ergo fructum dignum paenitentiae [9]et ne velitis dicere intra vos: "Patrem habemus Abraham"; dico enim vobis quoniam potest Deus de lapidibus istis suscitare Abrahae filios. [10]Iam enim securis ad radicem arborum posita est; omnis ergo arbor, quae non facit fructum bonum, exciditur et in ignem mittitur. [11]Ego quidem vos baptizo in aqua in paenitentiam; qui autem post me venturus est, fortior me est, cuius non sum dignus calceamenta portare; ipse vos baptizabit in Spiritu Sancto et igni, [12]cuius ventilabrum in manu sua, et permundabit aream suam et congregabit triticum suum in horreum, paleas autem comburet igni inexstinguibili». [13]Tunc venit Iesus a Galilaea in Iordanem ad Ioannem, ut baptizaretur ab eo. [14]Ioannes autem prohibebat eum dicens: «Ego a te debeo baptizari, et tu venis ad me?». [15]Respondens autem Iesus dixit ei: «Sine modo, sic enim decet nos implere omnem iustitiam». Tunc dimittit eum. [16]Baptizatus autem Iesus, confestim ascendit de aqua; et ecce aperti sunt ei caeli, et vidit Spiritum Dei descendentem sicut columbam et venientem super se. [17]Et ecce vox de caelis dicens: «Hic est Filius meus dilectus, in quo mihi complacui». **[4]** [1]Tunc Iesus ductus est in desertum a Spiritu, ut tentaretur a Diabolo. [2]Et cum ieiunasset quadraginta diebus et quadraginta noctibus, postea esuriit. [3]Et accedens tentator dixit ei: «Si Filius Dei es, dic, ut lapides isti panes fiant». [4]Qui respondens dixit: «Scriptum est: / "*Non in pane solo vivet homo, / sed in omni verbo, quod procedit de ore Dei*"». [5]Tunc assumit eum Diabolus in sanctam civitatem et statuit eum supra pinnaculum templi [6]et dicit ei: «Si Filius Dei es, mitte te deorsum. Scriptum est enim: "*Angelis suis mandabit de te, / et in manibus tollent te, / ne forte offendas ad lapidem pedem tuum*"». [7]Ait illi Iesus: «Rursum scriptum est: "*Non tentabis Dominum Deum tuum*"». [8]Iterum assumit eum Diabolus in montem excelsum valde et ostendit ei omnia regna mundi et gloriam eorum [9]et dicit illi: «Haec tibi omnia dabo, si cadens adoraveris me». [10]Tunc dicit ei Iesus: «Vade, Satanas! Scriptum est enim: / "*Dominum Deum tuum adorabis / et illi soli servies*"». [11]Tunc reliquit eum Diabolus, et ecce angeli accesserunt et ministrabant ei. [12]Cum autem audisset quod Ioannes traditus esset, secessit in Galilaeam. [13]Et relicta Nazareth, venit et habitavit in Capharnaum maritimam [14]in finibus Zabulon et Nephthali, ut impleretur, quod dictum est per Isaiam prophetam dicentem: [15]«*Terra Zabulon et terra Nephthali, / ad viam maris, trans Iordanem, / Galilaea gentium*; / [16]*populus, qui sedebat in tenebris, / lucem vidit magnam, / et sedentibus in regione et umbra mortis / lux orta est eis*». [17]Exinde coepit Iesus praedicare et dicere: «Paenitentiam agite; appropinquavit enim regnum caelorum». [18]Ambulans autem iuxta mare Galilaeae, vidit duos fratres, Simonem, qui vocatur Petrus, et Andream fratrem eius, mittentes rete in mare; erant enim piscatores. [19]Et ait illis: «Venite post me, et faciam vos piscatores hominum». [20]At illi continuo, relictis retibus, secuti sunt eum. [21]Et procedens inde vidit alios duos fratres, Iacobum Zebedaei et Ioannem fratrem eius, in navi cum Zebedaeo patre eorum reficientes retia sua, et vocavit eos. [22]Illi autem statim, relicta navi et patre suo, secuti sunt eum. [23]Et circumibat Iesus totam Galilaeam, docens in synagogis eorum et praedicans evangelium regni et sanans omnem languorem et omnem infirmitatem in populo. [24]Et abiit opinio eius in totam Syriam; et obtulerunt ei omnes male habentes, variis languoribus et tormentis comprehensos, et qui daemonia habebant, et lunaticos et paralyticos, et curavit eos. [25]Et secutae sunt eum turbae multae de Galilaea et Decapoli et Hierosolymis et Iudaea et de trans Iordanem. **[5]** [1]Videns autem turbas, ascendit in montem; et cum sedisset, accesserunt ad eum discipuli eius; [2]et aperiens os suum docebat eos dicens: [3]«Beati pauperes spiritu, quoniam ipsorum est regnum caelorum. [4]Beati, qui lugent, quoniam ipsi consolabuntur. [5]Beati mites, quoniam ipsi possidebunt terram. [6]Beati, qui esuriunt et sitiunt iustitiam, quoniam ipsi saturabuntur. [7]Beati misericordes, quia ipsi

misericordiam consequentur. [8]Beati mundo corde, quoniam ipsi Deum videbunt. [9]Beati pacifici,
quoniam filii Dei vocabuntur. [10]Beati, qui persecutionem patiuntur propter iustitiam, quoniam ipsorum
est regnum caelorum. [11]Beati estis cum maledixerint vobis et persecuti vos fuerint et dixerint omne
malum adversum vos, mentientes, propter me. [12]Gaudete et exsultate, quoniam merces vestra copiosa
est in caelis; sic enim persecuti sunt prophetas, qui fuerunt ante vos. [13]Vos estis sal terrae; quod si sal
evanuerit, in quo salietur? Ad nihilum valet ultra, nisi ut mittatur foras et conculcetur ab hominibus.
[14]Vos estis lux mundi. Non potest civitas abscondi supra montem posita; [15]neque accendunt lucernam
et ponunt eam sub modio, sed super candelabrum, ut luceat omnibus, qui in domo sunt. [16]Sic luceat lux
vestra coram hominibus, ut videant vestra bona opera et glorificent Patrem vestrum, qui in caelis est.
[17]Nolite putare quoniam veni solvere Legem aut Prophetas; non veni solvere, sed adimplere. [18]Amen
quippe dico vobis: Donec transeat caelum et terra, iota unum aut unus apex non praeteribit a Lege,
donec omnia fiant. [19]Qui ergo solverit unum de mandatis istis minimis et docuerit sic homines, minimus
vocabitur in regno caelorum; qui autem fecerit et docuerit, hic magnus vocabitur in regno caelorum.
[20]Dico enim vobis: Nisi abundaverit iustitia vestra plus quam scribarum et pharisaeorum, non intrabitis
in regnum caelorum. [21]Audistis quia dictum est antiquis: "*Non occides*; qui autem occiderit, reus erit
iudicio". [22]Ego autem dico vobis: Omnis, qui irascitur fratri suo, reus erit iudicio; qui autem dixerit fratri
suo: "Racha", reus erit concilio; qui autem dixerit: "Fatue", reus erit gehennae ignis. [23]Si ergo offeres
munus tuum ad altare, et ibi recordatus fueris quia frater tuus habet aliquid adversum te, [24]relinque ibi
munus tuum ante altare et vade prius, reconciliare fratri tuo et tunc veniens offer munus tuum. [25]Esto
consentiens adversario tuo cito, dum es in via cum eo, ne forte tradat te adversarius iudici, et iudex
tradat te ministro, et in carcerem mittaris. [26]Amen dico tibi: Non exies inde, donec reddas novissimum
quadrantem. [27]Audistis quia dictum est: "*Non moechaberis*". [28]Ego autem dico vobis: Omnis, qui viderit
mulierem ad concupiscendum eam, iam moechatus est eam in corde suo. [29]Quod si oculus tuus dexter
scandalizat te, erue eum et proice abs te; expedit enim tibi, ut pereat unum membrorum tuorum, quam
totum corpus tuum mittatur in gehennam. [30]Et si dextera manus tua scandalizat te, abscide eam et proice
abs te; expedit enim tibi, ut pereat unum membrorum tuorum, quam totum corpus tuum abeat in
gehennam. [31]Dictum est autem: "*Quicumque dimiserit uxorem suam, det illi libellum repudii*". [32]Ego
autem dico vobis: Omnis, qui dimiserit uxorem suam, excepta fornicationis causa, facit eam moechari;
et, qui dimissam duxerit, adulterat. [33]Iterum audistis quia dictum est antiquis: "*Non periurabis*; *reddes*
autem *Domino iuramenta tua*". [34]Ego autem dico vobis: Non iurare omnino, neque per *caelum*, quia
thronus Dei est, [35]neque per *terram*, quia *scabellum est pedum eius*, neque per Hierosolymam, quia
civitas est *magni Regis*; [36]neque per caput tuum iuraveris, quia non potes unum capillum album facere
aut nigrum. [37]Sit autem sermo vester: "Est, est", "Non, non"; quod autem his abundantius est, a Malo
est. [38]Audistis quia dictum est: "*Oculum pro oculo* et *dentem pro dente*". [39]Ego autem dico vobis: Non
resistere malo; sed si quis te percusserit in dextera maxilla tua, praebe illi et alteram; [40]et ei, qui vult
tecum iudicio contendere et tunicam tuam tollere, remitte ei et pallium; [41]et quicumque te angariaverit
mille passus, vade cum illo duo. [42]Qui petit a te, da ei; et volenti mutuari a te, ne avertaris. [43]Audistis
quia dictum est: "*Diliges proximum tuum* et odio habebis inimicum tuum". [44]Ego autem dico vobis:
Diligite inimicos vestros et orate pro persequentibus vos, [45]ut sitis filii Patris vestri, qui in caelis est, quia
solem suum oriri facit super malos et bonos et pluit super iustos et iniustos. [46]Si enim dilexeritis eos,
qui vos diligunt, quam mercedem habetis? Nonne et publicani hoc faciunt? [47]Et si salutaveritis fratres
vestros tantum, quid amplius facitis? Nonne et ethnici hoc faciunt? [48]Estote ergo vos perfecti, sicut Pater
vester caelestis perfectus est. **[6]** [1]Attendite, ne iustitiam vestram faciatis coram hominibus, ut videamini
ab eis; alioquin mercedem non habetis apud Patrem vestrum, qui in caelis est.[2]Cum ergo facies
eleemosynam, noli tuba canere ante te, sicut hypocritae faciunt in synagogis et in vicis, ut honorificentur
ab hominibus. Amen dico vobis: Receperunt mercedem suam. [3]Te autem faciente eleemosynam, nesciat
sinistra tua quid faciat dextera tua, [4]ut sit eleemosyna tua in abscondito, et Pater tuus, qui videt in
abscondito, reddet tibi. [5]Et cum oratis, non eritis sicut hypocritae, qui amant in synagogis et in angulis
platearum stantes orare, ut videantur ab hominibus. Amen dico vobis: Receperunt mercedem suam. [6]Tu
autem cum orabis, intra in cubiculum tuum et, clauso ostio tuo, ora Patrem tuum, qui est in abscondito;
et Pater tuus, qui videt in abscondito, reddet tibi. [7]Orantes autem nolite multum loqui sicut ethnici:
putant enim quia in multiloquio suo exaudiantur. [8]Nolite ergo assimilari eis; scit enim Pater vester,
quibus opus sit vobis, antequam petatis eum. [9]Sic ergo vos orabitis: Pater noster, qui es in caelis, /
sanctificetur nomen tuum, / [10]adveniat regnum tuum, / fiat voluntas tua, / sicut in caelo, et in terra. /
[11]Panem nostrum supersubstantialem da nobis hodie; / [12]et dimitte nobis debita nostra, / sicut et nos
dimittimus debitoribus nostris; / [13]et ne inducas nos in tentationem, / sed libera nos a Malo. [14]Si enim
dimiseritis hominibus peccata eorum, dimittet et vobis Pater vester caelestis; [15]si autem non dimiseritis

hominibus, nec Pater vester dimittet peccata vestra. [16]Cum autem ieiunatis, nolite fieri sicut hypocritae tristes; demoliuntur enim facies suas, ut pareant hominibus ieiunantes. Amen dico vobis: Receperunt mercedem suam. [17]Tu autem cum ieiunas, unge caput tuum et faciem tuam lava, [18]ne videaris hominibus ieiunans sed Patri tuo, qui est in abscondito; et Pater tuus, qui videt in abscondito, reddet tibi. [19]Nolite thesaurizare vobis thesauros in terra, ubi aerugo et tinea demolitur, et ubi fures effodiunt et furantur; [20]thesaurizate autem vobis thesauros in caelo, ubi neque aerugo neque tinea demolitur, et ubi fures non effodiunt nec furantur; [21]ubi enim est thesaurus tuus, ibi erit et cor tuum. [22]Lucerna corporis est oculus. Si ergo fuerit oculus tuus simplex, totum corpus tuum lucidum erit; [23]si autem oculus tuus nequam fuerit, totum corpus tuum tenebrosum erit. Si ergo lumen, quod in te est, tenebrae sunt, tenebrae quantae erunt! [24]Nemo potest duobus dominis servire: aut enim unum odio habebit et alterum diliget aut unum sustinebit et alterum contemnet; non potestis Deo servire et mammonae. [25]Ideo dico vobis: Ne solliciti sitis animae vestrae quid manducetis, neque corpori vestro quid induamini. Nonne anima plus est quam esca, et corpus quam vestimentum? [26]Respicite volatilia caeli, quoniam non serunt neque metunt neque congregant in horrea, et Pater vester caelestis pascit illa. Nonne vos magis pluris estis illis? [27]Quis autem vestrum cogitans potest adicere ad aetatem suam cubitum unum? [28]Et de vestimento quid solliciti estis? Considerate lilia agri quomodo crescunt: non laborant neque nent. [29]Dico autem vobis quoniam nec Salomon in omni gloria sua coopertus est sicut unum ex istis. [30]Si autem fenum agri, quod hodie est et cras in clibanum mittitur, Deus sic vestit, quanto magis vos, modicae fidei? [31]Nolite ergo solliciti esse dicentes: "Quid manducabimus?", aut: "Quid bibemus?", aut: "Quo operiemur?". [32]Haec enim omnia gentes inquirunt; scit enim Pater vester caelestis quia his omnibus indigetis. [33]Quaerite autem primum regnum Dei et iustitiam eius, et haec omnia adicientur vobis. [34]Nolite ergo esse solliciti in crastinum; crastinus enim dies sollicitus erit sibi ipse. Sufficit diei malitia sua. **[7]** [1]Nolite iudicare, ut non iudicemini; [2]in quo enim iudicio iudicaveritis, iudicabimini, et in qua mensura mensi fueritis, metietur vobis. [3]Quid autem vides festucam in oculo fratris tui, et trabem in oculo tuo non vides? [4]Aut quomodo dices fratri tuo: 'Sine, eiciam festucam de oculo tuo', et ecce trabes est in oculo tuo? [5]Hypocrita, eice primum trabem de oculo tuo, et tunc videbis eicere festucam de oculo fratris tui. [6]Nolite dare sanctum canibus, neque mittatis margaritas vestras ante porcos, ne forte conculcent eas pedibus suis et conversi dirumpant vos. [7]Petite, et dabitur vobis; quaerite et invenietis; pulsate, et aperietur vobis. [8]Omnis enim qui petit, accipit; et, qui quaerit, invenit; et pulsanti aperietur. [9]Aut quis est ex vobis homo, quem si petierit filius suus panem, numquid lapidem porriget ei? [10]Aut si piscem petierit, numquid serpentem porriget ei? [11]Si ergo vos, cum sitis mali, nostis dona bona dare filiis vestris, quanto magis Pater vester, qui in caelis est, dabit bona petentibus se. [12]Omnia ergo, quaecumque vultis ut faciant vobis homines, ita et vos facite eis; haec est enim Lex et Prophetae. [13]Intrate per angustam portam, quia lata porta et spatiosa via, quae ducit ad perditionem, et multi sunt, qui intrant per eam; [14]quam angusta porta et arta via, quae ducit ad vitam, et pauci sunt, qui inveniunt eam! [15]Attendite a falsis prophetis, qui veniunt ad vos in vestimentis ovium, intrinsecus autem sunt lupi rapaces. [16]A fructibus eorum cognoscetis eos: numquid colligunt de spinis uvas aut de tribulis ficus? [17]Sic omnis arbor bona fructus bonos facit, mala autem arbor fructus malos facit: [18]non potest arbor bona fructus malos facere, neque arbor mala fructus bonos facere. [19]Omnis arbor, quae non facit fructum bonum, exciditur et in ignem mittitur. [20]Igitur ex fructibus eorum cognoscetis eos. [21]Non omnis, qui dicit mihi: "Domine Domine", intrabit in regnum caelorum, sed qui facit voluntatem Patris mei, qui in caelis est. [22]Multi dicent mihi in illa die: "Domine, Domine, nonne in tuo nomine prophetavimus, et in tuo nomine daemonia eiecimus, et in tuo nomine virtutes multas fecimus?". [23]Et tunc confitebor illis: Numquam novi vos; discedite a me, qui operamini iniquitatem. [24]Omnis ergo, qui audit verba mea haec et facit ea, assimilabitur viro sapienti, qui aedificavit domum suam supra petram. [25]Et descendit pluvia, et venerunt flumina, et flaverunt venti et irruerunt in domum illam, et non cecidit; fundata enim erat supra petram. [26]Et omnis, qui audit verba mea haec et non facit ea, similis erit viro stulto, qui aedificavit domum suam supra arenam. [27]Et descendit pluvia, et venerunt flumina, et flaverunt venti et irruerunt in domum illam, et cecidit, et fuit ruina eius magna». [28]Et factum est cum consummasset Iesus verba haec, admirabantur turbae super doctrinam eius; [29]erat enim docens eos sicut potestatem habens et non sicut scribae eorum. **[8]** [1]Cum autem descendisset de monte, secutae sunt eum turbae multae. [2]Et ecce leprosus veniens adorabat eum dicens: «Domine, si vis, potes me mundare». [3]Et extendens manum, tetigit eum dicens: «Volo, mundare!»; et confestim mundata est lepra eius. [4]Et ait illi Iesus: «Vide, nemini dixeris; sed vade, ostende te sacerdoti et offer munus, quod praecepit Moyses, in testimonium illis». [5]Cum autem introisset Capharnaum, accessit ad eum centurio rogans eum [6]et dicens: «Domine, puer meus iacet in domo paralyticus et male torquetur». [7]Et ait illi: «Ego veniam et curabo eum». [8]Et respondens centurio ait: «Domine, non sum dignus, ut intres sub tectum meum, sed tantum dic verbo,

et sanabitur puer meus. 9Nam et ego homo sum sub potestate, habens sub me milites, et dico huic:
"Vade", et vadit; et alii: "Veni", et venit; et servo meo: "Fac hoc", et facit». 10Audiens autem Iesus,
miratus est et sequentibus se dixit: «Amen dico vobis: Apud nullum inveni tantam fidem in Israel!
11Dico autem vobis quod multi ab oriente et occidente venient et recumbent cum Abraham et Isaac et
Iacob in regno caelorum; 12filii autem regni eicientur in tenebras exteriores: ibi erit fletus et stridor
dentium». 13Et dixit Iesus centurioni: «Vade; sicut credidisti fiat tibi». Et sanatus est puer in hora illa.
14Et cum venisset Iesus in domum Petri, vidit socrum eius iacentem et febricitantem; 15et tetigit manum
eius, et dimisit eam febris; et surrexit et ministrabat ei. 16Vespere autem facto, obtulerunt ei multos
daemonia habentes; et eiciebat spiritus verbo et omnes male habentes curavit, 17ut adimpleretur, quod
dictum est per Isaiam prophetam dicentem: «*Ipse infirmitates nostras accepit / et aegrotationes
portavit*». 18Videns autem Iesus turbas multas circum se, iussit ire trans fretum. 19Et accedens unus
scriba ait illi: «Magister, sequar te quocumque ieris». 20Et dicit ei Iesus: «Vulpes foveas habent et
volucres caeli tabernacula, Filius autem hominis non habet, ubi caput reclinet». 21Alius autem de
discipulis eius ait illi: «Domine, permitte me primum ire et sepelire patrem meum». 22Iesus autem ait
illi: «Sequere me et dimitte mortuos sepelire mortuos suos». 23Et ascendente eo in naviculam, secuti
sunt eum discipuli eius. 24Et ecce motus magnus factus est in mari, ita ut navicula operiretur fluctibus;
ipse vero dormiebat. 25Et accesserunt et suscitaverunt eum dicentes: «Domine, salva nos, perimus!».
26Et dicit eis: «Quid timidi estis, modicae fidei?». Tunc surgens increpavit ventis et mari, et facta est
tranquillitas magna. 27Porro homines mirati sunt dicentes: «Qualis est hic, quia et venti et mare
oboediunt ei?». 28Et cum venisset trans fretum in regionem Gadarenorum, occurrerunt ei duo habentes
daemonia, de monumentis exeuntes, saevi nimis, ita ut nemo posset transire per viam illam. 29Et ecce
clamaverunt dicentes: «Quid nobis et tibi, Fili Dei? Venisti huc ante tempus torquere nos?». 30Erat
autem longe ab illis grex porcorum multorum pascens. 31Daemones autem rogabant eum dicentes: «Si
eicis nos, mitte nos in gregem porcorum». 32Et ait illis: «Ite». Et illi exeuntes abierunt in porcos; et ecce
impetu abiit totus grex per praeceps in mare, et mortui sunt in aquis. 33Pastores autem fugerunt et
venientes in civitatem nuntiaverunt omnia et de his, qui daemonia habuerant. 34Et ecce tota civitas exiit
obviam Iesu, et viso eo rogabant, ut transiret a finibus eorum. **[9]** 1Et ascendens in naviculam
transfretavit et venit in civitatem suam. 2Et ecce offerebant ei paralyticum iacentem in lecto. Et videns
Iesus fidem illorum, dixit paralytico: «Confide, fili; remittuntur peccata tua». 3Et ecce quidam de scribis
dixerunt intra se: «Hic blasphemat». 4Et cum vidisset Iesus cogitationes eorum, dixit: «Ut quid cogitatis
mala in cordibus vestris? 5Quid enim est facilius, dicere: "Dimittuntur peccata tua", aut dicere: "Surge
et ambula"? 6Ut sciatis autem quoniam Filius hominis habet potestatem in terra dimittendi peccata —
tunc ait paralytico—: Surge, tolle lectum tuum et vade in domum tuam». 7Et surrexit et abiit in domum
suam. 8Videntes autem turbae timuerunt et glorificaverunt Deum, qui dedit potestatem talem hominibus.
9Et cum transiret inde Iesus, vidit hominem sedentem in teloneo, Matthaeum nomine, et ait illi:
«Sequere me». Et surgens secutus est eum. 10Et factum est, discumbente eo in domo, ecce multi
publicani et peccatores venientes simul discumbebant cum Iesu et discipulis eius. 11Et videntes pharisaei
dicebant discipulis eius: «Quare cum publicanis et peccatoribus manducat magister vester?». 12At ille
audiens ait: «Non est opus valentibus medico sed male habentibus. 13Euntes autem discite quid est:
"*Misericordiam volo et non sacrificium*". Non enim veni vocare iustos, sed peccatores». 14Tunc
accedunt ad eum discipuli Ioannis dicentes: «Quare nos et pharisaei ieiunamus frequenter, discipuli
autem tui non ieiunant?». 15Et ait illis Iesus: «Numquid possunt convivae nuptiarum lugere, quamdiu
cum illis est sponsus? Venient autem dies, cum auferetur ab eis sponsus, et tunc ieiunabunt. 16Nemo
autem immittit commissuram panni rudis in vestimentum vetus; tollit enim supplementum eius a
vestimento, et peior scissura fit. 17Neque mittunt vinum novum in utres veteres, alioquin rumpuntur
utres, et vinum effunditur, et utres pereunt; sed vinum novum in utres novos mittunt, et ambo
conservantur». 18Haec illo loquente ad eos, ecce princeps unus accessit et adorabat eum dicens: «Filia
mea modo defuncta est; sed veni, impone manum tuam super eam, et vivet». 19Et surgens Iesus
sequebatur eum et discipuli eius. 20Et ecce mulier, quae sanguinis fluxum patiebatur duodecim annis,
accessit retro et tetigit fimbriam vestimenti eius. 21Dicebat enim intra se: «Si tetigero tantum
vestimentum eius, salva ero». 22At Iesus conversus et videns eam dixit: «Confide, filia; fides tua te
salvam fecit». Et salva facta est mulier ex illa hora. 23Et cum venisset Iesus in domum principis et
vidisset tibicines et turbam tumultuantem, 24dicebat: «Recedite; non est enim mortua puella, sed
dormit». Et deridebant eum. 25At cum eiecta esset turba, intravit et tenuit manum eius, et surrexit puella.
26Et exiit fama haec in universam terram illam. 27Et transeunte inde Iesu, secuti sunt eum duo caeci
clamantes et dicentes: «Miserere nostri, fili David!». 28Cum autem venisset domum, accesserunt ad eum
caeci, et dicit eis Iesus: «Creditis quia possum hoc facere?». Dicunt ei: «Utique, Domine». 29Tunc tetigit

oculos eorum dicens: «Secundum fidem vestram fiat vobis». [30]Et aperti sunt oculi illorum. Et comminatus est illis Iesus dicens: «Videte, ne quis sciat». [31]Illi autem exeuntes diffamaverunt eum in universa terra illa. [32]Egressis autem illis, ecce obtulerunt ei hominem mutum, daemonium habentem. [33]Et eiecto daemone, locutus est mutus. Et miratae sunt turbae dicentes: «Numquam apparuit sic in Israel!». [34]Pharisaei autem dicebant: «In principe daemoniorum eicit daemones». [35]Et circumibat Iesus civitates omnes et castella, docens in synagogis eorum et praedicans evangelium regni et curans omnem languorem et omnem infirmitatem. [36]Videns autem turbas, misertus est eis quia erant vexati et iacentes sicut oves non habentes pastorem. [37]Tunc dicit discipulis suis: «Messis quidem multa, operarii autem pauci; [38]rogate ergo Dominum messis, ut mittat operarios in messem suam». **[10]** [1]Et convocatis Duodecim discipulis suis, dedit illis potestatem spirituum immundorum, ut eicerent eos et curarent omnem languorem et omnem infirmitatem. [2]Duodecim autem apostolorum nomina sunt haec: primus Simon, qui dicitur Petrus, et Andreas frater eius, et Iacobus Zebedaei et Ioannes frater eius, [3]Philippus et Bartholomaeus, Thomas et Matthaeus publicanus, Iacobus Alphaei et Thaddaeus, [4]Simon Chananaeus et Iudas Iscariotes, qui et tradidit eum. [5]Hos Duodecim misit Iesus praecipiens eis et dicens: «In viam gentium ne abieritis et in civitates Samaritanorum ne intraveritis; [6]sed potius ite ad oves, quae perierunt domus Israel. [7]Euntes autem praedicate dicentes: «Appropinquavit regnum caelorum. [8]Infirmos curate, mortuos suscitate, leprosos mundate, daemones eicite; gratis accepistis, gratis date. [9]Nolite possidere aurum neque argentum neque pecuniam in zonis vestris, [10]non peram in via neque duas tunicas neque calceamenta neque virgam; dignus enim est operarius cibo suo. [11]In quamcumque civitatem aut castellum intraveritis, interrogate quis in ea dignus sit; et ibi manete donec exeatis. [12]Intrantes autem in domum, salutate eam; [13]et siquidem fuerit domus digna, veniat pax vestra super eam; si autem non fuerit digna, pax vestra ad vos revertatur. [14]Et quicumque non receperit vos neque audierit sermones vestros, exeuntes foras de domo vel de civitate illa, excutite pulverem de pedibus vestris. [15]Amen dico vobis: Tolerabilius erit terrae Sodomorum et Gomorraeorum in die iudicii quam illi civitati. [16]Ecce ego mitto vos sicut oves in medio luporum; estote ergo prudentes sicut serpentes et simplices sicut columbae. [17]Cavete autem ab hominibus; tradent enim vos in conciliis, et in synagogis suis flagellabunt vos; [18]et ad praesides et ad reges ducemini propter me in testimonium illis et gentibus. [19]Cum autem tradent vos, nolite cogitare quomodo aut quid loquamini; dabitur enim vobis in illa hora quid loquamini. [20]Non enim vos estis, qui loquimini, sed Spiritus Patris vestri, qui loquitur in vobis. [21]Tradet autem frater fratrem in mortem, et pater filium; et insurgent filii in parentes et morte eos afficient. [22]Et eritis odio omnibus propter nomen meum; qui autem perseveraverit in finem, hic salvus erit. [23]Cum autem persequentur vos in civitate ista, fugite in aliam; amen enim dico vobis: Non consummabitis civitates Israel, donec veniat Filius hominis. [24]Non est discipulus super magistrum nec servus super dominum suum. [25]Sufficit discipulo, ut sit sicut magister eius, et servus sicut dominus eius. Si patrem familias Beelzebul vocaverunt, quanto magis domesticos eius! [26] Ne ergo timueritis eos. Nihil enim est opertum, quod non revelabitur, et occultum, quod non scietur. [27]Quod dico vobis in tenebris, dicite in lumine; et quod in aure auditis, praedicate super tecta. [28]Et nolite timere eos, qui occidunt corpus, animam autem non possunt occidere; sed potius eum timete, qui potest et animam et corpus perdere in gehenna. [29]Nonne duo passeres asse veneunt? Et unus ex illis non cadet super terram sine Patre vestro. [30]Vestri autem et capilli capitis omnes numerati sunt. [31]Nolite ergo timere; multis passeribus meliores estis vos. [32]Omnis ergo qui confitebitur me coram hominibus, confitebor et ego eum coram Patre meo, qui est in caelis; [33]qui autem negaverit me coram hominibus, negabo et ego eum coram Patre meo, qui est in caelis. [34]Nolite arbitrari quia venerim mittere pacem in terram; non veni pacem mittere sed gladium. [35]Veni enim separare hominem *adversus patrem suum / et filiam adversus matrem suam / et nurum adversus socrum suam: /* [36]et *inimici hominis domestici eius.* [37]Qui amat patrem aut matrem plus quam me, non est me dignus; et, qui amat filium aut filiam super me, non est me dignus; [38]et, qui non accipit crucem suam et sequitur me, non est me dignus. [39]Qui invenerit animam suam, perdet illam; et, qui perdiderit animam suam propter me, inveniet eam. [40]Qui recipit vos, me recipit; et, qui me recipit, recipit eum, qui me misit. [41]Qui recipit prophetam in nomine prophetae, mercedem prophetae accipiet; et, qui recipit iustum in nomine iusti, mercedem iusti accipiet. [42]Et, quicumque potum dederit uni ex minimis istis calicem aquae frigidae tantum in nomine discipuli, amen dico vobis: Non perdet mercedem suam». **[11]** [1]Et factum est cum consummasset Iesus praecipiens Duodecim discipulis suis, transiit inde, ut doceret et praedicaret in civitatibus eorum. [2]Ioannes autem, cum audisset in vinculis opera Christi, mittens per discipulos suos [3]ait illi: «Tu es qui venturus es, an alium exspectamus?». [4]Et respondens Iesus ait illis: «Euntes renuntiate Ioanni, quae auditis et videtis: [5]*caeci vident* et claudi ambulant, leprosi mundantur et surdi audiunt et mortui resurgunt et *pauperes evangelizantur*; [6]et beatus est, qui non fuerit scandalizatus in me». [7]Illis autem abeuntibus, coepit Iesus dicere ad turbas de Ioanne:

«Quid existis in desertum videre? Arundinem vento agitatam? 8Sed quid existis videre? Hominem
mollibus vestitum? Ecce, qui mollibus vestiuntur, in domibus regum sunt. 9Sed quid existis videre?
Prophetam? Etiam, dico vobis, et plus quam prophetam. 10Hic est, de quo scriptum est: "*Ecce ego mitto
angelum meum ante faciem tuam, / qui praeparabit viam* tuam *ante* te". 11Amen dico vobis: Non
surrexit inter natos mulierum maior Ioanne Baptista; qui autem minor est in regno caelorum, maior est
illo. 12A diebus autem Ioannis Baptistae usque nunc regnum caelorum vim patitur, et violenti rapiunt
illud. 13Omnes enim Prophetae et Lex usque ad Ioannem prophetaverunt; 14et si vultis recipere, ipse est
Elias, qui venturus est. 15Qui habet aures, audiat. 16Cui autem similem aestimabo generationem istam?
Similis est pueris sedentibus in foro, qui clamantes coaequalibus 17dicunt: "Cecinimus vobis, et non
saltastis; / lamentavimus, et non planxistis". 18Venit enim Ioannes neque manducans neque bibens, et
dicunt: "Daemonium habet!"; 19venit Filius hominis manducans et bibens, et dicunt: "Ecce homo vorax
et potator vini, publicanorum amicus et peccatorum!". Et iustificata est sapientia ab operibus suis».
20Tunc coepit exprobrare civitatibus, in quibus factae sunt plurimae virtutes eius, quia non egissent
paenitentiam: 21«Vae tibi, Chorazin! Vae tibi, Bethsaida! Quia si in Tyro et Sidone factae essent virtutes,
quae factae sunt in vobis, olim in cilicio et cinere paenitentiam egissent. 22Verumtamen dico vobis: Tyro
et Sidoni remissius erit in die iudicii quam vobis. 23Et tu, Capharnaum, numquid *usque in caelum
exaltaberis? Usque in infernum descendes!* Quia si in Sodomis factae fuissent virtutes, quae factae sunt
in te, mansissent usque in hunc diem. 24Verumtamen dico vobis: Terrae Sodomorum remissius erit in
die iudicii quam tibi». 25In illo tempore respondens Iesus dixit: «Confiteor tibi, Pater, Domine caeli et
terrae, quia abscondisti haec a sapientibus et prudentibus et revelasti ea parvulis. 26Ita, Pater, quoniam
sic fuit placitum ante te. 27Omnia mihi tradita sunt a Patre meo; et nemo novit Filium nisi Pater, neque
Patrem quis novit nisi Filius et cui voluerit Filius revelare. 28Venite ad me, omnes, qui laboratis et
onerati estis, et ego reficiam vos. 29Tollite iugum meum super vos et discite a me, quia mitis sum et
humilis corde, et invenietis requiem animabus vestris. 30Iugum enim meum suave et onus meum leve
est». **[12]** 1In illo tempore abiit Iesus sabbatis per sata; discipuli autem eius esurierunt et coeperunt
vellere spicas et manducare. 2Pharisaei autem videntes dixerunt ei: «Ecce discipuli tui faciunt, quod non
licet facere sabbato». 3At ille dixit eis: «Non legistis quid fecerit David, quando esuriit, et qui cum eo
erant? 4Quomodo intravit in domum Dei et panes propositionis comedit, quod non licebat ei edere
neque his, qui cum eo erant, nisi solis sacerdotibus? 5Aut non legistis in Lege quia sabbatis sacerdotes
in templo sabbatum violant et sine crimine sunt? 6Dico autem vobis quia templo maior est hic. 7Si
autem sciretis quid est: "*Misericordiam volo et non sacrificium*", numquam condemnassetis innocentes.
8Dominus est enim Filius hominis sabbati». 9Et cum inde transisset, venit in synagogam eorum; 10et
ecce homo manum habens aridam. Et interrogabant eum dicentes: «Licet sabbatis curare?», ut
accusarent eum. 11Ipse autem dixit illis: «Quis erit ex vobis homo, qui habeat ovem unam et, si ceciderit
haec sabbatis in foveam, nonne tenebit et levabit eam? 12Quanto igitur melior est homo ove! Itaque licet
sabbatis bene facere». 13Tunc ait homini: «Extende manum tuam». Et extendit, et restituta est sana sicut
altera. 14Exeuntes autem pharisaei consilium faciebant adversus eum, quomodo eum perderent. 15Iesus
autem sciens secessit inde. Et secuti sunt eum multi, et curavit eos omnes 16et comminatus est eis, ne
manifestum eum facerent, 17ut adimpleretur, quod dictum est per Isaiam prophetam dicentem: 18«*Ecce
puer meus, quem elegi, / dilectus meus, in quo bene placuit animae meae; / ponam Spiritum meum
super eum, / et iudicium gentibus nuntiabit. / 19 Non contendet neque clamabit, / neque audiet aliquis
in plateis vocem eius. / 20Arundinem quassatam non confringet / et linum fumigans non exstinguet, /
donec eiciat ad victoriam iudicium; / 21et in nomine eius gentes sperabunt*». 22Tunc oblatus est ei
daemonium habens, caecus et mutus, et curavit eum, ita ut mutus loqueretur et videret. 23Et stupebant
omnes turbae et dicebant: «Numquid hic est filius David?». 24Pharisaei autem audientes dixerunt: «Hic
non eicit daemones nisi in Beelzebul, principe daemonum». 25Sciens autem cogitationes eorum dixit
eis: «Omne regnum divisum contra se desolatur, et omnis civitas vel domus divisa contra se non stabit.
26Et si Satanas Satanam eicit, adversus se divisus est; quomodo ergo stabit regnum eius? 27Et si ego in
Beelzebul eicio daemones, filii vestri in quo eiciunt? Ideo ipsi iudices erunt vestri. 28Si autem in Spiritu
Dei ego eicio daemones, igitur pervenit in vos regnum Dei. 29Aut quomodo potest quisquam intrare in
domum fortis et vasa eius diripere, nisi prius alligaverit fortem? Et tunc domum illius diripiet. 30Qui non
est mecum, contra me est; et, qui non congregat mecum, spargit. 31Ideo dico vobis: Omne peccatum
et blasphemia remittetur hominibus, Spiritus autem blasphemia non remittetur. 32Et quicumque dixerit
verbum contra Filium hominis, remittetur ei; qui autem dixerit contra Spiritum Sanctum, non remittetur
ei neque in hoc saeculo neque in futuro. 33Aut facite arborem bonam et fructum eius bonum, aut facite
arborem malam et fructum eius malum: siquidem ex fructu arbor agnoscitur. 34Progenies viperarum,
quomodo potestis bona loqui, cum sitis mali? Ex abundantia enim cordis os loquitur. 35Bonus homo de

bono thesauro profert bona, et malus homo de malo thesauro profert mala. 36Dico autem vobis: Omne
verbum otiosum, quod locuti fuerint homines, reddent rationem de eo in die iudicii: 37ex verbis enim
tuis iustificaberis, et ex verbis tuis condemnaberis». 38Tunc responderunt ei quidam de scribis et
pharisaeis dicentes: «Magister, volumus a te signum videre». 39Qui respondens ait illis: «Generatio mala
et adultera signum requirit, et signum non dabitur ei nisi signum Ionae prophetae. 40Sicut enim *fuit*
Ionas in ventre ceti tribus diebus et tribus noctibus, sic erit Filius hominis in corde terrae tribus diebus
et tribus noctibus. 41Viri Ninevitae surgent in iudicio cum generatione ista et condemnabunt eam, quia
paenitentiam egerunt in praedicatione Ionae; et ecce plus quam Iona hic! 42Regina austri surget in
iudicio cum generatione ista et condemnabit eam, quia venit a finibus terrae audire sapientiam
Salomonis; et ecce plus quam Salomon hic! 43Cum autem immundus spiritus exierit ab homine, ambulat
per loca arida quaerens requiem et non invenit. 44Tunc dicit: 'Revertar in domum meam unde exivi'; et
veniens invenit vacantem, scopis mundatam et ornatam. 45Tunc vadit et assumit secum septem alios
spiritus nequiores se, et intrantes habitant ibi; et fiunt novissima hominis illius peiora prioribus. Sic erit
et generationi huic pessimae». 46Adhuc eo loquente ad turbas, ecce mater et fratres eius stabant foris
quaerentes loqui ei. 47Dixit autem ei quidam: «Ecce mater tua et fratres tui foris stant quaerentes loqui
tecum». 48At ille respondens dicenti sibi ait: «Quae est mater mea, et qui sunt fratres mei?». 49Et
extendens manum suam in discipulos suos dixit: «Ecce mater mea et fratres mei. 50Quicumque enim
fecerit voluntatem Patris mei, qui in caelis est, ipse meus frater et soror et mater est». **[13]** 1In illo die
exiens Iesus de domo sedebat secus mare; 2et congregatae sunt ad eum turbae multae, ita ut in
naviculam ascendens sederet, et omnis turba stabat in litore. 3Et locutus est eis multa in parabolis
dicens: «Ecce exiit, qui seminat, seminare. 4Et dum seminat, quaedam ceciderunt secus viam, et
venerunt volucres et comederunt ea. 5Alia autem ceciderunt in petrosa, ubi non habebant terram
multam, et continuo exorta sunt, quia non habebant altitudinem terrae; 6sole autem orto, aestuaverunt
et, quia non habebant radicem, aruerunt. 7Alia autem ceciderunt in spinas, et creverunt spinae et
suffocaverunt ea. 8Alia vero ceciderunt in terram bonam et dabant fructum: aliud centesimum, aliud
sexagesimum, aliud tricesimum. 9Qui habet aures, audiat». 10Et accedentes discipuli dixerunt ei: «Quare
in parabolis loqueris eis?». 11Qui respondens ait illis: «Quia vobis datum est nosse mysteria regni
caelorum, illis autem non est datum. 12Qui enim habet, dabitur ei, et abundabit; qui autem non habet, et
quod habet, auferetur ab eo. 13Ideo in parabolis loquor eis, quia videntes non vident et audientes non
audiunt neque intellegunt; 14et adimpletur eis prophetia Isaiae dicens: "*Auditu audietis et non intellegetis*
/ et videntes videbitis et non videbitis. / 15 Incrassatum est enim cor populi huius, / et auribus graviter
audierunt / et oculos suos clauserunt, / ne quando oculis videant / et auribus audiant / et corde
intellegant et convertantur, / et sanem eos". 16Vestri autem beati oculi, quia vident, et aures vestrae, quia
audiunt. 17Amen quippe dico vobis: Multi prophetae et iusti cupierunt videre, quae videtis, et non
viderunt, et audire, quae auditis, et non audierunt! 18Vos ergo audite parabolam seminantis. 19Omnis,
qui audit verbum regni et non intellegit, venit Malus et rapit, quod seminatum est in corde eius; hic est,
qui secus viam seminatus est. 20Qui autem supra petrosa seminatus est, hic est, qui verbum audit et
continuo cum gaudio accipit illud, 21non habet autem in se radicem, sed est temporalis; facta autem
tribulatione vel persecutione propter verbum, continuo scandalizatur. 22Qui autem est seminatus in
spinis, hic est, qui verbum audit, et sollicitudo saeculi et fallacia divitiarum suffocat verbum, et sine
fructu efficitur. 23Qui vero in terra bona seminatus est, hic est, qui audit verbum et intellegit et fructum
affert et facit aliud quidem centum, aliud autem sexaginta, porro aliud triginta». 24Aliam parabolam
proposuit illis dicens: «Simile factum est regnum caelorum homini, qui seminavit bonum semen in agro
suo. 25Cum autem dormirent homines, venit inimicus eius et superseminavit zizania in medio tritici et
abiit. 26Cum autem crevisset herba et fructum fecisset, tunc apparuerunt et zizania. 27Accedentes autem
servi patris familias dixerunt ei: "Domine, nonne bonum semen seminasti in agro tuo? Unde ergo habet
zizania?". 28Et ait illis: "Inimicus homo hoc fecit". Servi autem dicunt ei: "Vis, imus et colligimus ea?".
29Et ait: "Non; ne forte colligentes zizania eradicetis simul cum eis triticum, 30sinite utraque crescere
usque ad messem. Et in tempore messis dicam messoribus: Colligite primum zizania et alligate ea in
fasciculos ad comburendum ea, triticum autem congregate in horreum meum"». 31Aliam parabolam
proposuit eis dicens: «Simile est regnum caelorum grano sinapis, quod accipiens homo seminavit in
agro suo. 32Quod minimum quidem est omnibus seminibus; cum autem creverit, maius est holeribus et
fit arbor, ita ut volucres caeli veniant et habitent in ramis eius». 33Aliam parabolam locutus est eis:
«Simile est regnum caelorum fermento, quod acceptum mulier abscondit in farinae satis tribus, donec
fermentatum est totum». 34Haec omnia locutus est Iesus in parabolis ad turbas et sine parabola nihil
loquebatur eis, 35ut adimpleretur, quod dictum erat per prophetam dicentem: «*Aperiam in parabolis os*
meum, / eructabo abscondita a constitutione mundi». 36Tunc dimissis turbis venit in domum, et

accesserunt ad eum discipuli eius dicentes: «Dissere nobis parabolam zizaniorum agri». [37]Qui
respondens ait: «Qui seminat bonum semen, est Filius hominis; [38]ager autem est mundus; bonum vero
semen, hi sunt filii regni; zizania autem filii sunt Mali; [39]inimicus autem, qui seminavit ea, est Diabolus;
messis vero consummatio saeculi est, messores autem angeli sunt. [40]Sicut ergo colliguntur zizania et
igni comburuntur, sic erit in consummatione saeculi: [41]mittet Filius hominis angelos suos, et colligent
de regno eius omnia scandala et eos, qui faciunt iniquitatem, [42]et mittent eos in caminum ignis; ibi erit
fletus et stridor dentium. [43]Tunc iusti fulgebunt sicut sol in regno Patris eorum. Qui habet aures, audiat.
[44]Simile est regnum caelorum thesauro abscondito in agro, quem qui invenit homo abscondit et prae
gaudio illius vadit et vendit universa, quae habet, et emit agrum illum. [45]Iterum simile est regnum
caelorum homini negotiatori quaerenti bonas margaritas. [46]Inventa autem una pretiosa margarita, abiit
et vendidit omnia, quae habuit, et emit eam. [47]Iterum simile est regnum caelorum sagenae missae in
mare et ex omni genere congreganti; [48]quam, cum impleta esset, educentes secus litus et sedentes
collegerunt bonos in vasa, malos autem foras miserunt. [49]Sic erit in consummatione saeculi: exibunt
angeli et separabunt malos de medio iustorum [50]et mittent eos in caminum ignis; ibi erit fletus et stridor
dentium. [51]Intellexistis haec omnia?». Dicunt ei: «Etiam». [52]Ait autem illis: «Ideo omnis scriba doctus
in regno caelorum similis est homini patri familias, qui profert de thesauro suo nova et vetera». [53]Et
factum est cum consummasset Iesus parabolas istas, transiit inde. [54]Et veniens in patriam suam, docebat
eos in synagoga eorum, ita ut mirarentur et dicerent: «Unde huic sapientia haec et virtutes? [55]Nonne hic
est fabri filius? Nonne mater eius dicitur Maria, et fratres eius Iacobus et Ioseph et Simon et Iudas? [56]Et
sorores eius nonne omnes apud nos sunt? Unde ergo huic omnia ista?». [57]Et scandalizabantur in eo.
Iesus autem dixit eis: «Non est propheta sine honore nisi in patria et in domo sua». [58]Et non fecit ibi
virtutes multas propter incredulitatem illorum. **[14]** [1]In illo tempore audivit Herodes tetrarcha famam
Iesu [2]et ait pueris suis: «Hic est Ioannes Baptista; ipse surrexit a mortuis, et ideo virtutes operantur in
eo». [3]Herodes enim tenuit Ioannem et alligavit eum et posuit in carcere propter Herodiadem uxorem
Philippi fratris sui. [4]Dicebat enim illi Ioannes: «Non licet tibi habere eam». [5]Et volens illum occidere,
timuit populum, quia sicut prophetam eum habebant. [6]Die autem natalis Herodis saltavit filia Herodiadis
in medio et placuit Herodi, [7]unde cum iuramento pollicitus est ei dare, quodcumque postulasset. [8]At
illa, praemonita a matre sua: «Da mihi, inquit, hic in disco caput Ioannis Baptistae». [9]Et contristatus rex
propter iuramentum et eos, qui pariter recumbebant, iussit dari [10]misitque et decollavit Ioannem in
carcere; [11]et allatum est caput eius in disco et datum est puellae, et tulit matri suae. [12]Et accedentes
discipuli eius tulerunt corpus et sepelierunt illud et venientes nuntiaverunt Iesu. [13]Quod cum audisset
Iesus, secessit inde in navicula in locum desertum seorsum; et cum audissent, turbae secutae sunt eum
pedestres de civitatibus. [14]Et exiens vidit turbam multam et misertus est eorum et curavit languidos
eorum. [15]Vespere autem facto, accesserunt ad eum discipuli dicentes: «Desertus est locus, et hora iam
praeteriit; dimitte turbas, ut euntes in castella emant sibi escas». [16]Iesus autem dixit eis: «Non habent
necesse ire; date illis vos manducare». [17]Illi autem dicunt ei: «Non habemus hic nisi quinque panes et
duos pisces». [18]Qui ait: «Afferte illos mihi huc». [19]Et cum iussisset turbas discumbere supra fenum,
acceptis quinque panibus et duobus piscibus, aspiciens in caelum benedixit et fregit et dedit discipulis
panes, discipuli autem turbis. [20]Et manducaverunt omnes et saturati sunt; et tulerunt reliquias
fragmentorum duodecim cophinos plenos. [21]Manducantium autem fuit numerus fere quinque milia
virorum, exceptis mulieribus et parvulis. [22]Et statim iussit discipulos ascendere in naviculam et
praecedere eum trans fretum, donec dimitteret turbas. [23]Et dimissis turbis, ascendit in montem solus
orare. Vespere autem facto, solus erat ibi. [24]Navicula autem iam multis stadiis a terra distabat, fluctibus
iactata; erat enim contrarius ventus. [25]Quarta autem vigilia noctis venit ad eos ambulans supra mare.
[26]Discipuli autem, videntes eum supra mare ambulantem, turbati sunt dicentes: «Phantasma est», et prae
timore clamaverunt. [27]Statimque Iesus locutus est eis dicens: «Habete fiduciam, ego sum; nolite
timere!». [28]Respondens autem ei Petrus dixit: «Domine, si tu es, iube me venire ad te super aquas». [29]At
ipse ait: «Veni!». Et descendens Petrus de navicula ambulavit super aquas et venit ad Iesum. [30]Videns
vero ventum validum timuit et, cum coepisset mergi, clamavit dicens: «Domine, salvum me fac!».
[31]Continuo autem Iesus extendens manum apprehendit eum et ait illi: «Modicae fidei, quare dubitasti?».
[32]Et cum ascendissent in naviculam, cessavit ventus. [33]Qui autem in navicula erant, adoraverunt eum
dicentes: «Vere Filius Dei es!». [34]Et cum transfretassent, venerunt in terram Gennesaret. [35]Et cum
cognovissent eum viri loci illius, miserunt in universam regionem illam et obtulerunt ei omnes male
habentes, [36]et rogabant eum, ut vel fimbriam vestimenti eius tangerent; et, quicumque tetigerunt, salvi
facti sunt. **[15]** [1]Tunc accedunt ad Iesum ab Hierosolymis pharisaei et scribae dicentes: [2]«Quare discipuli
tui transgrediuntur traditionem seniorum? Non enim lavant manus suas, cum panem manducant». [3]Ipse
autem respondens ait illis: «Quare et vos transgredimini mandatum Dei propter traditionem vestram?

4Nam Deus dixit: "*Honora patrem tuum et matrem*" et: "*Qui maladixerit patri vel matri, morte moriatur*". 5Vos autem dicitis: "Quicumque dixerit patri vel matri: Munus est, quodcumque ex me profuerit, 6non honorificabit patrem suum"; et irritum fecistis verbum Dei propter traditionem vestram. 7Hypocritae! Bene prophetavit de vobis Isaias dicens: 8"*Populus hic labiis me honorat, / cor autem eorum longe est a me*; / 9 *sine causa autem colunt me, / docentes doctrinas mandata hominum*"». 10Et convocata ad se turba, dixit eis: «Audite et intellegite: 11Non quod intrat in os, coinquinat hominem; sed quod procedit ex ore, hoc coinquinat hominem!». 12Tunc accedentes discipuli dicunt ei: «Scis quia pharisaei, audito verbo, scandalizati sunt?». 13At ille respondens ait: «Omnis plantatio, quam non plantavit Pater meus caelestis, eradicabitur. 14Sinite illos: caeci sunt duces caecorum. Caecus autem si caeco ducatum praestet, ambo in foveam cadent». 15Respondens autem Petrus dixit ei: «Edissere nobis parabolam istam». 16At ille dixit: «Adhuc et vos sine intellectu estis? 17Non intellegitis quia omne quod in os intrat, in ventrem vadit et in secessum emittitur? 18Quae autem procedunt de ore, de corde exeunt, et ea coinquinant hominem. 19De corde enim exeunt cogitationes malae, homicidia, adulteria, fornicationes, furta, falsa testimonia, blasphemiae. 20Haec sunt, quae coinquinant hominem; non lotis autem manibus manducare non coinquinat hominem». 21Et egressus inde Iesus, secessit in partes Tyri et Sidonis. 22Et ecce mulier Chananaea a finibus illis egressa clamavit dicens: «Miserere mei, Domine, fili David! Filia mea male a daemonio vexatur». 23Qui non respondit ei verbum. Et accedentes discipuli eius rogabant eum dicentes: «Dimitte eam, quia clamat post nos». 24Ipse autem respondens ait: «Non sum missus nisi ad oves, quae perierunt domus Israel». 25At illa venit et adoravit eum dicens: «Domine, adiuva me!». 26Qui respondens ait: «Non est bonum sumere panem filiorum et mittere catellis». 27At illa dixit: «Etiam, Domine, nam et catelli edunt de micis, quae cadunt de mensa dominorum suorum». 28Tunc respondens Iesus ait illi: «O mulier, magna est fides tua! Fiat tibi, sicut vis». Et sanata est filia illius ex illa hora. 29Et cum transisset inde, Iesus venit secus mare Galilaeae et ascendens in montem sedebat ibi. 30Et accesserunt ad eum turbae multae habentes secum claudos, caecos, debiles, mutos et alios multos et proiecerunt eos ad pedes eius, et curavit eos, 31ita ut turba miraretur videntes mutos loquentes, debiles sanos, et claudos ambulantes, et caecos videntes. Et magnificabant Deum Israel. 32Iesus autem convocatis discipulis suis dixit: «Misereor turbae, quia triduo iam perseverant mecum et non habent, quod manducent; et dimittere eos ieiunos nolo, ne forte deficiant in via». 33Et dicunt ei discipuli: «Unde nobis in deserto panes tantos, ut saturemus turbam tantam?». 34Et ait illis Iesus: «Quot panes habetis?». At illi dixerunt: «Septem et paucos pisciculos». 35Et praecepit turbae, ut discumberet super terram; 36et accipiens septem panes et pisces et gratias agens fregit et dedit discipulis, discipuli autem turbis. 37Et comederunt omnes et saturati sunt; et, quod superfuit de fragmentis, tulerunt septem sportas plenas. 38Erant autem, qui manducaverant, quattuor milia hominum extra mulieres et parvulos. 39Et dimissis turbis, ascendit in naviculam et venit in fines Magadan. **[16]** 1Et accesserunt ad eum pharisaei et sadducaei tentantes et rogaverunt eum, ut signum de caelo ostenderet eis. 2At ille respondens ait eis: «Facto vespere dicitis: 'Serenum erit, rubicundum est enim caelum'; 3et mane: 'Hodie tempestas, rutilat enim triste caelum'. Faciem quidem caeli diiudicare nostis, signa autem temporum non potestis. 4Generatio mala et adultera signum quaerit, et signum non dabitur ei nisi signum Ionae». Et, relictis illis, abiit. 5Et cum venissent discipuli trans fretum, obliti sunt panes accipere. 6Iesus autem dixit illis: «Intuemini et cavete a fermento pharisaeorum et sadducaeorum». 7At illi cogitabant inter se dicentes: «Panes non accepimus!». 8Sciens autem Iesus dixit: «Quid cogitatis inter vos, modicae fidei, quia panes non habetis? 9Nondum intellegitis neque recordamini quinque panum quinque milium hominum, et quot cophinos sumpsistis? 10Neque septem panum quattuor milium hominum, et quot sportas sumpsistis? 11Quomodo non intellegitis quia non de panibus dixi vobis? Sed cavete a fermento pharisaeorum et sadducaeorum». 12Tunc intellexerunt quia non dixerit cavendum a fermento panum, sed a doctrina pharisaeorum et sadducaeorum. 13Venit autem Iesus in partes Caesareae Philippi et interrogabat discipulos suos dicens: «Quem dicunt homines esse Filium hominis?». 14At illi dixerunt: «Alii Ioannem Baptistam, alii autem Eliam, alii vero Ieremiam, aut unum ex prophetis». 15Dicit illis: «Vos autem quem me esse dicitis?». 16Respondens Simon Petrus dixit: «Tu es Christus, Filius Dei vivi». 17Respondens autem Iesus dixit ei: «Beatus es, Simon Bariona, quia caro et sanguis non revelavit tibi, sed Pater meus, qui in caelis est. 18Et ego dico tibi: Tu es Petrus, et super hanc petram aedificabo Ecclesiam meam; et portae inferi non praevalebunt adversum eam. 19Tibi dabo claves regni caelorum; et quodcumque ligaveris super terram, erit ligatum in caelis, et quodcumque solveris super terram, erit solutum in caelis». 20Tunc praecepit discipulis, ut nemini dicerent quia ipse esset Christus. 21Exinde coepit Iesus ostendere discipulis suis quia oporteret eum ire Hierosolymam et multa pati a senioribus et principibus sacerdotum et scribis et occidi et tertia die resurgere. 22Et assumens eum Petrus coepit increpare illum dicens: «Absit a te, Domine, non erit tibi hoc». 23Qui

conversus dixit Petro: «Vade post me, Satana! Scandalum es mihi, quia non sapis ea, quae Dei sunt, sed
ea quae hominum!». [24]Tunc Iesus dixit discipulis suis: «Si quis vult post me venire, abneget semetipsum
et tollat crucem suam et sequatur me. [25]Qui enim voluerit animam suam salvam facere, perdet eam; qui
autem perdiderit animam suam propter me, inveniet eam. [26]Quid enim prodest homini, si mundum
universum lucretur, animae vero suae detrimentum patiatur? Aut quam dabit homo commutationem pro
anima sua? [27]Filius enim hominis venturus est in gloria Patris sui cum angelis suis, et tunc reddet
unicuique secundum opus eius. [28]Amen dico vobis: Sunt quidam de hic stantibus, qui non gustabunt
mortem, donec videant Filium hominis venientem in regno suo». **[17]** [1]Et post dies sex assumit Iesus
Petrum et Iacobum et Ioannem fratrem eius et ducit illos in montem excelsum seorsum. [2]Et
transfiguratus est ante eos; et resplenduit facies eius sicut sol, vestimenta autem eius facta sunt alba sicut
lux. [3]Et ecce apparuit illis Moyses et Elias cum eo loquentes. [4]Respondens autem Petrus dixit ad Iesum:
«Domine, bonum est nos hic esse. Si vis, faciam hic tria tabernacula: tibi unum et Moysi unum et Eliae
unum». [5]Adhuc eo loquente, ecce nubes lucida obumbravit eos; et ecce vox de nube dicens: «Hic est
Filius meus dilectus, in quo mihi bene complacui; ipsum audite». [6]Et audientes discipuli ceciderunt in
faciem suam et timuerunt valde. [7]Et accessit Iesus et tetigit eos dixitque eis: «Surgite et nolite timere».
[8]Levantes autem oculos suos, neminem viderunt nisi solum Iesum. [9]Et descendentibus illis de monte,
praecepit eis Iesus dicens: «Nemini dixeritis visionem, donec Filius hominis a mortuis resurgat». [10]Et
interrogaverunt eum discipuli dicentes: «Quid ergo scribae dicunt quod Eliam oporteat primum
venire?». [11]At ille respondens ait: «Elias quidem venturus est et restituet omnia. [12]Dico autem vobis
quia Elias iam venit, et non cognoverunt eum, sed fecerunt in eo, quaecumque voluerunt; sic et Filius
hominis passurus est ab eis». [13]Tunc intellexerunt discipuli quia de Ioanne Baptista dixisset eis. [14]Et
cum venissent ad turbam, accessit ad eum homo genibus provolutus ante eum [15]et dicens: «Domine,
miserere filii mei, quia lunaticus est et male patitur; nam saepe cadit in ignem et crebro in aquam. [16]Et
obtuli eum discipulis tuis, et non potuerunt curare eum». [17]Respondens autem Iesus ait: «O generatio
incredula et perversa, quousque ero vobiscum? Usquequo patiar vos? Afferte huc illum ad me». [18]Et
increpavit eum Iesus, et exiit ab eo daemonium, et curatus est puer ex illa hora. [19]Tunc accesserunt
discipuli ad Iesum secreto et dixerunt: «Quare nos non potuimus eicere illum?». [20]Ille autem dicit illis:
«Propter modicam fidem vestram. Amen quippe dico vobis: Si habueritis fidem sicut granum sinapis,
dicetis monti huic: "Transi hinc illuc!", et transibit, et nihil impossibile erit vobis». [(21)] [22]Conversantibus
autem eis in Galilaea, dixit illis Iesus: «Filius hominis tradendus est in manus hominum, [23]et occident
eum, et tertio die resurget». Et contristati sunt vehementer. [24]Et cum venissent Capharnaum,
accesserunt, qui didrachma accipiebant, ad Petrum et dixerunt: «Magister vester non solvit
didrachma?». [25]Ait: «Etiam». Et cum intrasset domum, praevenit eum Iesus dicens: «Quid tibi videtur,
Simon? Reges terrae a quibus accipiunt tributum vel censum? A filiis suis an ab alienis?». [26]Cum autem
ille dixisset: «Ab alienis», dixit illi Iesus: «Ergo liberi sunt filii. [27]Ut autem non scandalizemus eos, vade
ad mare et mitte hamum; et eum piscem, qui primus ascenderit, tolle, et aperto ore eius invenies
staterem. Illum sumens, da eis pro me et te». **[18]** [1]In illa hora accesserunt discipuli ad Iesum dicentes:
«Quis putas maior est in regno caelorum?». [2]Et advocans parvulum, statuit eum in medio eorum [3]et
dixit: «Amen dico vobis: Nisi conversi fueritis et efficiamini sicut parvuli, non intrabitis in regnum
caelorum. [4]Quicumque ergo humiliaverit se sicut parvulus iste, hic est maior in regno caelorum. [5]Et qui
susceperit unum parvulum talem in nomine meo, me suscipit. [6]Qui autem scandalizaverit unum de
pusillis istis, qui in me credunt, expedit ei, ut suspendatur mola asinaria in collo eius et demergatur in
profundum maris. [7]Vae mundo ab scandalis! Necesse est enim ut veniant scandala; verumtamen vae
homini, per quem scandalum venit! [8]Si autem manus tua vel pes tuus scandalizat te, abscide eum et
proice abs te: bonum tibi est ad vitam ingredi debilem vel claudum, quam duas manus vel duos pedes
habentem mitti in ignem aeternum. [9]Et si oculus tuus scandalizat te, erue eum et proice abs te: bonum
tibi est unoculum in vitam intrare, quam duos oculos habentem mitti in gehennam ignis. [10]Videte, ne
contemnatis unum ex his pusillis; dico enim vobis quia angeli eorum in caelis semper vident faciem
Patris mei, qui in caelis est. [(11)] [12]Quid vobis videtur? Si fuerint alicui centum oves, et erraverit una ex
eis, nonne relinquet nonaginta novem in montibus et vadit quaerere eam, quae erravit? [13]Et si contigerit
ut inveniat eam, amen dico vobis quia gaudebit super eam magis quam super nonaginta novem, quae
non erraverunt. [14]Sic non est voluntas ante Patrem vestrum, qui in caelis est, ut pereat unus de pusillis
istis. [15]Si autem peccaverit in te frater tuus, vade, corripe eum inter te et ipsum solum. Si te audierit,
lucratus es fratrem tuum; [16]si autem non audierit, adhibe tecum adhuc unum vel duos, *ut in ore duorum
testium vel trium stet omne verbum*; [17]quod si noluerit audire eos, dic ecclesiae; si autem et ecclesiam
noluerit audire, sit tibi sicut ethnicus et publicanus. [18]Amen dico vobis: Quaecumque alligaveritis super
terram, erunt ligata in caelo, et quaecumque solveritis super terram, erunt soluta in caelo. [19]Iterum dico

vobis: Si duo ex vobis consenserint super terram de omni re, quamcumque petierint, fiet illis a Patre
meo, qui in caelis est. 20 Ubi enim sunt duo vel tres congregati in nomine meo, ibi sum in medio eorum».
21 Tunc accedens Petrus dixit ei: «Domine, quotiens peccabit in me frater meus, et dimittam ei? Usque
septies?». 22 Dicit illi Iesus: «Non dico tibi usque septies sed usque septuagies septies. 23 Ideo
assimilatum est regnum caelorum homini regi, qui voluit rationem ponere cum servis suis. 24 Et cum
coepisset rationem ponere, oblatus est ei unus, qui debebat decem milia talenta. 25 Cum autem non
haberet, unde redderet, iussit eum dominus venumdari et uxorem et filios et omnia, quae habebat, et
reddi. 26 Procidens igitur servus ille adorabat eum dicens: "Patientiam habe in me, et omnia reddam tibi".
27 Misertus autem dominus servi illius dimisit eum et debitum dimisit ei. 28 Egressus autem servus ille
invenit unum de conservis suis, qui debebat ei centum denarios, et tenens suffocabat eum dicens:
"Redde, quod debes!". 29 Procidens igitur conservus eius rogabat eum dicens: "Patientiam habe in me,
et reddam tibi". 30 Ille autem noluit, sed abiit et misit eum in carcerem, donec redderet debitum.
31 Videntes autem conservi eius, quae fiebant, contristati sunt valde et venerunt et narraverunt domino
suo omnia, quae facta erant. 32 Tunc vocavit illum dominus suus et ait illi: "Serve nequam, omne
debitum illud dimisi tibi, quoniam rogasti me; 33 non oportuit et te misereri conservi tui, sicut et ego tui
misertus sum?". 34 Et iratus dominus eius tradidit eum tortoribus, quoadusque redderet universum
debitum. 35 Sic et Pater meus caelestis faciet vobis, si non remiseritis unusquisque fratri suo de cordibus
vestris». **[19]** 1 Et factum est cum consummasset Iesus sermones istos, migravit a Galilaea et venit in
fines Iudaeae trans Iordanem. 2 Et secutae sunt eum turbae multae, et curavit eos ibi. 3 Et accesserunt ad
eum pharisaei tentantes eum et dicentes: «Licet homini dimittere uxorem suam quacumque ex causa?».
4 Qui respondens ait: «Non legistis quia, qui creavit ab initio, *masculum et feminam fecit eos* 5 et dixit:
"*Propter hoc dimittet homo patrem et matrem et adhaerebit uxori suae, et erunt duo in carne una*?".
6 Itaque iam non sunt duo sed una caro. Quod ergo Deus coniunxit, homo non separet». 7 Dicunt illi:
«Quid ergo Moyses mandavit *dari libellum repudii et dimittere*?». 8 Ait illis: «Moyses ad duritiam cordis
vestri permisit vobis dimittere uxores vestras; ab initio autem non sic fuit. 9 Dico autem vobis quia
quicumque dimiserit uxorem suam, nisi ob fornicationem, et aliam duxerit, moechatur». 10 Dicunt ei
discipuli eius: «Si ita est causa hominis cum uxore, non expedit nubere». 11 Qui dixit eis: «Non omnes
capiunt verbum istud, sed quibus datum est. 12 Sunt enim eunuchi, qui de matris utero sic nati sunt; et
sunt eunuchi, qui facti sunt ab hominibus; et sunt eunuchi, qui seipsos castraverunt propter regnum
caelorum. Qui potest capere, capiat». 13 Tunc oblati sunt ei parvuli, ut manus eis imponeret et oraret;
discipuli autem increpabant eis. 14 Iesus vero ait: «Sinite parvulos et nolite eos prohibere ad me venire;
talium est enim regnum caelorum». 15 Et cum imposuisset eis manus, abiit inde. 16 Et ecce unus accedens
ait illi: «Magister, quid boni faciam, ut habeam vitam aeternam?». Qui dixit ei: 17 «Quid me interrogas
de bono? Unus est bonus. Si autem vis ad vitam ingredi, serva mandata». 18 Dicit illi: «Quae?». Iesus
autem dixit: «*Non homicidium facies, non adulterabis, non facies furtum, non falsum testimonium dices,*
19 *honora patrem et matrem et diliges proximum tuum sicut teipsum*». 20 Dicit illi adulescens: «Omnia
haec custodivi. Quid adhuc mihi deest?». 21 Ait illi Iesus: «Si vis perfectus esse, vade, vende, quae
habes, et da pauperibus, et habebis thesaurum in caelo; et veni, sequere me». 22 Cum audisset autem
adulescens verbum, abiit tristis; erat enim habens multas possessiones. 23 Iesus autem dixit discipulis
suis: «Amen dico vobis: Dives difficile intrabit in regnum caelorum. 24 Et iterum dico vobis: Facilius est
camelum per foramen acus transire, quam divitem intrare in regnum Dei». 25 Auditis autem his, discipuli
mirabantur valde dicentes: «Quis ergo poterit salvus esse?». 26 Aspiciens autem Iesus dixit illis: «Apud
homines hoc impossibile est, apud Deum autem omnia possibilia sunt». 27 Tunc respondens Petrus dixit
ei: «Ecce nos reliquimus omnia et secuti sumus te. Quid ergo erit nobis?». 28 Iesus autem dixit illis:
«Amen dico vobis quod vos, qui secuti estis me, in regeneratione, cum sederit Filius hominis in throno
gloriae suae, sedebitis et vos super thronos duodecim, iudicantes duodecim tribus Israel. 29 Et omnis, qui
reliquit domos vel fratres aut sorores aut patrem aut matrem aut filios aut agros propter nomen meum,
centuplum accipiet et vitam aeternam possidebit. 30 Multi autem erunt primi novissimi et novissimi
primi. **[20]** 1 Simile est enim regnum caelorum homini patri familias, qui exiit primo mane conducere
operarios in vineam suam; 2 conventione autem facta cum operariis ex denario diurno, misit eos in
vineam suam. 3 Et egressus circa horam tertiam vidit alios stantes in foro otiosos 4 et illis dixit: "Ite et
vos in vineam; et, quod iustum fuerit, dabo vobis". 5 Illi autem abierunt. Iterum autem exiit circa sextam
et nonam horam et fecit similiter. 6 Circa undecimam vero exiit et invenit alios stantes et dicit illis: "Quid
hic statis tota die otiosi?". 7 Dicunt ei: "Quia nemo nos conduxit". Dicit illis: "Ite et vos in vineam".
8 Cum sero autem factum esset, dicit dominus vineae procuratori suo: "Voca operarios et redde illis
mercedem incipiens a novissimis usque ad primos". 9 Et cum venissent, qui circa undecimam horam
venerant, acceperunt singuli denarium. 10 Venientes autem primi arbitrati sunt quod plus essent

accepturi; acceperunt autem et ipsi singuli denarium. 11Accipientes autem murmurabant adversus
patrem familias 12dicentes: "Hi novissimi una hora fecerunt, et pares illos nobis fecisti, qui portavimus
pondus diei et aestum!". 13At ille respondens uni eorum dixit: "Amice, non facio tibi iniuriam; nonne
ex denario convenisti mecum? 14Tolle, quod tuum est, et vade; volo autem et huic novissimo dare sicut
et tibi. 15Aut non licet mihi, quod volo, facere de meis? An oculus tuus nequam est, quia ego bonus
sum?". 16Sic erunt novissimi primi, et primi novissimi». 17Et ascendens Iesus Hierosolymam assumpsit
Duodecim discipulos secreto et ait illis in via: 18«Ecce ascendimus Hierosolymam, et Filius hominis
tradetur principibus sacerdotum et scribis, et condemnabunt eum morte 19et tradent eum gentibus ad
illudendum et flagellandum et crucifigendum, et tertia die resurget». 20Tunc accessit ad eum mater
filiorum Zebedaei cum filiis suis, adorans et petens aliquid ab eo. 21Qui dixit ei: «Quid vis?». Ait illi:
«Dic ut sedeant hi duo filii mei unus ad dexteram tuam et unus ad sinistram in regno tuo». 22Respondens
autem Iesus dixit: «Nescitis quid petatis. Potestis bibere calicem, quem ego bibiturus sum?». Dicunt ei:
«Possumus». 23Ait illis: «Calicem quidem meum bibetis, sedere autem ad dexteram meam et sinistram
non est meum dare illud, sed quibus paratum est a Patre meo». 24Et audientes decem indignati sunt de
duobus fratribus. 25Iesus autem vocavit eos ad se et ait: «Scitis quia principes gentium dominantur
eorum et, qui magni sunt, potestatem exercent in eos. 26Non ita erit inter vos, sed quicumque voluerit
inter vos magnus fieri, erit vester minister; 27et, quicumque voluerit inter vos primus esse, erit vester
servus; 28sicut Filius hominis non venit ministrari sed ministrare et dare animam suam redemptionem
pro multis». 29Et egredientibus illis ab Iericho, secuta est eum turba multa. 30Et ecce duo caeci sedentes
secus viam audierunt quia Iesus transiret et clamaverunt dicentes: «Domine, miserere nostri, fili
David!». 31Turba autem increpabat eos, ut tacerent; at illi magis clamabant dicentes: «Domine, miserere
nostri, fili David!». 32Et stetit Iesus et vocavit eos et ait: «Quid vultis, ut faciam vobis?». 33Dicunt illi:
«Domine, ut aperiantur oculi nostri». 34Misertus autem Iesus, tetigit oculos eorum; et confestim viderunt
et secuti sunt eum. **[21]** 1Et cum appropinquassent Hierosolymis et venissent Bethfage, ad montem
Oliveti, tunc Iesus misit duos discipulos 2dicens eis: «Ite in castellum, quod contra vos est, et statim
invenietis asinam alligatam et pullum cum ea; solvite et adducite mihi. 3Et si quis vobis aliquid dixerit,
dicite: "Dominus eos necessarios habet", et confestim dimittet eos». 4Hoc autem factum est, ut
impleretur, quod dictum est per prophetam dicentem: 5«*Dicite filiae Sion: / Ecce Rex tuus venit tibi, /*
mansuetus et sedens super asinam / et super pullum filium subiugalis». 6Euntes autem discipuli
fecerunt, sicut praecepit illis Iesus, 7et adduxerunt asinam et pullum, et imposuerunt super eis
vestimenta sua, et sedit super ea. 8Plurima autem turba straverunt vestimenta sua in via; alii autem
caedebant ramos de arboribus et sternebant in via. 9Turbae autem, quae praecedebant eum et quae
sequebantur, clamabant dicentes: «*Hosanna* filio David! *Benedictus, qui venit in nomine Domini!*
Hosanna in altissimis!». 10Et cum intrasset Hierosolymam, commota est universa civitas dicens: «Quis
est hic?». 11Turbae autem dicebant: «Hic est Iesus propheta a Nazareth Galilaeae». 12Et intravit Iesus
in templum et eiciebat omnes vendentes et ementes in templo, et mensas nummulariorum evertit et
cathedras vendentium columbas, 13et dicit eis: «Scriptum est: "*Domus mea domus orationis vocabitur*".
Vos autem facitis eam *speluncam latronum*». 14Et accesserunt ad eum caeci et claudi in templo, et
sanavit eos. 15Videntes autem principes sacerdotum et scribae mirabilia, quae fecit, et pueros clamantes
in templo et dicentes: «Hosanna filio David», indignati sunt 16et dixerunt ei: «Audis quid isti dicant?».
Iesus autem dicit eis: «Utique; numquam legistis: "*Ex ore infantium et lactantium perfecisti laudem*"?».
17Et relictis illis, abiit foras extra civitatem in Bethaniam ibique mansit. 18Mane autem revertens in
civitatem, esuriit. 19Et videns fici arborem unam secus viam, venit ad eam; et nihil invenit in ea nisi folia
tantum et ait illi: «Numquam ex te fructus nascatur in sempiternum». Et arefacta est continuo ficulnea.
20Et videntes discipuli mirati sunt dicentes: «Quomodo continuo aruit ficulnea?». 21Respondens autem
Iesus ait eis: «Amen dico vobis: Si habueritis fidem et non haesitaveritis, non solum de ficulnea facietis,
sed et si monti huic dixeritis: "Tolle et iacta te in mare", fiet. 22Et omnia, quaecumque petieritis in
oratione credentes, accipietis». 23Et cum venisset in templum, accesserunt ad eum docentem principes
sacerdotum et seniores populi dicentes: «In qua potestate haec facis? Et quis tibi dedit hanc
potestatem?». 24Respondens autem Iesus dixit illis: «Interrogabo vos et ego unum sermonem, quem si
dixeritis mihi, et ego vobis dicam, in qua potestate haec facio: 25Baptismum Ioannis unde erat? A caelo
an ex hominibus?». At illi cogitabant inter se dicentes: «Si dixerimus: "E caelo", dicet nobis: "Quare
ergo non credidistis illi?"; 26si autem dixerimus: "Ex hominibus", timemus turbam; omnes enim habent
Ioannem sicut prophetam». 27Et respondentes Iesu dixerunt: «Nescimus». Ait illis et ipse: «Nec ego dico
vobis in qua potestate haec facio». 28«Quid autem vobis videtur? Homo quidam habebat duos filios. Et
accedens ad primum dixit: "Fili, vade hodie, operare in vinea". 29Ille autem respondens ait: "Nolo";
postea autem paenitentia motus abiit. 30Accedens autem ad alterum dixit similiter. At ille respondens

ait: "Eo, domine"; et non ivit. 31Quis ex duobus fecit voluntatem patris?». Dicunt: «Primus». Dicit illis
Iesus: «Amen dico vobis: Publicani et meretrices praecedunt vos in regnum Dei. 32Venit enim ad vos
Ioannes in via iustitiae, et non credidistis ei; publicani autem et meretrices crediderunt ei. Vos autem
videntes nec paenitentiam habuistis postea, ut crederetis ei. 33Aliam parabolam audite. Homo erat pater
familias, qui *plantavit vineam et saepem circumdedit ei et fodit in ea torcular et aedificavit turrim* et
locavit eam agricolis et peregre profectus est. 34Cum autem tempus fructuum appropinquasset, misit
servos suos ad agricolas, ut acciperent fructus eius. 35Et agricolae, apprehensis servis eius, alium
ceciderunt, alium occiderunt, alium vero lapidaverunt. 36Iterum misit alios servos plures prioribus, et
fecerunt illis similiter. 37Novissime autem misit ad eos filium suum dicens: "Verebuntur filium meum".
38Agricolae autem videntes filium dixerunt intra se: "Hic est heres. Venite, occidamus eum et habebimus
hereditatem eius". 39Et apprehensum eum eiecerunt extra vineam et occiderunt. 40Cum ergo venerit
dominus vineae, quid faciet agricolis illis?». 41Aiunt illi: «Malos male perdet et vineam locabit aliis
agricolis, qui reddant ei fructum temporibus suis». 42Dicit illis Iesus: «Numquam legistis in Scripturis:
/ "*Lapidem, quem reprobaverunt aedificantes, / hic factus est in caput anguli; / a Domino factum est*
istud / et est mirabile in oculis nostris"? 43Ideo dico vobis quia auferetur a vobis regnum Dei et dabitur
genti facienti fructus eius. 44Et, qui ceciderit super lapidem istum confringetur; super quem vero
ceciderit, conteret eum». 45Et cum audissent principes sacerdotum et pharisaei parabolas eius,
cognoverunt quod de ipsis diceret; 46et quaerentes eum tenere, timuerunt turbas, quoniam sicut
prophetam eum habebant. **[22]** 1Et respondens Iesus dixit iterum in parabolis eis dicens: 2«Simile
factum est regnum caelorum homini regi, qui fecit nuptias filio suo. 3Et misit servos suos vocare
invitatos ad nuptias, et nolebant venire. 4Iterum misit alios servos dicens: "Dicite invitatis: Ecce
prandium meum paravi, tauri mei et altilia occisa, et omnia parata; venite ad nuptias". 5Illi autem
neglexerunt et abierunt, alius in villam suam, alius vero ad negotiationem suam; 6reliqui vero tenuerunt
servos eius et contumelia affectos occiderunt. 7Rex autem iratus est et, missis exercitibus suis, perdidit
homicidas illos et civitatem illorum succendit. 8Tunc ait servis suis: "Nuptiae quidem paratae sunt, sed
qui invitati erant, non fuerunt digni; 9ite ergo ad exitus viarum et quoscumque inveneritis, vocate ad
nuptias". 10Et egressi servi illi in vias, congregaverunt omnes, quos invenerunt, malos et bonos; et
impletae sunt nuptiae discumbentium. 11Intravit autem rex, ut videret discumbentes, et vidit ibi
hominem non vestitum veste nuptiali 12et ait illi: "Amice, quomodo huc intrasti, non habens vestem
nuptialem?". At ille obmutuit. 13Tunc dixit rex ministris: "Ligate pedes eius et manus et mittite eum
in tenebras exteriores: ibi erit fletus et stridor dentium". 14Multi enim sunt vocati, pauci vero electi».
15Tunc abeuntes pharisaei consilium inierunt, ut caperent eum in sermone. 16Et mittunt ei discipulos
suos cum herodianis dicentes: «Magister, scimus quia verax es et viam Dei in veritate doces et non est
tibi cura de aliquo; non enim respicis personam hominum. 17Dic ergo nobis quid tibi videatur: Licet
censum dare Caesari an non?». 18Cognita autem Iesus nequitia eorum, ait: «Quid me tentatis,
hypocritae? 19Ostendite mihi nomisma census». At illi obtulerunt ei denarium. 20Et ait illis: «Cuius est
imago haec et suprascriptio?». 21Dicunt ei: «Caesaris». Tunc ait illis: «Reddite ergo, quae sunt Caesaris,
Caesari et, quae sunt Dei, Deo». 22Et audientes mirati sunt et relicto eo abierunt. 23In illo die accesserunt
ad eum sadducaei, qui dicunt non esse resurrectionem, et interrogaverunt eum 24dicentes: «Magister,
Moyses dixit, *si quis mortuus fuerit non habens filios, ut ducat frater eius uxorem illius et suscitet semen*
fratri suo. 25Erant autem apud nos septem fratres: et primus, uxore ducta, defunctus est et non habens
semen reliquit uxorem suam fratri suo; 26similiter secundus et tertius usque ad septimum. 27Novissime
autem omnium mulier defuncta est. 28In resurrectione ergo cuius erit de septem uxor? Omnes enim
habuerunt eam». 29Respondens autem Iesus ait illis: «Erratis nescientes Scripturas neque virtutem Dei;
30in resurrectione enim neque nubent neque nubentur, sed sunt sicut angeli in caelo. 31De resurrectione
autem mortuorum non legistis, quod dictum est vobis a Deo dicente: 32"*Ego sum Deus Abraham et Deus*
Isaac et Deus Iacob"? Non est Deus mortuorum sed viventium». 33Et audientes turbae mirabantur in
doctrina eius. 34Pharisaei autem audientes quod silentium imposuisset sadducaeis, convenerunt in unum.
35Et interrogavit unus ex eis legis doctor tentans eum: 36«Magister, quod est mandatum magnum in
Lege?». 37Ait autem illi: «*Diliges Dominum Deum tuum in toto corde tuo et in tota anima tua* et in tota
mente tua: 38hoc est magnum et primum mandatum. 39Secundum autem simile est huic: *Diliges*
proximum tuum sicut teipsum. 40In his duobus mandatis universa Lex pendet et Prophetae».
41Congregatis autem pharisaeis, interrogavit eos Iesus 42dicens: «Quid vobis videtur de Christo? Cuius
filius est?». Dicunt ei: «David». 43Ait illis: «Quomodo ergo David in Spiritu vocat eum Dominum
dicens: 44"*Dixit Dominus Domino meo: Sede a dextris meis, / donec ponam inimicos tuos sub pedibus*
tuis"? 45Si ergo David vocat eum Dominum, quomodo filius eius est?». 46Et nemo poterat respondere
ei verbum, neque ausus fuit quisquam ex illa die eum amplius interrogare. **[23]** 1Tunc Iesus locutus

est ad turbas et ad discipulos suos 2dicens: «Super cathedram Moysis sederunt scribae et pharisaei. 3Omnia ergo, quaecumque dixerint vobis, facite et servate; secundum opera vero eorum nolite facere: dicunt enim et non faciunt. 4Alligant autem onera gravia et importabilia et imponunt in umeros hominum, ipsi autem digito suo nolunt ea movere. 5Omnia vero opera sua faciunt, ut videantur ab hominibus: dilatant enim phylacteria sua et magnificant fimbrias, 6amant autem primum recubitum in cenis et primas cathedras in synagogis 7et salutationes in foro et vocari ab hominibus Rabbi. 8Vos autem nolite vocari Rabbi; unus enim est Magister vester, omnes autem vos fratres estis. 9Et Patrem nolite vocare vobis super terram, unus enim est Pater vester, caelestis. 10Nec vocemini Magistri, quia Magister vester unus est, Christus. 11Qui maior est vestrum, erit minister vester. 12Qui autem se exaltaverit, humiliabitur; et, qui se humiliaverit, exaltabitur. 13Vae autem vobis, scribae et pharisaei hypocritae, quia clauditis regnum caelorum ante homines! Vos enim non intratis nec introeuntes sinitis intrare. (14) 15Vae vobis, scribae et pharisaei hypocritae, quia circuitis mare et aridam, ut faciatis unum proselytum, et cum fuerit factus, facitis eum filium gehennae duplo quam vos! 16Vae vobis, duces caeci, qui dicitis: "Quicumque iuraverit per templum, nihil est; quicumque autem iuraverit in auro templi, debet". 17Stulti et caeci! Quid enim maius est: aurum an templum, quod sanctificat aurum? 18Et: "Quicumque iuraverit in altari, nihil est; quicumque autem iuraverit in dono, quod est super illud, debet". 19Caeci! Quid enim maius est: donum an altare, quod sanctificat donum? 20Qui ergo iuraverit in altari, iurat in eo et in omnibus, quae super illud sunt; 21et, qui iuraverit in templo, iurat in illo et in eo, qui inhabitat in ipso; 22et, qui iuraverit in caelo, iurat in throno Dei et in eo, qui sedet super eum. 23Vae vobis, scribae et pharisaei hypocritae, quia decimatis mentam et anethum et cyminum et reliquistis, quae graviora sunt legis: iudicium et misericordiam et fidem! Haec oportuit facere et illa non omittere. 24Duces caeci, excolantes culicem, camelum autem glutientes. 25Vae vobis, scribae et pharisaei hypocritae, quia mundatis, quod de foris est calicis et paropsidis, intus autem pleni sunt rapina et immunditia! 26Pharisaee caece, munda prius, quod intus est calicis, ut fiat et id, quod de foris eius est, mundum. 27Vae vobis, scribae et pharisaei hypocritae, quia similes estis sepulcris dealbatis, quae a foris quidem parent speciosa, intus vero plena sunt ossibus mortuorum et omni spurcitia! 28Sic et vos a foris quidem paretis hominibus iusti, intus autem pleni estis hypocrisi et iniquitate. 29Vae vobis, scribae et pharisaei hypocritae, qui aedificatis sepulcra prophetarum et ornatis monumenta iustorum 30et dicitis: "Si fuissemus in diebus patrum nostrorum, non essemus socii eorum in sanguine prophetarum"! 31Itaque testimonio estis vobismetipsis quia filii estis eorum, qui prophetas occiderunt. 32Et vos implete mensuram patrum vestrorum. 33Serpentes, genimina viperarum, quomodo fugietis a iudicio gehennae? 34Ideo ecce ego mitto ad vos prophetas et sapientes et scribas; ex illis occidetis et crucifigetis et ex eis flagellabitis in synagogis vestris et persequemini de civitate in civitatem, 35ut veniat super vos omnis sanguis iustus, qui effusus est super terram a sanguine Abel iusti usque ad sanguinem Zachariae filii Barachiae, quem occidistis inter templum et altare. 36Amen dico vobis: Venient haec omnia super generationem istam. 37Ierusalem, Ierusalem, quae occidis prophetas et lapidas eos, qui ad te missi sunt, quotiens volui congregare filios tuos, quemadmodum gallina congregat pullos suos sub alas, et noluistis! *38Ecce relinquitur vobis domus vestra deserta!* 39Dico enim vobis: Non me videbitis amodo, donec dicatis: "*Benedictus, qui venit in nomine Domini!*"». **[24]** 1Et egressus Iesus de templo ibat, et accesserunt discipuli eius, ut ostenderent ei aedificationes templi; 2ipse autem respondens dixit eis: «Non videtis haec omnia? Amen dico vobis: Non relinquetur hic lapis super lapidem, qui non destruetur». 3Sedente autem eo super montem Oliveti, accesserunt ad eum discipuli secreto dicentes: «Dic nobis: Quando haec erunt, et quod signum adventus tui et consummationis saeculi?». 4Et respondens Iesus dixit eis: «Videte, ne quis vos seducat. 5Multi enim venient in nomine meo dicentes: "Ego sum Christus", et multos seducent. 6Audituri enim estis proelia et opiniones proeliorum. Videte, ne turbemini; oportet enim fieri, sed nondum est finis. 7Consurget enim gens in gentem, et regnum in regnum, et erunt fames et terrae motus per loca; 8haec autem omnia initia sunt dolorum. 9Tunc tradent vos in tribulationem et occident vos, et eritis odio omnibus gentibus propter nomen meum. 10Et tunc scandalizabuntur multi et invicem tradent et odio habebunt invicem; 11et multi pseudoprophetae surgent et seducent multos. 12Et, quoniam abundavit iniquitas, refrigescet caritas multorum; 13qui autem permanserit usque in finem, hic salvus erit. 14Et praedicabitur hoc evangelium regni in universo orbe in testimonium omnibus gentibus; et tunc veniet consummatio. 15Cum ergo videritis *abominationem desolationis*, quae dicta est a Daniele propheta, stantem *in loco sancto*, qui legit, intellegat: 16tunc qui in Iudaea sunt, fugiant ad montes; 17qui in tecto, non descendat tollere aliquid de domo sua; 18et, qui in agro, non revertatur tollere pallium suum. 19Vae autem praegnantibus et nutrientibus in illis diebus! 20Orate autem, ut non fiat fuga vestra hieme vel sabbato: 21erit enim tunc *tribulatio* magna, *qualis non fuit ab initio mundi usque modo* neque fiet. 22Et nisi breviati fuissent dies illi, non fieret salva omnis caro; sed propter electos breviabuntur dies

illi. [23]Tunc si quis vobis dixerit: “Ecce hic Christus” aut: “Hic”, nolite credere. [24]Surgent enim
pseudochristi et pseudoprophetae et dabunt signa magna et prodigia, ita ut in errorem inducantur, si fieri
potest, etiam electi. [25]Ecce praedixi vobis. [26]Si ergo dixerint vobis: “Ecce in deserto est”, nolite exire;
“Ecce in penetralibus”, nolite credere: [27]sicut enim fulgur exit ab oriente et paret usque in occidentem,
ita erit adventus Filii hominis. [28]Ubicumque fuerit corpus, illuc congregabuntur aquilae. [29]Statim autem
post tribulationem dierum illorum, *sol obscurabitur, et luna non dabit lumen suum, et stellae cadent* de
caelo, *et virtutes caelorum* commovebuntur. [30]Et tunc parebit signum Filii hominis in caelo, et tunc
plangent omnes tribus terrae et videbunt *Filium hominis venientem in nubibus caeli* cum virtute et
gloria multa; [31]et mittet angelos suos cum tuba magna, et congregabunt electos eius a quattuor ventis,
a summis caelorum usque ad terminos eorum. [32]Ab arbore autem fici discite parabolam: cum iam ramus
eius tener fuerit, et folia nata, scitis quia prope est aestas. [33]Ita et vos, cum videritis haec omnia, scitote
quia prope est in ianuis. [34]Amen dico vobis: Non praeteribit haec generatio, donec omnia haec fiant.
[35]Caelum et terra transibunt, verba vero mea non praeteribunt. [36]De die autem illa et hora nemo scit,
neque angeli caelorum neque Filius, nisi Pater solus. [37]Sicut enim dies Noe, ita erit adventus Filii
hominis. [38]Sicut enim erant in diebus ante diluvium comedentes et bibentes, nubentes et nuptum
tradentes, usque ad eum diem, quo introivit in arcam Noe, [39]et non cognoverunt, donec venit diluvium
et tulit omnes, ita erit et adventus Filii hominis. [40]Tunc duo erunt in agro: unus assumitur, et unus
relinquitur; [41]duae molentes in mola: una assumitur, et una relinquitur. [42]Vigilate ergo, quia nescitis qua
die Dominus vester venturus sit. [43]Illud autem scitote quoniam si sciret pater familias qua hora fur
venturus esset, vigilaret utique et non sineret perfodi domum suam. [44]Ideo et vos estote parati, quia, qua
nescitis hora, Filius hominis venturus est. [45]Quis putas est fidelis servus et prudens, quem constituit
dominus supra familiam suam, ut det illis cibum in tempore? [46]Beatus ille servus, quem cum venerit
dominus eius invenerit sic facientem. [47]Amen dico vobis quoniam super omnia bona sua constituet eum.
[48]Si autem dixerit malus servus ille in corde suo: “Moram facit dominus meus venire”, [49]et coeperit
percutere conservos suos, manducet autem et bibat cum ebriis, [50]veniet dominus servi illius in die, qua
non sperat, et in hora, qua ignorat, [51]et dividet eum partemque eius ponet cum hypocritis; illic erit fletus
et stridor dentium. **[25]** [1]Tunc simile erit regnum caelorum decem virginibus, quae accipientes lampades
suas exierunt obviam sponso. [2]Quinque autem ex eis erant fatuae et quinque prudentes. [3]Fatuae enim,
acceptis lampadibus suis, non sumpserunt oleum secum; [4]prudentes vero acceperunt oleum in vasis cum
lampadibus suis. [5]Moram autem faciente sponso, dormitaverunt omnes et dormierunt. [6]Media autem
nocte clamor factus est: “Ecce sponsus! Exite obviam ei”. [7]Tunc surrexerunt omnes virgines illae et
ornaverunt lampades suas. [8]Fatuae autem sapientibus dixerunt: “Date nobis de oleo vestro, quia
lampades nostrae exstinguuntur”. [9]Responderunt prudentes dicentes: “Ne forte non sufficiat nobis et
vobis, ite potius ad vendentes et emite vobis”. [10]Dum autem irent emere, venit sponsus, et quae paratae
erant, intraverunt cum eo ad nuptias; et clausa est ianua. [11]Novissime autem veniunt et reliquae virgines
dicentes: “Domine, Domine, aperi nobis”. [12]At ille respondens ait: “Amen dico vobis: Nescio vos”.
[13]Vigilate itaque, quia nescitis diem neque horam. [14]Sicut enim homo peregre proficiscens vocavit
servos suos et tradidit illis bona sua. [15]Et uni dedit quinque talenta, alii autem duo, alii vero unum,
unicuique secundum propriam virtutem, et profectus est. Statim [16]abiit, qui quinque talenta acceperat,
et operatus est in eis et lucratus est alia quinque; [17]similiter qui duo acceperat, lucratus est alia duo.
[18]Qui autem unum acceperat, abiens fodit in terra et abscondit pecuniam domini sui. [19]Post multum vero
temporis venit dominus servorum illorum et ponit rationem cum eis. [20]Et accedens, qui quinque talenta
acceperat, obtulit alia quinque talenta dicens: “Domine, quinque talenta tradidisti mihi; ecce alia
quinque superlucratus sum”. [21]Ait illi dominus eius: “Euge, serve bone et fidelis. Super pauca fuisti
fidelis; supra multa te constituam: intra in gaudium domini tui”. [22]Accessit autem et qui duo talenta
acceperat, et ait: “Domine, duo talenta tradidisti mihi; ecce alia duo lucratus sum”. [23]Ait illi dominus
eius: “Euge, serve bone et fidelis. Super pauca fuisti fidelis; supra multa te constituam: intra in gaudium
domini tui”. [24]Accedens autem et qui unum talentum acceperat, ait: “Domine, novi te quia homo durus
es: metis, ubi non seminasti, et congregas, ubi non sparsisti; [25]et timens abii et abscondi talentum tuum
in terra. Ecce habes, quod tuum est”. [26]Respondens autem dominus eius dixit ei: “Serve male et piger!
Sciebas quia meto, ubi non seminavi, et congrego, ubi non sparsi? [27]Oportuit ergo te mittere pecuniam
meam nummulariis, et veniens ego recepissem, quod meum est cum usura. [28]Tollite itaque ab eo
talentum et date ei, qui habet decem talenta: [29]omni enim habenti dabitur, et abundabit; ei autem, qui
non habet, et quod habet, auferetur ab eo. [30]Et inutilem servum eicite in tenebras exteriores: illic erit fletus
et stridor dentium”. [31]Cum autem venerit Filius hominis in gloria sua, et omnes angeli cum eo, tunc sedebit
super thronum gloriae suae. [32]Et congregabuntur ante eum omnes gentes; et separabit eos ab invicem, sicut
pastor segregat oves ab haedis, [33]et statuet oves quidem a dextris suis, haedos autem a sinistris. [34]Tunc

dicet Rex his, qui a dextris eius erunt: “Venite, benedicti Patris mei; possidete paratum vobis regnum
a constitutione mundi. [35]Esurivi enim, et dedistis mihi manducare; sitivi, et dedistis mihi bibere; hospes
eram, et collegistis me; [36]nudus, et operuistis me; infirmus, et visitastis me; in carcere eram, et venistis
ad me”. [37]Tunc respondebunt ei iusti dicentes: “Domine, quando te vidimus esurientem et pavimus, aut
sitientem et dedimus tibi potum? [38]Quando autem te vidimus hospitem et collegimus, aut nudum et
cooperuimus? [39]Quando autem te vidimus infirmum aut in carcere et venimus ad te?”. [40]Et respondens
Rex dicet illis: “Amen dico vobis: Quamdiu fecistis uni de his fratribus meis minimis, mihi fecistis”.
[41]Tunc dicet et his, qui a sinistris erunt: “Discedite a me, maledicti, in ignem aeternum, qui praeparatus
est Diabolo et angelis eius. [42]Esurivi enim, et non dedistis mihi manducare; sitivi, et non dedistis mihi
potum; [43]hospes eram, et non collegistis me; nudus, et non operuistis me; infirmus et in carcere, et non
visitastis me”. [44]Tunc respondebunt et ipsi dicentes: “Domine, quando te vidimus esurientem aut
sitientem aut hospitem aut nudum aut infirmum vel in carcere et non ministravimus tibi?”. [45]Tunc
respondebit illis dicens: “Amen dico vobis: Quamdiu non fecistis uni de minimis his, nec mihi fecistis”.
[46]Et ibunt hi in supplicium aeternum, iusti autem in vitam aeternam». **[26]** [1]Et factum est cum
consummasset Iesus sermones hos omnes, dixit discipulis suis: [2]«Scitis quia post biduum Pascha fiet,
et Filius hominis traditur, ut crucifigatur». [3]Tunc congregati sunt principes sacerdotum et seniores populi
in aulam principis sacerdotum, qui dicebatur Caiphas, [4]et consilium fecerunt, ut Iesum dolo tenerent et
occiderent; [5]dicebant autem: «Non in die festo, ne tumultus fiat in populo». [6]Cum autem esset Iesus in
Bethania, in domo Simonis leprosi, [7]accessit ad eum mulier habens alabastrum unguenti pretiosi et
effudit super caput ipsius recumbentis. [8]Videntes autem discipuli, indignati sunt dicentes: «Ut quid
perditio haec? [9]Potuit enim istud venumdari multo et dari pauperibus». [10]Sciens autem Iesus ait illis:
«Quid molesti estis mulieri? Opus enim bonum operata est in me; [11]nam semper pauperes habetis
vobiscum, me autem non semper habetis. [12]Mittens enim haec unguentum hoc supra corpus meum, ad
sepeliendum me fecit. [13]Amen dico vobis: Ubicumque praedicatum fuerit hoc evangelium in toto
mundo, dicetur et quod haec fecit in memoriam eius». [14]Tunc abiit unus de Duodecim, qui dicebatur
Iudas Iscariotes, ad principes sacerdotum [15]et ait: «Quid vultis mihi dare, et ego vobis eum tradam?».
At illi constituerunt ei triginta argenteos. [16]Et exinde quaerebat opportunitatem, ut eum traderet. [17]Prima
autem Azymorum accesserunt discipuli ad Iesum dicentes: «Ubi vis paremus tibi comedere Pascha?».
[18]Ille autem dixit: «Ite in civitatem ad quendam et dicite ei: “Magister dicit: Tempus meum prope est;
apud te facio Pascha cum discipulis meis”». [19]Et fecerunt discipuli, sicut constituit illis Iesus, et
paraverunt Pascha. [20]Vespere autem facto, discumbebat cum Duodecim. [21]Et edentibus illis, dixit:
«Amen dico vobis: Unus vestrum me traditurus est». [22]Et contristati valde, coeperunt singuli dicere ei:
«Numquid ego sum, Domine?». [23]At ipse respondens ait: «Qui intingit mecum manum in paropside,
hic me tradet. [24]Filius quidem hominis vadit, sicut scriptum est de illo; vae autem homini illi, per quem
Filius hominis traditur! Bonum erat ei, si natus non fuisset homo ille». [25]Respondens autem Iudas, qui
tradidit eum, dixit: «Numquid ego sum, Rabbi?». Ait illi: «Tu dixisti». [26]Cenantibus autem eis, accepit
Iesus panem et benedixit ac fregit deditque discipulis et ait: «Accipite, comedite: hoc est corpus meum».
[27]Et accipiens calicem, gratias egit et dedit illis dicens: «Bibite ex hoc omnes: [28]hic est enim sanguis
meus novi testamenti, qui pro multis effunditur in remissionem peccatorum. [29]Dico autem vobis: Non
bibam amodo de hoc genimine vitis usque in diem illum, cum illud bibam vobiscum novum in regno
Patris mei». [30]Et hymno dicto, exierunt in montem Oliveti. [31]Tunc dicit illis Iesus: «Omnes vos
scandalum patiemini in me in ista nocte. Scriptum est enim: “*Percutiam pastorem, et dispergentur oves
gregis*”. [32]Postquam autem resurrexero, praecedam vos in Galilaeam». [33]Respondens autem Petrus ait
illi: «Et si omnes scandalizati fuerint in te, ego numquam scandalizabor». [34]Ait illi Iesus: «Amen dico
tibi: In hac nocte, antequam gallus cantet, ter me negabis». [35]Ait illi Petrus: «Etiam si oportuerit me
mori tecum, non te negabo». Similiter et omnes discipuli dixerunt. [36]Tunc venit Iesus cum illis in
praedium, quod dicitur Gethsemani. Et dicit discipulis: «Sedete hic, donec vadam illuc et orem». [37]Et
assumpto Petro et duobus filiis Zebedaei, coepit contristari et maestus esse. [38]Tunc ait illis: «Tristis est
anima mea usque ad mortem; sustinete hic et vigilate mecum». [39]Et progressus pusillum, procidit in
faciem suam orans et dicens: «Pater mi, si possibile est, transeat a me calix iste; verumtamen non sicut
ego volo, sed sicut tu». [40]Et venit ad discipulos et invenit eos dormientes; et dicit Petro: «Sic non
potuistis una hora vigilare mecum? [41]Vigilate et orate, ut non intretis in tentationem; spiritus quidem
promptus est, caro autem infirma». [42]Iterum secundo abiit et oravit dicens: «Pater mi, si non potest hoc
transire, nisi bibam illud, fiat voluntas tua». [43]Et venit iterum et invenit eos dormientes: erant enim oculi
eorum gravati. [44]Et relictis illis, iterum abiit et oravit tertio, eundem sermonem iterum dicens. [45]Tunc
venit ad discipulos et dicit illis: «Dormite iam et requiescite; ecce appropinquavit hora, et Filius hominis
traditur in manus peccatorum. [46]Surgite, eamus; ecce appropinquavit, qui me tradit». [47]Et adhuc ipso

loquente, ecce Iudas, unus de Duodecim, venit et cum eo turba multa cum gladiis et fustibus, missi a
principibus sacerdotum et senioribus populi. 48Qui autem tradidit eum, dedit illis signum dicens:
«Quemcumque osculatus fuero, ipse est; tenete eum!». 49Et confestim accedens ad Iesum dixit: «Ave,
Rabbi!» et osculatus est eum. 50Iesus autem dixit illi: «Amice, ad quod venisti!». Tunc accesserunt et
manus iniecerunt in Iesum et tenuerunt eum. 51Et ecce unus ex his, qui erant cum Iesu, extendens
manum exemit gladium suum et percutiens servum principis sacerdotum amputavit auriculam eius.
52Tunc ait illi Iesus: «Converte gladium tuum in locum suum. Omnes enim, qui acceperint gladium,
gladio peribunt. 53An putas quia non possum rogare Patrem meum, et exhibebit mihi modo plus quam
duodecim legiones angelorum? 54Quomodo ergo implebuntur Scripturae quia sic oportet fieri?». 55In
illa hora dixit Iesus turbis: «Tamquam ad latronem existis cum gladiis et fustibus comprehendere me?
Cotidie sedebam docens in templo, et non me tenuistis». 56Hoc autem totum factum est, ut implerentur
scripturae Prophetarum. Tunc discipuli omnes, relicto eo, fugerunt. 57Illi autem tenentes Iesum duxerunt
ad Caipham principem sacerdotum, ubi scribae et seniores convenerant. 58Petrus autem sequebatur eum
a longe usque in aulam principis sacerdotum; et ingressus intro sedebat cum ministris, ut videret finem.
59Principes autem sacerdotum et omne concilium quaerebant falsum testimonium contra Iesum, ut eum
morti traderent, 60et non invenerunt, cum multi falsi testes accessissent. Novissime autem venientes duo
61dixerunt: «Hic dixit: "Possum destruere templum Dei et post triduum aedificare illud"». 62Et surgens
princeps sacerdotum ait illi: «Nihil respondes? Quid isti adversum te testificantur?». 63Iesus autem
tacebat. Et princeps sacerdotum ait illi: «Adiuro te per Deum vivum, ut dicas nobis, si tu es Christus
Filius Dei». 64Dicit illi Iesus: «Tu dixisti. Verumtamen dico vobis: Amodo videbitis *Filium hominis
sedentem a dextris Virtutis et venientem in nubibus caeli*». 65Tunc princeps sacerdotum scidit vestimenta
sua dicens: «Blasphemavit! Quid adhuc egemus testibus? Ecce nunc audistis blasphemiam. 66Quid
vobis videtur?». Illi autem respondentes dixerunt: «Reus est mortis!». 67Tunc exspuerunt in faciem eius
et colaphis eum ceciderunt; alii autem palmas in faciem ei dederunt 68dicentes: «Prophetiza nobis,
Christe: Quis est, qui te percussit?». 69Petrus vero sedebat foris in atrio; et accessit ad eum una ancilla
dicens: «Et tu cum Iesu Galilaeo eras!». 70At ille negavit coram omnibus dicens: «Nescio quid dicis!».
71Exeunte autem illo ad ianuam, vidit eum alia et ait his, qui erant ibi: «Hic erat cum Iesu Nazareno!».
72Et iterum negavit cum iuramento: «Non novi hominem!». 73Post pusillum autem accesserunt, qui
stabant et dixerunt Petro: «Vere et tu ex illis es, nam et loquela tua manifestum te facit». 74Tunc coepit
detestari et iurare: «Non novi hominem!». Et continuo gallus cantavit; 75et recordatus est Petrus verbi
Iesu, quod dixerat: «Priusquam gallus cantet, ter me negabis». Et egressus foras ploravit amare.
[27] 1Mane autem facto, consilium inierunt omnes principes sacerdotum et seniores populi adversus
Iesum, ut eum morti traderent. 2Et vinctum adduxerunt eum et tradiderunt Pilato praesidi. 3Tunc videns
Iudas, qui eum tradidit, quod damnatus esset, paenitentia ductus, rettulit triginta argenteos principibus
sacerdotum et senioribus 4dicens: «Peccavi tradens sanguinem innocentem». At illi dixerunt: «Quid ad
nos? Tu videris!». 5Et proiectis argenteis in templo, recessit et abiens laqueo se suspendit. 6Principes
autem sacerdotum, acceptis argenteis, dixerunt: «Non licet mittere eos in corbanam, quia pretium
sanguinis est». 7Consilio autem inito, emerunt ex illis agrum Figuli in sepulturam peregrinorum.
8Propter hoc vocatus est ager ille ager Sanguinis usque in hodiernum diem. 9Tunc impletum est quod
dictum est per Ieremiam prophetam dicentem: «*Et acceperunt triginta argenteos, pretium appretiati
quem appretiaverunt a filiis Israel*, 10*et dederunt eos in agrum Figuli, sicut constituit mihi Dominus*».
11Iesus autem stetit ante praesidem; et interrogavit eum praeses dicens: «Tu es Rex Iudaeorum?». Dixit
autem Iesus: «Tu dicis». 12Et cum accusaretur a principibus sacerdotum et senioribus, nihil respondit.
13Tunc dicit illi Pilatus: «Non audis quanta adversum te dicant testimonia?». 14Et non respondit ei ad
ullum verbum, ita ut miraretur praeses vehementer. 15Per diem autem sollemnem consueverat praeses
dimittere turbae unum vinctum, quem voluissent. 16Habebant autem tunc vinctum insignem, qui
dicebatur Barabbas. 17Congregatis ergo illis dixit Pilatus: «Quem vultis dimittam vobis: Barabbam an
Iesum, qui dicitur Christus?». 18Sciebat enim quod per invidiam tradidissent eum. 19Sedente autem illo
pro tribunali, misit ad illum uxor eius dicens: «Nihil tibi et iusto illi. Multa enim passa sum hodie per
visum propter eum». 20Principes autem sacerdotum et seniores persuaserunt turbis, ut peterent
Barabbam, Iesum vero perderent. 21Respondens autem praeses ait illis: «Quem vultis vobis de duobus
dimittam?». At illi dixerunt: «Barabbam!». 22Dicit illis Pilatus: «Quid igitur faciam de Iesu, qui dicitur
Christus?». Dicunt omnes: «Crucifigatur!». 23Ait autem: «Quid enim mali fecit?». At illi magis
clamabant dicentes: «Crucifigatur!». 24Videns autem Pilatus quia nihil proficeret, sed magis tumultus
fieret, accepta aqua, lavit manus coram turba dicens: «Innocens ego sum a sanguine hoc; vos videritis!».
25Et respondens universus populus dixit: «Sanguis eius super nos et super filios nostros». 26Tunc dimisit
illis Barabbam; Iesum autem flagellatum tradidit, ut crucifigeretur. 27Tunc milites praesidis suscipientes

Iesum in praetorio congregaverunt ad eum universam cohortem. [28]Et exuentes eum, clamydem coccineam circumdederunt ei [29]et plectentes coronam de spinis posuerunt super caput eius et arundinem in dextera eius et, genu flexo ante eum, illudebant ei dicentes: «Ave, rex Iudaeorum!». [30]Et exspuentes in eum acceperunt arundinem et percutiebant caput eius. [31]Et postquam illuserunt ei, exuerunt eum clamyde et induerunt eum vestimentis eius et duxerunt eum, ut crucifigerent. [32]Exeuntes autem invenerunt hominem Cyrenaeum nomine Simonem; hunc angariaverunt, ut tolleret crucem eius. [33]Et venerunt in locum, qui dicitur Golgotha, quod est Calvariae locus, [34]et *dederunt* ei vinum *bibere* cum *felle* mixtum; et cum gustasset, noluit bibere. [35]Postquam autem crucifixerunt eum, *diviserunt vestimenta* eius *sortem mittentes* [36]et sedentes servabant eum ibi. [37]Et imposuerunt super caput eius causam ipsius scriptam: «Hic est Iesus Rex Iudaeorum». [38]Tunc crucifiguntur cum eo duo latrones: unus a dextris et unus a sinistris. [39]Praetereuntes autem blasphemabant eum *moventes capita sua* [40]et dicentes: «Qui destruis templum et in triduo illud reaedificas, salva temetipsum; si Filius Dei es, descende de cruce!». [41]Similiter et principes sacerdotum illudentes cum scribis et senioribus dicebant: [42]«Alios salvos fecit, seipsum non potest salvum facere. Rex Israel est; descendat nunc de cruce, et credemus in eum. [43]*Confidit in Deo*; *liberet* nunc, *si vult eum*. Dixit enim: "Dei Filius sum"». [44]Idipsum autem et latrones, qui crucifixi erant cum eo, improperabant ei. [45]A sexta autem hora tenebrae factae sunt super universam terram usque ad horam nonam. [46]Et circa horam nonam clamavit Iesus voce magna dicens: «*Eli, Eli, lema sabacthani*?», hoc est: «*Deus meus, Deus meus, ut quid dereliquisti me*?». [47]Quidam autem ex illic stantibus audientes dicebant: «Eliam vocat iste». [48]Et continuo currens unus ex eis acceptam spongiam implevit aceto et imposuit arundini et *dabat* ei *bibere*. [49]Ceteri vero dicebant: «Sine, videamus an veniat Elias liberans eum». [50]Iesus autem iterum clamans voce magna emisit spiritum. [51]Et ecce velum templi scissum est a summo usque deorsum in duas partes, et terra mota est, et petrae scissae sunt, [52]et monumenta aperta sunt et multa corpora sanctorum, qui dormierant, surrexerunt [53]et exeuntes de monumentis post resurrectionem eius venerunt in sanctam civitatem et apparuerunt multis. [54]Centurio autem et, qui cum eo erant custodientes Iesum, viso terrae motu et his, quae fiebant, timuerunt valde dicentes: «Vere Dei Filius erat iste!». [55]Erant autem ibi mulieres multae a longe aspicientes, quae secutae erant Iesum a Galilaea ministrantes ei; [56]inter quas erat Maria Magdalene et Maria Iacobi et Ioseph mater et mater filiorum Zebedaei. [57]Cum sero autem factum esset, venit homo dives ab Arimathaea nomine Ioseph, qui et ipse discipulus erat Iesu. [58]Hic accessit ad Pilatum et petiit corpus Iesu. Tunc Pilatus iussit reddi. [59]Et accepto corpore, Ioseph involvit illud in sindone munda [60]et posuit illud in monumento suo novo, quod exciderat in petra, et advolvit saxum magnum ad ostium monumenti et abiit. [61]Erat autem ibi Maria Magdalene et altera Maria sedentes contra sepulcrum. [62]Altera autem die, quae est post Parascevem, convenerunt principes sacerdotum et pharisaei ad Pilatum [63]dicentes: «Domine, recordati sumus quia seductor ille dixit adhuc vivens: 'Post tres dies resurgam'. [64]Iube ergo custodiri sepulcrum usque in diem tertium, ne forte veniant discipuli eius et furentur eum et dicant plebi: 'Surrexit a mortuis', et erit novissimus error peior priore». [65]Ait illis Pilatus: «Habetis custodiam; ite, custodite, sicut scitis». [66]Illi autem abeuntes munierunt sepulcrum, signantes lapidem, cum custodia. **[28]** [1]Sero autem post sabbatum, cum illucesceret in primam sabbati, venit Maria Magdalene et altera Maria videre sepulcrum. [2]Et ecce terrae motus factus est magnus: angelus enim Domini descendit de caelo et accedens revolvit lapidem et sedebat super eum. [3]Erat autem aspectus eius sicut fulgur, et vestimentum eius candidum sicut nix. [4]Prae timore autem eius exterriti sunt custodes et facti sunt velut mortui. [5]Respondens autem angelus dixit mulieribus: «Nolite timere vos! Scio enim quod Iesum, qui crucifixus est, quaeritis. [6]Non est hic: surrexit enim, sicut dixit. Venite, videte locum, ubi positus erat. [7]Et cito euntes dicite discipulis eius: "Surrexit a mortuis et ecce praecedit vos in Galilaeam; ibi eum videbitis". Ecce dixi vobis». [8]Et exeuntes cito de monumento cum timore et magno gaudio cucurrerunt nuntiare discipulis eius. [9]Et ecce Iesus occurrit illis dicens: «Avete». Illae autem accesserunt et tenuerunt pedes eius et adoraverunt eum. [10]Tunc ait illis Iesus: «Nolite timere; ite, nuntiate fratribus meis, ut eant in Galilaeam et ibi me videbunt». [11]Quae cum abiissent, ecce quidam de custodia venerunt in civitatem et nuntiaverunt principibus sacerdotum omnia, quae facta fuerant. [12]Et congregati cum senioribus, consilio accepto, pecuniam copiosam dederunt militibus [13]dicentes: «Dicite: "Discipuli eius nocte venerunt et furati sunt eum, nobis dormientibus". [14]Et si hoc auditum fuerit a praeside, nos suadebimus ei et securos vos faciemus». [15]At illi, accepta pecunia, fecerunt, sicut erant docti. Et divulgatum est verbum istud apud Iudaeos usque in hodiernum diem. [16]Undecim autem discipuli abierunt in Galilaeam, in montem ubi constituerat illis Iesus, [17]et videntes eum adoraverunt; quidam autem dubitaverunt. [18]Et accedens Iesus locutus est eis dicens: «Data est mihi omnis potestas in caelo et in terra. [19]Euntes ergo docete omnes gentes, baptizantes eos in nomine Patris et Filii et Spiritus Sancti, [20]docentes eos servare omnia, quaecumque mandavi vobis. Et ecce ego vobiscum sum omnibus diebus usque ad consummationem saeculi».

EVANGELIUM SECUNDUM MARCUM

[1] [1]Initium evangelii Iesu Christi Filii Dei. [2]Sicut scriptum est in Isaia propheta: «*Ecce mitto angelum*
meum ante faciem tuam, / qui praeparabit viam tuam; / [3]*vox clamantis in deserto: / "Parate viam*
Domini, rectas facite semitas eius"», [4]fuit Ioannes Baptista in deserto praedicans baptismum
paenitentiae in remissionem peccatorum. [5]Et egrediebatur ad illum omnis Iudaeae regio et
Hierosolymitae universi et baptizabantur ab illo in Iordane flumine confitentes peccata sua. [6]Et erat
Ioannes vestitus pilis cameli, et zona pellicea circa lumbos eius, et locustas et mel silvestre edebat. [7]Et
praedicabat dicens: «Venit fortior me post me, cuius non sum dignus procumbens solvere corrigiam
calceamentorum eius. [8]Ego baptizavi vos aqua; ille vero baptizabit vos in Spiritu Sancto». [9]Et factum
est in diebus illis, venit Iesus a Nazareth Galilaeae et baptizatus est in Iordane ab Ioanne. [10]Et statim
ascendens de aqua vidit apertos caelos et Spiritum tamquam columbam descendentem in ipsum; [11]et
vox facta est de caelis: «Tu es Filius meus dilectus; in te complacui». [12]Et statim Spiritus expellit eum
in desertum. [13]Et erat in deserto quadraginta diebus et tentabatur a Satana; eratque cum bestiis, et angeli
ministrabant illi. [14]Postquam autem traditus est Ioannes, venit Iesus in Galilaeam praedicans evangelium
Dei [15]et dicens: «Impletum est tempus, et appropinquavit regnum Dei; paenitemini et credite
evangelio». [16]Et praeteriens secus mare Galilaeae vidit Simonem et Andream fratrem Simonis mittentes
in mare; erant enim piscatores. [17]Et dixit eis Iesus: «Venite post me, et faciam vos fieri piscatores
hominum». [18]Et protinus, relictis retibus, secuti sunt eum. [19]Et progressus pusillum vidit Iacobum
Zebedaei et Ioannem fratrem eius, et ipsos in navi componentes retia, [20]et statim vocavit illos. Et, relicto
patre suo Zebedaeo in navi cum mercennariis, abierunt post eum. [21]Et ingrediuntur Capharnaum. Et
statim sabbatis ingressus synagogam docebat. [22]Et stupebant super doctrina eius: erat enim docens eos
quasi potestatem habens et non sicut scribae. [23]Et statim erat in synagoga eorum homo in spiritu
immundo; et exclamavit [24]dicens: «Quid nobis et tibi, Iesu Nazarene? Venisti perdere nos? Scio qui sis:
Sanctus Dei». [25]Et comminatus est ei Iesus dicens: «Obmutesce et exi de homine!». [26]Et discerpens eum
spiritus immundus et exclamans voce magna exivit ab eo. [27]Et mirati sunt omnes, ita ut conquirerent
inter se dicentes: «Quidnam est hoc? Doctrina nova cum potestate; et spiritibus immundis imperat, et
oboediunt ei». [28]Et processit rumor eius statim ubique in omnem regionem Galilaeae. [29]Et protinus
egredientes de synagoga venerunt in domum Simonis et Andreae cum Iacobo et Ioanne. [30]Socrus autem
Simonis decumbebat febricitans; et statim dicunt ei de illa. [31]Et accedens elevavit eam apprehensa
manu; et dimisit eam febris, et ministrabat eis. [32]Vespere autem facto, cum occidisset sol, afferebant ad
eum omnes male habentes et daemonia habentes; [33]et erat omnis civitas congregata ad ianuam. [34]Et
curavit multos, qui vexabantur variis languoribus, et daemonia multa eiecit et non sinebat loqui
daemonia, quoniam sciebant eum. [35]Et diluculo valde mane surgens egressus est et abiit in desertum
locum ibique orabat. [36]Et persecutus est eum Simon et, qui cum illo erant; [37]et cum invenissent eum,
dixerunt ei: «Omnes quaerunt te!». [38]Et ait illis: «Eamus alibi in proximos vicos, ut et ibi praedicem: ad
hoc enim veni». [39]Et venit praedicans in synagogis eorum per omnem Galilaeam et daemonia eiciens.
[40]Et venit ad eum leprosus deprecans eum et genu flectens et dicens ei: «Si vis, potes me mundare». [41]Et
misertus extendens manum suam tetigit eum et ait illi: «Volo, mundare!»; [42]et statim discessit ab eo
lepra, et mundatus est. [43]Et infremuit in eum statimque eiecit illum [44]et dicit ei: «Vide, nemini quidquam
dixeris; sed vade, ostende te sacerdoti et offer pro emundatione tua, quae praecepit Moyses, in
testimonium illis». [45]At ille egressus coepit praedicare multum et diffamare sermonem, ita ut iam non
posset manifesto in civitatem introire, sed foris in desertis locis erat; et conveniebant ad eum undique.
[2] [1]Et iterum intravit Capharnaum post dies, et auditum est quod in domo esset. [2]Et convenerunt multi,
ita ut non amplius caperentur neque ad ianuam, et loquebatur eis verbum. [3]Et veniunt ferentes ad eum
paralyticum, qui a quattuor portabatur. [4]Et cum non possent offerre eum illi prae turba, nudaverunt
tectum, ubi erat, et perfodientes summittunt grabatum, in quo paralyticus iacebat. [5]Cum vidisset autem
Iesus fidem illorum, ait paralytico: «Fili, dimittuntur peccata tua». [6]Erant autem illic quidam de scribis
sedentes et cogitantes in cordibus suis: [7]«Quid hic sic loquitur? Blasphemat! Quis potest dimittere
peccata nisi solus Deus?». [8]Quo statim cognito Iesus spiritu suo quia sic cogitarent intra se, dicit illis:
«Quid ista cogitatis in cordibus vestris? [9]Quid est facilius, dicere paralytico: 'Dimittuntur peccata tua',
an dicere: 'Surge et tolle grabatum tuum et ambula'? [10]Ut autem sciatis quia potestatem habet Filius
hominis in terra dimittendi peccata—ait paralytico—: [11]Tibi dico: Surge, tolle grabatum tuum et vade
in domum tuam». [12]Et surrexit et protinus sublato grabato abiit coram omnibus, ita ut admirarentur
omnes et glorificarent Deum dicentes: «Numquam sic vidimus!». [13]Et egressus est rursus ad mare;
omnisque turba veniebat ad eum, et docebat eos. [14]Et cum praeteriret, vidit Levin Alphaei sedentem ad

teloneum et ait illi: «Sequere me». Et surgens secutus est eum. 15Et factum est cum accumberet in domo
illius, et multi publicani et peccatores simul discumbebant cum Iesu et discipulis eius; erant enim multi
et sequebantur eum. 16Et scribae pharisaeorum, videntes quia manducaret cum peccatoribus et
publicanis, dicebant discipulis eius: «Quare cum publicanis et peccatoribus manducat?». 17Et Iesus hoc
audito ait illis: «Non necesse habent sani medicum, sed qui male habent; non veni vocare iustos, sed
peccatores». 18Et erant discipuli Ioannis et pharisaei ieiunantes. Et veniunt et dicunt illi: «Cur discipuli
Ioannis et discipuli pharisaeorum ieiunant, tui autem discipuli non ieiunant?». 19Et ait illis Iesus:
«Numquid possunt convivae nuptiarum, quamdiu sponsus cum illis est, ieiunare? Quanto tempore
habent secum sponsum, non possunt ieiunare; 20venient autem dies cum auferetur ab eis sponsus, et tunc
ieiunabunt in illa die. 21Nemo assumentum panni rudis assuit vestimento veteri; alioquin supplementum
aufert aliquid ab eo, novum a veteri, et peior scissura fit. 22Et nemo mittit vinum novellum in utres
veteres, alioquin dirumpet vinum utres et vinum perit et utres; sed vinum novum in utres novos». 23Et
factum est cum ipse sabbatis ambularet per sata, discipuli eius coeperunt praegredi vellentes spicas.
24Pharisaei autem dicebant ei: «Ecce, quid faciunt sabbatis, quod non licet?». 25Et ait illis: «Numquam
legistis quid fecerit David, quando necessitatem habuit et esuriit ipse et qui cum eo erant? 26Quomodo
introivit in domum Dei sub Abiathar principe sacerdotum et panes propositionis manducavit, quos non
licet manducare nisi sacerdotibus, et dedit etiam eis, qui cum eo erant?». 27Et dicebat eis: «Sabbatum
propter hominem factum est, et non homo propter sabbatum; 28itaque dominus est Filius hominis etiam
sabbati». **[3]** 1Et introivit iterum in synagogam. Et erat ibi homo habens manum aridam; 2et observabant
eum, si sabbatis curaret illum, ut accusarent eum. 3Et ait homini habenti manum aridam: «Surge in
medium». 4Et dicit eis: «Licet sabbatis bene facere an male? Animam salvam facere an perdere?». At
illi tacebant. 5Et circumspiciens eos cum ira, contristatus super caecitate cordis eorum, dicit homini:
«Extende manum». Et extendit, et restituta est manus eius. 6Et exeuntes pharisaei statim cum herodianis
consilium faciebant adversus eum quomodo eum perderent. 7Et Iesus cum discipulis suis secessit ad
mare. Et multa turba a Galilaea secuta est et a Iudaea 8et ab Hierosolymis et ab Idumaea; et, qui trans
Iordanem et circa Tyrum et Sidonem, multitudo magna, audientes, quae faciebat, venerunt ad eum. 9Et
dixit discipulis suis, ut navicula sibi praesto esset propter turbam, ne comprimerent eum. 10Multos enim
sanavit, ita ut irruerent in eum, ut illum tangerent, quotquot habebant plagas. 11Et spiritus immundi, cum
illum videbant, procidebant ei et clamabant dicentes: «Tu es Filius Dei!». 12Et vehementer
comminabatur eis, ne manifestarent illum. 13Et ascendit in montem et vocat ad se, quos voluit ipse, et
venerunt ad eum. 14Et fecit Duodecim, ut essent cum illo, et ut mitteret eos praedicare 15habentes
potestatem eiciendi daemonia: 16et imposuit Simoni nomen Petrum; 17et Iacobum Zebedaei et Ioannem
fratrem Iacobi, et imposuit eis nomina Boanerges, quod est Filii tonitrui; 18et Andream et Philippum
et Bartholomaeum et Matthaeum et Thomam et Iacobum Alphaei et Thaddaeum et Simonem
Chananaeum 19et Iudam Iscarioth, qui et tradidit illum. 20Et venit ad domum; et convenit iterum turba,
ita ut non possent neque panem manducare. 21Et cum audissent sui, exierunt tenere eum; dicebant enim:
«In furorem versus est». 22Et scribae, qui ab Hierosolymis descenderant, dicebant: «Beelzebul habet»
et: «In principe daemonum eicit daemonia». 23Et convocatis eis, in parabolis dicebat illis: «Quomodo
potest Satanas Satanam eicere? 24Et si regnum in se dividatur, non potest stare regnum illud; 25et si
domus in semetipsam dispertiatur, non poterit domus illa stare. 26Et si Satanas consurrexit in
semetipsum et dispertitus est, non potest stare, sed finem habet. 27Nemo autem potest in domum fortis
ingressus vasa eius diripere, nisi prius fortem alliget; et tunc domum eius diripiet. 28Amen dico vobis:
Omnia dimittentur filiis hominum peccata et blasphemiae, quibus blasphemaverint; 29qui autem
blasphemaverit in Spiritum Sanctum, non habet remissionem in aeternum, sed reus est aeterni delicti».
30Quoniam dicebant: «Spiritum immundum habet». 31Et venit mater eius et fratres eius et foris stantes
miserunt ad eum vocantes eum. 32Et sedebat circa eum turba, et dicunt ei: «Ecce mater tua et fratres tui
et sorores tuae foris quaerunt te». 33Et respondens eis ait: «Quae est mater mea et fratres mei?». 34Et
circumspiciens eos, qui in circuitu eius sedebant, ait: «Ecce mater mea et fratres mei. 35Qui enim fecerit
voluntatem Dei, hic frater meus et soror mea et mater est». **[4]** 1Et iterum coepit docere ad mare. Et
congregatur ad eum turba plurima, ita ut in navem ascendens sederet in mari, et omnis turba circa mare
super terram erant. 2Et docebat eos in parabolis multa et dicebat illis in doctrina sua: 3«Audite. Ecce
exiit seminans ad seminandum. 4Et factum est dum seminat, aliud cecidit circa viam, et venerunt
volucres et comederunt illud. 5Aliud cecidit super petrosa, ubi non habebat terram multam, et statim
exortum est, quoniam non habebat altitudinem terrae; 6et quando exortus est sol, exaestuavit et, eo quod
non haberet radicem, exaruit. 7Et aliud cecidit in spinas, et ascenderunt spinae et suffocaverunt illud, et
fructum non dedit. 8Et alia ceciderunt in terram bonam et dabant fructum: ascendebant et crescebant et
afferebant unum triginta et unum sexaginta et unum centum». 9Et dicebat: «Qui habet aures audiendi,

audiat». [10]Et cum esset singularis, interrogaverunt eum hi, qui circa eum erant cum Duodecim,
parabolas. [11]Et dicebat eis: «Vobis datum est mysterium regni Dei; illis autem, qui foris sunt, in
parabolis omnia fiunt, [12]*ut videntes videant et non videant, / et audientes audiant et non intellegant, / ne
quando convertantur, / et dimittatur eis*». [13]Et ait illis: «Nescitis parabolam hanc, et quomodo omnes
parabolas cognoscetis? [14]Qui seminat, verbum seminat. [15]Hi autem sunt, qui circa viam, ubi seminatur
verbum: et cum audierint, confestim venit Satanas et aufert verbum, quod seminatum est in eos. [16]Et hi
sunt, qui super petrosa seminantur: qui cum audierint verbum, statim cum gaudio accipiunt illud [17]et
non habent radicem in se, sed temporales sunt; deinde orta tribulatione vel persecutione propter verbum,
confestim scandalizantur. [18]Et alii sunt, qui in spinis seminantur: hi sunt, qui verbum audierunt, [19]et
aerumnae saeculi et deceptio divitiarum et circa reliqua concupiscentiae introeuntes suffocant verbum,
et sine fructu efficitur. [20]Et hi sunt, qui super terram bonam seminati sunt: qui audiunt verbum et
suscipiunt et fructificant unum triginta et unum sexaginta et unum centum». [21]Et dicebat illis:
«Numquid venit lucerna, ut sub modio ponatur aut sub lecto? Nonne ut super candelabrum ponatur?
[22]Non enim est aliquid absconditum, nisi ut manifestetur, nec factum est occultum, nisi ut in palam
veniat. [23]Si quis habet aures audiendi, audiat». [24]Et dicebat illis: «Videte quid audiatis. In qua mensura
mensi fueritis, remetietur vobis et adicietur vobis. [25]Qui enim habet, dabitur illi; et, qui non habet, etiam
quod habet, auferetur ab illo». [26]Et dicebat: «Sic est regnum Dei, quemadmodum si homo iaciat
sementem in terram [27]et dormiat et exsurgat nocte ac die, et semen germinet et increscat, dum nescit
ille. [28]Ultro terra fructificat primum herbam, deinde spicam, deinde plenum frumentum in spica. [29]Et
cum se produxerit fructus, statim mittit falcem, quoniam adest messis». [30]Et dicebat: «Quomodo
assimilabimus regnum Dei aut in qua parabola ponemus illud? [31]Sicut granum sinapis, quod cum
seminatum fuerit in terra, minus est omnibus seminibus, quae sunt in terra; [32]et cum seminatum fuerit,
ascendit et fit maius omnibus holeribus et facit ramos magnos, ita ut possint sub umbra eius aves caeli
habitare». [33]Et talibus multis parabolis loquebatur eis verbum, prout poterant audire; [34]sine parabola
autem non loquebatur eis. Seorsum autem discipulis suis disserebat omnia. [35]Et ait illis illa die, cum
sero esset factum: «Transeamus contra». [36]Et dimittentes turbam, assumunt eum, ut erat in navi; et aliae
naves erant cum illo. [37]Et exoritur procella magna venti, et fluctus se mittebant in navem, ita ut iam
impleretur navis. [38]Et erat ipse in puppi supra cervical dormiens; et excitant eum et dicunt ei: «Magister,
non ad te pertinet quia perimus?». [39]Et exsurgens comminatus est vento et dixit mari: «Tace,
obmutesce!». Et cessavit ventus, et facta est tranquillitas magna. [40]Et ait illis: «Quid timidi estis?
Necdum habetis fidem?». [41]Et timuerunt magno timore et dicebant ad alterutrum: «Quis putas est iste,
quia et ventus et mare oboediunt ei?». **[5]** [1]Et venerunt trans fretum maris in regionem Gerasenorum.
[2]Et exeunte eo de navi, statim occurrit ei de monumentis homo in spiritu immundo, [3]qui domicilium
habebat in monumentis; et neque catenis iam quisquam eum poterat ligare, [4]quoniam saepe compedibus
et catenis vinctus dirupisset catenas et compedes comminuisset, et nemo poterat eum domare; [5]et
semper nocte ac die in monumentis et in montibus erat clamans et concidens se lapidibus. [6]Et videns
Iesum a longe cucurrit et adoravit eum [7]et clamans voce magna dicit: «Quid mihi et tibi, Iesu, fili Dei
Altissimi? Adiuro te per Deum, ne me torqueas». [8]Dicebat enim illi: «Exi, spiritus immunde, ab
homine». [9]Et interrogabat eum: «Quod tibi nomen est?». Et dicit ei: «Legio nomen mihi est, quia multi
sumus». [10]Et deprecabatur eum multum, ne se expelleret extra regionem. [11]Erat autem ibi circa montem
grex porcorum magnus pascens; [12]et deprecati sunt eum dicentes: «Mitte nos in porcos, ut in eos
introeamus». [13]Et concessit eis. Et exeuntes spiritus immundi introierunt in porcos. Et magno impetu
grex ruit per praecipitium in mare, ad duo milia, et suffocabantur in mari. [14]Qui autem pascebant eos,
fugerunt et nuntiaverunt in civitatem et in agros; et egressi sunt videre quid esset facti. [15]Et veniunt ad
Iesum; et vident illum, qui a daemonio vexabatur, sedentem, vestitum et sanae mentis, eum qui
legionem habuerat, et timuerunt. [16]Et qui viderant, narraverunt illis qualiter factum esset ei, qui
daemonium habuerat, et de porcis. [17]Et rogare eum coeperunt, ut discederet a finibus eorum. [18]Cumque
ascenderet navem, qui daemonio vexatus fuerat, deprecabatur eum, ut esset cum illo. [19]Et non admisit
eum, sed ait illi: «Vade in domum tuam ad tuos, et annuntia illis quanta tibi Dominus fecerit et misertus
sit tui». [20]Et abiit et coepit praedicare in Decapoli quanta sibi fecisset Iesus, et omnes mirabantur. [21]Et
cum transcendisset Iesus in navi rursus trans fretum, convenit turba multa ad illum, et erat circa mare.
[22]Et venit quidam de archisynagogis nomine Iairus et videns eum procidit ad pedes eius [23]et deprecatur
eum multum dicens: «Filiola mea in extremis est; veni, impone manus super eam, ut salva sit et vivat».
[24]Et abiit cum illo. Et sequebatur eum turba multa et comprimebant illum. [25]Et mulier, quae erat in
profluvio sanguinis annis duodecim [26]et fuerat multa perpessa a compluribus medicis et erogaverat
omnia sua nec quidquam profecerat sed magis deterius habebat, [27]cum audisset de Iesu, venit in turba
retro et tetigit vestimentum eius; [28]dicebat enim: «Si vel vestimenta eius tetigero, salva ero». [29]Et

confestim siccatus est fons sanguinis eius, et sensit corpore quod sanata esset a plaga. [30]Et statim Iesus cognoscens in semetipso virtutem, quae exierat de eo, conversus ad turbam aiebat: «Quis tetigit vestimenta mea?». [31]Et dicebant ei discipuli sui: «Vides turbam comprimentem te et dicis: 'Quis me tetigit?'». [32]Et circumspiciebat videre eam, quae hoc fecerat. [33]Mulier autem timens et tremens, sciens quod factum esset in se, venit et procidit ante eum et dixit ei omnem veritatem. [34]Ille autem dixit ei: «Filia, fides tua te salvam fecit. Vade in pace et esto sana a plaga tua». [35]Adhuc eo loquente, veniunt ab archisynagogo dicentes: «Filia tua mortua est; quid ultra vexas magistrum?». [36]Iesus autem, verbo, quod dicebatur, audito, ait archisynagogo: «Noli timere; tantummodo crede!». [37]Et non admisit quemquam sequi se nisi Petrum et Iacobum et Ioannem fratrem Iacobi. [38]Et veniunt ad domum archisynagogi; et videt tumultum et flentes et eiulantes multum, [39]et ingressus ait eis: «Quid turbamini et ploratis? Puella non est mortua, sed dormit». [40]Et irridebant eum. Ipse vero, eiectis omnibus, assumit patrem puellae et matrem et, qui secum erant, et ingreditur, ubi erat puella; [41]et tenens manum puellae ait illi: «Talitha, qum!» —quod est interpretatum: «Puella, tibi dico: Surge!»—. [42]Et confestim surrexit puella et ambulabat; erat enim annorum duodecim. Et obstupuerunt continuo stupore magno. [43]Et praecepit illis vehementer, ut nemo id sciret, et dixit dari illi manducare. **[6]** [1]Et egressus est inde et venit in patriam suam, et sequuntur illum discipuli sui. [2]Et facto sabbato, coepit in synagoga docere; et multi audientes admirabantur dicentes: «Unde huic haec, et quae est sapientia, quae data est illi, et virtutes tales, quae per manus eius efficiuntur? [3]Nonne iste est faber, filius Mariae et frater Iacobi et Iosetis et Iudae et Simonis? Et nonne sorores eius hic nobiscum sunt?». Et scandalizabantur in illo. [4]Et dicebat eis Iesus: «Non est propheta sine honore nisi in patria sua et in cognatione sua et in domo sua». [5]Et non poterat ibi virtutem ullam facere, nisi paucos infirmos impositis manibus curavit; [6]et mirabatur propter incredulitatem eorum. Et circumibat castella in circuitu docens. [7]Et convocat Duodecim et coepit eos mittere binos et dabat illis potestatem in spiritus immundos; [8]et praecepit eis, ne quid tollerent in via nisi virgam tantum: non panem, non peram neque in zona aes, [9]sed ut calcearentur sandaliis et ne induerentur duabus tunicis. [10]Et dicebat eis: «Quocumque introieritis in domum, illic manete, donec exeatis inde. [11]Et quicumque locus non receperit vos nec audierint vos, exeuntes inde excutite pulverem de pedibus vestris in testimonium illis». [12]Et exeuntes praedicaverunt, ut paenitentiam agerent; [13]et daemonia multa eiciebant et ungebant oleo multos aegrotos et sanabant. [14]Et audivit Herodes rex; manifestum enim factum est nomen eius. Et dicebant: «Ioannes Baptista resurrexit a mortuis, et propterea inoperantur virtutes in illo». [15]Alii autem dicebant: «Elias est». Alii vero dicebant: «Propheta est, quasi unus ex prophetis». [16]Quo audito, Herodes aiebat: «Quem ego decollavi Ioannem, hic resurrexit!». [17]Ipse enim Herodes misit ac tenuit Ioannem et vinxit eum in carcere propter Herodiadem uxorem Philippi fratris sui, quia duxerat eam. [18]Dicebat enim Ioannes Herodi: «Non licet tibi habere uxorem fratris tui». [19]Herodias autem insidiabatur illi et volebat occidere eum nec poterat: [20]Herodes enim metuebat Ioannem, sciens eum virum iustum et sanctum, et custodiebat eum, et audito eo multum haesitabat et libenter eum audiebat. [21]Et cum dies opportunus accidisset, quo Herodes natali suo cenam fecit principibus suis et tribunis et primis Galilaeae, [22]cumque introisset filia ipsius Herodiadis et saltasset, placuit Herodi simulque recumbentibus. Rex ait puellae: «Pete a me, quod vis, et dabo tibi». [23]Et iuravit illi multum: «Quidquid petieris a me, dabo tibi, usque ad dimidium regni mei». [24]Quae cum exisset, dixit matri suae: «Quid petam?». At illa dixit: «Caput Ioannis Baptistae». [25]Cumque introisset statim cum festinatione ad regem, petivit dicens: «Volo ut protinus des mihi in disco caput Ioannis Baptistae». [26]Et contristatus rex propter iusiurandum et propter recumbentes noluit eam decipere [27]et statim misso spiculatore rex praecepit afferri caput eius. Et abiens decollavit eum in carcere [28]et attulit caput eius in disco et dedit illud puellae et puella dedit illud matri suae. [29]Quo audito discipuli eius venerunt et tulerunt corpus eius et posuerunt illud in monumento. [30]Et convenientes apostoli ad Iesum renuntiaverunt illi omnia, quae egerant et docuerant. [31]Et ait illis: «Venite vos ipsi seorsum in desertum locum et requiescite pusillum». Erant enim, qui veniebant et redibant multi, et nec manducandi spatium habebant. [32]Et abierunt in navi in desertum locum seorsum. [33]Et viderunt eos abeuntes et cognoverunt multi, et pedestre de omnibus civitatibus concurrerunt illuc et praevenerunt eos. [34]Et exiens vidit multam turbam et misertus est super eos, quia erant sicut oves non habentes pastorem, et coepit docere illos multa. [35]Et cum iam hora multa facta esset, accesserunt discipuli eius dicentes: «Desertus est locus hic, et hora iam est multa; [36]dimitte illos, ut euntes in villas et vicos in circuitu emant sibi, quod manducent». [37]Respondens autem ait illis: «Date illis vos manducare». Et dicunt ei: «Euntes emamus denariis ducentis panes et dabimus eis manducare?». [38]Et dicit eis: «Quot panes habetis? Ite, videte». Et cum cognovissent, dicunt: «Quinque et duos pisces». [39]Et praecepit illis, ut accumbere facerent omnes secundum contubernia super viride fenum. [40]Et discubuerunt secundum areas per centenos et per quinquagenos. [41]Et acceptis quinque panibus et duobus piscibus, intuens in caelum benedixit et fregit panes et dabat discipulis suis, ut ponerent ante eos; et duos pisces divisit omnibus. 42Et manducaverunt omnes et saturati sunt; 43et sustulerunt fragmenta duodecim cophinos plenos, et de piscibus. 44Et erant, qui manducaverunt panes, quinque milia virorum. 45Et statim coegit discipulos suos ascendere navem, ut praecederent trans fretum ad Bethsaidam, dum ipse dimitteret populum. 46Et cum dimisisset eos, abiit in montem orare. 47Et cum sero factum esset, erat navis in medio mari, et ipse solus in terra. 48Et videns eos laborantes in remigando, erat enim ventus contrarius eis, circa quartam vigiliam noctis venit ad eos ambulans super mare et volebat praeterire eos. 49At illi, ut viderunt eum ambulantem super mare, putaverunt phantasma esse et exclamaverunt; 50omnes enim eum viderunt et conturbati sunt. Statim autem locutus est cum eis et dicit illis: «Confidite, ego sum; nolite timere!». 51Et ascendit ad illos in navem, et cessavit ventus. Et valde nimis intra se stupebant: 52non enim intellexerant de panibus, sed erat cor illorum obcaecatum. 53Et cum transfretassent in terram, pervenerunt Gennesaret et applicuerunt. 54Cumque egressi essent de navi, continuo cognoverunt eum 55et percurrentes universam regionem illam coeperunt in grabatis eos, qui se male habebant, circumferre, ubi audiebant eum esse. 56Et quocumque introibat in vicos aut in civitates vel in villas, in plateis ponebant infirmos, et deprecabantur eum ut vel fimbriam vestimenti eius tangerent; et quotquot tangebant eum, salvi fiebant. **[7]** 1Et conveniunt ad eum pharisaei et quidam de scribis venientes ab Hierosolymis; 2et cum vidissent quosdam ex discipulis eius communibus manibus, id est non lotis, manducare panes 3—pharisaei enim et omnes Iudaei, nisi pugillo lavent manus, non manducant, tenentes traditionem seniorum; 4et a foro nisi baptizentur, non comedunt; et alia multa sunt, quae acceperunt servanda: baptismata calicum et urceorum et aeramentorum et lectorum— 5et interrogant eum pharisaei et scribae: «Quare discipuli tui non ambulant iuxta traditionem seniorum, sed communibus manibus manducant panem?». 6At ille dixit eis: «Bene prophetavit Isaias de vobis hypocritis, sicut scriptum est: "*Populus hic labiis me honorat, / cor autem eorum longe est a me*; / 7*in vanum autem me colunt / docentes doctrinas praecepta hominum*". 8Relinquentes mandatum Dei tenetis traditionem hominum». 9Et dicebat illis: «Bene irritum facitis praeceptum Dei, ut traditionem vestram servetis. 10Moyses enim dixit: "*Honora patrem tuum et matrem tuam*" et: "*Qui maledixerit patri aut matri, morte moriatur*"; 11vos autem dicitis: "Si dixerit homo patri aut matri: Corban, quod est donum, quodcumque ex me tibi profuerit", 12ultra non permittitis ei facere quidquam patri aut matri 13rescindentes verbum Dei per traditionem vestram, quam tradidistis; et similia huiusmodi multa facitis». 14Et advocata iterum turba, dicebat illis: «Audite me, omnes, et intellegite: 15Nihil est extra hominem introiens in eum, quod possit eum coinquinare; sed quae de homine procedunt, illa sunt, quae coinquinant hominem!». 17Et cum introisset in domum a turba, interrogabant eum discipuli eius parabolam. 18Et ait illis: «Sic et vos imprudentes estis? Non intellegitis quia omne extrinsecus introiens in hominem non potest eum coinquinare, 19quia non introit in cor eius sed in ventrem et in secessum exit?», purgans omnes escas. 20Dicebat autem: «Quod de homine exit, illud coinquinat hominem; 21ab intus enim de corde hominum cogitationes malae procedunt, fornicationes, furta, homicidia, 22adulteria, avaritiae, nequitiae, dolus, impudicitia, oculus malus, blasphemia, superbia, stultitia: 23omnia haec mala ab intus procedunt et coinquinant hominem». 24Inde autem surgens abiit in fines Tyri et Sidonis. Et ingressus domum neminem voluit scire et non potuit latere. 25Sed statim ut audivit de eo mulier, cuius habebat filia spiritum immundum, veniens procidit ad pedes eius. 26Erat autem mulier Graeca, Syrophoenissa genere. Et rogabat eum, ut daemonium eiceret de filia eius. 27Et dicebat illi: «Sine prius saturari filios; non est enim bonum sumere panem filiorum et mittere catellis». 28At illa respondit et dicit ei: «Domine, etiam catelli sub mensa comedunt de micis puerorum». 29Et ait illi: «Propter hunc sermonem vade; exiit daemonium de filia tua». 30Et cum abisset domum suam, invenit puellam iacentem supra lectum et daemonium exisse. 31Et iterum exiens de finibus Tyri venit per Sidonem ad mare Galilaeae inter medios fines Decapoleos. 32Et adducunt ei surdum et mutum et deprecantur eum, ut imponat illi manum. 33Et apprehendens eum de turba seorsum misit digitos suos in auriculas eius et exspuens tetigit linguam eius 34et suspiciens in caelum ingemuit et ait illi: «Effetha», quod est: «Adaperire». 35Et statim apertae sunt aures eius, et solutum est vinculum linguae eius, et loquebatur recte. 36Et praecepit illis, ne cui dicerent; quanto autem eis praecipiebat, tanto magis plus praedicabant. 37Et eo amplius admirabantur dicentes: «Bene omnia fecit, et surdos facit audire et mutos loqui!». **[8]** 1In illis diebus iterum cum turba multa esset, nec haberent, quod manducarent, convocatis discipulis, ait illis: 2«Misereor super turbam, quia iam triduo sustinent me, nec habent, quod manducent; 3et si dimisero eos ieiunos in domum suam, deficient in via; et quidam ex eis de longe venerunt». 4Et responderunt ei discipuli sui: «Unde istos poterit quis hic saturare panibus in solitudine?». 5Et interrogabat eos: «Quot panes habetis?». Qui dixerunt: «Septem». 6Et praecipit turbae discumbere supra terram; et accipiens septem panes, gratias agens fregit et dabat discipulis suis, ut apponerent; et apposuerunt turbae. 7Et habebant pisciculos paucos; et benedicens eos, iussit hos quoque apponi. 8Et

manducaverunt et saturati sunt; et sustulerunt, quod superaverat de fragmentis, septem sportas. [9]Erant
autem quasi quattuor milia. Et dimisit eos. [10]Et statim ascendens navem cum discipulis suis venit in
partes Dalmanutha. [11]Et exierunt pharisaei et coeperunt conquirere cum eo quaerentes ab illo signum
de caelo, tentantes eum. [12]Et ingemiscens spiritu suo ait: «Quid generatio ista quaerit signum? Amen
dico vobis: Non dabitur generationi isti signum». [13]Et dimittens eos, iterum ascendens, abiit trans
fretum. [14]Et obliti sunt sumere panes et nisi unum panem non habebant secum in navi. [15]Et praecipiebat
eis dicens: «Videte, cavete a fermento pharisaeorum et fermento Herodis!». [16]Et disputabant ad invicem,
quia panes non haberent. [17]Quo cognito ait illis: «Quid disputatis, quia panes non habetis? Nondum
cognoscitis nec intellegitis? Caecatum habetis cor vestrum? [18]Oculos habentes non videtis, et aures
habentes non auditis? Nec recordamini, [19]quando quinque panes fregi in quinque milia, quot cophinos
fragmentorum plenos sustulistis?». Dicunt ei: «Duodecim». [20]«Quando illos septem in quattuor milia,
quot sportas plenas fragmentorum tulistis?». Et dicunt ei: «Septem». [21]Et dicebat eis: «Nondum
intellegitis?». [22]Et veniunt Bethsaida. Et adducunt ei caecum et rogant eum, ut illum tangat. [23]Et
apprehendens manum caeci eduxit eum extra vicum et exspuens in oculos eius, impositis manibus ei,
interrogabat eum: «Vides aliquid?». [24]Et aspiciens dicebat: «Video homines, quia velut arbores video
ambulantes». [25]Deinde iterum imposuit manus super oculos eius; et coepit videre et restitutus est et
videbat clare omnia. [26]Et misit illum in domum suam dicens: «Nec in vicum introieris». [27]Et egressus
est Iesus et discipuli eius in castella Caesareae Philippi; et in via interrogabat discipulos suos dicens eis:
«Quem me dicunt esse homines?». [28]Qui responderunt illi dicentes: «Ioannem Baptistam, alii Eliam,
alii vero unum de prophetis». [29]Et ipse interrogabat eos: «Vos vero quem me dicitis esse?». Respondens
Petrus ait ei: «Tu es Christus». [30]Et comminatus est eis, ne cui dicerent de illo. [31]Et coepit docere illos:
«Oportet Filium hominis multa pati et reprobari a senioribus et a summis sacerdotibus et scribis et
occidi et post tres dies resurgere»; [32]et palam verbum loquebatur. Et apprehendens eum Petrus coepit
increpare eum. [33]Qui conversus et videns discipulos suos comminatus est Petro et dicit: «Vade retro me,
Satana, quoniam non sapis, quae Dei sunt, sed quae sunt hominum». [34]Et convocata turba cum
discipulis suis, dixit eis: «Si quis vult post me sequi, deneget semetipsum et tollat crucem suam et
sequatur me. [35]Qui enim voluerit animam suam salvam facere, perdet eam; qui autem perdiderit animam
suam propter me et evangelium, salvam eam faciet. [36]Quid enim prodest homini, si lucretur mundum
totum et detrimentum faciat animae suae? [37]Quid enim dabit homo commutationem pro anima sua?
[38]Qui enim me confusus fuerit et mea verba in generatione ista adultera et peccatrice, et Filius hominis
confundetur eum, cum venerit in gloria Patris sui cum angelis sanctis». **[9]** [1]Et dicebat illis: «Amen
dico vobis: Sunt quidam de hic stantibus, qui non gustabunt mortem, donec videant regnum Dei venisse
in virtute». [2]Et post dies sex assumit Iesus Petrum et Iacobum et Ioannem, et ducit illos in montem
excelsum seorsum solos. Et transfiguratus est coram ipsis; [3]et vestimenta eius facta sunt splendentia,
candida nimis, qualia fullo super terram non potest tam candida facere. [4]Et apparuit illis Elias cum
Moyse, et erant loquentes cum Iesu. [5]Et respondens Petrus ait Iesu: «Rabbi, bonum est nos hic esse;
et faciamus tria tabernacula: tibi unum et Moysi unum et Eliae unum». [6]Non enim sciebat quid
responderet, erant enim exterriti. [7]Et facta est nubes obumbrans eos, et venit vox de nube: «Hic est
Filius meus dilectus; audite illum». [8]Et statim circumspicientes neminem amplius viderunt nisi Iesum
tantum secum. [9]Et descendentibus illis de monte, praecepit illis, ne cui, quae vidissent, narrarent, nisi
cum Filius hominis a mortuis resurrexerit. [10]Et verbum continuerunt apud se, conquirentes quid esset
illud: «a mortuis resurgere». [11]Et interrogabant eum dicentes: «Quid ergo dicunt scribae quia Eliam
oporteat venire primum?». [12]Qui ait illis: «Elias veniens primo, restituit omnia; et quomodo scriptum
est super Filio hominis, ut multa patiatur et contemnatur? [13]Sed dico vobis: Et Elias venit; et fecerunt
illi, quaecumque volebant, sicut scriptum est de eo». [14]Et venientes ad discipulos viderunt turbam
magnam circa eos et scribas conquirentes cum illis. [15]Et confestim omnis populus videns eum
stupefactus est, et accurrentes salutabant eum. [16]Et interrogavit eos: «Quid inter vos conquiritis?». [17]Et
respondit ei unus de turba: «Magister, attuli filium meum ad te habentem spiritum mutum; [18]et
ubicumque eum apprehenderit, allidit eum, et spumat et stridet dentibus et arescit. Et dixi discipulis tuis,
ut eicerent illum, et non potuerunt». [19]Qui respondens eis dicit: «O generatio incredula, quamdiu apud
vos ero? Quamdiu vos patiar? Afferte illum ad me». [20]Et attulerunt illum ad eum. Et cum vidisset illum,
spiritus statim conturbavit eum, et corruens in terram volutabatur spumans. [21]Et interrogavit patrem
eius: «Quantum temporis est, ex quo hoc ei accidit?». At ille ait: «Ab infantia; [22]et frequenter eum etiam
in ignem et in aquas misit, ut eum perderet; sed si quid potes, adiuva nos, misertus nostri». [23]Iesus
autem ait illi: «'Si potes!'. Omnia possibilia credenti». [24]Et continuo exclamans pater pueri aiebat:
«Credo; adiuva incredulitatem meam». [25]Et cum videret Iesus concurrentem turbam, comminatus est
spiritui immundo dicens illi: «Mute et surde spiritus, ego tibi praecipio: Exi ab eo et amplius ne introeas

in eum». [26]Et clamans et multum discerpens eum exiit; et factus est sicut mortuus, ita ut multi dicerent:
«Mortuus est!». [27]Iesus autem tenens manum eius elevavit illum, et surrexit. [28]Et cum introisset in
domum, discipuli eius secreto interrogabant eum: «Quare nos non potuimus eicere eum?». [29]Et dixit
illis: «Hoc genus in nullo potest exire nisi in oratione». [30]Et inde profecti peragrabant Galilaeam; nec
volebat quemquam scire. [31]Docebat enim discipulos suos et dicebat illis: «Filius hominis traditur in
manus hominum, et occident eum, et occisus post tres dies resurget». [32]At illi ignorabant verbum et
timebant eum interrogare. [33]Et venerunt Capharnaum. Qui cum domi esset, interrogabat eos: «Quid in
via tractabatis?». [34]At illi tacebant. Siquidem inter se in via disputaverant, quis esset maior. [35]Et residens
vocavit Duodecim et ait illis: «Si quis vult primus esse, erit omnium novissimus et omnium minister».
[36]Et accipiens puerum, statuit eum in medio eorum; quem ut complexus esset, ait illis: [37]«Quisquis
unum ex huiusmodi pueris receperit in nomine meo, me recipit; et, quicumque me susceperit, non me
suscipit, sed eum qui me misit». [38]Dixit illi Ioannes: «Magister, vidimus quendam in nomine tuo
eicientem daemonia, et prohibebamus eum, quia non sequebatur nos». [39]Iesus autem ait: «Nolite
prohibere eum. Nemo est enim, qui faciat virtutem in nomine meo et possit cito male loqui de me; [40]qui
enim non est adversum nos, pro nobis est. [41]Quisquis enim potum dederit vobis calicem aquae in
nomine, quia Christi estis, amen dico vobis: Non perdet mercedem suam. [42]Et quisquis scandalizaverit
unum ex his pusillis credentibus in me, bonum est ei magis, ut circumdetur mola asinaria collo eius,
et in mare mittatur. [43]Et si scandalizaverit te manus tua, abscide illam: bonum est tibi debilem introire
in vitam, quam duas manus habentem ire in gehennam, in ignem inexstinguibilem. [45]Et si pes tuus te
scandalizat, amputa illum: bonum est tibi claudum introire in vitam, quam duos pedes habentem mitti
in gehennam. [47]Et si oculus tuus scandalizat te, eice eum: bonum est tibi luscum introire in regnum Dei,
quam duos oculos habentem mitti in gehennam, [48]ubi vermis eorum non moritur et ignis non
exstinguitur; [49]omnis enim igne salietur. [50]Bonum est sal; quod si sal insulsum fuerit, in quo illud
condietis? Habete in vobis sal et pacem habete inter vos». **[10]** [1]Et inde exsurgens venit in fines Iudaeae
ultra Iordanem, et conveniunt iterum turbae ad eum, et, sicut consueverat, iterum docebat illos. [2]Et
accedentes pharisaei interrogabant eum, si licet viro uxorem dimittere, tentantes eum. [3]At ille
respondens dixit eis: «Quid vobis praecepit Moyses?». [4]Qui dixerunt: «Moyses permisit *libellum repudii
scribere et dimittere*». [5]Iesus autem ait eis: «Ad duritiam cordis vestri scripsit vobis praeceptum istud.
[6]Ab initio autem creaturae *masculum et feminam fecit eos*. [7]*Propter hoc relinquet homo patrem suum
et matrem et adhaerebit ad uxorem suam*, [8]*et erunt duo in carne una*; itaque iam non sunt duo sed una
caro. [9]Quod ergo Deus coniunxit, homo non separet». [10]Et domo iterum discipuli de hoc interrogabant
eum. [11]Et dicit illis: «Quicumque dimiserit uxorem suam et aliam duxerit, adulterium committit in eam;
[12]et si ipsa dimiserit virum suum et alii nupserit, moechatur». [13]Et offerebant illi parvulos, ut tangeret
illos; discipuli autem comminabantur eis. [14]At videns Iesus, indigne tulit et ait illis: «Sinite parvulos
venire ad me. Ne prohibueritis eos; talium est enim regnum Dei. [15]Amen dico vobis: Quisquis non
receperit regnum Dei velut parvulus, non intrabit in illud». [16]Et complexans eos benedicebat imponens
manus super illos. [17]Et cum egrederetur in viam, accurrens quidam et, genu flexo ante eum, rogabat
eum: «Magister bone, quid faciam ut vitam aeternam percipiam?». [18]Iesus autem dixit ei: «Quid me
dicis bonum? Nemo bonus nisi unus Deus. [19]Praecepta nosti: *ne occidas, ne adulteres, ne fureris, ne
falsum testimonium dixeris*, ne fraudem feceris, honora patrem tuum et matrem». [20]Ille autem dixit ei:
«Magister, haec omnia conservavi a iuventute mea». [21]Iesus autem intuitus eum dilexit eum et dixit illi:
«Unum tibi deest: vade, quaecumque habes, vende et da pauperibus et habebis thesaurum in caelo et
veni, sequere me». [22]Qui contristatus in hoc verbo, abiit maerens: erat enim habens possessiones multas.
[23]Et circumspiciens Iesus ait discipulis suis: «Quam difficile, qui pecunias habent, in regnum Dei
introibunt». [24]Discipuli autem obstupescebant in verbis eius. At Iesus rursus respondens ait illis: «Filii,
quam difficile est in regnum Dei introire. [25]Facilius est camelum per foramen acus transire quam
divitem intrare in regnum Dei». [26]Qui magis admirabantur dicentes ad semetipsos: «Et quis potest
salvus fieri?». [27]Intuens illos Iesus ait: «Apud homines impossibile est sed non apud Deum: omnia enim
possibilia sunt apud Deum». [28]Coepit Petrus ei dicere: «Ecce nos dimisimus omnia et secuti sumus te».
[29]Ait Iesus: «Amen dico vobis: Nemo est, qui reliquerit domum aut fratres aut sorores aut matrem aut
patrem aut filios aut agros propter me et propter evangelium, [30]qui non accipiat centies tantum nunc in
tempore hoc, domos et fratres et sorores et matres et filios et agros cum persecutionibus, et in saeculo
futuro vitam aeternam. [31]Multi autem erunt primi novissimi et novissimi primi». [32]Erant autem in via
ascendentes in Hierosolymam, et praecedebat illos Iesus, et stupebant; illi autem sequentes timebant.
Et assumens iterum Duodecim coepit illis dicere, quae essent ei eventura: [33]«Ecce ascendimus in
Hierosolymam; et Filius hominis tradetur principibus sacerdotum et scribis, et damnabunt eum morte
et tradent eum gentibus [34]et illudent ei et conspuent eum et flagellabunt eum et interficient eum, et post

tres dies resurget». 35Et accedunt ad eum Iacobus et Ioannes filii Zebedaei dicentes ei: «Magister,
volumus, ut quodcumque petierimus a te, facias nobis». 36At ille dixit eis: «Quid vultis, ut faciam
vobis?». 37Illi autem dixerunt ei: «Da nobis, ut unus ad dexteram tuam et alius ad sinistram sedeamus
in gloria tua». 38Iesus autem ait eis: «Nescitis quid petatis. Potestis bibere calicem, quem ego bibo, aut
baptismum, quo ego baptizor, baptizari?». 39At illi dixerunt ei: «Possumus». Iesus autem ait eis:
«Calicem quidem, quem ego bibo, bibetis et baptismum, quo ego baptizor, baptizabimini; 40sedere
autem ad dexteram meam vel ad sinistram non est meum dare, sed quibus paratum est». 41Et audientes
decem coeperunt indignari de Iacobo et Ioanne. 42Et vocans eos Iesus ait illis: «Scitis quia hi, qui
videntur principari gentibus, dominantur eis, et principes eorum potestatem habent ipsorum. 43Non ita
est autem in vobis, sed quicumque voluerit fieri maior inter vos, erit vester minister; 44et, quicumque
voluerit in vobis primus esse, erit omnium servus; 45nam et Filius hominis non venit, ut ministraretur
ei, sed ut ministraret et daret animam suam redemptionem pro multis». 46Et veniunt Ierichum. Et
proficiscente eo de Iericho et discipulis eius et plurima multitudine, filius Timaei Bartimaeus caecus
sedebat iuxta viam mendicans. 47Qui, cum audisset quia Iesus Nazarenus est, coepit clamare et dicere:
«Fili David Iesu, miserere mei!». 48Et comminabantur ei multi, ut taceret; at ille multo magis clamabat:
«Fili David, miserere mei!». 49Et stans Iesus dixit: «Vocate illum». Et vocant caecum dicentes ei:
«Animaequior esto. Surge, vocat te». 50Qui, proiecto vestimento suo, exsiliens venit ad Iesum. 51Et
respondens ei Iesus dixit: «Quid vis tibi faciam?». Caecus autem dixit ei: «Rabboni, ut videam». 52Et
Iesus ait illi: «Vade; fides tua te salvum fecit». Et confestim vidit et sequebatur eum in via. **[11]** 1Et cum
appropinquarent Hierosolymae, Bethphage et Bethaniae ad montem Olivarum, mittit duos ex discipulis
suis 2et ait illis: «Ite in castellum, quod est contra vos, et statim introeuntes illud invenietis pullum
ligatum, super quem nemo adhuc hominum sedit; solvite illum et adducite. 3Et si quis vobis dixerit:
"Quid facitis hoc?", dicite: "Domino necessarius est, et continuo illum remittit iterum huc"». 4Et
abeuntes invenerunt pullum ligatum ante ianuam foris in bivio et solvunt eum. 5Et quidam de illic
stantibus dicebant illis: «Quid facitis solventes pullum?». 6Qui dixerunt eis, sicut dixerat Iesus; et
dimiserunt eis. 7Et ducunt pullum ad Iesum et imponunt illi vestimenta sua; et sedit super eum. 8Et multi
vestimenta sua straverunt in via, alii autem frondes, quas exciderant in agris. 9Et qui praeibant et qui
sequebantur, clamabant: «*Hosanna! Benedictus, qui venit in nomine Domini!* 10Benedictum, quod venit
regnum patris nostri David! *Hosanna* in excelsis!». 11Et introivit Hierosolymam in templum; et
circumspectis omnibus, cum iam vespera esset hora, exivit in Bethaniam cum Duodecim. 12Et altera die
cum exirent a Bethania, esuriit. 13Cumque vidisset a longe ficum habentem folia, venit si quid forte
inveniret in ea; et cum venisset ad eam, nihil invenit praeter folia: non enim erat tempus ficorum. 14Et
respondens dixit ei: «Iam non amplius in aeternum quisquam fructum ex te manducet». Et audiebant
discipuli eius. 15Et veniunt Hierosolymam. Et cum introisset in templum, coepit eicere vendentes et
ementes in templo et mensas nummulariorum et cathedras vendentium columbas evertit, 16et non
sinebat, ut quisquam vas transferret per templum. 17Et docebat dicens eis: «Non scriptum est: "*Domus
mea domus orationis vocabitur omnibus gentibus*"? Vos autem fecistis eam *speluncam latronum*».
18Quo audito, principes sacerdotum et scribae quaerebant quomodo eum perderent; timebant enim eum,
quoniam universa turba admirabatur super doctrina eius. 19Et cum vespera facta esset, egrediebantur de
civitate. 20Et cum mane transirent, viderunt ficum aridam factam a radicibus. 21Et recordatus Petrus dicit
ei: «Rabbi, ecce ficus, cui maledixisti, aruit». 22Et respondens Iesus ait illis: «Habete fidem Dei! 23Amen
dico vobis: Quicumque dixerit huic monti: "Tollere et mittere in mare", et non haesitaverit in corde suo,
sed crediderit quia, quod dixerit, fiat, fiet ei. 24Propterea dico vobis: Omnia, quaecumque orantes petitis,
credite quia iam accepistis, et erunt vobis. 25Et cum statis in oratione, dimittite, si quid habetis adversus
aliquem, ut et Pater vester, qui in caelis est, dimittat vobis peccata vestra». 27Et veniunt rursus
Hierosolymam. Et cum ambularet in templo, accedunt ad eum summi sacerdotes et scribae et seniores
28et dicebant illi: «In qua potestate haec facis? Vel quis tibi dedit hanc potestatem, ut ista facias?».
29Iesus autem ait illis: «Interrogabo vos unum verbum, et respondete mihi, et dicam vobis, in qua
potestate haec faciam: 30Baptismum Ioannis de caelo erat an ex hominibus? Respondete mihi». 31At illi
cogitabant secum dicentes: «Si dixerimus: "De caelo", dicet: "Quare ergo non credidistis ei?"; 32si
autem dixerimus: "Ex hominibus?"». Timebant populum: omnes enim habebant Ioannem quia vere
propheta esset. 33Et respondentes dicunt Iesu: «Nescimus». Et Iesus ait illis: «Neque ego dico vobis in
qua potestate haec faciam». **[12]** 1Et coepit illis in parabolis loqui: «*Vineam pastinavit* homo *et
circumdedit saepem et fodit lacum et aedificavit turrim* et locavit eam agricolis et peregre profectus est.
2Et misit ad agricolas in tempore servum, ut ab agricolis acciperet de fructu vineae; 3qui apprehensum
eum caeciderunt et dimiserunt vacuum. 4Et iterum misit ad illos alium servum; et illum in capite
vulneraverunt et contumeliis affecerunt. 5Et alium misit, et illum occiderunt, et plures alios, quosdam

caedentes, alios vero occidentes. 6Adhuc unum habebat, filium dilectum. Misit illum ad eos novissimum
dicens: "Reverebuntur filium meum". 7Coloni autem illi dixerunt ad invicem: "Hic est heres. Venite,
occidamus eum, et nostra erit hereditas". 8Et apprehendentes eum occiderunt et eiecerunt extra vineam.
9Quid ergo faciet dominus vineae? Veniet et perdet colonos et dabit vineam aliis. 10Nec Scripturam hanc
legistis: "*Lapidem quem reprobaverunt aedificantes, / hic factus est in caput anguli*; / 11*a Domino
factum est istud / et est mirabile in oculis nostris*"?». 12Et quaerebant eum tenere et timuerunt turbam;
cognoverunt enim quoniam ad eos parabolam hanc dixerit. Et relicto eo abierunt. 13Et mittunt ad eum
quosdam ex pharisaeis et herodianis, ut eum caperent in verbo. 14Qui venientes dicunt ei: «Magister,
scimus quia verax es et non curas quemquam, nec enim vides in faciem hominum, sed in veritate viam
Dei doces. Licet dare tributum Caesari an non? Dabimus an non dabimus?». 15Qui sciens versutiam
eorum ait illis: «Quid me tentatis? Afferte mihi denarium, ut videam». 16At illi attulerunt. Et ait illis:
«Cuius est imago haec et inscriptio?». Illi autem dixerunt ei: «Caesaris». 17Iesus autem dixit illis: «Quae
sunt Caesaris, reddite Caesari et, quae sunt Dei, Deo». Et mirabantur super eo. 18Et veniunt ad eum
sadducaei, qui dicunt resurrectionem non esse, et interrogabant eum dicentes: 19«Magister, Moyses
nobis scripsit, ut *si cuius frater mortuus fuerit* et reliquerit uxorem *et filium non reliquerit, accipiat
frater eius uxorem et resuscitet semen fratri suo*. 20Septem fratres erant: et primus accepit uxorem et
moriens non reliquit semen; 21et secundus accepit eam et mortuus est, non relicto semine; et tertius
similiter; 22et septem non reliquerunt semen. Novissima omnium defuncta est et mulier. 23In
resurrectione, cum resurrexerint, cuius de his erit uxor? Septem enim habuerunt eam uxorem». 24Ait
illis Iesus: «Non ideo erratis, quia non scitis Scripturas neque virtutem Dei? 25Cum enim a mortuis
resurrexerint, neque nubent neque nubentur, sed sunt sicut angeli in caelis. 26De mortuis autem quod
resurgant, non legistis in libro Moysis super rubum, quomodo dixerit illi Deus inquiens: "*Ego sum Deus
Abraham et Deus Isaac et Deus Iacob*"? 27Non est Deus mortuorum sed vivorum! Multum erratis». 28Et
accessit unus de scribis, qui audierat illos conquirentes, videns quoniam bene illis responderit,
interrogavit eum: «Quod est primum omnium mandatum?». 29Iesus respondit: «Primum est: "*Audi,
Israel: Dominus Deus noster Dominus unus est*, 30*et diliges Dominum Deum tuum ex toto corde tuo et
ex tota anima tua et ex tota mente tua et ex tota virtute tua*". 31Secundum est illud: "*Diliges proximum
tuum tamquam teipsum*". Maius horum aliud mandatum non est». 32Et ait illi scriba: «Bene, Magister,
in veritate dixisti: "*Unus est, et non est alius praeter eum*, 33et *diligere eum ex toto corde et ex toto
intellectu et ex tota fortitudine*" et: "*Diligere proximum tamquam seipsum*" maius est omnibus
holocautomatibus et sacrificiis». 34Et Iesus videns quod sapienter respondisset, dixit illi: «Non es longe
a regno Dei». Et nemo iam audebat eum interrogare. 35Et respondens Iesus dicebat docens in templo:
«Quomodo dicunt scribae Christum filium esse David? 36Ipse David dixit in Spiritu Sancto: "*Dixit
Dominus Domino meo: Sede a dextris meis, / donec ponam inimicos tuos sub pedibus tuis*". 37Ipse
David dicit eum Dominum, et unde est filius eius?». Et multa turba eum libenter audiebat. 38Et dicebat
in doctrina sua: «Cavete a scribis, qui volunt in stolis ambulare et salutari in foro 39et in primis cathedris
sedere in synagogis et primos discubitus in cenis; 40qui devorant domos viduarum et ostentant prolixas
orationes. Hi accipient amplius iudicium». 41Et sedens contra gazophylacium aspiciebat quomodo turba
iactaret aes in gazophylacium; et multi divites iactabant multa. 42Et cum venisset una vidua pauper,
misit duo minuta, quod est quadrans. 43Et convocans discipulos suos ait illis: «Amen dico vobis: Vidua
haec pauper plus omnibus misit, qui miserunt in gazophylacium: 44omnes enim ex eo, quod abundabat
illis, miserunt; haec vero de penuria sua omnia, quae habuit, misit, totum victum suum». **[13]** 1Et cum
egrederetur de templo, ait illi unus ex discipulis suis: «Magister, aspice quales lapides et quales
structurae». 2Et Iesus ait illi: «Vides has magnas aedificationes? Hic non relinquetur lapis super lapidem,
qui non destruatur». 3Et cum sederet in montem Olivarum contra templum, interrogabat eum separatim
Petrus et Iacobus et Ioannes et Andreas: 4«Dic nobis: Quando ista erunt, et quod signum erit, quando
haec omnia incipient consummari?». 5Iesus autem coepit dicere illis: «Videte, ne quis vos seducat.
6Multi venient in nomine meo dicentes: "Ego sum", et multos seducent. 7Cum audieritis autem bella et
opiniones bellorum, ne timueritis; oportet fieri sed nondum finis. 8Exsurget enim gens super gentem, et
regnum super regnum, erunt terrae motus per loca, erunt fames; initium dolorum haec. 9Videte autem
vosmetipsos. Tradent vos conciliis et in synagogis vapulabitis et ante praesides et reges stabitis propter
me in testimonium illis. 10Et in omnes gentes primum oportet praedicari evangelium. 11Et cum duxerint
vos tradentes, nolite praecogitare quid loquamini, sed, quod datum vobis fuerit in illa hora, id loquimini:
non enim estis vos loquentes sed Spiritus Sanctus. 12Et tradet frater fratrem in mortem, et pater filium;
et consurgent filii in parentes et morte afficient eos; 13et eritis odio omnibus propter nomen meum. Qui
autem sustinuerit in finem, hic salvus erit. 14Cum autem videritis *abominationem desolationis* stantem,
ubi non debet, qui legit intellegat: tunc, qui in Iudaea sunt, fugiant in montes; 15qui autem super tectum,

ne descendat nec introeat, ut tollat quid de domo sua; 16et, qui in agro erit, non revertatur retro tollere vestimentum suum. 17Vae autem praegnantibus et nutrientibus in illis diebus! 18Orate vero, ut hieme non fiat: 19erunt enim dies illi *tribulatio talis, qualis non fuit ab initio creaturae*, quam condidit Deus, *usque nunc*, neque fiet. 20Et nisi breviasset Dominus dies, non fuisset salva omnis caro. Sed propter electos, quos elegit, breviavit dies. 21Et tunc, si quis vobis dixerit: 'Ecce hic est Christus, ecce illic', ne credideritis. 22Exsurgent enim pseudochristi et pseudoprophetae et dabunt signa et portenta ad seducendos, si potest fieri, electos. 23Vos autem videte; praedixi vobis omnia. 24Sed in illis diebus post tribulationem illam *sol contenebrabitur, et luna non dabit splendorem suum*, 25*et erunt stellae* de caelo decidentes, *et virtutes, quae sunt in caelis*, movebuntur. 26Et tunc videbunt *Filium hominis venientem in nubibus* cum virtute multa et gloria. 27Et tunc mittet angelos et congregabit electos suos a quattuor ventis, a summo terrae usque ad summum caeli. 28A ficu autem discite parabolam: cum iam ramus eius tener fuerit et germinaverit folia cognoscitis quia in proximo sit aestas. 29Sic et vos, cum videritis haec fieri, scitote quod in proximo sit in ostiis. 30Amen dico vobis: Non transiet generatio haec, donec omnia ista fiant. 31Caelum et terra transibunt, verba autem mea non transibunt. 32De die autem illo vel hora nemo scit, neque angeli in caelo neque Filius, nisi Pater. 33Videte, vigilate; nescitis enim, quando tempus sit. 34Sicut homo, qui peregre profectus reliquit domum suam et dedit servis suis potestatem, unicuique opus suum, ianitori quoque praecepit, ut vigilaret. 35Vigilate ergo; nescitis enim quando dominus domus veniat, sero an media nocte an galli cantu an mane; 36ne, cum venerit repente, inveniat vos dormientes. 37Quod autem vobis dico, omnibus dico: Vigilate!». **[14]** 1Erat autem Pascha et Azyma post biduum. Et quaerebant summi sacerdotes et scribae, quomodo eum dolo tenerent et occiderent; 2dicebant enim: «Non in die festo, ne forte tumultus fieret populi». 3Et cum esset Bethaniae in domo Simonis leprosi et recumberet, venit mulier habens alabastrum unguenti nardi puri pretiosi; fracto alabastro, effudit super caput eius. 4Erant autem quidam indigne ferentes intra semetipsos: «Ut quid perditio ista unguenti facta est? 5Poterat enim unguentum istud veniri plus quam trecentis denariis et dari pauperibus». Et fremebant in eam. 6Iesus autem dixit: «Sinite eam; quid illi molesti estis? Bonum opus operata est in me. 7Semper enim pauperes habetis vobiscum et, cum volueritis, potestis illis bene facere; me autem non semper habetis. 8Quod habuit, operata est: praevenit ungere corpus meum in sepulturam. 9Amen autem dico vobis: Ubicumque praedicatum fuerit evangelium in universum mundum, et, quod fecit haec, narrabitur in memoriam eius». 10Et Iudas Iscarioth, unus de Duodecim, abiit ad summos sacerdotes, ut proderet eum illis. 11Qui audientes gavisi sunt et promiserunt ei pecuniam se daturos. Et quaerebat quomodo illum opportune traderet. 12Et primo die Azymorum, quando Pascha immolabant, dicunt ei discipuli eius: «Quo vis eamus et paremus, ut manduces Pascha?». 13Et mittit duos ex discipulis suis et dicit eis: «Ite in civitatem, et occurret vobis homo lagoenam aquae baiulans; sequimini eum 14et, quocumque introierit, dicite domino domus: "Magister dicit: Ubi est refectio mea, ubi Pascha cum discipulis meis manducem?". 15Et ipse vobis demonstrabit cenaculum grande stratum paratum; et illic parate nobis». 16Et abierunt discipuli et venerunt in civitatem et invenerunt, sicut dixerat illis, et paraverunt Pascha. 17Et vespere facto venit cum Duodecim. 18Et discumbentibus eis et manducantibus, ait Iesus: «Amen dico vobis: Unus ex vobis me tradet, *qui manducat mecum*». 19Coeperunt contristari et dicere ei singillatim: «Numquid ego?». 20Qui ait illis: «Unus ex Duodecim, qui intingit mecum in catino. 21Nam Filius quidem hominis vadit, sicut scriptum est de eo. Vae autem homini illi, per quem Filius hominis traditur! Bonum est ei, si non esset natus homo ille». 22Et manducantibus illis, accepit panem et benedicens fregit et dedit eis et ait: «Sumite: hoc est corpus meum». 23Et accepto calice, gratias agens dedit eis, et biberunt ex illo omnes. 24Et ait illis: «Hic est sanguis meus novi testamenti, qui pro multis effunditur. 25Amen dico vobis: Iam non bibam de genimine vitis usque in diem illum, cum illud bibam novum in regno Dei». 26Et hymno dicto, exierunt in montem Olivarum. 27Et ait eis Iesus: «Omnes scandalizabimini, quia scriptum est: "*Percutiam pastorem, et dispergentur oves*". 28Sed posteaquam resurrexero, praecedam vos in Galilaeam». 29Petrus autem ait ei: «Et si omnes scandalizati fuerint, sed non ego». 30Et ait illi Iesus: «Amen dico tibi: Tu hodie, in nocte hac, priusquam bis gallus vocem dederit, ter me es negaturus». 31At ille amplius loquebatur: «Et si oportuerit me commori tibi, non te negabo». Similiter autem et omnes dicebant. 32Et veniunt in praedium, cui nomen Gethsemani, et ait discipulis suis: «Sedete hic, donec orem». 33Et assumit Petrum et Iacobum et Ioannem secum et coepit pavere et taedere 34et ait illis: «Tristis est anima mea usque ad mortem; sustinete hic et vigilate». 35Et cum processisset paululum, procidebat super terram et orabat, ut, si fieri posset, transiret ab eo hora, 36et dicebat: «Abba, Pater! Omnia tibi possibilia sunt. Transfer calicem hunc a me; sed non quod ego volo, sed quod tu». 37Et venit et invenit eos dormientes et ait Petro: «Simon, dormis? Non potuisti una hora vigilare? 38Vigilate et orate, ut non intretis in tentationem; spiritus quidem promptus, caro vero infirma». 39Et iterum abiens oravit, eundem sermonem dicens. 40Et veniens denuo invenit eos dormientes; erant enim oculi illorum ingravati, et ignorabant quid responderent ei. [41]Et venit tertio et ait illis: «Dormite iam et requiescite? Sufficit, venit hora: ecce traditur Filius hominis in manus peccatorum. [42]Surgite, eamus; ecce, qui me tradit, prope est». [43]Et confestim, adhuc eo loquente, venit Iudas unus ex Duodecim, et cum illo turba cum gladiis et lignis a summis sacerdotibus et scribis et senioribus. [44]Dederat autem traditor eius signum eis dicens: «Quemcumque osculatus fuero, ipse est; tenete eum et ducite caute». [45]Et cum venisset, statim accedens ad eum ait: «Rabbi», et osculatus est eum. [46]At illi manus iniecerunt in eum et tenuerunt eum. [47]Unus autem quidam de circumstantibus educens gladium percussit servum summi sacerdotis et amputavit illi auriculam. [48]Et respondens Iesus ait illis: «Tamquam ad latronem existis cum gladiis et lignis comprehendere me? [49]Cotidie eram apud vos in templo docens et non me tenuistis; sed adimpleantur Scripturae». [50]Et relinquentes eum omnes fugerunt. [51]Et adulescens quidam sequebatur eum amictus sindone super nudo, et tenent eum; [52]at ille, reiecta sindone, nudus profugit. [53]Et adduxerunt Iesum ad summum sacerdotem, et conveniunt omnes summi sacerdotes et seniores et scribae. [54]Et Petrus a longe secutus est eum usque intro in atrium summi sacerdotis et sedebat cum ministris et calefaciebat se ad ignem. [55]Summi vero sacerdotes et omne concilium quaerebant adversus Iesum testimonium, ut eum morte afficerent, nec inveniebant. [56]Multi enim testimonium falsum dicebant adversus eum, et convenientia testimonia non erant. [57]Et quidam surgentes falsum testimonium ferebant adversus eum dicentes: [58]«Nos audivimus eum dicentem: "Ego dissolvam templum hoc manu factum et intra triduum aliud non manu factum aedificabo"». [59]Et ne ita quidem conveniens erat testimonium illorum. [60]Et exsurgens summus sacerdos in medium interrogavit Iesum dicens: «Non respondes quidquam ad ea, quae isti testantur adversum te?». [61]Ille autem tacebat et nihil respondit. Rursum summus sacerdos interrogabat eum et dicit ei: «Tu es Christus filius Benedicti?». [62]Iesus autem dixit: «Ego sum, et *videbitis Filium hominis a dextris sedentem Virtutis et venientem cum nubibus caeli*». [63]Summus autem sacerdos scindens vestimenta sua ait: «Quid adhuc necessarii sunt nobis testes? [64]Audistis blasphemiam. Quid vobis videtur?». Qui omnes condemnaverunt eum esse reum mortis. [65]Et coeperunt quidam conspuere eum et velare faciem eius et colaphis eum caedere et dicere ei: «Prophetiza»; et ministri alapis eum caedebant. [66]Et cum esset Petrus in atrio deorsum, venit una ex ancillis summi sacerdotis [67]et, cum vidisset Petrum calefacientem se, aspiciens illum ait: «Et tu cum hoc Nazareno, Iesu, eras!». [68]At ille negavit dicens: «Neque scio neque novi quid tu dicas!». Et exiit foras ante atrium, et gallus cantavit. [69]Et ancilla, cum vidisset illum, rursus coepit dicere circumstantibus: «Hic ex illis est!». [70]At ille iterum negabat. Et post pusillum rursus, qui astabant, dicebant Petro: «Vere ex illis es, nam et Galilaeus es». [71]Ille autem coepit anathematizare et iurare: «Nescio hominem istum, quem dicitis!». [72]Et statim iterum gallus cantavit; et recordatus est Petrus verbi, sicut dixerat ei Iesus: «Priusquam gallus cantet bis, ter me negabis». Et coepit flere. **[15]** [1]Et confestim mane consilium facientes summi sacerdotes cum senioribus et scribis, id est universum concilium, vincientes Iesum duxerunt et tradiderunt Pilato. [2]Et interrogavit eum Pilatus: «Tu es rex Iudaeorum?». At ille respondens ait illi: «Tu dicis». [3]Et accusabant eum summi sacerdotes in multis. [4]Pilatus autem rursum interrogabat eum dicens: «Non respondes quidquam? Vide in quantis te accusant». [5]Iesus autem amplius nihil respondit, ita ut miraretur Pilatus. [6]Per diem autem festum dimittere solebat illis unum ex vinctis, quem peterent. [7]Erat autem qui dicebatur Barabbas, vinctus cum seditiosis, qui in seditione fecerant homicidium. [8]Et cum ascendisset turba, coepit rogare, sicut faciebat illis. [9]Pilatus autem respondit eis et dixit: «Vultis dimittam vobis regem Iudaeorum?». [10]Sciebat enim quod per invidiam tradidissent eum summi sacerdotes. [11]Pontifices autem concitaverunt turbam, ut magis Barabbam dimitteret eis. [12]Pilatus autem iterum respondens aiebat illis: «Quid ergo vultis faciam regi Iudaeorum?». [13]At illi iterum clamaverunt: «Crucifige eum!». [14]Pilatus vero dicebat eis: «Quid enim mali fecit?». At illi magis clamaverunt: «Crucifige eum!». [15]Pilatus autem, volens populo satisfacere, dimisit illis Barabbam et tradidit Iesum flagellis caesum, ut crucifigeretur. [16]Milites autem duxerunt eum intro in atrium, quod est praetorium, et convocant totam cohortem. [17]Et induunt eum purpuram et imponunt ei plectentes spineam coronam, [18]et coeperunt salutare eum: «Ave, rex Iudaeorum!», [19]et percutiebant caput eius arundine et conspuebant eum et ponentes genua adorabant eum. [20]Et postquam illuserunt ei, exuerunt illum purpuram et induerunt eum vestimentis suis. Et educunt illum, ut crucifigerent eum. [21]Et angariant praetereuntem quempiam Simonem Cyrenaeum venientem de villa, patrem Alexandri et Rufi, ut tolleret crucem eius. [22]Et perducunt illum in Golgotha locum, quod est interpretatum Calvariae locus. [23]Et dabant ei myrrhatum vinum, ille autem non accepit. [24]Et crucifigunt eum et *dividunt vestimenta* eius, *mittentes sortem super eis* quis quid tolleret. [25]Erat autem hora tertia, et crucifixerunt eum. [26]Et erat titulus causae eius inscriptus: «Rex Iudaeorum». [27]Et cum eo crucifigunt duos latrones, unum a dextris et alium a sinistris eius. [29]Et praetereuntes blasphemabant eum *moventes capita* sua et dicentes: «Vah, qui destruit templum et in tribus diebus

aedificat; 30salvum fac temetipsum descendens de cruce!». 31Similiter et summi sacerdotes ludentes ad
alterutrum cum scribis dicebant: «Alios salvos fecit, seipsum non potest salvum facere. 32Christus rex
Israel descendat nunc de cruce, ut videamus et credamus». Etiam qui cum eo crucifixi erant,
conviciabantur ei. 33Et, facta hora sexta, tenebrae factae sunt per totam terram usque in horam nonam.
34Et hora nona exclamavit Iesus voce magna: «*Heloi, Heloi, lema sabacthani?*», quod est interpretatum:
«*Deus meus, Deus meus, ut quid dereliquisti me?*». 35Et quidam de circumstantibus audientes dicebant:
«Ecce Eliam vocat». 36Currens autem unus et implens spongiam *aceto* circumponensque calamo *potum*
dabat ei dicens: «Sinite, videamus, si veniat Elias ad deponendum eum». 37Iesus autem, emissa voce
magna, exspiravit. 38Et velum templi scissum est in duo a sursum usque deorsum. 39Videns autem
centurio, qui ex adverso stabat, quia sic clamans exspirasset, ait: «Vere homo hic Filius Dei erat».
40Erant autem et mulieres de longe aspicientes, inter quas et Maria Magdalene et Maria Iacobi minoris
et Iosetis mater et Salome, 41quae, cum esset in Galilaea, sequebantur eum et ministrabant ei, et aliae
multae, quae simul cum eo ascenderant Hierosolymam. 42Et cum iam sero esset factum, quia erat
Parasceve, quod est ante sabbatum, 43venit Ioseph ab Arimathaea nobilis decurio, qui et ipse erat
exspectans regnum Dei, et audacter introivit ad Pilatum et petiit corpus Iesu. 44Pilatus autem miratus est
si iam obisset, et, accersito centurione, interrogavit eum si iam mortuus esset, 45et, cum cognovisset a
centurione, donavit corpus Ioseph. 46Is autem mercatus sindonem et deponens eum involvit sindone et
posuit eum in monumento, quod erat excisum de petra, et advolvit lapidem ad ostium monumenti.
47Maria autem Magdalene et Maria Iosetis aspiciebant, ubi positus esset. **[16]** 1Et cum transisset
sabbatum, Maria Magdalene et Maria Iacobi et Salome emerunt aromata, ut venientes ungerent eum.
2Et valde mane, prima sabbatorum, veniunt ad monumentum, orto iam sole. 3Et dicebant ad invicem:
«Quis revolvet nobis lapidem ab ostio monumenti?». 4Et respicientes vident revolutum lapidem; erat
quippe magnus valde. 5Et introeuntes in monumentum viderunt iuvenem sedentem in dextris,
coopertum stola candida, et obstupuerunt. 6Qui dicit illis: «Nolite expavescere! Iesum quaeritis
Nazarenum crucifixum. Surrexit, non est hic; ecce locus, ubi posuerunt eum. 7Sed ite, dicite discipulis
eius et Petro: "Praecedit vos in Galilaeam. Ibi eum videbitis, sicut dixit vobis"». 8Et exeuntes fugerunt
de monumento; invaserat enim eas tremor et pavor, et nemini quidquam dixerunt, timebant enim.
9Surgens autem mane, prima sabbati, apparuit primo Mariae Magdalenae, de qua eiecerat septem
daemonia. 10Illa vadens nuntiavit his, qui cum eo fuerant, lugentibus et flentibus; 11et illi audientes quia
viveret et visus esset ab ea, non crediderunt. 12Post haec autem duobus ex eis ambulantibus ostensus est
in alia effigie euntibus in villam; 13et illi euntes nuntiaverunt ceteris, nec illis crediderunt. 14Novissime
recumbentibus illis Undecim apparuit, et exprobravit incredulitatem illorum et duritiam cordis, quia his,
qui viderant eum resuscitatum, non crediderant. 15Et dixit eis: «Euntes in mundum universum praedicate
evangelium omni creaturae. 16Qui crediderit et baptizatus fuerit, salvus erit; qui vero non crediderit,
condemnabitur. 17Signa autem eos, qui crediderint, haec sequentur: in nomine meo daemonia eicient,
linguis loquentur novis, 18serpentes tollent, et, si mortiferum quid biberint, non eos nocebit, super
aegrotos manus imponent et bene habebunt». 19Et Dominus quidem Iesus, postquam locutus est eis,
assumptus est in caelum et sedit a dextris Dei. 20Illi autem profecti praedicaverunt ubique, Domino
cooperante et sermonem confirmante, sequentibus signis.

EVANGELIUM SECUNDUM LUCAM

[1] 1Quoniam quidem multi conati sunt ordinare narrationem, quae in nobis completae sunt, rerum,
2sicut tradiderunt nobis, qui ab initio ipsi viderunt et ministri fuerunt verbi, 3visum est et mihi, adsecuto
a principio omnia, diligenter ex ordine tibi scribere, optime Theophile, 4ut cognoscas eorum verborum,
de quibus eruditus es, firmitatem. 5Fuit in diebus Herodis regis Iudaeae sacerdos quidam nomine
Zacharias de vice Abiae et uxor illi de filiabus Aaron, et nomen eius Elisabeth. 6Erant autem iusti ambo
ante Deum, incedentes in omnibus mandatis et iustificationibus Domini, irreprehensibiles. 7Et non erat
illis filius eo quod esset Elisabeth sterilis, et ambo processissent in diebus suis. 8Factum est autem, cum
sacerdotio fungeretur in ordine vicis suae ante Deum, 9secundum consuetudinem sacerdotii sorte exiit,
ut incensum poneret ingressus in templum Domini; 10et omnis multitudo erat populi orans foris hora
incensi. 11Apparuit autem illi angelus Domini stans a dextris altaris incensi; 12et Zacharias turbatus est
videns, et timor irruit super eum. 13Ait autem ad illum angelus: «Ne timeas, Zacharia, quoniam exaudita
est deprecatio tua, et uxor tua Elisabeth pariet tibi filium, et vocabis nomen eius Ioannem. 14Et erit
gaudium tibi et exsultatio, et multi in nativitate eius gaudebunt: 15erit enim magnus coram Domino et

vinum et siceram non bibet et Spiritu Sancto replebitur adhuc ex utero matris suae [16]et multos filiorum Israel convertet ad Dominum Deum ipsorum. [17]Et ipse praecedet ante illum in spiritu et virtute Eliae, *ut convertat corda patrum in filios* et incredibiles ad prudentiam iustorum, parare Domino plebem perfectam». [18]Et dixit Zacharias ad angelum: «Unde hoc sciam? Ego enim sum senex et uxor mea processit in diebus suis». [19]Et respondens angelus dixit ei: «Ego sum Gabriel, qui adsto ante Deum, et missus sum loqui ad te et haec tibi evangelizare. [20]Et ecce eris tacens et non poteris loqui usque in diem, quo haec fiant, pro eo quod non credidisti verbis meis, quae implebuntur in tempore suo». [21]Et erat plebs exspectans Zachariam, et mirabantur quod tardaret ipse in templo. [22]Egressus autem non poterat loqui ad illos, et cognoverunt quod visionem vidisset in templo; et ipse erat innuens illis et permansit mutus. [23]Et factum est ut impleti sunt dies officii eius, abiit in domum suam. [24]Post hos autem dies concepit Elisabeth uxor eius et occultabat se mensibus quinque dicens: [25]«Sic mihi fecit Dominus in diebus, quibus respexit auferre opprobrium meum inter homines». [26]In mense autem sexto missus est angelus Gabriel a Deo in civitatem Galilaeae, cui nomen Nazareth, [27]ad virginem desponsatam viro, cui nomen erat Ioseph de domo David, et nomen virginis Maria. [28]Et ingressus ad eam dixit: «Ave, gratia plena, Dominus tecum». [29]Ipsa autem turbata est in sermone eius et cogitabat qualis esset ista salutatio. [30]Et ait angelus ei: «Ne timeas, Maria; invenisti enim gratiam apud Deum. [31]Et ecce concipies in utero et paries filium, et vocabis nomen eius Iesum. [32]Hic erit magnus et Filius Altissimi vocabitur, et dabit illi Dominus Deus sedem David patris eius, [33]et regnabit super domum Iacob in aeternum, et regni eius non erit finis». [34]Dixit autem Maria ad angelum: «Quomodo fiet istud, quoniam virum non cognosco?». [35]Et respondens angelus dixit ei: «Spiritus Sanctus superveniet in te, et virtus Altissimi obumbrabit tibi: ideoque et quod nascetur sanctum, vocabitur Filius Dei. [36]Et ecce Elisabeth cognata tua et ipsa concepit filium in senecta sua, et hic mensis est sextus illi, quae vocatur sterilis, [37]quia *non erit impossibile apud Deum omne verbum*». [38]Dixit autem Maria: «Ecce ancilla Domini; fiat mihi secundum verbum tuum». Et discessit ab illa angelus. [39]Exsurgens autem Maria in diebus illis abiit in montana cum festinatione in civitatem Iudae [40]et intravit in domum Zachariae et salutavit Elisabeth. [41]Et factum est ut audivit salutationem Mariae Elisabeth, exsultavit infans in utero eius, et repleta est Spiritu Sancto Elisabeth [42]et exclamavit voce magna et dixit: «Benedicta tu inter mulieres, et benedictus fructus ventris tui. [43]Et unde hoc mihi, ut veniat mater Domini mei ad me? [44]Ecce enim ut facta est vox salutationis tuae in auribus meis, exsultavit in gaudio infans in utero meo. [45]Et beata, quae credidit, quoniam perficientur ea, quae dicta sunt ei a Domino». [46]Et ait Maria: «Magnificat *anima mea Dominum*, / [47]et *exsultavit* spiritus meus *in Deo salvatore meo*, / [48]quia *respexit humilitatem ancillae* suae. / Ecce enim ex hoc beatam me dicent omnes generationes, / [49]quia fecit mihi magna, qui potens est, / et sanctum nomen eius, / [50]et misericordia eius in progenies et progenies / timentibus eum. / [51]Fecit potentiam in brachio suo, / dispersit superbos mente cordis sui; / [52]deposuit potentes de sede / et exaltavit humiles; / [53]esurientes implevit bonis / et divites dimisit inanes. / [54]Suscepit Israel puerum suum, / recordatus misericordiae, / [55]sicut locutus est ad patres nostros, / Abraham et semini eius in saecula». [56]Mansit autem Maria cum illa quasi mensibus tribus et reversa est in domum suam. [57]Elisabeth autem impletum est tempus pariendi, et peperit filium. [58]Et audierunt vicini et cognati eius quia magnificavit Dominus misericordiam suam cum illa, et congratulabantur ei. [59]Et factum est in die octavo venerunt circumcidere puerum et vocabant eum nomine patris eius Zachariam. [60]Et respondens mater eius dixit: «Nequaquam, sed vocabitur Ioannes». [61]Et dixerunt ad illam: «Nemo est in cognatione tua, qui vocetur hoc nomine». [62]Innuebant autem patri eius quem vellet vocari eum. [63]Et postulans pugillarem scripsit dicens: «Ioannes est nomen eius». Et mirati sunt universi. [64]Apertum est autem ilico os eius et lingua eius, et loquebatur benedicens Deum. [65]Et factus est timor super omnes vicinos eorum, et super omnia montana Iudaeae divulgabantur omnia verba haec. [66]Et posuerunt omnes, qui audierant, in corde suo dicentes: «Quid putas puer iste erit?». Etenim manus Domini erat cum illo. [67]Et Zacharias pater eius impletus est Spiritu Sancto et prophetavit dicens: [68]«*Benedictus Dominus, Deus Israel*, / quia visitavit et fecit redemptionem plebi suae / [69]et erexit cornu salutis nobis / in domo David pueri sui, / [70]sicut locutus est per os sanctorum, / qui a saeculo sunt, prophetarum eius, / [71]salutem ex inimicis nostris / et de manu omnium, qui oderunt nos; / [72]ad faciendam misericordiam cum patribus nostris / et memorari testamenti sui sancti, / [73]iusiurandum, quod iuravit ad Abraham patrem nostrum, / daturum se nobis, / [74]ut sine timore, de manu inimicorum liberati, / serviamus illi / [75]in sanctitate et iustitia coram ipso / omnibus diebus nostris. / [76]Et tu, puer, propheta Altissimi vocaberis: / praeibis enim *ante faciem Domini parare vias eius*, / [77]ad dandam scientiam salutis plebi eius / in remissionem peccatorum eorum, / [78]per viscera misericordiae Dei nostri, / in quibus visitabit nos oriens ex alto, / [79]*illuminare his, qui in tenebris et in umbra mortis sedent*, / ad dirigendos pedes nostros in viam pacis». [80]Puer autem crescebat et confortabatur spiritu et erat in deserto usque in diem ostensionis suae ad Israel. **[2]** [1]Factum est autem

in diebus illis exiit edictum a Caesare Augusto, ut describeretur universus orbis. [2]Haec descriptio prima
facta est praeside Syriae Quirino. [3]Et ibant omnes, ut profiterentur, singuli in suam civitatem. [4]Ascendit
autem et Ioseph a Galilaea de civitate Nazareth in Iudaeam in civitatem David, quae vocatur Bethlehem,
eo quod esset de domo et familia David, [5]ut profiteretur cum Maria desponsata sibi, uxore praegnante.
[6]Factum est autem cum essent ibi, impleti sunt dies, ut pareret, [7]et peperit filium suum primogenitum;
et pannis eum involvit et reclinavit eum in praesepio, quia non erat eis locus in deversorio. [8]Et pastores
erant in regione eadem vigilantes et custodientes vigilias noctis supra gregem suum. [9]Et angelus Domini
stetit iuxta illos, et claritas Domini circumfulsit illos, et timuerunt timore magno. [10]Et dixit illis angelus:
«Nolite timere; ecce enim evangelizo vobis gaudium magnum, quod erit omni populo, [11]quia natus est
vobis hodie Salvator, qui est Christus Dominus, in civitate David. [12]Et hoc vobis signum: invenietis
infantem pannis involutum et positum in praesepio». [13]Et subito facta est cum angelo multitudo militiae
caelestis laudantium Deum et dicentium: [14]«Gloria in altissimis Deo, et super terram pax in hominibus
bonae voluntatis». [15]Et factum est ut discesserunt ab eis angeli in caelum, pastores loquebantur ad
invicem: «Transeamus usque Bethlehem et videamus hoc verbum, quod factum est, quod Dominus
ostendit nobis». [16]Et venerunt festinantes et invenerunt Mariam et Ioseph et infantem positum in
praesepio. [17]Videntes autem notum fecerunt verbum, quod dictum erat illis de puero hoc. [18]Et omnes,
qui audierunt, mirati sunt de his, quae dicta erant a pastoribus ad ipsos. [19]Maria autem conservabat
omnia verba haec conferens in corde suo. [20]Et reversi sunt pastores glorificantes et laudantes Deum in
omnibus, quae audierant et viderant, sicut dictum est ad illos. [21]Et postquam consummati sunt dies octo,
ut circumcideretur, vocatum est nomen eius Iesus, quod vocatum est ab angelo, priusquam in utero
conciperetur. [22]Et postquam impleti sunt dies purgationis eorum secundum legem Moysis, tulerunt illum
in Hierosolymam, ut sisterent Domino, [23]sicut scriptum est in lege Domini: «*Omne masculinum
adaperiens vulvam sanctum Domino vocabitur*», [24]et ut darent hostiam secundum quod dictum est in
lege Domini: *par turturum aut duos pullos columbarum.* [25]Et ecce homo erat in Ierusalem, cui nomen
Simeon, et homo iste iustus et timoratus, exspectans consolationem Israel, et Spiritus Sanctus erat super
eum, [26]et responsum acceperat ab Spiritu Sancto non visurum se mortem nisi prius videret Christum
Domini. [27]Et venit in Spiritu in templum. Et cum inducerent puerum Iesum parentes eius, ut facerent
secundum consuetudinem legis pro eo, [28]et ipse accepit eum in ulnas suas et benedixit Deum et dixit:
[29]«Nunc dimittis servum tuum, Domine, / secundum verbum tuum in pace, / [30]quia viderunt oculi mei
/ salutare tuum, / [31]quod parasti / ante faciem omnium populorum, / [32]lumen ad revelationem gentium
/ et gloriam plebis tuae Israel». [33]Et erat pater eius et mater mirantes super his, quae dicebantur de illo.
[34]Et benedixit illis Simeon et dixit ad Mariam matrem eius: «Ecce positus est hic in ruinam et
resurrectionem multorum in Israel et in signum, cui contradicetur [35]—et tuam ipsius animam pertransiet
gladius— ut revelentur ex multis cordibus cogitationes». [36]Et erat Anna prophetissa, filia Phanuel, de
tribu Aser. Haec processerat in diebus multis et vixerat cum viro annis septem a virginitate sua; [37]et haec
vidua usque ad annos octoginta quattuor, quae non discedebat de templo, ieiuniis et obsecrationibus
serviens nocte ac die. [38]Et haec ipsa hora superveniens confitebatur Deo et loquebatur de illo omnibus,
qui exspectabant redemptionem Ierusalem. [39]Et ut perfecerunt omnia secundum legem Domini, reversi
sunt in Galilaeam in civitatem suam Nazareth. [40]Puer autem crescebat et confortabatur plenus sapientia;
et gratia Dei erat super illum. [41]Et ibant parentes eius per omnes annos in Ierusalem in die festo Paschae.
[42]Et cum factus esset annorum duodecim, ascendentibus illis secundum consuetudinem diei festi,
[43]consummatisque diebus, cum redirent, remansit puer Iesus in Ierusalem, et non cognoverunt parentes
eius. [44]Existimantes autem illum esse in comitatu, venerunt iter diei et requirebant eum inter cognatos
et notos [45]et non invenientes regressi sunt in Ierusalem requirentes eum. [46]Et factum est post triduum
invenerunt illum in templo sedentem in medio doctorum, audientem illos et interrogantem eos;
[47]stupebant autem omnes, qui eum audiebant, super prudentia et responsis eius. [48]Et videntes eum
admirati sunt, et dixit Mater eius ad illum: «Fili, quid fecisti nobis sic? Ecce pater tuus et ego dolentes
quaerebamus te». [49]Et ait ad illos: «Quid est quod me quaerebatis? Nesciebatis quia in his, quae Patris
mei sunt, oportet me esse?». [50]Et ipsi non intellexerunt verbum, quod locutus est ad illos. [51]Et descendit
cum eis et venit Nazareth et erat subditus illis. Et mater eius conservabat omnia verba in corde suo. [52]Et
Iesus *proficiebat* sapientia et aetate *et gratia apud Deum et homines.* **[3]** [1]Anno autem quinto decimo
imperii Tiberii Caesaris, procurante Pontio Pilato Iudaeam, tetrarcha autem Galilaeae Herode, Philippo
autem fratre eius tetrarcha Ituraeae et Trachonitidis regionis, et Lysania Abilinae tetrarcha, [2]sub principe
sacerdotum Anna et Caipha, factum est verbum Dei super Ioannem Zachariae filium in deserto. [3]Et venit
in omnem regionem circa Iordanem praedicans baptismum paenitentiae in remissionem peccatorum,
[4]sicut scriptum est in libro sermonum Isaiae prophetae: «*Vox clamantis in deserto: / "Parate viam
Domini, / rectas facite semitas eius. / [5]Omnis vallis implebitur / et omnis mons et collis humiliabitur;*

/ et erunt prava in directa, / et aspera in vias planas: / 6et videbit omnis caro salutare Dei"». 7Dicebat
ergo ad turbas, quae exibant, ut baptizarentur ab ipso: «Genimina viperarum, quis ostendit vobis fugere
a ventura ira? 8Facite ergo fructus dignos paenitentiae et ne coeperitis dicere in vobis ipsis: "Patrem
habemus Abraham"; dico enim vobis quia potest Deus de lapidibus istis suscitare Abrahae filios. 9Iam
enim et securis ad radicem arborum posita est; omnis ergo arbor non faciens fructum bonum exciditur
et in ignem mittitur». 10Et interrogabant eum turbae dicentes: «Quid ergo faciemus?». 11Respondens
autem dicebat illis: «Qui habet duas tunicas, det non habenti; et qui habet escas, similiter faciat».
12Venerunt autem et publicani, ut baptizarentur, et dixerunt ad illum: «Magister, quid faciemus?». 13At
ille dixit ad eos: «Nihil amplius quam constitutum est vobis, faciatis». 14Interrogabant autem eum et
milites dicentes: «Quid faciemus et nos?». Et ait illis: «Neminem concutiatis, neque calumniam faciatis
et contenti estote stipendiis vestris». 15Existimante autem populo et cogitantibus omnibus in cordibus
suis de Ioanne, ne forte ipse esset Christus, 16respondit Ioannes dicens omnibus: «Ego quidem aqua
baptizo vos. Venit autem fortior me, cuius non sum dignus solvere corrigiam calceamentorum eius; ipse
vos baptizabit in Spiritu Sancto et igni, 17cuius ventilabrum in manu eius ad purgandam aream suam et
ad congregandum triticum in horreum suum, paleas autem comburet igni inexstinguibili». 18Multa
quidem et alia exhortans evangelizabat populum. 19Herodes autem tetrarcha, cum corriperetur ab illo
de Herodiade uxore fratris sui et de omnibus malis, quae fecit Herodes, 20adiecit et hoc supra omnia
et inclusit Ioannem in carcere. 21Factum est autem cum baptizaretur omnis populus et Iesu baptizato et
orante, apertum est caelum, 22et descendit Spiritus Sanctus corporali specie sicut columba super ipsum;
et vox de caelo facta est: «Tu es Filius meus dilectus; in te complacui mihi». 23Et ipse Iesus erat
incipiens quasi annorum triginta, ut putabatur, filius Ioseph, qui fuit Heli, 24qui fuit Matthat, qui fuit
Levi, qui fuit Melchi, qui fuit Iannae, qui fuit Ioseph, 25qui fuit Matthathiae, qui fuit Amos, qui fuit
Nahum, qui fuit Esli, qui fuit Naggae, 26qui fuit Maath, qui fuit Matthathiae, qui fuit Semei, qui fuit
Iosech, qui fuit Ioda, 27qui fuit Ioanna, qui fuit Resa, qui fuit Zorobabel, qui fuit Salathiel, qui fuit Neri,
28qui fuit Melchi, qui fuit Addi, qui fuit Cosam, qui fuit Elmadam, qui fuit Her, 29qui fuit Iesu, qui fuit
Eliezer, qui fuit Iorim, qui fuit Matthat, qui fuit Levi, 30qui fuit Simeon, qui fuit Iudae, qui fuit Ioseph,
qui fuit Iona, qui fuit Eliachim, 31qui fuit Melea, qui fuit Menna, qui fuit Matthatha, qui fuit Nathan, qui
fuit David, 32qui fuit Iesse, qui fuit Obed, qui fuit Booz, qui fuit Salmon, qui fuit Naasson, 33qui fuit
Aminadab, qui fuit Admin, qui fuit Arni, qui fuit Esrom, qui fuit Phares, qui fuit Iudae, 34qui fuit Iacob,
qui fuit Isaac, qui fuit Abrahae, qui fuit Thare, qui fuit Nachor, 35qui fuit Seruch, qui fuit Ragau, qui fuit
Phaleg, qui fuit Heber, qui fuit Sala, 36qui fuit Cainan, qui fuit Arphaxad, qui fuit Sem, qui fuit Noe, qui
fuit Lamech, 37qui fuit Mathusala, qui fuit Henoch, qui fuit Iared, qui fuit Malaleel, qui fuit Cainan,
38qui fuit Enos, qui fuit Seth, qui fuit Adam, qui fuit Dei. **[4]** 1Iesus autem plenus Spiritu Sancto
regressus est ab Iordane et agebatur in Spiritu in deserto 2diebus quadraginta et tentabatur a Diabolo. Et
nihil manducavit in diebus illis et, consummatis illis, esuriit. 3Dixit autem illi Diabolus: «Si Filius Dei
es, dic lapidi huic, ut panis fiat». 4Et respondit ad illum Iesus: «Scriptum est: "*Non in pane solo vivet
homo*"». 5Et sustulit illum et ostendit illi omnia regna orbis terrae in momento temporis; 6et ait ei
Diabolus: «Tibi dabo potestatem hanc universam et gloriam illorum, quia mihi tradita est, et, cui volo,
do illam: 7tu ergo, si adoraveris coram me, erit tua omnis». 8Et respondens Iesus dixit illi: «Scriptum
est: "*Dominum Deum tuum adorabis et illi soli servies*"». 9Duxit autem illum in Ierusalem et statuit eum
supra pinnam templi et dixit illi: «Si Filius Dei es, mitte te hinc deorsum. 10Scriptum est enim: "*Angelis
suis mandabit de te, / ut conservent te*" / 11et: "*In manibus tollent te, / ne forte offendas ad lapidem
pedem tuum*"». 12Et respondens Iesus ait illi: «Dictum est: "*Non tentabis Dominum Deum tuum*"». 13Et
consummata omni tentatione, Diabolus recessit ab illo usque ad tempus. 14Et regressus est Iesus in
virtute Spiritus in Galilaeam. Et fama exiit per universam regionem de illo. 15Et ipse docebat in
synagogis eorum et magnificabatur ab omnibus. 16Et venit Nazareth, ubi erat nutritus, et intravit
secundum consuetudinem suam die sabbati in synagogam et surrexit legere. 17Et traditus est illi liber
prophetae Isaiae; et ut revolvit librum, invenit locum, ubi scriptum erat: 18«*Spiritus Domini super me*; /
*propter quod unxit me / evangelizare pauperibus, / misit me praedicare captivis remissionem / et caecis
visum, / dimittere confractos in remissione, / 19praedicare annum Domini acceptum*». 20Et cum
plicuisset librum, reddidit ministro et sedit; et omnium in synagoga oculi erant intendentes in eum.
21Coepit autem dicere ad illos: «Hodie impleta est haec Scriptura in auribus vestris». 22Et omnes
testimonium illi dabant et mirabantur in verbis gratiae, quae procedebant de ore ipsius, et dicebant:
«Nonne hic filius est Ioseph?». 23Et ait illis: «Utique dicetis mihi hanc similitudinem: "Medice, cura
teipsum; quanta audivimus facta in Capharnaum, fac et hic in patria tua"». 24Ait autem: «Amen dico
vobis: Nemo propheta acceptus est in patria sua. 25In veritate autem dico vobis: Multae viduae erant
in diebus Eliae in Israel, quando clausum est caelum annis tribus et mensibus sex, cum facta est fames

magna in omni terra; [26]et ad nullam illarum missus est Elias nisi in Sarepta Sidoniae ad mulierem
viduam. [27]Et multi leprosi erant in Israel sub Eliseo propheta; et nemo eorum mundatus est nisi Naaman
Syrus». [28]Et repleti sunt omnes in synagoga ira haec audientes [29]et surrexerunt et eiecerunt illum extra
civitatem et duxerunt illum usque ad supercilium montis, supra quem civitas illorum erat aedificata, ut
praecipitarent eum. [30]Ipse autem transiens per medium illorum ibat. [31]Et descendit in Capharnaum
civitatem Galilaeae. Et docebat illos sabbatis, [32]et stupebant in doctrina eius, quia in potestate erat sermo
ipsius. [33]Et in synagoga erat homo habens spiritum daemonii immundi; et exclamavit voce magna:
[34]«Sine; quid nobis et tibi, Iesu Nazarene? Venisti perdere nos? Scio te qui sis: Sanctus Dei». [35]Et
increpavit illi Iesus dicens: «Obmutesce et exi ab illo!». Et cum proiecisset illum daemonium in
medium, exiit ab illo nihilque illum nocuit. [36]Et factus est pavor in omnibus; et colloquebantur ad
invicem dicentes: «Quod est hoc verbum, quia in potestate et virtute imperat immundis spiritibus, et
exeunt?». [37]Et divulgabatur fama de illo in omnem locum regionis. [38]Surgens autem de synagoga
introivit in domum Simonis. Socrus autem Simonis tenebatur magna febri; et rogaverunt illum pro ea.
[39]Et stans super illam imperavit febri, et dimisit illam; et continuo surgens ministrabat illis. [40]Cum sol
autem occidisset, omnes, qui habebant infirmos variis languoribus, ducebant illos ad eum; at ille singulis
manus imponens curabat eos. [41]Exibant autem daemonia a multis clamantia et dicentia: «Tu es Filius
Dei». Et increpans non sinebat ea loqui, quia sciebant ipsum esse Christum. [42]Facta autem die, egressus
ibat in desertum locum; et turbae requirebant eum et venerunt usque ad ipsum et detinebant illum, ne
discederet ab eis. [43]Quibus ille ait: «Et aliis civitatibus oportet me evangelizare regnum Dei, quia ideo
missus sum». [44]Et erat praedicans in synagogis Iudaeae. **[5]** [1]Factum est autem cum turba urgeret
illum ut audiret verbum Dei, et ipse stabat secus stagnum Genesareth [2]et vidit duas naves stantes secus
stagnum; piscatores autem descenderant de illis et lavabant retia. [3]Ascendens autem in unam navem,
quae erat Simonis, rogavit eum a terra reducere pusillum; et sedens docebat de navicula turbas. [4]Ut
cessavit autem loqui, dixit ad Simonem: «Duc in altum et laxate retia vestra in capturam». [5]Et
respondens Simon dixit: «Praeceptor, per totam noctem laborantes nihil cepimus; in verbo autem tuo
laxabo retia». [6]Et cum hoc fecissent, concluserunt piscium multitudinem copiosam; rumpebantur autem
retia eorum. [7]Et annuerunt sociis, qui erant in alia navi, ut venirent et adiuvarent eos; et venerunt, et
impleverunt ambas naviculas, ita ut mergerentur. [8]Quod cum videret Simon Petrus, procidit ad genua
Iesu dicens: «Exi a me, quia homo peccator sum, Domine». [9]Stupor enim circumdederat eum et omnes,
qui cum illo erant, in captura piscium, quos ceperant; [10]similiter autem et Iacobum et Ioannem, filios
Zebedaei, qui erant socii Simonis. Et ait ad Simonem Iesus: «Noli timere; ex hoc iam homines eris
capiens». [11]Et subductis ad terram navibus, relictis omnibus, secuti sunt illum. [12]Et factum est cum esset
in una civitatum, et ecce vir plenus lepra; et videns Iesum et procidens in faciem rogavit eum dicens:
«Domine, si vis, potes me mundare». [13]Et extendens manum tetigit illum dicens: «Volo, mundare!»; et
confestim lepra discessit ab illo. [14]Et ipse praecepit illi, ut nemini diceret, sed: «Vade, ostende te
sacerdoti et offer pro emundatione tua, sicut praecepit Moyses, in testimonium illis». [15]Perambulabat
autem magis sermo de illo, et conveniebant turbae multae, ut audirent et curarentur ab infirmitatibus
suis; [16]ipse autem secedebat in desertis et orabat. [17]Et factum est in una dierum, et ipse erat docens, et
erant pharisaei sedentes et legis doctores, qui venerant ex omni castello Galilaeae et Iudaeae et
Ierusalem; et virtus Domini erat ei ad sanandum. [18]Et ecce viri portantes in lecto hominem, qui erat
paralyticus, et quaerebant eum inferre et ponere ante eum. [19]Et non invenientes qua parte illum inferrent
prae turba, ascenderunt supra tectum et per tegulas summiserunt illum cum lectulo in medium ante
Iesum. [20]Quorum fidem ut vidit, dixit: «Homo, remittuntur tibi peccata tua». [21]Et coeperunt cogitare
scribae et pharisaei dicentes: «Quis est hic, qui loquitur blasphemias? Quis potest dimittere peccata nisi
solus Deus?». [22]Ut cognovit autem Iesus cogitationes eorum, respondens dixit ad illos: «Quid cogitatis
in cordibus vestris? [23]Quid est facilius, dicere: "Dimittuntur tibi peccata tua", an dicere: "Surge et
ambula"? [24]Ut autem sciatis quia Filius hominis potestatem habet in terra dimittere peccata—ait
paralytico—: Tibi dico: Surge, tolle lectulum tuum et vade in domum tuam». [25]Et confestim surgens
coram illis tulit, in quo iacebat, et abiit in domum suam magnificans Deum. [26]Et stupor apprehendit
omnes, et magnificabant Deum, et repleti sunt timore dicentes: «Vidimus mirabilia hodie». [27]Et post
haec exiit et vidit publicanum nomine Levi sedentem ad teloneum et ait illi: «Sequere me». [28]Et relictis
omnibus, surgens secutus est eum. [29]Et fecit ei convivium magnum Levi in domo sua; et erat turba
multa publicanorum et aliorum, qui cum illis erant discumbentes. [30]Et murmurabant pharisaei et scribae
eorum adversus discipulos eius dicentes: «Quare cum publicanis et peccatoribus manducatis et bibitis?».
[31]Et respondens Iesus dixit ad illos: «Non egent, qui sani sunt, medico, sed qui male habent. [32]Non veni
vocare iustos sed peccatores in paenitentiam». [33]At illi dixerunt ad eum: «Discipuli Ioannis ieiunant
frequenter et obsecrationes faciunt, similiter et pharisaeorum; tui autem edunt et bibunt». [34]Quibus Iesus

ait: «Numquid potestis convivas nuptiarum, dum cum illis est sponsus, facere ieiunare? [35]Venient autem dies, et cum ablatus fuerit ab illis sponsus, tunc ieiunabunt in illis diebus». [36]Dicebat autem et similitudinem ad illos: «Nemo abscindit commissuram a vestimento novo et immittit in vestimentum vetus; alioquin et novum rumpet, et veteri non conveniet commissura a novo. [37]Et nemo mittit vinum novum in utres veteres; alioquin rumpet vinum novum utres, et ipsum effundetur, et utres peribunt; [38]sed vinum novum in utres novos mittendum est. [39]Et nemo bibens vetus vult novum; dicit enim: "Vetus melius est!"». **[6]** [1]Factum est autem in sabbato cum transiret per sata, et vellebant discipuli eius spicas et manducabant confricantes manibus. [2]Quidam autem pharisaeorum dixerunt: «Quid facitis, quod non licet in sabbatis?». [3]Et respondens Iesus ad eos dixit: «Nec hoc legistis, quod fecit David, cum esurisset ipse et qui cum eo erant? [4]Quomodo intravit in domum Dei et panes propositionis sumpsit et manducavit et dedit his, qui cum ipso erant, quos non licet manducare nisi tantum sacerdotibus?». [5]Et dicebat illis: «Dominus est sabbati Filius hominis». [6]Factum est autem in alio sabbato ut intraret in synagogam et doceret; et erat ibi homo, et manus eius dextra erat arida. [7]Observabant autem illum scribae et pharisaei si sabbato curaret, ut invenirent accusare illum. [8]Ipse vero sciebat cogitationes eorum et ait homini, qui habebat manum aridam: «Surge et sta in medium». Et surgens stetit. [9]Ait autem ad illos Iesus: «Interrogo vos si licet sabbato bene facere an male, animam salvam facere an perdere?». [10]Et circumspectis omnibus illis, dixit illi: «Extende manum tuam». Et fecit, et restituta est manus eius. [11]Ipsi autem repleti sunt insipientia et colloquebantur ad invicem quidnam facerent Iesu. [12]Factum est autem in illis diebus, exiit in montem orare et erat pernoctans in oratione Dei. [13]Et cum dies factus esset, vocavit discipulos suos et elegit Duodecim ex ipsis, quos et apostolos nominavit: [14]Simonem, quem et cognominavit Petrum, et Andream fratrem eius et Iacobum et Ioannem et Philippum et Bartholomaeum [15]et Matthaeum et Thomam et Iacobum Alphaei et Simonem, qui vocatur Zelotes, [16]et Iudam Iacobi et Iudam Iscarioth, qui fuit proditor. [17]Et descendens cum illis stetit in loco campestri, et turba multa discipulorum eius, et multitudo copiosa plebis ab omni Iudaea et Ierusalem et maritima Tyri et Sidonis, [18]qui venerunt, ut audirent eum et sanarentur a languoribus suis; et qui vexabantur a spiritibus immundis, curabantur. [19]Et omnis turba quaerebant eum tangere, quia virtus de illo exibat et sanabat omnes. [20]Et ipse, elevatis oculis suis in discipulos suos, dicebat: «Beati pauperes, quia vestrum est regnum Dei. [21]Beati, qui nunc esuritis, quia saturabimini. Beati, qui nunc fletis, quia ridebitis. [22]Beati eritis, cum vos oderint homines et cum separaverint vos et exprobraverint et eiecerint nomen vestrum tamquam malum propter Filium hominis. [23]Gaudete in illa die et exsultate, ecce enim merces vestra multa in caelo; secundum haec enim faciebant prophetis patres eorum. [24]Verumtamen vae vobis divitibus, quia habetis consolationem vestram! [25]Vae vobis, qui saturati estis nunc, quia esurietis! Vae vobis, qui ridetis nunc, quia lugebitis et flebitis! [26]Vae, cum bene vobis dixerint omnes homines! Secundum haec enim faciebant pseudoprophetis patres eorum. [27]Sed vobis dico, qui auditis: Diligite inimicos vestros, bene facite his, qui vos oderunt; [28]benedicite maledicentibus vobis, orate pro calumniantibus vos. [29]Ei qui te percutit in maxillam, praebe et alteram; et ab eo, qui aufert tibi vestimentum, etiam tunicam noli prohibere. [30]Omni petenti te tribue; et ab eo, qui aufert, quae tua sunt, ne repetas. [31]Et prout vultis, ut faciant vobis homines, facite illis similiter. [32]Et si diligitis eos, qui vos diligunt, quae vobis est gratia? Nam et peccatores diligentes se diligunt. [33]Et si bene feceritis his, qui vobis bene faciunt, quae vobis est gratia? Siquidem et peccatores idem faciunt. [34]Et si mutuum dederitis his, a quibus speratis recipere, quae vobis gratia est? Nam et peccatores peccatoribus fenerantur, ut recipiant aequalia. [35]Verumtamen diligite inimicos vestros et bene facite et mutuum date nihil desperantes; et erit merces vestra multa, et eritis filii Altissimi, quia ipse benignus est super ingratos et malos. [36]Estote misericordes, sicut et Pater vester misericors est. [37]Et nolite iudicare et non iudicabimini; et nolite condemnare et non condemnabimini. Dimittite et dimittemini; [38]date, et dabitur vobis: mensuram bonam, confertam, coagitatam, supereffluentem dabunt in sinum vestrum; eadem quippe mensura, qua mensi fueritis, remetietur vobis». [39]Dixit autem illis et similitudinem: «Numquid potest caecus caecum ducere? Nonne ambo in foveam cadent? [40]Non est discipulus super magistrum; perfectus autem omnis erit sicut magister eius. [41]Quid autem vides festucam in oculo fratris tui, trabem autem, quae in oculo tuo est, non consideras? [42]Quomodo potes dicere fratri tuo: "Frater, sine eiciam festucam, quae est in oculo tuo", ipse in oculo tuo trabem non videns? Hypocrita, eice primum trabem de oculo tuo et tunc perspicies, ut educas festucam, quae est in oculo fratris tui. [43]Non est enim arbor bona faciens fructum malum, neque iterum arbor mala faciens fructum bonum. [44]Unaquaeque enim arbor de fructu suo cognoscitur; neque enim de spinis colligunt ficus, neque de rubo vindemiant uvam. [45]Bonus homo de bono thesauro cordis profert bonum, et malus homo de malo profert malum: ex abundantia enim cordis os eius loquitur. [46]Quid autem vocatis me: "Domine, Domine", et non facitis, quae dico? [47]Omnis, qui venit ad me et audit sermones meos et facit eos, ostendam vobis cui similis sit:

48similis est homini aedificanti domum, qui fodit in altum et posuit fundamentum supra petram;
inundatione autem facta, illisum est flumen domui illi, et non potuit eam movere, bene enim aedificata
erat. 49Qui autem audivit et non fecit, similis est homini aedificanti domum suam supra terram sine
fundamento, in quam illisus est fluvius, et continuo cecidit, et facta est ruina domus illius magna».
[7] 1Cum autem implesset omnia verba sua in aures plebis, intravit Capharnaum. 2Centurionis autem
cuiusdam servus male habens erat moriturus, qui illi erat pretiosus. 3Et cum audisset de Iesu, misit ad
eum seniores Iudaeorum, rogans eum, ut veniret et salvaret servum eius. 4At illi cum venissent ad
Iesum, rogabant eum sollicite dicentes: «Dignus est, ut hoc illi praestes: 5diligit enim gentem nostram
et synagogam ipse aedificavit nobis». 6Iesus autem ibat cum illis. At cum iam non longe esset a domo,
misit centurio amicos dicens ei: «Domine, noli vexari; non enim dignus sum, ut sub tectum meum
intres, 7propter quod et meipsum non sum dignum arbitratus, ut venirem ad te; sed dic verbo, et sanetur
puer meus. 8Nam et ego homo sum sub potestate constitutus, habens sub me milites, et dico huic:
"Vade", et vadit; et alii: "Veni", et venit; et servo meo: "Fac hoc", et facit». 9Quo audito, Iesus miratus
est eum et conversus sequentibus se turbis dixit: «Dico vobis, nec in Israel tantam fidem inveni!». 10Et
reversi, qui missi fuerant domum, invenerunt servum sanum. 11Et factum est deinceps, ivit in civitatem,
quae vocatur Naim, et ibant cum illo discipuli eius et turba copiosa. 12Cum autem appropinquaret portae
civitatis, et ecce defunctus efferebatur filius unicus matri suae, et haec vidua erat, et turba civitatis multa
cum illa. 13Quam cum vidisset Dominus, misericordia motus super ea dixit illi: «Noli flere!». 14Et
accessit et tetigit loculum; hi autem, qui portabant, steterunt. Et ait: «Adulescens, tibi dico: Surge!».
15Et resedit, qui erat mortuus, et coepit loqui; et dedit illum matri suae. 16Accepit autem omnes timor,
et magnificabant Deum dicentes: «Propheta magnus surrexit in nobis» et: «Deus visitavit plebem
suam». 17Et exiit hic sermo in universam Iudaeam de eo et omnem circa regionem. 18Et nuntiaverunt
Ioanni discipuli eius de omnibus his. 19Et convocavit duos de discipulis suis Ioannes et misit ad
Dominum dicens: «Tu es qui venturus es, an alium exspectamus?». 20Cum autem venissent ad eum viri,
dixerunt: «Ioannes Baptista misit nos ad te dicens: 'Tu es qui venturus es, an alium exspectamus?'».
21In ipsa hora curavit multos a languoribus et plagis et spiritibus malis et caecis multis donavit visum.
22Et respondens dixit illis: «Euntes nuntiate Ioanni, quae vidistis et audistis: *caeci vident*, claudi
ambulant, leprosi mundantur et surdi audiunt, mortui resurgunt, *pauperes evangelizantur*; 23et beatus
est, quicumque non fuerit scandalizatus in me». 24Et cum discessissent nuntii Ioannis, coepit dicere de
Ioanne ad turbas: «Quid existis in desertum videre? Arundinem vento moveri? 25Sed quid existis videre?
Hominem mollibus vestimentis indutum? Ecce, qui in veste pretiosa sunt et deliciis, in domibus regum
sunt. 26Sed quid existis videre? Prophetam? Utique, dico vobis, et plus quam prophetam. 27Hic est, de
quo scriptum est: "*Ecce mitto angelum meum ante faciem tuam, / qui praeparabit viam tuam ante te*".
28Dico vobis: Maior inter natos mulierum Ioanne nemo est; qui autem minor est in regno Dei, maior est
illo. 29Et omnis populus audiens et publicani iustificaverunt Deum, baptizati baptismo Ioannis;
30pharisaei autem et legis periti consilium Dei spreverunt in semetipsos, non baptizati ab eo. 31Cui ergo
similes dicam homines generationis huius, et cui similes sunt? 32Similes sunt pueris sedentibus in foro
et loquentibus ad invicem, quod dicit: "Cantavimus vobis tibiis, et non saltastis; / lamentavimus, et non
plorastis!". 33Venit enim Ioannes Baptista neque manducans panem neque bibens vinum, et dicitis:
'Daemonium habet!'; 34venit Filius hominis manducans et bibens, et dicitis: 'Ecce homo devorator et
bibens vinum, amicus publicanorum et peccatorum!'. 35Et iustificata est sapientia ab omnibus filiis
suis». 36Rogabat autem illum quidam de pharisaeis, ut manducaret cum illo; et ingressus domum
pharisaei discubuit. 37Et ecce mulier, quae erat in civitate peccatrix, ut cognovit quod accubuit in domo
pharisaei, attulit alabastrum unguenti 38et stans retro secus pedes eius flens lacrimis coepit rigare pedes
eius et capillis capitis sui tergebat, et osculabatur pedes eius et unguento ungebat. 39Videns autem
pharisaeus, qui vocaverat eum, ait intra se dicens: «Hic si esset propheta sciret utique quae et qualis
mulier, quae tangit eum, quia peccatrix est». 40Et respondens Iesus dixit ad illum: «Simon, habeo tibi
aliquid dicere». At ille ait: «Magister, dic». 41«Duo debitores erant cuidam feneratori: unus debebat
denarios quingentos, alius quinquaginta. 42Non habentibus illis, unde redderent, donavit utrisque. Quis
ergo eorum plus diliget eum?». 43Respondens Simon dixit: «Aestimo quia is, cui plus donavit». At ille
dixit ei: «Recte iudicasti». 44Et conversus ad mulierem, dixit Simoni: «Vides hanc mulierem? Intravi in
domum tuam: aquam pedibus meis non dedisti; haec autem lacrimis rigavit pedes meos et capillis suis
tersit. 45Osculum mihi non dedisti; haec autem, ex quo intravi, non cessavit osculari pedes meos. 46Oleo
caput meum non unxisti; haec autem unguento unxit pedes meos. 47Propter quod dico tibi: Remissa sunt
peccata eius multa, quoniam dilexit multum; cui autem minus dimittitur, minus diligit». 48Dixit autem
ad illam: «Remissa sunt peccata tua». 49Et coeperunt, qui simul accumbebant, dicere intra se: «Quis est
hic, qui etiam peccata dimittit?». 50Dixit autem ad mulierem: «Fides tua te salvam fecit; vade in pace!».

[8] [1]Et factum est deinceps, et ipse iter faciebat per civitatem et castellum praedicans et evangelizans regnum Dei, et Duodecim cum illo [2]et mulieres aliquae, quae erant curatae ab spiritibus malignis et infirmitatibus, Maria, quae vocatur Magdalene, de qua daemonia septem exierant, [3]et Ioanna uxor Chuza, procuratoris Herodis, et Susanna et aliae multae, quae ministrabant eis de facultatibus suis. [4]Cum autem turba plurima conveniret et de singulis civitatibus properarent ad eum, dixit per similitudinem: [5]«Exiit, qui seminat, seminare semen suum. Et dum seminat ipse, aliud cecidit secus viam et conculcatum est, et volucres caeli comederunt illud. [6]Et aliud cecidit super petram et natum aruit, quia non habebat umorem. [7]Et aliud cecidit inter spinas, et simul exortae spinae suffocaverunt illud. [8]Et aliud cecidit in terram bonam et ortum fecit fructum centuplum». Haec dicens clamabat: «Qui habet aures audiendi, audiat». [9]Interrogabant autem eum discipuli eius quae esset haec parabola. [10]Quibus ipse dixit: «Vobis datum est nosse mysteria regni Dei, ceteris autem in parabolis, ut *videntes non videant et audientes non intellegant*. [11]Est autem haec parabola: Semen est verbum Dei. [12]Qui autem secus viam, sunt qui audiunt; deinde venit Diabolus et tollit verbum de corde eorum, ne credentes salvi fiant. [13]Qui autem supra petram: qui cum audierint, cum gaudio suscipiunt verbum; et hi radices non habent, qui ad tempus credunt, et in tempore tentationis recedunt. [14]Quod autem in spinis cecidit: hi sunt, qui audierunt et a sollicitudinibus et divitiis et voluptatibus vitae euntes suffocantur et non referunt fructum. [15]Quod autem in bonam terram: hi sunt, qui in corde bono et optimo audientes verbum retinent et fructum afferunt in patientia. [16]Nemo autem lucernam accendens operit eam vaso aut subtus lectum ponit, sed supra candelabrum ponit, ut intrantes videant lumen. [17]Non enim est occultum, quod non manifestetur, nec absconditum, quod non cognoscatur et in palam veniat. [18]Videte ergo quomodo auditis: qui enim habet, dabitur illi; et quicumque non habet, etiam quod putat se habere, auferetur ab illo». [19]Venerunt autem ad illum mater et fratres eius, et non poterant adire ad eum prae turba. [20]Et nuntiatum est illi: «Mater tua et fratres tui stant foris volentes te videre». [21]Qui respondens dixit ad eos: «Mater mea et fratres mei hi sunt, qui verbum Dei audiunt et faciunt». [22]Factum est autem in una dierum, et ipse ascendit in navem et discipuli eius, et ait ad illos: «Transfretemus trans stagnum». Et ascenderunt. [23]Navigantibus autem illis, obdormivit. Et descendit procella venti in stagnum, et complebantur et periclitabantur. [24]Accedentes autem suscitaverunt eum dicentes: «Praeceptor, praeceptor, perimus!». At ille surgens increpavit ventum et tempestatem aquae, et cessaverunt, et facta est tranquillitas. [25]Dixit autem illis: «Ubi est fides vestra?». Qui timentes mirati sunt dicentes ad invicem: «Quis putas hic est, quia et ventis imperat et aquae, et oboediunt ei?». [26]Enavigaverunt autem ad regionem Gergesenorum, quae est contra Galilaeam. [27]Et cum egressus esset ad terram, occurrit illi vir quidam de civitate, qui habebat daemonia et iam tempore multo vestimento non induebatur, neque in domo manebat sed in monumentis. [28]Is ut vidit Iesum, exclamans procidit ante illum et voce magna dixit: «Quid mihi et tibi est, Iesu, Fili Dei Altissimi? Obsecro te, ne me torqueas». [29]Praecipiebat enim spiritui immundo, ut exiret ab homine. Multis enim temporibus arripiebat illum, et vinciebatur catenis et compedibus custoditus; et ruptis vinculis, agebatur a daemonio in deserta. [30]Interrogavit autem illum Iesus dicens: «Quod tibi nomen est?». At ille dixit: «Legio», quia intraverunt daemonia multa in eum. [31]Et rogabant eum, ne imperaret illis, ut in abyssum irent. [32]Erat autem ibi grex porcorum multorum pascentium in monte; et rogaverunt eum, ut permitteret eis in illos ingredi. Et permisit illis. [33]Exierunt ergo daemonia ab homine et intraverunt in porcos, et impetu abiit grex per praeceps in stagnum et suffocatus est. [34]Quod ut viderunt factum, qui pascebant, fugerunt et nuntiaverunt in civitatem et in villas. [35]Exierunt autem videre, quod factum est, et venerunt ad Iesum, et invenerunt hominem sedentem, a quo daemonia exierant, vestitum ac sana mente ad pedes Iesu, et timuerunt. [36]Nuntiaverunt autem illis hi, qui viderant, quomodo sanus factus esset, qui a daemonio vexabatur. [37]Et rogaverunt illum omnis multitudo regionis Gergesenorum, ut discederet ab ipsis, quia timore magno tenebantur. Ipse autem ascendens navem reversus est. [38]Et rogabat illum vir, a quo daemonia exierant, ut cum eo esset. Dimisit autem eum dicens: [39]«Redi domum tuam et narra quanta tibi fecit Deus». Et abiit per universam civitatem praedicans quanta illi fecisset Iesus. [40]Cum autem rediret Iesus, excepit illum turba; erant enim omnes exspectantes eum. [41]Et ecce venit vir, cui nomen Iairus, et ipse princeps synagogae erat, et cecidit ad pedes Iesu rogans eum, ut intraret in domum eius, [42]quia filia unica erat illi fere annorum duodecim, et haec moriebatur. Et dum iret, a turbis comprimebatur. [43]Et mulier quaedam erat in fluxu sanguinis ab annis duodecim, quae in medicos erogaverat omnem substantiam suam, nec ab ullo potuit curari; [44]accessit retro et tetigit fimbriam vestimenti eius, et confestim stetit fluxus sanguinis eius. [45]Et ait Iesus: «Quis est qui me tetigit?». Negantibus autem omnibus, dixit Petrus: «Praeceptor, turbae te comprimunt et affligunt». [46]At dixit Iesus: «Tetigit me aliquis; nam et ego novi virtutem de me exisse». [47]Videns autem mulier quia non latuit, tremens venit et procidit ante eum et ob quam causam tetigerit eum indicavit coram omni populo et quemadmodum confestim sanata sit. [48]At ipse dixit illi:

«Filia, fides tua te salvam fecit. Vade in pace». [49]Adhuc illo loquente, venit quidam e domo principis synagogae dicens: «Mortua est filia tua; noli amplius vexare magistrum». [50]Iesus autem, audito hoc verbo, respondit ei: «Noli timere; crede tantum, et salva erit». [51]Et cum venisset domum, non permisit intrare secum quemquam nisi Petrum et Ioannem et Iacobum et patrem puellae et matrem. [52]Flebant autem omnes et plangebant illam. At ille dixit: «Nolite flere; non est enim mortua, sed dormit». [53]Et deridebant eum scientes quia mortua esset. [54]Ipse autem tenens manum eius clamavit dicens: «Puella, surge!». [55]Et reversus est spiritus eius, et surrexit continuo; et iussit illi dari manducare. [56]Et stupuerunt parentes eius, quibus praecepit, ne alicui dicerent, quod factum erat. **[9]** [1]Convocatis autem Duodecim, dedit illis virtutem et potestatem super omnia daemonia et ut languores curarent, [2]et misit illos praedicare regnum Dei et sanare infirmos; [3]et ait ad illos: «Nihil tuleritis in via, neque virgam neque peram neque panem neque pecuniam, neque duas tunicas habeatis. [4]Et in quamcumque domum intraveritis, ibi manete et inde exite. [5]Et quicumque non receperint vos, exeuntes de civitate illa pulverem pedum vestrorum excutite in testimonium supra illos». [6]Egressi autem circumibant per castella evangelizantes et curantes ubique. [7]Audivit autem Herodes tetrarcha omnia, quae fiebant, et haesitabat, eo quod diceretur a quibusdam: «Ioannes surrexit a mortuis»; [8]a quibusdam vero: «Elias apparuit»; ab aliis autem: «Propheta unus de antiquis surrexit». [9]Et ait Herodes: «Ioannem ego decollavi; quis autem est iste, de quo audio ego talia?». Et quaerebat videre eum. [10]Et reversi apostoli narraverunt illi, quaecumque fecerunt. Et assumptis illis, secessit seorsum ad civitatem, quae vocatur Bethsaida. [11]Quod cum cognovissent turbae, secutae sunt illum. Et excepit illos et loquebatur illis de regno Dei, et eos, qui cura indigebant, sanabat. [12]Dies autem coeperat declinare; et accedentes Duodecim dixerunt illi: «Dimitte turbam, ut euntes in castella villasque, quae circa sunt, divertant et inveniant escas, quia hic in loco deserto sumus». [13]Ait autem ad illos: «Vos date illis manducare». At illi dixerunt: «Non sunt nobis plus quam quinque panes et duo pisces, nisi forte nos eamus et emamus in omnem hanc turbam escas». [14]Erant enim fere viri quinque milia. Ait autem ad discipulos suos: «Facite illos discumbere per convivia ad quinquagenos». [15]Et ita fecerunt et discumbere fecerunt omnes. [16]Acceptis autem quinque panibus et duobus piscibus, respexit in caelum et benedixit illis et fregit et dabat discipulis suis, ut ponerent ante turbam. [17]Et manducaverunt et saturati sunt omnes; et sublatum est, quod superfuit illis, fragmentorum cophini duodecim. [18]Et factum est cum solus esset orans, erant cum illo discipuli, et interrogavit illos dicens: «Quem me dicunt esse turbae?». [19]At illi responderunt et dixerunt: «Ioannem Baptistam, alii autem Eliam, alii vero: Propheta unus de prioribus surrexit». [20]Dixit autem illis: «Vos autem quem me esse dicitis?». Respondens Petrus dixit: «Christum Dei». [21]At ille increpans illos praecepit, ne cui dicerent hoc, [22]dicens: «Oportet Filium hominis multa pati et reprobari a senioribus et principibus sacerdotum et scribis et occidi et tertia die resurgere». [23]Dicebat autem ad omnes: «Si quis vult post me venire, abneget semetipsum et tollat crucem suam cotidie et sequatur me. [24]Qui enim voluerit animam suam salvam facere, perdet illam; qui autem perdiderit animam suam propter me, hic salvam faciet illam. [25]Quid enim proficit homo, si lucretur universum mundum, se autem ipsum perdat vel detrimentum sui faciat? [26]Nam qui me erubuerit et meos sermones, hunc Filius hominis erubescet, cum venerit in gloria sua et Patris et sanctorum angelorum. [27]Dico autem vobis vere: Sunt aliqui hic stantes, qui non gustabunt mortem, donec videant regnum Dei». [28]Factum est autem post haec verba fere dies octo, et assumpsit Petrum et Ioannem et Iacobum et ascendit in montem, ut oraret. [29]Et facta est, dum oraret, species vultus eius altera, et vestitus eius albus refulgens. [30]Et ecce duo viri loquebantur cum illo, et erant Moyses et Elias, [31]qui visi in gloria dicebant exodum eius, quem completurus erat in Ierusalem. [32]Petrus vero et qui cum illo gravati erant somno; et evigilantes viderunt gloriam eius et duos viros, qui stabant cum illo. [33]Et factum est cum discederent ab illo, ait Petrus ad Iesum: «Praeceptor, bonum est nos hic esse; et faciamus tria tabernacula: unum tibi et unum Moysi et unum Eliae», nesciens quid diceret. [34]Haec autem illo loquente, facta est nubes et obumbravit eos; et timuerunt intrantibus illis in nubem. [35]Et vox facta est de nube dicens: «Hic est Filius meus electus; ipsum audite». [36]Et dum fieret vox, inventus est Iesus solus. Et ipsi tacuerunt et nemini dixerunt in illis diebus quidquam ex his, quae viderant. [37]Factum est autem in sequenti die, descendentibus illis de monte, occurrit illi turba multa. [38]Et ecce vir de turba exclamavit dicens: «Magister, obsecro te, respice in filium meum, quia unicus est mihi; [39]et ecce spiritus apprehendit illum, et subito clamat et dissipat eum cum spuma et vix discedit ab eo dilanians eum; [40]et rogavi discipulos tuos, ut eicerent illum, et non potuerunt». [41]Respondens autem Iesus dixit: «O generatio infidelis et perversa, usquequo ero apud vos et patiar vos? Adduc huc filium tuum». [42]Et cum accederet, elisit illum daemonium et dissipavit. Et increpavit Iesus spiritum immundum et sanavit puerum et reddidit illum patri eius. [43]Stupebant autem omnes in magnitudine Dei. Omnibusque mirantibus in omnibus, quae faciebat, dixit ad discipulos suos: [44]«Ponite vos in auribus vestris sermones istos: Filius enim hominis futurum est ut tradatur in manus hominum». [45]At illi ignorabant verbum istud, et erat velatum ante eos, ut non sentirent illud, et timebant interrogare eum de hoc verbo. [46]Intravit autem cogitatio in eos, quis eorum maior esset. [47]At Iesus sciens cogitationem cordis illorum, apprehendens puerum statuit eum secus se [48]et ait illis: «Quicumque susceperit puerum istum in nomine meo, me recipit; et, quicumque me receperit, recipit eum, qui me misit; nam qui minor est inter omnes vos, hic maior est». [49]Respondens autem Ioannes dixit: «Praeceptor, vidimus quendam in nomine tuo eicientem daemonia, et prohibuimus eum, quia non sequitur nobiscum». [50]Et ait ad illum Iesus: «Nolite prohibere; qui enim non est adversus vos, pro vobis est». [51]Factum est autem dum complerentur dies assumptionis eius, et ipse faciem suam firmavit, ut iret Ierusalem, [52]et misit nuntios ante conspectum suum. Et euntes intraverunt in castellum Samaritanorum, ut pararent illi. [53]Et non receperunt eum, quia facies eius erat euntis Ierusalem. [54]Cum vidissent autem discipuli Iacobus et Ioannes dixerunt: «Domine, vis dicamus, ut *ignis descendat de caelo et consumat* illos?». [55]Et conversus increpavit illos. [56]Et ierunt in aliud castellum. [57]Et euntibus illis in via, dixit quidam ad illum: «Sequar te, quocumque ieris». [58]Et ait illi Iesus: «Vulpes foveas habent et volucres caeli nidos, Filius autem hominis non habet, ubi caput reclinet». [59]Ait autem ad alterum: «Sequere me». Ille autem dixit: «Domine, permitte mihi primum ire et sepelire patrem meum». [60]Dixitque ei Iesus: «Sine, ut mortui sepeliant mortuos suos; tu autem vade, annuntia regnum Dei». [61]Et ait alter: «Sequar te, Domine, sed primum permitte mihi renuntiare his, qui domi sunt». [62]Ait ad illum Iesus: «Nemo mittens manum suam in aratrum et aspiciens retro, aptus est regno Dei». **[10]** [1]Post haec autem designavit Dominus alios septuaginta duos et misit illos binos ante faciem suam in omnem civitatem et locum, quo erat ipse venturus. [2]Et dicebat illis: «Messis quidem multa, operarii autem pauci; rogate ergo Dominum messis, ut mittat operarios in messem suam. [3]Ite; ecce ego mitto vos sicut agnos inter lupos. [4]Nolite portare sacculum, neque peram neque calceamenta, et neminem per viam salutaveritis. [5]In quamcumque domum intraveritis, primum dicite: "Pax huic domui". [6]Et si ibi fuerit filius pacis, requiescet super illam pax vestra; sin autem ad vos revertetur. [7]In eadem autem domo manete edentes et bibentes, quae apud illos sunt: dignus enim est operarius mercede sua. Nolite transire de domo in domum. [8]Et in quamcumque civitatem intraveritis, et susceperint vos, manducate, quae apponuntur vobis, [9]et curate infirmos, qui in illa sunt, et dicite illis: "Appropinquavit in vos regnum Dei". [10]In quamcumque civitatem intraveritis, et non receperint vos, exeuntes in plateas eius dicite: [11]"Etiam pulverem, qui adhaesit nobis ad pedes de civitate vestra, extergimus in vos; tamen hoc scitote quia appropinquavit regnum Dei". [12]Dico vobis quia Sodomis in die illa remissius erit quam illi civitati. [13]Vae tibi, Chorazin! Vae tibi, Bethsaida! Quia si in Tyro et Sidone factae fuissent virtutes, quae in vobis factae sunt, olim in cilicio et cinere sedentes paeniterent. [14]Verumtamen Tyro et Sidoni remissius erit in iudicio quam vobis. [15]Et tu, Capharnaum, numquid *usque in caelum exaltaberis? Usque ad infernum demergeris!* [16]Qui vos audit, me audit; et qui vos spernit, me spernit; qui autem me spernit, spernit eum, qui me misit». [17]Reversi sunt autem septuaginta duo cum gaudio dicentes: «Domine, etiam daemonia subiciuntur nobis in nomine tuo!». [18]Et ait illis: «Videbam Satanam sicut fulgur de caelo cadentem. [19]Ecce dedi vobis potestatem calcandi supra serpentes et scorpiones et supra omnem virtutem inimici; et nihil vobis nocebit. [20]Verumtamen in hoc nolite gaudere quia spiritus vobis subiciuntur; gaudete autem quod nomina vestra scripta sunt in caelis». [21]In ipsa hora exsultavit Spiritu Sancto et dixit: «Confiteor tibi, Pater, Domine caeli et terrae, quod abscondisti haec a sapientibus et prudentibus et revelasti ea parvulis; etiam, Pater, quia sic placuit ante te. [22]Omnia mihi tradita sunt a Patre meo; et nemo scit qui sit Filius nisi Pater, et qui sit Pater nisi Filius et cui voluerit Filius revelare». [23]Et conversus ad discipulos seorsum dixit: «Beati oculi, qui vident, quae videtis. [24]Dico enim vobis: Multi prophetae et reges voluerunt videre, quae vos videtis, et non viderunt, et audire, quae auditis, et non audierunt». [25]Et ecce quidam legis peritus surrexit tentans illum dicens: «Magister, quid faciendo vitam aeternam possidebo?». [26]At ille dixit ad eum: «In Lege quid scriptum est? Quomodo legis?». [27]Ille autem respondens dixit: «*Diliges Dominum Deum tuum ex toto corde tuo et ex tota anima tua et ex omnibus viribus tuis* et ex omni mente tua et *proximum tuum sicut teipsum*». [28]Dixitque illi: «Recte respondisti; hoc fac et vives». [29]Ille autem, volens iustificare seipsum, dixit ad Iesum: «Et quis est meus proximus?». [30]Suscipiens autem Iesus dixit: «Homo quidam descendebat ab Ierusalem in Iericho et incidit in latrones, qui etiam despoliaverunt eum et, plagis impositis, abierunt, semivivo relicto. [31]Accidit autem, ut sacerdos quidam descenderet eadem via et, viso illo, praeterivit; [32]similiter et Levita, cum esset secus locum et videret eum, pertransiit. [33]Samaritanus autem quidam iter faciens, venit secus eum et videns eum misericordia motus est, [34]et appropians alligavit vulnera eius infundens oleum et vinum; et imponens illum in iumentum suum duxit in stabulum et curam eius egit. [35]Et altera die protulit duos denarios et dedit stabulario et ait: "Curam illius habe, et, quodcumque supererogaveris, ego, cum rediero, reddam tibi". [36]Quis horum trium videtur tibi proximus fuisse illi, qui incidit in

latrones?». [37]At ille dixit: «Qui fecit misericordiam in illum». Et ait illi Iesus: «Vade et tu fac similiter».
[38]Cum autem irent, ipse intravit in quoddam castellum, et mulier quaedam Martha nomine excepit
illum. [39]Et huic erat soror nomine Maria, quae etiam sedens secus pedes Domini audiebat verbum illius.
[40]Martha autem satagebat circa frequens ministerium; quae stetit et ait: «Domine, non est tibi curae
quod soror mea reliquit me solam ministrare? Dic ergo illi, ut me adiuvet». [41]Et respondens dixit illi
Dominus: «Martha, Martha, sollicita es et turbaris erga plurima, [42]porro unum est necessarium; Maria
enim optimam partem elegit, quae non auferetur ab ea». **[11]** [1]Et factum est cum esset in loco quodam
orans, ut cessavit, dixit unus ex discipulis eius ad eum: «Domine, doce nos orare, sicut et Ioannes docuit
discipulos suos». [2]Et ait illis: «Cum oratis, dicite: Pater, sanctificetur nomen tuum, / adveniat regnum
tuum; / [3]panem nostrum cotidianum da nobis cotidie, / [4]et dimitte nobis peccata nostra, / siquidem et
ipsi dimittimus omni debenti nobis, / et ne nos inducas in tentationem». [5]Et ait ad illos: «Quis vestrum
habebit amicum et ibit ad illum media nocte et dicet illi: "Amice, commoda mihi tres panes, [6]quoniam
amicus meus venit de via ad me, et non habeo, quod ponam ante illum"; [7]et ille de intus respondens
dicat: "Noli mihi molestus esse; iam ostium clausum est, et pueri mei mecum sunt in cubili; non possum
surgere et dare tibi". [8]Dico vobis: Et si non dabit illi surgens, eo quod amicus eius sit, propter
improbitatem tamen eius surget et dabit illi, quotquot habet necessarios. [9]Et ego vobis dico: Petite, et
dabitur vobis; quaerite, et invenietis; pulsate, et aperietur vobis. [10]Omnis enim qui petit, accipit; et, qui
quaerit, invenit; et pulsanti aperietur. [11]Quem autem ex vobis patrem filius petierit piscem, numquid pro
pisce serpentem dabit illi? [12]Aut si petierit ovum, numquid porriget illi scorpionem? [13]Si ergo vos, cum
sitis mali, nostis dona bona dare filiis vestris, quanto magis Pater de caelo dabit Spiritum Sanctum
petentibus se». [14]Et erat eiciens daemonium, et illud erat mutum; et factum est cum daemonium exisset,
locutus est mutus. Et admiratae sunt turbae; [15]quidam autem ex eis dixerunt: «In Beelzebul principe
daemoniorum eicit daemonia». [16]Et alii tentantes signum de caelo quaerebant ab eo. [17]Ipse autem sciens
cogitationes eorum dixit eis: «Omne regnum in seipsum divisum desolatur, et domus supra domum
cadit. [18]Si autem et Satanas in seipsum divisus est, quomodo stabit regnum ipsius? Quia dicitis in
Beelzebul eicere me daemonia. [19]Si autem ego in Beelzebul eicio daemonia, filii vestri in quo eiciunt?
Ideo ipsi iudices vestri erunt. [20]Porro si in digito Dei eicio daemonia, profecto pervenit in vos regnum
Dei. [21]Cum fortis armatus custodit atrium suum, in pace sunt ea, quae possidet; [22]si autem fortior illo
superveniens vicerit eum, universa arma eius auferet, in quibus confidebat, et spolia eius distribuet.
[23]Qui non est mecum, adversum me est; et, qui non colligit mecum, dispergit. [24]Cum immundus spiritus
exierit de homine, perambulat per loca inaquosa quaerens requiem et non inveniens dicit: 'Revertar in
domum meam unde exivi'. [25]Et cum venerit, invenit scopis mundatam et exornatam. [26]Et tunc vadit et
assumit septem alios spiritus nequiores se, et ingressi habitant ibi; et sunt novissima hominis illius
peiora prioribus». [27]Factum est autem cum haec diceret, extollens vocem quaedam mulier de turba dixit
illi: «Beatus venter, qui te portavit, et ubera, quae suxisti!». [28]At ille dixit: «Quinimmo beati, qui audiunt
verbum Dei et custodiunt!». [29]Turbis autem concurrentibus, coepit dicere: «Generatio haec generatio
nequam est; signum quaerit, et signum non dabitur illi nisi signum Ionae. [30]Nam sicut Ionas fuit signum
Ninevitis, ita erit et Filius hominis generationi isti. [31]Regina austri surget in iudicio cum viris
generationis huius et condemnabit illos, quia venit a finibus terrae audire sapientiam Salomonis, et ecce
plus Salomone hic. [32]Viri Ninevitae surgent in iudicio cum generatione hac et condemnabunt illam, quia
paenitentiam egerunt ad praedicationem Ionae, et ecce plus Iona hic. [33]Nemo lucernam accendit et in
abscondito ponit, neque sub modio, sed supra candelabrum, ut, qui ingrediuntur, lumen videant.
[34]Lucerna corporis est oculus tuus. Si oculus tuus fuerit simplex, totum corpus tuum lucidum erit; si
autem nequam fuerit, etiam corpus tuum tenebrosum erit. [35]Vide ergo, ne lumen, quod in te est, tenebrae
sint. [36]Si ergo corpus tuum totum lucidum fuerit, non habens aliquam partem tenebrarum, erit lucidum
totum, sicut quando lucerna in fulgore suo illuminat te». [37]Et cum loqueretur, rogavit illum quidam
pharisaeus, ut pranderet apud se; et ingressus recubuit. [38]Pharisaeus autem videns miratus est quod non
baptizatus esset ante prandium. [39]Et ait Dominus ad illum: «Nunc vos pharisaei, quod de foris est calicis
et catini, mundatis, quod autem intus est vestrum, plenum est rapina et iniquitate. [40]Stulti! Nonne, qui
fecit, quod de foris est, etiam id, quod de intus est, fecit? [41]Verumtamen, quae insunt, date
eleemosynam, et ecce omnia munda sunt vobis. [42]Sed vae vobis pharisaeis, quia decimatis mentam et
rutam et omne holus et praeteritis iudicium et caritatem Dei! Haec autem oportuit facere et illa non
omittere. [43]Vae vobis pharisaeis, quia diligitis primam cathedram in synagogis et salutationes in foro!
[44]Vae vobis, quia estis ut monumenta, quae non parent, et homines ambulantes supra nesciunt!».
[45]Respondens autem quidam ex legis peritis ait illi: «Magister, haec dicens etiam nobis contumeliam
facis». [46]At ille ait: «Et vobis legis peritis: Vae, quia oneratis homines oneribus, quae portari non
possunt, et ipsi uno digito vestro non tangitis sarcinas! [47]Vae vobis, quia aedificatis monumenta

prophetarum, patres autem vestri occiderunt illos! [48]Profecto testificamini et consentitis operibus patrum
vestrorum, quoniam ipsi quidem eos occiderunt, vos autem aedificatis. [49]Propterea et sapientia Dei dixit:
Mittam ad illos prophetas et apostolos, et ex illis occident et persequentur, [50]ut requiratur sanguis
omnium prophetarum, qui effusus est a constitutione mundi, a generatione ista, [51]a sanguine Abel usque
ad sanguinem Zachariae, qui periit inter altare et aedem. Ita dico vobis: Requiretur ab hac generatione.
[52]Vae vobis legis peritis, quia tulistis clavem scientiae! Ipsi non introistis et eos, qui introibant,
prohibuistis». [53]Cum autem inde exisset, coeperunt scribae et pharisaei graviter insistere et eum allicere
in sermone de multis [54]insidiantes ei, ut caperent aliquid ex ore eius. **[12]** [1]Interea multis
circumstantibus, ita ut se invicem conculcarent, coepit dicere ad discipulos suos primum: «Attendite a
fermento pharisaeorum, quod est hypocrisis. [2]Nihil autem opertum est, quod non reveletur, neque
absconditum, quod non sciatur. [3]Quoniam, quae in tenebris dixistis, in lumine audientur, et quod in
aurem locuti estis in cubiculis, praedicabitur in tectis. [4]Dico autem vobis amicis meis: Ne terreamini ab
his, qui occidunt corpus, et post haec non habent amplius, quod faciant. [5]Ostendam autem vobis quem
timeatis: Timete eum, qui postquam occiderit, habet potestatem mittere in gehennam. Ita dico vobis:
Hunc timete. [6]Nonne quinque passeres veneunt dipundio? Et unus ex illis non est in oblivione coram
Deo. [7]Sed et capilli capitis vestri omnes numerati sunt. Nolite timere; multis passeribus pluris estis.
[8]Dico autem vobis: Omnis, quicumque confessus fuerit in me coram hominibus, et Filius hominis
confitebitur in illo coram angelis Dei; [9]qui autem negaverit me coram hominibus, denegabitur coram
angelis Dei. [10]Et omnis, qui dicet verbum in Filium hominis, remittetur illi; ei autem qui in Spiritum
Sanctum blasphemaverit, non remittetur. [11]Cum autem inducent vos in synagogas et ad magistratus et
potestates, nolite solliciti esse qualiter aut quid respondeatis aut quid dicatis: [12]Spiritus enim Sanctus
docebit vos in ipsa hora, quae oporteat dicere». [13]Ait autem quidam ei de turba: «Magister, dic fratri
meo, ut dividat mecum hereditatem». [14]At ille dixit ei: «Homo, quis me constituit iudicem aut divisorem
super vos?». [15]Dixitque ad illos: «Videte et cavete ab omni avaritia, quia si cui res abundant, vita eius
non est ex his, quae possidet». [16]Dixit autem similitudinem ad illos dicens: «Hominis cuiusdam divitis
uberes fructus ager attulit. [17]Et cogitabat intra se dicens: "Quid faciam, quod non habeo, quo congregem
fructus meos?". [18]Et dixit: "Hoc faciam: destruam horrea mea et maiora aedificabo, et illuc congregabo
omne triticum et bona mea, [19]et dicam animae meae: Anima, habes multa bona posita in annos
plurimos; requiesce, comede, bibe, epulare". [20]Dixit autem illi Deus: "Stulte! Hac nocte animam tuam
repetunt a te; quae autem parasti, cuius erunt?". [21]Sic est qui sibi thesaurizat et non fit in Deum dives».
[22]Dixitque ad discipulos suos: «Ideo dico vobis: nolite solliciti esse animae quid manducetis, neque
corpori quid vestiamini. [23]Anima enim plus est quam esca, et corpus quam vestimentum. [24]Considerate
corvos quia non seminant neque metunt, quibus non est cellarium neque horreum, et Deus pascit illos;
quanto magis vos pluris estis volucribus. [25]Quis autem vestrum cogitando potest adicere ad aetatem
suam cubitum? [26]Si ergo neque, quod minimum est, potestis, quid de ceteris solliciti estis?
[27]Considerate lilia quomodo crescunt: non laborant, neque nent; dico autem vobis: Nec Salomon in
omni gloria sua vestiebatur sicut unum ex istis. [28]Si autem fenum, quod hodie in agro est et cras in
clibanum mittitur, Deus sic vestit, quanto magis vos, pusillae fidei. [29]Et vos nolite quaerere quid
manducetis aut quid bibatis, et nolite solliciti esse. [30]Haec enim omnia gentes mundi quaerunt; Pater
autem vester scit quoniam his indigetis. [31]Verumtamen quaerite regnum eius; et haec adicientur vobis.
[32]Noli timere, pusillus grex, quia complacuit Patri vestro dare vobis regnum. [33]Vendite, quae possidetis,
et date eleemosynam. Facite vobis sacculos, qui non veterescunt, thesaurum non deficientem in caelis,
quo fur non appropiat, neque tinea corrumpit; [34]ubi enim thesaurus vester est, ibi et cor vestrum erit.
[35]Sint lumbi vestri praecincti et lucernae ardentes, [36]et vos similes hominibus exspectantibus dominum
suum, quando revertatur a nuptiis, ut, cum venerit et pulsaverit, confestim aperiant ei. [37]Beati servi illi,
quos cum venerit dominus invenerit vigilantes. Amen dico vobis, quod praecinget se et faciet illos
discumbere, et transiens ministrabit illis. [38]Et si venerit in secunda vigilia et si in tertia vigilia venerit et
ita invenerit, beati sunt illi. [39]Hoc autem scitote quia, si sciret pater familias qua hora fur veniret, non
sineret perfodi domum suam. [40]Et vos estote parati, quia, qua hora non putatis, Filius hominis venit».
[41]Ait autem Petrus: «Domine, ad nos dicis hanc parabolam an et ad omnes?». [42]Et dixit Dominus: «Quis
putas est fidelis dispensator et prudens, quem constituet dominus super familiam suam, ut det illis in
tempore tritici mensuram? [43]Beatus ille servus, quem cum venerit dominus eius invenerit ita facientem.
[44]Vere dico vobis: Supra omnia, quae possidet, constituet illum. [45]Quod si dixerit servus ille in corde
suo: "Moram facit dominus meus venire", et coeperit percutere pueros et ancillas et edere et bibere et
inebriari, [46]veniet dominus servi illius in die, qua non sperat, et hora, qua nescit, et dividet eum
partemque eius cum infidelibus ponet. [47]Ille autem servus, qui cognovit voluntatem domini sui et non
praeparavit vel non fecit secundum voluntatem eius, vapulabit multis; [48]qui autem non cognovit et fecit

digna plagis, vapulabit paucis. Omni autem, cui multum datum est, multum quaeretur ab eo, et cui
commendaverunt multum, plus petent ab eo. 49Ignem veni mittere in terram et quid volo? Si iam
accensus esset! 50Baptisma autem habeo baptizari et quomodo coartor, usque dum perficiatur! 51Putatis
quia pacem veni dare in terram? Non, dico vobis, sed separationem. 52Erunt enim ex hoc quinque in
domo una divisi: tres in duo et duo in tres; 53dividentur pater in filium et *filius in patrem*, mater in filiam
et *filia in matrem*, socrus in nurum suam et *nurus in socrum*». 54Dicebat autem et ad turbas: «Cum
videritis nubem orientem ab occasu, statim dicitis: "Nimbus venit", et ita fit; 55et cum austrum flantem,
dicitis: "Aestus erit", et fit. 56Hypocritae, faciem terrae et caeli nostis probare, hoc autem tempus
quomodo nescitis probare? 57Quid autem et a vobis ipsis non iudicatis, quod iustum est? 58Cum autem
vadis cum adversario tuo ad principem, in via da operam liberari ab illo, ne forte trahat te apud iudicem,
et iudex tradat te exactori, et exactor mittat te in carcerem. 59Dico tibi: Non exies inde, donec etiam
novissimum minutum reddas». **[13]** 1Aderant autem quidam ipso in tempore nuntiantes illi de
Galilaeis, quorum sanguinem Pilatus miscuit cum sacrificiis eorum. 2Et respondens dixit illis: «Putatis
quod hi Galilaei prae omnibus Galilaeis peccatores fuerunt, quia talia passi sunt? 3Non, dico vobis, sed
nisi paenitentiam egeritis, omnes similiter peribitis. 4Vel illi decem et octo, supra quos cecidit turris in
Siloam et occidit eos, putatis quia et ipsi debitores fuerunt praeter omnes homines habitantes in
Ierusalem? 5Non, dico vobis, sed si non paenitentiam egeritis, omnes similiter peribitis». 6Dicebat autem
hanc similitudinem: «Arborem fici habebat quidam plantatam in vinea sua et venit quaerens fructum in
illa et non invenit. 7Dixit autem ad cultorem vineae: "Ecce anni tres sunt, ex quo venio quaerens fructum
in ficulnea hac, et non invenio. Succide ergo illam. Ut quid etiam terram evacuat?". 8At ille respondens
dicit illi: "Domine, dimitte illam et hoc anno, usque dum fodiam circa illam et mittam stercora, 9et
siquidem fecerit fructum in futurum; sin autem succides eam"». 10Erat autem docens in una
synagogarum sabbatis. 11Et ecce mulier, quae habebat spiritum infirmitatis annis decem et octo, et erat
inclinata nec omnino poterat sursum respicere. 12Quam cum vidisset Iesus vocavit et ait illi: «Mulier,
dimissa es ab infirmitate tua», 13et imposuit illi manus; et confestim erecta est et glorificabat Deum.
14Respondens autem archisynagogus, indignans quia sabbato curasset Iesus, dicebat turbae: «Sex dies
sunt, in quibus oportet operari; in his ergo venite et curamini et non in die sabbati». 15Respondit autem
ad illum Dominus et dixit: «Hypocritae, unusquisque vestrum sabbato non solvit bovem suum aut
asinum a praesepio et ducit adaquare? 16Hanc autem filiam Abrahae, quam alligavit Satanas ecce decem
et octo annis, non oportuit solvi a vinculo isto die sabbati?». 17Et cum haec diceret, erubescebant omnes
adversarii eius, et omnis populus gaudebat in universis, quae gloriose fiebant ab eo. 18Dicebat ergo:
«Cui simile est regnum Dei, et cui simile existimabo illud? 19Simile est grano sinapis, quod acceptum
homo misit in hortum suum, et crevit et factum est in arborem, et volucres caeli requieverunt in ramis
eius». 20Et iterum dixit: «Cui simile aestimabo regnum Dei? 21Simile est fermento, quod acceptum
mulier abscondit in farinae sata tria, donec fermentaretur totum». 22Et ibat per civitates et castella
docens et iter faciens in Hierosolymam. 23Ait autem illi quidam: «Domine, pauci sunt, qui salvantur?».
Ipse autem dixit ad illos: 24«Contendite intrare per angustam portam, quia multi, dico vobis, quaerent
intrare et non poterunt. 25Cum autem surrexerit pater familias et clauserit ostium, et incipietis foris stare
et pulsare ostium dicentes: "Domine, aperi nobis"; et respondens dicet vobis: "Nescio vos unde sitis".
26Tunc incipietis dicere: "Manducavimus coram te et bibimus, et in plateis nostris docuisti"; 27et dicet
loquens vobis: "Nescio vos unde sitis; discedite a me, omnes operarii iniquitatis". 28Ibi erit fletus et
stridor dentium, cum videritis Abraham et Isaac et Iacob et omnes prophetas in regno Dei, vos autem
expelli foras. 29Et venient ab oriente et occidente et aquilone et austro et accumbent in regno Dei. 30Et
ecce sunt novissimi, qui erunt primi, et sunt primi, qui erunt novissimi». 31In ipsa hora accesserunt
quidam pharisaeorum dicentes illi: «Exi et vade hinc, quia Herodes vult te occidere». 32Et ait illis: «Ite,
dicite vulpi illi: "Ecce eicio daemonia et sanitates perficio hodie et cras et tertia consummor.
33Verumtamen oportet me hodie et cras et sequenti ambulare, quia non capit prophetam perire extra
Ierusalem". 34Ierusalem, Ierusalem, quae occidis prophetas et lapidas eos, qui missi sunt ad te, quotiens
volui congregare filios tuos, quemadmodum avis nidum suum sub pinnis, et noluistis. 35Ecce *relinquitur
vobis domus vestra*. Dico autem vobis: Non videbitis me, donec veniat cum dicetis: "*Benedictus, qui
venit in nomine Domini*"». **[14]** 1Et factum est, cum intraret in domum cuiusdam principis
pharisaeorum sabbato manducare panem, et ipsi observabant eum. 2Et ecce homo quidam hydropicus
erat ante illum. 3Et respondens Iesus dixit ad legis peritos et pharisaeos dicens: «Licet sabbato curare
an non?». 4At illi tacuerunt. Ipse vero apprehensum sanavit eum ac dimisit. 5Et ad illos dixit: «Cuius
vestrum filius aut bos in puteum cadet, et non continuo extrahet illum die sabbati?». 6Et non poterant
ad haec respondere illi. 7Dicebat autem ad invitatos parabolam, intendens quomodo primos accubitus
eligerent, dicens ad illos: 8«Cum invitatus fueris ab aliquo ad nuptias, non discumbas in primo loco, ne

forte honoratior te sit invitatus ab eo, [9]et veniens is, qui te et illum vocavit, dicat tibi: “Da huic locum”;
et tunc incipias cum rubore novissimum locum tenere. [10]Sed cum vocatus fueris, vade, recumbe in
novissimo loco, ut, cum venerit qui te invitavit, dicat tibi: “Amice, ascende superius”; tunc erit tibi gloria
coram omnibus simul discumbentibus. [11]Quia omnis, qui se exaltat, humiliabitur; et, qui se humiliat,
exaltabitur». [12]Dicebat autem et ei, qui se invitaverat: «Cum facis prandium aut cenam, noli vocare
amicos tuos neque fratres tuos neque cognatos neque vicinos divites, ne forte et ipsi te reinvitent et fiat
tibi retributio. [13]Sed cum facis convivium, voca pauperes, debiles, claudos, caecos; [14]et beatus eris, quia
non habent retribuere tibi. Retribuetur enim tibi in resurrectione iustorum». [15]Haec cum audisset quidam
de simul discumbentibus, dixit illi: «Beatus, qui manducabit panem in regno Dei». [16]At ipse dixit ei:
«Homo quidam fecit cenam magnam et vocavit multos; [17]et misit servum suum hora cenae dicere
invitatis: “Venite, quia iam paratum est”. [18]Et coeperunt simul omnes excusare. Primus dixit ei: “Villam
emi et necesse habeo exire et videre illam; rogo te, habe me excusatum”. [19]Et alter dixit: “Iuga boum
emi quinque et eo probare illa; rogo te, habe me excusatum”. [20]Et alius dixit: “Uxorem duxi et ideo non
possum venire”. [21]Et reversus servus nuntiavit haec domino suo. Tunc iratus pater familias dixit servo
suo: “Exi cito in plateas et vicos civitatis et pauperes ac debiles et caecos et claudos introduc huc”. [22]Et
ait servus: “Domine, factum est ut imperasti, et adhuc locus est”. [23]Et ait dominus servo: “Exi in vias et
saepes, et compelle intrare, ut impleatur domus mea. [24]Dico autem vobis quod nemo virorum illorum,
qui vocati sunt, gustabit cenam meam”». [25]Ibant autem turbae multae cum eo, et conversus dixit ad illos:
[26]«Si quis venit ad me et non odit patrem suum et matrem et uxorem et filios et fratres et sorores, adhuc
et animam suam, non potest esse meus discipulus. [27]Et, qui non baiulat crucem suam et venit post me,
non potest esse meus discipulus. [28]Quis enim ex vobis volens turrem aedificare, non prius sedens
computat sumptus, si habet ad perficiendum? [29]Ne, posteaquam posuerit fundamentum et non potuerit
perficere, omnes, qui vident, incipiant illudere ei [30]dicentes: “Hic homo coepit aedificare et non potuit
consummare”. [31]Aut quis rex, iturus committere bellum adversus alium regem, non sedens prius cogitat
si possit cum decem milibus occurrere ei, qui cum viginti milibus venit ad se? [32]Alioquin, adhuc illo
longe agente, legationem mittens rogat ea, quae pacis sunt. [33]Sic ergo omnis ex vobis, qui non renuntiat
omnibus, quae possidet, non potest meus esse discipulus. [34]Bonum est sal; si autem sal quoque
evanuerit, in quo condietur? [35]Neque in terram neque in sterquilinium utile est, sed foras proiciunt illud.
Qui habet aures audiendi, audiat». **[15]** [1]Erant autem appropinquantes ei omnes publicani et
peccatores, ut audirent illum. [2]Et murmurabant pharisaei et scribae dicentes: «Hic peccatores recipit et
manducat cum illis». [3]Et ait ad illos parabolam istam dicens: [4]«Quis ex vobis homo, qui habet centum
oves, et si perdiderit unam ex illis, nonne dimittit nonaginta novem in deserto et vadit ad illam, quae
perierat, donec inveniat illam? [5]Et cum invenerit eam, imponit in umeros suos gaudens [6]et veniens
domum convocat amicos et vicinos dicens illis: “Congratulamini mihi, quia inveni ovem meam, quae
perierat”. [7]Dico vobis: Ita gaudium erit in caelo super uno peccatore paenitentiam agente quam super
nonaginta novem iustis, qui non indigent paenitentia. [8]Aut quae mulier habens drachmas decem, si
perdiderit drachmam unam, nonne accendit lucernam et everrit domum et quaerit diligenter, donec
inveniat? [9]Et cum invenerit, convocat amicas et vicinas dicens: “Congratulamini mihi, quia inveni
drachmam, quam perdideram”. [10]Ita dico vobis: Gaudium fit coram angelis Dei super uno peccatore
paenitentiam agente». [11]Ait autem: «Homo quidam habebat duos filios. [12]Et dixit adulescentior ex illis
patri: “Pater, da mihi portionem substantiae, quae me contingit”. Et divisit illis substantiam. [13]Et non
post multos dies, congregatis omnibus, adulescentior filius peregre profectus est in regionem
longinquam et ibi dissipavit substantiam suam vivendo luxuriose. [14]Et postquam omnia consummasset,
facta est fames valida in regione illa, et ipse coepit egere. [15]Et abiit et adhaesit uni civium regionis illius,
et misit illum in villam suam, ut pasceret porcos; [16]et cupiebat saturari de siliquis, quas porci
manducabant, et nemo illi dabat. [17]In se autem reversus dixit: “Quanti mercennarii patris mei abundant
panibus, ego autem hic fame pereo. [18]Surgam et ibo ad patrem meum et dicam illi: Pater, peccavi in
caelum et coram te [19]et iam non sum dignus vocari filius tuus; fac me sicut unum de mercennariis tuis”.
[20]Et surgens venit ad patrem suum. Cum autem adhuc longe esset, vidit illum pater ipsius et
misericordia motus est et accurrens cecidit supra collum eius et osculatus est illum. [21]Dixitque ei filius:
“Pater, peccavi in caelum et coram te; iam non sum dignus vocari filius tuus”. [22]Dixit autem pater ad
servos suos: “Cito proferte stolam primam et induite illum et date anulum in manum eius et calceamenta
in pedes [23]et adducite vitulum saginatum, occidite et manducemus et epulemur, [24]quia hic filius meus
mortuus erat et revixit, perierat et inventus est”. Et coeperunt epulari. [25]Erat autem filius eius senior in
agro et, cum veniret et appropinquaret domui, audivit symphoniam et choros, [26]et vocavit unum de
servis et interrogavit quae haec essent. [27]Isque dixit illi: “Frater tuus venit, et occidit pater tuus vitulum
saginatum, quia salvum illum recepit”. [28]Indignatus est autem et nolebat introire. Pater ergo illius

egressus coepit rogare illum. 29At ille respondens dixit patri suo: "Ecce tot annis servio tibi et numquam
mandatum tuum praeterii, et numquam dedisti mihi haedum, ut cum amicis meis epularer, 30sed
postquam filius tuus hic, qui devoravit substantiam tuam cum meretricibus, venit, occidisti illi vitulum
saginatum". 31At ipse dixit illi: "Fili, tu semper mecum es, et omnia mea tua sunt; 32epulari autem et
gaudere oportebat, quia frater tuus hic mortuus erat et revixit, perierat et inventus est"». **[16]** 1Dicebat
autem et ad discipulos: «Homo quidam erat dives, qui habebat vilicum, et hic diffamatus est apud illum
quasi dissipasset bona ipsius. 2Et vocavit illum et ait illi: "Quid hoc audio de te? Redde rationem
vilicationis tuae; iam enim non poteris vilicare". 3Ait autem vilicus intra se: "Quid faciam, quia dominus
meus aufert a me vilicationem? Fodere non valeo, mendicare erubesco. 4Scio quid faciam, ut, cum
amotus fuero a vilicatione, recipiant me in domos suas". 5Convocatis itaque singulis debitoribus domini
sui, dicebat primo: "Quantum debes domino meo?". 6At ille dixit: "Centum cados olei". Dixitque illi:
"Accipe cautionem tuam et sede cito, scribe quinquaginta". 7Deinde alii dixit: "Tu vero quantum
debes?". Qui ait: "Centum coros tritici". Ait illi: "Accipe litteras tuas et scribe octoginta". 8Et laudavit
dominus vilicum iniquitatis, quia prudenter fecisset, quia filii huius saeculi prudentiores filiis lucis in
generatione sua sunt. 9Et ego vobis dico: Facite vobis amicos de mammona iniquitatis, ut, cum defecerit,
recipiant vos in aeterna tabernacula. 10Qui fidelis est in minimo, et in maiori fidelis est; et qui in modico
iniquus est, et in maiori iniquus est. 11Si ergo in iniquo mammona fideles non fuistis, quod verum est,
quis credet vobis? 12Et si in alieno fideles non fuistis, quod vestrum est, quis dabit vobis? 13Nemo servus
potest duobus dominis servire: aut enim unum odiet et alterum diliget, aut uni adhaerebit et alterum
contemnet. Non potestis Deo servire et mammonae». 14Audiebant autem omnia haec pharisaei, qui erant
avari, et deridebant illum. 15Et ait illis: «Vos estis qui iustificatis vos coram hominibus; Deus autem
novit corda vestra, quia, quod hominibus altum est, abominatio est ante Deum. 16Lex et Prophetae usque
ad Ioannem; ex tunc regnum Dei evangelizatur, et omnis in illud vim facit. 17Facilius est autem caelum
et terram praeterire, quam de Lege unum apicem cadere. 18Omnis, qui dimittit uxorem suam et ducit
alteram, moechatur; et qui dimissam a viro ducit, moechatur. 19Homo quidam erat dives et induebatur
purpura et bysso et epulabatur cotidie splendide. 20Quidam autem pauper nomine Lazarus iacebat ad
ianuam eius ulceribus plenus 21et cupiens saturari de his, quae cadebant de mensa divitis; sed et canes
veniebant et lingebant ulcera eius. 22Factum est autem ut moreretur pauper et portaretur ab angelis in
sinum Abrahae; mortuus est autem et dives et sepultus est. 23Et in inferno elevans oculos suos cum esset
in tormentis, videbat Abraham a longe et Lazarum in sinu eius. 24Et ipse clamans dixit: "Pater Abraham,
miserere mei et mitte Lazarum, ut intingat extremum digiti sui in aquam, ut refrigeret linguam meam,
quia crucior in hac flamma". 25At dixit Abraham: "Fili, recordare quia recepisti bona tua in vita tua, et
Lazarus similiter mala; nunc autem hic consolatur, tu vero cruciaris. 26Et in his omnibus inter nos et vos
chaos magnum firmatum est, ut hi, qui volunt hinc transire ad vos, non possint, neque inde ad nos
transmeare". 27Et ait: "Rogo ergo te, Pater, ut mittas eum in domum patris mei 28 —habeo enim quinque
fratres— ut testetur illis, ne et ipsi veniant in locum hunc tormentorum". 29Ait autem Abraham: "Habent
Moysen et Prophetas; audiant illos". 30At ille dixit: "Non, pater Abraham, sed si quis ex mortuis ierit ad
eos, paenitentiam agent". 31Ait autem illi: "Si Moysen et Prophetas non audiunt, neque si quis ex
mortuis resurrexerit, credent"». **[17]** 1Et ad discipulos suos ait: «Impossibile est ut non veniant
scandala; vae autem illi, per quem veniunt! 2Utilius est illi si lapis molaris imponatur circa collum eius
et proiciatur in mare, quam ut scandalizet unum de pusillis istis. 3Attendite vobis! Si peccaverit frater
tuus, increpa illum, et si paenitentiam egerit, dimitte illi; 4et si septies in die peccaverit in te et septies
conversus fuerit ad te dicens: "Paenitet me", dimittes illi». 5Et dixerunt apostoli Domino: «Adauge nobis
fidem!». 6Dixit autem Dominus: «Si haberetis fidem sicut granum sinapis, diceretis huic arbori moro:
"Eradicare et transplantare in mare", et oboediret vobis. 7Quis autem vestrum habens servum arantem
aut pascentem, qui regresso de agro dicet illi: "Statim transi, recumbe", 8et non dicet ei: "Para, quod
cenem, et praecinge te et ministra mihi, donec manducem et bibam, et post haec tu manducabis et
bibes"? 9Numquid gratiam habet servo illi, quia fecit, quae praecepta sunt? 10Sic et vos, cum feceritis
omnia, quae praecepta sunt vobis, dicite: "Servi inutiles sumus; quod debuimus facere, fecimus"». 11Et
factum est dum iret in Ierusalem, et ipse transibat per mediam Samariam et Galilaeam. 12Et cum
ingrederetur quoddam castellum, occurrerunt ei decem viri leprosi, qui steterunt a longe, 13et levaverunt
vocem dicentes: «Iesu praeceptor, miserere nostri!». 14Quos ut vidit, dixit: «Ite, ostendite vos
sacerdotibus». Et factum est dum irent, mundati sunt. 15Unus autem ex illis, ut vidit quia sanatus est,
regressus est cum magna voce magnificans Deum 16et cecidit in faciem ante pedes eius gratias agens ei;
et hic erat Samaritanus. 17Respondens autem Iesus dixit: «Nonne decem mundati sunt? Et novem ubi
sunt? 18Non sunt inventi qui redirent, ut darent gloriam Deo, nisi hic alienigena?». 19Et ait illi: «Surge,
vade; fides tua te salvum fecit». 20Interrogatus autem a pharisaeis: «Quando venit regnum Dei?»,

respondit eis et dixit: «Non venit regnum Dei cum observatione, 21neque dicent: "Ecce hic" aut: "Illic";
ecce enim regnum Dei intra vos est». 22Et ait ad discipulos: «Venient dies, quando desideretis videre
unum diem Filii hominis et non videbitis. 23Et dicent vobis: "Ecce hic", "Ecce illic"; nolite ire neque
sectemini. 24Nam sicut fulgur coruscans de sub caelo in ea, quae sub caelo sunt, fulget, ita erit Filius
hominis in die sua. 25Primum autem oportet illum multa pati et reprobari a generatione hac. 26Et sicut
factum est in diebus Noe, ita erit et in diebus Filii hominis: 27edebant, bibebant, uxores ducebant,
dabantur ad nuptias, usque in diem, qua intravit Noe in arcam, et venit diluvium et perdidit omnes.
28Similiter sicut factum est in diebus Lot: edebant, bibebant, emebant, vendebant, plantabant,
aedificabant; 29qua die autem exiit Lot a Sodomis, pluit ignem et sulphur de caelo et omnes perdidit.
30Secundum haec erit, qua die Filius hominis revelabitur. 31In illa die, qui fuerit in tecto et vasa eius in
domo, ne descendat tollere illa, et qui in agro, similiter non redeat retro. 32Memores estote uxoris Lot.
33Quicumque quaesierit animam suam salvam facere, perdet illam; et, quicumque perdiderit illam,
vivificabit eam. 34Dico vobis: Illa nocte erunt duo in lecto uno: unus assumetur, et alter relinquetur;
35duae erunt molentes in unum: una assumetur, et altera relinquetur». 37Respondentes dicunt illi: «Ubi,
Domine?». Qui dixit eis: «Ubicumque fuerit corpus, illuc congregabuntur et aquilae». **[18]** 1Dicebat
autem parabolam ad illos quoniam oportet semper orare et non deficere, 2dicens: «Iudex quidam erat in
quadam civitate, qui Deum non timebat et hominem non reverebatur. 3Vidua autem erat in civitate illa
et veniebat ad eum dicens: "Vindica me de adversario meo". 4Et nolebat per multum tempus; post haec
autem dixit intra se: "Etsi Deum non timeo nec hominem revereor, 5tamen quia molesta est mihi haec
vidua, vindicabo illam, ne in novissimo veniens suggillet me"». 6Ait autem Dominus: «Audite quid
iudex iniquitatis dicit; 7Deus autem non faciet vindictam electorum suorum clamantium ad se die ac
nocte, et patientiam habebit in illis? 8Dico vobis: Cito faciet vindictam illorum. Verumtamen Filius
hominis veniens, putas, inveniet fidem in terra?». 9Dixit autem et ad quosdam, qui in se confidebant
tamquam iusti et aspernabantur ceteros, parabolam istam: 10«Duo homines ascenderunt in templum, ut
orarent: unus pharisaeus et alter publicanus. 11Pharisaeus stans haec apud se orabat: "Deus, gratias ago
tibi quia non sum sicut ceteri hominum, raptores, iniusti, adulteri, velut etiam hic publicanus; 12ieiuno
bis in sabbato, decimas do omnium, quae possideo". 13Et publicanus a longe stans nolebat nec oculos
ad caelum levare, sed percutiebat pectus suum dicens: "Deus, propitius esto mihi peccatori". 14Dico
vobis: Descendit hic iustificatus in domum suam ab illo. Quia omnis, qui se exaltat, humiliabitur; et, qui
se humiliat, exaltabitur». 15Afferebant autem ad illum et infantes, ut eos tangeret; quod cum viderent,
discipuli increpabant illos. 16Iesus autem convocans illos dixit: «Sinite pueros venire ad me et nolite eos
vetare; talium est enim regnum Dei. 17Amen dico vobis: Quicumque non acceperit regnum Dei sicut
puer, non intrabit in illud». 18Et interrogavit eum quidam princeps dicens: «Magister bone, quid faciens
vitam aeternam possidebo?». 19Dixit autem ei Iesus: «Quid me dicis bonum? Nemo bonus nisi solus
Deus. 20Mandata nosti: *non moechaberis, non occides, non furtum facies, non falsum testimonium dices,*
honora patrem tuum et matrem». 21Qui ait: «Haec omnia custodivi a iuventute». 22Quo audito Iesus ait
ei: «Adhuc unum tibi deest: omnia, quaecumque habes, vende et da pauperibus et habebis thesaurum in
caelo et veni, sequere me». 23His ille auditis, contristatus est, quia dives erat valde. 24Videns autem illum
Iesus tristem factum dixit: «Quam difficile, qui pecunias habent, in regnum Dei intrant. 25Facilius est
enim camelum per foramen acus transire, quam divitem intrare in regnum Dei». 26Et dixerunt, qui
audiebant: «Et quis potest salvus fieri?». 27Ait autem illis: «Quae impossibilia sunt apud homines,
possibilia sunt apud Deum». 28Ait autem Petrus: «Ecce nos dimisimus nostra et secuti sumus te». 29Qui
dixit eis: «Amen dico vobis: Nemo est, qui reliquit domum aut uxorem aut fratres aut parentes aut filios
propter regnum Dei, 30et non recipiat multo plura in hoc tempore et in saeculo venturo vitam aeternam».
31Assumpsit autem Duodecim et ait illis: «Ecce ascendimus Ierusalem, et consummabuntur omnia, quae
scripta sunt per Prophetas de Filio hominis: 32tradetur enim gentibus et illudetur et contumeliis afficietur
et conspuetur, 33et, postquam flagellaverint, occident eum, et die tertia resurget». 34Et ipsi nihil horum
intellexerunt; et erat verbum istud absconditum ab eis, et non intellegebant, quae dicebantur. 35Factum
est autem cum appropinquaret Iericho, caecus quidam sedebat secus viam mendicans. 36Et cum audiret
turbam praetereuntem, interrogabat quid hoc esset. 37Dixerunt autem ei: «Iesus Nazarenus transit». 38Et
clamavit dicens: «Iesu, fili David, miserere mei!». 39Et qui praeibant, increpabant eum, ut taceret; ipse
vero multo magis clamabat: «Fili David, miserere mei!». 40Stans autem Iesus iussit illum adduci ad se.
Et cum appropinquasset, interrogavit illum: 41«Quid tibi vis faciam?». At ille dixit: «Domine, ut
videam». 42Et Iesus dixit illi: «Respice! Fides tua te salvum fecit». 43Et confestim vidit et sequebatur
illum magnificans Deum. Et omnis plebs, ut vidit, dedit laudem Deo. **[19]** 1Et ingressus perambulabat
Iericho. 2Et ecce vir nomine Zacchaeus, et hic erat princeps publicanorum et ipse dives. 3Et quaerebat
videre Iesum quis esset, et non poterat prae turba, quia statura pusillus erat. 4Et praecurrens ascendit in

arborem sycomorum, ut videret illum, quia inde erat transiturus. [5]Et cum venisset ad locum, suspiciens
Iesus dixit ad eum: «Zacchaee, festinans descende, nam hodie in domo tua oportet me manere». [6]Et
festinans descendit et excepit illum gaudens. [7]Et cum viderent, omnes murmurabant dicentes: «Ad
hominem peccatorem divertit!». [8]Stans autem Zacchaeus dixit ad Dominum: «Ecce dimidium bonorum
meorum, Domine, do pauperibus, et, si quid aliquem defraudavi, reddo quadruplum». [9]Ait autem Iesus
ad eum: «Hodie salus domui huic facta est, eo quod et ipse filius sit Abrahae; [10]venit enim Filius
hominis quaerere et salvum facere, quod perierat». [11]Haec autem illis audientibus, adiciens dixit
parabolam, eo quod esset prope Ierusalem, et illi existimarent quod confestim regnum Dei
manifestaretur. [12]Dixit ergo: «Homo quidam nobilis abiit in regionem longinquam accipere sibi regnum
et reverti. [13]Vocatis autem decem servis suis, dedit illis decem minas, et ait ad illos: "Negotiamini, dum
venio". [14]Cives autem eius oderant illum et miserunt legationem post illum dicentes: "Nolumus hunc
regnare super nos!". [15]Et factum est ut rediret, accepto regno, et iussit ad se vocari servos illos, quibus
dedit pecuniam, ut sciret quantum negotiati essent. [16]Venit autem primus dicens: "Domine, mina tua
decem minas acquisivit". [17]Et ait illi: "Euge, bone serve; quia in modico fidelis fuisti, esto potestatem
habens supra decem civitates". [18]Et alter venit dicens: "Mina tua, domine, fecit quinque minas". [19]Et
huic ait: "Et tu esto supra quinque civitates". [20]Et alter venit dicens: "Domine, ecce mina tua, quam
habui repositam in sudario; [21]timui enim te, quia homo austerus es: tollis, quod non posuisti, et metis,
quod non seminasti". [22]Dicit ei: "De ore tuo te iudico, serve nequam! Sciebas quod ego austerus homo
sum, tollens quod non posui et metens quod non seminavi? [23]Et quare non dedisti pecuniam meam ad
mensam? Et ego veniens cum usuris utique exegissem illud". [24]Et adstantibus dixit: "Auferte ab illo
minam et date illi, qui decem minas habet". [25]Et dixerunt ei: "Domine, habet decem minas!". [26]Dico
vobis: "Omni habenti dabitur; ab eo autem, qui non habet, et, quod habet, auferetur". [27]Verumtamen
inimicos meos illos, qui noluerunt me regnare super se, adducite huc et interficite ante me!». [28]Et his
dictis, praecedebat ascendens Hierosolymam. [29]Et factum est cum appropinquasset ad Bethfage et
Bethaniam, ad montem, qui vocatur Oliveti, misit duos discipulos [30]dicens: «Ite in castellum, quod
contra est, in quod introeuntes invenietis pullum asinae alligatum, cui nemo umquam hominum sedit;
solvite illum et adducite. [31]Et si quis vos interrogaverit: "Quare solvitis?", sic dicetis: "Dominus eum
necessarium habet"». [32]Abierunt autem, qui missi erant, et invenerunt, sicut dixit illis. [33]Solventibus
autem illis pullum, dixerunt domini eius ad illos: «Quid solvitis pullum?». [34]At illi dixerunt: «Dominus
eum necessarium habet». [35]Et duxerunt illum ad Iesum; et iactantes vestimenta sua supra pullum
imposuerunt Iesum. [36]Eunte autem illo, substernebant vestimenta sua in via. [37]Et cum appropinquaret
iam ad descensum montis Oliveti, coeperunt omnis multitudo discipulorum gaudentes laudare Deum
voce magna super omnibus, quas viderant, virtutibus [38]dicentes: «*Benedictus, qui venit rex in nomine
Domini!* / Pax in caelo et gloria in excelsis!». [39]Et quidam pharisaeorum de turbis dixerunt ad illum:
«Magister, increpa discipulos tuos!». [40]Et respondens dixit: «Dico vobis: Si hi tacuerint, lapides
clamabunt!». [41]Et ut appropinquavit, videns civitatem flevit super illam [42]dicens: «Si cognovisses et
tu in hac die, quae ad pacem tibi! Nunc autem abscondita sunt ab oculis tuis. [43]Quia venient dies in te,
et circumdabunt te inimici tui vallo et obsidebunt te et coangustabunt te undique [44]et ad terram
prosternent te et filios tuos, qui in te sunt, et non relinquent in te lapidem super lapidem, eo quod non
cognoveris tempus visitationis tuae». [45]Et ingressus in templum, coepit eicere vendentes [46]dicens illis:
«Scriptum est: "*Et erit domus mea domus orationis*". Vos autem fecistis illam *speluncam latronum*».
[47]Et erat docens cotidie in templo. Principes autem sacerdotum et scribae et principes plebis quaerebant
illum perdere [48]et non inveniebant quid facerent; omnis enim populus suspensus erat audiens illum.
[20] [1]Et factum est in una dierum, docente illo populum in templo et evangelizante, supervenerunt
principes sacerdotum et scribae cum senioribus [2]et aiunt dicentes ad illum: «Dic nobis: In qua potestate
haec facis aut quis est qui dedit tibi hanc potestatem?». [3]Respondens autem dixit ad illos: «Interrogabo
vos et ego verbum; et dicite mihi: [4]Baptismum Ioannis de caelo erat an ex hominibus?». [5]At illi
cogitabant inter se dicentes: «Si dixerimus: "De caelo", dicet: "Quare non credidistis illi?"; [6]si autem
dixerimus: "Ex hominibus", plebs universa lapidabit nos; certi sunt enim Ioannem prophetam esse». [7]Et
responderunt se nescire unde esset. [8]Et Iesus ait illis: «Neque ego dico vobis in qua potestate haec
facio». [9]Coepit autem dicere ad plebem parabolam hanc: «Homo *plantavit vineam* et locavit eam
colonis et ipse peregre fuit multis temporibus. [10]Et in tempore misit ad cultores servum, ut de fructu
vineae darent illi; cultores autem caesum dimiserunt eum inanem. [11]Et addidit alterum servum mittere;
illi autem hunc quoque caedentes et afficientes contumelia dimiserunt inanem. [12]Et addidit tertium
mittere; qui et illum vulnerantes eiecerunt. [13]Dixit autem dominus vineae: "Quid faciam? Mittam filium
meum dilectum; forsitan hunc verebuntur". [14]Quem cum vidissent coloni, cogitaverunt inter se dicentes:
"Hic est heres. Occidamus illum, ut nostra fiat hereditas". [15]Et eiectum illum extra vineam occiderunt.

Quid ergo faciet illis dominus vineae? [16]Veniet et perdet colonos istos et dabit vineam aliis». Quo
audito, dixerunt: «Absit!». [17]Ille autem aspiciens eos ait: «Quid est ergo hoc, quod scriptum est: /
"*Lapidem, quem reprobaverunt aedificantes, / hic factus est in caput anguli*"? [18]Omnis, qui ceciderit
supra illum lapidem, conquassabitur; supra quem autem ceciderit, comminuet illum». [19]Et quaerebant
scribae et principes sacerdotum mittere in illum manus in illa hora et timuerunt populum; cognoverunt
enim quod ad ipsos dixerit similitudinem istam. [20]Et observantes miserunt insidiatores, qui se iustos
simularent, ut caperent eum in sermone, et sic traderent illum principatui et potestati praesidis. [21]Et
interrogaverunt illum dicentes: «Magister, scimus quia recte dicis et doces et non accipis personam, sed
in veritate viam Dei doces. [22]Licet nobis dare tributum Caesari an non?». [23]Considerans autem dolum
illorum dixit ad eos: [24]«Ostendite mihi denarium. Cuius habet imaginem et inscriptionem?». [25]At illi
dixerunt: «Caesaris». Et ait illis: «Reddite ergo, quae Caesaris sunt, Caesari et, quae Dei sunt, Deo».
[26]Et non potuerunt verbum eius reprehendere coram plebe et mirati in responso eius tacuerunt.
[27]Accesserunt autem quidam sadducaeorum, qui negant esse resurrectionem, et interrogaverunt eum
[28]dicentes: «Magister, Moyses scripsit nobis, si frater alicuius mortuus fuerit habens uxorem et hic sine
filiis fuerit, ut accipiat eam frater eius uxorem et suscitet semen fratri suo. [29]Septem ergo fratres erant:
et primus accepit uxorem et mortuus est sine filiis; [30]et sequens [31]et tertius accepit illam, similiter autem
et septem non reliquerunt filios et mortui sunt. [32]Novissima mortua est et mulier. [33]Mulier ergo in
resurrectione cuius eorum erit uxor? Siquidem septem habuerunt eam uxorem». [34]Et ait illis Iesus: «Filii
saeculi huius nubunt et traduntur ad nuptias; [35]illi autem, qui digni habentur saeculo illo et resurrectione
ex mortuis, neque nubunt, neque ducunt uxores. [36]Neque enim ultra mori possunt: aequales enim
angelis sunt et filii sunt Dei, cum sint filii resurrectionis. [37]Quia vero resurgant mortui et Moyses
ostendit secus rubum, sicut dicit: "*Dominum Deum Abraham et Deum Isaac et Deum Iacob*". [38]Deus autem
non est mortuorum sed vivorum: omnes enim vivunt ei». [39]Respondentes autem quidam scribarum dixerunt:
«Magister, bene dixisti». [40]Et amplius non audebant eum quidquam interrogare. [41]Dixit autem ad illos:
«Quomodo dicunt Christum filium David esse? [42]Ipse enim David dicit in libro Psalmorum: "*Dixit Dominus
Domino meo: Sede a dextris meis, /* [43]*donec ponam inimicos tuos scabellum pedum tuorum*". [44]David ergo
Dominum illum vocat; et quomodo filius eius est?». [45]Audiente autem omni populo, dixit discipulis suis:
[46]«Attendite a scribis, qui volunt ambulare in stolis et amant salutationes in foro et primas cathedras in
synagogis et primos discubitus in conviviis, [47]qui devorant domos viduarum et simulant longam orationem.
Hi accipient damnationem maiorem». **[21]** [1]Respiciens autem vidit eos, qui mittebant munera sua in
gazophylacium, divites. [2]Vidit autem quandam viduam pauperculam mittentem illuc minuta duo [3]et dixit:
«Vere dico vobis: Vidua haec pauper plus quam omnes misit. [4]Nam omnes hi ex abundantia sua miserunt
in munera; haec autem ex inopia sua omnem victum suum, quem habebat, misit». [5]Et quibusdam dicentibus
de templo quod lapidibus bonis et donis ornatum esset dixit: [6]«Haec, quae videtis, venient dies in quibus non
relinquetur lapis super lapidem, qui non destruatur». [7]Interrogaverunt autem illum dicentes: «Praeceptor,
quando ergo haec erunt, et quod signum, cum fieri incipient?». [8]Qui dixit: «Videte, ne seducamini.
Multi enim venient in nomine meo dicentes: "Ego sum" et: "Tempus appropinquavit". Nolite ergo ire
post illos. [9]Cum autem audieritis proelia et seditiones, nolite terreri; oportet enim primum haec fieri, sed
non statim finis». [10]Tunc dicebat illis: «Surget gens contra gentem et regnum adversus regnum; [11]et
terrae motus magni et per loca fames et pestilentiae erunt, terroresque et de caelo signa magna erunt.
[12]Sed ante haec omnia inicient vobis manus suas et persequentur tradentes in synagogas et custodias, et
trahemini ad reges et praesides propter nomen meum; [13]continget autem vobis in testimonium. [14]Ponite
ergo in cordibus vestris non praemeditari quemadmodum respondeatis; [15]ego enim dabo vobis os et
sapientiam, cui non poterunt resistere vel contradicere omnes adversarii vestri. [16]Trademini autem et
a parentibus et fratribus et cognatis et amicis, et morte afficient ex vobis, [17]et eritis odio omnibus propter
nomen meum. [18]Et capillus de capite vestro non peribit. [19]In patientia vestra possidebitis animas vestras.
[20]Cum autem videritis circumdari ab exercitu Ierusalem, tunc scitote quia appropinquavit desolatio eius.
[21]Tunc, qui in Iudaea sunt, fugiant in montes; et, qui in medio eius, discedant; et, qui in regionibus, non
intrent in eam. [22]Quia dies ultionis hi sunt, ut impleantur omnia, quae scripta sunt. [23]Vae autem
praegnantibus et nutrientibus in illis diebus! Erit enim pressura magna super terram et ira populo huic,
[24]et cadent in ore gladii et captivi ducentur in omnes gentes, et Ierusalem calcabitur a gentibus, donec
impleantur tempora nationum. [25]Et erunt signa in sole et luna et stellis, et super terram pressura gentium
prae confusione sonitus maris et fluctuum, [26]arescentibus hominibus prae timore et exspectatione
eorum, quae supervenient orbi, nam *virtutes caelorum* movebuntur. [27]Et tunc videbunt *Filium hominis
venientem in nube* cum potestate et gloria magna. [28]His autem fieri incipientibus, respicite et levate
capita vestra, quoniam appropinquat redemptio vestra». [29]Et dixit illis similitudinem: «Videte ficulneam
et omnes arbores: [30]cum iam germinaverint, videntes vosmetipsi scitis quia iam prope est aestas. [31]Ita

et vos, cum videritis haec fieri, scitote quoniam prope est regnum Dei. [32]Amen dico vobis: Non praeteribit generatio haec, donec omnia fiant. [33]Caelum et terra transibunt, verba autem mea non transibunt. [34]Attendite autem vobis, ne forte graventur corda vestra in crapula et ebrietate et curis huius vitae, et superveniat in vos repentina dies illa; [35]tamquam laqueus enim superveniet in omnes, qui sedent super faciem omnis terrae. [36]Vigilate itaque omni tempore orantes, ut possitis fugere ista omnia, quae futura sunt, et stare ante Filium hominis». [37]Erat autem diebus docens in templo, noctibus vero exiens morabatur in monte, qui vocatur Oliveti. [38]Et omnis populus manicabat ad eum in templo audire eum. **[22]** [1]Appropinquabat autem dies festus Azymorum, qui dicitur Pascha. [2]Et quaerebant principes sacerdotum et scribae quomodo eum interficerent; timebant vero plebem. [3]Intravit autem Satanas in Iudam, qui cognominabatur Iscarioth, unum de Duodecim; [4]et abiit et locutus est cum principibus sacerdotum et magistratibus quemadmodum illum traderet eis. [5]Et gavisi sunt et pacti sunt pecuniam illi dare. [6]Et spopondit et quaerebat opportunitatem, ut eis traderet illum sine turba. [7]Venit autem dies Azymorum, in qua necesse erat occidi Pascha. [8]Et misit Petrum et Ioannem dicens: «Euntes parate nobis Pascha, ut manducemus». [9]At illi dixerunt ei: «Ubi vis paremus?». [10]Et dixit ad eos: «Ecce introeuntibus vobis in civitatem occurret vobis homo amphoram aquae portans; sequimini eum in domum, in quam intrat. [11]Et dicetis patri familias domus: "Dicit tibi Magister: Ubi est deversorium ubi Pascha cum discipulis meis manducem?". [12]Ipse vobis ostendet cenaculum magnum stratum; ibi parate». [13]Euntes autem invenerunt, sicut dixit illis, et paraverunt Pascha. [14]Et cum facta esset hora, discubuit, et apostoli cum eo. [15]Et ait illis: «Desiderio desideravi hoc Pascha manducare vobiscum, antequam patiar. [16]Dico enim vobis: Non manducabo illud, donec impleatur in regno Dei». [17]Et accepto calice, gratias egit et dixit: «Accipite hoc et dividite inter vos. [18]Dico enim vobis: Non bibam amodo de generatione vitis, donec regnum Dei veniat». [19]Et accepto pane, gratias egit et fregit et dedit eis dicens: «Hoc est corpus meum, quod pro vobis datur. Hoc facite in meam commemorationem». [20]Similiter et calicem, postquam cenavit, dicens: «Hic calix novum testamentum est in sanguine meo, qui pro vobis funditur. [21]Verumtamen ecce manus tradentis me mecum est in mensa; [22]et quidem Filius hominis, secundum quod definitum est, vadit; verumtamen vae illi homini, per quem traditur!». [23]Et ipsi coeperunt quaerere inter se quis esset ex eis, qui hoc facturus esset. [24]Facta est autem et contentio inter eos, quis eorum videretur esse maior. [25]Dixit autem eis: «Reges gentium dominantur eorum et, qui potestatem habent super eos, benefici vocantur. [26]Vos autem non sic, sed qui maior est in vobis, fiat sicut iunior; et, qui praecessor est, sicut ministrator. [27]Nam quis maior est: qui recumbit, an qui ministrat? Nonne qui recumbit? Ego autem in medio vestrum sum sicut qui ministrat. [28]Vos autem estis qui permansistis mecum in tentationibus meis; [29]et ego dispono vobis, sicut disposuit mihi Pater meus regnum, [30]ut edatis et bibatis super mensam meam in regno meo, et sedeatis super thronos iudicantes duodecim tribus Israel. [31]Simon, Simon, ecce Satanas expetivit vos, ut cribraret sicut triticum; [32]ego autem rogavi pro te, ut non deficiat fides tua. Et tu, aliquando conversus, confirma fratres tuos». [33]Qui dixit ei: «Domine, tecum paratus sum et in carcerem et in mortem ire». [34]Et ille dixit: «Dico tibi, Petre, non cantabit hodie gallus donec ter abneges nosse me». [35]Et dixit eis: «Quando misi vos sine sacculo et pera et calceamentis, numquid aliquid defuit vobis?». At illi dixerunt: «Nihil». [36]Dixit ergo eis: «Sed nunc, qui habet sacculum, tollat, similiter et peram; et, qui non habet, vendat tunicam suam et emat gladium. [37]Dico enim vobis: Hoc, quod scriptum est, oportet impleri in me, illud: "*Cum iniustis deputatus est*". Etenim ea, quae sunt de me, adimpletionem habent». [38]At illi dixerunt: «Domine, ecce gladii duo hic». At ille dixit eis: «Satis est». [39]Et egressus ibat secundum consuetudinem in montem Olivarum; secuti sunt autem illum et discipuli. [40]Et cum pervenisset ad locum, dixit illis: «Orate, ne intretis in tentationem». [41]Et ipse avulsus est ab eis, quantum iactus est lapidis, et, positis genibus, orabat [42]dicens: «Pater, si vis, transfer calicem istum a me; verumtamen non mea voluntas sed tua fiat». [43]Apparuit autem illi angelus de caelo confortans eum. Et factus in agonia prolixius orabat. [44]Et factus est sudor eius sicut guttae sanguinis decurrentis in terram. [45]Et cum surrexisset ab oratione et venisset ad discipulos, invenit eos dormientes prae tristitia [46]et ait illis: «Quid dormitis? Surgite; orate, ne intretis in tentationem». [47]Adhuc eo loquente, ecce turba, et qui vocabatur Iudas, unus de Duodecim, antecedebat eos, et appropinquavit Iesu, ut oscularetur eum. [48]Iesus autem dixit ei: «Iuda, osculo Filium hominis tradis?». [49]Videntes autem hi, qui circa ipsum erant, quod futurum erat, dixerunt: «Domine, si percutimus in gladio?». [50]Et percussit unus ex illis servum principis sacerdotum et amputavit auriculam eius dextram. [51]Respondens autem Iesus ait: «Sinite usque huc!». Et cum tetigisset auriculam eius, sanavit eum. [52]Dixit autem Iesus ad eos, qui venerant ad se principes sacerdotum et magistratus templi et seniores: «Quasi ad latronem existis cum gladiis et fustibus? [53]Cum cotidie vobiscum fuerim in templo, non extendistis manus in me; sed haec est hora vestra et potestas tenebrarum». [54]Comprehendentes autem eum, duxerunt et introduxerunt in domum principis sacerdotum. Petrus vero

sequebatur a longe. 55Accenso autem igni in medio atrio et circumsedentibus illis, sedebat Petrus in
medio eorum. 56Quem cum vidisset ancilla quaedam sedentem ad lumen et eum fuisset intuita, dixit:
57«Et hic cum illo erat!». At ille negavit eum dicens: 58«Mulier, non novi illum!». Et post pusillum alius
videns eum dixit: «Et tu de illis es!». Petrus vero ait: «O homo, non sum!». 59Et intervallo facto quasi
horae unius, alius quidam affirmabat dicens: «Vere et hic cum illo erat, nam et Galilaeus est!». 60Et ait
Petrus: «Homo, nescio quid dicis!». Et continuo adhuc illo loquente cantavit gallus. 61Et conversus
Dominus respexit Petrum; et recordatus est Petrus verbi Domini, sicut dixit ei: «Priusquam gallus cantet
hodie, ter me negabis». 62Et egressus foras flevit amare. 63Et viri, qui tenebant illum, illudebant ei
caedentes, 64et velaverunt eum et interrogabant eum dicentes: «Prophetiza: Quis est, qui te percussit?».
65Et alia multa blasphemantes dicebant in eum. 66Et ut factus est dies, convenerunt seniores plebis et
principes sacerdotum et scribae et duxerunt illum in concilium suum 67dicentes: «Si tu es Christus, dic
nobis». Et ait illis: «Si vobis dixero, non credetis; 68si autem interrogavero, non respondebitis mihi. 69Ex
hoc autem erit *Filius hominis sedens a dextris virtutis Dei*». 70Dixerunt autem omnes: «Tu ergo es Filius
Dei?». Qui ait ad illos: «Vos dicitis quia ego sum». 71At illi dixerunt: «Quid adhuc desideramus
testimonium? Ipsi enim audivimus de ore eius!». **[23]** 1Et surgens omnis multitudo eorum, duxerunt
illum ad Pilatum. 2Coeperunt autem accusare illum dicentes: «Hunc invenimus subvertentem gentem
nostram et prohibentem tributa dare Caesari et dicentem se Christum regem esse». 3Pilatus autem
interrogavit eum dicens: «Tu es rex Iudaeorum?». At ille respondens ait: «Tu dicis». 4Ait autem Pilatus
ad principes sacerdotum et turbas: «Nihil invenio causae in hoc homine». 5At illi invalescebant dicentes:
«Commovet populum docens per universam Iudaeam et incipiens a Galilaea usque huc!». 6Pilatus
autem audiens interrogavit si homo Galilaeus esset 7et ut cognovit quod de Herodis potestate esset,
remisit eum ad Herodem, qui et ipse Hierosolymis erat illis diebus. 8Herodes autem, viso Iesu, gavisus
est valde: erat enim cupiens ex multo tempore videre eum, eo quod audiret de illo et sperabat signum
aliquod videre ab eo fieri. 9Interrogabat autem illum multis sermonibus; at ipse nihil illi respondebat.
10Stabant etiam principes sacerdotum et scribae constanter accusantes eum. 11Sprevit autem illum
Herodes cum exercitu suo et illusit indutum veste alba et remisit ad Pilatum. 12Facti sunt autem amici
inter se Herodes et Pilatus in ipsa die, nam antea inimici erant ad invicem. 13Pilatus autem, convocatis
principibus sacerdotum et magistratibus et plebe, 14dixit ad illos: «Obtulistis mihi hunc hominem quasi
avertentem populum, et ecce ego coram vobis interrogans nullam causam inveni in homine isto ex his,
in quibus eum accusatis, 15sed neque Herodes: remisit enim illum ad nos. Et ecce nihil dignum morte
actum est ei. 16Emendatum ergo illum dimittam». 18Exclamavit autem universa turba dicens: «Tolle
hunc et dimitte nobis Barabbam!», 19qui erat propter seditionem quandam factam in civitate et
homicidium missus in carcerem. 20Iterum autem Pilatus locutus est ad illos volens dimittere Iesum, 21at
illi succlamabant dicentes: «Crucifige, crucifige illum!». 22Ille autem tertio dixit ad illos: «Quid enim
mali fecit iste? Nullam causam mortis invenio in eo; corripiam ergo illum et dimittam». 23At illi
instabant vocibus magnis postulantes, ut crucifigeretur, et invalescebant voces eorum. 24Et Pilatus
adiudicavit fieri petitionem eorum: 25dimisit autem eum, qui propter seditionem et homicidium missus
fuerat in carcerem, quem petebant, Iesum vero tradidit voluntati eorum. 26Et cum abducerent eum,
apprehenderunt Simonem quendam Cyrenensem venientem de villa et imposuerunt illi crucem portare
post Iesum. 27Sequebatur autem illum multa turba populi et mulierum, quae plangebant et lamentabant
eum. 28Conversus autem ad illas Iesus dixit: «Filiae Ierusalem, nolite flere super me, sed super vos ipsas
flete et super filios vestros, 29quoniam ecce venient dies, in quibus dicent: "Beatae steriles et ventres,
qui non genuerunt, et ubera, quae non lactaverunt!". 30Tunc incipient *dicere montibus*: "*Cadite super
nos!*", *et collibus*: "*Operite nos!*", 31quia si in viridi ligno haec faciunt, in arido quid fiet?».
32Ducebantur autem et alii duo nequam cum eo, ut interficerentur. 33Et postquam venerunt in locum, qui
vocatur Calvariae, ibi crucifixerunt eum et latrones, unum a dextris et alterum a sinistris. 34Iesus autem
dicebat: «Pater, dimitte illis, non enim sciunt quid faciunt». *Dividentes* vero *vestimenta eius miserunt
sortes*. 35Et stabat populus *exspectans*. Et *deridebant* illum et principes dicentes: «Alios salvos fecit; se
salvum faciat, si hic est Christus Dei electus!». 36Illudebant autem ei et milites accedentes, *acetum*
offerentes illi 37et dicentes: «Si tu es rex Iudaeorum, salvum te fac!». 38Erat autem et superscriptio super
illum: «Hic est rex Iudaeorum». 39Unus autem de his, qui pendebant, latronibus blasphemabat eum
dicens: «Nonne tu es Christus? Salvum fac temetipsum et nos!». 40Respondens autem alter increpabat
illum dicens: «Neque tu times Deum, quod in eadem damnatione es? 41Et nos quidem iuste, nam digna
factis recipimus! Hic vero nihil mali gessit». 42Et dicebat: «Iesu, memento mei cum veneris in regnum
tuum». 43Et dixit illi: «Amen dico tibi: Hodie mecum eris in paradiso». 44Et erat iam fere hora sexta, et
tenebrae factae sunt in universa terra usque in horam nonam, 45et obscuratus est sol, et velum templi
scissum est medium. 46Et clamans voce magna Iesus ait: «Pater, *in manus tuas commendo spiritum*

meum»; et haec dicens exspiravit. [47]Videns autem centurio, quod factum fuerat, glorificavit Deum
dicens: «Vere hic homo iustus erat!». [48]Et omnis turba eorum, qui simul aderant ad spectaculum istud, et
videbant, quae fiebant, percutientes pectora sua revertebantur. [49]Stabant autem omnes noti eius a longe, et
mulieres, quae secutae erant eum a Galilaea, haec videntes. [50]Et ecce vir nomine Ioseph, qui erat decurio,
vir bonus et iustus [51]—hic non consenserat consilio et actibus eorum— ab Arimathaea civitate Iudaeorum,
qui exspectabat regnum Dei, [52]hic accessit ad Pilatum et petiit corpus Iesu, [53]et depositum involvit sindone
et posuit eum in monumento exciso, in quo nondum quisquam positus fuerat. [54]Et dies erat Parasceves, et
sabbatum illucescebat. [55]Subsecutae autem mulieres, quae cum ipso venerant de Galilaea, viderunt
monumentum et quemadmodum positum erat corpus eius, [56]et revertentes paraverunt aromata et unguenta
et sabbato quidem siluerunt secundum mandatum. **[24]** [1]Prima autem sabbatorum, valde diluculo
venerunt ad monumentum portantes, quae paraverant, aromata. [2]Et invenerunt lapidem revolutum a
monumento [3]et ingressae non invenerunt corpus Domini Iesu. [4]Et factum est, dum mente haesitarent de
isto, ecce duo viri steterunt secus illas in veste fulgenti. [5]Cum timerent autem et declinarent vultum in
terram, dixerunt ad illas: «Quid quaeritis viventem cum mortuis? [6]Non est hic, sed surrexit. Recordamini
qualiter locutus est vobis, cum adhuc in Galilaea esset, [7]dicens: "Oportet Filium hominis tradi in manus
hominum peccatorum et crucifigi et die tertia resurgere"». [8]Et recordatae sunt verborum eius [9]et regressae
a monumento nuntiaverunt haec omnia illis Undecim et ceteris omnibus. [10]Erat autem Maria Magdalene
et Ioanna et Maria Iacobi; et ceterae cum eis dicebant ad apostolos haec. [11]Et visa sunt ante illos sicut
deliramentum verba ista, et non credebant illis. [12]Petrus autem surgens cucurrit ad monumentum et
procumbens videt linteamina sola; et rediit ad sua mirans, quod factum fuerat. [13]Et ecce duo ex illis ibant
ipsa die in castellum, quod erat in spatio stadiorum sexaginta ab Ierusalem nomine Emmaus, [14]et ipsi
loquebantur ad invicem de his omnibus, quae acciderant. [15]Et factum est, dum fabularentur et secum
quaererent, et ipse Iesus appropinquans ibat cum illis; [16]oculi autem illorum tenebantur, ne eum
agnoscerent. [17]Et ait ad illos: «Qui sunt hi sermones, quos confertis ad invicem ambulantes?». Et steterunt
tristes. [18]Et respondens unus, cui nomen Cleopas, dixit ei: «Tu solus peregrinus es in Ierusalem et non
cognovisti, quae facta sunt in illa his diebus?». [19]Quibus ille dixit: «Quae?». Et illi dixerunt ei: «De Iesu
Nazareno, qui fuit vir propheta, potens in opere et sermone coram Deo et omni populo, [20]et quomodo eum
tradiderunt summi sacerdotes et principes nostri in damnationem mortis, et crucifixerunt eum. [21]Nos autem
sperabamus quia ipse esset redempturus Israel; at nunc super haec omnia tertia dies hodie quod haec facta
sunt. [22]Sed et mulieres quaedam ex nostris terruerunt nos, quae ante lucem fuerunt ad monumentum [23]et,
non invento corpore eius, venerunt dicentes se etiam visionem angelorum vidisse, qui dicunt eum vivere.
[24]Et abierunt quidam ex nostris ad monumentum et ita invenerunt, sicut mulieres dixerunt, ipsum vero non
viderunt». [25]Et ipse dixit ad eos: «O stulti et tardi corde ad credendum in omnibus, quae locuti sunt
Prophetae! [26]Nonne haec oportuit pati Christum et intrare in gloriam suam?». [27]Et incipiens a Moyse et
omnibus Prophetis interpretabatur illis in omnibus Scripturis, quae de ipso erant. [28]Et appropinquaverunt
castello, quo ibant, et ipse se finxit longius ire. [29]Et coegerunt illum dicentes: «Mane nobiscum, quoniam
advesperascit et inclinata est iam dies». Et intravit, ut maneret cum illis. [30]Et factum est, dum recumberet
cum illis, accepit panem et benedixit ac fregit et porrigebat illis. [31]Et aperti sunt oculi eorum et
cognoverunt eum; et ipse evanuit ab eis. [32]Et dixerunt ad invicem: «Nonne cor nostrum ardens erat in
nobis, dum loqueretur nobis in via et aperiret nobis Scripturas?». [33]Et surgentes eadem hora regressi sunt
in Ierusalem et invenerunt congregatos Undecim et eos, qui cum ipsis erant, [34]dicentes: «Surrexit Dominus
vere et apparuit Simoni». [35]Et ipsi narrabant, quae gesta erant in via, et quomodo cognoverunt eum in
fractione panis. [36]Dum haec autem loquuntur, ipse stetit in medio eorum et dicit eis: «Pax vobis!».
[37]Conturbati vero et conterriti existimabant se spiritum videre. [38]Et dixit eis: «Quid turbati estis, et quare
cogitationes ascendunt in corda vestra? [39]Videte manus meas et pedes meos, quia ipse ego sum! Palpate
me et videte, quia spiritus carnem et ossa non habet, sicut me videtis habere». [40]Et cum hoc dixisset,
ostendit eis manus et pedes. [41]Adhuc autem illis non credentibus prae gaudio et mirantibus, dixit eis:
«Habetis hic aliquid, quod manducetur?». [42]At illi obtulerunt ei partem piscis assi. [43]Et sumens coram eis
manducavit. [44]Et dixit ad eos: «Haec sunt verba, quae locutus sum ad vos, cum adhuc essem vobiscum,
quoniam necesse est impleri omnia, quae scripta sunt in Lege Moysis et Prophetis et Psalmis de me».
[45]Tunc aperuit illis sensum, ut intellegerent Scripturas. [46]Et dixit eis: «Sic scriptum est, Christum pati et
resurgere a mortuis die tertia, [47]et praedicari in nomine eius paenitentiam in remissionem peccatorum in
omnes gentes, incipientibus ab Ierusalem. [48]Vos estis testes horum. [49]Et ecce ego mitto promissum Patris
mei in vos; vos autem sedete in civitate, quoadusque induamini virtutem ex alto». [50]Eduxit autem eos foras
usque in Bethaniam et, elevatis manibus suis, benedixit eis. [51]Et factum est dum benediceret illis, recessit
ab eis et ferebatur in caelum. [52]Et ipsi adoraverunt eum et regressi sunt in Ierusalem cum gaudio magno
[53]et erant semper in templo benedicentes Deum.

EVANGELIUM SECUNDUM IOANNEM

[1] 1In principio erat Verbum, et Verbum erat apud Deum, et Deus erat Verbum. 2Hoc erat in principio
apud Deum. 3Omnia per ipsum facta sunt, et sine ipso factum est nihil, quod factum est; 4in ipso vita
erat, et vita erat lux hominum, 5et lux in tenebris lucet, et tenebrae eam non comprehenderunt. 6Fuit
homo missus a Deo, cui nomen erat Ioannes; 7hic venit in testimonium, ut testimonium perhiberet de
lumine, ut omnes crederent per illum. 8Non erat ille lux, sed ut testimonium perhiberet de lumine. 9Erat
lux vera, quae illuminat omnem hominem, veniens in mundum. 10In mundo erat, et mundus per ipsum
factus est, et mundus eum non cognovit. 11In propria venit, et sui eum non receperunt. 12Quotquot autem
acceperunt eum, dedit eis potestatem filios Dei fieri, his, qui credunt in nomine eius, 13qui non ex
sanguinibus neque ex voluntate carnis neque ex voluntate viri, sed ex Deo nati sunt. 14Et Verbum caro
factum est et habitavit in nobis; et vidimus gloriam eius, gloriam quasi Unigeniti a Patre, plenum gratiae
et veritatis. 15Ioannes testimonium perhibet de ipso, et clamat dicens: «Hic erat, quem dixi: Qui post
me venturus est, ante me factus est, quia prior me erat». 16Et de plenitudine eius nos omnes accepimus,
et gratiam pro gratia; 17quia lex per Moysen data est, gratia et veritas per Iesum Christum facta est.
18Deum nemo vidit umquam; Unigenitus Deus, qui est in sinum Patris, ipse enarravit. 19Et hoc est
testimonium Ioannis, quando miserunt ad eum Iudaei ab Hierosolymis sacerdotes et Levitas, ut
interrogarent eum: «Tu quis es?». 20Et confessus est et non negavit; et confessus est: «Non sum ego
Christus». 21Et interrogaverunt eum: «Quid ergo? Elias es tu?». Et dicit: «Non sum». «Propheta es tu?».
Et respondit: «Non». 22Dixerunt ergo ei: «Quis es? Ut responsum demus his, qui miserunt nos. Quid
dicis de teipso?». 23Ait: «*Ego vox clamantis in deserto: /* "*Dirigite viam Domini*", sicut dixit Isaias
propheta». 24Et qui missi fuerant, erant ex pharisaeis; 25et interrogaverunt eum et dixerunt ei: «Quid ergo
baptizas, si tu non es Christus neque Elias neque propheta?». 26Respondit eis Ioannes dicens: «Ego
baptizo in aqua; medius vestrum stat, quem vos non scitis, 27qui post me venturus est, cuius ego non
sum dignus, ut solvam eius corrigiam calceamenti». 28Haec in Bethania facta sunt trans Iordanem, ubi
erat Ioannes baptizans. 29Altera die videt Iesum venientem ad se et ait: «Ecce agnus Dei, qui tollit
peccatum mundi. 30Hic est, de quo dixi: Post me venit vir, qui ante me factus est, quia prior me erat.
31Et ego nesciebam eum, sed ut manifestetur Israel, propterea veni ego in aqua baptizans». 32Et
testimonium perhibuit Ioannes dicens: «Vidi Spiritum descendentem quasi columbam de caelo, et
mansit super eum; 33et ego nesciebam eum, sed, qui misit me baptizare in aqua, ille mihi dixit: 'Super
quem videris Spiritum descendentem et manentem super eum, hic est qui baptizat in Spiritu Sancto'.
34Et ego vidi et testimonium perhibui quia hic est Filius Dei». 35Altera die iterum stabat Ioannes et ex
discipulis eius duo, 36et respiciens Iesum ambulantem dicit: «Ecce agnus Dei». 37Et audierunt eum duo
discipuli loquentem et secuti sunt Iesum. 38Conversus autem Iesus et videns eos sequentes se dicit eis:
«Quid quaeritis?». Qui dixerunt ei: «Rabbi —quod dicitur interpretatum Magister— ubi manes?».
39Dicit eis: «Venite et videbitis». Venerunt ergo et viderunt, ubi maneret, et apud eum manserunt die
illo; hora erat quasi decima. 40Erat Andreas, frater Simonis Petri, unus ex duobus, qui audierant ab
Ioanne et secuti fuerant eum. 41Invenit hic primum fratrem suum Simonem et dicit ei: «Invenimus
Messiam» —quod est interpretatum Christus—; 42adduxit eum ad Iesum. Intuitus eum Iesus dixit: «Tu
es Simon filius Ioannis; tu vocaberis Cephas» —quod interpretatur Petrus—. 43In crastinum voluit exire
in Galilaeam et invenit Philippum. Et dicit ei Iesus: «Sequere me». 44Erat autem Philippus a Bethsaida,
civitate Andreae et Petri. 45Invenit Philippus Nathanael et dicit ei: «Quem scripsit Moyses in Lege et
Prophetae invenimus, Iesum filium Ioseph a Nazareth». 46Et dixit ei Nathanael: «A Nazareth potest
aliquid boni esse?». Dicit ei Philippus: «Veni et vide». 47Vidit Iesus Nathanael venientem ad se et dicit
de eo: «Ecce vere Israelita, in quo dolus non est». 48Dicit ei Nathanael: «Unde me nosti?». Respondit
Iesus et dixit ei: «Priusquam te Philippus vocaret, cum esses sub ficu, vidi te». 49Respondit ei Nathanael:
«Rabbi, tu es Filius Dei, tu rex es Israel!». 50Respondit Iesus et dixit ei: «Quia dixi tibi: Vidi te sub ficu,
credis? Maiora his videbis». 51Et dicit ei: «Amen, amen dico vobis: Videbitis *caelum* apertum et *angelos
Dei ascendentes et descendentes* supra Filium hominis». [2] 1Et die tertio nuptiae factae sunt in Cana
Galilaeae, et erat mater Iesu ibi; 2vocatus est autem et Iesus et discipuli eius ad nuptias. 3Et deficiente
vino, dicit mater Iesu ad eum: «Vinum non habent». 4Et dicit ei Iesus: «Quid mihi et tibi, mulier?
Nondum venit hora mea». 5Dicit mater eius ministris: «Quodcumque dixerit vobis, facite». 6Erant autem
ibi lapideae hydriae sex positae secundum purificationem Iudaeorum, capientes singulae metretas binas
vel ternas. 7Dicit eis Iesus: «Implete hydrias aqua». Et impleverunt eas usque ad summum. 8Et dicit eis:
«Haurite nunc et ferte architriclino». Illi autem tulerunt. 9Ut autem gustavit architriclinus aquam vinum
factam et non sciebat unde esset, ministri autem sciebant, qui haurierant aquam, vocat sponsum

architriclinus [10]et dicit ei: «Omnis homo primum bonum vinum ponit et, cum inebriati fuerint, id quod deterius est; tu servasti bonum vinum usque adhuc». [11]Hoc fecit initium signorum Iesus in Cana Galilaeae et manifestavit gloriam suam, et crediderunt in eum discipuli eius. [12]Post hoc descendit Capharnaum ipse et mater eius et fratres eius et discipuli eius, et ibi manserunt non multis diebus. [13]Et prope erat Pascha Iudaeorum, et ascendit Hierosolymam Iesus. [14]Et invenit in templo vendentes boves et oves et columbas, et nummularios sedentes; [15]et, cum fecisset flagellum de funiculis, omnes eiecit de templo, oves quoque et boves, et nummulariorum effudit aes et mensas subvertit; [16]et his, qui columbas vendebant, dixit: «Auferte ista hinc! Nolite facere domum Patris mei domum negotiationis». [17]Recordati sunt discipuli eius quia scriptum est: «*Zelus domus tuae comedit me*». [18]Responderunt ergo Iudaei et dixerunt ei: «Quod signum ostendis nobis, quia haec facis?». [19]Respondit Iesus et dixit eis: «Solvite templum hoc et in tribus diebus excitabo illud». [20]Dixerunt ergo Iudaei: «Quadraginta et sex annis aedificatum est templum hoc, et tu tribus diebus excitabis illud?». [21]Ille autem dicebat de templo corporis sui. [22]Cum ergo resurrexisset a mortuis, recordati sunt discipuli eius quia hoc dicebat, et crediderunt Scripturae et sermoni, quem dixit Iesus. [23]Cum autem esset Hierosolymis in Pascha, in die festo, multi crediderunt in nomine eius, videntes signa eius, quae faciebat. [24]Ipse autem Iesus non credebat semetipsum eis, eo quod ipse nosset omnes, [25]et quia opus ei non erat, ut quis testimonium perhiberet de homine: ipse enim sciebat quid esset in homine. **[3]** [1]Erat autem homo ex pharisaeis, Nicodemus nomine, princeps Iudaeorum; [2]hic venit ad eum nocte et dixit ei: «Rabbi, scimus quia a Deo venisti magister: nemo enim potest haec signa facere, quae tu facis, nisi fuerit Deus cum eo». [3]Respondit Iesus et dixit ei: «Amen, amen dico tibi: Nisi quis natus fuerit desuper, non potest videre regnum Dei». [4]Dicit ad eum Nicodemus: «Quomodo potest homo nasci, cum senex sit? Numquid potest in ventrem matris suae iterato introire et nasci?». [5]Respondit Iesus: «Amen, amen dico tibi: Nisi quis natus fuerit ex aqua et Spiritu, non potest introire in regnum Dei. [6]Quod natum est ex carne, caro est; et, quod natum est ex Spiritu, spiritus est. [7]Non mireris quia dixi tibi: Oportet vos nasci denuo. [8]Spiritus, ubi vult, spirat, et vocem eius audis, sed non scis unde veniat et quo vadat; sic est omnis, qui natus est ex Spiritu». [9]Respondit Nicodemus et dixit ei: «Quomodo possunt haec fieri?». [10]Respondit Iesus et dixit ei: «Tu es magister Israel et haec ignoras? [11]Amen, amen dico tibi: Quod scimus, loquimur et, quod vidimus, testamur, et testimonium nostrum non accipitis. [12]Si terrena dixi vobis, et non creditis, quomodo, si dixero vobis caelestia, credetis? [13]Et nemo ascendit in caelum, nisi qui descendit de caelo, Filius hominis. [14]Et sicut Moyses exaltavit serpentem in deserto, ita exaltari oportet Filium hominis, [15]ut omnis, qui credit, in ipso habeat vitam aeternam». [16]Sic enim dilexit Deus mundum, ut Filium suum unigenitum daret, ut omnis, qui credit in eum, non pereat, sed habeat vitam aeternam. [17]Non enim misit Deus Filium in mundum, ut iudicet mundum, sed ut salvetur mundus per ipsum. [18]Qui credit in eum, non iudicatur; qui autem non credit, iam iudicatus est, quia non credidit in nomen Unigeniti Filii Dei. [19]Hoc est autem iudicium: Lux venit in mundum, et dilexerunt homines magis tenebras quam lucem; erant enim eorum mala opera. [20]Omnis enim, qui mala agit, odit lucem et non venit ad lucem, ut non arguantur opera eius; [21]qui autem facit veritatem, venit ad lucem, ut manifestentur eius opera, quia in Deo sunt facta. [22]Post haec venit Iesus et discipuli eius in Iudaeam terram, et illic demorabatur cum eis et baptizabat. [23]Erat autem et Ioannes baptizans in Enon iuxta Salim, quia aquae multae erant illic, et adveniebant et baptizabantur; [24]nondum enim missus fuerat in carcerem Ioannes. [25]Facta est ergo quaestio ex discipulis Ioannis cum Iudaeo de purificatione. [26]Et venerunt ad Ioannem et dixerunt ei: «Rabbi, qui erat tecum trans Iordanem, cui tu testimonium perhibuisti, ecce hic baptizat et omnes veniunt ad eum!». [27]Respondit Ioannes et dixit: «Non potest homo accipere quidquam, nisi fuerit ei datum de caelo. [28]Ipsi vos mihi testimonium perhibetis quod dixerim: Non sum ego Christus, sed: Missus sum ante illum. [29]Qui habet sponsam, sponsus est; amicus autem sponsi, qui stat et audit eum, gaudio gaudet propter vocem sponsi. Hoc ergo gaudium meum impletum est. [30]Illum oportet crescere, me autem minui». [31]Qui de sursum venit, supra omnes est; qui est de terra, de terra est et de terra loquitur. Qui de caelo venit, supra omnes est; [32]et quod vidit et audivit, hoc testatur, et testimonium eius nemo accipit. [33]Qui accipit eius testimonium, signavit quia Deus verax est. [34]Quem enim misit Deus, verba Dei loquitur, non enim ad mensuram dat Spiritum. [35]Pater diligit Filium et omnia dedit in manu eius. [36]Qui credit in Filium, habet vitam aeternam; qui autem incredulus est Filio, non videbit vitam, sed ira Dei manet super eum. **[4]** [1]Ut ergo cognovit Iesus quia audierunt pharisaei quia Iesus plures discipulos facit et baptizat quam Ioannes, [2]—quamquam Iesus ipse non baptizaret sed discipuli eius— [3]reliquit Iudaeam et abiit iterum in Galilaeam. [4]Oportebat autem eum transire per Samariam. [5]Venit ergo in civitatem Samariae, quae dicitur Sichar, iuxta praedium, quod dedit Iacob Ioseph filio suo; [6]erat autem ibi fons Iacob. Iesus ergo fatigatus ex itinere sedebat sic super fontem; hora erat quasi sexta. [7]Venit mulier de Samaria haurire aquam. Dicit ei Iesus: «Da mihi bibere»; [8]discipuli enim eius abierant

in civitatem, ut cibos emerent. 9Dicit ergo ei mulier illa Samaritana: «Quomodo tu Iudaeus cum sis,
bibere a me poscis, quae sum mulier Samaritana?». Non enim coutuntur Iudaei Samaritanis.
10Respondit Iesus et dixit ei: «Si scires donum Dei et quis est, qui dicit tibi: "Da mihi bibere", tu forsitan
petisses ab eo et dedisset tibi aquam vivam». 11Dicit ei mulier: «Domine, neque in quo haurias habes,
et puteus altus est; unde ergo habes aquam vivam? 12Numquid tu maior es patre nostro Iacob, qui dedit
nobis puteum, et ipse ex eo bibit et filii eius et pecora eius?». 13Respondit Iesus et dixit ei: «Omnis, qui
bibit ex aqua hac, sitiet iterum; 14qui autem biberit ex aqua, quam ego dabo ei, non sitiet in aeternum,
sed aqua, quam dabo ei, fiet in eo fons aquae salientis in vitam aeternam». 15Dicit ad eum mulier:
«Domine, da mihi hanc aquam, ut non sitiam, neque veniam huc haurire». 16Dicit ei: «Vade, voca virum
tuum et veni huc». 17Respondit mulier et dixit ei: «Non habeo virum». Dicit ei Iesus: «Bene dixisti:
"Non habeo virum"; 18quinque enim viros habuisti, et nunc, quem habes, non est tuus vir. Hoc vere
dixisti». 19Dicit ei mulier: «Domine, video quia propheta es tu. 20Patres nostri in monte hoc adoraverunt,
et vos dicitis quia in Hierosolymis est locus, ubi adorare oportet». 21Dicit ei Iesus: «Crede mihi, mulier,
quia venit hora quando neque in monte hoc neque in Hierosolymis adorabitis Patrem. 22Vos adoratis,
quod nescitis; nos adoramus, quod scimus, quia salus ex Iudaeis est. 23Sed venit hora et nunc est,
quando veri adoratores adorabunt Patrem in Spiritu et veritate; nam et Pater tales quaerit, qui adorent
eum. 24Spiritus est Deus, et eos, qui adorant eum, in Spiritu et veritate oportet adorare». 25Dicit ei
mulier: «Scio quia Messias venit —qui dicitur Christus—; cum venerit ille, nobis annuntiabit omnia».
26Dicit ei Iesus: «Ego sum, qui loquor tecum». 27Et continuo venerunt discipuli eius et mirabantur quia
cum muliere loquebatur; nemo tamen dixit: «Quid quaeris aut quid loqueris cum ea?». 28Reliquit ergo
hydriam suam mulier et abiit in civitatem et dicit illis hominibus: 29«Venite, videte hominem, qui dixit
mihi omnia, quaecumque feci; numquid ipse est Christus?». 30Exierunt de civitate et veniebant ad eum.
31Interea rogabant eum discipuli dicentes: «Rabbi, manduca». 32Ille autem dixit eis: «Ego cibum habeo
manducare, quem vos nescitis». 33Dicebant ergo discipuli ad invicem: «Numquid aliquis attulit ei
manducare?». 34Dicit eis Iesus: «Meus cibus est, ut faciam voluntatem eius, qui misit me, et ut perficiam
opus eius. 35Nonne vos dicitis: "Adhuc quattuor menses sunt, et messis venit"? Ecce dico vobis: Levate
oculos vestros et videte regiones quia albae sunt ad messem! Iam 36qui metit, mercedem accipit et
congregat fructum in vitam aeternam, ut et qui seminat, simul gaudeat et qui metit. 37In hoc enim est
verbum verum: Alius est qui seminat, et alius est qui metit. 38Ego misi vos metere, quod vos non
laborastis; alii laboraverunt, et vos in laborem eorum introistis». 39Ex civitate autem illa multi
crediderunt in eum Samaritanorum propter verbum mulieris testimonium perhibentis: «Dixit mihi
omnia, quaecumque feci!». 40Cum venissent ergo ad illum Samaritani, rogaverunt eum, ut apud ipsos
maneret; et mansit ibi duos dies. 41Et multo plures crediderunt propter sermonem eius; 42et mulieri
dicebant: «Iam non propter tuam loquelam credimus; ipsi enim audivimus et scimus quia hic est vere
Salvator mundi!». 43Post duos autem dies exiit inde in Galilaeam; 44ipse enim Iesus testimonium
perhibuit quia propheta in sua patria honorem non habet. 45Cum ergo venisset in Galilaeam, exceperunt
eum Galilaei, cum omnia vidissent, quae fecerat Hierosolymis in die festo; et ipsi enim venerant in diem
festum. 46Venit ergo iterum in Cana Galilaeae, ubi fecit aquam vinum. Et erat quidam regius, cuius filius
infirmabatur Capharnaum; 47hic cum audisset quia Iesus advenerit a Iudaea in Galilaeam, abiit ad eum
et rogabat ut descenderet et sanaret filium eius; incipiebat enim mori. 48Dixit ergo Iesus ad eum: «Nisi
signa et prodigia videritis, non credetis». 49Dicit ad eum regius: «Domine, descende priusquam moriatur
puer meus». 50Dicit ei Iesus: «Vade. Filius tuus vivit». Credidit homo sermoni, quem dixit ei Iesus, et
ibat. 51Iam autem eo descendente, servi eius occurrerunt ei dicentes quia puer eius vivit. 52Interrogabat
ergo horam ab eis, in qua melius habuerit. Dixerunt ergo ei: «Heri hora septima reliquit eum febris».
53Cognovit ergo pater quia illa hora erat, in qua dixit ei Iesus: «Filius tuus vivit», et credidit ipse et
domus eius tota. 54Hoc iterum secundum signum fecit Iesus, cum venisset a Iudaea in Galilaeam.
[5] 1Post haec erat dies festus Iudaeorum, et ascendit Iesus Hierosolymam. 2Est autem Hierosolymis,
super Probatica, piscina, quae cognominatur Hebraice Bethsatha, quinque porticus habens. 3In his
iacebat multitudo languentium, caecorum, claudorum, aridorum. 5Erat autem quidam homo ibi triginta
et octo annos habens in infirmitate sua. 6Hunc cum vidisset Iesus iacentem, et cognovisset quia multum
iam tempus habet, dicit ei: «Vis sanus fieri?». 7Respondit ei languidus: «Domine, hominem non habeo,
ut, cum turbata fuerit aqua, mittat me in piscinam; dum autem venio ego, alius ante me descendit».
8Dicit ei Iesus: «Surge, tolle grabatum tuum et ambula». 9Et statim sanus factus est homo, et sustulit
grabatum suum et ambulabat. Erat autem sabbatum in illo die. 10Dicebant ergo Iudaei illi, qui sanatus
fuerat: «Sabbatum est, et non licet tibi tollere grabatum tuum». 11Ille autem respondit eis: «Qui me fecit
sanum, ille mihi dixit: "Tolle grabatum tuum et ambula"». 12Interrogaverunt eum: «Quis est ille homo,
qui dixit tibi: "Tolle et ambula"?». 13Is autem, qui sanus fuerat effectus, nesciebat quis esset; Iesus enim

declinavit a turba constituta in loco. 14Postea invenit eum Iesus in templo, et dixit illi: «Ecce sanus
factus es; iam noli peccare, ne deterius tibi aliquid contingat». 15Abiit ille homo et nuntiavit Iudaeis quia
Iesus esset, qui fecit eum sanum. 16Et propterea persequebantur Iudaei Iesum, quia haec faciebat in
sabbato. 17Iesus autem respondit eis: «Pater meus usque modo operatur, et ego operor». 18Propterea ergo
magis quaerebant eum Iudaei interficere, quia non solum solvebat sabbatum, sed et Patrem suum
dicebat Deum, aequalem se faciens Deo. 19Respondit itaque Iesus et dixit eis: «Amen, amen dico vobis:
Non potest Filius a se facere quidquam, nisi quod viderit Patrem facientem; quaecumque enim ille
faciat, haec et Filius similiter facit. 20Pater enim diligit Filium et omnia demonstrat ei, quae ipse facit,
et maiora his demonstrabit ei opera, ut vos miremini. 21Sicut enim Pater suscitat mortuos et vivificat,
sic et Filius, quos vult, vivificat. 22Neque enim Pater iudicat quemquam, sed iudicium omne dedit Filio,
23ut omnes honorificent Filium, sicut honorificant Patrem. Qui non honorificat Filium, non honorificat
Patrem, qui misit illum. 24Amen, amen dico vobis: Qui verbum meum audit et credit ei, qui misit me,
habet vitam aeternam et in iudicium non venit, sed transiit a morte in vitam. 25Amen, amen dico vobis:
Venit hora, et nunc est, quando mortui audient vocem Filii Dei et, qui audierint, vivent. 26Sicut enim
Pater habet vitam in semetipso, sic dedit et Filio vitam habere in semetipso; 27et potestatem dedit ei
iudicium facere, quia Filius hominis est. 28Nolite mirari hoc, quia venit hora, in qua omnes, qui in
monumentis sunt, audient vocem eius 29et procedent, qui bona fecerunt, in resurrectionem vitae, qui
vero mala egerunt, in resurrectionem iudicii. 30Non possum ego a meipso facere quidquam; sicut audio,
iudico, et iudicium meum iustum est, quia non quaero voluntatem meam, sed voluntatem eius, qui misit
me. 31Si ego testimonium perhibeo de meipso, testimonium meum non est verum; 32alius est, qui
testimonium perhibet de me, et scio quia verum est testimonium, quod perhibet de me. 33Vos misistis
ad Ioannem, et testimonium perhibuit veritati; 34ego autem non ab homine testimonium accipio, sed
haec dico, ut vos salvi sitis. 35Ille erat lucerna ardens et lucens, vos autem voluistis exsultare ad horam
in luce eius. 36Ego autem habeo testimonium maius Ioanne; opera enim, quae dedit mihi Pater, ut
perficiam ea, ipsa opera, quae ego facio, testimonium perhibent de me quia Pater me misit; 37et, qui
misit me, Pater, ipse testimonium perhibuit de me. Neque vocem eius umquam audistis, neque speciem
eius vidistis, 38et verbum eius non habetis in vobis manens, quia, quem misit ille, huic vos non creditis.
39Scrutamini Scripturas, quia vos putatis in ipsis vitam aeternam habere; et illae sunt, quae testimonium
perhibent de me. 40Et non vultis venire ad me, ut vitam habeatis. 41Gloriam ab hominibus non accipio,
42sed cognovi vos, quia dilectionem Dei non habetis in vobis. 43Ego veni in nomine Patris mei, et non
accipitis me; si alius venerit in nomine suo, illum accipietis. 44Quomodo potestis vos credere, qui
gloriam ab invicem accipitis, et gloriam, quae a solo est Deo, non quaeritis? 45Nolite putare quia ego
accusaturus sim vos apud Patrem; est qui accuset vos: Moyses, in quo vos speratis. 46Si enim crederetis
Moysi, crederetis forsitan et mihi; de me enim ille scripsit. 47Si autem illius litteris non creditis,
quomodo meis verbis credetis?». **[6]** 1Post haec abiit Iesus trans mare Galilaeae, quod est Tiberiadis.
2Et sequebatur eum multitudo magna, quia videbant signa, quae faciebat super his, qui infirmabantur.
3Subiit autem in montem Iesus et ibi sedebat cum discipulis suis. 4Erat autem proximum Pascha, dies
festus Iudaeorum. 5Cum sublevasset ergo oculos Iesus et vidisset quia multitudo magna venit ad eum,
dicit ad Philippum: «Unde ememus panes, ut manducent hi?». 6Hoc autem dicebat tentans eum; ipse
enim sciebat quid esset facturus. 7Respondit ei Philippus: «Ducentorum denariorum panes non
sufficiunt eis, ut unusquisque modicum quid accipiat!». 8Dicit ei unus ex discipulis eius, Andreas frater
Simonis Petri: 9«Est puer hic, qui habet quinque panes hordeaceos et duos pisces; sed haec quid sunt
propter tantos?». 10Dixit Iesus: «Facite homines discumbere». Erat autem fenum multum in loco.
Discubuerunt ergo viri numero quasi quinque milia. 11Accepit ergo panes Iesus et, cum gratias egisset,
distribuit discumbentibus, similiter et ex piscibus, quantum volebant. 12Ut autem impleti sunt, dicit
discipulis suis: «Colligite, quae superaverunt, fragmenta, ne quid pereat». 13Collegerunt ergo et
impleverunt duodecim cophinos fragmentorum ex quinque panibus hordeaceis, quae superfuerunt his,
qui manducaverunt. 14Illi ergo homines, cum vidissent quod fecerat signum, dicebant: «Hic est vere
propheta, qui venit in mundum!». 15Iesus ergo, cum cognovisset quia venturi essent, ut raperent eum et
facerent eum regem, secessit iterum in montem ipse solus. 16Ut autem sero factum est, descenderunt
discipuli eius ad mare 17et, cum ascendissent navem, veniebant trans mare in Capharnaum. Et tenebrae
iam factae erant, et nondum venerat ad eos Iesus. 18Mare autem, vento magno flante, exsurgebat. 19Cum
remigassent ergo quasi stadia viginti quinque aut triginta, vident Iesum ambulantem super mare et
proximum navi fieri, et timuerunt. 20Ille autem dicit eis: «Ego sum, nolite timere!». 21Volebant ergo
accipere eum in navem, et statim fuit navis ad terram, in quam ibant. 22Altera die turba, quae stabat trans
mare, vidit quia navicula alia non erat ibi nisi una et quia non introisset cum discipulis suis Iesus in
navem, sed soli discipuli eius abiissent; 23aliae supervenerunt naves a Tiberiade iuxta locum, ubi

manducaverant panem, gratias agente Domino. [24]Cum ergo vidisset turba quia Iesus non esset ibi neque
discipuli eius, ascenderunt ipsi naviculas et venerunt Capharnaum quaerentes Iesum. [25]Et cum
invenissent eum trans mare, dixerunt ei: «Rabbi, quando huc venisti?». [26]Respondit eis Iesus et dixit:
«Amen, amen dico vobis: Quaeritis me non quia vidistis signa, sed quia manducastis ex panibus et
saturati estis. [27]Operamini non cibum, qui perit, sed cibum, qui permanet in vitam aeternam, quem
Filius hominis vobis dabit; hunc enim Pater signavit Deus!». [28]Dixerunt ergo ad eum: «Quid faciemus,
ut operemur opera Dei?». [29]Respondit Iesus et dixit eis: «Hoc est opus Dei, ut credatis in eum, quem
misit ille». [30]Dixerunt ergo ei: «Quod ergo tu facis signum, ut videamus et credamus tibi? Quid
operaris? [31]Patres nostri manna manducaverunt in deserto, sicut scriptum est: "*Panem de caelo dedit eis
manducare*"». [32]Dixit ergo eis Iesus: «Amen, amen dico vobis: Non Moyses dedit vobis panem de
caelo, sed Pater meus dat vobis panem de caelo verum: [33]panis enim Dei est, qui descendit de caelo et
dat vitam mundo». [34]Dixerunt ergo ad eum: «Domine, semper da nobis panem hunc».[35]Dixit eis Iesus:
«Ego sum panis vitae. Qui venit ad me, non esuriet; et, qui credit in me, non sitiet umquam. [36]Sed dixi
vobis quia et vidistis me, et non creditis. [37]Omne, quod dat mihi Pater, ad me veniet, et eum, qui venit
ad me, non eiciam foras, [38]quia descendi de caelo, non ut faciam voluntatem meam sed voluntatem eius,
qui misit me. [39]Haec est autem voluntas eius, qui misit me, ut omne, quod dedit mihi, non perdam ex
eo, sed resuscitem illud in novissimo die. [40]Haec est enim voluntas Patris mei, ut omnis, qui videt
Filium et credit in eum, habeat vitam aeternam; et resuscitabo ego eum in novissimo die».
[41]Murmurabant ergo Iudaei de illo quia dixisset: «Ego sum panis, qui de caelo descendi», [42]et dicebant:
«Nonne hic est Iesus filius Ioseph, cuius nos novimus patrem et matrem? Quomodo dicit nunc: "De
caelo descendi"?». [43]Respondit Iesus et dixit eis: «Nolite murmurare in invicem. [44]Nemo potest venire
ad me, nisi Pater, qui misit me, traxerit eum; et ego resuscitabo eum in novissimo die. [45]Est scriptum in
Prophetis: "*Et erunt omnes docibiles Dei*". Omnis, qui audivit a Patre et didicit, venit ad me. [46]Non quia
Patrem vidit quisquam, nisi is qui est a Deo, hic vidit Patrem. [47]Amen, amen dico vobis: Qui credit,
habet vitam aeternam. [48]Ego sum panis vitae. [49]Patres vestri manducaverunt in deserto manna et mortui
sunt. [50]Hic est panis de caelo descendens, ut, si quis ex ipso manducaverit, non moriatur. [51]Ego sum
panis vivus, qui de caelo descendi. Si quis manducaverit ex hoc pane, vivet in aeternum; panis autem,
quem ego dabo, caro mea est pro mundi vita». [52]Litigabant ergo Iudaei ad invicem dicentes: «Quomodo
potest hic nobis carnem suam dare ad manducandum?». [53]Dixit ergo eis Iesus: «Amen, amen dico
vobis: Nisi manducaveritis carnem Filii hominis et biberitis eius sanguinem, non habetis vitam in
vobismetipsis. [54]Qui manducat meam carnem et bibit meum sanguinem, habet vitam aeternam; et ego
resuscitabo eum in novissimo die. [55]Caro enim mea verus est cibus, et sanguis meus verus est potus.
[56]Qui manducat meam carnem et bibit meum sanguinem, in me manet, et ego in illo. [57]Sicut misit me
vivens Pater, et ego vivo propter Patrem; et, qui manducat me, et ipse vivet propter me. [58]Hic est panis,
qui de caelo descendit, non sicut manducaverunt patres et mortui sunt; qui manducat hunc panem, vivet
in aeternum». [59]Haec dixit in synagoga docens in Capharnaum. [60]Multi ergo audientes ex discipulis eius
dixerunt: «Durus est hic sermo! Quis potest eum audire?». [61]Sciens autem Iesus apud semetipsum quia
murmurarent de hoc discipuli eius, dixit eis: «Hoc vos scandalizat? [62]Si ergo videritis Filium hominis
ascendentem, ubi erat prius? [63]Spiritus est, qui vivificat, caro non prodest quidquam; verba, quae ego
locutus sum vobis, Spiritus sunt et vita sunt. [64]Sed sunt quidam ex vobis, qui non credunt». Sciebat enim
ab initio Iesus, qui essent non credentes, et quis traditurus esset eum. [65]Et dicebat: «Propterea dixi vobis:
Nemo potest venire ad me, nisi fuerit ei datum a Patre». [66]Ex hoc multi discipulorum eius abierunt retro
et iam non cum illo ambulabant. [67]Dixit ergo Iesus ad Duodecim: «Numquid et vos vultis abire?».
[68]Respondit ei Simon Petrus: «Domine, ad quem ibimus? Verba vitae aeternae habes; [69]et nos
credidimus et cognovimus quia tu es Sanctus Dei». [70]Respondit eis Iesus: «Nonne ego vos Duodecim
elegi? Et ex vobis unus Diabolus est?». [71]Dicebat autem Iudam Simonis Iscariotis: hic enim erat
traditurus eum, cum esset unus ex Duodecim. **[7]** [1]Et post haec ambulabat Iesus in Galilaeam; non
enim volebat in Iudaeam ambulare, quia quaerebant eum Iudaei interficere. [2]Erat autem in proximo dies
festus Iudaeorum, Scenopegia. [3]Dixerunt ergo ad eum fratres eius: «Transi hinc et vade in Iudaeam, ut
et discipuli tui videant opera tua, quae facis. [4]Nemo quippe in occulto quid facit et quaerit ipse in palam
esse. Si haec facis, manifesta teipsum mundo». [5]Neque enim fratres eius credebant in eum. [6]Dicit ergo
eis Iesus: «Tempus meum nondum adest, tempus autem vestrum semper est paratum. [7]Non potest
mundus odisse vos, me autem odit, quia ego testimonium perhibeo de illo quia opera eius mala sunt.
[8]Vos ascendite ad diem festum, ego non ascendo ad diem festum istum, quia meum tempus nondum
impletum est». [9]Haec autem cum dixisset, ipse mansit in Galilaea. [10]Ut autem ascenderunt fratres eius
ad diem festum, tunc et ipse ascendit, non manifeste sed quasi in occulto. [11]Iudaei ergo quaerebant eum
in die festo et dicebant: «Ubi est ille?». [12]Et murmur multus de eo erat in turba. Alii quidem dicebant:

«Bonus est!»; alii autem dicebant: «Non, sed seducit turbam!». 13Nemo tamen palam loquebatur de illo
propter metum Iudaeorum. 14Iam autem die festo mediante, ascendit Iesus in templum et docebat.
15Mirabantur ergo Iudaei dicentes: «Quomodo hic litteras scit, cum non didicerit?». 16Respondit ergo
eis Iesus et dixit: «Mea doctrina non est mea sed eius, qui misit me. 17Si quis voluerit voluntatem eius
facere, cognoscet de doctrina utrum ex Deo sit, an ego a meipso loquar. 18Qui a semetipso loquitur,
gloriam propriam quaerit; qui autem quaerit gloriam eius, qui misit illum, hic verax est, et iniustitia in
illo non est. 19Nonne Moyses dedit vobis legem? Et nemo ex vobis facit legem. Quid me quaeritis
interficere?». 20Respondit turba: «Daemonium habes! Quis te quaerit interficere?». 21Respondit Iesus
et dixit eis: «Unum opus feci, et omnes miramini. 22Propterea Moyses dedit vobis circumcisionem —
non quia ex Moyse est sed ex patribus— et in sabbato circumciditis hominem. 23Si circumcisionem
accipit homo in sabbato, ut non solvatur lex Moysis, mihi indignamini quia totum hominem sanum feci
in sabbato? 24Nolite iudicare secundum faciem, sed iustum iudicium iudicate». 25Dicebant ergo quidam
ex Hierosolymitis: «Nonne hic est, quem quaerunt interficere? 26Et ecce palam loquitur, et nihil ei
dicunt. Numquid vere cognoverunt principes quia hic est Christus? 27Sed hunc scimus unde sit, Christus
autem cum venerit, nemo scit unde sit». 28Clamavit ergo docens in templo Iesus et dicens: «Et me scitis
et unde sim scitis. Et a meipso non veni, sed est verus, qui misit me, quem vos non scitis. 29Ego scio
eum, quia ab ipso sum, et ipse me misit». 30Quaerebant ergo eum apprehendere, et nemo misit in illum
manus, quia nondum venerat hora eius. 31De turba autem multi crediderunt in eum et dicebant:
«Christus cum venerit, numquid plura signa faciet quam quae hic fecit?». 32Audierunt pharisaei turbam
murmurantem de illo haec et miserunt pontifices et pharisaei ministros, ut apprehenderent eum. 33Dixit
ergo Iesus: «Adhuc modicum tempus vobiscum sum et vado ad eum, qui misit me. 34Quaeretis me et
non invenietis; et ubi sum ego, vos non potestis venire». 35Dixerunt ergo Iudaei ad seipsos: «Quo hic
iturus est, quia nos non inveniemus eum? Numquid in dispersionem Graecorum iturus est et docturus
Graecos? 36Quis est hic sermo, quem dixit: "Quaeretis me et non invenietis" et: "Ubi sum ego, vos non
potestis venire"?». 37In novissimo autem die magno festivitatis stabat Iesus et clamavit dicens: «Si quis
sitit, veniat ad me et bibat, 38qui credit in me. Sicut dixit Scriptura, flumina de ventre eius fluent aquae
vivae». 39Hoc autem dixit de Spiritu, quem accepturi erant qui crediderant in eum. Nondum enim erat
Spiritus, quia Iesus nondum fuerat glorificatus. 40Ex illa ergo turba, cum audissent hos sermones,
dicebant: «Hic est vere propheta!»; 41alii dicebant: «Hic est Christus!»; quidam autem dicebant:
«Numquid a Galilaea Christus venit? 42Nonne Scriptura dixit: "*Ex semine David*, et *de Bethlehem*
castello, ubi erat David, *venit* Christus"?». 43Dissensio itaque facta est in turba propter eum. 44Quidam
autem ex ipsis volebant apprehendere eum, sed nemo misit super illum manus. 45Venerunt ergo ministri
ad pontifices et pharisaeos, et dixerunt eis illi: «Quare non adduxistis eum?». 46Responderunt ministri:
«Numquam sic locutus est homo». 47Responderunt ergo eis pharisaei: «Numquid et vos seducti estis?
48Numquid aliquis ex principibus credidit in eum aut ex pharisaeis? 49Sed turba haec, quae non novit
legem, maledicti sunt!». 50Dicit Nicodemus ad eos, ille qui venit ad eum antea, qui unus erat ex ipsis:
51«Numquid lex nostra iudicat hominem, nisi audierit ab ipso prius et cognoverit quid faciat?».
52Responderunt et dixerunt ei: «Numquid et tu ex Galilaea es? Scrutare et vide quia propheta a Galilaea
non surgit!». 53Et reversi sunt unusquisque in domum suam. **[8]** 1Iesus autem perrexit in montem
Oliveti. 2Diluculo autem iterum venit in templum, et omnis populus veniebat ad eum, et sedens docebat
eos. 3Adducunt autem scribae et pharisaei mulierem in adulterio deprehensam et statuerunt eam in
medio 4et dicunt ei: «Magister, haec mulier manifesto deprehensa est in adulterio. 5In lege autem
Moyses mandavit nobis huiusmodi lapidare; tu ergo quid dicis?». 6Hoc autem dicebant tentantes eum,
ut possent accusare eum. Iesus autem inclinans se deorsum digito scribebat in terra. 7Cum autem
perseverarent interrogantes eum, erexit se et dixit eis: «Qui sine peccato est vestrum, primus in illam
lapidem mittat»; 8et iterum se inclinans scribebat in terra. 9Audientes autem unus post unum exibant,
incipientes a senioribus, et remansit solus, et mulier in medio stans. 10Erigens autem se Iesus dixit ei:
«Mulier, ubi sunt? Nemo te condemnavit?». 11Quae dixit: «Nemo, Domine». Dixit autem Iesus: «Nec
ego te condemno; vade et amplius iam noli peccare». 12Iterum ergo locutus est eis Iesus dicens: «Ego
sum lux mundi; qui sequitur me, non ambulabit in tenebris, sed habebit lucem vitae». 13Dixerunt ergo
ei pharisaei: «Tu de teipso testimonium perhibes; testimonium tuum non est verum». 14Respondit Iesus
et dixit eis: «Et si ego testimonium perhibeo de meipso, verum est testimonium meum, quia scio unde
veni et quo vado; vos autem nescitis unde venio aut quo vado. 15Vos secundum carnem iudicatis, ego
non iudico quemquam. 16Et si iudico ego, iudicium meum verum est, quia solus non sum, sed ego et,
qui me misit, Pater. 17Sed et in lege vestra scriptum est quia duorum hominum testimonium verum est.
18Ego sum, qui testimonium perhibeo de meipso, et testimonium perhibet de me, qui misit me, Pater».
19Dicebant ergo ei: «Ubi est Pater tuus?». Respondit Iesus: «Neque me scitis neque Patrem meum; si

me sciretis, forsitan et Patrem meum sciretis». [20]Haec verba locutus est in gazophylacio docens in
templo; et nemo apprehendit eum, quia necdum venerat hora eius. [21]Dixit ergo iterum eis: «Ego vado,
et quaeretis me et in peccato vestro moriemini! Quo ego vado, vos non potestis venire». [22]Dicebant ergo
Iudaei: «Numquid interficiet semetipsum, quia dicit: "Quo ego vado, vos non potestis venire"?». [23]Et
dicebat eis: «Vos de deorsum estis, ego de supernis sum; vos de mundo hoc estis, ego non sum de hoc
mundo. [24]Dixi ergo vobis quia moriemini in peccatis vestris; si enim non credideritis quia ego sum,
moriemini in peccatis vestris». [25]Dicebant ergo ei: «Tu quis es?». Dixit eis Iesus: «In principio: id quod
et loquor vobis! [26]Multa habeo de vobis loqui et iudicare; sed, qui misit me, verax est, et ego, quae
audivi ab eo, haec loquor ad mundum». [27]Non cognoverunt quia Patrem eis dicebat. [28]Dixit ergo eis
Iesus: «Cum exaltaveritis Filium hominis, tunc cognoscetis quia ego sum, et a meipso facio nihil, sed,
sicut docuit me Pater, haec loquor. [29]Et qui me misit, mecum est; non reliquit me solum, quia ego, quae
placita sunt ei, facio semper». [30]Haec illo loquente, multi crediderunt in eum. [31]Dicebat ergo Iesus ad
eos, qui crediderunt ei, Iudaeos: «Si vos manseritis in sermone meo, vere discipuli mei estis [32]et
cognoscetis veritatem, et veritas liberabit vos». [33]Responderunt ei: «Semen Abrahae sumus et nemine
servivimus umquam? Quomodo tu dicis: "Liberi fietis"?». [34]Respondit eis Iesus: «Amen, amen dico
vobis: Omnis, qui facit peccatum, servus est. [35]Servus autem non manet in domo in aeternum; filius
manet in aeternum. [36]Si ergo Filius vos liberaverit, vere liberi eritis. [37]Scio quia semen Abrahae estis;
sed quaeritis me interficere, quia sermo meus non capit in vobis. [38]Ego, quae vidi apud Patrem, loquor;
et vos ergo, quae audivistis a patre, facitis». [39]Responderunt et dixerunt ei: «Pater noster Abraham est».
Dicit eis Iesus: «Si filii Abrahae essetis, opera Abrahae faceretis. [40]Nunc autem quaeritis me interficere,
hominem, qui veritatem vobis locutus sum, quam audivi a Deo; hoc Abraham non fecit. [41]Vos facitis
opera patris vestri». Dixerunt itaque ei: «Nos ex fornicatione non sumus nati; unum patrem habemus
Deum!». [42]Dixit eis Iesus: «Si Deus pater vester esset, diligeretis me; ego enim ex Deo processi et veni,
neque enim a meipso veni, sed ille me misit. [43]Quare loquelam meam non cognoscitis? Quia non
potestis audire sermonem meum. [44]Vos ex patre Diabolo estis et desideria patris vestri vultis facere. Ille
homicida erat ab initio et in veritate non stabat, quia non est veritas in eo. Cum loquitur mendacium, ex
propriis loquitur, quia mendax est et pater eius. [45]Ego autem quia veritatem dico non creditis mihi.
[46]Quis ex vobis arguit me de peccato? Si veritatem dico, quare vos non creditis mihi? [47]Qui est ex Deo,
verba Dei audit; propterea vos non auditis, quia ex Deo non estis». [48]Responderunt Iudaei et dixerunt
ei: «Nonne bene dicimus nos quia Samaritanus es tu et daemonium habes?». [49]Respondit Iesus: «Ego
daemonium non habeo, sed honorifico Patrem meum, et vos inhonoratis me. [50]Ego autem non quaero
gloriam meam; est qui quaerit et iudicat. [51]Amen, amen dico vobis: Si quis sermonem meum servaverit,
mortem non videbit in aeternum». [52]Dixerunt ergo ei Iudaei: «Nunc cognovimus quia daemonium
habes. Abraham mortuus est et prophetae, et tu dicis: "Si quis sermonem meum servaverit, non gustabit
mortem in aeternum". [53]Numquid tu maior es patre nostro Abraham, qui mortuus est? Et prophetae
mortui sunt! Quem teipsum facis?». [54]Respondit Iesus: «Si ego glorifico meipsum, gloria mea nihil est;
est Pater meus, qui glorificat me, quem vos dicitis: "Deus noster est!", [55]et non cognovistis eum. Ego
autem novi eum. Et si dixero: Non scio eum, ero similis vobis, mendax; sed scio eum et sermonem eius
servo. [56]Abraham pater vester exsultavit, ut videret diem meum, et vidit et gavisus est». [57]Dixerunt ergo
Iudaei ad eum: «Quinquaginta annos nondum habes et Abraham vidisti?». [58]Dixit eis Iesus: «Amen,
amen dico vobis: Antequam Abraham fieret, ego sum». [59]Tulerunt ergo lapides, ut iacerent in eum; Iesus
autem abscondit se et exivit de templo. **[9]** [1]Et praeteriens vidit hominem caecum a nativitate. [2]Et
interrogaverunt eum discipuli sui dicentes: «Rabbi, quis peccavit, hic aut parentes eius, ut caecus
nasceretur?». [3]Respondit Iesus: «Neque hic peccavit neque parentes eius, sed ut manifestentur opera
Dei in illo. [4]Nos oportet operari opera eius, qui misit me, donec dies est; venit nox, quando nemo potest
operari. [5]Quamdiu in mundo sum, lux sum mundi». [6]Haec cum dixisset, exspuit in terram et fecit lutum
ex sputo et linivit lutum super oculos eius [7]et dixit ei: «Vade, lava in natatoria Siloae!»—quod
interpretatur Missus—. Abiit ergo et lavit et venit videns. [8]Itaque vicini et, qui videbant eum prius quia
mendicus erat, dicebant: «Nonne hic est, qui sedebat et mendicabat?»; [9]alii dicebant: «Hic est!»; alii
dicebant: «Nequaquam, sed similis est eius!». Ille dicebat: «Ego sum!». [10]Dicebant ergo ei: «Quomodo
igitur aperti sunt oculi tibi?». [11]Respondit ille: «Homo, qui dicitur Iesus, lutum fecit et unxit oculos
meos et dixit mihi: 'Vade ad Siloam et lava!'. Abii ergo et lavi et vidi». [12]Et dixerunt ei: «Ubi est ille?».
Ait: «Nescio». [13]Adducunt eum ad pharisaeos, qui caecus fuerat. [14]Erat autem sabbatum, in qua die
lutum fecit Iesus et aperuit oculos eius. [15]Iterum ergo interrogabant et eum pharisaei quomodo vidisset.
Ille autem dixit eis: «Lutum posuit super oculos meos, et lavi et video». [16]Dicebant ergo ex pharisaeis
quidam: «Non est hic homo a Deo, quia sabbatum non custodit!»; alii autem dicebant: «Quomodo
potest homo peccator haec signa facere?». Et schisma erat in eis. [17]Dicunt ergo caeco iterum: «Tu quid

dicis de eo quia aperuit oculos tuos?». Ille autem dixit: «Propheta est!». [18]Non crediderunt ergo Iudaei
de illo quia caecus fuisset et vidisset, donec vocaverunt parentes eius, qui viderat. [19]Et interrogaverunt
eos dicentes: «Hic est filius vester, quem vos dicitis quia caecus natus est? Quomodo ergo nunc videt?».
[20]Responderunt ergo parentes eius et dixerunt: «Scimus quia hic est filius noster et quia caecus natus
est. [21]Quomodo autem nunc videat nescimus, aut quis eius aperuit oculos nos nescimus; ipsum
interrogate. Aetatem habet; ipse de se loquetur!». [22]Haec dixerunt parentes eius, quia timebant Iudaeos;
iam enim conspiraverant Iudaei, ut, si quis eum confiteretur Christum, extra synagogam fieret.
[23]Propterea parentes eius dixerunt: «Aetatem habet; ipsum interrogate!». [24]Vocaverunt ergo rursum
hominem, qui fuerat caecus, et dixerunt ei: «Da gloriam Deo! Nos scimus quia hic homo peccator est».
[25]Respondit ergo ille: «Si peccator est nescio; unum scio quia caecus cum essem, modo video».
[26]Dixerunt ergo illi: «Quid fecit tibi? Quomodo aperuit oculos tuos?». [27]Respondit eis: «Dixi vobis iam,
et non audistis; quid iterum vultis audire? Numquid et vos vultis discipuli eius fieri?». [28]Et maledixerunt
ei et dixerunt: «Tu discipulus illius es, nos autem Moysis discipuli sumus. [29]Nos scimus quia Moysi
locutus est Deus, hunc autem nescimus unde sit». [30]Respondit homo et dixit eis: «In hoc enim mirabile
est quia vos nescitis unde sit, et aperuit meos oculos! [31]Scimus quia peccatores Deus non audit, sed si
quis Dei cultor est et voluntatem eius facit, hunc exaudit. [32]A saeculo non est auditum quia aperuit quis
oculos caeci nati; [33]nisi esset hic a Deo, non poterat facere quidquam». [34]Responderunt et dixerunt ei:
«In peccatis tu natus es totus et tu doces nos?». Et eiecerunt eum foras. [35]Audivit Iesus quia eiecerunt
eum foras et, cum invenisset eum, dixit ei: «Tu credis in Filium hominis?». [36]Respondit ille et dixit: «Et
quis est, Domine, ut credam in eum?». [37]Dixit ei Iesus: «Et vidisti eum et, qui loquitur tecum, ipse est».
[38]At ille ait: «Credo, Domine!»; et adoravit eum. [39]Et dixit Iesus: «In iudicium ego in hunc mundum
veni, ut, qui non vident, videant, et, qui vident, caeci fiant». [40]Audierunt haec ex pharisaeis, qui cum
ipso erant, et dixerunt ei: «Numquid et nos caeci sumus?». [41]Dixit eis Iesus: «Si caeci essetis, non
haberetis peccatum. Nunc vero dicitis: "Videmus!"; peccatum vestrum manet». **[10]** [1]«Amen, amen
dico vobis: Qui non intrat per ostium in ovile ovium, sed ascendit aliunde, ille fur est et latro; [2]qui autem
intrat per ostium, pastor est ovium. [3]Huic ostiarius aperit, et oves vocem eius audiunt, et proprias oves
vocat nominatim et educit eas. [4]Cum proprias omnes emiserit, ante eas vadit, et oves illum sequuntur,
quia sciunt vocem eius; [5]alienum autem non sequentur, sed fugient ab eo, quia non noverunt vocem
alienorum». [6]Hoc proverbium dixit eis Iesus; illi autem non cognoverunt quid esset, quod loquebatur
eis. [7]Dixit ergo iterum Iesus: «Amen, amen dico vobis: Ego sum ostium ovium. [8]Omnes, quotquot
venerunt ante me, fures sunt et latrones, sed non audierunt eos oves. [9]Ego sum ostium: per me si quis
introierit, salvabitur et ingredietur et egredietur et pascua inveniet. [10]Fur non venit, nisi ut furetur et
mactet et perdat; ego veni, ut vitam habeant et abundantius habeant. [11]Ego sum pastor bonus: bonus
pastor animam suam ponit pro ovibus; [12]mercennarius et, qui non est pastor, cuius non sunt oves
propriae, videt lupum venientem et dimittit oves et fugit —et lupus rapit eas et dispergit— [13]quia
mercennarius est, et non pertinet ad eum de ovibus. [14]Ego sum pastor bonus: et cognosco meas, et
cognoscunt me meae, [15]sicut cognoscit me Pater, et ego cognosco Patrem; et animam meam pono pro
ovibus. [16]Et alias oves habeo, quae non sunt ex hoc ovili, et illas oportet me adducere, et vocem meam
audient et fient unus grex, unus pastor. [17]Propterea me Pater diligit, quia ego pono animam meam, ut
iterum sumam eam. [18]Nemo tollit eam a me, sed ego pono eam a meipso. Potestatem habeo ponendi
eam et potestatem habeo iterum sumendi eam. Hoc mandatum accepi a Patre meo». [19]Dissensio iterum
facta est inter Iudaeos propter sermones hos. [20]Dicebant autem multi ex ipsis: «Daemonium habet et
insanit! Quid eum auditis?». [21]Alii dicebant: «Haec verba non sunt daemonium habentis! Numquid
daemonium potest caecorum oculos aperire?». [22]Facta sunt tunc Encaenia in Hierosolymis. Hiems erat;
[23]et ambulabat Iesus in templo in porticu Salomonis. [24]Circumdederunt ergo eum Iudaei et dicebant ei:
«Quousque animam nostram tollis? Si tu es Christus, dic nobis palam!». [25]Respondit eis Iesus: «Dixi
vobis, et non creditis; opera, quae ego facio in nomine Patris mei, haec testimonium perhibent de me.
[26]Sed vos non creditis, quia non estis ex ovibus meis. [27]Oves meae vocem meam audiunt, et ego
cognosco eas, et sequuntur me, [28]et ego vitam aeternam do eis, et non peribunt in aeternum, et non
rapiet eas quisquam de manu mea. [29]Pater meus quod dedit mihi, maius omnibus est, et nemo potest
rapere de manu Patris. [30]Ego et Pater unum sumus». [31]Sustulerunt iterum lapides Iudaei, ut lapidarent
eum. [32]Respondit eis Iesus: «Multa opera bona ostendi vobis ex Patre; propter quod eorum opus me
lapidatis?». [33]Responderunt ei Iudaei: «De bono opere non lapidamus te sed de blasphemia, et quia tu,
homo cum sis, facis teipsum Deum». [34]Respondit eis Iesus: «Nonne scriptum est in lege vestra: "*Ego
dixi: Dii estis?*" [35]Si illos dixit deos ad quos sermo Dei factus est, et non potest solvi Scriptura, [36]quem
Pater sanctificavit et misit in mundum, vos dicitis: "Blasphemas!", quia dixi: Filius Dei sum? [37]Si non
facio opera Patris mei, nolite credere mihi; [38]si autem facio, et si mihi non vultis credere, operibus

credite, ut cognoscatis et sciatis quia in me est Pater, et ego in Patre». 39Quaerebant ergo iterum eum prehendere; et exivit de manibus eorum. 40Et abiit iterum trans Iordanem, in eum locum, ubi erat Ioannes baptizans primum, et mansit illic. 41Et multi venerunt ad eum et dicebant: «Ioannes quidem signum fecit nullum; omnia autem, quaecumque dixit Ioannes de hoc, vera erant». 42Et multi crediderunt in eum illic. **[11]** 1Erat autem quidam languens Lazarus a Bethania, de castello Mariae et Marthae sororis eius. 2Maria autem erat, quae unxit Dominum unguento et extersit pedes eius capillis suis, cuius frater Lazarus infirmabatur. 3Miserunt ergo sorores ad eum dicentes: «Domine, ecce, quem amas, infirmatur». 4Audiens autem Iesus dixit: «Infirmitas haec non est ad mortem sed pro gloria Dei, ut glorificetur Filius Dei per eam».5Diligebat autem Iesus Martham et sororem eius et Lazarum. 6Ut ergo audivit quia infirmabatur, tunc quidem mansit in loco, in quo erat, duobus diebus; 7deinde post hoc dicit discipulis: «Eamus in Iudaeam iterum». 8Dicunt ei discipuli: «Rabbi, nunc quaerebant te Iudaei lapidare, et iterum vadis illuc?». 9Respondit Iesus: «Nonne duodecim horae sunt diei? Si quis ambulaverit in die, non offendit, quia lucem huius mundi videt; 10si quis autem ambulaverit in nocte, offendit, quia lux non est in eo». 11Haec ait et post hoc dicit eis: «Lazarus amicus noster dormit, sed vado, ut a somno exsuscitem eum». 12Dixerunt ergo ei discipuli: «Domine, si dormit, salvus erit». 13Dixerat autem Iesus de morte eius, illi autem putaverunt quia de dormitione somni diceret. 14Tunc ergo dixit eis Iesus manifeste: «Lazarus mortuus est, 15et gaudeo propter vos, ut credatis, quoniam non eram ibi; sed eamus ad eum». 16Dixit ergo Thomas, qui dicitur Didymus, ad condiscipulos: «Eamus et nos, ut moriamur cum eo!». 17Venit itaque Iesus et invenit eum quattuor dies iam in monumento habentem. 18Erat autem Bethania iuxta Hierosolymam quasi stadiis quindecim. 19Multi autem ex Iudaeis venerant ad Martham et Mariam, ut consolarentur eas de fratre. 20Martha ergo ut audivit quia Iesus venit, occurrit illi; Maria autem domi sedebat. 21Dixit ergo Martha ad Iesum: «Domine, si fuisses hic, frater meus non esset mortuus! 22Sed et nunc scio quia, quaecumque poposceris a Deo, dabit tibi Deus». 23Dicit illi Iesus: «Resurget frater tuus». 24Dicit ei Martha: «Scio quia resurget in resurrectione in novissimo die». 25Dixit ei Iesus: «Ego sum resurrectio et vita. Qui credit in me, et si mortuus fuerit, vivet; 26et omnis, qui vivit et credit in me, non morietur in aeternum. Credis hoc?». 27Ait illi: «Utique, Domine; ego credidi quia tu es Christus Filius Dei, qui in mundum venisti». 28Et cum haec dixisset, abiit et vocavit Mariam sororem suam silentio dicens: «Magister adest et vocat te». 29Illa autem ut audivit, surrexit cito et venit ad eum; 30nondum enim venerat Iesus in castellum, sed erat adhuc in illo loco, ubi occurrerat ei Martha. 31Iudaei igitur, qui erant cum ea in domo et consolabantur eam, cum vidissent Mariam quia cito surrexit et exiit, secuti sunt eam putantes: «Vadit ad monumentum, ut ploret ibi». 32Maria ergo, cum venisset, ubi erat Iesus, videns eum cecidit ad pedes eius dicens ei: «Domine, si fuisses hic, non esset mortuus frater meus!». 33Iesus ergo, ut vidit eam plorantem et Iudaeos, qui venerant cum ea, plorantes, fremuit spiritu et turbavit seipsum 34et dixit: «Ubi posuistis eum?». Dicunt ei: «Domine, veni et vide». 35Lacrimatus est Iesus. 36Dicebant ergo Iudaei: «Ecce quomodo amabat eum!». 37Quidam autem dixerunt ex ipsis: «Non poterat hic, qui aperuit oculos caeci, facere, ut et hic non moreretur?». 38Iesus ergo rursum fremens in semetipso, venit ad monumentum; erat autem spelunca, et lapis superpositus erat ei. 39Ait Iesus: «Tollite lapidem!». Dicit ei Martha, soror eius, qui mortuus fuerat: «Domine, iam foetet; quatriduanus enim est!». 40Dicit ei Iesus: «Nonne dixi tibi quoniam si credideris, videbis gloriam Dei?». 41Tulerunt ergo lapidem. Iesus autem, elevatis sursum oculis, dixit: «Pater, gratias ago tibi quoniam audisti me. 42Ego autem sciebam quia semper me audis, sed propter populum, qui circumstat dixi, ut credant quia tu me misisti». 43Et haec cum dixisset, voce magna clamavit: «Lazare, veni foras!». 44Prodiit, qui fuerat mortuus, ligatus pedes et manus institis; et facies illius sudario erat ligata. Dicit Iesus eis: «Solvite eum et sinite eum abire». 45Multi ergo ex Iudaeis, qui venerant ad Mariam et viderant, quae fecit, crediderunt in eum; 46quidam autem ex ipsis abierunt ad pharisaeos et dixerunt eis, quae fecit Iesus. 47Collegerunt ergo pontifices et pharisaei concilium et dicebant: «Quid facimus, quia hic homo multa signa facit? 48Si dimittimus eum sic, omnes credent in eum, et venient Romani et tollent nostrum et locum et gentem!». 49Unus autem ex ipsis, Caiphas, cum esset pontifex anni illius, dixit eis: «Vos nescitis quidquam, 50nec cogitatis quia expedit vobis, ut unus moriatur homo pro populo, et non tota gens pereat!». 51Hoc autem a semetipso non dixit, sed cum esset pontifex anni illius, prophetavit quia Iesus moriturus erat pro gente 52et non tantum pro gente sed et ut filios Dei, qui erant dispersi, congregaret in unum. 53Ab illo ergo die cogitaverunt, ut interficerent eum. 54Iesus ergo iam non in palam ambulabat apud Iudaeos, sed abiit inde in regionem iuxta desertum, in civitatem, quae dicitur Ephraim, et ibi morabatur cum discipulis. 55Proximum autem erat Pascha Iudaeorum, et ascenderunt multi Hierosolymam de regione ante Pascha, ut sanctificarent seipsos. 56Quaerebant ergo Iesum et colloquebantur ad invicem in templo stantes: «Quid videtur vobis? Numquid veniet ad diem festum?». 57Dederant autem pontifices et pharisaei mandatum, ut si quis cognoverit, ubi sit, indicet, ut

apprehendant eum. **[12]** 1Iesus ergo ante sex dies Paschae venit Bethaniam, ubi erat Lazarus, quem
suscitavit a mortuis Iesus. 2Fecerunt ergo ei cenam ibi, et Martha ministrabat, Lazarus vero unus erat ex
discumbentibus cum eo. 3Maria ergo accepit libram unguenti nardi puri, pretiosi et unxit pedes Iesu et
extersit capillis suis pedes eius; domus autem impleta est ex odore unguenti. 4Dicit autem Iudas
Iscariotes, unus ex discipulis eius, qui erat eum traditurus: 5«Quare hoc unguentum non veniit trecentis
denariis et datum est egenis?». 6Dixit autem hoc, non quia de egenis pertinebat ad eum, sed quia fur erat
et, loculos habens, ea, quae mittebantur, portabat. 7Dixit ergo Iesus: «Sine illam, ut in diem sepulturae
meae servet illud. 8Pauperes enim semper habetis vobiscum, me autem non semper habetis». 9Cognovit
ergo turba multa ex Iudaeis quia illic est, et venerunt non propter Iesum tantum, sed ut et Lazarum
viderent, quem suscitavit a mortuis. 10Cogitaverunt autem principes sacerdotum, ut et Lazarum
interficerent, 11quia multi propter illum abibant ex Iudaeis et credebant in Iesum. 12In crastinum turba
multa, quae venerat ad diem festum, cum audissent quia venit Iesus Hierosolymam, 13acceperunt ramos
palmarum et processerunt obviam ei et clamabant: «*Hosanna! / Benedictus, qui venit in nomine Domini,*
/ et rex Israel!». 14Invenit autem Iesus asellum et sedit super eum, sicut scriptum est: 15«*Noli timere,
filia Sion.* / Ecce rex tuus venit / *sedens super pullum asinae*». 16Haec non cognoverunt discipuli eius
primum, sed quando glorificatus est Iesus, tunc recordati sunt quia haec erant scripta de eo, et haec
fecerunt ei. 17Testimonium ergo perhibebat turba, quae erat cum eo, quando Lazarum vocavit de
monumento et suscitavit eum a mortuis. 18Propterea et obviam venit ei turba, quia audierunt eum fecisse
hoc signum. 19Pharisaei ergo dixerunt ad semetipsos: «Videtis quia nihil proficitis? Ecce mundus post
eum abiit!». 20Erant autem Graeci quidam ex his, qui ascenderant, ut adorarent in die festo; 21hi ergo
accesserunt ad Philippum, qui erat a Bethsaida Galilaeae, et rogabant eum dicentes: «Domine, volumus
Iesum videre». 22Venit Philippus et dicit Andreae; venit Andreas et Philippus et dicunt Iesu. 23Iesus
autem respondet eis dicens: «Venit hora, ut glorificetur Filius hominis. 24Amen, amen dico vobis: Nisi
granum frumenti cadens in terram mortuum fuerit, ipsum solum manet; si autem mortuum fuerit,
multum fructum affert. 25Qui amat animam suam, perdit eam; et, qui odit animam suam in hoc mundo,
in vitam aeternam custodiet eam. 26Si quis mihi ministrat, me sequatur, et ubi sum ego, illic et minister
meus erit; si quis mihi ministraverit, honorificabit eum Pater. 27Nunc anima mea turbata est. Et quid
dicam? Pater, salvifica me ex hora hac? Sed propterea veni in horam hanc. 28Pater, glorifica tuum
nomen!». Venit ergo vox de caelo: «Et glorificavi et iterum glorificabo». 29Turba ergo, quae stabat et
audierat, dicebat tonitruum factum esse; alii dicebant: «Angelus ei locutus est». 30Respondit Iesus et
dixit: «Non propter me vox haec facta est sed propter vos. 31Nunc iudicium est huius mundi, nunc
princeps huius mundi eicietur foras; 32et ego, si exaltatus fuero a terra, omnes traham ad meipsum».
33Hoc autem dicebat significans, qua morte esset moriturus. 34Respondit ergo ei turba: «Nos audivimus
ex lege quia Christus manet in aeternum; et quomodo tu dicis: "Oportet exaltari Filium hominis"? Quis
est iste Filius hominis?». 35Dixit ergo eis Iesus: «Adhuc modicum tempus lumen in vobis est. Ambulate,
dum lucem habetis, ut non tenebrae vos comprehendant; et qui ambulat in tenebris, nescit quo vadat.
36Dum lucem habetis, credite in lucem, ut filii lucis fiatis». Haec locutus est Iesus et abiit et abscondit
se ab eis. 37Cum autem tanta signa fecisset coram eis, non credebant in eum, 38ut sermo Isaiae prophetae
impleretur, quem dixit: «*Domine, quis credidit auditui nostro, / et brachium Domini cui revelatum est?*».
39Propterea non poterant credere, quia iterum dixit Isaias: 40«*Excaecavit oculos eorum / et induravit
eorum cor, / ut non videant oculis / et intellegant corde et convertantur, / et sanem eos*». 41Haec dixit
Isaias, quia vidit gloriam eius et locutus est de eo. 42Verumtamen et ex principibus multi crediderunt in
eum, sed propter pharisaeos non confitebantur, ut de synagoga non eicerentur; 43dilexerunt enim gloriam
hominum magis quam gloriam Dei. 44Iesus autem clamavit et dixit: «Qui credit in me, non credit in me
sed in eum, qui misit me; 45et, qui videt me, videt eum, qui misit me. 46Ego lux in mundum veni, ut
omnis, qui credit in me, in tenebris non maneat. 47Et si quis audierit verba mea et non custodierit, ego
non iudico eum; non enim veni, ut iudicem mundum, sed ut salvificem mundum. 48Qui spernit me et
non accipit verba mea, habet, qui iudicet eum: sermo, quem locutus sum, ille iudicabit eum in novissimo
die, 49quia ego ex meipso non sum locutus, sed, qui misit me, Pater, ipse mihi mandatum dedit quid
dicam et quid loquar. 50Et scio quia mandatum eius vita aeterna est. Quae ergo ego loquor, sicut dixit
mihi Pater, sic loquor». **[13]** 1Ante diem autem festum Paschae, sciens Iesus quia venit eius hora, ut
transeat ex hoc mundo ad Patrem, cum dilexisset suos, qui erant in mundo, in finem dilexit eos. 2Et in
cena, cum Diabolus iam misisset in corde, ut traderet eum Iudas Simonis Iscariotis, 3sciens quia omnia
dedit ei Pater in manus et quia a Deo exivit et ad Deum vadit, 4surgit a cena et ponit vestimenta sua et,
cum accepisset linteum, praecinxit se. 5Deinde mittit aquam in pelvem et coepit lavare pedes
discipulorum et extergere linteo, quo erat praecinctus. 6Venit ergo ad Simonem Petrum. Dicit ei:
«Domine, tu mihi lavas pedes?». 7Respondit Iesus et dixit ei: «Quod ego facio, tu nescis modo, scies

autem postea». [8]Dicit ei Petrus: «Non lavabis mihi pedes in aeternum!». Respondit Iesus ei: «Si non lavero te, non habes partem mecum». [9]Dicit ei Simon Petrus: «Domine, non tantum pedes meos, sed et manus et caput!». [10]Dicit ei Iesus: «Qui lotus est non indiget nisi ut pedes lavet, sed est mundus totus; et vos mundi estis, sed non omnes». [11]Sciebat enim quisnam esset, qui traderet eum; propterea dixit: «Non estis mundi omnes». [12]Postquam ergo lavit pedes eorum et accepit vestimenta sua, cum recubuisset iterum, dixit eis: «Scitis quid fecerim vobis? [13]Vos vocatis me: "Magister" et: "Domine", et bene dicitis; sum etenim. [14]Si ergo ego lavi vestros pedes, Dominus et Magister, et vos debetis alter alterius lavare pedes. [15]Exemplum enim dedi vobis, ut, quemadmodum ego feci vobis, et vos faciatis. [16]Amen, amen dico vobis: Non est servus maior domino suo, neque apostolus maior eo, qui misit illum. [17]Si haec scitis, beati estis, si facitis ea. [18]Non de omnibus vobis dico, ego scio, quos elegerim, sed ut impleatur Scriptura: "*Qui manducat meum panem, levavit contra me calcaneum suum*". [19]Amodo dico vobis priusquam fiat, ut credatis cum factum fuerit, quia ego sum. [20]Amen, amen dico vobis: Qui accipit, si quem misero, me accipit; qui autem me accipit, accipit eum, qui me misit». [21]Cum haec dixisset Iesus, turbatus est spiritu et protestatus est et dixit: «Amen, amen dico vobis: Unus ex vobis tradet me». [22]Aspiciebant ad invicem discipuli, haesitantes de quo diceret. [23]Erat recumbens unus ex discipulis eius in sinu Iesu, quem diligebat Iesus. [24]Innuit ergo huic Simon Petrus, ut interrogaret: «Quis est, de quo dicit?». [25]Cum ergo recumberet ille ita supra pectus Iesu, dicit ei: «Domine, quis est?». [26]Respondet Iesus: «Ille est, cui ego intinctam buccellam porrexero». Cum ergo intinxisset buccellam dat Iudae Simonis Iscariotis. [27]Et post buccellam tunc introivit in illum Satanas. Dicit ergo ei Iesus: «Quod facis, fac citius». [28]Hoc autem nemo scivit discumbentium ad quid dixerit ei; [29]quidam enim putabant quia loculos habebat Iudas, quia dicit ei Iesus: «Eme ea, quae opus sunt nobis ad diem festum», aut egenis ut aliquid daret. [30]Cum ergo accepisset ille buccellam, exivit continuo; erat autem nox. [31]Cum ergo exisset, dicit Iesus: «Nunc clarificatus est Filius hominis, et Deus clarificatus est in eo; [32]si Deus clarificatus est in eo, et Deus clarificabit eum in semetipso, et continuo clarificabit eum. [33]Filioli, adhuc modicum vobiscum sum; quaeretis me, et sicut dixi Iudaeis: Quo ego vado, vos non potestis venire, et vobis dico modo. [34]Mandatum novum do vobis, ut diligatis invicem; sicut dilexi vos, ut et vos diligatis invicem. [35]In hoc cognoscent omnes quia mei discipuli estis: si dilectionem habueritis ad invicem». [36]Dicit ei Simon Petrus: «Domine, quo vadis?». Respondit Iesus: «Quo vado, non potes me modo sequi, sequeris autem postea». [37]Dicit ei Petrus: «Domine, quare non possum te sequi modo? Animam meam pro te ponam». [38]Respondet Iesus: «Animam tuam pro me pones? Amen, amen dico tibi: Non cantabit gallus, donec me ter neges. **[14]** [1]Non turbetur cor vestrum. Creditis in Deum et in me credite. [2]In domo Patris mei mansiones multae sunt; si quo minus, dixissem vobis quia vado parare vobis locum? [3]Et si abiero et praeparavero vobis locum, iterum venio et accipiam vos ad meipsum, ut, ubi sum ego, et vos sitis. [4]Et quo ego vado, scitis viam». [5]Dicit ei Thomas: «Domine, nescimus quo vadis; quomodo possumus viam scire?». [6]Dicit ei Iesus: «Ego sum via et veritas et vita; nemo venit ad Patrem nisi per me. [7]Si cognovistis me, et Patrem meum utique cognoscetis; et amodo cognoscitis eum et vidistis eum». [8]Dicit ei Philippus: «Domine, ostende nobis Patrem, et sufficit nobis». [9]Dicit ei Iesus: «Tanto tempore vobiscum sum, et non cognovisti me, Philippe? Qui vidit me, vidit Patrem. Quomodo tu dicis: "Ostende nobis Patrem"? [10]Non credis quia ego in Patre, et Pater in me est? Verba, quae ego loquor vobis, a meipso non loquor; Pater autem in me manens facit opera sua. [11]Credite mihi quia ego in Patre, et Pater in me est; alioquin propter opera ipsa credite. [12]Amen, amen dico vobis: Qui credit in me, opera, quae ego facio, et ipse faciet et maiora horum faciet, quia ego ad Patrem vado. [13]Et quodcumque petieritis in nomine meo, hoc faciam, ut glorificetur Pater in Filio; [14]si quid petieritis me in nomine meo, ego faciam. [15]Si diligitis me, mandata mea servabitis; [16]et ego rogabo Patrem, et alium Paraclitum dabit vobis, ut maneat vobiscum in aeternum, [17]Spiritum veritatis, quem mundus non potest accipere, quia non videt eum nec cognoscit. Vos cognoscitis eum, quia apud vos manet; et in vobis erit. [18]Non relinquam vos orphanos, venio ad vos. [19]Adhuc modicum, et mundus me iam non videt; vos autem videtis me, quia ego vivo et vos vivetis. [20]In illo die vos cognoscetis quia ego sum in Patre meo, et vos in me et ego in vobis. [21]Qui habet mandata mea et servat ea, ille est qui diligit me; qui autem diligit me, diligetur a Patre meo, et ego diligam eum et manifestabo ei meipsum». [22]Dicit ei Iudas, non ille Iscariotes: «Domine, et quid factum est, quia nobis manifestaturus es teipsum et non mundo?». [23]Respondit Iesus et dixit ei: «Si quis diligit me, sermonem meum servabit, et Pater meus diliget eum, et ad eum veniemus et mansionem apud eum faciemus; [24]qui non diligit me, sermones meos non servat. Et sermo quem auditis, non est meus, sed eius qui misit me, Patris. [25]Haec locutus sum vobis apud vos manens. [26]Paraclitus autem, Spiritus Sanctus, quem mittet Pater in nomine meo, ille vos docebit omnia et suggeret vobis omnia, quae dixi vobis. [27]Pacem relinquo vobis, pacem meam do vobis; non quomodo mundus dat, ego do vobis. Non turbetur cor vestrum neque formidet. [28]Audistis quia ego dixi vobis:

Vado et venio ad vos. Si diligeretis me, gauderetis quia vado ad Patrem, quia Pater maior me est. 29Et
nunc dixi vobis, priusquam fiat, ut, cum factum fuerit, credatis. 30Iam non multa loquar vobiscum, venit
enim princeps mundi et in me non habet quidquam, 31sed, ut cognoscat mundus quia diligo Patrem, et
sicut mandatum dedit mihi Pater, sic facio. Surgite, eamus hinc. **[15]** 1Ego sum vitis vera, et Pater
meus agricola est. 2Omnem palmitem in me non ferentem fructum, tollit eum; et omnem, qui fert
fructum, purgat eum, ut fructum plus afferat. 3Iam vos mundi estis propter sermonem, quem locutus
sum vobis. 4Manete in me, et ego in vobis. Sicut palmes non potest ferre fructum a semetipso, nisi
manserit in vite, sic nec vos, nisi in me manseritis. 5Ego sum vitis, vos palmites. Qui manet in me, et
ego in eo, hic fert fructum multum, quia sine me nihil potestis facere. 6Si quis in me non manserit,
missus est foras sicut palmes et aruit, et colligunt eos et in ignem mittunt, et ardent. 7Si manseritis in
me, et verba mea in vobis manserint, quodcumque volueritis, petite, et fiet vobis. 8In hoc clarificatus est
Pater meus, ut fructum multum afferatis et efficiamini mei discipuli. 9Sicut dilexit me Pater, et ego dilexi
vos; manete in dilectione mea. 10Si praecepta mea servaveritis, manebitis in dilectione mea, sicut ego
Patris mei praecepta servavi et maneo in eius dilectione. 11Haec locutus sum vobis, ut gaudium meum
in vobis sit, et gaudium vestrum impleatur. 12Hoc est praeceptum meum, ut diligatis invicem, sicut dilexi
vos; 13maiorem hac dilectionem nemo habet, ut animam suam quis ponat pro amicis suis. 14Vos amici
mei estis, si feceritis, quae ego praecipio vobis. 15Iam non dico vos servos, quia servus nescit quid facit
dominus eius; vos autem dixi amicos, quia omnia, quae audivi a Patre meo, nota feci vobis. 16Non vos
me elegistis, sed ego elegi vos et posui vos, ut vos eatis et fructum afferatis, et fructus vester maneat, ut
quodcumque petieritis Patrem in nomine meo, det vobis. 17Haec mando vobis, ut diligatis invicem. 18Si
mundus vos odit, scitote quia me priorem vobis odio habuit. 19Si de mundo essetis, mundus, quod suum
est, diligeret; quia vero de mundo non estis, sed ego elegi vos de mundo, propterea odit vos mundus.
20Mementote sermonis, quem ego dixi vobis: Non est servus maior domino suo. Si me persecuti sunt,
et vos persequentur; si sermonem meum servaverunt, et vestrum servabunt. 21Sed haec omnia facient
vobis propter nomen meum, quia nesciunt eum, qui misit me. 22Si non venissem et locutus fuissem eis,
peccatum non haberent; nunc autem excusationem non habent de peccato suo. 23Qui me odit, et Patrem
meum odit. 24Si opera non fecissem in eis, quae nemo alius fecit, peccatum non haberent; nunc autem
et viderunt et oderunt et me et Patrem meum. 25Sed ut impleatur sermo, qui in lege eorum scriptus est:
"*Odio me habuerunt gratis*". 26Cum autem venerit Paraclitus, quem ego mittam vobis a Patre, Spiritum
veritatis, qui a Patre procedit, ille testimonium perhibebit de me; 27sed et vos testimonium perhibetis,
quia ab initio mecum estis. **[16]** 1Haec locutus sum vobis, ut non scandalizemini. 2Absque synagogis
facient vos; sed venit hora, ut omnis, qui interficit vos, arbitretur obsequium se praestare Deo. 3Et haec
facient, quia non noverunt Patrem neque me. 4Sed haec locutus sum vobis, ut, cum venerit hora eorum,
reminiscamini eorum, quia ego dixi vobis. Haec autem vobis ab initio non dixi, quia vobiscum eram.
5At nunc vado ad eum, qui me misit, et nemo ex vobis interrogat me: "Quo vadis?". 6Sed quia haec
locutus sum vobis, tristitia implevit cor vestrum. 7Sed ego veritatem dico vobis: Expedit vobis, ut ego
vadam. Si enim non abiero, Paraclitus non veniet ad vos; si autem abiero, mittam eum ad vos. 8Et cum
venerit ille, arguet mundum de peccato et de iustitia et de iudicio: 9de peccato quidem, quia non credunt
in me; 10de iustitia vero, quia ad Patrem vado, et iam non videtis me; 11de iudicio autem, quia princeps
mundi huius iudicatus est. 12Adhuc multa habeo vobis dicere, sed non potestis portare modo. 13Cum
autem venerit ille, Spiritus veritatis, deducet vos in omnem veritatem; non enim loquetur a semetipso,
sed quaecumque audiet, loquetur et, quae ventura sunt, annuntiabit vobis. 14Ille me clarificabit, quia de
meo accipiet et annuntiabit vobis. 15Omnia, quaecumque habet Pater, mea sunt; propterea dixi quia de
meo accipit et annuntiabit vobis. 16Modicum, et iam non videtis me, et iterum modicum, et videbitis
me». 17Dixerunt ergo ex discipulis eius ad invicem: «Quid est hoc, quod dicit nobis: "Modicum, et non
videtis me, et iterum modicum et videbitis me" et: "Vado ad Patrem"?». 18Dicebant ergo: «Quid est hoc,
quod dicit: "Modicum"? Nescimus quid loquitur». 19Cognovit Iesus quia volebant eum interrogare et
dixit eis: «De hoc quaeritis inter vos quia dixi: "Modicum, et non videtis me, et iterum modicum, et
videbitis me"? 20Amen, amen dico vobis quia plorabitis et flebitis vos, mundus autem gaudebit; vos
contristabimini, sed tristitia vestra vertetur in gaudium. 21Mulier, cum parit, tristitiam habet, quia venit
hora eius; cum autem pepererit puerum, iam non meminit pressurae propter gaudium quia natus est
homo in mundum. 22Et vos igitur nunc quidem tristitiam habetis; iterum autem videbo vos, et gaudebit
cor vestrum, et gaudium vestrum nemo tollit a vobis. 23Et in illo die me non rogabitis quidquam. Amen,
amen dico vobis: Si quid petieritis Patrem in nomine meo, dabit vobis. 24Usque modo non petistis
quidquam in nomine meo. Petite et accipietis, ut gaudium vestrum sit plenum. 25Haec in proverbiis
locutus sum vobis; venit hora, cum iam non in proverbiis loquar vobis, sed palam de Patre annuntiabo
vobis. 26Illo die in nomine meo petetis, et non dico vobis quia ego rogabo Patrem de vobis; 27ipse enim

Pater amat vos, quia vos me amastis et credidistis quia ego a Deo exivi. 28Exivi a Patre et veni in
mundum; iterum relinquo mundum et vado ad Patrem». 29Dicunt discipuli eius: «Ecce nunc palam
loqueris, et proverbium nullum dicis. 30Nunc scimus quia scis omnia et non opus est tibi, ut quis te
interroget; in hoc credimus quia a Deo existi». 31Respondit eis Iesus: «Modo creditis? 32Ecce venit hora
et iam venit, ut dispergamini unusquisque in propria et me solum relinquatis; et non sum solus, quia
Pater mecum est. 33Haec locutus sum vobis, ut in me pacem habeatis; in mundo pressuram habetis, sed
confidite, ego vici mundum». **[17]** 1Haec locutus est Iesus; et sublevatis oculis suis in caelum dixit:
«Pater, venit hora: clarifica Filium tuum, ut Filius clarificet te, 2sicut dedisti ei potestatem omnis carnis,
ut omne, quod dedisti ei, det eis vitam aeternam. 3Haec est autem vita aeterna, ut cognoscant te solum
verum Deum et, quem misisti, Iesum Christum. 4Ego te clarificavi super terram: opus consummavi,
quod dedisti mihi, ut faciam; 5et nunc clarifica me tu, Pater, apud temetipsum claritate, quam habebam,
priusquam mundus esset, apud te. 6Manifestavi nomen tuum hominibus, quos dedisti mihi de mundo.
Tui erant, et mihi eos dedisti, et sermonem tuum servaverunt. 7Nunc cognoverunt quia omnia, quae
dedisti mihi, abs te sunt, 8quia verba, quae dedisti mihi, dedi eis, et ipsi acceperunt et cognoverunt vere
quia a te exivi, et crediderunt quia tu me misisti. 9Ego pro eis rogo; non pro mundo rogo, sed pro his,
quos dedisti mihi, quia tui sunt, 10et mea omnia tua sunt et tua mea; et clarificatus sum in eis. 11Et iam
non sum in mundo, et hi in mundo sunt, et ego ad te venio. Pater sancte, serva eos in nomine tuo, quod
dedisti mihi, ut sint unum sicut nos. 12Cum essem cum eis, ego servabam eos in nomine tuo, quod
dedisti mihi et custodivi, et nemo ex his periit nisi filius perditionis, ut Scriptura impleatur. 13Nunc
autem ad te venio et haec loquor in mundo, ut habeant gaudium meum impletum in semetipsis. 14Ego
dedi eis sermonem tuum, et mundus odio eos habuit, quia non sunt de mundo, sicut ego non sum de
mundo. 15Non rogo, ut tollas eos de mundo, sed ut serves eos ex Malo. 16De mundo non sunt, sicut ego
non sum de mundo. 17Sanctifica eos in veritate; sermo tuus veritas est. 18Sicut me misisti in mundum,
et ego misi eos in mundum; 19et pro eis ego sanctifico meipsum, ut sint et ipsi sanctificati in veritate.
20Non pro his autem rogo tantum, sed et pro eis, qui credituri sunt per verbum eorum in me, 21ut omnes
unum sint, sicut tu, Pater, in me et ego in te, ut et ipsi in nobis unum sint: ut mundus credat quia tu me
misisti. 22Et ego claritatem, quam dedisti mihi, dedi illis, ut sint unum, sicut nos unum sumus; 23ego
in eis, et tu in me, ut sint consummati in unum: ut cognoscat mundus quia tu me misisti et dilexisti eos,
sicut me dilexisti. 24Pater, quod dedisti mihi, volo, ut ubi ego sum, et illi sint mecum, ut videant
claritatem meam, quam dedisti mihi, quia dilexisti me ante constitutionem mundi. 25Pater iuste, et
mundus te non cognovit; ego autem te cognovi et hi cognoverunt quia tu me misisti, 26et notum feci eis
nomen tuum et notum faciam, ut dilectio, qua dilexisti me, in ipsis sit, et ego in ipsis». **[18]** 1Haec cum
dixisset Iesus, egressus est cum discipulis suis trans torrentem Cedron, ubi erat hortus, in quem introivit
ipse et discipuli eius. 2Sciebat autem et Iudas, qui tradebat eum, locum, quia frequenter Iesus convenerat
illuc cum discipulis suis. 3Iudas ergo, cum accepisset cohortem et a pontificibus et pharisaeis ministros,
venit illuc cum lanternis et facibus et armis. 4Iesus itaque, sciens omnia, quae ventura erant super eum,
processit et dicit eis: «Quem quaeritis?». 5Responderunt ei: «Iesum Nazarenum». Dicit eis: «Ego sum!».
Stabat autem et Iudas, qui tradebat eum, cum ipsis. 6Ut ergo dixit eis: «Ego sum!», abierunt retrorsum
et ceciderunt in terram. 7Iterum ergo eos interrogavit: «Quem quaeritis?». Illi autem dixerunt: «Iesum
Nazarenum». 8Respondit Iesus: «Dixi vobis: Ego sum! Si ergo me quaeritis, sinite hos abire», 9ut
impleretur sermo quem dixit: «Quos dedisti mihi, non perdidi ex ipsis quemquam». 10Simon ergo
Petrus, habens gladium, eduxit eum et percussit pontificis servum et abscidit eius auriculam dextram.
Erat autem nomen servo Malchus. 11Dixit ergo Iesus Petro: «Mitte gladium in vaginam; calicem, quem
dedit mihi Pater, non bibam illum?». 12Cohors ergo et tribunus et ministri Iudaeorum comprehenderunt
Iesum et ligaverunt eum 13et adduxerunt ad Annam primum; erat enim socer Caiphae, qui erat pontifex
anni illius. 14Erat autem Caiphas, qui consilium dederat Iudaeis: «Expedit unum hominem mori pro
populo». 15Sequebatur autem Iesum Simon Petrus et alius discipulus. Discipulus autem ille erat notus
pontifici et introivit cum Iesu in atrium pontificis; 16Petrus autem stabat ad ostium foris. Exivit ergo
discipulus alius, qui erat notus pontifici, et dixit ostiariae et introduxit Petrum. 17Dicit ergo Petro ancilla
ostiaria: «Numquid et tu ex discipulis es hominis istius?». Dicit ille: «Non sum!». 18Stabant autem servi
et ministri, qui prunas fecerant, quia frigus erat, et calefaciebant se; erat autem cum eis et Petrus stans
et calefaciens se. 19Pontifex ergo interrogavit Iesum de discipulis suis et de doctrina eius. 20Respondit
ei Iesus: «Ego palam locutus sum mundo; ego semper docui in synagoga et in templo, quo omnes Iudaei
conveniunt, et in occulto locutus sum nihil. 21Quid me interrogas? Interroga eos, qui audierunt quid
locutus sum ipsis; ecce hi sciunt, quae dixerim ego». 22Haec autem cum dixisset, unus assistens
ministrorum dedit alapam Iesu dicens: «Sic respondes pontifici?». 23Respondit ei Iesus: «Si male
locutus sum, testimonium perhibe de malo; si autem bene, quid me caedis?». 24Misit ergo eum Annas

ligatum ad Caipham pontificem. 25Erat autem Simon Petrus stans et calefaciens se. Dixerunt ergo ei:
«Numquid et tu ex discipulis eius es?». Negavit ille et dixit: «Non sum!». 26Dicit unus ex servis
pontificis, cognatus eius, cuius abscidit Petrus auriculam: «Nonne ego te vidi in horto cum illo?».
27Iterum ergo negavit Petrus; et statim gallus cantavit. 28Adducunt ergo Iesum a Caipha in praetorium.
Erat autem mane. Et ipsi non introierunt in praetorium, ut non contaminarentur, sed manducarent
Pascha. 29Exivit ergo Pilatus ad eos foras et dicit: «Quam accusationem affertis adversus hominem
hunc?». 30Responderunt et dixerunt ei: «Si non esset hic malefactor, non tibi tradidissemus eum».
31Dixit ergo eis Pilatus: «Accipite eum vos et secundum legem vestram iudicate eum!». Dixerunt ei
Iudaei: «Nobis non licet interficere quemquam», 32ut sermo Iesu impleretur, quem dixit, significans qua
esset morte moriturus. 33Introivit ergo iterum in praetorium Pilatus et vocavit Iesum et dixit ei: «Tu es
rex Iudaeorum?». 34Respondit Iesus: «A temetipso tu hoc dicis, an alii tibi dixerunt de me?».
35Respondit Pilatus: «Numquid ego Iudaeus sum? Gens tua et pontifices tradiderunt te mihi; quid
fecisti?». 36Respondit Iesus: «Regnum meum non est de mundo hoc; si ex hoc mundo esset regnum
meum, ministri mei decertarent, ut non traderer Iudaeis; nunc autem meum regnum non est hinc».
37Dixit itaque ei Pilatus: «Ergo rex es tu?». Respondit Iesus: «Tu dicis quia rex sum. Ego in hoc natus
sum et ad hoc veni in mundum, ut testimonium perhibeam veritati; omnis, qui est ex veritate, audit
meam vocem». 38Dicit ei Pilatus: «Quid est veritas?». Et cum hoc dixisset, iterum exivit ad Iudaeos et
dicit eis: «Ego nullam invenio in eo causam. 39Est autem consuetudo vobis, ut unum dimittam vobis
in Pascha; vultis ergo dimittam vobis regem Iudaeorum?». 40Clamaverunt ergo rursum dicentes: «Non
hunc, sed Barabbam!». Erat autem Barabbas latro. **[19]** 1Tunc ergo apprehendit Pilatus Iesum et
flagellavit. 2Et milites, plectentes coronam de spinis, imposuerunt capiti eius et veste purpurea
circumdederunt eum; 3et veniebant ad eum et dicebant: «Ave, rex Iudaeorum!», et dabant ei alapas. 4Et
exiit iterum Pilatus foras et dicit eis: «Ecce adduco vobis eum foras, ut cognoscatis quia in eo invenio
causam nullam». 5Exiit ergo Iesus foras, portans spineam coronam et purpureum vestimentum. Et dicit
eis: «Ecce homo!». 6Cum ergo vidissent eum pontifices et ministri, clamaverunt dicentes: «Crucifige,
crucifige!». Dicit eis Pilatus: «Accipite eum vos et crucifigite; ego enim non invenio in eo causam».
7Responderunt ei Iudaei: «Nos legem habemus, et secundum legem debet mori, quia Filium Dei se
fecit». 8Cum ergo audisset Pilatus hunc sermonem, magis timuit 9et ingressus est praetorium iterum et
dicit ad Iesum: «Unde es tu?». Iesus autem responsum non dedit ei. 10Dicit ergo ei Pilatus: «Mihi non
loqueris? Nescis quia potestatem habeo dimittere te et potestatem habeo crucifigere te?». 11Respondit
Iesus: «Non haberes potestatem adversum me ullam, nisi tibi esset datum desuper; propterea qui tradidit
me tibi, maius peccatum habet». 12Exinde quaerebat Pilatus dimittere eum; Iudaei autem clamabant
dicentes: «Si hunc dimittis, non es amicus Caesaris! Omnis, qui se regem facit, contradicit Caesari».
13Pilatus ergo, cum audisset hos sermones, adduxit foras Iesum et sedit pro tribunali in locum, qui
dicitur Lithostrotos, Hebraice autem Gabbatha. 14Erat autem Parasceve Paschae, hora erat quasi sexta.
Et dicit Iudaeis: «Ecce rex vester!». 15Clamaverunt ergo illi: «Tolle, tolle, crucifige eum!». Dicit eis
Pilatus: «Regem vestrum crucifigam?». Responderunt pontifices: «Non habemus regem nisi Caesarem».
16Tunc ergo tradidit eis illum, ut crucifigeretur. Susceperunt ergo Iesum. 17Et baiulans sibi crucem exivit
in eum, qui dicitur Calvariae locum, quod Hebraice dicitur Golgotha, 18ubi eum crucifixerunt et cum eo
alios duos hinc et hinc, medium autem Iesum. 19Scripsit autem et titulum Pilatus et posuit super crucem;
erat autem scriptum: «Iesus Nazarenus Rex Iudaeorum». 20Hunc ergo titulum multi legerunt Iudaeorum,
quia prope civitatem erat locus, ubi crucifixus est Iesus; et erat scriptum Hebraice, Latine, Graece.
21Dicebant ergo Pilato pontifices Iudaeorum: «Noli scribere: Rex Iudaeorum, sed: Ipse dixit: 'Rex sum
Iudaeorum'». 22Respondit Pilatus: «Quod scripsi, scripsi!». 23Milites ergo cum crucifixissent Iesum,
acceperunt vestimenta eius et fecerunt quattuor partes, unicuique militi partem, et tunicam. Erat autem
tunica inconsutilis, desuper contexta per totum. 24Dixerunt ergo ad invicem: «Non scindamus eam, sed
sortiamur de illa, cuius sit», ut Scriptura impleatur dicens: «*Partiti sunt vestimenta mea sibi / et in
vestem meam miserunt sortem*». Et milites quidem haec fecerunt. 25Stabant autem iuxta crucem Iesu
mater eius et soror matris eius, Maria Cleopae, et Maria Magdalene. 26Cum vidisset ergo Iesus matrem
et discipulum stantem, quem diligebat, dicit matri: «Mulier, ecce filius tuus». 27Deinde dicit discipulo:
«Ecce mater tua». Et ex illa hora accepit eam discipulus in sua. 28Post hoc sciens Iesus quia iam omnia
consummata sunt, ut consummaretur Scriptura, dicit: «Sitio». 29Vas positum erat aceto plenum;
spongiam ergo plenam aceto hyssopo circumponentes, obtulerunt ori eius. 30Cum ergo accepisset
acetum, Iesus dixit: «Consummatum est!». Et inclinato capite tradidit spiritum. 31Iudaei ergo, quoniam
Parasceve erat, ut non remanerent in cruce corpora sabbato, erat enim magnus dies illius sabbati,
rogaverunt Pilatum, ut frangerentur eorum crura, et tollerentur. 32Venerunt ergo milites et primi quidem
fregerunt crura et alterius, qui crucifixus est cum eo; 33ad Iesum autem cum venissent, ut viderunt eum

iam mortuum, non fregerunt eius crura, [34]sed unus militum lancea latus eius aperuit, et continuo exivit sanguis et aqua. [35]Et qui vidit, testimonium perhibuit, et verum est eius testimonium, et ille scit quia vera dicit, ut et vos credatis. [36]Facta sunt enim haec, ut Scriptura impleatur: «*Os non comminuetur eius*», [37]et iterum alia Scriptura dicit: «*Videbunt in quem transfixerunt*». [38]Post haec autem rogavit Pilatum Ioseph ab Arimathaea, qui erat discipulus Iesu, occultus autem propter metum Iudaeorum, ut tolleret corpus Iesu; et permisit Pilatus. Venit ergo et tulit corpus eius. [39]Venit autem et Nicodemus, qui venerat ad eum nocte primum, ferens mixturam myrrhae et aloes quasi libras centum. [40]Acceperunt ergo corpus Iesu et ligaverunt illud linteis cum aromatibus, sicut mos Iudaeis est sepelire. [41]Erat autem in loco, ubi crucifixus est, hortus, et in horto monumentum novum, in quo nondum quisquam positus erat. [42]Ibi ergo propter Parascevem Iudaeorum, quia iuxta erat monumentum, posuerunt Iesum. **[20]** [1]Prima autem sabbatorum Maria Magdalene venit mane, cum adhuc tenebrae essent, ad monumentum, et videt lapidem sublatum a monumento. [2]Currit ergo et venit ad Simonem Petrum et ad alium discipulum, quem amabat Iesus, et dicit eis: «Tulerunt Dominum de monumento, et nescimus, ubi posuerunt eum!». [3]Exiit ergo Petrus et ille alius discipulus, et veniebant ad monumentum. [4]Currebant autem duo simul, et ille alius discipulus praecucurrit citius Petro et venit primus ad monumentum; [5]et cum se inclinasset, videt posita linteamina, non tamen introivit. [6]Venit ergo et Simon Petrus sequens eum et introivit in monumentum; et videt linteamina posita [7]et sudarium, quod fuerat super caput eius, non cum linteaminibus positum, sed separatim involutum in unum locum. [8]Tunc ergo introivit et alter discipulus, qui venerat primus ad monumentum, et vidit et credidit. [9]Nondum enim sciebant Scripturam quia oportet eum a mortuis resurgere. [10]Abierunt ergo iterum ad semetipsos discipuli. [11]Maria autem stabat ad monumentum foris plorans. Dum ergo fleret, inclinavit se in monumentum [12]et videt duos angelos in albis sedentes, unum ad caput et unum ad pedes, ubi positum fuerat corpus Iesu. [13]Et dicunt ei illi: «Mulier, quid ploras?». Dicit eis: «Tulerunt Dominum meum, et nescio, ubi posuerunt eum». [14]Haec cum dixisset, conversa est retrorsum et videt Iesum stantem et non sciebat quia Iesus est. [15]Dicit ei Iesus: «Mulier, quid ploras? Quem quaeris?». Illa, existimans quia hortulanus esset, dicit ei: «Domine, si tu sustulisti eum, dicito mihi, ubi posuisti eum, et ego eum tollam». [16]Dicit ei Iesus: «Maria!». Conversa illa dicit ei Hebraice: «Rabbuni!»—quod dicitur Magister—. [17]Dicit ei Iesus: «Iam noli me tenere, nondum enim ascendi ad Patrem; vade autem ad fratres meos et dic eis: Ascendo ad Patrem meum et Patrem vestrum, et Deum meum et Deum vestrum». [18]Venit Maria Magdalene annuntians discipulis: «Vidi Dominum!», et quia haec dixit ei. [19]Cum esset ergo sero die illa prima sabbatorum, et fores essent clausae, ubi erant discipuli propter metum Iudaeorum, venit Iesus et stetit in medio et dicit eis: «Pax vobis!». [20]Et hoc cum dixisset, ostendit eis manus et latus. Gavisi sunt ergo discipuli, viso Domino. [21]Dixit ergo eis iterum: «Pax vobis! Sicut misit me Pater, et ego mitto vos». [22]Et cum hoc dixisset, insufflavit et dicit eis: «Accipite Spiritum Sanctum. [23]Quorum remiseritis peccata, remissa sunt eis; quorum retinueritis, retenta sunt». [24]Thomas autem, unus ex Duodecim, qui dicitur Didymus, non erat cum eis, quando venit Iesus. [25]Dicebant ergo ei alii discipuli: «Vidimus Dominum!». Ille autem dixit eis: «Nisi videro in manibus eius signum clavorum et mittam digitum meum in signum clavorum et mittam manum meam in latus eius, non credam». [26]Et post dies octo iterum erant discipuli eius intus, et Thomas cum eis. Venit Iesus ianuis clausis et stetit in medio et dixit: «Pax vobis!». [27]Deinde dicit Thomae: «Infer digitum tuum huc et vide manus meas et affer manum tuam et mitte in latus meum, et noli fieri incredulus sed fidelis!». [28]Respondit Thomas et dixit ei: «Dominus meus et Deus meus!». [29]Dicit ei Iesus: «Quia vidisti me, credidisti. Beati, qui non viderunt et crediderunt!». [30]Multa quidem et alia signa fecit Iesus in conspectu discipulorum suorum, quae non sunt scripta in libro hoc; [31]haec autem scripta sunt, ut credatis quia Iesus est Christus Filius Dei, et ut credentes vitam habeatis in nomine eius. **[21]** [1]Postea manifestavit se iterum Iesus discipulis ad mare Tiberiadis; manifestavit autem sic. [2]Erant simul Simon Petrus et Thomas, qui dicitur Didymus, et Nathanael, qui erat a Cana Galilaeae, et filii Zebedaei et alii ex discipulis eius duo. [3]Dicit eis Simon Petrus: «Vado piscari». Dicunt ei: «Venimus et nos tecum». Exierunt et ascenderunt in navem; et illa nocte nihil prendiderunt. [4]Mane autem iam facto, stetit Iesus in litore; non tamen sciebant discipuli quia Iesus est. [5]Dicit ergo eis Iesus: «Pueri, numquid pulmentarium habetis?». Responderunt ei: «Non». [6]Ille autem dixit eis: «Mittite in dexteram navigii rete et invenietis». Miserunt ergo et iam non valebant illud trahere a multitudine piscium. [7]Dicit ergo discipulus ille, quem diligebat Iesus, Petro: «Dominus est!». Simon ergo Petrus, cum audisset quia Dominus est, tunicam succinxit se, erat enim nudus, et misit se in mare; [8]alii autem discipuli navigio venerunt, non enim longe erant a terra, sed quasi cubitis ducentis, trahentes rete piscium. [9]Ut ergo descenderunt in terram, vident prunas positas et piscem superpositum et panem. [10]Dicit eis Iesus: «Afferte de piscibus, quos prendidistis nunc». [11]Ascendit ergo Simon Petrus et traxit rete in terram, plenum magnis piscibus centum quinquaginta tribus; et cum tanti essent, non est scissum rete. [12]Dicit eis Iesus: «Venite, prandete». Nemo autem audebat discipulorum interrogare eum: «Tu quis es?», scientes quia Dominus est. [13]Venit Iesus et accipit panem et dat eis et piscem similiter. [14]Hoc iam tertio manifestatus est Iesus discipulis, cum resurrexisset a mortuis. [15]Cum ergo prandissent, dicit Simoni Petro Iesus: «Simon Ioannis, diligis me plus his?». Dicit ei: «Etiam, Domine, tu scis quia amo te». Dicit ei: «Pasce agnos meos». [16]Dicit ei iterum secundo: «Simon Ioannis, diligis me?». Ait illi: «Etiam, Domine, tu scis quia amo te». Dicit ei: «Pasce oves meas». [17]Dicit ei tertio: «Simon Ioannis, amas me?». Contristatus est Petrus quia dixit ei tertio: «Amas me?», et dicit ei: «Domine, tu omnia scis, tu cognoscis quia amo te». Dicit ei: «Pasce oves meas. [18]Amen, amen dico tibi: Cum esses iunior, cingebas teipsum et ambulabas, ubi volebas; cum autem senueris, extendes manus tuas, et alius te cinget et ducet, quo non vis». [19]Hoc autem dixit significans qua morte clarificaturus esset Deum. Et hoc cum dixisset, dicit ei: «Sequere me». [20]Conversus Petrus videt illum discipulum, quem diligebat Iesus, sequentem, qui et recubuit in cena super pectus eius et dixit: «Domine, quis est qui tradit te?». [21]Hunc ergo cum vidisset Petrus, dicit Iesu: «Domine, hic autem quid?». [22]Dicit ei Iesus: «Si eum volo manere donec veniam, quid ad te? Tu me sequere». [23]Exivit ergo sermo iste in fratres quia discipulus ille non moritur. Non autem dixit ei Iesus: «Non moritur», sed: «Si eum volo manere donec veniam, quid ad te?». [24]Hic est discipulus, qui testimonium perhibet de his et scripsit haec, et scimus quia verum est testimonium eius. [25]Sunt autem et alia multa, quae fecit Iesus, quae si scribantur per singula, nec ipsum arbitror mundum capere eos, qui scribendi sunt, libros.

LIBER ACTUUM APOSTOLORUM

[1] [1]Primum quidem sermonem feci de omnibus, o Theophile, quae coepit Iesus facere et docere, [2]usque in diem, qua, cum praecepisset apostolis per Spiritum Sanctum, quos elegit, assumptus est; [3]quibus et praebuit seipsum vivum post passionem suam in multis argumentis, per dies quadraginta apparens eis et loquens ea, quae sunt de regno Dei. [4]Et convescens praecepit eis ab Hierosolymis ne discederent, sed exspectarent promissionem Patris: «Quam audistis a me, [5]quia Ioannes quidem baptizavit aqua, vos autem baptizabimini in Spiritu Sancto non post multos hos dies». [6]Igitur qui convenerant, interrogabant eum dicentes: «Domine, si in tempore hoc restitues regnum Israeli?». [7]Dixit autem eis: «Non est vestrum nosse tempora vel momenta, quae Pater posuit in sua potestate, [8]sed accipietis virtutem superveniente Sancto Spiritu in vos et eritis mihi testes et in Ierusalem et in omni Iudaea et Samaria et usque ad ultimum terrae». [9]Et cum haec dixisset, videntibus illis, elevatus est, et nubes suscepit eum ab oculis eorum. [10]Cumque intuerentur in caelum eunte illo, ecce duo viri astiterunt iuxta illos in vestibus albis, [11]qui et dixerunt: «Viri Galilaei, quid statis aspicientes in caelum? Hic Iesus, qui assumptus est a vobis in caelum, sic veniet quemadmodum vidistis eum euntem in caelum». [12]Tunc reversi sunt in Ierusalem a monte, qui vocatur Oliveti, qui est iuxta Ierusalem sabbati habens iter. [13]Et cum introissent, in cenaculum ascenderunt, ubi manebant et Petrus et Ioannes et Iacobus et Andreas, Philippus et Thomas, Bartholomaeus et Matthaeus, Iacobus Alphaei et Simon Zelotes et Iudas Iacobi. [14]Hi omnes erant perseverantes unanimiter in oratione cum mulieribus et Maria matre Iesu et fratribus eius. [15]Et in diebus illis exsurgens Petrus in medio fratrum dixit—erat autem turba hominum simul fere centum viginti—: [16]«Viri fratres, oportebat impleri Scripturam, quam praedixit Spiritus Sanctus per os David de Iuda, qui fuit dux eorum, qui comprehenderunt Iesum, [17]quia connumeratus erat in nobis et sortitus est sortem ministerii huius. [18]Hic quidem possedit agrum de mercede iniquitatis et pronus factus crepuit medius, et diffusa sunt omnia viscera eius. [19]Et notum factum est omnibus habitantibus Ierusalem, ita ut appellaretur ager ille lingua eorum Aceldamach, hoc est ager Sanguinis. [20]Scriptum est enim in libro Psalmorum: "*Fiat commoratio eius deserta, / et non sit qui inhabitet in ea*" / et: "*Episcopatum eius accipiat alius*". [21]Oportet ergo ex his viris, qui nobiscum congregati erant in omni tempore, quo intravit et exivit inter nos Dominus Iesus, [22]incipiens a baptismate Ioannis usque in diem, qua assumptus est a nobis, testem resurrectionis eius nobiscum fieri unum ex istis». [23]Et statuerunt duos, Ioseph, qui vocabatur Barsabbas, qui cognominatus est Iustus, et Matthiam. [24]Et orantes dixerunt: «Tu, Domine, qui corda nosti omnium, ostende quem elegeris ex his duobus unum [25]accipere locum ministerii huius et apostolatus, de quo praevaricatus est Iudas, ut abiret in locum suum». [26]Et dederunt sortes eis, et cecidit sors super Matthiam, et annumeratus est cum undecim apostolis. **[2]** [1]Et cum compleretur dies Pentecostes, erant omnes pariter in eodem loco. [2]Et factus est repente de caelo sonus tamquam advenientis spiritus vehementis et replevit totam domum, ubi erant sedentes. [3]Et apparuerunt illis dispertitae linguae tamquam ignis, seditque supra singulos eorum; [4]et repleti sunt omnes Spiritu Sancto et coeperunt loqui aliis linguis, prout Spiritus dabat eloqui illis. 5Erant autem in Ierusalem habitantes Iudaei, viri religiosi ex omni natione, quae sub caelo est; 6facta autem hac voce, convenit multitudo et confusa est, quoniam audiebat unusquisque lingua sua illos loquentes. 7Stupebant autem et mirabantur dicentes: «Nonne ecce omnes isti, qui loquuntur, Galilaei sunt? 8Et quomodo nos audimus unusquisque propria lingua nostra, in qua nati sumus? 9Parthi et Medi et Elamitae, et qui habitant Mesopotamiam, Iudaeam quoque et Cappadociam, Pontum et Asiam, 10Phrygiam quoque et Pamphyliam, Aegyptum et partes Libyae, quae est circa Cyrenem, et advenae Romani, 11Iudaei quoque et proselyti, Cretes et Arabes, audimus loquentes eos nostris linguis magnalia Dei». 12Stupebant autem omnes et haesitabant ad invicem dicentes: «Quidnam hoc vult esse?»; 13alii autem irridentes dicebant: «Musto pleni sunt isti». 14Stans autem Petrus cum Undecim levavit vocem suam et locutus est eis: «Viri Iudaei et, qui habitatis Ierusalem universi, hoc vobis notum sit, et auribus percipite verba mea. 15Non enim, sicut vos aestimatis, hi ebrii sunt, est enim hora diei tertia, 16sed hoc est, quod dictum est per prophetam Ioel: 17"*Et erit:* in novissimis diebus, dicit Deus, / *effundam de Spiritu meo super omnem carnem, / et prophetabunt filii vestri et filiae vestrae, / et iuvenes vestri visiones videbunt, / et seniores vestri somnia somniabunt*; / 18*et quidem super servos meos et super ancillas meas / in diebus illis effundam de Spiritu meo,* / et prophetabunt. / 19*Et dabo prodigia in caelo* sursum *et* signa *in terra* deorsum, / *sanguinem et ignem et vaporem fumi*; / 20*sol convertetur in tenebras / et luna in sanguinem, / antequam veniat dies Domini / magnus et manifestus. /* 21*Et erit: / omnis quicumque invocaverit nomen Domini, salvus erit*". 22Viri Israelitae, audite verba haec: Iesum Nazarenum, virum approbatum a Deo apud vos virtutibus et prodigiis et signis, quae fecit per illum Deus in medio vestri, sicut ipsi scitis, 23hunc definito consilio et praescientia Dei traditum per manum iniquorum affigentes interemistis, 24quem Deus suscitavit solutis doloribus mortis, iuxta quod impossibile erat teneri illum ab ea. 25David enim dicit circa eum: "*Providebam Dominum coram me semper, / quoniam a dextris meis est, ne commovear. /* 26*Propter hoc laetatum est cor meum, / et exsultavit lingua mea*; */ insuper et caro mea requiescet in spe. /* 27*Quoniam non derelinques animam meam in inferno / neque dabis Sanctum tuum videre corruptionem. /* 28*Notas fecisti mihi vias vitae, / replebis me iucunditate cum facie tua*". 29Viri fratres, liceat audenter dicere ad vos de patriarcha David quoniam et defunctus est et sepultus est et sepulcrum eius est apud nos usque in hodiernum diem; 30propheta igitur cum esset et sciret quia iure iurando *iurasset illi* Deus *de fructu lumbi eius sedere super sedem eius*, 31providens locutus est de resurrectione Christi quia *neque derelictus est in inferno, neque* caro eius *vidit corruptionem.* 32Hunc Iesum resuscitavit Deus, cuius omnes nos testes sumus. 33Dextera igitur Dei exaltatus et, promissione Spiritus Sancti accepta a Patre, effudit hunc, quem vos videtis et auditis. 34Non enim David ascendit in caelos; dicit autem ipse: "*Dixit Dominus Domino meo: Sede a dextris meis,* / 35*donec ponam inimicos tuos scabellum pedum tuorum*". 36Certissime ergo sciat omnis domus Israel quia et Dominum eum et Christum Deus fecit, hunc Iesum, quem vos crucifixistis». 37His auditis, compuncti sunt corde et dixerunt ad Petrum et reliquos apostolos: «Quid faciemus, viri fratres?». 38Petrus vero ad illos: «Paenitentiam, inquit, agite, et baptizetur unusquisque vestrum in nomine Iesu Christi in remissionem peccatorum vestrorum, et accipietis donum Sancti Spiritus; 39vobis enim est repromissio et filiis vestris et omnibus, qui longe sunt, quoscumque advocaverit Dominus Deus noster». 40Aliis etiam verbis pluribus testificatus est et exhortabatur eos dicens: «Salvamini a generatione ista prava». 41Qui ergo, recepto sermone eius, baptizati sunt; et appositae sunt in illa die animae circiter tria milia. 42Erant autem perseverantes in doctrina apostolorum et communicatione, in fractione panis et orationibus. 43Fiebat autem omni animae timor; multa quoque prodigia et signa per apostolos fiebant. 44Omnes autem, qui crediderant erant pariter et habebant omnia communia 45et possessiones et substantias vendebant et dividebant illas omnibus, prout cuique opus erat; 46cotidie quoque perdurantes unanimiter in templo et frangentes circa domos panem, sumebant cibum cum exsultatione et simplicitate cordis, 47collaudantes Deum et habentes gratiam ad omnem plebem. Dominus autem augebat, qui salvi fierent cotidie in idipsum. **[3]** 1Petrus autem et Ioannes ascendebant in templum ad horam orationis nonam. 2Et quidam vir, qui erat claudus ex utero matris suae, baiulabatur, quem ponebant cotidie ad portam templi, quae dicitur Speciosa, ut peteret eleemosynam ab introeuntibus in templum; 3is cum vidisset Petrum et Ioannem incipientes introire in templum, rogabat, ut eleemosynam acciperet. 4Intuens autem in eum Petrus cum Ioanne dixit: «Respice in nos». 5At ille intendebat in eos, sperans se aliquid accepturum ab eis. 6Petrus autem dixit: «Argentum et aurum non est mihi; quod autem habeo, hoc tibi do: In nomine Iesu Christi Nazareni surge et ambula!». 7Et apprehensa ei manu dextera, allevavit eum; et protinus consolidatae sunt bases eius et tali, 8et exsiliens stetit et ambulabat et intravit cum illis in templum, ambulans et exsiliens et laudans Deum. 9Et vidit omnis populus eum ambulantem et laudantem Deum; 10cognoscebant autem illum quoniam ipse erat, qui ad eleemosynam sedebat ad Speciosam portam templi, et impleti sunt stupore et exstasi

in eo, quod contigerat illi. [11]Cum teneret autem Petrum et Ioannem, concurrit omnis populus ad eos ad
porticum, qui appellatur Salomonis, stupentes. [12]Videns autem Petrus respondit ad populum: «Viri
Israelitae, quid miramini in hoc aut nos quid intuemini, quasi nostra virtute aut pietate fecerimus hunc
ambulare? [13]*Deus Abraham et Deus Isaac et Deus Iacob, Deus patrum nostrorum* glorificavit puerum
suum Iesum, quem vos quidem tradidistis et negastis ante faciem Pilati, iudicante illo dimitti; [14]vos
autem Sanctum et Iustum negastis et petistis virum homicidam donari vobis, [15]ducem vero vitae
interfecistis, quem Deus suscitavit a mortuis, cuius nos testes sumus. [16]Et in fide nominis eius hunc,
quem videtis et nostis, confirmavit nomen eius, et fides, quae per eum est, dedit huic integritatem istam
in conspectu omnium vestrum. [17]Et nunc, fratres, scio quia per ignorantiam fecistis, sicut et principes
vestri; [18]Deus autem, quae praenuntiavit per os omnium prophetarum pati Christum suum, implevit sic.
[19]Paenitemini igitur et convertimini, ut deleantur vestra peccata, [20]ut veniant tempora refrigerii a
conspectu Domini, et mittat eum, qui praedestinatus est vobis Christus, Iesum, [21]quem oportet caelum
quidem suscipere usque in tempora restitutionis omnium, quae locutus est Deus per os sanctorum a
saeculo suorum prophetarum. [22]Moyses quidem dixit: "*Prophetam vobis suscitabit Dominus Deus
vester de fratribus vestris tamquam me; ipsum audietis iuxta omnia, quaecumque locutus fuerit* vobis.
[23]*Erit autem: omnis anima, quae non audierit prophetam illum, exterminabitur de plebe*". [24]Et omnes
prophetae a Samuel et deinceps quotquot locuti sunt, etiam annuntiaverunt dies istos. [25]Vos estis filii
prophetarum et testamenti, quod disposuit Deus ad patres vestros dicens ad Abraham: "*Et in semine tuo
benedicentur omnes familiae terrae*". [26]Vobis primum Deus suscitans Puerum suum, misit eum
benedicentem vobis in avertendo unumquemque a nequitiis vestris». **[4]** [1]Loquentibus autem illis ad
populum, supervenerunt eis sacerdotes et magistratus templi et sadducaei, [2]dolentes quod docerent
populum et annuntiarent in Iesu resurrectionem ex mortuis, [3]et iniecerunt in eos manus et posuerunt
in custodiam in crastinum; erat enim iam vespera. [4]Multi autem eorum, qui audierant verbum,
crediderunt; et factus est numerus virorum quinque milia. [5]Factum est autem in crastinum, ut
congregarentur principes eorum et seniores et scribae in Ierusalem, [6]et Annas princeps sacerdotum et
Caiphas et Ioannes et Alexander et quotquot erant de genere sacerdotali, [7]et statuentes eos in medio
interrogabant: «In qua virtute aut in quo nomine fecistis hoc vos?». [8]Tunc Petrus repletus Spiritu Sancto
dixit ad eos: «Principes populi et seniores, [9]si nos hodie diiudicamur in benefacto hominis infirmi, in
quo iste salvus factus est, [10]notum sit omnibus vobis et omni plebi Israel quia in nomine Iesu Christi
Nazareni, quem vos crucifixistis, quem Deus suscitavit a mortuis, in hoc iste astat coram vobis sanus.
[11]Hic est *lapis, qui reprobatus est a vobis aedificatoribus, / qui factus est in caput anguli.* [12]Et non est
in alio aliquo salus, nec enim nomen aliud est sub caelo datum in hominibus, in quo oportet nos salvos
fieri». [13]Videntes autem Petri fiduciam et Ioannis, et comperto quod homines essent sine litteris et
idiotae, admirabantur et cognoscebant eos quoniam cum Iesu fuerant; [14]hominem quoque videntes
stantem cum eis, qui curatus fuerat, nihil poterant contradicere. [15]Iubentes autem eos foras extra
concilium secedere, conferebant ad invicem [16]dicentes: «Quid faciemus hominibus istis? Quoniam
quidem notum signum factum est per eos omnibus habitantibus in Ierusalem manifestum, et non
possumus negare; [17]sed ne amplius divulgetur in populum, comminemur eis, ne ultra loquantur in
nomine hoc ulli hominum». [18]Et vocantes eos denuntiaverunt, ne omnino loquerentur neque docerent
in nomine Iesu. [19]Petrus vero et Ioannes respondentes dixerunt ad eos: «Si iustum est in conspectu Dei
vos potius audire quam Deum, iudicate; [20]non enim possumus nos, quae vidimus et audivimus, non
loqui». [21]At illi ultra comminantes dimiserunt eos, nequaquam invenientes, quomodo punirent eos,
propter populum, quia omnes glorificabant Deum in eo, quod acciderat; [22]annorum enim erat amplius
quadraginta homo, in quo factum erat signum istud sanitatis. [23]Dimissi autem venerunt ad suos et
annuntiaverunt quanta ad eos principes sacerdotum et seniores dixissent. [24]Qui cum audissent
unanimiter levaverunt vocem ad Deum et dixerunt: «Domine, tu, qui *fecisti caelum et terram et mare et
omnia, quae in eis sunt,* [25]qui Spiritu Sancto per os patris nostri David pueri tui dixisti: "*Quare
fremuerunt gentes, / et populi meditati sunt inania? /* [26]*Astiterunt reges terrae, / et principes convenerunt
in unum / adversus Dominum et adversus Christum eius*". [27]Convenerunt enim vere in civitate ista
adversus sanctum puerum tuum Iesum, quem unxisti, Herodes et Pontius Pilatus cum gentibus et
populis Israel [28]facere, quaecumque manus tua et consilium praedestinavit fieri. [29]Et nunc, Domine,
respice in minas eorum et da servis tuis cum omni fiducia loqui verbum tuum, [30]in eo quod manum
tuam extendas ad sanitatem et signa et prodigia facienda per nomen sancti pueri tui Iesu». [31]Et cum
orassent, motus est locus, in quo erant congregati, et repleti sunt omnes Sancto Spiritu et loquebantur
verbum Dei cum fiducia. [32]Multitudinis autem credentium erat cor et anima una, nec quisquam eorum,
quae possidebant, aliquid suum esse dicebat, sed erant illis omnia communia. [33]Et virtute magna
reddebant apostoli testimonium resurrectionis Domini Iesu, et gratia magna erat super omnibus illis.

[34]Neque enim quisquam egens erat inter illos; quotquot enim possessores agrorum aut domorum erant,
vendentes afferebant pretia eorum, quae vendebant, [35]et ponebant ante pedes apostolorum; dividebatur
autem singulis, prout cuique opus erat. [36]Ioseph autem, qui cognominatus est Barnabas ab apostolis—
quod est interpretatum filius Consolationis—Levites, Cyprius genere, [37]cum haberet agrum, vendidit et
attulit pecuniam et posuit ante pedes apostolorum. **[5]** [1]Vir autem quidam nomine Ananias cum
Sapphira uxore sua vendidit agrum [2]et subtraxit de pretio, conscia quoque uxore, et afferens partem
quandam ad pedes apostolorum posuit. [3]Dixit autem Petrus: «Anania, cur implevit Satanas cor tuum
mentiri te Spiritui Sancto et subtrahere de pretio agri? [4]Nonne manens tibi manebat et venumdatum in
tua erat potestate? Quare posuisti in corde tuo hanc rem? Non es mentitus hominibus sed Deo!».
[5]Audiens autem Ananias haec verba cecidit et exspiravit; et factus est timor magnus in omnes audientes.
[6]Surgentes autem iuvenes involverunt eum et efferentes sepelierunt. [7]Factum est autem quasi horarum
trium spatium, et uxor ipsius nesciens, quod factum fuerat, introivit. [8]Respondit autem ei Petrus: «Dic
mihi si tanti agrum vendidistis?». At illa dixit: «Etiam, tanti». [9]Petrus autem ad eam: «Quid est quod
convenit vobis tentare Spiritum Domini? Ecce pedes eorum, qui sepelierunt virum tuum, ad ostium et
efferent te». [10]Confestim cecidit ante pedes eius et exspiravit; intrantes autem iuvenes invenerunt illam
mortuam et efferentes sepelierunt ad virum suum. [11]Et factus est timor magnus super universam
ecclesiam et in omnes, qui audierunt haec. [12]Per manus autem apostolorum fiebant signa et prodigia
multa in plebe; et erant unanimiter omnes in porticu Salomonis. [13]Ceterorum autem nemo audebat
coniungere se illis, sed magnificabat eos populus; [14]magis autem addebantur credentes Domino,
multitudines virorum ac mulierum, [15]ita ut et in plateas efferrent infirmos et ponerent in lectulis et
grabatis, ut, veniente Petro, saltem umbra illius obumbraret quemquam eorum. [16]Concurrebat autem et
multitudo vicinarum civitatum Ierusalem, afferentes aegros et vexatos ab spiritibus immundis, qui
curabantur omnes. [17]Exsurgens autem princeps sacerdotum et omnes, qui cum illo erant, quae est
haeresis sadducaeorum, repleti sunt zelo [18]et iniecerunt manus in apostolos et posuerunt illos in custodia
publica. [19]Angelus autem Domini per noctem aperuit ianuas carceris et educens eos dixit: [20]«Ite et
stantes loquimini in templo plebi omnia verba vitae huius». [21]Qui cum audissent, intraverunt diluculo
in templum et docebant. Adveniens autem princeps sacerdotum et, qui cum eo erant, convocaverunt
concilium et omnes seniores filiorum Israel et miserunt in carcerem, ut adducerentur illi. [22]Cum
venissent autem ministri, non invenerunt illos in carcere; reversi autem nuntiaverunt [23]dicentes:
«Carcerem invenimus clausum cum omni diligentia et custodes stantes ad ianuas, aperientes autem intus
neminem invenimus!». [24]Ut audierunt autem hos sermones, magistratus templi et principes sacerdotum
ambigebant de illis quidnam fieret illud. [25]Adveniens autem quidam nuntiavit eis: «Ecce viri, quos
posuistis in carcere, sunt in templo stantes et docentes populum». [26]Tunc abiens magistratus cum
ministris adducebat illos, non per vim, timebant enim populum, ne lapidarentur. [27]Et cum adduxissent
illos, statuerunt in concilio. Et interrogavit eos princeps sacerdotum [28]dicens: «Nonne praecipiendo
praecepimus vobis, ne doceretis in nomine isto? Et ecce replevistis Ierusalem doctrina vestra et vultis
inducere super nos sanguinem hominis istius». [29]Respondens autem Petrus et apostoli dixerunt:
«Oboedire oportet Deo magis quam hominibus. [30]Deus patrum nostrorum suscitavit Iesum, quem vos
interemistis suspendentes in ligno; [31]hunc Deus Ducem et Salvatorem exaltavit dextera sua ad dandam
paenitentiam Israel et remissionem peccatorum. [32]Et nos sumus testes horum verborum, et Spiritus
Sanctus, quem dedit Deus oboedientibus sibi». [33]Haec cum audissent, dissecabantur et volebant
interficere illos. [34]Surgens autem quidam in concilio pharisaeus nomine Gamaliel, legis doctor
honorabilis universae plebi, iussit foras ad breve homines fieri [35]dixitque ad illos: «Viri Israelitae,
attendite vobis super hominibus istis quid acturi sitis. [36]Ante hos enim dies exstitit Theudas dicens esse
se aliquem, cui consensit virorum numerus circiter quadringentorum; qui occisus est, et omnes,
quicumque credebant ei, dissipati sunt et redacti sunt ad nihilum. [37]Post hunc exstitit Iudas Galilaeus in
diebus census et avertit populum post se; et ipse periit, et omnes, quotquot consentiebant ei, dispersi
sunt. [38]Et nunc dico vobis: Discedite ab hominibus istis et sinite illos. Quoniam si est ex hominibus
consilium hoc aut opus hoc, dissolvetur; [39]si vero ex Deo est, non poteritis dissolvere eos, ne forte et
adversus Deum pugnantes inveniamini!». Consenserunt autem illi [40]et convocantes apostolos, caesis
denuntiaverunt, ne loquerentur in nomine Iesu, et dimiserunt eos. [41]Et illi quidem ibant gaudentes a
conspectu concilii quoniam digni habiti sunt pro nomine contumeliam pati; [42]et omni die in templo et
circa domos non cessabant docentes et evangelizantes Christum, Iesum. **[6]** [1]In diebus autem illis,
crescente numero discipulorum, factus est murmur Graecorum adversus Hebraeos, eo quod
neglegerentur in ministerio cotidiano viduae eorum. [2]Convocantes autem Duodecim multitudinem
discipulorum, dixerunt: «Non est aequum nos derelinquentes verbum Dei ministrare mensis;
[3]considerate vero, fratres, viros ex vobis boni testimonii septem plenos Spiritu et sapientia, quos

constituemus super hoc opus; 4nos vero orationi et ministerio verbi instantes erimus». 5Et placuit sermo
coram omni multitudine, et elegerunt Stephanum, virum plenum fide et Spiritu Sancto, et Philippum et
Prochorum et Nicanorem et Timonem et Parmenam et Nicolaum proselytum Antiochenum, 6quos
statuerunt ante conspectum apostolorum, et orantes imposuerunt eis manus. 7Et verbum Dei crescebat,
et multiplicabatur numerus discipulorum in Ierusalem valde; multa etiam turba sacerdotum oboediebat
fidei. 8Stephanus autem plenus gratia et virtute faciebat prodigia et signa magna in populo. 9Surrexerunt
autem quidam de synagoga, quae appellatur Libertinorum et Cyrenensium et Alexandrinorum et eorum,
qui erant a Cilicia et Asia, disputantes cum Stephano, 10et non poterant resistere sapientiae et Spiritui,
quo loquebatur. 11Tunc submiserunt viros, qui dicerent: «Audivimus eum dicentem verba blasphema in
Moysen et Deum»; 12et commoverunt plebem et seniores et scribas, et concurrentes rapuerunt eum et
adduxerunt in concilium 13et statuerunt testes falsos dicentes: «Homo iste non cessat loqui verba
adversus locum sanctum et legem; 14audivimus enim eum dicentem quoniam Iesus Nazarenus hic
destruet locum istum et mutabit consuetudines, quas tradidit nobis Moyses». 15Et intuentes eum omnes,
qui sedebant in concilio, viderunt faciem eius tamquam faciem angeli. **[7]** 1Dixit autem princeps
sacerdotum: «Si haec ita se habent?». 2Qui ait: «Viri fratres et patres, audite. Deus gloriae apparuit patri
nostro Abraham, cum esset in Mesopotamia, priusquam moraretur in Charran, 3*et dixit ad illum:* "*Exi
de terra tua et de cognatione tua, et veni in terram, quam tibi monstravero*". 4Tunc egressus de terra
Chaldaeorum habitavit in Charran. Et inde postquam mortuus est pater eius, transtulit illum in terram
istam, in qua nunc vos habitatis, 5et non dedit illi hereditatem in ea nec passum pedis et repromisit *dare
illi eam in possessionem et semini eius post ipsum,* cum non haberet filium. 6Locutus est autem sic
Deus: "*Erit semen eius accola in terra aliena, et servituti eos subicient et male tractabunt annis
quadringentis*; 7*et gentem, cui servierint, iudicabo ego*, dixit Deus, *et post haec exibunt et deservient
mihi in* loco *isto*". 8Et dedit illi testamentum circumcisionis; et sic genuit Isaac et circumcidit eum die
octava, et Isaac Iacob, et Iacob duodecim patriarchas. 9Et patriarchae aemulantes Ioseph vendiderunt in
Aegyptum; et erat Deus cum eo, 10et eripuit eum ex omnibus tribulationibus eius, et *dedit ei gratiam* et
sapientiam *in conspectu pharaonis regis Aegypti, et constituit eum praepositum super Aegyptum et super
omnem domum suam.* 11*Venit autem fames in universam Aegyptum et Chanaan* et tribulatio magna, et
non inveniebant cibos patres nostri. 12Cum audisset autem Iacob esse frumentum in Aegypto, misit
patres nostros primum; 13et in secundo cognitus est Ioseph a fratribus suis, et manifestatum est pharaoni
genus Ioseph. 14Mittens autem Ioseph accersivit Iacob patrem suum et omnem cognationem in
animabus septuaginta quinque, 15et descendit Iacob in Aegyptum. Et defunctus est ipse et patres nostri,
16et translati sunt in Sichem et positi sunt in sepulcro, quod emit Abraham pretio argenti a filiis Hemmor
in Sichem. 17Cum appropinquaret autem tempus repromissionis, quam confessus erat Deus Abrahae,
crevit populus et multiplicatus est in Aegypto, 18quoadusque *surrexit rex alius super Aegypto, qui non
sciebat Ioseph.* 19Hic circumveniens genus nostrum, afflixit patres, ut exponerent infantes suos, ne vivi
servarentur. 20Eodem tempore natus est Moyses et erat formosus coram Deo; qui nutritus est tribus
mensibus in domo patris. 21Exposito autem illo, sustulit eum filia pharaonis et enutrivit eum sibi in
filium; 22et eruditus est Moyses in omni sapientia Aegyptiorum et erat potens in verbis et in operibus
suis. 23Cum autem impleretur ei quadraginta annorum tempus, ascendit in cor eius, ut visitaret fratres
suos filios Israel. 24Et cum vidisset quendam iniuriam patientem, vindicavit et fecit ultionem ei, qui
opprimebatur, percusso Aegyptio. 25Existimabat autem intellegere fratres quoniam Deus per manum
ipsius daret salutem illis, at illi non intellexerunt. 26Atque sequenti die apparuit illis litigantibus et
reconciliabat eos in pacem dicens: "Viri, fratres estis; ut quid nocetis alterutrum?". 27Qui autem iniuriam
faciebat proximo, reppulit eum dicens: "*Quis te constituit principem et iudicem super nos?* 28*Numquid
interficere me tu vis, quemadmodum interfecisti heri Aegyptium?*". 29Fugit autem Moyses propter
verbum istud et factus est advena in terra Madian, ubi generavit filios duos. 30Et expletis annis
quadraginta, *apparuit illi in deserto montis* Sinai *angelus in ignis flamma rubi.* 31Moyses autem videns
admirabatur visum; accedente autem illo, ut consideraret, facta est vox Domini: 32"*Ego Deus patrum
tuorum, Deus Abraham et Isaac et Iacob*". Tremefactus autem Moyses non audebat considerare. 33*Dixit
autem illi Dominus:* "*Solve calceamentum pedum tuorum; locus enim, in quo stas, terra sancta est.*
34*Videns vidi afflictionem populi mei, qui est in Aegypto, et gemitum eorum audivi et descendi liberare
eos; et nunc veni, mittam te in Aegyptum*". 35Hunc Moysen, quem negaverunt dicentes: "*Quis te
constituit principem et iudicem*?", hunc Deus et principem et redemptorem misit cum manu angeli, qui
apparuit illi in rubo. 36Hic eduxit illos faciens prodigia et signa in terra Aegypti et in Rubro mari et in
deserto annis quadraginta. 37Hic est Moyses, qui dixit filiis Israel: "*Prophetam vobis suscitabit Deus de
fratribus vestris tamquam me*". 38Hic est qui fuit in ecclesia in solitudine cum angelo, qui loquebatur ei
in monte Sinai et cum patribus nostris, qui accepit verba viva dare nobis, 39cui noluerunt oboedire patres

nostri, sed reppulerunt et aversi sunt in cordibus suis in Aegyptum [40]dicentes ad Aaron: "*Fac nobis deos,
qui praecedant nos; Moyses enim hic, qui eduxit nos de terra Aegypti, nescimus quid factum sit ei*". [41]Et
vitulum fecerunt in illis diebus et obtulerunt hostiam simulacro et laetabantur in operibus manuum
suarum. [42]Convertit autem Deus et tradidit eos servire militiae caeli, sicut scriptum est in libro
Prophetarum: "*Numquid victimas et hostias obtulistis mihi / annis quadraginta in deserto, domus
Israel? /* [43]*Et suscepistis tabernaculum Moloch / et sidus dei vestri Rhaephan, / figuras, quas fecistis* ad
adorandum eas. / *Et transferam vos trans* Babylonem". [44]Tabernaculum testimonii erat patribus nostris
in deserto, sicut disposuit, qui loquebatur ad Moysen, ut faceret illud secundum formam, quam viderat;
[45]quod et induxerunt suscipientes patres nostri cum Iesu in possessionem gentium, quas expulit Deus a
facie patrum nostrorum usque in diebus David, [46]qui invenit gratiam ante Deum et petiit, ut inveniret
tabernaculum domui Iacob. [47]Salomon autem aedificavit illi domum. [48]Sed non Altissimus in
manufactis habitat, sicut propheta dicit: [49]"*Caelum mihi thronus est, / terra autem scabellum pedum
meorum. / Quam domum aedificabitis mihi, dicit Dominus, / aut quis locus requietionis meae? /* [50]*Nonne
manus mea fecit haec omnia?*". [51]Duri cervice et incircumcisi cordibus et auribus, vos semper Spiritui
Sancto resistitis, sicut patres vestri et vos. [52]Quem prophetarum non sunt persecuti patres vestri? Et
occiderunt eos, qui praenuntiabant de adventu Iusti, cuius vos nunc proditores et homicidae fuistis, [53]qui
accepistis legem in dispositionibus angelorum et non custodistis». [54]Audientes autem haec,
dissecabantur cordibus suis et stridebant dentibus in eum. [55]Cum autem esset plenus Spiritu Sancto,
intendens in caelum vidit gloriam Dei et Iesum stantem a dextris Dei [56]et ait: «Ecce video caelos apertos
et Filium hominis a dextris stantem Dei». [57]Exclamantes autem voce magna continuerunt aures suas et
impetum fecerunt unanimiter in eum [58]et eicientes extra civitatem lapidabant. Et testes deposuerunt
vestimenta sua secus pedes adulescentis, qui vocabatur Saulus. [59]Et lapidabant Stephanum invocantem
et dicentem: «Domine Iesu, suscipe spiritum meum». [60]Positis autem genibus clamavit voce magna:
«Domine, ne statuas illis hoc peccatum»; et cum hoc dixisset, obdormivit. **[8]** [1]Saulus autem erat
consentiens neci eius. Facta est autem in illa die persecutio magna in ecclesiam, quae erat Hierosolymis;
et omnes dispersi sunt per regiones Iudaeae et Samariae praeter apostolos. [2]Sepelierunt autem
Stephanum viri timorati et fecerunt planctum magnum super illum. [3]Saulus vero devastabat ecclesiam
per domos intrans et trahens viros ac mulieres tradebat in custodiam. [4]Igitur qui dispersi erant,
pertransierunt evangelizantes verbum. [5]Philippus autem descendens in civitatem Samariae praedicabat
illis Christum. [6]Intendebant autem turbae his, quae a Philippo dicebantur, unanimiter, audientes et
videntes signa, quae faciebat: [7]ex multis enim eorum, qui habebant spiritus immundos clamantes voce
magna exibant; multi autem paralytici et claudi curati sunt. [8]Factum est autem magnum gaudium in illa
civitate. [9]Vir autem quidem nomine Simon iampridem erat in civitate magias faciens et dementans
gentem Samariae, dicens esse se aliquem magnum, [10]cui attendebant omnes a minimo usque ad
maximum dicentes: «Hic est virtus Dei, quae vocatur Magna». [11]Attendebant autem eum propter quod
multo tempore magiis dementasset eos. [12]Cum vero credidissent Philippo evangelizanti de regno Dei et
nomine Iesu Christi, baptizabantur viri ac mulieres. [13]Tunc Simon et ipse credidit et, cum baptizatus
esset, adhaerebat Philippo; videns etiam signa et virtutes magnas fieri stupens admirabatur. [14]Cum
autem audissent apostoli, qui erant Hierosolymis, quia recepit Samaria verbum Dei, miserunt ad illos
Petrum et Ioannem, [15]qui cum descendissent, oraverunt pro ipsis, ut acciperent Spiritum Sanctum;
[16]nondum enim super quemquam illorum venerat, sed baptizati tantum erant in nomine Domini Iesu.
[17]Tunc imposuerunt manus super illos, et accipiebant Spiritum Sanctum. [18]Cum vidisset autem Simon
quia per impositionem manuum apostolorum daretur Spiritus, obtulit eis pecuniam [19]dicens: «Date et
mihi hanc potestatem, ut cuicumque imposuero manus, accipiat Spiritum Sanctum». [20]Petrus autem
dixit ad eum: «Argentum tuum tecum sit in perditionem, quoniam donum Dei existimasti pecunia
possideri! [21]Non est tibi pars neque sors in verbo isto, cor enim tuum non est rectum coram Deo.
[22]Paenitentiam itaque age ab hac nequitia tua et roga Dominum, si forte remittatur tibi haec cogitatio
cordis tui; [23]in felle enim amaritudinis et obligatione iniquitatis video te esse». [24]Respondens autem
Simon dixit: «Precamini vos pro me ad Dominum, ut nihil veniat super me horum, quae dixistis». [25]Et
illi quidem testificati et locuti verbum Domini, redibant Hierosolymam, et multis vicis Samaritanorum
evangelizabant. [26]Angelus autem Domini locutus est ad Philippum dicens: «Surge et vade contra
meridianum ad viam, quae descendit ab Ierusalem in Gazam; haec est deserta». [27]Et surgens abiit; et
ecce vir Aethiops eunuchus potens Candacis reginae Aethiopum, qui erat super omnem gazam eius, qui
venerat adorare in Ierusalem [28]et revertebatur sedens super currum suum et legebat prophetam Isaiam.
[29]Dixit autem Spiritus Philippo: «Accede et adiunge te ad currum istum». [30]Accurrens autem Philippus
audivit illum legentem Isaiam prophetam et dixit: «Putasne intellegis, quae legis?». [31]Qui ait: «Et
quomodo possum, si non aliquis ostenderit mihi?». Rogavitque Philippum, ut ascenderet et sederet

secum. [32]Locus autem Scripturae, quem legebat, erat hic: «*Tamquam ovis ad occisionem ductus est / et sicut agnus coram tondente se sine voce, / sic non aperit os suum. /* [33]*In humilitate eius iudicium eius sublatum est. / Generationem illius quis enarrabit? / Quoniam tollitur de terra vita eius*». [34]Respondens autem eunuchus Philippo dixit: «Obsecro te, de quo propheta dicit hoc? De se an de alio aliquo?». [35]Aperiens autem Philippus os suum et incipiens a Scriptura ista, evangelizavit illi Iesum. [36]Et dum irent per viam, venerunt ad quandam aquam, et ait eunuchus: «Ecce aqua; quid prohibet me baptizari?». [38]Et iussit stare currum, et descenderunt uterque in aquam Philippus et eunuchus, et baptizavit eum. [39]Cum autem ascendissent de aqua, Spiritus Domini rapuit Philippum, et amplius non vidit eum eunuchus; ibat autem per viam suam gaudens. [40]Philippus autem inventus est in Azoto et pertransiens evangelizabat civitatibus cunctis, donec veniret Caesaream. **[9]** [1]Saulus autem, adhuc spirans minarum et caedis in discipulos Domini, accessit ad principem sacerdotum [2]et petiit ab eo epistulas in Damascum ad synagogas, ut si quos invenisset huius viae, viros ac mulieres, vinctos perduceret in Ierusalem. [3]Et cum iter faceret, contigit ut appropinquaret Damasco, et subito circumfulsit eum lux de caelo, [4]et cadens in terram audivit vocem dicentem sibi: «Saul, Saul, quid me persequeris?». [5]Qui dixit: «Quis es, Domine?». Et ille: «Ego sum Iesus, quem tu persequeris! [6]Sed surge et ingredere civitatem, et dicetur tibi quid te oporteat facere». [7]Viri autem illi, qui comitabantur cum eo, stabant stupefacti, audientes quidem vocem, neminem autem videntes. [8]Surrexit autem Saulus de terra apertisque oculis nihil videbat; ad manus autem illum trahentes introduxerunt Damascum. [9]Et erat tribus diebus non videns et non manducavit, neque bibit. [10]Erat autem quidam discipulus Damasci nomine Ananias, et dixit ad illum in visu Dominus: «Anania». At ille ait: «Ecce ego, Domine». [11]Et Dominus ad illum: «Surgens vade in vicum, qui vocatur Rectus, et quaere in domo Iudae Saulum nomine Tarsensem; ecce enim orat [12]et vidit virum Ananiam nomine introeuntem et imponentem sibi manus, ut visum recipiat». [13]Respondit autem Ananias: «Domine, audivi a multis de viro hoc, quanta mala sanctis tuis fecerit in Ierusalem; [14]et hic habet potestatem a principibus sacerdotum alligandi omnes, qui invocant nomen tuum». [15]Dixit autem ad eum Dominus: «Vade, quoniam vas electionis est mihi iste, ut portet nomen meum coram gentibus et regibus et filiis Israel; [16]ego enim ostendam illi quanta oporteat eum pro nomine meo pati». [17]Et abiit Ananias et introivit in domum et imponens ei manus dixit: «Saul frater, Dominus misit me, Iesus qui apparuit tibi in via, qua veniebas, ut videas et implearis Spiritu Sancto». [18]Et confestim ceciderunt ab oculis eius tamquam squamae, et visum recepit. Et surgens baptizatus est [19]et, cum accepisset cibum, confortatus est. Fuit autem cum discipulis, qui erant Damasci, per dies aliquot [20]et continuo in synagogis praedicabat Iesum, quoniam hic est Filius Dei. [21]Stupebant autem omnes, qui audiebant et dicebant: «Nonne hic est, qui expugnabat in Ierusalem eos, qui invocabant nomen istud, et huc ad hoc venerat, ut vinctos illos duceret ad principes sacerdotum?». [22]Saulus autem magis convalescebat et confundebat Iudaeos, qui habitabant Damasci, affirmans quoniam hic est Christus. [23]Cum implerentur autem dies multi, consilium fecerunt Iudaei, ut eum interficerent; [24]notae autem factae sunt Saulo insidiae eorum. Custodiebant autem et portas die ac nocte, ut eum interficerent; [25]accipientes autem discipuli eius nocte per murum dimiserunt eum submittentes in sporta. [26]Cum autem venisset in Ierusalem, tentabat iungere se discipulis; et omnes timebant eum, non credentes quia esset discipulus. [27]Barnabas autem apprehensum illum duxit ad apostolos, et narravit illis quomodo in via vidisset Dominum et quia locutus est ei, et quomodo in Damasco fiducialiter egerit in nomine Iesu. [28]Et erat cum illis intrans et exiens in Ierusalem, fiducialiter agens in nomine Domini. [29]Loquebatur quoque et disputabat cum Graecis; illi autem quaerebant occidere eum. [30]Quod cum cognovissent, fratres deduxerunt eum Caesaream et dimiserunt Tarsum. [31]Ecclesia quidem per totam Iudaeam et Galilaeam et Samariam habebat pacem, aedificabatur et ambulabat in timore Domini et consolatione Sancti Spiritus crescebat. [32]Factum est autem Petrum, dum pertransiret universos, devenire et ad sanctos, qui habitabant Lyddae. [33]Invenit autem ibi hominem quendam nomine Aeneam ab annis octo iacentem in grabato, qui erat paralyticus. [34]Et ait illi Petrus: «Aenea, sanat te Iesus Christus; surge et sterne tibi». Et continuo surrexit. [35]Et viderunt illum omnes, qui inhabitabant Lyddam et Saron, qui conversi sunt ad Dominum. [36]In Ioppe autem erat quaedam discipula nomine Tabitha, quae interpretata dicitur Dorcas; haec erat plena operibus bonis et eleemosynis, quas faciebat. [37]Factum est autem in diebus illis ut infirmata moreretur; quam cum lavissent posuerunt in cenaculo. [38]Cum autem prope esset Lydda ab Ioppe, discipuli audientes quia Petrus esset in ea, miserunt duos viros ad eum rogantes: «Ne pigriteris venire usque ad nos!». [39]Exsurgens autem Petrus venit cum illis; et cum advenisset, duxerunt illum in cenaculum et circumsteterunt illum omnes viduae flentes et ostendentes tunicas et vestes, quas faciebat Dorcas, cum esset cum illis. [40]Eiectis autem omnibus foras Petrus, et ponens genua oravit et conversus ad corpus dixit: «Tabitha, surge!». At illa aperuit oculos suos et, viso Petro, resedit. [41]Dans autem illi manum erexit eam et, cum vocasset sanctos et viduas, exhibuit eam vivam. [42]Notum autem

factum est per universam Ioppen, et crediderunt multi in Domino. 43Factum est autem ut dies multos
moraretur in Ioppe apud quendam Simonem coriarium. **[10]** 1Vir autem quidam in Caesarea nomine
Cornelius, centurio cohortis, quae dicitur Italica, 2religiosus et timens Deum cum omni domo sua,
faciens eleemosynas multas plebi et deprecans Deum semper, 3vidit in visu manifeste quasi hora nona
diei angelum Dei introeuntem ad se et dicentem sibi: «Corneli». 4At ille intuens eum et timore correptus
dixit: «Quid est, domine?». Dixit autem illi: «Orationes tuae et eleemosynae tuae ascenderunt in
memoriam in conspectu Dei. 5Et nunc mitte viros in Ioppen et accersi Simonem quendam, qui
cognominatur Petrus; 6hic hospitatur apud Simonem quendam coriarium, cui est domus iuxta mare».
7Ut autem discessit angelus, qui loquebatur illi, cum vocasset duos domesticos suos et militem
religiosum ex his, qui illi parebant, 8et narrasset illis omnia, misit illos in Ioppen. 9Postera autem die
iter illis facientibus et appropinquantibus civitati, ascendit Petrus super tectum, ut oraret circa horam
sextam. 10Et cum esuriret, voluit gustare; parantibus autem eis, cecidit super eum mentis excessus, 11et
videt caelum apertum et descendens vas quoddam velut linteum magnum quattuor initiis submitti in
terram, 12in quo erant omnia quadrupedia et serpentia terrae et volatilia caeli. 13Et facta est vox ad eum:
«Surge, Petre, occide et manduca!». 14Ait autem Petrus: «Nequaquam, Domine, quia numquam
manducavi omne commune et immundum». 15Et vox iterum secundo ad eum: «Quae Deus purificavit,
ne tu commune dixeris». 16Hoc autem factum est per ter, et statim receptum est vas in caelum. 17Et dum
intra se haesitaret Petrus quidnam esset visio, quam vidisset, ecce viri, qui missi erant a Cornelio,
inquirentes domum Simonis astiterunt ad ianuam 18et, cum vocassent, interrogabant si Simon, qui
cognominatur Petrus, illic haberet hospitium. 19Petro autem cogitante de visione, dixit Spiritus ei: «Ecce
viri tres quaerunt te; 20surge itaque et descende et vade cum eis nihil dubitans, quia ego misi illos».
21Descendens autem Petrus ad viros dixit: «Ecce ego sum, quem quaeritis; quae causa est, propter quam
venistis?». 22Qui dixerunt: «Cornelius centurio, vir iustus et timens Deum et testimonium habens ab
universa gente Iudaeorum, responsum accepit ab angelo sancto accersire te in domum suam et audire
verba abs te». 23Invitans igitur eos recepit hospitio. Sequenti autem die surgens profectus est cum eis,
et quidam ex fratribus ab Ioppe comitati sunt eum. 24Altera autem die introivit Caesaream; Cornelius
vero exspectabat illos, convocatis cognatis suis et necessariis amicis. 25Et factum est cum introisset
Petrus, obvius ei Cornelius procidens ad pedes adoravit. 26Petrus vero levavit eum dicens: «Surge, et
ego ipse homo sum». 27Et loquens cum illo intravit et invenit multos, qui convenerant, 28dixitque ad
illos: «Vos scitis quomodo illicitum sit viro Iudaeo coniungi aut accedere ad alienigenam. Et mihi
ostendit Deus neminem communem aut immundum dicere hominem; 29propter quod sine dubitatione
veni accersitus. Interrogo ergo quam ob causam accersistis me». 30Et Cornelius ait: «A nudius quarta
die usque in hanc horam orans eram hora nona in domo mea, et ecce vir stetit ante me in veste candida
31et ait: "Corneli, exaudita est oratio tua, et eleemosynae tuae commemoratae sunt in conspectu Dei.
32Mitte ergo in Ioppen et accersi Simonem, qui cognominatur Petrus; hic hospitatur in domo Simonis
coriarii iuxta mare". 33Confestim igitur misi ad te, et tu bene fecisti veniendo. Nunc ergo omnes nos
in conspectu Dei adsumus audire omnia, quaecumque tibi praecepta sunt a Domino». 34Aperiens autem
Petrus os dixit: «In veritate comperio quoniam non est personarum acceptor Deus, 35sed in omni gente,
qui timet eum et operatur iustitiam, acceptus est illi. 36Verbum misit filiis Israel evangelizans pacem per
Iesum Christum; hic est omnium Dominus. 37Vos scitis quod factum est verbum per universam Iudaeam
incipiens a Galilaea post baptismum, quod praedicavit Ioannes: 38Iesum a Nazareth, quomodo unxit
eum Deus Spiritu Sancto et virtute, qui pertransivit benefaciendo et sanando omnes oppressos a
Diabolo, quoniam Deus erat cum illo. 39Et nos testes sumus omnium, quae fecit in regione Iudaeorum
et Ierusalem; quem et occiderunt suspendentes in ligno. 40Hunc Deus suscitavit tertia die et dedit eum
manifestum fieri 41non omni populo, sed testibus praeordinatis a Deo, nobis, qui manducavimus et
bibimus cum illo postquam resurrexit a mortuis; 42et praecepit nobis praedicare populo et testificari quia
ipse est, qui constitutus est a Deo iudex vivorum et mortuorum. 43Huic omnes Prophetae testimonium
perhibent remissionem peccatorum accipere per nomen eius omnes, qui credunt in eum». 44Adhuc
loquente Petro verba haec, cecidit Spiritus Sanctus super omnes, qui audiebant verbum. 45Et
obstupuerunt, qui ex circumcisione fideles, qui venerant cum Petro, quia et in nationes gratia Spiritus
Sancti effusa est; 46audiebant enim illos loquentes linguis et magnificantes Deum. Tunc respondit
Petrus: 47«Numquid aquam quis prohibere potest, ut non baptizentur hi, qui Spiritum Sanctum
acceperunt sicut et nos?». 48Et iussit eos in nomine Iesu Christi baptizari. Tunc rogaverunt eum, ut
maneret aliquot diebus. **[11]** 1Audierunt autem apostoli et fratres, qui erant in Iudaea, quoniam et
gentes receperunt verbum Dei. 2Cum ascendisset autem Petrus in Ierusalem, disceptabant adversus
illum, qui erant ex circumcisione, 3dicentes: «Introisti ad viros praeputium habentes et manducasti cum
illis!». 4Incipiens autem Petrus exponebat illis ex ordine dicens: 5«Ego eram in civitate Ioppe orans et

vidi in excessu mentis visionem, descendens vas quoddam velut linteum magnum quattuor initiis
submitti de caelo, et venit usque ad me; 6in quod intuens considerabam et vidi quadrupedia terrae et
bestias et reptilia et volatilia caeli. 7Audivi autem et vocem dicentem mihi: "Surgens, Petre, occide et
manduca!". 8Dixi autem: Nequaquam, Domine, quia commune aut immundum numquam introivit in
os meum. 9Respondit autem vox secundo de caelo: "Quae Deus mundavit, tu ne commune dixeris".
10Hoc autem factum est per ter, et retracta sunt rursum omnia in caelum. 11Et ecce confestim tres viri
astiterunt in domo, in qua eramus, missi a Caesarea ad me. 12Dixit autem Spiritus mihi, ut irem cum illis
nihil haesitans. Venerunt autem mecum et sex fratres isti, et ingressi sumus in domum viri. 13Narravit
autem nobis quomodo vidisset angelum ad domum suam stantem et dicentem: "Mitte in Ioppen et
accersi Simonem, qui cognominatur Petrus, 14qui loquetur tibi verba, in quibus salvus eris tu et universa
domus tua". 15Cum autem coepissem loqui, decidit Spiritus Sanctus super eos sicut et super nos in
initio. 16Recordatus sum autem verbi Domini sicut dicebat: "Ioannes quidem baptizavit aqua, vos autem
baptizabimini in Spiritu Sancto". 17Si ergo aequale donum dedit illis Deus sicut et nobis, qui credidimus
in Dominum Iesum Christum, ego quis eram qui possem prohibere Deum?». 18His autem auditis
acquieverunt et glorificaverunt Deum dicentes: «Ergo et gentibus Deus paenitentiam ad vitam dedit».
19Et illi quidem, qui dispersi fuerant a tribulatione, quae facta fuerat sub Stephano, perambulaverunt
usque Phoenicen et Cyprum et Antiochiam, nemini loquentes verbum nisi solis Iudaeis. 20Erant autem
quidam ex eis viri Cyprii et Cyrenaei, qui cum introissent Antiochiam, loquebantur et ad Graecos
evangelizantes Dominum Iesum. 21Et erat manus Domini cum eis; multusque numerus credentium
conversus est ad Dominum. 22Auditus est autem sermo in auribus ecclesiae, quae erat in Ierusalem,
super istis, et miserunt Barnabam usque Antiochiam; 23qui cum pervenisset et vidisset gratiam Dei,
gavisus est et hortabatur omnes proposito cordis permanere in Domino, 24quia erat vir bonus et plenus
Spiritu Sancto et fide. Et apposita est turba multa Domino. 25Profectus est autem Tarsum, ut quaereret
Saulum; 26quem cum invenisset, perduxit Antiochiam. Factum est autem eis ut annum totum
conversarentur in ecclesia et docerent turbam multam, et cognominarentur primum Antiochiae discipuli
Christiani. 27In his autem diebus supervenerunt ab Hierosolymis prophetae Antiochiam; 28et surgens
unus ex eis nomine Agabus, significavit per Spiritum famem magnam futuram in universo orbe
terrarum; quae facta est sub Claudio. 29Discipuli autem, prout quis habebat, proposuerunt singuli eorum
in ministerium mittere habitantibus in Iudaea fratribus; 30quod et fecerunt, mittentes ad presbyteros per
manum Barnabae et Sauli. **[12]** 1Illo autem tempore misit Herodes rex manus, ut affligeret quosdam
de ecclesia. 2Occidit autem Iacobum fratrem Ioannis gladio. 3Videns autem quia placeret Iudaeis,
apposuit apprehendere et Petrum—erant autem dies Azymorum—4quem cum apprehendisset, misit in
carcerem tradens quattuor quaternionibus militum custodire eum, volens post Pascha producere eum
populo. 5Et Petrus quidem servabatur in carcere; oratio autem fiebat sine intermissione ab ecclesia ad
Deum pro eo. 6Cum autem producturus eum esset Herodes, in ipsa nocte erat Petrus dormiens inter duos
milites vinctus catenis duabus, et custodes ante ostium custodiebant carcerem. 7Et ecce angelus Domini
astitit, et lumen refulsit in habitaculo; percusso autem latere Petri, suscitavit eum dicens: «Surge
velociter!». Et ceciderunt catenae de manibus eius. 8Dixit autem angelus ad eum: «Praecingere et calcea
te sandalia tua!». Et fecit sic. Et dicit illi: «Circumda tibi vestimentum tuum et sequere me!». 9Et exiens
sequebatur et nesciebat quia verum est, quod fiebat per angelum; aestimabat autem se visum videre.
10Transeuntes autem primam custodiam et secundam venerunt ad portam ferream, quae ducit ad
civitatem, quae ultro aperta est eis, et exeuntes processerunt vicum unum, et continuo discessit angelus
ab eo. 11Et Petrus ad se reversus dixit: «Nunc scio vere quia misit Dominus angelum suum et eripuit me
de manu Herodis et de omni exspectatione plebis Iudaeorum». 12Consideransque venit ad domum
Mariae matris Ioannis, qui cognominatur Marcus, ubi erant multi congregati et orantes. 13Pulsante
autem eo ostium ianuae, processit puella ad audiendum, nomine Rhode; 14et ut cognovit vocem Petri
prae gaudio non aperuit ianuam, sed intro currens nuntiavit stare Petrum ante ianuam. 15At illi dixerunt
ad eam: «Insanis!». Illa autem affirmabat sic se habere. Illi autem dicebant: «Angelus eius est». 16Petrus
autem perseverabat pulsans; cum autem aperuissent, viderunt eum et obstupuerunt. 17Annuens autem
eis manu, ut tacerent, enarravit quomodo Dominus eduxisset eum de carcere dixitque: «Nuntiate Iacobo
et fratribus haec». Et egressus abiit in alium locum. 18Facta autem die erat non parva turbatio inter
milites, quidnam de Petro factum esset. 19Herodes autem cum requisisset eum et non invenisset,
interrogatis custodibus iussit eos abduci; descendensque a Iudaea in Caesaream ibi commorabatur.
20Erat autem iratus Tyriis et Sidoniis; at illi unanimes venerunt ad eum et persuaso Blasto, qui erat super
cubiculum regis, postulabant pacem, eo quod aleretur regio eorum ab annona regis. 21Statuto autem die,
Herodes, vestitus veste regia, sedens pro tribunali, contionabatur ad eos; 22populus autem acclamabat:
«Dei vox et non hominis!». 23Confestim autem percussit eum angelus Domini, eo quod non dedisset

gloriam Deo, et consumptus a vermibus exspiravit. [24]Verbum autem Dei crescebat et multiplicabatur.
[25]Barnabas autem et Saulus reversi sunt in Ierusalem expleto ministerio, assumpto Ioanne, qui
cognominatus est Marcus. **[13]** [1]Erant autem in ecclesia, quae erat Antiochiae, prophetae et doctores:
Barnabas et Simeon, qui vocabatur Niger, et Lucius Cyrenensis, et Manaen, qui erat Herodis tetrarchae
collactaneus, et Saulus. [2]Ministrantibus autem illis Domino et ieiunantibus, dixit Spiritus Sanctus:
«Separate mihi Barnabam et Saulum in opus, ad quod vocavi eos». [3]Tunc ieiunantes et orantes
imponentesque eis manus dimiserunt illos. [4]Et ipsi quidem missi ab Spiritu Sancto devenerunt
Seleuciam et inde navigaverunt Cyprum [5]et, cum venissent Salamina, praedicabant verbum Dei in
synagogis Iudaeorum; habebant autem et Ioannem ministrum. [6]Et cum perambulassent universam
insulam usque Paphum, invenerunt quendam virum magum pseudoprophetam Iudaeum, cui nomen
Bariesu, [7]qui erat cum proconsule Sergio Paulo, viro prudente. Hic accitis Barnaba et Saulo, quaesivit
audire verbum Dei; [8]resistebat autem illis Elymas, magus, sic enim interpretatur nomen eius, quaerens
avertere proconsulem a fide. [9]Saulus autem, qui et Paulus, repletus Spiritu Sancto, intuens in eum
[10]dixit: «O plene omni dolo et omni fallacia, fili Diaboli, inimice omnis iustitiae, non desines subvertere
vias Domini rectas? [11]Et nunc ecce manus Domini super te: et eris caecus, non videns solem usque ad
tempus». Et confestim cecidit in eum caligo et tenebrae, et circumiens quaerebat, qui eum manum
darent. [12]Tunc proconsul, cum vidisset factum, credidit admirans super doctrinam Domini. [13]Et cum a
Papho navigassent, qui erant cum Paulo, venerunt Pergen Pamphyliae; Ioannes autem discedens ab eis
reversus est Hierosolymam. [14]Illi vero pertranseuntes, a Perge venerunt Antiochiam Pisidiae, et ingressi
synagogam die sabbatorum sederunt. [15]Post lectionem autem Legis et Prophetarum, miserunt principes
synagogae ad eos dicentes: «Viri fratres, si quis est in vobis sermo exhortationis ad plebem, dicite!».
[16]Surgens autem Paulus et manu silentium indicens ait: «Viri Israelitae et qui timetis Deum, audite.
[17]Deus plebis huius Israel elegit patres nostros et plebem exaltavit, cum essent incolae in terra Aegypti,
et in brachio excelso eduxit eos ex ea [18]et per quadraginta fere annorum tempus mores eorum sustinuit
in deserto [19]et destruens gentes septem in terra Chanaan sorte distribuit terram eorum, [20]quasi
quadringentos et quinquaginta annos. Et post haec dedit iudices usque ad Samuel prophetam. [21]Et
exinde postulaverunt regem, et dedit illis Deus Saul filium Cis, virum de tribu Beniamin, annis
quadraginta. [22]Et amoto illo, suscitavit illis David in regem, cui et testimonium perhibens dixit: "*Inveni
David* filium Iesse, *virum secundum cor meum*, qui faciet omnes voluntates meas". [23]Huius Deus ex
semine secundum promissionem eduxit Israel salvatorem Iesum, [24]praedicante Ioanne ante adventum
eius baptismum paenitentiae omni populo Israel. [25]Cum impleret autem Ioannes cursum suum, dicebat:
"Quid me arbitramini esse? Non sum ego; sed ecce venit post me, cuius non sum dignus calceamenta
pedum solvere". [26]Viri fratres, filii generis Abraham et qui in vobis timent Deum, nobis verbum salutis
huius missum est. [27]Qui enim habitabant Ierusalem et principes eorum, hunc ignorantes et voces
Prophetarum, quae per omne sabbatum leguntur, iudicantes impleverunt, [28]et nullam causam mortis
invenientes petierunt a Pilato, ut interficeretur; [29]cumque consummassent omnia, quae de eo scripta
erant, deponentes eum de ligno posuerunt in monumento. [30]Deus vero suscitavit eum a mortuis; [31]qui
visus est per dies multos his, qui simul ascenderant cum eo de Galilaea in Ierusalem, qui nunc sunt
testes eius ad plebem. [32]Et nos vobis evangelizamus eam, quae ad patres promissio facta est, [33]quoniam
hanc Deus adimplevit filiis eorum, nobis resuscitans Iesum, sicut et in Psalmo secundo scriptum est:
"*Filius meus es tu; ego hodie genui te*". [34]Quod autem suscitaverit eum a mortuis, amplius iam non
reversurum in corruptionem, ita dixit: "*Dabo vobis sancta David fidelia*". [35]Ideoque et in alio dicit:
"*Non dabis Sanctum tuum videre corruptionem*". [36]David enim sua generatione cum administrasset
voluntati Dei, dormivit et appositus est ad patres suos et vidit corruptionem; [37]quem vero Deus
suscitavit, non vidit corruptionem. [38]Notum igitur sit vobis, viri fratres, quia per hunc vobis remissio
peccatorum annuntiatur; ab omnibus, quibus non potuistis in lege Moysi iustificari, [39]in hoc omnis, qui
credit, iustificatur. [40]Videte ergo, ne superveniat, quod dictum est in Prophetis: [41]"*Videte, contemptores,
/ et admiramini et disperdimini, / quia opus operor ego in diebus vestris, / opus, quod non credetis, si
quis enarraverit vobis!*"». [42]Exeuntibus autem illis, rogabant, ut sequenti sabbato loquerentur sibi verba
haec. [43]Cumque dimissa esset synagoga, secuti sunt multi Iudaeorum et colentium proselytorum Paulum
et Barnabam, qui loquentes suadebant eis, ut permanerent in gratia Dei. [44]Sequenti vero sabbato paene
universa civitas convenit audire verbum Domini. [45]Videntes autem turbas Iudaei repleti sunt zelo et
contradicebant his, quae a Paulo dicebantur, blasphemantes. [46]Tunc audenter Paulus et Barnabas
dixerunt: «Vobis oportebat primum loqui verbum Dei; sed quoniam repellitis illud et indignos vos
iudicatis aeternae vitae, ecce convertimur ad gentes. [47]Sic enim praecepit nobis Dominus: "*Posui te in
lumen gentium, / ut sis in salutem usque ad extremum terrae*"». [48]Audientes autem gentes gaudebant et
glorificabant verbum Domini, et crediderunt, quotquot erant praeordinati ad vitam aeternam; [49]ferebatur

autem verbum Domini per universam regionem. [50]Iudaei autem concitaverunt honestas inter colentes
mulieres et primos civitatis et excitaverunt persecutionem in Paulum et Barnabam et eiecerunt eos de
finibus suis. [51]At illi, excusso pulvere pedum in eos, venerunt Iconium; [52]discipuli quoque replebantur
gaudio et Spiritu Sancto. **[14]** [1]Factum est autem Iconii, ut eodem modo introirent synagogam
Iudaeorum et ita loquerentur, ut crederet Iudaeorum et Graecorum copiosa multitudo. [2]Qui vero
increduli fuerunt Iudaei, suscitaverunt et exacerbaverunt animas gentium adversus fratres. [3]Multo igitur
tempore demorati sunt, fiducialiter agentes in Domino, testimonium perhibente verbo gratiae suae, dante
signa et prodigia fieri per manus eorum. [4]Divisa est autem multitudo civitatis: et quidam quidem erant
cum Iudaeis, quidam vero cum apostolis. [5]Cum autem factus esset impetus gentilium et Iudaeorum cum
principibus suis, ut contumeliis afficerent et lapidarent eos, [6]intellegentes confugerunt ad civitates
Lycaoniae, Lystram et Derben et ad regionem in circuitu, [7]et ibi evangelizantes erant. [8]Et quidam vir in
Lystris infirmus pedibus sedebat, claudus ex utero matris suae, qui numquam ambulaverat. [9]Hic audivit
Paulum loquentem; qui intuitus eum et videns quia haberet fidem, ut salvus fieret, [10]dixit magna voce:
«Surge super pedes tuos rectus!». Et exsilivit et ambulabat. [11]Turbae autem cum vidissent, quod fecerat
Paulus, levaverunt vocem suam Lycaonice dicentes: «Dii similes facti hominibus descenderunt ad nos!»;
[12]et vocabant Barnabam Iovem, Paulum vero Mercurium, quoniam ipse erat dux verbi. [13]Sacerdos
quoque templi Iovis, quod erat ante civitatem, tauros et coronas ad ianuas afferens cum populis, volebat
sacrificare. [14]Quod ubi audierunt apostoli Barnabas et Paulus, conscissis tunicis suis, exsilierunt in
turbam clamantes [15]et dicentes: «Viri, quid haec facitis? Et nos mortales sumus similes vobis homines,
evangelizantes vobis ab his vanis converti ad Deum vivum, *qui fecit caelum et terram et mare et omnia,
quae in eis sunt*. [16]Qui in praeteritis generationibus permisit omnes gentes ambulare in viis suis; [17]et
quidem non sine testimonio semetipsum reliquit benefaciens, de caelo dans vobis pluvias et tempora
fructifera, implens cibo et laetitia corda vestra». [18]Et haec dicentes vix sedaverunt turbas, ne sibi
immolarent. [19]Supervenerunt autem ab Antiochia et Iconio Iudaei et persuasis turbis lapidantesque
Paulum trahebant extra civitatem aestimantes eum mortuum esse. [20]Circumdantibus autem eum
discipulis, surgens intravit civitatem. Et postera die profectus est cum Barnaba in Derben. [21]Cumque
evangelizassent civitati illi et docuissent multos, reversi sunt Lystram et Iconium et Antiochiam
[22]confirmantes animas discipulorum, exhortantes, ut permanerent in fide, et quoniam per multas
tribulationes oportet nos intrare in regnum Dei. [23]Et cum ordinassent illis per singulas ecclesias
presbyteros et orassent cum ieiunationibus, commendaverunt eos Domino, in quem crediderant.
[24]Transeuntesque Pisidiam venerunt Pamphyliam, [25]et loquentes in Perge verbum descenderunt in
Attaliam. [26]Et inde navigaverunt Antiochiam, unde erant traditi gratiae Dei in opus, quod compleverunt.
[27]Cum autem venissent et congregassent ecclesiam, rettulerunt quanta fecisset Deus cum illis et quia
aperuisset gentibus ostium fidei. [28]Morati sunt autem tempus non modicum cum discipulis. **[15]** [1]Et
quidam descendentes de Iudaea docebant fratres: «Nisi circumcidamini secundum morem Moysis, non
potestis salvi fieri». [2]Facta autem seditione et conquisitione non minima Paulo et Barnabae adversum
illos, statuerunt, ut ascenderent Paulus et Barnabas et quidam alii ex illis ad apostolos et presbyteros in
Ierusalem super hac quaestione. [3]Illi igitur deducti ab ecclesia pertransiebant Phoenicen et Samariam
narrantes conversionem gentium et faciebant gaudium magnum omnibus fratribus. [4]Cum autem
venissent Hierosolymam, suscepti sunt ab ecclesia et apostolis et presbyteris et annuntiaverunt quanta
Deus fecisset cum illis. [5]Surrexerunt autem quidam de haeresi pharisaeorum, qui crediderant, dicentes:
«Oportet circumcidere eos, praecipere quoque servare legem Moysis!». [6]Conveneruntque apostoli et
presbyteri videre de verbo hoc. [7]Cum autem magna conquisitio fieret, surgens Petrus dixit ad eos: «Viri
fratres, vos scitis quoniam ab antiquis diebus in vobis elegit Deus per os meum audire gentes verbum
evangelii et credere; [8]et qui novit corda, Deus testimonium perhibuit illis dans Spiritum Sanctum sicut
et nobis [9]et nihil discrevit inter nos et illos fide purificans corda eorum. [10]Nunc ergo quid tentatis Deum
imponere iugum super cervicem discipulorum, quod neque patres nostri neque nos portare potuimus?
[11]Sed per gratiam Domini Iesu credimus salvari quemadmodum et illi». [12]Tacuit autem omnis
multitudo, et audiebant Barnabam et Paulum narrantes quanta fecisset Deus signa et prodigia in
gentibus per eos. [13]Et postquam tacuerunt, respondit Iacobus dicens: «Viri fratres, audite me. [14]Simeon
narravit quemadmodum primum Deus visitavit sumere ex gentibus populum nomini suo, [15]et huic
concordant verba Prophetarum, sicut scriptum est: [16]"*Post haec revertar / et reaedificabo tabernaculum
David, quod decidit, / et diruta eius reaedificabo et erigam illud, /* [17]*ut requirant reliqui hominum
Dominum / et omnes gentes, super quas invocatum est nomen meum, / dicit Dominus faciens haec* [18]nota
a saeculo". [19]Propter quod ego iudico non inquietari eos, qui ex gentibus convertuntur ad Deum, [20]sed
scribere ad eos, ut abstineant se a contaminationibus simulacrorum et fornicatione et suffocato et
sanguine. [21]Moyses enim a generationibus antiquis habet in singulis civitatibus, qui eum praedicent in

synagogis, ubi per omne sabbatum legitur». [22]Tunc placuit apostolis et presbyteris cum omni ecclesia
electos viros ex eis mittere Antiochiam cum Paulo et Barnaba: Iudam, qui cognominatur Barsabbas,
et Silam, viros primos in fratribus, [23]scribentes per manum eorum: «Apostoli et presbyteri fratres his,
qui sunt Antiochiae et Syriae et Ciliciae fratribus ex gentibus, salutem! [24]Quoniam audivimus quia
quidam ex nobis quibus non mandavimus, exeuntes turbaverunt vos verbis evertentes animas vestras,
[25]placuit nobis collectis in unum eligere viros et mittere ad vos cum carissimis nobis Barnaba et Paulo,
[26]hominibus, qui tradiderunt animas suas pro nomine Domini nostri Iesu Christi. [27]Misimus ergo Iudam
et Silam, qui et ipsi verbis referent eadem. [28]Visum est enim Spiritui Sancto et nobis nihil ultra
imponere vobis oneris quam haec necessario: [29]abstinere ab idolothytis et sanguine et suffocatis et
fornicatione; a quibus custodientes vos bene agetis. Valete». [30]Illi igitur dimissi descenderunt
Antiochiam et, congregata multitudine, tradiderunt epistulam; [31]quam cum legissent, gavisi sunt super
consolatione. [32]Iudas quoque et Silas, cum et ipsi essent prophetae, verbo plurimo consolati sunt fratres
et confirmaverunt. [33]Facto autem tempore, dimissi sunt cum pace a fratribus ad eos, qui miserant illos.
[35]Paulus autem et Barnabas demorabantur Antiochiae docentes et evangelizantes cum aliis pluribus
verbum Domini. [36]Post aliquot autem dies dixit ad Barnabam Paulus: «Revertentes visitemus fratres per
universas civitates, in quibus praedicavimus verbum Domini, quomodo se habeant». [37]Barnabas autem
volebat secum assumere et Ioannem, qui cognominatur Marcus; [38]Paulus autem iudicabat eum, qui
discessisset ab eis a Pamphylia et non isset cum eis in opus, non debere recipi eum. [39]Facta est autem
exacerbatio, ita ut discederent ab invicem, et Barnabas assumpto Marco navigaret Cyprum. [40]Paulus
vero, electo Sila, profectus est traditus gratiae Domini a fratribus; [41]perambulabat autem Syriam et
Ciliciam confirmans ecclesias. **[16]** [1]Pervenit autem in Derben et Lystram. Et ecce discipulus quidam
erat ibi nomine Timotheus, filius mulieris Iudaeae fidelis, patre autem Graeco; [2]huic testimonium
reddebant, qui in Lystris erant et Iconii fratres. [3]Hunc voluit Paulus secum proficisci et assumens
circumcidit eum propter Iudaeos, qui erant in illis locis; sciebant enim omnes quod pater eius Graecus
esset. [4]Cum autem pertransirent civitates, tradebant eis custodire dogmata, quae erant decreta ab
apostolis et presbyteris, qui essent Hierosolymis. [5]Ecclesiae quidem confirmabantur fide et abundabant
numero cotidie. [6]Transierunt autem Phrygiam et Galatiae regionem, vetati a Sancto Spiritu loqui verbum
in Asia; [7]cum venissent autem circa Mysiam, tentabant ire Bithyniam, et non permisit eos Spiritus Iesu;
[8]cum autem praeterissent Mysiam, descenderunt Troadem. [9]Et visio per noctem Paulo ostensa est: vir
Macedo quidam erat stans et deprecans eum et dicens: «Transiens in Macedoniam, adiuva nos!». [10]Ut
autem visum vidit, statim quaesivimus proficisci in Macedoniam, certi facti quia vocasset nos Deus
evangelizare eis. [11]Navigantes autem a Troade recto cursu venimus Samothraciam et sequenti die
Neapolim [12]et inde Philippos, quae est prima partis Macedoniae civitas, colonia. Eramus autem in hac
urbe diebus aliquot commorantes. [13]Die autem sabbatorum egressi sumus foras portam iuxta flumen,
ubi putabamus orationem esse, et sedentes loquebamur mulieribus, quae convenerant. [14]Et quaedam
mulier nomine Lydia, purpuraria civitatis Thyatirenorum colens Deum, audiebat, cuius Dominus aperuit
cor intendere his, quae dicebantur a Paulo. [15]Cum autem baptizata esset et domus eius, deprecata est
dicens: «Si iudicastis me fidelem Domino esse, introite in domum meam et manete»; et coegit nos.
[16]Factum est autem euntibus nobis ad orationem, puellam quandam habentem spiritum pythonem
obviare nobis, quae quaestum magnum praestabat dominis suis divinando. [17]Haec subsecuta Paulum et
nos clamabat dicens: «Isti homines servi Dei Altissimi sunt, qui annuntiant vobis viam salutis». [18]Hoc
autem faciebat multis diebus. Dolens autem Paulus et conversus spiritui dixit: «Praecipio tibi in nomine
Iesu Christi exire ab ea»; et exiit eadem hora. [19]Videntes autem domini eius quia exivit spes quaestus
eorum, apprehendentes Paulum et Silam traxerunt in forum ad principes [20]et producentes eos
magistratibus dixerunt: «Hi homines conturbant civitatem nostram, cum sint Iudaei, [21]et annuntiant
mores, quos non licet nobis suscipere neque facere cum simus Romani». [22]Et concurrit plebs adversus
eos, et magistratus scissis tunicis eorum iusserunt virgis caedi [23]et, cum multas plagas eis imposuissent,
miserunt eos in carcerem, praecipientes custodi, ut caute custodiret eos; [24]qui cum tale praeceptum
accepisset, misit eos in interiorem carcerem et pedes eorum strinxit in ligno. [25]Media autem nocte
Paulus et Silas orantes laudabant Deum, et audiebant eos, qui in custodia erant; [26]subito vero
terraemotus factus est magnus, ita ut moverentur fundamenta carceris, et aperta sunt statim ostia omnia,
et universorum vincula soluta sunt. [27]Expergefactus autem custos carceris et videns apertas ianuas
carceris, evaginato gladio volebat se interficere, aestimans fugisse vinctos. [28]Clamavit autem Paulus
magna voce dicens: «Nihil feceris tibi mali; universi enim hic sumus». [29]Petitoque lumine intro cucurrit
et tremefactus procidit Paulo et Silae [30]et producens eos foras ait: «Domini, quid me oportet facere, ut
salvus fiam?». [31]At illi dixerunt: «Crede in Domino Iesu et salvus eris tu et domus tua». [32]Et locuti sunt
ei verbum Domini cum omnibus, qui erant in domo eius. [33]Et tollens eos in illa hora noctis lavit eos a

plagis, et baptizatus est ipse et omnes eius continuo; [34]cumque perduxisset eos in domum, apposuit mensam et laetatus est cum omni domo sua credens Deo. [35]Et cum dies factus esset, miserunt magistratus lictores dicentes: «Dimitte homines illos!». [36]Nuntiavit autem custos carceris verba haec Paulo: «Miserunt magistratus, ut dimittamini; nunc igitur exeuntes ite in pace». [37]Paulus autem dixit eis: «Caesos nos publice indemnatos, cum homines Romani essemus, miserunt in carcerem; et nunc occulte nos eiciunt? Non ita, sed veniant et ipsi nos educant». [38]Nuntiaverunt autem magistratibus lictores verba haec. Timueruntque audito quod Romani essent, [39]et venientes deprecati sunt eos et educentes rogabant, ut egrederentur urbem. [40]Exeuntes autem de carcere introierunt ad Lydiam et, visis fratribus, consolati sunt eos et profecti sunt. **[17]** [1]Cum autem perambulassent Amphipolim et Apolloniam, venerunt Thessalonicam, ubi erat synagoga Iudaeorum. [2]Secundum consuetudinem autem suam Paulus introivit ad eos et per sabbata tria disserebat eis de Scripturis [3]adaperiens et comprobans quia Christum oportebat pati et resurgere a mortuis, et: «Hic est Christus, Iesus, quem ego annuntio vobis». [4]Et quidam ex eis crediderunt et adiuncti sunt Paulo et Silae et de colentibus Graecis multitudo magna et mulieres nobiles non paucae. [5]Zelantes autem Iudaei assumentesque de foro viros quosdam malos et turba facta concitaverunt civitatem, et assistentes domui Iasonis quaerebant eos producere in populum. [6]Et cum non invenissent eos, trahebant Iasonem et quosdam fratres ad politarchas clamantes: «Qui orbem concitaverunt, isti et huc venerunt, [7]quos suscepit Iason; et hi omnes contra decreta Caesaris faciunt, regem alium dicentes esse, Iesum». [8]Concitaverunt autem plebem et politarchas audientes haec; [9]et accepto satis ab Iasone et a ceteris, dimiserunt eos. [10]Fratres vero confestim per noctem dimiserunt Paulum et Silam in Beroeam; qui cum advenissent, in synagogam Iudaeorum introierunt. [11]Hi autem erant nobiliores eorum, qui sunt Thessalonicae, qui susceperunt verbum cum omni aviditate, cotidie scrutantes Scripturas si haec ita se haberent. [12]Et multi quidem crediderunt ex eis et Graecarum mulierum honestarum et virorum non pauci. [13]Cum autem cognovissent in Thessalonica Iudaei quia et Beroeae annuntiatum est a Paulo verbum Dei, venerunt et illuc commoventes et turbantes multitudinem. [14]Statimque tunc Paulum dimiserunt fratres, ut iret usque ad mare; Silas autem et Timotheus remanserunt ibi. [15]Qui autem deducebant Paulum, perduxerunt usque Athenas, et accepto mandato ad Silam et Timotheum, ut quam celerrime venirent ad illum, profecti sunt. [16]Paulus autem cum Athenis eos exspectaret, irritabatur spiritus eius in ipso videns idololatriae deditam civitatem. [17]Disputabat igitur in synagoga cum Iudaeis et colentibus et in foro per omnes dies ad eos, qui aderant. [18]Quidam autem ex Epicureis et Stoicis philosophi disserebant cum eo. Et quidam dicebant: «Quid vult seminiverbius hic dicere?»; alii vero: «Novorum daemoniorum videtur annuntiator esse», quia Iesum et resurrectionem evangelizabat. [19]Et apprehensum eum ad Areopagum duxerunt dicentes: «Possumus scire quae est haec nova, quae a te dicitur doctrina? [20]Mira enim quaedam infers auribus nostris; volumus ergo scire quidnam velint haec esse». [21]Athenienses autem omnes et advenae hospites ad nihil aliud vacabant nisi aut dicere aut audire aliquid novi. [22]Stans autem Paulus in medio Areopagi ait: «Viri Athenienses, per omnia quasi superstitiosiores vos video; [23]praeteriens enim et videns simulacra vestra inveni et aram in qua scriptum erat: "Ignoto deo". Quod ergo ignorantes colitis, hoc ego annuntio vobis. [24]Deus, qui fecit mundum et omnia, quae in eo sunt, hic, caeli et terrae cum sit Dominus, non in manufactis templis inhabitat, [25]nec manibus humanis colitur indigens aliquo, cum ipse det omnibus vitam et inspirationem et omnia; [26]fecitque ex uno omne genus hominum inhabitare super universam faciem terrae, definiens statuta tempora et terminos habitationis eorum, [27]quaerere Deum si forte attrectent eum et inveniant, quamvis non longe sit ab unoquoque nostrum. [28]In ipso enim vivimus et movemur et sumus, sicut et quidam vestrum poetarum dixerunt: "Ipsius enim et genus sumus". [29]Genus ergo cum simus Dei, non debemus aestimare auro aut argento aut lapidi, sculpturae artis et cogitationis hominis, divinum esse simile. [30]Et tempora quidem ignorantiae despiciens Deus, nunc annuntiat hominibus, ut omnes ubique paenitentiam agant, [31]eo quod statuit diem, in qua iudicaturus est orbem in iustitia in viro, quem constituit, fidem praebens omnibus suscitans eum a mortuis». [32]Cum audissent autem resurrectionem mortuorum, quidam quidem irridebant, quidam vero dixerunt: «Audiemus te de hoc iterum». [33]Sic Paulus exivit de medio eorum. [34]Quidam vero viri adhaerentes ei crediderunt, in quibus et Dionysius Areopagita et mulier nomine Damaris et alii cum eis. **[18]** [1]Post haec discedens ab Athenis venit Corinthum. [2]Et inveniens quendam Iudaeum nomine Aquilam, Ponticum genere, qui nuper venerat ab Italia, et Priscillam uxorem eius, eo quod praecepisset Claudius discedere omnes Iudaeos a Roma, accessit ad eos [3]et, quia eiusdem erat artis, manebat apud eos et operabatur; erant autem scenofactoriae artis. [4]Disputabat autem in synagoga per omne sabbatum suadebatque Iudaeis et Graecis. [5]Cum venissent autem de Macedonia Silas et Timotheus, instabat verbo Paulus testificans Iudaeis esse Christum Iesum. [6]Contradicentibus autem eis et blasphemantibus, excutiens vestimenta dixit ad eos: «Sanguis vester super caput vestrum! Mundus ego. Ex hoc nunc ad

gentes vadam». 7 Et migrans inde intravit in domum cuiusdam nomine Titi Iusti, colentis Deum, cuius
domus erat coniuncta synagogae. 8 Crispus autem archisynagogus credidit Domino cum omni domo sua,
et multi Corinthiorum audientes credebant et baptizabantur. 9 Dixit autem Dominus nocte per visionem
Paulo: «Noli timere, sed loquere et ne taceas, 10 quia ego sum tecum, et nemo apponetur tibi, ut noceat
te, quoniam populus est mihi multus in hac civitate». 11 Sedit autem annum et sex menses docens apud
eos verbum Dei. 12 Gallione autem proconsule Achaiae, insurrexerunt uno animo Iudaei in Paulum et
adduxerunt eum ad tribunal 13 dicentes: «Contra legem hic persuadet hominibus colere Deum».
14 Incipiente autem Paulo aperire os, dixit Gallio ad Iudaeos: «Si quidem esset iniquum aliquid aut
facinus pessimum, o Iudaei, merito vos sustinerem; 15 si vero quaestiones sunt de verbo et nominibus
et lege vestra, vos ipsi videritis; iudex ego horum nolo esse». 16 Et minavit eos a tribunali.
17 Apprehendentes autem omnes Sosthenen, principem synagogae, percutiebant ante tribunal; et nihil
horum Gallioni curae erat. 18 Paulus vero, cum adhuc sustinuisset dies multos, fratribus valefaciens
navigabat Syriam, et cum eo Priscilla et Aquila, qui sibi totonderat in Cenchreis caput; habebat enim
votum. 19 Deveneruntque Ephesum, et illos ibi reliquit, ipse vero ingressus synagogam disputabat cum
Iudaeis. 20 Rogantibus autem eis, ut ampliore tempore maneret, non consensit, 21 sed valefaciens et
dicens: «Iterum revertar ad vos Deo volente», navigavit ab Epheso; 22 et descendens Caesaream ascendit
et salutavit ecclesiam et descendit Antiochiam. 23 Et facto ibi aliquanto tempore, profectus est
perambulans ex ordine Galaticam regionem et Phrygiam, confirmans omnes discipulos. 24 Iudaeus autem
quidam Apollo nomine, Alexandrinus natione, vir eloquens, devenit Ephesum, potens in Scripturis.
25 Hic erat catechizatus viam Domini et fervens spiritu loquebatur et docebat diligenter ea, quae sunt de
Iesu, sciens tantum baptisma Ioannis. 26 Hic ergo coepit fiducialiter agere in synagoga; quem cum
audissent Priscilla et Aquila, assumpserunt eum et diligentius exposuerunt ei viam Dei. 27 Cum autem
vellet transire in Achaiam, exhortati fratres scripserunt discipulis, ut susciperent eum; qui cum venisset,
contulit multum his, qui crediderant per gratiam; 28 vehementer enim Iudaeos revincebat publice
ostendens per Scripturas esse Christum Iesum. **[19]** 1 Factum est autem cum Apollo esset Corinthi,
ut Paulus, peragratis superioribus partibus, veniret Ephesum et inveniret quosdam discipulos, 2 dixitque
ad eos: «Si Spiritum Sanctum accepistis credentes?». At illi ad eum: «Sed neque si Spiritus Sanctus est
audivimus». 3 Ille vero ait: «In quo ergo baptizati estis?». Qui dixerunt: «In Ioannis baptismate». 4 Dixit
autem Paulus: «Ioannes baptizavit baptisma paenitentiae, populo dicens in eum, qui venturus esset post
ipsum ut crederent, hoc est in Iesum». 5 His auditis, baptizati sunt in nomine Domini Iesu; 6 et cum
imposuisset illis manus Paulus, venit Spiritus Sanctus super eos, et loquebantur linguis et prophetabant.
7 Erant autem omnes viri fere duodecim. 8 Introgressus autem synagogam cum fiducia loquebatur per tres
menses disputans et suadens de regno Dei. 9 Cum autem quidam indurarentur et non crederent
maledicentes viam coram multitudine, discedens ab eis segregavit discipulos, cotidie disputans in schola
Tyranni. 10 Hoc autem factum est per biennium, ita ut omnes, qui habitabant in Asia, audirent verbum
Domini, Iudaei atque Graeci. 11 Virtutesque non quaslibet Deus faciebat per manus Pauli, 12 ita ut etiam
super languidos deferrentur a corpore eius sudaria vel semicinctia, et recederent ab eis languores, et
spiritus nequam egrederentur. 13 Tentaverunt autem quidam et de circumeuntibus Iudaeis exorcistis
invocare super eos, qui habebant spiritus malos, nomen Domini Iesu dicentes: «Adiuro vos per Iesum,
quem Paulus praedicat». 14 Erant autem cuiusdam Scevae Iudaei principis sacerdotum septem filii, qui
hoc faciebant. 15 Respondens autem spiritus nequam dixit eis: «Iesum novi et Paulum scio, vos autem
qui estis?». 16 Et insiliens homo in eos, in quo erat spiritus malus, dominatus amborum invaluit contra
eos, ita ut nudi et vulnerati effugerent de domo illa. 17 Hoc autem notum factum est omnibus Iudaeis
atque Graecis, qui habitabant Ephesi, et cecidit timor super omnes illos, et magnificabatur nomen
Domini Iesu. 18 Multique credentium veniebant confitentes et annuntiantes actus suos. 19 Multi autem ex
his, qui fuerant curiosa sectati, conferentes libros combusserunt coram omnibus; et computaverunt pretia
illorum et invenerunt argenti quinquaginta milia. 20 Ita fortiter verbum Domini crescebat et
convalescebat. 21 His autem expletis, proposuit Paulus in Spiritu, transita Macedonia et Achaia, ire
Hierosolymam, dicens: «Postquam fuero ibi, oportet me et Romam videre». 22 Mittens autem in
Macedoniam duos ex ministrantibus sibi, Timotheum et Erastum, ipse remansit ad tempus in Asia.
23 Facta est autem in illo tempore turbatio non minima de via. 24 Demetrius enim quidam nomine,
argentarius, faciens aedes argenteas Dianae praestabat artificibus non modicum quaestum; 25 quos
congregans et eos, qui eiusmodi erant opifices, dixit: «Viri, scitis quia de hoc artificio acquisitio est
nobis 26 et videtis et auditis quia non solum Ephesi, sed paene totius Asiae Paulus hic suadens avertit
multam turbam dicens quoniam non sunt dii, qui manibus fiunt. 27 Non solum autem haec periclitatur
nobis pars in redargutionem venire, sed et magnae deae Dianae templum in nihilum reputari, et destrui
incipiet maiestas eius, quam tota Asia et orbis colit». 28 His auditis, repleti sunt ira et clamabant dicentes:

«Magna Diana Ephesiorum!», [29]et impleta est civitas confusione, et impetum fecerunt uno animo in
theatrum, rapto Gaio et Aristarcho Macedonibus, comitibus Pauli. [30]Paulo autem volente intrare in
populum, non permiserunt discipuli; [31]quidam autem de Asiarchis, qui erant amici eius, miserunt ad
eum rogantes, ne se daret in theatrum. [32]Alii autem aliud clamabant; erat enim ecclesia confusa, et
plures nesciebant qua ex causa convenissent. [33]De turba autem instruxerunt Alexandrum, propellentibus
eum Iudaeis; Alexander ergo, manu silentio postulato, volebat rationem reddere populo. [34]Quem ut
cognoverunt Iudaeum esse, vox facta est una omnium quasi per horas duas clamantium: «Magna Diana
Ephesiorum!». [35]Et cum sedasset scriba turbam dixit: «Viri Ephesii, quis enim est hominum, qui nesciat
Ephesiorum civitatem cultricem esse magnae Dianae et simulacri a Iove delapsi? [36]Cum ergo his
contradici non possit, oportet vos sedatos esse et nihil temere agere. [37]Adduxistis enim homines istos
neque sacrilegos neque blasphemantes deam nostram. [38]Quod si Demetrius et, qui cum eo sunt, artifices
habent adversus aliquem causam, conventus forenses aguntur, et proconsules sunt: accusent invicem.
[39]Si quid autem ulterius quaeritis, in legitima ecclesia poterit absolvi. [40]Nam et periclitamur argui
seditionis hodiernae, cum nullus obnoxius sit, de quo non possimus reddere rationem concursus istius».
Et cum haec dixisset, dimisit ecclesiam. **[20]** [1]Postquam autem cessavit tumultus, accersitis Paulus
discipulis et exhortatus eos, valedixit et profectus est, ut iret in Macedoniam. [2]Cum autem
perambulasset partes illas et exhortatus eos fuisset multo sermone, venit ad Graeciam; [3]cumque fecisset
menses tres, factae sunt illi insidiae a Iudaeis navigaturo in Syriam, habuitque consilium, ut reverteretur
per Macedoniam. [4]Comitabatur autem eum Sopater Pyrrhi Beroeensis, Thessalonicensium vero
Aristarchus et Secundus et Gaius Derbeus et Timotheus, Asiani vero Tychicus et Trophimus. [5]Hi cum
praecessissent, sustinebant nos Troade; [6]nos vero navigavimus post dies Azymorum a Philippis, et
venimus ad eos Troadem in diebus quinque, ubi demorati sumus diebus septem. [7]In una autem
sabbatorum cum convenissemus ad frangendum panem, Paulus disputabat eis, profecturus in crastinum,
protraxitque sermonem usque in mediam noctem. [8]Erant autem lampades copiosae in cenaculo, ubi
eramus congregati; [9]sedens autem quidam adulescens nomine Eutychus super fenestram, cum
mergeretur somno gravi disputante diutius Paulo, eductus somno cecidit de tertio cenaculo deorsum
et sublatus est mortuus. [10]Cum descendisset autem Paulus incubuit super eum et complexus dixit:
«Nolite turbari, anima enim ipsius in eo est!». [11]Ascendens autem frangensque panem et gustans
satisque allocutus usque in lucem, sic profectus est. [12]Adduxerunt autem puerum viventem et consolati
sunt non minime. [13]Nos autem praecedentes navi enavigavimus in Asson, inde suscepturi Paulum, sic
enim disposuerat volens ipse per terram iter facere. [14]Cum autem convenisset nos in Asson, assumpto
eo, venimus Mitylenen [15]et inde navigantes sequenti die pervenimus contra Chium et alia applicuimus
Samum et sequenti venimus Miletum. [16]Proposuerat enim Paulus transnavigare Ephesum, ne qua mora
illi fieret in Asia; festinabat enim, si possibile sibi esset, ut diem Pentecosten faceret Hierosolymis. [17]A
Mileto autem mittens Ephesum convocavit presbyteros ecclesiae. [18]Qui cum venissent ad eum, dixit eis:
«Vos scitis a prima die, qua ingressus sum in Asiam, qualiter vobiscum per omne tempus fuerim,
[19]serviens Domino cum omni humilitate et lacrimis et tentationibus, quae mihi acciderunt in insidiis
Iudaeorum; [20]quomodo nihil subtraxerim utilium, quominus annuntiarem vobis et docerem vos publice
et per domos, [21]testificans Iudaeis atque Graecis in Deum paenitentiam et fidem in Dominum nostrum
Iesum. [22]Et nunc ecce alligatus ego Spiritu vado in Ierusalem, quae in ea eventura sint mihi ignorans,
[23]nisi quod Spiritus Sanctus per omnes civitates protestatur mihi dicens quoniam vincula et tribulationes
me manent. [24]Sed nihili facio animam meam pretiosam mihi, dummodo consummem cursum meum et
ministerium, quod accepi a Domino Iesu, testificari evangelium gratiae Dei. [25]Et nunc ecce ego scio
quia amplius non videbitis faciem meam vos omnes, per quos transivi praedicans regnum; [26]quapropter
contestor vos hodierna die quia mundus sum a sanguine omnium, [27]non enim subterfugi, quominus
annuntiarem omne consilium Dei vobis. [28]Attendite vobis et universo gregi, in quo vos Spiritus Sanctus
posuit episcopos, pascere ecclesiam Dei, quam acquisivit sanguine suo. [29]Ego scio quoniam intrabunt
post discessionem meam lupi graves in vos non parcentes gregi, [30]et ex vobis ipsis exsurgent viri
loquentes perversa, ut abstrahant discipulos post se. [31]Propter quod vigilate memoria retinentes quoniam
per triennium nocte et die non cessavi cum lacrimis monens unumquemque vestrum. [32]Et nunc
commendo vos Deo et verbo gratiae ipsius, qui potens est aedificare et dare hereditatem in sanctificatis
omnibus. [33]Argentum aut aurum aut vestem nullius concupivi; [34]ipsi scitis quoniam ad ea, quae mihi
opus erant et his, qui mecum sunt, ministraverunt manus istae. [35]Omnia ostendi vobis quoniam sic
laborantes oportet suscipere infirmos, ac meminisse verborum Domini Iesu, quoniam ipse dixit:
"Beatius est magis dare quam accipere!"». [36]Et cum haec dixisset, positis genibus suis, cum omnibus
illis oravit. [37]Magnus autem fletus factus est omnium, et procumbentes super collum Pauli osculabantur
eum [38]dolentes maxime in verbo, quod dixerat, quoniam amplius faciem eius non essent visuri. Et

deducebant eum ad navem. **[21]** 1Cum autem factum esset ut navigaremus abstracti ab eis, recto cursu
venimus Cho et sequenti die Rhodum et inde Patara; 2et cum invenissemus navem transfretantem in
Phoenicen, ascendentes navigavimus. 3Cum paruissemus autem Cypro, et relinquentes eam ad sinistram
navigabamus in Syriam et venimus Tyrum, ibi enim navis erat expositura onus. 4Inventis autem
discipulis, mansimus ibi diebus septem; qui Paulo dicebant per Spiritum, ne iret Hierosolymam. 5Et
explicitis diebus, profecti ibamus, deducentibus nos omnibus cum uxoribus et filiis usque foras
civitatem; et positis genibus in litore orantes, 6valefecimus invicem et ascendimus in navem, illi autem
redierunt in sua. 7Nos vero navigatione explicita, a Tyro devenimus Ptolemaida et salutatis fratribus
mansimus die una apud illos. 8Alia autem die profecti venimus Caesaream et intrantes in domum
Philippi evangelistae, qui erat de septem, mansimus apud eum. 9Huic autem erant filiae quattuor
virgines prophetantes. 10Et cum moraremur plures dies, supervenit quidam a Iudaea propheta nomine
Agabus; 11is cum venisset ad nos et tulisset zonam Pauli, alligans sibi pedes et manus dixit: «Haec dicit
Spiritus Sanctus: Virum, cuius est zona haec, sic alligabunt in Ierusalem Iudaei et tradent in manus
gentium». 12Quod cum audissemus, rogabamus nos et, qui loci illius erant, ne ipse ascenderet Ierusalem.
13Tunc respondit Paulus: «Quid facitis flentes et affligentes cor meum? Ego enim non solum alligari sed
et mori in Ierusalem paratus sum propter nomen Domini Iesu». 14Et cum ei suadere non possemus,
quievimus dicentes: «Domini voluntas fiat!». 15Post dies autem istos praeparati ascendebamus
Hierosolymam; 16venerunt autem et ex discipulis a Caesarea nobiscum adducentes apud quem
hospitaremur, Mnasonem quendam Cyprium, antiquum discipulum. 17Et cum venissemus Hierosolymam,
libenter exceperunt nos fratres. 18Sequenti autem die introibat Paulus nobiscum ad Iacobum, omnesque
collecti sunt presbyteri. 19Quos cum salutasset, narrabat per singula, quae fecisset Deus in gentibus per
ministerium ipsius. 20At illi cum audissent, glorificabant Deum dixeruntque ei: «Vides, frater, quot milia
sint in Iudaeis, qui crediderunt, et omnes aemulatores sunt legis; 21audierunt autem de te quia
discessionem doceas a Moyse omnes, qui per gentes sunt, Iudaeos, dicens non debere circumcidere eos
filios suos, neque secundum consuetudines ambulare. 22Quid ergo est? Utique audient te supervenisse.
23Hoc ergo fac, quod tibi dicimus. Sunt nobis viri quattuor votum habentes super se; 24his assumptis,
sanctifica te cum illis et impende pro illis, ut radant capita, et scient omnes quia, quae de te audierunt,
nihil sunt, sed ambulas et ipse custodiens legem. 25De his autem, qui crediderunt, gentibus nos
scripsimus iudicantes, ut abstineant ab idolothyto et sanguine et suffocato et fornicatione». 26Tunc
Paulus, assumptis viris, postera die purificatus cum illis intravit in templum annuntians expletionem
dierum purificationis, donec offerretur pro unoquoque eorum oblatio. 27Dum autem septem dies
consummarentur, hi, qui de Asia erant, Iudaei cum vidissent eum in templo, concitaverunt omnem
turbam et iniecerunt ei manus 28clamantes: «Viri Israelitae, adiuvate! Hic est homo, qui adversus
populum et legem et locum hunc omnes ubique docens, insuper et Graecos induxit in templum et polluit
sanctum locum istum». 29Viderant enim Trophimum Ephesium in civitate cum ipso, quem aestimabant
quoniam in templum induxisset Paulus. 30Commotaque est civitas tota, et facta est concursio populi, et
apprehendentes Paulum trahebant eum extra templum, et statim clausae sunt ianuae. 31Quaerentibus
autem eum occidere, nuntiatum est tribuno cohortis quia tota confunditur Ierusalem, 32qui statim,
assumptis militibus et centurionibus, decucurrit ad illos; qui cum vidissent tribunum et milites,
cessaverunt percutere Paulum. 33Tunc accedens tribunus apprehendit eum et iussit alligari catenis
duabus et interrogabat quis esset et quid fecisset. 34Alii autem aliud clamabant in turba; et cum non
posset certum cognoscere prae tumultu, iussit duci eum in castra. 35Et cum venisset ad gradus, contigit
ut portaretur a militibus propter vim turbae; 36sequebatur enim multitudo populi clamantes: «Tolle
eum!». 37Et cum coepisset induci in castra, Paulus dicit tribuno: «Si licet mihi loqui aliquid ad te?». Qui
dixit: «Graece nosti? 38Nonne tu es Aegyptius, qui ante hos dies tumultum concitasti et eduxisti in
desertum quattuor milia virorum sicariorum?». 39Et dixit Paulus: «Ego homo sum quidem Iudaeus a
Tarso Ciliciae, non ignotae civitatis municeps; rogo autem te, permitte mihi loqui ad populum». 40Et
cum ille permisisset, Paulus stans in gradibus annuit manu ad plebem et, magno silentio facto, allocutus
est Hebraea lingua dicens: **[22]** 1«Viri fratres et patres, audite a me, quam ad vos nunc reddo,
rationem». 2Cum audissent autem quia Hebraea lingua loquebatur ad illos, magis praestiterunt
silentium. Et dixit: 3«Ego sum vir Iudaeus, natus Tarso Ciliciae, enutritus autem in ista civitate, secus
pedes Gamaliel eruditus iuxta veritatem paternae legis, aemulator Dei sicut et vos omnes estis hodie.
4Qui hanc viam persecutus sum usque ad mortem, alligans et tradens in custodias viros ac mulieres,
5sicut et princeps sacerdotum testimonium mihi reddit et omne concilium; a quibus et epistulas
accipiens ad fratres, Damascum pergebam, ut adducerem et eos, qui ibi essent, vinctos in Ierusalem, uti
punirentur. 6Factum est autem eunte me et appropinquante Damasco, circa mediam diem subito de caelo
circumfulsit me lux copiosa, 7et decidi in terram et audivi vocem dicentem mihi: "Saul, Saul, quid me

persequeris?”. [8]Ego autem respondi: “Quis es, Domine?”. Dixitque ad me: “Ego sum Iesus Nazarenus,
quem tu persequeris”. [9]Et qui mecum erant, lumen quidem viderunt, vocem autem non audierunt eius,
qui loquebatur mecum. [10]Et dixi: “Quid faciam, Domine?”. Dominus autem dixit ad me: “Surgens vade
Damascum, et ibi tibi dicetur de omnibus, quae statutum est tibi, ut faceres”. [11]Et cum non viderem prae
claritate luminis illius, ad manum deductus a comitibus veni Damascum. [12]Ananias autem quidam vir
religiosus secundum legem testimonium habens ab omnibus habitantibus Iudaeis, [13]veniens ad me et
astans dixit mihi: “Saul frater, respice!”. Et ego eadem hora respexi in eum. [14]At ille dixit: “Deus patrum
nostrorum praeordinavit te, ut cognosceres voluntatem eius et videres Iustum et audires vocem ex ore
eius, [15]quia eris testis illi ad omnes homines eorum, quae vidisti et audisti. [16]Et nunc quid moraris?
Exsurgens baptizare et ablue peccata tua, invocato nomine ipsius”. [17]Factum est autem revertenti mihi
in Ierusalem et oranti in templo fieri me in stupore mentis [18]et videre illum dicentem mihi: “Festina et
exi velociter ex Ierusalem, quoniam non recipient testimonium tuum de me”. [19]Et ego dixi: “Domine,
ipsi sciunt quia ego eram concludens in carcerem et caedens per synagogas eos, qui credebant in te; [20]et
cum funderetur sanguis Stephani testis tui, et ipse astabam et consentiebam et custodiebam vestimenta
interficientium illum”. [21]Et dixit ad me: “Vade, quoniam ego in nationes longe mittam te”». [22]Audiebant
autem eum usque ad hoc verbum et levaverunt vocem suam dicentes: «Tolle de terra eiusmodi, non
enim fas est eum vivere!». [23]Vociferantibus autem eis et proicientibus vestimenta sua et pulverem
iactantibus in aerem, [24]iussit tribunus induci eum in castra dicens flagellis eum interrogari, ut sciret
propter quam causam sic acclamarent ei. [25]Et cum astrinxissent eum loris, dixit astanti centurioni
Paulus: «Si hominem Romanum et indemnatum licet vobis flagellare?». [26]Quo audito, centurio
accedens ad tribunum nuntiavit dicens: «Quid acturus es? Hic enim homo Romanus est». [27]Accedens
autem tribunus dixit illi: «Dic mihi, tu Romanus es?». At ille dixit: «Etiam». [28]Et respondit tribunus:
«Ego multa summa civitatem hanc consecutus sum». Et Paulus ait: «Ego autem et natus sum».
[29]Protinus ergo discesserunt ab illo, qui eum interrogaturi erant; tribunus quoque timuit, postquam
rescivit quia Romanus esset et quia alligasset eum. [30]Postera autem die volens scire diligenter qua ex
causa accusaretur a Iudaeis, solvit eum et iussit principes sacerdotum convenire et omne concilium et
producens Paulum statuit coram illis. **[23]** [1]Intendens autem concilium Paulus ait: «Viri fratres, ego
omni conscientia bona conversatus sum ante Deum usque in hodiernum diem». [2]Princeps autem
sacerdotum Ananias praecepit astantibus sibi percutere os eius. [3]Tunc Paulus ad eum dixit: «Percutiet
te Deus, paries dealbate! Et tu sedes iudicans me secundum legem et contra legem iubes me percuti?».
[4]Et qui astabant, dixerunt: «Summum sacerdotem Dei maledicis?». [5]Dixit autem Paulus: «Nesciebam,
fratres, quia princeps est sacerdotum; scriptum est enim: “*Principem populi tui non maledices*”».
[6]Sciens autem Paulus quia una pars esset sadducaeorum et altera pharisaeorum, exclamabat in concilio:
«Viri fratres, ego pharisaeus sum, filius pharisaeorum; de spe et resurrectione mortuorum ego iudicor».
[7]Et cum haec diceret, facta est dissensio inter pharisaeos et sadducaeos, et divisa est multitudo.
[8]Sadducaei enim dicunt non esse resurrectionem neque angelum neque spiritum; pharisaei autem
utrumque confitentur. [9]Factus est autem clamor magnus, et surgentes scribae quidam partis
pharisaeorum pugnabant dicentes: «Nihil mali invenimus in homine isto: quod si spiritus locutus est ei
aut angelus»; [10]et cum magna dissensio facta esset, timens tribunus ne discerperetur Paulus ab ipsis,
iussit milites descendere, ut raperent eum de medio eorum ac deducerent in castra. [11]Sequenti autem
nocte assistens ei Dominus ait: «Constans esto! Sicut enim testificatus es, quae sunt de me in Ierusalem,
sic te oportet et Romae testificari». [12]Facta autem die, faciebant concursum Iudaei et devoverunt se
dicentes neque manducaturos neque bibituros, donec occiderent Paulum. [13]Erant autem plus quam
quadraginta, qui hanc coniurationem fecerant; [14]qui accedentes ad principes sacerdotum et seniores
dixerunt: «Devotione devovimus nos nihil gustaturos, donec occidamus Paulum. [15]Nunc ergo vos notum
facite tribuno cum concilio, ut producat illum ad vos, tamquam aliquid certius cognituri de eo; nos vero
priusquam appropiet, parati sumus interficere illum». [16]Quod cum audisset filius sororis Pauli insidias,
venit et intravit in castra nuntiavitque Paulo. [17]Vocans autem Paulus ad se unum ex centurionibus ait:
Adulescentem hunc perduc ad tribunum, habet enim aliquid indicare illi». [18]Et ille quidem assumens
eum duxit ad tribunum et ait: «Vinctus Paulus vocans rogavit me hunc adulescentem perducere ad te
habentem aliquid loqui tibi». [19]Apprehendens autem tribunus manum illius, secessit cum eo seorsum et
interrogabat: «Quid est quod habes indicare mihi?». [20]Ille autem dixit: «Iudaei constituerunt rogare te,
ut crastina die Paulum producas in concilium, quasi aliquid certius inquisiturum sit de illo. [21]Tu ergo ne
credideris illis; insidiantur enim ei ex eis viri amplius quadraginta, qui se devoverunt non manducare
neque bibere, donec interficiant eum, et nunc parati sunt exspectantes promissum tuum». [22]Tribunus
igitur dimisit adulescentem praecipiens, ne cui eloqueretur quoniam «haec nota mihi fecisti». [23]Et
vocatis duobus centurionibus, dixit: «Parate milites ducentos, ut eant usque Caesaream, et equites

septuaginta et lancearios ducentos, a tertia hora noctis, 24et iumenta praeparate», ut imponentes Paulum
salvum perducerent ad Felicem praesidem, 25scribens epistulam habentem formam hanc: 26«Claudius
Lysias optimo praesidi Felici salutem. 27Virum hunc comprehensum a Iudaeis et incipientem interfici
ab eis, superveniens cum exercitu eripui, cognito quia Romanus est. 28Volensque scire causam, propter
quam accusabant illum, deduxi in concilium eorum; 29quem inveni accusari de quaestionibus legis
ipsorum, nihil vero dignum morte aut vinculis habentem crimen. 30Et cum mihi perlatum esset de
insidiis, quae in virum pararentur, confestim misi ad te denuntians et accusatoribus, ut dicant adversum
eum apud te». 31Milites ergo, secundum praeceptum sibi assumentes Paulum, duxerunt per noctem in
Antipatridem; 32et postera die dimissis equitibus, ut abirent cum eo, reversi sunt ad castra. 33Qui cum
venissent Caesaream et tradidissent epistulam praesidi, statuerunt ante illum et Paulum. 34Cum legisset
autem et interrogasset de qua provincia esset et cognoscens quia de Cilicia: 35«Audiam te, inquit, cum
et accusatores tui venerint»; iussitque in praetorio Herodis custodiri eum. **[24]** 1Post quinque autem
dies descendit princeps sacerdotum Ananias cum senioribus quibusdam et Tertullo quodam oratore, qui
adierunt praesidem adversus Paulum. 2Et citato eo coepit accusare Tertullus dicens: «Cum in multa pace
agamus per te, et multa corrigantur genti huic per tuam providentiam, 3semper et ubique suscipimus,
optime Felix, cum omni gratiarum actione. 4Ne diutius autem te protraham, oro breviter audias nos pro
tua clementia. 5Invenimus enim hunc hominem pestiferum et concitantem seditiones omnibus Iudaeis,
qui sunt in universo orbe, et auctorem seditionis sectae Nazarenorum, 6qui etiam templum violare
conatus est, quem et apprehendimus, 8a quo poteris ipse diiudicans de omnibus istis cognoscere, de
quibus nos accusamus eum». 9Adiecerunt autem et Iudaei dicentes haec ita se habere. 10Respondit
autem Paulus, annuente sibi praeside dicere: «Ex multis annis esse te iudicem genti huic sciens bono
animo de causa mea rationem reddam, 11cum possis cognoscere quia non plus sunt dies mihi quam
duodecim, ex quo ascendi adorare in Ierusalem, 12et neque in templo invenerunt me cum aliquo
disputantem aut concursum facientem turbae neque in synagogis neque in civitate, 13neque probare
possunt tibi, de quibus nunc accusant me. 14Confiteor autem hoc tibi quod secundum viam, quam dicunt
haeresim, sic deservio patrio Deo credens omnibus, quae secundum Legem sunt et in Prophetis scripta,
15spem habens in Deum, quam et hi ipsi exspectant, resurrectionem futuram iustorum et iniquorum. 16In
hoc et ipse studeo sine offendiculo conscientiam habere ad Deum et ad homines semper. 17Post annos
autem plures eleemosynas facturus in gentem meam veni et oblationes, 18in quibus invenerunt me
purificatum in templo, non cum turba neque cum tumultu; 19quidam autem ex Asia Iudaei, quos
oportebat apud te praesto esse et accusare si quid haberent adversum me 20aut hi ipsi dicant quid
invenerint iniquitatis, cum starem in concilio, 21nisi de una hac voce, qua clamavi inter eos stans: De
resurrectione mortuorum ego iudicor hodie apud vos!». 22Distulit autem illos Felix certissime sciens ea,
quae de hac via sunt, dicens: «Cum tribunus Lysias descenderit, cognoscam causam vestram», 23iubens
centurioni custodiri eum et habere mitigationem, nec quemquam prohibere de suis ministrare ei. 24Post
aliquot autem dies adveniens Felix cum Drusilla uxore sua, quae erat Iudaea, vocavit Paulum et audivit
ab eo de fide, quae est in Christum Iesum. 25Disputante autem illo de iustitia et continentia et de iudicio
futuro, timefactus Felix respondit: «Quod nunc attinet, vade; tempore autem opportuno accersiam te»,
26simul et sperans quia pecunia daretur sibi a Paulo; propter quod et frequenter accersiens eum
loquebatur cum eo. 27Biennio autem expleto, accepit successorem Felix Porcium Festum; volensque
gratiam praestare Iudaeis, Felix reliquit Paulum vinctum. **[25]** 1Festus ergo cum venisset in provinciam,
post triduum ascendit Hierosolymam a Caesarea; 2adieruntque eum principes sacerdotum et primi
Iudaeorum adversus Paulum, et rogabant eum 3postulantes gratiam adversum eum, ut iuberet perduci
eum in Ierusalem, insidias tendentes, ut eum interficerent in via. 4Festus igitur respondit servari Paulum
in Caesarea, se autem maturius profecturum: 5«Qui ergo in vobis, ait, potentes sunt, descendentes simul,
si quod est in viro crimen, accusent eum». 6Demoratus autem inter eos dies non amplius quam octo aut
decem, descendit Caesaream, et altera die sedit pro tribunali et iussit Paulum adduci. 7Qui cum
perductus esset, circumsteterunt eum, qui ab Hierosolyma descenderant, Iudaei, multas et graves causas
obicientes, quas non poterant probare, 8Paulo rationem reddente: «Neque in legem Iudaeorum neque in
templum neque in Caesarem quidquam peccavi». 9Festus autem volens Iudaeis gratiam praestare,
respondens Paulo dixit: «Vis Hierosolymam ascendere et ibi de his iudicari apud me?». 10Dixit autem
Paulus: «Ad tribunal Caesaris sto, ubi me oportet iudicari. Iudaeis nihil nocui, sicut et tu melius nosti.
11Si ergo iniuste egi et dignum morte aliquid feci, non recuso mori; si vero nihil est eorum, quae hi
accusant me, nemo potest me illis donare. Caesarem appello!». 12Tunc Festus cum consilio locutus
respondit: «Caesarem appellasti; ad Caesarem ibis». 13Et cum dies aliquot transacti essent, Agrippa rex
et Berenice descenderunt Caesaream et salutaverunt Festum. 14Et cum dies plures ibi demorarentur,
Festus regi indicavit de Paulo dicens: «Vir quidam est derelictus a Felice vinctus, 15de quo cum essem

Hierosolymis, adierunt me principes sacerdotum et seniores Iudaeorum postulantes adversus illum
damnationem; 16ad quos respondi quia non est consuetudo Romanis donare aliquem hominem,
priusquam is, qui accusatur, praesentes habeat accusatores locumque defendendi se ab accusatione
accipiat. 17Cum ergo huc convenissent, sine ulla dilatione sequenti die sedens pro tribunali iussi adduci
virum; 18de quo cum stetissent accusatores, nullam causam deferebant, de quibus ego suspicabar malis,
19quaestiones vero quasdam de sua superstitione habebant adversus eum et de quodam Iesu defuncto,
quem affirmabat Paulus vivere. 20Haesitans autem ego de huiusmodi quaestione, dicebam si vellet ire
Hierosolymam et ibi iudicari de istis. 21Paulo autem appellante, ut servaretur ad Augusti cognitionem,
iussi servari eum, donec mittam eum ad Caesarem». 22Agrippa autem ad Festum: «Volebam et ipse
hominem audire!». «Cras, inquit, audies eum». 23Altera autem die, cum venisset Agrippa et Berenice
cum multa ambitione, et introissent in auditorium cum tribunis et viris principalibus civitatis, et iubente
Festo, adductus est Paulus. 24Et dicit Festus: «Agrippa rex et omnes, qui simul adestis nobiscum viri,
videtis hunc, de quo omnis multitudo Iudaeorum interpellavit me Hierosolymis et hic, clamantes non
oportere eum vivere amplius. 25Ego vero comperi nihil dignum eum morte fecisse, ipso autem hoc
appellante Augustum, iudicavi mittere. 26De quo quid certum scribam domino, non habeo; propter quod
produxi eum ad vos et maxime ad te, rex Agrippa, ut, interrogatione facta, habeam quid scribam: 27sine
ratione enim mihi videtur mittere vinctum et causas eius non significare». **[26]** 1Agrippa vero ad
Paulum ait: «Permittitur tibi loqui pro temetipso». Tunc Paulus, extenta manu, coepit rationem reddere:
2«De omnibus, quibus accusor a Iudaeis, rex Agrippa, aestimo me beatum, apud te cum sim defensurus
me hodie, 3maxime te sciente omnia, quae apud Iudaeos sunt consuetudines et quaestiones; propter
quod obsecro patienter me audias. 4Et quidem vitam meam a iuventute, quae ab initio fuit in gente mea
et in Hierosolymis, noverunt omnes Iudaei, 5praescientes me ab initio, si velint testimonium perhibere,
quoniam secundum diligentissimam sectam nostrae religionis vixi pharisaeus. 6Et nunc propter spem
eius, quae ad patres nostros repromissionis facta est a Deo, sto iudicio subiectus, 7in quam duodecim
tribus nostrae cum perseverantia nocte ac die deservientes sperant devenire; de qua spe accusor a
Iudaeis, rex! 8Quid incredibile iudicatur apud vos, si Deus mortuos suscitat? 9Et ego quidem
existimaveram me adversus nomen Iesu Nazareni debere multa contraria agere; 10quod et feci
Hierosolymis, et multos sanctorum ego in carceribus inclusi, a principibus sacerdotum potestate accepta,
et cum occiderentur, detuli sententiam, 11et per omnes synagogas frequenter puniens eos compellebam
blasphemare, et abundantius insaniens in eos persequebar usque in exteras civitates. 12In quibus dum
irem Damascum cum potestate et permissu principum sacerdotum, 13die media in via vidi, rex, de caelo
supra splendorem solis circumfulgens me lumen et eos, qui mecum simul ibant; 14omnesque nos cum
decidissemus in terram, audivi vocem loquentem mihi Hebraica lingua: "Saul, Saul, quid me
persequeris? Durum est tibi contra stimulum calcitrare". 15Ego autem dixi: "Quis es, Domine?".
Dominus autem dixit: "Ego sum Iesus, quem tu persequeris. 16Sed exsurge et sta super pedes tuos; ad
hoc enim apparui tibi, ut constituam te ministrum et testem eorum, quae vidisti, et eorum, quibus
apparebo tibi, 17eripiens te de populo et de gentibus, in quas ego mitto te 18aperire oculos eorum, ut
convertantur a tenebris ad lucem et de potestate Satanae ad Deum, ut accipiant remissionem peccatorum
et sortem inter sanctificatos per fidem, quae est in me". 19Unde, rex Agrippa, non fui incredulus caelestis
visionis, 20sed his, qui sunt Damasci primum et Hierosolymis, et in omnem regionem Iudaeae et
gentibus annuntiabam, ut paenitentiam agerent et converterentur ad Deum digna paenitentiae opera
facientes. 21Hac ex causa me Iudaei, cum essem in templo comprehensum, tentabant interficere.
22Auxilium igitur assecutus a Deo usque in hodiernum diem sto testificans minori atque maiori, nihil
extra dicens quam ea, quae prophetae sunt locuti futura esse et Moyses, 23si passibilis Christus, si
primus ex resurrectione mortuorum lumen annuntiaturus est populo et gentibus». 24Sic autem eo
rationem reddente, Festus magna voce dixit: «Insanis, Paule; multae te litterae ad insaniam
convertunt!». 25At Paulus: «Non insanio, inquit, optime Feste, sed veritatis et sobrietatis verba eloquor.
26Scit enim de his rex, ad quem et audenter loquor; latere enim eum nihil horum arbitror, neque enim in
angulo hoc gestum est. 27Credis, rex Agrippa, prophetis? Scio quia credis». 28Agrippa autem ad Paulum:
«In modico suades me Christianum fieri!». 29Et Paulus: «Optarem apud Deum et in modico et in magno
non tantum te sed et omnes hos, qui audiunt me hodie, fieri tales, qualis et ego sum, exceptis vinculis
his!». 30Et exsurrexit rex et praeses et Berenice et, qui assidebant eis, 31et cum secessissent, loquebantur
ad invicem dicentes: «Nihil morte aut vinculis dignum quid facit homo iste». 32Agrippa autem Festo
dixit: «Dimitti poterat homo hic, si non appellasset Caesarem». **[27]** 1Ut autem iudicatum est navigare
nos in Italiam, tradiderunt et Paulum et quosdam alios vinctos centurioni nomine Iulio, cohortis
Augustae. 2Ascendentes autem navem Hadramyttenam, incipientem navigare circa Asiae loca,
sustulimus, perseverante nobiscum Aristarcho Macedone Thessalonicensi; 3sequenti autem die

devenimus Sidonem, et humane tractans Iulius Paulum permisit ad amicos ire et curam sui agere. [4]Et
inde cum sustulissemus, subnavigavimus Cypro, propterea quod essent venti contrarii, [5]et pelagus
Ciliciae et Pamphyliae navigantes venimus Myram, quae est Lyciae. [6]Et ibi inveniens centurio navem
Alexandrinam navigantem in Italiam transposuit nos in eam. [7]Et cum multis diebus tarde navigaremus
et vix devenissemus contra Cnidum, prohibente nos vento, subnavigavimus Cretae secundum
Salmonem, [8]et vix iuxta eam navigantes venimus in locum quendam, qui vocatur Boni Portus, cui iuxta
erat civitas Lasaea. [9]Multo autem tempore peracto, et cum iam non esset tuta navigatio, eo quod et
ieiunium iam praeterisset, monebat Paulus [10]dicens eis: «Viri, video quoniam cum iniuria et multo
damno non solum oneris et navis sed etiam animarum nostrarum incipit esse navigatio». [11]Centurio
autem gubernatori et nauclero magis credebat quam his, quae a Paulo dicebantur. [12]Et cum aptus portus
non esset ad hiemandum, plurimi statuerunt consilium enavigare inde, si quo modo possent devenientes
Phoenicen hiemare, portum Cretae respicientem ad africum et ad caurum. [13]Aspirante autem austro,
aestimantes propositum se tenere, cum sustulissent, propius legebant Cretam. [14]Non post multum autem
misit se contra ipsam ventus typhonicus, qui vocatur euroaquilo; [15]cumque arrepta esset navis et non
posset conari in ventum, data nave flatibus, ferebamur. [16]Insulam autem quandam decurrentes, quae
vocatur Cauda, potuimus vix obtinere scapham, [17]qua sublata, adiutoriis utebantur accingentes navem;
et timentes, ne in Syrtim inciderent, submisso vase, sic ferebantur. [18]Valide autem nobis tempestate
iactatis, sequenti die iactum fecerunt [19]et tertia die suis manibus armamenta navis proiecerunt. [20]Neque
sole autem neque sideribus apparentibus per plures dies, et tempestate non exigua imminente, iam
auferebatur spes omnis salutis nostrae. [21]Et cum multa ieiunatio fuisset, tunc stans Paulus in medio
eorum dixit: «Oportebat quidem, o viri, audito me, non tollere a Creta lucrique facere iniuriam hanc
et iacturam. [22]Et nunc suadeo vobis bono animo esse, nulla enim amissio animae erit ex vobis
praeterquam navis; [23]astitit enim mihi hac nocte angelus Dei, cuius sum ego, cui et deservio, [24]dicens:
"Ne timeas, Paule; Caesari te oportet assistere, et ecce donavit tibi Deus omnes, qui navigant tecum".
[25]Propter quod bono animo estote, viri; credo enim Deo quia sic erit, quemadmodum dictum est mihi.
[26]In insulam autem quandam oportet nos incidere». [27]Sed posteaquam quarta decima nox supervenit,
cum ferremur in Hadria, circa mediam noctem suspicabantur nautae apparere sibi aliquam regionem.
[28]Qui submittentes bolidem invenerunt passus viginti et pusillum inde separati et rursum submittentes
invenerunt passus quindecim; [29]timentes autem, ne in aspera loca incideremus, de puppi mittentes
ancoras quattuor optabant diem fieri. [30]Nautis vero quaerentibus fugere de navi, cum demisissent
scapham in mare sub obtentu, quasi a prora inciperent ancoras extendere, [31]dixit Paulus centurioni et
militibus: «Nisi hi in navi manserint, vos salvi fieri non potestis». [32]Tunc absciderunt milites funes
scaphae et passi sunt eam excidere. [33]Donec autem lux inciperet fieri, rogabat Paulus omnes sumere
cibum dicens: «Quarta decima hodie die exspectantes ieiuni permanetis nihil accipientes; [34]propter quod
rogo vos accipere cibum, hoc enim pro salute vestra est, quia nullius vestrum capillus de capite peribit».
[35]Et cum haec dixisset et sumpsisset panem, gratias egit Deo in conspectu omnium et, cum fregisset,
coepit manducare. [36]Animaequiores autem facti omnes et ipsi assumpserunt cibum. [37]Eramus vero
universae animae in navi ducentae septuaginta sex. [38]Et satiati cibo alleviabant navem iactantes triticum
in mare. [39]Cum autem dies factus esset, terram non agnoscebant, sinum vero quendam considerabant
habentem litus, in quem cogitabant si possent eicere navem. [40]Et cum ancoras abstulissent,
committebant mari simul laxantes iuncturas gubernaculorum et, levato artemone, secundum flatum
aurae tendebant ad litus. [41]Et cum incidissent in locum dithalassum, impegerunt navem; et prora quidem
fixa manebat immobilis, puppis vero solvebatur a vi fluctuum. [42]Militum autem consilium fuit, ut
custodias occiderent, ne quis, cum enatasset, effugeret; [43]centurio autem volens servare Paulum
prohibuit eos a consilio, iussitque eos, qui possent natare, mittere se primos et ad terram exire [44]et
ceteros, quosdam in tabulis, quosdam vero super ea, quae de navi essent; et sic factum est ut omnes
evaderent ad terram. **[28]** [1]Et cum evasissemus, tunc cognovimus quia Melita insula vocatur. [2]Barbari
vero praestabant non modicam humanitatem nobis; accensa enim pyra suscipiebant nos omnes propter
imbrem, qui imminebat et frigus. [3]Cum congregasset autem Paulus sarmentorum aliquantam
multitudinem et imposuisset super ignem, vipera, a calore cum processisset, invasit manum eius. [4]Ut
vero viderunt barbari pendentem bestiam de manu eius, ad invicem dicebant: «Utique homicida est
homo hic, qui cum evaserit de mari, Ultio non permisit vivere». [5]Et ille quidem excutiens bestiam in
ignem, nihil mali passus est; [6]at illi exspectabant eum in tumorem convertendum aut subito casurum et
mori. Diu autem illis exspectantibus et videntibus nihil mali in eo fieri, convertentes se dicebant eum
esse deum. [7]In locis autem illis erant praedia principis insulae nomine Publii, qui nos suscipiens triduo
benigne hospitio recepit. [8]Contigit autem patrem Publii febribus et dysenteria vexatum iacere, ad quem
Paulus intravit et, cum orasset et imposuisset ei manus, sanavit eum. [9]Quo facto et ceteri, qui in insula

habebant infirmitates, accedebant et curabantur; [10]qui etiam multis honoribus nos honoraverunt et
navigantibus imposuerunt, quae necessaria erant. [11]Post menses autem tres navigavimus in navi
Alexandrina, quae in insula hiemaverat, cui erat insigne Castorum. [12]Et cum venissemus Syracusam,
mansimus ibi triduo; [13]inde solventes devenimus Rhegium. Et post unum diem, superveniente austro,
secunda die venimus Puteolos, [14]ubi inventis fratribus rogati sumus manere apud eos dies septem; et sic
venimus Romam. [15]Et inde cum audissent de nobis fratres, occurrerunt nobis usque ad Appii Forum
et Tres Tabernas; quos cum vidisset Paulus, gratias agens Deo, accepit fiduciam. [16]Cum introissemus
autem Romam, permissum est Paulo manere sibimet cum custodiente se milite. [17]Factum est autem ut
post tertium diem convocaret primos Iudaeorum; cumque convenissent dicebat eis: «Ego, viri fratres,
nihil adversus plebem faciens aut mores paternos, vinctus ab Hierosolymis traditus sum in manus
Romanorum, [18]qui cum interrogationem de me habuissent, volebant dimittere eo quod nulla causa esset
mortis in me; [19]contradicentibus autem Iudaeis, coactus sum appellare Caesarem, non quasi gentem
meam habens aliquid accusare. [20]Propter hanc igitur causam rogavi vos videre et alloqui; propter spem
enim Israel catena hac circumdatus sum». [21]At illi dixerunt ad eum: «Nos neque litteras accepimus de
te a Iudaea, neque adveniens aliquis fratrum nuntiavit aut locutus est quid de te malum. [22]Rogamus
autem a te audire quae sentis, nam de secta hac notum est nobis quia ubique ei contradicitur». [23]Cum
constituissent autem illi diem, venerunt ad eum in hospitium plures, quibus exponebat testificans
regnum Dei, suadensque eos de Iesu ex Lege Moysis et Prophetis a mane usque ad vesperam. [24]Et
quidam credebant his quae dicebantur, quidam vero non credebant; [25]cumque invicem non essent
consentientes, discedebant, dicente Paulo unum verbum: «Bene Spiritus Sanctus locutus est per Isaiam
prophetam ad patres vestros [26]dicens: "*Vade ad populum istum et dic: / Auditu audietis et non
intellegetis, / et videntes videbitis et non perspicietis. /* [27]*Incrassatum est enim cor populi huius, / et
auribus graviter audierunt, / et oculos suos compresserunt, / ne forte videant oculis / et auribus audiant
/ et corde intellegant et convertantur, / et sanabo illos*". [28]Notum ergo sit vobis quoniam gentibus
missum est hoc salutare Dei; ipsi et audient!».[(29)] [30]Mansit autem biennio toto in suo conducto; et
suscipiebat omnes qui ingrediebantur ad eum, [31]praedicans regnum Dei et docens quae sunt de Domino
Iesu Christo cum omni fiducia sine prohibitione.

Explanatory Notes

Asterisks in the text of the New Testament refer to these RSVCE "Explanatory Notes".

THE GOSPEL ACCORDING TO MATTHEW

1:1: The genealogy is given to show that Jesus had the descent required for Messiahship, i.e. from Abraham and, in particular, from David the king.

1:16: Joseph's, not Mary's, descent is given here, as the Jews did not usually reckon descent through the mother. Joseph was the legal and presumed father, and it was this fact that conferred rights of inheritance, in this case, the fulfilment of the Messianic promises.

1:25: This means only that Joseph had nothing to do with the conception of Jesus. It implies nothing as to what happened afterwards.

3:2, *Repent* implies an internal change of heart.

3:6: Not a Christian baptism but a preparation for it.

3:15: Though without sin, Jesus wished to be baptized by John, as this was the final preparation for his Messianic mission.

5:17: Jesus came to bring the old law to its natural fulfilment in the new while discarding what had become obsolete; cf. Jn 4:21.

5:29: An exaggeration to emphasize the need to avoid occasions of sin.

5:32, *unchastity*: The Greek word used here appears to refer to marriages which were not legally marriages, because they were either within the forbidden degrees of consanguinity (Lev 18:6–16) or contracted with a Gentile. The phrase *except on the ground of unchastity* does not occur in the parallel passage in Lk 16:18. See also Mt 19:9 (Mk 10:11–12), and especially 1 Cor 7:10–11, which shows that the prohibition is unconditional.

6:6: This does not, of course, exclude public worship but ostentatious prayer.

6:24, *mammon*: i.e., riches.

8:3: The miracles of Jesus were never performed to amaze people and shock them into belief. They were worked with a view to a real strengthening of faith in the recipient or beholder, from whom the proper dispositions were required.

8:29, *before the time:* Before the day of judgment the demons are permitted by God to tempt men and even to possess them.

10:5: The gospel, the Messianic salvation, had first to be preached and offered to the chosen people, Israel. Later it would be offered to the Gentiles.

11:3: The Baptist expected more obvious signs of the Messiah. By quoting the prophet Isaiah, Jesus showed that he was indeed inaugurating the Messianic kingdom—but by doing good rather than by glorious manifestations or sudden punishments.

11:27: This shows a profound relationship between the Son and the Father, far superior to adoptive sonship.

12:14: The Pharisees regarded healing as work and so forbade it on the sabbath.

12:24, *Beel-zebul:* Name of a Canaanite god meaning "the Prince-god". The Jews interpreted this name as "Prince of demons", because for them all false gods were demons.

12:31: To attribute to the devil the works of the Holy Spirit seems to imply a hardness of heart which precludes repentance.

12:46, *brethren*: The Greek word or its Semitic equivalent was used for varying degrees of blood relationship; cf. Gen 14:14; 29:12; Lev 10:4.

12:48: Jesus puts the work of salvation before family relationships. It is not said, however, that he refused to see them.

13:12: To those well-disposed Jews who have made good use of the old covenant will now be given the perfection of the new. On the other hand, from those who have rejected God's advances will now be taken away even that which they have, because the old covenant is passing away.

13:52: This is Matthew's ideal: that the learned Jew should become the disciple of Jesus and so add the riches of the new covenant to those of the old, which he already possesses; cf. verse 12.

13:55: See note on Mt 12:46.

Explanatory Notes

14:33: Their realization of his Godhead was the prelude to Peter's confession of faith at Caesarea Philippi (Mt 16:16).

15:5: By dedicating his property to God, i.e. to the temple, a man could avoid having to help his parents, without actually giving up what he had. The scribes held such a vow to be valid without necessarily approving it.

15:24: See note on 10:5.

16:14: The title of prophet had a Messianic significance because the gift of prophecy, which had been extinct since Malachi, was expected to return at the beginning of the Messianic era, especially by an outpouring of the Spirit as foretold by the prophet Joel and as realized in Acts 2:16.

16:16: The context shows that Peter recognizes the sonship of Jesus as divine and not adoptive like ours. Mark and Luke in the parallel passages mention only the confession of the Messiahship.

16:18: The name "Peter" comes from the Greek word for "rock". Jesus makes him the foundation on which the Church is to be built. The word "church" means "assembly" or "society" of believers. The Hebrew equivalent is used in the Old Testament to indicate the chosen people. In applying it to the church Jesus shows it to be the Messianic community foretold by the prophets. See note on Mt 18:18.

16:19, *the kingdom of heaven*: Peter has the key to the gates of the city of God. This power is exercised through the church. "Binding" and "loosing" are rabbinic terms referring to excommunication, then later to forbidding or allowing something. Not only can Peter admit to the kingdom; he also has power to make authoritative decisions in matters of faith or morals.

16:25, *life* (both times): A play on the word "life"—natural and supernatural; cf. Mk 8:35–36.

17:4: Peter thought the glorious Messianic kingdom had come. In fact, Jesus allowed this glimpse of his glory to strengthen them for the coming passion.

18:9, *Gehenna* (see footnote **b**) was the name of a valley south of Jerusalem where human sacrifice had once been practised; cf. 2 Chron 33:6. Later it became a cursed place and refuse dump, and the name came to symbolize the Christian place of punishment.

18:18: To the other apostles is given a share in the authority given to Peter.

19:9: This appears to refer to the case in Mt 5:32, though the Greek word for "except" is different.

19:11–12: Jesus means that a life of continence is to be chosen only by those who are called to it for the sake of the kingdom of God.

21:9: The crowd openly recognize Jesus as the Messiah and he allows it for the first time.

21:23: They object to the assumption of authority implicit in the manner of his entry into the city and in his expulsion of the sellers from the temple.

21:33–44: This parable is really an allegory in which almost every detail represents something in God's dealings with Israel.

22:11: The wedding garment represents the dispositions necessary for admission to the kingdom.

23:5, *phylacteries*: Little leather boxes containing, on a very small scroll, the principal words of the law; cf. Deut 6:4–9. Taking the command literally, they fastened these to their arms and their foreheads.

23:9: i.e., "Do not use the title without reference to God's universal fatherhood." He cannot mean that the title is never to be used by a son to his father.

24:1—25:46: The "Eschatological Discourse," as it is called, deals with the fall of Jerusalem and the end of the world. The two themes seem to be inextricably intermingled in the Gospels as we now have it, but it is possible that originally they were in separate discourses. However, the fusion of the two does bring out their connection. The one prefigures the other. Moreover, in the reverse direction, so to speak, the language used to describe the day of the Lord in Joel and elsewhere is here applied to the fall of Jerusalem, the details of which must therefore not be taken too literally (24:29).

25:29: See note on 13:12.

26:17: The passover was celebrated this year on the Friday evening (Jn 18:28). Jesus must have anticipated the passover meal because he would be dead the following day and because the meal prefigured his death.

26:26: The details of the Eucharist are superimposed on the ritual of the passover.

26:51: It was Peter, as John in his later Gospel tells us (Jn 18:10), though Matthew is reluctant to say so.

26:59: They sought evidence against him and this was necessarily false.

26:64–65: For the first time Jesus speaks clearly of his own identity. Caiaphas evidently understands him to claim divinity.

27:46: Jesus applies Psalm 22 (Vulgate 21) to himself.

27:66: The sealing and guarding only helped to make the subsequent resurrection more obvious.

28:1–20: The resurrection appearances. There are divergent traditions in the Gospels, Galilean and Judean. Paul adds his own record (1 Cor 15). The accounts do not easily fit together, but this is surely evidence of their genuineness. There is no attempt to produce an artificial conformity.

THE GOSPEL ACCORDING TO MARK

1:34: Throughout his ministry Jesus forbade the demons and those he healed of their infirmities to reveal his identity as Messiah, because the people, with their ideas of a national leader to come, were only too prone to mistake his true mission.
2:14, *Levi*: Mark does not identify him with Matthew the apostle; cf. Mt 9:9.
3:31, *brethren*: See note on Mt 12:46.
4:12, *so that . . .* : One might rephrase this: "So that the scripture might be fulfilled"; cf. Jn 18:32; 19:24, 28. It was not God's intention to prevent their understanding. Matthew avoids this difficulty by writing, "I speak to them in parables, *because* seeing they do not see" (Mt 13:13).
5:43: Knowing their nationalistic views about the Messiah to come, Jesus wished to avoid a tumult.
7:3: Mark, writing for Gentiles, explains these Jewish customs.
8:36, *life*: See note on Mt 16:25.
9:13, *Elijah has come*: i.e., in the person of the Baptist (Mt 11:14).
10:24, *amazed at his words*: The Old Testament often records God's offers of material rewards for observance of his laws. This was because the future life was not yet revealed. It was therefore taken for granted, in spite of contrary evidence, that riches were a sign of God's favour.
10:30: Some of the reward will be given in this life.
14:13: It was unusual for a man to carry water; it was a woman's task.
14:51–52: This young man is usually supposed to have been the evangelist himself.
15:1: The Jews could not execute Jesus without the Roman governor's permission.
15:40, *the younger*, or "the Less".
16:1: There had been no time on the Friday to anoint him before the sabbath rest.
16:9–20: This passage is regarded as inspired and canonical scripture even if not written by Mark. As it is missing from some important manuscripts, it is possible that Mark did not write it. On the other hand, he would hardly have left his Gospel unfinished at verse 8. Many think that the original ending was lost at a very early date and that this ending was composed at the end of the apostolic period to take its place.

THE GOSPEL ACCORDING TO LUKE

1:3, *Theophilus* is again referred to in Acts 1:1, but nothing is known of him.
1:5—2:52: The "Infancy Gospel;" as it is called, is written in a markedly Semitic style which differs from that of the rest of the Gospel. It appears to be based on the reminiscences of Mary.
1:30: The words of the angel are drawn from Messianic passages in the Old Testament.
1:46–55; The *Magnificat* is based on the Song of Hannah (1 Sam 2:1–10), and other Old Testament passages which describes God's favour towards Israel and especially towards the poor and lowly.
1:69, *a horn of salvation*: i.e., a mighty saviour.
2:7, *first-born*: The term connotes possession of certain rights, privileges and obligations; cf. Ex 13:1–2, 11–16. The word is used even in modern times without necessarily implying subsequent births.
2:34, *for the fall*: i.e., in the sense that by rejecting his claims many would sin grievously.
2:49: Jesus stresses the priority of his duty to his Father, which involves a high degree of independence of earthly ties.
3:2: See note on Jn 18:13.
3:7, *brood of vipers*: This epithet seems to have been directed mainly at the Pharisees; cf. Mt 3:7.
3:23: This genealogy, more universalist than that of Matthew, goes back to Adam, the ancestor of all men, and then to God, his Maker. Like Matthew, however, it gives the genealogy of Joseph, though Mary may well have been of the family of David.
4:16–30: This account of the visit to the synagogue seems to be composed of the details of more than one visit. Luke is trying here to underline the contrast between Christ's offer of salvation and the people's refusal of it.

6:20–49: Luke's discourse is shorter than that of Matthew because it does not contain Matthew's additional material collected from other occasions, or his details which would interest only Jews.
7:28: John, by virtue of his office, belonged to the old dispensation, the time of preparation for the kingdom. In terms of spiritual status, even the humbler members of the kingdom were superior to him.
7:47: The preceding parable suggests that she loved much because she had been forgiven much. Jesus now implies that her love is a sign rather than a cause of forgiveness, thus confirming the point of the parable.
8:19, *brethren*: See note on Mt 12:46.
8:39: There was no reason for secrecy (to avoid popular disturbance) in a non-Jewish area.
9:51: Here begins the "travel narrative" of Luke, which continues up to the Passion.
received up: i.e., into heaven; cf. 2 Kings 2:9–11; Acts 1:2, 11. The term here includes his passion, death, resurrection and ascension.
9:53: The Samaritans worshiped on Mount Gerizim, while orthodox Jews, of course, went to Jerusalem, and to Jerusalem only for sacrifice.
10:18: Jesus refers to the fall of the angels (cf. Rev 12:9), while he speaks of his conquest of the forces of evil.
14:26: Christ's disciples must be prepared to part from anyone who prevents them from serving him.
16:8: The master commended his foresight without approving what he actually did.
17:20: At that time, many people were expecting to see the kingdom inaugurated with striking manifestations; cf. 19:11.
19:41–44: These moving words spoken over the city are full of scriptural allusions. Moreover, the details given could apply as well to the siege of 587 BC as to that of AD 70. It is not safe, therefore, to argue from this passage that the fall of the city had already taken place when Luke wrote his Gospel.
20:37: As elsewhere (1 Cor 15:13–19), survival after death is linked with the resurrection of the body.
21:24, *the times of the Gentiles*: i.e., those during which the Gentiles will take the place of the unbelieving people of Israel. Evidently, therefore, the end of the world does not coincide with the fall of Jerusalem. St Paul says that the Jews will be converted before the end (Rom 11:26).
22:52: Matthew and Mark describe the arrest first, before Christ's words. Luke and John both put his address to the soldiers and officials before the arrest, doubtless to stress his command over events.
23:2: They purposely produce political charges, as these alone would interest Pilate.
23:14: Luke, writing for Gentiles, makes it clear that Pilate wanted to release Jesus.
23:31: One does not burn green wood. The meaning is that, if an innocent man is thus punished, what must the guilty (dry wood) expect.
24:38: Luke stresses this episode for the benefit of his Greek readers, for whom the resurrection of the body was both impossible and absurd; cf. Acts 17:32.

THE GOSPEL ACCORDING TO JOHN

1:1: John begins by giving his Gospel a theological background. By speaking at once of "the Word" he implies that his readers are familiar with the term. To Gentiles it indicated some form of divine revelation or self-expression. Jews would equate it with the divine Wisdom described in Proverbs, which already appears as something more than a divine quality and has some relation with the visible world. In Sirach and Wisdom the idea is further developed. In the last-named book, Wisdom appears as a pre-existing person, taking part in the creation of the world and having a mission to reveal God to his creatures; cf. Wisdom 7:22—8:1.
1:5, *light . . . darkness*: One of the familiar themes of the Gospel.
1:29: John applies to Jesus the Messianic prophecy of Is 53:6–7, perhaps worded more explicitly by the evangelist in later years.
2:4, *what have you to do with me?* While this expression always implies a divergence of view, the precise meaning is to be determined by the context, which here shows that it is not an unqualified refusal, still less a rebuke.
2:12, *brethren*: See note on Mt 12:46.
3:22, *baptized*: A baptism like that of John. The time for baptism "in the Spirit" had not yet come.
3:24: From the other Gospels we learn that, after John was arrested, Jesus withdrew from Judea.
4:20, *this mountain*: Gerizim, on which the Samaritans worshiped.
5:18, *broke the sabbath*: i.e., broke the sabbath as interpreted by them; see note on Mt 12:14.

6:51: Jesus is the "living bread," both as Word of God (verses 32ff) and as sacrificial victim for the salvation of man.

6:52: A natural question to ask. Jesus answers, not by explaining it away, but by re-emphasizing the reality, though not, of course, in the crude sense implied in their question.

6:62: When Jesus ascends into heaven they will know that he spoke the truth.

7:3, *brethren*: See note on Mt 12:46.

7:53—8:11: This passage, though absent from some of the most ancient manuscripts, is regarded as inspired and canonical by the Church. The style suggests that it is not by St John, and that it belongs to the Synoptic Tradition.

8:21, *die in your sin*: Theirs is that sin against the truth which is the sin against the Holy Spirit; cf. Mt 12:31.

8:41: They mean, "We are not idolaters," and protest their fidelity to God their Father: see notes on Rev 14:4 and 17:2.

8:56, *he saw it* either in prophetic vision while on earth or by some special privilege after death.

8:58: The present tense indicates Christ's eternal existence as God.

9:4: Jesus explains in advance the purpose of the miracle.

10:14, *the good shepherd*: The name has Messianic significance; cf. Ezek 34.

10:18: Throughout the Gospel, Jesus insists that he is master of his own life and no one takes it from him; cf. 18:6 (at his arrest); 19:11 (before Pilate); 19:30 (on the cross).

11:6, *stayed two days longer*: This is explained in verse 15.

11:50: Caiaphas agreed that, as Jesus was not (in their opinion) the Messiah, any popular insurrection now could only end in disaster; so it was better, he argued, to do away with him. He was unconscious of the deeper meaning of his words, namely that Jesus must die for the salvation of man.

12:1: Here begins the last week of Jesus' public life. This is described in great detail, as was the first week in chapter 1.

12:32, *lifted up*: i.e., on the cross; but the words also contain a reference to his going up into heaven. The two mysteries are inseparable.

13:1: John begins here to unfold the mystery of the love of Jesus for "his own". Note the solemn introduction to the "hour" of his passion and death.

13:34, *new commandment*: Jesus gives a new depth to the familiar commandment of the Old Testament. The standard now is, "as I have loved you".

14:26, *all things*: After Jesus has gone to his Father, the Holy Spirit will complete his revelation to the world.

15:18: Jesus contrasts the love his disciples have with the hatred the world bears them.

16:10: Jesus is taken from them because they did not receive him.

17:1–26: The priestly prayer of Jesus, before his sacrifice.

17:5: Declares his pre-existence.

18:13: According to Jewish law the high-priesthood was for life. The Romans had deposed Annas, the legal holder, in AD 15, and appointed another in his place, but many Jews continued to recognize Annas.

18:28: They would have contracted a legal impurity by entering the house of a pagan.

18:29: See note on Lk 23:2.

18:31: Crucifixion was a Roman not a Jewish punishment.

19:7: At last, because of Pilate's reluctance, they produce the real charge.

19:8–9: Pilate is afraid and asks Jesus where he comes from—not his country but his mysterious origins, as implied in the charge.

19:27, *took her to his own home*: Joseph must now have been dead.

20:17: The death and resurrection of Jesus had put an end to the ordinary familiar relationships of human life, and the time of lasting companionship had not yet come.

21:1–25: This chapter was added later, either by the evangelist or by a disciple; cf. 20:30–31 and 21:24.

21:7: John remembered a similar miracle before; cf. Lk 5:6.

21:15–17: The threefold question addressed to Peter alone corresponds to the threefold denial. Jesus gives Peter charge over his flock.

THE ACTS OF THE APOSTLES

1:1, *the first book*: i.e., St Luke's Gospel.

1:14, *brethren*: See note on Mt 12:46.

1:22: An apostle must be a witness to Christ's resurrection.

Explanatory Notes

2:14: Peter assumes the leadership in public. In this discourse we have the earliest form of the apostolic preaching.
3:1: In the early days, the first Christians observed the prescriptions of the Jewish Law.
4:2: The Sadducees did not believe in the resurrection of the dead.
4:32, *everything in common*: They freely shared what was theirs individually; cf. Acts 5:4.
5:11 *church*: i.e., the Christian and Messianic community, a term borrowed from the Old Testament.
5:20, *Life*: cf. Acts 9:2, "the Way". These terms recall the words of Jesus, "I am the way, and the truth, and the life" (Jn 14:6).
5:34, *Gamaliel*: teacher of St Paul; cf. Acts 22:3.
6:1, *Hellenists*: Greek-speaking Jews of the Dispersion, who had their own synagogues in Jerusalem and read the scriptures in Greek.
8:20: Hence the word "simony", meaning "buying and selling spiritual powers and privileges".
9:5: Jesus identifies himself with his followers.
9:13, *saints*: i.e., Christians, made holy by baptism.
10:16: The vision was to prepare Peter for his reception of Cornelius the Gentile and his household into the church; cf. also Acts 15.
12:1: The second wave of persecution; cf. Acts 8:1.
13:16–41: This first recorded sermon of Paul is similar to that of Peter in Acts 2:14–36.
16:10: This is the first of the passages in Acts in which the story is told in the first person plural, indicating that Luke, the author, was there. The manuscript Codex Bezae, however, has a "we" passage in 11:28.
16:13: Being a Roman colony, Philippi had no synagogue within its walls.
19:35, *the sacred stone* or statue of the goddess which according to legend came down from heaven. Possibly a meteorite.
20:7: Celebration of the Eucharist on the Lord's day, i.e., Saturday evening, according to the Jewish way of reckoning a day from sunset to sunset.
20:34: Paul insisted on working for his living, though recognizing the apostle's right to support by the faithful; cf. 1 Cor 9:4–7.
21:4, *told Paul not to go*: This was not a command. The Holy Spirit enlightened them about what lay before Paul and they naturally wished to spare him; cf. verse 11.
22:20, *thy witness*: Greek, "martyr". Witnessing by one's death (i.e., martyrdom) is the supreme example.

List of changes in the Revised Standard Version for the Catholic Edition

For "brothers" read "brethren" in Mt 12:46, 47 (note), 48, 49; 13:55; Mk 3:31, 32, 33, 34; Lk 8:19, 20, 21; Jn 2:12; 7:3, 5, 10; Acts 1:14.

	TEXT		FOOTNOTES	
	RSV	RSVCE	RSV	RSVCE
Mt 1:19	divorce her	send her away		
Mt 18:24			[f]Delete existing note and substitute:	[f]A talent was more than fifteen years' wages of a labourer
Mt 18:28			[g]Delete existing note and substitute:	[g]The denarius was a day's wage for a labourer
Mt 19:9		. . . commits adultery; and he who marries a divorced woman commits adultery."[k]		[k]Other ancient authorities omit *and he . . . adultery*

Changes in the RSV for the Catholic Edition

	TEXT		FOOTNOTES	
	RSV	RSVCE	RSV	RSVCE
Mt 20:2			[m]Delete existing note and substitute:	[m]The denarius was a day's wage for a labourer
Mt 21:44		[q]+[44] And he who falls on this stone will be broken to pieces; but when it falls on any one, it will crush him		[q]Other ancient authorities omit verse 44
Mt 25:15			[d]Delete existing note and substitute:	[d]A talent was more than fifteen years' wages of a labourer
Mt 27:24		[l]this righteous man's blood		[l]Other ancient authorities omit *righteous* or *man's*
Mk 6:37			[u]Delete existing note and substitute:	[u]The denarius was a day's wage for a labourer
Mk 9:29		[j]+ and fasting		[j]Other ancient authorities omit *and fasting*
Mk 10:24		[r]+ for those who trust in riches		[r]Other ancient authorities omit *for those . . . in riches*
Mk 13:33		[a]+ and pray		[a]Other ancient authorities omit *and pray*
Mk 14:5			[b]Delete existing note and substitute:	[b]The denarius was a day's wage for a labourer
Mk 16:9–20		[k](Insert into the text after verse 8) [9]Now when he rose early on the first day of the week, he appeared first to Mary Magdalene, from whom he had cast out seven demons. [10]She went and told those who had been with him, as they mourned and wept. [11]But when they heard that he was alive and had been seen by her, they would not believe it.		[k]Other ancient authorities omit verses 9–20. Some ancient authorities conclude Mark instead with the following: *But they reported briefly to Peter and those with him all that they had been told. And after this, Jesus*

Changes in the RSV for the Catholic Edition

	TEXT		FOOTNOTES	
	RSV	RSVCE	RSV	RSVCE
		[12]After this he appeared in another form to two them, as they were walking into the country. [13]And they went back and told the rest, but they did not believe them. [14]Afterwards he appeared to the eleven themselves as they sat at a table; and he upbraided them for their unbelief and hardness of heart, because they had not believed those who saw him after he had risen. [15]And he said to them, "Go into all the world and preach the gospel to the whole creation. [16]He who believes and is baptized will be saved; but he who does not believe will be condemned. [17]And these signs will accompany those who believe: in my name they will cast out demons; they will speak in new tongues; [18]they will pick up serpents, and if they drink any deadly thing, it will not hurt them; they will lay their hands on the sick, and they will recover." [19]So then the Lord Jesus, after he had spoken to them, was taken up into heaven, and sat down at the right hand of God. [20]And they went forth and preached everywhere, while the Lord worked with them and confirmed the message by the signs that attended it. Amen.		*himself sent out by means of them, from east to west, the sacred and imperishable proclamation of eternal salvation*
Lk 1:28	O favoured one	full of grace[b2]		[b2]Or *O favoured one*
Lk 8:43		[b]+ and had spent all her living upon physicians		[b]Other ancient authorities omit *and had spent . . . physicians*

Changes in the RSV for the Catholic Edition

	TEXT		FOOTNOTES	
	RSV	RSVCE	RSV	RSVCE
Lk 10:35			[i]Delete existing note and substitute:	[i]The denarius was a day's wage for a labourer
Lk 15:8			[t]Delete existing note and substitute:	[t]The dracma, rendered here by *silver coin*, was about a day's wage for a labourer
Lk 19:13			[e]Delete existing note and substitute:	[e]The mina, rendered here by *pound*, was about three months' wages for a labourer
Lk 22:19–20		[j]+ which is given for you. Do this in remembrance of me." [20]And likewise the cup after supper, saying, "This cup which is poured out for you is the new covenant in my blood."		[j]Some ancient authorities omit *which is given . . . blood*
Lk 24:5		[u]+ He is not here, but has risen.		[u]Other ancient authorities omit *He is . . . has risen*
Lk 24:12		[v]+[12] But Peter rose and ran to the tomb; stooping and looking in, he saw the linen cloths by themselves; and he went home wondering at what had happened.		[v]Other ancient authorities omit verse 12
Lk 24:36		[x] + and said to them, "Peace to you!"		[x]Other ancient authorities omit *and said . . . to you*
Lk 24:40		[y]+[40]And when he had said this, he showed them his hands and feet.		[y]Other ancient authorities omit verse 40
Lk 24:51		[a]+ and was carried up into heaven.		[a]Other ancient authorities omit *and was . . . heaven*
Lk 24:52		[b] + worshipped him, and		[b]Other ancient authorities omit *worshipped him, and*

Changes in the RSV for the Catholic Edition

	TEXT		FOOTNOTES	
	RSV	RSVCE	RSV	RSVCE
Jn 6:7			[l]Delete existing note and substitute:	[l]The denarius was a day's wage for a labourer
Jn 7:52		[r](Insert into the text here) 53 They went each to his 8 own house, 1 but Jesus went to the Mount of Olives. 2 Early in the morning he came again to the temple; and he sat down and taught them. 3 The scribes and the Pharisees brought a woman who had been caught in adultery, and placing her in the midst 4 they said to him, "Teacher, this woman has been caught in the act of adultery. 5 Now in the law Moses commanded us to stone such. What do you say about her?" 6 This they said to test him, that they might have some charge to bring against him. Jesus bent down and wrote with his finger on the ground. 7 And as they continued to ask him, he stood up and said to them, "Let him who is without sin among you be the first to throw a stone at her." 8 And once more he bent down and wrote with his finger on the ground. 9 But when they heard it, they went away, one by one, beginning with the eldest, and Jesus was left alone with the woman standing before him. 10 Jesus looked up and said to her, "Woman, where are they? Has no one condemned you?" 11 She said, "No one, Lord." And Jesus said, "Neither do I condemn you: go, and do not sin again."		[r]Some ancient authorities insert 7:53–8:11 either at the end of this gospel or after Lk 21:38, with variations of the text. Others omit it altogether.
Jn 12:5			[b]Delete existing note and substitute:	[b]The denarius was a day's wage for a labourer

Headings added to the Biblical Text

THE GOSPEL ACCORDING TO MATTHEW

1. BIRTH AND INFANCY OF JESUS
The ancestry of Jesus Christ 1:1
The virginal conception of Jesus, and his birth 1:18
The adoration of the Magi 2:1
The flight into Egypt. The massacre of the Innocents 2:13
Return to Nazareth 2:19

2. PRELUDE TO THE PUBLIC MINISTRY OF JESUS
John the Baptist preaching in the wilderness 3:1
Jesus is baptized 3:13
Jesus fasts and is tempted 4:1

Part One: Jesus' ministry in Galilee

Jesus begins to preach 4:12
The first disciples are called 4:18

3. THE SERMON ON THE MOUNT
The Beatitudes 5:1
Salt of the earth and light of the world 5:13
Jesus and his teaching, the fullness of the Law 5:17
An upright intention in almsgiving, prayer and fasting 6:1
Trust in God's fatherly providence 6:19
Various precepts. Do not judge 7:1
Respect for holy things 7:6
Effectiveness of prayer 7:7
The golden rule 7:12
The narrow gate 7:13
False prophets 7:15
Doing the will of God 7:21
Building on rock 7:24
Jesus teaches with authority 7:28

4. MIRACLES OF THE MESSIAH
Curing of a leper 8:1
The centurion's faith 8:5
Curing of Peter's mother-in-law 8:14
Other cures 8:16
Following Christ is not easy 8:18
The calming of the storm 8:23
The demoniacs of Gadara 8:28
Curing of a paralyzed man 9:1
The call of Matthew 9:9
A discussion on fasting 9:14
The raising of Jairus' daughter and the curing of the woman with a haemorrhage 9:18
Curing of two blind men. The dumb devil 9:27
The need for good pastors 9:35

5. FROM THE OLD TO THE NEW PEOPLE OF GOD
The calling of the twelve apostles 10:1
The apostles' first mission 10:5
Jesus' instructions to the apostles 10:16
Messengers from John the Baptist 11:1
Jesus reproaches his contemporaries 11:16
Jesus reproaches cities for their unbelief 11:20
Jesus thanks his Father 11:25
The law of the sabbath 12:1
Curing of the man with a withered hand 12:9
Jesus, the servant of God 12:15
Allegations by the Pharisees. The sin against the Holy Spirit 12:22
The sign of Jonah 12:38
The true kinsmen of Jesus 12:46

6. THE PARABLES OF THE KINGDOM
Parable of the sower. The meaning of parables 13:1
The parable of the weeds 13:24
The mustard seed; the leaven 13:31
The parable of the weeds explained 13:36
The hidden treasure; the pearl; the net 13:44

7. JESUS WITHDRAWS TO THE BORDER COUNTRY
No one is a prophet in his own country 13:53
The martyrdom of John the Baptist 14:1
First miracle of the loaves and fish 14:13
Jesus walks on the water 14:22
Cures in Gennesaret 14:34
The tradition of the elders. True cleanness 15:1
The Canaanite woman 15:21
Curing of many sick people 15:29
Second miracle of the loaves and fish 15:32
The Pharisees and Sadducees try to test Jesus 16:1
Peter's profession of faith and his primacy 16:13

Headings added to the Biblical Text

Part Two: Jesus' ministry on the way to Jerusalem

8. TOWARDS JUDEA AND JERUSALEM
Jesus foretells his passion and resurrection. The law of Christian renunciation 16:21
The Transfiguration 17:1
Curing of an epileptic boy 17:14
Second announcement of the Passion. The temple tax 17:22

9. THE DISCOURSE ON THE CHURCH
The "little ones" and the Kingdom. On leading others astray. The lost sheep 18:1
Fraternal correction. The apostles' authority 18:15
Forgiveness of injuries. Parable of the unforgiving servant 18:21
Marriage and virginity 19:1
Jesus blesses the children 19:13
The rich young man. Christian poverty and renunciation 19:16
Parable of the labourers in the vineyard 20:1
Third announcement of the Passion 20:17
The mother of the sons of Zebedee makes her request 20:20
Curing of the blind men of Jericho 20:29

Part Three: Jesus' ministry in Jerusalem

10. CLEANSING OF THE TEMPLE. CONTROVERSIES
The Messiah enters the Holy City 21:1
Jesus in the temple 21:12
The cursing of the fig tree 21:18
The authority of Jesus is questioned 21:23
Parable of the two sons 21:28
Parable of the wicked tenants 21:33
Parable of the marriage feast 22:1
Paying tax to Caesar 22:15
The resurrection of the dead 22:23
The greatest commandment of all 22:34
The divinity of the Messiah 22:41
Jesus berates the scribes and Pharisees 23:1
Jerusalem admonished 23:37

11. THE ESCHATOLOGICAL DISCOURSE
Announcement of the destruction of the temple 24:1
The beginning of tribulations. Persecution on account of the Gospel 24:3
The great tribulation 24:15
The coming of the Son of man 24:29
The end will surely come. The lesson of the fig tree 24:32
The time of the second coming of Christ 24:36
Parable of the faithful servant 24:45
Parable of the wise and foolish maidens 25:1
Parable of the talents 25:14
The Last Judgment 25:31

12. THE PASSION, DEATH AND RESURRECTION OF JESUS
Last announcement of the Passion. The conspiracy against Jesus 26:1
The anointing at Bethany. Judas betrays Jesus 26:6
Preparations for the Last Supper and announcement of Judas' treachery 26:17
The institution of the Eucharist 26:26
The disciples' desertion foretold 26:30
Gethsemane—the agony in the garden 26:36
Arrest of Jesus 26:47
Jesus before the chief priests 26:57
Peter's denials 26:69
Jesus is brought before Pilate 27:1
Judas' despair and death 27:3
Jesus' trial before Pilate 27:11
The crowning with thorns 27:27
The crucifixion and death of Jesus 27:32
The burial of Jesus 27:57
Jesus rises from the dead and appears to the women 28:1
The soldiers are bribed 28:11
Appearance in Galilee. The mission to the world 28:16

THE GOSPEL ACCORDING TO MARK

1. PRELUDE TO THE PUBLIC MINISTRY OF JESUS
The ministry of John the Baptist 1:1
Jesus is baptized 1:9
The tempting of Jesus 1:12

Part One: Jesus' ministry in Galilee

2. JESUS BEGINS HIS MINISTRY
Jesus begins to preach 1:14
Jesus calls his first disciples 1:16
Jesus in the synagogue of Capernaum 1:21
Curing of Peter's mother-in-law 1:29
Jesus cures many sick people 1:32
Jesus goes to a lonely place to pray 1:35
Curing of a leper 1:40
Curing of a paralyzed man 2:1
The calling of Matthew 2:13
A discussion on fasting 2:18
The law of the sabbath 2:23
Curing of the man with a withered hand 3:1
Cures beside the Sea of Galilee 3:7
Jesus chooses twelve apostles 3:13
Jesus' relatives are concerned about him 3:19
Allegations of the scribes. Sin against the Holy Spirit 3:22
The true kinsmen of Jesus 3:31

3. PARABLES OF THE KINGDOM OF GOD
Parable of the sower. The meaning of parables 4:1
Parables of the lamp and the measure 4:21
Parables of the seed and of the mustard seed 4:26
The end of the Parables Discourse 4:33

Headings added to the Biblical Text

Part Two: Jesus' ministry on the way to Jerusalem

Part Three: Jesus' ministry in Jerusalem

THE GOSPEL ACCORDING TO LUKE

Headings added to the Biblical Text

2. PRELUDE TO THE PUBLIC MINISTRY OF JESUS
John the Baptist preaching in the wilderness 3:1
John the Baptist imprisoned 3:19
Jesus is baptized 3:21
The ancestry of Jesus 3:23
Jesus fasts and is tempted in the wilderness 4:1

Part One: Jesus' ministry in Galilee

3. THE START OF HIS MINISTRY IN GALILEE
Preaching in Nazareth 4:16
In the synagogue in Capernaum 4:31
Curing of Peter's mother-in-law 4:38
Other cures 4:40
Jesus preaches in other cities in Judea 4:42
The miraculous catch of fish and the calling of the first disciples 5:1
Curing of a leper 5:12
Curing of a paralyzed man 5:17
The calling of Matthew 5:27
A discussion on fasting 5:33
The law of the sabbath 6:1
Curing of man with a withered hand 6:6

4. JESUS' MIRACLES AND PREACHING IN GALILEE
Jesus chooses twelve apostles 6:12
Preaching on the plain 6:17
The Beatitudes and the Woes 6:20
Love of enemies 6:27
Integrity 6:39
The centurion's faith 7:1
The son of the widow of Nain restored to life 7:11
Messengers from John the Baptist 7:18
Jesus reproaches his contemporaries 7:31
Forgiveness for a sinful woman 7:36
The holy women 8:1
Parable of the sower. The meaning of parables 8:4
Parable of the lamp 8:16
The true kinsmen of Jesus 8:19
The calming of the storm 8:22
The Gerasene demoniac 8:26
Jairus' daughter is restored to life. Curing of a woman with a haemorrhage 8:40

5. JESUS TRAVELS WITH HIS APOSTLES
The mission of the apostles 9:1
Herod's opinion about Jesus 9:7
Return of the apostles. First miracle of the loaves and fish 9:10
Peter's profession of faith 9:18
First announcement of the Passion 9:21
The need for self-denial 9:23
The Transfiguration 9:28
Curing of an epileptic boy 9:37
Second announcement of the Passion 9:43
Humility and tolerance 9:46

Part Two: Jesus' ministry on the way to Jerusalem

6. THE JOURNEY BEGINS
Samaritans refuse to receive Jesus 9:51
Requirements for following Jesus 9:57
The mission of the seventy disciples 10:1
Jesus reproaches cities for their unbelief 10:13
The seventy return from their mission 10:17
Jesus gives thanks 10:21

7. FURTHER PREACHING
Parable of the good Samaritan 10:25
Martha and Mary welcome our Lord 10:38
The Our Father 11:1
Effective prayer 11:5
The Kingdom of God and the kingdom of Satan 11:14
Responding to the word of God 11:27
The sign of Jonah 11:29
The lamp of the body, the light of the soul 11:33
Jesus reproaches scribes and Pharisees 11:37

8. ANNOUNCEMENT OF THE END
Various teachings 12:1
Parable of the rich fool 12:13
Trust in God's fatherly providence 12:22
The need for vigilance; the parable of the steward 12:35
Jesus brings division, not peace 12:49
The signs of the times 12:54
The need for repentance 13:1
Parable of the barren fig tree 13:6
Jesus cures a woman on the sabbath 13:10
Parables of the mustard seed and of the leaven 13:18
The narrow gate 13:22
Jesus' reply to Herod 13:31
Jerusalem admonished 13:34
Jesus cures a dropsical man on the sabbath 14:1
A lesson about humility 14:7
The right attitude to the poor 14:12
Parable of the invited guests 14:15
Conditions for following Jesus 14:25

9. PARABLES OF GOD'S MERCY
The lost sheep 15:1
The lost coin 15:8
The prodigal son 15:11

10. VARIOUS TEACHINGS
The unjust steward 16:1
The law and the Gospel 16:16
Lazarus and the rich man 16:19
On leading others astray 17:1
Forgiving offences 17:3
The power of faith 17:5
Humble service 17:7
Cure of ten lepers 17:11
The coming of the Kingdom of God 17:20
The day of Christ's coming 17:22
Persevering prayer. Parable of the unjust judge 18:1
Parable of the Pharisee and the tax collector 18:9
Jesus blesses the children 18:15
The rich young man. Christian poverty and renunciation 18:18

Part Three: The Jerusalem ministry

THE GOSPEL ACCORDING TO JOHN

Part One: Jesus is manifested as the Messiah by his signs and words

8. JESUS IS ACCLAIMED AS THE MESSIANIC KING
Mary anoints our Lord at Bethany 12:1
The Messiah's entry into Jerusalem 12:12
Jesus announces his glorification 12:20
Jesus appeals for faith in himself 12:37

Part Two: Jesus is manifested as the Messiah Son of God in his passion, death and resurrection

9. THE LAST SUPPER
Jesus washes his disciples' feet 13:1
The treachery of Judas foretold 13:21
The new commandment. The disciples' desertion foretold 13:31
Jesus reveals the Father 14:1
Promise of the Holy Spirit 14:15
The vine and the branches 15:1
The law of love 15:9
A hostile world 15:18
The action of the Holy Spirit 16:1
Fullness of joy 16:16
The priestly prayer of Jesus 17:1

10. THE PASSION AND DEATH OF JESUS
Arrest of Jesus 18:1
Jesus before the chief priests. Peter's denials 18:13
The trial before Pilate: Jesus is King 18:28
The scourging at the pillar and the crowning with thorns 19:1
Pilate hands Jesus over 19:12
The crucifixion and death of Jesus 19:17
Jesus' side is pierced. The burial 19:31

11. APPEARANCES OF THE RISEN CHRIST
The empty tomb 20:1
The appearance to Mary Magdalene 20:11
Jesus' first appearance to the disciples 20:19
A second appearance with Thomas present 20:24
The miraculous catch of fish 21:1
Peter's primacy 21:15
Conclusion 21:24

THE GOSPEL ACCORDING TO ACTS

Prologue 1:1
The Ascension 1:6

Part One: The Church in Jerusalem

1. THE DISCIPLES IN JERUSALEM
The apostolic college 1:12
The election of Matthias 1:15

2. PENTECOST
The coming of the Holy Spirit 2:1
Peter's address 2:14
Many baptisms 2:37
The early Christians 2:42

3. THE APOSTLES' WORK IN JERUSALEM
Curing of a man lame from birth 3:1
Peter's address in the temple 3:11
Peter and John are arrested 4:1
Address to the Sanhedrin 4:5
The Church's thanksgiving prayer 4:23
The way of life of the early Christians 4:32
Deception by Ananias and Sapphira 5:1
Growth of the Church 5:12
The apostles are arrested and miraculously freed 5:17
The apostles before the Sanhedrin 5:26
Gamaliel's intervention 5:34
The apostles are flogged 5:40

4. THE "DEACONS". ST STEPHEN
Appointment of the seven deacons 6:1
Stephen's arrest 6:8
Stephen's address to the Sanhedrin 7:1
Martyrdom of St Stephen 7:54

Part Two: The Church spreads beyond Jerusalem

5. THE CHURCH IN SAMARIA
Persecution of the Church 8:1b
Philip's preaching in Samaria 8:5
Simon the magician 8:9
Peter and John in Samaria 8:14
The sin of simony 8:18
Philip baptizes an Ethiopian official 8:26

6. THE CONVERSION OF ST PAUL
Saul on his way to Damascus 9:1
Ananias baptizes Saul 9:10
Paul begins his apostolate 9:19
Paul flees from Damascus 9:23
Barnabas and Paul in Jerusalem 9:26
Growth of the Church 9:31

7. ST PETER'S ACTIVITY
Curing of a paralyzed man at Lydda 9:32
Peter raises Tabitha to life 9:36
The vision of the centurion Cornelius 10:1
Peter's vision 10:9
Peter in the house of Cornelius 10:23
Peter preaches to Cornelius 10:34
The baptism of Cornelius and his household 10:44
In Jerusalem Peter justifies his conduct 11:1
Beginning of the Church in Antioch 11:19
Antioch helps the Church in Judea 11:27
Persecution by Herod. Peter's arrest and miraculous deliverance 12:1
Death of Herod 12:20
Barnabas and Paul return 12:24

Headings added to the Biblical Text

Part Three: The spread of the Church among the Gentiles. Missionary journeys of St Paul

8. ST PAUL'S FIRST APOSTOLIC JOURNEY
Paul and Barnabas are sent on a mission 13:1
Paul and Barnabas in Cyprus 13:4
Paul and Barnabas cross into Asia Minor 13:13
Preaching in the synagogue of Antioch of Pisidia 13:14
Paul and Barnabas preach to the pagans 13:44
Iconium evangelized. Persecution 14:1
Curing of a cripple at Lystra 14:8
Paul is stoned 14:19
Return journey to Antioch 14:21

9. THE COUNCIL OF JERUSALEM
Dissension at Antioch; Judaizers 15:1
Paul and Barnabas go to Jerusalem 15:3
Peter's address to the council 15:6
James' speech 15:12
The council's decision 15:22
Reception of the council's decree 15:30

10. ST PAUL'S SECOND APOSTOLIC JOURNEY
Silas, Paul's new companion 15:36
Timothy joins Paul 16:1
Tour of the churches of Asia Minor 16:4
Macedonia 16:11
The conversion of Lydia 16:12
Curing of a possessed girl. Imprisonment of Paul 16:16
Baptism of the jailer 16:25
Release from jail and departure from Philippi 16:35
Difficulties with Jews in Thessalonica 17:1
Reception in Beroea 17:10
Paul in Athens 17:16
Paul's speech in the Areopagus 17:22
Paul in Corinth, with Aquila and Priscilla 18:1
Preaching to Jews and Gentiles 18:5
Paul before Gallio 18:12
Return to Antioch via Ephesus 18:18

11. ST PAUL'S THIRD APOSTOLIC JOURNEY
Galatia and Phrygia 18:23
Apollos in Ephesus and Corinth 18:24
Disciples of John the Baptist at Ephesus 19:1
Paul's preaching and miracles at Ephesus 19:8
Books of magic burned 19:17
Paul's plans for further journeys 19:21
The silversmiths' riot in Ephesus 19:23
Paul goes into Macedonia and begins his return journey 20:1
Celebration of the Eucharist. Eutychus' fall and recovery 20:7
From Troas to Miletus 20:13
Farewell address to the elders of Ephesus 20:17

Part Four: St Paul, in imprisonment, bears witness to Christ

12. ST PAUL IN JERUSALEM
From Miletus to Caesarea 21:1
The prophet Agabus 21:10
Paul arrives in Jerusalem and meets the Christians 21:15
Paul is arrested in the temple 21:27
Paul defends himself before the crowd 22:1
Paul, the Roman citizen 22:22
Speech before the Sanhedrin 22:30
A Jewish plot against Paul 23:12

13. FROM JERUSALEM TO ROME
Paul is moved to Caesarea 23:22
The trial before Felix 24:1
A further appearance before Felix 24:24
Festus resumes the trial. Paul appeals to Caesar 25:1
Festus briefs Agrippa 25:13
Paul before Agrippa 25:23
Paul's speech in the presence of Agrippa 26:1
Reactions to Paul's speech 26:24
Departure for Rome. Voyage to Crete 27:1
The voyage is resumed against Paul's advice 27:9
A storm 27:13
Paul's vision. He rallies his companions 27:21
Shipwreck and rescue 27:39
Waiting in Malta 28:1
Arrival in Rome 28:11
Paul and the Roman Jews 28:17
Paul's ministry in Rome 28:30

Sources quoted in the Navarre Bible New Testament Commentary

1. DOCUMENTS OF THE CHURCH AND OF POPES

Benedict XII
Const. *Benedictus Deus*, 29 January 1336
Benedict XV
Enc. *Humani generis redemptionem*, 15 June 1917
Enc. *Spiritus Paraclitus*, 1 September 1920
Clement of Rome, St
Letter to the Corinthians
Constantinople, First Council of
Nicene-Constantinopolitan Creed
Constantinople, Third Council of
Definitio de duabus in Christo voluntatibus et operationibus
Florence, Council of
Decree *Pro Jacobitis*
Laetentur coeli
Decree *Pro Armeniis*
John Paul II
Addresses and homilies
Apos. Exhort. *Catechesi tradendae*, 16 October 1979
Apos. Exhort. *Familiaris consortio*, 22 November 1981
Apos. Exhort. *Reconciliatio et paenitentia*, 2 December 1984
Apos. Letter. *Salvifici doloris*, 11 February 1984
Bull, *Aperite portas*, 6 January 1983
Enc. *Redemptor hominis*, 4 March 1979
Enc. *Dives in misercordia*, 30 November 1980
Enc. *Dominum et Vivificantem*, 30 May 1986
Enc. *Laborem exercens*, 14 September 1981
Letter to all priests, 8 April 1979
Letter to all bishops, 24 February 1980
Gelasius I
Ne forte
Gregory the Great, St
Epistula ad Theodorum medicum contra Fabianum
Exposition on the Seven Penitential
Ne forte
In Evangelia homiliae
In Ezechielem homiliae
Moralia in Job
Regulae pastoralis liber
Innocent III
Letter *Eius exemplo*, 18 December 1208
John XXIII
Pacem in terris, 11 April 1963
Enc. *Ad Petri cathedram*, 29 June 1959
Lateran Council (649)
Canons
Leo the Great, St
Homilies and sermons
Licet per nostros
Promisisse mememeni
Leo IX
Creed
Leo XIII
Enc. *Aeterni Patris*, 4 August 1879
Enc. *Immortale Dei*, 1 November 1885
Enc. *Libertas praestantissimum*, 20 June 1888
Enc. *Sapientiae christianae*, 18 January 1890
Enc. *Rerum novarum*, 15 May 1891
Enc. *Providentissimus Deus*, 18 November 1893
Enc. *Divinum illud munus*, 9 May 1897
Lateran, Fourth Council of (1215)
De fide catholica
Lyons, Second Council of (1274)
Doctrina de gratia
Profession of faith of Michael Palaeologue
Orange, Second Council of (529)
De gratia
Paul IV
Const. *Cum quorumdam*, 7 August 1555
Paul VI
Enc. *Ecclesiam suam*, 6 August 1964
Enc. *Mysterium fidei*, 9 September 1965
Apos. Exhort. *Marialis cultus*, 2 February 1967
Apos. Letter *Petrum et Paulum*, 27 February 1967
Enc. *Populorum progressio*, 26 March 1967
Enc. *Sacerdotalis coelibatus*, 24 June 1967
Creed of the People of God: Solemn Profession of Faith, 30 June 1968
Apos. Letter *Octagesima adveniens*, 14 June 1971

Sources quoted in the Commentary

Apos. Exhort. *Gaudete in Domino*, 9 May 1975
Apos. Exhort. *Evangelii nuntiandi*, 8 Dec. 1975
Homilies and addresses
Pius V, St
Catechism of the Council of Trent for Parish Priests or *Pius V Catechism*
Pius IX, Bl.
Bull *Ineffabilis Deus*, 8 December 1854
Syllabus of Errors
Pius X, St
Enc. *E supreme apostolatus*, 4 October 1903
Enc. *Ad Diem illum*, 2 February 1904
Enc. *Acerbo nimis*, 15 April 1905
Catechism of Christian Doctrine, 15 July 1905
Decree *Lamentabili*, 3 July 1907
Enc. *Haerent animo*, 4 August 1908
Pius XI
Enc. *Quas primas*, 11 December 1925
Enc. *Divini illius magistri*, 31 December 1929
Enc. *Mens nostra*, 20 December 1929
Enc. *Casti connubii*, 31 December 1930
Enc. *Quadragesimo anno*, 15 May 1931
Enc. *Ad catholici sacerdotii*, 20 December 1935
Pius XII
Enc. *Mystici Corporis*, 29 June 1943
Enc. *Mediator Dei*, 20 November 1947
Enc. *Divino afflante Spiritu*, 30 September 1943
Enc. *Humani generis*, 12 August 1950
Apost. Const. *Menti nostrae*, 23 September 1950
Enc. *Sacra virginitas*, 25 March 1954
Enc. *Ad caeli Reginam*, 11 October 1954
Homilies and addresses
Quierzy, Council of (833)
Doctrina de libero arbitrio hominis et de praedestinatione
Trent, Council of (1545–1563)
De sacris imaginibus
De Purgatorio
De reformatione
De sacramento ordinis
De libris sacris
De peccato originale
De SS. Eucharistia
De iustificatione
De SS. Missae sacrificio
De sacramento matrimonio
Doctrina de peccato originali
Doctrina de sacramento extremae unctionis
Doctrina de sacramento paenitentiae
Toledo, Ninth Council of (655)
De Redemptione
Toledo, Eleventh Council of (675)
De Trinitate Creed
Valence, Third Council of (855)
De praedestinatione
Vatican, First Council of the (1869–1870)
Dogm. Const. *Dei Filius*
Dogm. Const. *Pastor aeternus*
Vatican, Second Council of the (1963–1965)
Const. *Sacrosanctum Concilium*
Decree *Christus Dominus*
Decl. *Dignitatis humanae*
Decl. *Gravissimum educationis*
Decl. *Nostrae aetate*
Decree *Optatam totius*
Decree *Ad gentes*
Decree *Apostolicam actuositatem*
Decree *Perfectae caritatis*
Decree *Presbyterorum ordinis*
Decree *Unitatis redintegratio*
Dogm. Const. *Dei Verbum*
Dogm. Const. *Lumen gentium*
Past. Const. *Gaudium et spes*

Liturgical Texts

Roman Missal: Missale Romanum, editio typica altera (Vatican City, 1975)
The Divine Office (London, Sydney, Dublin, 1974)

Other Church Documents

Code of Canon Law
Codex Iuris Canonici (Vatican City, 1983)
Congregation for the Doctrine of the Faith
Declaration concerning Sexual Ethics, December 1975
Instruction on Infant Baptism, 20 October 1980
Inter insigniores, 15 October 1976
Letter on certain questions concerning Eschatology, 17 May 1979
Libertatis conscientia, 22 March 1986
Sacerdotium ministeriale, 6 August 1983
Libertatis nuntius, 6 August 1984
Mysterium Filii Dei, 21 February 1972
Pontifical Biblical Commission
Replies
New Vulgate
Nova Vulgata Bibliorum Sacrorum editio typica altera (Vatican City, 1986)

Sources quoted in the Commentary

2. THE FATHERS, ECCLESIASTICAL WRITERS AND OTHER AUTHORS

Alphonsus Mary Liguori, St
Christmas Novena
The Love of Our Lord Jesus Christ reduced to practice
Meditations for Advent
Thoughts on the Passion
Shorter Sermons
Sunday Sermons
Treasury of Teaching Material
Ambrose, St
De sacramentis
De mysteriis
De officiis ministrorum
Exameron
Expositio Evangelii secundum Lucam
Expositio in Ps 118
Treatise on the Mysteries
Anastasius of Sinai, St
Sermon on the Holy Synaxis
Anon.
Apostolic Constitutions
Didache, or *Teaching of the Twelve Apostles*
Letter to Diognetus
Shepherd of Hermas
Anselm, St
Prayers and Meditations
Aphraates
Demonstratio
Athanasius, St
Adversus Antigonum
De decretis nicaenae synodi
De Incarnatio contra arianos
Historia arianorum
Oratio I contra arianos
Oratio II contra arianos
Oratio contra gentes
Augustine, St
The City of God
Confessions
Contra Adimantum Manichaei discipulum
De Actis cum Felice Manicheo
De agone christiano
De bono matrimonii
De bono viduitatis
De catechizandis rudibus
De civitate Dei
De coniugiis adulterinis
De consensu Evangelistarum
De correptione et gratia
De doctrina christiana
De dono perseverantiae
De fide et operibus
De fide et symbolo
De Genesi ad litteram
De gratia et libero arbitrio
De natura et gratia
De praedestinatione sanctorum
De sermo Domini in monte
De spiritu et littera
De Trinitate
De verbis Domini sermones
Enarrationes in Psalmos
Enchiridion
Expositio epistulae ad Galatas
In I Epist. Ioann. ad Parthos
In Ioannis Evangelium tractatus
Letters
Quaestiones in Heptateuchum
Sermo ad Cassariensis Ecclesiae plebem
Sermo de Nativitate Domini
Sermons
Basil, St
De Spiritu Sancto
Homilia in Julittam martyrem
In Psalmos homiliae
Bede, St
Explanatio Apocalypsis
In Ioannis Evangelium expositio
In Lucae Evangelium expositio
In Marci Evangelium expositio
In primam Epistolam Petri
In primam Epistolam S. Ioanis
Sermo super Qui audientes gavisi sunt
Super Acta Apostolorum expositio
Super divi Iacobi Epistolam
Bernal, Salvador
Monsignor Josemaría Escrivá de Balaguer, Dublin, 1977
Bernard, St
Book of Consideration
De Beata Virgine
De fallacia et brevitate vitae
De laudibus novae militiae
Divine amoris
Meditationes piissimae de cognitionis humanae conditionis
Sermons on Psalm 90
Sermon on Song of Songs
Sermons
Bonaventure, St
In IV Libri sententiarum
Speculum Beatae Virgine
Borromeo, St Charles
Homilies

Sources quoted in the Commentary

Catherine of Siena, St
Dialogue
Cano, Melchor
De locis
Cassian, John
Collationes
De institutis coenobiorum
Clement of Alexandria
Catechesis III, De Baptismo
Commentary on Luke
Quis dives salvetur?
Stromata
Cyprian, St
De bono patientiae
De dominica oratione
De mortalitate
De opere et eleemosynis
De unitate Ecclesiae
De zelo et livore
Epist. ad Fortunatum
Quod idola dii non sint
Cyril of Alexandria, St
Commentarium in Lucam
Explanation of Hebrews
Homilia XXVIII in Mattheum
Cyril of Jerusalem, St
Catecheses
Mystagogical Catechesis
Diadochus of Photike
Chapters on Spiritual Perfection
Ephrem, St
Armenian Commentary on Acts
Commentarium in Epistolam ad Haebreos
Eusebius of Caesarea
Ecclesiastical History
Francis de Sales, St
Introduction to the Devout Life
Treatise on the Love of God
Francis of Assisi, St
Little Flowers
Reflections on Christ's Wounds
Fulgentius of Ruspe
Contra Fabianum libri decem
De fide ad Petrum
Gregory Nazianzen, St
Orationes theologicae
Sermons
Gregory of Nyssa, St
De instituto christiano
De perfecta christiana forma
On the Life of Moses
Oratio catechetica magna
Oratio I in beatitudinibus
Oratio I in Christi resurrectionem

Hippolytus, St
De consummatione saeculi
Ignatius of Antioch, St
Letter to Polycarp
Letters to various churches
Ignatius, Loyola, St
Spiritual Exercises
Irenaeus, St
Against Heresies
Proof of Apostolic Preaching
Jerome, St
Ad Nepotianum
Adversus Helvidium
Comm. in Ionam
Commentary on Galatians
Commentary on St Mark's Gospel
Contra Luciferianos
Dialogus contra pelagianos
Expositio in Evangelium secundum Lucam
Homilies to neophytes on Psalm 41
Letters
On Famous Men
John of Avila, St
Audi, filia
Lecciones sobre Gálatas
Sermons
John Chrysostom, St
Ante exilium homilia
Adversus Iudaeos
Baptismal Catechesis
De coemeterio et de cruce
De incomprehensibile Dei natura
De sacerdotio
De virginitate
Fifth homily on Anna
Hom. De Cruce et latrone
Homilies on St Matthew's Gospel, St John's Gospel, Acts of the Apostles, Romans, Ephesians, 1 and 2 Corinthians, Colossians, 1 and 2 Timothy, 1 and 2 Thessalonians, Philippians, Philemon, Hebrews
II Hom. De proditione Iudae
Paraeneses ad Theodorum lapsum
Second homily in praise of St Paul
Sermon recorded by Metaphrastus
John of the Cross, St
A Prayer of the Soul enkindled by Love
Ascent of Mount Carmel
Dark Night of the Soul
Spiritual Canticle
John Damascene, St
De fide orthodoxa
John Mary Vianney, St
Sermons

Sources quoted in the Commentary

Josemaría Escrivá, St
Christ Is Passing By
Conversations
The Forge
Friends of God
Furrow
Holy Rosary
In Love with the Church
The Way
The Way of the Cross
Josephus, Flavius
Against Apion
Jewish Antiquities
The Jewish War
Justin Martyr, St
Dialogue with Tryphon
First and Second Apologies
à Kempis, Thomas
The Imitation of Christ
Luis de Granada, Fray
Book of Prayer and Meditation
Guide for Sinners
Introduccíon al símbolo de la fe
Life of Jesus Christ
Sermon on Public Sins
Suma de la vida cristiana
Luis de Léon, Fray
Exposición del Libro de Job
Minucius Felix
Octavius
Newman, J.H.
Biglietto Speech
Discourses to Mixed Congregations
Historical Sketches
Origen
Contra Celsum
Homilies on Genesis
Homilies on St John
In Exodum homiliae
Homiliae in Iesu nave
In Leviticum homiliae
In Matth. comm.
In Rom. comm.
Philo of Alexandria
De sacrificio Abel
Photius
Ad Amphilochium
Polycarp, St
Letter to the Philippians
del Portillo, A.
On Priesthood, Chicago, 1974
Primasius
Commentariorum super Apocalypsim B. Ioannis libri quinque
Prosper of Aquitaine, St
De vita contemplativa
Pseudo-Dionysius
De divinis nominibus
Pseudo-Macarius
Homilies
Severian of Gabala
Commentary on 1 Thessalonians
Teresa of Avila, St
Book of Foundations
Exclamations of the Soul to God
Interior Castle
Life
Poems
Way of Perfection
Tertullian
Against Marcion
Apologeticum
De baptismo
De oratione
Theodore the Studite, St
Oratio in adorationis crucis
Theodoret of Cyrrhus
Interpretatio Ep. ad Haebreos
Theophylact
Enarratio in Evangelium Marci
Thérèse de Lisieux, St
The Autobiography of a Saint
Thomas Aquinas, St
Adoro te devote
Commentary on St John = Super Evangelium S. Ioannis lectura
Commentaries on St Matthew's Gospel, Romans, 1 and 2 Corinthians, Galatians, Ephesians, Colossians, Philippians, 1 and 2 Timothy, 1 and 2 Thessalonians, Titus, Hebrews
De veritate
Expositio quorumdam propositionum ex Epistola ad Romanos
On the Lord's Prayer
On the two commandments of Love and the ten commandments of the Law
Summa contra gentiles
Summa theologiae
Super Symbolum Apostolorum
Thomas More, St
De tristitia Christi
Victorinus of Pettau
Commentary on the Apocalypse
Vincent Ferrer, St
Treatise on the Spiritual Life
Vincent of Lerins, St
Commonitorium
Zosimus, St
Epist. Enc. "Tractoria" ad Ecclesias Orientales